2017
Medicare
Explained

. Wolters Kluwer

D1371978

Managing Editor
Paul Clark
Assistant Managing Editor
Kelly J. Rooney, J.D., M.P.H.

Contributing Editors

Kathryn S. Beard, J.D.
Assistant Managing Editor
Sheila Lynch-Afryl, J.D., M.A.

Kayla R. Bryant, J.D.
Bryant Storm, J.D.

Amy Styka
Production

2700 Lake Cook Road
Riverwoods, IL 60015
866 529-6600
wolterskluwerlb.com

Printed in the United States of America

ISBN: 978-1-4548-8543-6

Foreword

This book has been prepared for Medicare beneficiaries and others who need a relatively thorough explanation of the Medicare program with particular emphasis on services covered in institutional settings and services provided by physicians and suppliers.

Published annually, this book includes changes made by law and regulation amendments and by updates to program manuals issued by the Centers for Medicare and Medicaid Services (CMS). This edition includes changes issued during 2016 that affect Medicare beneficiaries and providers in 2017.

The 2017 highlights are as follows:

Medicare Part A (hospital insurance). For 2017, the inpatient hospital deductible will be $1,316 per each beneficiary "spell of illness," an increase from the $1,288 inpatient deductible in 2016. Patients are responsible for a coinsurance amount for each day after the 60th and through the 90th day per spell of illness, and in 2017 daily coinsurance amounts will be $329 for the 61st through 90th day of hospitalization. When Medicare patients use their lifetime reserve days in 2017, their coinsurance will be $658 per day. When Medicare patients are patients in skilled nursing facilities in 2017, their coinsurance will be $164.50 for the 21st through 100th day of skilled nursing facility care (see ¶ 220, ¶ 242).

Medicare Part B (supplementary medical insurance). Most people with Medicare Part B will be "held harmless" from any increase in premiums in 2017 and will pay about $109. The Part B premium for beneficiaries not subject to the "hold harmless" provision, i.e., those not collecting Social Security benefits, those who will enroll in Part B for the first time in 2017, dual-eligible beneficiaries who have their premiums paid by Medicaid, and beneficiaries who pay an additional income-related premium, will be $134.

Income-adjusted premiums for 2017 are as follows: Individuals with modified adjusted gross income (MAGI) greater than $85,000 but less than or equal to $107,000 and couples with MAGI greater than $170,000 but less than or equal to $214,000 will pay a monthly premium of $187.50. Individuals with MAGI greater than $107,000 but less than or equal to $160,000 and couples with MAGI greater than $214,000 and less than or equal to $320,000 will pay a monthly premium of $267.90. Individuals with MAGI greater than $160,000 but less than or equal to $214,000 and couples with MAGI greater than $320,000 and less than or equal to $428,000 will pay a monthly premium of $348.30. Individuals with MAGI greater than $214,000 and couples with MAGI greater than $428,000 will pay a monthly premium of $398.80. The rates are modified slightly for beneficiaries who are married and lived with their spouse at any time during the taxable year but file a separate tax return from their spouse (see ¶ 320).

For 2017, the Part B deductible will be $183 (see ¶ 335).

Beginning January 1, 2017, Part B covers renal dialysis services furnished by a renal dialysis facility or provider of services to an individual with acute kidney injury, defined as an individual who has acute loss of renal function and does not receive renal dialysis services for which payment is made under the end-stage renal disease (ESRD) prospective payment system (see ¶ 389).

The 21st Century Cures Act (P.L. 114-255) provides separate coverage of home infusion therapy effective January 1, 2021, which includes the following services furnished in a beneficiary's home: (1) professional services, including nursing services, furnished in accordance with the plan of care; and (2) training and education (not otherwise paid for as durable medical equipment), remote monitoring, and monitoring services for the provision of home infusion therapy and home infusion drugs furnished by a qualified home infusion therapy supplier. Home infusion therapy will be specifically excluded from the definition of home health services (see ¶ 390).

Physician reimbursement. The physician fee schedule payment amount for a service is determined by a formula that takes into consideration the relative value unit for the service, the conversion factor for the year, and the geographic adjustment factor for the service. The Medicare Access and CHIP Reauthorization Act of 2015 (MACRA) (P.L. 114-10) changed how the conversion factor is updated. Under MACRA, starting in 2019, the amounts paid to individual providers will be subject to adjustment through one of two mechanisms, depending on whether the physician chooses to participate in an Advanced Alternative Payment Model (APM) program or the Merit-Based Incentive Payment System (MIPS) program (see ¶ 855).

Medicare Part C (managed care plans). The 21st Century Cures Act also made several significant changes to the Part C program. Beginning in 2021, individuals with ESRD will be permitted to enroll in MA plans. Starting in 2019, there will be an open enrollment period during the first three months of the year for Medicare Advantage (MA)-eligible individuals, during which an individual who is enrolled in an MA plan will be permitted to change his or her election at any time (see ¶ 401). Beginning January 1, 2021, organ acquisitions for kidney transplants will no longer be covered under Part C and instead will be covered by Parts A and B (see ¶ 402).

Medicare Part D (prescription drug plans). The Comprehensive Addiction and Recovery Act of 2016 (P.L. 114-198) provides, effective for plan years beginning after January 1, 2019, for two programs intended to prevent drug abuse under Part D: (1) a drug management programs for at-risk beneficiaries; and (2) utilization management tools to prevent drug abuse (see ¶ 525).

For 2017, beneficiaries in standard prescription drug plans (PDPs) will be subject to a $400 deductible. In 2017, beneficiaries in the coverage gap will continue to receive a 50 percent discount on brand-name drugs. PDPs also must pay another 5 percent, providing Part D beneficiaries with total coverage of 55 percent in the donut hole (see ¶ 507).

For 2017, the national average monthly bid amount for a PDP will be $61.08, down from $64.66 in 2016. The 2017 base beneficiary premium is $35.63, up from $34.10 in 2016. High-income beneficiaries are subject to income-adjusted premiums for Part D, just as they are for Part B. For 2017, the income-related monthly adjustment amount for a PDP premium will be $13.30 for an individual with MAGI greater that $85,000, but not more than $107,000; $34.20 for an individual with MAGI greater than $107,000, but not more than $160,000; $55.20 for an individual with MAGI greater than $160,000, but not more than $214,000; and $76.20 for an individual with MAGI greater than $214,000. In the case of a joint tax return, the MAGI dollar amounts are doubled (see ¶ 505).

Quality of care. CMS will continue to implement a number of quality of care initiatives in 2017, many of which will affect provider and facility reimbursement.

MACRA consolidates and replaces the electronic health record meaningful use program, Physician Quality Reporting System, and the value-based payment modifier into the MIPS program. MACRA will sunset the three programs at the end of 2018 (see ¶ 855).

Inpatient hospitals that do not submit required quality data on specific quality indicators to the Medicare program each year will have their applicable hospital market basket percentage increase reduced by 2 percent. Similarly, Medicare payments to hospitals can be reduced under the Hospital Readmissions Reduction Program and the Hospital-Acquired

Condition Reduction Program, and hospitals can earn incentives under the Hospital Inpatient Value-Based Purchasing Program (see ¶ 810).

Outpatient hospitals that fail to report on quality measures in 2017 will have their payments reduced by 2.0 percent in calendar year 2019. To ensure that hospitals are accurately reporting quality of care measures for chart-abstracted data, CMS may validate one or more measures by reviewing documentation of patient encounters submitted by selected participating hospitals. CMS requires outpatient hospitals to achieve a minimum 75 percent validation score based on this validation process to receive the full update (see ¶ 820).

Other Wolters Kluwer publications:

Further details on the topics covered in this book, together with the texts of pertinent laws, regulations, policy guidelines, court decisions, etc., may be found in Wolters Kluwer's MEDICARE AND MEDICAID GUIDE. The GUIDE is available as a six-volume, loose-leaf print product as well as electronically on the Internet. Other electronic databases, including the full text of the CMS program manuals and the codes and complete descriptions contained in the physician fee schedule, are offered as part of Wolters Kluwer's electronic Health Law Library. Wolters Kluwer also has an easy-to-read electronic reporter specializing in Part B issues entitled the PHYSICIANS' MEDICARE GUIDE. Wolters Kluwer also offers, in print and electronic form, a comprehensive guide to the landmark health care reform legislation passed in 2010, entitled LAW, EXPLANATION AND ANALYSIS OF THE PATIENT PROTECTION AND AFFORDABLE CARE ACT (2014 UPDATE), VOLUMES 1 AND 2.

Finally, Wolters Kluwer publishes the following related paperback books:

2017 Master Medicare Guide

2017 Social Security Benefits (Including Medicare)

2017 Social Security Explained

To find out more about these publications, call 1-888-224-7377 or visit www.WKLawBusiness.com.

A note about the citations in the text:

Throughout the text, statements are documented, when possible, by citations to the law, regulations, and program manuals issued by the federal government. In the interests of simplicity and conservation of space, citations generally have been made only to the highest authority available for the statement in the text, although, when appropriate, multiple citations (i.e., citations both to a law provision and its implementing regulation) are included. In some instances, when there is no clear ranking of authorities, only the most widely available source is cited.

January 2017

Table of Contents

Detailed Table of Contents

Chapter 1—Introduction

Chapter 2—Medicare Part A—Hospital Insurance

Eligibility and Enrollment

Inpatient Hospital Services

Nursing Home Services

Home Health Services

Chapter 3—Medicare Part B—Supplemental Insurance

Eligibility and Enrollment

Benefits

Chapter 1- INTRODUCTION

[¶ 100] Introduction to Medicare

As part of the Social Security Amendments of 1965, Congress established two new programs to cover the cost of medical care for the elderly and disabled. The first of these programs, largely financed through the hospital insurance taxes, provides basic protection against the costs of inpatient hospital and other institutional provider care. Officially, this program is called "Hospital Insurance Benefits for the Aged and Disabled," although it includes much more than hospital benefits. Unofficially it is sometimes called "basic Medicare," "hospital insurance," or "Medicare Part A" (because the authorization for the program is Part A of Title XVIII of the Social Security Act).

The second of these programs is a voluntary program covering the costs of physician and other health care practitioner services and items and supplies not covered under the basic program. It is financed through monthly premiums from enrollees and contributions from the federal government. Officially, this program is called "Supplementary Medical Insurance Benefits for the Aged and Disabled," but unofficially it is called "supplementary Medicare," the "medical insurance program," or "Medicare Part B."

A third Medicare program that expands managed care options for beneficiaries who are entitled to Part A and enrolled in Part B was created under the Balanced Budget Act of 1997 (BBA) (P.L. 105-33) and expanded under the Medicare Modernization Act of 2003 (MMA) (P.L. 108-173); it is now commonly referred to as "Medicare Part C" or "Medicare Advantage." Since January 1, 1999, beneficiaries have had the option of choosing to receive their health benefits through the traditional Medicare "fee-for-service" program or through a managed care plan certified under the Medicare Advantage program. Payments Medicare makes to a Medicare Advantage plan replace the amounts Medicare otherwise would have paid under Parts A and B.

The Medicare program was also expanded by the MMA to include a prescription drug benefit, under Part D of Title XVIII of the Social Security Act. The prescription drug benefit became available to eligible individuals on January 1, 2006, and is called Medicare Part D.

Together, the four programs are known officially as "Health Insurance for the Aged and Disabled," the name of Title XVIII of the Social Security Act, which contains the basic law governing the Medicare program.

Contents of this Book

Medicare Part A, the hospital insurance program, is discussed in Chapter 2, and Medicare Part B, supplementary medical insurance, is discussed in Chapter 3. Medicare Part C, the Medicare Advantage program, is discussed in Chapter 4, and Medicare Part D, the prescription drug benefit, is discussed in Chapter 5. Certain items that are specifically excluded from coverage by Medicare are discussed in Chapter 6. Miscellaneous administrative features of the Medicare program are discussed in Chapter 7, including quality improvement organizations, recovery audit contractors, electronic health data privacy, "Medigap" insurance, and initiatives used to curb health care fraud and abuse. Payment to providers, physicians, and suppliers by Medicare is discussed in Chapter 8. Claims filing procedures and appeals of adverse determinations are discussed in Chapter 9.

Rules concerning eligibility and applications for Medicare are discussed at the beginning of Chapter 2 in the case of Part A, and at the beginning of Chapter 3 in the case of Part B. Election and enrollment in Medicare Part C are discussed in Chapter 4 (¶ 401). Eligibility and enrollment in Medicare Part D are discussed in Chapter 5 (¶ 503).

Chapter 2– MEDICARE PART A—HOSPITAL INSURANCE

Eligibility and Enrollment

[¶ 200] Entitlement to Part A Hospital Insurance Benefits

Most individuals automatically become entitled to hospital insurance benefits under Part A of the Medicare program when they reach age 65 if they are eligible for monthly Social Security retirement or survivor benefits or railroad retirement benefits as "qualified railroad retirement beneficiaries." [Soc. Sec. Act § 226; 42 C.F.R. § § 406.5, 406.10.]

Entitlement to Medicare for these individuals begins in the month in which they become 65 years old, regardless of whether they have elected to receive Social Security (or other) retirement benefits. [42 C.F.R. § 406.10(b)(1).] Individuals electing to receive Social Security benefits earlier than age 65 do not need not file an application for Medicare when they become 65; they will automatically receive an application. Individuals electing not to receive Social Security, however, need to file an application for Medicare (see below under "Part A Application Requirements"). [42 C.F.R. § 406.6.]

Individuals under age 65 also are entitled to benefits under Part A if they are entitled to: (1) Social Security or railroad retirement disability benefits for at least the previous 24 months (see ¶ 204); or (2) end-stage renal disease (ESRD) benefits (see ¶ 205). [Soc. Sec. Act § § 226(a), 226A(a); 42 C.F.R. § § 406.5(a), 406.12, 406.13.]

Individuals age 65 or over who are not entitled to Part A benefits on one of the bases outlined above can enroll voluntarily in the Part A program by paying a monthly premium (see ¶ 203). [Soc. Sec. Act § 1818(a); 42 C.F.R. § § 406.5(b), 406.20(b).]

Individuals entitled to benefits under Part A (except persons with ESRD) and enrolled in the supplementary medical insurance program (Medicare Part B—see ¶ 300–¶ 320) may choose to receive benefits under the traditional fee-for-service programs, or they may choose to enroll in a Medicare Advantage managed care plan, which offers additional benefits. [Soc. Sec. Act § 1851(a)(3).] The Medicare Advantage program, also called Medicare Part C, is discussed in detail in ¶ 400–¶ 412.

In addition, individuals entitled to benefits under Part A (except persons with ESRD) and enrolled in Part B may choose to enroll in Part D, which provides coverage for prescription drugs (see ¶ 500–¶ 535). [Soc. Sec. Act § 1860D-1 *et seq.*]

Coverage Period for Part A

Medicare entitlement usually begins on the first day of the month when an individual reaches age 65. Therefore, an individual whose 65th birthday is on January 6, 2017, is eligible for benefits on January 1, 2017. [Soc. Sec. Act § 226(c)(1); 42 C.F.R. § 406.10(b)(1).]

The Social Security and Medicare programs follow the rule that a person reaches a given age on the day before the anniversary of birth. A person born on April 1, 1952, for example, is considered to have reached age 65 on March 31, 2017, and Medicare hospital benefits begin March 1, 2017. [*Medicare General Information, Eligibility, and Entitlement Manual*, Pub. 100-01, Ch. 2, § 10.2.]

A Social Security applicant who applies for monthly benefits after reaching age 65 can be entitled to Part A benefits retroactively beginning with the first day of the first month in which all the requirements for benefits otherwise are met, but not more than six months (12

¶200

months for disabled widow's or widower's benefits) before the month in which the application is filed. [42 C.F.R. § 406.6(d)(2), (4).]

Suspended Part A Benefits of Aliens

An individual whose cash Social Security benefits have been suspended under section 202(t)(1) of the Social Security Act (relating to suspension of the benefits of certain aliens who are outside the United States for more than six months) is not entitled to Part A benefits furnished in any month for which such a suspension is applicable. [Soc. Sec. Act § 202(t)(9); 42 C.F.R § 406.50.]

Conviction of Subversive Activities

If a person is convicted of espionage, sabotage, treason, sedition, subversive action, or conspiracy to establish a dictatorship, his or her income (or the income of the insured individual on whose earnings record he or she became or seeks to become entitled) for the year of conviction and any previous year may not be counted in determining the insured status necessary for entitlement to hospital insurance. [Soc. Sec. Act § 202(u); 42 C.F.R § 406.52.]

Part A Application Requirements

A person age 65 or over who has filed an application and established entitlement to monthly Social Security benefits or who is a qualified railroad retirement beneficiary ordinarily does not need to file any additional application for Part A. It comes automatically with these other benefits. [42 C.F.R. § 406.6(a).]

However, an application for Medicare benefits is required for those who have not applied for Social Security benefits. An application also is required for an individual who seeks entitlement on the basis of: (1) ESRD (¶ 205); (2) "Medicare-qualified government employment" (¶ 206); (3) deemed entitlement to disabled widow's or widower's benefits under certain circumstances; or (4) voluntary Part A enrollment (¶ 203). [42 C.F.R. § 406.6(c), (e).]

Form CMS-18-F-5, "Application for Hospital Insurance Entitlement," is the most commonly used to apply for Part A entitlement, and may also be used for enrollment in the Part B program (¶ 310). ESRD applicants use Form CMS-43, "Application for Health Insurance Benefits Under Medicare for Individuals with End-Stage Renal Disease." [42 C.F.R. § 406.7.]

Except in the case of individuals seeking entitlement on the basis of ESRD, an application for Part A must be filed by an individual before death—a relative or legal representative may not file for retroactive entitlement after the individual has died. [42 C.F.R. §§ 406.10(b)(2), 406.13(d)(3).]

Filing claims for Medicare benefits by Medicare beneficiaries is discussed at ¶ 900 *et seq.*

Health Insurance Card

As evidence of entitlement to Medicare benefits, CMS issues each beneficiary a "Health Insurance Card" (in the case of railroad retirement beneficiaries, the Railroad Retirement Board issues the health insurance card). This card includes the name of the beneficiary, the Health Insurance Claim number, sex of the beneficiary, and the effective date of entitlement. When receiving covered services, the cardholder should show the card to the health care provider. [Pub. 100-01, Ch. 2, § 50.]

Social Security numbers. By April 16, 2019, the HHS Secretary is required to ensure that Social Security numbers (or any derivative thereof) are not displayed, coded, or embedded on Medicare cards issued to an individual who is entitled to Part A benefits or enrolled under Part B. HHS must also ensure that any other identifier displayed on the card is not identifiable as a Social Security account number or derivative thereof. [Soc. Sec. Act 205(c)(2)(C)(xiii); Medicare Access and CHIP Reauthorization Act of 2015 (MACRA) (P.L. 114-10) § 501(d).]

[¶ 203] Voluntary Enrollment in the Hospital Insurance Program

Hospital insurance (Part A) coverage is available on a voluntary basis, for a premium, to individuals 65 or over who are not entitled to Social Security or other Medicare-qualifying benefits (see ¶ 200). This is called premium hospital insurance.

Eligibility. An individual is eligible to enroll voluntarily in Part A if he or she:

> (1) has attained age 65;
>
> (2) is enrolled in Medicare Part B;
>
> (3) is a resident of the United States and is either:
>
> > a. a citizen of the United States; or
> >
> > b. an alien lawfully admitted for permanent residence who has continuously resided in the United States for the five years immediately before the month in which application for enrollment is made; and
>
> (4) is not otherwise entitled to Part A benefits.

[Soc. Sec. Act § 1818(a); 42 C.F.R. § § 406.5(b), 406.20.]

For purposes of determining U.S. residency, the term "United States" includes the District of Columbia, Commonwealth of Puerto Rico, the Virgin Islands, Guam, American Samoa, and the Northern Mariana Islands. [Soc. Sec. Act § § 210(i), 1861(x); Northern Mariana Islands Covenant Implementation Act (P.L. 94-241).]

Enrollment. An individual may accomplish voluntary enrollment in Part A only during an "enrollment period." [Soc. Sec. Act § 1818(b).] For individuals 65 years of age or older, the initial enrollment period extends for three months before and three months after the first month the individual would be eligible for Part A. Following this initial enrollment period, an individual is able to enroll for Part A benefits from January 1 to March 31 of each subsequent year. If the individual enrolls during one of the annual enrollment periods following his or her initial enrollment, the benefits are effective on July 1 of that year. [42 C.F.R. § 406.21.] Note that these enrollment periods do not apply to the majority of individuals who are automatically enrolled upon reaching the age 65 and enrolling for Social Security benefits.

In general, the provisions governing enrollment (see ¶ 310–¶ 312), coverage periods (see ¶ 313), and premiums (see ¶ 320) under Part B—excluding premium increases for late enrollment (see below)—also are applicable to voluntary enrollment in Part A. [Soc. Sec. Act § 1818(c).]

An individual meeting the conditions for voluntary enrollment and paying the appropriate premium may elect coverage under a Medicare Advantage managed care plan under Part C (see ¶ 401). [Soc. Sec. Act § 1851(a)(3).]

Payment of Premiums for Voluntary Enrollees

Voluntary enrollees must pay a monthly premium based on the total cost of Part A protection for the enrolled group. The premium is updated annually according to a formula established by law. [Soc. Sec. Act § 1818(d)(2).] For 2017, the monthly Part A premium is $413. [*Notice*, 81 FR 80071, Nov. 15, 2016.]

The following table shows the monthly premium rates in effect during the past few years:

Year	$ Amount
2017	413
2016	411
2015	407
2014	426

There is a 45 percent Part A premium reduction available to certain individuals with 30 or more quarters of Social Security coverage. One who has had at least 30 months of such coverage—or who was married to, widowed from, or divorced from such an individual for certain periods of time—is entitled to the reduction. [Soc. Sec. Act § 1818(d)(4)(A).] The reduced premium for eligible individuals in 2017 is $227, an increase of $1 over 2016. [*Notice*, 81 FR 80071, Nov. 15, 2016; *Notice*, 80 FR 70805, Nov. 16, 2015.]

The Part A premium is zero for certain public retirees. [Soc. Sec. Act § 1818(d)(5).] Government employees are discussed in detail at ¶ 206.

Part A Late Enrollment and Reenrollment Penalties

There is a 10 percent late enrollment penalty for individuals who enroll voluntarily in Part A 12 months or more after the expiration of the initial enrollment period. The penalty is based on the date when an individual first meets the eligibility requirements for enrollment and continues for twice the number of years (i.e., full 12-month periods) that the enrollment was delayed. [Soc. Sec. Act § 1818(c)(6); 42 C.F.R. § § 406.32(d), 406.33.]

If an individual drops out of the program and then reenrolls, the months during which the individual was out of the program are counted in determining the re-enrollment penalty. [42 C.F.R. § 406.34.]

Example • • • _____

Agnes Williams was eligible to enroll during an initial enrollment period that ended May 31, 2014. She waited, and enrolled in the 2017 general enrollment period (January 1, 2017—March 31, 2017). Thirty-four months elapsed after the close of her initial enrollment period and before March 31, 2017, the close of the period in which she actually enrolled. (Delinquent enrollment is counted from the end of the initial enrollment period to the end of the enrollment period in which the individual actually enrolls—see ¶ 320.) There were, therefore, two 12-month periods during which she could have been, but was not, enrolled. She is assessed a 10 percent premium penalty, and that penalty expires after she has paid it for 48 months.

_____

State and local government retirees who retired before January 1, 2002, can be exempt from the Part A delayed enrollment penalties. Their exemption depends on the total amount of payroll taxes they or their employers paid. [Soc. Sec. Act § 1818(d)(6).]

Group Premium Payments

A state or any other public or private organization can pay monthly premiums on a group basis for its retired or active employees age 65 and over. For group coverage, the agency or organization may make premium payments under a contract or other arrangements. The Secretary may refuse to enter into a group premium payment contract if such a method of payment is not administratively feasible. [Soc. Sec. Act § 1818(e).]

¶203

Termination of Entitlement to Voluntary Part A Benefits

An individual's entitlement to the voluntary Part A program terminates if he or she: (1) files a request for termination; (2) becomes entitled to regular Part A benefits in one of the ways described at ¶ 200; (3) is no longer entitled to Part B; (4) fails to pay voluntary Part A premiums; or (5) dies. [Soc. Sec. Act § 1818(c)(4), (5); 42 C.F.R. § 406.28.]

If the voluntary enrollee stops paying the premium, entitlement will end on the last day of the third month after the billing month. CMS will reinstate entitlement, however, if the individual can show good cause for failing to pay the premiums on time, as long as all overdue premiums are paid within three calendar months after the date entitlement would have been terminated. [42 C.F.R. § 406.28(d).]

[¶ 204] Disability Beneficiaries

An individual under age 65 is entitled to hospital insurance benefits if, for 24 months, he or she has been: (1) entitled or deemed entitled to Social Security disability benefits as an insured individual, child, widow, or widower who is "under a disability;" or (2) a disabled qualified beneficiary certified under section 7(d) of the Railroad Retirement Act. [Soc. Sec. Act § 226(b); 42 C.F.R. § 406.12(a).]

"Medicare-qualified government employment" (see ¶ 206) is treated as Social Security qualifying employment for the purpose of the provision of Medicare disability benefits. [Soc. Sec. Act § 226(a)(2)(C).]

Exhaustion of entitlement. Disabled beneficiaries who are not yet 65 and continue to be disabled, and who no longer are entitled to benefits solely because their earnings are in excess of the amount permitted, may purchase Part A coverage. Enrollment can occur during special enrollment periods, as provided by law. Premiums are similar to the premiums required for voluntary enrollees (see ¶ 203). [Soc. Sec. Act § 1818A.]

Social Security retirees. Upon reaching the age of 65, beneficiaries who are disabled can become eligible for Medicare as Social Security retirees if they satisfy the requirements for that status (see ¶ 200).

Waiting Period

Disabled individuals may not receive Part A benefits until they have satisfied a 24-month "waiting period" during which they have continuously been disabled. An exception to this rule applies for individuals with amyotrophic lateral sclerosis (ALS), who have no waiting period. [Soc. Sec. Act § 226(b), (h).]

Months of a previous period of entitlement or deemed entitlement to disability benefits count toward the 24-month requirement if any of the following conditions is met:

(1) entitlement was an insured individual or a disabled qualified railroad retirement beneficiary, and the previous period ended within the 60 months preceding the month in which the current disability began;

(2) entitlement was as a disabled child, widow, or widower, and the previous period ended within the 84 months preceding the month in which the current disability began; or

(3) the previous period ended on or after March 1, 1988, and the current impairment is the same as, or directly related to, the impairment on which the previous period of entitlement was based.

[Soc. Sec. Act § 226(f); 42 C.F.R. § 406.12(b).]

Termination of Coverage

Generally, entitlement to Part A ends with the earliest of the following:

• the last day of the last month in which the beneficiary was entitled or deemed entitled to disability benefits or was qualified as a disabled railroad retirement beneficiary, if he or she was notified of the termination of entitlement before that month;

• the last day of the month following the month in which he or she is mailed a notice that his or her entitlement or deemed entitlement to disability benefits, or his or her status as a qualified disabled railroad retirement beneficiary, has ended;

• the last day of the month before the month he or she attains age 65; or

• the day of death.

[Soc. Sec. Act § 226(b); 42 C.F.R. § 406.12(d)(2).]

Returning to work. If an individual's entitlement to disability benefits or status as a qualified disabled railroad retirement beneficiary ends because he or she engaged in, or demonstrated the ability to engage in, substantial gainful activity after the 36 months following the nine-month trial work period provided for by Soc. Sec. Act § 222(c)(4), Medicare entitlement continues until the earlier of the following:

(1) the last day of the 78th month following the first month of substantial gainful activity occurring after the 15th month of the individual's reentitlement period or, if later, the end of the month following the month the individual's disability benefit entitlement ends; or

(2) the last day of the month following the month in which notice is mailed to the individual indicating that he or she is no longer entitled to hospital insurance because of an event or circumstance (for example, there has been medical improvement, or the disabled widow has remarried) that would terminate disability benefit entitlement if it had not already been terminated because of substantial gainful activity.

[Soc. Sec. Act § 226(b); 42 C.F.R. § 406.12(e).]

Employer Group Health Plan Coverage

Medicare is the secondary payer for disability beneficiaries who are covered by a large group health plan (an employer with 100 or more employees) as a current employee (or as a family member of a current employee). Thus, when an employee (or a member of the employee's family) becomes disabled, the large employer's group health plan has primary coverage responsibility and Medicare has secondary coverage responsibility. The law provides that either the federal government or the individual has a cause of action against a plan that does not meet its coverage responsibilities and that double damages may be recovered. [Soc. Sec. Act § 1862(b)(1)(B), (b)(2)(B)(iii).]

Employer group health plans are discussed in more detail at ¶ 636.

[¶ 205] End-Stage Renal Disease Beneficiaries

Medicare covers individuals who have not reached age 65 and are suffering from end-stage renal (kidney) disease (ESRD) if they are: (1) fully or currently insured for Social Security or railroad retirement benefits (see ¶ 200); (2) entitled either to monthly Social Security or railroad retirement benefits; or (3) spouses or dependent children of eligible individuals. ESRD benefits are available only after an application for Medicare benefits is filed, and the application may be filed after the individual's death. [Soc. Sec. Act § 226A(a); 42 C.F.R. §§ 406.6(c), 406.13(c) and (d).]

"End-stage renal disease" is defined as "that stage of kidney impairment that appears irreversible and permanent and requires a regular course of dialysis or kidney transplantation to maintain life." [42 C.F.R. § 406.13(b).] Payment for ESRD benefits is discussed at ¶ 845.

Waiting period. Coverage for dialysis patients normally begins the third month after the month in which a course of renal dialysis is initiated. However, entitlement begins on the first day of the month in which a regular course of renal dialysis began if, before the end of the waiting period, the beneficiary participates in a self-dialysis training program offered by a participating Medicare facility. For kidney transplant candidates, coverage can begin as early as the month in which the candidate is hospitalized for transplantation, provided the surgery takes place in that month or in the following two months. [Soc. Sec. Act § 226A(b), (c); 42 C.F.R. § 406.13(e).]

Termination of coverage. Coverage ends at the end of the 12th month after the month in which a course of dialysis ends, unless the individual receives a kidney transplant during that period or begins another regular course of dialysis. For a kidney transplant recipient, coverage ends with the end of the 36th month after the month in which the individual has received a kidney transplant, unless he or she receives another kidney transplant or begins a regular course of dialysis during that period. [Soc. Sec. Act § 226A(b)(2); 42 C.F.R. § 406.13(f).]

[¶ 206] Government Employees

An individual who has worked in Medicare-qualified government employment (or any related individual who would be entitled to Social Security cash benefits on the employee's record if Medicare-qualified government employment qualified for those benefits) is entitled to hospital insurance benefits if he or she: (1) would meet the requirements of 42 C.F.R. §§ 406.10 (see ¶ 200), 406.12 (see ¶ 204), or 406.13 (see ¶ 205) if Medicare-qualified government employment were Social Security covered employment; and (2) has filed an application for hospital insurance. [Soc. Sec. Act § 226(a)(2)(C); 42 C.F.R. § 406.15(e).]

"Medicare-qualified government employment" means federal, state, or local government employment that is subject only to the hospital insurance portion of the tax imposed by the Federal Insurance Contributions Act (FICA), including (1) wages paid for federal employment after December 1982; (2) wages paid to state and local government employees hired after March 31, 1986; and (3) wages paid to state and local government employees hired before April 1, 1986, but whose employment after March 31, 1986, is covered, for Medicare purposes only, under an agreement under Soc. Sec. Act § 218. [Soc. Sec. Act § 210(p); 42 C.F.R. § 406.15(a).]

Individuals entitled to Medicare by virtue of their Medicare-qualified government employment also are entitled to Medicare disability benefits (¶ 204) and end-stage renal disease benefits (¶ 205). [Soc. Sec. Act §§ 226(b)(2)(C), 226A(a)(1).]

Government Employment Not Considered "Medicare-Qualified"

Federal employees who are not considered "Medicare-qualified" include:

(1) inmates in federal penal institutions;

(2) certain interns (other than medical or dental interns or medical or dental residents in training) and student nurses employed by the federal government; and

(3) employees serving on a temporary basis in case of fire, storm, earthquake, flood, or other similar emergency.

[Soc. Sec. Act § 210(a)(6).]

State and local government employees who are not "Medicare-qualified" include:

(1) individuals employed to relieve them from unemployment;

(2) patients or inmates in a hospital, home, or other institution;

(3) employees serving on a temporary basis in case of fire, storm, snow, earthquake, flood, or other similar emergency;

(4) interns (other than medical or dental interns or medical or dental residents in training), student nurses, and other student employees of hospitals of the District of Columbia; and

(5) an election official or election worker if the remuneration paid for services performed in a calendar year is less than $1,000.

[Soc. Sec. Act § 210(p)(2).]

As noted above, state and local government employees hired before April 1, 1986, are exempt from the hospital portion of the FICA tax, so their employment is not considered to be "Medicare-qualified." A state, however, may ask the Commissioner of Social Security to enter into an agreement whereby these employees also would have their employment treated as "Medicare-qualified." In such cases, only employment occurring after March 31, 1986, is considered "Medicare-qualified." [Soc. Sec. Act § 218(n).]

Payment of Premiums

Government employees who have retired but are unable to qualify for Medicare benefits in the manner described above are entitled to enroll voluntarily in the Part A program and pay the appropriate premium (see ¶ 203). [42 C.F.R. § 406.11.]

Additionally, public retirees meeting certain statutory conditions are entitled to avoid the payment of the monthly premium. The methodology for determining whether a public retiree is exempt from Part A premium payment is similar to determining the reduced premium required of individuals having 30 or more quarters of Social Security coverage (see "Payment of Premiums for Voluntary Enrollees" at ¶ 203). Specifically, the premium is zero for any individual receiving cash benefits under a qualified state or local government retirement system on the basis of the individual's employment for at least 40 calendar quarters (or a combination of such quarters and Social Security-covered quarters totalling 40). As is the case with reduced premiums, individuals who have been married to, widowed from, or divorced from such an individual for certain periods of time also are entitled to a zero premium. [Soc. Sec. Act § 1818(d)(5)(B).]

To be covered under this provision, certain conditions must be met: (1) the individual's Part A premium may not be payable in whole or part by a state (including a state Medicaid program) or a political subdivision of a state; and (2) in the preceding 84 months, the individual was enrolled in Part A and did not have had the Part A premium paid in whole or part by any governmental entity described above. [Soc. Sec. Act § 1818(d)(5)(A).]

A "qualified state or local government retirement system" is defined as a system established or maintained by a state or political subdivision (or agency thereof) that covers positions of some or all employees of the governmental entity and that does not adjust cash benefits based on eligibility for the premium relief described above. [Soc. Sec. Act § 1818(d)(5)(C).]

Inpatient Hospital Services

[¶ 210] Inpatient Hospital Services: Coverage in General

Medicare Part A covers services provided to beneficiaries who are inpatients in qualified hospitals participating in the Medicare program for up to 90 days in any one "spell of illness." In addition, each beneficiary has a lifetime reserve of 60 days that can be used after the 90 days have been exhausted (see ¶ 224). [Soc. Sec. Act § 1812(a)(1).]

Ordinarily, for hospital services to be covered under Part A, the hospital that provides the services must be *participating* in Medicare (to "participate" a hospital must have signed a Medicare participation agreement—see ¶ 730). In emergency situations, however, Medicare will cover the services provided by a nonparticipating hospital (see ¶ 227). Part A will also pay for nonemergency inpatient services furnished in a hospital located outside the United States if the beneficiary resides in the United States and the foreign hospital is closer to, or more accessible from, the beneficiary's home than the nearest adequately equipped hospital in the United States (see ¶ 610). [*Medicare Benefit Policy Manual*, Pub. 100-02, Ch. 16, § 60.]

Covered Inpatient Hospital Services

Medicare covers the following services or supplies provided while the beneficiary is an inpatient in the hospital:

(1) bed and board;

(2) nursing services (other than the services of a private-duty nurse or attendant) and other related services that ordinarily are furnished by the hospital for the care and treatment of inpatients;

(3) use of hospital facilities;

(4) medical social services;

(5) drugs, biologics, supplies, appliances, and equipment for use in the hospital that ordinarily are furnished by the hospital for the care and treatment of inpatients;

(6) certain other diagnostic and therapeutic items and services that ordinarily are furnished to inpatients; and

(7) transportation services, including transport by ambulance.

[Soc. Sec. Act § 1861(b); 42 C.F.R. § 409.10.]

To be covered, these services must be provided directly by the hospital or under an arrangement made by the hospital with an outside contractor. Further, when payment can be made for an inpatient hospital stay under Part A, all Medicare-covered services furnished during that stay are paid under Part A.

Limitations and exclusions related to inpatient hospital services. Covered services do not include: (1) the services of physicians and certain other health care practitioners, which are covered under Part B (see ¶ 350); (2) services of private-duty nurses (see ¶ 217); and (3) pneumococcal, influenza, and hepatitis B vaccine and their administration, which are covered under Part B even when provided to an inpatient during a hospital stay covered under Part A. [Soc. Sec. Act § 1861(b)(4), (5); 42 C.F.R. § 409.10; Pub. 100-02, Ch. 1, §§ 1–60; *Medicare Claims Processing Manual*, Pub. 100-04, Ch. 18, § 10.1.]

General exclusions from Medicare coverage can be found in Chapter 6, explanations of deductible and coinsurance limitations are at ¶ 220, coverage of services in a hospital after exhaustion of Part A benefits is discussed at ¶ 361, and the lifetime limit on inpatient psychiatric hospital services is explained at ¶ 225.

"Inpatient" Defined

An "inpatient" is a person who has been admitted to a hospital for bed occupancy to receive inpatient hospital services. A person is considered an inpatient if formally admitted as a patient with the expectation of remaining at least overnight and occupying a bed, even if a hospital bed actually is not used overnight due to discharge or transfer. [Pub. 100-02, Ch. 1, § 10.]

When a patient with a known diagnosis enters a hospital for a specific minor surgical procedure that is expected to keep him or her in the hospital for only a few hours (fewer than 24) and this expectation is realized, the individual will be considered an outpatient regardless of the hour of admission, whether a bed is used, or the hospital stay extends past midnight. [Pub. 100-02, Ch. 1, § 10.]

Special rules apply when a patient needs only extended care services but actually is placed in a hospital bed, including a "swing bed" (see ¶ 229).

"Spell of Illness" Defined

The duration of inpatient hospital services and post-hospital services in a skilled nursing facility (SNF) is limited according to the beginning and ending of a "spell of illness"—also commonly called a "benefit period."

Beginning a "spell." A "spell of illness" is a period of consecutive days that begins with the first day (that is not included in a previous spell of illness) on which a patient is furnished inpatient hospital or SNF services by a "qualified" provider during a period in which the patient is entitled to Part A benefits. [Soc. Sec. Act § 1861(a)(1); 42 C.F.R. § 409.60(a).]

A "qualified" provider is a hospital (including a psychiatric hospital) or SNF that has been certified as satisfying the requirements of the definition of such an institution (see ¶ 229 and ¶ 249). A hospital that meets the requirements related to emergency services, which are outlined at ¶ 227, is a qualified hospital for purposes of beginning a spell of illness when it furnishes the patient covered inpatient emergency services. [*Medicare General Information, Eligibility, and Entitlement Manual*, Pub. 100-01, Ch. 3, § 10.4.1; Ch. 5, § 20.2.]

Admission to a qualified SNF will begin a spell of illness, even if payment for the services cannot be made because the prior hospitalization or transfer requirement has not been met (see ¶ 230).

Ending a "spell." The spell of illness ends with the close of a period of 60 consecutive days during which the patient was neither an inpatient of a hospital nor an inpatient of a SNF. The 60-consecutive-day period begins with the day on which the individual is discharged. [Soc. Sec. Act § 1861(a)(2); Pub. 100-01, Ch. 3, § 10.4.2.]

It is important to note that a stay in a nonparticipating hospital will result in continuing a spell of illness even if the services received are not covered. For example, a stay in a nonparticipating hospital is counted as a qualified stay for purposes of determining whether a spell of illness has ended, even if the nonparticipating hospital did not furnish covered emergency services. A stay in a SNF does not continue a spell of illness unless the stay meets Medicare skilled nursing care requirements. Thus, a beneficiary who is transferred from a hospital to a SNF, but receives only "custodial care" (see ¶ 244) at the SNF, would begin counting the 60-consecutive-day period on the day of discharge from the hospital. [42 C.F.R. § 409.60(b).]

An individual may be discharged from and readmitted to a hospital or SNF several times during a spell of illness and still be in the same spell if 60 days have not elapsed between discharge and readmission. The stay does not need to be for related physical or mental conditions. [Pub. 100-01, Ch. 3, § 10.4.3.2.]

Example • • • _____

(1) John White was entitled to Part A benefits and was hospitalized in a participating general hospital on June 1. He previously had not established a spell of illness. He remained in the hospital for 30 days and then was transferred to a SNF for 50 days, after which he was discharged to his home on August 18. John's spell of illness began on June 1 and ended on October 17, the end of the 60-day period beginning with the date of his last discharge.

(2) Assume the same set of facts as above, except that John was rehospitalized after 50 days in the SNF and remained in the hospital for another 60 days, after which he was discharged to his home on October 17. John's spell of illness still began on June 1, but it ended on December 16, the end of the 60-day period beginning with the date of his last discharge.

(3) Assume the same set of facts as in example (2), except that John was required to enter the hospital for a third time, *before* exhaustion of the 60-day period following his last hospital discharge. Assume further that he remained in the hospital until his death. No new spell of illness could begin regardless of how long John remained in the hospital during his terminal illness. The crossing from one calendar year to another does not end an ongoing spell of illness.

_____

Once a spell of illness has ended, the beneficiary's next admission to a qualified hospital or SNF will start a new spell of illness. [42 C.F.R. § 409.60.]

Note that when a beneficiary begins a new spell of illness as a hospital inpatient, a new inpatient hospital deductible (see ¶ 220) must be paid, even if it is within the same calendar year. [42 C.F.R. § 409.60.]

"Inpatient Day of Care" Defined

The number of days of care charged to a beneficiary for inpatient hospital services is always in units of full days. A day begins at midnight and ends 24 hours later. A part of a day, including the day of admission, counts as a full day, but the day of discharge or death, or a day on which a patient begins a leave of absence, is not counted as a day. If admission and discharge occur on the same day, the day is considered a day of admission and counts as one day. As noted, the day on which a patient begins a leave of absence is treated as a day of discharge and not counted (unless the patient returns to the hospital by midnight of the same day), each day during the leave is not counted as an inpatient day, and the day the patient returns to the hospital from the leave is treated as a day of admission and counted if the patient is present at midnight of that day. [Pub. 100-02, Ch. 3, § § 20.1, 20.1.2.]

Notice of Rights and Coverage

Hospitals must provide beneficiaries, including those enrolled in Medicare Advantage plans, the "Important Message from Medicare" (IM) notice within two days of admission, and the beneficiary or a representative must sign the notice. The IM explains a Medicare beneficiary's rights as a hospital patient, including appeal rights at discharge. Hospitals must deliver a copy of the signed notice within two days prior to discharge. Beneficiaries who request an appeal must be provided a more detailed notice. [42 C.F.R. § § 405.1205, 422.620.]

Advance Beneficiary Notices

If a hospital determines that items or services will no longer be covered by Medicare, the hospital must issue an Advance Beneficiary Notice (ABN). The ABN informs a Medicare beneficiary, before he or she receives specified items or services, that Medicare certainly or probably will not provide for items or services provided on that visit. The ABN provides the

¶210

beneficiary with the information necessary to decide whether to receive items or services that may require out-of-pocket payment or payment through other insurance. [42 C.F.R. § 411.408(f) (1); Pub. 100-04, Ch. 30, § § 10, 50.1.] ABNs are discussed at ¶ 900.

An ABN must: (1) be in writing, in the CMS-approved format and using approved notice language; (2) cite the particular service or services for which payment is likely to be denied; and (3) cite the notifier's reasons for believing Medicare payment will be denied. Providers, practitioners, or suppliers must issue an ABN as soon as they make an assessment that Medicare payment certainly or probably will not be made. [Pub. 100-04, Ch. 30, § § 40.3, 40.3.8.]

Discharge Planning

Hospitals must have in effect a discharge planning process that applies to all patients and is specified in writing. A registered nurse, social worker, or other appropriately qualified personnel must administer a discharge planning evaluation, which includes an assessment of post-hospital services the patient is likely to need, the availability of the services, and the likelihood of the patient's capacity for self-care and the possibility of returning to the patient's pre-hospitalization environment. The hospital must counsel the patient and family members for post-hospital care if needed. [42 C.F.R. § 482.43.]

In addition, the evaluation must be completed on a timely basis and be included in the patient's medical record. If the hospital finds that the patient does not need a discharge plan, the patient's physician may request one. The hospital must reassess the discharge plan if any factors may affect continuing care needs or if the discharge plan is found not to be appropriate. Finally, the discharge plan must include a list of home health agencies or SNFs that participate in Medicare and that serve the geographic area in which the patient resides. [42 C.F.R. § 482.43.]

Late Discharge

A stay beyond the checkout time for the comfort or convenience of the patient is not covered under the program, and the hospital's agreement to participate in the program does not preclude it from charging the patient. Medicare expects that a hospital will not impose late charges on a beneficiary unless it has given the beneficiary reasonable notice (for example, 24 hours) of impending discharge. When the patient's medical condition is the cause of the stay past the checkout time (for example, the patient needs further services, is bedridden and awaiting transportation to his or her home or a SNF, or dies in the hospital), the stay beyond the discharge hour is covered under the program and the hospital may not charge the patient. [Pub. 100-02, Ch. 3, § 20.1.1.]

[¶ 211] Accommodations

Part A generally will pay only for *semi-private* accommodations (rooms of two to four beds) or ward accommodations (five or more beds) in connection with inpatient hospital care or nursing care in a skilled nursing facility (see ¶ 232). [42 C.F.R. § 409.11(a); *Medicare Benefit Policy Manual*, Pub. 100-02, Ch. 1, § 10.1.1.]

Private Rooms

Medicare will make extra payment for a private room or other accommodations more expensive than semi-private only when such accommodations are medically necessary. Private rooms are considered medically necessary in the following circumstances:

(1) the patient's condition requires isolation for the patient's health or that of others;

(2) the facility has no semi-private or less expensive accommodations; or

(3) all such accommodations are occupied, *and* the patient needs hospitalization immediately—that is, inpatient treatment cannot be deferred until less expensive accommodations become available.

In the situations specified in (1) and (3), Medicare pays for a private room until the patient's condition no longer requires isolation or until semi-private or ward accommodations are available. [42 C.F.R. § 409.11(b)(1), (b)(2).]

The hospital may charge the beneficiary the difference between its customary charge for the private room and its most prevalent charge for a semi-private room if (1) none of the conditions described above is met; and (2) the private room was requested by the patient or a member of the family, who, at the time of the request, was informed what the hospital's charge would be. [42 C.F.R. § 409.11(b)(3).]

Payment also will be made for intensive care facilities when medically indicated.

Example • • •
_____

At the time Mary Green is admitted to the hospital, she requests a private room. It is not medically necessary that she be in a private room, and she is told by the hospital that she will be charged the difference between its "customary charge" (see below) for a private room ($2,000 per day) and the customary charge for a semi-private room at the hospital's "most prevalent rate" (see below) at the time of admission ($1,300 per day). The hospital may charge Mary $700 per day for the private room, and the rest of her bill for bed and board—less any required deductible or coinsurance amount—is covered by Part A.

_____

"Customary charges" are the current amounts that the institution uniformly charges patients for specific services and accommodations. The "most prevalent rate" for semi-private accommodations is the rate that applies to the greatest number of semi-private beds. [Pub. 100-02, Ch. 1, § 10.1.7.]

Deluxe Private Rooms

A beneficiary in need of a private room (either because isolation is needed for medical reasons or because immediate admission is needed when no other accommodations are available) may be assigned to any private room in the hospital. Part A does not pay for personal comfort items (see ¶ 616), nor does it pay for deluxe accommodations or services, such as a suite or a room that is substantially more spacious than required for treatment, specially equipped or decorated, or serviced for the comfort and convenience of persons willing to pay a differential. If a beneficiary (or the beneficiary's representative) requests deluxe accommodations, the hospital should advise that there will be a charge, not covered by Medicare, of a specified amount for each day the beneficiary occupies the deluxe accommodations. The maximum amount the beneficiary may be charged is the differential between the most prevalent private room rate at the time of admission and the customary charge for the room occupied. [Pub. 100-02, Ch. 1, § 10.1.4.]

The beneficiary may not be charged a differential in private room rates if that differential is based on factors other than personal comfort items. These factors might include, but are not limited to: differences between older and newer wings, proximity to a lounge, elevators or nursing stations, or a desirable view. [Pub. 100-02, Ch. 1, § 10.1.4.]

All-Private Room Hospitals

If the patient is admitted to a hospital that has only private rooms and no semi-private or ward accommodations, medical necessity will be deemed to exist for the accommodations furnished. Beneficiaries may not be subjected to an extra charge for a private room in an all-private room hospital. [Pub. 100-02, Ch. 1, § 10.1.5.]

[¶ 212] Drugs and Biologics

Drugs and biologics furnished to an inpatient are covered under Part A if they: (1) represent a cost to the institution in rendering services to the beneficiary; (2) are ordinarily furnished by the hospital for the care and treatment of inpatients; and (3) are furnished to an inpatient for use in the hospital. Medicare will, however, pay for a limited supply of drugs for use outside the hospital if it is medically necessary to facilitate the beneficiary's departure from the hospital and required until he or she can obtain a continuing supply. [Soc. Sec. Act. § 1861(b)(2); 42 C.F.R. § 409.13.]

For a drug or biologic furnished by a hospital to be a covered hospital service, it must be included or approved for inclusion in the latest official edition or revision of certain drug compendia (including the *United States Pharmacopeia - National Formulary*, the *United States Pharmacopeia-Drug Information*, or the *American Dental Association Guide to Dental Therapeutics*). This does not include any drugs or biologics unfavorably evaluated in the *American Dental Association Guide to Dental Therapeutics* or expressly approved by the pharmacy and drug therapeutics committee (or equivalent committee) of the medical staff of the hospital for use in the hospital. [*Medicare Benefit Policy Manual*, Pub. 100-02, Ch. 1, § 30.]

Combination drugs are covered if the combination itself or all of the active ingredients are listed or approved for listing in any of the compendia named. Similarly, any combination drugs approved by the pharmacy and therapeutics committee for use in the hospital are covered. [Pub. 100-02, Ch. 1, § 30.3.]

Coverage is not limited to drugs and biologics routinely stocked by the hospital. A drug or biologic not stocked by the hospital that the hospital obtains from an outside source, such as a community pharmacy, also is covered if the facility rather than the patient is responsible for making payment to the supplier. [Pub. 100-02, Ch. 1, § 30.4.]

An investigational drug is not considered to meet the "reasonable and necessary" test that applies to all services (see ¶ 601) because its efficacy has not yet been established. Even if approved by an appropriate hospital committee, an investigational drug or biologic cannot be reimbursed. [Pub. 100-02, Ch. 1, § 30.2.]

Part D. The Medicare prescription drug benefit (Medicare Part D) permits eligible individuals to choose from at least two prescription drug plans (PDPs) in their region, with a standard coverage plan or an alternative coverage plan with actuarial-equivalent benefits (see ¶ 510). See Chapter 5 for a complete description of the prescription drug coverage provided under Medicare Part D. Drugs and biologics covered under Medicare Part B are discussed at ¶ 362.

[¶ 213] Supplies, Appliances, and Equipment

Supplies, appliances, and equipment ordinarily furnished by the hospital for the beneficiary's care and treatment during an inpatient stay are covered inpatient hospital services. [Soc. Sec. Act. § 1861(b)(2).]

Under certain circumstances, supplies, appliances, and equipment used during the beneficiary's stay are covered even when the items leave the hospital with the patient at the time of discharge. Medicare pays for items to be used beyond the hospital stay if: (1) the item is one that the beneficiary must continue to use after he or she leaves the hospital (for example, heart valves or a heart pacemaker); or (2) the item is medically necessary to permit or facilitate the beneficiary's departure from the hospital and is required until he or she can obtain a continuing supply (for example, tracheostomy or draining tubes). [42 C.F.R. § 409.14; *Medicare Benefit Policy Manual*, Pub. 100-02, Ch. 1, § 40.]

Routine Personal Hygiene Items and Services

Hospital "admission packs," containing primarily toilet articles (such as soap, toothbrushes, toothpaste, and combs), are covered if routinely furnished by the hospital to all of its inpatients. If not routinely furnished, the packs are not covered and the hospital may charge the beneficiary. The beneficiary may not be charged, however, unless the beneficiary requests the pack with the knowledge of what is requested and what will be charged. [Pub. 100-02, Ch. 1, § 40.]

[¶ 214] Diagnostic and Therapeutic Items and Services

Medicare covers "other diagnostic or therapeutic items or services" that ordinarily are furnished to inpatients by the hospital. [Soc. Sec. Act § 1861(b)(3).] The services must be furnished by the hospital or by others under arrangements made by the hospital. Billing for the services must be through the hospital. Included in this benefit are a number of of diagnostic and therapeutic techniques, such as blood tests and x-rays. [42 C.F.R. § 409.16; *Medicare Benefit Policy Manual*, Pub. 100-02, Ch. 1, § § 50, 50.1.]

Many diagnostic and therapeutic items and services also are covered when furnished as outpatient hospital services (see ¶ 352).

Therapeutic Items

Therapeutic items are covered when ordinarily furnished by the hospital to its inpatients or when furnished to hospital inpatients by others under agreements made with the hospital. These items include, but are not limited to:

- surgical dressings, splints, casts, and other devices used for the reduction of fractures and dislocations;

- prosthetic devices (non-dental) that replace all or part of an internal body organ, including continuous tissue, or replace all or part of the function of a permanently inoperative or malfunctioning internal body organ; and

- leg, arm, back, and neck braces, trusses, and artificial legs, arms, and eyes.

Therapeutic items that leave the hospital with the patient upon discharge, such as splints or casts, are covered if they are not furnished for use only outside the hospital. Temporary or disposable items medically necessary to permit or facilitate the patient's departure from the hospital and required until the patient can obtain a continuing supply are covered. [Pub. 100-02, Ch. 1, § 50.1.]

Psychologists and Physical Therapists

When a psychologist, clinical psychologist, or physical therapist is a salaried member of the staff of a hospital, that person's diagnostic or therapeutic services to inpatients of the hospital are covered in the same manner as the services of other nonphysician hospital employees. [Pub. 100-02, Ch. 1, § 50.2.]

Rehabilitative Care

A patient may be eligible for Medicare inpatient hospital coverage solely on the basis of the need for rehabilitative services. For an inpatient rehabilitative facility (IRF) claim to be considered reasonable and necessary, there must be a reasonable expectation that the patient meets the following requirements at the time of admission:

- requires the active and ongoing therapeutic intervention of multiple therapy disciplines (including physical therapy, occupational therapy, speech-language pathology, or prosthetics/orthotics therapy), one of which must be physical or occupational therapy;

* generally requires and can reasonably be expected to actively participate in, and benefit from, an intensive therapy program;

* is sufficiently stable at the time of admission to actively participate in the intensive rehabilitation therapy program; and

* requires physician supervision by a rehabilitation physician.

[42 C.F.R. § 412.622(a)(3).]

A patient can be expected to benefit significantly from the intensive rehabilitation therapy program only if his or her condition and functional status are such that he or she can reasonably be expected to make measurable improvement as a result of the rehabilitation treatment and if such improvement can be expected to be made within a prescribed period of time. To meet this standard, however, the patient need not be expected to achieve complete independence in self-care or be expected to return to his or her prior level of functioning. [Pub. 100-02, Ch. 1, § 110.2.]

Documentation. The patient's medical record must include documentation of a pre-admission screening performed by qualified clinicians within the 48 hours immediately preceding the admission. The record should include a detailed and comprehensive review of the patient's condition and medical history; it serves as a basis for the initial determination of whether the patient meets the requirements of admission. A rehabilitation physician must document concurrence with the findings and results of the pre-admission screening. The record must also document that a rehabilitation physician performed a post-admission evaluation within 24 hours of admission. [42 C.F.R. § 412.622(a)(4); Pub. 100-02, Ch. 1, §§ 110.1.1, 110.1.2.]

The patient's medical record must contain an individualized overall plan of care that was developed by a rehabilitation physician with input from the interdisciplinary team within four days of the patient's admission to the IRF. It must also include documentation of weekly interdisciplinary team meetings led by a rehabilitation physician and attended by a registered nurse with training or experience in rehabilitation, a social worker or case manager, and a therapist from each therapy discipline. [42 C.F.R. § 412.622(a)(4), (5); Pub. 100-02, Ch. 1, § 110.1.3.]

Rehabilitation services are also discussed at ¶ 244.

Independent Clinical Laboratory Services

Part A also covers diagnostic services furnished to an inpatient by an independent clinical laboratory under arrangements with the hospital, provided the lab is certified under the Clinical Laboratory Improvement Amendments of 1988 (CLIA) (P.L. 100-578) to perform the services. An "independent laboratory" is independent of the attending or consulting physician's office and the hospital. [Pub. 100-02, Ch. 1, § 50.3.]

A "clinical laboratory" is where microbiological, serological, chemical, hematological, radiobioassay, cytological, immunohematological, or pathological examinations are performed on materials derived from the human body to provide information for the diagnosis, prevention, or treatment of a disease or assessment of a medical condition. [Pub. 100-02, Ch. 1, § 50.3.]

¶214

Alcoholism and Drug Abuse (Chemical Dependency) Treatments

Alcohol detoxification and rehabilitation services are covered by Medicare when furnished as inpatient hospital services under Part A and as physician services under Part B. [*Medicare National Coverage Determinations Manual*, Pub. 100-03, Ch. 1, § § 130.1, 130.2.]

Inpatient hospital stays for alcohol detoxification. Inpatient hospital stays for alcohol detoxification are covered during the more acute stages of alcoholism or alcohol withdrawal when medical complications occur or are highly probable. Detoxification can usually be accomplished within two to three days with an occasional need for up to five days where the patient's condition dictates. Following detoxification, a patient may be transferred to an inpatient rehabilitation unit or discharged to a residential treatment program or outpatient treatment setting. [Pub. 100-03, Ch. 1, § § 130.1, 130.2.]

Inpatient hospital stays for alcohol rehabilitation. Part A covers inpatient hospital stays for alcohol rehabilitation for treatment of chronic alcoholism. Because alcohol rehabilitation can be provided in a variety of settings, an inpatient hospital stay for alcohol rehabilitation is only covered when it is medically necessary that care be provided in an inpatient hospital setting, not in a less costly setting or on an outpatient basis. Further, because alcoholism is classifiable as a psychiatric condition, the beneficiary must be receiving "active treatment." Generally, 16 to 19 days of rehabilitation services are considered sufficient prior to continuing care on a basis other than an inpatient hospital setting. [Pub. 100-03, Ch. 1, § § 130.1, 130.2.]

Outpatient hospital coverage. Medicare covers both diagnostic and therapeutic services furnished to hospital outpatients for the treatment of alcoholism. The same rules that apply to outpatient hospital services in general (see ¶ 352) also apply here. All services must be reasonable and necessary for diagnosis or treatment of the patient's condition. In addition, alcoholism treatment services such as drug therapy, psychotherapy, and patient education that are provided incident to a physician's services in a freestanding clinic are covered under the same rules as clinic services (see ¶ 351). The psychiatric services limitation discussed at ¶ 387 also applies to these services. [Pub. 100-03, Ch. 1, § § 130.2, 130.5.]

Aversion therapy. Chemical aversion therapy for the treatment of alcoholism is a covered service. Electrical aversion therapy is not covered, however, because it has not been shown to be safe and effective. [Pub. 100-03, Ch. 1, § § 130.3, 130.4.]

Drug abuse. Treatment for drug abuse or other chemical dependency, when medically necessary, is covered by Medicare in all of the settings described above as long as the services provided are reasonable and necessary for the treatment of the patient's condition. [Pub. 100-03, Ch. 1, § § 130.5, 130.6, 130.7.]

Mental Health Benefits

Medicare covers inpatient psychiatric hospital benefits, subject to some important limitations (see ¶ 225). Partial hospitalization services, which are mental health services for outpatients, are covered under Part B when they would prevent the need for inpatient psychiatric care (see ¶ 387).

[¶ 215] Services of Interns, Residents-in-Training, and Teaching Physicians

Physician services for inpatients are generally covered under Part B and excluded under Part A (see ¶ 226). Medicare Part A covers the services of interns and residents-in-training who participate in teaching programs approved by the appropriate accrediting associations. If the intern or resident is not providing services as part of an approved teaching program, those services are covered under Part B (see further ¶ 340). [Soc. Sec. Act § 1861(b)(4), (6).]

The administrative and teaching services of teaching physicians are also covered under Part A. [42 C.F.R. §415.55.] The services of teaching physicians to individual patients are covered under Part B (see ¶ 340 and ¶ 855).

[¶ 217] Nursing and Related Services; Private-Duty Exclusion

Nursing and other related services are covered as inpatient hospital services if ordinarily furnished by the hospital for the care and treatment of inpatients. However, the services of a private-duty nurse or other private-duty attendant are expressly excluded. [Soc. Sec. Act § 1861(b)(2), (5); 42 C.F.R. § 409.12.]

Private-duty nurses or private-duty attendants are registered professional nurses, licensed practical nurses, or any other trained attendants whose services ordinarily are rendered to, and restricted to, a particular patient by arrangement between the patient and the private-duty nurse or attendant. Private-duty services are engaged or paid by an individual patient or by someone acting on the patient's behalf, including a hospital that initially incurs the cost and seeks reimbursement for noncovered services from the patient.. When the hospital acts on behalf of a patient, the services of the private-duty nurse or other attendant are not inpatient hospital services, regardless of the control the hospital may exercise over the private services. [*Medicare Benefit Policy Manual*, Pub. 100-02, Ch. 1, § 20.]

[¶ 218] Inpatient Services Connected with Dental Services

Although the law contains a general exclusion of services performed in connection with the care, treatment, filling, removal, or replacement of teeth or structures directly supporting teeth (see ¶ 634), Part A covers inpatient hospital services for dental procedures when the beneficiary, due to his or her underlying medical condition and clinical status or the severity of the dental procedure, requires hospitalization in connection with the provision of these services. [Soc. Sec. Act § 1862(a)(12).]

Therefore, if a beneficiary is hospitalized for a noncovered dental procedure but the hospitalization is required due to the severity of the procedure or to assure proper medical management, control, or treatment of a nondental impairment, the inpatient hospital services are covered. Similarly, when the beneficiary is hospitalized because of a non-dental impairment and the need for the noncovered dental procedure is determined after admission (for example, a beneficiary requires hospitalization because of diabetes and after admission a decision is made to extract teeth), the inpatient hospital services also are covered. [Soc. Sec. Act § 1862(a)(12).]

When Medicare covers the hospital services, then all ancillary services furnished by the hospital (such as x-rays, administration of anesthesia, use of the operating room) also are covered. [*Medicare Benefit Policy Manual*, Pub. 100-02, Ch. 1, § 70.]

When a beneficiary is hospitalized for a covered dental procedure and the dentist's services are covered under Part B (see ¶ 340), the inpatient hospital services furnished during the stay are covered under Part A. Both the professional services of the dentist and the inpatient hospital expenses are covered when, for example, the dentist reduces a jaw fracture of a beneficiary who is an inpatient of a participating hospital. [Pub. 100-02, Ch. 1, § 70.]

A qualified dentist may certify, for purposes of inpatient hospital coverage in connection with a dental procedure, that the beneficiary suffers from impairments of such severity as to require hospitalization (see ¶ 350).

[¶ 220] Inpatient Hospital Deductible and Coinsurance

Beneficiaries with hospital insurance coverage under Medicare Part A are entitled to coverage for up to 90 or more days of covered inpatient hospital services in each "spell of illness" (see ¶ 210). In addition, a beneficiary is entitled to a lifetime total of 60 days of inpatient hospital coverage after exhaustion of the 90 days of entitlement during a spell of illness—commonly called "lifetime reserve days." [Soc. Sec. Act § 1812(a)(1).] See ¶ 224 for a detailed discussion of lifetime reserve days.

The amount payable by Part A is reduced by the deductible and coinsurances described below.

Inpatient Hospital Deductible

For inpatient hospital services furnished in each "spell of illness" (defined at ¶ 210), the patient is responsible for an inpatient hospital deductible. The amount of the deductible is determined by the year in which the patient's spell of illness begins. In 2017, the deductible is $1,316 per spell of illness. There can be more than one spell of illness and, thus, more than one required deductible, in a calendar year. [*Notice*, 81 FR 80060, Nov. 15, 2016.]

The inpatient hospital deductible for each successive year is calculated by modifying the previous year's deductible by the same percentage used to determine Medicare payments to prospective payment system (PPS) hospitals. The amount calculated is rounded to the nearest multiple of $4 (an amount midway between two multiples is rounded up). Once the deductible is determined, the coinsurance amounts are adjusted accordingly. [Soc. Sec. Act § 1813(b)(1), (2).]

If the hospital stay spans two calendar years, the deductible in effect on the first day of the hospitalization is applicable. The coinsurance, however, is based on the coinsurance in effect for the year in which the cost-sharing days are incurred. [Soc. Sec. Act § 1813(b)(3).]

The deductible is satisfied only by charges for *covered* services. Expenses for covered services count toward the deductible on an incurred, rather than a paid, basis, and expenses incurred during one spell of illness cannot be applied toward the deductible in a later spell of illness. The inpatient hospital deductible is imposed only once during a "spell of illness," even though the beneficiary may have been hospitalized more than once during that spell of illness (see the examples at ¶ 210). Neither expenses incurred in meeting the blood deductible (see below) nor the monthly premiums paid by those voluntarily enrolled for hospital insurance coverage (see ¶ 203) count toward the inpatient hospital deductible. [Soc. Sec. Act § 1813(a)(2).]

A reduction in benefit days resulting from the application of the psychiatric hospital carryover restriction, on and immediately preceding the date of entitlement, does not affect the amount of the deductible for which the patient is responsible. [*Medicare General Information, Eligibility, and Entitlement Manual*, Pub. 100-01, Ch. 3, § 10.1.] For a discussion of the psychiatric hospital carryover restriction, see ¶ 225.

Inpatient Hospital Coinsurance

When a beneficiary receives inpatient hospital services for more than 60 days during a spell of illness, he or she is responsible for a coinsurance amount for each day after the 60th and through the 90th day on which these services are furnished. There also is a coinsurance amount for each day, after the 90th and through the 150th in any spell of illness, that is chargeable against the individual's 60-day lifetime reserve (see ¶ 224). [Soc. Sec. Act § 1813(a)(1).]

The coinsurance amount for the 61st through 90th days is equal to one-fourth of the inpatient hospital deductible, as annually adjusted ($329 in 2017), and one-half of such deductible for lifetime reserve days ($658 in 2017). [Soc. Sec. Act § 1813(a)(1); *Notice*, 81 FR 80060, Nov. 15, 2016.] When a patient's hospitalization spans two calendar years, the coinsurance in effect for the year in which the cost-sharing days are incurred applies. [Soc. Sec. Act § 1813(b)(3); 42 C.F.R. § 409.83(a).]

In the determination of the amount of the coinsurance met, the coinsurance charge for a day of inpatient hospital services may not exceed the charges imposed for that day with respect to the individual beneficiary. Customary charges are considered actual charges if they are greater than the charges imposed. [Soc. Sec. Act § 1813(a)(1).] In connection with the lifetime reserve days provision, however, when the actual charge is equal to or less than the coinsurance amount, the beneficiary is deemed to have elected not to use one of the lifetime reserve days. Thus, the day is treated as a noncovered day and no coinsurance amount is chargeable to the patient (see ¶ 224). [42 C.F.R. § 409.83(c)(2).]

Deductible for Whole Blood and Packed Red Blood Cells

In addition to the inpatient hospital deductible, there is another deductible, equal to the cost of the first three pints of whole blood (or packed red blood cells) received by a beneficiary in a calendar year. This blood deductible can be satisfied under either Part A or Part B (see ¶ 335), or a combination of the two. [Soc. Sec. Act § 1813(a)(2).]

"Whole blood" is human blood from which none of the liquid or cellular components have been removed. Components of whole blood such as plasma and gamma globulin are not subject to the blood deductible because they are covered as biologics (see ¶ 212). [Pub. 100-01, Ch. 3, § 20.5.3.]

The difference, if any, between the cost of the whole blood (or equivalent quantities of packed red blood cells) to the provider and the charge to the beneficiary will be deducted from the payments that otherwise would be made to the provider under Part A. Thus, a hospital cannot make a profit on the blood or packed red blood cells for which it charges a beneficiary, nor may it charge the patient for the cost of administering, storing, and processing the blood. [Soc. Sec. Act § 1866(a)(2)(C); Pub. 100-01, Ch. 3, § 20.5.]

Replacement. A hospital may not charge a patient for the first three pints of whole blood or equivalent quantities of packed red blood cells if he or she arranges for their replacement on a pint-for-pint basis. [Soc. Sec. Act § 1866(a)(2)(C); Pub. 100-01, Ch. 3, § 20.5.4.1.]

When a beneficiary elects to replace deductible pints or units, they are considered replaced if the beneficiary, another individual, or a group or organization acting on the beneficiary's behalf (e.g., a blood assurance plan) offers replacement pints or units, regardless of whether the provider actually accepts the offer. Thus, a provider may not charge a beneficiary merely because its policy is not to accept blood from a particular organization that has offered to replace blood on behalf of the beneficiary. However, a provider may charge a beneficiary for deductible blood if there is a reasonable basis for believing the replacement blood would endanger the health of either the donor or a recipient. [Pub. 100-01, Ch. 3, § § 20.5.4, 20.5.4.1.]

When a provider accepts blood donated in advance for or by a beneficiary in anticipation of need, such donations are considered as replacement for any deductible pints or units subsequently furnished to the beneficiary. [Pub. 100-01, Ch. 3, § 20.5.4.1.]

[¶ 224] Use of Lifetime Reserve Days

Beneficiaries who are covered under Part A are entitled to have payment made on their behalf for up to 150 days of inpatient hospital services during a single "spell of illness" (see ¶ 210). These 150 days of entitlement are calculated as follows: the first 60 days of coverage are fully paid, subject only to the initial deductible amount; the next 30 days of coverage are subject to a coinsurance amount; and the last 60 days of coverage are subject to a coinsurance amount double the coinsurance amount for days 61 through 90 (see ¶ 220 for the current amount of deductible and coinsurance). The last 60 days are "lifetime reserve" days, which may be used only once in an individual's lifetime. Therefore, if a beneficiary is hospitalized for 150 days during the first covered spell of illness, all lifetime reserve days will be expended. If a beneficiary is hospitalized for only 100 days during the first spell of illness, 50 lifetime reserve days would be left for use during a subsequent spell of illness that requires hospitalization for more than 90 days. Medicare will pay for lifetime reserve days used on the basis of the beneficiary's request for payment unless the individual elects in writing not to have the program pay for the additional days, thereby saving reserve days for a later time. [Soc. Sec. Act § 1812(a)(1), (b)(1); *Medicare Benefit Policy Manual*, Pub. 100-02, Ch. 5, § § 20, 30.1.]

These rules for lifetime reserve days may not apply in certain situations when a hospital is paid under the prospective payment system (see the discussion under "Period Covered by Election Not to Use Reserve Days" below).

There is an additional lifetime limitation of 190 days on inpatient psychiatric hospital services (see ¶ 225). [Soc. Sec. Act § 1812(b)(3).]

For coverage under Part B of inpatient "ancillary" services furnished after a beneficiary's days of entitlement under Part A are exhausted, see ¶ 361.

Election by Beneficiary Not to Use Reserve Days

The beneficiary (or someone acting on the beneficiary's behalf) may make an election not to use lifetime reserve days at the time of admission to a hospital or at any time thereafter, subject to the limitations on retroactive elections described below.

Election made prospectively. Ordinarily, an election *not* to use reserve days will apply prospectively. If the beneficiary files the election at the time of admission to a hospital, it may be made effective on the first day of hospitalization or on any day thereafter. If the election is filed later, it may be made effective on any day after the day it is filed. [42 C.F.R. § 409.65; Pub. 100-02, Ch. 5, § § 30.2, 30.3.]

Retroactive election. A beneficiary, while still in the hospital or within 90 days following discharge, may elect retroactively not to use reserve days, provided: (1) the beneficiary (or some other source) offers to pay the hospital for any of the services not payable under Part B; or (2) the hospital agrees to accept the retroactive election. [42 C.F.R. § 409.65; Pub. 100-02, Ch. 5, § § 30.2, 30.3.]

A beneficiary may file an election not to use the lifetime reserve days later than 90 days following discharge only if benefits are available from a third-party payer and the hospital agrees to the retroactive election. [42 C.F.R. § 409.65; Pub. 100-02, Ch. 5, § § 30.2, 30.3.]

Examples • • • _____

Before July 1, Henry Wong had used 90 days of inpatient hospital services in a spell of illness. Beginning July 1, he was hospitalized for 10 more days during the same spell of illness. On July 1, at the time of his admission, Henry indicated that he wanted to use his reserve days for that stay. One month after being discharged from the hospital, Henry informed the hospital that he now wished to save his reserve days for a future stay. Henry agreed to pay the hospital for the services he received during the 10 days of hospitalization and was permitted to file a retroactive election not to use his reserve days for those 10 days.

On July 1, Walter Brown was discharged from a hospital after being hospitalized for 105 days. The hospital billed Medicare for 90 regular days plus 15 lifetime reserve days. On October 20 (more than 90 days following discharge), Walter learned that a private insurer could pay for the last 15 days of the stay. Walter informed the hospital that he wished to file a retroactive election not to use lifetime reserve days for the last 15 days of the stay. The hospital agreed to the request, and Walter filed an election form. The hospital refunded the Medicare payment and billed the private carrier instead.

Period Covered by Election Not to Use Reserve Days

A beneficiary election *not* to use reserve days for a particular hospital stay may apply to the entire stay or to a single period of consecutive days in the stay, but it cannot apply to selected days in a stay. If an election (whether made prospectively or retroactively) not to use reserve days is made effective with the first day for which reserve days are available, it may be terminated at any time. After termination of the election, all hospital days would be covered to the extent that reserve days are available. (Thus, an individual who has private insurance that covers hospitalization beginning with the first day after 90 days of benefits have been exhausted may terminate the election as of the first day not covered by the insurance plan). If an election not to use reserve days is made effective beginning with any day after the first day for which reserve days are available, it must remain in effect until the end of that stay unless the entire election is revoked. [42 C.F.R. § 409.65.]

A beneficiary is deemed to have elected not to use lifetime reserve days if the charges for those days are less than the beneficiary's coinsurance obligation. [42 C.F.R. § 409.65.]

Exception for hospitals reimbursed under the prospective payment system. For hospitals reimbursed under the prospective payment system (PPS), the rules stated above apply with the following exceptions:

One or more regular benefit days available at time of admission. If the beneficiary has one or more regular benefit (non-lifetime reserve) days remaining in the benefit period upon entering the hospital, Medicare will pay the entire prospective payment amount for non-outlier days (see ¶ 810 for an explanation of the term "outlier days"). Thus, there will be no advantage to a beneficiary in using any lifetime reserve days for non-outlier days if at least one day of the regular 90 days of coverage remains when the beneficiary enters the hospital. In this situation, the beneficiary will be deemed to have elected *not* to use any lifetime reserve days for the non-outlier part of the stay. The beneficiary also may elect not to use lifetime reserve days for outlier days, but such an election must apply to all outlier days. [42 C.F.R. § 409.65; Pub. 100-02, Ch. 5, § § 30.1, 30.4.1, 30.4.2.1.]

Example • • • _____

Olivia Gonzalez was admitted to a hospital on April 1 and discharged on June 29, utilizing 89 regular days of inpatient care. On August 1, Olivia entered the hospital again. For this Medicare severity diagnosis-related group (MS-DRG), outlier days would have begun August 26, but Olivia was discharged on August 23, before the commencement of outlier days. Because the first two days of the second stay were regular coverage days, Medicare will reimburse the hospital the prospective payment amount for the entire stay. Because no outlier days are involved, there is no advantage to the beneficiary in using lifetime reserve days. Therefore, Olivia will be deemed to have elected *not* to use any lifetime reserve days for that stay.

Although lifetime reserve days are not used for non-outlier days when the beneficiary has at least one regular day available at the time of admission, payment will be made for outlier days occurring after regular coverage days have been exhausted unless: (1) the beneficiary elects not to use lifetime reserve days for the outlier days; or (2) the beneficiary is deemed to have elected not to use lifetime reserve days for the outlier days. A beneficiary is deemed to have elected not to use lifetime reserve days for outlier days if the average daily charge for the outlier days for which lifetime reserve days otherwise would be available is equal to or less than the daily coinsurance amount for the lifetime reserve days. In that situation, the beneficiary would be required to pay for all of the hospital's charges for such outlier days regardless of election and, therefore, would not benefit from the use of lifetime reserve days. If the beneficiary elects *not* to use lifetime reserve days for outlier days, such an election must apply to all outlier days. If the beneficiary elects not to use lifetime reserve days for outlier days, Medicare will pay for the non-outlier portion of the stay and will make no payment for the outlier days. [42 C.F.R. § 409.65; Pub. 100-02, Ch. 5, § 30.1.]

Example • • • _____

Stuart Desmond, who had never used any of his lifetime reserve days, was admitted to the hospital on April 1, 2016, and discharged on June 29, utilizing 89 regular days of covered inpatient care. On August 1, Stuart entered the hospital again; he was discharged on September 5. For this MS-DRG, outlier days began on August 26. Medicare must reimburse the hospital the prospective payment amount for the non-outlier portion of the stay. The average daily charges were $800 for the outlier portion of the stay. The lifetime reserve day coinsurance amount was $644 in 2016. Because the average daily charge for the outlier days was more than the daily coinsurance amount for lifetime reserve days, there was no deemed election not to use lifetime reserve days for the outlier portion of the stay. For outlier days Stuart had the option: (1) to make no election and, therefore, use his lifetime reserve days, in which case Medicare pays for the non-outlier portion of the stay and for the 10 outlier days, August 26 through September 4, with Stuart utilizing 10 lifetime reserve days; or (2) to elect *not* to use his lifetime reserve days for the 10 outlier days, in which case Medicare pays only for the non-outlier portion of the stay, and Stuart would not use any lifetime reserve days.

Exhaustion of regular benefit days. An election by a beneficiary not to use lifetime reserve days must apply to the entire hospital stay when no regular benefit days are available. If the beneficiary elects not to use lifetime reserve days, Medicare will not pay for any portion of the stay. A beneficiary whose 90 days of benefits are exhausted before cost outlier status is reached must elect to use lifetime reserve days for the hospital to be paid cost outlier payments. Cost outlier status is reached the day that charges reach the cost outlier status for the applicable MS-DRG under the inpatient prospective payment system (IPPS) (see ¶ 810). Use of reserve days must begin on the day following that day, to permit payment for outlier charges. If the beneficiary elects not to use lifetime reserve days when benefits are exhausted, the hospital may charge the beneficiary for the charges that would have been paid as cost outlier. [42 C.F.R. § 409.65(e)(2); Pub. 100-02, Ch. 5, § 30.4.2.]

Example • • • _____

Frances McDonald was admitted to a hospital on March 10, 2016, and discharged on June 8, utilizing 90 regular days of coverage. On August 1, Frances entered the hospital again; she was discharged on September 10. For this MS-DRG, outlier days began on August

26. At the time of the second admission, Frances still had 60 lifetime reserve days available. The hospital charges for this stay were $35,000. The sum of the coinsurance amounts for the lifetime reserve days needed to pay for this stay was $25,760 ($644 per day × 40 days). Because the charges for the stay were greater than the sum of lifetime reserve days coinsurance amounts, there was no deemed election not to use lifetime reserve days. Frances had the option: (1) of making no lifetime reserve election, in which case Medicare pays for the entire stay, including the outlier days, and she would use 40 lifetime reserve days; or (2) of electing *not* to use lifetime reserve days, in which case Medicare does not pay for any portion of the stay.

[¶ 225] Psychiatric Hospital Restrictions

If an individual is an inpatient of a participating psychiatric hospital on the first day for which he or she is entitled to hospital insurance benefits (see ¶ 200–¶ 206), the days (not necessarily consecutive) on which the individual was an inpatient of a psychiatric hospital in the 150-day period immediately before this first day are deducted from the 150 days of inpatient hospital services for which the individual otherwise is entitled to have payment made during the first spell of illness. [Soc. Sec. Act § 1812(c); 42 C.F.R. § 409.63; *Medicare Benefit Policy Manual*, Pub. 100-02, Ch. 4, § 10.]

When an individual subject to a reduction in days is an inpatient in a general hospital, the contractor will apply the reduction only if it has determined that the individual was an inpatient primarily for the diagnosis or treatment of mental illness. The term "mental illness" means the specific psychiatric conditions described in the American Psychiatric Association's "Diagnostic and Statistical Manual—Mental Disorders." [Pub. 100-02, Ch. 4, § 30.]

In determining the number of days to be deducted, the days of admission and the days on which the patient returned from leave of absence are included. Days of discharge, days on which the patient began a leave of absence, and the days of leave during all of which the individual is absent from the hospital are not counted. [Pub. 100-02, Ch. 3, § 20.1.]

Payment may not be made for more than a total of 190 days of inpatient psychiatric hospital services during the patient's lifetime. The period spent in a psychiatric hospital before entitlement does not count against the patient's 190-day lifetime limitation, however, even though pre-entitlement days may have been counted against the 150 days in the first spell of illness. [Pub. 100-02, Ch. 4, § 50.]

Example • • • _____

Mark DeSoto was an inpatient of a participating psychiatric hospital on his first day of entitlement on February 1. He had been in such a hospital in the pre-entitlement period for 20 days. Therefore, Medicare payment can be made for 130 days during the patient's first spell of illness. Payment will be made in the following order: 60 full benefit days, 30 coinsurance days, 40 coinsurance (lifetime reserve) days.

Outpatient "partial hospitalization" services are covered under Part B when these services would prevent the need for inpatient psychiatric care (see ¶ 387). Payment for inpatient psychiatric services under the inpatient psychiatric hospital prospective payment system is discussed at ¶ 840.

[¶ 226] Physicians' Professional Services

The medical and surgical services provided to inpatients by physicians and other health care professionals (e.g., physician assistants, nurse practitioners, psychologists, clinical social workers) normally are covered under Part B and are, therefore, excluded from coverage under Part A. [Soc. Sec. Act § 1861(b)(4).]

The exclusion of physicians' professional services under Part A also applies to the services rendered to individual patients by such hospital-based physicians as radiologists, anesthesiologists, pathologists, and psychiatrists; however, the services of non-physician technicians (e.g., an x-ray technician) aiding hospital-based physicians in these services generally are covered under Part A. [*Medicare Benefit Policy Manual*, Pub. 100-02, Ch. 15, §§ 30.1, 30.2.]

The services of hospital-based physicians that are not related to the care of an individual patient—e.g., research, administration, supervision of professional or technical personnel, or service on hospital committees—are covered under Part A and no charge can be made to the patient for these services. [Pub. 100-02, Ch. 15, §§ 30.1, 30.2.]

As discussed at ¶ 215, the services of interns and residents in an approved teaching program also are covered under Part A.

Coverage and payment for the services of hospital-based physicians are further discussed at ¶ 350 and ¶ 855, respectively.

[¶ 227] Emergency Services

There are emergency situations in which an individual who is eligible for Medicare goes or is taken to a hospital that does not participate in the program. For example, an accident victim might have to be taken immediately to the nearest hospital, either for outpatient diagnosis and treatment or for admission as an inpatient. The law permits the payment of benefits for emergency outpatient services or inpatient care in the United States in such cases until it is no longer medically necessary to care for the patient in the nonparticipating institution. Payment will be made only when the nonparticipating facility was the most accessible hospital able to furnish necessary emergency care. [Soc. Sec. Act § 1814(d)(1).]

The following discussion applies *only* to emergency services in a hospital *not participating* in Medicare. Emergency services in a participating hospital are covered under Medicare in the same manner as nonemergency services. The special requirements applicable to participating hospitals with respect to the treatment of emergency room cases are discussed at ¶ 730.

Payment for Emergency Services in Nonparticipating Hospitals

There are two possible methods of payment to a nonparticipating hospital for emergency services. Payment can be made to the hospital if it so elects and meets the conditions described below. Otherwise, payment is made to the individual on the basis of an itemized bill. For payment to be made to the hospital:

(1) the services must be emergency services;

(2) the services must be covered inpatient hospital services under Part A or covered outpatient services;

(3) the hospital must meet the definition of "emergency services hospital" (see below);

(4) the hospital must agree to not charge the patient or any other individual for covered items or services (except to the extent that a participating hospital would be permitted to charge for these services (see ¶ 730)), and must agree to return any money incorrectly collected; and

(5) the hospital must have signed a statement of election to claim payment for all inpatient and outpatient services furnished during the year.

[Soc. Sec. Act §§ 1814(d)(1), 1835(b)(1), 1866(a); 42 C.F.R. §§ 424.104, 424.108; *Medicare General Information, Eligibility, and Entitlement Manual*, Pub. 100-01, Ch. 5, § 20.1.]

If the hospital does not elect to claim payment as discussed above, payment may be made to the beneficiary on the basis of an itemized bill, subject to applicable deductible and coinsurance amounts. [Soc. Sec. Act §§ 1814(d)(2), 1835(b)(2).]

Definition of "Emergency Services Hospital"

A facility qualifies as an "emergency services hospital" if it is licensed as a hospital under applicable state or local laws, has a full-time nursing service, is engaged primarily in furnishing medical care under the supervision of a physician, and is not engaged primarily in providing skilled nursing care and related services for inpatients who require medical or nursing care. Psychiatric hospitals that meet these requirements also can qualify as emergency services hospitals. A federal hospital need not be licensed under state or local licensing laws to meet this definition. [Soc. Sec. Act § 1861(e); 42 C.F.R. § 424.101; Pub. 100-01, Ch. 5, § 20.2.]

Definition of "Emergency Services"

"Emergency services" are inpatient or outpatient hospital services that are necessary to prevent the death or serious impairment an individual's health and that, because of the threat to the life or health, necessitate the use of the most accessible hospital available and equipped to furnish the services. [42 C.F.R. § 424.101.]

The following situations do not in themselves indicate a need for emergency services, unless there also is an immediate threat to the patient's life or health: (1) the death of the patient during hospitalization; (2) a lack of adequate care at home; or (3) a lack of transportation to a participating hospital. [42 C.F.R. § 424.102.]

Termination of Emergency Services

Payment to a nonparticipating hospital for emergency services under Part A ceases when the emergency has ended. Payment under Part B may be made, however, for certain ancillary services furnished during nonemergency inpatient stays (see ¶ 361). An emergency no longer exists when it becomes medically safe to move the patient to a participating institution or to discharge the patient, whichever occurs first. The physician's supporting statement will ordinarily serve as the basis for determining that an emergency has ended. [42 C.F.R. § 424.103(b)(3).]

Emergency Services Outside the United States

Under certain circumstances, Medicare will pay for emergency inpatient hospital services furnished to a beneficiary outside the United States by a foreign hospital. See ¶ 610.

[¶ 228] Religious Nonmedical Health Care Institutions

Providers qualifying as religious nonmedical health care institutions are included as hospitals and skilled nursing facilities for Medicare purposes. [Soc. Sec. Act § 1861(e), (y), (ss).] To qualify, an institution must:

(1) be a tax-exempt organization under section 501(c)(3) of the Internal Revenue Code;

(2) be lawfully operated under all applicable federal, state, and local laws and regulations;

(3) provide only nonmedical nursing items and services exclusively to individuals who choose to rely solely upon a religious method of healing, through experienced nonmedical personnel, and on a 24-hour basis;

(4) not provide medical items or services (including screening, examination, diagnosis, or administration of drugs) to its patients, or be affiliated by common ownership or otherwise with an institution that provides such services; and

(5) have in effect a specialized utilization review plan and provide the Secretary with information required to monitor quality of care and to provide for coverage determinations.

[Soc. Sec. Act § 1861(ss); 42 C.F.R. § 403.720.]

Patients being treated in a religious nonmedical health care institution must make an election to receive such benefits. Additionally, Medicare reimbursement in these institutions is available only to individuals with a condition that would require them to be inpatients in a hospital or skilled nursing facility were it not for their religious beliefs. [Soc. Sec. Act § 1821(a), (b).]

Payment is on a reasonable cost basis and may be made only for items and services normally furnished in such institutions (i.e., nonmedical nursing services and related items). [Soc. Sec. Act § 1861(e), (y); 42 C.F.R. § 403.752.]

Medicare will cover specified durable medical equipment and intermittent religious nonmedical health care institution nursing visits provided in the home to beneficiaries. However, payment for nonmedical care is subject to the requirements for reasonableness and necessity. [Soc. Sec. Act § 1862(a)(1)(A).] Religious nonmedical nursing personnel may not engage in any activities that are medical in nature. The remainder of the services covered under the Medicare home health benefit are medical in nature and must be provided under the order of a physician. The specified durable medical equipment items include canes, crutches, walkers, commodes, a standard wheelchair, hospital beds, bedpans, and urinals. [*Medicare Benefit Policy Manual*, Pub. 100-02, Ch. 1, § 130.4.]

[¶ 229] "Hospital" Defined—Qualified Hospitals

As a general rule, Medicare will not cover a beneficiary's stay in a hospital unless the hospital is "participating" in the Medicare program (see ¶ 730). Services provided in a nonparticipating hospital, however, may be covered by Medicare in emergency situations (see ¶ 227).

To participate as a hospital in the Medicare program, an institution must be a "hospital" within the meaning of section 1861(e) of the Social Security Act. The section lists several requirements hospitals must meet, the most important of which is that the hospital is primarily engaged in providing the following services to inpatients by or under the supervision of physicians: (1) diagnostic services and therapeutic services for medical diagnosis, treatment, and care of injured, disabled, or sick persons; or (2) services for the rehabilitation of injured, disabled, or sick persons. [Soc. Sec. Act § 1861(e)(1).] In addition, section 1861(e) requires hospitals to provide 24-hour nursing care, have a utilization review plan in effect, and meet certain health and safety requirements.

Psychiatric hospitals must participate in Medicare for the services they furnish to be covered. The requirements for these hospitals are similar to the requirements for other hospitals, although they differ in some respects due to their different purpose. Section 1861(f) of the Social Security Act lists the requirements psychiatric hospitals must meet, the most important of which is that the hospital be primarily engaged in providing, by or under the supervision of a physician, psychiatric services for the diagnosis and treatment of mentally ill persons. [Soc. Sec. Act § 1861(f)(1).]

Medicare regulations describing the conditions of participation for hospitals are found at 42 C.F.R. Part 482.

Hospital Providers of Extended Care Services ("Swing-Bed" Facilities)

Because of the shortage of rural skilled nursing facility (SNF) beds for Medicare patients, rural hospitals with fewer than 100 beds may be paid under Part A for furnishing covered nursing home services to Medicare beneficiaries. Such a hospital, known as a swing-bed facility, can "swing" its beds between hospital and SNF levels of care on an as-needed basis if it has obtained a swing-bed approval from CMS. [Soc. Sec. Act § 1883; *Medicare General Information, Eligibility, and Entitlement Manual*, Pub. 100-01, Ch. 5, § 30.3.]

A hospital providing extended care services will be treated as a SNF for purposes of applying coverage rules. This means that those services are subject to all of the Part A coverage, physician certification, deductible, and coinsurance provisions that are applicable to SNF extended care services. For example:

(1) SNF level of care days in a swing-bed facility are counted against total SNF benefit days available to Medicare beneficiaries;

(2) Medicare beneficiaries receiving a SNF level of care in a swing-bed facility must first meet the three-day prior hospital stay requirement; and

(3) services needed and provided must be of the type and at the level to constitute extended care or SNF level services.

[Soc. Sec. Act § 1883(d); 42 C.F.R. § 409.30; *Medicare Benefit Policy Manual*, Pub. 100-02, Ch. 8, §§ 10.3, 20.1, 30.]

Nursing Home Services

[¶ 230] Extended Care Services

Medicare Part A covers extended care services furnished to inpatients of a skilled nursing facility (SNF). A SNF is an institution or a distinct part of an institution, such as a skilled nursing home or rehabilitation center, that has a transfer agreement in effect with one or more participating hospitals and that is primarily engaged in providing skilled nursing care and related services for residents who require medical or nursing care, or rehabilitation services for the rehabilitation of injured, disabled, or sick persons. [Soc. Sec. Act § 1819(a); 42 C.F.R. § 483.5(a); *Medicare General Information, Eligibility, and Entitlement Manual*, Pub. 100-01, Ch. 5, § 30.] Conditions of participation for SNFs are discussed at ¶ 249.

Part A covers care in a SNF if the following requirements are met:

(1) the beneficiary requires skilled nursing services or skilled rehabilitation services, which are ordered by a physician and rendered for a condition for which the patient received inpatient hospital services or for a condition that arose while receiving care in a SNF for a condition for which he or she received inpatient hospital services;

(2) the beneficiary requires these skilled services on a daily basis;

(3) as a practical matter, considering economy and efficiency, the daily skilled services can be provided only on an inpatient basis in a SNF; and

(4) the services delivered are reasonable and necessary for the treatment of a patient's illness or injury.

[Soc. Sec. Act § 1814(a)(2)(B); 42 C.F.R. § 409.31(b).]

A physician, nurse practitioner, clinical nurse specialist, or physician assistant must certify that these requirements are met. [Soc. Sec. Act § 1814(a)(2).]

Documentation. Claims for skilled care coverage must include sufficient documentation to enable a reviewer to determine whether (1) skilled involvement is required for the services in question to be furnished safely and effectively; and (2) the services themselves are, in fact, reasonable and necessary for the treatment of a patient's illness or injury. [*Medicare Benefit Policy Manual*, Pub. 100-02, Ch. 8, § 30.2.2.1.]

Covered Services

Extended care services include the following:

• nursing care provided by or under the supervision of a registered professional nurse, but excluding the services of a private duty nurse or attendant (see 42 C.F.R. § 409.21);

• bed and board in connection with furnishing of such nursing care (see ¶ 232);

• physical or occupational therapy and/or speech-language pathology services furnished by the SNF or by others under arrangements with them made by the facility (see ¶ 233);

• medical social services (see 42 C.F.R. § 409.24);

• drugs, biologics, supplies, appliances, and equipment furnished for use in the SNF, as are ordinarily furnished by such facility for the care and treatment of inpatients (see ¶ 235 and ¶ 236);

• medical services provided by an intern or resident-in-training of a hospital with which the facility has in effect a transfer agreement under an approved teaching program of the hospital, and other diagnostic or therapeutic services provided by a hospital with which the facility has such an agreement in effect (see ¶ 237); and

• other services necessary to the health of the patients as are generally provided by SNFs, or by others under arrangements, including respiratory therapy services and medically necessary ambulance transportation (see 42 C.F.R. § 409.27).

[Soc. Sec. Act § 1861(h).]

Services furnished to an inpatient of a SNF for which payment cannot be made under Part A (usually because the beneficiary has exhausted his entitlement to benefits) are reimbursable under Part B if they constitute "medical and other health services" and the beneficiary is otherwise entitled to Part B benefits. [Pub. 100-02, Ch. 8, § 70.]

Prior Hospitalization Requirement

An individual must be an inpatient of a hospital for at least three consecutive calendar days and then transfer to a participating SNF usually within 30 days after discharge from the hospital to qualify for Medicare reimbursement of post-hospital extended care services. [Soc. Sec. Act § 1861(i); 42 C.F.R. § 409.30; Pub. 100-02, Ch. 8, § 10.]

Three-day prior hospitalization. In the determination of whether the individual's prior hospital stay meets the required minimum of three consecutive calendar days, the day of admission is counted as a hospital inpatient day, but the day of discharge is not. The hospital discharge must have occurred on or after the first day of the month in which an individual attains age 65 or becomes entitled to Medicare benefits under the disability or end-stage renal disease provisions. [42 C.F.R. § 409.30(a)(2); Pub. 100-02, Ch. 8, § 20.1.]

A three-day stay in a psychiatric hospital satisfies the prior hospital stay requirement. A three-day stay in a foreign hospital also satisfies the prior hospital stay requirement if the foreign hospital meets the requirements of an emergency hospital. However, stays in religious nonmedical health care institutions and time spent in observation status or in the emergency room prior to (or in lieu of) an inpatient admission to the hospital do not count toward the three-day qualifying inpatient hospital stay. [Pub. 100-02, Ch. 8, §§ 20.1, 20.1.1.]

¶230

A patient who is transferred directly from an acute care hospital to a SNF and is correctly assigned a resource utilization group (RUG) will be presumed to require the SNF level of care. This presumption continues through the five-day period allowed for patient assessment under 42 C.F.R. § 413.343(b) if the assessment is completed timely. [42 C.F.R. § 409.30; Pub. 100-02, Ch. 8, § 30.1.]

To be covered, the post-hospital extended care services must have been for the treatment of a condition for which the beneficiary was receiving inpatient hospital services, or by a condition that arose while in the facility for treatment of a condition for which the patient was previously hospitalized. The condition need not have been the principal diagnosis that precipitated the beneficiary's admission to the hospital; it could be any one of the conditions present during the qualifying hospital stay. In addition, the qualifying hospital stay must have been medically necessary. [Soc. Sec. Act § 1814(a)(2)(B); 42 C.F.R. § 409.31(b)(2); Pub. 100-02, Ch. 8, § 20.1.]

CMS will cover SNF care for beneficiaries involuntarily unenrolled from Medicare Advantage (MA) plans as a result of a MA plan termination when they do not have a three-day hospital stay before SNF admission, if the beneficiary was admitted to the SNF before the effective date of disenrollment. [Pub. 100-02, Ch. 8, § 10.]

Thirty-day transfer requirement. Post-hospital extended care services represent an extension of care for a condition for which the individual received inpatient hospital services. Extended care services are "post-hospital" if initiated within 30 days after the date of discharge from a hospital. [Soc. Sec. Act § 1861(i); 42 C.F.R. § 409.30(b).]

The day of discharge from the hospital is not counted in the determination of the 30-day transfer period. For example, a patient discharged from a hospital on August 1 and admitted to a SNF on August 31 was admitted within 30 days. [Pub. 100-02, Ch. 8, § 20.2.1.]

An individual who is admitted to a SNF within 30 days after discharge from a hospital but does not require a covered level of care until more than 30 days after such discharge does not meet the 30-day requirement. [Pub. 100-02, Ch. 8, § 20.2.1.]

If an individual whose SNF stay was covered upon admission is later determined not to require a covered level of care for a period that continues for more than 30 days, payment will not be resumed for any extended care services he or she may subsequently require, even though the individual has remained in the facility, until the occurrence of a new qualifying hospital stay. In the absence of a new qualifying hospital stay, such services are not deemed to be "post-hospital" extended care services. [Pub. 100-02, Ch. 8, § 20.2.1.]

The period of extended care services may be interrupted briefly and then resumed, if necessary, without hospitalization preceding the readmission to the facility. The 30-day transfer requirement is satisfied if, for example, the beneficiary: (1) leaves the SNF and is readmitted to the same or any other participating SNF within 30 days; or (2) remains in the SNF to receive custodial care following a covered stay and subsequently develops a renewed need for covered care there within 30 consecutive days. [Pub. 100-02, Ch. 8, § 20.2.3.]

The law provides an exception to the 30-day transfer requirement. If a patient is not admitted to a SNF within 30 days after discharge from a hospital because to admit him or her within that time would not be medically appropriate, the admission to the SNF will be covered if it is within such time as would be medically appropriate to begin an active course of treatment. [Soc. Sec. Act § 1861(i); 42 C.F.R. § 409.30(b)(2)(i); Pub. 100-02, Ch. 8, § 20.2.2.]

[¶ 232] Accommodations

The coverage of ward, semi-private, and private accommodations in a skilled nursing facility (SNF) is treated in the same way as the coverage of hospital accommodations (see ¶ 211). [Soc. Sec. Act § 1861(h)(2); 42 C.F.R. § 409.22.]

Medicare covers a private room if:

(1) the patient's condition requires him or her to be isolated;

(2) the SNF has no semiprivate or ward accommodations; or

(3) the SNF semiprivate and ward accommodations are fully occupied by other patients, were so occupied at the time the patient was admitted to the SNF for treatment of a condition that required immediate inpatient SNF care, and have been so occupied during the interval.

The beneficiary is responsible for the difference between the SNF's charge for the private room and its most prevalent charge for a semi-private room if none of these conditions is met and the private room was requested by the patient or a member of the family who, at the time of request, was informed what the charge would be. [42 C.F.R. § 409.22(b).]

Unlike the Medicaid program, Medicare does not make payments to a nursing facility to hold a bed for a patient who takes a temporary leave of absence from the facility. [42 C.F.R. § 489.22(d).]

Patients in inappropriate beds. When patients requiring inpatient hospital services occupy beds in a SNF or in the hospital's distinct part SNF, they are considered inpatients of the SNF. In such cases, the services furnished in the SNF may not be considered inpatient hospital services, and payment may not be made under the Medicare program for those services. Such a situation may arise where the SNF is a distinct part of an institution, the remainder of which is a hospital, and either there is no bed available in the hospital, or for any other reason the institution fails to place the patient in the appropriate bed. The same rule applies where the SNF is a separate institution. [*Medicare Benefit Policy Manual*, Pub. 100-02, Ch. 8, § 50.]

In the special case of patients who require extended care services but occupy beds in a hospital, the general rule is that no payment will be made on their behalf for the hospital services furnished to them. However, when such patients occupy hospital beds because there are no SNF beds available to them, the general rule may not apply. A physician or a utilization review committee may certify to the need for continued hospitalization in these situations. [42 C.F.R. § 424.13(c).]

Similarly, under Soc. Sec. Act § 1861(v)(1)(G), a quality improvement organization or the HHS Secretary may also require continued coverage for the extended care services at a special nursing home rate of payment. Rural hospitals entering into "swing-bed" agreements, as well as other hospitals without such agreements, are eligible for special rates of reimbursement for patients inappropriately occupying hospital beds because there are no SNF beds available. [Pub. 100-02, Ch. 8, § 10.3.]

Patients who are denied coverage because they have been placed in the wrong bed may nevertheless be entitled to Medicare coverage under the "waiver of liability" provision (see ¶ 915). The law recognizes that the patient is not in a position to make a choice or influence an incorrect action taken by hospital or SNF. [Soc. Sec. Act § 1879; Pub. 100-02, Ch. 8, § 50.]

[¶ 233] Physical and Occupational Therapy and Speech-Language Pathology Services

Physical and occupational therapy and speech-language pathology furnished by a skilled nursing facility (SNF) or by others under arrangements made by the facility are covered when provided in accordance with a physician's orders, by or under the supervision of a qualified therapist, and in accordance with a plan satisfying the requirements of 42 C.F.R. § 409.17. [Soc. Sec. Act §§ 1832(a)(2)(C), 1833(a)(8), 1861(h)(3); 42 C.F.R. § 409.23.]

Coverage for skilled therapy services turns on the beneficiary's need for skilled care, not on the presence or absence of a beneficiary's potential for improvement from therapy services. Therapy services are considered skilled when they are so inherently complex that they can be safely and effectively performed only by, or under the supervision of, a qualified therapist. These skilled services may be necessary to improve the patient's current condition, to maintain the patient's current condition, or to prevent or slow further deterioration of the patient's condition. [*Medicare Benefit Policy Manual*, Pub. 100-02, Ch. 8, § 30.4.]

Limits on the amount Medicare will pay for outpatient rehabilitation therapy services, generally called therapy caps, apply to outpatient physical therapy, speech-language pathology services, and occupational therapy services under Medicare Part B (see ¶ 860). [Soc. Sec. Act § 1833(g).] Since the limitations apply to outpatient services, they do not apply to SNF residents in a covered Part A stay, including patients occupying swing beds. Rehabilitation services are included within the global Part A per diem payment that the SNF receives under the prospective payment system for the covered stay. [*Medicare Claims Processing Manual*, Pub. 100-04, Ch. 5, § 10.2.]

[¶ 235] Drugs and Biologics

Medicare covers drugs and biologics as post-hospital SNF care if they: (1) represent a cost to the facility; (2) are ordinarily furnished by the facility for the care and treatment of inpatients; and (3) are furnished to an inpatient for use in the facility. Medicare will, however, pay for a limited supply of drugs for use outside the facility if it is medically necessary to facilitate the beneficiary's departure from the facility and required until he or she can obtain a continuing supply. [Soc. Sec. Act § 1861(h)(3); 42 C.F.R. § 409.25(a), (b).]

Because the provision of drugs and biologics is considered an essential part of skilled nursing care, a facility must ensure their availability to inpatients. When a facility secures drugs and biologics from an outside source, their availability is ensured only if the facility assumes financial responsibility for the necessary drugs and biologics, i.e., the supplier looks to the facility, not the patient, for payment. [*Medicare Benefit Policy Manual*, Pub. 100-02, Ch. 8, § 50.5.]

Payment may not be made for particular uses of drugs that the Food and Drug Administration (FDA) has expressly disapproved or that do not meet the coverage requirements specified in Pub. 100-02, Ch. 1, section 30. If the Medicare administrative contractor has reason to question whether the FDA has approved a drug or biologic for marketing, it must obtain satisfactory evidence of the FDA's approval. [Pub. 100-02, Ch. 8, § 50.5.]

A drug that is not approved by Medicare can still be covered in a SNF if the drug:

(1) was furnished to the patient during his or her prior hospitalization;

(2) was approved for use in the hospital by the hospital's pharmacy and drug therapeutics committee;

(3) is required for the continuing treatment of the patient in the SNF; and

(4) is reasonable and necessary.

Under these limited circumstances, a combination drug approved by a hospital pharmacy and drug therapeutics committee also may be covered as an extended care service. [Pub. 100-02, Ch. 8, § 50.5.]

Rules for drugs and biologics applicable to hospital inpatients and inpatients of SNFs are found in the *Medicare Benefit Policy Manual*, Pub. 100-02, Ch. 1, sections 30 through 30.4. [Pub. 100-02, Ch. 8, § 50.5.]

With respect to drugs or biologics furnished to an *inpatient* for use *outside* a SNF, see the comparable provisions pertaining to hospital inpatients at ¶ 212. Special limitations on payment for certain "less than effective" drugs applicable under the Part B program are described at ¶ 644.

[¶ 236] Supplies, Appliances, and Equipment

Supplies, appliances, and equipment are covered as extended care services only if they: (1) are ordinarily furnished by the skilled nursing facility (SNF) for the care and treatment of inpatients; and (2) are furnished to an inpatient for use in the SNF. Examples of covered SNF supplies include oxygen, surgical dressings, splints, casts, and personal hygiene items and services. [Soc. Sec. Act § 1861(h)(5); 42 C.F.R. § 409.25(c); *Medicare Benefit Policy Manual*, Pub. 100-02, Ch. 1, § 40; Ch. 8, § 50.6.]

Under certain circumstances, supplies, appliances, and equipment used during the beneficiary's stay are covered even though they leave the facility with the patient when discharged. Medicare pays for items to be used after the individual leaves the facility if the item: (1) is one that the beneficiary must continue to use after leaving, such as a leg brace; or (2) is necessary to permit or facilitate the beneficiary's departure from the facility and is required until he or she can obtain a continuing supply. [42 C.F.R. § 409.25(d); Pub. 100-02, Ch. 1, § 40.]

A temporary or disposable item, such as a sterile dressing, that is medically necessary to permit or facilitate a patient's departure from the facility and is required until such time as the patient can obtain a continuing supply, is covered as an extended care service. [Pub. 100-02, Ch. 1, § 40; Ch. 8, § 50.6.]

[¶ 237] Interns and Residents-in-Training

Medicare pays for medical services that are furnished by an intern or a resident-in-training under a hospital teaching program as post-hospital skilled nursing facility (SNF) care if the intern or resident is in: (1) a participating hospital with which the SNF has in effect a transfer agreement; or (2) a hospital that has swing-bed approval and is furnishing services to a SNF-level inpatient of that hospital. [Soc. Sec. Act § 1861(h)(6); 42 C.F.R. § 409.26(a).]

The medical and surgical services furnished to the facility's patients by interns and residents-in-training of a hospital with which the facility has a transfer agreement are covered under Part B if the services are not covered under Part A. [*Medicare Benefit Policy Manual*, Pub. 100-02, Ch. 8, § 50.7.]

[¶ 238] Whole Blood and Packed Red Blood Cells

Medicare coverage includes the cost of unreplaced blood (after satisfaction of the three-pint blood deductible discussed at ¶ 220) and the cost of administering the blood to inpatients of participating skilled nursing facilities. [Soc. Sec. Act § 1866(a)(2)(C); *Medicare General Information, Eligibility, and Entitlement Manual*, Pub. 100-01, Ch. 3, § 20.5.]

[¶ 239] Services Payable Under Part B

The medical and other health services listed below are covered under Part B when furnished by a participating skilled nursing facility (SNF), either directly or under arrangements to inpatients who are not entitled to have payment made under Part A, or to outpatients:

- diagnostic x-ray tests, diagnostic laboratory tests, and other diagnostic tests;

- x-ray, radium, and radioactive isotope therapy, including materials and services of technicians;

- surgical dressings, and splints, casts, and other devices used for reduction of fractures and dislocations;

- prosthetic devices (other than dental) that replace all or part of an internal body organ (including contiguous tissue), or all or part of the function of a permanently inoperative or malfunctioning internal body organ, including replacement or repairs of such devices;

- leg, arm, back, and neck braces; trusses; and artificial legs, arms, and eyes, including adjustments, repairs, and replacements required because of breakage, wear, loss, or a change in the patient's physical condition;

- outpatient physical and occupational and speech-language pathology services;

- screening mammography services;

- screening pap smears and pelvic exams;

- influenza, pneumococcal pneumonia, and hepatitis B vaccines;

- some colorectal screening;

- diabetes self-management;

- prostate screening;

- ambulance services;

- hemophilia clotting factors; and

- Epoetin Alfa (EPO) for end-stage renal disease beneficiaries when given in conjunction with dialysis.

[42 C.F.R. §§ 409.27(a), 410.60(b); *Medicare Benefit Policy Manual*, Pub. 100-02, Ch. 8, § 70.]

[¶ 242] Skilled Nursing Facility Coinsurance

The beneficiary is required to pay a coinsurance amount equal to one-eighth of the inpatient hospital deductible for each day after the 20th and before the 101st day of skilled nursing facility (SNF) services furnished during a spell of illness (see ¶ 210). [Soc. Sec. Act § 1813(a)(3).]

This coinsurance amount, like the inpatient hospital deductible on which it is dependent, is subject to annual change. Daily coinsurance for the 21st through 100th day in a SNF is $164.50 in 2017, up from $161.00 in 2016. [*Medicare General Information, Eligibility and Entitlement Manual*, Pub. 100-01, Ch. 3, § 10.3; *Notices*, 81 FR 80060, Nov. 15, 2016; 80 FR 70808, Nov. 16, 2015.]

[¶ 243] Duration of Covered SNF Services

A patient who has Part A coverage is entitled to have payment made on his or her behalf for up to 100 days of covered inpatient extended care services in each spell of illness subject to the coinsurance requirement discussed at ¶ 242. [Soc. Sec. Act § 1812(a)(2), (b)(2).]

The number of days of care charged to a beneficiary for inpatient skilled nursing facility (SNF) services is counted in units of full days. A day begins at midnight and ends 24 hours later. A part of a day, including the day of admission, counts as a full day. [*Medicare Benefit Policy Manual*, Pub. 100-02, Ch. 3, § 20.1.]

However, the day of discharge or death or a day on which a patient begins a leave of absence is not counted as a day. Charges for ancillary services on the day of discharge or death or the day on which a patient begins a leave of absence are covered. If admission and discharge or death occur on the same day, the day is considered a day of admission and counts as one inpatient day. [Pub. 100-02, Ch. 3, §§ 20.1, 20.1.3.]

Late discharge. When a patient chooses to occupy accommodations in a SNF beyond the normal check-out time for personal reasons, the facility may charge the patient for a continued stay. The SNF, however, must provide the beneficiary with an Advance Beneficiary Notice (ABN) before the non-covered services are provided (see ¶ 210). When the patient's medical condition is the cause of the stay past the checkout time (e.g., the patient needs further services, is bedridden and awaiting transportation to his or her home, or dies in the SNF), the stay beyond the discharge hour is covered under the program and the SNF may not charge the patient. [Pub. 100-02, Ch. 3, § 20.1.1.]

The imposition of a late checkout charge by a hospital or SNF does not affect the counting of days for: (1) ending a benefit period; (2) the number of days of inpatient care available to the individual in a SNF; and (3) the three-day prior hospitalization requirement for coverage of post-hospital extended care services and Part A home health services. A late charge by a hospital does not affect counting of days for meeting the prior inpatient stay requirement for coverage of extended care services. [Pub. 100-02, Ch. 3, § 20.1.1.]

Leaves of absence. The day on which the patient begins a leave of absence is treated as a day of discharge and is not counted as an inpatient day unless the patient returns to the facility by midnight of the same day. The day the patient returns to the facility from a leave of absence is treated as a day of admission and is counted as an inpatient day if he or she is present at midnight of that day. [Pub. 100-02, Ch. 3, § 20.1.2.]

Charges to the beneficiary for admission or readmission are not allowable. However, when temporarily leaving a SNF, a resident may choose to make bed-hold payments to the SNF. Under Soc. Sec. Act § 1819(c)(1)(B)(iii) and 42 C.F.R. § 483.10(b)(5)–(6), the SNF must inform residents in advance of their option to make bed-hold payments, as well as the amount of the facility's charge. [*Medicare Claims Processing Manual*, Pub. 100-04, Ch. 1, § 30.1.1.1.]

Days counting toward maximum. Post-hospital extended care services count toward the maximum number of benefit days payable per benefit period only if: (1) payment for the services is made; or (2) payment for the services would be made if a request for payment were properly filed, the physician certified that the services were medically necessary, if that is a requirement, and the provider submitted all necessary evidence. When payment cannot be made because of the extended care coinsurance requirement, the days used nevertheless count toward the beneficiary's maximum days of extended care. [Pub. 100-02, Ch. 3, § 30.]

[¶ 244] Levels of Care

Medicare covers post-hospital extended care only if a physician, nurse practitioner, clinical nurse specialist, or physician assistant certifies—and recertifies when required—that the services are or were necessary because the individual needs or needed on a daily basis skilled nursing care or other skilled rehabilitation services, which as a practical matter can be provided only in a skilled nursing facility (SNF) on an inpatient basis for any of the conditions with respect to which he or she was receiving inpatient hospital services. [Soc. Sec. Act § 1814(a)(2)(B).]

Thus, for a patient to be eligible for post-hospital extended care as an inpatient of a SNF, he or she must require the type and level of care that is defined as "post-hospital extended care," a level of care often distinguished from "custodial care," which is excluded (see ¶ 625). [42 C.F.R. § 411.15(g).]

Three criteria must be met to satisfy the level-of-care requirement under the extended care benefit: (1) the beneficiary must require skilled nursing services or skilled rehabilitation services on a daily basis; (2) the services must be furnished for a condition: (a) for which the beneficiary received inpatient hospital or inpatient critical access hospital (CAH) care, or (b) that arose while the beneficiary was receiving care in a SNF for a condition for which the beneficiary had received inpatient hospital or inpatient CAH services; and (3) as a practical matter, the service can be provided only in a SNF on an inpatient basis. [42 C.F.R. § 409.31(b).]

See ¶ 915 for a discussion of waiver of liability when a beneficiary is improperly transferred to a lower level of care.

"Skilled Nursing/Rehabilitation Services" Defined

Skilled nursing and skilled rehabilitation services are services that: (1) are ordered by a physician; (2) require the skills of technical or professional personnel, for example, a registered nurse, licensed practical (vocational) nurse, physical therapist, occupational therapist, speech-language pathologist, or audiologist; and (3) are provided either directly by or under the supervision of such personnel. [42 C.F.R. § 409.31(a).]

In the determination of whether a service is skilled, the inherent complexity of the service and special medical complications are considered. The restoration potential of a patient is not the deciding factor in determining whether skilled services are needed. Even when full recovery or medical improvement is not possible, skilled care may be needed to prevent, to the extent possible, deterioration of the patient's condition or to sustain current capacities. [42 C.F.R. § 409.32.]

Inherent complexity. If the inherent complexity of a service prescribed for a patient is such that it can be performed safely and effectively only by or under the supervision of technical or professional personnel, the service constitutes a skilled service. For example, certain intravenous or intramuscular injections, types of aspiration, insertion of catheters, and other inherently complex services qualify as SNF services. [42 C.F.R. §§ 409.32, 409.33.]

Special medical complications. A service that is usually nonskilled may be considered skilled when, because of special medical complications, its performance or supervision, or the observation of the patient, requires the use of skilled nursing or skilled rehabilitation personnel. For example, while heat treatments are usually unskilled, they may be considered skilled when specifically ordered by a physician as part of active treatment that requires a nurse's observation to adequately evaluate the patient's progress. [42 C.F.R. §§ 409.32, 409.33.]

Personal care services. Personal care services that do not require the skills of qualified technical or professional personnel are not skilled services and, therefore, not covered, except when special medical complications are involved. Personal care services include administration of routine medications, changes of dressings for noninfected conditions, and other general or routine care services. [42 C.F.R. §§ 409.32(b), 409.33(d).]

"Daily Basis" Requirement

Skilled nursing services or skilled rehabilitation services must be required and provided on a "daily basis." To meet the daily basis requirement, the following frequency is required: (1) skilled nursing services or skilled rehabilitation services must be needed and provided seven days a week; or (2) as an exception, if skilled rehabilitation services are not available seven days a week, those services must be needed and provided at least five days a week. A break of one or two days in the furnishing of rehabilitation services will not preclude coverage if discharge would not be practical for the one or two days during which, for instance, the physician has suspended the therapy sessions because the patient exhibited extreme fatigue. [42 C.F.R. § 409.34.]

[¶ 248] Rights of SNF Residents

A skilled nursing facility (SNF) must promote and protect the rights of each resident, including a resident's:

(1) self-respect;

(2) dignity;

(3) free choice with respect to medical care and treatment;

(4) right to be informed of and participate in his or her treatment;

(5) freedom from restraints;

(6) privacy;

(7) communication;

(8) confidentiality;

(9) accommodation of needs;

(10) grievance procedures;

(11) participation in resident and family groups;

(12) participation in social, religious, and community activities;

(13) access of his or her medical records;

(14) refusal of treatment, including formulation of advance directives;

(15) receipt of information regarding significant changes in his or her treatment;

(16) management of his or her financial affairs;

(17) refusal or choice to perform work services for the SNF;

(18) examination of state certification survey results; and

(19) refusal of a transfer to a nonskilled nursing part of the facility.

[Soc. Sec. Act § 1819(c)(1)(A); 42 C.F.R. § 483.10.]

Notice of rights. The facility is required to: (1) give notice, orally and in writing at the time of admission to the facility, of the resident's legal rights during the stay at the facility; (2) make available to each resident, upon reasonable request, a written statement of such rights; and (3) inform each resident, in writing before or at the time of admission and periodically during the resident's stay, of services available in the facility and of related charges for such services, including any charges for services not covered under Medicare or by the facility's basic per diem charge. [Soc. Sec. Act § 1819(c)(1)(B); 42 C.F.R. § 483.10(g)(4).]

The written description of legal rights must include a description of the SNF's protection of personal funds (see Soc. Sec. Act § 1819(c)(6)) and a statement that a resident may file a complaint with a state survey and certification agency regarding resident abuse and neglect or misappropriation of resident property in the facility. [Soc. Sec. Act § 1819(c)(1)(B).]

Payment Issues

If a beneficiary requests a noncovered service or a service that is more expensive than the amount of Medicare payment, the provider must inform the beneficiary that there will be a specific charge for that service. [42 C.F.R. § 489.32.] However, providers, including a SNF, may not impose any of the following prepayment requirements:

    (1) require an individual entitled to hospital insurance benefits to prepay in part or in whole for inpatient services as a condition of admittance as an inpatient, except where it is clear upon admission that payment under Medicare Part A cannot be made;

    (2) deny covered inpatient services to an individual entitled to have payment made for those services on the ground of inability or failure to pay a requested amount at or before admission;

    (3) evict, or threaten to evict, an individual for inability to pay a deductible or a coinsurance amount required under Medicare;

    (4) charge an individual for an agreement to admit or readmit the individual on some specified future date for covered inpatient services; or

    (5) charge a resident for failure to remain an inpatient for any agreed-upon length of time or for failure to give advance notice of departure from the provider's facilities.

[42 C.F.R. § 489.22.]

Privacy Issues

HHS regulations protect the privacy of individually identifiable information in accordance with the Health Insurance Portability and Accountability Act (HIPAA) (P.L. 104-191). Under these regulations, a facility must provide notice to a patient on the first service visit regarding the facility's use of the beneficiary's medical data and the beneficiary's right to access that data. [45 C.F.R. § 164.520.] See ¶ 715 for a full description of HIPAA protections.

Residents of SNFs are entitled to personal privacy and confidentiality of their personal and medical records. Personal privacy includes accommodations, treatment, written and telephone communications, personal care, visits, and family and resident group meetings. However, personal privacy does not require the facility to provide a private room for each resident. Residents are also entitled to a safe, clean, comfortable, and homelike environment. [42 C.F.R. § 483.10(i), (j).]

Discharge or Transfer from a SNF

    A facility's discharge planning process must focus on residents' discharge goals and the preparation of residents for discharge. Discharge plans must identify the needs of each resident. [42 C.F.R. § 483.15.]

    A SNF cannot discharge or transfer a resident from the facility unless: (1) the transfer or discharge is necessary to meet the resident's welfare; (2) the resident's health has improved to the extent that the resident no longer needs the SNF's services; (3) the safety or health of other residents is endangered; (4) the resident has failed, after reasonable and appropriate notice, to pay for a stay at the facility; or (5) the facility ceases to operate. If a transfer or discharge is warranted, the reason must be documented in the resident's clinical record. [Soc. Sec. Act § 1819(c)(2)(A); 483.15(c)(1), (2).]

    Before the discharge or transfer occurs, the SNF must notify the resident (or family member or legal representative) about the transfer and discharge, as well as the reasons for it, generally 30 days in advance. [Soc. Sec. Act § 1819(c)(2)(B)(ii); 42 C.F.R. § 483.15(c)(3), (4).]

[¶ 249] "Skilled Nursing Facility"—Conditions of Participation

    As a general rule, a beneficiary's stay in a skilled nursing facility (SNF) will not be covered by Medicare unless the SNF is "participating" in the Medicare program, that is, the

SNF has been approved for Medicare participation by the government and has signed a participation agreement (see ¶ 730).

To participate as a SNF in the Medicare program, an institution must fit the statutory definition at Soc. Sec. Act § 1819(a). The law defines "skilled nursing facility" as an institution or a distinct part (see below) of an institution that:

(1) is primarily engaged in providing skilled nursing care and related services for residents who require medical or nursing care, or rehabilitation services for the rehabilitation of injured, disabled, or sick residents;

(2) has in effect a transfer agreement with one or more participating hospitals; and

(3) meets detailed requirements relating to services provided, residents' rights, professional standards, health and safety standards, and notification to the state of changes in ownership or control.

Facilities that primarily treat mental illness are specifically excluded from the SNF definition. [Soc. Sec. Act § 1819(a); 42 C.F.R. § 483.5(a).]

The term "skilled nursing facility" includes institutions operated or listed as religious nonmedical health care institutions. A Medicare beneficiary may choose to have services in these facilities covered as post-hospital extended care services. [Soc. Sec. Act § 1861(y).] See ¶ 228 for a discussion of religious nonmedical health care institutions.

A SNF must comply with the conditions of participation (CoPs) for SNFs set out at 42 C.F.R. 483 Subpart B. The CoPs impose specific requirements regarding admission standards, care planning, resident rights, the provision of services, care quality, facilities, and administration.

Planning. Upon admission, a SNF must make a comprehensive assessment of a resident's needs, strengths, goals, life history, and preferences. [42 C.F.R. § 483.20(b)(1).] Within 48 hours, the SNF must develop and implement a baseline care plan, to be followed, within seven days, by a comprehensive care plan including measurable objectives and time frames to meet a resident's medical, nursing, mental, and psychosocial needs. [42 C.F.R. § 483.21.]

Compliance. Beginning November 28, 2017, the operating organization for each SNF must have in operation a compliance and ethics program, which includes, among other mandates, the assignment of compliance staff, the development of compliance policies and procedures, and enforcement of those procedures. [42 C.F.R. § 483.85.]

Quality. Every SNF must develop, implement, and maintain an effective comprehensive, data-driven quality assurance and performance improvement (QAPI) program. The program may include, but is not limited to, systems and reports demonstrating systematic identification, reporting, investigation, analysis, and prevention of adverse events, as well as documentation demonstrating the development, implementation, and evaluation of corrective actions or performance improvement activities. SNFs must present their QAPI plan to the state survey agency no later than October 4, 2017. [42 C.F.R. § 483.75(a).] The Nursing Home Compare website contains searchable SNF quality information. [Soc. Sec. Act § 1819(i).]

Administration. SNFs must be licensed under state and local law and, in addition to satisfying Medicare CoPs, are required to meet applicable provisions of other HHS regulations, including those pertaining to nondiscrimination (45 C.F.R. Parts 80, 84, 91, and 92), protection of human subjects of research (45 C.F.R. Part 46), fraud and abuse (42 C.F.R. Part 455), and the protection of individually identifiable health information (45 C.F.R. Parts 160 and 164). [42 C.F.R. § 483.70(c).] Additionally, SNFs are prohibited from entering into pre-dispute agreements for binding arbitration with any resident or resident's representative. [42 C.F.R. § 483.70(n).]

Staffing. SNFs must develop, implement, and maintain an effective training program for all new and existing staff, as well as individuals providing services under a contractual arrangement, and volunteers, consistent with their expected roles. The training must focus on topics including, but not limited to: abuse, neglect, residents' rights, behavioral health, fraud, compliance, ethics, and infection control. [42 C.F.R. § 483.95.]

Other requirements. A state may require higher health and safety standards of SNFs than those mandated by accrediting bodies or by the federal government; a state's higher Medicaid standards then become Medicare standards. [42 C.F.R. § 488.3(b).]

A SNF of the Indian Health Service (IHS), whether operated by the IHS or a tribal organization, is eligible for Medicare payments if it meets all of the Medicare requirements for SNFs. [Soc. Sec. Act § 1880(a).]

A single set of requirements is applicable to SNFs under both Medicare and Medicaid. Thus, a SNF eligible to participate under one program is eligible to participate under the other, provided it agrees to the contract terms. The identical definition also permits a single consolidated survey to determine a facility's qualifications to participate in either program. [Soc. Sec. Act § 1919(a); 42 C.F.R. § 483.1(b).]

Skilled Nursing Beds in Hospitals

It is possible to treat part of an institution as a SNF. This may be done either by having a "distinct part" of the institution certified as a SNF or by having an agreement with the HHS Secretary under which inpatient hospital beds may be used for skilled nursing care on a "swing" basis (see ¶ 229). [Soc. Sec. Act § 1819(a); 42 C.F.R. § 483.5(a); *Medicare Claims Processing Manual*, Pub. 100-04, Ch. 6, § 100.]

To qualify for participation in the program as a "distinct part" SNF, the "distinct part" must be physically separated from the rest of the institution, that is, it must represent an entire, physically identifiable unit consisting of all the beds within that unit, such as a separate building, floor, wing, or ward. A distinct part must include all of the beds within the designated area and cannot consist of a random collection of individual rooms or beds that are scattered throughout the physical plant. [42 C.F.R. § 483.5(b)(1); *Medicare General Information, Eligibility, and Entitlement Manual*, Pub. 100-01, Ch. 5, § 30.1.]

Transfer Agreements

To participate in Medicare, a SNF must have a written transfer agreement with one or more participating hospitals providing for the transfer of patients between the hospital and the facility and for the interchange of medical and other information. If an otherwise qualified SNF has attempted in good faith, but without success, to enter into a transfer agreement, this requirement may be waived. [Soc. Sec. Act §§ 1819(a)(2), 1861(l); 42 C.F.R. § 483.70(j); Pub. 100-01, Ch. 5, § 30.2.]

Home Health Services

[¶ 250] Home Health Services: Qualifying Conditions for Coverage

Home health services are covered only if furnished by a home health agency (HHA) participating in the Medicare program. The HHA must act on a physician's certification that the individual: (1) is confined to the home (see ¶ 264); (2) needs intermittent skilled nursing care or physical or occupational therapy or speech-language pathology services; and (3) is under the care of a physician who has established a plan of care (see ¶ 260, ¶ 262). [Soc. Sec. Act § 1814(a)(2)(C); 42 C.F.R. §§ 409.42, 424.22.]

Coverage of skilled nursing care or therapy to perform a maintenance program is based on the patient's need for skilled care and does not require the patient to have the potential for improvement as a result of the nursing care or therapy. Skilled care may be necessary to improve or maintain a patient's current condition or to prevent or slow further deterioration of the patient's condition. [*Medicare Benefit Policy Manual*, Pub. 100-02, Ch. 7, § 20.1.2.]

Part A finances up to 100 visits during one home health spell of illness if the following criteria are met:

(1) the beneficiary is enrolled in Part A and B and qualifies for home health benefits;

(2) the beneficiary meets the three-consecutive-day-stay requirement; and

(3) the home health services are initiated, and the first covered home health visit is rendered, within 14 days of discharge from a three-consecutive-day stay in a hospital or rural primary care hospital, or within 14 days of discharge from a skilled nursing facility (SNF) in which the patient was provided post-hospital extended care services.

If the first home health visit is not initiated within 14 days of discharge or if the three-consecutive-day stay requirement is not met, then the services are covered under Part B. See ¶ 383 for a discussion of coverage of home health services under Part B. [Soc. Sec. Act § 1812(a)(3); Pub. 100-02, Ch. 7, § 60.1.]

If a beneficiary is enrolled only in Part A and qualifies for the Medicare home health benefit, then all of the home health services are financed under Part A. The 100-visit limit does not apply to beneficiaries who are only enrolled in Part A. If a beneficiary is enrolled only in Part B and qualifies for the Medicare home health benefit, then all of the home health services are financed under Part B. There is no 100-visit limit under Part B. [Soc. Sec. Act § 1812(a)(3); Pub. 100-02, Ch. 7, § 60.3.]

Home Health Definitions

"Post-institutional home health services" are defined as services initiated within 14 days after discharge from (1) a three-day hospital inpatient stay; or (2) a SNF stay in which post-hospital extended care services were provided. [Soc. Sec. Act § 1861(tt)(1).]

"Home health spell of illness" refers to a period of consecutive days, starting with the first day the beneficiary receives post-institutional home health services during a month in which he or she is entitled to Part A benefits. This period ends when the beneficiary has not received hospital, critical access hospital, SNF, or home health services for 60 days. [Soc. Sec. Act § 1861(tt)(2).]

A "home health episode of care" is a 60-day period starting on the day that the first billable services are provided to a beneficiary under a plan of care and ending 60 days later. On the 61st day that services are provided, a new home health episode of care begins, regardless of whether a service was delivered on that day. A beneficiary may have an unlimited number of non-overlapping episodes of care, and an episode can be shorter than 60 days. The 60-day episode of care is used to determine the amount of payment made on behalf of a beneficiary, and shorter episodes of care are pro-rated (see payment rates at ¶ 830). [*Medicare Claims Processing Manual*, Pub. 100-04, Ch. 10, § 10.1.5.]

"Home health services" are defined as the following items and services, provided on a visiting basis in a residence used as the patient's home, except as noted in item (7), below:

(1) part-time or intermittent nursing care provided by or under the supervision of a registered professional nurse;

(2) physical or occupational therapy or speech-language pathology services;

(3) medical social services under the direction of a physician;

(4) part-time or intermittent services of a home health aide who has completed an approved training program successfully;

(5) medical supplies (other than drugs and biologics), durable medical equipment, and, effective January 1, 2017, applicable disposable devices while under the plan of care;

(6) medical services of interns and residents-in-training under an approved teaching program of a hospital with which the HHA is affiliated; and

(7) any of the items and services that: (a) are provided on an outpatient basis under arrangements made by the HHA at a hospital or SNF, or at a qualified rehabilitation center, and (b) involve the use of equipment that cannot be made readily available in the patient's residence, or that are furnished at the facility while the patient is there to receive any item or service involving the use of such equipment. Transportation of the individual is not covered (see ¶ 257).

[Soc. Sec. Act § 1861(m); 42 C.F.R. § § 409.44, 409.45.]

[¶ 251] Skilled Nursing Care

If a patient qualifies for home health services, Medicare covers either part-time or intermittent skilled nursing services. For purposes of receiving home health care, "part-time or intermittent care" means skilled nursing and home health aide services furnished for up to 28 hours per week combined over any number of days per week so long as they are furnished for fewer than eight hours per day. Medicare may approve additional time of up to 35 hours per week, but for fewer than eight hours per day, on a case-by-case basis. For purposes of an individual qualifying for home health benefits and payment for provider claims, when the individual needs intermittent skilled nursing care, the term "intermittent" means skilled nursing care that is either provided or needed fewer than seven days each week, or fewer than eight hours of each day for periods up to and including 21 days, with extensions in exceptional circumstances. [Soc. Sec. Act § 1861(m); 42 C.F.R. § 409.44(b); *Medicare Benefit Policy Manual*, Pub. 100-02, Ch. 7, § 50.7.1.]

Skilled nursing care in excess of the amounts of care that meet the definitions of "part-time" or "intermittent" may be provided to a home care patient or purchased by other payers without bearing on whether the care is covered to the extent allowed by Medicare. The HHA may bill the home care patient or other payer for care that exceeds the hours of care that Medicare allows as reasonable and necessary. [Pub. 100-02, Ch. 7, § 50.7.1.]

Skilled nursing services are services that:

(1) require the skills of a registered nurse or a licensed practical nurse (or licensed vocational nurse) under the supervision of a registered nurse;

(2) are reasonable and necessary to the treatment of the patient's illness or injury; and

(3) are needed on an intermittent basis.

Coverage of skilled nursing care is based on the patient's need for skilled care, not on the potential for improvement from the nursing care. [42 C.F.R. § 409.44(b); Pub. 100-02, Ch. 7, § 40.1.] Skilled nursing services are covered when they are necessary to maintain the patient's current condition or prevent or slow further deterioration, as long as the beneficiary requires skilled care for the services to be safely and effectively provided. [Pub. 100-02, Ch. 7, § 40.1.1.]

In general, the intermittent basis requirement is met if a patient needs skilled nursing care at least once every 60 days. A one-time nursing service, such as giving a gamma globulin injection following exposure to hepatitis, for example, is not considered a need for intermittent skilled nursing care because a recurrence of the problem every 60 days is not medically predictable. If the need for a skilled nursing visit at least once every 60 days is medically predictable, but a situation arises after the first visit making additional visits unnecessary—for example, the patient is institutionalized or dies—the one visit is covered. [Pub. 100-02, Ch. 7, § 40.1.3.]

Home health records for every visit should reflect the need for the skilled medical care provided, including objective measurements of physical outcomes of treatment. [Pub. 100-02, Ch. 7, § 40.1.1.]

[¶ 252] Home Health Physical and Occupational Therapy and Speech-Language Pathology Services

Physical and occupational skilled therapy and speech-language pathology services furnished by a home health agency (HHA) or by others under arrangements made by the HHA are covered when provided in accordance with a physician's orders and by, or under the supervision of, a qualified therapist. To be covered as skilled therapy, the services must require the skills of a qualified therapist and must be reasonable and necessary for the treatment of the beneficiary's illness or injury, or for the restoration or maintenance of the function affected by the illness or injury. Coverage depends on the beneficiary's need for skilled care, not on the presence or absence of the beneficiary's potential for improvement. [42 C.F.R. § 409.44(c); *Medicare Benefit Policy Manual*, Pub. 100-02, Ch. 7, § § 40.2, 40.2.1.]

For therapy services to qualify for Medicare coverage, the following requirements must be met:

(1) the patient's plan of care must describe a course of therapy treatment and therapy goals that are consistent with the evaluation of the patient's function, and both must be included in the clinical record;

(2) the therapy goals must be established by a qualified therapist in conjunction with the physician;

(3) the patient's clinical record must include documentation describing how the course of therapy treatment for the patient's illness or injury is in accordance with accepted professional standards of clinical practice;

(4) therapy treatment goals described in the plan of care must be measurable and must pertain directly to the patient's illness or injury and the patient's resultant impairments; and

(5) the patient's clinical record must demonstrate that the method used to assess his or her function includes objective measurements of function in accordance with accepted professional standards of clinical practice that will allow for a comparison of successive measurements to determine the effectiveness of therapy goals. The objective measurements that assess activities of daily living may include but are not limited to eating, swallowing, bathing, dressing, toileting, walking, climbing stairs, or using assistive devices, and mental and cognitive factors.

[42 C.F.R. § 409.44(c) (1).]

Reasonableness and necessity. To be considered reasonable and necessary, the services must be considered under accepted standards of professional clinical practice to be a specific, safe, and effective treatment for the beneficiary's condition. In addition, the patient's function must be initially assessed and periodically reassessed by a qualified therapist of the corresponding discipline for the type of therapy being provided, using a method that includes objective measurements. If more than one discipline of therapy is being provided, a qualified therapist from each of the disciplines must perform the assessment and periodic reassessments. The measurement results and corresponding effectiveness of the therapy, or lack thereof, must be documented in the clinical record. [42 C.F.R. § 409.44(c)(2)(i)(A).]

In addition, one of the following three criteria must be met:

(1) there is an expectation that the beneficiary's condition will improve materially in a reasonable (and generally predictable) period of time based on the physician's assessment of the beneficiary's restoration potential and unique medical condition;

(2) the unique clinical condition of the patient may require the specialized skills, knowledge, and judgment of a qualified therapist to design or establish a safe and effective maintenance program required in connection with the patient's specific illness or injury; or

(3) the unique clinical condition of the patient may require the specialized skills of a qualified therapist to perform a safe and effective maintenance program required in connection with the patient's specific illness or injury.

[42 C.F.R. § 409.44(c)(2)(iii); Pub. 100-02, Ch. 7, § 40.2.1.]

For each therapy discipline, a qualified therapist (not an assistant) must assess and reassess the patient's function at least once every 30 calendar days. [42 C.F.R. § 409.44(c)(2)(i); Pub. 100-02, Ch. 7, § 40.2.1.]

Payment for therapy services. Payment for therapy services is included in the home health prospective payment amount received by the HHA for the episode of care. The Part B outpatient limitations on the total amount of therapy services that can be claimed in a year do not apply to therapy furnished by HHAs. See ¶ 830 for a discussion on the home health prospective payment system. [Pub. 100-02, Ch. 7, § 30.4; *Medicare Claims Processing Manual*, Pub. 100-04, Ch. 5, § 10.2.]

[¶ 253] Home Health Medical Social Services

Medical social services are covered as home health services if ordered by a physician and included in the plan of care. The frequency and nature of the services must be reasonable and necessary for the treatment of the beneficiary's condition. Medical social services are "dependent" services that are covered only if the beneficiary needs: (1) skilled nursing care on an intermittent basis; (2) physical therapy or speech-language pathology services; or (3) occupational therapy services on a continuing basis. [42 C.F.R. § 409.45(a), (c)(1).]

Medical social services are covered under Part A only if: (1) the services are necessary to resolve social or emotional problems that are, or are expected to become, an impediment to the effective treatment of the patient's medical condition or rate of recovery; (2) the frequency and nature of the services are reasonable and necessary for the treatment of the patient's conditions; (3) the medical social services are furnished by a qualified social worker or qualified social work assistant under the supervision of a social worker; and (4) the services needed to resolve the problems that are impeding the beneficiary's recovery require the skills of a qualified social worker or social worker assistant under the supervision of a qualified medical social worker. [42 C.F.R. § 409.45(c).]

Covered services include, but are not limited to, the following:

(1) assessment of the social and emotional factors related to the patient's illness, need for care, response to treatment, and adjustment to care;

(2) appropriate action to obtain community services to assist in resolving problems in these areas;

(3) assessment of the relationship of the patient's medical and nursing requirements to the home situation, financial resources, and availability of community resources; and

(4) counseling services required by the patient.

[*Medicare Benefit Policy Manual*, Pub. 100-02, Ch. 7, § 50.3.]

Counseling services furnished to the patient's family are covered only when the home health agency (HHA) can demonstrate that a brief intervention (about two or three visits) by a medical social worker is necessary to remove a clear and direct impediment to the effective treatment of the patient's medical condition or to his or her rate of recovery. [42 C.F.R. § 409.45(c)(2)(ii); Pub. 100-02, Ch. 7, § 50.3.]

[¶ 254] Home Health Aides

Medicare covers part-time or intermittent services of a home health aide who has successfully completed a training program approved by the HHS Secretary. To be covered, these services must be ordered by a physician in the plan of care for a beneficiary who qualifies for home health services. The reason for the visits by the home health aide must be to provide hands-on personal care to the beneficiary or services that are needed to maintain the beneficiary's health or to facilitate treatment of the beneficiary's illness or injury. Services provided by the home health aide must be reasonable and necessary. The physician's order should indicate the frequency of the home health aide services required. [Soc. Sec. Act §§ 1861(m)(4), 1891(a)(3); 42 C.F.R. § 409.45(b).]

To be considered reasonable and necessary, the services must: (1) meet the requirements for home health aide services; (2) be of a type that the patient cannot perform himself or herself; and (3) be of a type that no able or willing caregiver can provide, or if there is a potential caregiver, the patient must be unwilling to receive care from that caregiver. [42 C.F.R. § 409.45(b)(3).]

Covered home health aide services include the following: (1) personal care of a patient; (2) simple dressing changes that do not require the skills of a licensed nurse; (3) assistance with medications that ordinarily are self-administered and do not require the skills of a licensed nurse; (4) assistance with activities that are directly supportive of skilled therapy, such as routine exercises and the practice of functional communication skills; and (5) routine care of prosthetic and orthotic devices. [42 C.F.R. § 409.45(b)(1); *Medicare Benefit Policy Manual*, Pub. 100-02, Ch. 7, § 50.2.]

The discussion on intermittent services at ¶ 251 is applicable also to home health aides.

[¶ 255] Medical Supplies and Durable Medical Equipment

Covered medical supplies are items that, due to their therapeutic or diagnostic characteristics, are essential to enable the home health agency (HHA) to effectively carry out the plan of care that the physician ordered for the treatment or diagnosis of the patient's illness or injury. This includes such items as: catheters and catheter supplies; ostomy bags and ostomy care supplies; dressings and wound care supplies, such as sterile gloves, gauze, and applicators; and intravenous supplies. [Soc. Sec. Act §§ 1861(m)(5), 1866(a)(1)(P); 42 C.F.R. §§ 409.45(f), 489.20(k); *Medicare Benefit Policy Manual*, Pub. 100-02, Ch. 7, §§ 50.4.1.1 and 50.4.2.]

Effective January 1, 2017, also included are applicable disposable devices, defined: (1) disposable negative pressure wound therapy devices that are integrated systems composed of a nonmanual vacuum pump, a receptacle for collecting exudate, and dressings for the purposes of wound therapy; and (2) devices that substitute for, and are used in lieu of, negative pressure wound therapy durable medical equipment items that are an integrated systems of a negative pressure vacuum pump, a separate exudate collection canister, and dressings that would otherwise be covered for individuals for such wound therapy. [Soc. Sec. Act §§ 1834(s)(2), 1861(m)(5).]

Limited amounts of medical supplies may be left in the home between visits when repeated applications are required and rendered by the patient or by caregivers. These items must be part of the plan of care in which the home health staff is actively involved. For example, if the patient is independent in giving himself or herself insulin injections but the nurse visits once a day to change wound dressings, the wound dressings/irrigation solution may be left in the home between visits. Supplies that require administration by a nurse, such as needles, syringes, and catheters, should not be left in the home between visits. [Pub. 100-02, Ch. 7, § 50.4.1.3.]

HHAs must offer to furnish catheters, catheter supplies, ostomy bags, and supplies related to ostomy care to any individual who needs them as part of the provision of health services. [Soc. Sec. Act § 1866(a)(1)(P); 42 C.F.R. § 489.20(k).]

Durable medical equipment (DME) may be covered under the home health benefit as either a Part A or Part B service. DME furnished by an HHA as a home health service is always covered by Part A if the beneficiary is entitled to Part A. The coinsurance for DME furnished as a home health service is 20 percent of the customary charge for the services. [42 C.F.R. §§ 409.45(e), 409.50.]

Exclusion of Drugs and biologics

Drugs and biologics are generally excluded from coverage as a home health benefit. [Soc. Sec. Act § 1861(m)(5); 42 C.F.R. § 409.49(a).] In certain cases they may be covered under Part B, such as when they are administered by a physician as a part of his or her professional services (see ¶ 351 and ¶ 362). The administration of medication also may be covered if the services of a licensed nurse are required to administer the medications safely and effectively for the reasonable and necessary treatment of the illness or injury. [Pub. 100-02, Ch. 7, § 40.1.2.4.]

Osteoporosis drugs. Injections of osteoporosis drugs are covered as non-routine medical supplies for homebound female beneficiaries in certain circumstances (the nursing visit to perform the injection may be the individual's qualifying service for home health coverage) if:

(1) the individual's physician certifies that the individual sustained a bone fracture that a physician certifies was related to post-menopausal osteoporosis and she is unable to learn the skills needed to self-administer the drug, and that her family or caregivers are unable or unwilling to administer the drug, or she is otherwise physically or mentally incapable of administering the drug; and

(2) the individual is confined to the home.

[Soc. Sec. Act § 1861(kk); Pub. 100-02, Ch. 7, § 50.4.3; *Medicare Claims Processing Manual*, Pub. 100-04, Ch. 10, § 90.1.]

[¶ 256] Interns and Residents-in-Training

Home health services include the medical services of interns and residents-in-training under an approved hospital teaching program, if the services are ordered by the physician who is responsible for the plan of care and the home health agency (HHA) is affiliated with, or under common control of, a hospital providing the medical services. "Approved" means:

(1) approved by the Accreditation Council for Graduate Medical Education;

(2) in the case of an osteopathic hospital, approved by the Committee on Hospitals of the Bureau of Professional Education of the American Osteopathic Association;

(3) in the case of an intern or resident-in-training in the field of dentistry, approved by the Council on Dental Education of the American Dental Association; or

(4) in the case of an intern or resident-in-training in the field of podiatry, approved by the Council on Podiatric Education of the American Podiatric Association.

[42 C.F.R. § 409.45(g); *Medicare Benefit Policy Manual*, Pub. 100-02, Ch. 7, § 50.5.]

[¶ 257] Outpatient Services

In certain instances, the services described in ¶ 251–¶ 256, provided on an outpatient basis, can be included as home health services (see ¶ 250, item (7)). While the beneficiary ordinarily must be homebound to be eligible for home health services, such services are covered if furnished under arrangements at a hospital, skilled nursing facility (SNF), rehabilitation center, or outpatient department associated with a medical school and if the services: (1) require the use of equipment (for example, hydrotherapy) that cannot be made available at the beneficiary's home; or (2) are furnished while the beneficiary is at the facility to receive services requiring the use of such equipment. The hospital, SNF, or outpatient department must be a qualified provider of services. [42 C.F.R. § 409.47(b); *Medicare Benefit Policy Manual*, Pub. 100-02, Ch. 7, § 50.6.]

In some cases, special transportation arrangements may have to be made to bring the homebound patient to the institution providing these special services. The cost of transporting an individual to a facility cannot be reimbursed as a home health service. [42 C.F.R. § 409.49(b); Pub. 100-02, Ch. 7, § 50.6.]

[¶ 260] Physician Certification and Recertification of Home Health Services

The home health patient must be under the care of a physician who established the plan of care (POC). [42 C.F.R. § 424.22(a)(1)(iv).] The physician must be qualified to sign the physician certification and the POC (see ¶ 262). Doctors of medicine, osteopathy, or podiatric medicine are considered qualified, but a podiatrist may establish a POC only if consistent with the functions authorized for that specialty by state law. [42 C.F.R. § 409.42(b).]

Home Health Certification and Recertification

As a condition for payment of home health services under Medicare Part A or Medicare Part B, a physician must certify the following:

(1) the patient needs or needed intermittent skilled nursing care, or physical therapy speech-language pathology services;

(2) home health services were required because the individual was confined to the home except when receiving outpatient services;

(3) a plan for furnishing the services has been established and is periodically reviewed by a physician who is a doctor of medicine, osteopathy, or podiatric medicine;

(4) the services were furnished while the individual was under the care of a physician who is a doctor of medicine, osteopathy, or podiatric medicine; and

(5) a face-to-face patient encounter (described below) occurred.

[Soc. Sec. Act §§ 1814(a)(2)(C), 1835(a)(2)(A); 42 C.F.R. § 424.22(a).]

The home health agency must obtain the certification of need for home health ser-vicesat the time the POC is established or as soon thereafter as possible. The physician who establishes the plan must sign and date the certification. Documentation in the certifying physician's medical records and/or the acute/post-acute care facility's medical records must used as the basis for certification of home health eligibility. [42 C.F.R. § 424.22(a), (c).]

Face-to-face encounter. The physician responsible for performing the initial certifica-tion must document that a face-to-face patient encounter, related to the primary reason the patient requires home health services, has occurred no more than 90 days prior to the home health start of care date, or within 30 days of the start of the home health care. The physician must include the date of the encounter and an explanation of the clinical findings supporting the patient's homebound status and the need for either intermittent skilled nursing services or therapy services. [Soc. Sec. Act § 1814(a)(2)(C); 42 C.F.R. § 424.22(a)(1)(v).]

The face-to-face encounter may be performed by one of the following:

(1) the certifying physician;

(2) a physician with privileges who cared for the patient in an acute or post-acute care facility from which the patient was directly admitted to home health;

(3) a nurse practitioner or a clinical nurse specialist working in collaboration with either of the above physicians; or

(4) a certified nurse-midwife or a physician assistant working under the supervi-sion of either of the above physicians.

[Soc. Sec. Act § 1814(a)(2)(C); 42 C.F.R. § 424.22(a)(1)(v)(A).]

The face-to-face patient encounter may occur through telehealth. [Soc. Sec. Act § 1814(a)(2)(C); 42 C.F.R. § 424.22(a)(1)(v)(B).]

Recertification of the Need for Home Health Services

Recertification must occur at least every 60 days, preferably at the time the plan is reviewed, when there is a need for continuous home health care after an initial 60-day episode. The physician who reviews the plan of care must sign and date the recertification. Recertification is required more often than every 60 days when there is a: (1) beneficiary-elected transfer; or (2) discharge with goals met and/or no expectation of a return to home health care. [42 C.F.R. § 424.22(b).]

The recertification statement must indicate the continuing need for services and esti-mate how much longer the services will be required. The need for occupational therapy may be the basis for continuing services that were initiated because the individual needed skilled nursing care or physical therapy or speech therapy. [42 C.F.R. § 424.22(b)(2).]

[¶ 262] Home Health Plan of Care Requirement

Home health items and services must be furnished under a plan of care (POC) established and periodically reviewed by a physician. [Soc. Sec. Act § 1861(m); 42 C.F.R. §§ 409.42(d), 409.43.] The same physician must certify the medical necessity of the home health services, signing the certification at the time the POC is established (see ¶ 260). [42 C.F.R. § 424.22(a).]

A physician that has a financial relationship with the home health agency (HHA) providing services may not establish a POC or certify and recertify services. [42 C.F.R. § 424.22(d).] See ¶ 720 on fraud and abuse.

Content of the Home Health Plan of Care

The POC must contain the following:

¶262

(1) all pertinent diagnoses, including the beneficiary's mental status;

(2) types of services, supplies, and equipment required;

(3) frequency of visits, prognosis, rehabilitation potential;

(4) functional limitations;

(5) activities permitted;

(6) nutritional requirements;

(7) all medications and treatments;

(8) safety measures to protect against injury;

(9) instructions for timely discharge or referral; and

(10) any additional items the HHA or physician choose to include.

[42 C.F.R. §§409.43(a), 484.18(a); *Medicare Benefit Policy Manual*, Pub. 100-02, Ch. 7, §30.2.1.]

The physician must consult with a qualified therapist as necessary before establishing therapy services in the POC. The course of treatment for therapy services in a POC must: (1) include measurable therapy treatment goals pertaining directly to the patient's illness or injury and the patient's resultant impairments; (2) include the expected duration of therapy services; and (3) describe a course of treatment consistent with the qualified therapist's assessment of the patient's function. [42 C.F.R. §484.18(a); Pub. 100-02, Ch. 7, §30.2.1.]

The physician's orders in the POC must specify the medical treatments to be furnished as well as the type of HH discipline who will furnish the ordered services and at what frequency the services will be furnished. Orders that are described as "as needed" or PRN must be accompanied by a description of the patient's medical signs and symptoms that would occasion the visit. These provisions in a POC also must include a specific number of such visits to be made under the order until an additional physician order must be obtained. [42 C.F.R. §409.43(b); Pub. 100-02, Ch. 7, §30.2.2.]

The physician must sign the POC before the HHA submits a claim for payment. Services may be provided before the POC is signed because a claim is not submitted until the end of a 60-day episode of care. The physician must sign and date any changes to the POC must also be signed and dated by the physician. [42 C.F.R. §409.43(c); Pub. 100-02, Ch. 7, §30.2.3.]

If any services are provided based on a physician's oral orders, the orders must be put in writing and signed and dated with the date of receipt by the registered nurse or qualified therapist responsible for furnishing or supervising the ordered services. The physician must countersign and date the oral orders before the HHA bills for the care. [42 C.F.R. §409.43(d); Pub. 100-02, Ch. 7, §30.2.4A.]

Plan of Care Review

The physician who established the plan of care must review and sign it at least every 60 days. The review must occur more frequently than every 60 days if there is: (1) a beneficiary-elected transfer; (2) a significant change in condition; or (3) a discharge with goals met and/or no expectation of a return to home health care and the patient returns to home health care during the 60-day episode. Each review of a beneficiary's plan of care must contain the signature of the physician who reviewed it and the date of review. [42 C.F.R. §§409.43(e), 484.18(b); Pub. 100-02, Ch. 7, §30.2.6.]

[¶ 264] Patient Confined to Home

For a beneficiary to be eligible to receive covered home health services, he or she must generally be confined to home. In all cases, a physician must certify this confinement. [Soc. Sec. Act § 1814(a)(2)(C); 42 C.F.R. §§ 409.42(a), 409.47.]

A beneficiary is considered "confined to home" if the following criteria are met:

    (1) The patient must either:

        • need the aid of supportive devices such as crutches, canes, wheelchairs, and walkers; the use of special transportation; or the assistance of another person in order to leave his or her place of residence because of illness or injury; or

        • have a condition such that leaving his or her home is medically contraindicated.

    (2) The patient must also:

        • have a normal inability to leave home; and

        • require a considerable and taxing effort to leave home.

[*Medicare Benefit Policy Manual*, Pub. 100-02, Ch. 7, § 30.1.1.]

Beneficiaries are considered homebound even if they take an occasional absence from the home for nonmedical purposes. The absences must be infrequent, relatively short in duration, and not indicate that the patient has the ability to obtain health care outside of the home. These determinations are made by assessing the patient's condition over a period of time. [Pub. 100-02, Ch. 7, § 30.1.1.]

Attendance at a religious service is considered an absence of infrequent or short duration. Beneficiaries can be considered homebound while receiving therapeutic, psychosocial, or medical treatment in a state-licensed adult day-care program on a regular basis. [Soc. Sec. Act §§ 1814(a), 1835(a).]

Patient's Place of Residence

Home health services must be furnished on a visiting basis in a place used as the patient's residence. This may be his or her own dwelling, an apartment, a relative's home, a home for the aged, or some other type of institution. However, an institution may not be considered a patient's place of residence if it meets at least the most important requirement in the definition of "hospital" (see ¶ 229) or in the definition of "skilled nursing facility" (see ¶ 249). [42 C.F.R. § 409.47(a); Pub. 100-02, Ch. 7, § 30.1.2.]

[¶ 266] Home Health Visits

A visit occurs when a home health worker makes personal contact with the patient in order to provide a covered service in the patient's residence. If the HHA furnishes services in an outpatient facility under arrangements with the facility, one visit may be covered for each type of service provided.. [42 C.F.R. § 409.48(c); *Medicare Benefit Policy Manual*, Pub. 100-02, Ch. 7, § 70.2.]

There is nothing to preclude an HHA from adopting telemedicine or other technologies in order to promote efficiency; however, those technologies will not be specifically recognized or reimbursed by Medicare under the home health benefit. [Soc. Sec. Act § 1895(e)(1)(B); Pub. 100-02, Ch. 7, § 110.]

Home Health Evaluation Visits

When HHA personnel make an initial evaluation visit, the cost of this visit is considered an administrative expense because the patient has not been accepted for care. If during the course of this initial evaluation visit the HHA determines that the patient is suitable for home health care, and provides the first skilled service as ordered under the physician's plan of treatment, the visit would become the first billable visit. An observation and evaluation or reevaluation visit ordered by the physician for the purpose of evaluating the patient's continuing need for skilled services is covered as a skilled visit. [Pub. 100-02, Ch. 7, § 70.2C.]

A supervisory visit made by a nurse or other personnel to evaluate the patient's specific personal care needs or to review whether the aide is meeting the patient's personal care needs is considered an administrative function and is not chargeable to the patient as a skilled visit. [Pub. 100-02, Ch. 7, § 70.2C.]

Home Health Patient-Specific Comprehensive Assessments

HHAs participating in Medicare are required to conduct patient-specific comprehensive assessments on certain patients using the "Outcomes and Assessment Information Set" (OASIS). HHAs must incorporate OASIS items in their own assessments, including information regarding demographics and patient history, living arrangements, supportive assistance, sensory status, integumentary status, elimination status, neuro/emotional/behavioral status, activities of daily living, medications, equipment management, emergent care, and discharge. [42 C.F.R. § 484.55(e).]

Initial assessment. Within 48 hours of the patient's referral or return home, or on the start-of-care date ordered by the physician, a registered nurse or an appropriate therapist must complete an initial assessment that includes an eligibility evaluation. [42 C.F.R. § 484.55(a).]

Comprehensive assessments. Except for a patient whose physician orders only physical, occupational, or speech therapy, the comprehensive assessment must be completed by a registered nurse within five calendar days of the start of care. A speech-language pathologist, physical therapist, or occupational therapist may conduct the assessment if the physician ordered only these types of therapy. [42 C.F.R. § 484.55(b).]

The comprehensive assessment should reflect the patient's current health status accurately and include information that demonstrates the patient's progress toward achievement of desired outcomes. Comprehensive assessments must be updated within the last five days of every 60 days beginning with the start-of-care date unless there is a:

(1) significant change in condition;

(2) transfer to another HHA elected by the beneficiary; or

(3) discharge and then a return to the same HHA during a 60-day episode.

[42 C.F.R. § 484.55(d).]

Comprehensive assessments also must be updated at discharge and within 48 hours of a beneficiary's return home from a hospital stay longer than 24 hours for any reason other than diagnostic testing. [42 C.F.R. § 484.55(d).]

Drug regimen review. The comprehensive assessment includes a review of all medications the patient is using at the time of the assessment. This review should identify any potential adverse effects and drug reactions, including ineffective drug therapy, duplicate drug therapy, significant side effects, significant drug interactions, and noncompliance with drug therapy. [42 C.F.R. § 484.55(c).]

Confidentiality. The HHA must ensure the confidentiality of all patient-identifiable information contained in the clinical record, including OASIS data, and may not release patient-identifiable OASIS information to the public. [42 C.F.R. § 484.11.] Under the conditions of participation for HHAs, patients whose data will be collected and used by the federal government must receive a notice of their privacy rights, including the right to refuse to answer questions. CMS has prepared standard statements notifying patients of their privacy rights, which are available on the CMS website at http://www.cms.gov/Center/Provider-Type/Home-Health-Agency-HHA-Center.html. The statements, which are available in English and Spanish in versions for Medicare/Medicaid beneficiaries and for non-Medicare/non-Medicaid patients, must be incorporated into HHAs' admission processes. [42 C.F.R. § 484.10.]

See ¶ 715 for more discussion on the privacy of beneficiaries' medical data and the requirements for providers, including the need to obtain authorizations from beneficiaries prior to the release of individually identifiable health information in certain circumstances.

Home health prospective payment system. The weighted answers to several OASIS items, including the need for therapy, provide a key element of Medicare reimbursement under the home health prospective payment system (HH PPS) (see ¶ 830).

Advance Directives

Advance medical directives are written instructions, such as a living will or durable power of attorney for health care, recognized under state law and governing provision of care when the individual is incapacitated. HHAs much inform beneficiaries about advance directives and document their choices in medical records. HHAs must provide the information to the beneficiary before care is provided during the initial visit. [Soc. Sec. Act § 1866(f)(3); 42 C.F.R. § 489.102(a).]

Beneficiaries are not *required* to make advance directives, and the amount and type of care may not be conditioned upon the completion or noncompletion of an advance directive. HHAs must provide written information to beneficiaries about their rights under state law to make decisions concerning their medical care, including the right to accept or refuse medical care and the right to formulate medical directives before care is started. [Soc. Sec. Act § 1866(f)(1); 42 C.F.R. § 489.102(a).]

[¶ 267] Specific Exclusions from Home Health Coverage

In addition to the general exclusions applicable to both parts of the Medicare program, which are discussed in Chapter 6, the following are excluded from home health services:

    (1) drugs and biologics, except for osteoporosis drugs (see ¶ 255);

    (2) transportation services from place of residence to a facility to receive home health services on an outpatient basis (see ¶ 257);

    (3) services that would not be covered as inpatient services (see ¶ 217);

    (4) housekeeping services the sole purpose of which is to enable the patient to continue residing in his or her home (e.g., cooking, shopping, Meals on Wheels, cleaning, laundry);

    (5) end-stage renal disease (ESRD) services covered under the ESRD prospective payment system;

    (6) prosthetic devices covered under Part B (catheters, ostomy bags, and supplies are not considered prosthetic devices if furnished under a home health plan of care and are not subject to this exclusion);

    (7) medical social services provided to members of the beneficiary's family that are not incidental to covered social services provided to the beneficiary;

    (8) respiratory care furnished by a respiratory therapist in a beneficiary's home;

    (9) in-home visits by dietitians or nutritionists; and

(10) effective January 1, 2021, home infusion therapy services.

[Soc. Sec. Act § § 1834, 1861(b), (m); 42 C.F.R. § 409.49; *Medicare Benefit Policy Manual*, Pub. 100-02, Ch. 7, § 80.]

[¶ 268] "Home Health Agency" Defined—Qualified Home Health Agencies

As a general rule, services furnished by a home health agency (HHA) will not be covered by Medicare unless the HHA has been approved for Medicare participation by the government and has signed a participation agreement (see ¶ 730). [42 C.F.R. § 409.41.]

To participate in Medicare as a "home health agency," an organization must:

(1) be a public agency or private organization, or a subdivision of such an agency or organization;

(2) be primarily engaged in providing skilled nursing and other therapeutic services;

(3) have policies established by a group of professional personnel (including at least one physician and one registered nurse) associated with the agency;

(4) maintain clinical records on all patients;

(5) provide for supervision of services by a physician or nurse;

(6) be licensed by the state licensing agency where required;

(7) have in effect an overall plan and budget that meets certain requirements;

(8) meet certain conditions of participation (COPs) and health and safety and financial stability requirements;

(9) provide the Secretary with a surety bond in the form specified by the HHS Secretary (in an amount of at least $50,000), which the Secretary determines is commensurate with the volume of payments made to the HHA; and

(10) meet an any additional requirements that the Secretary finds necessary for the effective and efficient implementation of the program.

[Soc. Sec. Act § 1861(o); *Medicare General Information, Eligibility, and Entitlement Manual*, Pub. 100-01, Ch. 5, § 50.]

For Part A, but not for Part B, the definition of an HHA does not include any agency or organization that is primarily for the care and treatment of mental diseases. [Soc. Sec. Act § 1861(o).]

Arrangements may be made by an HHA with other HHAs to furnish items or services under certain circumstances. Any HHA providing items and services must agree not to charge the patient for covered services or items and must agree to return money incorrectly collected (see ¶ 830). [Pub. 100-01, Ch. 5, § 50.2.]

Home Health Conditions of Participation

The requirements for participating HHAs and the additional health and safety requirements prescribed by the HHS Secretary are incorporated into conditions of participation (COPs) for HHAs. These conditions are included in the regulations governing the Medicare program. [42 C.F.R. Part 484.]

HHAs that are out of compliance with COPs may correct their performance and achieve prompt compliance through new methods, such as directed plans of correction or directed in-service training. CMS may impose sanctions on and terminate HHAs that are out of compliance with COPs. [42 C.F.R. § § 488.810, 488.850, 488.855.]

Hospice Care

[¶ 270] Hospice Care: Coverage in General

Hospice care is an interdisciplinary approach to caring for terminally ill patients by treating pain and providing comfort, rather than seeking a cure for the terminal disease. A hospice program must be a public agency or private organization that meets Medicare conditions of participation in order to qualify as a Medicare provider. [Soc. Sec. Act § 1861(dd).]

A Medicare beneficiary becomes eligible for hospice care upon a physician's certification that he or she has a terminal illness, i.e., is expected to live six months or less if the illness proceeds at its normal course. The prognosis is based on the physician's clinical judgment regarding the normal course of the patient's illness. [Soc. Sec. Act §§ 1814(a)(7)(A), 1861(dd)(3)(A); 42 C.F.R. § 418.20.]

When electing hospice care, the patient must be informed of the palliative, rather than curative, nature of the treatment Palliative care is defined as patient- and family-centered care that optimizes quality of life by anticipating, preventing, and treating suffering. Palliative care addresses physical, intellectual, emotional, social, and spiritual needs and facilitates patient autonomy, access to information, and choice. [42 C.F.R. §§ 418.3, 418.24(b)(2).]

Covered Hospice Services

"Hospice care" includes the following services and supplies:

(1) nursing care provided by or under the supervision of a registered professional nurse;

(2) physical or occupational therapy or speech-language pathology services;

(3) medical social services under the direction of a physician;

(4) homemaker services and the services of a home health aide (also known as a hospice aide) who has successfully completed an approved training program;

(5) medical supplies (including drugs and biologics) and the use of medical appliances;

(6) physicians' and nurse practitioners' services;

(7) short-term inpatient care, including both procedures necessary for pain control and symptom management and occasional respite care for periods up to five days;

(8) counseling (including dietary counseling) with respect to care of the terminally ill beneficiary and the family's and caregivers' adjustment to the beneficiary's death; and

(9) any other item or service that is specified in the plan of care and otherwise covered by Medicare.

[Soc. Sec. Act § 1861(dd)(1), (3)(B); 42 C.F.R. § 418.202.]

Nursing, home health aide, and homemaker services may be provided on a 24-hour, continuous basis during periods of crisis as necessary to allow the patient to remain at home. Respite care is short-term inpatient care provided to the patient only when necessary to relieve family members or other caregivers. Bereavement counseling is a required hospice service, available to the family before and up to one year after the patient's death, but it is not separately reimbursable. [Soc. Sec. Act § 1861(dd)(1); 42 C.F.R. § 418.204; *Medicare Benefit Policy Manual*, Pub. 100-02, Ch. 9, § 40.2.3.]

¶270

Custodial care and personal comfort items, while generally excluded by Medicare (see ¶ 616 and ¶ 625), are covered when the beneficiary is under the care of a hospice. [Soc. Sec. Act § 1862(a)(1)(C); 42 C.F.R. § 411.15(g), (j).]

A beneficiary who is denied coverage for hospice care because services received were determined not to be reasonable or necessary may nevertheless be entitled to Medicare coverage under the waiver-of-liability rules discussed at ¶ 915.

[¶ 272] Benefit Periods

A Medicare beneficiary may elect to receive hospice care for up to two periods of 90 days each, followed by an unlimited number of periods up to 60 days each. [Soc. Sec. Act § 1812(a)(4); 42 C.F.R. § 418.21(a).] A beneficiary electing to receive hospice care must choose to receive it through a particular hospice program. [Soc. Sec. Act § 1812(d)(1); 42 C.F.R. § 418.24(a)(1).]

Election of Hospice Benefits

In order to receive hospice care, a Medicare beneficiary (or, in the event of physical or mental incapacitation, his or her representative) must file an election statement with a particular hospice. Election statements must include all of the following:

(1) identification of the particular hospice and of the attending physician that will provide care to the individual (the individual or representative must acknowledge that the identified attending physician was his or her choice);

(2) the individual's or representative's acknowledgment that he or she has been given a full understanding of the palliative rather than curative nature of hospice care, as it relates to the individual's terminal illness;

(3) acknowledgment that certain Medicare services (see below) are waived by the election;

(4) the effective date of the election, which may be the first day of hospice care or a later date, but cannot be earlier than the date of the election statement; and

(5) the signature of the individual or representative.

[42 C.F.R. § 418.24(b).]

The election to receive hospice care continues through the initial election period and through subsequent election periods without a break in care as long as the beneficiary remains in the care of a hospice, does not revoke the election, and is not discharged from the hospice. [42 C.F.R. § 418.24(c).]

Revocation of election. The Medicare beneficiary or his or her representative may revoke the election of hospice care at any time during an election period by filing a signed statement that includes the revocation's effective date. Upon revocation, the beneficiary is no longer covered under Medicare for hospice care and resumes Medicare coverage of the benefits waived by election. If the beneficiary remains (or later becomes) eligible for hospice coverage, he or she may file an election statement to receive hospice coverage at any time. [Soc. Sec. Act § 1812(d)(2)(B); 42 C.F.R. §§ 418.24(e), 418.28.]

Attending physician. A beneficiary receiving hospice benefits may change the designated attending physician by filing a signed statement with the hospice. The statement must identify the new attending physician and include both the effective date of the change and the date signed. The effective date cannot be before the date the statement is signed. The statement must also acknowledge that the change in the attending physician is the beneficiary's choice. [42 C.F.R. § 418.24(f).]

Beneficiary Rights During A Hospice Benefit Period

When a beneficiary elects hospice care, he or she waives all rights to Medicare payments for certain services. Medicare will not pay for hospice care provided by a different hospice than the one designated by the patient (unless provided under arrangements made by the designated hospice). The beneficiary also waives the right to payment for any Medicare services that are related to the treatment of the terminal condition or a related condition, as well as to services that are equivalent to hospice care, unless the services are provided by the designated hospice, provided by another hospice under arrangements made by the designated hospice, or provided by the individual's attending physician if that physician is not an employee of the designated hospice or receiving compensation from the hospice for those services. [Soc. Sec. Act § 1812(d)(2)(A); 42 C.F.R. § 418.24(d).]

Medicare will pay for any item or service that is specified in the hospice plan of care as reasonable and necessary for the palliation and management of the patient's terminal illness and related conditions and for which Medicare payment would otherwise be made. [Soc. Sec. Act § 1861(dd)(1)(I); 42 C.F.R. § 418.202(i).]

A beneficiary also is entitled to change from one hospice program to another hospice program once per period. Such a change is not considered to be a revocation of an election if the individual is otherwise entitled to hospice care benefits within that period. [Soc. Sec. Act § 1812(d)(2)(C); 42 C.F.R. § 418.30.]

Example _____

Sam Green has elected to receive hospice care for a 90-day period at Hospice A. He now wants to move to Hospice B. During the 90-day period, he may elect to change programs to Hospice B, or Hospice A can make arrangements for services to be provided by Hospice B. If Sam changes to Hospice B, he cannot change to Hospice C within that 90-day period, but Hospice B can make arrangements for Hospice C to provide services for the remainder of the period. At the end of the period, Sam may change to Hospice C for the next period.

[¶ 274] Certification and Care Requirements

The hospice must obtain written certification of the beneficiary's terminal illness for each election period. In addition, the hospice medical director must recommend the patient for admission to the hospice in consultation with, or with input from, the patient's attending physician, if any. The recommendation must be signed by the physician and included in the patient's medical records. [42 C.F.R. §§ 418.22, 418.25.]

Certification and Recertification of Terminal Illness

At the beginning of the initial 90-day hospice benefit period, both the patient's attending physician, if any, and the medical director or physician member of the hospice interdisciplinary group must certify in writing that the patient is terminally ill. At the beginning of each subsequent period, only the hospice physician or the physician member of the hospice interdisciplinary group must recertify the patient's terminally ill status. [Soc. Sec. Act § 1814(a)(7)(A); 42 C.F.R. § 418.22(a)(1), (c).]

The hospice must obtain an initial certification of terminal illness within two days of admission to the hospice. If the hospice cannot obtain a written certification within two days, it must obtain an oral certification, and the written certification must be obtained before submission of a claim for payment. Subsequent certifications may be made orally, but the written certification must be made before the claim is submitted for payment. Certifications must be supported by documentation. [42 C.F.R. § 418.22(a)(3).]

Face-to-face encounter. If a beneficiary elects to continue to receive hospice care, a hospice physician or nurse practitioner must have a face-to-face encounter with the individual to determine continued eligibility for hospice care, before the 180th-day recertification and then each subsequent recertification. [Soc. Sec. Act § 1814(a)(7)(D); 42 C.F.R. § 418.22(a)(4).]

Content of certification. Certification of terminal illness must be based on the physician's or medical director's clinical judgment regarding the normal course of the individual's illness. The certification must:

(1) specify that the prognosis is for a life expectancy of six months or less if the terminal illness runs its normal course;

(2) contain clinical information and other documentation that supports the medical prognosis;

(3) include a brief narrative explanation of the clinical findings that supports a life expectancy of six months or less;

(4) include a written attestation by the physician or nurse practitioner who performed the face-to-face encounter; and

(5) be signed and dated by the physicians, and include the benefit period dates to which the certification or recertification applies.

[42 C.F.R. §§ 418.22(b), 418.25.]

Although nurse practitioners may serve as the attending physician, they may not certify or recertify the beneficiary's terminal illness or prognosis. [Soc. Sec. Act § 1814(a)(7)(A)(i)(I).]

Mandatory medical review. If a certain percentage of a hospice's patients receive care for over 180 days, CMS must conduct a medical review for any patient receiving care for this amount of time. The HHS Secretary establishes this percentage. [Soc. Sec. Act § 1814(a)(7)(E).]

Written Plan of Care

All hospice care must be provided according to a written plan of care (POC), established by the hospice medical director in conjunction with the hospice's interdisciplinary staff, before hospice care begins. Both the beneficiary's attending physician and the hospice medical director and interdisciplinary staff must periodically review the POC. [Soc. Sec. Act § 1814(a)(7)(B), (C); 42 C.F.R. §§ 418.56, 418.200.]

The hospice must develop an individualized POC reflecting patient and family goals and interventions based on the problems identified in initial and updated comprehensive assessments. The plan must include all services necessary for the palliation and management of the terminal illness and related conditions, including: (1) interventions to manage pain and symptoms; (2) a detailed statement of the scope and frequency of services necessary to meet the specific patient and family needs; (3) measurable outcomes anticipated from implementing and coordinating the POC; (4) drugs and treatment necessary to meet the needs of the patient; (5) medical supplies and appliances necessary to meet the needs of the patient; and (6) the interdisciplinary group's documentation of the patient's or representative's level of understanding, involvement, and agreement with the POC. [42 C.F.R. § 418.56(c).]

The hospice interdisciplinary group (in collaboration with the individual's attending physician, if any) must review, revise, and document the individualized POC as frequently as the patient's condition requires, but no less frequently than every 15 calendar days. A revised POC must include information from the patient's updated comprehensive assessment and must note the patient's progress toward outcomes and goals specified in the plan. [42 C.F.R. §418.56(d).]

Coordination of Services

The hospice must develop and maintain a system of communication and integration that: (1) ensures that the interdisciplinary group maintains responsibility for directing, coordinating, and supervising the care and services provided; (2) ensures that the care and services are provided in accordance with the POC; (3) ensures that the care and services provided are based on all assessments of the patient and family needs; (4) provides for and ensures the ongoing sharing of information between all disciplines providing care and services in all settings; and (5) provides for an ongoing sharing of information with other non-hospice health care providers furnishing services unrelated to the terminal illness and related conditions. [42 C.F.R. §418.56(e).]

[¶ 276] Discharge from Hospice Care

A patient may be discharged from a hospice program in three situations:

(1) the hospice determines that the patient is no longer terminally ill;

(2) the patient moves out of the hospice service area or transfers to another hospice; or

(3) for cause, because the behavior of the patient (or another individual in the patient's home) is disruptive, abusive, or uncooperative to the extent that delivery of care to the patient or the ability of the hospice to operate effectively is seriously impaired.

[42 C.F.R. §418.26(a).]

Before discharging a patient for any of these reasons, the hospice must obtain a written physician's discharge order from the hospice medical director. If a patient has an attending physician, this physician should be consulted before discharge and his or her review and decision included in the discharge note. [42 C.F.R. §418.26(b).]

Before discharging a patient for cause, the hospice must:

(1) advise the patient that discharge is being considered;

(2) ascertain that the patient's proposed discharge is not due to the patient's use of necessary hospice services;

(3) make a serious effort to resolve the problems presented by the patient or family; and

(4) document in the patient's records both the problems and the efforts made to resolve them.

[42 C.F.R. §418.26(a)(3).]

Discharge planning. Hospices must have a process for discharge planning and must initiate this process when the staff begins to consider discharge. The discharge planning process must include planning for any necessary family counseling, patient education, or other services before the patient is discharged because he or she is no longer terminally ill. [42 C.F.R. §418.26(d).]

Effect of discharge. A patient who has been discharged from hospice care no longer has an election of hospice care in effect. A patient whose condition remains terminal or becomes terminal again may make a new election of hospice care. Until a new election is made, the patient is not eligible for hospice care and Medicare coverage resumes for any benefits waived during hospice election. [42 C.F.R. §418.26(c).]

[¶ 278] Deductibles and Coinsurance

During the period of election for hospice care, no copayments or deductibles other than those for drugs, biologics, and respite care apply for hospice care services provided to the patient, regardless of the setting where care is provided. [Soc. Sec. Act § 1813(a)(4).]

Drugs and biologics. The beneficiary is liable for a coinsurance payment for each palliative drug and biologic prescription provided by the hospice except when the individual is an inpatient. The amount of coinsurance for each prescription must be about 5 percent of the cost of the drug or biologic to the hospice, up to $5, in accordance with the hospice's established drug copayment schedule approved by the Medicare contractor. The cost of the drug or biologic may not exceed what a prudent buyer would pay in similar circumstances. [Soc. Sec. Act § 1813(a)(4)(A)(i); 42 C.F.R. § 418.400(a).]

Respite care. The amount of coinsurance for each respite care day is 5 percent of the Medicare payment for a respite care day. The amount of the individual's coinsurance liability for respite care during a hospice coinsurance period may not exceed the inpatient hospital deductible applicable for the year that the hospice coinsurance period began (see ¶ 220). A "hospice coinsurance period" is the period of consecutive days beginning with the first day the patient's hospice election is in effect and ending after 14 consecutive days of the election no longer being in effect. [Soc. Sec. Act § 1813(a)(4)(A)(ii); 42 C.F.R. § 418.400(b).]

[¶ 280] Hospice Program Requirements

To qualify as a Medicare provider, a hospice program must be a public agency or a private organization that is primarily engaged in providing the care and services described above and that makes these services available as needed, on a 24-hour basis. The hospice program must provide care and services in individuals' homes, on an outpatient basis, and on a short-term inpatient basis. The total number of days of short-term inpatient care provided in any 12-month period to patients with a hospice election in effect with respect to that hospice may not exceed 20 percent of the days during that period during which hospice elections are in effect. [Soc. Sec. Act § 1861(dd)(2)(A).]

Hospices must have an interdisciplinary group of staff that includes at least a physician medical director, a registered nurse, a social worker, and a pastoral or other counselor. All must be hospice employees except the physician, who can be under contract with the hospice, and the pastoral counselor. The functions of the group are to:

- establish and review the plan of care for each patient;
- maintain central records on each patient;
- provide or supervise the provision of hospice care and services;
- govern and set policy for the hospice;
- continue providing service even if the patient is no longer able to pay;
- use volunteers in accordance with standards set by the HHS Secretary;
- maintain records on the use of volunteers and the costs savings and expanded services achieved; and
- ensure that the hospice complies with state licensing laws and state and federal regulations.

[Soc. Sec. Act § 1861(dd)(2)(B)–(G); 42 C.F.R. §§ 418.56, 418.58.]

In addition, a hospice program is required to make reasonable efforts to arrange for volunteer clergy or other members of religious organizations to visit patients who desire such visits and to advise patients of this opportunity. Hospice programs are also required to provide counseling services. [42 C.F.R. § 418.64(d)(3).]

Generally, hospice employees and volunteer staff must provide hospice services directly. The nursing, counseling, and medical social service obligations are considered "core services," which must be provided directly by hospice employees, except that the hospice may use contracted physicians. Hospices may contract with other hospices to provide nursing or medical social services in exigent circumstances, such as an unanticipated period of high patient load, staffing shortages due to illness or other events, when a patient temporarily travels outside a hospice program's service area, and to provide highly specialized services that are not frequently required. [42 C.F.R. § 418.64.]

A hospice in a non-urban area may apply for a waiver to contract for nursing services if it: (1) was operating before January 1, 1983; and (2) demonstrates that it has made a good-faith effort to hire a sufficient number of nurses to directly provide nursing care. [Soc. Sec. Act § 1861(dd)(5).]

A hospice that contracts for services remains responsible for providing and supervising those services professionally, administratively, and financially. All authorizations and all services provided by the contractor must be documented as necessary. [42 C.F.R. § 418.310.] If a hospice makes arrangements with another hospice to provide services under exigent circumstances, the hospice that the beneficiary elected is reimbursed. [Soc. Sec. Act § 1861(dd)(5)(D); 42 C.F.R. § 418.302(d)(2).]

A provider that is certified for Medicare participation as a hospital, skilled nursing facility, or home health agency may also be certified as a hospice. If so, the provider must have separate provider agreements and must file separate cost reports. [Soc. Sec. Act § 1861(dd)(4).]

A certified hospice program is surveyed by its state or local survey agency (see ¶ 703) at least once every three years. [Soc. Sec. Act § 1861(dd)(4)(C).]

Chapter 3– MEDICARE PART B—SUPPLEMENTAL MEDICAL INSURANCE

Eligibility and Enrollment

[¶ 300] Eligibility for Part B Benefits

Unlike the inpatient hospital insurance benefits program (Part A of Title XVIII of the Social Security Act), which is largely financed by Federal Insurance Contributions Act (FICA) taxes, the Supplementary Medical Insurance (SMI) Benefits for the Aged and Disabled (Part B) program is financed by monthly premium payments by enrollees and federal contributions to the SMI Trust Fund from the federal government. Medicare Part B covers physician services, medical supplies, and other outpatient services, which are not paid by Medicare Part A. [Soc. Sec. Act § 1844; 42 C.F.R. § 407.2.]

For most individuals who are entitled to Part A benefits, enrollment in Part B occurs automatically, unless they elect to decline enrollment (see ¶ 312).

Enrollment for Part B benefits is open to all persons who are entitled to Part A benefits (see ¶ 200). An individual also may enroll in Part B even if he or she is not entitled to Part A benefits if the individual is: (1) age 65 or over; (2) a resident of the United States; and (3) either (a) a citizen of the United States, or (b) an alien lawfully admitted to the United States for permanent residence who has resided in the United States continuously during the five years immediately preceding he or she applies for enrollment. [Soc. Sec. Act § 1836; 42 C.F.R. § 407.10(a).] The term "United States" includes the Commonwealth of Puerto Rico, the Virgin Islands, Guam, American Samoa, and the Northern Mariana Islands. [Soc. Sec. Act § § 210(i), 1861(x).]

For the disabled under age 65 (see ¶ 204), neither Part A nor Part B coverage can begin before the 25th month of the individual's entitlement to disability benefits, except for Amyotrophic Lateral Sclerosis (ALS) patients (see ¶ 204) and individuals exposed to public health hazards (see below). [Soc. Sec. Act § § 226(b) and (h), 1881A.]

The Medicare coverage period for persons diagnosed with end-stage renal disease (ESRD) generally begins in the third month after the month when dialysis begins. Specific coverage rules for ESRD patients are described at ¶ 205.

Exposure to Health Hazards

"Environmental exposure affected individuals" are deemed immediately eligible for Medicare benefits, regardless of age. Part A entitlement is immediate, while Part B enrollment eligibility is available the first month the individual is deemed affected. [Soc. Sec. Act § 1881A(a).]

An "environmental exposure affected individual" means an individual who:

(1) is diagnosed with one or more medical conditions such as asbestosis, pleural thickening, or pleural plaques;

(2) has been present for an aggregate total of six months in a geographic area subject to an emergency declaration during a period not less than 10 years prior to such diagnosis and before the implementation of all remedial and removal actions; and

(3) has filed an application for benefits.

[Soc. Sec. Act § 1881A(e).]

Suspended Benefits for Aliens Outside of the U.S.

Part B benefits are suspended in the same manner they are suspended under Part A in the case of certain aliens who are or were outside the United States (see ¶ 200). [Soc. Sec. Act § 202(t)(9).]

Conviction of Subversive Activities

An individual convicted of any of the offenses stipulated in section 202(u)(1) of the Social Security Act, relating to subversive activities, cannot enroll in the Part B plan. [Soc. Sec. Act § 202(u); 42 C.F.R. § 407.10(b).]

[¶ 310] Enrollment in Part B

Persons entitled to Medicare benefits under Part A are enrolled automatically and covered for Medicare benefits under Part B, unless they indicate they do not want to be enrolled in the Part B plan (see ¶ 312). [Soc. Sec. Act § 1837(f); 42 C.F.R. § 407.17.]

If an individual declines immediate enrollment, he or she must later file a signed written enrollment request during an initial, general, or special enrollment period (see ¶ 311). [42 C.F.R. § 407.22.]

To request enrollment, an individual may complete one of the following CMS forms (which may be obtained by mail from CMS or at any local Social Security office): (1) Application for Enrollment in the Supplementary Medical Insurance Program (CMS-4040 or CMS 40-D); (2) Application for Medical Insurance (CMS-40-B or CMS 40-F); or (3) Application for Hospital Insurance Entitlement (CMS-18-F-5). Alternatively, an individual may request enrollment by either answering the Part B enrollment questions on an application for monthly Social Security benefits or signing a simple statement of request. [42 C.F.R. § 407.11.]

Note that the coverage period—the period during which premiums are due and during which an individual is entitled to benefits under Part B—is not the same as the enrollment period (see ¶ 313).

Health Insurance Card

As evidence of eligibility, each beneficiary entitled to Part A or Part B benefits is issued a Health Insurance Card. This card gives the beneficiary's name, claim number, sex, extent of entitlement, and effective date(s) of entitlement—the beginning dates of the beneficiary's Part A and Part B coverage. [*Medicare General Information, Eligibility, and Entitlement Manual*, Pub. 100-01, Ch. 2, § 50.]

Beneficiaries may order a replacement for a lost or damaged Medicare card by visiting the Medicare Card Replacement section of the Social Security Administration's (SSA) website at https://faq.ssa.gov/link/portal/34011/34019/Article/3708/How-do-I-get-a-replacement-Medicare-card. The new card will be mailed within 30 days to the address the SSA has on record. An individual needing immediate proof of Medicare coverage can call 1-800-772-1213 or contact a local SSA office.

Social Security numbers. By April 16, 2019, the HHS Secretary is required to ensure that Social Security numbers (or any derivative thereof) are not displayed, coded, or embedded on Medicare cards issued to an individual who is entitled to Part A benefits or enrolled under Part B. HHS must also ensure that any other identifier displayed on the card is not identifiable as a Social Security account number or derivative thereof. [Soc. Sec. Act § 205(c)(2)(C)(xiii); Medicare Access and CHIP Reauthorization Act of 2015 (MACRA) (P.L. 114-10) § 501.]

[¶ 311] Enrollment Periods

An individual ordinarily may enroll in the Part B program, either by a positive act or through automatic enrollment (see ¶ 312), only during an "enrollment period." There are three kinds of enrollment periods:

(1) the "initial enrollment period," which is based on the date when an individual first meets the eligibility requirements for enrollment (see ¶ 300);

(2) the "general enrollment period," during which individuals may enroll if they have missed their initial enrollment period; and

(3) certain special enrollment periods (see below).

[Soc. Sec. Act § 1837; 42 C.F.R. § 407.12.]

Initial enrollment period. The "initial enrollment period" is seven months long. It begins three months before the month in which an individual first meets the eligibility requirements (see ¶ 300) and ends three months after the first month of eligibility. For example, an individual first meeting the eligibility requirements in July 2017 would have a seven-month enrollment period beginning April 1, 2017, and ending October 31, 2017. An individual age 65 qualifying solely on the basis of hospital insurance entitlement is deemed to meet the eligibility requirements on the first day on which he or she becomes entitled to hospital insurance benefits. [Soc. Sec. Act § 1837(d); 42 C.F.R. § 407.14(a).]

The Social Security Administration (SSA) or CMS will establish a deemed initial enrollment period for an individual who fails to enroll during the initial enrollment period because of a belief, based on erroneous documentary evidence, that he or she had not yet attained age 65. The period will be established as though the individual had attained age 65 on the date indicated by the incorrect information. [Soc. Sec. Act § 1837(d); 42 C.F.R. § 407.14(b).]

In most cases, individuals who do not enroll in the supplementary medical insurance program within a year of the close of their initial enrollment period will be required to pay a permanently increased premium. Individuals who drop out of the program and re-enroll later also will have to pay an increased premium in most cases. [Soc. Sec. Act § 1839(b).] Increased premiums are discussed at ¶ 320.

General enrollment period. The law also provides a "general enrollment period" for those who failed to enroll in their initial enrollment period, or for those who terminated their enrollment but want to re-enroll. The "general enrollment period" is from January 1 through March 31 of each year. [Soc. Sec. Act § 1837(e); 42 C.F.R. § 407.15(a).]

An individual who fails to enroll during the initial enrollment period, or whose enrollment has been terminated, may enroll thereafter only during a general enrollment period or, if he or she meets the specified conditions, during a special enrollment period. There is no limit on how many times an individual can unenroll and re-enroll. [42 C.F.R. §§ 407.12(a)(2), 407.30(b).]

Example • • • _____

Roger Green became a Social Security beneficiary when he reached age 65 in May 2016. His initial enrollment period was February 1, 2016, through August 31, 2016. Because he failed to enroll during this period, his next chance to enroll will be during the next general enrollment period, January 1, 2017, through March 31, 2017. Assuming that he also fails to enroll in 2017, he may now enroll during any subsequent general enrollment period (January 1 to March 31 of each year), but he will be required to pay an increased premium due to his late enrollment (see ¶ 320).

Special Enrollment Periods

Individuals who fail to enroll during their initial enrollment period or whose enrollment has been terminated may enroll or reenroll during a special enrollment period if they meet the required conditions.

Employer group health plans. Elderly or disabled employees and their spouses who receive primary health coverage under an employer group health plan, as discussed at ¶ 636, are not required to enroll in the same enrollment period applicable to other individuals. They may wish to delay enrollment because Part B benefits may duplicate the employer plan's benefits. A special enrollment period applicable to these individuals is available for eight full months after they terminate participation in the employer plan (or six months in the case of disabled individuals whose group plan is involuntarily terminated). [Soc. Sec. Act § 1837(i); 42 C.F.R. § 407.20(b).]

If the individual enrolls in the first month of the special enrollment period, coverage begins on the first day of that month. If enrollment occurs in a later month, coverage will begin on the first day of the following month. [Soc. Sec. Act § 1838(e).]

Volunteers. Beneficiaries who volunteer outside of the United States for at least 12 months through a program sponsored by a tax-exempt organization also may enroll during a special enrollment period, provided they can demonstrate health coverage while serving in the program. This also includes individuals who terminated enrollment while in a volunteer program. The special enrollment period is the six-month period beginning on the first day of the month that includes the date that the individual no longer satisfies these requirements. [Soc. Sec. Act § 1837(k); 42 C.F.R. § 407.21.] Coverage for an individual enrolling during this type of special enrollment period begins on the first day of the month following the month in which he or she enrolls. [Soc. Sec. Act § 1838(f); 42 C.F.R. § 407.21(c).]

TRICARE beneficiaries. TRICARE is a managed health care program for active duty and retired members of the uniformed services and their families and survivors. Section 3110(a) of the Patient Protection and Affordable Care Act (ACA) (P.L. 111-148) established a special Part B enrollment period for military retirees, their spouses (including widows/widowers), and their dependent children, who are otherwise eligible for TRICARE and entitled to Medicare Part A based on disability or end-stage renal disease (ESRD), but who have declined Part B by not enrolling during their initial enrollment period for Medicare. These individuals may elect to enroll in Medicare Part B during the 12-month period beginning on the day after the last day of the initial enrollment period of the individual or, if later, the 12-month period beginning with the month the individual is notified of deemed enrollment in Medicare Part A. This special enrollment period may be used only once during an individual's lifetime. [Soc. Sec. Act § 1837(l).]

[¶ 312] Automatic Enrollment

As individuals become entitled to Medicare Part A, they also become entitled to Part B. They are automatically enrolled in Part B by the Social Security Administration, unless they elect to decline coverage. [42 C.F.R. § 407.17.]

To be automatically enrolled in Part B, the enrollee must reside in the United States, excluding Puerto Rico. [Soc. Sec. Act § 1837(f).] Persons eligible for automatic enrollment are, to the extent possible, fully informed of the automatic enrollment provisions and given at least two months to decline coverage. Those who do not decline coverage before it is scheduled to begin are deemed to have enrolled automatically. [42 C.F.R. § 407.17.]

An individual who:

(1) is receiving Social Security retirement or disability benefits or otherwise is entitled to Medicare benefits on the first day of the initial enrollment period (see ¶ 311); or

(2) becomes entitled to Social Security retirement benefits during any one of the first three months of the initial enrollment period

is *deemed* to have enrolled in the third month of the initial enrollment period, and coverage begins with the first day of the following month. [Soc. Sec. Act § 1837(f), (g).]

An individual who first becomes entitled to Social Security retirement or survivors benefits during the last four months of the seven-month initial enrollment period will be deemed to have enrolled automatically in the month in which he or she files the application establishing entitlement to Medicare. A person who defers establishing entitlement to Medicare until after the end of the initial enrollment period will be deemed to have enrolled in Part B on the first day of the general enrollment period in effect at the time, or immediately following the time, at which the individual establishes entitlement to Part A. [Soc. Sec. Act § 1837(g)(2)(B), (g)(3).]

Disability beneficiaries. In the case of disability beneficiaries, the initial enrollment period cannot be determined on the basis of attainment of age 65. The law provides that the initial enrollment period for an individual eligible for Part B by reason of entitlement to disability benefits for a period of 24 months will begin on the first day of the third month before the 25th month of entitlement to disability benefits. Enrollment periods will recur with each continuous period of eligibility and upon attainment of age 65. [Soc. Sec. Act § 1837(g)(1).]

Examples • • • _____

(1) Bill Miller, a Social Security retirement beneficiary who elected to receive Social Security benefits at age 62, reached age 65 and became automatically entitled to Medicare Part A in May 2017. His initial enrollment period under Part B (see ¶ 311) began February 1, 2017, and extends through August 31, 2017. Bill automatically is deemed to have enrolled in the Part B program in the third month (April) of his enrollment period, and coverage begins May 1, 2017.

(2) Jennifer Green became age 65 and potentially entitled to Social Security benefits in August 2016. She did not file an application for Social Security benefits, however, until January 2017. Because her application for Medicare benefits, which was made automatically when she filed for Social Security benefits (see ¶ 200), did not occur until after the end of her first enrollment period (November 30, 2016, see ¶ 311), her enrollment in Part B is deemed to have occurred on January 1, 2017, the first day of the general enrollment period. Her coverage period begins on July 1, 2017 (see ¶ 313).

[¶ 313] Coverage Period

The "coverage period" of an individual enrolled in the Part B program is the period during which the individual is entitled to Part B benefits. Except in the case of an individual who is enrolled automatically (see ¶ 312), the earliest possible coverage can be obtained if an individual enrolls during the three months of the initial enrollment period that are *before* the month in which the individual reaches age 65. [Soc. Sec. Act § 1838(a).]

An individual's coverage period begins on whichever of the following dates is the *latest*:

(1) For an individual who enrolls in the initial enrollment period: (a) if the individual enrolls during the first three months, coverage begins with the first month of

eligibility; (b) if the individual enrolls during the fourth month, coverage begins with the following month; (c) if the individual enrolls during the fifth month, coverage begins with the second month after the month of enrollment; and (d) if the individual enrolls in either the sixth or seventh month, coverage begins with the third month after the month of enrollment.

(2) For an individual who enrolls in a general enrollment period, coverage becomes effective the July 1 following the month of enrollment.

(3) For an individual deemed to have enrolled automatically in the first three months of the enrollment period (see ¶ 312), Part B coverage begins on the first day of the month in which the individual meets the eligibility requirements (see ¶ 300). If an individual is automatically enrolled but is deemed to have enrolled after the first three months of his or her enrollment period, then his or her coverage period will begin as described in (1) and (2), above.

[Soc. Sec. Act § 1838(a); 42 C.F.R. § § 407.18, 407.25.]

Example • • • _____

Donna first meets the eligibility requirements for enrollment in April. Therefore, the initial enrollment period runs from January through July of that year. Depending upon the month of enrollment, the coverage period will begin as follows:

Enrolls in—	*Coverage period begins on—*
Initial enrollment period:	
January	April 1 (month eligibility requirements first met)
February	April 1
March	April 1
April	May 1 (month following month of enrollment)
May	July 1 (second month after month of enrollment)
June	September 1 (third month after month of enrollment)
July	October 1 (third month after month of enrollment)

The beginning of coverage for end-stage renal disease (ESRD) beneficiaries is described at ¶ 205. For details on the coverage period for elderly and disabled employees and their spouses who receive primary health coverage under an employer group health plan, see ¶ 311.

Termination or Cancellation of Coverage

An individual's coverage period continues until enrollment is terminated or the individual's death. An individual's enrollment may be terminated: (1) by the filing of notice that the individual no longer wishes to participate in the program; or (2) for nonpayment of premiums. If an enrollment is terminated by the filing of a notice, the termination will take effect at the close of the month following the month in which the notice is filed. A termination for nonpayment of premiums will take effect with the end of the grace period (see ¶ 320) during which overdue premiums may be paid and coverage continued. [Soc. Sec. Act § 1838(b); 42 C.F.R. § § 407.27, 408.8.]

Automatically enrolled beneficiaries. A termination request filed by an individual deemed to have enrolled automatically (see ¶ 312) before the month in which Part B coverage becomes effective will cancel the coverage. A termination request filed by an automatically enrolled individual on or after the first day coverage will cancel the coverage as

¶313

of the close of the month following the month in which the notice is filed. [Soc. Sec. Act § 1838(b).]

Disability beneficiaries. In the case of an individual entitled to Medicare on the basis of 24 or more months of disability, rather than on the basis of having reached age 65, coverage and enrollment under Part B ends with the close of the last month for which the individual is entitled to hospital insurance benefits. [Soc. Sec. Act § 1838(c).]

Reenrollment. An individual whose enrollment has terminated may reenroll only during a general enrollment period or a special enrollment period, if the requirements are met (see ¶ 311). [Soc. Sec. Act § 1837.]

[¶ 320] Premiums

The following table shows the standard monthly premium rates in effect under the Part B program during the past several years:

Year	Premium	Year	Premium
2017	134.00	2015	104.90
2016	121.80	2014	104.90

[*Notice*, 81 FR 80063, Nov. 15, 2016.]

Part B premiums are set by actuaries to cover 50 percent of the monthly actuarial rate. [Soc. Sec. Act § 1839(a)(3); 42 C.F.R. § 408.20.] The federal government is required by statute to supplement the remainder of Part B costs out of general revenues. [Soc. Sec. Act § 1844(a).]

Income-related monthly adjustment. Beneficiaries with modified adjusted gross incomes (MAGIs) above a specified threshold must pay a higher percentage of the cost of Medicare Part B medical coverage than those with MAGIs below the threshold. This beneficiary premium adjustment is called an income-related monthly adjustment amount (IRMAA). Premiums are calculated based on MAGI for the second year before the year for which the premium is being determined; accordingly, 2017 premiums are based on 2015 MAGI. [Soc. Sec. Act § 1839(i); 42 C.F.R. § 408.28.]

For 2017, for beneficiaries who filed an individual tax return with income—

- less than or equal to $85,000, there is no IRMAA and the monthly premium is $134.00;

- greater than $85,000 and less than or equal to $107,000, the monthly premium is $187.50;

- greater than $107,000 and less than or equal to $160,000, the monthly premium is $267.90;

- greater than $160,000 and less than or equal to $214,000, the monthly premium is $348.30;

- greater than $214,000, the monthly premium is $398.80.

For beneficiaries who file a joint tax return with income—

- less than or equal to $170,000, there is no IRMAA and the monthly premium is $134.00 per beneficiary;

- greater than $170,000 and less than or equal to $214,000, the monthly premium is $187.50 per beneficiary;

- greater than $214,000 and less than or equal to $320,000, the monthly premium is $267.90 per beneficiary;

- greater than $320,000 and less than or equal to $428,000, the monthly premium is $348.30 per beneficiary;

- greater than $428,000, the monthly premium is $398.80 per beneficiary.

Other rates apply to beneficiaries who are married and lived with their spouse at any time during the taxable year but file a separate tax return. [*Notice*, 81 FR 80063, Nov. 15, 2016.]

Income thresholds used in determining Part B premiums are frozen at 2010 amounts from January 1, 2011, through December 31, 2017. [Soc. Sec. Act § 1839(i)(3)(C), (i)(6).]

Beneficiaries "held harmless." Most people with Medicare Part B will be "held harmless" from any increase in premiums in 2017, and the average 2017 premium paid by Part B enrollees who are held harmless will be about $109. This provision protects individuals from an increase that would result in a reduction in monthly Social Security benefits when the Social Security cost-of-living increase is insufficient to cover the amount of the premium increase. [Soc. Sec. Act 1839(f); *Notice*, 80 FR 70811, Nov. 16, 2015.]

Increased Premium for Late Enrollment

If an individual who enrolls after the "initial enrollment period" (see ¶ 311) or re-enrolls after terminating enrollment, the monthly premium otherwise applicable will be increased by 10 percent for each full 12 months (in the same "continuous period of eligibility") in which the individual could have been, but was not, enrolled. For these purposes, the length of the period of delay is computed by totalling:

(1) the months that elapsed between the close of the initial enrollment period and the close of the enrollment period in which enrollment occurred, plus

(2) in the case of an individual who re-enrolls, the months that elapsed between the date of the termination of the previous coverage period and the close of the enrollment period in which reenrollment occurred. Any premium that is not a multiple of 10 cents is rounded to the nearest multiple of 10 cents.

[Soc. Sec. Act § 1839(b)–(c); 42 C.F.R. § § 408.22, 408.27.]

The beginning of a disabled individual's "continuous period of eligibility" serves as the beginning of an initial enrollment period for purposes of determining whether the premium increase applicable to late enrollees should apply. In general, a "continuous period of eligibility" is:

(1) the period beginning with the first day a person is eligible to enroll in Part B (see ¶ 300) and ending with the person's death; or

(2) a period during all of which an individual is entitled to disability benefits and that ended in or before the month preceding the month in which the individual became 65 years of age.

[Soc. Sec. Act § 1839(d).]

Examples• • • _____

(1) Paul Jones was eligible to enroll in an initial enrollment period that ended May 31, 2014. He actually enrolled in the general enrollment period January 1, 2016, through March 31, 2016. There were 22 months between the close of his initial enrollment period (May 31, 2014) and the close of the period in which he actually enrolled (March 31, 2016). Because there was only one full 12-month period during which he could have been, but was not, enrolled, his premium was (permanently) increased 10 percent.

(2) Marlene Blum became age 65 in July 2008 and first enrolled in March 2010. She paid premiums increased by 10 percent above the regular rate because there was one 12-month

period (17 total months) between the end of her initial enrollment period, October 2008 (see ¶ 311), and the end of the general enrollment period, March 2010, in which she actually enrolled. A few years later, she failed to pay the premiums and her coverage was terminated (after the end of her grace period) on June 30, 2015. She enrolled for a second time in January 2016.

Added to her previous 17 months of delinquency is the period of nine months between July 2015 through March 2016 (the end of the general enrollment period in which she reenrolled), for a total of 26 months. Because this amounts to two full 12-month periods, her monthly premium is (permanently) increased 20 percent.

(3) John Foley was late in enrolling by 38 months. Accordingly, his Part B premium was permanently increased by 30 percent. Thus, in 2017, when the standard premium is $134 per month, he is required to pay $174.20 per month ($134 × 130 percent = $174.20).

Elderly and disabled employees and their spouses who delay enrollment in the Part B program because they elect primary health coverage under an employer group plan, as discussed at ¶ 636, have been accorded a special enrollment period (see ¶ 311). Therefore, the months in which they are enrolled in such a plan are not counted in determining the penalty for delinquent enrollment. Beneficiaries who volunteer outside of the United States for at least 12 months through a program sponsored by a tax-exempt organization also have a special enrollment period and will not incur a delayed enrollment penalty. [Soc. Sec. Act § 1839(b).]

Collection of Premiums

Premiums are payable for the period beginning with the first month of the individual's coverage and ending with the month in which the individual dies or, if earlier, in which the individual's coverage ends. [Soc. Sec. Act § 1840(g); 42 C.F.R. § 408.4.]

Social Security and railroad retirement beneficiaries, and civil service annuitants—except those enrolled by a state as public assistance recipients—have their premiums deducted, when possible, from their monthly benefit, annuity, or pension checks paid in the preceding month. [Soc. Sec. Act § 1840(a)–(d); 42 C.F.R. § 408.40.] In the case of beneficiaries who have premiums deducted from their Social Security checks, if there is a Social Security cost-of-living adjustment that is less than the amount of the increased premium, the premium increase otherwise applicable will be reduced to avoid a reduction in the beneficiaries' Social Security checks. [Soc. Sec. Act § 1839(f); 42 C.F.R. § 408.6(a)(2)(ii).]

The premiums of public assistance recipients enrolled under a state "buy-in" agreement are paid by the state that enrolled them. [Soc. Sec. Act §§ 1840(h), 1843; 42 C.F.R. § 408.6(c).]

Premiums are paid by direct remittance in certain circumstances. Direct payment must be made by individuals who are: (1) not entitled to a monthly cash Social Security benefit, a railroad retirement annuity or pension, or a federal civil service annuity; or (2) entitled to one of these benefits, but for some reason the benefit cannot be paid during the period in question. These individuals are sent premium notices, together with a card and envelope for use in sending payment to the proper servicing center. [42 C.F.R. § 408.60 *et seq.*]

Refund of Excess Premiums

CMS refunds premiums received for any month after the month in which a Part B enrollee dies. Refunds are paid to: (1) the person or persons who paid the premiums; (2) the legal representative of the estate, if the enrollee paid the premiums before death; or (3) the person or persons in the priorities specified in the law, if there is no person meeting the requirements in (1) or (2). [Soc. Sec. Act § 1870(g); 42 C.F.R. § 408.112.]

Failure to Pay Premiums

CMS terminates a beneficiary's enrollment for nonpayment of premiums. However, a grace period extending from the date payment is due through the last day of the third month following the month in which such payment is due applies for beneficiaries who are billed directly. For example, if an enrollee's premium payment became due on March 1 of any given year, the grace period would extend to June 30 of that year. If the beneficiary does not make payment on or before the end of the grace period, coverage and enrollment terminate. [Soc. Sec. Act § 1838(b); 42 C.F.R. §§ 408.8(a), (c), 408.100.]

The initial grace period may be extended for up to an additional three months if there is a finding that the enrollee had good cause for not paying the overdue premiums during the initial grace period. Good cause will be found if the enrollee establishes that the failure to pay within the initial grace period was due to conditions over which he or she had no control or reasonably could not have been expected to foresee. [Soc. Sec. Act § 1838(b); 42 C.F.R. § 408.8(d).] For example, good cause may be found if the enrollee was mentally or physically incapable of paying premiums on a timely basis or had some reasonable basis to believe that payment had been made, or if the failure to pay was due to administrative error. [*Medicare General Information, Eligibility, and Entitlement Manual*, Pub. 100-01, Ch. 2, § 40.7.4.]

Reinstatement. Coverage may be reinstated without interruption of benefits if the enrollee: (1) appeals the termination of benefits by the end of the month following the month in which the notice of termination was sent; (2) the enrollee alleges, and it is found to be true, that he or she did not receive timely and adequate notice that the payments were overdue; and (3) within 30 days of a subsequent request for payment, pays all premiums due through the month in which the enrollee appealed the termination. If the evidence establishes that the enrollee acted diligently to pay the premiums and the delay in payment was not the fault of the enrollee or if the enrollee reasonably believed that the premiums were being paid by deduction from benefits or by some other means, coverage may be reinstated. Coverage may not be reinstated if it is found that the enrollee failed to make payment within the grace period due to insufficient income or or the termination was appealed more than one month after the termination notice was sent. [42 C.F.R. §§ 408.102, 408.104.]

Benefits

[¶ 330] Part B Benefits: In General

Medicare medical insurance benefits (Part B) supplement the coverage provided by Medicare hospital insurance benefits (Part A). Part A covers inpatient institutional services at hospitals, skilled nursing facilities, hospices, and home health services after hospitalization. Part B covers the services of physicians and other health practitioners, as well as a variety of "medical and other health services" not covered under Part A. The kinds of "medical and other health services" included in Part B are described beginning at ¶ 340.

Methods of Payment

In general, there are two methods of payment for items or services covered by the Medicare program:

> (1) Medicare pays the provider or facility on the patient's behalf for services including hospital and skilled nursing care, home health services, medical and other health services, outpatient physical therapy services, and rural health clinic services, among others. [Soc. Sec. Act § 1832(a)(2); 42 C.F.R. § 410.150.] The provider or facility files the claim for payment, and the patient's obligation is fully satisfied once he or she

has paid any required deductible or coinsurance amounts (see ¶ 335). The Medicare payment amount is based on prospective payment rates, reasonable costs, fee schedules, and in some cases, competitive bidding by providers (see ¶ 800 *et seq.*).

(2) In the case of all other Part B services, Medicare may pay the provider or the patient. If assignment is accepted, Medicare pays the supplier or practitioner, and the patient's obligation is fully satisfied once he or she has paid any required deductible or coinsurance amounts (see ¶ 868). If the supplier or practitioner does not accept assignment, Medicare pays the patient, and the patient is responsible for paying the supplier or practitioner.

[Soc. Sec. Act § 1832(a)(1); 42 C.F.R. § 424.53(e).]

Medicare payment and assignment rules are discussed in Chapter 8.

Limitations to Part B Coverage

Benefits provided under the Part B program have limitations. Financial limitations include an annual deductible and 20 percent coinsurance payments applicable to most services covered under Part B, as well as a deductible for the cost of outpatient blood transfusions (see ¶ 335).

Benefits are limited to named items and services listed as covered by the Medicare program. Coverage is often limited to certain kinds of services or frequencies and must be reasonable and necessary for the diagnosis or symptoms presented by the beneficiary. In addition, a number of items and services are listed as excluded from Medicare coverage. Exclusions are discussed in Chapter 6.

Payment also may not be made under Part B for services furnished to an individual if he or she is entitled to have payment made for those services under Part A. [Soc. Sec. Act § 1833(d).] In general, all services provided to an inpatient of a hospital will be paid for by Part A if they are covered Medicare services, with the exception of certain services that are only covered under Part B, such as physician services, the influenza vaccine, and screening mammography, among others. [*Medicare Benefit Policy Manual*, Pub. 100-02, Ch. 6, § 10.]

[¶ 335] Deductible and Coinsurance

In addition to the monthly premium charged to individuals enrolled in Part B (see ¶ 320), an annual deductible and a 20 percent "coinsurance" or "copayment" normally are required. The Part B deductible is $183 for 2017. It was $166 for 2016. The law requires the deductible to be indexed to the growth in Part B expenditures. [Soc. Sec. Act § 1833(b); *Notice* 81 FR 80063, Nov. 15, 2016;*Notice*, 80 FR 70811, Nov. 16, 2015.]

Application of the Deductible and Coinsurance

The Part B annual deductible applies only to services covered by Medicare. If the deductible is not applied because the service is not covered or because the service is included in the list under "Exceptions" below, the deductible for that year remains unsatisfied. [42 C.F.R. § 410.160.]

The deductible is satisfied by the initial expenses incurred in each calendar year. Even in cases in which an individual is not eligible for the entire calendar year (for example, when coverage begins after the first month of the year), the individual is subject to the full deductible. The date of service generally determines when expenses were incurred, but expenses are allocated to the deductible in the order in which the bills are received by the Medicare administrative contractor administering the Part B program. [*Medicare General Information, Eligibility, and Entitlement Manual*, Pub. 100-01, Ch. 3, § 20.2.]

Medicare patients normally are required to pay 20 percent of the cost of each Medicare covered service, their coinsurance amount. Medicare pays the other 80 percent. For Medicare purposes, the cost of a Medicare service is the "Medicare-approved charge" for that service. The coinsurance percentage applies to the Medicare-approved charge. [Soc. Sec. Act § 1833(a), (b).]

Examples • • • _____

(1) Robert White visited his doctor in January 2016 for his annual routine checkup, which is covered as his annual "wellness visit." No deductible or copayment applies. In February, a dental checkup, which indicated that Mr. White's teeth were in good condition, cost $150. Later in the year, it was discovered that he had high blood pressure. Successive visits to the doctor during the remainder of the year in connection with the treatment for this condition resulted in a total of $600 in Medicare-approved charges for the doctor's services. The $150 for the dental checkup cannot be counted toward Mr. White's Part B deductible because it is not a covered expense. Services in connection with the care and treatment of teeth or structures directly supporting the teeth are generally not covered, with some exceptions such as treatment of an oral infection (see ¶ 634). Of the remaining $600 in covered expenses, $166 satisfies the deductible for the year and 80 percent of the remaining $434 ($347) is paid by Medicare. Mr. White's charges total $402 ($150 (noncovered dental checkup) + $166 deductible + $86 coinsurance).

Note the exception to deductible and copayments for prevention services described below.

(2) Sarah visits her doctor in 2016 and has various clinical diagnostic laboratory tests performed in the doctor's office lab. Because the doctor accepts assignment for these tests and is paid under the fee schedule applicable to these services, no deductible (or coinsurance) is required (see "Exceptions" below) for the lab tests. Later, Sarah visits the doctor on another matter, incurring $250 in Medicare-approved charges for the doctor's services. She then has to pay the $166 deductible and an additional $17 as coinsurance ([$250 – $166] × 20 percent = $17). Medicare pays $67.

(3) Mary needs emergency surgery in 2016. She is taken to a participating hospital in an ambulance. She has no previous medical expenses of any kind for the year, and she has no previous "spell of illness" (see ¶ 210). Her hospital stay lasts 16 days. Her expenses are as follows:

Hospital costs (including room and board, nursing services, drugs, and use of the operating room)	$9,000
Fees for services to her of personal physician, surgeon, and anesthesiologist	$2,500
Emergency ambulance services	$300
Follow-up visits to personal physician following hospital discharge	$300
	$12,100

After payment of the $1,288 inpatient hospital deductible (¶ 220), the remainder of Mary's hospital costs are paid for under Part A (see ¶ 210 *et seq.*). The nonhospital portion of her expenses ($3,100) is covered under Part B, except that Mary is required to pay the $166 Part B deductible, plus 20 percent of the remaining $2934 in expenses, or $587. Mary pays a total of $2,041 ($1,288 + $166 + $587). The rest is paid for by Medicare.

Note that if Mary has Medicare supplement (or "Medigap") insurance (see ¶ 740), some or all of what she is required to pay in the above example will be paid by her Medigap insurance.

¶335

Exceptions

Several exceptions apply to the deductible and coinsurance requirements.

Noncovered services. No deductible or coinsurance is required for items or services that are not reasonable and medically necessary. If the provider knew, or should have known, that Medicare considered such services medically unnecessary, but failed to inform the beneficiary before furnishing them, the provider is held liable for their cost. If the beneficiary made payment for such items or services, he or she can be indemnified for them. [Pub. 100-01, Ch. 3, § 20.4.1.]

Clinical diagnostic laboratory tests. Medicare payment for clinical diagnostic laboratory tests (other than tests performed by a hospital or other provider for its inpatients) is made according to fee schedules established by the HHS Secretary (see ¶ 875 for details). In the case of tests provided on an assignment basis (see ¶ 868), Medicare pays for 100 percent of the fee schedule rate, and the deductible and coinsurance are waived. [Soc. Sec. Act § 1833 (a) (1) (D), (a) (2) (D), (b) (3), (h) (1).]

In the case of a diagnostic laboratory test that is paid on the basis of a negotiated rate instead of a fee schedule, the amount paid under the negotiated rate is considered the full charge for the test, and the deductible and coinsurance do not apply. Otherwise, the payment is equal to 80 percent of the lesser of:

(1) the amount determined under such fee schedule;

(2) the determined limitation amount for a clinical diagnostic laboratory test performed; or

(3) the amount of charges billed for the tests.

[Soc. Sec. Act § § 1833 (a) (1) (D), (a) (2) (D), (b) (3), (h) (4) (B), (h) (6).]

Note that the Protecting Access to Medicare Act of 2014 (PAMA) (P.L. 113-93) requires CMS to implement a new Medicare payment system for clinical diagnostic laboratory tests based on private payer rates beginning January 1, 2017. [Soc. Sec. Act § 1834A, as added by PAMA § 216.]

Home health services. No deductible or coinsurance generally is applied to home health services. When a home health agency furnishes services that are not included in the definition of "home health services," however, the deductible and coinsurance do apply. The coinsurance also applies to supplies, drugs, durable medical equipment, and prosthetics/orthotics furnished by home health agencies. [Soc. Sec. Act § 1833 (a) (1), (a) (2) (A), (b) (2); Pub. 100-01, Ch. 3, § 20.4.]

Donation of kidney for transplant surgery. There are no deductible or coinsurance requirements with respect to services furnished to an individual who donates a kidney for transplant surgery. [42 C.F.R. § 410.163.]

Federally qualified health center services. No deductible is required for federally qualified health center services (see ¶ 382). [Soc. Sec. Act § 1833 (b) (4).]

Blood Deductibles

Part B requires a deductible for the expenses incurred during any calendar year for the first three pints of whole blood (or equivalent quantities of packed red blood cells) furnished to outpatients. As in the case of the similar deductible for inpatients under Part A, this deductible is reduced to the extent that the blood (or equivalent quantities of packed red blood cells) has been appropriately replaced. [42 C.F.R. §410.161.] Satisfaction of the deductible through replacement is discussed in greater detail at ¶ 220.

The blood deductible under Part B is not required to the extent it has been satisfied under Part A. [Soc. Sec. Act §§1813(a)(2), 1833(b).]

"Welcome to Medicare" Exam and Preventive Services

No deductible applies to an initial preventive physical exam (IPPE), also called the "Welcome to Medicare" exam (see ¶ 369), including IPPE services rendered in rural health clinics. Similarly, no deductible is required for screening mammography services, screening pap smears, screening pelvic exams, ultrasound screening for abdominal aortic aneurysm, or colorectal cancer screening tests. [Soc. Sec. Act §1833(b); 42 C.F.R. §§410.152(l)(12), 410.160(b)(9).]

Coinsurance amounts are waived for most preventive services, including medical nutrition therapy, IPPEs, and personalized preventive plan services in connection with an annual wellness visit. [Soc. Sec. Act §1833(a)(1)(B), (W), (X), (Y), (b)(1).]

Pneumococcal and influenza vaccines. Pneumococcal and influenza vaccines and their administration are covered without imposition of deductible or coinsurance requirements. [Soc. Sec. Act §§1833(a)(1)(B), (b)(1), 1861(s)(10)(A).]

[¶ 340] Medical and Other Health Services

The law divides the kinds of services covered under Part B into various categories, one of which is "medical and other health services" (see ¶ 330). [Soc. Sec. Act §1832(a).]

"Medical and other health services" includes the following items or services identified at Soc. Sec. Act §1861(s):

- physicians' services (see ¶ 350);

- services and supplies furnished incident to a physician's professional services, of kinds that commonly are furnished in physicians' offices and that commonly either are rendered without charge or are included in the physician's bills (see ¶ 351);

- outpatient hospital services furnished incident to physicians' services (see ¶ 352) and partial hospitalization (mental health) services incident to such services (see ¶ 387);

- outpatient diagnostic services furnished by a hospital (see ¶ 352);

- outpatient physical and occupational therapy and speech-language pathology services (see ¶ 381);

- rural health clinic and federally qualified health center services (see ¶ 382);

- home dialysis supplies and equipment, self-care home dialysis support services, institutional dialysis services and supplies, renal dialysis services, and kidney disease education services (see ¶ 845);

- services of nonphysician health care practitioners, including physician assistants, nurse practitioners and clinical nurse specialists, certified registered nurse anesthetists and anesthesia assistants, nurse-midwives, clinical psychologists, and clinical social workers (see ¶ 351 and ¶ 366);

- diagnostic x-ray tests, laboratory tests, and other diagnostic tests (see ¶ 353);

- x-ray, radium, and radioactive isotope therapy, including materials and services of technicians (see ¶ 354);

- surgical dressings, splints, casts, and other devices used for reduction of fractures and dislocations (see ¶ 359);

- durable medical equipment (see ¶ 356);

- prosthetic devices (other than dental) that replace all or part of an internal body organ (including colostomy bags and supplies directly related to colostomy care), and replacement of such devices (see ¶ 357);

- leg, arm, back, and neck braces, and artificial legs, arms, and eyes (including required adjustments, repairs, and replacements) (see ¶ 357);

- certain drugs and biologics, including pneumococcal pneumonia, influenza, and hepatitis B vaccines, antigens, blood clotting factors for hemophilia patients, immunosuppressant therapy drugs furnished to an individual who receives an organ transplant, erythropoietin (EPO) for dialysis patients, oral anti-cancer drugs, anti-emetic drugs used in conjunction with chemotherapy treatments, and intravenous immune globulin administered in the home for the treatment of primary immune deficiency diseases (see ¶ 362);

- ambulance services, if the use of other methods of transportation is contraindicated by the individual's condition (see ¶ 355);

- certain preventive and screening services (if specifically exempted from the exclusion for routine checkups), including an initial preventive physical exam, personalized prevention plan services, cardiovascular screening blood tests, pap smears, pelvic exams, mammograms, bone mass measurement tests, and screening tests and services for diabetes, colorectal cancer, prostate cancer, and glaucoma (see ¶ 369);

- diabetes outpatient self-management training services or medical nutrition therapy services for beneficiaries who have not received diabetes self-management training (see ¶ 369);

- therapeutic shoes for individuals with severe diabetic conditions (see ¶ 370 and ¶ 619);

- ultrasound screening for abdominal aortic aneurysm (see ¶ 369);

- items and services furnished under a cardiac or pulmonary rehabilitation program, or an intensive cardiac rehabilitation program; and

- home infusion therapy.

All "medical and other health services" provided to an inpatient of a qualified hospital (except for the services of physicians and other practitioners and pneumococcal and hepatitis B vaccine) are paid for by Part A if Part A coverage is available. Payment may not be made under Part B for services furnished to an inpatient if the inpatient is entitled to have payment made for services under Part A. [*Medicare Benefit Policy Manual*, Pub. 100-02, Ch. 15, § 10.]

[¶ 350] Physicians' Services

Part B covers reasonable and medically necessary physicians' services. [Soc. Sec. Act § § 1832(a)(2)(B), 1861(s)(1).] Physicians' services are the professional services performed by physicians for a patient, including diagnosis, therapy, surgery, consultation, and care plan oversight. A service may be considered to be a physician's service when the physician either examines the patient in person or is able to visualize (e.g., by means of x-rays, electrocardiogram and electroencephalogram tapes, and tissue samples) some aspect of the patient's condition without the interposition of a third person's judgment. [42 C.F.R. § 410.20(a), (b); *Medicare Benefit Policy Manual*, Pub. 100-02, Ch. 15, § 30.]

Services by means of a telephone call between a physician and a beneficiary or between a physician and a member of a beneficiary's family are covered under Part B; however, because the physician work resulting from telephone calls is considered to be an integral part of the prework and postwork of other physician services, the fee schedule amount for these services includes payment for the telephone calls. [Pub. 100-02, Ch. 15, § 30B.]

"Concurrent care" refers to services more extensive than consultative services and rendered by more than one physician during a period of time. The reasonable and necessary services of each physician rendering concurrent care may be covered when each physician is required to play an active role in the patient's treatment, for example, because of the existence of more than one medical condition requiring diverse specialized medical services. [Pub. 100-02, Ch. 15, § 30.]

Part B covers patient-initiated "second opinions" related to the medical need for surgery or for major nonsurgical diagnostic and therapeutic procedures. [Pub. 100-02, Ch. 15, § 30D.]

Physicians' services furnished to a patient are ordinarily paid by Medicare according to the physician fee schedule discussed at ¶ 855.

"Physician" Defined

The term "physician" means a licensed doctor of medicine, osteopathy (including an osteopathic practitioner), dental surgery or dental medicine, podiatric medicine, chiropractic services, or optometry. [Soc. Sec. Act § 1861(q), (r); 42 C.F.R. § 410.20(b).] However, as discussed below, only certain services of dentists, podiatrists, chiropractors, and optometrists are covered. The term "physician" does not include a Christian Science practitioner or naturopath. [*Medicare General Information, Eligibility, and Entitlement Manual*, Pub. 100-01, Ch. 5, § 70.]

For services to be covered as services of a "physician," the doctor performing them must have "legal authorization"; that is, the doctor must be licensed to practice by the state. Coverage does not extend to services that the practitioner is not legally authorized to perform. For example, if state licensing law limits the scope of practice of osteopaths and osteopathic practitioners to the manipulation of bones and muscles, only these authorized osteopathic services are covered. [Pub. 100-01, Ch. 5, § 70.1.]

Part B Coverage of Dentists' Services

A dentist qualifies as a physician if he or she is a doctor of dental surgery or dental medicine who is legally authorized to practice dentistry by the state in which he or she performs such functions and who is acting within the scope of his or her license when performing such functions. Such services include any otherwise covered service that may legally and alternatively be performed by doctors of medicine, osteopathy, and dentistry, e.g., dental examinations to detect infections prior to certain surgical procedures, treatment of oral infections, and interpretations of diagnostic x-ray examinations in connection with covered services. [Soc. Sec. Act § 1861(r)(2); Pub. 100-01, Ch. 5, § 70.2.]

Because of the general exclusion of payment for dental services (see ¶ 634), payment for the services of dentists is limited to those procedures that are not primarily provided for the care, treatment, removal, or replacement of teeth or structures directly supporting teeth. The coverage or exclusion of any given dental service is not affected by the professional designation of the physician rendering the services; i.e., an excluded dental service remains excluded, and a covered dental service is covered, whether furnished by a dentist or a doctor of medicine or osteopathy. [Pub. 100-01, Ch. 5, § 70.2.]

A dentist also qualifies as a physician for purposes of (1) providing the physician's certification required for inpatient hospital services connected with a dental procedure when the patient requires hospitalization; and (2) performing outpatient ambulatory surgical procedures that can be safely performed on an ambulatory basis in the dentist's office. [42 C.F.R. § 424.13(d)(2).]

¶350

A description of inpatient hospital services connected with dental procedures is at ¶ 218.

Dental care in rural facilities. In an effort to increase access to dental care in rural and other underserved communities, section 5304 of the Patient Protection and Affordable Care Act (ACA) (P.L. 111-148) required HHS to establish a demonstration program to award grants to eligible entities to create training programs to train or employ alternative dental health care providers beginning March 23, 2012, and ending by March 23, 2017. [Public Health Service Act § 340G-1.]

Part B Coverage of Optometrists' Services

A doctor of optometry is considered a physician for all the covered vision care services he or she is legally authorized to perform in the state in which he or she performs them. To be covered under Medicare, the services must be medically reasonable and necessary for the diagnosis or treatment of illness or injury and must meet all applicable coverage requirements. [Soc. Sec. Act § 1861(r)(4); 42 C.F.R. § 410.22; Pub. 100-01, Ch. 5, § 70.5.] Note, however, that many vision care services are excluded from Medicare coverage (see ¶ 619).

Part B Coverage of Podiatrists' Services

A doctor of podiatric medicine is included within the definition of "physician," but only with respect to functions he or she is legally authorized to perform by the state in which he or she performs them. [Soc. Sec. Act § 1861(r)(3); 42 C.F.R. § 410.25; Pub. 100-01, Ch. 5, § 70.3.] Certain types of foot treatment or foot care, however, are excluded from Medicare coverage (see ¶ 619), whether performed by a doctor of medicine or a doctor of podiatric medicine.

A doctor of podiatric medicine also is considered a "physician" with respect to satisfying the physician certification and recertification requirements, for establishing and reviewing a home health plan of treatment, and utilization review. A podiatrist, however, is not considered a "physician" for purposes of the physician activities required to qualify an institution or organization as a skilled nursing facility. [Pub. 100-01, Ch. 5, § 70.3.]

Part B Coverage of Chiropractors' Services

A chiropractor licensed by the state—or, if the state does not license chiropractors, a chiropractor legally authorized to practice in the jurisdiction in which he or she performs services—is included in the definition of physician, but only with respect to the coverage of his or her own professional services, services and supplies "incident" to the services, and treatment by means of manual manipulation of the spine. In addition, a chiropractor's services are covered only if the treatment is to correct a subluxation demonstrated to exist by x-ray. No reimbursement may be made, however, for x-rays or other diagnostic or therapeutic services furnished or ordered by a chiropractor. [Soc. Sec. Act § 1861(r)(5); 42 C.F.R. § 410.21; Pub. 100-01, Ch. 5, § 70.6.]

Provider-Based Physician Services

The services of hospital- and other provider-based physicians (e.g., radiologists, anesthesiologists, and pathologists) include two distinct elements: the professional component and the provider component.

The *professional component* of provider-based physicians' services includes those services directly related to the medical care of the individual patient. Payment for those services is made according to the Medicare physician fee schedule (see ¶ 855) by the Part B Medicare administrative contractor. The *provider component* of provider-based physicians' services includes those services not directly related to the medical care of individual patients (e.g., teaching, administrative, and autopsy services, and other services that benefit the provider's patients as a group). Those services are reimbursed to the provider as provider services under Part A. [Pub. 100-02, Ch. 15, § 30.1.]

Physicians in federal hospitals. Physicians' services performed in hospitals operated by the federal government—military hospitals, Veterans Administration hospitals, and Public Health Service hospitals—are normally reimbursable only when that hospital provides services to the public generally as a community institution. A physician working in the scope of his or her federal employment may be considered as coming within the statutory definition of "physician" even though the physician may not have a license to practice in the state in which he or she is employed. [Pub. 100-01, Ch. 5, § 70.4.]

Interns and residents. The services of interns and residents-in-training provided in the hospital setting as part of an approved training program are normally paid under Part A as hospital services and not under Part B as physicians' services. Services not part of the training program or provided outside the hospital or in the hospital's outpatient department or emergency room are covered under Part B. [42 C.F.R. § § 415.200–415.208; Pub. 100-01, Ch. 5, § 70.7.]

Teaching physician services. Physicians teaching or supervising in an approved teaching program are normally regarded as providing Part A provider services, reimbursable to the hospital. If the teaching or supervising physician is the patient's attending physician, however, his or her services usually will be covered under Part B as physicians' services. [Pub. 100-02, Ch. 15, § 30.2.]

Payment for the services of provider-based physicians is discussed in greater detail at ¶ 855.

Psychiatrists and Psychologists

Psychiatrists are medical doctors and their services are covered by Medicare to the same extent as other physicians' services. Note, however, that there are special limits on Medicare coverage of psychiatric services (see ¶ 225 and ¶ 387). Psychiatric services also may be covered as incident to physicians' services as an outpatient hospital benefit (see ¶ 352).

Clinical psychologists generally are not considered physicians. Their services can be covered as incident to physicians' services (see ¶ 351), and their diagnostic services can be covered additionally as "other diagnostic tests" (see ¶ 353). The services of a "qualified psychologist" are covered as a separate Part B benefit (see ¶ 366).

Care Management Services

Beginning in calendar year 2015, CMS will make a separate payment for non-face-to-face chronic care management services furnished to patients with multiple chronic conditions that are expected to last at least 12 months or until the death of the patient, and that place the patient at significant risk of death, acute exacerbation/decompensation, or functional decline. [Soc. Sec. Act § 1848(b)(8); *Final rule*, 79 FR 67548, Nov. 13, 2014; *Final rule*, 78 FR 74230, Dec. 10, 2013.]

Part B also covers transitional care management services for a patient whose medical and/or psychosocial problems require moderate or high complexity medical decision making during transitions in care from an inpatient hospital setting (including acute hospital, rehabilitation hospital, long-term acute care hospital), partial hospital, observation status in a hospital, or skilled nursing facility/nursing facility, to the patient's community setting (home, domiciliary, rest home, or assisted living). Transitional care management starts on the date of discharge and continues for the next 29 days. [*Final rule*, 77 FR 68892, Nov. 16, 2012.]

¶350

[¶ 351] Services and Supplies Furnished Incident to Physicians' Services

Medicare Part B covers services and supplies furnished incident to a physician's professional services, of kinds that are commonly furnished in physicians' offices and are commonly either furnished without charge or are included in the physicians' bills. [Soc. Sec. Act § 1861(s)(2)(A); 42 C.F.R. §§ 410.10(b), 410.26(b).]

"Incident to a physician's professional services" means that the services or supplies are furnished as an integral, although incidental, part of the physician's or nonphysician practitioner's personal professional services in the course of diagnosis or treatment of an injury or illness. To be covered incident to the services of a physician, services and supplies (including drugs and biologics not usually self-administered by the patient) must be:

(1) furnished in a noninstitutional setting to noninstitutional patients;

(2) integral, although incidental, parts of the physician's professional services;

(3) rendered without charge or included in the physician's bill;

(4) of a type that are commonly furnished in physician's offices or clinics;

(5) furnished by the physician, practitioner with an incident-to benefit, or auxiliary personnel; and

(6) furnished in accordance with applicable state law.

[Soc. Sec. Act § 1861(s)(2)(A); 42 C.F.R. § 410.26(b).]

Auxiliary personnel performing incident-to services must meet state licensing requirements. [42 C.F.R. § 410.26(a)(1).]

This provision does not apply when supplies are clearly of a type a physician would not be expected to have on hand in the office or the services are of a type not considered medically appropriate to provide in the office setting. Supplies usually furnished by the physician in the course of diagnosis and treatment, such as gauze, ointments, bandages (including ace bandages), and oxygen, are covered, but charges for the supplies must be included in the physician's bills. To be covered, supplies must represent an expense to the physician. [*Medicare Benefit Policy Manual*, Pub. 100-02, Ch. 15, § 60.1.]

See ¶ 810 for a discussion of services furnished in a prospective payment system hospital to hospital inpatients that are incident to a physician's services.

Incident-to Drugs and Biologics

To meet all the general requirements for coverage under the incident-to provision, a Food and Drug Administration-approved drug or biologic must be:

• be of a form that is not usually self-administered;

• furnished by a physician; and

• administered by the physician, or by auxiliary personnel employed by the physician and under the physician's personal supervision.

[Pub. 100-02, Ch. 15, § 50.3.]

While Medicare Part B does generally not cover drugs that can be self-administered, such as those in pill form or used for self-injection, some self-administered drugs are covered under Part B. Examples of self-administered drugs that are covered include blood-clotting factors, drugs used in immunosuppressive therapy, erythropoietin (EPO) for dialysis patients, osteoporosis drugs for certain homebound patients, and certain oral cancer drugs. [42 C.F.R. §§ 410.26(c)(1), 410.29(a); Pub. 100-02, Ch. 15, § 50.]

Furthermore, the administration of a drug, regardless of the source, is a service that represents an expense to the physician. Therefore, administration of the drug is payable if the drug would have been covered if the physician purchased it. [Pub. 100-02, Ch. 15, § 60.1.]

Claims for drugs payable administered by a physician to refill an implanted item of durable medical equipment (DME) may only be paid under Part B to the physician as a drug incident to a physician's service and are not payable to a pharmacy/supplier as DME under Soc. Sec. Act § 1861(s)(6). [42 C.F.R. § 410.26(b)(9).]

Drugs and biologics are also subject to the limitations specified in 42 C.F.R. § 410.29. [42 C.F.R. § 410.26(c)(1).]

Direct Supervision Requirement

To be covered, incident-to services and supplies must generally be furnished under the direct supervision of the physician or other practitioner. The supervising physician/practitioner supervising the auxiliary personnel need not be the same physician/practitioner upon whose professional service the incident-to service is based; however, only the supervising physician (or other practitioner) may bill Medicare for incident-to services. [42 C.F.R. § 410.26(b)(5).]

"Auxiliary personnel" includes any individual who is acting under the supervision of a physician (or other practitioner), regardless of whether the individual is an employee, leased employee, or independent contractor of the physician (or other practitioner) or of the same entity that employs or contracts with the physician (or other practitioner). Auxiliary personnel who have been excluded from Medicare, Medicaid, and all other federally funded health care programs or who have had their enrollment revoked for any reason are prohibited from providing incident-to services. [42 C.F.R. § 410.26(a)(1).]

"Direct supervision" in the office setting means the physician is present in the office suite and immediately available to furnish assistance and direction throughout the performance of the procedure. It does not mean that the physician must be present in the room when the procedure is performed. [42 C.F.R. §§ 410.26(a)(1) and (a)(2), 410.32(b)(3)(ii); Pub. 100-02, Ch. 15, § 60.1.]

If auxiliary personnel perform services outside the office setting, their services are covered as incident to the physician's services only if there is direct supervision by the physician. For example, if a nurse accompanies the physician on house calls and administers an injection, the nurse's services are covered; if the same nurse makes the calls alone and administers the injection, the services are not covered (even when billed by the physician) because the physician is not providing direct personal supervision. [Pub. 100-02, Ch. 15, § 60.1.]

Homebound patients. There are exceptions to the direct supervision requirement for homebound patients when home health services are not readily available. Homebound patients may receive services such as injections, venipuncture, and EKGs furnished by qualified personnel who are not under a physician's direct supervision. (See Pub. 100-02, Ch. 15, § 60.4, for the complete list of such services.)

Designated care management services. Designated care management services can be furnished under general supervision of the physician (or other practitioner) when these services or supplies are provided incident to the services of a physician or other practitioner. General supervision means the service is furnished under the physician's or other practitioner's overall direction and control, but the physician's or other practitioner's presence is not required during the performance of the service. [42 C.F.R. § 410.26(a)(3), (b)(5).]

¶351

Nonphysician Practitioners

Medicare Part B covers services and supplies incident to the services of clinical psychologists (CPs), physicians assistants (PAs), nurse practitioners (NPs), clinical nurse specialists (CNSs), and certified nurse-midwives (CNMs) if the requirements of 42 C.F.R. §410.26 are met. [Soc. Sec. Act §1861(gg)(1), (ii); 42 C.F.R. §§410.71(a)(2), 410.74(b), 410.75(d), 410.76(d), 410.77(c).] See ¶366 for a discussion of coverage of nonphysician practitioners' services.

Further, Part B covers the services of certain nonphysician practitioners, including CNMs, CPs, clinical social workers, PAs, NPs, and CNSs, as services incident to a physician's professional services. For services of a nonphysician practitioner to be covered as incident to the services of a physician, they must meet all of the requirements for coverage, as described in 42 C.F.R. §410.26 and Pub. 100-02, Ch. 15, §60. [Pub. 100-02, Ch. 15, §60.2.]

The amount of separate Medicare payment for the services of nonphysician practitioners is discussed at ¶860.

Incident-to Services in Outpatient and Clinic Settings

Services furnished in a prospective payment system hospital to hospital inpatients that are "incident to" a physician's services are included within the hospital's prospective payment rate and are paid under Part A.

All hospital outpatient services that are not diagnostic are services that aid the physician or practitioner in the treatment of the patient. Such therapeutic services include clinic services, emergency room services, and observation services. Coverage of outpatient *therapeutic* services incident to a physician's service furnished on or after January 1, 2010, is described at 42 C.F.R. §410.27 and Pub. 100-02, Ch. 6, §20.5.2.

Except in the case of rural health clinics, to which special rules apply (see ¶382), the guidelines for coverage of services and supplies incident to a physician's service in a "physician-directed clinic" or group association are generally the same as the general rules described above. A "physician-directed clinic" is one in which (1) a physician (or a number of physicians) is present to perform medical (rather than administrative) services at all times the clinic is open; (2) each patient is under the care of a clinic physician; and (3) the nonphysician services are under medical supervision. [Pub. 100-02, Ch. 15, §60.3.]

In highly organized clinics, however, "direct personal physician supervision" may be the responsibility of several physicians as opposed to an individual attending physician. The physician ordering a particular service need not be the physician who is supervising the service. Therefore, services performed by therapists and other aides are covered even though they are performed in another department of the clinic. [Pub. 100-02, Ch. 15, §60.3.]

Supplies provided by the clinic during the course of treatment also are covered. When auxiliary personnel perform services outside the clinic premises, the services are covered as "incident to" the professional services of a physician only if performed under the direct personal supervision of a clinic physician. If the clinic refers a patient for auxiliary services performed by personnel who are not employed by the clinic, such services are not "incident to" a physician's service. [Pub. 100-02, Ch. 15, §60.3.]

Outpatient hospital services are discussed at ¶352. Special rules concerning ambulatory surgical centers are discussed at ¶386.

[¶352] Outpatient Hospital Services

Hospitals and critical access hospitals (CAHs) provide two distinct types of services to outpatients: (1) *therapeutic* services that aid the physician in the treatment of the patient, and

(2) *diagnostic* services such as diagnostic x-rays or diagnostic laboratory services. Both kinds of services furnished by hospitals to outpatients are covered under Part B. The following rules pertaining to the coverage of outpatient hospital services are not applicable to physical therapy, speech-language pathology, occupational therapy, or end-stage renal disease (ESRD) services furnished by hospitals to outpatients. [Soc. Sec. Act § 1861(s)(2)(B) and (C); 42 C.F.R. §§ 410.27, 410.28; *Medicare Benefit Policy Manual*, Pub. 100-02, Ch. 6, § 20.] See ¶ 381 for a description of coverage for therapy services.

"Outpatient services" defined. A "hospital outpatient" is a person who has not been admitted by the hospital as an inpatient, is registered on the hospital records as an outpatient, and receives services (rather than supplies alone) from hospital personnel. An inpatient of a participating hospital may not be considered an outpatient of that or any other hospital. An inpatient of a skilled nursing facility (SNF), however, may be considered an outpatient of a participating hospital. [Pub. 100-02, Ch. 6, § 20.2.]

When a tissue sample, blood sample, or specimen is taken by personnel that are neither employed nor arranged for by the hospital and is sent to the hospital for the performance of tests, the test is not an outpatient hospital service because the patient does not receive services directly from the hospital. Similarly, supplies provided by a hospital supply room for use by physicians in the treatment of private patients are not covered as an outpatient service because the patients receiving the supplies are not outpatients of the hospital. [Pub. 100-02, Ch. 6, § 20.2.]

Outpatient observation services. Outpatient observation services are covered only when provided by the order of a physician or another individual authorized by state licensure law and hospital staff bylaws to admit patients to the hospital or order outpatient tests. In the majority of cases, the decision whether to discharge a patient from the hospital following resolution of the reason for the observation care or admit the patient as an inpatient can be made in less than 48 hours, usually in less than 24 hours. In only rare and exceptional cases do reasonable and necessary outpatient observation services span more than 48 hours. [Pub. 100-02, Ch. 6, § 20.6.]

Beginning August 6, 2016, a hospital or CAH must provide each individual who receives observation services as an outpatient at such hospital or CAH for more than 24 hours an oral and written notification that explains the status of the individual as an outpatient receiving observation services and the implications of such status (such as implications for cost-sharing requirements and subsequent eligibility for coverage for services furnished by a SNF). The notification must occur within 36 hours of the time the individual begins receiving observation services (or, if sooner, upon release), and the written notification must be signed by the beneficiary. [Soc. Sec. Act § 1866(a)(1)(Y); 42 C.F.R. § 489.20(y).]

Outpatient Hospital Therapeutic Services

Medicare Part B pays for therapeutic hospital services and supplies furnished incident to a physician's or nonphysician practitioner's service, which are defined as all services and supplies furnished to hospital outpatients that are not diagnostic services and that aid the physician or nonphysician practitioner in the treatment of the patient, including drugs and biologics that are not usually self-administered. [Soc. Sec. Act § 1861(s)(2)(B); 42 C.F.R. § 410.27(a).] These services include clinic services, emergency room services, and observation services. [Pub. 100-02, Ch. 6, § 20.5.2.]

To be covered, the services must be furnished (1) by or under arrangements made by the participating hospital or CAH, except in the case of a SNF resident (see 42 C.F.R. § 411.15(p)); (2) as an integral although incidental part of a physician's or nonphysician

¶352

practitioner's services; and (3) in the hospital or CAH or in a department of the hospital or CAH. [42 C.F.R. § 410.27(a)(1).]

Physician supervision. Therapeutic hospital services must be furnished under the direct supervision (or other level of supervision as specified by CMS for the particular service) of a physician or a nonphysician practitioner. For services furnished in the hospital or CAH, or in an outpatient department of the hospital or CAH, both on- and off-campus, "direct supervision" means that the physician or nonphysician practitioner must be immediately available to furnish assistance and direction throughout the performance of the procedure (see ¶ 351). It does not mean that the physician or nonphysician practitioner must be present in the room when the procedure is performed. [42 C.F.R. § 410.27(a)(1)(iv)(A).]

Pulmonary rehabilitation, cardiac rehabilitation, and intensive cardiac rehabilitation services must be performed under the direct supervision of a doctor of medicine or a doctor of osteopathy. [42 C.F.R. § 410.27(a)(1)(iv)(D).]

For nonsurgical extended duration therapeutic services, which are hospital or CAH outpatient therapeutic services that can last a significant period of time, have a substantial monitoring component that is typically performed by auxiliary personnel, have a low risk of requiring the physician's or appropriate nonphysician practitioner's immediate availability after the initiation of the service, and are not primarily surgical in nature, Medicare requires a minimum of direct supervision during the initiation of the service, which may be followed by general supervision at the discretion of the supervising physician or the appropriate nonphysician practitioner. [42 C.F.R. § 410.27(a)(1)(iv)(E).]

CMS has delayed enforcement of the direct supervision requirement for CAHs and small and rural hospitals with fewer than 100 beds. Most recently, Congress extended the enforcement delay through calendar year 2016. [21st Century Cures Act (P.L. 114-255) § 16004(a), amending P.L. 113-198.]

Outpatient Hospital Diagnostic Services

Medicare Part B covers hospital or CAH diagnostic services furnished to outpatients, including drugs and biologics required in the performance of the services (even if those drugs or biologics are self-administered), if the services: (1) are furnished by or under arrangements made by a participating hospital or participating CAH, except in the case of a SNF resident as provided in 42 C.F.R. § 411.15(p); (2) are ordinarily furnished by, or under arrangements made by, the hospital or CAH to its outpatients for the purpose of diagnostic study; and (3) would be covered as inpatient hospital services if furnished to an inpatient. The services must also be provided under the appropriate level of supervision. [Soc. Sec. Act § 1861(s)(2)(C); 42 C.F.R. § 410.28(a), (e).]

A service is "diagnostic" if it is an examination or procedure to which the patient is subjected, or that is performed on materials derived from the patient, to obtain information to aid in the assessment of a medical condition or the identification of a disease. Among these examinations and tests are diagnostic laboratory services such as hematology and chemistry, diagnostic x-rays, isotope studies, electrocardiograms (EKGs), pulmonary function studies, thyroid function tests, psychological tests, and other tests given to determine the nature and severity of an ailment or injury. [Pub. 100-02, Ch. 6, § 20.4.1.]

Covered diagnostic services to outpatients include: the services of nurses, psychologists, and technicians; drugs and biologics necessary for diagnostic study; and the use of supplies and equipment. When a hospital sends hospital personnel and hospital equipment to a patient's home to furnish a diagnostic service, the service is covered as if the patient had received the service in the hospital outpatient department. [Pub. 100-02, Ch. 6, § 20.4.4.]

Under arrangements. When the hospital makes arrangements with another facility for diagnostic services furnished on an outpatient basis, the services may be covered whether furnished in the hospital or in the other facility. Independent laboratory services furnished to an outpatient under an arrangement with the hospital are covered under the diagnostic laboratory tests provision of Part B. Laboratory services also may be furnished to a hospital outpatient under arrangements by the laboratory of another participating hospital or by the laboratory of an emergency hospital or participating SNF that meets the hospital conditions of participation relating to laboratory services. [Pub. 100-02, Ch. 6, § 20.4.5.]

Outpatient Surgery

The rules on coverage of outpatient surgery in hospital outpatient departments, free-standing ambulatory surgical centers, and hospital-affiliated ambulatory surgical centers are described at ¶ 386.

Psychiatric Services

For a discussion of services and programs that a hospital may provide to its outpatients who need psychiatric care, see ¶ 387.

Payment Rules

For a discussion of payment methods for outpatient hospital items and services, see ¶ 820.

[¶ 353] Diagnostic X-Ray, Laboratory, and Other Diagnostic Tests

Diagnostic x-ray, laboratory, and other diagnostic tests are covered under Part B. [Soc. Sec. Act § 1861(s)(3); 42 C.F.R. § 410.10(e).]

Ordering diagnostic tests. In most cases, the services must be furnished by a physician or must be incident to a physician's services. As a general rule, diagnostic tests must be ordered by the physician who is treating the beneficiary—that is, the physician furnishes a consultation or treats the beneficiary for a specific medical problem and uses the test results in the management of the beneficiary's medical problem. Nonphysician practitioners licensed to provide physician services under state law also are subject to the physician ordering requirement. [42 C.F.R. § 410.32(a).]

An order from a physician may be delivered via the following forms of communication: (1) a written document signed by the physician, which is hand-delivered, mailed, or faxed to the testing facility; (2) a telephone call from the physician's office to the testing facility documented in their respective copies of the beneficiary's medical records; or (3) an electronic mail from the physician's office to the testing facility. No signature is required, however, on orders for clinical diagnostic tests paid under the clinical laboratory fee schedule or the physician fee schedule. [*Medicare Benefit Policy Manual*, Pub. 100-02, Ch. 15, § 80.6.1.]

There is an exception to the treating physician requirement: a physician who meets the qualification requirements for an interpreting physician may order a diagnostic mammogram based on the findings of a screening mammogram, even though the physician does not treat the patient. [42 C.F.R. § 410.32(a).]

Physician supervision. Generally, to be considered reasonable and necessary, all diagnostic x-ray and other diagnostic tests covered under Soc. Sec. Act § 1861(s)(3) and payable under the physician fee schedule must be furnished under the appropriate level of supervision by a physician. The degree of physician supervision (general supervision, direct supervision, or personal supervision) required at the time the test is conducted depends on the difficulty and risk of the test. [42 C.F.R. § 410.32(b)(1), (3).]

Exceptions to the basic rule include the following diagnostic tests:

(1) mammography procedures;

(2) audiology tests personally furnished by a qualified audiologist;

(3) psychological testing services when personally furnished by a clinical psychologist or an independently practicing psychologist or furnished under the general supervision of a physician or a clinical psychologist;

(4) tests personally performed by a physical therapist certified by the American Board of Physical Therapy Specialties as a qualified electrophysiologic clinical specialist and permitted to provide the service under state law;

(5) diagnostic tests performed by a nurse practitioner or clinical nurse specialist authorized to perform the tests under applicable state laws;

(6) certain pathology and laboratory procedures; and

(7) diagnostic tests performed by a certified nurse-midwife authorized to perform the tests under applicable state laws.

[42 C.F.R. § 410.32(b)(2).]

Nurse practitioners, clinical nurse specialists, and physician assistants may not function as supervisory physicians under the diagnostic tests benefit. When these practitioners personally perform diagnostic tests, however, they may perform diagnostic tests pursuant to state scope of practice laws and under the applicable state requirements for physician supervision or collaboration. [Pub. 100-02, Ch. 15, § 80.]

Appropriate use criteria. Section 218(b) of the Protecting Access to Medicare Act of 2014 (PAMA) (P.L. 113-93) requires the HHS Secretary to establish a program to promote the use of appropriate use criteria for certain diagnostic imaging services to assist ordering and furnishing professionals in making the most appropriate treatment decision for a specific clinical condition for an individual. Beginning in 2020, outlier ordering professionals must begin applying for prior authorization to order imaging services. [Soc. Sec. Act § 1834(q); 42 C.F.R. § 414.94.]

Portable X-ray Suppliers

Diagnostic x-ray services furnished by a portable x-ray supplier are covered when furnished in a place of residence used as the patient's home or in nonparticipating institutions. Diagnostic x-ray services also are covered under Part B when provided in participating skilled nursing facilities (SNFs) and hospitals under circumstances in which they cannot be covered under Part A. [Soc. Sec. Act § 1861(s)(3); 42 C.F.R. § 410.32(c); Pub. 100-02, Ch. 15, § 80.4.1.]

Portable x-ray services must be ordered by a physician licensed to practice in the state or a nonphysician practitioner (including a nurse practitioner, clinical nurse specialist, physician assistant, certified nurse-midwife, or clinical psychologist) acting within the scope of the law. They must be performed under the general supervision of a physician or nonphysician practitioner by a supplier that meets the conditions of participation described to 42 C.F.R. Part 486, Subpart C. [42 C.F.R. § 410.32(c).]

Coverage for portable x-ray services is limited to: (1) skeletal films involving the extremities, pelvis, vertebral column, and skull; (2) chest and abdominal films that do not involve the use of contrast media; and (3) diagnostic mammograms if the supplier is approved for this service. [42 C.F.R. § 410.32(c)(4); Pub. 100-02, Ch. 15, § 80.4.3.]

A physician or nonphysician practitioner's written, signed order must specify the reason a portable x-ray test is required, the area of the body to be exposed, the number of radiographs to be obtained, the views needed, and a statement concerning the condition of the patient that indicates why portable x-ray services are necessary. For each patient, the supplier must make a record of the date of the portable x-ray examination, the name of the patient, a description of the procedures ordered and performed, the referring physician or nonphysician practitioner, the operator of the portable x-ray equipment who performed the examination, the physician to whom the radiograph was sent, and the date it was sent. [42 C.F.R. § 486.106.]

Diagnostic Laboratory Tests

Part B covers diagnostic laboratory tests when furnished by a qualified hospital, physician's office laboratory, rural health clinic, federally qualified health center, a SNF to its residents, or a laboratory that meets the applicable requirements for laboratories of 42 C.F.R. Part 493. [Soc. Sec. Act § 1861(s)(3); 42 C.F.R. §§ 410.10(e), 410.32(d).]

Clinical laboratory services involve the biological, microbiological, serological, chemical, immunohematological, hematological, biophysical, cytological, pathological, or other examination of materials derived from the human body for the diagnosis, prevention, or treatment of a disease or assessment of a medical condition. These examinations also include procedures to determine, measure, or otherwise describe the presence or absence of various substances or organisms in the body. Facilities only collecting or preparing specimens (or both) or only serving as a mailing service and not performing testing are not considered laboratories. [42 C.F.R. § 493.2; 100-02, Ch. 15, § 80.1.]

Prohibited referrals. The law prohibits Medicare payment to a laboratory that has a financial relationship with the referring physician. Violators are subject to civil money penalties and exclusion from the program. Laboratories are required to include information on referring physicians when submitting claims for payment (see "Stark Law" at ¶ 720). [Soc. Sec. Act §§ 1833(q), 1877.]

Licensing requirements. Diagnostic laboratory services furnished by laboratories in physician offices or independent laboratories are covered under Part B only if the laboratories are licensed pursuant to state or local law or are approved as meeting the requirements for licensing by the state or local agency responsible for licensing laboratories. These laboratories also must meet the standards prescribed in the Medicare regulations (42 C.F.R. Part 493) pursuant to the Clinical Laboratory Improvement Amendments of 1988 (CLIA) (P.L. 100-578).

Payment for clinical diagnostic laboratory tests is discussed at ¶ 875.

Other Diagnostic Tests

"Other diagnostic tests" are covered under Part B if the services are furnished by physicians or nonphysician practitioners operating within the scope of their authority under state law. [Soc. Sec. Act § 1861(s)(3); 42 C.F.R. § 410.10(e).] Some examples of "other diagnostic tests" are psychological and neuropsychological tests and hearing and balance assessment services performed by a qualified audiologist. [Pub. 100-02, Ch. 15, §§ 80.2, 80.3.]

Psychological tests. Part B covers diagnostic testing services when performed by a qualified psychologist (who is not a clinical psychologist) practicing independently of an institution, agency, or physician's office, if a physician orders such testing. Examples of psychologists whose services are covered under this provision include educational psychologists and counseling psychologists. [Pub. 100-02, Ch. 15, § 80.2.]

Hearing evaluations. Diagnostic testing performed by a qualified audiologist (or a nurse practitioner or clinical nurse specialist authorized to perform the tests under applicable state laws) is covered when a physician orders such testing to evaluate the need for, or appropriate type of, treatment of a hearing deficit or related medical problem. Diagnostic services performed only to determine the need for, or the appropriate type of, a hearing aid are not covered. If a physician refers a beneficiary to an audiologist for evaluation of signs or symptoms associated with hearing loss or ear injury, however, the audiologist's diagnostic services are covered even if the only outcome is the prescription of a hearing aid. [Pub. 100-02, Ch. 15, § 80.3.]

Audiologists may not bill Medicare for nonaudiology services such as nonauditory evoked potentials or cerumen removal; however, the labor of certain other diagnostic tests or treatment services may qualify to be billed when furnished by audiologists under physician supervision when all the appropriate policies are followed. [Pub. 100-02, Ch. 15, § 80.3.]

Screening for HIV infection. CMS has determined that screening for HIV infection, which is recommended with a grade of A by the U.S. Preventive Services Task Force (USPSTF) for certain individuals, is reasonable and necessary for early detection of HIV and is appropriate for individuals entitled to benefits under Part A or enrolled under Part B. CMS, therefore, covers both standard Food and Drug Administration-approved HIV rapid screening tests for:

(1) annual voluntary HIV screening of Medicare beneficiaries at increased risk for HIV infection per USPSTF guidelines; and

(2) a maximum of three voluntary HIV screening of pregnant Medicare beneficiaries: (a) when the diagnosis of pregnancy is known, (b) during the third trimester, and (c) at labor.

[*Medicare National Determinations Manual*, Pub. 100-03, Ch. 1, § 210.7.]

Independent Diagnostic Testing Facilities

Diagnostic tests provided by an independent diagnostic testing facility (IDTF) are covered and paid under the physician fee schedule. An IDTF may be a fixed location, a mobile entity, or an individual nonphysician practitioner. An IDTF is independent of a physician's office or hospital, but it may furnish diagnostic procedures in a physician's office. In most cases, an IDTF must have one or more supervising physicians who are responsible for direct and ongoing oversight of the quality of the testing performed, proper operation and calibration of testing equipment, and the qualification of nonphysician personnel who use the equipment. [42 C.F.R. § 410.33(a), (b).]

All procedures performed by the IDTF must be ordered in writing by the physician who is treating the beneficiary, although nonphysician practitioners may order tests in accordance with the scope of their licenses. The supervising physician for the IDTF may not order tests to be performed by the IDTF unless the IDTF's supervising physician is the beneficiary's treating physician. [42 C.F.R. § 410.33(d).]

With the exception of hospital-based and mobile IDTFs, a fixed-base IDTF may not share a practice location with another Medicare-enrolled individual or organization, lease or sublease its operations or its practice location to another Medicare-enrolled individual or organization, or share diagnostic testing equipment used in the initial diagnostic test with another Medicare-enrolled individual or organization. [42 C.F.R. § 410.33(g)(15).]

[¶ 354] X-Ray, Radium, and Radioactive Isotope Therapy

X-ray, radium, and radioactive isotope therapy are covered under the Part B program. These services also include materials and the services of technicians. [Soc. Sec. Act § 1861(s)(4); 42 C.F.R. § 410.35.]

X-ray, radium, and radioactive isotope therapy furnished in a nonprovider facility require direct personal supervision of a physician. The physician need not be in the same room, but must be in the area and immediately available to provide assistance and direction throughout the time the procedure is being performed. This level of physician involvement does not represent a physician's service and cannot be billed as a Part B service. Radiologists' weekly treatment management services, however, are covered. [*Medicare Benefit Policy Manual*, Pub. 100-02, Ch. 15, § 90.]

A separate charge for the services of a physicist is not recognized unless such services are covered under the "incident to" provision (see Pub. 100-02, Ch. 15, § 60.1) or the services are included as part of a technical component service billed by a freestanding radiation therapy center. The "incident to" provision also may be extended to include all necessary and appropriate services supplied by a radiation physicist assisting a radiologist when the physicist is in the physician's employ and working under his or her direct supervision. [Pub. 100-02, Ch. 15, § 90.]

[¶ 355] Ambulance Services

Medicare Part B covers ambulance services when the use of other methods of transportation is contraindicated by the individual's condition. [Soc. Sec. Act § 1861(s)(7); 42 C.F.R. § 410.10(i).] For Part B to cover ambulance services, the following conditions must be met: (1) the supplier meets the requirements of 42 C.F.R. § 410.41; (2) the services meet the medical necessity and origin and destination requirements of 42 C.F.R. § 410.40; and (2) Medicare Part A payment is not made directly or indirectly for the services. [42 C.F.R. § 410.40(a).] See ¶ 880 for information on payment for ambulance services.

Medical Necessity Requirements

Medicare covers ambulance services only if they are furnished to a beneficiary whose medical condition is such that other means of transportation are contraindicated. To satisfy the medical necessity requirement, the beneficiary's condition must require both the ambulance transportation itself and the level of service provided. [42 C.F.R. § 410.40(d); *Medicare Benefit Policy Manual*, Pub. 100-02, Ch. 10, § 10.2.]

Nonemergency transportation. For nonemergency ambulance transportation, medical necessity is satisfied if either:

    (1) the beneficiary is bed-confined and it is documented that other methods of transportation are contraindicated; or

    (2) the beneficiary's medical condition, regardless of bed confinement, is such that ambulance transportation is medically required.

For a beneficiary to be considered bed-confined, he or she must be unable to: (1) get up from bed without assistance; (2) ambulate; or (3) sit in a chair or wheelchair. [42 C.F.R. § 410.40(d).]

Medicare covers nonemergency, scheduled, repetitive ambulance services if the ambulance provider or supplier, before furnishing the service, obtains a written order from the beneficiary's attending physician certifying that the medical necessity requirements discussed above are met. The physician's order must be dated no earlier than 60 days before the date the service is furnished. Under certain circumstances, Medicare also covers medically necessary nonemergency ambulance services that are either unscheduled or that are scheduled on a nonrepetitive basis. [42 C.F.R. § 410.40(d)(2).]

Effect of beneficiary death. In general, if the beneficiary dies before being transported in a ground ambulance, no Medicare payment may be made. Medicare does, however, allow payment for an air ambulance service when the ambulance is dispatched to pick up a beneficiary but he or she is pronounced dead before being loaded onto the ambulance. The allowed amount is the appropriate base rate, but no allowance is made for mileage or for rural adjustment. If the beneficiary dies after pickup, before or upon arrival at the receiving facility, the entire ambulance service is covered. [Pub. 100-02, Ch. 10, §§ 10.2.6, 10.4.9.]

Covered Levels of Ambulance Transportation

Ambulance services are divided into different levels of ground (including water) and air ambulance services based on the medically necessary treatment provided during transport. These services include several different levels of service for ground and air transport of patients.

Medicare covers the following levels of ambulance service:

- basic life support (BLS) (emergency and nonemergency);
- advanced life support, level 1 (ALS1) (emergency and nonemergency);
- advanced life support, level 2 (ALS2);
- paramedic ALS intercept (PI);
- specialty care transport (SCT);
- fixed wing air ambulance (FW); and
- rotary wing air ambulance (RW) (helicopter).

[42 C.F.R. § 410.40(b).]

Paramedic ALS intercept services are covered under specific conditions in small towns and rural areas. Intercept services are ALS services furnished by a paramedic in connection with the services of a volunteer BLS ambulance supplier. The coverage applies only if there is a state law prohibiting the volunteer ambulance supplier from billing for any services. [42 C.F.R. § 410.40(c).]

Air ambulance services. There are two categories of air ambulance services: fixed wing (airplane) and rotary wing (helicopter) aircraft. Medicare covers medically appropriate air ambulance transportation only if the beneficiary's medical condition is such that transportation by basic or advanced life support ground ambulance is not appropriate, and either (1) the point of pickup is inaccessible by ground vehicle (e.g., in Hawaii, Alaska, and remote or sparsely populated areas of the continental United States); or (2) great distances or other obstacles are involved in getting the patient to the nearest hospital with appropriate facilities. [42 C.F.R. § 410.40(b)(6), (7); Pub. 100-02, Ch. 10, § 10.4.]

A "rural air ambulance service" means fixed wing and rotary wing air ambulance service in which the point of pick up occurs in a rural area or in a rural census tract of a metropolitan statistical area. To be covered, the service must be reasonable and necessary based on the health condition of the individual being transported at or immediately before the time of transport and must comply with equipment and crew requirements established by the Secretary. [Soc. Sec. Act § 1834(l)(14).]

Origin and Destination Requirements

Medicare covers the following ambulance transportation:

(1) from any point of origin to the nearest hospital, critical access hospital (CAH), or skilled nursing facility (SNF) that is capable of furnishing the required level and type of care for the beneficiary's illness or injury;

(2) from a hospital, CAH, or SNF to the beneficiary's home;

¶355

(3) from a SNF to the nearest supplier of medically necessary services not available at the SNF where the beneficiary is a resident, including the return trip; and

(4) for a beneficiary who is receiving renal dialysis for treatment of end-stage renal disease (ESRD), from the beneficiary's home to the nearest facility that furnishes renal dialysis, including the return trip.

[42 C.F.R. § 410.40(e).]

The reference in 42 C.F.R. § 410.40(e) to the "nearest" facility continues a long-standing policy that the Medicare beneficiary must be taken to the "nearest appropriate facility." This means that the patient must be transported to a Medicare-participating institution that is generally equipped to provide the needed hospital or skilled nursing care for the illness or injury involved. That a more distant institution is better equipped to care for the patient does not warrant a finding that a closer institution does not have "appropriate facilities." Such a finding is warranted, however, if the beneficiary's condition requires a higher level of trauma care or other specialized service available only at the more distant hospital. [Pub. 100-02, Ch. 10, § 10.3.6.]

If two or more facilities that meet the destination requirements can treat the patient appropriately and the locality of each facility encompasses the place where the ambulance transportation of the patient began, then the full mileage to any one of the facilities to which the beneficiary is taken is covered. [Pub. 100-02, Ch. 10, § 10.3.]

Requests by a home health agency. When a home health agency finds it necessary to have a beneficiary transported by ambulance to a hospital or SNF to obtain services not otherwise available, the trip is covered as a Part B service only if all the usual coverage requirements are met for ambulance transportation from wherever the patient is located. Such transportation is not covered as a home health service. [Pub. 100-02, Ch. 10, § 10.3.9.]

Ambulance Services Outside the United States

If services are furnished outside the United States, Medicare Part B covers ambulance transportation to a foreign hospital only as part of the beneficiary's admission for medically necessary inpatient services, as specified in 42 C.F.R. §§ 424.120–424.127. [42 C.F.R. § 410.40(f).] See ¶ 610.

[¶ 356] Durable Medical Equipment

Medicare Part B pays for the rental or purchase of durable medical equipment (DME) if the equipment is used in the patient's home or in an institution that is used as a home. [Soc. Sec. Act § 1861(s)(6); 42 C.F.R. §§ 410.10(h), 410.38(a).]

For a list of DME and the coverage status of each item, see § 280.1 in the *Medicare National Coverage Determinations Manual*, Pub. 100-03.

"Durable Medical Equipment" Defined

DME is equipment that: (1) can withstand repeated use; (2) is primarily and customarily used to serve a medical purpose; (3) generally is not useful to a person in the absence of illness or injury; and (4) is appropriate for use in the home. [*Medicare Benefit Policy Manual*, Pub. 100-02, Ch. 15, § 110.1.]

DME includes iron lungs, oxygen tents, hospital beds, and wheelchairs used in the patient's home (including an institution used as his or her home), whether furnished on a rental basis or purchased. It also includes blood-testing strips and blood glucose monitors for individuals with diabetes regardless of whether the beneficiary has Type I or Type II diabetes or his or her use of insulin. With respect to a seat-lift chair, only the seat-lift mechanism (and not the chair) is considered DME. [Soc. Sec. Act § 1861(n); 42 C.F.R. § 410.38(a).]

Medical supplies of an expendable nature, such as incontinence pads, catheters, bandages, and elastic stockings, are not considered durable (although they may fall into other coverage categories). There are other items that, although durable in nature, may fall into other Medicare coverage categories such as prosthetic devices, braces, or artificial arms, legs, and eyes. Implantable items for which payment may be made under Soc. Sec. Act § 1833(t), such as intraocular lenses, are not considered DME. [Soc. Sec. Act § 1834(a)(13).]

Equipment presumptively nonmedical. Equipment that is used primarily and customarily for a nonmedical purpose may not be considered "medical" equipment for which payment may be made under Medicare, even though the item has some remote medically related use. For example, devices and equipment used for environmental control or to enhance the environmental setting in which the beneficiary is placed are not considered covered DME. [Pub. 100-02, Ch. 15, § 110.1.]

Special exception items. Specified items of equipment may be covered under certain conditions even though they do not meet the definition of DME because they are not used primarily and customarily to serve a medical purpose and/or are generally useful in the absence of illness or injury. These items are covered if it is clearly established that they serve a therapeutic purpose in an individual case. Examples include heat lamps for a medical rather than a soothing or cosmetic purpose, and gel pads and pressure and water mattresses when prescribed for a patient who has bed sores or if there is medical evidence indicating the patient is highly susceptible to ulceration. [Pub. 100-02, Ch. 15, § 110.1.]

Supplies and accessories. Medicare covers supplies such as oxygen that are necessary for the effective use of DME. Such supplies include those drugs and biologics that must be put directly into the equipment to achieve the therapeutic benefit of the DME or to ensure the proper functioning of the equipment, e.g., tumor chemotherapy agents used with an infusion pump or heparin used with a home dialysis system. The coverage of such drugs or biologics, however, does not preclude the need for a determination that the drug or biologic itself is reasonable and necessary for treatment of the illness or injury or to improve the functioning of a malformed body member. [Pub. 100-02, Ch. 15, § 110.3.]

Definition of Beneficiary's Home

To be covered as DME the item must be used in the patient's home. For purposes of rental or purchase of DME, a patient's home may be his or her own dwelling, an apartment, a relative's home, a home for the aged, or some other type of institution. An institution may not be considered a beneficiary's home, however, if it is a hospital, critical access hospital, or skilled nursing facility. [Pub. 100-02, Ch. 15, § 110.1.]

Medical Necessity for DME

To be covered, the DME must be necessary and reasonable for treatment of an illness or injury, or to improve the functioning of a malformed body member. In most cases the physician's prescription for the equipment and other medical information available to the durable medical equipment Medicare administrative contractor (DME MAC) will be sufficient to establish that the equipment meets this requirement. [Pub. 100-02, Ch. 15, § 110.1.]

Reasonableness. Even though an item of DME may serve a useful medical purpose, the DME MAC also will consider to what extent, if any, it would be reasonable for the Medicare program to pay for the item prescribed. In determining reasonableness, the MAC will consider the following:

(1) Would the expense of the item to the program be clearly disproportionate to the therapeutic benefits that could ordinarily be derived from use of the equipment?

(2) Is the item substantially more costly than a medically appropriate and realistically feasible alternative pattern of care?

(3) Does the item serve essentially the same purpose as equipment already available to the beneficiary?

[Pub. 100-02, Ch. 15, § 110.1.]

Certificate of medical necessity. For items or services billed to a DME MAC, the supplier must receive a signed certificate of medical necessity (CMN) from the treating physician. A supplier must have a signed original, faxed, photocopied, or electronic CMN in its records before it can submit a claim for payment to Medicare. [*Medicare Program Integrity Manual*, Pub. 100-08, Ch. 5, § 5.3.]

Advance Beneficiary Notice. Suppliers must provide Advance Beneficiary Notices (ABNs) that advise beneficiaries, before items or services such as DME are furnished, when Medicare is likely to deny payment for them due to lack of medical necessity. [*Medicare Claims Processing Manual*, Pub. 100-04, Ch. 1, § 60.]

Written Order Requirements for DME

In addition to the CMN requirement and in an effort to prevent fraud, waste, and abuse, CMS has designated a list of certain covered DME items, referred to as Specified Covered Items, that require a written order. Specified Covered Items include:

- transcutaneous electrical nerve stimulation units, rollabout chairs, oxygen and respiratory equipment, hospital beds and accessories, and traction-cervical;

- any item of DME that appears on the durable medical equipment, prosthetics, orthotics, and supplies fee schedule with a price ceiling at or greater than $1,000; and

- any other item of DME that CMS adds to the list of Specified Covered Items through the notice and comment rulemaking process to reduce the risk of fraud, waste, and abuse.

[Soc. Sec. Act § 1834(a)(11)(B)(i); 42 C.F.R. § 410.38(g)(1), (2); *Program Integrity Manual*, Pub. 100-08, Ch. 5, § 5.2.]

Written orders issued for Specified Covered Items must include all of the following:

(1) beneficiary's name,

(2) item of DME ordered,

(3) signature of the prescribing practitioner,

(4) prescribing practitioner's National Provider Identifier, and

(5) the date of the order.

[42 C.F.R. § 410.38(g)(4).]

A supplier must maintain the written order and the supporting documentation provided by the physician, physician assistant (PA), nurse practitioner (NP), or clinical nurse specialist (CNS) and make them available to CMS upon request for seven years from the date of service. [42 C.F.R. § § 410.38(g)(5), 424.516(f).]

Face-to-face encounter requirement. For orders issued for Specified Covered Items pursuant to 42 C.F.R. § 410.38(g)(1) and (2), the physician must document and communicate to the DME supplier that the physician or a PA, NP, or CNS has had a face-to-face encounter with the beneficiary within six months before the written order. During the face-to-face encounter the physician or practitioner must conduct a needs assessment and evaluate and/or treat the beneficiary for the medical condition that supports the need for each covered item of DME ordered. [Soc. Sec. Act § 1834(a)(11)(B)(ii); 42 C.F.R. § 410.38(g)(3).]

Repairs, Maintenance, Replacement, and Delivery

Under certain circumstances, payment may be made for repair, maintenance, and replacement of medically required DME, including equipment that had been in use before the beneficiary enrolled in the Part B program. [Pub. 100-02, Ch. 15, § 110.2.]

Repairs. Repairs to equipment that a beneficiary owns are covered when necessary to make the equipment serviceable. If the expense for repairs exceeds the estimated expense of purchasing or renting another item of equipment for the remaining period of medical need, no payment can be made for the amount of the excess. Because renters of equipment recover from the rental charge the expenses they incur in maintaining the equipment they rent out, separately itemized charges for repair of rented equipment are not covered. [Pub. 100-02, Ch. 15, § 110.2.]

Maintenance. Routine periodic servicing, such as testing, cleaning, regulating, and checking of the beneficiary's equipment, is not covered. The owner is expected to perform such routine maintenance rather than a retailer or some other person who charges the beneficiary. More extensive maintenance, which, based on the manufacturers' recommendations, is to be performed by authorized technicians, is covered as repairs. This might include, for example, breaking down sealed components and performing tests that require specialized testing equipment not available to the beneficiary. Because renters of equipment recover from the rental charge the expenses they incur in maintaining in working order the equipment they rent out, separately itemized charges for maintenance of rented equipment are generally not covered. [Pub. 100-02, Ch. 15, § 110.2.]

Replacement. Equipment that the beneficiary owns or that is a capped rental item may be replaced in cases of loss or irreparable damage, e.g., as a result of a specific accident or a natural disaster. Replacement of equipment due to irreparable wear takes into consideration the reasonable useful lifetime of the equipment. [Pub. 100-02, Ch. 15, § 110.2.]

If equipment or a device is replaced free of charge by the warrantor, no program payment may be made because there was no charge involved. If the warrantor supplied the replaced equipment or device, but some charge or a pro rata payment was imposed, program payment may be made for the partial payment imposed for the device furnished by the warrantor. [Pub. 100-02, Ch. 16, § 40.4.]

Cases suggesting malicious damage, culpable neglect, or wrongful disposition of equipment will be investigated and denied when the MAC determines that it would be unreasonable to make program payment under the circumstances. [Pub. 100-02, Ch. 15, § 110.2.]

Delivery. Payment for delivery of DME whether rented or purchased generally is included in the fee schedule allowance for the item. [Pub. 100-02, Ch. 15, § 110.2.]

Coverage Rules for Power Mobility Devices

Special rules apply to coverage of power mobility devices (PMDs), DME that is in a class of wheelchairs that includes a power wheelchair (a four-wheeled motorized vehicle whose steering is operated by an electronic device or a joystick to control direction and turning) or a power-operated vehicle (a three- or four-wheeled motorized scooter that is operated by a tiller) that a beneficiary uses in the home. [42 C.F.R. § 410.38(c)(1).]

For Medicare Part B to cover PMDs, the physician or treating practitioner must:

(1) conduct a face-to-face examination of the beneficiary to determine the medical necessity for the PMD as part of an appropriate overall treatment plan;

(2) write a prescription, which is received by the supplier within 45 days after the face-to-face examination;

(3) provide supporting documentation, including pertinent parts of the beneficiary's medical record, that supports the medical necessity for the device, which is received by the supplier within 45 days after the face-to-face examination.

Beneficiaries discharged from a hospital do not need to receive a separate face-to-face examination as long as the physician or treating practitioner who performed the face-to-face examination in the hospital issues a PMD prescription and supporting documentation that is received by the supplier within 45 days after the date of discharge. In addition, the physician or treating practitioner may order accessories for PMDs without conducting a face-to-face examination. [42 C.F.R. § 410.38(c)(2), (3).]

Oxygen Services in the Home

Oxygen and oxygen equipment provided in the home are covered by Medicare under the DME benefit. Oxygen is considered reasonable and necessary only for patients with significant hypoxemia if requirements for medical documentation, laboratory evidence, and health conditions are met. [*Medicare National Coverage Determinations Manual*, Pub. 100-03, Ch. 1, § 240.2.]

A patient may qualify for coverage of a portable oxygen system either by itself or to use in addition to a stationary oxygen system. Portable oxygen is not covered when it is provided only as a backup to a stationary oxygen system. A portable oxygen system is covered for a particular patient if medical documentation indicates that the patient is mobile in the home and would benefit from the use of a portable oxygen system in the home. [Pub. 100-03, Ch. 1, § 240.2.]

A new physician certification is required every 90 days for certain patients receiving home oxygen therapy. The recertification must be made if, at the time the home oxygen therapy is initiated, the patient has an initial arterial blood gas value at or above a partial pressure of 56 or an arterial oxygen saturation at or above 89 percent. The recertification must be based on a follow-up test of these indications within the final 30 days of the 90-day period. [Soc. Sec. Act § 1834(a)(5)(E).]

Payments for maintenance and servicing (for parts and labor not covered by the supplier's or manufacturer's warranty) will be made if the Secretary determines them to be reasonable and necessary. [Soc. Sec. Act § 1834(a)(5)(F)(ii)(III).]

After the 36th continuous month during which payment is made for oxygen equipment, the supplier must continue to furnish the equipment during any period of medical need for the remainder of the reasonable useful lifetime of the equipment. [Soc. Sec. Act § 1834(a)(5)(F)(ii).]

Change in the Patient's Condition

A beneficiary may sell or otherwise dispose of DME purchased under the program and for which there is no further use, for example, because of recovery from the illness or injury that gave rise to the need for the equipment. There is no authority for Medicare to repossess the equipment. If, after disposal, there is again medical need for similar equipment, payment can be made for the rental or purchase of that equipment. When, however, an arrangement is motivated solely by a desire to profit from artificial expenses to be met by the program and realize a profit thereby, such expenses are not covered. [Pub. 100-02, Ch. 15, § 110.4.]

¶356

When payments stop because the beneficiary's condition has changed and the equipment is no longer medically necessary or because the beneficiary dies, the individual or his or her estate is responsible for the remaining noncovered charges. [Pub. 100-02, Ch. 15, § 110.4.]

[¶ 357] Prosthetic Devices and Prosthetics/Orthotics

Medicare Part B covers prosthetic devices, other than dental, that replace all or part of an internal body organ, including colostomy bags and supplies directly related to colostomy care. Coverage includes replacement of prosthetic devices and one pair of conventional eyeglasses or conventional contact lenses furnished after each cataract surgery during which an intraocular lens is inserted. A written physician order is required. [Soc. Sec. Act § 1861(s)(8); 42 C.F.R. § 410.36(a)(2), (b).]

Examples of prosthetic devices include parenteral and enteral nutrition (PEN), cardiac pacemakers, prosthetic lenses, breast prostheses, maxillofacial devices, and devices that replace all or part of the ear or nose as well as urinary collection and retention systems with or without a tube and a Foley catheter that replace bladder function in cases of permanent urinary incontinence. Medicare does not cover a prosthetic device dispensed before the beneficiary undergoes the procedure that makes the use of the device necessary. [*Medicare Benefit Policy Manual*, Pub. 100-02, Ch. 15, § 120; *Medicare Coverage Determinations Manual*, Pub. 100-03, Ch. 1, § 20.8.]

No payment may be made for prosthetics and certain custom-fabricated orthotics unless they are furnished by a qualified practitioner and fabricated by a qualified practitioner or a qualified supplier at an approved facility. Affected custom-fabricated orthotics are items requiring education, training, and experience to custom fabricate. [Soc. Sec. Act § 1834(h)(1)(F).]

Vacuum erection systems. Effective for claims with dates of service on or after July 1, 2015, Medicare Part B no longer covers vacuum erection system prosthetic devices and related accessories, in the same manner that erectile dysfunction drugs are excluded under Part D. [Soc. Sec. Act § 1834(a)(1)(I).]

Dentures. Dentures are excluded from coverage; however, when a denture or a portion thereof is an integral part (built-in) of a covered prosthesis (e.g., an obturator to fill an opening in the palate), it is covered as part of that prosthesis. [Pub. 100-02, Ch. 15, § 120.]

Prosthetic lenses. Prostheses replacing the lens of an eye include post-surgical lenses customarily used during convalescence from eye surgery in which the lens of the eye was removed. In addition, permanent lenses are also covered when required by an individual lacking the organic lens of the eye because of surgical removal or congenital absence. Prosthetic lenses obtained on or after the beneficiary's date of entitlement to supplementary medical insurance benefits may be covered even though the surgical removal of the crystalline lens occurred before entitlement. [42 C.F.R. § 411.15(b); Pub. 100-02, Ch. 15, § 120.]

The general exclusion applicable to refractive services regardless of the reason for them, however, means that refractive services for the purpose of prescribing or providing prosthetic lenses are not covered. [42 C.F.R. § 411.15(c).]

Repair and replacement. Replacements of prosthetic devices that are artificial limbs or the replacement of any parts of artificial limbs are covered when there is a change in the condition of the patient or a change in the condition of the device. The physician's determination in these situations is controlling, except that confirmation may be required for devices or parts that are less than three years old. [Soc. Sec. Act § 1834(h)(1)(G).] Necessary supplies, adjustments, repairs, and replacements are covered even when the device had been in use before the user enrolled in Part B of the program, so long as the device continues to be medically required. [Pub. 100-02, Ch. 15, § 120.]

Enteral and Parenteral Nutrition Therapy

For PEN to be covered under Part B, the beneficiary must have a permanently inoperative internal body organ or function thereof. Coverage of such therapy, however, does not require a medical judgment that the impairment giving rise to the therapy will persist throughout the patient's remaining years. If the medical record, including the judgment of the attending physician, indicates that the impairment will be of long and indefinite duration, the test of permanence is considered met. [Pub. 100-03, Ch. 1, § 180.2.]

The claim for PEN therapy must contain a physician's written order or prescription and sufficient medical documentation to permit an independent conclusion that the requirements of the prosthetic device benefit are met and that PEN therapy is medically necessary. If the coverage requirements for PEN therapy are met, related supplies, equipment, and nutrients are also covered. [Pub. 100-02, Ch. 15, § 120; Pub. 100-03, Ch. 1, § 180.2.]

Braces, Trusses, and Artificial Limbs

Part B covers leg, arm, back, and neck braces, trusses, and artificial legs, arms, and eyes when furnished incident to a physician's services or on a physician's order. [Soc. Sec. Act § 1861(s)(9); 42 C.F.R. § 410.36(a)(3); Pub. 100-02, Ch. 15, § 130.]

Braces include rigid and semi-rigid devices that support weak or deformed body member or restrict or eliminate motion in diseased or injured parts of the body. Back braces include, but are not limited to, special corsets, including sacroiliac, sacrolumbar and dorsolumbar corsets, and belts. Elastic stockings, garter belts, and similar devices do not come within the scope of the definition of a brace. [Pub. 100-02, Ch. 15, § 130.]

Although orthopedic shoes or other supportive devices for the feet generally are excluded from coverage, the exclusion does not apply to such a shoe if it is an integral part of a leg brace. [42 C.F.R. § 411.15(f); Pub. 100-02, Ch. 15, § 290.]

A terminal device (e.g., hand or hook) is covered under this provision regardless of whether an artificial limb is required by the patient. Stump stockings and harnesses (including replacements) also are covered when these appliances are essential to the effective use of the artificial limb. [Pub. 100-02, Ch. 15, § 130.]

Adjustments to an artificial limb or other appliance required by wear or a change in the patient's condition are covered when ordered by a physician. Adjustments, repairs, and replacements are covered even when the item had been in use before the user enrolled in Part B of the program as long as the device continues to be medically required. [Soc. Sec. Act § 1861(s)(9); 42 C.F.R. § 410.36(a)(3); Pub. 100-02, Ch. 15, § 130.]

[¶ 359] Surgical Dressings, Splints, and Casts

Medicare Part B covers surgical dressings, splints, casts, and other devices used for reduction of fractures and dislocations. [Soc. Sec. Act § 1861(s)(5); 42 C.F.R. §§ 410.10(g), 410.36(a).]

The coverage of splints and casts includes dental splints. [*Medicare Benefit Policy Manual*, Pub. 100-02, Ch. 15, § 100.]

Surgical dressings are limited to primary and secondary dressings required for the treatment of a wound caused by, or treated by, a surgical procedure performed by a physician or other health care professional. In addition, surgical dressings required after debridement of a wound are covered. [Pub. 100-02, Ch. 15, § 100.]

¶359

"Primary dressings" are therapeutic or protective coverings applied directly to wounds or lesions either on the skin or caused by an opening to the skin. Secondary dressing materials that serve a therapeutic or protective function and are needed to secure a primary dressing are also covered. Secondary dressings include adhesive tape, roll gauze, bandages, and disposable compression material. [Pub. 100-02, Ch. 15, § 100.]

Examples of items *not* ordinarily covered as surgical dressings include elastic stockings, support hose, foot coverings, leotards, knee supports, surgical leggings, gauntlets, and pressure garments for the arms and hands. Some items, such as transparent film, may be used as a primary or secondary dressing. [Pub. 100-02, Ch. 15, § 100.]

If a physician, certified nurse-midwife, physician assistant, nurse practitioner, or clinical nurse specialist applies surgical dressings as part of a professional service that is billed to Medicare, the surgical dressings are considered incident to the practitioner's professional services. When surgical dressings are not covered incident to the services of a health care practitioner and are obtained by a patient from a supplier pursuant to an order from a physician or other health care professional, the dressings are covered separately under Part B. [Pub. 100-02, Ch. 15, § 100.]

[¶ 361] Inpatient Ancillary Services

No payment may be made under Part B with respect to any services furnished to an individual to the extent that the individual is entitled (or would be entitled, except for the deductible and coinsurances) to have payment made for these services under Part A. [Soc. Sec. Act § 1833(d).] This precludes payment under Part B and Part A for the same services. When such payment is not precluded, however—for example, when an inpatient has exhausted his or her 90 days of entitlement in a "spell of illness"— payment may be made for certain "medical and other health services" under Part B, even though they are furnished to an inpatient of a skilled nursing facility (SNF). These services are usually referred to as "Part B ancillary services."

The following medical and other health services are covered under Part B when furnished by a participating SNF either directly or under arrangements to inpatients who are not entitled to have payment made under Part A (e.g., benefits exhausted or three-day prior-stay requirement not met):

- diagnostic x-ray tests, diagnostic laboratory tests, and other diagnostic tests;

- x-ray, radium, and radioactive isotope therapy, including materials and services of technicians;

- surgical dressings and splints, casts, and other devices used for reduction of fractures and dislocations;

- prosthetic devices (other than dental) that replace all or part of an internal body organ (including contiguous tissue), or all or part of the function of a permanently inoperative or malfunctioning internal body organ, including replacement or repair of such devices;

- leg, arm, back, and neck braces; trusses; and artificial legs, arms, and eyes, including adjustments, repairs, and replacements required because of breakage, wear, loss, or a change in the patient's physical condition;

- outpatient physical and occupational therapy and outpatient speech-language pathology services;

- screening mammography services;

- screening pap smears and pelvic exams;

- influenza, pneumococcal pneumonia, and hepatitis B vaccines;
- some colorectal screening;
- prostate screening;
- ambulance services;
- hemophilia clotting factors; and
- Epoetin Alfa (EPO) for end-stage renal disease beneficiaries when given in conjunction with dialysis.

[42 C.F.R. § § 409.27(a), 410.60(b); *Medicare Benefit Policy Manual*, Pub. 100-02, Ch. 8, § 70.]

Medical and Other Services Furnished to Hospital Inpatients

If a Medicare Part A claim for inpatient hospital services is denied because the inpatient admission was not reasonable and necessary, or if a hospital determines after a beneficiary is discharged that the inpatient admission was not reasonable and necessary, and if waiver of liability payment is not made, the hospital may be paid for the following Part B inpatient services that would have been reasonable and necessary if the beneficiary had been treated as a hospital outpatient:

(1) Part B services paid under the outpatient prospective payment system (OPPS), excluding observation services and hospital outpatient visits that require an outpatient status; and

(2) the following services excluded from OPPS payment that are instead paid under the respective Part B fee schedules or prospectively determined rates for which payment is made when provided to hospital outpatients:

(a) physical therapy services, speech-language pathology services, and occupational therapy services;

(b) ambulance services;

(c) prosthetic devices, prosthetic supplies, and orthotic devices paid under the durable medical equipment, prosthetics/orthotics, and supplies (DMEPOS) fee schedule (excludes implantable prosthetic devices (other than dental) that replace all or part of an internal body organ (including colostomy bags and supplies directly related to colostomy care) and replacement of such devices);

(d) durable medical equipment (DME) supplied by the hospital for the patient to take home, except DME that is implantable;

(e) certain clinical diagnostic laboratory services;

(f) screening and diagnostic mammography services; and

(g) annual wellness visit providing personalized prevention plan services.

[42 C.F.R. § 414.5(a); Pub. 100-02, Ch. 6, § 10.1.]

Hospitals also may be paid under Part B for services included in the payment window before the point of inpatient admission for outpatient services treated as inpatient services, including services requiring an outpatient status. [42 C.F.R. § 414.5(b); Pub. 100-02, Ch. 6, § 10.1.]

Other circumstances. Part B payment can be made to a hospital for certain medical and other services for inpatients enrolled in Part B if: (1) no Part A prospective payment is made at all for the hospital stay because of patient exhaustion of benefit days before or during the admission; or (2) the patient was not otherwise eligible for or entitled to coverage under Part A. For hospitals paid under the OPPS, certain Part B inpatient services (including diagnostic tests; x-ray, radium, and radioactive isotope therapy; certain screening tests; acute dialysis of a hospital inpatient; and immunosuppressive and oral anti-cancer drugs) are separately payable under Part B and are excluded from OPPS packaging if the primary service with which the service would otherwise be bundled is not a payable Part B inpatient service. [Pub. 100-02, Ch. 6, § 10.2.]

The following inpatient services are payable under the non-OPPS Part B fee schedules or prospectively determined rates:

(1) surgical dressings and splints, casts, and other devices used for reduction of fractures and dislocations;

(2) prosthetic devices (other than dental) that replace all or part of an internal body organ (including contiguous tissue) or all or part of the function of a permanently inoperative or malfunctioning internal body organ, including replacement of such devices;

(3) leg, arm, back, and neck braces; trusses; and artificial legs, arms, and eyes, including replacements required because of a change in the patient's physical condition;

(4) physical and occupational therapy services and outpatient speech-language pathology services;

(5) screening mammography services; and

(6) ambulance services.

[Pub. 100-02, Ch. 6, § 10.2.]

The services listed below, when provided to a hospital inpatient, may be covered under Part B even if the patient has Part A coverage for the hospital stay, because these services are covered under Part B and not covered under Part A:

- physicians' services (including the services of residents and interns in unapproved teaching programs) and the services of physician assistants, certified nurse-midwives, and qualified clinical psychologists;

- influenza, pneumococcal pneumonia, and hepatitis B vaccines and their administration;

- screening mammography services, screening pap smears and pelvic exams, glaucoma screening, colorectal screening, and prostate screening;

- bone mass measurements; and

- diabetes self-management training services.

[Pub. 100-02, Ch. 6, § 10.3; Ch. 15, § 250.]

To have any Medicare coverage at all (Part A or Part B), any nonphysician service rendered to a hospital inpatient must be provided directly or arranged for by the hospital. [Pub. 100-02, Ch. 6, § 10.]

[¶ 362] Drugs and biologics

Drugs and biologics must meet the same Medicare criteria for coverage under Part B as under Part A. These requirements are discussed at ¶ 212.

There are, however, significant limitations on Part B coverage of drugs and biologics that do not apply under Part A. Drugs and biologics generally are covered under Part B only if they: (1) meet the specific definition of drugs and biologics; (2) are of the type that are not usually self-administered by the patient; (3) are reasonable and necessary to diagnose or treat an existing illness or condition; (4) are administered by a physician or other health professional as an "incident to" service (see ¶ 351); (5) are not excluded as noncovered immunizations; and (6) are not found by the Food and Drug Administration (FDA) to be "less than effective" (see ¶ 644). [Soc. Sec. Act § 1861(s)(2); 42 C.F.R. § 410.29; *Medicare Benefit Policy Manual*, Pub. 100-02, Ch. 15, § 50.]

A drug or biologic may be covered only where it is included, or approved for inclusion, in the latest official edition of the United States Pharmacopoeia National Formulary, the United States Pharmacopoeia-Drug Information, or the American Dental Association Guide to Dental Therapeutics. The term "drugs" also includes any drugs or biologics used in an anticancer chemotherapeutic regimen for a medically accepted indication. Combination drugs are also included in the definition of drugs if the combination itself or all of the therapeutic ingredients of the combination are included, or approved for inclusion, in any of these drug compendia. [Soc. Sec. Act § 1861(t)(1); Pub. 100-02, Ch. 15, § 50.1.]

Prescription drugs are covered under Medicare Part D. A description of Medicare coverage of prescription drugs begins at ¶ 500.

See ¶ 885 for a discussion of payment rules for drugs and biologics.

Determining Self-Administration

Whether a drug or biologic is a type not usually self-administered by the patient is based on the usual method of administration of the form of that drug or biologic as furnished by the physician. Injectable drugs, including intravenously administered drugs, are typically covered; with limited exceptions, other routes of administration including oral drugs, suppositories, and topical medications are considered to be usually self-administered by the patient. [Pub. 100-02, Ch. 15, § 50.2.]

The *Medicare Benefit Policy Manual* defines "usually administered" as meaning a route of administration used more than 50 percent of the time. Thus, if a drug is self-administered by more than 50 percent of Medicare beneficiaries, the drug is excluded from Medicare coverage. [Pub. 100-02, Ch. 15, § 50.2.]

Reliable statistical information on the extent of self-administration by patients may not always be available. In the absence of reliable statistical information on the extent of self-administration by patients, contractors are to consider the following presumptions:

- Drugs delivered intravenously are not usually self-administered.

- Drugs delivered by intramuscular injection are not usually self-administered. The contractor may consider the depth and nature of the particular intramuscular injection in applying this presumption. However, contractors should examine use of the particular drug and consider: (1) whether the drug is used for an acute condition (if so, it is less likely that a patient would self-administer the drug); and (2) how often the injection is given (for example, if the drug is administered once or more per week, it is likely to be self-administered by the patient).

- Drugs delivered by subcutaneous injection are self-administered; however, contractors should examine use of the particular drug and consider whether it is used for an acute condition and the frequency of administration, as described above.

[Pub. 100-02, Ch. 15, § 50.2.]

Drugs as supplies. Some drugs that usually are self-administered by the patient may, nevertheless, be covered by Medicare Part B when they function as supplies, such as when they are provided as an integral component of a procedure or when they facilitate the performance of or recovery from a particular procedure. Except for the applicable copayment, hospitals may not bill beneficiaries for these types of drugs because their costs, as supplies, are packaged into the prospective payment system payment for the procedure with which they are used. [Pub. 100-02, Ch. 15, § 50.2.]

Exclusion of Immunizations

Vaccinations and inoculations are excluded as "immunizations" unless they are directly related to the treatment of an injury or direct exposure to a disease or condition, such as antirabies treatment, tetanus antitoxin or booster vaccine, botulin antitoxin, antivenin sera, or immune globulin. In the absence of injury or direct exposure, preventive immunizations (vaccinations or inoculations) against such diseases as smallpox, polio, and diphtheria are not covered. Pneumococcal pneumonia, hepatitis B, and influenza virus vaccines are exceptions to this rule and are covered (see below). [Pub. 100-02, Ch. 15, § 50.4.4.2.]

Statutory Exceptions to Above Rules

There are a number of exceptions to the rule against self-administered drugs and preventive immunizations:

Antigens. Payment may be made for a reasonable supply of antigens that have been prepared for a particular patient if: (1) the antigens are prepared by a physician who is a doctor of medicine or osteopathy; and (2) the physician who prepared the antigens has examined the patient and has determined a plan of treatment and a dosage regimen. Antigens must be administered in accordance with the plan of treatment and by a physician or by a properly instructed person (who could be the patient) under the supervision of the physician. A reasonable supply of antigens is considered to be not more than a 12-month supply of antigens that has been prepared for a particular patient at any one time. [Soc. Sec. Act § 1861(s)(2)(G); 42 C.F.R. § 410.68.]

Pneumococcal pneumonia vaccine. To protect the elderly from pneumococcal pneumonia, a disease to which they are particularly susceptible, pneumococcal pneumonia vaccine and its administration are covered without deductible or coinsurance. Coverage includes revaccination of patients at highest risk of pneumococcal infection. The vaccine may be requested by the patient; neither a physician's order nor physician supervision is required. [Soc. Sec. Act § 1861(s)(10)(A); 42 C.F.R. § 410.57; Pub. 100-02, Ch. 15, § 50.4.4.2.]

Hepatitis B vaccine. Hepatitis B vaccine and its administration are covered when furnished to an individual who is at high or intermediate risk of contracting Hepatitis B. [Soc. Sec. Act § 1861(s)(10)(B).]

High-risk groups include: (1) end-stage renal disease (ESRD) patients; (2) hemophiliacs who receive Factor VIII or IX concentrates; (3) clients of institutions for individuals with intellectual disabilities; (4) persons who live in the same household as a hepatitis B carrier; (5) homosexual men; (6) illicit injectable drug abusers; (7) Pacific Islanders; and (8) persons diagnosed with diabetes mellitus. Intermediate risk groups include: (1) staff in institutions for individuals with intellectual disabilities and classroom employees who work with individuals with intellectual disabilities; (2) health care workers who have frequent contact with blood or blood-derived body fluids during their routine work; and (3) heterosexually active persons with multiple sexual partners (which means those Medicare beneficiaries who have had at least two documented episodes of sexually transmitted diseases within the past five years). Persons in these groups, however, are not considered at high or intermediate risk of contracting Hepatitis B if they have undergone a prevaccination screening and been found to be currently positive for antibodies to hepatitis B. [42 C.F.R. § 410.63; Pub. 100-02, Ch. 15, § 50.4.4.2.]

Payment for hepatitis B vaccine and its administration for ESRD beneficiaries is made on a reasonable-charge basis and is not included in the prospective payment amount paid to

ESRD facilities or in the comprehensive fee amount paid to physicians for treating ESRD patients. [Soc. Sec. Act § 1881(b)(11)(A).]

Influenza virus vaccine. Influenza virus vaccine and its administration are covered without deductible or coinsurance when furnished in compliance with applicable state law by any provider of services or any entity or individual with a supplier number. Typically, these vaccines are administered once a year in the fall or winter. Medicare does not require for coverage purposes that the vaccine be ordered by a physician. Therefore, the beneficiary may receive the vaccine upon request without a physician's order and without physician supervision. [Soc. Sec. Act § 1861(s)(10)(A); 42 C.F.R. § 410.57(b); Pub. 100-02, Ch. 15, § 50.4.4.2.]

Blood clotting factors. Medicare covers blood clotting factors for hemophilia patients competent to use such factors to control bleeding without medical or other supervision. Items related to the administration of the factors also are covered. This coverage is subject to utilization controls deemed necessary by the Medicare program for the efficient use of the factors. [Soc. Sec. Act § 1861(s)(2)(I); Pub. 100-02, Ch. 15, § 50.5.5.] Medicare will make a separate payment for administration of clotting factors. The separate payment may take into account the mixing and delivery of clotting factors to a beneficiary, including special inventory management and storage requirements, as well as ancillary supplies and patient training necessary for self-administration. [Soc. Sec. Act § 1842(o)(5).]

Immunosuppressive drugs. Medicare covers prescription drugs used in immunosuppressive therapy when furnished to an individual who receives a covered organ transplant. [Soc. Sec. Act § 1861(s)(2)(J).] There is no time limit on Medicare coverage for immunosuppressive drugs. [Pub. 100-02, Ch. 15, § 50.5.1.]

Coverage is limited to those immunosuppressive drugs that specifically are labeled as such and approved for marketing by the FDA. Also included are prescription drugs, such as prednisone, that are used in conjunction with immunosuppressive drugs as part of a therapeutic regimen reflected in FDA-approved labeling for immunosuppressive drugs. Antibiotics, hypertensives, and other drugs not directly related to preventing organ rejection are not covered. [Pub. 100-02, Ch. 15, § 50.5.1.]

IVIG for immune deficiency diseases. Medicare covers intravenous immune globulin (IVIG), a pooled plasma derivative, for the treatment of primary immune deficiency diseases in a patient's home. The benefit does not include coverage for items or services related to the administration of the derivative. For coverage of IVIG under this benefit, it is not necessary for the derivative to be administered through a piece of durable medical equipment. [Soc. Sec. Act § 1861(s)(2)(Z), (zz); 42 C.F.R. § 410.10(y); Pub. 100-02, Ch. 15, § 50.6.]

Erythropoietin. Erythropoietin (EPO) is covered, even when self-administered, for the treatment of anemia for patients with chronic renal failure who are on dialysis. It is covered for self-administration by a home dialysis patient if the patient (or an appropriate caregiver) is trained to inject EPO. The patient's doctor or the renal dialysis facility also must develop a protocol for follow-up review and reevaluation of the patient's condition and the patient's ability to use the drug safely and effectively. [Soc. Sec. Act § 1861(s)(2)(O); Pub. 100-02, Ch. 15, § 50.5.2.]

Osteoporosis drugs. Medicare covers injectable drugs approved for the treatment of a bone fracture related to post-menopausal osteoporosis if: (1) the drugs are administered by a home health agency, (2) the patient's attending physician certifies that the patient has suffered a bone fracture related to post-menopausal osteoporosis and the patient is incapable of self-administering the drugs, and (3) the patient is confined to her home. [Soc. Sec. Act § 1861(m)(5), (kk).]

¶362

Oral anti-cancer and anti-emetic drugs. Oral anti-cancer chemotherapeutic drugs are covered, even when self-administered, if they contain the same active ingredients as intravenously administered anti-cancer drugs. [Soc. Sec. Act § 1861(s)(2)(Q), (t)(2); Pub. 100-02, Ch. 15, § 50.5.3.] Off-label uses of FDA-approved drugs and biologics for anti-cancer chemotherapeutic regimens are covered by Medicare when they are clinically recognized for the treatment of a specific type of cancer and are listed by CMS in its benefits manual under one or more compendia or under peer-reviewed medical literature. [Pub. 100-02, Ch. 15, § 50.4.5.]

Part B also covers self-administered anti-emetic drugs when they are prescribed by a physician for use with a covered anti-cancer drug when necessary for the administration and absorption of the oral anti-cancer drug (for example, when a high likelihood of vomiting exists). The anti-emetic must be used during the period that begins immediately before and ends within 48 hours after the time of the administration of the anti-cancer drug and it must be used as a full replacement for the anti-emetic therapy that otherwise would be administered intravenously. [Soc. Sec. Act § 1861(s)(2)(T); Pub. 100-02, Ch. 15, § 50.5.4.]

[¶ 366] Other Health Care Practitioners

Over the years Medicare has expanded coverage for the services of nonphysician health care practitioners. Included in this group are physician assistants (PAs), nurse practitioners (NPs) and clinical nurse specialists (CNSs), certified registered nurse anesthetists (CRNAs) and anesthesia assistants (AAs), certified nurse-midwives, clinical psychologists, and clinical social workers (CSWs). (See ¶ 860 for the details of payment rules for these practitioners.)

Physician Assistants, Nurse Practitioners, and Clinical Nurse Specialists

Medicare Part B covers the services of PAs, NPs, and CNSs if the services would be covered as physicians' services if furnished by a physician. Such services are covered if the PA, NP, or CNS is legally authorized to perform them in the state in which they are performed and does not perform services that are otherwise excluded from coverage because of one of the statutory exclusions. Medicare covers these services in all settings in both rural and urban areas. [Soc. Sec. Act § 1861(s)(2)(K); 42 C.F.R. §§ 410.74(a), 410.75(c), 410.76(c).]

Examples of the types of services that PAs, NPs, and CNSs may furnish include services that traditionally have been reserved to physicians, such as physical examinations, minor surgery, setting casts for simple fractures, interpreting x-rays, and other activities that involve an independent evaluation or treatment of the patient's condition. Also included are PAs', NPs', and CNSs' performance of the initial preventive physical examination and the annual wellness visit. [Soc. Sec. Act § 1861(s)(2)(K); *Medicare Benefit Policy Manual*, Pub. 100-02, Ch. 15, §§ 190, 200, 210.]

Personal performance. PA, NP, and CNS professional services are covered only when they have been personally performed by the PA, NP, or CNS. Supervision of other nonphysician staff does not constitute personal performance of a professional service. [42 C.F.R. §§ 410.74(d)(1), 410.75(e)(1), 410.76(e)(1).]

Physician assistants. To be covered, PA services must be performed under the general supervision of a physician. The supervising physician need not be physically present when the physician assistant is performing the services unless required by state law; however, the supervising physician must be immediately available to the PA for consultation. [Soc. Sec. Act § 1861(s)(2)(K)(i); 42 C.F.R. § 410.74(a)(2)(iv).]

CNSs and NPs. Both NPs and CNSs must perform services while working in collaboration with a physician. Collaboration is a process in which the practitioner works with one or more physicians to deliver health care services within the scope of the practitioner's expertise, with medical direction and appropriate supervision as provided for in jointly developed guidelines or other mechanisms as provided by the law of the state in which the services are performed. The collaborating physician does not need to be present with the NP when the services are furnished or to make an independent evaluation of each patient who is seen by the NP. [Soc. Sec. Act § 1861(s)(2)(K)(ii), (aa)(6); 42 C.F.R. §§ 410.75(c)(3), 410.76(c)(3).]

CRNAs and Anesthesia Assistants

Medicare Part B covers anesthesia services and related care furnished by a CRNA or an AA who is legally authorized to perform the services by the state in which the services are furnished. [Soc. Sec. Act § 1861(s)(11), (bb); 42 C.F.R. § 410.69(a).]

Nurse-Midwife Services

Medicare Part B covers certified nurse-midwife services. The term "certified nurse-midwife services" means such services furnished by a certified nurse-midwife and such services and supplies furnished as an incident to the nurse-midwife's service that the certified nurse-midwife is legally authorized to perform under state law as would otherwise be covered if furnished by a physician or as an incident to a physicians' service. [Soc. Sec. Act § 1861(s)(2)(L), (gg); 42 C.F.R. § 410.77.]

Covered services are those furnished by a certified nurse-midwife that are within the scope of practice authorized by the law of the state in which they are furnished and would otherwise be covered if furnished by a physician, including obstetrical and gynecological services. Coverage of service to the newborn continues only to the point that the newborn is or would normally be treated medically as a separate individual. [42 C.F.R. § 410.77(b)(1); Pub. 100-02, Ch. 15, § 180.]

Incident-to services. Part B covers services and supplies incident to the services of a certified nurse-midwife if the requirements of 42 C.F.R. § 410.26 are met. [42 C.F.R. § 410.77(b), (c).]

Personal performance. A nurse-midwife can be paid for professional services only when the services have been performed personally by the nurse-midwife. Supervision of other nonphysician staff by a nurse-midwife does not constitute personal performance of a professional service by the nurse-midwife. [42 C.F.R. § 410.77(d); Pub. 100-02, Ch. 15, § 180.]

Place of service. There is no restriction on place of service. Nurse-midwife services are covered if provided in the nurse-midwife's office, the patient's home, or a hospital or other facility, such as a clinic or birthing center owned or operated by a nurse-midwife. [Pub. 100-02, Ch. 15, § 180.]

Relationship with physician. Unless required by state law, nurse-midwife services are covered regardless of whether he or she is under the supervision of, or associated with, a physician or other health care provider. [42 C.F.R. § 410.77(b)(2); Pub. 100-02, Ch. 15, § 180.]

Clinical Psychologists

Medicare Part B covers services furnished by a clinical psychologist that are within the scope of his or her state license, if the services would be covered if furnished by a physician or as an incident to a physician's services. [Soc. Sec. Act § 1861(s)(2)(M), (ii).]

Incident-to services and supplies. Part B also covers services and supplies furnished "incident to" a CP's services if the requirements of 42 C.F.R. § 410.26 are met. [42 C.F.R. § 410.71(a)(2).]

Requirement for consultation. A CP must agree that, upon the beneficiary's consent, the CP will attempt to consult with the beneficiary's attending or primary care physician

¶366

within a reasonable time to consider any conditions contributing to the beneficiary's symptoms. If the CP's attempts to consult directly with the physician are not successful, the CP must notify the physician within a reasonable time that he or she is furnishing services to the patient. Neither the CP nor the attending or primary care physician may bill Medicare or the beneficiary for this consultation. [42 C.F.R. § 410.71(c), (e); Pub. 100-02, Ch. 15, § 160.]

Noncovered services. The services of CPs are not covered if they are otherwise excluded from Medicare coverage even though a clinical psychologist is authorized by state law to perform them. In addition, any therapeutic services that are billed by CPs under Current Procedural Terminology® (CPT®) psychotherapy codes that include medical evaluation and management services are not covered. [Pub. 100-02, Ch. 15, § 160.]

Clinical Social Workers

Part B coverage of CSW services includes the diagnosis and treatment of mental illnesses that the CSW is legally authorized to perform under state law and would otherwise be covered if performed by a physician or as incident to a physician's services. [Soc. Sec. Act § 1861(s)(2)(N), (hh)(2); 42 C.F.R. § 410.73(b)(1).]

Noncovered services. Part B does not cover services furnished to an inpatient of a hospital or skilled nursing facility that the facility is required to provide, or to a patient in a Medicare-participating dialysis facility if the services are those required by the conditions for coverage for end-stage renal disease facilities. CSW services are not covered if they are otherwise excluded from Medicare coverage even though a CSW is authorized by state law to perform them. [42 C.F.R. § 410.73(b)(2); Pub. 100-02, Ch. 15, § 170.]

Requirement for consultation. A CSW must agree that, upon the patient's consent, the CSW will attempt to consult with the patient's attending or primary care physician. Neither the CSW nor the attending or primary care physician may bill Medicare or the beneficiary for this consultation. [42 C.F.R. § 410.73(c), (d)(2).]

Registered Dietitians and Nutrition Professionals

Medicare covers medical nutrition therapy (MNT) services for certain beneficiaries who have diabetes or a renal disease when furnished by registered dietitians or nutritional professionals. [Soc. Sec. Act § 1861(s)(2)(V); 42 C.F.R. §§ 410.130–410.134; *Medicare National Coverage Determinations Manual*, Pub. 100-03, Ch. 1, § 180.1.] MNT services are included in the physician fee schedule. The definition of "practitioner" in the regulations includes registered dietitians and nutrition professionals. [Soc. Sec. Act § 1842(b)(18)(C); 42 C.F.R. § 405.400.]

[¶ 369] Preventive Services

Medicare Part B covers specific preventive screening services and tests. The initial preventive physical exam (IPPE), performed within the first year of Part B enrollment, begins the process. Medicare beneficiaries are eligible to receive personalized prevention plan services every year after their IPPEs as long as they have not received either an IPPE or personalized prevention plan services within the preceding 12-month period.

The Patient Protection and Affordable Care Act (ACA) (P.L. 111-148) expanded coverage of preventive services. The ACA added a definition of "preventive services" and removed barriers to Medicare beneficiaries' use of such services by waiving coinsurance and deductibles for most preventive services. Under section 4104(a) of the ACA, "preventive services" are defined as: (1) the screening and preventive services currently listed in Soc. Sec. Act § 1861(ww)(2); (2) an IPPE; and (3) personalized preventive plan services. [Soc. Sec. Act § 1861(ddd)(3).]

Sections 4103(c)(1), 4104(b) and 10406 of the ACA waive coinsurance amounts for most preventive services; thus, Medicare will be responsible for 100 percent of the costs. [Soc. Sec. Act § 1833(a)(1)(B).] Preventive services for which no coinsurance amount will be charged to beneficiaries are those services given a grade of "A" or "B" by the United States Preventive Services Task Force (USPSTF). [Soc. Sec. Act § 1833(b)(1).]

"Welcome to Medicare" Exams

Medicare pays for one IPPE, also called the "Welcome to Medicare Physical," within the first year after the effective date of the beneficiary's first Part B coverage period, if the coverage began on or after January 1, 2009. [Soc. Sec. Act §§ 1861(s)(2)(W) and (ww), 1862(a)(1)(K); 42 C.F.R. §§ 410.16, 411.15(a)(1) and (k)(11).]

The IPPE includes: (1) a physical examination, including measurement of height, weight, body mass index, and blood pressure, with the goal of health promotion and disease detection; (2) end-of-life planning; and (3) education, counseling, and referral for screening and other covered preventive benefits separately authorized under Part B. The statutory screening and other preventive services authorized under Part B include:

- pneumococcal, influenza, and hepatitis B vaccine and their administration;
- screening mammography;
- screening pap smear and screening pelvic exam services;
- prostate cancer screening services;
- colorectal cancer screening tests;
- diabetes outpatient self-management training services;
- bone mass measurements;
- screening for glaucoma;
- medical nutrition therapy services for individuals with diabetes or renal disease;
- cardiovascular screening tests;
- diabetes screening tests;
- ultrasound screening for abdominal aortic aneurysm;
- an electrocardiogram; and
- additional preventive services, as defined by Soc. Sec. Act § 1861(ddd)(1).

[Soc. Sec. Act § 1861(ww).] The IPPE also includes screening for depression and a review of the beneficiary's medical and social history and functional abilities. A physician or qualified nonphysician practitioner must perform the IPPE as a condition for coverage. [42 C.F.R. § 410.16; *Medicare Claims Processing Manual*, Pub. 100-04, Ch. 12, § 30.6.1.1.]

The deductible and coinsurance for the IPPE are waived. [Soc. Sec. Act § 1833(b)(9); 42 C.F.R. §§ 410.152(l)(12), 410.160(b)(9); Pub. 100-04, Ch. 12, § 30.6.1.1.]

Excluded coverage. Excluded routine physical checkups include: (1) examinations performed for a purpose other than the treatment or diagnosis of a specific illness, symptom, complaint, or injury (such as routine chest x-rays); and (2) examinations required by third parties such as insurance companies, business establishments, or government agencies. [42 C.F.R. § 411.15(a); *Medicare Benefit Policy Manual*, Pub. 100-02, Ch. 16, § 90.]

The routine services exclusion does not apply to services furnished in a federally qualified health center. [Soc. Sec. Act § 1862(a).]

Annual Wellness Exams

Medicare beneficiaries are eligible to receive an annual wellness visit (AWV) providing personalized prevention plan services. [Soc. Sec. Act § 1861(s)(2)(FF) and (hhh)(1); 42 C.F.R. § 410.15(c).]

"Personalized prevention plan services" means the creation of a plan for an individual that includes a health risk assessment. A plan must take into account the results of the assessment and may include elements such as:

(1) the individual's medical and family history;

(2) a list of his or her current providers or suppliers;

(3) the individual's height, weight, body mass index, blood pressure, and other measurements;

(4) detection of any cognitive impairments;

(5) establishment of a screening schedule for the next five years based on recommendations of the USPSTF and a list of risk factors and conditions for which preventive measures or treatment are recommended;

(6) personalized health advice and a referral, as necessary, to address risk factors; and

(7) any other element identified by the HHS Secretary.

Beginning January 1, 2016, at the discretion of the beneficiary, AWVs include advance care planning services, including discussions about future care decisions that might need to be made, how the beneficiary can let others know about care preferences, and an explanation of advance directives that may involve the completion of standard forms. [Soc. Sec. Act § 1861(hhh); 42 C.F.R. § 410.15(a).]

The health risk assessment must be performed by a health professional, which includes a physician, physician assistant, nurse practitioner, clinical nurse specialist, or other medical professionals or teams of professionals. [42 C.F.R. § 410.15(b).]

Medicare pays for an AWV for a beneficiary who is no longer within 12 months after the effective date of his or her first Medicare Part B coverage period and who has not received either an IPPE or an AWV providing personalized prevention plan services within the past 12 months. The deductible and coinsurance for personalized prevention plan services, including those performed in the outpatient department of a hospital, are waived. [Soc. Sec. Act § 1833(a)(1)(X) and (b)(10), (t)(1)(B)(iv); 42 C.F.R. §§ 410.152(l)(13), 410.160(b)(12); Pub. 100-04, Ch. 12, § 30.6.1.1.]

Mammograms

Medicare Part B covers screening mammography, which includes the radiological procedure itself as well as a physician's interpretation of the results of the procedure. [Soc. Sec. Act § 1861(s)(13), (jj); 42 C.F.R. §§ 410.10(r), 410.34.]

Women between the ages of 35 and 39 are covered for one screening mammogram during that five-year age period. Women age 40 and over are covered for one screening mammogram per 12-month period. [Soc. Sec. Act § 1834(c)(2)(A); 42 C.F.R. § 410.34(d).] Division H Title II section 229 of the Consolidated Appropriations Act, 2016 requires the HHS Secretary, from November 1, 2015, through January 1, 2018, to cover annual screening mammograms starting at age 40, despite federal recommendations that screenings start at 50.

The usual Part B deductible is waived for screening mammograms. [Soc. Sec. Act § 1833(b)(5); 42 C.F.R. §§ 410.152(l)(2), 410.160(b)(5).]

Pap Smears and Pelvic Exams

Medicare covers screening pap smears and screening pelvic examinations. Screening pap smear coverage includes routine exfoliative cytology tests and the physician's interpretation of the results of the tests. Screening pelvic exam coverage includes testing for the early detection of cervical or vaginal cancer and includes clinical breast examinations. [Soc. Sec. Act § 1861(s)(14), (nn); 42 C.F.R. § 410.56; Pub. 100-02, Ch. 15, § 280.4.]

Pap smears and pelvic exams are covered at two-year intervals. Annual exams, however, are covered for women identified as being at high risk for developing cervical or vaginal cancer and for women of childbearing age who have had an abnormality detected during any of the three preceding years. [Soc. Sec. Act §§ 1861(nn), 1862(a)(1)(F); 42 C.F.R. § 410.56(b).]

The usual Part B deductible is waived for these exams. [Soc. Sec. Act § 1833(b)(6); 42 C.F.R. §§ 410.152(l)(3), 410.160(b)(6); Pub. 100-04, Ch. 18, § 30.3.]

Colorectal Cancer Screening Tests

Part B covers colorectal cancer screening tests. [Soc. Sec. Act § 1861(s)(2)(R), (pp); Pub. 100-02, Ch. 15, § 280.2.2.] Covered screening procedures include: (1) one annual fecal-occult blood test every 12 months for individuals age 50 and older; (2) flexible sigmoidos-copy every four years for individuals age 50 and older; (3) colonoscopy for high-risk individuals every two years and for other individuals every 10 years, including anesthesia furnished in conjunction with the service; and (4) screening barium enemas every four years for individuals age 50 and older who are not at high risk of developing colorectal cancer or every two years for individuals who are at high risk. [Soc. Sec. Act §§ 1834(d), 1861(pp); 42 C.F.R. § 410.37.]

An individual is at high risk for developing colorectal cancer if he or she has one or more of the following characteristics: (1) a close relative (sibling, parent, or child) who has had colorectal cancer or an adenomatous polyp; (2) a family history of familial adenomatous polyposis; (3) a family history of hereditary nonpolyposis colorectal cancer; (4) a personal history of colorectal cancer; (5) a personal history of adenomatous polyps; or (6) inflammatory bowel disease, including Crohn's Disease and ulcerative colitis. [42 C.F.R. § 410.37(a)(3); Pub. 100-02, Ch. 15, § 280.2.3.]

Physician assistants, nurse practitioners, and clinical nurse specialists, in addition to the beneficiary's attending physician, are allowed to order screening fecal-occult blood tests. [42 C.F.R. § 410.37(b).]

Deductibles are waived for colorectal cancer screening tests. The deductible is also waived for surgical and anesthesia services furnished in connection with, as a result of, and in the same clinical encounter (i.e., furnished on the same date) as a planned colorectal cancer screening test. [Soc. Sec. Act § 1833(b)(8); 42 C.F.R. §§ 410.152(l)(5), 410.160(b)(7); Pub. 100-04, Ch. 18, § 60.1.1.]

Diabetes Screening and Self-Management Services

Medicare covers diabetes outpatient self-management educational and training services furnished by a certified provider who meets certain quality standards. This program is intended to educate beneficiaries in the successful self-management of diabetes. [Soc. Sec. Act § 1861(qq).] The program includes instructions in self-monitoring of blood glucose, education about diet and exercise, an insulin treatment plan developed specifically for the patient who is insulin-dependent, and motivation for patients to use these skills for self-management. [42 C.F.R. § 410.141(c); Pub. 100-02, Ch. 15, § 300.]

The doctor or qualified nonphysician practitioner who is managing the beneficiary's diabetic condition must certify that these services are needed. The services must be provided under a comprehensive plan of care to ensure therapy compliance or provide the patient with the necessary skills and knowledge (including the skill to self-administer injectable drugs) to participate in the management of his or her own condition. Up to 10 hours of initial training and two hours of annual additional training are authorized. [Pub. 100-02, Ch. 15, § § 300, 300.1, 300.3.]

Diabetes screening. Part B covers also diabetes screening tests after a referral from a physician or qualified nonphysician practitioner to an individual at risk for diabetes for the purpose of early detection of diabetes. Medicare covers diabetes screening once every 12 months for a beneficiary who is not pre-diabetic and once every six months for a beneficiary who is pre-diabetic. [Soc. Sec. Act § 1861(s)(2)(Y), (yy); 42 C.F.R. § 410.18.]

Medicare Diabetes Prevention Program services. Beginning January 1, 2018, CMS will cover Medicare Diabetes Prevention Program (MDPP) services for beneficiaries who: (1) are enrolled in Part B; (2) have as of the date of attendance at the first core session a body mass index (BMI) of at least 25 if not self-identified as Asian and a BMI of at least 23 if self-identified as Asian; (3) have, within the 12 months before attending the first core session, a hemoglobin A1c test with a value between 5.7 and 6.4 percent, a fasting plasma glucose of 110–125 mg/dL, or a two-hour plasma glucose of 140–199 mg/ dL (oral glucose tolerance test); (4) have no previous diagnosis of type 1 or type 2 diabetes; and (5) do not have end-stage renal disease. MDPP suppliers must furnish to beneficiaries 16 core sessions at least a week apart over a period of at least 16 weeks to 26 weeks and at least one core maintenance session in each of the second six months. [42 C.F.R. § 410.79.]

Bone Mass Measurement Tests

Medicare covers biannual bone mass measurement tests ordered by physicians or qualified nonphysician practitioners to identify bone mass, detect bone loss, or determine bone quality for: (1) estrogen-deficient women at clinical risk for osteoporosis; (2) individuals with vertebral abnormalities; (3) individuals receiving long-term glucocorticoid steroid therapy; (4) individuals with primary hyperparathyroidism; and (5) individuals being monitored to assess the response to or efficacy of an approved osteoporosis drug therapy. A physician must interpret these test results. [Soc. Sec. Act § 1861(s)(15), (rr); 42 C.F.R. § 410.31.]

Prostate Cancer Screening Tests

Medicare covers annual prostate cancer screening tests, including digital rectal examinations and prostate-specific antigen (PSA) blood tests, for men over age 50. The tests must be performed (or in the case of the PSA blood test, ordered) by the patient's physician, physician assistant, nurse practitioner, clinical nurse specialist, or certified nurse-midwife. [Soc. Sec. Act § 1861(s)(2)(P), (oo); 42 C.F.R. § 410.39.]

The screening PSA test is not subject to the Part B deductible and coinsurance requirements. The deductible and coinsurance requirements apply to screening rectal examinations. [Pub. 100-04, Ch. 18, § 50.2.]

Screening Glaucoma Tests

Medicare covers annual screening glaucoma tests for individuals determined to be at high risk for glaucoma, including: (1) individuals with diabetes mellitus; (2) individuals with a family history of glaucoma; (3) African-Americans age 50 and over; and (4) Hispanic-

Americans age 65 and over. [Soc. Sec. Act § 1861(s)(2)(U), (uu); 42 C.F.R. § 410.23; Pub. 100-02, Ch. 15, § 280.1.]

Covered screening tests include: (1) a dilated eye exam with an intraocular pressure measurement; and (2) a direct ophthalmoscopy exam or a slit-lamp biomicroscopic exam. Glaucoma screening examinations must be furnished by, or under the direct supervision of, an optometrist or opthalmologist. "Direct supervision" means the optometrist or opthalmologist must be present in the office suite and be immediately available to furnish assistance and direction throughout the performance of the procedure. [42 C.F.R. § 410.23; Pub. 100-02, Ch. 15, § 280.1.]

Abdominal Aortic Ultrasound

Medicare covers a one-time ultrasound screening for abdominal aortic aneurysm for an individual who, after a referral from a physician or a qualified nonphysician practitioner: (1) has not been previously furnished such an ultrasound screening; and (2) is included in at least one of the following risk categories: (a) has a family history of abdominal aortic aneurysm, (b) is a man age 65 to 75 who has smoked at least 100 cigarettes in his lifetime, or (c) is a beneficiary with other factors specified in national coverage determinations. The test must be performed by a supplier or supplier who is authorized to provide covered diagnostic services. [Soc. Sec. Act § 1861(s)(2)(AA), (bbb); 42 C.F.R. § 410.19; Pub. 100-04, Ch. 18, § 110.2.]

Effective January 27, 2014, CMS eliminated the requirement that an eligible beneficiary must receive a referral for aortic aneurism screening as a result of an IPPE. [*Final rule*, 78 FR 74230, Dec. 10, 2013.]

Medical Nutrition Therapy Services

Medicare covers medical nutrition therapy (MNT) services for beneficiaries with diabetes or a renal disease who: (1) have not received diabetes outpatient maintenance self-management training services within a specified time period; and (2) are not receiving maintenance dialysis benefits. Services covered include nutritional diagnostic, therapy, and counseling services for the purpose of disease management. The services must be provided by a registered dietitian or nutritional professional pursuant to a referral by the beneficiary's treating physician. [Soc. Sec. Act § 1861(s)(2)(V), (vv); 42 C.F.R. §§ 410.130–410.134.]

Basic coverage of MNT for the first year a beneficiary receives MNT is three hours, and basic coverage for subsequent years is two hours. If the beneficiary's treating physician determines that both MNT and diabetes self-management training are medically necessary in the same episode of care, Medicare will cover both services without decreasing either benefit as long as MNT and diabetes self-management training are not provided on the same date of service. Additional hours are covered if the treating physician determines that there is a change in medical condition, diagnosis, or treatment regimen that requires a change in MNT and orders additional hours during that episode of care. [Pub. 100-03, Ch. 1, § 180.1.]

The Part B deductible is waived for this test. [42 C.F.R. § 410.160(b)(11).]

Cardiovascular Screening

Medicare covers cardiovascular screening tests once every five years for an asymptomatic individual. These blood tests measure cholesterol levels and other lipid or triglyceride levels. [Soc. Sec. Act § 1861(s)(2)(X), (xx); 42 C.F.R. § 410.17.]

[¶ 370] Therapeutic Shoes

Therapeutic shoes and inserts are covered for beneficiaries with severe diabetic foot disease. The beneficiary's treating physician, either a doctor of medicine or a doctor of osteopathy who is responsible for diagnosing and treating the patient's diabetic condition, must certify the need for diabetic shoes. [Soc. Sec. Act § 1861(s)(12); *Medicare Benefit Policy Manual*, Pub. 100-02, Ch. 15, § 140.]

The treating physician must:

(1) document in the medical record that the beneficiary has diabetes;

(2) certify that the beneficiary is being treated under a comprehensive plan of care for diabetes and needs diabetic shoes; and

(3) document in the patient's record that the patient has one or more of the following conditions: peripheral neuropathy with evidence of callus formation, a history of pre-ulcerative calluses, a history of previous ulceration, foot deformity, previous amputation, or poor circulation.

[Soc. Sec. Act § 1861(s)(12)(A); Pub. 100-02, Ch. 15, § 140.]

After the physician managing the beneficiary's systemic diabetic condition certifies the need for therapeutic shoes, a podiatrist or other qualified physician who is knowledgeable in the fitting of diabetic shoes and inserts may prescribe the particular type of footwear necessary. A podiatrist or other qualified individual must fit and furnish the footwear. The certifying physician may not furnish the therapeutic shoes unless he or she is the only qualified individual in the area. [Soc. Sec. Act § 1861(s)(12)(B), (C); Pub. 100-02, Ch. 15, § 140.]

Limitations. Coverage is limited to one of the following within a calendar year: (1) one pair of custom-molded shoes (including inserts provided with such shoes) and two additional pairs of inserts; or (2) one pair of depth shoes and three pairs of inserts (not including the noncustomized inserts provided with such shoes). [Pub. 100-02, Ch. 15, § 140.]

[¶ 381] Physical Therapy, Occupational Therapy, and Speech-Language Pathology Services

The Part B program covers physical therapy, occupational therapy, and speech-language pathology services. [Soc. Sec. Act § 1861(s)(2)(D).] The following discussion refers to physical therapy, occupational therapy, and speech-language pathology services, collectively, as "therapy" services.

Providers of Outpatient Therapy Services

Outpatient physical and occupational therapy and speech-language pathology services (including audiology services) must be furnished by a provider of services, a clinic, rehabilitation agency, or public health agency, or by others under an "arrangement" with, and under the supervision of, such provider, clinic, or agency. The services must be furnished to an individual: (1) who is under the care of a physician; and (2) with respect to whom a plan describing the type, amount, and duration of therapy services that are to be furnished has been established by a physician or the therapist providing the services, and is periodically reviewed by the physician. Excluded, however, are: (1) any item or service if it would not be included if furnished to an inpatient of a hospital; and (2) any such service furnished by a clinic, rehabilitation agency, or by others under arrangements with a clinic or agency, unless the clinic or agency meets Medicare standards and requirements. [Soc. Sec. Act § 1861(g), (p), (ll).]

Therapy services are payable under the physician fee schedule when furnished by:

(1) a provider to its outpatients in the patient's home;

(2) a provider to patients who come to the facility's outpatient department;

(3) a provider to inpatients of other institutions; or

(4) a supplier to patients in the office or in the patient's home.

[*Medicare Benefit Policy Manual*, Pub. 100-02, Ch. 15, § 220.1.4.]

Part B coverage includes therapy services furnished by participating hospitals and skilled nursing facilities (SNFs) to inpatients who have exhausted their Part A inpatient benefits or who are otherwise not eligible for Part A benefits. Providers of outpatient therapy services that have inpatient facilities but are not participating hospitals and SNFs may not furnish covered outpatient therapy services to their own inpatients. Providers of therapy services that have inpatient facilities, other than participating hospitals and SNFs, may not furnish covered therapy services to their own inpatients. However, since the inpatients of one institution may be considered the outpatients of another institution, all providers of therapy services may furnish such services to inpatients of another health facility. [42 C.F.R. § § 410.59(b), 410.60(b), 410.62; Pub. 100-02, Ch. 15, § 220.1.4.]

Comprehensive outpatient rehabilitation facilities. Comprehensive outpatient rehabilitation facilities (CORFs) may provide these outpatient therapy services in the home as long as the patient also does not receive home health benefits. The CORF plan of treatment must be reviewed every 60 days for respiratory therapy and every 90 days for physical therapy, occupational therapy, and speech-language pathology. [42 C.F.R. § 410.105(b)(3)(i), (c)(2); Pub. 100-02, Ch. 12, § § 10, 30.]

Rehabilitation agencies. Rehabilitation agencies that are Medicare Part B providers must have a physician's signature in the clinical record of a rehabilitation plan within 30 days of an initial therapy visit and within each 90-day recertification period thereafter, or as often as the patient's condition changes. [42 C.F.R. § § 424.24(c)(2), 485.711(b)(3).]

Private practice therapists. The Part B program covers the services of a "qualified" physical therapist, speech-language pathologist, or occupational therapist in "private practice" if the therapist or speech-language pathologist: (1) is legally authorized to engage in private practice by the state in which he or she practices and practices only within the scope of his or her license; (2) engages in private practice on a regular basis as an individual in a solo practice, partnership, or group practice, or as an employee of one of these; (3) bills Medicare only for services furnished in his or her private practice office space or in the patient's home (excluding any institution that is a hospital, a critical access hospital (CAH), or a SNF); and (4) treats individuals who are patients of the practice and for whom the practice collects fees for the services furnished. [Soc. Sec. Act § 1861(p); 42 C.F.R. § § 410.59(c), 410.60(c), 410.62(c).]

The services must be provided either by or under the direct personal supervision of the therapist in private practice, and the supporting personnel, including other therapists, must be employees of the therapist in private practice. Services furnished by a therapist in the therapist's office under arrangements with hospitals in rural communities and public health agencies, or services provided in the beneficiary's home under arrangements with a provider of therapy services, are not covered under this provision. [Pub. 100-02, Ch. 15, § 230.4.]

Reasonableness and Necessity of Outpatient Therapy Services

To be considered reasonable and necessary to treat an illness or an injury, therapy services must meet all of the following conditions:

(1) the services must be considered under accepted standards of medical practice to be a specific and effective treatment for the patient's condition;

(2) the services must be of such a level of complexity and sophistication, or the condition of the patient must be such, that the services required can be safely and effectively performed only by a qualified therapist or under a therapist's supervision;

(3) while a beneficiary's particular medical condition is a valid factor in deciding if skilled therapy services are needed, a beneficiary's diagnosis or prognosis cannot be the sole factor in deciding that a service is or is not skilled; the key issue is whether the skills of a therapist are needed to treat the illness or injury, or whether the services can be carried out by nonskilled personnel; and

(4) the amount, frequency, and duration of services must be reasonable.

Services related to activities for the general good and welfare of patients, e.g., general exercises to promote overall fitness and flexibility and activities to provide diversion or general motivation, do not constitute therapy services for Medicare purposes. [Pub. 100-02, Ch. 15, § 220.2.]

Medicare coverage does not turn on the presence or absence of a beneficiary's potential for improvement from the therapy but, rather, on the beneficiary's need for skilled care. Skilled therapy services may be necessary to improve a patient's current condition, to maintain the patient's current condition, or to prevent or slow further deterioration of the patient's condition. [Pub. 100-02, Ch. 15, § 220.2.]

Maintenance therapy. If the specialized skill, knowledge, and judgment of a qualified therapist are required to establish or design a maintenance program to maintain the patient's current condition or to prevent or slow further deterioration, the establishment or design of a maintenance program by a qualified therapist is covered. Once a maintenance program is established, coverage of therapy services to carry out a maintenance program turns on the beneficiary's need for skilled care. [Pub. 100-02, Ch. 15, § 220.2.]

Types of Covered Outpatient Therapy Services

Part B covers the following types of therapy services:

Occupational therapy. Occupational therapy may involve:

(1) evaluation of a patient's level of function by administering diagnostic and prognostic tests;

(2) teaching task-oriented therapeutic activities designed to restore physical function, such as woodworking activities on an inclined table to restore shoulder, elbow, and wrist range of motion lost as a result of burns;

(3) individualized therapeutic activity programs for patients with a diagnosed psychiatric illness, such as sewing activities following a pattern to reduce confusion and restore reality orientation in a schizophrenic patient;

(4) activities to increase sensory input and improve response for stroke patients with functional loss resulting in a distorted body image; and

(5) teaching compensatory technique to improve the level of independence in daily activities or adapt to an evolving deterioration in health and function.

[42 C.F.R. § 410.59; Pub. 100-02, Ch. 15, § 230.2.]

Physical therapy. Covered physical therapy services are not limited to services typically provided in clinics. They may include services such as aquatic therapy in a community center pool or functional electrical stimulation to enhance walking in spinal cord injury patients. The *Medicare Benefit Policy Manual* discusses types of covered physical therapy services in Chapter 15, § § 220 and 230. [42 C.F.R. § 410.60; Pub. 100-02, Ch. 15, § 230.1.]

Speech-language pathology. Speech-language pathology services are those services necessary for the diagnosis and treatment of speech and language disorders, which result in communication disabilities and for the diagnosis and treatment of swallowing disorders (dysphagia), regardless of the presence of a communication disability. [42 C.F.R. § 410.62; Pub. 100-02, Ch. 15, § 230.3.]

Conditions for Coverage of Outpatient Therapy

Outpatient rehabilitation services must be furnished under a written plan of treatment established and certified by a physician or qualified nonphysician practitioner (NPP). Services must also be furnished while the beneficiary is under the care of a physician. An order, while not required by Medicare, provides evidence that the patient both needs therapy services and is under the care of a physician. [Pub. 100-02, Ch. 15, § 220.1.1; 42 C.F.R. §§ 410.60–410.62.]

Plan of treatment. Outpatient physical, occupational, and speech therapy must be furnished under a plan of care established by a physician, nurse practitioner, clinical nurse specialist, or physician assistant, or the therapist providing the services. The plan must be established before treatment is begun. It must prescribe the type, amount, frequency, and duration of the physical therapy, occupational therapy, or speech-language pathology services to be furnished to the individual and indicate the diagnosis and anticipated goals that are consistent with the patient function reporting on claims for services. [42 C.F.R. §§ 410.59(a)(2), 410.60(a)(2), 410.61, 410.62(a)(2).]

Physician certification. As soon as possible after the plan of care is established, the physician/NPP or therapist/pathologist that established the plan must by sign the plan, certifying that: (1) the beneficiary needs therapy or speech-language pathology services; (2) the services were furnished while the beneficiary was under the care of a physician, nurse practitioner, clinical nurse specialist, or physician assistant; and (3) the services were furnished under a plan of treatment that meets the requirements of 42 C.F.R. § 410.61. Recertification is required at least every 90 days. [42 C.F.R. § 424.24(c); Pub. 100-02, Ch. 15, § 220.1.3.]

Outpatient Therapy Provided Under Arrangements

A provider may make arrangements with other providers to furnish covered outpatient physical, occupational, or speech therapy. [Soc. Sec. Act § 1861(p).] Services under "arrangements" are services for which receipt of payment by the provider for the arranged services must (as with services provided directly) relieve the beneficiary or any other person of further liability to pay for the services.

The provider must assume professional responsibility for the services and put into place many of the same controls applied to services furnished by salaried employees. The provider must:

(1) accept the patient for treatment in accordance with its admission policies;

(2) maintain a complete and timely clinical record on the patient that includes diagnosis, medical history, orders, and progress notes relating to all services received;

(3) maintain liaison with the attending physician or NPP with regard to the progress of the patient and to assure that the required plan of treatment is periodically reviewed by the physician;

(4) secure from the physician/NPP the required certifications and recertifications; and

(5) ensure that the medical necessity of such service is reviewed on a sample basis by the agency's staff or an outside review group.

[Pub. 100-02, Ch. 15, § 230.6.]

Providers "under an arrangement" must furnish services in accordance with the terms of a written contract specifying that the provider retains responsibility for and control and supervision of such services. The contract also must:

(1) provide that the therapy services be furnished in accordance with a plan of care;

(2) specify the geographic areas in which the services are to be furnished;

(3) provide that personnel and services meet the same requirements as if furnished directly by the provider;

(4) provide that the therapist will participate in conferences required to coordinate patient care;

(5) provide for the preparation of treatment records that will be incorporated into clinical records;

(6) specify the financial arrangements, i.e., the contracting organization or individual may not bill the patient or the health insurance program; and

(7) specify the contract's time period and manner of termination or renewal.

[Pub. 100-02, Ch. 15, § 230.6.]

Hospital billing "under arrangements." A hospital may bill Medicare for outpatient therapy (physical therapy, occupational therapy, or speech-language pathology) services that it furnishes to its outpatients, either directly or under arrangements in the hospital's outpatient department. Services provided to residents of a Medicare-certified SNF may not be billed by the hospital as services to its outpatients; these services are covered under a SNF's global prospective payment system payment for the covered Part A stay. [Pub. 100-02, Ch. 15, § 230.6.]

Payment Methodology

Except for outpatient therapy services furnished by critical access hospitals, payment for therapy services furnished to outpatients, hospital, or SNF patients not in a covered Part A stay, or individuals provided therapy services by a home health agency who are not homebound or under a home health plan of care (see ¶ 860), is made under the Medicare physician fee schedule. Reimbursement for therapy provided to Part A inpatients of hospitals or SNFs is included in the prospective payment system (PPS) rate (see ¶ 810). Reimbursement for therapy provided by home health agencies under a home health plan of care is included in the home health PPS rate. Outpatient therapy services furnished by CAHs are paid on a reasonable cost basis. [Soc. Sec. Act § 1832(a)(2)(C).]

[¶ 382] Rural Health Clinics and Federally Qualified Health Centers

Part B covers rural health clinic (RHC) and federally qualified health center (FQHC) services in medically underserved areas. [Soc. Sec. Act §§ 1832(a)(2)(D), 1861(aa); 42 C.F.R. § 410.10(j), (s).]

RHCs are clinics located in areas designated by the Bureau of the Census as rural and the Secretary of HHS as medically underserved or having an insufficient number of physicians. FQHCs are defined similarly but are usually in urban areas. [Soc. Sec. Act § 1861(aa); 42 C.F.R. § 491.2.]

RHC and FQHC services reimbursable under Part B include:

(1) physicians' services (and services and supplies incident to a physician's services);

(2) similar services furnished by a physician assistant, nurse practitioner, certified nurse-midwife, clinical psychologist, or clinical social worker (and services and supplies incident to their services);

(3) visiting nurse services furnished to homebound patients in areas where there is a shortage of home health agencies; and

(4) otherwise covered drugs furnished by, and incident to, services of physicians and nonphysician practitioners.

[42 C.F.R. §§ 405.2411, 405.2446, 410.45(a); *Medicare Benefit Policy Manual*, Pub. 100-02, Ch. 13, §40.]

Medical nutrition therapy services and diabetes outpatient self-management training services also are included FQHC services. [42 C.F.R. § 405.2446(b)(9).]

In addition, Medicare covers certain preventive primary services furnished by FQHCs, including physical examinations targeted to risk, visual acuity screening, hearing screening, cholesterol screening, blood pressure measurement, and nutritional assessment and referral. Preventive primary services furnished by FQHCs do *not* include group or mass information programs, health education classes, group education activities, eyeglasses, hearing aids, or preventive dental services. Screening mammography is not considered an FQHC service but may be provided at an FQHC if the center meets the applicable regulatory requirements. [Soc. Sec. Act § 1861(aa)(3)(A); 42 C.F.R. § 405.2448; Pub. 100-02, Ch. 13, §§ 50.1, 50.2.]

In the case of an RHC located in an area in which there exists a shortage of home health agencies, the term "rural health service" includes part-time or intermittent nursing care and related medical supplies (other than drugs and biologics) furnished by a registered professional nurse or licensed practical nurse to a homebound individual under a written plan of treatment. [Soc. Sec. Act § 1861(aa)(1)(C).]

RHC and FQHC services are reimbursable when furnished to a patient at the clinic or other outpatient setting, including a patient's place of residence, or the scene of an accident. RHC and FQHC services are not covered in a hospital. [42 C.F.R. §§ 405.2411(b), 405.2446(c) and (d); Pub. 100-02, Ch. 13, § 40.1.]

A clinic certified as an RHC or FQHC may furnish services beyond the scope of the services covered under the RHC or FQHC benefit. If the services are authorized to be furnished by a RHC or FQHC and covered under another separate Medicare benefit category, they must be separately billed to the Medicare administrative contractor under the payment rules that apply to the service. Items and services that are *not* RHC or FQHC services include: certain laboratory services; durable medical equipment; prosthetic devices; leg, arm, back, and neck braces; ambulance services; and the technical component of certain services. [Pub. 100-02, Ch. 13, §§ 60, 60.1.]

Except for preventive services, for which Medicare pays 100 percent, FQHC and RHC services are subject to the Part B coinsurance requirements. The deductible applies to RHC services but not to FQHC services. [42 C.F.R. §§ 405.2410, 405.2462(d).]

As discussed at ¶ 607, services paid for directly or indirectly by a government entity usually are excluded from coverage under the Medicare program. The law, however, makes a specific exception to this exclusion in the case of RHC and FQHC services. [Soc. Sec. Act § 1862(a)(3).]

See ¶ 847 for a discussion of payment for RHC services and ¶ 850 for a discussion of payment for FQHC services.

[¶ 383] Home Health Services

For Medicare beneficiaries that are enrolled in both Medicare Part A and Part B, Part A pays home health services for the first 100 visits following a "spell of illness" that required a hospital or skilled nursing home (SNF) stay, referred to as a "post institutional" stay. Part A finances up to 100 visits during one home health spell of illness if the following criteria are met:

> (1) the beneficiary is enrolled in Part A and Part B and qualifies for home health benefits;

> (2) the beneficiary meets the three-consecutive-day stay requirement; and

> (3) the home health services are initiated and the first covered home health visit is rendered within 14 days of discharge from a three-consecutive-day stay in a hospital or rural primary care hospital or within 14 days of discharge from a skilled nursing facility in which post-hospital extended care services were provided.

If the first home health visit is not initiated within 14 days of discharge or if the three-consecutive-day stay requirement is not met, then services are covered under Part B. [Soc. Sec. Act § 1812(a)(3); *Medicare Benefit Policy Manual*, Pub. 100-02, Ch. 7, § § 60.1, 60.2, 60.3.]

After a beneficiary exhausts 100 visits of Part A post-institutional home health services, Part B finances the balance of the home health spell of illness. [Pub. 100-02, Ch. 7, § 60.1.]

Post-institutional defined. Home health services are considered "post-institutional" if they were furnished to a beneficiary within 14 days of discharge from: (1) a hospital in which the individual was an inpatient for at least three consecutive days before discharge; or (2) a SNF in which the beneficiary received post-hospital extended care services. [Soc. Sec. Act § 1861(tt)(1); Pub. 100-02, Ch. 7, § 60.3.]

Spell of illness defined. For home health services, a "spell of illness" is a period of consecutive days beginning with the first day that the beneficiary receives post-institutional home health services during a month in which the patient is entitled to Part A benefits.. The home health spell of illness ends when the individual has not received inpatient hospital, SNF, or home health services for 60 consecutive days. [Soc. Sec. Act § 1861(tt)(2); Pub. 100-02, Ch. 7, § 60.1.]

Requirements for home health benefits. To qualify for home health benefits, a beneficiary must: (1) be confined to the home; (2) be under a physician's care; (3) be receiving services under a plan of care established and periodically reviewed by a physician; (4) be in need of skilled nursing care on an intermittent basis, or physical therapy or speech-language pathology services; or (5) have a continued need for occupational therapy. [Soc. Sec. Act § 1835(a)(2)(A); Pub. 100-02, Ch. 7, § 30.]

Face-to-face encounter. A physician, nurse practitioner, clinical nurse specialist, certified nurse-midwife, or physician assistant must have a face-to-face encounter with the beneficiary related to the reason for the beneficiary's admission into home health at least 90 days before or within 30 days after home health care begins. The encounter must be documented by the certifying physician. Documentation must include:

> (1) the date of the encounter;

> (2) an explanation of why the clinical findings of the encounter, which was related to the primary reason for home care, support that the patient is homebound and in need of Medicare covered home health services; and

> (3) a physician signature.

[Soc. Sec. Act § 1814(a)(2)(C); 42 C.F.R. § 424.22(a)(1)(v).]

Part A home health benefits are discussed beginning at ¶ 250. The home health prospective payment system is discussed at ¶ 830.

[¶ 385] Comprehensive Outpatient Rehabilitation Facility Services

Medicare Part B covers comprehensive outpatient rehabilitation facility (CORF) services. [Soc. Sec. Act § 1832(a)(2)(E).] A CORF is a public or private institution that is capable of providing a broad array of rehabilitation services on an outpatient basis at a central location in a coordinated fashion. Outpatient therapy services furnished by a CORF may be provided in a patient's home (absent any home health benefits) and other off-site locations. CORFs cover items and services such as:

(1) physicians' services;

(2) physical, occupational, and respiratory therapy and speech-language pathology services;

(3) prosthetic and orthotic devices, including testing, fitting, or training in the use of such devices;

(4) social and psychological services;

(5) nursing care provided by or under the supervision of a registered professional nurse;

(6) drugs and biologics that are administered by or under the supervision of a physician or registered nurse, and are not usually self-administered by the patient;

(7) supplies and durable medical equipment; and

(8) home environment evaluation visits.

[Soc. Sec. Act § 1861(cc)(1); 42 C.F.R. § 410.100.]

Except for a home environment evaluation and physical, occupational, and speech-language pathology services, all CORF services must be provided on the premises of the CORF. [42 C.F.R. § 410.105(b).]

None of the services listed above is covered as a CORF service if it: (1) would not be covered as an inpatient hospital service if furnished to a hospital inpatient; or (2) is not reasonable and necessary for the diagnosis or treatment of illness or injury or to improve the functioning of a malformed body member. [Soc. Sec. Act § 1861(cc)(1); 42 C.F.R. § 410.102.]

There must be potential for restoration or improvement of lost or impaired functions for CORF services to be covered. For example, treatments involving repetitive exercises (i.e., maintenance programs, general conditioning, or ambulation) that do not require the skilled services of therapists or other professional rehabilitation practitioners are not covered because nonmedical personnel such as family members or exercise instructors could perform these services in the patient's residence. [*Medicare Benefit Policy Manual*, Pub. 100-02, Ch. 12, § 10.]

Written plan of treatment. CORF services must be furnished under a written plan of treatment that (1) is established and signed by a physician before treatment is begun; and (2) prescribes the type, amount, frequency, and duration of the services to be furnished and indicates the diagnosis and anticipated rehabilitation goals that are consistent with the patient function reporting on the claims for services. A facility physician or the referring physician must review the CORF plan of treatment every 60 days for respiratory therapy and every 90 days for physical therapy, occupational therapy, and speech-language pathology services. [42 C.F.R. § 410.105(c).]

Functional reporting. At the beginning of treatment, specified reporting intervals consistent with progress reporting, and discharge from therapy, claims for CORF physical therapy, occupational therapy, and speech-language pathology services must include nonpayable G-codes and severity modifiers, which report the functional status of CORF patients. [42 C.F.R. § 410.105(d); Pub. 100-02, Ch. 12, § 30.]

Administrative services. Certain administrative services provided by physicians associated with a CORF are considered CORF physician services, which are not billable by the CORF. These services include consultation with and medical supervision of nonphysician staff, team conferences, case reviews, and other facility medical and administration activities relating to the comprehensive coordinated skilled rehabilitation service. [Pub. 100-02, Ch. 12, § 40.1.]

Diagnostic and therapeutic services. Physicians' diagnostic and therapeutic services furnished to an individual patient are not CORF physicians' services. The physician must bill the Medicare administrative contractor for these services, and payment is based on the Medicare physician fee schedule. [Pub. 100-02, Ch. 12, § 40.1.]

Payment. CORF services are paid under a special prospective payment system and are subject to the same annual payment limitation rules applicable to other therapy and rehabilitation services. The Medicare physician fee schedule constitutes the prospective payment system for these services. [Soc. Sec. Act § 1834(k); *Medicare Claims Processing Manual*, Pub. 100-04, Ch. 5, § 10.2.]

The conditions of participation applicable to CORFs are contained in 42 C.F.R. Chapter IV (Subchapter G, Part 485, Subpart B) of the regulations.

[¶ 386] Ambulatory Surgical Services

There are a number of surgical procedures covered by Medicare that, though usually performed on an inpatient basis, may be performed on an outpatient basis, consistent with sound medical practice. Medicare covers surgical procedures that do not have a significant safety risk when performed in an outpatient ambulatory surgical center (ASC) and do not require an overnight stay. [42 C.F.R. § 416.166.]

ASC Definition

An ASC is a distinct entity that operates exclusively for the purpose of furnishing outpatient surgical services to patients not requiring hospitalization and in which the expected duration of services would not exceed 24 hours following admission. It must enter into an agreement with CMS to participate in Medicare as an ASC and meet the conditions of participation set forth in 42 C.F.R. § § 416.40–416.49. [42 C.F.R. § 416.2.]

An ASC is either independent (that is, not part of a provider of services or any other facility), or operated by a hospital. To be considered an ASC operated by a hospital, a facility must:

(1) elect to be covered as an ASC;

(2) constitute a separately identifiable entity that is physically, administratively, and financially independent and distinct from the hospital's other operations, with costs for the ASC treated as a nonreimbursable cost center on the hospital's cost report;

(3) meet all health and safety requirements and agree to the assignment, coverage, and payment rules that apply to independent ASCs; and

(4) be surveyed and approved as complying with the ASC conditions of coverage.

[*Medicare Benefit Policy Manual*, Pub. 100-02, Ch. 15, § 260.1; *Medicare Claims Processing Manual*, Pub. 100-04, Ch. 14, § 10.1.]

An ASC must meet several conditions for coverage to be reimbursed by Medicare for services provided. The ASC conditions for coverage are comparable to the conditions of participation for other providers, including compliance with state licensure requirements. [42 C.F.R. §§416.40–416.52.]

Admissions and discharge planning. Within 30 days before a scheduled surgery, each patient must have a complete medical history and physical assessment by a physician or other qualified practitioner, and upon admission each patient must have a pre-surgical assessment. The patient's post-surgical condition must be assessed and documented in the patient's medical record. Each patient must have a discharge order signed by the physician who performed the surgery along with instructions about follow-up care and must be discharged into the company of a responsible adult unless exempted by the attending physician. [42 C.F.R. §416.52.]

Surgical services. The ASC must have an effective procedure for the immediate transfer to a qualified hospital of a patient requiring emergency medical care beyond the capabilities of the ASC. The ASC must have a written transfer agreement with such a hospital, or all physicians performing surgery in the ASC must have admitting privileges with such a hospital. [42 C.F.R. §416.41(b).]

Surgical procedures must be performed in a safe manner by qualified physicians who have been granted clinical privileges by the governing body of the ASC. The center must ensure that a physician will evaluate a patient's anesthetic risk and anesthetic recovery, anesthesia is administered only by qualified personnel, and proper discharge procedures are followed. [42 C.F.R. §416.42.]

Evaluation of quality. The center must conduct an ongoing self-assessment of the quality, medical necessity, and appropriateness of care provided and use these findings to revise policies if necessary. The ASC must measure, analyze, and track quality indicators, adverse patient events, infection control, and other aspects of performance. Performance improvement priorities must focus on high-risk, high-volume, and problem-prone areas. Performance improvement projects must be implemented and documented. [42 C.F.R. §416.43.]

Patients' rights. ASCs must provide patients and the patient's representative with both verbal and written notice of the patient's rights in advance of the date of the procedure and in a language that the patient and the patient's representative understand. A notice of patients' rights must be posted in the facility. Patients have a right to personal privacy, receive care in a safe setting, and be free from all forms of abuse or harassment. [42 C.F.R. §416.50(a), (f).]

Grievance procedure. The ASC must establish a grievance procedure that has time frames for review and response. All allegations, including, but not limited to, mistreatment; neglect; and verbal, mental, sexual, or physical abuse must be immediately reported, documented, investigated, and disposed of in an appropriate manner. Only substantial allegations must be reported to the state or local authority. [42 C.F.R. §416.50(d).]

Advance directives. The ASC must provide the patient or the patient's representative with information concerning its policies on advance directives before the date of admission. The ASC must document in the patient's record whether he or she has executed an advance directive. [42 C.F.R. §416.50(c).] The fees of physicians and other health care practitioners for surgery and anesthesia are paid under the physician fee schedule (see ¶855); reimbursement for ASC or hospital outpatient facility costs is described at ¶825.

Covered ASC Services

Subject to specified exclusions, covered surgical procedures are surgical procedures specified by the HHS Secretary and published in the *Federal Register* and/or on the CMS website that are separately paid under the hospital outpatient prospective payment system (OPPS), that would not be expected to pose a significant safety risk to a Medicare beneficiary when performed in an ASC, and for which standard medical practice dictates that the beneficiary would not typically be expected to require active medical monitoring and care at midnight following the procedure. [42 C.F.R. § 416.166(b).]

Covered procedures do not include procedures that:

(1) generally result in extensive blood loss;

(2) require major or prolonged invasion of body cavities;

(3) directly involve major blood vessels;

(4) are generally emergent or life-threatening in nature;

(5) commonly require systemic thrombolytic therapy;

(6) are designated as requiring inpatient care under 42 C.F.R. § 419.22(n);

(7) can only be reported using a CPT® unlisted surgical procedure code; or

(8) are otherwise excluded under 42 C.F.R. § 411.15.

[42 C.F.R. § 416.166(c).]

Included facility services. The regulations list the services for which payment is packaged into the ASC payment for a covered surgical procedure under 42 C.F.R. § 416.166. Examples include nursing, technician, and related services; use of the facility where the surgical procedures are performed; equipment; and surgical dressings. [42 C.F.R. § 416.164(a).]

Ancillary services. Medicare makes separate payments to ASCs for certain covered ancillary services that are provided integral to a covered ASC surgical procedure. Covered ancillary services include the following:

(1) brachytherapy sources;

(2) certain implantable items with pass-through status under the OPPS;

(3) certain items and services that CMS designates as contractor-priced, including, but not limited to, the acquisition or procurement of corneal tissue for corneal transplant procedures;

(4) certain drugs and biologics for which separate payment is allowed under the OPPS; and

(5) certain radiology services for which separate payment is allowed under the OPPS.

[42 C.F.R. § 416.164(b).]

Excluded services. ASC services do not include items and services outside the scope of ASC services for which payment may be made under 42 C.F.R. Part 414 in accordance with 42 C.F.R. § 410.152, including, but not limited to (1) physicians' services (including surgical procedures and all pre-operative and post-operative services that are performed by a physician); (2) anesthetists' services; (3) radiology services (other than those integral to performance of a covered surgical procedure); (4) diagnostic procedures (other than those directly related to performance of a covered surgical procedure); (5) ambulance services; (6) leg, arm, back, and neck braces other than those that serve the function of a cast or splint;

(7) artificial limbs; and (8) nonimplantable prosthetic devices and durable medical equipment. [42 C.F.R. § 416.164(c).]

[¶ 387] Mental Health Services

Services generally covered by Medicare Part B for the treatment of psychiatric patients include:

- individual and group therapy with physicians, psychologists, or other mental health professionals authorized by the state;

- occupational therapy services, if the patient requires the skills of a qualified occupational therapist and the services are performed by or under the supervision of a qualified occupational therapist or by an occupational therapy assistant;

- services of social workers, trained psychiatric nurses, and other staff trained to work with psychiatric patients;

- drugs and biologics furnished to outpatients for therapeutic purposes, but only if they are of a type that cannot be self-administered;

- activity therapies, but only those that are individualized and essential for the treatment of the patient's condition; the treatment plan must clearly justify the need for each particular therapy utilized and explain how it fits into the patient's treatment;

- family counseling services (counseling services with members of the household are covered only when the primary purpose of such counseling is the treatment of the patient's condition);

- patient education programs, but only when the educational activities are closely related to the care and treatment of the patient; and

- diagnostic services for the purpose of diagnosing those individuals for whom an extended or direct observation is necessary to determine functioning and interactions, identify problem areas, and formulate a treatment plan.

[*Medicare Benefit Policy Manual*, Pub. 100-02, Ch. 6, § 70.1.]

The following are generally not covered: (1) meals and transportation; (2) activity therapies, group activities, or other services and programs that are primarily recreational or diversional in nature; (3) psychosocial programs; and (4) vocational training. [Pub. 100-02, Ch. 6, § 70.1.]

There are no specific limits on the length of time that services may be covered. There are many factors that affect the outcome of treatment, including the nature of the illness, prior history, goals of treatment, and a patient's response. As long as a patient continues to show improvement in accordance with his or her individualized treatment plan and the frequency of services is within accepted norms of medical practice, coverage may be continued, but if a patient reaches a point in treatment when further improvement does not appear to be indicated, mental health treatment must be reevaluated. [Pub. 100-02, Ch. 6, § 70.1.]

Partial Hospitalization Coverage

Medicare covers partial hospitalization services connected with the treatment of mental illness. Outpatient partial hospitalization services are covered only if the individual otherwise would require inpatient psychiatric care. The treatment offered by partial hospitalization programs closely resembles that of a highly structured, short-term hospital inpatient program. [Soc. Sec. Act § § 1835(a)(2)(F), 1861(s)(2)(B).]

Under this benefit, Medicare covers:

(1) individual and group therapy with physicians or psychologists (or other authorized mental health professionals);

(2) occupational therapy;

(3) services of social workers, trained psychiatric nurses, and other staff trained to work with psychiatric patients;

(4) drugs and biologics furnished for therapeutic purposes that cannot be self-administered;

(5) individualized activity therapies that are not primarily recreational or diversionary;

(6) family counseling (for treatment of the patient's condition);

(7) patient training and education; and

(8) diagnostic services.

[Soc. Sec. Act § 1861(ff)(2); 42 C.F.R. § 410.43(a)(4).]

Meals and transportation are specifically excluded from coverage. Programs involving primarily social, recreational, or diversionary activities are not considered partial hospitalization. [Pub. 100-02, Ch. 6, § 70.3.]

The services must be reasonable and necessary for the diagnosis or active treatment of the individual's condition. They also must be reasonably expected to improve or maintain the individual's condition and functional level and prevent relapse or hospitalization. The course of treatment must be prescribed, supervised, and reviewed by a physician. Patients must require a minimum of 20 hours per week of therapeutic services, as evidenced by their plan of care. The program must be hospital-based or hospital-affiliated and must be a distinct and organized intensive ambulatory treatment service offering less than 24-hour daily care. The program also is covered when provided in a community health center (see ¶ 382). [Soc. Sec. Act § 1861(ff); 42 C.F.R. § 410.43; Pub. 100-02, Ch. 6, § 70.3.]

[¶ 388] Telehealth Services

Medicare covers consultations furnished by means of interactive telecommunications systems if the consultation services are provided for a Medicare patient located in certain rural areas. These services are also known as "telehealth services." [Soc. Sec. Act § 1834(m); 42 C.F.R. § 410.78.]

The teleconsultation must be referred and performed by a physician, physician assistant, nurse practitioner, clinical nurse specialist, nurse-midwife, clinical psychologist, clinical social worker, registered dietitian or nutrition professional, or, effective January 1, 2016, a certified registered nurse anesthetist. The medical examination of the patient must be under the control of the consulting practitioner. [Soc. Sec. Act § 1834(m); 42 C.F.R. § 410.78(b).]

Telecommunication system. An "interactive telecommunications system" means multimedia communications equipment that includes, at a minimum, audio and video equipment permitting two-way, real-time interactive communication between the patient and the distant site physician or practitioner. Telephones, fax machines, and e-mail systems do not meet this definition. [42 C.F.R. § 410.78(a)(3).]

For any federal telemedicine demonstration program conducted in Alaska or Hawaii, the use of store-and-forward technologies that provide for the asynchronous transmission of health care information in single or multimedia formats is permitted. [Soc. Sec. Act § 1834(m)(1); 42 C.F.R. § 410.78(a).]

Originating site. Facilities that may act as the originating site (the location of the beneficiary at the time the telehealth service is furnished) include the office of a physician or practitioner, a critical access hospital (CAH), a rural health clinic, a federally qualified health center, a hospital, a hospital-based or CAH-based renal dialysis center (including satellites), a skilled nursing facility, or a community mental health center. [Soc. Sec. Act § 1834(m)(4)(C)(ii); 42 C.F.R. § 410.78(b)(3).]

The originating site must be: (1) located in a rural Health Professional Shortage Area (HPSA) that is either outside of an Metropolitan Statistical Area (MSA) as of December 31 of the preceding calendar year or within rural census tracts as determined by the Office of Rural Health Policy as of December 31 of the preceding calendar year; (2) in a county that is not included in an MSA as of December 31 of the preceding year; or (3) participating in a federal telemedicine demonstration project that was approved by HHS as of December 31, 2000. [Soc. Sec. Act § 1834(m)(4)(C)(i); 42 C.F.R. § 410.78(b)(4).]

List of covered telehealth services. Changes to the list of covered Medicare telehealth services are made through the annual physician fee schedule rulemaking process. [Soc. Sec. Act § 1834(m)(4)(F)(ii); 42 C.F.R. § 410.78(f).] A list of covered telehealth services is available on the CMS website at http://www.cms.gov/Medicare/Medicare-General-Information/Telehealth/Telehealth-Codes.html.

For example, the physician fee schedule final rule for calendar year 2017 added certain codes for end-stage renal disease (ESRD)-related dialysis services, advance care planning services, and mammography services to the list of telehealth services. The final rule for 2016 added certain codes for prolonged services in the inpatient or observation setting and ESRD-related services for home dialysis. [*Final rule*, 81 FR 80170, Nov. 15, 2016; *Final rule*, 80 FR 70886, Nov. 16, 2015; *Medicare Claims Processing Manual*, Pub. 100-04, Ch. 12, § 190.3.]

[¶ 389] End-Stage Renal Disease Services

Part B covers home dialysis supplies and equipment, self-care home dialysis support services, institutional dialysis services and supplies, and renal dialysis services. Beginning January 1, 2017, Part B covers renal dialysis services furnished by a renal dialysis facility or provider of services paid under Soc. Sec. Act § 1881(b)(14) to an individual with acute kidney injury (as defined in Soc. Sec. Act § 1834(r)(2)). [Soc. Sec. Act § 1861(s)(2)(F); 42 C.F.R. § 410.10(k).]

Dialysis treatments are covered in various settings, including hospital outpatient ESRD facilities, independent renal dialysis facilities, or the patient's home. Items and services furnished at ESRD facilities differ according to the types of patients being treated, the types of equipment and supplies used, the preferences of the treating physician, and the capability and makeup of the staff. [*Medicare Benefit Policy Manual*, Pub. 100-02, Ch. 11, § 20.]

Medicare covers the rental or purchase of home dialysis equipment for home use, all necessary supplies, and a wide range of home support services. This coverage includes delivery and installation service charges and maintenance expenses for the equipment. [Soc. Sec. Act § 1881(b)(8).]

The home dialysis support services covered by Medicare include periodic monitoring of the patient's home adaptation, visits by qualified provider or facility personnel in accordance with a plan prepared and periodically reviewed by a professional team (including the individual's physician), installation and maintenance of dialysis equipment, and testing and treatment of the water used during dialysis. [Soc. Sec. Act § 1881(b)(9).]

Education services. Medicare covers kidney disease education services that are: (1) furnished to an individual with stage IV chronic kidney disease who will require dialysis or a kidney transplant; and (2) designed to provide comprehensive information about the management of comorbidities, the prevention of uremic complications, and each option for renal replacement therapy (including hemodialysis and peritoneal dialysis at home and in-center as well as vascular access options and transplantation). Medicare Part B makes payment for up to six sessions of kidney disease education services. A session is one hour long and may be provided individually or in group settings of two to 20 individuals who need not all be Medicare beneficiaries. [Soc. Sec. Act § 1861(s)(2)(EE), (ggg); 42 C.F.R. § 410.48.]

Transplantation services. Medicare covers the cost of kidney transplantation surgery only if the surgery is performed in a renal transplantation center. [42 C.F.R. § 482.72.] Medicare also covers the costs of care for actual or potential kidney donors, including all reasonable preparatory, operation, and post-operation recovery expenses associated with the donation, without regard to the usual Medicare deductible, coinsurances, and premium payments. Payments for post-operation recovery expenses are limited, however, to the actual period of recovery. [Soc. Sec. Act § 1881(d); Pub. 100-02, Ch. 11, § 140.]

[¶ 390] Home Infusion Therapy

Pursuant to section 5012(a) of the 21st Century Cures Act (P.L. 114-255), effective January 1, 2021, Medicare Part B will separately cover home infusion therapy, which includes the following items and services furnished by a qualified home infusion therapy supplier: (1) professional services, including nursing services, furnished in accordance with the plan of care; and (2) training and education (not otherwise paid for as durable medical equipment), remote monitoring, and monitoring services for the provision of home infusion therapy and home infusion drugs furnished by a qualified home infusion therapy supplier. [Soc. Sec. Act § 1861(s)(2)(GG), (iii).]

The services must be furnished in the home of a beneficiary: (1) who is under the care of an applicable provider (i.e., a physician, nurse practitioner, or physician assistant); and (2) with respect to whom a plan prescribing the type, amount, and duration of infusion therapy services that are to be furnished such individual has been established by a physician and is periodically reviewed by a physician in coordination with the furnishing of home infusion drugs under Part B. [Soc. Sec. Act § 1861(iii).]

Home infusion therapy will be specifically excluded from the definition of home health services. [Soc. Sec. Act § 1861(m), as amended by 21st Century Cures Act § 5012(c)(3).]

[¶ 395] National and Local Coverage Determinations

The Secretary of HHS has the authority to make coverage decisions, within a broad range of categories, for specific items or services not mentioned in the law. For these items and services to be covered, the Secretary must determine them to be reasonable and necessary for the diagnosis and treatment of illnesses and injuries, or to improve the functioning of a malformed body member items and services. HHS decisions as to whether Medicare will cover new services are issued as national coverage determinations (NCDs). [Soc. Sec. Act § 1862(l).]

CMS develops NCDs to describe the circumstances for Medicare coverage nationwide for an item or service. NCDs generally outline the conditions for which an item or service is considered to be covered (or not covered) under Soc. Sec. Act § 1862(a)(1) or other applicable provisions of the Social Security Act. NCDs are usually issued as a program instruction. Once published in a CMS program instruction, an NCD is binding on all Medicare contractors and Medicare Advantage organizations. NCDs are binding on administrative law judges (ALJs) during the claim appeal process. [*Medicare Program Integrity Manual*, Pub. 100-08, Ch. 13, § 13.1.1.]

The NCD development process includes:

(1) the internal and external processes for requesting an NCD or an NCD reconsideration;

(2) a tracking system that provides public notice of acceptance of a complete, formal request and subsequent actions in a web-based format;

(3) a process to allow notice and opportunity to comment before implementation of an NCD;

(4) standardization of the information required to complete a formal request; and

(5) publication of a decision memorandum explaining the purpose and basis of the decision.

CMS considers coverage of additional services with the help of the Medicare Evidence Development & Coverage Advisory Committee, which is composed of members of the health care industry and consumer groups, or other consultants. [*Notice*, 78 FR 48164, Aug. 7, 2013.]

Local coverage determinations. Medicare administrative contractors (MACs) that process claims can issue local coverage determinations (LCDs). LCDs are made only on the reasonableness and necessity of an item or service, not addressing statutory and other exclusions. Providers may ask the contractor to review an LCD or consider a new item or service. [Pub. 100-08, Ch. 13, § 13.1.3.]

Section 4009 of the 21st Century Cures Act (P.L. 114-255) requires MACs that develop an LCD to post information about the LCD on the MAC's website and on Medicare.gov. [Soc. Sec. Act § 1862(l)(5)(D).]

Reconsiderations and reviews of NCDs and LCDs. For a discussion of LCD and NCD reconsiderations and reviews, see ¶ 928.

Recent announcements of coverage decisions. In 2016, CMS announced new or expanded coverage of the following services as a result of the NCD process:

- Effective January 27, 2016, the use of allogeneic hematopoietic stem cell transplantation (HSCT) for treatment of multiple myeloma, myelofibrosis, and sickle cell disease is covered by Medicare only if provided in the context of a Medicare-approved clinical study meeting specific criteria under the Coverage with Evidence Development paradigm. [*Medicare National Coverage Determinations Manual*, Pub. 100-03, Ch. 1, § 110.23; Transmittal No. 193, July 1, 2016.]

- Effective April 13, 2015, CMS covers HIV screening for all individuals enrolled in Part A or Part B between the ages of 15 and 65 years. [Pub. 100-03, Ch. 1, § 210.7; Transmittal No. 190, February 5, 2016.]

- Effective July 9, 2015, CMS covers Human Papillomavirus (HPV) testing under specified conditions. [Pub. 100-03, Ch. 1, § 220.2.1; Transmittal No. 1789, February 5, 2016.]

¶395

Chapter 4– MEDICARE PART C—MEDICARE ADVANTAGE

[¶ 400] Overview

The Medicare Advantage (MA) program—also known as Medicare Part C—offers beneficiaries the option of receiving all of their Medicare benefits from health plans run by private companies. According to Kaiser Family Foundation data, in 2016 17.6 million beneficiaries were enrolled in MA plans, a 5 percent increase between 2015 and 2016. About 31 percent of Medicare beneficiaries were enrolled in MA plans in 2016, with increased enrollment in these plans in almost every state. [*Medicare Advantage 2016 Spotlight: Enrollment Market Update*, Kaiser Family Foundation, May 2016.]

The MA program is administered according to federal regulations found at 42 C.F.R. Part 422. CMS also publishes updates to information regarding the administration of the MA program in the *Medicare Managed Care Manual*, CMS Pub. 100-16.

Types of Medicare Advantage Plans

MA organizations can offer three types of plans to beneficiaries: (1) a coordinated care plan (which includes special needs plans); (2) a combination of a medical savings account (MSA) plan and a contribution into a MSA; and (3) a private fee-for-service (PFFS) plan. [Soc. Sec. Act § 1851(a)(2); 42 C.F.R. § 422.4(a).] **WK Note:** "Medicare cost plans," which are available in some areas of the country and have some of the same rules as MA plans, are not MA plans and are not covered in detail in this chapter.

Coordinated care plans. Coordinated care plans include a network of providers that are under contract or arrangement with the MA organization to deliver a benefit package approved by CMS. The plans may include health maintenance organizations (HMOs), provider-sponsored organizations (PSOs), regional or local preferred provider organizations (PPOs), and other network plans (other than PFFS plans). [42 C.F.R. § 422.4(a)(1), (a)(1)(iii).] In 2016, 64 percent of MA plan beneficiaries were in HMOs. [*Medicare Advantage 2016 Spotlight: Enrollment Market Update*, Kaiser Family Foundation, May 2016.]

Special needs plans (SNPs), mostly HMOs, are an option for three groups of beneficiaries with significant or relatively specialized care needs. "Special needs individual" means an MA eligible individual who: (1) is dually eligible for Medicare and Medicaid; (2) requires a nursing home or institutional level of care; or (3) has severe chronic or disabling conditions. SNPs offer the same benefits as traditional Medicare, but they also must provide the Part D prescription drug benefit as well as additional services tailored to the special needs population. Section 206 of the Medicare Access and CHIP Reauthorization Act of 2015 (P.L. 114-10) extended the SNP program through December 31, 2018. [Soc. Sec. Act § 1859(b)(6), (f)(1); 42 C.F.R. §§ 422.2, 422.4(a)(1)(iv).] See ¶ 402 for more information about SNPs.

Private fee-for-service plans. Similar to fee-for-service Medicare, PFFS plans reimburse providers at a rate determined by the plan on a fee-for-service basis, without putting the provider at risk. These plans do not vary reimbursement based on utilization, and they do not limit the selection of providers. [Soc. Sec. Act § 1859(b)(2); 42 C.F.R. § 422.4(a)(3).]

Medical savings accounts. MSA plans have two parts: (1) an MA medical savings account health insurance plan that pays for a basic set of health benefits approved by CMS and includes a uniform premium and a uniform level of cost-sharing for beneficiaries in the plan's service area, and (2) an MSA, which is a trust or custodial account into which CMS will make deposits. [Soc. Sec. Act § 1859(b)(3); 42 C.F.R. § 422.4(a)(2).]

Part D coverage. An organization that offers an MA coordinated plan in a specific area must offer qualified Part D prescription drug coverage in that plan or in another MA plan in the same area. MA organizations offering MSA plans generally are not permitted to offer prescription drug coverage. MA organizations offering PFFS plans can choose whether to offer Part D coverage. [42 C.F.R. §§422.4(c), 422.114.]

MA Regional Plans

CMS has established 26 regions for MA plans. [*Medicare Managed Care Manual*, Pub. 100-16, Ch. 1, §30.2.3.] The purpose of the regions is to maximize the availability of MA regional plans to all MA-eligible individuals without regard to health status or geographic location, especially to individuals in rural areas. CMS may periodically review and revise the regions if it determines it is appropriate. By regulation, there must be no fewer than 10 regions and no more than 50 regions. [Soc. Sec. Act §1858(a); 42 C.F.R. §422.455.]

Medical Loss Ratio Requirements for MA Plans

MA plans must have a medical loss ratio (MLR) of at least 85 percent for contracts beginning in 2014 or later. The minimum MLR requirement is intended to create incentives for MA organizations to reduce administrative costs such as for marketing costs, profits, and other uses of the funds earned by MA organizations and to help ensure that taxpayers and enrolled beneficiaries receive value from Medicare health plans. [Soc. Sec. Act §1857(e)(4); 42 C.F.R. §422.2410.]

An MLR is determined based on the percentage of Medicare contract revenue spent on clinical services, prescription drugs, quality improving activities, and direct benefits to beneficiaries in the form of reduced Part B premiums. If an MA organization has an MLR of less than 85 percent, it is subject to several levels of sanctions, including remittance of funds to CMS, a prohibition on enrolling new members, and contract termination. [Soc. Sec. Act §1857(e)(4); 42 C.F.R. §422.2410.]

CMS releases to the public Part C MLR data, for each contract for each contract year, no earlier than 18 months after the end of the applicable contract year. [42 C.F.R. §422.2490.]

[¶401] Eligibility, Election, Enrollment, and Disenrollment

An individual's eligibility for a Medicare Advantage (MA) plan is determined, in part, by his or her eligibility for Medicare Part A and Part B. [42 C.F.R. §422.50.] CMS has issued guidance for MA eligibility and enrollment on its website at: http://www.cms.hhs.gov/home/medicare.asp under the "Eligibility and Enrollment" heading.

Eligibility to Elect an MA Plan

In general, an individual is eligible to elect an MA plan if he or she is a U.S. citizen or is lawfully present in the U.S. and:

(1) is entitled to Medicare Part A and enrolled under Part B;

(2) either resides in the service area of the MA plan or resides outside this service area but is enrolled in a health plan offered by the MA organization during the month immediately preceding the month in which the individual is entitled to both Medicare Part A and Part B; and

(3) has not been medically determined to have end-stage renal disease (ESRD).

[Soc. Sec. Act §1851(a)(3); 42 C.F.R. §422.50.]

Special rules for ESRD. An individual medically determined to have ESRD is not currently eligible to elect an MA plan, except that: (1) an individual who develops ESRD while enrolled in an MA plan or in a health plan offered by an MA organization may continue to be enrolled in that plan; and (2) an individual with ESRD whose enrollment in an MA plan was terminated or discontinued after December 31, 1998, because CMS or the MA organization terminated the MA organization's contract for the plan or discontinued the plan in the area in which the individual resides, is eligible to elect another MA plan; and (3) an individual with ESRD may elect an MA special needs plan (SNP) as long as that plan has chosen to enroll ESRD individuals. [Soc. Sec. Act § 1851(a)(3)(B); 42 C.F.R. § 422.50(a)(2).]

Beginning in 2021, however, individuals with ESRD will be permitted to enroll in MA plans. [Soc. Sec. Act § 1853(a)(3), as amended by 21st Century Cures Act (P.L. 114-255) § 17006.]

SNP eligibility. To elect a special needs plan for a special needs individual, an individual must: (1) meet the definition of a special needs individual, i.e., an individual who is institutionalized, is entitled to assistance under a state Medicaid plan, or has a severe or disabling condition and would benefit from enrollment in a specialized MA plan; (2) meet the eligibility requirements for that specific SNP; and (3) be eligible to elect an MA plan. If a SNP determines that an enrollee no longer meets the eligibility criteria but can reasonably be expected to again meet the criteria within a six-month period, the enrollee is deemed to continue to be eligible for the MA plan for a period of not less than 30 days but not to exceed six months. [Soc. Sec. Act § 1859(f); 42 C.F.R. §§ 422.2, 422.52.]

Hospice patients. MA organizations do not provide hospice care but must inform each Medicare enrollee eligible to select hospice care about the availability of hospice care under certain circumstances. [Soc. Sec. Act §§ 1852(a)(1)(B)(i), 1853(h); 42 C.F.R. §§ 422.100(c)(1), 422.320.]

Continuation of enrollment. An MA organization may offer a continuation of enrollment option to enrollees when they no longer reside in the service area of a plan and permanently move into the area designated as the MA organization's "continuation area." The beneficiary may choose whether to continue enrollment in the plan after the move or to disenroll. [Soc. Sec. Act § 1851(b)(1); 42 C.F.R. § 422.54.]

Election and Enrollment in MA Plans

Generally, each MA organization must accept without restriction individuals who are eligible to elect an MA plan that the MA organization offers and who elect the plan during initial coverage election periods and annual election periods. If CMS determines that a plan has a capacity limit, the MA organization may limit enrollment in the plan under certain circumstances. [42 C.F.R. §§ 422.60, 422.62.]

Beneficiaries may currently make elections during three different types of election periods:

- the initial coverage election period (ICEP);
- the annual election period (AEP); or
- a special election period (SEP).

[Soc. Sec. Act § 1851(e); 42 C.F.R. § 422.62.]

Initial coverage election period. The ICEP is the period during which a newly MA-eligible individual may make an initial election. The ICEP begins three months before the month an individual is first entitled to Medicare Part A and Part B and ends the last day of the individual's Part B initial enrollment period. [Soc. Sec. Act § 1851(e)(1); 42 C.F.R. § 422.62(a)(1).] An individual who fails to make an election during the initial coverage election period is deemed to have elected original fee-for-service Medicare. [Soc. Sec. Act § 1851(c)(3)(A); 42 C.F.R. § 422.66(c).]

Annual election period. The AEP for MA and Part D prescription drug plans (PDPs) runs from October 15 through December 7. During the AEP, individuals may switch to a different MA plan, or from original Medicare to an MA plan. [Soc. Sec. Act § 1851(e)(3)(B)(v); 42 C.F.R. § 422.62(a)(2).]

Open enrollment period. Section 17005 of the 21st Century Cures Act provides for an open enrollment period for MA-eligible individuals starting in 2019. An MA-eligible individual who is enrolled in an MA plan will be permitted to change his or her election at any time during the first three months of the year. An individual who first becomes an MA-eligible individual during a year beginning with 2019 and enrolls in an MA plan will be permitted to change his or her election at any time during the first thee months during such year in which the individual is an MA-eligible individual. This change may occur only once during the applicable three-month period in each year. [Soc. Sec. Act § 1851(e)(2)(G).]

Open enrollment for institutionalized individuals. An individual who is eligible to elect an MA plan and who is institutionalized is not limited in the number of elections or changes he or she may make. An MA-eligible institutionalized individual may at any time elect an MA plan or change his or her election from an MA plan to original Medicare, to a different MA plan, or from original Medicare to an MA plan. [Soc. Sec. Act § 1851(e)(2)(D); 42 C.F.R. § 422.62(a)(6).]

Annual 45-day period for disenrollment from MA plans to original Medicare. During the first 45 days of each calendar year (January 1 to February 14) from 2011 to 2018, MA beneficiaries may choose to disenroll from an MA plan and return to traditional fee-for-service Medicare coverage, and they also may choose Part D prescription drug coverage. [Soc. Sec. Act § 1851(e)(2)(C); 42 C.F.R. §§ 422.62(a)(7), 423.38(d).]

Special election periods. SEPs constitute periods outside of the usual enrollment periods when an individual may elect a plan or change his or her current plan election. SEPs include situations when:

(1) CMS or the MA organization has terminated the organization's contract for the plan or discontinued the plan in the area in which the individual resides, or the organization has notified the individual of the impending termination of the plan or the impending discontinuation of the plan in the area in which he or she resides;

(2) an individual has made a change in residence outside of the service area or continuation area or has experienced another change in circumstances as determined by CMS (other than termination for non-payment of premiums or disruptive behavior) that causes the individual to no longer be eligible to elect the MA plan;

(3) the individual demonstrates that the MA organization offering the plan substantially violated a material provision of its contract under MA in relation to the individual, including, but not limited to, failure to provide medical services in accordance with quality standards or failure to provide medically necessary services in a timely fashion;

(4) the individual demonstrates that the MA organization materially misrepresented the plan's contract provision in marketing the plan to the individual; or

(5) the individual meets other exceptional conditions as CMS may provide.

[Soc. Sec. Act § 1851(e)(4); 42 C.F.R. § 422.62(b).]

Forms. An individual who wishes to elect an MA plan may make or change his or her election during the election periods specified above by filing the appropriate election forms with the MA organization or through other mechanisms approved by CMS. An individual who wishes to disenroll from an MA plan may change his or her election during the election periods by either filing a new election form or by filing the appropriate disenrollment form with the MA organization or through other mechanisms determined by CMS. [42 C.F.R. § 422.66(a), (b).]

Alternate employer or union election mechanism. MA organizations that offer MA plans to employers or unions may choose to accept voluntary elections directly from that group without obtaining an MA election form from each individual. The employer or union reports to the MA organization individuals' choices of coverage. MA organizations may specify the employers or unions, if any, from which they will accept this election format and may choose to accept enrollment and/or voluntary disenrollment elections. [*Medicare Managed Care Manual*, Pub. 100-16, Ch. 2, § 20.4.1.]

Conversion of enrollment. An MA plan must accept any individual (even if the individual has ESRD) who is enrolled in a health plan offered by the MA organization during the month immediately preceding the month in which he or she is eligible for Medicare. [42 C.F.R. § 422.66(d).]

Plan closure. An MA organization has the option to voluntarily close one or more of its MA plans to open enrollment period enrollment elections. However, if an MA organization has an MA plan that is open during an open enrollment period and decides to change this process, it must notify CMS and the general public 30 calendar days in advance of the new limitations on the open enrollment process. When an MA plan is voluntarily closed for the open enrollment period, it is closed to all open enrollment period requests, but it must still accept elections made during the ICEP and SEP and be open for the AEP, unless an approved capacity limit applies and has been reached. [Pub. 100-16, Ch. 2, § 30.9.1.]

Passive enrollment. When MA plans immediately terminate or when CMS determines that continued enrollment in an MA plan poses potential harm to the members, CMS may implement passive enrollment procedures. Under passive enrollment procedures, individuals are considered to have elected a plan selected by CMS unless they: (1) decline the plan selected by CMS, or (2) request enrollment in another plan. The MA organization that receives the passive enrollment must provide notice, before the enrollment effective date, to the potential enrollee that describes the costs and benefits of the plan and the process for accessing care under the plan and clearly explains the beneficiary's ability to decline the enrollment or choose another plan. [42 C.F.R. § 422.60(g).]

Effective dates of elections.

(1) An election made during an ICEP is effective as of the first day of the month of entitlement to both Part A and Part B.

(2) Elections or changes of election made during the AEP are effective the first day of the following calendar year.

(3) Elections made during an open enrollment period are effective the first day of the first month following the month in which the election is made (note: open enrollment periods are currently available only to institutionalized individuals).

(4) The effective date of elections made during SEPs depend on the circumstances and are made by CMS in a manner consistent with protecting the continuity of health benefits coverage.

(5) The effective date for an election of coverage under original Medicare made during a SEP for an individual age 65 is the first day of the first calendar month following the month in which the election is made.

(6) The effective date for an election made from January 1 through February 14 to disenroll from an MA plan to original Medicare is effective the first day of the first month following the month in which the election is made.

[Soc. Sec. Act § 1851(f); 42 C.F.R. § 422.68.]

Disenrollment from MA Plans

An individual may disenroll from an MA plan only during one of the election periods noted above. The individual may disenroll by: (1) enrolling in another plan during a valid enrollment period; (2) giving or faxing a signed written notice to the MA organization, or through his or her employer or union where applicable; (3) submitting a request via the Internet to the MA organization, if the MA organization offers such an option; or (4) calling 1-800-MEDICARE. If an enrollee makes a verbal request, the MA organization must instruct the individual to make the request in one of the ways described above. [42 C.F.R. § 422.66(b); Pub. 100-16, Ch. 2, § 50.1.]

Disenrollment by the MA organization. Generally, an MA organization may not disenroll an individual from any MA plan it offers or request or encourage disenrollment. The organization may, however, disenroll an individual if he or she: (1) does not pay any monthly basic or supplementary premium in a timely manner; (2) engages in disruptive behavior; or (3) provides fraudulent information on an election form or permits the fraudulent use of an enrollment card. [42 C.F.R. § 422.74(a), (b)(1).]

The MA organization *must* disenroll an individual under the following circumstances:

(1) the individual no longer resides in the MA plan's service area (including when the individual is incarcerated and does not reside in the service area of the MA plan);

(2) the individual loses entitlement to Part A or Part B benefits;

(3) the individual dies;

(4) for special needs individuals enrolled in a specialized MA plan, the individual no longer meets the special needs status of that plan; or

(5) the individual is not lawfully present in the United States.

[42 C.F.R. § 422.74(b)(2), (d).]

The MA organization also *must* disenroll enrollees: if the organization has its contract with CMS terminated; if it terminates the MA plan; or if it discontinues the plan in an area where it had previously been available. However, when an MA organization discontinues offering an MA plan in a portion of its service area, it may elect to offer enrollees residing in all or portions of the affected area the option to continue enrollment in an MA plan offered by the organization, as long as there is no other MA plan offered in the affected area at the time of the organization's election. The organization may require an enrollee who chooses to continue enrollment to agree to receive the full range of basic benefits (excluding emergency and urgently needed care) exclusively through facilities designated by the organization within the plan service area. [42 C.F.R. § 422.74(b)(3).]

Notice of disenrollment. If the disenrollment is for any of the reasons other than death or loss of entitlement to Medicare Part A or Part B benefits, the MA organization must give the individual a written notice of the disenrollment with an explanation of why the MA organization is planning to disenroll the individual. The organization must provide the individual with a notice of disenrollment before submitting the disenrollment to CMS, and it must include an explanation of the individual's right to a hearing under the MA organization's grievance procedures. [42 C.F.R. § 422.74(c).]

¶401

Consequences of disenrollment. An individual who is disenrolled for nonpayment of premiums, disruptive behavior, fraud and abuse, or loss of Part A or B benefits is deemed to have elected original Medicare. If the individual is disenrolled because the plan was terminated, the area covered by the plan was reduced, or the individual no longer resides in the MA plan's service area, he or she will have a SEP to make a new choice. If the individual fails to make an election during the SEP, he or she will be enrolled in original Medicare. [42 C.F.R. § 422.74(e).] MA organizations are required to notify members of their Medigap-guaranteed issue rights when members disenroll to original Medicare during a special election period. [Pub. 100-16, Ch. 2, § 50.1.7.]

[¶ 402] Benefits and Beneficiary Protections

A Medicare Advantage (MA) organization offering an MA plan must provide enrollees, at a minimum, with all basic Medicare-covered services (except hospice benefits) by furnishing the benefits directly or through arrangements, or by paying for the benefits. MA organizations also may provide supplemental benefits through their plans. [42 C.F.R. § 422.100.] MA organizations must comply with CMS national coverage decisions (NCDs), general coverage guidelines included in original Medicare manuals and instructions (unless superseded by regulations), and written coverage decisions of local Medicare contractors. If an MA organization covers geographic areas encompassing more than one local coverage policy area, it may elect to uniformly apply to plan enrollees in all areas the coverage policy that is the most beneficial to MA enrollees. [42 C.F.R. § 422.101(b).]

Medicare as secondary payer. CMS does not pay for services to the extent that Medicare is not the primary payer (see ¶ 636). An MA organization must, for each MA plan: (1) identify payers that are primary to Medicare; (2) identify the amounts payable by those payers; and (3) coordinate its benefits to Medicare enrollees with the benefits of the primary payers. [42 C.F.R. § 422.108.]

Benefits Provided by MA Plans

An MA plan must include basic benefits and also may include supplemental benefits. Basic benefits are all Medicare-covered services, except hospice services; they must be provided through providers meeting the requirements of the Medicare conditions of participation. Beginning January 1, 2021, pursuant to section 17006(c) of the 21st Century Cures Act (P.L. 114-255), organ acquisitions for kidney transplants will no longer be covered under Part C and instead will be covered by Parts A and B. Supplemental benefits consist of: (1) mandatory supplemental benefits not covered by Medicare that an MA enrollee must purchase as part of an MA plan that are paid for in full, directly by Medicare enrollees, in the form of premiums or cost-sharing; and (2) optional supplemental benefits not covered by Medicare that are purchased at the option of the MA enrollee and paid for in full, directly by the Medicare enrollee, in the form of premiums or cost-sharing. [Soc. Sec. Act § 1852(a)(1)– (3); 42 C.F.R. §§ 422.100(a), (c), (h), 422.101–422.104.]

Noncontracting providers and suppliers. An MA organization must make timely and reasonable payment to or on behalf of the plan enrollee for the following services obtained from a provider or supplier that does not contract with the MA organization to provide services covered by the MA plan:

    (1) ambulance services dispatched through 911 or its local equivalent;

    (2) emergency and urgently needed services;

    (3) maintenance and post-stabilization care services;

    (4) renal dialysis services provided while the enrollee was temporarily outside the plan's service area; and

(5) services for which coverage has been denied by the MA organization and found upon appeal to be services the enrollee was entitled to have furnished, or paid for, by the MA organization.

[42 C.F.R. § 422.100(b)(1).]

An MA plan and an MA medical savings account (MSA) plan offered by an MA organization, after the annual deductible has been met, satisfy the basic requirements with respect to benefits for services furnished by a noncontracting provider if that MA plan provides payment in an amount the provider would have received under original Medicare, including balance billing permitted under Medicare Part A and Part B. [42 C.F.R. § 422.100(b)(2).]

Availability of plans. An MA organization must offer an MA plan to all Medicare beneficiaries residing in the service area of the MA plan. The organization must offer the plan at a uniform premium, with uniform benefits and level of cost-sharing throughout the plan's service area or segment of service area. [42 C.F.R. § 422.100(d).]

Review and approval of benefits and cost-sharing. CMS reviews and approves MA benefits and associated cost-sharing using written policy guidelines and requirements and other CMS instructions to ensure:

- Medicare-covered services meet CMS fee-for-service guidelines.

- MA organizations are not designing benefits to discriminate against beneficiaries, promote discrimination, discourage enrollment or encourage disenrollment, steer subsets of Medicare beneficiaries to particular MA plans, or inhibit access to services.

- Benefit design meets other MA program requirements.

- MA local plans have an out-of-pocket maximum for Medicare Parts A and B services that is no greater than the annual limit set by CMS.

- With respect to a local preferred provider organization (PPO) plan, the annual out-of-pocket limit applies only to use of network providers. Such local PPO plans must include a total catastrophic limit on beneficiary out-of-pocket expenditures for both in-network and out-of-network Parts A and B services that is: (1) consistent with the requirements applicable to MA regional plans; and (2) not greater than the annual limit set by CMS.

- Cost-sharing for Medicare Part A and B services specified by CMS does not exceed levels annually determined by CMS to be discriminatory for such services.

[42 C.F.R. § 422.100(f).]

Mammography, influenza, and pneumococcal benefits. Enrollees of MA organizations may directly access (through self-referral) mammography screening and influenza and pneumococcal vaccines. MA organizations may not impose cost-sharing for influenza vaccines and pneumococcal vaccines. [42 C.F.R. § 422.100(g).]

Coverage of durable medical equipment. An MA organization must cover and ensure enrollee access to all categories of durable medical equipment (DME) covered under Medicare Part B. However, an MA organization may, within specific categories of DME, limit coverage to certain brands, items, and supplies of preferred manufacturers, provided that:

(1) its contracts with DME suppliers ensure that enrollees have access to all DME brands, items, and supplies of preferred manufacturers;

(2) its enrollees have access to all medically necessary DME brands, items, and supplies of non-preferred manufacturers;

¶402

(3) at the request of new enrollees, it provides for a 90-day transition period during which the MA organization will ensure a supply of DME brands, items, and supplies of non-preferred manufacturers, and provide for the repair of same;

(4) it makes no negative changes to its DME brands, items, and supplies of preferred manufacturers during the plan year;

(5) it treats denials of DME brands, items, and supplies of non-preferred manufacturers as organization determinations subject to appeal;

(6) it discloses, as part of its description of benefits, DME coverage limitations and beneficiary appeal rights in the case of a denial of a DME brand, item, or supply of a non-preferred manufacturer; and

(7) it provides full coverage, without limitation on brand and manufacturer, to all DME categories or subcategories annually determined by CMS to require full coverage.

[42 C.F.R. § 422.100(l).]

Special rules for ambulance, emergency, and urgently needed services. The MA organization is financially responsible for ambulance services, including ambulance services dispatched through 911 or its local equivalent, where other means of transportation would endanger the beneficiary's health. The MA organization is also financially responsible for emergency and urgently needed services regardless of whether the services are obtained within or outside the MA organization, and regardless of whether there is prior authorization for the services. [42 C.F.R. § 422.113(a), (b).]

Special rules for maintenance and post-stabilization care services. In addition, the MA organization is financially responsible for post-stabilization care services obtained within or outside the MA organization that: (1) are pre-approved by a plan provider or other MA organization representative; (2) are not pre-approved by a plan provider or other MA organization representative, but are administered to maintain the enrollee's stabilized condition within one hour of a request to the MA organization for pre-approval of further post-stabilization care services; and (3) are not pre-approved by a plan provider or other MA organization representative, but are administered to maintain, improve, or resolve the enrollee's stabilized condition under certain conditions. [Soc. Sec. Act § 1852(d)(2); 42 C.F.R. § 422.113(c)(2).]

Requirements during a disaster or emergency. When a state of disaster is declared, an MA organization must ensure access to benefits by covering Part A, Part B, and supplemental Part B benefits furnished at non-contracted facilities, waive requirements for gatekeeper referrals where applicable, provide the same cost-sharing for enrollees as if the service or benefit had been furnished at a plan-contracted facility, and make changes that benefit the enrollee effective immediately without the 30-day notification requirement. [42 C.F.R. § 422.100(m).]

Return to home skilled nursing facility services. MA plans must provide coverage of post-hospital extended care services to Medicare enrollees through a home skilled nursing facility (SNF) if the enrollee elects to receive the coverage through the home SNF, and if the home SNF either has a contract with the MA organization or agrees to accept substantially similar payment under the same terms and conditions that apply to similar SNFs that contract with the MA organization. A home SNF is: (1) the SNF in which the enrollee resided at the time of admission to the hospital preceding the receipt of post-hospital extended care services; (2) a SNF that is providing post-hospital extended care services through a continuing care retirement community in which the MA plan enrollee was a resident at the time of admission to the hospital; or (3) the SNF in which the spouse of the enrollee is residing at the time of discharge from the hospital. [42 C.F.R. § 422.133.]

Effect of NCDs and legislative changes in benefits. If CMS determines and announces that an individual NCD or legislative change in benefits meets the criteria for "significant cost," an MA organization is not required to assume risk for the costs of that service or benefit until the contract year for which payments are appropriately adjusted to take into account the cost of the NCD service or legislative change in benefits. If CMS determines that an NCD or legislative change in benefits does not meet the "significant cost" threshold, the MA organization is required to provide coverage for the NCD or legislative change in benefits and assume risk for the costs of that service or benefit as of the effective date stated in the NCD or specified in the legislation. [Soc. Sec. Act § 1852(a)(5); 42 C.F.R. § 422.109(b).]

"Significant cost" is defined as either: (1) the average cost of furnishing a single service that exceeds a cost threshold of the preceding year's dollar threshold adjusted to reflect the national per capita growth percentage; or (2) the estimated cost of all Medicare services furnished as a result of a particular NCD or legislative change in benefits representing at least 0.1 percent of the national average per capita costs. [42 C.F.R. § 422.109(a).]

Special Rules for Self-Referral and Point-of-Service Option

If an MA plan member receives an item or service of the plan that is covered upon referral or pre-authorization from a contracted provider of that plan, the member cannot be financially liable for more than the normal in-plan cost-sharing if he or she correctly identifies himself or herself as a member of that plan to the contracted provider before receiving the covered item or service. However, if the contracted provider can show that the enrollee was notified before receiving the item or service that the item or service is covered only if further action is taken by the enrollee, then this requirement does not apply. [42 C.F.R. § 422.105(a).]

Point-of-service option. As a general rule, a point-of-service (POS) benefit is an option that an MA organization may offer in a health maintenance organization (HMO) plan to provide enrollees with additional choice in obtaining specified health care services. The organization may offer a POS option under a coordinated care plan as an additional benefit under an HMO plan as a mandatory or optional supplemental benefit. [42 C.F.R. § 422.105(b).]

Access to Services

An MA organization offering a coordinated care plan may specify the networks of providers that enrollees can use, as long as the organization ensures that all covered services, including supplemental services contracted for the Medicare enrollee, are available and accessible under the plan. [42 C.F.R. § 422.112(a).]

To accomplish this, the MA organization must do the following:

(1) maintain and monitor a network of appropriate providers supported by written agreements that is sufficient to provide necessary access to meet the needs of enrollees (except that MA regional plans can use methods other than written agreements with CMS approval);

(2) establish a panel of primary care providers (PCPs) from which an enrollee may choose a PCP;

(3) provide or arrange for necessary specialty care and, in particular, give female enrollees the option of direct access to a women's health specialist;

(4) demonstrate, if seeking to expand the service area of an MA plan, that the number and type of providers available to the plan are sufficient to meet the needs of the population;

(5) demonstrate to CMS that its providers in a plan are credentialed;

(6) establish written standards for timely access to care, medical necessity determinations, and provider consideration of enrollee input for treatment plans;

(7) establish convenient and non-discriminatory hours of operation and make plan services available 24 hours per day, seven days per week, when medically necessary;

(8) ensure that services are provided in a culturally competent manner to all enrollees;

(9) provide coverage for ambulance services, emergency and urgently needed services, and post-stabilization care services; and

(10) ensure that coordinated care and private fee-for-service (PFFS) MA plans that meet Medicare access and availability requirements through direct contracting network providers are consistent with the prevailing community pattern of health care delivery in the areas where the network is being offered.

[Soc. Sec. Act § 1852(d)(1); 42 C.F.R. § 422.112(a).]

MA organizations also must ensure continuity of care and integration of services through arrangements with contracted providers. [42 C.F.R. § 422.112(b).]

Access to services under private fee-for-service plans. An MA organization that offers a PFFS plan must demonstrate to CMS that it has a sufficient number and range of providers willing to furnish services under the plan. An MA organization meets this requirement if it has: (1) payment rates that are not less than the rates that apply under original Medicare for the provider in question; and (2) contracts or agreements with a sufficient number and range of providers to furnish the services covered under the plan or meet the required access standards. [Soc. Sec. Act § 1852(d)(4); 42 C.F.R. § 422.114(a)(1), (2).]

Reward and Incentive Programs

MA organizations may create reward and incentive programs that focus on promoting improved health, preventing illness and injuries, and encouraging the efficient use of health care resources. These rewards or incentives must: (1) be offered in connection with an entire service or activity; (2) be offered without discrimination; (3) have a monetary cap that is determined by CMS and that is expected to affect enrollee behavior but not exceed the value of the activity or service; and (4) be compliant with all relevant fraud and abuse laws. [42 C.F.R. § 422.134.]

To be considered nondiscriminatory, a reward or incentive program must be designed so that all enrollees may earn rewards and not discriminate based on race, national origin (including limited English proficiency), gender, disability, chronic disease, whether a person resides in an institutional setting, frailty, health status, or any other prohibited basis. Moreover, reward and incentive programs within MA organizations may not offer items in the form of cash or other monetary rebates and may not be used to target potential enrollees. [42 C.F.R. § 422.134.]

Special Needs Plans

MA organizations seeking to offer a special needs plan (SNP) serving beneficiaries eligible for both Medicare and Medicaid (dual eligibles) must have a contract with the state Medicaid agency. The MA organization retains responsibility under the contract for providing benefits for individuals entitled to receive medical assistance. Such benefits may include long-term care services. At a minimum, the contract must document:

(1) the MA organization's responsibility, including financial obligations, to provide or arrange for Medicaid benefits;

(2) the category (or categories) of eligibility for dual-eligible beneficiaries to be enrolled under the SNP;

(3) the Medicaid benefits covered under the SNP;

(4) the cost-sharing protections covered under the SNP;

(5) the identification and sharing of information on Medicaid provider participation;

(6) the verification of enrollees' eligibility for both Medicare and Medicaid;

(7) the service area covered by the SNP; and

(8) the contract period for the SNP.

[42 C.F.R. § 422.107.]

SNPs that meet a high standard of integration and minimum performance and quality-based standards may offer additional supplemental benefits when CMS finds that such benefits could better integrate care for the dual-eligible population. To offer these additional benefits, the SNP must: (1) have operated in the MA contract year prior to the MA contract year for which it is submitting its bid; and (2) offer its enrollees such benefits without cost-sharing or additional premium charges. [42 C.F.R. § 422.102(e).]

Model of care for SNPs. MA organizations offering SNPs must implement an evidence-based model of care (MOC) with appropriate networks of providers and specialists. The organization must: (1) conduct a comprehensive initial health risk assessment of each enrollee's physical, psychosocial, and functional needs as well as an annual health risk reassessment, using a comprehensive risk assessment tool that CMS will review during oversight activities; (2) develop and implement a comprehensive individualized plan of care through an interdisciplinary care team in consultation with the beneficiary, identifying goals and objectives, including measurable outcomes as well as specific services and benefits to be provided; and (3) use an interdisciplinary team in the management of care. [42 C.F.R. § 422.101(f)(1).]

MA organizations offering SNPs must also ensure an effective management structure by developing and implementing the following MOC components: (1) target one of the three SNP populations; (2) have appropriate staff trained on the SNP plan MOC to coordinate and deliver all services and benefits; (3) coordinate the delivery of care across health care settings, providers, and services to ensure continuity of care; (4) coordinate the delivery of specialized benefits and services that meet the needs of the most vulnerable beneficiaries among the three target special needs populations, including frail or disabled beneficiaries and beneficiaries near the end of life; and (5) coordinate communication among plan personnel, providers, and beneficiaries. All MA organizations wishing to offer or continue to offer an SNP must be approved by the National Committee for Quality Assurance. [42 C.F.R. § 422.101(f)(2).]

Coordination of Benefits

If an MA organization contracts with an employer group health plan (EGHP) or labor union that covers enrollees in an MA plan, or with a state Medicaid agency to provide Medicaid benefits to enrollees who are eligible for both Medicare and Medicaid and who are enrolled in an MA plan, the enrollees must be provided the same benefits as all other enrollees in the MA plan, with the EGHP, labor union, or Medicaid benefits supplementing the MA plan benefits. [42 C.F.R. § 422.106(a).]

Permissible employer, labor organization, or Medicaid plan benefits include: (1) payment of a portion or all of the MA basic and supplemental premiums; (2) payment of a portion or all of other cost-sharing amounts approved for the MA plan; or (3) other employer-sponsored benefits that may require additional premium and cost-sharing, or other benefits provided by the organization under a contract with the state Medicaid agency. [42 C.F.R. § 422.106(b).]

MA organizations may request a CMS waiver or modification of those requirements that hinder the design of, the offering of, or the enrollment in MA plans under contracts between MA organizations and employers, labor organizations, or the trustees of funds established by one or more employers or labor organizations to furnish benefits to the entity's employees, former employees, or members or former members of the labor organizations. [42 C.F.R. § 422.106(c).]

Beneficiary Protections

An MA organization may not deny, limit, or condition coverage or benefits to beneficiaries on the basis of health status, including medical condition, claims experience, receipt of health care, medical history, genetic information, evidence of insurability (including conditions arising out of acts of domestic violence), or disability. [42 C.F.R. § 422.110(a).]

An MA organization may not currently enroll an individual who has been medically determined to have end-stage renal disease (ESRD). However, if an individual is diagnosed with ESRD while enrolled in an MA plan, he or she may not be disenrolled for that reason. [42 C.F.R. § 422.110(b).]

Advance directives. An MA organization must maintain written policies and procedures concerning advance directives with respect to all adults receiving medical care by or through the MA organization. [42 C.F.R. § 422.128.]

Disclosure requirements. An MA organization must disclose to each beneficiary enrolling in one of its plans a plan description, including the plan's service area, benefits, access (including out-of-area coverage), emergency coverage, supplemental benefits, prior authorization and review rules, grievance and appeals procedures, quality improvement program, disenrollment rights and responsibilities, catastrophic caps and single deductible, and claims information. This information must be provided at the time of enrollment and at least annually thereafter, 15 days before the annual coordinated election period, in a clear, accurate, and standardized form. [Soc. Sec. Act § 1852(c); 42 C.F.R. § 422.111.]

The plan description for a SNP for dual-eligible individuals must include a comprehensive written statement describing cost-sharing protections and benefits that the individual is entitled to under Medicare and Medicaid. [42 C.F.R. § 422.111(b)(2)(iii).]

Confidentiality of enrollee records. For any medical records or enrollment information it maintains, an MA organization must abide by all federal and state laws regarding confidentiality and disclosure of medical records; ensure that medical information is released only in accordance with federal or state laws or under court orders or subpoenas; maintain the records in an accurate manner; and ensure timely access by enrollees to their own records. [42 C.F.R. § 422.118.]

[¶ 403] Beneficiary Grievances, Organizational Determinations, and Appeals

Medicare Advantage (MA) plans must provide meaningful procedures for hearing and resolving grievances between the plan and enrolled beneficiaries and for organization determinations and appeals. [Soc. Sec. Act § 1852(f), (g); 42 C.F.R. § 422.560.]

Grievance procedures are separate and distinct from appeal procedures, which address organization determinations. For the purposes of these procedures:

- An *"appeal"* is a procedure that deals with the review of an adverse organization determination on the health care services an enrollee believes he or she is entitled to receive. The basis of this process includes delay in providing, arranging for, or approving health care services (such that a delay would adversely affect the health of the enrollee), or disputes of any amounts the enrollee must pay for a service. These procedures include reconsiderations by the MA organization and, if necessary, an independent review entity (IRE), hearings before administrative law judges (ALJs), review by the Medicare Appeals Council, and judicial review. Disputes involving optional supplemental benefits offered by cost plans and health care prepayment plans (HCPPs) are treated as appeals.

- A *"grievance"* is any complaint or dispute, other than one involving an organization determination, expressing dissatisfaction with any aspect of an MA organization's or provider's operation, activities, or behavior, regardless of whether remedial action is requested. Grievances may include complaints regarding access to or the timeliness, appropriateness, or setting of a provided health service, procedure, or item. Grievance issues also may include complaints that a covered health service procedure or item during a course of treatment did not meet accepted standards for delivery of health care.

[42 C.F.R. § § 422.561, 422.564(b); *Medicare Managed Care Manual*, Pub. 100-16, Ch. 13, § 10.1.]

Grievance Procedures for MA Organizations

Each MA organization must provide meaningful procedures for timely hearing and resolving grievances between enrollees and the organization or any other entity or individual through which the organization provides health care services under any MA plan it offers. Upon receiving a complaint, an MA organization must promptly determine and inform the enrollee whether the complaint is subject to its grievance or appeal procedures. [Soc. Sec. Act § 1852(f); 42 C.F.R. § 422.564(a), (b).]

Grievance disposition. An MA organization must notify the enrollee of its decision as expeditiously as the case requires, based on the enrollee's health status, but no later than 30 days after the date the organization receives the oral or written grievance. The notification time frame may be extended by up to 14 days if the enrollee requests the extension or if the organization justifies a need for additional information and documents how the delay is in the interest of the enrollee. If the organization extends the deadline, it must immediately notify the enrollee in writing of the reasons for the delay. [42 C.F.R. § 422.564(e).]

The MA organization must notify the enrollee of the disposition of the grievance as follows: (1) it must respond in writing to all grievances submitted in writing; (2) it may respond either orally or in writing to grievances submitted orally, unless the enrollee requests a written response; and (3) it must respond in writing to all grievances related to quality of care, regardless of how the grievance is filed. The response must also include a description of the enrollee's right to file a written complaint with the quality improvement organization (QIO). [42 C.F.R. § 422.564(e)(3).]

Expedited grievances. An MA organization must respond to an enrollee's grievance within 24 hours if the complaint involves an MA organization's: (1) decision to invoke an extension relating to an organization determination or reconsideration; or (2) refusal to grant an enrollee's request for an expedited organization determination or reconsideration. [42 C.F.R. § 422.564(f).]

MA Organization Determinations

Each MA organization must have a procedure for making timely organization determinations regarding the benefits an enrollee is entitled to receive under an MA plan, including basic benefits and mandatory and optional supplemental benefits, and the amount, if any, that the enrollee is required to pay for a health service. The MA organization must have a standard procedure for making determinations and an expedited procedure for situations in which applying the standard procedure could seriously jeopardize the enrollee's life, health, or ability to regain maximum function. [Soc. Sec. Act § 1852(g)(1); 42 C.F.R. § 422.566(a).]

Organization determinations. An organization determination is any determination made by an MA organization regarding any of the following:

(1) payment for temporarily out-of-the-area renal dialysis services, emergency services, post-stabilization care, or urgently needed services;

(2) payment for any other health services furnished by a provider other than the MA organization that the enrollee believes are covered under Medicare or, if not covered under Medicare, should have been furnished, arranged for, or reimbursed by the MA organization;

(3) the MA organization's refusal to provide or pay for services, in whole or in part, including the type or level of services, that the enrollee believes should be furnished or arranged for by the MA organization;

(4) reduction or premature discontinuation of a previously authorized ongoing course of treatment; or

(5) failure of the MA organization to approve, furnish, arrange for, or provide payment for health care services in a timely manner, or to provide the enrollee with timely notice of an adverse determination, such that a delay would adversely affect the health of the enrollee.

[42 C.F.R. § 422.566(b).]

Individuals or entities who can request an organization determination include the enrollee or his or her representative; any provider that furnishes, or intends to furnish, services to the enrollee; or the legal representative of a deceased enrollee's estate. An enrollee or a physician (regardless of whether the physician is affiliated with the MA organization) can request an expedited determination. [42 C.F.R. § 422.566(c).]

Generally, an enrollee makes an oral or written request with the MA organization or, if applicable, to the entity responsible for making the determination. The enrollee must make requests for payment in writing, unless the MA organization or entity responsible for making the determination has implemented a voluntary policy of accepting verbal payment requests. [42 C.F.R. § 422.568(a).]

Notice requirements. When a party makes a request for a service, the MA organization must notify the enrollee of its determination as expeditiously as the enrollee's health condition requires, but no later than 14 calendar days after receiving the request for a standard organization determination. The MA organization may extend the time frame by up to 14 calendar days if (1) the enrollee requests the extension; (2) the extension is justified and in the enrollee's interest due to the need for additional medical evidence from a noncontract provider that may change an MA organization's decision to deny an item or service; or (3) the extension is justified due to extraordinary, exigent, or other non-routine circumstances and is in the enrollee's interest. When the MA organization extends the time frame, it must notify the enrollee in writing of the reasons for the delay and inform the enrollee of the right to file an expedited grievance if he or she disagrees with the decision to grant an extension. The MA organization must notify the enrollee of its determination as expeditiously as the enrollee's health condition requires, but no later than upon expiration of the extension. [42 C.F.R. § 422.568(b).]

Reconsiderations by MA Organizations and Outside Entities

Any party to an organization determination may, within 60 days of receipt of the request for reconsideration, request that the MA organization reconsider the determination. [Soc. Sec. Act § 1852(g)(2); 42 C.F.R. § 422.578.]

Expedited determinations and reconsiderations. MA plans must have procedures for expediting determinations and reconsiderations when, on the request of an enrollee or a physician, the organization determines that the normal time frame for a determination or reconsideration could seriously jeopardize the affected enrollee's life or health. When it has received such a request, the MA organization must notify the enrollee or the physician, as appropriate, of its determination. If the MA organization denies the request for expedited reconsideration, it must make the determination within the standard 14-day time frame. If it grants the request, it must make the determination no later than 72 hours after receiving the request. [Soc. Sec. Act § 1852(g)(3); 42 C.F.R. §§ 422.570(d), 422.572(a).]

Independent outside entities. When the MA organization affirms, in whole or in part, its adverse organization determination, an independent, outside entity that contracts with CMS must review and resolve the issues that remain in dispute. The independent outside entity must conduct the review as expeditiously as the enrollee's health condition requires but must not exceed the deadlines specified in the contract. [42 C.F.R. § 422.592.]

Administrative Law Judge Hearings

If the amount remaining in controversy after reconsideration meets the threshold requirement, any party to the reconsideration (except the MA organization) who is dissatisfied with the reconsidered determination has a right to a hearing before an ALJ. A request for an ALJ hearing must be in writing and filed with the entity specified in the reconsideration notice within 60 days. The parties to a hearing are the parties to the reconsideration, the MA organization, and any other person or entity whose rights with respect to the reconsideration may be affected by the hearing. [42 C.F.R. §§ 422.600, 422.602; Pub. 100-16, Ch. 13, §§ 100.1, 100.2.]

Amount in controversy. In 2017, plan enrollees who are dissatisfied, either because they have not received health care to which they believe they are entitled, or because they contest the cost of a service they have received, are entitled to a hearing before an ALJ if the amount in controversy is $160 or more, which is a $10 increase over the 2016 requirements. [*Notice*, 81 FR 65651, Sept. 23, 2016.]

Medicare Appeals Council Review

Any party to an ALJ hearing, including the MA organization, who is dissatisfied with the ALJ hearing decision may request that the Medicare Appeals Council review the ALJ's decision or dismissal (see ¶ 924). [42 C.F.R. § 422.608.]

¶403

Judicial Review

Any party, including the MA organization, may request judicial review of an ALJ's decision if the Medicare Appeals Council denied the party's request for review and the amount in controversy meets the threshold requirement established annually. Any party may also request judicial review of a Medicare Appeals Council decision if it is the final decision of CMS and the amount in controversy meets the threshold requirement. [Soc. Sec. Act § 1852(g)(5); 42 C.F.R. § 422.612.]

To request judicial review, a party must file a civil action in a district court of the United States. The minimum amount in controversy for judicial review of Medicare claims made on or after January 1, 2017, is $1,560, up from $1,500 in 2016. [*Notice*, 81 FR 65651, Sept. 23, 2016.]

Effectuating Reconsidered Determinations or Decisions

If, on reconsideration of a *request for service*, the MA organization completely reverses its organization determination, the organization must authorize or provide the service under dispute as expeditiously as the enrollee's health condition requires, but no later than 30 calendar days after the date the MA organization receives the request for reconsideration. [42 C.F.R. § 422.618(a)(1).]

If, on reconsideration of a *request for payment*, the MA organization completely reverses its organization determination, the organization must pay for the service no later than 60 calendar days after the date the MA organization receives the request for reconsideration. [42 C.F.R. § 422.618(a)(2).]

Reversals by the independent outside entity. If, on reconsideration of a *request for service*, the MA organization's determination is reversed in whole or in part by the independent outside entity, the MA organization must authorize the service under dispute within 72 hours from the date it receives notice reversing the determination or provide the service under dispute as expeditiously as the enrollee's health condition requires, but no later than 14 calendar days from that date. [42 C.F.R. § 422.618(b)(1).]

If, on reconsideration of a *request for payment*, the MA organization's determination is reversed in whole or in part by the independent outside entity, the MA organization must pay for the service no later than 30 calendar days from the date it receives notice reversing the organization determination. [42 C.F.R. § 422.618(b)(2).]

Other reversals. If the independent outside entity's determination is reversed in whole or in part by the ALJ or at a higher level of appeal, the MA organization must pay for, authorize, or provide the service under dispute as expeditiously as the enrollee's health condition requires, but no later than 60 calendar days from the date it receives notice reversing the determination. However, if the MA organization requests Medicare Appeals Council review, the organization may await the outcome of the review before it pays for, authorizes, or provides the service under dispute. [42 C.F.R. § 422.618(c).]

Expedited requests. If, on reconsideration of an expedited request for service, the MA organization completely reverses its organization determination, the MA organization must authorize or provide the service under dispute as expeditiously as the enrollee's health condition requires, but no later than 72 hours after the date the MA organization receives the request for reconsideration. [42 C.F.R. § 422.619(a).]

If the MA organization's determination is reversed in whole or in part by the independent outside entity, the MA organization must authorize or provide the service under dispute as expeditiously as the enrollee's health condition requires, but no later than 72 hours from the date it receives notice reversing the determination. [42 C.F.R. § 422.619(b).]

If the independent outside entity's expedited determination is reversed in whole or in part by the ALJ, or at a higher level of appeal, the MA organization must authorize or provide the service under dispute as expeditiously as the enrollee's health condition requires, but no later than 60 days from the date it receives notice reversing the determination. The MA organization must inform the independent outside entity that the organization has effectuated the decision. [42 C.F.R. § 422.619(c)(1).]

If the MA organization requests Medicare Appeals Council review consistent with 42 C.F.R. § 422.608, it may await the outcome of the review before it authorizes or provides the service under dispute. An MA organization that files an appeal with the Medicare Appeals Council must concurrently send a copy of its appeal request and any accompanying documents to the enrollee and must notify the independent outside entity that it has requested an appeal. [42 C.F.R. § 422.619(c)(2).]

Notification of Hospital Discharge Appeal Rights

Hospitals must deliver a standardized written notice of an MA enrollee's rights as a hospital inpatient, including discharge appeal rights, within two calendar days of the enrollee's admission to the hospital. The notice of rights must include: (1) the enrollee's rights as a hospital inpatient, including the right to benefits for inpatient services and for post-hospital services; (2) the enrollee's right to request an immediate review, including a description of the process and the availability of other appeals processes if the enrollee fails to meet the deadline for an immediate review; (3) the circumstances under which an enrollee will or will not be liable for charges for continued stay in the hospital; (4) the enrollee's right to receive additional information; and (5) any other information required by CMS. [42 C.F.R. § 422.620(b)(1), (2).]

For delivery of the written notice of rights to be valid, the enrollee (or the enrollee's representative) must sign and date the notice to indicate that he or she has received the notice and can understand its contents. [42 C.F.R. § 422.620(b)(3).]

Follow-up notification. The hospital must present a copy of the signed notice to the enrollee (or enrollee's representative) at least two calendar days before discharge. Before the MA organization can discharge an enrollee from the inpatient hospital level of care, the physician who is responsible for the enrollee's inpatient care must concur. [42 C.F.R. § 422.620(c), (d).]

QIO review of the decision to discharge. An enrollee who wishes to appeal a determination by an MA organization or hospital that inpatient care is no longer necessary must request immediate QIO review of the determination in writing or by telephone no later than the day of discharge. An enrollee who requests immediate QIO review may remain in the hospital with no additional financial liability for inpatient services received before noon of the day after the QIO notifies the enrollee of its review determination. [42 C.F.R. § 422.622.]

Termination of Provider Services

Before any termination of service, the provider of the service must deliver valid written notice to the enrollee of the MA organization's decision to terminate services. "Termination of service" is defined as the discharge of an enrollee from covered provider services, or discontinuation of covered provider services, when the enrollee has been authorized by the MA organization to receive an ongoing course of treatment from that provider (including home health agencies, skilled nursing facilities, and comprehensive outpatient rehabilitation facilities). Termination includes cessation of coverage at the end of a course of treatment preauthorized in a discrete increment, regardless of whether the enrollee agrees that such services should end. [42 C.F.R. § 422.624(a).]

The provider must notify the enrollee of the MA organization's decision to terminate covered services no later than two days before the proposed end of the services and must use a standardized notice. The standardized termination notice must include: (1) the date that coverage of services ends; (2) the date that the enrollee's financial liability for continued services begins; (3) a description of the enrollee's right to a fast-track appeal, including information on how to contact an IRE, an enrollee's right to submit evidence showing that services should continue, and the availability of other MA appeal procedures if the enrollee fails to meet the deadline for a fast-track IRE appeal; (4) the enrollee's right to receive detailed information about the termination notice and all documents sent by the provider to the IRE; and (5) any other information required by the Secretary. [42 C.F.R. § 422.624(b).]

Enrollees have a right to a fast-track appeal of an MA organization's decision to terminate provider services. Enrollees must submit a request for appeal to an IRE under contract with CMS, in writing or by telephone, by noon of the first day after the day the termination notice was delivered. [42 C.F.R. § 422.626(a).]

[¶ 405] Contracts with Medicare Advantage Organizations

Entities seeking a contract as a Medicare organization offering a Medicare Advantage (MA) plan must fulfill certain application requirements. MA organizations offering prescription drug plans must, in addition to these requirements, follow the requirements in Chapter 5 related to the prescription drug benefit. [Soc. Sec. Act § 1857(a); 42 C.F.R. § 422.500.]

Minimum enrollment requirements. CMS will not enter into a contract with a managed care organization unless the organization enrolls: (1) at least 5,000 individuals (or 1,500 individuals if the organization is a provider-sponsored organization (PSO)) for the purpose of receiving health benefits from the organization; (2) or at least 1,500 individuals (or 500 individuals if the organization is a PSO) for the purpose of receiving health benefits from the organization and this organization primarily serves patients in rural areas. CMS may waive the minimum enrollment requirement at the time of application or during the first three years of the contract if the organization demonstrates that it is capable of administering and managing an MA contract and is able to manage the level of risk required under the contract. [Soc. Sec. Act § 1857(b); 42 C.F.R. § 422.514.]

Application Requirements for MA Organizations

An organization submitting an application for a particular contract year must first submit a completed Notice of Intent to Apply by the date established by CMS. Submitting a Notice of Intent to Apply does not bind that organization to submit an application for the applicable contract year, and failure to submit a Notice will not form the basis of any CMS action against the organization. [42 C.F.R. § 422.501(b).]

Content of application. To become an MA organization and be qualified to provide a particular type of MA plan, the applicant must fully complete all parts of a certified application, in the form and manner required by CMS, including: (1) documentation of appropriate state licensure or certification that the applicant is able to offer health insurance or health benefits coverage that meets state-specified standards applicable to MA plans, and is authorized by the state to accept prepaid capitation for providing, arranging, or paying for the comprehensive health care services to be offered under the MA contract; (2) for regional plans, documentation of application for state licensure in any state in the region that the organization is not already licensed; and (3) for specialized MA plans for special needs individuals (SNPs), documentation that the entity meets the SNP requirements of 42 C.F.R. §§ 422.2, 422.4(a)(1)(iv); 422.101(f), 422.107 (if applicable), and 422.152(g). [42 C.F.R. § 422.501(c).]

CMS use of information from a current or prior contract. If, during the 14 months preceding the application deadline, an MA organization fails to comply with the requirements of the MA program under any current or prior contract with CMS, or if it fails to complete a corrective action plan during the 14 months preceding the application deadline, CMS may deny an application even if the applicant currently meets all of the requirements. In the absence of 14 months of performance history, CMS may deny an application based on a lack of information available to determine an applicant's capacity to comply with the requirements of the MA program. [42 C.F.R. § 422.502(b).]

Notice of CMS determination. CMS must notify each applicant that applies for an MA contract or to be designated a SNP of its determination and the basis for the determination. If CMS finds that the applicant does not appear to meet the requirements for an MA organization and has not provided enough information to evaluate the application, it must give the applicant notice of intent to deny the application and allow the applicant 10 days to respond in writing. [42 C.F.R. § 422.502(c).]

Contract period. CMS contracts with MA plans are for a term of at least 12 months. Contracts are renewed annually only if the MA organization has not notified CMS of its intention not to renew and CMS has not provided the MA organization with a notice of its intention not to renew. Renewal of a contract is contingent on the parties reaching an agreement on the bid. [Soc. Sec. Act § 1857(c)(1); 42 C.F.R. § 422.505.]

Contract provisions. The MA organization agrees to comply with all applicable requirements and conditions, including to accept new enrollments, make enrollments effective, process voluntary disenrollments, and limit involuntary disenrollments. Other requirements include the prohibition on discrimination in beneficiary enrollment, the provision of basic and supplemental benefits, and the operation of a quality assurance and performance improvement program. [42 C.F.R. § 422.504(a).]

Contract Nonrenewal, Modification, and Termination

An MA organization may elect not to renew its contract with CMS as of the end of the term of the contract for any reason. If an MA organization does not intend to renew its contract, it must notify: (1) CMS in writing, by the first Monday in June of the year in which the contract would end; and (2) each Medicare enrollee by mail at least 90 calendar days before the date on which the nonrenewal is effective. [42 C.F.R. § 422.506(a).]

If an MA organization does not renew its contract, CMS may deny an application for a new contract or a service area expansion for two years unless there are special circumstances that warrant special consideration. During this two-year period, CMS will not contract with an organization whose covered persons also served as covered persons for the non-renewing sponsor. [42 C.F.R. § 422.506(a).]

CMS decision not authorize renewal. CMS may decide not to authorize renewal of an MA contract: (1) if the MA organization has not fully implemented or shown discernible progress in implementing quality improvement projects; (2) for any of the reasons that would also permit CMS to terminate the contract; and (3) if the MA organization has committed acts that would support the imposition of intermediate sanctions or civil money penalties. The contract must be nonrenewed as to an individual MA plan if that plan does not have a sufficient number of enrollees to establish that it is a viable independent plan option. CMS must provide notice of its decision not to authorize renewal of a contract to the MA organization by August 1 of the contract year, and to each of the MA organization's Medicare enrollees by mail at least 90 calendar days before the date on which the nonrenewal is effective, or at the conclusion of the appeals process, if applicable. [42 C.F.R. § 422.506(b).]

¶405

Modification or termination by mutual consent. CMS and an MA organization may modify or terminate a contract at any time by written mutual consent. If the contract is terminated by mutual consent, the MA organization must provide notice to its Medicare enrollees and the general public; the MA organization is not required to provide such notice, however, if the contract is replaced the following day by a new contract. If the contract is modified by mutual consent, the MA organization must notify its Medicare enrollees of any changes that CMS determines are appropriate for notification. [42 C.F.R. § 422.508(a), (b).]

As a condition of a consent to a mutual termination, CMS will prohibit the MA organization from applying for new contracts or service area expansions for a period of two years, absent circumstances warranting special consideration. During the same two-year period, CMS will not contract with an organization whose covered persons also served as covered persons for the mutually terminating sponsor. [42 C.F.R. § 422.508(c), (d).]

Termination of contract by CMS. The HHS Secretary may cancel a contract at any time if an MA plan: (1) substantially fails to carry out the terms of its contract with CMS; (2) carries out the terms of the contract in a manner that is inconsistent with the efficient, effective administration of the MA program; or (3) no longer substantially meets applicable requirements of a contracting organization under the MA program. CMS may find that one of these three preceding events has occurred upon a finding that the MA organization did any of the following:

- based on credible evidence, has committed or participated in false, fraudulent, or abusive activities affecting the Medicare, Medicaid, or other state or federal health care programs, including submission of false or fraudulent data;

- substantially fails to comply with the requirements relating to grievances and appeals;

- fails to provide CMS with valid data;

- fails to implement an acceptable quality assessment and performance improvement program;

- substantially fails to comply with prompt payment requirements;

- substantially fails to comply with service access requirements;

- fails to comply with the requirements regarding physician incentive plans;

- fails to meet provider and supplier enrollment requirements;

- fails to comply with the regulatory requirements contained in Part C or Part D;

- fails to meet CMS performance requirements in carrying out the regulatory requirements contained in Part C or Part D or both;

- achieves a Part C summary plan rating of less than three stars for three consecutive contract years (plan ratings issued by CMS before September 1, 2012, are not included in the calculation of the three-year period); or

- fails to report medical loss ratio data in a timely and accurate manner.

[Soc. Sec. Act § 1857(c)(2); 42 C.F.R. § 422.510(a).]

Termination of contract by the MA organization. The MA organization may terminate the contract if CMS fails to substantially carry out the terms of the contract. The MA organization must give advance notice to CMS at least 90 days before the intended date of termination and to its Medicare enrollees and the general public at least 60 days before the termination effective date. The notice to beneficiaries must include a written description of alternatives available for obtaining Medicare services within the services area, including alternative MA plans, Medigap options, and original Medicare. [42 C.F.R. § 422.512(a), (b).]

¶405

CMS's liability for payment to the MA organization ends as of the first day of the month after the last month for which the contract is in effect. CMS may deny an application for a new contract or a service area expansion from an MA organization that has terminated its contract within the preceding two years unless there are circumstances that warrant special consideration. During the same two-year period, CMS will not contract with an organization whose covered persons also served as covered persons for the terminating sponsor. [42 C.F.R. § 422.512(d), (e).]

Medicare Advantage Contract Determinations

CMS can make four types of contract determinations:

(1) that an entity is not qualified to enter into a contract with CMS;

(2) to terminate a contract with an MA organization;

(3) not to authorize a renewal of a contract with an MA organization; and

(4) that an entity is not qualified to offer a specialized MA plan for special needs individuals.

[42 C.F.R. § 422.641.]

Notice of contract determination. When CMS makes a contract determination, it gives the MA organization written notice specifying the reasons for the determination and the organization's right to request a hearing. Generally, for CMS-initiated terminations, CMS mails a notice 45 calendar days before the anticipated effective date of the termination. When CMS determines that it will not authorize a contract renewal, CMS mails the notice to the MA organization by August 1 of the current contract year. [42 C.F.R. § 422.644.]

Effect of contract determination. A contract determination is final and binding unless the organization files a timely request for a hearing with a CMS office within 15 calendar days. [42 C.F.R. § § 422.646, 422.662(b).]

Right to a hearing. Parties entitled to a hearing include: (1) a contract applicant that has been determined to be unqualified to enter into a contract with CMS; (2) an MA organization whose contract has been terminated or not renewed or has had an intermediate sanction imposed; or (3) an applicant that has been determined to be unqualified to offer a specialized MA plan for special needs individuals. [42 C.F.R. § 422.660.]

Notice and effect of hearing decision. The hearing officer's decision must be based upon the evidence of record and must contain separately numbered findings of fact and conclusions of law. A copy of the hearing decision is provided to each party. The decision is final and binding unless it is reversed or modified by the Administrator following review or it is reopened and revised. [42 C.F.R. § 422.690.]

Review by Administrator. CMS or an MA organization that has received a hearing decision regarding a contract determination may request review by the Administrator within 15 calendar days of receiving the hearing decision. Both CMS and the MA organization may provide written arguments to the Administrator. The Administrator has the discretion to elect to review the hearing decision or to decline review and must notify both parties of his or her determination regarding review within 30 calendar days of receiving the request. [42 C.F.R. § 422.692.]

Reopenings. CMS may reopen and revise an initial contract determination on its own motion. The hearing officer may, on his or her own motion, reopen and revise a decision that is unfavorable to any party, but is otherwise final, within one year of the notice of the hearing decision. A decision by the Administrator that is otherwise final may be reopened and revised by the Administrator upon the Administrator's own motion within one year of the notice of the Administrator's decision. The notice of reopening and of any revisions following the reopening must be mailed to the parties and specify the reasons for revisions. [42 C.F.R. §422.696.]

[¶ 406] Medicare Advantage Bids and Benchmarks

This section discusses the requirements for Medicare Advantage (MA) bidding payment methodology, including the submission of plan bids by MA organizations, the negotiation and approval of bids by CMS, and the calculation of benchmarks by CMS. [42 C.F.R. §422.250.]

Submission of Bids by MA Organizations

By the first Monday in June, each MA organization must submit to CMS an aggregate monthly bid amount for each MA plan (other than a medical savings account (MSA) plan) the organization intends to offer in the upcoming year in a given service area. An MA organization's bid submissions must reflect differences in benefit packages or plan costs that CMS determines represent substantial differences in relation to the sponsor's other bid submissions. [42 C.F.R. §422.254(a).]

Bid requirements. The monthly aggregate bid amount submitted by an MA organization for each plan is the organization's estimate of the revenue required for the following categories for providing coverage to an MA-eligible beneficiary with a national average risk profile:

- the unadjusted MA statutory non-drug monthly bid amount, which is the MA plan's estimated average monthly required revenue for providing benefits under the original Medicare fee-for-service program option;

- the amount to provide basic prescription drug coverage, if any; and

- the amount to provide supplemental health care benefits, if any.

Each bid is for a uniform benefit package for the service area and must contain all estimated revenue required by the plan, including administrative costs and return on investment. [42 C.F.R. §422.254(b).] Bids for coordinated care plans, including regional MA plans and specialized MA plans for special needs beneficiaries, and for MA private fee-for-service plans must include specific information, including the plan type and the actuarial basis for determining the bid amount. [42 C.F.R. §422.254(c).]

Beneficiary rebate information. If the plan is required to provide a monthly rebate for a year, the MA organization offering the plan must inform CMS how the plan will distribute the beneficiary rebate. [42 C.F.R. §422.254(d).]

Medical savings account plan information. MA organizations intending to offer MA MSA plans must submit: (1) the enrollment capacity (if any) for the plan; (2) the amount of the MSA monthly premium for basic benefits under the original Medicare fee-for-service program option; (3) the amount of the plan deductible; and (4) the amount of the beneficiary supplemental premium, if any. [42 C.F.R. §422.254(e).]

Separate bids must be submitted for Part A and Part B enrollees and Part B-only enrollees for each MA plan offered. [42 C.F.R. §422.254(f).]

Review, Negotiation, and Approval of Bids Submitted by MA Organizations

CMS reviews the aggregate bid amounts submitted by MA organizations and conducts negotiations regarding the bids (including the supplemental benefits) and the proportions of the aggregate bid attributable to basic benefits, supplemental benefits, and prescription drug benefits. CMS may deny a bid if the plan sponsor proposes significant increases in cost-sharing or decreases in benefits offered under the plan. [42 C.F.R. § 422.256(a).]

Standards of bid review. CMS can accept bid amounts or proportions only if it determines that the bid amount and proportions are supported by actuarial bases and that the bid amount and proportions reasonably and equitably reflect the plan's estimated revenue requirements for providing the benefits under that plan. For coordinated care plans (including regional MA plans and specialized MA plans) and private fee-for-service plans, the actuarial value of plan basic cost-sharing, reduced by any supplemental benefits, may not exceed the actuarial value of deductibles, coinsurance, and copayments that would be applicable for the benefits to individuals entitled to benefits under Part A and enrolled under Part B in the plan's service area if they were not members of an MA organization for the year. [42 C.F.R. § 422.256(b).]

Substantial differences between bids. CMS will approve a bid only if it finds that the benefit package and plan costs represented by that bid are substantially different from the MA organization's other bid submissions. To be "substantially different," each bid must be significantly different from other plans of its plan type with respect to premiums, benefits, or cost-sharing structure. [42 C.F.R. § 422.256(b)(4).]

Negotiation process. The negotiation process may include the resubmission of information to allow MA organizations to modify their initial bid submissions to account for the outcome of CMS's regional benchmark calculations and CMS's calculation of the national average monthly bid amount. [42 C.F.R. § 422.256(c).]

Exceptions. For private fee-for-service plans, CMS will not review, negotiate, or approve the bid amount, proportions of the bid, or the amounts of the basic beneficiary premium and supplemental premium. In addition, CMS does not review, negotiate, or approve amounts submitted with regard to MA MSA plans, except to determine that the deductible does not exceed the statutory maximum. [42 C.F.R. § 422.256(d), (e).]

Release of MA bid pricing data. CMS will release to the public MA bid pricing data for MA plan bids accepted or approved by CMS for a contract year under 42 C.F.R. § 422.256. The annual release will contain MA bid pricing data from the final list of MA plan bids accepted or approved by CMS for a contract year that is at least five years before the upcoming calendar year. [42 C.F.R. § 422.272.]

Calculation of Medicare Advantage Benchmarks

CMS uses MA plan bid information to arrive at an amount to pay MA plans in each region, the monthly "benchmark" amount.

Area plans. The term "MA area-specific non-drug monthly benchmark amount" means, for a month in a year:

  • for MA local plans with service areas entirely within a single MA local area, $\frac{1}{12}$ of the blended benchmark amount, adjusted as appropriate for the purpose of risk adjustment; or

  • for MA local plans with service areas including more than one MA local area, an amount equal to the weighted average of the amount described above for the year for each local area (county) in the plan's service area, using as weights the projected number of enrollees in each MA local area that the plan used to calculate the bid amount, and adjusted as appropriate for the purpose of risk adjustment.

[Soc. Sec. Act § 1853(j); 42 C.F.R. § 422.258(a).]

¶406

Regional plans. For MA regional plans, the term "MA region-specific non-drug monthly benchmark amount" is the sum of two components: (1) the statutory component (based on a weighted average of local benchmarks in the region), and (2) the plan bid component (based on a weighted average of regional plan bids in the region). [42 C.F.R. § 422.258(b).] CMS calculates the monthly regional non-drug benchmark amount for each MA region using the components of described in 42 C.F.R. § 422.258(c).

"Blended benchmark" calculation. Beginning in 2012, a "blended benchmark" is used to determine payments for all MA plans except for MA plans under the Program of All-inclusive Care of the Elderly (PACE). [Soc. Sec. Act § 1853(n)(1); 42 C.F.R. § 422.258(d).]

The use of the "blended benchmark" was to be phased in over a four-year period if the benchmark amount was at least $30 and less than $50. If the benchmark amount is greater than $50, then the new blended benchmark will be phased in over six years. In no case will the blended benchmark for an MA area for the year be greater than the applicable amount for an MA area for the year. [Soc. Sec. Act § 1853(n)(3), (4).]

Applicable amount. The "applicable amount" is equal to the amount for the area for the previous year increased by the national per capita MA growth percentage, for that succeeding year. [Soc. Sec. Act § 1853(k); 42 C.F.R. § 422.258(d)(2).]

Specified amount. The specified amount is the product of the base payment amount for an area for a year (adjusted as required) multiplied by the applicable percentage for an area for a year. [Soc. Sec. Act § 1853(n)(2); 42 C.F.R. § 422.258(d)(3).]

Base payment amount. The "base payment amount" is calculated by taking the previous year's base payment amount and increasing it by the national per capita MA growth percentage taking into account the phase-out in indirect cost of medical education from capitation rates. [Soc. Sec. Act § 1853(n)(2)(E); 42 C.F.R. § 422.258(d)(4).]

Applicable percentage. The "applicable percentage" is as follows:

- for MA plans in the highest quartile ranking of payments for the previous year, the applicable percentage is 95 percent;

- for MA plans in the second highest quartile ranking of payments for the previous year, the applicable percentage is 100 percent;

- for MA plans in the third highest quartile ranking of payments for the previous year, the applicable percentage is 107.5 percent; and

- for MA plans in the fourth highest quartile ranking of payments for the previous year, the applicable percentage is 115 percent.

[Soc. Sec. Act § 1853(n)(2)(B); 42 C.F.R. § 422.258(d)(5).]

Increases to the applicable percentage for quality of care. Plans rated at least four stars based on a five-star system stemming from the data collected under Soc. Sec. Act § 1852(e) receive bonus payments. Plans that fail to report data receive a rating of fewer than 3.5 stars. [Soc. Sec. Act § 1853(o)(4)(B); 42 C.F.R. § 422.258(d)(7)(iii).]

For 2014 and later, MA plans that have a quality rating of four stars or higher will have their applicable percentage increased by 5.0 percent. A new plan (i.e., an organization that has not had a contract as a MA provider in the previous three years) that meets the criteria to be considered a qualifying plan will have its applicable percentage increased by 3.5 percent. [Soc. Sec. Act § 1853(o); 42 C.F.R. § 422.258(d)(7).]

Calculation of Savings for MA Plans

The average per capita monthly savings for an MA local plan is 100 percent of the difference between the plan's risk-adjusted statutory non-drug monthly bid amount and the plan's risk-adjusted area-specific non-drug monthly benchmark amount. Plans with bids equal to or greater than plan benchmarks will have zero savings. [42 C.F.R. § 422.264(b).]

The risk-adjusted MA statutory non-drug monthly bid amount is the unadjusted plan bid amount for coverage of original Medicare benefits adjusted using the factors for local and regional plans. [42 C.F.R. § 422.264(a)(1).]

The risk-adjusted MA *area-specific* and *region-specific* non-drug monthly benchmark amounts are the unadjusted benchmark amount for coverage of original Medicare benefits by a local MA plan. [42 C.F.R. § 422.264(a)(2), (3).]

For MA local plans, CMS has the authority to apply risk adjustment factors that are plan-specific average risk adjustment factors or statewide average risk adjustment factors or to use other factors. If CMS applies statewide average risk adjustment factors, the statewide factor for each state is the average of the risk factors based on all enrollees in MA local plans in that state in the previous year. [42 C.F.R. § 422.264(c).]

MA regional plan computation. The average per capita monthly savings for an MA regional plan and year is 100 percent of the difference between the plan's risk-adjusted statutory non-drug monthly bid amount and the plan's risk-adjusted region-specific non-drug monthly benchmark amount, using the risk adjustment factors described below. Plans with bids equal to or greater than plan benchmarks will have zero savings. [42 C.F.R. § 422.264(d).]

Risk adjustment factors for regional plan savings. For regional plans, CMS has the authority to apply risk adjustment factors that are plan-specific average risk adjustment factors, region-wide average risk adjustment factors, or factors determined on a basis other than MA regions. In the event that CMS applies region-wide average risk adjustment factors, the region-wide factor for each MA region is the average of all risk factors, based on all enrollees in MA regional plans in that region in the previous year. [42 C.F.R. § 422.264(e).]

Medicare Advantage Beneficiary Rebates

An MA organization must provide to the enrollee a monthly rebate equal to a specified percentage of the average per capita savings for MA local plans and regional plans. For 2014 and later, this percentage is determined based on the following final rebate percentage:

- for plans with at least 4.5 stars, 70 percent of the average per capita savings;
- for plans with at least 3.5 stars and fewer than 4.5 stars, 65 percent of the average per capita savings; and
- for plans with fewer than 3.5 stars, 50 percent of the average per capita savings.

[Soc. Sec. Act § 1854(b)(1)(C); 42 C.F.R. § 422.266(a).]

New MA plans. A new MA plan is treated as having a rating of 3.5 stars for purposes of determining the beneficiary rebate amount. [Soc. Sec. Act § 1854(b)(1)(C)(vi); 42 C.F.R. § 422.266(a)(2)(iv).]

Form of rebate. MA organizations must provide the rebate by crediting the amount to the enrollee's supplemental health care benefits, payment of the premium for prescription drug coverage, or payment toward the Part B premium. [42 C.F.R. § 422.266(b).]

Disclosure of rebate. MA organizations must disclose to CMS information on the amount of the rebate provided. MA organizations must also distinguish, for each MA plan, the amount of rebate applied to enhance original Medicare benefits from the amount of rebate applied to enhance Part D benefits. [Soc. Sec. Act § 1854(b)(1)(C)(vii); 42 C.F.R. § 422.266(c).]

[¶ 407] Beneficiary Premiums and Cost-Sharing

Medicare Advantage (MA) enrollees are responsible for cost-sharing, including copayments, coinsurance, and deductibles, and premiums, which vary by plan.

Beneficiary Cost-Sharing

There are three forms of beneficiary cost-sharing under the MA program: copayments, coinsurance, and deductibles. A copayment is a fixed amount that can be charged for a service; coinsurance is a fixed percentage of the total cost of a service that can be charged. [42 C.F.R. § 422.2.]

Balance billing. "Balance billing" is the amount billed by a provider that is the difference between the amount the provider charges an individual for a service, and the sum of the amount the individual's health insurer will pay, plus any cost-sharing by the individual. [42 C.F.R. § 422.2.]

An MA organization that offers a private fee-for-service plan must furnish enrolled beneficiaries with an appropriate explanation of benefits, including a clear statement of the beneficiary's liability. The organization also must require that hospitals provide notice to beneficiaries before they receive inpatient hospital or other services when the amount of balance billing could be $500 or more. This notice must include a good faith estimate of the balance billing. [42 C.F.R. § 422.216(d).]

Services of noncontracting providers. An MA organization must make timely and reasonable payment to, or on behalf of, the plan enrollee for certain services obtained from a provider or supplier that does not contract with the MA organization to provide services covered by the MA plan. These services are outlined in ¶ 402. An MA plan (and an MA medical savings account (MSA) plan, after the annual deductible has been met) offered by an MA organization satisfies the timely and reasonable payment requirements with respect to benefits for services furnished by a noncontracting provider if that MA plan provides payment in an amount the provider would have received under original Medicare, including balance billing permitted under Medicare Part A and Part B. [42 C.F.R. § 422.100(b).] An MA plan may charge a higher copayment if a beneficiary chooses to receive covered health care services from providers who do not have contracts or agreements with the MA plan. [Soc. Sec. Act § 1852(d)(4)(b).]

Cost-sharing for certain benefits. MA beneficiaries who need: (1) chemotherapy administration services; (2) renal dialysis services; (3) skilled nursing care; and (4) other services that the HHS Secretary determines appropriate generally will not be subjected to higher cost-sharing for these services than traditional fee-for-service Medicare (Medicare Parts A and B) beneficiaries pay. [Soc. Sec. Act § 1852(a)(1)(B)(iii).]

In the case of an individual who is a full-benefit dual eligible or a qualified Medicare beneficiary enrolled in an MA special needs plan (SNP), the plan may not impose cost-sharing that exceeds the amount of cost-sharing that would be permitted under Medicaid. [Soc. Sec. Act § 1852(a)(7).]

Deductibles. MA regional and local preferred provider organization (PPO) plans, to the extent they apply a deductible: (1) must have a single deductible related to all in-network and out-of-network Medicare Part A and Part B services; (2) may specify separate deductible amounts for specific in-network Medicare Part A and Part B services, to the extent these deductible amounts apply to that single deductible amount; (3) may waive other plan-covered items and services from the single deductible; and (4) must waive all Medicare-covered preventive services from the single deductible. [42 C.F.R. § 422.101(d)(1).]

Refunds. An MA organization must agree to refund all amounts incorrectly collected from its Medicare enrollees, or from others on behalf of the enrollees, and to pay any other amounts due the enrollees or others on their behalf. The MA organization must use lump-sum payments for: (1) amounts incorrectly collected that were not collected as premiums; (2) other amounts due; and (3) all amounts due if the MA organization is going out of business or terminating its MA contract for an MA plan. If the amounts incorrectly collected were in the form of premiums or included premiums as well as other charges, the MA organization may refund by adjustment of future premiums or by a combination of premium adjustment and lump-sum payments. If an enrollee has died or cannot be located after reasonable effort, the MA organization must make the refund in accordance with state law. [42 C.F.R. § 422.270(b), (c).]

If the MA organization does not make the required refund by the end of the contract period following the contract period during which an amount was determined to be due to an enrollee, CMS will reduce the premium the MA organization is allowed to charge an MA plan enrollee by the amounts incorrectly collected or otherwise due. In addition, the MA organization is subject to sanction for failure to refund amounts incorrectly collected from MA plan enrollees. [42 C.F.R. § 422.270(d).]

Beneficiary Premiums

If an MA plan has an unadjusted statutory non-drug bid amount that is less than the relevant unadjusted CMS non-drug benchmark amount (see ¶ 406), the monthly basic beneficiary premium is zero. If the plan's bid amount is equal to or greater than the relevant unadjusted non-drug benchmark amount, the basic beneficiary premium is the amount by which the bid amount exceeds the benchmark amount. The benchmark is a bidding target used by CMS and based on rates paid to MA plans before 2006. [42 C.F.R § 422.262(a).]

Consolidated monthly premium. MA organizations must charge enrollees a consolidated monthly MA premium, which is equal to the sum of the MA monthly basic beneficiary premium (if any), the MA monthly supplementary beneficiary premium (if any), and the MA monthly prescription drug beneficiary premium (if any). For MSA plans offered by an MA organization, the monthly beneficiary premium is the supplemental premium. [Soc. Sec. Act § 1854(b); 42 C.F.R § 422.262(b).]

Uniformity of premiums. Except as permitted for supplemental premiums for MA contracts with employers and labor organizations, the MA monthly bid amount, the MA monthly basic beneficiary premium, the MA monthly supplemental beneficiary premium, the MA monthly prescription drug premium, and the monthly MSA premium of an MA organization may not vary among individuals enrolled in an MA plan. In addition, the MA organization cannot vary the level of cost-sharing charged for basic benefits or supplemental benefits among individuals enrolled in an MA plan. An MA organization may apply these uniformity requirements to segments of an MA local plan service area (rather than to the entire service area) as long as such a segment is composed of one or more MA payment areas. The bid information required by 42 C.F.R. § 422.254 (see ¶ 406) is submitted separately for each segment. This rule does not apply to MA regional plans. [42 C.F.R § 422.262(c).]

Monetary inducement prohibited. An MA organization may not provide cash or other monetary rebates as an inducement for enrollment or for any other reason or purpose. [42 C.F.R § 422.262(d).]

¶407

Timing of payments. The MA organization must permit payments of MA monthly basic and supplemental beneficiary premiums and monthly prescription drug beneficiary premiums on a monthly basis. [42 C.F.R § 422.262(e).]

Method of payment. An MA organization must permit each enrollee, at his or her option, to make payment of premiums to the organization through: (1) withholding from the enrollee's Social Security benefit payments, or benefit payments by the Railroad Retirement Board or the Office of Personnel Management, in the manner that the Part B premium is withheld (a charge may not be imposed on beneficiaries for the election of this withholding option); (2) an electronic funds transfer mechanism; or (3) by other means that CMS may specify, including payment by an employer or under employment-based retiree health coverage on behalf of an employee, former employee, or by other third parties such as a state. An enrollee may opt to make a direct payment of premium to the plan. [42 C.F.R § 422.262(f).]

Retroactive premium collection. In circumstances where retroactive collection of premium amounts is necessary and the enrollee is without fault in creating the premium arrearage, the MA organization must offer the enrollee the option of payment either by lump sum, by equal monthly installment spread out over at least the same period for which the premiums were due, or through other arrangements mutually acceptable to the enrollee and the MA organization. For example, for monthly installments, if seven months of premiums are due, the member would have at least seven months to repay. [42 C.F.R § 422.262(h).]

[¶ 408] Payments to Medicare Advantage Organizations

CMS makes advance monthly payments to Medicare Advantage (MA) plans for coverage of original fee-for-service (FFS) benefits for an individual in an MA payment area for a month. [Soc. Sec. Act § 1853(a)(1); 42 C.F.R. § 422.304(a)(1).]

For MA plans that have average per capita monthly savings, i.e., bids below the benchmark (see ¶ 406), CMS pays:

- the unadjusted MA statutory non-drug monthly bid amount risk-adjusted and adjusted (if applicable) for variations in rates within the plan's service area and for the effects of risk adjustment on beneficiary premiums; and

- the amount (if any) of any rebate.

[Soc. Sec. Act § 1853(a)(1)(B)(i); 42 C.F.R. § 422.304(a).]

For MA plans that do not have average per capita monthly savings, i.e., plans with bids at or above benchmark, CMS pays the unadjusted MA area-specific non-drug monthly benchmark amount, risk-adjusted and adjusted (if applicable) for variations in rates within the plan's service area and for the effects of risk adjustment on beneficiary premiums. [Soc. Sec. Act § 1853(a)(1)(B)(ii); 42 C.F.R. § 422.304(a).]

Federal drug subsidies. MA organizations offering an MA prescription drug (MA-PD) plan also receive: (1) direct and reinsurance subsidy payments for qualified prescription drug coverage; and (2) reimbursement for premium and cost-sharing reductions for low-income individuals. [Soc. Sec. Act § 1853(a)(1)(D); 42 C.F.R. § 422.304(b).]

Enrollees with ESRD. For enrollees with end-stage renal disease (ESRD), CMS establishes special rates that are actuarially equivalent to rates in effect before the enactment of the Medicare Modernization Act of 2003 (MMA) (P.L. 108-173). CMS publishes annual changes in these capitation rates no later than the first Monday in April each year. [Soc. Sec. Act § 1853(a)(1)(H); 42 C.F.R. § 422.304(c)(1).]

Medical savings account enrollees. For medical savings account (MSA) plans, CMS pays the unadjusted MA area-specific non-drug monthly benchmark amount for the service area, subject to risk adjustment as set forth at 42 C.F.R. § 422.308(c), less $\frac{1}{12}$ of the annual lump sum amount (if any) CMS deposits to the enrollee's MA MSA. [Soc. Sec. Act § 1853(e); 42 C.F.R. § 422.304(c)(2).]

Religious fraternal benefit plan enrollees. For enrollees in religious fraternal benefit (RFB) plans, CMS adjusts the capitation payments, either on an individual or organization basis, to ensure that the payment level is appropriate for the actuarial characteristics and experience of these enrollees. [Soc. Sec. Act § 1859(e)(4); 42 C.F.R. § 422.304(c)(3).]

Annual Capitation Rates for MA Local Areas

Except for years when CMS rebases the FFS rates, the annual capitation rate for each MA local area is equal to the minimum percentage increase rate, which is the annual capitation rate for the area for the preceding year increased by the national per capita MA growth percentage for the year. [42 C.F.R. § 422.306(a); *Medicare Managed Care Manual*, Pub. 100-16, Ch. 8, § 20.2.]

In rebasing years, the annual capitation rate for each MA local area is the greater of: (1) the minimum percentage increase rate; or (2) the amount determined, no less frequently than every three years, to be the adjusted average per capita cost for the MA local area, based on 100 percent of FFS costs for individuals who are not enrolled in an MA plan for the year, adjusted: (a) as appropriate for the purpose of risk adjustment; (b) to exclude costs attributable to payments for the costs of direct graduate medical education; (c) to include CMS's estimate of the amount of additional per capita payments that would have been made in the MA local area if individuals entitled to benefits under this title had not received services from facilities of the Department of Defense or the Department of Veterans Affairs; and (d) to exclude costs attributable to Medicare FFS incentive payments for meaningful use of electronic health records. [42 C.F.R. § 422.306(b).]

Phase-out of the indirect cost of medical education as an MA capitation rate component. After CMS determines the annual capitation rate for each MA local area, it adjusts the amount to exclude the phase-in percentage for the year of the estimated costs for payments of indirect medical education costs in the area for the year. [Soc. Sec. Act § 1853(k)(4); 42 C.F.R. § 422.306(c).]

Announcement of annual capitation rate. All payment rates are annual rates, determined and promulgated by HHS. The HHS Secretary will determine and announce, not later than the first Monday in April before the calendar year concerned, the annual capitation rate, payment area, and risk adjustment factors. HHS must publish proposed changes to the payment methodology no later than 60 days (before 2017, at least 45 days) before annual announcement of rates. Beginning in 2017, MA organizations have at least 30 days to comment on the proposed changes. [Soc. Sec. Act § 1853(b)(2); 42 C.F.R. § 422.312.]

2017 capitation rates. In accordance with section 1853(b)(1) of the Social Security Act, CMS notified MA organizations of the annual MA capitation rate for each MA payment area for calendar year 2017 and the risk and other factors to be used in adjusting such rates. The capitation rate tables for 2017 are posted on the CMS website at http://www.cms.gov/ Medicare/Health-Plans/MedicareAdvtgSpecRateStats/index.html under Ratebooks and Supporting Data. The statutory component of the regional benchmarks, transitional phase-in periods for the rates from the Patient Protection and Affordable Care Act (ACA) (P.L. 111-148), qualifying counties, and each county's applicable percentage are also posted at this website. CMS issued final capitation rates on April 4, 2016, which are found at the website noted above.

¶408

Special Rules for Payments to MA Organizations

Services for beneficiaries enrolled in MA plans that are subject to a plan's moral or religious exception approved by CMS (see ¶ 411) are billable as fee-for-service to Medicare contractors for coverage and payment determinations. The lists of services may vary between MA plans. Beneficiaries enrolled in such plans are responsible for applicable coinsurance for the excepted services, but the deductible will be deemed met. [42 C.F.R. § 422.206(b); *Medicare Claims Processing Manual*, Pub. 100-04, Ch. 1, § 91.]

Rules for MSA plans. A beneficiary who elects coverage under an MA MSA plan must establish an MA MSA with a trustee that meets certain requirements and, if he or she has more than one MA MSA, designate the particular account to which payments under the MA MSA plan are to be made. [42 C.F.R. § 422.314.]

Payments to the MA MSA are calculated by comparing the monthly MA MSA premium with $1/12$ of the annual capitation rate for the area. If the monthly MA MSA premium is less than $1/12$ of the annual capitation rate applied for the area, the difference is the amount to be deposited in the MA MSA for each month for which the beneficiary is enrolled in the MSA plan. CMS deposits the full amount to which a beneficiary is entitled for the calendar year, beginning with the month in which MA MSA coverage begins. If the beneficiary's coverage under the MA MSA plan ends before the end of the calendar year, CMS recovers the amount that corresponds to the remaining months of that year. [Soc. Sec. Act § 1853(e); 42 C.F.R. § 422.314.]

Special rules for payments to federally qualified health centers. If an enrollee in an MA plan receives a service from a federally qualified health center (FQHC) that has a written agreement with the MA organization offering services to the plan, CMS will pay the FQHC directly for the services at a minimum on a quarterly basis, less the amount the FQHC would receive for the MA enrollee from the MA organization and taking into account the cost-sharing amount paid by the enrollee. [Soc. Sec. Act § 1853(a)(4); 42 C.F.R. § 422.316.]

Special rules for coverage that begins or ends during an inpatient hospital stay. If coverage under an MA plan begins while the beneficiary is an inpatient, the previous MA organization or original Medicare, as appropriate, makes payment for inpatient services until the date of the beneficiary's discharge. The MA organization offering the newly elected MA plan is not responsible for the inpatient services until the date after the beneficiary's discharge. The MA organization offering the newly elected MA plan is paid the full amount otherwise payable. [Soc. Sec. Act § 1853(g); 42 C.F.R. § 422.318(b).]

If coverage under an MA plan ends while the beneficiary is an inpatient, the MA organization is responsible for the inpatient services until the date of the beneficiary's discharge. Neither original Medicare nor any succeeding MA organization offering a newly elected MA plan will make payment for those services during the remainder of the stay. The MA organization that no longer provides coverage receives no payment for the beneficiary for the period after coverage ends. [Soc. Sec. Act § 1853(g); 42 C.F.R. § 422.318(c).]

Special rules for hospice care. MA organizations do not cover hospice care. An MA organization must inform each Medicare enrollee eligible to elect hospice care about the availability of hospice care if a Medicare hospice program is located within the plan's service area or it is common practice to refer patients to hospice programs outside that area. Unless the enrollee disenrolls from the MA plan, a beneficiary electing hospice continues his or her enrollment in the MA plan and is entitled to receive, through the MA plan, any benefits other than those that are the responsibility of the Medicare hospice. No payment is made to an MA organization on behalf of a Medicare enrollee who has elected hospice care, except for the portion of the payment attributable to the beneficiary rebate for the MA plan plus the amount of the monthly prescription drug payment, if any. This no-payment rule is effective from the first day of the month following the month of election to receive hospice care until the first day of the month following the month in which the election is terminated. [Soc. Sec. Act § 1853(h); 42 C.F.R. § 422.320.]

[¶ 409] Marketing Requirements

A Medicare Advantage (MA) organization may not distribute any marketing materials or election forms or make such materials or forms available to individuals eligible to elect an MA organization unless it submits the material or form to CMS for review and CMS did not disapprove the distribution. [Soc. Sec. Act § 1851(h); 42 C.F.R. § 422.2262(a).]

Definition of "Marketing Materials"

Marketing materials include any informational materials targeted to Medicare beneficiaries that: (1) promote the MA organization or MA plan; (2) inform beneficiaries that they may enroll, or remain enrolled, in a plan; (3) explain the benefits of enrollment or the rules that apply to enrollees; and (4) explain how Medicare services are covered under an MA plan, including coverage conditions. These marketing materials may include:

(1) general audience materials in such mediums as general circulation brochures, newspapers, magazines, television, radio, billboards, yellow pages, or the Internet;

(2) marketing representative materials such as scripts or outlines for telemarketing or other presentations;

(3) presentation materials such as slides and charts;

(4) promotional materials such as brochures or leaflets, including materials for circulation by third parties such as physicians or other providers;

(5) membership communication materials such as membership rules, subscriber agreements, member handbooks, and wallet card instructions;

(6) letters to members about contractual changes, changes in providers, premiums, benefits, and plan procedures; and

(7) membership activities, such as materials on rules involving non-payment of premiums, confirmation of enrollment or disenrollment, or non-claim specific notification information.

[42 C.F.R. 422.2260.]

Ad hoc materials excluded. Marketing materials exclude ad hoc enrollee communications materials, meaning materials: (1) targeted to current enrollees, (2) customized or limited to a subset of enrollees or that apply to a specific situation, (3) that do not include information about the plan's benefit structure, and (4) that apply to a specific situation or cover claims processing or other operational issues. [42 C.F.R. 422.2260(6).] CMS may review such ad hoc enrollee communication materials and determine whether they must be modified or may no longer be used. [42 C.F.R. § 422.2262(d).]

CMS Review of MA Organizations' Marketing Materials

An MA organization may not distribute any marketing materials or election forms or make such materials or forms available to individuals eligible to elect an MA organization unless, at least 45 days before the date of distribution, the organization submitted the material or form to CMS for review and CMS did not disapprove the distribution. The time period may be reduced to 10 days if the materials use CMS proposed model language and format. [Soc. Sec. Act § 1851(h)(1), (3), (5); 42 C.F.R. § 422.2262(a).]

File and use. The MA organization may distribute certain CMS-designated marketing materials five days following their submission to CMS if the organization certifies that it followed all applicable marketing guidelines and, when applicable, used CMS-specified model language without modification. When specified by CMS, organizations must use standardized formats and language in model materials. [42 C.F.R. § 422.2262(b), (c).]

Review guidelines. In reviewing marketing material or election forms, CMS determines whether the materials provide: (1) adequate written description of rules, procedures, basic benefits and services, and fees and other charges; (2) adequate written description of any supplemental benefits and services; (3) adequate written explanation of the grievance and appeals process (including differences between the two, and when it is appropriate to use each); and (4) any other information necessary to enable beneficiaries to make an informed enrollment decision. [42 C.F.R. § 422.2264(a).]

CMS must also make sure that the materials: (1) notify the general public of its enrollment period in an appropriate manner, through appropriate media, throughout its service area and, if applicable, continuation areas; (2) include a written notice that the MA organization is authorized by law to refuse to renew its contract with CMS, that CMS also may refuse to renew the contract, and that termination or non-renewal may result in termination of the beneficiary's enrollment in the plan; (3) are not materially inaccurate or misleading or otherwise make material misrepresentations; and (4) for markets with a significant non-English-speaking population, are provided in the language of these individuals. [42 C.F.R. § 422.2264(b)–(e).]

Marketing Prohibitions for MA Organizations

When conducting marketing activities, an MA plan or organization may not:

• provide cash or other monetary rebates as an inducement for enrollment or otherwise;

• offer gifts to potential enrollees, unless the gifts are of nominal value, are offered to all potential enrollees without regard to whether they enroll, and are not in the form of cash or other monetary rebates;

• engage in any discriminatory activity, such as attempts to recruit Medicare beneficiaries from higher income areas without making comparable efforts to enroll Medicare beneficiaries from lower income areas;

• solicit door-to-door for Medicare beneficiaries or through other unsolicited means of direct contact, including calling a beneficiary when the beneficiary did not initiate the contact;

• engage in activities that could mislead or confuse Medicare beneficiaries or misrepresent the MA organization, such as claiming it is recommended or endorsed by CMS or Medicare or that CMS or Medicare recommends that the beneficiary enroll in the MA plan;

• market non-health care-related products to prospective enrollees during any MA or Part D sales activity or presentation;

• market any health care-related product during a marketing appointment beyond the scope agreed upon by the beneficiary, and documented by the plan, before the appointment (48 hours in advance, when practicable);

• market additional health-related lines of plan business not identified before an individual appointment without a separate appointment identifying the additional lines of business to be discussed;

¶409

- distribute marketing materials for which, before expiration of the 45-day period, the MA organization receives from CMS written notice of disapproval because it is inaccurate or misleading or misrepresents the MA organization, its marketing representatives, or CMS;

- use providers or provider groups to distribute printed information comparing the benefits of different health plans unless the providers, provider groups, or pharmacies accept and display materials from all health plans with which the providers, provider groups, or pharmacies contract;

- conduct sales presentations or distribute and accept MA plan enrollment forms in provider offices or other areas where health care is delivered to individuals, except in the case where such activities are conducted in common areas in health care settings;

- conduct sales presentations or distribute and accept plan applications at educational events;

- employ MA plan names that suggest that a plan is not available to all Medicare beneficiaries (this prohibition does not apply to MA plan names in effect on July 31, 2000);

- display the names and/or logos of co-branded network providers on the organization's member identification card, unless the provider names and/or logos are related to the member selection of specific provider organizations (other marketing materials that include names and/or logos of provider co-branding partners must clearly indicate that other providers are available in the network);

- engage in any other marketing activity prohibited by CMS in its marketing guidance;

- provide meals for potential enrollees, regardless of value; and

- use a plan name that does not include the name of the plan type at the end of the plan name.

[Soc. Sec. Act § 1851(h)(4) and (6), (j); 42 C.F.R. § 422.2268.]

Confirmation of MA Organizations' Marketing Resources

The MA organization must demonstrate to CMS that its marketing resources are allocated to marketing to the disabled Medicare population as well as to beneficiaries age 65 and over. MA organizations must also establish and maintain a system for confirming that enrolled beneficiaries have, in fact, enrolled in the MA plan and understand the rules applicable under the plan. [42 C.F.R. § 422.2272(a), (b).]

Licensing of Marketing Representatives

MA organizations must employ as marketing representatives only individuals who are licensed by the state to conduct marketing activities in that state. The organization must inform the state that it has appointed these individuals as marketing representatives as required by the appointment process provided for under state law. [Soc. Sec. Act § 1851(h)(7); 42 C.F.R. § 422.2272(c).]

The MA organization must also report the termination of any such agent or broker to the state, including the reasons for such termination if the state requires that the reasons for the termination be reported. Finally, an MA organization must terminate any unlicensed agent or broker employed as a marketing representative and notify any beneficiaries who have been enrolled by an unqualified agent or broker of the agent's or broker's termination and, if requested, of their options to confirm enrollment or make a plan change, including a special election period. [Soc. Sec. Act § 1851(h)(7); 42 C.F.R. § 422.2272(d), (e).]

Broker and Agent Requirements

If an MA organization uses agents and brokers to sell its plans, it must: (1) follow compensation rules established by CMS; (2) ensure agents selling Medicare products are trained annually on Medicare rules and regulations and details specific to the plan products they intend to sell; and (3) ensure agents selling Medicare products are tested annually to ensure appropriate knowledge and understanding of Medicare rules and regulations and details specific to the plan products they intend to sell. [Soc. Sec. Act § 1851(j)(2); 42 C.F.R. § 422.2274(b)–(f).]

"Compensation" defined. Compensation includes monetary or nonmonetary remuneration of any kind relating to the sale or renewal of the policy, including commissions, bonuses, gifts, prizes, awards, and referral or finder fees. Compensation does *not* include: (1) the payment of fees to comply with state appointment laws, training, certification, and testing costs; (2) reimbursement for mileage to and from appointments with beneficiaries; or (3) reimbursement for actual costs associated with beneficiary sales appointments such as venue rent, snacks, and materials. [42 C.F.R. § 422.2274(a).]

Compensation amounts. An MA organization must compensate independent brokers and agents, if it pays compensation, as follows. For an initial year enrollment of a Medicare beneficiary into an MA plan, the compensation must be at or below the fair market value of such services, published annually as a cut-off amount by CMS. For renewal years, compensation may be up to 50 percent of the current fair market value cut-off amounts published annually by CMS. [Soc. Sec. Act § 1851(j)(2)(D); 42 C.F.R. § 422.2274(b)(1).]

If the MA organization contracts with a third-party entity such as a field management organization or similar type entity to sell its insurance products or perform services: (1) the amount paid to the third party and its agents for enrollment of a beneficiary into a plan must be the same as paid to non-third-party agents and brokers; and (2) the amount paid to the third party for services other than selling insurance products, if any, must be fair market value and must not exceed an amount that is commensurate with the amounts paid by the MA organization to a third party for similar services during each of the previous two years. [42 C.F.R. § 422.2274(b)(1).]

Aggregate compensation. An entity must not provide aggregate compensation to its agents or brokers greater than the renewal compensation payable by the replacing plan on renewal policies if an existing policy is replaced with a "like plan type" at any time. The initial compensation is paid for replacements between unlike plan types. [42 C.F.R. § 422.2274(b)(2).]

Plan year compensation. Compensation may be paid only for the beneficiary's months of enrollment during a plan year. Compensation payments may be made up front for the entire current plan year or in installments throughout the year. When a beneficiary disenrolls from an MA plan, the MA organization must recover compensation paid to agents and brokers for those months of the plan year for which the beneficiary is not enrolled. For disenrollments occurring within the first three months, the entire compensation must be recovered unless CMS determines that recoupment is not in the best interests of the Medicare program. [42 C.F.R. § 422.2274(b)(3).]

Finder's fees. Finder's (referral) fees paid to all agents and brokers (1) may not exceed an amount that CMS determines could reasonably be expected to provide financial incentive for an agent or broker to recommend or enroll a beneficiary into a plan that is not the most appropriate to meet his or her needs; and (2) must be included in the total compensation not to exceed the fair market value for that calendar year. [42 C.F.R. § 422.2274(h).]

Compensation structure. MA organizations must establish a compensation structure for new and replacement enrollments and renewals effective in a given plan year. Compensation structures must be in place by the beginning of the plan marketing period, October 1. [42 C.F.R. § 422.2274(b)(4).]

Employer Group Retiree Marketing

MA organizations may develop marketing materials designed for members of an employer group who are eligible for employer-sponsored benefits through the MA organization and furnish these materials only to the group members. These materials are not subject to CMS prior review and approval. [42 C.F.R. § 422.2276.]

[¶ 410] Quality Improvement Programs

Medicare Advantage (MA) organizations that offer one or more MA plans must have, for each of those plans, an ongoing quality improvement program for services provided to enrollees. An MA plan must: (1) create a quality improvement program plan that sufficiently outlines the elements of the plan's quality improvement program; (2) have a chronic care improvement program; (3) conduct quality improvement projects that can be expected to have a favorable effect on health outcomes and enrollee satisfaction; and (4) encourage its providers to participate in CMS and HHS quality improvement initiatives. [Soc. Sec. Act § 1852(e); 42 C.F.R. § 422.152(a), (c), (d); *Medicare Managed Care Manual*, Pub. 100-16, Ch. 5, § 20.1.]

Requirements for all plan types. For all types of plans that it offers, an organization must: (1) maintain a health information system that collects, analyzes, and integrates the data necessary to implement its quality improvement program; (2) ensure that the information it receives from providers of services is reliable and complete; and (3) make all collected information available to CMS. For each plan, there must be in effect a process for formal evaluation, at least annually, of the impact and effectiveness of its quality improvement program. In addition, the organization must correct all problems that come to its attention through internal surveillance, complaints, or other mechanisms. [42 C.F.R. § 422.152(f); Pub. 100-16, Ch. 5, § § 20, 20.1.]

Requirements for MA coordinated care plans. An MA coordinated care plan (except for local and regional preferred provider organization (PPO) plans) must have a quality improvement program that: (1) in processing requests for initial or continued authorization of services, follows written policies and procedures that reflect current standards of medical practice; (2) has in effect mechanisms to detect both under-utilization and over-utilization of service; and (3) measures and reports performance. These requirements also apply to MA local PPO-type plans that are offered by an organization that is licensed or organized under state law as a health maintenance organization. [42 C.F.R. § 422.152(b).]

All coordinated care contracts (including local and regional PPOs, contracts with exclusively special needs plan (SNP) benefit packages, private fee-for-service (PFFS) contracts, and medical savings account (MSA) contracts) and all cost contracts under section 1876 of the Social Security Act with 600 or more enrollees in July of the prior year must contract with approved Medicare Consumer Assessment of Healthcare Providers and Systems (CAHPS) survey vendors to conduct the Medicare CAHPS satisfaction survey of plan enrollees and submit the survey data to CMS. [42 C.F.R. § 422.152(b)(5).]

Requirements for MA regional plans and MA local plans. MA organizations offering an MA regional plan or local PPO plan must: (1) measure performance under the plan using standard measures required by CMS and report its performance to CMS; (2) collect, analyze, and report the data; and (3) evaluate the continuity and coordination of care furnished to enrollees. If the organization uses written protocols for utilization review, the organization must: (1) base those protocols on current standards of medical practice; and (2) have mechanisms to evaluate utilization of services and to inform enrollees and providers of services of the results of the evaluation. [Soc. Sec. Act § 1852(e)(3)(A)(iii); 42 C.F.R. § 422.152(e).]

Requirements for MA PFFS plans and Medicare MSA plans. MA PFFS and MSA plans are subject to requirements that may not exceed the requirement specified for MA regional plans and MA local plans. [42 C.F.R. § 422.152(h).]

Specialized MA plans for special needs individuals. All SNPs for special needs individuals must be approved by the National Committee for Quality Assurance (NCQA) and must submit their model of care to CMS for NCQA evaluation and approval. A SNP, in addition to the requirements of 42 C.F.R. § 422.152(a) and (f), must conduct a quality improvement program that: (1) provides for the collection, analysis, and reporting of data that measures health outcomes and indices of quality pertaining to its targeted special needs population (i.e., dual eligible, institutionalized, or chronic condition) at the plan level; (2) makes available information on quality and outcomes measures that will enable beneficiaries to compare health coverage options and CMS to monitor the plan's model of care performance; and (3) measures the effectiveness of its model of care through the collection, aggregation, analysis, and reporting of data that demonstrate the following:

- access to care as evidenced by measures from the care coordination domain (e.g., service and benefit utilization rates);

- improvement in beneficiary health status as evidenced by measures from functional, psychosocial, or clinical domains (e.g., quality of life indicators, depression scales, or chronic disease outcomes);

- staff implementation of the SNP model of care as evidenced by measures of care structure and process from the continuity of care domain (e.g., NCQA accreditation measures or medication reconciliation associated with care setting transitions indicators);

- comprehensive health risk assessment as evidenced by measures from the care coordination domain (e.g., accuracy of acuity stratification, safety indicators, or timeliness of initial assessments or annual reassessments);

- implementation of an individualized plan of care as evidenced by measures from functional, psychosocial, or clinical domains;

- a provider network that has targeted clinical expertise as evidenced by measures from medication management, disease management, or behavioral health domains;

- delivery of services across the continuum of care;

- delivery of extra services and benefits that meet the specialized needs of the most vulnerable beneficiaries as evidenced by measures from the psychosocial, functional, and end-of-life domains;

- use of evidence-based practices and nationally recognized clinical protocols; and

- use of integrated systems of communication as evidenced by measures from the care coordination domain (e.g., call center utilization rates and rates of beneficiary involvement in care plan development).

[Soc. Sec. Act § 1852(e)(3)(A)(ii); 42 C.F.R. § 422.152(g).]

Compliance Deemed on the Basis of Accreditation

CMS has the authority to deem MA organizations compliant with Medicare requirements. An MA organization is deemed to meet any of the following requirements if it is fully accredited, and periodically reaccredited, for the standards by a private, national accreditation organization approved by CMS and the accreditation organization used the standards approved by CMS for the purposes of assessing the MA organization's compliance with Medicare requirements:

(1) quality improvement;

(2) antidiscrimination;

(3) access to services;

(4) confidentiality and accuracy of enrollee records;

(5) information on advance directives;

(6) provider participation rules; and

(7) certain requirements for Part D prescription drug benefit programs offered by MA programs, including access to covered drugs, drug utilization management programs, quality assurance measures and methods, medication therapy management programs, and privacy, confidentiality, and accuracy of enrollee records.

[Soc. Sec. Act § 1852(e)(4); 42 C.F.R. §§ 422.156(a) and (b), 423.165(b).]

[¶ 411] Relationships with Providers

CMS has established requirements and standards for the Medicare Advantage (MA) organization's relationships with providers, including physicians, other health care professionals, and institutional providers and suppliers, under contracts or arrangements or deemed contracts under MA private fee-for-service (PFFS) plans. [Soc. Sec. Act § 1852(j)(1); 42 C.F.R. § 422.200.]

The term "providers" means individuals who are licensed or certified by a state to deliver health care services, such as doctors, nurse practitioners, and clinical social workers. The term also refers to the entities that deliver those services, including hospitals, nursing homes, and home health agencies. [42 C.F.R. § 422.2.]

Antidiscrimination rules. In selecting practitioners, an MA organization may not discriminate, in terms of participation, reimbursement, or indemnification, against any health care professional who is acting within the scope of his or her license or certification under state law solely on the basis of the license or certification. If an organization declines to include a given provider or group of providers in its network, it must furnish written notice to the affected providers of the reason for the decision. This antidiscrimination prohibition does not preclude the MA organization from: (1) refusing to grant participation to health care professionals in excess of the number necessary to meet the needs of the plan's enrollees (except for MA PFFS plans, which may not refuse to contract on this basis); (2) using different reimbursement amounts for different specialties or for different practitioners in the same specialty; or (3) implementing measures designed to maintain quality and control costs. [Soc. Sec. Act § 1852(b)(2); 42 C.F.R. § 422.205.]

Physician incentive plans. Any physician incentive plan operated by an MA organization must meet the following basic requirements:

(1) The MA organization may not make any specific payment, directly or indirectly, to a physician or physician group as an inducement to reduce or limit medically necessary services furnished to any particular enrollee. Indirect payments may include offerings of monetary value measured in the present or future.

(2) If the physician incentive plan places a physician or physician group at substantial financial risk for services that the physician or physician group does not

furnish itself, the MA organization must ensure that all physicians and physician groups at substantial financial risk have either aggregate or per-patient stop-loss protection. [Soc. Sec. Act § 1852(j)(4); 42 C.F.R. § 422.208(c).]

An MA organization may not operate a physician incentive plan unless it provides satisfactory assurance to the HHS Secretary that these requirements are met. An MA organization must provide the following information to any Medicare beneficiary who requests it: (1) whether the organization uses a physician incentive plan that affects the use of referral services; (2) the type of incentive arrangement; and (3) whether it provides stop-loss protection. [42 C.F.R. §§ 422.208(c)(3), 422.210.]

Limits on provider indemnification. An MA organization is prohibited from having a provider or a provider group indemnify the organization against civil liability for damage arising from the organization's denial of medically necessary care. [Soc. Sec. Act § 1852(j)(5); 42 C.F.R. § 422.212.]

Special rules for noncontract providers. A provider that does not have a contract establishing the amount of payment for services furnished to a Medicare beneficiary enrolled in an MA plan must accept the amount that would have been paid under the original Medicare program as payment in full. [Soc. Sec. Act § 1852(k); 42 C.F.R. § 422.214(a)(1).]

Special rules for MA PFFS plans. For MA PFFS plans, the MA organization: (1) must establish payment rates for plan-covered items and services that apply to deemed providers; (2) may vary payment rates for providers; (3) must reimburse providers on a fee-for-service basis; and (4) must make information on its payment rates available to providers that furnish services that may be covered under the MA PFFS plan. [Soc. Sec. Act § 1852(j)(6); 42 C.F.R. § 422.216(a).]

Private contracting. An MA organization may not pay a physician or other practitioner for services (other than emergency or urgently needed services) furnished to a Medicare enrollee by a health care professional who has filed with the Medicare administrative contractor an affidavit promising to furnish Medicare-covered services to Medicare beneficiaries only through private contracts (see ¶ 872). An MA organization must pay for emergency or urgently needed services furnished by a physician or practitioner who has not signed a private contract with the beneficiary. [Soc. Sec. Act § 1852(k)(2)(B); 42 C.F.R. § 422.220.]

Provider Participation Requirements

An MA organization that operates a coordinated care plan or network medical savings account (MSA) plan must provide for the participation of individual physicians, and the management and members of groups of physicians, through reasonable procedures that include:

- written notice of rules of participation, including terms of payment, credentialing, and other rules directly related to participation decisions;
- written notice of material changes in participation rules before the changes are put in effect;
- written notice of participation decisions that are adverse to physicians; and
- a process for appealing adverse participation decisions, including the right of physicians to present information and their views on the decision.

[Soc. Sec. Act § 1852(j)(1); 42 C.F.R. § 422.202(a).]

Formal consultation with physicians. An MA organization must establish a formal mechanism to consult with the physicians who have agreed to provide services under the

MA plan, regarding the organization's medical policy, quality improvement programs, and medical management procedures. The organization must ensure that practice guidelines and utilization management guidelines communicated to providers and enrollees: (1) are based on reasonable medical evidence or a consensus of health care professionals in the particular field; (2) consider the needs of the enrolled population; (3) are developed in consultation with contracting health care professionals; and (4) are reviewed and updated periodically. [Soc. Sec. Act § 11852(j)(2); 42 C.F.R. § 422.202(b).]

Subcontracted groups. These provider participation procedures extend not only to direct contracting health care professionals, but also to those with subcontracted agreements. [42 C.F.R. § 422.202(c).]

Provider Selection and Credentialing

An MA organization must have written policies and procedures for the selection and evaluation of providers. The organization must follow a documented process with respect to providers and suppliers who have signed contracts or participation agreements.

- For providers (other than physicians and other health care professionals), the documented process requires determination, and redetermination at specified intervals, that each provider: (1) is licensed to operate in the state and is in compliance with any other applicable state or federal requirements; and (2) has been reviewed and approved by an accrediting body or meets the standards established by the organization itself. [42 C.F.R. § 422.204(b)(1).]

- For physicians and other health care professionals, including members of physician groups, the process must include: (1) initial credentialing that includes written application, verification of licensure or certification from primary sources, disciplinary status, eligibility for payment under Medicare, and site visits; (2) recredentialing at least every three years that updates information obtained during initial credentialing, considers performance indicators such as those collected through quality improvement programs, utilization management systems, handling of grievances and appeals, enrollee satisfaction surveys, and other plan activities, and includes an attestation of the correctness and completeness of the new information; and (3) a process for consulting with contracting health care professionals with respect to criteria for credentialing and recredentialing. [42 C.F.R. § 422.204(b)(2).]

The documented process must also require that basic benefits be provided through, or payments be made to, providers and suppliers that meet applicable Medicare requirements. [42 C.F.R. § 422.204(b)(3).]

An MA organization may not employ or contract with a provider excluded from participation in the Medicare program. [42 C.F.R. §§ 422.204(b)(4), 422.752(a)(8).] HHS's investigatory arm, the Office of Inspector General, maintains a list of excluded providers on its website at https://exclusions.oig.hhs.gov/.

Interference with Health Care Professional Advice Prohibited

An MA organization may not prohibit or restrict a health care professional from advising, or advocating on behalf of, a patient enrolled under an MA plan regarding: (1) health status, medical care, or treatment options, including the provision of sufficient information to the patient to provide an opportunity to decide among all relevant treatment options; (2) the risks, benefits, and consequences of treatment or non-treatment; or (3) the opportunity for the patient to refuse treatment and to express preferences about future treatment. Health care professionals must provide information regarding treatment options, including the option of no treatment, in a culturally competent manner, and must ensure that individuals with disabilities have effective communications with participants throughout the health system in making decisions regarding treatment options. [Soc. Sec. Act § 1852(j)(3); 42 C.F.R. § 422.206(a).]

However, an MA plan is not required to cover, furnish, or pay for a particular counseling or referral service if the MA organization that offers the plan: (1) objects to that service on moral or religious grounds; and (2) through appropriate written means, makes information available regarding those policies available to CMS (through its Medicare application) and current and prospective enrollees. [Soc. Sec. Act § 1852(j)(3)(B); 42 C.F.R. § 422.206(b).]

[¶ 412] Intermediate Sanctions and Civil Money Penalties

The following sanctions may be imposed on Medicare Advantage (MA) organizations for certain deficiencies: (1) suspension of enrollment of Medicare beneficiaries; (2) suspension of payment to the MA organization for Medicare beneficiaries who are enrolled in the plan after the notice of the intermediate sanction; and (3) suspension of all marketing activities to Medicare beneficiaries by the MA organization for specified MA plans. CMS may also terminate an MA organization's contract or impose civil money penalties (CMPs). [Soc. Sec. Act § 1857(g)(2), (3); 42 C.F.R. §§ 422.750, 422.752.]

Intermediate sanctions. CMS may impose one or more of the intermediate sanctions listed in 42 C.F.R. § 422.750(a) on an MA organization for the following violations:

(1) failing to provide a beneficiary with medically necessary services and the beneficiary is adversely affected;

(2) imposing premiums that exceed the MA monthly basic and supplemental beneficiary premiums;

(3) expelling or refusing to re-enroll a beneficiary in violation of MA requirements;

(4) engaging in any practice that would have the effect of denying or discouraging the enrollment of eligible individuals whose medical condition or history indicates a need for substantial future medical services;

(5) misrepresenting or falsifying information to CMS, an individual, or any other entity;

(6) interfering with practitioners' advice to enrollees;

(7) failing to enforce the limit on balance billing under a private fee-for service plan;

(8) employing or contracting with providers who are excluded from Medicare participation for the provision of health care, utilization review, medical social work, or administrative services;

(9) enrolling an individual in an MA plan without his or her prior consent;

(10) transferring an individual enrolled in an MA plan to another plan without his or her prior consent or solely for the purposes of making a commission;

(11) failing to comply with applicable marketing requirements or implementing guidance;

(12) employing or contracting with any individual, agent, provider, supplier, or entity that engages in any of the conduct described above; or

(13) failing to ensure that providers and suppliers are enrolled in Medicare and not making payment to excluded or revoked individuals or entities.

[Soc. Sec. Act § 1857(g)(1); 42 C.F.R. § 422.752(a).]

Procedures for imposing intermediate sanctions. Before imposing intermediate sanctions, CMS must send a written notice to the MA organization stating the nature and basis of the proposed intermediate sanction and the organization's right to a hearing and send the HHS Office of Inspector General (OIG) a copy of the notice. CMS allows the MA organization 10 calendar days from receipt of the notice to provide a written rebuttal. The MA organization may request a hearing within 15 calendar days of receipt of the intent to impose an intermediate sanction. [42 C.F.R. § 422.756(a), (b).]

Effective date and duration of sanction. The effective date of the sanction is the date specified by CMS in the notice. If, however, CMS determines that the MA organization's conduct poses a serious threat to an enrollee's health and safety, CMS may make the sanction effective on an earlier date. The sanction remains in effect until CMS is satisfied that the deficiencies that are the basis for the sanction determination have been corrected and are not likely to recur. If an immediate sanction has been imposed, CMS may require the MA organization to market and/or accept enrollments for a certain period of time in order to assess whether the deficiencies have been cured and are not like to recur. [42 C.F.R. § 422.756(c).]

Contract nonrenewal or termination. In addition to or as an alternative to the intermediate sanctions described above, CMS may decline to authorize the renewal of an organization's contract or terminate the contract. [42 C.F.R. § 422.756(d).] However, through the end of plan year 2018, the HHS Secretary may not terminate a contract solely because the MA plan failed to achieve a minimum quality rating under the 5-star rating system under Soc. Sec. Act § 1853(o)(4). [Soc. Sec. Act § 1857(h)(3), as added by 21st Century Cures Act (P.L. 114-255) § 17001(b).]

Imposition of Civil Money Penalties Against MA Organization

In addition to, or in place of, any intermediate sanctions, CMS may impose CMPs for any of the reasons for contract terminations contained in 42 C.F.R. § 422.510(a), except by reason of the existence of credible evidence that the MA organization committed or participated in false, fraudulent, or abusive activities affecting the Medicare program under 42 C.F.R. § 422.510(a)(4)(i). [42 C.F.R. § 422.752(c)(1).]

In addition to or in place of any intermediate sanctions imposed by CMS, the OIG may impose CMPs for any of the 13 bases for intermediate sanctions listed above (see 42 C.F.R. § 422.752(a)) or determinations made based on the existence of credible evidence that the MA organization committed or participated in false, fraudulent, or abusive activities affecting the Medicare program under 42 C.F.R. § 422.510(a)(4)(i). [42 C.F.R. § 422.752(c)(2).]

If CMS makes a determination to impose a CMP, it must send a written notice of the decision containing a description of the basis for the determination, the basis for the penalty, the amount of the penalty, the date the penalty is due, the MA organization's right to a hearing, and information about where to file the hearing request. [42 C.F.R. § 422.756(e).]

Collection of CMPs. When an MA organization does not request an administrative law judge (ALJ) hearing, CMS initiates collection of the CMP following the expiration of the time frame for requesting the ALJ hearing. If an MA organization requests a hearing and the ALJ upholds CMS's decision to impose a CMP, CMS may initiate collection of the CMP once the administrative decision is final. [42 C.F.R. § 422.758.]

Determining the amount of CMPs. In determining the amount of the CMP, CMS will consider the following:

(1) the nature of the conduct;

(2) the degree of culpability;

(3) the harm that resulted or could have resulted from the conduct;

(4) the financial condition of the organization;

(5) the history of prior offenses by the organization or its principals; and

(6) such other matters as justice may require.

[42 C.F.R. § 422.760(a)]

If the deficiency on which the determination is based has directly adversely affected one or more MA enrollees, CMS may assess CMPs of up to $25,000 for each determination. For each week that a deficiency remains uncorrected after the week in which the MA organization receives notice of the determination, CMS may assess up to $10,000. If CMS makes a determination that an MA organization has failed to substantially carry out the terms of its contract, CMS may assess $250 per Medicare enrollee from the terminated MA plan or plans at the time the MA organization terminated its contract, or $100,000, whichever is greater. [42 C.F.R. § 422.760(b).]

Chapter 5– MEDICARE PART D—PRESCRIPTION DRUG BENEFIT

[¶ 500] Overview

Beneficiaries entitled to Part A and enrolled in Part B, enrollees in Medicare Advantage (MA) private fee-for-service plans, and enrollees in Part C medical savings account plans are eligible for the Part D prescription drug benefit. Under the prescription drug benefit, eligible individuals have access to at least two prescription drug plans (PDPs) in their region. In regions where eligible individuals do not have access to at least two PDPs, limited risk or fallback prescription drug plans must be offered. [Soc. Sec. Act §§ 1860D-1(a), 1860D-3(a).] As a practical matter, however, fallback plans have not been necessary since the Part D program started in 2006 as at least two qualified PDPs have been offered in each region.

An individual eligible for the prescription drug benefit may enroll in a private plan during specified enrollment periods by filing the appropriate enrollment form with the PDP. Full benefit dual-eligible individuals (those eligible for both Medicare and Medicaid) who fail to enroll in a plan will be automatically enrolled by CMS (see ¶ 503).

Under the PDP program, eligible individuals have the choice of either a standard coverage plan or an alternative coverage plan with actuarially equivalent benefits. In addition to the standard coverage plan, participating plans may offer a supplemental benefit (see ¶ 510). Coinsurance and deductibles for 2017 are discussed at ¶ 507, and premium and cost-sharing subsidies for low-income individuals are discussed at ¶ 508.

Establishment of Prescription Drug Service Areas

CMS established 26 MA regions and 34 PDP regions consisting of the 50 states and the District of Columbia, as well as five separate PDP regions for the territories. PDP regions were established in a manner that was consistent, to the extent practicable, with MA regions, usually on a state-by-state basis. [Soc. Sec. Act § 1860D-11(a); 42 C.F.R. § 423.112; *Final rule*, 70 FR 4194, 4246, Jan. 28, 2005.]

Covered Part D Drugs

To be covered, a Part D drug must be approved by the U.S. Food and Drug Administration (FDA) for use and sale in the U.S. and be prescribed and used for a medically accepted reason. Part D drugs include biological products, insulin, medical supplies associated with the injection of insulin (including syringes, needles, alcohol swabs, and gauze), vaccines and their administration, supplies directly associated with delivering insulin into the body (such as an inhalation chamber used to deliver the insulin through inhalation), and combination products approved and regulated by the FDA as a drug, vaccine, or biologic. [Soc. Sec. Act § 1860D-2(e)(1); 42 C.F.R. § 423.100.]

Excluded drugs. Part D cannot pay for drugs when they would be covered under Medicare Part A or Part B. In addition, the following drugs cannot be included in standard coverage: (1) drugs or classes of drugs, or their medical uses, that may be excluded from coverage or otherwise restricted under Medicaid under Soc. Sec. Act § 1927(d)(2) or (d)(3), except for smoking cessation agents; (2) medical foods, defined as foods that are formulated to be consumed or administered enterally under the supervision of a physician and are intended for the specific dietary management of a disease or condition for which distinctive nutritional requirements, are established by medical evaluation, and are not regulated as drugs under section 505 of the Federal Food, Drug, and Cosmetic Act; (3) drugs for erectile dysfunction; (4) drugs for relief of cough and colds; (5) non-prescription drugs; (6) drugs used for cosmetic purposes or hair growth; (7) drugs used to promote fertility; and (8) prescription vitamins and minerals, except prenatal vitamins and fluoride preparation products. [Soc. Sec. Act § 1860D-2(e)(2); 42 C.F.R. § 423.100; *Medicare Prescription Drug Manual*, Pub. 100-18, Ch. 6, § 20.1.]

Part D Medical Loss Ratio Requirements

Pursuant to the Patient Protection and Affordable Care Act (ACA) (P.L. 111-148), for contracts beginning in 2014 or later, Medicare Part D sponsors are required to report their medical loss ratio (MLR), which represents the percentage of revenue used for patient care, rather than for such other items as administrative expenses or profit.

The minimum MLR requirement is intended to (1) create incentives for Part D sponsors to reduce administrative costs such as those for marketing, profits, and other uses of the funds earned by Part D sponsors; and (2) help ensure that taxpayers and enrolled beneficiaries receive value from Medicare health plans. An MLR is determined based on the percentage of Medicare contract revenue spent on clinical services, prescription drugs, quality improving activities, and direct benefits to beneficiaries in the form of reduced Part B premiums. Part D sponsors must remit payment to CMS when their spending on clinical services, prescription drugs, quality improving activities, and Part B premium rebates, in relation to their total revenue, is less than the 85 percent MLR requirement. If a Part D sponsor fails to meet MLR requirements for more than three consecutive years, it will also be subject to enrollment sanctions and, after five consecutive years, to contract termination. [Soc. Sec. Act §§ 1857(e)(4), 1860D-12(b)(3)(D); 42 C.F.R. § 423.2410.]

CMS will release to the public Part D MLR data, for each contract for each contract year, no earlier than 18 months after the end of the applicable contract year. [42 C.F.R. § 423.2490.]

[¶ 503] Eligibility and Enrollment

To be eligible for prescription drug benefits under Part D, an individual must (1) be entitled to Medicare benefits under Part A or enrolled in Medicare Part B; (2) live in the service area of a Part D plan; and (3) be a U.S. citizen or be lawfully present in the U.S. Except for those enrolled in a Medicare Advantage prescription drug plan (MA-PD), a Program of All-inclusive Care for the Elderly (PACE) plan, or a cost-based health maintenance organization (HMO) or competitive medical plan (CMP), individuals may enroll in prescription drug plans (PDPs) if they are eligible for Part D, live in the PDP service area, and are not enrolled in another Part D plan. [42 C.F.R. § 423.30(a).]

Medicare Advantage plan enrollees. A Part D eligible individual enrolled in an MA-PD plan must obtain qualified prescription drug coverage from that plan. Medicare Advantage enrollees may not enroll in a PDP unless they are enrolled in a MA private fee-for-services plan that does not provide qualified prescription drug coverage or they are enrolled in a medical savings account plan. [42 C.F.R. § 423.30(b).]

PACE plan enrollees. A Part D eligible individual enrolled in a PACE plan offering qualified prescription drug coverage must obtain coverage through that PACE plan. [42 C.F.R. § 423.30(c).]

Cost-based HMO or CMP enrollees. A Part D eligible individual enrolled in a cost-based HMO or CMP that provides qualified prescription drug coverage is eligible to enroll in a PDP only if the individual does not elect prescription drug coverage under the cost-based HMO or CMP and otherwise meets general PDP eligibility requirements. [42 C.F.R. § 423.30(d).]

Incarcerated individuals. Individuals incarcerated in correctional facilities are not eligible to enroll in PDPs, even when they are located within a PDP service area. [*Medicare Prescription Drug Benefit Manual*, Pub. 100-18, Ch. 3, § 20.2.]

State mental institution patients. Unlike incarcerated individuals, individuals who are residing in state mental institutions are not considered by CMS to be out of service areas. Medicare beneficiaries residing in such institutions have access to Medicare benefits under Part A and Part B and are entitled to enroll in Part D plans. However, because individuals in state mental institutions may be limited to enrolling in the pharmacy network that contracts with their institution, CMS provides a special enrollment period to enable them to join the appropriate Part D plan based upon their situation. [Pub. 100-18, Ch. 3, § § 20.2, 30.3.8.]

Enrollment in Prescription Drug Plans

An individual eligible for a Part D benefit may enroll in a private PDP during the specified regulatory enrollment periods by filing the appropriate enrollment form with the PDP or through other CMS-approved enrollment mechanisms. [42 C.F.R. § 423.32(a).]

Enrollment forms. The beneficiary must complete the enrollment form, which includes an acknowledgment of the disclosure and exchange of necessary information between CMS and the PDP sponsor. Individuals who assist in the completion of an enrollment, including authorized representatives of the beneficiary, must indicate that they provided assistance and disclose their relationship to the beneficiary. Part D eligible individuals must provide information regarding reimbursement through other insurance, group health plans, other third-party payment arrangements, or other sources, and consent to the release of such information. [42 C.F.R. § 423.32(b).]

Timely processing and prompt notice. A PDP sponsor must timely process an enrollment request in accordance with CMS enrollment guidelines and enroll a Part D eligible individual who elects to enroll or is enrolled in the plan during the specified enrollment periods. A sponsor also must provide an individual with prompt notice of acceptance or denial of an enrollment request. [42 C.F.R. § 423.32(c), (d).]

Maintenance of enrollment. An enrolled individual remains enrolled in a PDP until: (1) the individual successfully enrolls in another PDP or MA-PD; (2) the individual voluntarily disenrolls from the PDP; (3) the individual is involuntarily disenrolled from the PDP; (4) the PDP is discontinued within the individual's area of residence; or (5) the individual is enrolled after the initial enrollment. [42 C.F.R. § 423.32(e).]

Cost-based HMOs, CMPs, and PACE plans. Individuals enrolled in cost-based HMOs, CMPs, and PACE plans that offered prescription drug coverage as of December 31, 2005, were permitted to remain enrolled in those plans and receive Part D benefits offered by the plans until one of the five conditions for disenrollment is met (see above). [42 C.F.R. § 423.32(f).]

Passive enrollment by CMS. In situations involving either immediate termination based on serious financial difficulties or other situations in which CMS determines that remaining enrolled in a plan poses potential harm to plan members, CMS may implement passive enrollment procedures. Under passive enrollment procedures, individuals are considered to have enrolled in the plan selected by CMS unless they decline the plan or request enrollment in another plan. Before the enrollment effective date (or as soon as possible after the effective date if prior notice is not practicable), the organization that receives the passive enrollment beneficiaries must provide them with notification that describes the costs and benefits of the new plan, the process for accessing care under the plan, and the beneficiary's ability to decline the enrollment or choose another plan. [42 C.F.R. § 423.32(g).]

Enrollment of Low-Income Subsidy Eligible Individuals

CMS must ensure the enrollment into Part D plans of low-income subsidy eligible individuals who fail to enroll in a Part D plan. A low-income subsidy eligible individual is an individual who meets the definition of full-subsidy eligible (see ¶ 508), including those eligible for both Medicare and Medicaid, or other subsidy-eligible individual. [42 C.F.R. § 423.34(a), (b).]

Automatic enrollment. Except for low-income subsidy eligible individuals who are qualifying covered retirees with a group health plan sponsor, CMS automatically enrolls individuals who fail to enroll in a Part D plan into a PDP offering basic prescription drug coverage in the area where the beneficiary resides. The PDP must have a monthly beneficiary premium amount that does not exceed the low-income subsidy amount. If there is more than one PDP in an area with a monthly beneficiary premium at or below the low-income premium subsidy amount, individuals are enrolled on a random basis. Low-income subsidy eligible individuals enrolled in an MA private fee-for-service plan, a cost-based HMO or CMP that does not offer qualified prescription drug coverage, or a medical savings account plan, and who fail to enroll in a Part D plan, also will be enrolled automatically. [Soc. Sec. Act § 1860D-1(b)(1)(C); 42 C.F.R. § 423.34(d).]

Exception for employer group health plans. Full-benefit dual-eligible individuals who are qualifying covered retirees, and for whom CMS has approved the group health plan sponsor to receive the retiree drug subsidy (see ¶ 530), also are automatically enrolled in a Part D plan, unless they elect to decline that enrollment. Before effectuating the enrollment, however, CMS will provide notice to such individuals of their choices and advise them to discuss the potential impact of Medicare Part D coverage on their group health plan coverage. The notice informs such individuals that they will be deemed to have declined to enroll in Part D unless they affirmatively enroll in a Part D plan or contact CMS and confirm that they wish to be auto-enrolled in a PDP. Individuals who elect not to be auto-enrolled may enroll in Medicare Part D at a later time if they choose to do so. All other low-income subsidy eligible beneficiaries who are qualified covered retirees are not automatically enrolled into PDPs. [42 C.F.R. § 423.34(d)(3).]

PDP plans that voluntarily waive a de minimis premium amount. CMS may include in the automatic enrollment process PDPs that voluntarily waive a *de minimis* premium amount if CMS determines that such inclusion is warranted. [Soc. Sec. Act § 1860D-1(b)(1)(D); 42 C.F.R. § 423.34(d)(4).]

Declining enrollment or disenrollment by dual-eligible individuals. A low-income subsidy eligible individual may decline enrollment in Part D or disenroll from a Part D plan and elect to enroll in another Part D plan during the special enrollment period. [42 C.F.R. § 423.34(e).]

Full-benefit dual eligibles' effective date of enrollment. Enrollment for full-benefit dual-eligible individuals must be effective: (1) for Part D for individuals who are Medicaid eligible and subsequently become newly eligible for Part D, the first day of the month the individual is eligible for Part D; and (2) for individuals who are eligible for Part D and subsequently become newly eligible for Medicaid, the first day of the month when the individual becomes eligible for both Medicaid and Part D. [42 C.F.R. § 423.34(f).]

Effective date of enrollment for non-full-benefit dual eligibles who are low-income subsidy eligible. The effective date for non-full-benefit dual-eligible individuals who are low-income subsidy eligible is no later than the first day of the second month after CMS determines that they meet the criteria for enrollment. [42 C.F.R. § 423.34(g).]

¶503

Reassigning low-income subsidy eligible individuals. During the annual coordinated election period, CMS may reassign certain low-income subsidy eligible individuals to another PDP if CMS determines that the further enrollment is warranted. However, if a PDP offering basic prescription drug coverage in the area where the beneficiary resides has a monthly beneficiary premium amount that exceeds the low-income subsidy amount by a *de minimis* amount and the PDP volunteers to waive the *de minimis* amount, then CMS will not reassign low-income subsidy individuals who would otherwise be enrolled on the basis that the monthly beneficiary premium exceeds the low-income subsidy by a *de minimis* amount. [Soc. Sec. Act § 1860D-14(a)(5); 42 C.F.R. § 423.34(c).]

Facilitation of reassignments. The HHS Secretary must, in the case of subsidy-eligible individuals enrolled in a PDP who subsequently are reassigned to a new PDP, provide the beneficiary, within 30 days of the reassignment, with: (1) information on formulary differences between the individual's former plan and the plan to which the individual is reassigned with respect to the individual's drug regimen; and (2) a description of the individual's right to request a coverage determination, exception, or reconsideration; bring an appeal; or resolve a grievance. [Soc. Sec. Act § 1860D-14(d).]

Voluntary Disenrollment from a Prescription Drug Plan

An individual may disenroll from a PDP during the specified enrollment periods by enrolling in a different PDP, submitting a disenrollment request to a PDP, or filing an appropriate disenrollment request through other mechanisms approved by CMS. The PDP sponsor must submit a disenrollment notice to CMS within the time frames CMS specifies, provide the enrollee with a CMS notice of disenrollment, and file and retain disenrollment requests for the period specified by CMS. CMS may grant retroactive disenrollment to an individual if there never was a legally valid enrollment or if a valid request for disenrollment was properly made but not processed or acted upon. [42 C.F.R. § 423.36.]

Part D Enrollment Periods

Law and regulations provide for an initial enrollment period (IEP), an annual coordinated election period (AEP), and special enrollment periods (SEPs) for PDPs.

Initial enrollment period. The IEP is the period during which an individual is first eligible to enroll in a Part D plan. [42 C.F.R. § 423.38(a).]

The IEP for an individual who is first eligible to enroll on or after March 2006 is the same as the IEP for Medicare Part B, i.e., a seven-month period beginning with the third month before the month in which an individual first meets the eligibility requirements and ending seven months later (see ¶ 311). An exception is made for individuals not eligible to enroll in Part D at any time during their IEP for Part B. Their IEP runs from three months before becoming eligible for Part D to three months following eligibility. In addition, the IEP under Part D for individuals who become entitled to Medicare Part A or enrolled in Part B for a retroactive effective date starts with the month in which notification of Medicare determination is received and ends on the last day of the third month following the month in which the notification was received. [42 C.F.R. § 423.38(a)(3).]

Annual coordinated election period. The Part D AEP for a calendar year runs from October 15 through December 7 of the preceding year. [42 C.F.R. § 423.38(b)(3).]

Special enrollment periods. SEPs allow an individual to enroll in a PDP or disenroll from a PDP and enroll in another PDP or MA-PD plan at any time under any of the following circumstances:

(1) creditable prescription drug coverage is lost or involuntarily reduced so that it is no longer creditable coverage (loss of coverage due to failure to pay premiums is not considered involuntary);

(2) the individual is not adequately informed that he or she has lost creditable prescription drug coverage, that he or she never had creditable prescription drug coverage, or that the coverage is involuntarily reduced so that the coverage is no longer creditable;

(3) the individual's enrollment or non-enrollment in a PDP is unintentional, inadvertent, or erroneous because of error, misrepresentation, or inaction of a federal employee or any person authorized to act on behalf of the federal government;

(4) the individual is a full-subsidy eligible or other subsidy eligible under 42 C.F.R. § 423.772;

(5) the individual elects to disenroll from an MA-PD plan and elects coverage under Medicare Part A and Part B;

(6) the PDP's contract is terminated by the PDP or CMS or the PDP plan no longer is offered in the area where the individual resides;

(7) the individual is no longer eligible for the PDP because of a change of residence; or

(8) the individual demonstrates in accordance with CMS guidelines that the PDP sponsor substantially violated a material provision of its contract, including: failure to provide benefits on a timely basis, failure to provide benefits in accordance with applicable quality standards, or material misrepresentation of the plan's provisions during marketing; or the individual meets other exceptional circumstances as determined by CMS, such as when an individual has a life-threatening condition or illness.

[42 C.F.R. § 423.38(c); Pub. 100-18, Ch. 3, § 30.3.8.]

Coordination with MA annual 45-day disenrollment period. An individual enrolled in an MA plan who switches to original Medicare between January 1 through February 14 also may elect a PDP during this time. [42 C.F.R. § 423.38(d).]

Effective Dates of Part D Coverage and Change of Coverage

CMS must apply the effective date requirements provided under the MA program to Part D enrollments.

(1) **Initial enrollment period.** An enrollment made before the month of entitlement to Medicare Part A or enrollment in Part B is effective the first day of the month the individual is entitled to or enrolled in Part A or enrolled in Part B. Except as indicated for full-benefit dual-eligible individuals, an enrollment made during or after the month of entitlement to Part A or enrollment in Part B is effective the first day of the calendar month following the month in which the enrollment in Part D is made. If the individual, however, is not eligible to enroll in Part D on the first day of the calendar month following the month in which the election to enroll is made, the enrollment is effective the first day of the month the individual is eligible for Part D. [42 C.F.R. § 423.40(a).]

(2) **Annual coordinated election period.** For an enrollment or change of enrollment in Part D made during an AEP, the coverage or change in coverage is effective as of the first day of the following calendar year. [42 C.F.R. § 423.40(b).]

(3) **Special enrollment periods.** For an enrollment or change of enrollment in Part D made during a SEP, the effective date is determined by CMS in a manner

consistent with protecting the continuity of health benefits coverage. [42 C.F.R. § 423.40(c).]

45-day MA annual disenrollment period. If an individual who has disenrolled from an MA plan enrolls in a PDP plan from January 1 through February 14, enrollment is effective the first day of the month following the month in which the enrollment in the PDP is made. [42 C.F.R. § 423.40(d).]

Involuntary Disenrollment from a Prescription Drug Plan

Generally, a PDP sponsor is prohibited from involuntarily disenrolling an individual from a PDP it offers or requesting or encouraging an individual to disenroll, either through verbal or written communication or through action or inaction. The PDP sponsor is, however, required to disenroll an individual under various conditions (see below) and may disenroll an individual for failing to timely pay monthly premiums or for disruptive behavior. [42 C.F.R. § 423.44(a), (b).]

Notice requirements. If the disenrollment is for any reason other than death or loss of Part D eligibility, the PDP sponsor must give the individual timely notice of the disenrollment with an explanation of why the PDP is planning to disenroll the individual. This sponsor must provide the notice to the individual before submitting the disenrollment notice to CMS, and it must explain the individual's right to file a grievance under the PDP's grievance procedures. [42 C.F.R. § 423.44(c).]

Mandatory disenrollment. A PDP sponsor must disenroll an individual from a PDP it offers if:

(1) the individual no longer resides in the PDP's service area;

(2) the individual loses eligibility for Part D;

(3) the individual dies;

(4) the PDP's contract is terminated by CMS, by the PDP, or through mutual consent;

(5) the individual materially misrepresents information to the PDP sponsor as to whether his or her costs are expected to be reimbursed through insurance or other third-party means; or

(6) the individual is not lawfully present in the United States.

[42 C.F.R. § 423.44(b)(2).]

Optional involuntary disenrollment for unpaid premiums. A PDP sponsor may disenroll an individual from a PDP it offers for failure to pay any monthly premium if the sponsor demonstrates to CMS that it made reasonable efforts to collect the unpaid premium and the PDP gives the enrollee proper notice of disenrollment. The PDP sponsor must give the enrollee a two-month grace period to pay the past due premiums, beginning on the first day of the month the premium is unpaid or the first day of the month following the date on which the premium is requested, whichever is later. When disenrollment occurs for failure to pay monthly premiums, the PDP may refuse reenrollment of the individual until all past premiums have been paid. A PDP sponsor must not disenroll an individual who has premiums withheld from his or her Social Security, Railroad Retirement Board, or Office of Personnel Management check, or who is in "premium withhold" as defined by CMS. [42 C.F.R. § 423.44(b)(1)(i), (d)(1)(i)–(v).]

Extension of grace period for good cause. When an individual is disenrolled for failure to pay the plan premium, CMS (or a third party to which CMS has assigned this responsibility, such as a Part D sponsor) may reinstate enrollment in the PDP without interruption of coverage if he or she shows good cause for failure to pay within the initial grace period and pays all overdue premiums within three calendar months after the disenrollment date. The individual must establish by a credible statement that failure to pay premiums within the initial grace period was due to circumstances for which the individual had no control or the individual could not reasonably have been expected to foresee. However, enrollment in the PDP cannot be reinstated if the only basis for the reinstatement is a change in the individual's circumstances after the involuntary disenrollment for nonpayment of premiums. [42 C.F.R. § 423.44(d)(1)(vi), (vii).]

Optional involuntary disenrollment for disruptive behavior. A PDP may disenroll an individual whose behavior is disruptive only after: (1) the PDP sponsor makes an effort to resolve the problem, (2) the PDP sponsor documents the enrollee's behavior, and (3) CMS has reviewed and approved the proposed disenrollment. A PDP enrollee is considered disruptive if his or her behavior substantially impairs the PDP's ability to arrange or provide for services to the individual or other plan members. An individual cannot be considered disruptive if the behavior is related to the use of medical services or compliance (or noncompliance) with medical advice or treatment. The PDP sponsor must make a serious effort to resolve the problems presented by the individual, including providing reasonable accommodations for individuals with mental or cognitive conditions. [42 C.F.R. § 423.44(d)(2).]

Involuntary disenrollment for failure to pay IRMAA. CMS will disenroll individuals who fail to pay the Part D income-related monthly adjustment amount (IRMAA) (see ¶ 505). For all Part D IRMAA amounts directly billed to an enrollee, the initial grace period ends with the last day of the third month after the billing month. When an individual is disenrolled for failing to pay the IRMAA within the initial grace period, CMS (or an entity acting for CMS) may reinstate enrollment, without interruption of coverage, if the individual shows good cause and pays all IRMAA arrearages and any overdue premiums due the Part D plan sponsor within three calendar months after the disenrollment date. When CMS has disenrolled an individual for failure to pay the IRMAA, the PDP sponsor must provide notice of termination in a form and manner determined by CMS. The effective date of disenrollment is the first day following the last day of the initial grace period. [42 C.F.R. § 423.44(e).]

Late Enrollment Penalty

A Part D eligible individual must pay a late enrollment penalty (LEP) if there is a continuous period of 63 days or longer at any time after the end of the individual's IEP during which the individual was eligible to enroll in a PDP, was not covered under any creditable prescription drug coverage, and was not enrolled in a Part D plan. [42 C.F.R. § 423.46(a).]

Part D plan sponsors are responsible for determining, at the time of enrollment, whether a member was previously enrolled in Part D or had other creditable coverage prior to applying to enroll in his or her plan and whether there were any lapses in coverage of 63 days or more. [42 C.F.R. § 423.46(b).]

Reconsideration. Individuals determined to be subject to a LEP may request reconsideration, which will be conducted by CMS or an independent review entity contracted by CMS. Decisions made through this review are not subject to appeal but may be reviewed and revised at the discretion of CMS. [42 C.F.R. § 423.46(c).]

Calculation of the late enrollment penalty. The LEP is equal to 1 percent of the base beneficiary premium or another amount specified by CMS based on available analysis or other information. [42 C.F.R. § 423.286(d)(3); Pub. 100-18, Ch. 4, § 40.1.]

Determining Creditable Status of Prescription Drug Coverage

A Part D enrollee who otherwise would be subject to a late enrollment penalty may avoid the penalty if his or her previous coverage meets the standards of "creditable prescription drug coverage." Previous coverage will meet those standards only if it is determined (in a manner specified by CMS) to provide coverage of the cost of prescription drugs the actuarial value of which (as defined by CMS) to the individual equals or exceeds the actuarial value of standard prescription drug coverage. [42 C.F.R. § 423.56(a).]

The following coverage is considered creditable:

(1) coverage under a PDP or a MA-PD;

(2) Medicaid;

(3) a group health plan (including coverage provided by a federal or a nonfederal government plan and by a church plan for its employees);

(4) a State Pharmaceutical Assistance Program;

(5) veterans' coverage (including survivors and dependents) of prescription drugs;

(6) prescription drug coverage under a Medigap policy;

(7) military coverage (including TRICARE);

(8) individual health insurance coverage that includes coverage for outpatient prescription drugs and that does not meet the definition of an excepted benefit;

(9) coverage provided by the medical care program of the Indian Health Service, tribe, or tribal organization, or Urban Indian organization;

(10) coverage provided by a PACE organization;

(11) coverage provided by a cost-based HMO or CMP;

(12) coverage provided through a state high-risk pool; and

(13) other coverage as CMS may determine appropriate.

[42 C.F.R. § 423.56(b).]

Calculation of actuarial equivalence standard. The basic actuarial equivalence value test for the determination of creditable coverage or alternative coverage is determined by calculating whether the expected plan payout on average will be at least equal to the expected plan payout under defined prescription drug coverage, not taking into account the value of any discount or coverage provided during the coverage gap ("donut hole"). [Soc. Sec. Act § 1860D-22(a)(2)(A); 42 C.F.R. § 423.884(d).]

Disclosure of creditable or non-creditable coverage status. With the exception of PDPs and MA-PD plans and PACE or cost-based HMO or CMP plans that provide qualified prescription drug coverage under Part D, each entity that offers prescription drug coverage must disclose to all enrolled or eligible individuals whether the coverage offered is creditable prescription drug coverage. If the coverage is not creditable, the entity also must disclose to eligible individuals that there are limitations on the periods in a year in which the individual may enroll in Part D plans and that the individual may be subject to a late enrollment penalty. [42 C.F.R. §§ 423.56(c), (d), 423.884(e).]

Clarifying notice of creditable coverage. An individual who is not adequately informed that his or her prescription drug coverage was not creditable may apply for CMS review. If CMS determines that the individual did not receive adequate notice or received incorrect information, CMS may deem the individual to have had creditable coverage, regardless of whether it was actually creditable, so that the LEP will not be imposed. [42 C.F.R. § 423.56(g).]

[¶ 505] Payment of Part D Premiums

Generally, the monthly beneficiary premium for a prescription drug plan (PDP) must be the same for all Part D eligible individuals enrolled in a plan. The monthly beneficiary premium is the base beneficiary premium adjusted to reflect the difference between the bid and the national average monthly bid amount, any supplemental benefits, and any late enrollment penalties. [Soc. Sec. Act § 1860D-13(a); 42 C.F.R. § 423.286(a).]

2017 national average monthly bid amount. For each coverage year, CMS computes the national average monthly bid amount from the applicable Part D plan bid submissions to calculate the base beneficiary premium. The national average monthly bid amount for 2017 is $61.08, which is down from the 2016 national average monthly bid amount of $64.66. [42 C.F.R. § 423.279; *Annual Release of Part D National Average Bid Amount and Other Part C & D Bid Information*, July 29, 2016.]

Calculation of the beneficiary premium. The beneficiary premium percentage for any year is a fraction, the numerator of which is 25.5 percent. The denominator is 100 percent minus a percentage equalling (1) the total estimated reinsurance payments for the coverage year, divided by (2) the total estimated reinsurance payments plus total estimated payments to Part D plans attributable to the standardized bid amount during the coverage year. [Soc. Sec. Act § 1860D-13(a)(3); 42 C.F.R. § 423.286(b).]

Base beneficiary premium. The base beneficiary premium for a month is equal to the product of the beneficiary premium percentage and the national average monthly bid amount. If the amount of the standardized bid amount exceeds the adjusted national average monthly bid amount, the monthly base beneficiary premium is increased by the amount of the excess. If the amount of the adjusted national average monthly bid amount exceeds the standardized bid amount, the monthly base beneficiary premium is decreased by the amount of the excess. [Soc. Sec. Act § 1860D-13(a)(2); 42 C.F.R. § 423.286(c)–(e).] The Part D base beneficiary premium for 2017 is $35.63, which is up from $34.10 in 2016. [*Annual Release of Part D National Average Bid Amount and Other Part C & D Bid Information*, July 29, 2016.]

Monthly beneficiary premium. Part D beneficiary premiums are calculated as the base beneficiary premium adjusted by the following factors: (1) the difference between the plan's standardized bid amount and the national average monthly bid amount; (2) an increase for any supplemental premium; (3) an increase for any late enrollment penalty; (4) an increase for income-related monthly adjustment amount (IRMAA) (see below); and (5) elimination or decrease with the application of the low-income premium subsidy. [Soc. Sec. Act § 1860D-13(a); 42 C.F.R. § 423.286(d), (e).]

Increase in individual monthly premium based on income. The monthly amount of the beneficiary premium applicable for each month after December 2010 is increased by an IRMAA for individuals whose modified adjusted gross income (MAGI) exceeds the threshold amount applicable under Soc. Sec. Act § 1839(i) for the calendar year. This IRMAA for an individual for a month in a year is equal to the product of: (1) the quotient obtained by dividing (a) the applicable percentage described below for the individual for the calendar year reduced by 25.5 percent, by (b) 25.5 percent; and (2) the base beneficiary premium. [Soc. Sec. Act § 1860D-13(a)(7)(A), (B); 42 C.F.R. § 423.286(d)(4).]

For 2017, the MAGI amounts, percentage increases, and monthly adjustment amounts are as follows for beneficiaries who filed an individual tax return in 2016:

- if the MAGI is less than or equal to $85,000, there is no monthly adjustment amount;

- if the MAGI is more than $85,000 but not more than $107,000, the applicable percentage is 35 percent, with a monthly adjustment of $13.30;

- if the MAGI is more than $107,000 but not more than $160,000, the applicable percentage is 50 percent, with a monthly adjustment of $34.20;

- if the MAGI is more than $160,000 but not more than $214,000, the applicable percentage is 65 percent, with a monthly adjustment of $55.20; and

- if the MAGI is more than $214,000, the applicable percentage is 80 percent, with a monthly adjustment of $76.20.

[Soc. Sec. Act § 1839(i)(3)(C); *Annual Release of Part D National Average Bid Amount and Other Part C & D Bid Information*, July 29, 2016.]

In the case of a joint return, the MAGI dollar amount is twice the dollar amounts otherwise applicable for the calendar year. [Soc. Sec. Act § 1839(i)(3)(C)(ii).]

Also, in 2017, for beneficiaries who are married but file separate tax returns from their spouses, with income: less than or equal to $85,000, there is no monthly adjustment amount; greater than $85,000 and less than or equal to $129,000, the monthly adjustment is $55.20; or, greater than $129,000, the monthly adjustment is $76.20. [*Annual Release of Part D National Average Bid Amount and Other Part C & D Bid Information*, July 29, 2016.]

Premium collection. Plan enrollees have the option to make premium payments to PDP sponsors using any of the methods available to enrollees in MA plans listed in 42 C.F.R. § 422.262(f), including withholding from Social Security payments, electronic funds transfers, or through employers or third parties specified by CMS. Medicare will pay a plan sponsor only the portion of a late enrollment penalty attributable to increased PDP actuarial costs not taken into account through risk adjustment. [42 C.F.R. § 423.293.]

Collection of the IRMAA. The IRMAA must be paid through withholding from the enrollee's Social Security benefit payments, or benefit payments by the Railroad Retirement Board or the Office of Personnel Management, in the same manner that the Part B premium is withheld. If an enrollee's benefit payment from one of the three sources above is insufficient to have the IRMAA withheld, or if an enrollee is not receiving any such benefits, the beneficiary must be billed directly. The beneficiary may pay the amount through an electronic funds transfer mechanism or by other means specified by CMS. CMS must terminate Part D coverage for any individual who fails to pay the IRMAA. [42 C.F.R. § 423.293(d).]

[¶ 507] Part D Deductible and Coinsurance Requirements

"Standard prescription drug coverage" consists of coverage of covered Part D drugs subject to an annual deductible, 25 percent coinsurance (or an actuarially equivalent structure) up to an initial coverage limit, and catastrophic coverage after an individual incurs out-of-pocket expenses above a certain annual threshold. [Soc. Sec. Act § 1860D-2(b); 42 C.F.R. § 423.104(d).]

Deductible. The annual deductible is increased over the previous year's amount by the annual percentage increase in average per capita aggregate expenditures for Part D drugs for the 12-month period ending in July of the previous year, rounded to the nearest multiple of $5. [Soc. Sec. Act § 1860D-2(b)(1); 42 C.F.R. § 423.104(d)(1)(ii).] For 2017, the annual deductible is $400, which is up from $360 in 2016. [*Announcement of Calendar Year 2017 Medicare Advantage Capitation Rates and Medicare Advantage and Part D Payment Policies and Final Call Letter*, April 4, 2016.]

Cost-sharing under the initial coverage limit. Coinsurance for actual costs for covered Part D drugs covered under the Part D plan above the annual deductible and up to the initial coverage limit is (1) 25 percent of the actual cost; or (2) actuarially equivalent to an average expected coinsurance of no more than 25 percent of actual cost. A Part D plan providing actuarially equivalent standard coverage may apply tiered copayments if certain requirements are met. [Soc. Sec. Act § 1860-2(b)(2)(A) and (B); 42 C.F.R. § 423.104(d)(2).]

Initial coverage limit. The initial coverage limit is increased over the previous year's amount by the annual percentage increase in average per capita aggregate expenditures for Part D drugs for the 12-month period ending in July of the previous year, rounded to the nearest multiple of $10. [Soc. Sec. Act § 1860D-2(b)(3); 42 C.F.R. § 423.104(d)(3).] For 2017, the initial coverage limit is $3,700, up from $3,310 in 2016. [*Announcement of Calendar Year 2017 Medicare Advantage Capitation Rates and Medicare Advantage and Part D Payment Policies and Final Call Letter*, April 4, 2016.]

Before the enactment of the Patient Protection and Affordable Care Act (ACA) (P.L. 111-148), as amended by the Health Care and Education Reconciliation Act of 2010 (HCERA) (P.L. 111-152), beneficiaries paid 100 percent of all costs in the coverage gap, also known as the "donut hole," which occurs between the initial coverage limit and the out-of-pocket threshold. [42 C.F.R. § 423.100.]

The ACA reduced the effect of the "donut hole" through:

(1) a rebate of $250 in 2010 only;

(2) a 50 percent discount for brand-name drugs;

(3) gradually increasing generic drug discounts; and

(4) increased Medicare coverage of brand-name drugs.

[Soc. Sec. Act § 1860D-2.]

See below for a discussion of the ACA's changes to close the coverage gap.

Annual out-of-pocket threshold. The annual out-of-pocket threshold for 2016 through 2019 is increased over the previous year's amount by: (1) the annual percentage increase in average per capita aggregate expenditures for Part D drugs for the 12-month period ending in July of the previous year; or (2) the annual percentage increase in the consumer price index for all urban consumers (U.S. city average) for the 12-month period ending in July of the previous year. [Soc. Sec. Act § 1860D-2(b)(4)(B); 42 C.F.R. § 423.104(d)(5)(iii).] For 2017, the annual out-of-pocket threshold is $4,950. [*Announcement of Calendar Year 2017 Medicare Advantage Capitation Rates and Medicare Advantage and Part D Payment Policies and Final Call Letter*, April 4, 2016.]

Once a beneficiary's "incurred costs" reach the annual out-of-pocket threshold, the beneficiary's cost-sharing equals the greater of (1) coinsurance of 5 percent of the actual cost, or (2) copayment amounts from the previous year increased by the annual percentage increase in average per capita aggregate expenditures for Part D drugs for the 12-month period ending in July of the previous year, rounded to the nearest multiple of $.05. [Soc. Sec. Act § 1860D-2(b)(4)(A); 42 C.F.R. § 423.104(d)(5)(i), (ii).]

In 2017, once the PDP enrollee reaches the annual out-of-pocket threshold, his or her nominal cost-sharing is equal to the greater of 5 percent coinsurance or a copayment of $3.30 for a generic drug or a preferred multiple source drug and $8.25 for any other drug. [*Announcement of Calendar Year 2017 Medicare Advantage Capitation Rates and Medicare Advantage and Part D Payment Policies and Final Call Letter*, April 4, 2016.]

¶507

For purposes of calculating the annual out-of-pocket threshold, costs are considered "incurred" if they are paid with respect to covered Part D drugs for the annual deductible, cost-sharing, and for amounts for which benefits were not provided due to the coverage gap (excluding costs for covered Part D drugs that are not included in the plan's formulary). Generally, costs are treated as incurred only if they are paid by the Part D eligible individual (or another person on behalf of the individual) and he or she is not reimbursed through insurance, a group health plan, or other third-party arrangement. Costs are considered incurred if they are paid (1) under Soc. Sec. Act § 1860D-14; (2) under a State Pharmaceutical Assistance Program; (3) by the Indian Health Service (IHS), an Indian tribe or tribal organization, or an urban Indian organization; or (4) by an AIDS Drug Assistance Program under Part B of Title XXVI of the Public Health Service Act. [Soc. Sec. Act § 1860D-2(b)(4)(C).]

Drug Costs in the Coverage Gap

The HHS Secretary provided a one-time rebate of $250 for certain beneficiaries whose incurred costs for covered Part D drugs exceeded the initial coverage limit in 2010. [Soc. Sec. Act § 1860D-42(c).]

Coverage gap discount program. For drugs to be covered under Part D, a manufacturer must participate in a coverage gap discount program that provides a 50 percent discount on applicable brand-name drugs provided to applicable beneficiaries while in the coverage gap. To participate, the manufacturer must enter into an agreement with the Secretary of HHS and with a third-party contractor designated by the Secretary to administer the program. [Soc. Sec. Act § 1860D-43(a), (b); 42 C.F.R. §§ 423.2315, 423.2325.]

Generic drugs in the coverage gap. The ACA provided for increased generic drug plan coverage starting in 2011. The coverage for an applicable beneficiary who has coinsurance for costs within the coverage gap for covered generic Part D drugs is equal to the generic-gap coinsurance percentage or actuarially equivalent to an average expected payment of such percentage of costs for covered Part D drugs that are not applicable drugs. [Soc. Sec. Act § 1860D-2(b)(2)(C)(i); 42 C.F.R. § 423.104(d)(4)(i).]

For 2012 through 2019, the generic-gap coinsurance percentage is the generic-gap coinsurance percentage for the previous year decreased by 7 percentage points. For 2020 and later, it is 25 percent. [Soc. Sec. Act § 1860D-2(b)(2)(C)(ii); 42 C.F.R. § 423.104(d)(4)(iii).]

Increased Part D coverage for applicable name-brand drugs in the coverage gap. In 2013 and later years, the Part D coverage for a beneficiary in the coverage gap also increases due to the ACA. The coinsurance is (1) the difference between the applicable gap percentage and the discount percentage for applicable drugs, or (2) actuarially equivalent to an average expected payment of such percentage of such costs, for covered Part D drugs that are applicable drugs. [Soc. Sec. Act § 1860D-2(b)(2)(D)(i); 42 C.F.R. § 423.104(d)(4)(ii).]

The applicable gap percentage for applicable drugs in the coverage gap is:

- in 2013 and 2014, 97.5 percent;
- in 2015 and 2016, 95 percent;
- in 2017, 90 percent;
- in 2018, 85 percent;
- in 2019, 80 percent; and
- in 2020 and each subsequent year, 75 percent.

[Soc. Sec. Act § 1860D-2(b)(2)(D)(ii); 42 C.F.R. § 423.104(d)(4)(iv).]

[¶ 508] Premium and Cost-Sharing Subsidies for Low-Income Individuals

CMS subsidizes the monthly beneficiary premium and cost-sharing amounts incurred by Part D eligible individuals with low income and resources. [Soc. Sec. Act § 1860D-14.]

For purposes of low-income subsidy eligibility, "income" includes the income of the applicant and spouse who is living in the same household, if any, regardless of whether the spouse is also an applicant. Support and maintenance is exempted from income. "Resources" include the liquid resources of the applicant (and, if married, his or her spouse who is living in the same household), such as checking and savings accounts, stocks, bonds, and other resources that can be readily converted to cash within 20 days, and real estate that is not the applicant's primary residence or the land on which the primary residence is located. The value of any life insurance policy is exempted from the definition of resources. [42 C.F.R. § 423.772.]

Eligibility for Part D Low-Income Subsidies

The primary goal under the low-income subsidy program is to have nationally uniform standards and rules for determining eligibility for a subsidy. CMS has not permitted states to use the more liberal methodologies that they use to determine eligibility for Medicare savings programs under Medicaid to determine Medicare Part D low-income subsidy eligibility because CMS does not have the authority to extend more liberal methodologies to the Social Security Administration. [*Final rule*, 70 FR 4194, 4374, Jan. 28, 2005.]

Determinations for the low-income subsidy can be made in advance of a person enrolling in a Part D plan. A subsidy-eligible individual is not entitled to the subsidy, however, until such time as the person's enrollment in the plan is effective. [*Final rule*, 70 FR 4194, 4374, Jan. 28, 2005.]

Subsidy-eligible individual. A subsidy-eligible individual is a Part D eligible individual residing in a state who: (1) is enrolled in, or seeking to enroll in a Part D plan; (2) has an income below 150 percent of the federal poverty level (FPL) applicable to the individual's family size; and (3) has resources that are at or below the resource thresholds described below. [42 C.F.R. § 423.773(a).]

Full-subsidy-eligible individual. A full-subsidy-eligible individual is a subsidy-eligible individual who: (1) has income below 135 percent of the FPL applicable to the individual's family size; and (2) has resources that do not exceed the amount of resources allowable for the previous year increased by the annual percentage increase in the consumer price index (all items, U.S. city average) as of September of that previous year, rounded to the nearest multiple of $10. [42 C.F.R. § 423.773(b).]

An individual must be treated as meeting the eligibility requirements for full-subsidy-eligible individuals described above if the individual is a: (1) full-benefit dual-eligible individual; (2) recipient of Social Security Income (SSI) benefits under Title XVI of the Social Security Act; or (3) eligible for Medicaid as a qualified Medicare beneficiary (QMB), specified low-income Medicare beneficiary (SLMB), or a qualifying individual (QI) under a state's plan. [42 C.F.R. § 423.773(c)(1).]

CMS will notify all individuals treated as full-subsidy eligible that they do not need to apply for the subsidies and they are deemed eligible. For an individual deemed eligible between January 1 and June 30 of a calendar year, he or she will be deemed eligible for a full subsidy for the rest of the calendar year. If deemed eligible between July 1 and December 1 of the calendar year, the individual will be deemed eligible for the rest of the calendar year and the following calendar year. [42 C.F.R. § 423.773(c)(2).]

¶508

Other low-income subsidy individuals. Other low-income subsidy individuals are subsidy-eligible individuals who: (1) have income less than 150 percent of the FPL applicable to the individual's family size; and (2) have resources that do not exceed the resource amount allowable for the previous year, increased by the annual percentage increase in the consumer price index (all items, U.S. city average) as of September of the previous year, rounded to the nearest multiple of $10. [42 C.F.R. § 423.773(d).]

Low-income Part D eligible individuals must reside in the 50 states or the District of Columbia to receive premium and cost-sharing subsidies. [42 C.F.R. § § 423.773(a), 423.907.]

Eligibility Determinations, Redeterminations, and Applications

An individual must file an application for subsidy assistance with a state's Medicaid program office or the Social Security Administration (SSA). Part D plans are to refer individual inquiries concerning application or eligibility for the low-income subsidy to state agencies or SSA. [42 C.F.R. § 423.774(d); *Medicare Prescription Drug Benefit Manual*, Pub. 100-18, Ch. 13, § 40.1.]

Eligibility determinations. If an individual applies with the state Medicaid agency, the determination of eligibility for subsidies is made by the state under its state plan under Title XIX of the Social Security Act. If an individual applies with the SSA, the Commissioner of Social Security will make the determination. [42 C.F.R. § 423.774(a).]

Effective date of initial eligibility determinations. Initial eligibility determinations are effective beginning with the first day of the month in which the individual applies, and they remain in effect for no more than one year. [42 C.F.R. § 423.774(b).]

Redeterminations and appeals of low-income subsidy eligibility. If the state makes an eligibility determination, it must make redeterminations and appeals of low-income subsidy eligibility determinations in the same manner and frequency as the redeterminations and appeals made under the state's Medicaid plan. Redeterminations and appeals of eligibility determinations made by the Commissioner will be made in the manner specified by the Commissioner of Social Security. [42 C.F.R. § 423.774(c).]

Application requirements. For subsidy applications to be considered complete, applicants or personal representatives applying on the applicants' behalf must: (1) complete all required elements of the application; (2) provide any statements from financial institutions, as requested, to support information in the application; and (3) certify, under penalty of perjury or similar sanction for false statements, as to the accuracy of the information provided on the application form. [42 C.F.R. § 423.774(d).]

Special eligibility rule for widows and widowers. Section 3304(a) of the Patient Protection and Affordable Care Act (ACA) (P.L. 111-148) created a special rule for widows and widowers regarding eligibility for the low-income subsidy. If the spouse dies during the effective period for a favorable determination or redetermination that has been made related to an individual's eligibility for a low-income subsidy, the effective period will be extended for one year after the date on which the determination or redetermination would otherwise cease to be effective. [Soc. Sec. Act § 1860D-14(a)(3)(B)(vi); Pub. 100-18, Ch. 13, § 40.1.]

Part D Premium Subsidy Amounts

The Part D premium subsidy amounts available to subsidy-eligible individuals vary depending upon the individual's income and resources/asset levels. [Soc. Sec. Act § 1860D-14(b); 42 C.F.R. § 423.780.]

Full-subsidy-eligible individuals are entitled to a premium subsidy equal to 100 percent of the premium subsidy amount. The premium subsidy amount is the lesser of:

- under the Part D plan selected by the beneficiary, the portion of the monthly beneficiary premium attributable to basic coverage for enrollees in prescription drug plans (PDPs) or the portion of the Medicare Advantage (MA) monthly beneficiary premium attributable to basic prescription drug coverage for enrollees in MA-PD plans; or

- the greater of the low-income benchmark premium amount for a PDP region or the lowest monthly beneficiary premium for a PDP that offers basic prescription drug coverage in the PDP region.

[42 C.F.R. § 423.780(a), (b)(1).]

The low-income benchmark premium amount for a PDP region is a weighted average of the monthly beneficiary premium amounts (see below) for the Part D plans, with the weight for each PDP and MA-PD plan equal to a percentage. The numerator of the percentage is the number of Part D eligible individuals enrolled in the plan in the reference month, and the denominator is the total number of Part D eligible individuals enrolled in all PDP and MA-PD plans in a PDP region in the reference month. [42 C.F.R. § 423.780(b)(2).]

CMS publishes the regional low-income premium subsidy amounts in a file on its website: https://www.cms.gov/Medicare/Health-Plans/MedicareAdvtgSpecRateStats/Downloads/RegionalRatesBenchmarks2017.pdf.

Premium amounts. The premium amounts used to calculate the low-income benchmark premium amount are as follows: (1) the monthly beneficiary premium for a PDP that is basic prescription drug coverage; (2) the portion of the monthly beneficiary premium attributable to basic prescription drug coverage for a PDP that is enhanced alternative coverage; or (3) the MA monthly prescription drug beneficiary premium for a MA-PD plan determined before application of the monthly rebate. [42 C.F.R. § 423.780(b)(2)(ii).]

Other low-income subsidy-eligible individuals—sliding scale premium. Other low-income subsidy-eligible individuals are entitled to a premium subsidy based on a linear sliding scale, as follows:

(1) a full premium subsidy amount (100 percent) for individuals with income at or below 135 percent of the FPL applicable to their family size;

(2) a premium subsidy equal to 75 percent of the premium subsidy amount for individuals with income greater than 135 percent but at or below 140 percent of the FPL applicable to the family size;

(3) a premium subsidy equal to 50 percent of the premium subsidy amount for individuals with income greater than 140 percent but at or below 145 percent of the FPL applicable to the family size; or

(4) a premium subsidy equal to 25 percent of the premium subsidy amount for individuals with income greater than 145 percent but below 150 percent of FPL applicable to the family size.

[42 C.F.R. § 423.780(d).]

Waiver of late enrollment penalty for subsidy-eligible individuals. Subsidy-eligible individuals are not subject to a late enrollment penalty. [42 C.F.R. § 423.780(e).]

Waiver of minimal monthly premiums. The Secretary of HHS will allow a PDP or MA-PD plan to waive the monthly beneficiary premium for a subsidy-eligible individual if the amount of the premium is minimal. If the premium is waived, the Secretary will not reassign subsidy-eligible individuals enrolled in the plan to other plans based on the fact that the monthly beneficiary premium under the plan was greater than the low-income benchmark premium amount. [Soc. Sec. Act § 1860D-14(a)(5); 42 C.F.R. § 423.780(f).]

Part D Cost-Sharing Subsidy

Full-subsidy-eligible individuals have no annual deductible, and there is no coverage gap for full-subsidy individuals. In addition, they are entitled to a reduction in cost-sharing for all covered Part D drugs covered under the PDP or MA-PD plan below the out-of-pocket limit, including Part D drugs covered under the PDP or MA-PD plan obtained after the initial coverage limit. Finally, all cost-sharing for covered Part D drugs covered under the PDP or MA-PD plan above the out-of-pocket limit is eliminated for full-subsidy-eligible individuals. In other words, Medicare pays the full benefit once the catastrophic level is reached. [42 C.F.R. § 423.782(a).]

Elimination of cost-sharing for noninstitutionalized full-benefit dual eligibles. Full-benefit dual-eligible individuals who are institutionalized or who are receiving home- and community-based services have no cost-sharing for Part D drugs covered under their PDP or MA-PD plans. [Soc. Sec. Act § 1860D-14(a)(1)(D)(i); 42 C.F.R. § 423.782(a)(2)(ii).]

2017 reductions in cost-sharing. Reductions in copayments are applied as follows:

(1) For full-benefit dual-eligible individuals who are not institutionalized and who have income above 100 percent of the FPL applicable to the individual's family size and for individuals who have income under 135 percent of the FPL applicable to the individual's family size who meet the resources test for costs up to the out-of-pocket threshold, copayment amounts must not exceed the copayment amounts specified for standard prescription drug coverage. For 2017, copayment amounts will not exceed $3.30 for a generic or preferred multiple source drug and $8.25 for any other drug (but see (2) below because such individuals who are receiving home- and community-based services have no cost-sharing as of January 1, 2012).

(2) Full-benefit dual-eligible individuals who are institutionalized or who are receiving home and community-based services have no cost-sharing for covered Part D drugs covered under their PDP or MA-PD plans. [Soc. Sec. Act § 1860D-14(a)(1)(D)(i); 42 C.F.R. § 423.782(a)(2)(ii).]

(3) Full-benefit dual-eligible individuals with incomes that do not exceed 100 percent of the FPL applicable to the individual's family size are subject to cost-sharing for covered Part D drugs equal to the lesser of: (1) the amount specified for the percentage increase in the consumer price index, rounded to the nearest multiple of 5 cents or 10 cents, respectively; or (2) the copayment amount charged to other individuals described in (1). For 2017, the costs for these individuals must be capped at $1.20 for a generic drug or preferred multiple source drug and $3.70 for any other drug (but see (2) above because such individuals who are receiving home and community-based services have no cost-sharing as of January 1, 2012).

[42 C.F.R. § 423.782(a); *Announcement of CY 2017 MA Capitation Rates and MA and Part D Payment Policies and Final Call Letter*, April 4, 2016.]

Other low-income subsidy-eligible individuals. In addition to continuation of coverage (no coverage gap), other low-income subsidy-eligible individuals are entitled to the following:

(1) For 2017, the annual deductible for these individuals is $82;

(2) 15 percent coinsurance for all covered Part D drugs obtained after the annual deductible under the plan up to the out-of-pocket limit; and

(3) For 2017, copayments may not exceed $3.30 for a generic drug and $8.25 for any other drug.

[42 C.F.R. § 423.782(b); *Announcement of CY 2017 MA Capitation Rates and MA and Part D Payment Policies and Final Call Letter*, April 4, 2016.]

Administration of Subsidy Program

CMS notifies the Part D sponsor offering the Part D plan in which a subsidy-eligible individual is enrolled of the individual's eligibility for a subsidy and the amount of the subsidy. [Soc. Sec. Act § 1860D-14(c); 42 C.F.R. § 423.800(a).]

Reduction of premium or cost-sharing by PDP sponsor or organization. The Part D sponsor offering the Part D plan in which a subsidy-eligible individual is enrolled must reduce the individual's premiums and cost-sharing as applicable and provide information to CMS on the amount of those reductions. The Part D sponsor must track the application of the subsidies to be applied to the out-of-pocket threshold. [42 C.F.R. § 423.800(b).]

Reimbursement for cost-sharing paid before notification of eligibility for low-income subsidy. The Part D sponsor must reimburse subsidy-eligible individuals and organizations that pay cost-sharing on behalf of such individuals after the effective date of the individual's eligibility for a subsidy. [42 C.F.R. § 423.800(c).]

Best available evidence. Part D sponsors must accept the best available evidence received from beneficiaries and respond to requests for assistance in securing acceptable evidence of subsidy eligibility from beneficiaries according to processes established by CMS and within the reasonable time frames as determined by CMS. [42 C.F.R. 423.800(d).]

Retroactive adjustment time frame. Sponsors must process retroactive adjustments to cost-sharing for low-income subsidy-eligible individuals and any resulting refunds and recoveries within 45 days of the sponsor's receipt of complete information. [42 C.F.R. 423.800(e).]

[¶ 510] Benefits and Beneficiary Protections

Requirements regarding standards for access to covered Part D drugs; Part D sponsor formularies; information dissemination by Part D sponsors; disclosure to beneficiaries of pricing information for generic versions of covered Part D drugs; and the privacy, confidentiality, and accuracy of prescription drug plan (PDP) sponsors' beneficiary records are implemented in Subpart C, Part 423 of the Part D regulations.

Requirements Related to Qualified Prescription Drug Coverage

CMS may approve as Part D sponsors only those entities proposing to offer qualified prescription drug coverage. Qualified prescription drug coverage may consist of either standard prescription drug coverage or alternative prescription drug coverage, both of which provide access to Part D drugs at negotiated prices. A sponsor offering a prescription drug plan (PDP) must offer that plan to all Part D eligible beneficiaries residing in the plan's service area with the same premium, benefits, and level of cost-sharing throughout the service area. [42 C.F.R. § 423.104(b), (d).]

Alternative prescription drug coverage. Alternative prescription drug coverage provides coverage for Part D drugs and includes access to negotiated prices. Alternative prescription drug coverage also must:

(1) have an annual deductible that does not exceed the annual deductible for standard prescription drug coverage;

(2) impose cost-sharing no greater than that specified for standard prescription drug coverage once the annual out-of-pocket threshold is met;

(3) have a total or gross value that is at least equal to the total or gross value of defined standard coverage;

(4) have an unsubsidized value that is at least equal to the unsubsidized value of standard prescription drug coverage (*Note:* The unsubsidized value of coverage is the amount by which the actuarial value of the coverage exceeds the actuarial value of the subsidy payments for the coverage); and

(5) provide coverage that is designed, based upon an actuarially representative pattern of utilization, to provide for the payment of costs that are equal to the initial coverage limit, in an amount at least equal to the product of: (a) the amount by which the initial coverage limit for the year exceeds the deductible and (b) 100 percent minus the coinsurance percentage specified for standard prescription drug coverage.

[42 C.F.R. § 423.104(e).]

Negotiated prices. A PDP sponsor is required to provide enrollees with access to negotiated prices for covered Part D drugs included in its formulary. [42 C.F.R. § 423.104(g).]

Access to Covered Part D Drugs

PDPs must secure the participation of a pharmacy network consisting of retail pharmacies sufficient to ensure that all beneficiaries residing in each state in a PDP's service area, each state in a regional Medicare Advantage (MA) organization's service area, the entire service area of a local MA organization, or the entire geographic area of a cost contract have convenient access to covered drugs. As a result, PDPs must establish pharmacy networks in which:

(1) in urban areas, at least 90 percent of Medicare beneficiaries in the PDP service area live, on average, within two miles of the retail pharmacy participating in the plan's network;

(2) in suburban areas, at least 90 percent of Medicare beneficiaries in the PDP service area live, on average, within five miles of a retail pharmacy participating in the plan's network; and

(3) in rural areas, at least 70 percent of Medicare beneficiaries in the PDP service area live, on average, within 15 miles of a retail pharmacy participating in the plan's network.

[Soc. Sec. Act § 1860D-4(b); 42 C.F.R. § 423.120(a)(1).]

Part D plans may count Indian tribes and tribal organizations, urban Indian organizations (I/T/U) pharmacies, and pharmacies operated by federally qualified health centers and rural health centers toward the required percentages for urban, suburban, and rural areas. [42 C.F.R. § 423.120(a)(2).]

A PDP's contracted pharmacy network must provide adequate access to home infusion pharmacies and convenient access and standard contracting terms and conditions to all long-term care and I/T/U pharmacies in its service area. [42 C.F.R. § 423.120(a)(4), (5), (6).]

Part D sponsors are required to permit the participation in their pharmacy networks of any pharmacy willing to accept the plan's standard terms and conditions, and they may not require a pharmacy to accept insurance risk as a condition of participation in the network. [Soc. Sec. Act § 1860D-4(b)(1)(A), (E); 42 C.F.R. § 423.120(a)(8).]

A PDP sponsor offering a plan that provides coverage other than defined standard coverage may reduce copayments or coinsurance for covered drugs obtained through a preferred pharmacy relative to the copayments or coinsurance applicable for such drugs when obtained through a non-preferred pharmacy. [Soc. Sec. Act § 1860D-4(b)(1)(B); 42 C.F.R. § 423.120(a)(9).]

A PDP sponsor must permit its enrollees to receive benefits, which may include an extended (90-day) supply of covered drugs, at any of its network pharmacies that are retail pharmacies. A Part D plan, however, may require an enrollee obtaining a covered drug at a retail network pharmacy to pay any higher cost-sharing applicable to that pharmacy instead of the cost-sharing applicable to the drug at the mail-order network pharmacy. [Soc. Sec. Act § 1860D-4(b)(1)(D); 42 C.F.R. § 423.120(a)(10).]

Part D Formulary Requirements

A Part D sponsor that uses a formulary under its qualified prescription drug coverage must meet the following requirements:

> (1) development and revision by a pharmacy and therapeutic committee;

> (2) provision of an adequate formulary;

> (3) a drug transition process for enrollees prescribed Part D drugs that are not on its Part D plan's formulary;

> (4) a limitation on changes in therapeutic classification;

> (5) the provision of notice regarding formulary changes;

> (6) a limitation on formulary changes before the beginning of a contract year; and

> (7) policies and procedures to educate and inform health care providers and enrollees concerning its formulary.

[Soc. Sec. Act § 1860D-4(b)(3); 42 C.F.R. § 423.120(b).]

A Part D plan's formulary must:

> (1) include within each therapeutic category and class of Part D drugs at least two Part D drugs that are not therapeutically equivalent and bioequivalent, with different strengths and dosage forms available for each of those drugs, except that only one Part D drug must be included in a particular category or class of covered Part D drugs if the category or class includes only one Part D drug;

> (2) include at least one Part D drug within a particular category or class of Part D drugs to the extent the Part D plan demonstrates, and CMS approves, that only two drugs are available in that category or class of Part D drugs, and that one drug is clinically superior to the other drug in that category or class of Part D drugs;

> (3) include adequate coverage of the types of drugs most commonly needed by Part D enrollees, as recognized in national treatment guidelines; and

> (4) be approved by CMS consistent with 42 C.F.R. § 423.272(b)(2).

[42 C.F.R. § 423.120(b)(2).]

Until the Secretary determines, through rulemaking, criteria to identify, as appropriate, categories and classes of clinical concern, the following six classes must be included in PDP formularies:

> (1) anticonvulsants;

> (2) antidepressants;

> (3) antineoplastics;

(4) antipsychotics

(5) antiretrovirals; and

(6) immunosuppressants for the treatment of transplant rejection.

[Soc. Sec. Act § 1860D-4(b)(3)(G); 42 C.F.R. § 423.120(b)(2)(v).]

Exceptions to the requirements related to the categories and classes of clinical concern are:

(1) drug products that are rated as therapeutically equivalent (under the FDA's most recent publication of "Approved Drug Products with Therapeutic Equivalence Evaluations," also known as the Orange Book);

(2) utilization management processes that limit the quantity of drugs due to safety; and

(3) other drugs that CMS specifies through a process that is based upon scientific evidence and medical standards of practice (and, in the case of antiretroviral medications, is consistent with HHS Guidelines for the Use of Antiretroviral Agents in HIV-1-Infected Adults and Adolescents) and that permits public notice and comment.

[42 C.F.R. § 423.120(b)(2)(vi).]

Transition process. A Part D sponsor must provide for an appropriate transition process for enrollees prescribed Part D drugs that are not on its Part D plan's formulary (including Part D drugs that are on a sponsor's formulary but require prior authorization or step therapy under a plan's utilization management rules). The transition process must:

(1) be applicable to new enrollees into Part D plans following the annual coordinated election period, newly eligible Medicare enrollees from other coverage, individuals who switch from one plan to another after the start of the contract year, and current enrollees remaining in the plan affected by formulary changes;

(2) ensure access to a temporary supply of drugs within the first 90 days of coverage under a new plan for retail, home infusion, long-term care, and mail-order pharmacies;

(3) ensure the provision of a temporary fill when an enrollee requests a fill of a non-formulary drug (including Part D drugs that are on a plan's formulary but require prior authorization or step therapy under a plan's utilization management rules);

(4) ensure written notice is provided to each affected enrollee within three business days after adjudication of the temporary fill;

(5) ensure that reasonable efforts are made to notify prescribers of affected enrollees who receive a transition notice; and

(6) charge cost-sharing for a temporary supply of drugs provided under its transition process such that the following conditions are met: (a) for low-income subsidy (LIS) enrollees, a sponsor must not charge higher cost-sharing for transition supplies than the statutory maximum copayment amounts; and (b) for non-LIS enrollees, a sponsor must charge the same cost-sharing for non-formulary Part D drugs provided during the transition that would apply for non-formulary drugs approved through a formulary exception; and the same cost-sharing for formulary drugs subject to utilization management edits provided during the transition that would apply once the utilization management criteria are met.

[42 C.F.R. § 423.120(b)(3).]

Limitation on changes in therapeutic classification. Except as CMS may permit to account for new therapeutic uses and newly approved Part D drugs, a Part D sponsor may not change the therapeutic categories and classes in a formulary other than at the beginning of each plan year. [42 C.F.R. § 423.120(b)(4).]

Provision of notice regarding formulary changes. Before removing a covered Part D drug from its Part D plan's formulary or making any change in the preferred or tiered cost-sharing status of a covered Part D drug, a Part D sponsor must provide at least 60 days' notice to CMS, State Pharmaceutical Assistance Programs, entities providing other prescription drug coverage, authorized prescribers, network pharmacies, and pharmacists. The sponsor must also either provide direct written notice to affected enrollees at least 60 days before the date the change becomes effective or, at the time an affected enrollee requests a refill of the Part D drug, provide such enrollee with a 60-day supply of the Part D drug under the same terms as previously allowed and written notice of the formulary change. [42 C.F.R. § 423.120(b)(5)(i).]

The written notice to the affected enrollee must contain:

(1) the name of the affected covered Part D drug;

(2) whether the plan is removing the covered Part D drug from the formulary or changing its preferred or tiered cost-sharing status;

(3) the reason why the plan is removing such covered Part D drug from the formulary or changing its preferred or tiered cost-sharing status;

(4) alternative drugs in the same therapeutic category or class or cost-sharing tier and expected cost-sharing for those drugs; and

(5) the means by which enrollees may obtain a coverage determination or exception.

[42 C.F.R. § 423.120(b)(5)(ii).]

Part D sponsors may immediately remove from their Part D plan formularies covered Part D drugs deemed unsafe by the Food and Drug Administration (FDA) or removed from the market by their manufacturer. Part D sponsors must provide retrospective notice of any such formulary changes to affected enrollees, CMS, State Pharmaceutical Assistance Programs, entities providing other prescription drug coverage, authorized prescribers, network pharmacies, and pharmacists consistent with the above requirements. [42 C.F.R. § 423.120(b)(5)(iii).]

Limitation on formulary changes before the beginning of a contract year. A Part D sponsor may not remove a covered Part D drug from its Part D plan's formulary, or make any change in the preferred or tiered cost-sharing status of a covered Part D drug on its plan's formulary, between the beginning of the annual coordinated election period and 60 days after the beginning of the contract year associated with that annual coordinated election period. [42 C.F.R. § 423.120(b)(6).]

Provider and patient education. A Part D sponsor must establish policies and procedures to educate and inform health care providers and enrollees concerning its formulary. [42 C.F.R. § 423.120(b)(7).]

Use of standardized technology. A Part D sponsor must issue and reissue, as necessary, a card or other type of technology that its enrollees may use to access negotiated prices for covered Part D drugs. When processing Part D claims, a sponsor or its intermediary must comply with the electronic transaction standards established by 45 C.F.R. § 162.1102. A sponsor must require its network pharmacies to submit claims to the sponsor or its intermediary whenever the card is presented or is on file at the pharmacy unless the enrollee expressly requests that a particular claim not be submitted to the sponsor or its intermediary. [42 C.F.R. § 423.120(c)(1)–(3).]

¶510

A Part D sponsor must assign and exclusively use a unique: (1) Part D bank identification number (BIN) or RxBIN and Part D processor control number (RxPCN) combination in its Medicare line of business; and (2) Part D cardholder identification number (RxID) to clearly identify its Medicare Part D beneficiaries. [42 C.F.R. § 423.120(c)(4).]

Beginning in plan year 2016, a claim for a covered Part D drug under a Part D PDP or a Medicare Advantage prescription drug plan (MA-PD) must include a valid prescriber national provider identifier (NPI). The physician or eligible professional who prescribed the drug must be enrolled in the Medicare program in an approved status or have a valid opt-out affidavit on file with a Medicare administrative contractor. However, pharmacy claims for Part D drugs prescribed by an "other authorized prescriber" (defined as an individual other than a physician or eligible professional who is authorized under state law to write prescriptions) are not subject to this requirement. [Soc. Sec. Act § 1860D-4(c)(4); 42 C.F.R. §§ 423.120(c)(6), 423.160(a)(4).]

Upon receipt of a pharmacy claim or beneficiary request for reimbursement for a drug that a Part D sponsor would otherwise be required to reject or deny for the reasons described in 42 C.F.R. § 423.120(c)(6)(ii) or (iii), the sponsor must provide the beneficiary with a three-month provisional supply of the drug (as prescribed by the prescriber and if allowed by applicable law) and written notice within three business days after adjudication of the claim or request in a form and manner specified by CMS. [42 C.F.R. § 423.120(c)(6)(v)(B).]

Compounded drug products. For multi-ingredient compounds, a Part D sponsor must determine whether the compound is covered under Part D. A compound that contains at least one ingredient covered under Part B is considered a Part B compound, regardless of whether other ingredients in the compound are covered under Part B. Only compounds that contain at least one ingredient that independently meets the definition of a Part D drug and do not contain any Part B ingredients may be considered Part D compounds and covered under Part D. For a Part D compound to be considered on-formulary, all ingredients that independently meet the definition of a Part D drug must be considered on-formulary. For a Part D compound to be considered off-formulary, transition rules apply such that all ingredients in the Part D compound that independently meet the definition of a Part D drug must become payable in the event of a transition fill and all ingredients that independently meet the definition of a Part D drug must be covered if an exception is approved for coverage of the compound. [42 C.F.R. § 423.120(d)(1).]

Compound payment liabilities. A Part D sponsor must establish consistent rules for beneficiary payment liabilities for both ingredients of the Part D compound that independently meet the definition of a Part D drug and non-Part D ingredients. For low-income subsidy beneficiaries, the copayment amount is based on whether the most expensive ingredient that independently meets the definition of a Part D drug in the Part D compound is a generic or brand name drug. For any non-Part D ingredient of the Part D compound, the Part D sponsor's contract with the pharmacy must prohibit balance billing the beneficiary for the cost of any such ingredients. [42 C.F.R. § 423.120(d)(2).]

Out-of-Network Access to Covered Part D Drugs

PDPs are required to ensure that their enrollees have adequate access to drugs dispensed at out-of-network pharmacies when enrollees cannot reasonably be expected to obtain covered drugs at a network pharmacy and do not access covered Part D drugs at an out-of-network pharmacy on a routine basis. [42 C.F.R. § 423.124(a)(1).] Provided the enrollees do not routinely access out-of-network pharmacies, CMS expects PDPs to guarantee out-of-network access if an enrollee:

(1) is traveling outside the plan's service area, runs out of or loses covered drugs or becomes ill and needs a covered drug, and cannot access a network pharmacy;

(2) cannot obtain a covered drug in a timely manner within a service area because, for example, there is no network pharmacy within a reasonable driving distance that provides 24 hour/7 day per week service;

(3) must fill a prescription for a covered drug and that particular drug is not regularly stocked at accessible network retail or mail-order pharmacies;

(4) is provided covered drugs dispensed by an out-of-network institution-based pharmacy while a patient in an emergency department, provider-based clinic, outpatient surgery, or other outpatient setting and, as a result, cannot get the medications filled at a network pharmacy; or

(5) experiences a declared federal disaster or other declared public health emergency in which Part D enrollees are evacuated or otherwise displaced from their place of residence and cannot reasonably be expected to obtain covered Part D drugs at a network pharmacy and, in addition, in circumstances in which normal distribution channels are unavailable.

[*Medicare Prescription Drug Benefit Manual*, Pub. 100-18, Ch. 5, § 60.1.]

In addition, plans must provide coverage for vaccines and other covered Part D drugs that are appropriately dispensed and administered in a physician's office. [42 C.F.R. § 423.124(a)(2).]

Limits on out-of-network access. CMS requires PDPs to establish reasonable rules to ensure that enrollees use out-of-network pharmacies in an appropriate manner, provided that the plans also ensure adequate access to out-of-network pharmacies on a non-routine basis when enrollees cannot reasonably access network pharmacies. For example, PDPs may wish to limit the amount of covered drugs dispensed at an out-of-network pharmacy and require that a beneficiary purchase maintenance medications via mail order for extended out-of-area travel or require a plan notification or authorization process for individuals who fill their prescriptions at out-of-network pharmacies. [42 C.F.R. § 423.124(a), (c); Pub. 100-18, Ch. 5, § 60.1.]

Financial responsibility for out-of-network access. Enrollees obtaining covered Part D drugs at out-of-network pharmacies must assume financial responsibility for any differential between the out-of-network pharmacy's (or provider's) usual and customary price and the Part D sponsor's plan allowance. [42 C.F.R. § 423.124(b).]

Dissemination of Part D Plan Information

To ensure that eligible or enrolled individuals in PDPs receive the information they need to make informed choices about their coverage options, sponsors must disclose a detailed description of each qualified PDP. The description must be provided in a clear, accurate, and standardized form at the time of enrollment and annually thereafter, 15 days before the annual coordinated election period. The information required is similar to the information MA plans must disclose to their enrollees. [Soc. Sec. Act § 1860D-4(a); 42 C.F.R. § 423.128(a).]

The description must include information regarding:

(1) service area;

(2) benefits, including applicable conditions and limitations, premiums, cost-sharing, cost-sharing for subsidy-eligible individuals, and other benefit-associated conditions;

(3) how to obtain more information on cost-sharing requirements, including tiered or other copayment levels applicable to each drug;

(4) the plan's formulary, including a list of included drugs, the manner in which the formulary functions, the process for obtaining an exception to the plan's formulary or tiered cost-sharing structure, and a description of how an eligible individual may obtain additional information on the formulary;

(5) the number, mix, and addresses of network pharmacies from which enrollees may reasonably be expected to obtain covered drugs and how the sponsor meets the access requirements;

(6) provisions for access to covered drugs at out-of-network pharmacies;

(7) all grievance, coverage determination, and appeal rights and procedures;

(8) policies and procedures for quality assurance and the medication therapy management program;

(9) disenrollment rights and responsibilities; and

(10) the fact that a sponsor may terminate or refuse to renew its contract, or reduce the service area, and the effect that this may have on plan enrollees.

[42 C.F.R. § 423.128(b).]

Information available on request of the eligible individual. Upon request of a Part D eligible individual, a Part D sponsor must provide: general coverage information; the procedures the sponsor uses to control utilization of services and expenditures; the number of grievances, appeals, and exceptions, and their disposition in the aggregate; and the financial condition of the Part D sponsor, including the most recently audited information regarding the sponsor offering the plan. "General coverage information" includes information on: (1) how to exercise election options, (2) procedural rights, (3) benefits, (4) premiums, (5) the plan's formulary, (6) the plan's service area, and (7) quality and performance indicators for benefits under the plan. [42 C.F.R. § 423.128(c).]

Mechanisms for providing specific information to enrollees. Part D sponsors must have mechanisms in place to provide specific information requested by current and prospective enrollees. The mechanisms must include: a toll-free customer call center, an Internet website, and responses in writing upon beneficiary request. The plans' customer call centers must:

(1) be open during usual business hours;

(2) provide telephone service to customers, including pharmacists, pursuant to standard business practices;

(3) provide interpreters for non-English speaking and limited-English-speaking individuals; and

(4) provide immediate access to the coverage determination and redetermination process.

[42 C.F.R. § 423.128(d).]

Explanation of benefits. Part D sponsors must furnish an explanation of benefits (EOB) to enrollees who receive covered Part D drugs. EOBs must be written in a form easily understandable to beneficiaries and must be provided at least monthly for those enrollees utilizing their prescription drug benefits in a given month. EOBs for Part D plans also must:

(1) include a listing of the item or service for which payment was made, as well as the amount of such payment for each item or service;

(2) include a notice of the individual's right to request an itemized statement;

(3) include information regarding the cumulative, year-to-date amount of benefits provided relative to the deductible, the initial coverage limit, and the annual out-of-pocket threshold for that year, and a beneficiary's cumulative, year-to-date total of incurred costs;

(4) include information regarding any applicable formulary changes; and

(5) be provided no later than the end of the month following any month when prescription drug benefits are provided, including for covered Part D spending between the initial coverage limit and the out-of-pocket threshold.

[42 C.F.R. § 423.128(e).]

Disclosure of deficiencies. CMS may require a Part D plan sponsor to disclose to its enrollees or potential enrollees the Part D plan sponsor's performance and contract compliance deficiencies in a manner specified by CMS. [42 C.F.R. § 423.128(f).]

Changes in rules. If a Part D sponsor intends to change its rules for a Part D plan, it must do all of the following: (1) submit the changes for CMS review; (2) for changes that take effect on January 1, notify all enrollees at least 15 days before the beginning of the annual coordinated election period; and (3) provide notice of all other changes in accordance with Part D notice requirements. [42 C.F.R. § 423.128(g).]

Disclosure of formulary and coverage information for auto-assigned subsidy eligibles. Subsidy-eligible individuals enrolled in a PDP who subsequently are reassigned to a new PDP by the HHS Secretary must be provided, within 30 days of the reassignment, with: (1) information on formulary differences between the individual's former plan and the plan to which the individual is reassigned with respect to the individual's drug regimen; and (2) a description of the individual's right to request a coverage determination, exception, or reconsideration, bring an appeal, or resolve a grievance. [Soc. Sec. Act § 1860D-14(d).]

Disclosure of Prices for Equivalent Drugs (Generic Differential Notice)

Part D sponsors must ensure that pharmacies inform enrollees of any differential between the price of a covered Part D drug and the price of the lowest-priced generic version available under the plan at that pharmacy. This generic price differential information must be provided at the time the plan enrollee purchases the drug or, in the case of drugs purchased by mail order, at the time of delivery. Disclosure of this information, however, is not necessary if the particular covered drug purchased by an enrollee is the lowest-priced generic version of that drug available at a particular pharmacy. [Soc. Sec. Act § 1860D-4(k); 42 C.F.R. § 423.132(a), (b).]

CMS is permitted to waive the generic differential notice requirement in the following cases:

(1) whenever a private fee-for-service MA plan offers qualified prescription drug coverage and provides plan enrollees with access to covered Part D drugs dispensed at all pharmacies, without regard to whether they are contracted network pharmacies, and does not charge additional cost-sharing for access to covered drugs dispensed at all pharmacies;

(2) at out-of-network pharmacies;

(3) at pharmacies of Indian tribes and tribal organizations, and urban Indian organizations' network pharmacies;

¶510

(4) at network pharmacies located in any of the U.S. territories (American Samoa, the Commonwealth of the Northern Mariana Islands, Guam, Puerto Rico, and the Virgin Islands);

(5) at long-term care network pharmacies; and

(6) at any other place, when CMS deems compliance is impossible or impracticable.

[Soc. Sec. Act § 1860D-4(k); 42 C.F.R. § 423.132(c).]

Privacy, Confidentiality, and Accuracy of Enrollee Records

To the extent that a PDP sponsor maintains medical records or other health information regarding Part D enrollees, the sponsor must meet the same requirements regarding confidentiality and accuracy of enrollee records as MA organizations offering MA plans. [Soc. Sec. Act § 1860D-4(i).]

PDP sponsors must:

(1) abide by all federal and state laws regarding confidentiality and disclosure of medical records or other health and enrollment information, including the Health Insurance Portability and Accountability Act of 1996 (HIPAA) and the privacy rule promulgated under HIPAA;

(2) ensure that medical information is released only in accordance with applicable federal or state law or under court orders or subpoenas;

(3) maintain the records and information in an accurate and timely manner; and

(4) ensure timely access by enrollees to records and information pertaining to them.

[42 C.F.R. § 423.136.]

PDPs are covered entities under the HIPAA privacy rule because they meet the definition of "health plan." Any violations by a PDP sponsor of its obligations under the privacy rule are subject to enforcement by the HHS Office for Civil Rights. [*Final rule*, 70 FR 4194, 4277, Jan. 28, 2005.]

[¶ 515] Grievances, Coverage Determinations, Redeterminations, and Reconsiderations

The law and regulations concerning grievances, coverage determinations, redeterminations, and reconsiderations under the Part D prescription drug benefit establish a process that largely mirrors the procedures required under the Medicare Advantage (MA) program (see ¶ 403). Definitions for these terms, as used in Part D, follow.

Grievance. A grievance is any complaint or dispute expressing dissatisfaction with a Part D plan sponsor's operations or behavior. Grievances do not include coverage determinations. [42 C.F.R. § 423.560.]

Coverage determination. A coverage determination is a decision by a Part D sponsor regarding the benefits an enrollee is entitled to receive for drug coverage. [42 C.F.R. § 423.566.]

Reconsideration. A reconsideration is a review of an adverse coverage determination by an independent review entity (IRE) and includes review of the evidence upon which the determination was based and any additional evidence the enrollee submits or the IRE obtains. [42 C.F.R. § 423.560.]

Redetermination. A redetermination is a review of an adverse coverage determination by a Part D plan sponsor and includes the review of evidence upon which the determination was based and any other evidence the enrollee submits or the plan obtains. [42 C.F.R. § 423.560.]

This section sets forth the requirements related to: (1) Part D plan sponsors with respect to grievances, coverage determinations, and redeterminations; (2) Part D IREs with respect to reconsiderations; and (3) Part D enrollees' rights with respect to grievances, coverage determinations, redeterminations, and reconsiderations. The requirements regarding reopenings, administrative law judge (ALJ) hearings, Medicare Appeals Council review, and judicial review are discussed in ¶ 516. [42 C.F.R. § 423.558.]

Responsibilities of Part D Plan Sponsors and Rights of Enrollees

For each prescription drug plan (PDP) that it offers, a Part D plan sponsor must establish and maintain:

(1) a grievance procedure addressing issues unrelated to coverage determinations;

(2) a single, uniform exceptions and appeals process that includes procedures for accepting oral and written requests for coverage determinations and redeterminations;

(3) a procedure for making timely coverage determinations, including determinations on requests for exceptions to a tiered cost-sharing formulary structure or exceptions to a formulary; and

(4) appeal procedures for issues related to coverage determinations that meet the requirements of the Part D regulations.

[Soc. Sec. Act § 1860D-4(b)(3)(H), (g), (h); 42 C.F.R. § 423.562(a)(1).]

A PDP must ensure that enrollees receive written information related to grievance and appeal procedures available to them through the plan and the complaint process available to them under the quality improvement organization process. In addition, a PDP must arrange with its network pharmacies to post or distribute notices instructing enrollees to contact their plans to obtain a coverage determination or request an exception. [42 C.F.R. § 423.562(a)(2), (3).]

Delegated responsibilities. If the Part D plan sponsor delegates any of its responsibilities to another entity or individual through which the sponsor provides covered benefits, the sponsor is ultimately responsible for ensuring that the entity or individual satisfies these requirements. [42 C.F.R. § 423.562(a)(4).]

Medical director requirement. A Part D plan sponsor must employ a medical director who is responsible for ensuring the clinical accuracy of all coverage determinations and redeterminations involving medical necessity. The medical director must be a physician with a current and unrestricted license to practice medicine in a state, territory, Puerto Rico, or the District of Columbia. [42 C.F.R. § 423.562(a)(5).]

Rights of enrollees. Enrollees have the right to: (1) have grievances between the enrollee and the Part D plan sponsor heard and resolved by the plan; (2) have the plan make a timely coverage determination, including a request for an exception to the plan's tiered cost-sharing structure or formulary; and (3) request an expedited coverage determination from the plan. [42 C.F.R. § 423.562(b).]

If an enrollee is dissatisfied with any part of a coverage determination, he or she has the right to:

(1) a redetermination of the adverse coverage determination by the PDP sponsor;

(2) request an expedited redetermination;

(3) a reconsideration or expedited reconsideration by an IRE contracted by CMS if, as a result of a redetermination, a plan affirms, in whole or in part, its adverse coverage determination;

(4) an ALJ hearing if the IRE affirms the plan's adverse coverage determination, in whole or in part, and the amount in controversy requirement is met;

(5) request a Medicare Appeals Council review of the ALJ hearing decision if the ALJ affirms the IRE's adverse coverage determination, in whole or in part; and

(6) judicial review of the Medicare Appeals Council hearing decision if it affirms the ALJ's adverse coverage determination, in whole or in part, and the amount-in-controversy requirement is met.

[42 C.F.R. § 423.562(b)(4).]

Part D Grievance Procedure

PDPs must have meaningful procedures for timely hearing and resolution of grievances from enrollees against PDP sponsors or any other entity or individual providing covered benefits under the such plans. The grievance procedures must be separate and distinct from appeals procedures. When the plan receives a complaint, it must promptly determine and inform the enrollee whether the complaint is subject to its grievance or appeal procedures. [42 C.F.R. § 423.564(a), (b).]

Method for filing a grievance. An enrollee must file any grievance with a plan either orally or in writing no later than 60 calendar days after the event or incident that precipitated the grievance. [42 C.F.R. § 423.564(d).]

Disposition and notification. The plan must notify the enrollee of its decision as expeditiously as the case requires based on the enrollee's health status, but no later than 30 calendar days after the date the plan receives the oral or written grievance. The 30-calendar-day time frame may be extended by up to 14 calendar days if the enrollee requests the extension or if the plan justifies a need for additional information and documents how the delay is in the interest of the enrollee. [42 C.F.R. § 423.564(e).]

Expedited grievances. A PDP is required to respond to an enrollee's grievance within 24 hours if the complaint involves a refusal by the plan to grant an enrollee's request for an expedited coverage determination or an expedited redetermination and the enrollee has not yet purchased or received the drug that is in dispute. [42 C.F.R. § 423.564(f).]

Recordkeeping. The PDP must maintain records on grievances received orally and in writing. Records minimally must include the date of receipt, final disposition of the grievance, and the date that the plan notified the enrollee of the disposition. [42 C.F.R. § 423.564(g).]

Complaint system. As part of its contract with CMS, the Part D plan sponsor must agree to address complaints received by CMS against the sponsor by (1) addressing and resolving complaints in the CMS complaint tracking system; and (2) displaying a link to the electronic complaint form on the Medicare.gov website on the Part D plan's main website. [42 C.F.R. § 423.505(b)(22).]

Coverage Determinations by Prescription Drug Plans

Each PDP must have a procedure for making timely coverage determinations regarding the prescription drug benefits an enrollee is entitled to receive under the plan, including basic coverage and supplemental benefits, and the amount, including cost-sharing, that the enrollee is required to pay. The plan must have a standard procedure and an expedited procedure when use of the standard procedure may seriously jeopardize the enrollee's life, health, or ability to regain maximum function. [Soc. Sec. Act § 1860D-4(g); 42 C.F.R. § 423.566(a).]

Only adverse coverage determinations are subject to the appeals process. Plan actions that constitute coverage decisions include:

(1) a decision not to provide or pay for a Part D drug that the enrollee believes may be covered by the plan, including a decision not to pay because: (a) the drug is not on the plan's formulary, (b) the drug is determined not to be medically necessary, (c) the drug is furnished by an out-of-network pharmacy, or (d) the PDP determines that the drug is otherwise excludable from coverage if applied to Medicare Part D;

(2) failure to provide a coverage determination in a timely manner when a delay would adversely affect the health of the enrollee;

(3) a decision concerning an exceptions request to the plan's tiered cost-sharing structure;

(4) a decision concerning an exceptions request involving a non-formulary Part D drug; or

(5) a decision on the amount of cost-sharing for a drug.

[42 C.F.R. § 423.566(b).]

The enrollee or the enrollee's appointed representative, on behalf of the enrollee, or the prescribing physician, on behalf of the enrollee, may request a standard or expedited coverage determination. [42 C.F.R. § 423.566(c).]

Medical review of coverage determinations. If a Part D plan sponsor expects to issue a partially or fully adverse medical necessity decision based on the initial review of a request, a physician or other appropriate health care professional with sufficient medical and other expertise, including knowledge of Medicare coverage criteria, must first review the coverage determination. The physician or other health care professional must have a current and unrestricted license to practice within the scope of his or her profession in a state, territory, Puerto Rico, or the District of Columbia. [42 C.F.R. § 423.566(d).]

Standard coverage determination requests. An enrollee must ask for a standard coverage determination by making a request with the Part D sponsor orally or in writing, except that requests for payment must be in writing unless the sponsor has implemented a policy of accepting oral requests. The sponsor must establish and maintain a method of documenting all oral request and retain documentation in the case file. [42 C.F.R. § 423.568(a).]

Time frames for notification. When a party makes a request for a drug benefit, the plan sponsor must notify the enrollee and the prescribing physician involved, if appropriate, of its determination as expeditiously as the enrollee's health condition requires, but no later than 72 hours after receipt of the request or, for an exceptions request, no later than 72 hours after receipt of the physician's or other prescriber's supporting statement. [42 C.F.R. § 423.568(b).]

When a party makes a request for payment, the Part D plan sponsor must notify the enrollee of its determination and make payment (when applicable) no later than 14 calendar days after receipt of the request. [42 C.F.R. § 423.568(c).]

If the plan fails to notify the enrollee of its determination in the appropriate time frame, the failure constitutes an adverse coverage determination, and the plan must forward the enrollee's request to the IRE within 24 hours of the expiration of the adjudication time frame. [42 C.F.R. § 423.568(h).]

Written notice. If a Part D plan sponsor makes a completely favorable decision regarding a request for drug benefits, it must give the enrollee written notice of the determination. The sponsor may provide the initial notice orally as long as it sends a written follow-up notice within three calendar days. The notice must explain the conditions of the approval in a readable and understandable form. [42 C.F.R. § 423.568(d) and (e).]

If a Part D plan sponsor decides to deny a drug benefit in whole or in part, it must give the enrollee written notice of the determination. The initial notice may be oral as long as the sponsor mails a written follow-up notice within three calendar days of the oral notice. The notice of denial must:

    (1) use approved notice language in a readable and understandable form;

    (2) state the specific reasons for the denial;

    (3) inform the enrollee of his or her right to a redetermination; and

    (4) comply with any other notice requirements specified by CMS.

For drug coverage denials, the denial notice must describe both the standard and expedited redetermination processes, including the enrollee's right to obtain and conditions for obtaining an expedited redetermination, and the rest of the appeals process. For payment denials, the denial notice must describe the standard redetermination process and the rest of the appeals process. [42 C.F.R. § 423.568(f) and (g).]

Effect of a coverage determination. A coverage determination is binding on the Part D plan and the enrollee unless it is reviewed and revised by a redetermination or it is reopened and revised. [42 C.F.R. § 423.576.]

Requirements for an Expedited Coverage Determination by the PDP

An enrollee or an enrollee's prescribing physician or other prescriber may request that a PDP expedite a coverage determination. An expedited review is not available for requests for payment of Part D drugs that have been furnished. An enrollee or an enrollee's prescribing physician or other prescriber on behalf of the enrollee must submit an oral or written request directly to the plan or, if applicable, to the entity responsible for making the determination, as directed by the plan. The prescribing physician or other prescriber may provide oral or written support for an enrollee's request for an expedited determination. [Soc. Sec. Act § 1860D-4(g); 42 C.F.R. § 423.570(a), (b).]

Processing the request. When a request for an expedited review is received, the PDP must provide for an expedited determination in the following situations:

    • when an enrollee makes the request, if the plan determines that applying the standard time frame for making a determination may seriously jeopardize the life or health of the enrollee or the enrollee's ability to regain maximum function; and

    • when the request has been made or is supported by an enrollee's prescribing physician or other prescriber, if the physician or other prescriber indicates that applying the standard time frame for making a determination may seriously jeopardize the life or health of the enrollee or the enrollee's ability to regain maximum function.

[42 C.F.R. § 423.570(c).]

Time frame and notice for denied requests. If a plan denies a request for expedited determination, it must make the determination within the 72-hour time frame established for a standard determination. The 72-hour period begins on the day the plan receives the request for expedited determination or, for an exceptions request, the day the plan receives the physician's or other prescriber's supporting statement. [42 C.F.R. § 423.570(d)(1).]

The PDP also must give the enrollee and prescribing physician or other prescriber prompt oral notice of the denial that explains that the plan must process the request using the 72-hour time frame for standard determinations and informs the enrollee of the right to file an expedited grievance if he or she disagrees with the plan's decision not to expedite. In addition, the PDP must inform the enrollee of the right to resubmit a request for an expedited determination with the prescribing physician's or other prescriber's support and provide instructions about the plan's grievance process and its time frames. Within three calendar days of the oral notice, the plan must deliver an equivalent written notice. [42 C.F.R. § 423.570(d)(2), (3).]

Time frame and notice requirements for expedited determinations. A plan that approves a request for expedited determination must make its determination and notify the enrollee and the prescribing physician or other prescriber involved, when appropriate, of its decision whether adverse or favorable, as expeditiously as the enrollee's health condition requires, but no later than 24 hours after receiving the request or, for an exceptions request, after the physician's or other prescriber's supporting statement. If the plan fails to notify the enrollee of its determination within the 24-hour time frame, the failure constitutes an adverse coverage determination and the plan must forward the enrollee's request to the IRE within 24 hours of the expiration of the adjudication time frame. [42 C.F.R. § 423.572(a), (d).]

If the Part D plan sponsor first notifies an enrollee of an adverse or favorable expedited determination orally, it must mail written confirmation to the enrollee within three calendar days of the oral notification. If the determination is completely favorable, the notice must explain the conditions of the approval in a readable and understandable form. If the determination is not completely favorable, the notice must:

(1) use approved language in a readable and understandable form;

(2) state the specific reasons for the denial;

(3) inform the enrollee of his or her right to a redetermination; and

(4) describe the standard and expedited redetermination processes, including the enrollee's right to request an expedited redetermination; conditions for obtaining an expedited redetermination; and other aspects of the appeal process.

[42 C.F.R. § 423.572(b), (c).]

Formulary Exceptions Processes

PDP sponsors must establish exceptions processes to a plan's tiered cost-sharing structure and for receipt of an off-formulary drug. [Soc. Sec. Act § 1860D-4(g)(2); 42 C.F.R. § 423.578(a), (b).] An enrollee may not, however, use the exceptions process to request or be granted coverage for a prescription drug that does not meet the definition of a Part D drug. [42 C.F.R. § 423.578(e).]

Exception process to tiered cost-sharing structure. Under a tiered cost-sharing structure, drugs are assigned to different copayment tiers based on cost-sharing, clinical considerations, or both. An enrollee's level of cost-sharing is based on the tier into which the prescribed drug falls. Typically, drugs fall into one of three tiers—generic drugs, preferred brand-name drugs, or non-preferred brand-name drugs. All of a plan's cost-sharing tiers make up its formulary. [42 C.F.R. § 423.4.]

A PDP's exception procedures must encompass all types of tiering exceptions requests. The plan must grant an exception to its tiered cost-sharing structure whenever it determines that the non-preferred drug for treatment of the enrollee's condition is medically necessary, consistent with the physician's statement. [Soc. Sec. Act § 1860D-4(g)(2); 42 C.F.R. § 423.578(a).]

The PDP's exceptions criteria must include, but are not limited to: (1) a description of the criteria the plan uses to evaluate a determination made by the enrollee's prescribing physician or other prescriber; (2) consideration of whether the requested Part D drug that is the subject of the exceptions request is the therapeutic equivalent of any other drug on the plan's formulary; and (3) consideration of the number of drugs on the plan's formulary that are in the same class and category as the requested prescription drug that is the subject of the exceptions request. [42 C.F.R. § 423.578(a)(2).]

An enrollee or the enrollee's prescribing physician or other prescriber may file a request for an exception. The prescribing physician or other prescriber must provide an oral or written supporting statement that the preferred drug for the treatment of the enrollee's condition:

    (1) would not be as effective for the enrollee as the requested drug; and/or

    (2) would have adverse effects for the enrollee.

If the physician or other prescriber provides an oral supporting statement, the plan subsequently may require the physician or other prescriber to provide a written supporting statement to demonstrate the medical necessity of the drug as well as provide additional supporting medical documentation. [42 C.F.R. § 423.578(a)(3)–(5).]

Request for exceptions involving a non-formulary Part D drug. Part D plan sponsors that offer PDPs with formularies must establish and maintain exceptions procedures subject to CMS's approval for PDP enrollees who require non-formulary drugs. A non-formulary drug is a drug that is not on a plan's formulary. Formulary use includes the application of cost utilization tools such as: (1) a dose restriction, including the dosage form, that causes a particular Part D drug not to be covered for the number of doses prescribed; or (2) a step therapy requirement that causes a particular Part D drug not to be covered until the requirements of the plan's coverage policy are met; or (3) a therapeutic substitution requirement. [42 C.F.R. § 423.578(b).]

The PDP must grant an exception whenever it determines that the drug is medically necessary, consistent with the physician's statement, and the drug would be covered but for the fact that it is an off-formulary drug. The plan's formulary exceptions process must address:

    (1) situations in which a formulary changes during the year and situations in which an enrollee is already using a given drug;

    (2) continued coverage of a particular Part D prescription drug that the PDP is discontinuing on the formulary for reasons other than safety or because the Part D prescription drug cannot be supplied by or was withdrawn from the market by the drug's manufacturer; and

    (3) an exception to a plan's coverage policy that causes a Part D prescription drug not to be covered because of cost utilization tools, such as a requirement for step therapy, dosage limitations, or therapeutic substitution.

[42 C.F.R. § 423.578(b)(1).]

An enrollee, the enrollee's appointed representative, or the prescribing physician or other prescriber on behalf of the enrollee may file a request for an exception. The prescribing physician or other prescriber must provide an oral or written supporting statement that the requested prescription drug is medically necessary to treat the enrollee's disease or medical condition. [42 C.F.R. § 423.578(b)(4), (5).]

If the plan covers a non-formulary drug, the costs incurred by the enrollee for that drug are treated as being included for purposes of calculating and meeting the annual out-of-pocket threshold. [42 C.F.R. § 423.578(b)(3).]

When a non-formulary exceptions request is approved, the plan may not require the enrollee to request approval for a refill, or a new prescription to continue using the Part D prescription drug after the refills for the initial prescription are exhausted, as long as: (1) the enrollee's prescribing physician or other prescriber continues to prescribe the drug; (2) the drug continues to be considered safe for treating the enrollee's disease or medical condition; and (3) the enrollment period has not expired. [42 C.F.R. § 423.578(c)(4).]

Coverage determination. A decision by a PDP concerning an exceptions request constitutes a coverage determination. If the plan fails to make a decision on an exceptions request and provide notice of the decision within the time frame required for a standard determination or an expedited determination, as applicable, the failure constitutes an adverse coverage determination and the plan must forward the enrollee's request to the IRE within 24 hours of the expiration of the adjudication time frame. [42 C.F.R. § 423.578(c)(1), (c)(2).]

Rules for Redeterminations

To appeal a coverage determination, an enrollee or an enrollee's prescribing physician or other prescriber must file a written request for redetermination with the plan that made the coverage determination within 60 calendar days from the date of the notice of the coverage determination. The plan may adopt a policy for accepting oral requests and may extend the time frame for filing the request if the enrollee can show good cause for late filing. [Soc. Sec. Act § 1860D-4(g); 42 C.F.R. §§ 423.580, 423.582.]

Who must conduct the review of an adverse coverage determination. A person who was not involved in making the coverage determination must conduct the redetermination. When the issue is the denial of coverage based on a lack of medical necessity, the redetermination must be made by a physician with expertise in the field of medicine that is appropriate for the services at issue. The physician making the redetermination need not, in all cases, be of the same specialty or subspecialty as the prescribing physician. [42 C.F.R. § 423.590(f).]

Time frames for standard redetermination requests. If the Part D plan sponsor makes a redetermination of a request for coverage that is completely favorable to the enrollee or a redetermination that affirms, in whole or in part, its adverse coverage determination, the sponsor must notify the enrollee in writing of its redetermination as expeditiously as the enrollee's health condition requires, but no later than seven calendar days from the date it receives the request for a standard redetermination. If the Part D plan sponsor makes a redetermination of a request for payment that is completely favorable to the enrollee or affirms, in whole or in part, its adverse coverage determination, the sponsor must issue its redetermination and effectuate it no later than seven calendar days from the date it receives the request for redetermination. [42 C.F.R. § 423.590(a), (b).]

If the PDP fails to provide the enrollee with a redetermination within these time frames, the failure constitutes an adverse redetermination decision and the plan must forward the enrollee's request to the IRE within 24 hours of the expiration of the adjudication time frame. [42 C.F.R. § 423.590(c).]

Notice of adverse redetermination. The notice of any adverse determination must use approved notice language in a readable and understandable form, state the specific reasons for the denial, and inform the enrollee of his or her right to a reconsideration. For adverse drug coverage redeterminations, the notice must describe the standard and expedited reconsideration processes, including the enrollee's right to, and conditions for, obtaining an expedited reconsideration, and the remainder of the appeals process. For adverse payment redeterminations, the notice must describe the standard reconsideration process and the remainder of the appeals process. [42 C.F.R. § 423.590(g).]

Notice of completely favorable redeterminations. The notice of any completely favorable determination must explain the conditions of the approval in a readable and understandable form. [42 C.F.R. § 423.590(h).]

Expedited Redeterminations

An enrollee or an enrollee's prescribing physician or other prescriber acting on behalf of an enrollee may request that a Part D plan sponsor expedite a redetermination of a coverage determination. Requests for redetermination on payment of drugs already received, however, may not be expedited because a medical emergency does not exist for an enrollee who has obtained the medication in dispute. [Soc. Sec. Act § 1860D-4(g); 42 C.F.R. § 423.584(a).]

The enrollee or prescribing physician or other prescriber must submit an oral or written request directly to the PDP or, if applicable, to the entity responsible for making the redetermination, as directed by the plan. A prescribing physician or other prescriber may provide oral or written support for an enrollee's request for an expedited redetermination. [42 C.F.R. § 423.584(b).]

Processing expedited redetermination requests. The PDP must: (1) establish an efficient and convenient means for individuals to submit oral or written expedited redetermination requests; (2) document all oral requests in writing; and (3) maintain the documentation in the case file. In addition, the PDP must decide promptly whether to expedite the redetermination or follow the time frame for standard redetermination based on the following requirements:

- for a request made by an enrollee, the plan must provide an expedited redetermination if it determines that applying the standard time frame for making a redetermination may seriously jeopardize the life or health of the enrollee or the enrollee's ability to regain maximum function; and

- for a request made or supported by a prescribing physician or other prescriber, the plan must provide an expedited redetermination if the physician indicates that applying the standard time frame for conducting a redetermination may seriously jeopardize the life or health of the enrollee or the enrollee's ability to regain maximum function.

[42 C.F.R. § 423.584(c).]

Denial of an expedited redetermination request. If a PDP denies a request for expedited redetermination, it must make the determination within the seven-calendar-day time frame that begins the day the plan receives the request for expedited redetermination. The plan must give the enrollee prompt oral notice of the denial that:

(1) explains that the plan processes the enrollee's request using the seven-calendar-day time frame for standard redetermination;

(2) informs the enrollee of the right to file an expedited grievance if he or she disagrees with the decision by the plan not to expedite;

(3) informs the enrollee of the right to resubmit a request for an expedited redetermination with the prescribing physician's or other prescriber's support; and

(4) provides instructions about the expedited grievance process and its time frames.

Within three calendar days of the oral notice to the enrollee, the PDP must deliver an equivalent written notice that contains the required information. [42 C.F.R. § 423.584(d).]

Time frame for expedited redeterminations. A Part D plan sponsor that approves a request for expedited redetermination must complete its redetermination and give the enrollee and the prescribing physician or other prescriber involved, when appropriate, notice of its decision as expeditiously as the enrollee's health condition requires, but no later than 72 hours after receiving the request. If notice of an adverse or favorable expedited redetermination is given orally, the sponsor must mail written confirmation within three calendar days of the oral notice. [42 C.F.R. § 423.590(d).]

Failure to meet time frame for expedited redetermination. If the PDP fails to provide the enrollee or the prescribing physician or other prescriber, when appropriate, with the results of its expedited redetermination within the 72-hour time frame, the failure constitutes an adverse redetermination decision and the plan must forward the enrollee's request to the IRE within 24 hours of the expiration of the adjudication time frame. [42 C.F.R. § 423.590(e).]

Reconsideration by an Independent Review Entity

An enrollee (or the prescribing physician or other prescriber, acting on behalf of the enrollee) who is dissatisfied with the redetermination of a PDP has a right to a reconsideration by an IRE that contracts with CMS. [Soc. Sec. Act § 1860D-4(h); 42 C.F.R. § 423.600(a).]

The enrollee, or the enrollee's prescribing physician or other prescriber, must file a written request for reconsideration with the IRE within 60 calendar days of the date of the redetermination by the plan. When an enrollee or an enrollee's prescribing physician or other prescriber files an appeal, the IRE is required to solicit the views of the prescribing physician or other prescriber, either orally or in writing. The IRE must maintain a written account of the prescribing physician's views, prepared by the prescribing physician, other prescriber, or IRE. [42 C.F.R. § 423.600(a), (b).]

Requirements for reconsideration for non-formulary drugs. For an enrollee to request an IRE reconsideration of a determination by a plan not to provide for a Part D drug that is not on the formulary, the prescribing physician or other prescriber must determine that all covered Part D drugs on any tier of the formulary for treatment of the same condition would not be as effective for the individual as the non-formulary drug, would have adverse effects for the individual, or both. [42 C.F.R. § 423.600(c).]

Time frame for reconsideration. The IRE must conduct the reconsideration as expeditiously as the enrollee's health condition requires but no later than seven calendar days from the date of a request for a reconsideration. When a request for an expedited reconsideration is received and granted, the IRE must conduct the reconsideration as expeditiously as the enrollee's health condition requires, but no later than 72 hours after receiving the request. [42 C.F.R. § 423.600(d).]

Medical necessity issues. When the issue is the denial of coverage based on a lack of medical necessity (or any substantively equivalent term used to describe the concept of medical necessity), the reconsideration must be made by a physician with expertise in the field of medicine that is appropriate for the services at issue. The physician making the reconsideration need not, in all cases, be of the same specialty or subspecialty as the prescribing physician or other prescriber. [42 C.F.R. § 423.600(e).]

Notice of reconsideration determination. The IRE is responsible for mailing a notice of its reconsideration determination to the enrollee and the PDP and sending a copy to CMS. When the prescribing physician or other prescriber requests the reconsideration on behalf of the enrollee, the IRE is also responsible for notifying the prescribing physician or other prescriber of its decision. The notice must state the specific reasons for the IRE's decision in understandable language. If the reconsideration determination is adverse, the notice must inform the enrollee of his or her right to an ALJ hearing if the amount in controversy meets the threshold requirement and describe the procedures that the enrollee must follow to obtain an ALJ hearing. [42 C.F.R. § 423.602.]

Effect of a reconsideration determination. A reconsideration determination is final and binding on the enrollee and the plan, unless the enrollee files a request for an ALJ hearing. [42 C.F.R. § 423.604.]

Effectuation of Standard and Expedited Determinations, Reconsiderations, and Decisions

If a PDP reverses its coverage determination in a redetermination of a request for benefits, the plan must authorize or provide the benefit under dispute as expeditiously as the enrollee's health condition requires, but no later than seven calendar days from the date it receives the request for redetermination. [42 C.F.R. § 423.636(a)(1).]

If the PDP reverses its coverage determination on a redetermination of a request for payment, the Part D plan sponsor must authorize payment for the benefit within seven calendar days from the date it receives the request for redetermination and make payment no later than 30 calendar days after the date the plan sponsor receives the request for redetermination. [42 C.F.R. § 423.636(a)(2).]

On an expedited redetermination of a request for benefits, if the plan reverses its coverage determination, the plan must authorize or provide the benefit under dispute as expeditiously as the enrollee's health condition requires, but no later than 72 hours after the date the Part D plan sponsor receives the request for redetermination. [42 C.F.R. § 423.638(a).]

Reversals other than by the Part D plan sponsor. On appeal of a request for benefit, if the plan's determination is reversed in whole or in part by the IRE or at a higher level of appeal, the PDP must authorize or provide the benefit under dispute within 72 hours from the date it receives notice reversing the determination. On appeal of a request for payment, if the plan's determination is reversed in whole or in part by the IRE or at a higher level of appeal, the Part D plan sponsor must authorize payment for the benefit within 72 hours and make payment no later than 30 calendar days from the date it receives notice reversing the coverage determination. [42 C.F.R. § 423.636(b).]

If the expedited determination or expedited redetermination for benefits by the plan is reversed in whole or in part by the IRE or at a higher level of appeal, the plan must authorize or provide the benefit under dispute as expeditiously as the enrollee's health condition requires, but no later than 24 hours from the date it receives notice reversing the determination. [42 C.F.R. § 423.638(b).]

In all cases, when a plan's determination is reversed in whole or in part by the IRE or at any higher level of appeal, the plan must inform the IRE that it has effectuated the decision. [42 C.F.R. §§ 423.636(b), 423.638(b).]

[¶ 516] Reopenings, ALJ Hearings, Medicare Appeals Council Review, and Judicial Review

The regulations at 42 C.F.R. Part 423 Subpart U set forth the regulatory requirements for: (1) Part D sponsors, the Part D independent review entity (IRE), administrative law judges (ALJs), and the Medicare Appeals Council with respect to reopenings; (2) ALJs with respect to hearings; (3) the Medicare Appeals Council with respect to review of Part D appeals; and (4) Part D enrollees' rights with respect to reopenings, ALJ hearings, Medicare Appeals Council reviews, and judicial review by a federal district court. [42 C.F.R. § 423.1968.] The requirements for Part D plan sponsors with respect to grievances, coverage determinations, redeterminations, and reconsiderations are covered in ¶ 515.

Reopenings

A reopening is a remedy designed to change a binding determination or decision, even though the determination or decision may have been correct at the time it was made. A reopening may be taken by:

(1) a Part D plan sponsor to revise the coverage determination or redetermination;

(2) an IRE to revise the reconsideration;

(3) an ALJ to revise the hearing decision; or

(4) the Medicare Appeals Council to revise the hearing or review decision.

[42 C.F.R. § § 423.1978(a), 423.1980(a).]

When an enrollee has filed a valid request for an appeal of a coverage determination, redetermination, reconsideration, hearing, or Medicare Appeals Council review, no adjudicator has jurisdiction to reopen an issue that is under appeal until all appeal rights for that issue are exhausted. The Part D plan sponsor's, IRE's, ALJ's, or Medicare Appeals Council's decision on whether to reopen is binding and not subject to appeal. [42 C.F.R. § § 423.1978(d), 423.1980(a).]

Reopening coverage determinations and redeterminations. A Part D plan sponsor may reopen its coverage determination or redetermination on its own motion: (1) within one year from the date of the coverage determination or redetermination for any reason; (2) within four years from the date of the coverage determination or redetermination for good cause; or (3) at any time if there exists reliable evidence that the coverage determination was procured by fraud or similar fault. [42 C.F.R. § 423.1980(b).]

"Good cause" for reopening may be established when: (1) there is new and material evidence that was unavailable or unknown at the time of the determination or decision and may result in a different conclusion; or (2) the evidence that was considered clearly shows on its face that an obvious error was made. Generally, a change of legal interpretation or policy by CMS in a regulation, CMS ruling, or CMS general instruction, whether made in response to judicial precedent or otherwise, is not a basis for reopening a determination or hearing decision. [42 C.F.R. § 423.1986.]

An enrollee may request that a Part D plan sponsor reopen its coverage determination or redetermination: (1) within one year from the date of the coverage determination or redetermination for any reason; or (2) within four years from the date of the coverage determination or redetermination for good cause. [42 C.F.R. § 423.1980(c).]

IRE, ALJ, and Medicare Appeals Council reopening of reconsiderations, hearings, and reviews. Reopenings of IRE reconsiderations, ALJ hearing decisions, and Medicare Appeals Council reviews may be requested by an IRE, ALJ, or the Medicare Appeals Council on its own motion within 180 calendar days from the date of the reconsideration, decision, or review for good cause, but if the action was procured by fraud or similar fault, the reopening may be made at any time. [42 C.F.R. § 423.1980(d).]

Enrollee or sponsor request for reopening of reconsiderations, hearings, and reviews. A Part D plan sponsor or an enrollee who received an IRE reconsideration, ALJ hearing decision, or Medicare Appeals Council review may request a reopening within 180 calendar days from the date of its reconsideration, hearing decision, or review for good cause. [42 C.F.R. § 423.1980(e).]

Notice requirement. Regardless of whether a reopening is initiated by an adjudicator, an enrollee, or the Part D plan sponsor, when any determination or decision is reopened and revised, the Part D plan sponsor, IRE, ALJ, or Medicare Appeals Council must mail its revised determination or decision to the enrollee at his or her last known address, and the IRE, ALJ, or Medicare Appeals Council must mail its revised determination or decision to the Part D plan sponsor. An adverse revised determination or decision must state the rationale and basis for the reopening and revision and any right to appeal. [42 C.F.R. § 423.1982.]

Effect of revised determination or decision. A revised determination or decision is binding unless it is appealed or otherwise reopened. [42 C.F.R. § 423.1978(c).] The methods of appeal are as follows:

- **Coverage determinations.** The revision of a coverage determination is binding unless an enrollee submits a request for a redetermination that is accepted and processed.

- **Redeterminations.** The revision of a redetermination is binding unless an enrollee submits a request for an IRE reconsideration that is accepted and processed.

- **Reconsiderations.** The revision of a reconsideration is binding unless an enrollee submits a request for an ALJ hearing that is accepted and processed.

- **ALJ hearing decisions.** The revision of an ALJ hearing decision is binding unless an enrollee submits a request for a Medicare Appeals Council review that is accepted and processed.

- **Medicare Appeals Council review.** The revision of a Medicare Appeals Council determination or decision is binding unless an enrollee files a civil action in a federal district court that accepts jurisdiction and issues a decision.

[42 C.F.R. § 423.1984.]

Administrative Law Judge Hearings

If the amount remaining in controversy after the IRE reconsideration meets the threshold requirement established annually by the HHS Secretary, an enrollee who is dissatisfied with the IRE reconsideration determination has a right to a hearing before an ALJ. The threshold amount for 2017, which is $160, is $10 more than the amount for 2015 and 2016. If the basis for the appeal is the refusal by the Part D plan sponsor to provide drug benefits, CMS uses the projected value of those benefits to compute the amount remaining in controversy. The projected value of a drug must include any costs the enrollee could incur based on the number of refills prescribed for the drug in dispute during the plan year. [42 C.F.R. § 423.1970(a), (b); *Notice*, 81 FR 65651, Sept. 23, 2016.]

Two or more appeals may be aggregated by a single enrollee or multiple enrollees to meet the amount in controversy for an ALJ hearing if: (1) the appeals have previously been reconsidered by an IRE; (2) the enrollee(s) requests aggregation at the same time the requests for hearing are filed, and the request for aggregation and requests for hearing are filed within 60 calendar days after receipt of the notice of reconsideration for each of the reconsiderations being appealed; and (3) the ALJ determines that the appeals the enrollee seeks to aggregate involve the delivery of prescription drugs to a single enrollee or, in the case of multiple enrollees, the ALJ determines that the appeals the enrollees seek to aggregate involve the same prescription drug. [42 C.F.R. § 423.1970(c); *Final rule*, 82 FR 4974, Jan. 17, 2017.]

Filing a request for an ALJ hearing. The enrollee must file a written request for an ALJ hearing with Office of Medicare Hearings and Appeals office specified in the IRE's reconsideration notice within 60 calendar days of the date of the notice of an IRE reconsideration determination. If a request for a hearing clearly shows that the amount in controversy is less than that required, the ALJ dismisses the request. If, after the hearing starts, the ALJ finds that the amount in controversy is less than the amount required, the ALJ must discontinue the hearing and must not rule on the substantive issues raised in the appeal. [42 C.F.R. § 423.1972.]

Expedited hearing request. An enrollee also may request that the hearing before an ALJ be expedited. An expedited hearing must involve an issue specified in 42 C.F.R. § 423.566(b), but must not include solely a request for payment of Part D drugs already furnished. The enrollee must submit a written or oral request for an expedited ALJ hearing within 60 calendar days of the date of the written notice of an IRE reconsideration determination. The request for an expedited ALJ hearing should also explain why the standard time frame may seriously jeopardize the life or health of the enrollee. [42 C.F.R. § 423.2002(b).]

Review of IRE dismissal. An enrollee has a right to have an IRE's dismissal of a request for reconsideration reviewed by an ALJ if the enrollee files a request within 60 calendar days after receipt of the written notice of the IRE's dismissal and meets the amount-in-controversy requirements. If the ALJ determines that the IRE's dismissal was in error, he or she must vacate the dismissal and remand the case to the IRE for reconsideration. An ALJ's decision regarding an IRE's dismissal of a reconsideration request is binding and not subject to further review. The dismissal of a request for ALJ review of an IRE's dismissal of a reconsideration request is also binding and not subject to further review, unless vacated by the Medicare Appeals Council. [42 C.F.R. § 423.2004.]

Time frames for ALJ decision. When a request for an ALJ hearing is filed after an IRE has issued a written reconsideration, the ALJ must issue a decision, dismissal order, or remand, as appropriate, no later than the end of the 90-calendar-day period beginning on the date the request for hearing is received by the entity specified in the IRE's notice of reconsideration, unless the 90-calendar-day period has been extended. The ALJ must provide an expedited hearing decision if the appeal involves an issue specified in 42 C.F.R. § 423.566(b), but not solely a request for payment of Part D drugs already furnished, and the enrollee's prescribing physician or other prescriber indicates, or the ALJ determines, that applying the standard time frame for making a decision may seriously jeopardize the enrollee's life, health, or ability to regain maximum function. [42 C.F.R. § 423.2016.]

Submission of evidence. An enrollee must submit any written evidence that he or she wishes to have considered at the ALJ hearing. An ALJ must not consider any evidence submitted regarding a change in condition of an enrollee after the appealed coverage determination was made. An ALJ will remand a case to the IRE when an enrollee wishes evidence on his or her change in condition after the coverage determination to be considered. A represented enrollee must submit all written evidence he or she wishes to have considered at the hearing with the request for hearing or within 10 calendar days of receiving the notice of hearing. For an expedited ALJ hearing, an enrollee must submit all written evidence with the request for hearing or within two calendar days of receiving the notice of hearing. [42 C.F.R. § 423.2018.]

Hearing notice. The ALJ must send a notice of hearing to the enrollee and other potential participants advising them of the proposed time and place of the hearing. The notice of the hearing must be mailed or otherwise transmitted to the enrollee and other potential participants at their last known addresses or given by personal service. The ALJ must mail or serve the notice at least 20 calendar days before the hearing, except for expedited hearings, when written notice is mailed or served at least three calendar days before the hearing. [42 C.F.R. § 423.2022.]

Permissible issues. The issues before the ALJ include all the issues brought out in the coverage determination, redetermination, or reconsideration that were not decided entirely in an enrollee's favor. The ALJ or the enrollee may raise a new issue; however, the ALJ may consider a new issue relating to a determination or appealed matter specified in the request for hearing only if its resolution could have a material impact on the appealed matter and (1) there is new and material evidence that was not available or known at the time of the determination and that may result in a different conclusion; or (2) the evidence that was considered in making the determination clearly shows on its face that an obvious error was made at the time of the determination. [42 C.F.R. § 423.2032; *Final rule*, 82 FR 4974, Jan. 17, 2017.]

Hearing process. An enrollee has the right to appear at the hearing before the ALJ to present evidence and state his or her position by video-teleconferencing or telephone or in person. An enrollee may waive his or her right to appear by sending the ALJ a written statement indicating that he or she does not wish to appear at the hearing. An enrollee (or an enrollee's appointed representative) may appear before the ALJ to state the enrollee's case, present a written summary of the case, or enter written statements about the facts and law material to the case in the record. The ALJ may receive evidence at the hearing even though the evidence is not admissible in court under the rules of evidence used by the court. The ALJ, however, may not consider evidence on any change in condition of an enrollee after a coverage determination. [42 C.F.R. § § 423.2000, 423.2036.]

ALJ subpoenas. An ALJ may, on his or her own initiative, issue subpoenas for the appearance and testimony of witnesses and for the enrollee or the Part D plan sponsor to make books, records, correspondence, papers, or other documents that are material to an issue at the hearing available for inspection and copying. An ALJ may not issue a subpoena to CMS or the IRE to compel an appearance, testimony, or the production of evidence, or to the Part D plan sponsor to compel an appearance or testimony. To the extent that a subpoena compels disclosure of a matter for which an objection based on privilege, or other protection from disclosure such as case preparation, confidentiality, or undue burden, was made before an ALJ, the Medicare Appeals Council may review immediately the ruling of the ALJ on the objections to the subpoena or that portion of the subpoena, as applicable. [42 C.F.R. § 423.2036(f).]

Notice and effect of ALJ decisions. Unless the ALJ dismisses the hearing, the ALJ must issue a written decision that gives the findings of fact, conclusions of law, and the reasons for the decision. For expedited hearings, the ALJ must issue a written decision within 10 calendar days of the hearing. [42 C.F.R. § 423.2046.]

The decision of the ALJ is binding unless:

(1) an enrollee requests a review of the decision by the Medicare Appeals Council within the stated time period or the Medicare Appeals Council reviews the ALJ decision and issues a final decision or remand order;

(2) the decision is reopened and revised by an ALJ or the Medicare Appeals Council;

(3) the expedited access to judicial review process is used;

(4) the ALJ's decision is a recommended decision directed to the Medicare Appeals Council and the Medicare Appeals Council issues a decision; or

(5) in a case remanded by a federal district court, the Medicare Appeals Council assumes jurisdiction and issues a decision.

[42 C.F.R. § 423.2048.]

Removal by the Medicare Appeals Council. If a request for hearing is pending before an ALJ, the Medicare Appeals Council may assume responsibility for the hearing by requesting that the ALJ forward the hearing request. If the Medicare Appeals Council holds a hearing, however, it must conduct the hearing according to the rules for ALJ hearings. [42 C.F.R. § 423.2050.]

Medicare Appeals Council Reviews

An enrollee who is dissatisfied with an ALJ hearing decision or dismissal may request Medicare Appeals Council review. The Medicare Appeals Council's review of an ALJ's written decision is a new review (conducted as though no review has yet taken place). After review, the Medicare Appeals Council must issue a final decision or dismissal order or remand the case. One of these actions must be issued no later than the end of the 90-calendar-day period beginning on the date the request for review is received by the entity specified in the ALJ's written notice of decision, unless the 90-calendar-day time frame is extended or the enrollee requests expedited Medicare Appeals Council review. If an enrollee requests expedited Medicare Appeals Council review, the Medicare Appeals Council must issue a final decision, dismissal order, or remand as expeditiously as the enrollee's health condition requires, but no later than the end of the 10-calendar-day period beginning on the date the request for review is received by the entity specified in the ALJ's written notice of decision, unless the 10-calendar-day period is extended. [42 C.F.R. §§ 423.1974, 423.2100.]

Filing the Medicare Appeals Council review request. An enrollee requests a Medicare Appeals Council review by submitting a written request for review within 60 calendar days after receipt of the ALJ's written decision or dismissal to the entity specified in the notice of the ALJ's action. An enrollee may request that Medicare Appeals Council review be expedited if the appeal involves an issue specified in 42 C.F.R. § 423.566(b) but does not include solely a request for payment of Part D drugs already furnished. If an enrollee is requesting that the Medicare Appeals Council review be expedited, the enrollee must submit an oral or written request within 60 calendar days after the receipt of the ALJ's written decision or dismissal. [42 C.F.R. §§ 423.2102, 423.2106.]

Reviews on Medicare Appeals Council's own motion. The Medicare Appeals Council may decide on its own motion to review a decision or dismissal issued by an ALJ. CMS or the IRE may refer a case to the Medicare Appeals Council to consider reviewing on its own motion any time within 60 calendar days after the ALJ's written decision or dismissal is issued if the decision or dismissal contains an error of law material to the outcome of the claim or presents a broad policy or procedural issue that may affect the public interest. CMS or the IRE also may request that the Medicare Appeals Council take own-motion review of a case if: (1) CMS or the IRE participated or requested to participate in the appeal at the ALJ level; and (2) the ALJ's decision or dismissal is not supported by the preponderance of evidence in the record or the ALJ abused his or her discretion. [42 C.F.R. § 423.2110.]

Dismissing review requests. The Medicare Appeals Council must dismiss a request for review if the enrollee did not file the request within the stated period of time and the time for filing has not been extended. The Medicare Appeals Council also must dismiss the request for review if: (1) the enrollee asks to withdraw the request for review; (2) the individual or entity does not have a right to request review; or (3) the enrollee dies while the request for review is pending and the enrollee's estate or representative either has no remaining financial interest in the case or does not want to continue the appeal. [42 C.F.R. § 423.2114.]

Briefs and evidence. Upon request, the Medicare Appeals Council must give the enrollee a reasonable opportunity to file a brief or other written statement. The Medicare Appeals Council also may request, but not require, CMS, the IRE, and/or the Part D plan sponsor to file a brief if it determines that it is necessary. [42 C.F.R. § 423.2120.] When the Medicare Appeals Council reviews an ALJ decision, it must consider the evidence contained in the record of the proceedings before the ALJ and any new evidence that relates to the period before the coverage determination. If the hearing decision decides a new issue that the enrollee was not afforded an opportunity to address at the ALJ level, the Medicare Appeals Council must consider any evidence related to that new issue. The Medicare Appeals Council must not consider any new evidence submitted regarding a change in condition of an enrollee after a coverage determination is made. [42 C.F.R. § 423.2122(a).]

Oral argument. An enrollee may request oral argument or the Medicare Appeals Council may decide on its own that oral argument is necessary to decide the case. The Medicare Appeals Council will grant oral argument if it decides that the case raises an important question of law, policy, or fact that cannot be decided based on written submissions alone. If it decides on its own to hear oral argument, it must inform the enrollee of the time and place of the oral argument at least 10 calendar days before the scheduled date or, in the case of an expedited review, at least two calendar days before the scheduled date. [42 C.F.R. § 423.2124.]

Medicare Appeals Council remand. The Medicare Appeals Council may remand a case when additional evidence is needed or additional action by the ALJ is required. The Medicare Appeals Council will designate in its remand order whether the ALJ will issue a decision or a recommended decision on remand. The case must be remanded to the appropriate Part D IRE if it determines that the enrollee wishes evidence on his or her change in condition after the coverage determination to be considered in the appeal. [42 C.F.R. § 423.2126.]

Final Medicare Appeals Council action. After it has reviewed the evidence in the administrative record and any additional evidence, the Medicare Appeals Council must make a decision or remand the case to an ALJ. The Medicare Appeals Council has the authority to adopt, modify, or reverse the ALJ hearing decision or recommended decision. A copy of the decision is mailed to the enrollee at his or her last known address, CMS, the IRE, and the Part D plan sponsor. The decision of the Medicare Appeals Council is final and binding unless a federal district court modifies it or it is revised as the result of a reopening. [42 C.F.R. § § 423.2128, 423.2130.]

Judicial Review

An enrollee may obtain court review of a Medicare Appeals Council decision if the amount in controversy meets the threshold requirement estimated annually by the HHS Secretary. The enrollee may request judicial review of an ALJ's decision if the Medicare Appeals Council denied the enrollee's request for review and the amount in controversy meets the threshold requirements. The threshold amount for filing for judicial review on or after January 1, 2017, is $1,560, up from $1,500 in 2016. [*Notice*, 81 FR 65651, Sept. 23, 2016.] A civil action for judicial review must be filed in the U.S. district court for the judicial district in which the enrollee resides. If the enrollee does not reside within any judicial district, the civil action must be filed in the District Court of the United States for the District of Columbia. [42 C.F.R. § § 423.1976, 423.2136(a), (b).]

In any civil action for judicial review, the proper party defendant is the Secretary of HHS, in his or her official capacity. Upon judicial review, the findings of the Secretary as to any fact, if supported by substantial evidence, are to be considered conclusive by the federal district court. [42 C.F.R. § 423.2136(d), (e).]

Filing requirements. Any civil action for judicial review must be filed with the appropriate federal district court within 60 calendar days after the date the enrollee receives written notice of the Medicare Appeals Council's decision. The date of receipt of the notice of the Medicare Appeals Council's decision is presumed to be five calendar days after the date of the notice, unless there is a reasonable showing to the contrary. Likewise, if a case is certified for judicial review in accordance with the expedited access to judicial review process, the civil action must be filed within 60 calendar days after receipt of the review entity's certification, unless the time for filing is extended by the ALJ or Medicare Appeals Council upon a showing of good cause. [42 C.F.R. § 423.2136(c).]

Remand of the case by the court. When a federal district court remands a case to the HHS Secretary for further consideration, the Medicare Appeals Council may (1) make a decision; or (2) remand the case to an ALJ with instructions to take action and either issue a decision, take other action, or return the case to the Medicare Appeals Council with a recommended decision. [42 C.F.R. § 423.2138.] When a federal district court remands a case for further consideration and the Medicare Appeals Council further remands the case to an ALJ, a decision subsequently issued by the ALJ becomes the final decision of the Secretary unless the Medicare Appeals Council assumes jurisdiction. [42 C.F.R. § 423.2140(a).]

Written exceptions to ALJ remand decision. If an enrollee disagrees with an ALJ decision (after remand of the case from the district court and further remand from the Medicare Appeals Council), he or she may file exceptions to the decision with the Medicare Appeals Council. The enrollee must submit a written statement setting forth the reasons for disagreeing with the ALJ decision within 30 calendar days of receiving the decision (and the Medicare Appeals Council will grant a timely request for a 30-day extension). [42 C.F.R. § 423.2140(b).]

If the Medicare Appeals Council concludes that there is no reason to change the ALJ's decision, it must issue a notice addressing the exceptions and explaining why no change is necessary. When this occurs, the decision of the ALJ is considered a final decision of the HHS Secretary. When an enrollee files written exceptions to the decision of the ALJ, the Medicare Appeals Council may decide to assume jurisdiction. If it assumes jurisdiction, it makes a new, independent decision based on its consideration of the entire record adopting, modifying, or reversing the decision of the ALJ or remanding the case to an ALJ for further proceedings, including a new decision. This new decision of the Medicare Appeals Council is the final decision of the Secretary. [42 C.F.R. § 423.2140(b).]

Medicare Appeals Council jurisdiction without written exceptions. Any time within 60 calendar days after the date of the written decision of the ALJ, the Medicare Appeals Council may decide to assume jurisdiction of the case even though no written exceptions have been filed by the enrollee. After giving notice to the enrollee and providing the opportunity to file a brief regarding the relevant facts and law in the case (usually 30 calendar days), the Medicare Appeals Council will either issue a final decision of the HHS Secretary affirming, modifying, or reversing the decision of the ALJ, or remand the case to an ALJ for further proceedings, including a new decision. [42 C.F.R. § 423.2140(c).]

Expedited Access to Judicial Review

To obtain expedited access to judicial review (EAJR), a "review entity" must certify that the Medicare Appeals Council does not have the authority to decide the question of law or regulation relevant to the matters in dispute and there is no material issue of fact in dispute.

For purposes of EAJR, a "review entity" is defined as an entity of up to three reviewers who are ALJs or members of the Departmental Appeals Board. [42 C.F.R. § 423.1990(a).]

An enrollee may request EAJR in place of an ALJ hearing or Medicare Appeals Council review if:

(1) an IRE has made a reconsideration determination and the enrollee has filed a request for an ALJ hearing and a final decision, dismissal order, or remand order of the ALJ has not been issued; or an ALJ has made a decision and the enrollee has filed a request for Medicare Appeals Council review and a final decision, dismissal order, or remand order of the Medicare Appeals Council has not been issued;

(2) the requestor is an enrollee;

(3) the amount remaining in controversy meets the threshold requirements;

(4) when there is more than one enrollee to the ALJ hearing or Medicare Appeals Council review, each enrollee concurs, in writing, with the request for the EAJR; and

(5) there are no material issues of fact in dispute.

[42 C.F.R. § 423.1990(b).]

Method of filing. An enrollee may include an EAJR request in his or her request for an ALJ hearing or Medicare Appeals Council review or, if an appeal is already pending, the enrollee may file a written EAJR request with the HHS Departmental Appeals Board. The ALJ hearing office or Medicare Appeals Council must forward the EAJR request to the review entity within five calendar days of receipt. The enrollee must file a request for EAJR: (1) any time before receipt of the notice of the ALJ's decision, if the enrollee has requested an ALJ hearing; or (2) any time before receipt of notice of the Medicare Appeals Council's decision, if the enrollee has requested Medicare Appeals Council review. [42 C.F.R. § 423.1990(d).]

Review entity's action on EAJR request. Within 60 calendar days after the date the review entity receives a EAJR request and the accompanying documents and materials, the review entity will issue either a certification or a denial of the request. The certification or denial by the review entity is binding and not subject to review by the HHS Secretary. If the review entity fails to certify or deny the EAJR request within the 60-calendar-day time frame, the enrollee may bring a civil action in federal district court within 60 calendar days. [42 C.F.R. § 423.1990(e).]

If the review entity certifies the EAJR request, the enrollee automatically waives any right to completion of the remaining steps in the administrative appeals process and has 60 calendar days, beginning on the date of the certification, to bring a civil action in federal district court. If a request for EAJR does not meet the conditions set forth above or if the review entity does not certify the request, the review entity must advise the enrollee in writing that the request has been denied and return the request to the Office of Medicare Hearings and Appeals or the Medicare Appeals Council. The ALJ or Medicare Appeals Council will treat the rejection as a request for an ALJ hearing or for Medicare Appeals Council review. [42 C.F.R. § 423.1990(g), (h).]

[¶ 525] Cost Control and Quality Improvement Requirements

Part D sponsors must implement certain cost control and quality improvement requirements, including the establishment of a drug utilization management program, quality assurance (QA) measures and systems, and a medication therapy management program (MTMP). Part 423 Subpart D of the Medicare Part D regulations and Chapter 7 of the *Medicare Prescription Drug Benefits Manual*, Pub. 100-18, implement these administrative provisions.

Drug Utilization Management, QA, and MTMPs

Each Part D sponsor must establish a drug utilization management program, QA measures and systems, and an MTMP. Each of these requirements affects the quality and cost of care provided to beneficiaries. [Soc. Sec. Act § 1860D-4(c); 42 C.F.R. § 423.153(a).] The drug utilization management and MTMP requirements, however, do not apply to private fee-for-service Medicare Advantage plans offering qualified prescription drug coverage. [Soc. Sec. Act § 1860D-21(d)(3); 42 C.F.R. § 423.153(e).]

Drug utilization management program. The Part D regulations provide minimum requirements and give considerable flexibility to sponsors in the design of their drug utilization management programs. The minimum requirements are that a plan must:

(1) maintain a program that includes incentives to reduce costs where medically appropriate;

(2) maintain policies and systems to assist in preventing over-utilization and under-utilization of prescribed medications;

(3) provide CMS with information concerning the procedures and performance of its drug utilization management program, according to guidelines specified by CMS; and

(4) establish a daily cost-sharing rate for drugs dispensed for a supply less than the approved month's supply, if the drug is in the form of a solid oral dose (except for solid oral doses of antibiotics and solid oral doses that are dispensed in their original container) and may be dispensed for less than the approved month's supply under applicable law; the co-payment is calculated by multiplying the applicable daily cost-sharing rate by the days' supply actually dispensed.

[42 C.F.R. § 423.153(b).]

Quality assurance measures and systems. A Part D sponsor must have established QA measures and systems to reduce medication errors and adverse drug interactions and improve medication use. The QA measures and systems must include:

(1) representation that network providers are required to comply with minimum standards for pharmacy practice as established by the states;

(2) concurrent drug utilization review systems, policies, and procedures designed to ensure that a review of the prescribed drug therapy is performed before each prescription is dispensed (the review must include, but not be limited to: screening for potential drug therapy problems due to therapeutic duplication; age/gender-related contraindications; over-utilization and under-utilization; drug-drug interactions; incorrect drug dosage or duration of drug therapy; drug-allergy contraindications; and clinical abuse/misuse);

(3) retrospective drug utilization review systems, policies, and procedures designed to ensure ongoing periodic examination of claims data and other records, through computerized drug claims processing and information retrieval systems, to identify patterns of inappropriate or medically unnecessary care among enrollees or patterns associated with specific drugs;

(4) internal medication error identification and reduction systems; and

(5) provision of information to CMS regarding quality assurance measures and systems.

[42 C.F.R. § 423.153(c).]

¶525

Medication therapy management programs. A Part D sponsor must establish a MTMP that is designed to:

(1) optimize therapeutic outcomes for targeted beneficiaries (described below) by improving medication use,

(2) reduce adverse drug events (including adverse drug interactions) for targeted beneficiaries,

(3) be furnished by a pharmacist or other qualified provider,

(4) distinguish between services in ambulatory and institutional settings,

(5) target beneficiaries using an opt-out method of enrollment only,

(6) target enrollees for enrollment in the MTMP at least quarterly, and

(7) offer a minimum level of MTMP services to each beneficiary.

[Soc. Sec. Act § 1860D-4(c); 42 C.F.R. § 423.153(d)(1); Pub. 100-18, Ch. 7, § 30.1.]

The minimum level of MTMP services include:

(1) interventions for both beneficiaries and prescribers;

(2) annual comprehensive medication review with written summaries, which must include an interactive, person-to-person, or telehealth consultation performed by a pharmacist or other qualified provider (unless the beneficiary is in a long-term care setting) and may result in a recommended medication action plan;

(3) quarterly targeted medication reviews with follow-up interventions when necessary; and

(4) standardized action plans and summaries that comply with requirements for the standardized format.

[Soc. Sec. Act § 1860D-4(c)(2)(C); 42 C.F.R. § 423.153(d)(1)(vii).]

Targeted beneficiaries. Targeted beneficiaries for the MTMP are enrollees in the sponsor's Part D plan who:

(1) have multiple chronic diseases, with three chronic diseases being the maximum number a Part D plan sponsor may require (sponsors must target at least four of the following core chronic conditions: hypertension; heart failure; diabetes; dyslipidemia; respiratory disease such as asthma, chronic obstructive pulmonary disease, or chronic lung disorders; bone disease-arthritis such as osteoporosis, osteoarthritis, or rheumatoid arthritis; and mental health such as depression, schizophrenia, bipolar disorder, or chronic and disabling disorders);

(2) are taking multiple Part D drugs, with eight Part D drugs being the maximum number of drugs a plan sponsor may require; and

(3) are likely to incur annual Part D drug costs in an amount greater than or equal to $3000 increased by the annual percentage specified in 42 C.F.R. 423.104(d)(5)(iv).

[Soc. Sec. Act § 1860D-4(c)(2)(A)(ii); 42 C.F.R. § 423.153(d)(2); Pub. 100-18, Ch. 7, § 30.2.]

Cooperation with pharmacists and physicians. The MTMP must be developed in cooperation with licensed and practicing pharmacists and physicians and coordinated with any care management plan established for a targeted individual under a chronic care improvement program (CCIP). A sponsor must provide drug claims data to CCIPs for those beneficiaries who are enrolled in CCIPs. [Soc. Sec. Act § 1860D-4(c)(2)(E), (F); 42 C.F.R. § 423.153(d)(3), (4); Pub. 100-18, Ch. 7, § 30.4.]

To become a Part D sponsor, an applicant must describe how it takes into account the resources used and time required to implement the MTMP it chooses to adopt in establishing fees for pharmacists or others providing MTMP services, and disclose to CMS upon request the amount of the management and dispensing fees and the portion paid for MTMP services to pharmacists. Reports of these amounts are protected. [Soc. Sec. Act § 1860D-4(c)(2)(G); 42 C.F.R. § 423.153(d)(5).]

Programs to Prevent Drug Abuse Under Part D

Section 704 of the Comprehensive Addiction and Recovery Act of 2016 (P.L. 114-198) provides, effective for plan years beginning after January 1, 2019, for two programs intended to prevent drug abuse under Part D: (1) a drug management programs for at-risk beneficiaries; and (2) utilization management tools to prevent drug abuse. [Soc. Sec. Act § 1860D-4(c)(5), (6).]

Drug management programs for at-risk beneficiaries. A PDP sponsor may establish a drug management program for at-risk beneficiaries under which sponsors may limit such beneficiaries' access to frequently abused drugs to certain prescribers and pharmacies. An "at-risk beneficiary for prescription drug abuse" is a Part D eligible individual who (1) is identified as such an at-risk beneficiary through the use of clinical guidelines developed by the Secretary in consultation with PDP sponsors and other stakeholders that indicate misuse or abuse of prescription drugs; or (2) with respect to whom the PDP sponsor of a prescription drug plan, upon enrolling such individual in such plan, received notice from the HHS Secretary that such individual was identified to be an at-risk beneficiary for prescription drug abuse under the prescription drug plan in which such individual was most recently previously enrolled and such identification has not been terminated. [Soc. Sec. Act § 1860D-4(c)(5).]

Utilization management tools to prevent drug abuse. A PDP sponsor must have in place a utilization management tool to prevent drug abuse. Such a tool includes any of the following: (1) a utilization tool designed to prevent the abuse of frequently abused drugs by individuals and to prevent the diversion of such drugs at pharmacies; (2) retrospective utilization review to identify (a) individuals that receive frequently abused drugs at a frequency or in amounts that are not clinically appropriate, and (b) providers or suppliers that may facilitate the abuse or diversion of frequently abused drugs by beneficiaries; or (3) consultation with the Medicare drug integrity contractor (MEDIC) to verify if an individual enrolling in a prescription drug plan offered by a PDP sponsor has been previously identified by another PDP sponsor as an individual that receives frequently abused drugs at a frequency or in amounts that are not clinically appropriate. [Soc. Sec. Act § 1860D-4(c)(1)(E), (c)(6).]

Medicare drug integrity contractors. Beginning January 1, 2019, the HHS Secretary is required to authorize MEDICs to directly accept prescription and necessary medical records from entities such as pharmacies, prescription drug plans, Medicare Advantage prescription drug plans (MA-PDs), and physicians to aid in the determination of whether such individual is an at-risk beneficiary for prescription drug abuse. MEDICs must respond to requests by prescription drug sponsors or MA-PDs within 15 days. [Soc. Sec. Act § 1893(j).]

Dispensing Drugs in Long-Term Care Facilities

Generally, when dispensing covered Part D drugs to enrollees who reside in long-term care (LTC) facilities, a Part D sponsor must:

(1) require all pharmacies servicing LTC facilities to dispense solid oral doses of brand-name drugs in no greater than 14-day increments at a time and permit the use of

uniform dispensing techniques as defined by the LTC facilities in which the enrollees reside;

(2) not penalize LTCs' choice of more efficient uniform dispensing techniques by prorating dispensing fees based on days' supply or quantity dispensed;

(3) ensure that any difference in payment methodology among LTC pharmacies incentivizes more efficient dispensing techniques; and

(4) collect and report information on the dispensing methodology used for each dispensing event described in (1).

[Soc. Sec. Act § 1860D-4(c)(3); 42 C.F.R. § 423.154(a).]

Excluded from the above LTC dispensing requirements are: (1) solid oral doses of antibiotics; and (2) solid oral doses that are dispensed in their original container as indicated in the Food and Drug Administration Prescribing Information or are customarily dispensed in their original packaging to assist patients with compliance (for example, oral contraceptives). [42 C.F.R. § 423.154(b).]

CMS waives these dispensing requirements, except for (2) and (3), for pharmacies when they service intermediate care facilities for the mentally retarded, institutes for mental disease, and Indian Tribe and Tribal Organization, and Urban Indian Organization (I/T/U) pharmacies. [42 C.F.R. § 423.154(c).]

The terms and conditions offered by a Part D sponsor must be in accordance with federal and state law and address the disposal of drugs that have been dispensed to an enrollee in a LTC facility, but not used, and that have been returned to the pharmacy. The terms for return for credit and reuse must also be permitted under state law. [42 C.F.R. § 423.154(d).]

Customer Satisfaction Surveys

Part D plans with 600 or more enrollees as of July of the prior year must contract with approved Medicare Consumer Assessment of Healthcare Providers and Systems (CAHPS) survey vendors to conduct the Medicare CAHPS satisfaction survey of Part D plan enrollees in accordance with CMS specifications and submit the survey data to CMS. [Soc. Sec. Act § 1860D-4(d); 42 C.F.R. § 423.156.]

Electronic Prescription Drug Program

Prescribers and dispensers who electronically transmit prescription and certain other information for covered drugs prescribed for Medicare Part D eligible beneficiaries are required to comply with any electronic prescription standards that are in effect. [Soc. Sec. Act § 1860D-4(e); 42 C.F.R. § 423.159(c).]

Promotion of electronic prescribing. A Medicare Advantage (MA) organization offering an MA prescription drug plan (MA-PD) may provide for a separate or differential payment to a participating physician who prescribes covered Part D drugs in accordance with electronic prescription standards. These electronic standards may include initial standards and any final standards established by CMS. Any separate or differential payments must be in compliance with applicable federal and state laws related to fraud and abuse, including the physician self-referral prohibition and the federal anti-kickback statute. [42 C.F.R. § 423.159(d).]

Part D sponsors, prescribers, and dispensers must maintain a regulatory-compliant electronic prescription drug program when transmitting, directly or through an intermediary, prescriptions and prescription-related information using electronic media for covered Part D drugs for Part D eligible individuals. The electronic prescription drug program standards supersede any state law or regulation that is contrary to the standards or restricts the ability to carry out Part D and that pertains to the electronic transmission of medication history and of information on eligibility, benefits, and prescriptions with respect to covered Part D drugs under Part D. [42 C.F.R. § 423.160(a); Pub. 100-18, Ch. 7, § § 50.1, 50.2.]

Assistance by QIOs

Quality improvement organizations (QIOs) must offer providers, practitioners, and Part D sponsors quality improvement assistance pertaining to health care services, including those related to prescription drug therapy. To accomplish this requirement, QIOs need access to data from transactions between pharmacies and Part D plans. Any such information collected by the QIOs is subject to CMS confidentiality requirements. Part D sponsors are required to provide information directly to QIOs and to CMS for distribution to QIOs. [42 C.F.R. § 423.162; Pub. 100-18, Ch. 7, § 20.8.]

Compliance Based on Accreditation

A Part D sponsor can be deemed to meet certain requirements if: (1) it is fully accredited (and periodically reaccredited) for the standards related to the applicable area by a private, national accreditation organization (AO) approved by CMS; and (2) the AO uses the standards approved by CMS for the purposes of assessing the Part D sponsor's compliance with Medicare requirements. [Soc. Sec. Act § 1860D-4(j); 42 C.F.R. § 423.165(a).]

The requirements related to the following areas are deemable:

(1) access to covered drugs (42 C.F.R. § § 423.120 and 423.124);

(2) drug utilization management programs, QA measures and systems, and MTMPs (42 C.F.R. § § 423.120 and 423.124); and

(3) privacy, confidentiality, and accuracy of enrollee records (42 C.F.R. § 423.136).

[Soc. Sec. Act § 1860D-4(j); 42 C.F.R. § 423.165(b).]

Deemed Part D sponsor obligations. A Part D sponsor that is deemed to meet Medicare requirements must submit to CMS surveys, which are intended to validate AO processes. CMS will remove part or all of a Part D sponsor's deemed status if: (1) CMS determines, on the basis of its own investigation, that the sponsor does not meet the Medicare requirements for which deemed status was granted; (2) CMS withdraws its approval of the AO that accredited the sponsor; or (3) the sponsor fails to meet the above requirements of a deemed Part D sponsor. [42 C.F.R. § 423.165(d), (e).]

Enforcement authority. CMS retains the authority to initiate enforcement action against any Part D sponsor that it determines, on the basis of a CMS survey or the results of the accreditation survey, no longer meets the Medicare requirements for which deemed status was granted. [42 C.F.R. § 423.165(f).]

Accreditation organizations. An AO may be approved by CMS for a given standard if the organization, in accrediting Part D sponsors and Part D plans, applies and enforces standards that are at least as stringent as Medicare requirements. Secondly, the AO must comply with CMS application and reapplication procedures. Finally, the AO must also ensure that: (1) any individual associated with it, or associated with an entity it accredits, does not influence the accreditation decision concerning that entity; (2) the majority of its governing body is not composed of managed care organizations, Part D sponsors, or their representatives; and (3) its governing body has a broad and balanced representation of interests and acts without bias. [42 C.F.R. § § 423.168(a), 423.171.]

¶525

[¶ 530] Payments to Sponsors of Retiree Prescription Drug Plans

The sponsors of qualified retiree prescription drug plans (PDPs) can receive an annual subsidy equal to 28 percent of specified retiree drug costs for each qualifying covered retiree. [Soc. Sec. Act § 1860D-22(a)(3); 42 C.F.R. § 423.886.]

Requirements for Qualified Retiree Prescription Drug Plans

Employment-based retiree health coverage is considered to be a qualified retiree PDP if all of the following requirements are satisfied:

(1) an actuarial attestation is submitted;

(2) Part D eligible individuals covered under the plan are provided with creditable coverage notices; and

(3) records are maintained and made available for audit.

[Soc. Sec. Act § 1860D-22(a)(2); 42 C.F.R. § 423.884(a).]

Disclosure of information. The sponsor must have a written agreement with its health insurance issuer or group health plan regarding disclosure of information to CMS, and the issuer or plan must disclose to CMS, on behalf of the sponsor, the information necessary for the sponsor to comply with CMS requirements. [42 C.F.R. § 423.884(b).]

Submitting an Application for Subsidy

The sponsor must submit an application for the subsidy to CMS along with the following information:

(1) employer tax ID number;

(2) sponsor name and address;

(3) contact name and e-mail address;

(4) actuarial attestation (see below) and any other supporting documentation required by CMS for each qualified retiree PDP for which the sponsor seeks subsidy payments;

(5) a list of all individuals the sponsor believes are qualifying covered retirees enrolled in each PDP, including spouses and dependents, if Medicare eligible, along with the listed individual's: (a) full name, (b) Health Insurance Claim (HIC) number or Social Security number, (c) date of birth, (d) gender, and (e) relationship to the retired employee (Note: a sponsor may satisfy this requirement by entering into a voluntary data sharing agreement with CMS);

(6) a signed sponsor agreement; and

(7) any other information specified by CMS.

[42 C.F.R. § 423.884(c)(1), (2).]

An authorized representative of the requesting sponsor must sign the completed application and certify that the information contained in the application is true and accurate. [42 C.F.R. § 423.884(c)(4).]

Terms and conditions for subsidy payment. To receive a subsidy payment, the sponsor must specifically accept and agree to:

(1) comply with the terms and conditions of eligibility for a subsidy payment;

(2) acknowledge that at the same time that CMS releases Part C and Part D summary payment data, it also will release Part D retiree drug subsidy payment data for

the most recently reconciled year, including the name of the eligible sponsor, the total gross aggregate dollar amount of the CMS subsidy, and the number of eligible retirees;

(3) acknowledge that the information in the application is being provided to obtain federal funds; and

(4) require that all subcontractors, including plan administrators, acknowledge that information provided in connection with the subcontract is used for purposes of obtaining federal funds.

[42 C.F.R. § 423.884(c)(3).]

Application timing and required updates. An application for a given plan year must be submitted before the beginning of the plan year, unless an extension has been filed and approved by CMS. The sponsor must provide updates of the application's information to CMS on a monthly basis or at a frequency specified by CMS. [42 C.F.R. § 423.884(c)(5), (6).]

CMS data match. Once the full application for the subsidy payment is submitted, CMS matches the names and identifying information of the individuals submitted as qualifying covered retirees with a CMS database to determine which retirees are Part D eligible individuals who are not enrolled in a Part D plan. CMS provides information concerning the results of the search (names and identifying information) to the sponsor. [42 C.F.R. § 423.884(c)(7).]

Actuarial Attestation Requirements

The sponsor of the plan must provide to CMS an attestation (in a form and manner specified by CMS) that must include the following assurances:

(1) the actuarial gross value of the retiree prescription drug coverage under the plan for the plan year is at least equal to the actuarial gross value of the defined standard prescription drug coverage under Part D for the plan year in question, not taking into account the value of any discount or coverage provided in the coverage gap;

(2) the actuarial net value of the retiree prescription drug coverage under the plan for that plan year is at least equal to the actuarial net value of the defined standard prescription drug coverage under Part D for the plan year in question, not taking into account the value of any discount or coverage provided in the coverage gap; and

(3) the actuarial values must be determined using the methodology described below.

[42 C.F.R. § 423.884(d)(1).]

Actuarial requirements. The attestation must be made and signed by a qualified actuary (member of the American Academy of Actuaries) and must state that the attestation is true and accurate. Applicants may use qualified outside actuaries, including actuaries employed by the plan administrator or an insurer providing benefits under the plan. The attestation must contain an acknowledgment that the information being provided in the attestation is being used to obtain federal funds. [42 C.F.R. § 423.884(d)(2)–(4).]

Methodology. The attestation must be based on generally accepted actuarial principles and any actuarial guidelines established by CMS. To the extent CMS has not provided guidance on a specific aspect of the actuarial equivalence standard, an actuary providing the attestation may rely on any reasonable interpretation of the CMS regulations and Soc. Sec. Act § 1860D-22(a) consistent with generally accepted actuarial principles in determining actuarial values. [42 C.F.R. § 423.884(d)(5).]

Timing. The sponsor must provide the attestation annually at the time it submits its subsidy application. If there is a material change to the drug coverage of the sponsor's retiree prescription drug plan, the sponsor must provide its the attestation within 90 days before the implementation of the change. The term "material change" means the addition of a benefit option that does not affect the actuarial value of the retiree prescription drug coverage under the sponsor's plan. [42 C.F.R. § 423.884(d)(6).]

Notice of a failure to continue to satisfy the actuarial equivalence standard. A sponsor must notify CMS no later than 90 days before the implementation of a change to the drug coverage that affects the actuarial value of the retiree prescription drug coverage under the sponsor's plan such that it no longer meets the actuarial equivalence standards. [42 C.F.R. § 423.884(d)(7).]

Retiree Drug Subsidy Amounts

For each qualifying covered retiree enrolled with the sponsor of a qualified retiree PDP in a plan year, the sponsor receives a subsidy payment in the amount of 28 percent of the allowable retiree costs in the plan year that are attributable to gross retiree costs that exceed the cost threshold and do not exceed the cost limit (see below). The subsidy payment is calculated by first determining gross retiree costs between the cost threshold and cost limit and then determining allowable retiree costs attributable to the gross retiree costs. [Soc. Sec. Act § 1860D-22(a)(3)(A); 42 C.F.R. § 423.886(a).]

Cost threshold and cost limit. The cost threshold and cost limit for qualified retiree prescription drug plans are adjusted in the same manner as the annual Part D deductible and out-of-pocket threshold are adjusted annually. For 2017, the cost threshold is $400 and the cost limit is $8,250. [Soc. Sec. Act § 1860D-22(a)(3)(B); 42 C.F.R. § 423.886(b)(3); *Announcement of Calendar Year 2017 Medicare Advantage Capitation Rates and Medicare Advantage and Part D Payment Policies and Final Call Letter*, April 4, 2016.]

Payment Methods and Providing Necessary Information

The provisions governing payment to Part D plan sponsors for qualified prescription drug coverage, including requirements to provide information necessary to ensure accurate subsidy payments, also govern the subsidy payment to sponsors of retiree PDPs. Payment by CMS is conditioned on provision of accurate information. The sponsor must submit the information in a form and manner and at the times provided by CMS. CMS will make payment after the sponsor submits the cost data. [42 C.F.R. § 423.888(a), (b)(3).]

Timing and submission of cost data. Payment can be on a monthly, quarterly, or annual basis, as elected by the plan sponsor, unless CMS decides to restrict the options because of operational limitations. If the plan sponsor elects for payment on a monthly or quarterly basis, it must provide cost data on the same monthly or quarterly basis, or at such time as CMS specifies. If the sponsor elects an annual payment, it must submit to CMS actual rebate and other price concession data within 15 months after the end of the plan year. [42 C.F.R. § 423.888(b).]

Special rule for insured plans. Sponsors of group health plans that provide benefits through health insurance coverage and choose monthly payments, quarterly payments, or an interim annual payment may elect to determine gross covered plan-related retiree prescription drug costs for purposes of the monthly, quarterly, or interim annual payments based on a portion of the premium costs paid by the sponsor or the qualifying covered retirees. Premium costs that are determined using generally accepted actuarial principles may be attributable to the gross prescription drug costs incurred by the health insurance issuer for the sponsor's qualifying covered retirees, except that administrative costs and risk charges must be subtracted from the premium. [42 C.F.R. § 423.888(b)(5)(i).]

Maintaining records. The sponsor of the qualified retiree PDP or a designee must maintain for a period of six years and furnish to CMS or the Office of Inspector General, upon request, the following records:

(1) reports and working documents of the actuaries who wrote the attestation;

(2) all documentation of costs incurred and other relevant information utilized for calculating the amount of the subsidy payment, including the underlying claims data; and

(3) any other records specified by CMS.

[42 C.F.R. § 423.888(d).]

Appeals by Retiree Prescription Drug Plans

A sponsor is entitled to an informal written reconsideration of an adverse initial determination by CMS regarding the amount of the subsidy payment; the actuarial equivalence of the sponsor's retiree PDP; whether an enrollee in a retiree PDP is a qualifying covered retiree; or any other similar determination affecting eligibility for, or the amount of, a subsidy payment. An initial determination is final and binding unless reconsidered. [42 C.F.R. § 423.890(a)(1), (2).]

Informal hearing request. A sponsor dissatisfied with the CMS reconsideration decision is entitled to an informal hearing. The sponsor must make file a written hearing request with CMS within 15 days of the date the sponsor receives the CMS reconsideration decision. The CMS hearing officer is limited to the review of the record that was before CMS when CMS made both its initial and reconsideration determinations. [42 C.F.R. § 423.890(b)(1), (2), (3).]

The CMS hearing officer decides the case and sends a written decision to the sponsor, explaining the basis for the decision. The hearing officer decision is final and binding, unless the decision is reversed or modified by the Administrator. [42 C.F.R. § 423.890(b)(4), (5).]

Review by the Administrator. A sponsor that has received a hearing officer decision upholding a CMS initial or reconsidered determination may request review by the Administrator within 15 days of receipt of the decision. The Administrator's determination is final and binding. [42 C.F.R. § 423.890(c).]

Reopening of initial or reconsidered determination. CMS may reopen and revise an initial or reconsidered determination upon its own motion or upon the request of a sponsor within one year of the date of the notice of determination for any reason, within four years for good cause, and at any time when the underlying decision was obtained through fraud or similar fault. [42 C.F.R. § 423.890(d)(1).]

A decision by CMS not to reopen an initial or reconsidered determination is final and binding and cannot be appealed. [42 C.F.R. § 423.890(d)(6).]

Change of Ownership Requirements for Retiree Prescription Drug Plan Sponsors

Sponsors who apply for a retiree drug subsidy payment must comply with certain change of ownership requirements. A change of ownership includes:

• the removal, addition, or substitution of a partner, unless the partners expressly agree otherwise as permitted by applicable state law;

• transfer of all or substantially all of the assets of the sponsor to another party; or

• the merger of the sponsor's corporation into another corporation or the consolidation of the sponsor's organization with one or more other corporations, resulting in a new corporate body.

The transfer of corporate stock or the merger of another corporation into the sponsor's corporation with the sponsor surviving does not ordinarily constitute change of ownership. [42 C.F.R. § 423.892(a), (b).]

Notice requirement. A sponsor that has a retiree PDP in effect and is considering or negotiating a change in ownership must notify CMS at least 60 days before the anticipated effective date of the change. [42 C.F.R. § 423.892(c).]

Automatic assignment. When there is a change of ownership that results in a transfer of the liability for prescription drug costs, the existing sponsor agreement is automatically assigned to the new owner. The new owner to whom a sponsor agreement is assigned is subject to all applicable statutes and regulations and to the terms and conditions of the sponsor agreement. [42 C.F.R. § 423.892(d), (e).]

[¶ 535] Marketing Requirements

CMS has established prohibitions and limitations on the sales and marketing activities of Medicare Advantage (MA) and prescription drug plans (PDPs).

Marketing materials include any information targeted to Medicare beneficiaries that: (1) promotes a Part D plan; (2) informs beneficiaries that they may enroll or remain enrolled in a plan; (3) explains the benefits or applicable rules of enrollment; or (4) explains how Medicare services are covered under a plan, including coverage conditions. [42 C.F.R. § 423.2260.]

Marketing materials may include:

(1) general audience materials such as general circulation brochures, newspapers, magazines, television, radio, billboards, yellow pages, or the Internet;

(2) scripts or outlines for telemarketing or other presentations;

(3) slides and charts;

(4) promotional materials such as brochures or leaflets, including materials for circulation by third parties (such as physicians or other providers);

(5) membership communication materials such as membership rules, subscriber agreements, member handbooks, and wallet card instructions to enrollees;

(6) letters to members about contractual changes and changes in providers, premiums, benefits, and plan procedures; and

(7) membership activities, such as materials on rules for nonpayment of premiums, confirmation of enrollment or disenrollment, or non-claim-specific notification information.

[42 C.F.R. § 423.2260.]

Excluded information. Marketing materials do not include ad hoc enrollee communications materials, such as informational materials that: (1) are targeted to current enrollees; (2) are customized or limited to a subset of enrollees or apply to a specific situation; (3) do not include information about the plan's benefit structure; and (4) apply to a specific situation or cover member-specific claims processing or other operational issues. [42 C.F.R. § 423.2260.]

CMS Review of Marketing Materials

A Part D plan may not distribute any marketing materials or make such materials or forms available to eligible individuals unless, at least 45 days before the date of distribution, the sponsor submits the material or form to CMS for review, and CMS does not disapprove of the distribution. This time period may be reduced to 10 days if the plan's marketing materials use, without modification, CMS-specified proposed model language and format, including standardized language and formatting. [Soc. Sec. Act §§ 1851(h)(1), (5), 1860D-1(b)(1)(B)(vi); 42 C.F.R. § 423.2262(a).]

The Part D sponsor may distribute certain designated marketing materials five days following their submission to CMS if the sponsor certifies that it followed all applicable marketing guidelines and, when applicable, used CMS model language without modification. [42 C.F.R. § 423.2262(b).]

CMS review guidelines. CMS examines marketing materials and enrollment forms to see that they provide information in a format, print size, and standard terminology specified by CMS. This information includes adequate written description of rules, procedures, basic benefits, services, fees, the grievance and appeals process, and any other information necessary to enable beneficiaries to make informed enrollment decisions. [Soc. Sec. Act §§ 1851(h)(2), 1860D-1(b)(1)(B)(vi); 42 C.F.R. § 423.2264(a).]

CMS also must make sure that the materials:

(1) notify the public of its enrollment period in an appropriate manner; including notice that (a) the plan may refuse to renew its contract with CMS, (b) CMS may refuse to renew the plan's contract, and (c) termination or nonrenewal may result in termination of the beneficiary's enrollment in the plan;

(2) include notice that the plan may reduce its service area and no longer be offered in the area where a beneficiary resides;

(3) are not materially inaccurate or misleading or otherwise make material misrepresentations; and

(4) in markets with a significant non-English-speaking population, are provided in the language of these individuals.

[42 C.F.R. § 423.2264.]

Materials "deemed" approved. If CMS does not disapprove marketing materials within the specified review time frame, the materials are deemed approved and the Part D sponsor may use them. [Soc. Sec. Act §§ 1851(h)(3), 1860D-1(b)(1)(B)(vi); 42 C.F.R. § 423.2262(a)(2).]

Marketing Standards

In conducting marketing activities, a Part D plan may not:

- provide cash or other remuneration as an inducement for enrollment;

- offer gifts to potential enrollees, unless the gifts are of nominal value, are offered to all potential enrollees without regard to whether the beneficiary enrolls, and are not in the form of cash or other monetary rebates;

- engage in any discriminatory activity such as attempts to recruit beneficiaries from higher income areas without making comparable efforts to enroll beneficiaries from lower income areas;

- solicit door-to-door or through other unsolicited means of direct contact, including calling a beneficiary without the beneficiary initiating the contact;

- engage in activities that could mislead or confuse Medicare beneficiaries, misrepresent the sponsor or its plan, or claim that it is recommended or endorsed by CMS or Medicare or that CMS or Medicare recommends that the beneficiary enroll in the Part D plan;

- cross-sell non-health-care-related products to prospective enrollees during any Part D sales activity or presentation;

- market any health-care-related product during a marketing appointment that is beyond the scope agreed upon by the beneficiary and documented by the plan, prior to the appointment (48 hours in advance, when practicable);

- market additional health-related lines of plan business not identified before an individual appointment without a separate appointment identifying the additional lines of business to be discussed;

- distribute marketing materials for which the sponsor receives from CMS written notice of disapproval because they are inaccurate or misleading or misrepresent the sponsor, its marketing representatives, or CMS;

- use providers, provider groups, or pharmacies to distribute printed information for beneficiaries to use when comparing the benefits of different plans unless the providers, provider groups, or pharmacies accept and display materials from all plan sponsors with which they contract;

- conduct sales presentations or distribute and accept plan enrollment forms in provider offices, pharmacies, or other areas where health care is delivered to individuals, except when such activities are conducted in common areas in health care settings;

- conduct sales presentations or distribute and accept plan applications at educational events;

- employ plan names that suggest that a plan is not available to all beneficiaries;

- display the names and logos of co-branded network providers on the organization's member identification card;

- engage in any other marketing activity prohibited by CMS in its marketing guidance;

- provide meals for potential enrollees, regardless of value; and

- use a plan name that does not include the plan type.

[Soc. Sec. Act §§ 1851(h)(4), (6), (j), 1860D-4(l); 42 C.F.R. § 423.2268.]

In its marketing, the Part D organization must demonstrate to the satisfaction of CMS that marketing resources are allocated to marketing to the disabled Medicare population (under age 65) as well as beneficiaries age 65 and over. A Part D plan also must establish and maintain a system for confirming that enrolled beneficiaries have enrolled in the PDP and understand the rules applicable under the plan. [42 C.F.R. § 423.2272(a), (b).]

Licensing of Marketing Representatives

A Part D organization must employ as marketing representatives only those individuals who are licensed by the state to conduct direct marketing activities in that state. The sponsor must inform the state that it has appointed these individuals as marketing representatives as required by the appointment process provided for under state law. [Soc. Sec. Act §§ 1851(h)(7), 1860D-4(l); 42 C.F.R. § 423.2272(c).]

The organization must also report the termination of any such agent or broker to the state, including the reasons for such termination if state law requires that the reasons for the termination be reported. Finally, an organization must terminate upon discovery any unlicensed agent or broker employed as a marketing representative and notify any beneficiaries enrolled by an unqualified agent or broker of the agent's or broker's status and, if requested, of their options to confirm enrollment or make a plan change, including a special election period. [Soc. Sec. Act §§ 1851(h)(7), 1860D-4(l); 42 C.F.R. § 423.2272(d), (e).]

Broker and Agent Requirements

A Part D sponsor must meet the following requirements if it markets Part D plan products through any broker or agent: (1) ensure agents selling Medicare products are trained and tested annually on Medicare rules and regulations and details specific to the plan products they sell; (2) at CMS's request, provide CMS the information necessary for it to conduct oversight of marketing activities; (3) comply with state requests for information about the performance of a licensed agent or broker as part of a state investigation into the individual's conduct; and (4) report to CMS annually on whether it intends to use independent agents or brokers or both in the upcoming plan year and, if applicable, the specific amount or range of amounts independent agents or brokers or both will be paid. [42 C.F.R. § 423.2274(c)–(g).]

Compensation requirements. Part D plan sponsor may provide compensation to an independent broker or agent for the sale of a Part D plan if the following compensation rules are followed:

- The compensation amount paid to an agent or broker for enrollment of a Medicare beneficiary into a PDP is: (1) for an initial enrollment, at or below the fair market value cut-off amounts published annually by CMS; and (2) for renewals, an amount equal to 50 percent of the current fair market value cut-off amounts.

- If the Part D sponsor contracts with a third-party entity such as a field marketing organization or similar type entity to sell its insurance products or perform services: (1) the amount paid to the third party, or its agents, for enrollment of a beneficiary into a plan must be the same as paid to non-third-party agents and brokers; and (2) the amount paid to the third party for services other than selling insurance products, if any, must be fair market value and must not exceed an amount that is commensurate with the amounts paid by the PDP organization to a third party for similar services during each of the previous two years.

[42 C.F.R. § 423.2274(b)(1).]

Aggregate compensation. No entity may provide, and no agent or broker shall receive, aggregate compensation greater than the renewal compensation payable by the replacing plan on renewal policies if an existing policy is replaced with a like plan type. The initial compensation is paid for replacements between unlike plan types. [42 C.F.R. § 423.2274(b)(2).]

Plan year compensation. Compensation may be paid only for the beneficiary's months of enrollment during a plan year. Compensation payments may be made up front for the entire current plan year or in installments throughout the year. When a beneficiary disenrolls from a plan, compensation paid to agents and brokers must be recovered for those months of the plan year for which the beneficiary is not enrolled. For disenrollments occurring within the first three months, the entire compensation must be recovered unless CMS determines that recoupment is not in the best interests of the Medicare program. [42 C.F.R. § 423.2274(b)(3).]

Compensation structure. A Part D sponsor must establish a compensation structure for new and replacement enrollments and renewals effective in a given plan year. They must be in place by October 1 and must be available upon CMS's request. [42 C.F.R. § 423.2274(b)(4).]

Finder's fees. Finder's (referral) fees paid to all agents and brokers may not exceed an amount that CMS determines could reasonably be expected to provide financial incentive for an agent or broker to recommend or enroll a beneficiary into a plan that is not the most appropriate to meet his or her needs. The fee must be included in the total compensation not to exceed the fair market value for that calendar year. [42 C.F.R. § 423.2274(h).]

"Compensation" defined. For the purposes of broker and agent requirements, "compensation" includes pecuniary or nonpecuniary remuneration of any kind relating to the sale or renewal of a policy including, but not limited to, commissions, bonuses, gifts, prizes, awards, and referral or finder's fees. Compensation does *not* include: (1) the payment of fees to comply with state appointment laws or training, certification, and testing costs; (2) reimbursement for mileage to and from appointments with beneficiaries; or (3) reimbursement for actual costs associated with beneficiary sales appointments such as venue rent, snacks, and materials. [42 C.F.R. § 423.2274(a).]

Employer Group Retirees

Part D sponsors may develop marketing materials for members of an employer group who are eligible for employer-sponsored benefits through the Part D sponsor. These materials may be furnished only to the employer group members. These marketing materials are exempt from prior review and approval by CMS. [42 C.F.R. § 423.2276.]

Chapter 6– EXCLUSIONS FROM COVERAGE

[¶ 600] Exclusions Under Part A and Part B

In addition to the limitations and exclusions discussed in the preceding chapters, other items or services are excluded under both Medicare Part A and Part B, as established by Soc. Sec. Act § 1862(a). In general, CMS will not cover items and services that are not reasonable or necessary for the diagnosis or treatment of illness or injury or to improve the functioning of a malformed body member. Particular services and items are also excluded from payment eligibility and are discussed in the following sections. [42 C.F.R. § 411.1 *et seq.*]

[¶ 601] Services Not Reasonable and Necessary

Items and services that are not reasonable and necessary for the diagnosis or treatment of illness or injury or to improve the functioning of a malformed body part are excluded from coverage. Many items and services are considered reasonable and necessary for some conditions but not for others. [Soc. Sec. Act § 1862(l)(1); 42 C.F.R. § 411.15(k).]

Medicare Coverage Determinations Manual, Pub. 100-03, discusses specific coverage decisions and exclusions.

Note that a beneficiary can be "held harmless" (not required to pay) in certain situations in which claims are disallowed under this exclusion. This "waiver of liability" provision is discussed at ¶ 915. [Soc. Sec. Act § 1879.]

Exclusion of Assisted Suicide

Procedures to assist a patient in committing suicide or to cause the patient's death are excluded, but this exclusion does not prevent the withholding or withdrawal of medical treatment, nutrition, or hydration or the provision of a service for the purpose of alleviating pain or discomfort, even if the use may increase the risk of death, as long as the service is not furnished for the specific purpose of causing death. [Soc. Sec. Act § 1862(a)(16); 42 C.F.R. § 411.15(q).]

Services Related to Non-Covered Services

Services related to services that are typically excluded from coverage under Medicare Parts A and B (for instance, cosmetic surgery, non-covered organ transplants, non-covered artificial organ implants), including follow-up services and those related to complications arising out of non-covered services, are also excluded. [*Medicare Benefit Policy Manual*, Pub. 100-02, Ch. 16, § 180.] For a list of examples of services that are considered "related to" non-covered services, see Pub. 100-02, Ch. 16, § 180.

Experimental and Investigational Devices and Treatments

Medicare generally does not cover experimental and investigational devices and treatments. However, Medicare does cover the routine costs of care furnished to a beneficiary in a qualifying Category A (experimental) clinical trial. [Soc. Sec. Act § 1862(m)(1).] Medicare also covers Category B (nonexperimental/investigational) devices and routine care items and services furnished in Food and Drug Administration-approved Category B investigational device exemption studies if specified criteria are met. [42 C.F.R. §§ 405.201–405.213, 411.15(o); Pub. 100-03, Ch. 1, § 310.1.]

[¶ 604] No Legal Obligation to Pay

Medicare will not make payment for items or services for which neither the beneficiary nor any other person or organization has a legal obligation to pay or to provide. This exclusion does not apply, however, to services furnished in a federally qualified community health center (see ¶ 382). [Soc. Sec. Act § 1862(a)(2); 42 C.F.R. § 411.4(a).]

Items/services furnished free of charge. This exclusion applies when items and services are furnished free of charge regardless of the beneficiary's ability to pay and without expectation of payment from any source. An example is free x-rays or immunizations provided by health organizations. The exclusion does not apply, however, where items and services are furnished to an indigent individual without charge because of his or her inability to pay, if the provider, physician, or supplier bills other patients to the extent that they are able to pay. If a provider, physician, or supplier waives his or her charges for individuals of limited means but also expects to be paid when the patient has insurance, a legal obligation to pay exists and benefits are payable for services rendered to patients with medical insurance if the provider, physician, or supplier customarily bills all insured patients, even though non-insured patients are not charged. [*Medicare Benefit Policy Manual*, Pub. 100-02, Ch. 16, § 40.]

Other health coverage. Except as discussed at ¶ 636 (involving workers' compensation, automobile and liability insurance, and certain employer group health plans), payment is not precluded under Medicare even though the patient is covered by another health insurance plan or program that is obligated to provide or pay for the same services. In these cases, the other plan pays the primary benefits and if it does not pay the entire bill, secondary Medicare benefits may be payable. [Pub. 100-02, Ch. 16, § 40.3.] The amount of secondary benefits Medicare will pay is determined by rules discussed at ¶ 636.

Items covered under a warranty. When a defective medical device such as a cardiac pacemaker is replaced under a warranty, Medicare may cover hospital and physician charges despite the warrantor's liability. If the warrantor replaces the device free of charge, Medicare will not make payment because there was no charge involved. [Pub. 100-02, Ch. 16, § 40.4.]

Members of religious orders. A legal obligation to pay exists when a religious order either pays for or furnishes services to members of the order. Medical services furnished in such a setting ordinarily would not be expressed in terms of a legal obligation; however, the religious order has an obligation to care for its members who have rendered life-long services, so the order pays for such services whether they are furnished by the religious order itself or by independent sources that customarily charge for their services. [Pub. 100-02, Ch. 16, § 40.5.]

State or local prisoners. Medicare payment may be made for services furnished to individuals who are in the custody of the police or other penal authorities only if: (1) state or local law requires the individuals to repay the cost of medical services they receive while in custody; and (2) the state or local government entity enforces the requirement to pay by billing all such individuals and by pursuing collection of the amounts they owe in the same way and with the same vigor that it pursues the collection of other debts. [42 C.F.R. § 411.4(b).]

[¶ 607] Services Paid for by Governmental Entity

Generally, Medicare does not pay for items or services that are paid for directly or indirectly by a governmental entity, including state and local governments. [Soc. Sec. Act § 1862(a)(3); 42 C.F.R. § 411.8(a).]

However, Medicare may make payment for:

(1) services furnished under a health insurance plan established for employees of the governmental entity;

(2) services furnished under a program based on a title of the Social Security Act other than Medicare, such as Medicaid;

(3) services furnished in or by a participating general or special hospital that is operated by a state or local governmental entity and serves the general community;

(4) services furnished by a hospital or elsewhere as a means of controlling infectious diseases or because of the individual's medical indigency;

(5) services furnished by participating hospitals and skilled nursing facilities of the Indian Health Service (IHS) (see below);

(6) services furnished by a public or private health facility (other than a federal provider or facility operated by a federal agency) that: (a) receives United States government funds under a federal program that provides support to facilities furnishing health care services, (b) customarily seeks reimbursement for items and services not covered under Medicare from all resources available for the health care of its patients—for example, private insurance and patients' cash resources, and (c) limits the amounts it collects or seeks to collect from a Part B beneficiary and others on the beneficiary's behalf;

(7) rural and community health clinic services (see ¶ 382);

(8) certain emergency services (see ¶ 227); and

(9) services furnished under arrangements made by a participating hospital.

[Soc. Sec. Act § 1862(a)(3); 42 C.F.R. §§ 411.6, 411.8(b).]

Indian Health Service

The IHS is the primary health care provider to the American Indian/Alaska Native Medicare population. The IHS, consisting of tribal, urban, and federally operated IHS health programs, delivers a spectrum of clinical and preventive health services to its beneficiaries via a network of hospitals, clinics, and other entities. Although sections 1814(c) and 1835(d) of the Social Security Act generally prohibit payment to any federal agency, an exception applies to the IHS/tribally owned and operated facilities. IHS facilities may bill for Medicare Part B covered services and items, including all screening and preventive services covered by Medicare, physician services, diagnostic x-ray and other diagnostic tests, anesthesia services, practitioner services, drugs and biologics incident to physician services, physical therapy services, occupational therapy services, speech-language pathology services, ambulance services, and telehealth services. [Soc. Sec. Act § 1880(e)(1)(A); *Medicare Claims Processing Manual*, Pub. 100-04, Ch. 19, §§ 10, 70.]

Social admissions. Services rendered to American Indian/Alaska Native beneficiaries admitted to IHS/tribal facilities for social reasons are not covered by Medicare. These social admissions are for the patients' and families' convenience and include occasions when IHS/tribal hospitals elect to admit patients before a scheduled day of surgery, or place a patient in a room after an inpatient discharge. [Pub. 100-04, Ch. 19, § 100.3.3.]

Department of Veterans Affairs

Medicare payment may not be made for any item or service that a provider, physician, or supplier provided pursuant to an authorization issued by the Department of Veterans Affairs (VA) under which the VA agrees to pay for the services. An authorization issued by the VA binds the VA to pay in full for the items and services provided. However, when the VA does not give an authorization to the party rendering the services, Medicare payment is not precluded even though the individual might have been entitled to have payment made by the VA if the individual had requested the authorization. [*Medicare Benefit Policy Manual*, Pub. 100-02, Ch. 16, § 50.1.1.]

If a physician accepts a veteran as a patient and bills the VA, the physician must accept the VA's "usual and customary" charge determination as payment in full and neither the patient nor any other party can be charged an additional amount. Therefore, Medicare cannot make payment if the physician's bill for authorized services exceeds the amount the VA paid the physician or reimbursed the beneficiary. Medicare can, however, pay secondary benefits to the beneficiary or physician to cover the VA copayment or deductible. Medicare also may pay for services not covered by the VA. [Pub. 100-02, Ch. 16, §§ 50.1.1, 50.1.4.]

Under certain circumstances, Medicare reimbursement for care provided to a nonveteran Medicare beneficiary in a VA hospital is authorized if the care was provided on the mistaken (but good faith) assumption that the beneficiary was an eligible veteran. [Soc. Sec. Act § 1814(h)(1).]

TRICARE and CHAMPVA

TRICARE is a Department of Defense health care program for all branches of the armed services. Civilian Health and Medical Program of the Veterans Administration (CHAMPVA) is a health program administered by the VA under which the VA shares the cost of covered services with eligible family members of certain veterans. If a TRICARE or CHAMPVA beneficiary also has Medicare coverage, Medicare is the primary payer. TRICARE or CHAMPVA covers the Medicare deductible and coinsurance amounts and portions of the bill not covered by Medicare. [Pub. 100-02, Ch. 16, § 50.4.]

TRICARE/CHAMPVA have established policies and procedures that provide for: (1) the identification of claimants who have coverage under both TRICARE/CHAMPVA and Medicare; and (2) the detection of duplicate payments under both programs. If TRICARE or CHAMPVA inadvertently pays amounts that duplicate Medicare payments for the same items or services, TRICARE/CHAMPVA will take steps to recover the incorrect payments. [Pub. 100-02, Ch. 16, § 50.4.]

Medicare-participating hospitals are required to participate in the programs and to accept patients from those programs. [Soc. Sec. Act § 1866(a)(1)(J).]

[¶ 610] Services Outside the United States

Generally, Medicare does not pay for services furnished outside the United States, which includes the 50 states, the District of Columbia, the Commonwealth of Puerto Rico, the Virgin Islands, Guam, the Northern Mariana Islands, American Samoa, and for purposes of services rendered on a ship, the territorial waters adjoining the land areas of the United States. For Medicare purposes, services rendered aboard a ship in an American port or within six hours of the time at which the ship arrives at, or departs from, that port will be considered to have been rendered in American waters. [Soc. Sec. Act §§ 210(h) and (i), 1862(a)(4); 42 C.F.R. § 411.9; *Medicare Claims Processing Manual*, Pub. 100-04, Ch. 32, § 350.1.]

Medicare will not make payment for a medical service (or a portion of it) that is subcontracted to a provider or supplier located outside the United States. For example, if a radiologist who practices in India analyzes imaging tests that were performed on a beneficiary in the United States, Medicare will not pay the radiologist or the U.S. facility that performed the imaging test for any of the services that were performed by the radiologist in India. [*Medicare Benefit Policy Manual*, Pub. 100-02, Ch. 16, § 60.]

Qualified railroad retirement beneficiaries submit their claims for inpatient services received in Canada to the Railroad Retirement Board (RRB) for a determination of coverage.

If the RRB finds the inpatient services are covered, it forwards the claim to a Medicare administrative contractor for consideration of whether the other requirements for Part B coverage are met and for further processing. The RRB does not cover services furnished in Mexico; Medicare rules apply to services received in Mexico. [Pub. 100-04, Ch. 32, § 350.7.]

Exceptions to Geographic Limits

There are some situations in which Medicare does pay for services rendered outside of the United States. Medicare pays for inpatient hospital services provided to beneficiaries entitled to Part A by a hospital located outside of the United States if: (1) the beneficiary is a resident of the United States; (2) the hospital is closer to or substantially more accessible to the beneficiary's residence than the nearest hospital within the United States; (3) the hospital is adequately equipped to deal with the beneficiary's illness or injury; and (4) the hospital is available for the treatment of the illness or injury. [Soc. Sec. Act §§ 1814(f)(1), 1862(a)(4).]

Emergency inpatient hospital services also are covered when the emergency occurred while the beneficiary was in the United States or, at the time of the emergency, the beneficiary was in Canada while traveling directly between Alaska and another state without unreasonable delay and by the most direct route and the Canadian hospital was closer or more accessible with adequate facilities to care for the beneficiary's needs. An emergency occurring within the Canadian inland waterway between the states of Washington and Canada is considered to have occurred in Canada. [Soc. Sec. Act § 1814(f)(2); 42 C.F.R. § 424.122(a), (b); Pub. 100-02, Ch. 16, § 60.]

Medicare will pay 100 percent of the foreign hospital's charges. [42 C.F.R. § 413.74(b).]

Physicians' services in connection with foreign hospitalization. Physicians' services provided to a Medicare beneficiary outside a hospital on the day of admission as an inpatient are covered, as long as the services were for the same condition for which the beneficiary was hospitalized. The physician must be legally licensed to practice in the country in which he or she furnished the services. This provision includes the services of a Canadian ship's physician who furnishes emergency treatment in Canadian waters on the day the beneficiary is admitted to a Canadian hospital for a covered emergency stay. [Soc. Sec. Act § 1862(a)(4); 42 C.F.R. § 424.124(a); Pub. 100-04, Ch. 32, § 350.6.]

Ambulance services in connection with foreign hospitalizations. Payment may be made for necessary ambulance service to a hospital in conjunction with a beneficiary's admission as an inpatient; however, return trips from a foreign hospital are not covered. [Soc. Sec. Act § 1862(a)(4); 42 C.F.R. § 424.124(a), (c); Pub. 100-04, Ch. 32, § 350.6.]

Regular deductible and coinsurance requirements apply to physicians' and ambulance services rendered outside the United States. [Pub. 100-04, Ch. 32, § 350.6.]

[¶ 613] Services Resulting from War

Medicare does not cover items and services that are required as a result of war, or an act of war, occurring after the effective date of the patient's current coverage for hospital insurance benefits or supplemental medical insurance benefits. [Soc. Sec. Act § 1862(a)(5); 42 C.F.R. § 411.10.]

[¶ 616] Personal Comfort Items

Personal comfort items, meaning those items that do not contribute meaningfully to the treatment of an illness or injury or the functioning of a malformed body member, are not covered except when provided in the course of hospice care (see ¶ 270). Charges for radios, televisions, telephones, or air conditioners are examples of personal comfort items excluded from Medicare coverage. [Soc. Sec. Act § 1862(a)(6); 42 C.F.R. § 411.15(j); *Medicare Benefit Policy Manual*, Pub. 100-02, Ch. 16, § 80.]

Basic personal services, such as simple barber and beautician services (for example, shaves, haircuts, shampoos, and simple hair sets) that patients need and cannot perform for themselves, may be viewed as ordinary patient care when furnished by a long-stay institution. Such services are included in the flat rate charge covered under Part A and provided routinely without charge to the patient by a hospital or skilled nursing facility. [Pub. 100-02, Ch. 16, § 80.]

Providers may charge patients for excluded personal comfort items that the patient requests only if the patient has knowledge that he or she will be charged for those items. [Pub. 100-02, Ch. 16, § 80.]

Providers also are allowed to charge patients when they request services that are more expensive than those covered by Medicare (see ¶ 730 under "Allowable Charges").

[¶ 619] Eye, Ear, and Foot Care

Medicare does not cover routine eye, ear, and foot care services. [Soc. Sec. Act § 1862(a)(7), (8), (13); 42 C.F.R. § 411.15.]

Eye Care

Excluded routine eye care includes: (1) eyeglasses; (2) most contact lenses; (3) eye examinations for the purpose of prescribing, fitting, or changing eyeglasses or contact lenses for refractive error only; and (4) procedures performed in the course of any eye examination to determine the refractive state of the eyes. [Soc. Sec. Act § 1862(a)(7); 42 C.F.R. § 411.15(b), (c).]

The eye care services exclusion does not apply to: (1) physicians' services (and services incident to a physician's service) performed in conjunction with an eye disease, for example, glaucoma or cataracts; (2) post-surgical prosthetic lenses customarily used during convalescence for eye surgery in which the lens of the eye was removed (for example, cataract surgery); (3) prosthetic intraocular lenses and one pair of conventional eyeglasses or contact lenses furnished after each cataract surgery with insertion of an intraocular lens; or (4) prosthetic lenses used by beneficiaries who are lacking the natural lens of the eye and who were not furnished with an intraocular lens. [42 C.F.R. § 411.15(b)(2); *Medicare Benefit Policy Manual*, Pub. 100-02, Ch. 16, § 90.]

Note that the law specifically authorizes coverage for one pair of conventional eyeglasses or contact lenses furnished subsequent to each cataract surgery in which an intraocular lens is inserted. [Soc. Sec. Act § 1861(s)(8).]

Ear Care

Hearing aids and examinations for the purpose of prescribing, fitting, or changing hearing aids are excluded from Medicare coverage. The scope of the hearing aid exclusion encompasses all types of air conduction hearing aids that provide acoustic energy to the cochlea via stimulation of the tympanic membrane with amplified sound, and bone conduction hearing aids that provide mechanical stimulation of the cochlea via stimulation of the scalp with amplified mechanical vibration or by direct contact with the tympanic membrane or middle ear ossicles. [Soc. Sec. Act § 1862(a)(7); 42 C.F.R. § 411.15(d).]

Certain devices that produce perception of sound by replacing the function of the middle ear, cochlea, or auditory nerve are payable by Medicare as prosthetic devices. These devices are indicated only when hearing aids are medically inappropriate or cannot be utilized due to congenital malformations, chronic disease, severe sensorineural hearing loss, or surgery. The following are covered as prosthetic devices: (1) osseointegrated implants in the skull bone that provide mechanical energy to the cochlea via a mechanical transducer; or (2) cochlear implants and auditory brainstem implants that replace the function of cochlear structures or auditory nerve and provide electrical energy to auditory nerve fibers and other neural tissue via implanted electrode arrays. [42 C.F.R. § 411.15(d)(2); Pub. 100-02, Ch. 16, § 100.]

Foot Care

Medicare does not cover the following foot-related services:

(1) routine foot care;

(2) the evaluation or treatment of subluxations (structural misalignments of the joints) of the feet; or

(3) the evaluation or treatment of flattened arches and the prescription of supportive devices.

[Soc. Sec. Act § 1862(a)(13); 42 C.F.R. § 411.15(l)(1).]

Routine foot care. Routine foot care includes the cutting or removal of corns or calluses, the trimming of nails (including mycotic nails), and other hygienic and preventive maintenance care in the realm of self-care, such as cleaning and soaking the feet, the use of skin creams to maintain skin tone of both ambulatory and bed-confined patients, and any services performed in the absence of localized illness, injury, or symptoms involving the foot. For example, foot care such as routine soaking and application of topical medication on a physician's order between required physician visits is not covered. [42 C.F.R. § 411.15(l)(1)(i); Pub. 100-02, Ch. 15, § 290.]

Exceptions to foot-care exclusion. Services may be covered: (1) for the treatment of warts; (2) for the treatment of mycotic toenails if furnished no more often than every 60 days or the billing physician documents the need for more frequent treatment; and (3) when they are incident to, at the same time as, or as a necessary integral part of a primary covered procedure performed on the foot, or initial diagnostic services (regardless of the resulting diagnosis) in connection with a specific symptom or complaint that might arise from a condition for which treatment would be covered. [42 C.F.R. § 411.15(l)(2); Pub. 100-02, Ch. 15, § 290.]

Orthopedic shoes. Expenses for orthopedic shoes or other supportive devices for the feet generally are not covered, except when the shoe is an integral part of a leg brace and its expense is included as part of the cost of the brace. [Soc. Sec. Act § 1862(a)(8); 42 C.F.R. § 411.15(f).] The exclusion also does not apply to therapeutic shoes and inserts for individuals with severe diabetic foot disease (see ¶ 370). [Soc. Sec. Act § 1861(s)(12).]

[¶ 625] Custodial Care

Custodial care, except in the case of hospice care (see ¶ 270), is excluded from Medicare coverage. [Soc. Sec. Act § 1862(a)(9); 42 C.F.R. § 411.15(g).]

Custodial care is personal care that does not require the continuing attention of trained medical or paramedical personnel and serves to assist the individual in meeting the activities of daily living. The following activities are considered custodial care: (1) help in walking and getting in or out of bed; (2) assistance in bathing, dressing, feeding, and using the toilet; (3) preparation of special diets; and (4) supervision over medication that usually can be self-administered. Institutional care that is below the level of care covered in a skilled nursing facility (SNF) is custodial care. [*Medicare Benefit Policy Manual*, Pub. 100-02, Ch. 16, § 110.] For a discussion of noncovered levels of care in a SNF, see ¶ 244.

Note that a beneficiary can be "held harmless" (i.e., not required to pay) in certain situations in which claims are disallowed under this exclusion. This provision is discussed at ¶ 915.

[¶ 628] Cosmetic Surgery

Medicare does not cover cosmetic surgery and expenses incurred in connection with such surgery. This exclusion applies to any surgical procedure directed at improving appearance, except when required for the prompt (i.e., as soon as medically feasible) repair of accidental injury or for the improvement of the functioning of a malformed body member. For example, this exclusion does not apply to surgery: (1) in connection with treatment of severe burns or repair of the face following a serious automobile accident; or (2) for therapeutic purposes that coincidentally also serve some cosmetic purpose. [Soc. Sec. Act § 1862(a)(10); 42 C.F.R. § 411.15(h); *Medicare Benefit Policy Manual*, Pub. 100-02, Ch. 16, § 120.]

[¶ 631] Charges by Immediate Relatives and Household Members

Medicare does not pay for charges imposed by physicians or other persons who are immediate relatives of the patient or members of the patient's household. The intent of this exclusion is to bar payment for items and services that would ordinarily be furnished gratuitously because of the relationship of the beneficiary to the person imposing the charge. [Soc. Sec. Act § 1862(a)(11); 42 C.F.R. § 411.12(a).]

Immediate relatives and household members. "Immediate relative" means spouse; natural or adoptive parent, child, and sibling; stepparent, stepchild, stepbrother, and stepsister; parent-in-law, child-in-law, brother-in-law, and sister-in-law; grandparent and grandchild; and spouse of grandparent and grandchild. "Members of the patient's household" means those persons sharing a common abode with the patient as part of a single family unit, including domestic employees and others who live together as part of a single family unit. A roommate or boarder is not included. [42 C.F.R. § 411.12(b).]

A brother-in-law or sister-in-law relationship does not exist between a physician (or supplier) and the spouse of his wife's (her husband's) brother or sister. A father-in-law or mother-in-law relationship does not exist between a physician and the stepfather or stepmother of the physician's spouse. A step-relationship or an in-law relationship continues to exist even if the marriage upon which the relationship is based is terminated through divorce or through the death of one of the parties. For example, if a physician provides services to a stepparent after the death of (or divorce by) the natural parent, or if the physician provides services to an in-law after the death of the spouse of the physician, the services are considered to have been furnished to an immediate relative and, therefore, excluded from coverage. [*Medicare Benefit Policy Manual*, Pub. 100-02, Ch. 16, § 130.]

Physicians' services. The exclusion applies to the charges for physicians' services furnished by an immediate relative of the beneficiary or member of the beneficiary's household, even if the bill or claim is submitted by another individual or by an entity such as a partnership or a professional corporation. It also applies to charges for services furnished incident to a physician's professional services (for example, by the physician's nurse or technician) only if the physician who ordered or supervised the services has an excluded relationship to the beneficiary. [42 C.F.R. § 411.12(c)(1).]

Services other than physicians' services. In the case of services other than physicians' services, charges are excluded if they are provided by: (1) an individually owned provider or supplier, if the owner has an excluded relationship with the patient; or (2) a partnership, if any of the partners has an excluded relationship with the patient. [42 C.F.R. § 411.12(c)(2).]

Corporations. This exclusion does not apply to charges imposed by a corporation, other than a professional corporation, regardless of the patient's relationship to any of the stockholders, officers, or directors of the corporation or to the person who furnished the service. [42 C.F.R. § 411.12(d); Pub. 100-02, Ch. 16, § 130.]

[¶ 634] Dental Services

Items and services in connection with the care, treatment, filling, removal, or replacement of teeth or structures directly supporting the teeth (i.e., the periodontium, which includes the gingivae, dentogingival junction, periodontal membrane, cementum of the teeth, and alveolar process) generally are not covered. Payment may, however, be made under Part A for inpatient hospital services in connection with the provision of such dental services if the beneficiary, because of his or her underlying medical condition and clinical status or because of the severity of the dental procedure, requires hospitalization in connection with the provision of such services (see ¶ 218). [Soc. Sec. Act § 1862(a)(12); 42 C.F.R. § 411.15(i); *Medicare Benefit Policy Manual*, Pub. 100-02, Ch. 16, § 140.]

Medicare makes payment for the wiring of teeth when this is done in connection with the reduction of a jaw fracture. The extraction of teeth to prepare the jaw for radiation treatments of neoplastic disease also is covered. [Pub. 100-02, Ch. 15, § 150; Ch. 16, § 140.]

Whether such services as the administration of anesthesia, diagnostic x-rays, and other related procedures are covered depends upon whether Medicare covers the primary procedure being performed by the dentist. An x-ray taken in connection with the reduction of a fracture of the jaw or facial bone is covered, but a single x-ray or x-ray survey taken in connection with the care or treatment of teeth or the periodontium is not covered. [Pub. 100-02, Ch. 15, § 150; Ch. 16, § 140.]

[¶ 635] Services Not Provided In-House

Any services furnished to an inpatient of a hospital or to a hospital outpatient during an encounter by an entity other than the hospital are not covered, unless the hospital has an arrangement with that entity to furnish that particular service to the hospital's patients. The Medicare program requires hospitals and skilled nursing facilities (SNFs) caring for Medicare patients to provide in-house all the services that are furnished to those patients. This requirement is satisfied if the hospital or SNF has made arrangements to have the services provided by another entity, such as an independent laboratory or physical therapy group. Services not provided in-house that are supposed to be provided in-house are excluded from coverage and will not be covered by Medicare. [Soc. Sec. Act § 1862(a)(14), (18); 42 C.F.R. § 411.15(m)(1).]

The reason for this exclusion is that under each prospective payment system (PPS), in-house services are included in the calculation of the hospital's and SNF's PPS diagnosis-related group (DRG) payment rate, and Medicare will not pay for these services twice (see ¶ 810 and ¶ 835).

This exclusion applies, but is not limited, to the following items and services: (1) clinical laboratory services; (2) pacemakers and other prostheses and prosthetic devices (other than dental) that replace all or part of an internal body organ (for example, intraocular lenses); (3) artificial limbs, knees, and hips; (4) equipment and supplies covered under the prosthetic device benefits; and (5) services furnished incident to physicians' services. [42 C.F.R. § 411.15(m)(2).]

This exclusion does *not* apply to physicians' services or to the services of the following health care practitioners: (1) physician assistants; (2) nurse practitioners and clinical nurse specialists; (3) certified nurse-midwives; (4) qualified psychologists; and (5) certified registered nurse anesthetists and anesthesiologist's assistants. [42 C.F.R. § 411.15(m)(3).]

Charges to Beneficiaries

Under the regulations governing provider agreements, hospitals are prohibited from charging beneficiaries for inpatient hospital services furnished by entities with which there is no arrangements agreement. Furthermore, because services furnished under arrangements are included in the hospital's DRG rate, if an entity other than the hospital charges the hospital inpatient for its services, that charge is treated as a charge by the hospital and is regarded as a violation of its provider agreement. [42 C.F.R. § 489.21(f).]

[¶ 636] Medicare as Secondary Payer

Medicare payment is excluded for services to the extent that payment has been made, or reasonably can be expected to be made, when the following alternate types of insurance are available:

    (1) workers' compensation;

    (2) automobile, no-fault, or liability insurance; and

    (3) employer group health plans (GHPs).

This exclusion is referred to as the Medicare Secondary Payer (MSP) rule. [Soc. Sec. Act § 1862(b)(2)(A); 42 C.F.R. § 411.20.]

Questionnaires to identify other coverage. To improve Medicare's identification of MSP situations, CMS mails questionnaires to individuals before they become entitled to benefits under Part A or enroll in Part B to determine possible coverage under a primary plan. Payment for otherwise covered services will not be denied, however, solely on the grounds that a beneficiary failed to complete the questionnaire properly. [Soc. Sec. Act § 1862(b)(2)(C), (b)(5)(D).]

Providers and suppliers also are required to furnish information concerning potential coverage under other plans. Payment may not be made for Part B claims if the provider or supplier fails to complete MSP questions on the claim form. Entities that knowingly, willfully, and repeatedly fail to complete a claim form or fail to provide accurate MSP information are subject to fines of up to $2,000 for each incident. [Soc. Sec. Act § 1862(b)(6).]

Coordination of benefits. In instances when Medicare is secondary payer to more than one primary insurer (e.g., an individual who is covered under his or her own GHP and under the GHP of an employed spouse or under no-fault insurance), the other primary payers will customarily coordinate benefits. If a portion of the charges remains unpaid after the other insurers have paid primary benefits, a secondary Medicare payment may be made. [*Medicare Secondary Payer Manual*, Pub. 100-05, Ch. 1, § 10.9.]

Workers' Compensation

Medicare payment is excluded for any items and services to the extent that payment has been made or reasonably can be expected to be made under a workers' compensation law or plan of the United States or a state. This exclusion also applies to the workers' compensation plans of the District of Columbia, American Samoa, Guam, the Virgin Islands, Puerto Rico, and the Virgin Islands. [Soc. Sec. Act § 1862(b)(2)(A)(ii); 42 C.F.R. § 411.40; Pub. 100-05, Ch. 1, § 10.4.]

The beneficiary is responsible for taking whatever action is necessary to obtain payment under workers' compensation when payment reasonably can be expected. Failure to take proper and timely action under such circumstances will preclude Medicare payment to the extent that payment reasonably could have been expected to be made under workers' compensation had the individual exhausted benefit rights under that system. [42 C.F.R. § 411.43(a).]

If a lump-sum workers' compensation award stipulates that the amount paid is intended to compensate the individual for all future medical expenses required because of the work-related injury or disease, Medicare payments for such services are excluded until medical expenses related to the injury or disease equal the amount of the lump-sum payment. [42 C.F.R. § 411.46(a).]

Medicare will not make payment if: (1) workers' compensation pays an amount that equals or exceeds the gross amount payable by Medicare without regard to deductible and coinsurance; (2) workers' compensation pays an amount that equals or exceeds the provider's, physician's, or supplier's charges for Medicare-covered services; or (3) the provider accepts or is required under the workers' compensation law to accept such workers' compensation payment as payment in full. If workers' compensation pays less than these amounts and the provider is not obligated to accept the amount as payment in full, secondary Medicare payments can be made. [42 C.F.R. § 411.32(b).]

Liability claims. Most state laws provide that if an employee is injured at work due to the negligent act of a third party, the employee cannot receive payments from both workers' compensation and the third party for the same injury. Generally, the workers' compensation carrier pays benefits while the third-party claim is pending. However, once a settlement of the third-party claim is reached or an award has been made, the workers' compensation carrier may recover the benefits it paid from the third-party settlement and may deny any future claims for that injury up to the amount of the liability payment made to the individual. Regardless of the liabilities of any other parties to one another, Medicare is the residual payer. [Soc. Sec. Act § 1862(b)(2)(B)(ii); Pub. 100-05, Ch. 1, § 10.9.]

Automobile and Liability Insurance Coverage

Medicare payment is excluded for any items and services to the extent that payment has been made or reasonably can be expected to be made under an automobile or liability insurance policy or plan, including a self-insured plan, or under no-fault insurance. [Soc. Sec. Act § 1862(b)(2)(A)(ii); 42 C.F.R. §§ 411.20(a)(2), 411.50(c).]

In no-fault insurance cases, the beneficiary is responsible for taking whatever action is necessary to obtain any payments from the no-fault insurer that reasonably can be expected. Medicare normally will not make any payments until the beneficiary has exhausted all remedies to obtain payments from the no-fault insurer. [42 C.F.R. § 411.51.]

It is common for insurance companies to settle claims without admitting liability. Therefore, any payment by a liability insurer constitutes a liability insurance payment regardless of whether there has been a determination of liability. Medicare is entitled to seek repayment of the amount it paid, less a proportionate share of procurement costs, from any payment a claimant receives from a liability insurer or self-insured party. [42 C.F.R. § 411.37(a).]

Generally, if settlement or other payment is greater than Medicare's claim, Medicare must be paid in full. If, however, a court or other adjudicator designates certain amounts as compensation for pain and suffering or other losses not related to medical services, Medicare will accept the designation and will not seek recovery from those portions of awards. [Pub. 100-05, Ch. 7, § 50.4.4.]

Employer Group Health Plans

Medicare payment is excluded for employees entitled to Medicare based on old age, disability, or (during a 30-month coordination-of-benefits period) end-stage renal disease (ESRD) to the extent that health care benefit payments have been made or reasonably can be expected to be made under a GHP. [Soc. Sec. Act §1862(b)(2)(A)(i); 42 C.F.R. §411.20(a)(1).]

Working aged. The working aged exclusion applies to Medicare-eligible individuals age 65 or over whose employer group health coverage is based on the current employment of the individual or spouse by an employer that employs 20 or more employees. Health insurance plans for retirees or spouses of retirees are not affected because retirement does not constitute "current employment." [Soc. Sec. Act §1862(b)(1)(A); 42 C.F.R. §411.20(a)(1)(ii); Pub. 100-05, Ch. 2, §§10, 10.3.]

Under this exclusion, employers are required to offer their employees age 65 or over the same GHP coverage offered to younger workers. Similarly, employers are required to offer their workers with Medicare-eligible spouses age 65 or over the same spousal GHP benefits they offer to workers with spouses that are not Medicare-eligible. [Soc. Sec. Act §1862(b)(1)(A)(i).] Employees and their spouses then have the option of choosing either the employer plan or Medicare as their primary health insurer. If the employee or spouse elects the employer plan, Medicare will assume back-up coverage. If the employee or spouse elects Medicare as the primary insurer, however, the employer plan may not offer back-up coverage. [42 C.F.R. §411.172(c); Pub. 100-05, Ch. 2, §10.]

Medicare may assume primary responsibility in paying for a beneficiary's health care if the services furnished are not covered under the employer plan or the beneficiaries have exhausted their benefits under the plan. Conditional Medicare payments can be made if the employer plan denies the claim or the beneficiary failed to file a claim due to physical or mental incapacity. [42 C.F.R. §411.175.]

The working aged employee provisions do not apply to disability beneficiaries or ESRD beneficiaries. [Soc. Sec. Act §1862(b)(1)(A)–(C).]

Disabled employees. Medicare is the secondary payer for individuals under age 65 entitled to Medicare based on disability (see ¶204) who are covered by a "large group health plan" (LGHP) and whose coverage is based on the current employment status of the individual or of a family member. When an employee (or a member of the employee's family) becomes disabled, the LGHP has primary coverage responsibility and Medicare has secondary coverage responsibility. [Soc. Sec. Act §1862(b)(1)(B); 42 C.F.R. §§411.200–411.206.]

An LGHP is defined as a group health plan of either: (1) a single employer or employee organization; or (2) at least one of two or more employers or employee organizations that employed at least 100 full-time employees or part-time employees on 50 percent or more of its regular business days during the previous calendar year. [Soc. Sec. Act §1862(b)(1)(B)(iii); Pub. 100-05, Ch. 2, §30.2.]

As in the case of elderly employees, there is a special enrollment period for disabled employees who do not enroll in Part B because they have chosen disability coverage under the employer's plan (see ¶311).

ESRD beneficiaries. Medicare benefits are secondary for a limited period of time, known as the coordination-of-benefits period, for individuals who are eligible or entitled to Medicare benefits because of ESRD (see ¶845) and who are entitled to primary health care coverage under an employer GHP regardless of the number of employees employed by the

¶636

employer and regardless of the individual's current employment status. [42 C.F.R. §411.162(a).]

The coordination-of-benefits period begins with the first month in which the individual becomes eligible for Medicare, or the first month in which the individual would have been eligible for Medicare if he or she had filed an application for Medicare ESRD benefits. The coordination-of-benefits period ends 30 months later. During the coordination-of-benefits period, Medicare has secondary payment responsibility. After the coordination-of-benefits period ends, Medicare has primary payment responsibility, as the patient becomes entitled to Medicare. [Soc. Sec. Act § 1862(b)(1)(C); 42 C.F.R. § 411.162.]

During the coordination-of-benefits period, Medicare will pay primary benefits for Medicare covered services that: (1) are furnished to Medicare beneficiaries who have declined to enroll in the GHP; (2) are not covered by the employer plan; (3) are covered under the GHP but not available to particular enrollees because they have exhausted their benefits; or (4) are furnished to individuals whose continuation coverage under the Consolidated Omnibus Budget Reconciliation Act of 1985 (COBRA) (P.L. 99-272) (i.e., continued health insurance coverage after leaving employment) has been terminated because of the individual's Medicare entitlement. Medicare will make secondary payments to supplement the amount paid by the employer plan if that plan pays only a portion of the charge for the service. [42 C.F.R. § 411.162(a).]

Medicare benefits are primary without a coordination-of-benefits period for ESRD-eligible individuals if the following conditions are met: (1) the beneficiary was already entitled to Medicare because of age or disability; (2) either the group health insurance was not based on current employment status, or the employer had fewer than 20 employees (in the case of the aged) or fewer than 100 employees (in the case of the disabled); and (3) the plan is paying secondary to Medicare because the plan had justifiably taken into account the age-based or disability-based entitlement. The employer health plan may continue to pay benefits secondary to Medicare but may not differentiate in the services covered and the payments made between persons who have ESRD and those who do not. [42 C.F.R. § 411.163(b)(4).]

Conditional Medicare Payments

If a primary plan has not made or cannot reasonably be expected to make payment with respect to such item or service promptly, Medicare may make a conditional payment. The conditional payment will be recovered later if it is determined that Medicare's liability is secondary. Regardless of any time limit on filing a claim under an employer group health plan, the government has three years to file a claim for recovery of conditional benefits paid by Medicare, beginning on the date the item or service was furnished. [Soc. Sec. Act § 1862(b)(2)(B); 42 C.F.R. §§ 411.45, 411.52, 411.53.]

A primary payer, and an entity that receives payment from a primary payer, must reimburse CMS for any payment if it is demonstrated that the primary payer has or had a responsibility to make payment, which is demonstrated by: (1) a judgment; (2) a payment conditioned upon the recipient's compromise, waiver, or release (whether or not there is a determination or admission of liability) of payment for items and services included in a claim against the primary plan or the primary plan's insured; or (3) by other means, including a settlement, award, or contractual obligation. [Soc. Sec. Act § 1862(b)(2)(B)(ii); 42 C.F.R. § 411.22.]

Prompt payment. In general, a payment is considered to be made promptly if it is made within 120 days after receipt of the claim. In the case of liability insurance, however, a claim is considered paid promptly if it is paid within 120 days after the earlier of: (1) the date a claim is filed; or (2) the date the services were furnished. In the case of inpatient hospital services, services are considered to be furnished, for purposes of this provision, on the date of discharge. [42 C.F.R. §§ 411.21, 411.50(b).]

Government action. If conditional Medicare payments are made, Medicare can bring an action to recover the payments it made against any entity that is responsible for payment under the MSP rules. In addition, it is possible for recovery to be made from a portion of the proceeds from the settlement of a lawsuit. The law further provides for subrogation, to the extent Medicare payment has been made for an item or service, to any right to payment for the item or service from the third party having primary payer responsibility. Medicare also is entitled to collect double damages against an alternate insurer that does not pay when it is required to do so. [Soc. Sec. Act § 1862(b)(2)(A), (b)(2)(B); 42 C.F.R. § 411.26.]

The beneficiary is required to cooperate in Medicare's attempt to recover conditional payments. Medicare is entitled to recover the payments from a beneficiary that fails to cooperate. If the beneficiary receives a payment from the alternate insurer, he or she must reimburse Medicare within 60 days. [42 C.F.R. §§ 411.23, 411.24(g) and (h).]

ESRD beneficiaries covered under a GHP. For ESRD beneficiaries who are also covered under a GHP, as a general rule, conditional primary Medicare payments may not be made if the claim is denied for one of the following reasons: (1) the GHP asserts it is secondary to Medicare or to the liability, no-fault, or workers' compensation insurer; (2) the GHP limits its payment when the individual is entitled to Medicare; (3) the services are covered by the GHP for younger employees and spouses but not for employees and spouses age 65 or over; or (4) the claim was not filed properly (including failure to file timely), if that failure is for any reason other than physical or mental incapacity of the beneficiary. Conditional primary Medicare benefits may be paid if the beneficiary, the provider, or the supplier that has accepted assignment files a proper claim under the GHP and the plan denies the claim in whole or in part; or the beneficiary, because of physical or mental incapacity, fails to file a proper claim. [42 C.F.R. § 411.165.]

Partial Payments by Alternate Insurer

If the alternate insurer pays less than the full amount of the charge for the services rendered, Medicare may make secondary payments to supplement the alternate insurer's payments. In no case, however, will the Medicare secondary payment exceed the amount that otherwise would have been payable if there were no alternate insurance. Medicare secondary payments also can be made to pay the alternate insurer's deductible and coinsurance requirements. [Soc. Sec. Act § 1862(b)(4); 42 C.F.R. §§ 411.32, 411.33.]

Some third-party payments obligate the provider, physician, or supplier to accept the payment as payment in full. No Medicare payment is payable in such a case. [42 C.F.R. § 411.32(b).]

For physicians and suppliers who are not obligated to accept the third-party payment as payment in full, the amount of the Medicare secondary benefit payable is the lowest of the following:

(1) the actual charge by the physician or supplier minus the amount paid by the third-party payer;

(2) the amount Medicare would pay if services were not covered by the third-party payer; or

(3) the higher of: (a) the Medicare fee schedule or other amount payable under Medicare (without regard to any deductible and/or coinsurance amounts), or (b) the third-party payer's allowable charge (without regard to any deductible and/or coinsur-

ance amounts imposed by the policy or plan), minus the amount actually paid by the third-party payer.

[42 C.F.R. § 411.33(a).]

For hospitals and other providers that are not obligated to accept third-party payments as payment in full, the Medicare secondary payment is the lowest of the following:

(1) the gross amount payable by Medicare minus the applicable deductible and coinsurance amount;

(2) the gross amount payable by Medicare minus the amount paid by the third-party payer for Medicare-covered services;

(3) the provider's charges (or the amount the provider is obligated to accept as payment in full) minus the amount paid by the third-party payer; or

(4) the provider's charges (or the amount the provider is obligated to accept as payment in full) minus the applicable Medicare deductible and coinsurance amount.

[42 C.F.R. § 411.33(e).]

[¶ 644] Excluded Drugs and Biologics

Prescription drugs that were approved before the 1962 amendments to the federal Food, Drug and Cosmetic Act (FDC Act) , and that the HHS Secretary subsequently determines to be "less than effective" in use, are excluded under Part B. Also, no payment can be made for drug products that are identical, related, or similar to a drug that is excluded. To exclude a drug under this provision, the Secretary must publish a notice of an opportunity for hearing in accordance with section 505(e) of the FDC Act. [Soc. Sec. Act § 1862(c); *Medicare Benefit Policy Manual*, Pub. 100-02, Ch. 15, § 50.4.6.] This provision applies only under Part B. There is no comparable provision for excluding such drugs under Part A.

Drugs and biologics (except for covered osteoporosis drugs) also are excluded from coverage as items or services administered by home health agencies. [Soc. Sec. Act § 1861(m)(5).]

Immunizations are also excluded, except for: (1) vaccinations or inoculations directly related to the treatment of an injury or direct exposure; (2) pneumococcal vaccinations that are reasonable and necessary for the prevention of an illness; (3) Hepatitis B vaccinations that are reasonable and necessary for the prevention of an illness for those individuals at high or intermediate risk of contracting Hepatitis B; and (4) influenza vaccinations that are reasonable and necessary for the prevention of an illness. [42 C.F.R. § 411.15(e).]

For a discussion of when drugs and biologics are covered under Medicare, see ¶ 212 and ¶ 235 with respect to Part A, and ¶ 351 and ¶ 362 with respect to Part B. The Part D prescription drug benefit is discussed in Chapter 5.

[¶ 646] Services of Excluded Individuals and Entities

No Medicare payment may be made, except in an emergency, to an entity or individual, such as a provider, supplier, physician, or other health care practitioner, who has been excluded from the Medicare program due to program abuses (see ¶ 720). Similarly, Medicare payment will not be made for items or services furnished at the medical direction or on the prescription of a physician who is excluded from program participation if the person furnishing the items or services knew or had reason to know of the exclusion. [Soc. Sec. Act § 1862(e)(1).]

If a beneficiary submits a claim for items or services received from a physician or supplier who has been excluded from program participation, Medicare will pay for the items or services if the beneficiary did not know or did not have reason to know about the exclusion. [Soc. Sec. Act § 1862(e)(2).]

[¶ 654] Certain Services of Surgery Assistants

The following assistant-at-surgery services are excluded: (1) services of an assistant at surgery in cataract operations, including subsequent insertions of intraocular lenses, unless, before the surgery is performed, the appropriate quality improvement organization (QIO) (see ¶ 710) or a Medicare administrative contractor (MAC) has approved the use of the assistant due to the existence of a complicating medical condition; and (2) services of an assistant at surgery in a surgical procedure (or class of surgical procedures) for which assistants at surgery on average are used in fewer than 5 percent of such procedures nationally. Services subject to this exclusion include, but are not limited to, clinical laboratory services, pacemakers, artificial limbs, knees, and hips, intraocular lenses, total parenteral nutrition, and services incident to physicians' services. [Soc. Sec. Act §§ 1848(i)(2)(B), 1862(a)(15); 42 C.F.R. § 411.15(n).]

The Office of Inspector General may exclude a physician that (1) knowingly and willfully presented or caused to be presented a claim, or billed an individual enrolled under Part B of the Medicare program (or his or her representative) for services of an assistant at surgery during a cataract operation, or charges that include a charge for an assistant at surgery during a cataract operation; and (2) failed to obtain prior approval for the use of such assistant from the appropriate QIO or MAC. [42 C.F.R. § 1001.1701(a).]

Chapter 7– ADMINISTRATIVE PROVISIONS

[¶ 700] HHS and CMS Organizational Structure

The Secretary of the U.S. Department of Health and Human Services (HHS) oversees the Medicare program. Within HHS, the Medicare program is administered by the Centers for Medicare and Medicaid Services (CMS). CMS is responsible for: enrolling providers; enforcing provider standards, called "conditions of participation"; evaluating and paying claims; reviewing utilization; developing and reviewing policies governing coverage of developing services; and preventing and prosecuting fraud and abuse by providers. HHS contracts with other entities to perform many of these functions, including Medicare administrative contractors (MACs) (see ¶ 705), state and local survey and Medicaid agencies (see ¶ 703), private insurance companies, and quality improvement organizations. In addition to using such agencies or organizations under the conditions described below, the HHS Secretary is authorized to purchase or contract separately for such services as auditing or cost analysis. [Soc. Sec. Act § 1874(b).]

CMS Programs

In addition to the Medicare program, CMS operates the state-federal Medicaid program, the Children's Health Insurance Program, and a variety of programs designed to control program costs, ensure appropriate utilization of health services by eligible beneficiaries and recipients, and eliminate provider fraud and abuse. CMS's goal is to ensure that the best possible care is delivered in the most economical manner to eligible beneficiaries and recipients. CMS also provides national policy planning for health care financing and for delivery of health services within these operating programs.

Medicare integrity. To ensure the integrity of the Medicare program, CMS has a number of fraud control and prevention initiatives, which work in collaboration with the HHS Office of Inspector General (OIG) and the Department of Justice. The HHS Secretary is also authorized to contract with private entities known as recovery audit contractors (RACs) to perform specified review and audit functions (see ¶ 711 for a full discussion of RACs). [Soc. Sec. Act § 1893(b).] The Social Security Administration is also involved in the administration of the Medicare program, primarily in the enrollment of beneficiaries in the program and the maintenance of beneficiary rolls.

Beneficiary information programs. The Secretary must issue all beneficiaries an "Explanation of Medicare Benefits" for all medical services or items furnished, including a notice of the right to request itemized statements. Within 30 days of a beneficiary's request, providers must furnish itemized statements of items or services or face a possible civil money penalty of not more than $100 for each such failure. Beneficiaries have 90 days after receiving the statement to submit written requests identifying billing irregularities to the Secretary, who must take all appropriate measures to recover any amounts unnecessarily paid. Beginning in 2016, a beneficiary may elect to receive an Explanation of Medicare Benefits in an electronic format instead of by mail. [Soc. Sec. Act § 1806.]

The Secretary must provide an annual notice to beneficiaries, including a statement of the beneficiary's right to request itemized statements of items or services provided, as well as an instruction to check explanations of benefits and itemized statements carefully for accuracy. The notice also must contain a description of the Medicare fraud and abuse information collection program (see below) and a toll-free telephone number to report errors or questionable charges. [Soc. Sec. Act § 1804(c).]

Reports of fraud or abuse. Pursuant to Health Insurance Portability and Accountability Act of 1996 (HIPAA) (P.L. 104-191) § 203(b), the HHS Secretary established a program to encourage individuals to report other individuals and entities who are engaging, or have engaged, in acts or omissions that qualify for the imposition of sanctions under the OIG's civil penalty, exclusion, or law enforcement authorities (see below). A portion of the amount collected as the result of this program is paid to the reporting individual when at least $100 is collected by the Secretary or the U.S. Attorney General. [42 C.F.R. § 420.405.]

Information on program efficiency. Individuals are also encouraged to submit suggestions for improving the efficiency of the Medicare program. As with the fraud and abuse reporting program, the Secretary may make an appropriate payment to individuals whose suggestions result in program savings. [HIPAA § 203(c); 42 C.F.R. § 420.410.]

The Center for Medicare Management serves as the focal point for CMS's interactions with providers and MACs concerning fee-for-service policies and procedures. It is responsible for policies concerning the scope of benefits and payment methods for all services covered by Medicare. [*Notice*, 78 FR 48164, Aug. 7, 2013.]

CMS Regional Offices

In addition to a central office in Baltimore, CMS maintains 10 regional offices, which are located in Atlanta, Boston, Chicago, Dallas, Denver, Kansas City (Mo.), New York, Philadelphia, San Francisco, and Seattle. CMS regional offices are often the first point of contact for beneficiaries, health care providers, state and local governments, and the general public. The regional offices provide customer service, program management, and education and outreach programs, and they develop partnerships with state and local health and social service agencies. Additional information on the CMS regional offices can be found at http://www.cms.gov/RegionalOffices/.

Medicare Beneficiary Ombudsman

The Medicare Beneficiary Ombudsman within HHS responds to beneficiaries' complaints, grievances, and inquiries. In addition, the ombudsman provides assistance: (1) collecting relevant information needed to file appeals; (2) terminating enrollment under Medicare Part C; and (3) presenting information related to income-related premium adjustments. The ombudsman cannot serve as an advocate for any increases in payments or new coverage of services but may identify issues and problems in payment or coverage policies. [Soc. Sec. Act § 1808(c).] The ombudsman's website is located at http://www.cms.gov/Center/Special-Topic/Ombudsman-Center.html.

HHS Office of Inspector General

The OIG is an independent unit within HHS that is headed by an Inspector General and a Deputy Inspector General. The OIG is charged with: (1) conducting audits and investigations relating to HHS programs and operations; (2) promoting economy and efficiency in the administration of HHS programs and operations, as well as preventing and detecting fraud and abuse; and (3) providing a means of keeping the Secretary and Congress fully and currently informed about problems and deficiencies relating to the administration and operation of HHS programs and the necessity of corrective action. Reports on OIG activities must be submitted annually to Congress and quarterly to the Secretary and appropriate congressional committees. The OIG must report immediately on any serious problems or abuses. [Inspector General Act of 1978 (P.L. 95-452).]

The OIG has primary responsibility for detecting abuses and applying sanctions against providers, physicians, entities, and suppliers of health care items and services that commit federal health care program abuses. The Health Care Fraud and Abuse Control Program, required by HIPAA, is administered under the joint direction of the U.S. Attorney General and the Secretary of HHS, acting through the OIG (see ¶ 720).

¶700

Health Care Reform Initiatives

The Patient Protection and Affordable Care Act (ACA) (P.L. 111-148) required the HHS Secretary to oversee various programs to enhance health care quality, some of which are administered by CMS and some of which are administered by other HHS agencies and entities.

National Quality Strategy. Pursuant to section 3011 of the ACA, the HHS Secretary established a national strategy to improve the delivery of health care and patient outcomes and created a comprehensive strategic plan to achieve those priorities. [Public Health Service Act § 399HH(a), (a)(2)(C) and (D).] HHS's Agency for Healthcare Research and Quality submitted its first national strategy to Congress in March 2011, and updates the report annually. The national priorities for improvement of health care quality and the agency-specific strategic plans are posted on an agency website available to the public (http://www.ahrq.gov/workingforquality/).

Center for Medicare and Medicaid Innovation. Section 3021 of the ACA established the Center for Medicare and Medicaid Innovation (CMMI) within CMS. Its purpose is to test systems of provider payment and delivery of services in order to cut costs while preserving or enhancing the quality of care delivered to Medicare and Medicaid beneficiaries. The HHS Secretary selects test models, giving preference to models that have the effect of improving the coordination, quality, and efficiency of health care services available to Medicare and Medicaid beneficiaries. [Soc. Sec. Act § 1115A.]

Independent Payment Advisory Board. Section 3403 of the ACA created an Independent Payment Advisory Board (IPAB), administered within HHS, composed of 15 independent members appointed by the President as well as the HHS Secretary, the CMS Administrator, and the Administrator of the Health Resources and Services Administration (HRSA) within HHS, to reduce the per capita rate of growth in Medicare spending. IPAB is intended to be an independent, nonpartisan body of doctors and other health experts. It was envisioned as a way to free Congress from the burdens of dealing with highly technical issues such as Medicare reimbursement rates. [Soc. Sec. Act § 1899A.]

As of December 2016, no members have been appointed to IPAB and the Board has never convened, because Medicare spending has not grown at a high enough rate to require IPAB action. The CMS Actuary publishes its IPAB determinations at https://www.cms.gov/Research-Statistics-Data-and-Systems/Research/ActuarialStudies/IPAB-Determination.html.

Railroad Retirement Board

CMS and the Railroad Retirement Board have agreed on a delegation of important responsibilities to the railroad agency in connection with Medicare Part B. Under this delegation, the Railroad Retirement Board has responsibility for enrolling railroad eligibles in Medicare, collecting their premiums, and selecting MACs (see ¶ 705) for railroad enrollees under Part B.

The Railroad Retirement Board applies the same policies and regulations as CMS in determining what expenses are covered and what payments are to be made. [Soc. Sec. Act § 226(a)(2)(B), (b)(2)(B).]

Private Accrediting Organizations

The HHS Secretary contracts with private national accreditation bodies to determine whether hospitals, skilled nursing facilities, home health agencies, ambulatory surgical centers, hospices, organ transplant centers, rural health clinics, laboratories, clinics, rehabilitation agencies (including comprehensive outpatient rehabilitation agencies), psychiatric hospitals, public health agencies, and suppliers of durable medical equipment, prosthetics, orthotics, and supplies meet Medicare requirements. [Soc. Sec. Act §§ 1834(a)(20)(F), 1865(a); 42 C.F.R § 488.6.]

[¶ 703] Role of the State and Local Agencies

The Social Security Act requires the HHS Secretary to enter into agreements with able and willing state agencies to determine whether a provider of services—a hospital, skilled nursing facility, home health agency, hospice, rural health clinic, critical access hospital, comprehensive outpatient rehabilitation facility, clinic, rehabilitation agency, public health agency, or ambulatory surgical center—meets the conditions of participation of federal health care programs. State agencies conduct investigations, called surveys, and certify to the Secretary that a provider meets the conditions of participation. [Soc. Sec. Act § 1864(a), (c).]

State agencies also certify compliance with respect to other health care entities, such as independent laboratories, suppliers of portable x-ray services, and public health agencies providing outpatient physical and occupational therapy or speech-language pathology services under Part B. If the state survey agency determines that a provider or facility is not in substantial compliance with the conditions of participation, it must give written notice of the deficiencies. [42 C.F.R. § 488.18.]

Providers and facilities are surveyed at the following times: on initial application to participate in Medicare; when certification or enrollment is up for renewal; when the provider or facility receives a complaint or allegation of a deficiency; and selectively, on a sample basis. [Soc. Sec. Act § 1864(a), (c).]

Public assistance recipients. State Medicaid agencies also determine eligibility of Medicare beneficiaries for the low-income subsidy, which pays for part or all of the beneficiaries' cost-sharing requirements for prescription drug plans under Medicare Part D (see ¶ 508). [Soc. Sec. Act § 1860D-14.]

If a state enters into an agreement with Medicare to pay the Part B premium on behalf of its public assistance recipients, the agreement may provide for a designated state agency to serve as a Medicare administrative contractor (MAC) on behalf of its public assistance recipients. [Soc. Sec. Act § 1843(f).]

Disclosure of Survey and Fraud Information

Within 90 days following the state agency's completion of a health facility survey, information from the survey is available to the public, including a statement of deficiencies or the survey report itself and any pertinent written statements furnished by the surveyed facility. [Soc. Sec. Act § 1864(a).]

Adverse fraud and abuse information. The National Practitioner Data Bank (NPDB), which includes the database formerly known as the Healthcare Integrity and Protection Data Bank, collects fraud and abuse data from state agencies and other sources and provides this data to authorized recipients. HHS's Health Resources and Services Administration administers the NPDB as a confidential clearinghouse for fraud and abuse information. The databank is located at http://www.npdb.hrsa.gov/ (see ¶ 720).

[¶ 705] Role of Medicare Administrative Contractors

Private organizations have a considerable role in the administration of Medicare. Medicare administrative contractors (MACs) process and pay both Part A and Part B claims from particular geographic areas of the country. MACs competitively bid on contracts with the federal government to perform administrative and operational tasks for the program. [Soc. Sec. Act §§ 1816, 1842(a), 1874A.]

MACs' functions include: (1) determining the amount of Medicare payments required to be made to providers and suppliers; (2) making Medicare payments; (3) providing beneficiary education and assistance; (4) providing consultative services to institutions, agencies, and other persons to enable them to establish and maintain necessary fiscal records; (5) communicating with providers and suppliers; (6) providing education and technical assistance to providers and suppliers; (7) having in place an improper payment outreach and education program; and (8) any additional functions as necessary. [Soc. Sec. Act § 1874A(a)(4).]

Requirements for Medicare Administrative Contractors

An entity is eligible to become a MAC only if it: (1) has demonstrated capability to carry out the MAC functions; (2) complies with conflict-of-interest standards as are generally applicable to federal acquisition and procurement; (3) has sufficient assets to financially support the performance of the functions; and (4) meets other requirements as the Secretary may impose. [Soc. Sec. Act § 1874A(a)(2).]

Contract requirements. The HHS Secretary must use competitive procedures when awarding MAC contracts. If a MAC has met or exceeded performance requirements, HHS may renew the contract from term to term without the application of competitive procedures, as long as it recompetes contracts at least once every 10 years. [Soc. Sec. Act § 1847A(b)(1)(A), (B).]

The Secretary is required to develop contract performance requirements and standards for measuring the extent to which a contractor has met the requirements. The Secretary must make contractor performance requirements and measurement standards available to the public. [Soc. Sec. Act § 1874A(b)(3).]

Beginning for contracts entered into or renewed on or after December 28, 2018, the HHS Secretary must provide incentives for MACs to reduce the improper payment error rates in their jurisdictions. [Soc. Sec. Act § 1874A(b)(1)(D).]

MAC Jurisdictions

Out of 15 original MAC jurisdictions, CMS is consolidating MAC workloads into five pairings, to form five consolidated Part A and Part B MAC contracts and its ultimate goal of 10 MAC jurisdictions. Jurisdictions that have already combined are as follows:

- Jurisdictions 2 and 3 were combined to form MAC Jurisdiction F (Alaska, Washington, Oregon, Idaho, North Dakota, South Dakota, Montana, Wyoming, Utah, and Arizona).

- Jurisdictions 4 and 7 were combined to form MAC Jurisdiction H (Louisiana, Arkansas, Mississippi, Texas, Oklahoma, Colorado, and New Mexico).

- Jurisdictions 13 and 14 were combined to form MAC Jurisdiction K (New York, Connecticut, Massachusetts, Rhode Island, Vermont, Maine, and New Hampshire).

[https://www.cms.gov/Medicare/Medicare-Contracting/Medicare-Administrative-Contractors/Who-are-the-MACs.html.]

CMS intends to keep the following five MAC jurisdictions unchanged:

- Jurisdiction E (formerly known as Jurisdiction 1) (California, Hawaii, Nevada, and Pacific Islands)

- Jurisdiction N (formerly known as Jurisdiction 9) (Florida, Puerto Rico, and U.S. Virgin Islands)

- Jurisdiction J (formerly known as Jurisdiction 10) (Alabama, Georgia, and Tennessee)

- Jurisdiction M (formerly known as Jurisdiction 11) (North Carolina, South Carolina, Virginia, and West Virginia)

- Jurisdiction L (formerly known as Jurisdiction 12) (Delaware, Maryland, Pennsylvania, New Jersey, and Washington, D.C.)

[https://www.cms.gov/Medicare/Medicare-Contracting/Medicare-Administrative-Contractors/Who-are-the-MACs.html.]

CMS has postponed the consolidation of the following jurisdictions:

- Jurisdictions 5 and 6 will be combined to form Jurisdiction G (Minnesota, Wisconsin, Illinois, Kansas, Nebraska, Iowa, and Missouri).

- Jurisdictions 8 and 15 will be combined to form Jurisdiction I (Kentucky, Ohio, Michigan, and Indiana).

[https://www.cms.gov/Medicare/Medicare-Contracting/Medicare-Administrative-Contractors/Downloads/RFI-Announcement-AB-MAC-March-2014.pdf.]

DME MACs. Durable medical equipment (DME) MACs are responsible for processing Medicare durable medical equipment, orthotics, and prosthetics claims for a jurisdiction. CMS has established four DME MAC jurisdictions. [https://www.cms.gov/Medicare/Medicare-Contracting/Medicare-Administrative-Contractors/Who-are-the-MACs.html.]

Home health and hospice. Four of the A/B MACs also process home health and hospice claims in addition to their typical Medicare Part A and Part B claims. [https://www.cms.gov/Medicare/Medicare-Contracting/Medicare-Administrative-Contractors/Who-are-the-MACs.html#ABandHH+H.]

[¶ 710] Quality Improvement Organizations

Quality improvement organizations (QIOs) review the professional activities of physicians and other health care practitioners and providers that furnish health care services and items that may be paid for by Medicare. QIOs are private organizations staffed by professionals, mostly doctors and other health care professionals, who are trained to review medical care, help beneficiaries with complaints about quality of care, and implement improvements in quality of care. [Soc. Sec. Act §§ 1153, 1154(a)(1); https://www.cms.gov/Medicare/Quality-Initiatives-Patient-Assessment-Instruments/QualityImprovementOrgs/index.html.]

The term of QIO contracts is five years, with each cycle referenced as an ordinal Statement of Work (SOW). [Soc. Sec. Act § 1153(c)(3).] As a condition of participation in Medicare, all hospitals, critical access hospitals (CAHs), skilled nursing facilities, and home health agencies are required to have an agreement with a QIO. [Soc. Sec. Act § 1866(a)(1)(F).]

Scope of QIO Review

QIOs review hospitals paid by the hospital inpatient prospective payment system (IPPS), under which hospitals are paid a fixed rate per discharge according to Medicare severity diagnosis-related groups (MS-DRGs) of illnesses (see ¶ 810). QIOs review the care and services provided to a beneficiary to determine the following:

(1) whether the services were reasonable and medically necessary;

(2) whether the quality of the services meets professionally recognized standards of health care;

(3) whether inpatient services could be effectively furnished more economically on an outpatient basis or in an inpatient health care facility of a different type;

(4) the validity of diagnostic and procedural information supplied by the hospital;

(5) the completeness, adequacy, and quality of hospital care provided;

(6) the medical necessity, reasonableness, and appropriateness of hospital admissions and discharges;

(7) the medical necessity, reasonableness, and appropriateness of inpatient hospital care for which additional payment is sought; and

(8) whether a hospital has misrepresented admission or discharge information or has taken an action that results in unnecessary admissions or other inappropriate practices.

[Soc. Sec. Act § 1154(a)(1); 42 C.F.R. § 476.71(a).]

The determinations of QIOs on these matters are binding for purposes of determining whether Medicare benefits should be paid, with some exceptions. [Soc. Sec. Act § 1154(a)(2).]

If a QIO finds that an IPPS hospital has taken an action that results in unnecessary admissions, unnecessary multiple admissions of the same such individuals, or other inappropriate medical or other practices with respect to such individuals, the Secretary may: (1) deny payment, in whole or in part, for the inappropriate services; (2) require the hospital to take other corrective action necessary to prevent or correct the inappropriate practice; or (3) in the case of a pattern of inappropriate admissions and billing practices that have the effect of circumventing the IPPS, terminate the provider participation agreement (see Soc. Sec. Act § 1128(c)–(g)). [Soc. Sec. Act § 1886(f)(2).]

Each QIO assumes review responsibilities in accordance with the schedule, functions, and negotiated objectives specified in its contract with CMS, including the review requirements detailed in the SOW, which are incorporated into the QIO contract. [42 C.F.R. § 476.74.] The SOW establishes specific tasks for QIOs in relation to hospitals, ambulatory surgical centers, clinics, rehabilitation facilities, home health agencies, and physicians. The emphasis is on collaboration with providers to develop and institute processes to improve the quality of care and eliminate unreasonable, unnecessary, and inappropriate care provided to beneficiaries. [*Notice*, 79 FR 46830, Aug. 11, 2014; *Medicare Quality Improvement Organization Manual*, Pub. 100-10, Ch. 1, § 1005.]

The eleventh SOW, which began on August 1, 2014, is scheduled to last five years. As a part of a restructuring of the QIO program in 2014, the QIO program separated medical case review from its quality improvement activities in each state under two types of regional contracts: (1) Beneficiary and Family Centered Care QIOs (BFCC-QIOs) contractors, who perform medical case review; and (2) Quality Innovation Network QIOs (QIN-QIOs) contractors, who perform quality improvement activities and provide technical assistance to providers and practitioners. In addition, the restructured QIO program uses a non-QIO a contractor to assist CMS in the monitoring and oversight of the BFCC-QIO case review activities. [*Notice*, 79 FR 46830, Aug. 11, 2014.] More information on the eleventh SOW is posted at https://www.fbo.gov/.

QIO Mandatory Case Review

QIOs must review the following:

Beneficiary complaints. QIOs review all written beneficiary complaints regarding quality of health care and services not meeting professionally recognized standards of health care, as well as oral complaints (see the "Alternative Dispute Resolution Process" discussion below). QIOs must receive written complaints within three years of the care giving rise to the complaint and treat all information submitted by the beneficiary or his or her representative as confidential. Providers must deliver all medical information requested in response to a

Medicare beneficiary complaint within 14 calendar days of the QIO's request. The QIO peer reviewer will complete the review and notify the practitioner and/or provider of the interim initial determination within 10 calendar days of the receipt of all medical information, giving the provider an opportunity for discussion. The QIO peer reviewer then must telephone the beneficiary within three days and issue a written final initial determination to all parties within five days after completion of the review. [Soc. Sec. Act § 1154(a)(14); 42 C.F.R. §§ 476.120, 476.130.]

A Medicare beneficiary, provider, or practitioner who is dissatisfied with a QIO's final initial determination may request a reconsideration by the QIO. [42 C.F.R. § 476.140.]

Noncoverage notices issued by hospitals. Hospitals issue noncoverage notices to Medicare beneficiaries informing them that Medicare will deny coverage of their continued stay if the hospital determines and the attending physician concurs that inpatient care no longer is required. QIOs are required to review noncoverage notices issued by a hospital on the request of the hospital, the beneficiary, or his or her representative. [Soc. Sec. Act § 1154(e); Pub. 100-10, Ch. 7, § 7000.]

Antidumping violations. QIOs review allegations of hospital emergency rooms turning away or transferring patients without screening for, or stabilizing, emergency medical conditions. [Soc. Sec. Act § 1867(d)(3); 42 C.F.R. § 489.24(h).]

Review of assistants at surgery in cataract operations. QIOs review requests for surgical assistants based on medical necessity. Medicare payment for the services of an assistant at cataract surgery is prohibited unless a QIO approves the services before the surgery based on the existence of a complicating medical condition. [Soc. Sec. Act § 1862(a)(15); Pub. 100-10, Ch. 4, § 4020.]

Requests for upward adjustment of MS-DRG. QIOs perform MS-DRG coding validation reviews of IPPS cases, including hospital requests for higher-weighted MS-DRG adjustments. The purpose of DRG validation is to ensure that diagnostic and procedural information and the discharge status of the patient as coded and reported by the hospital on its claim match the attending physician's description and the information contained in the patient's medical record. [Soc. Sec. Act § 1866(a)(1)(F); 42 C.F.R. § 476.71(a)(4); Pub. 100-10, Ch. 4, § 4130.]

Referrals. QIOs review all cases referred by CMS, HHS, the Office of Inspector General, Medicare contractors, clinical data abstraction centers, Medicare Advantage organization contractors, or state Medicaid and survey and certification agencies. [Pub. 100-10, Ch. 4, § 4070.]

CAH patient records. QIOs evaluate CAHs for quality of care, the appropriateness of admissions and discharge, Medicare coverage issues, accuracy of coding, or appropriateness of medical services. [Pub. 100-10, Ch. 3, § 3010.]

Alternative Dispute Resolution Process

QIOs offer an alternative dispute resolution option called "Immediate Advocacy" to quickly resolve an oral complaint a Medicare beneficiary or his or her representative has regarding the quality of Medicare covered health care. This process involves a QIO representative's direct contact with the provider and/or practitioner. A QIO may offer the option of resolving an oral complaint through the use of immediate advocacy if:

(1) the QIO receives the complaint within six months of the incident;

(2) after initial screening of the complaint, the QIO makes a preliminary determination that it is unrelated to the clinical quality of health care itself but relates to items or services that accompany or are incidental to the medical care and are provided by a

practitioner and/or provider; or the complaint, while related to the clinical quality of health care received by the beneficiary, does not rise to the level of being a gross and flagrant, substantial, or significant quality of care concern;

(3) the beneficiary agrees to the disclosure of his or her name to the involved provider and/or practitioner;

(4) all parties orally consent to the use of immediate advocacy; and

(5) all parties agree to confidentiality limitations on redisclosure.

The QIO or either party may discontinue participation in immediate advocacy at any time. The QIO may determine that a complaint has been abandoned and then inform the parties that immediate advocacy will be discontinued and inform the Medicare beneficiary of his or her right to submit a written complaint. [42 C.F.R. §§ 476.1, 476.110.]

Appeals from QIO Coverage Determinations

If a QIO's determination denies coverage or a requested MS-DRG as a result of MS-DRG validation, the beneficiary, provider, or practitioner is entitled to notice and reconsideration of the determination by the QIO. An initial denial determination consists of a finding that the health care services provided were unnecessary, unreasonable, or at an inappropriate level of care. [Soc. Sec. Act §§ 1154(a)(3), 1155; 42 C.F.R. §§ 478.12, 478.15, 478.16.]

A beneficiary, provider, or attending practitioner who is dissatisfied with an initial denial determination may obtain reconsideration of the initial review by filing a written request within 60 days after the date of the initial denial determination, unless the time is extended for good cause. The date of receipt of the initial denial determination notice is presumed to be five days after the date listed on the notice unless there is a showing to the contrary. [42 C.F.R. §§ 478.12, 478.20, 478.22.]

If the QIO's reconsidered determination is adverse to the beneficiary and the amount in controversy is at least $200, the beneficiary (but not a provider or practitioner) may request a hearing by an administrative law judge (ALJ) within 60 days after the date of receipt of the notice of reconsidered determination. If the amount in controversy is $2,000 or greater, the beneficiary is entitled to judicial review of the ALJ's decision. [Soc. Sec. Act § 1155; 42 C.F.R. §§ 478.12, 478.20, 478.40, 478.46.]

Limitations on Beneficiary Liability

The law prohibits physicians, in the case of assigned claims, from billing beneficiaries for services for which payment has been denied by a QIO on the basis of substandard quality of care. [Soc. Sec. Act § 1842(b)(3)(B)(ii).] CMS also indemnifies the beneficiary in the case of any deductible and coinsurance paid if a QIO has denied Medicare payment for services. [Soc. Sec. Act § 1879(b).]

QIO-Recommended Sanctions

If a QIO determines that a practitioner or provider has violated its obligations to furnish services that are economical, medically necessary, of proper quality, and properly documented, the QIO may recommend sanctions. Practitioners and providers are entitled to reasonable notice of a sanction determination and must be provided the opportunity for a hearing as well as judicial review. The first step is to give the provider or practitioner the opportunity to meet with three members of the QIO to discuss the potential violation and agree to a corrective action plan approved by the QIO. [Soc. Sec. Act § 1156(a), (b); 42 C.F.R. § 1004.30.]

If the practitioner or provider fails to complete its corrective action plan and the QIO determines that the provider or practitioner has violated the requirements in a substantial number of cases or has violated one or more requirements "grossly and flagrantly," the QIO must submit a report and recommendation to the Secretary on the imposition of sanctions, including exclusion from Medicare and Medicaid participation or assessment of fines. A QIO recommendation of exclusion automatically becomes effective if the Secretary fails to act within a 120-day review period. [Soc. Sec. Act § 1156(b); 42 C.F.R. §§ 1004.30, 1004.40; Pub. 100-10, Ch. 9, § 9000.]

[¶ 711] Recovery Audit Contractors

The HHS Secretary is authorized to contract with eligible private entities known as recovery audit contractors (RACs) to perform specified review and audit functions. The RAC program was designed is to identify and correct Medicare improper payments through the efficient detection and collection of overpayments made on claims of health care services provided to Medicare beneficiaries, and the identification of underpayments to providers so that the CMS can implement actions that will prevent future improper payments. [Soc. Sec. Act § 1893(h).]

RACs perform a variety of review and audit functions, including:

(1) review of activities of providers of services or other individuals and entities furnishing items and services for which Medicare payment may be made, including medical and utilization review and fraud review;

(2) audit of cost reports;

(3) determinations as to whether Medicare payment should not be or should not have been made, and recovery of payments that should not have been made;

(4) education of providers, beneficiaries, and other persons with respect to payment integrity and benefit quality assurance issues;

(5) developing and updating a list of items of durable medical equipment that are subject to prior authorization under Soc. Sec. Act § 1834(a)(15); and

(6) the Medicare-Medicaid Data Match Program.

[Soc. Sec. Act § 1893(b).]

RACs are paid on a contingency basis from the recovered funds. The amount of the contingency fee is a percentage of the improper payment recovered from, or reimbursed to, providers. [Soc. Sec. Act § 1893(h).]

CMS also has the authority to enter into contracts with RACs to identify and reconcile overpayments and underpayments in Medicare Parts C and D. In addition to their other responsibilities, RACs must: ensure that MA and prescription drug plans (PDPs) have antifraud plans in effect and review the effectiveness of the plans; review PDPs' estimates on enrollment of high-cost beneficiaries; and examine claims for reinsurance payments to determine whether PDPs submitting such claims incurred costs in excess of the allowable reinsurance costs permitted. [Soc. Sec. Act § 1893(h)(9).]

RAC Program Operation

The RAC program originated as a demonstration project but was later expanded to include all 50 states. Five RACs cover specific geographic areas of the nation. [https://www.cms.gov/research-statistics-data-and-systems/monitoring-programs/medicare-ffs-compliance-programs/recovery-audit-program/.]

Requirements. RACs must comply with the following requirements:

(1) have a medical director;

(2) look back only three years when reviewing claims;

(3) not look back for any improper payments on claims paid before October 1, 2007;

(4) RACs are allowed to review claims during the current fiscal year;

(5) have certified coders on staff;

(6) provide credentials of reviewers upon request;

(7) there is a limit on the number of medical records that a RAC may request in any 45-day period, based on the size and/or volume of the provider or practitioner;

(8) include the reason(s) for the review on the request for record letters and overpayment demands;

(9) grant the provider/practitioner a discussion with the medical director on request;

(10) report frequent problem areas;

(11) pay back the contingency fee if they lose at any level of appeal;

(12) have a web-based application that allows providers to customize addresses and contact information or see the status of cases;

(13) publicly disclose contingency fees; and

(14) participate in the external validation process, a uniform process among the states.

[Recovery Auditing in Medicare for Fiscal Year 2014 Report to Congress, Oct. 15, 2015.]

An entity is eligible to enter into a contract under the RAC program if it meets certain requirements, one of which is to demonstrate to the Secretary that the entity's financial holdings, interests, or relationships will not interfere with its ability to perform as required. Medicare administrative contractors (MACs) (see ¶ 705) are prohibited from entering into contracts under this provision. [Soc. Sec. Act § 1893(c), (h)(6)(B).]

RACs work with Medicare contractors in determining the amount of any overpayments. RACs collect the overpayments using the same procedures as other contractors, subject to the same requirements and limits on recoupment. [*Medicare Financial Management Manual*, Pub. 100-06, Ch. 4, § 100.6.]

Appeals of RAC Determinations

Appeals of RAC determinations regarding fee-for-service claims are handled with other overpayment determinations under the regular Medicare appeals process. [42 C.F.R. § 405.902; Pub. 100-06, Ch. 4, § 100.7.] There are five levels of appeals for claim denials, including those resulting from RAC audits: (1) redetermination by the MAC; (2) reconsideration by a qualified independent contractor; (3) administrative law judge hearing; (4) Medicare Appeals Council review; and (5) judicial review in federal court. [Soc. Sec. Act § 1869; http://www.cms.gov/Outreach-and-Education/Medicare-Learning-Network-MLN/MLN-Products/Downloads/MedicareAppealsProcess.pdf.]

If the Part C or Part D RAC did not apply its stated payment methodology correctly, MA organizations and Part D plan sponsors may appeal the findings of the applied methodology. [42 C.F.R. §§ 422.2600, 423.2600.]

See ¶ 924 for a detailed discussion of the claims appeals process.

[¶ 715] Privacy of Health Data

Pursuant to the Health Insurance Portability and Accountability Act of 1996 (HIPAA) (P.L. 104-191), HHS implemented national standards to protect individually identifiable health information. The HIPAA privacy and security standards apply to all health care plans, health care clearinghouses, and health care providers who transmit any health information in electronic form (collectively called "covered entities"). [45 C.F.R. §§ 160.102, 160.103.]

Business associates. Health care providers and other covered entities are responsible for the use of protected health information (PHI) released to other organizations and must have a contract (or other written agreement) with each business associate detailing how the business associate will protect the individually identifiable information. [45 C.F.R. § 164.502(e)(2).] Business associates must provide the same protection to individually identifiable data as health care providers or other covered entities. [45 C.F.R. § 164.504(e).]

Individually Identifiable Health Information

"Individually identifiable health information" is defined as data that is created or received by a health care provider, health plan, employer, or health care clearinghouse that relates to any of the following: (1) the past, present, or future physical or mental health condition of an individual; (2) the provision of health care to an individual; or (3) the past, present, or future payment for the provision of health care. It identifies the individual or could reasonably be used to identify the individual. [45 C.F.R. § 160.103.]

"Protected health information" (PHI) is defined as individually identifiable health information that is transmitted or maintained in an electronic format or any other medium. The regulations cover all health data, including written records and oral communications, and not just electronically maintained or transmitted data. The disclosure of health information includes the release, transfer, provision of, access to, or divulging of patient health information, in any manner, to others outside of the entity holding the information. [45 C.F.R. § 160.103.]

The term "health care" as it relates to HIPAA means care, services, or supplies related to the health of an individual, including the following services: (1) preventive, diagnostic, therapeutic, rehabilitative, counseling, service assessments, or any other procedure with respect to the physical, mental, or functional condition of a patient; and (2) the sale or dispensing of prescription drugs, equipment, or devices in accordance with a prescription. [45 C.F.R. § 160.103.] For example, the disclosure of information for something as simple as an eyeglass prescription or the cost of services paid by a patient is prohibited under HIPAA.

Notice of Privacy Practices

Health care providers must issue a notice to patients during the first delivery of service describing the provider's privacy policy. Providers are required to conduct a good faith effort to obtain written acknowledgment from a patient of the receipt of the privacy notice. In an emergency situation, the provider may obtain the acknowledgment as soon as reasonably practicable. The notice also must be available at any time and publicly displayed in a clear and prominent location in the provider's office. [45 C.F.R. § 164.520(c)(2).]

The notice must describe how the patient's medical information will be used and disclosed. The notice is required to inform patients that they have a right to inspect, copy, amend, and receive a list of people and organizations that have requested access to their PHI and must contain the name, title, and telephone number of a contact person in the provider's office, as well as a description of the provider's legal duties with respect to the patient's PHI. [45 C.F.R. § 164.520(a)(1), (b).]

The notice must contain the following header statement in all capital letters (or otherwise be prominently displayed):

¶715

"THIS NOTICE DESCRIBES HOW MEDICAL INFORMATION ABOUT YOU MAY BE USED AND DISCLOSED AND HOW YOU CAN GET ACCESS TO THIS INFORMATION. PLEASE REVIEW IT CAREFULLY."

[45 C.F.R. § 164.520(b)(1)(i).] In addition, providers must retain copies of the notices issued and, if applicable, any written acknowledgments of the patient's receipt of the notice, or any other documentation of the provider's good faith efforts to obtain a written acknowledgment of the patient's privacy rights. [45 C.F.R. § 164.520(e).]

Exception for inmates. Because inmates do not have a right to notice under the provisions of 45 C.F.R. § 164.520, these notice requirements do not apply to a correctional institution that is also a covered entity. [45 C.F.R. § 164.520(a)(3).]

Authorization to Release Individually Identifiable Health Information

Health care providers may not release individually identifiable health information without an authorization unless the information is released: (1) for the provider's own treatment, payment, or health care operations; (2) for treatment activities of another health care provider; (3) for payment activities of another covered entity; (4) to other providers of the patient's care; or (5) to other providers in the provider's organized health care arrangement for the purposes of treating the patient. [45 C.F.R. § 164.506.] Patients have the right to request that providers restrict the use or disclosure of their personally identifiable health data, although the provider does not have to agree to a patient's requested restriction. [45 C.F.R. § 164.522.]

Patients may grant providers authorization to disclose individually identifiable health information for the following specific purposes:

- marketing;
- sale of PHI;
- any use or disclosure of psychotherapy notes, except: (1) to carry out treatment, payment, or health care operations, or (2) for permitted uses by the originator of the psychotherapy notes;

Disclosures must be consistent with the authorization, and providers may not condition the provision of health care based on a patient's signing of such an authorization. [45 C.F.R. § 164.508(a).]

Requirements for authorizations. Authorizations must contain: (1) a description of the information to be disclosed and how it will be used; (2) the name of the person or organization authorized to make the disclosure; (3) the name of the person or organization or a description of the class of organization to which the information will be disclosed; (4) a description of the purpose of the release ("at the request of the individual" is a sufficient description of the purpose when the patient initiates the authorization); (5) an expiration date or event; and (6) the dated signature of the patient. [45 C.F.R. § 164.508(c).]

Exemptions to Privacy Rule

Under certain circumstances a covered entity may use or disclose PHI, as long as the individual is informed before the use or disclosure and has the opportunity to agree to or prohibit or restrict the use or disclosure. [45 C.F.R. § 164.510.]

Facility directories. Health care facilities may provide a directory of patients that includes the patient's name, location in the facility, the general condition of the patient that does not communicate specific medical information, and the individual's religious affiliation. A patient must be given the opportunity to restrict or prohibit the information placed in this directory. [45 C.F.R. § 164.510(a)(1), (2).]

Limited use and disclosure. If the patient is unable to agree or object to the use or disclosure of PHI because he or she is not present, incapacitated, or in an emergency circumstance, health care facilities may use their professional judgment to determine whether disclosure is in the best interests of the patient. If so, the facility may disclose only the PHI that is directly relevant. [45 C.F.R. § 164.510(b)(3).]

Disaster relief. Health care facilities may use or disclose PHI to a public or private entity authorized by law or by its charter to assist in disaster relief efforts, for the purpose of coordinating with such entities permitted uses or disclosures of PHI, only to the extent the facility, in the exercise of professional judgment, determines that the requirements do not interfere with the ability to respond to the emergency circumstances. [45 C.F.R. § 164.510(b)(4).]

Deceased patient. If the patient is deceased, a health care facility may disclose the patient's relevant PHI to a family member, or other identified individuals who were involved in the patient's care or payment for health care prior to the patient's death, unless doing so is inconsistent with any prior expressed preference of the patient that is known to the facility. [45 C.F.R. § 164.510(b)(5).]

Public welfare. Health care facilities may use or disclose a patient's PHI without authorization when the use or disclosure is: (1) required by law; (2) for public health activities; (3) to protect victims of abuse, neglect, or domestic violence; (4) for health oversight activities; (5) in judicial and administrative proceedings; (6) for law enforcement purposes; (7) about decedents; (8) for cadaveric organ, eye, or tissue donation purposes; (9) for research purposes; (10) to avert a serious threat to health or safety; (11) for specialized government functions; (12) for purposes of reporting to the National Instant Criminal Background Check System the identity of an individual who is prohibited from possessing a firearm under 18 U.S.C. § 922(g)(4); or (13) related to workers' compensation. Public welfare exceptions are limited and often require informing the patient about the disclosure. [45 C.F.R. § 164.512.]

Fundraising. Health care facilities may release limited PHI data to a business associate without authorization from the patient for the purpose of raising funds for the benefit of the facility. Health care facilities must remove personally identifiable data from fundraising lists upon request of the individual. [45 C.F.R. § 164.514(f).]

Minors. Health care providers may release PHI regarding a minor to the minor's parents, or individual acting as a parent, only if allowed by state law. If a minor can consent to a medical procedure and does not require the consent of any other individual, then the PHI concerning that procedure may not be released to a parent or individual acting as a parent unless the minor agrees or has signed an authorization for the release. [45 C.F.R. § 164.502(g).]

Patients' Rights Under HIPAA

Patients may view or request a copy (including electronic copies) of their PHI. A provider may, however, deny access to a patient's records if it believes that release of that information will endanger the life or physical safety of the individual. Providers, with the consent of the patient, may provide a summary of the data instead of the actual data itself and may charge a fee for providing access or copies. [45 C.F.R. § 164.524.]

Upon request, a laboratory may provide patients and their personal representatives with access to completed test reports belonging to that patient. [42 C.F.R. § 493.1291(l).]

An individual has the right to have a covered entity amend PHI or a record about that individual, but the provider does not have to include material submitted by a patient as an amendment if it was generated by another provider, is inaccurate, or is not part of the requested records. [45 C.F.R. §164.526.] An individual also has a right to receive an accounting of disclosures of PHI made by a covered entity in the six years before the date on which the accounting is requested. Providers do not have to provide an accounting of the release of individually identifiable health information under certain circumstances, such as pursuant to a valid authorization. [45 C.F.R. §164.528.]

HIPAA Breach Notification

HIPAA-covered entities, such as hospitals, doctors' offices, and health insurance plans, are required to notify an individual when his or her unsecured PHI has been or is reasonably believed to have been accessed, acquired, used, or disclosed as the result of a breach. This notice must be sent without unreasonable delay and in no case later than 60 days after the discovery of a breach. [45 C.F.R. §164.404.] The covered entity must also notify the HHS Secretary and, for breaches that involve more than 500 residents of a state or jurisdiction, the media. [45 C.F.R. §§164.406, 164.408.] Business associates, as defined by HIPAA, are also subject to breach notification procedures. [45 C.F.R. §164.410.]

16 C.F.R. Part 318 requires vendors of personal health records to notify individuals in the event of a security breach.

HIPAA Complaints

Health care providers must designate a privacy official who is responsible for the development and implementation of privacy policies and procedures and a contact person who receives complaints and requests. All staff members must be trained on privacy policies and procedures. [45 C.F.R. §164.530(a)(1), (b)(1).]

A covered entity must also provide a process for individuals to make complaints concerning the entity's HIPAA privacy policies and procedures or its compliance with such policies and procedures. [45 C.F.R. §164.530(d).]

A HIPAA complaint must:

 • be filed in writing by mail, fax, e-mail, or via the Office of Civil Rights (OCR) Complaint Portal;

 • name the covered entity involved and describe the acts or omissions that violated the requirements of the Privacy, Security, or Breach Notification Rules; and

 • be filed within 180 days of when the act or omission complained of occurred.

OCR may extend the 180-day deadline for complaints if "good cause" is shown. Directions for filing a complaint, including forms, are provided on the OCR website at http://www.hhs.gov/hipaa/filing-a-complaint/complaint-process/index.html.

Penalties for HIPAA Violations

CMS imposes tiered penalties against any person who violates the requirements and standards of HIPAA Administration Simplification (Soc. Sec. Act §§1171–1180). Penalties range from $100 to $50,000 per violation. [Soc. Sec. Act §1176; 45 C.F.R. §160.404.]

Preemption of State Law

Most states have laws regulating the use and release of PHI. State law that provides more stringent regulation on the use and release of PHI preempts the HIPAA regulations, so providers must follow the state's laws in these cases. In all other cases, the HIPAA privacy regulations preempt state law. [45 C.F.R. §160.203.]

Protection of Genetic Information

Title I of the Genetic Information Nondiscrimination Act of 2008 (GINA) (P.L. 110-233) prohibits group health plans and issuers in the group market from increasing premiums for a group based on the results of an enrollee's genetic information, denying enrollment, imposing pre-existing condition exclusions, and other forms of underwriting based on genetic information. In the individual health insurance market, GINA prohibits issuers from using genetic information to deny coverage, raise premiums, or impose pre-existing condition exclusions. [45 C.F.R. § § 146.121, 146.122.]

Further, group health plans and health insurance issuers in both the group and individual markets cannot request, require, or buy genetic information for underwriting purposes or prior to and in connection with enrollment. Plans and issuers are generally prohibited from asking individuals or family members to undergo a genetic test. [45 C.F.R. § 146.122(a)–(c).]

[¶ 717] Electronic Health Records

The Health Information Technology for Economic and Clinical Health (HITECH) Act (enacted as part of the American Recovery and Reinvestment Act of 2009 (ARRA) (P.L. 111-5)) provided for financial incentives and penalties to encourage the use of electronic health record (EHR) technology by physicians and hospitals to better manage patient care.

Certification of Electronic Health Record Technology

The HHS Office of the National Coordinator (ONC) for Health Information Technology identified the standards and certification criteria for certified EHR technology so that eligible professionals and hospitals can be assured that the systems they adopt are capable of performing the required functions (see 42 C.F.R. § § 495.2–495.370). Regulations on certification criteria and the certification program for EHR are found at 45 C.F.R. Part 170.

Meaningful Use of EHR Technology

To improve the use of EHR technology, CMS developed a three-stage measure known as "meaningful use." Each stage includes a series of specific objectives tied to a measure to allow health care providers to demonstrate that they are "meaningful users" of EHR technology. The first stage is data capture and sharing, the second stage is advance clinical processes, and the third stage is improved outcomes. [Soc. Sec. Act § § 1848(a)(7) and (o), 1886(n).]

For 2015 through 2017, all eligible professionals (EPs), eligible hospitals, and critical access hospitals (CAHs) must meet the modified Stage 2 meaningful use criteria of 42 C.F.R. § 492.22. For 2017 only, EPs, eligible hospitals, and CAHs have the option to use the criteria specified for 2018. In 2018 and later, all EPs, eligible hospitals, and CAHs must meet the Stage 3 meaningful use measures and objectives specified in 42 C.F.R. § 492.24. [42 C.F.R. § § 492.22, 492.24.]

CMS maintains a website for providers seeking information on the EHR incentive program at: http://www.cms.gov/Regulations-and-Guidance/Legislation/EHRIncentivePrograms/index.html.

Penalties for EPs and Hospitals

EPs such as physicians who do not make meaningful use of health information technology are subject to a payment adjustment to their Medicare physician fee schedule payment of 3 percent in 2017 and 2018. The HHS Secretary may, on a case-by-case basis, exempt an eligible professional from the application of the payment adjustment if compliance with the requirement for being a meaningful EHR user would result in a significant hardship. [Soc. Sec. Act § 1848(a)(7), (o); 42 C.F.R. § 495.102(d).]

The Medicare Access and CHIP Reauthorization Act of 2015 (MACRA) (P.L. 114-10) consolidates and replaces the EHR meaningful use program, the Physician Quality Reporting System (PQRS), and the value-based payment modifier into the new Merit-Based Incentive Payment System (MIPS) program. MACRA will sunset the three programs at the end of 2018. Under MACRA, starting in 2019, the amounts paid to individual providers will be subject to adjustment through one of two mechanisms, depending on whether the physician chooses to participate in an Alternative Payment Model (APM) program or MIPS. [MACRA § 101(b), (c), (e)(2).] See ¶ 855 for a discussion of MACRA.

Eligible hospitals and critical access hospitals that do not successfully demonstrate meaningful use of certified EHR technology are subject to Medicare payment adjustments beginning in 2015. [Soc. Sec. Act § 1886(b)(3)(B)(ix); 42 C.F.R. § 495.104.]

[¶ 720] Fraud and Abuse Penalties

"Fraud" is defined as obtaining something of value unlawfully through willful misrepresentation. It includes theft, embezzlement, false statements, illegal commissions, kickbacks, conspiracies, and obtaining contracts through collusive arrangements and similar devices. "Abuse" is defined as the administrative violation of agency regulations, which impair the effective and efficient execution of the program. Violations may result in federal monetary losses or in denial or reduction in lawfully authorized benefits to participants, but they do not involve fraud. [*Financial Management Manual*, Pub. 100-06, Ch. 8, § 140.1.]

The laws used to combat health care fraud and abuse under government-funded health care programs include, among others:

- the federal criminal statutes under Title 18, Criminal Penalties for Acts Involving Federal Health Care Programs;

- the False Claims Act (FCA);

- sections of the Health Insurance Portability and Accountability Act of 1996 (HIPAA) (P.L. 104-191); and

- provisions of the Social Security Act including: (1) "Criminal Penalties for Acts Involving Federal Health Care Programs," Soc. Sec. Act § 1128B(a) and (c)–(h), including the anti-kickback provisions (Soc. Sec. Act § 1128B(b)), and "Limitation on Certain Physician Self-referrals," Soc. Sec. Act § 1877 (referred to as the Stark law).

Health Care Fraud and Abuse Control Program

The Health Care Fraud and Abuse Control Program is under the joint direction of the Attorney General and HHS acting through the Office of Inspector General (OIG). Under the Health Care Fraud and Abuse Control Program, the OIG and the Attorney General are required to: (1) coordinate federal, state, and local law enforcement programs to control fraud and abuse with respect to health plans; (2) conduct investigations, audits, evaluations, and inspections relating to the delivery of and payment for health care in the United States; (3) facilitate the enforcement of the provisions of the exclusion provisions, civil money penalties (CMPs) statute, and false statements and anti-kickback provisions, as well as other statutes applicable to health care fraud and abuse; and (4) provide for the establishment and modification of safe harbors and issue advisory opinions and special fraud alerts. [Soc. Sec. Act § 1128C.]

Fraud and Abuse Data Collection Program

The National Practitioner Data Bank (NPDB) (see http://www.npdb.hrsa.gov/) collects and releases data related to the professional competence of physicians, dentists, and certain other health care practitioners. The types of information included in the NPDB are medical malpractice claims payments, certain adverse licensure actions, adverse clinical privileging actions, adverse professional society membership actions, and exclusions from Medicare and Medicaid. [Soc. Sec. Act § § 1128E, 1921.]

Anti-kickback Statute

The anti-kickback statute is intended to curb the corrupting monetary influence on a physician's decision as to when and where to refer patients. It forbids the solicitation, receipt, offer, or payment of any kind of remuneration (including any kickback, bribe, or rebate) in return for referring an individual or for recommending or arranging the purchase, lease, or ordering of an item or service that may be wholly or partially paid for under a federal health care program. In addition to criminal prosecution and civil fines, violation of these laws subjects the violator to exclusion from Medicare, Medicaid, and other state health care programs. [Soc. Sec. Act § 1128B.]

Conviction under the anti-kickback statute may be punishable by a fine of up to $25,000, imprisonment for up to five years, or both. [Soc. Sec. Act § 1128B(b).] Claims that include items or services resulting from a violation of the anti-kickback statute constitute false claims under the federal FCA. [Soc. Sec. Act § 1128B(g).]

Safe harbors. Congress created several exceptions to the anti-kickback prohibitions (referred to as "statutory safe harbors") to address certain permissible activities and carve out exceptions to what can be considered remuneration under the statute. HHS also created regulatory safe harbors that immunize various payment practices and business arrangements from criminal prosecution or civil sanctions under the anti-kickback statute. [Soc. Sec. Act § 1128B(b)(3); 42 C.F.R. § 1001.952.]

Criminal Medicare and Medicaid Fraud

Anyone convicted of a felony related to activities involving federal health care programs may be subject to criminal penalties, including imprisonment and fines between $1,000 and $25,000. Felonies include making false statements and false representations. [Soc. Sec. Act § § 1107 and 1128B.]

In addition, a physician or supplier who knowingly, willfully, and repeatedly violates Medicare assignment agreement terms (see ¶ 868) by improperly charging beneficiaries will be guilty of a misdemeanor and, when convicted, will be fined a maximum of $2,000 or imprisoned for not more than six months, or both. [Soc. Sec. Act § 1128B(e).]

A person need not have specific intent to commit a violation of section 1128B. [Soc. Sec. Act § 1128B(h).]

Federal health care offenses. Title 18 of the United States Code, regarding Crimes and Criminal Procedures, includes the term "federal health care offense," which involves certain offenses or criminal conspiracies to commit such offenses. [18 U.S.C. § 24.]

"Stark" Law: Physician Self-Referral Prohibitions

The "Limitation on Certain Physician Referrals" statute, commonly known as the "Stark" law, prohibits a physician from making referrals for certain designated health care services (DHS) to entities with which the physician (or an immediate family member) has a financial relationship. If a financial relationship exists between a referring physician and an entity providing a DHS that does not meet an exception, the Stark law is violated and no claims from the referring physician to the entity providing DHS may be submitted to Medicare. The Stark law further prohibits an entity from presenting or causing to be presented a Medicare claim or bill to any individual, third-party payer, or other entity, for clinical laboratory services furnished under a prohibited referral. [Soc. Sec. Act § 1877.]

Financial relationship. For purposes of the physician self-referral prohibition statute, a "financial relationship" includes a physician's or a physician's immediate family member's ownership or investment interest in, or compensation arrangements (i.e., contractual arrangements) with, any entity that furnishes DHS. A compensation arrangement is any arrangement involving remuneration, direct or indirect, whether cash or in kind, between a physician and an entity. [42 C.F.R. § 411.354.]

Exceptions to physician self-referral prohibitions. CMS has established categories of exceptions to the physician self-referral prohibitions. [42 C.F.R. §§ 411.355–411.357.]

Stark law penalties. The penalties for making prohibited self-referrals include: (1) denial of payment for the DHS; (2) refund of amounts collected from the government for DHS claims; (3) imposition of CMPs of up to $15,000 for each DHS for which a claim was submitted; (4) imposition of a CMP of up to $100,000 and exclusion from participation in Medicare and other federal health care programs for circumvention schemes or arrangements that the physician or entity knows or should know violates the self-referral prohibitions; and (5) imposition of CMPs up to $10,000 per day for failing to meet the reporting requirements of Soc. Sec. Act § 1877(f). [Soc. Sec. Act § 1877(g)(1)–(5); 42 C.F.R. §§ 411.361(f), 1003.103, 1003.105(a).]

CMS advisory opinions. Any individual or entity may request a written advisory opinion from CMS concerning whether a physician's referral relating to DHS (other than clinical laboratory services) is prohibited. In the advisory opinion, CMS determines whether a business arrangement described by the parties appears to constitute a "financial relationship" that could potentially restrict a physician's referrals and whether the arrangement or the DHS at issue appear to qualify for any of the exceptions to the referral prohibition. An advisory opinion issued by CMS is binding as to the Secretary and the party requesting the opinion. [Soc. Sec. Act § 1877(g)(6)(A); 42 C.F.R. § 411.370.]

Civil Actions Under the False Claims Act

The FCA authorizes federal prosecutors to file a civil action against any person or entity that knowingly files a false claim with a federal health care program, including Medicare or Medicaid. [31 U.S.C. § 3729 et seq.] The term "claim" refers to an application for payment for items and services under a "federal health care program," such as Medicare or Medicaid. [Soc. Sec. Act § 1128A(i)(2).]

A person or entity may be prosecuted under the FCA for any of the following:

- knowingly presenting, or causing to be presented, a false or fraudulent claim for payment or approval;

- knowingly making, using, or causing to be made or used a false record or statement material to a false or fraudulent claim;

- knowingly making, using, or causing to be made or used a false record or statement, or concealing, avoiding, or decreasing an obligation to pay or transmit money or property to the government; or

- conspiring to commit any of the above violations.

[31 U.S.C. §§ 3729(a)(1), 3730(a).]

Knowledge. The FCA does not require proof of specific intent to defraud a federal health care program. It is sufficient for the person to (1) have actual knowledge of the information; (2) act in deliberate ignorance of the truth or falsity of the information; or (3) act in reckless disregard of the truth or falsity of the information provided or submitted. [31 U.S.C. § 3729(b).]

***Qui tam* actions.** The FCA authorizes private persons to bring *qui tam* actions (also known as "whistleblower" actions). The FCA's *qui tam* provisions empower private persons to sue on behalf of the government and to share in the recovery of such actions. The amount of recovery for a *qui tam* plaintiff depends on whether the government decides to intervene in the case and the extent to which the *qui tam* plaintiff contributed to the prosecution of the claim. [31 U.S.C. § 3730.]

Penalties. A party that commits any prohibited acts under the FCA is liable to the federal government for a civil penalty of not less than $5,500 and not more than $11,000, plus three times the amount of damages that the government sustains because of the act of that party (also known as treble damages). [31 U.S.C. § 3729(a).] In addition to CMPs, parties that file false claims may also be subject to criminal prosecution and exclusion from participation in federal and state health care programs.

Civil Money Penalties

Under the provisions of Social Security Act section 1128A, the HHS Secretary is authorized to impose administrative sanctions in the form of CMPs and assessments against any person, organization, agency, or public or private entity that commits any of the acts described in Soc. Sec. Act § 1128A. [Soc. Sec. Act § 1128A(a); 42 C.F.R. § 1003.102(a), (b).] The law also permits an individual upon whom the Secretary imposes a CMP or assessment to be excluded from participation in the Medicare and Medicaid programs. [Soc. Sec. Act § 1128(b).]

CMPs will not be imposed in connection with certain charitable and other innocuous programs. [Soc. Sec. Act § 1128A(i)(6)(F)–(I).]

Exclusion from Program Participation

The OIG has the authority to exclude individuals and entities that have engaged in fraud or abuse from participation in Medicare, Medicaid, and other federal health care programs. The OIG imposes a mandatory exclusionary period for those individuals or entities convicted of a health care-related offense and has the discretion to exclude providers that have engaged in civil fraud, kickbacks, or other prohibited activities, including quality of care deficiencies. [Soc. Sec. Act § 1128(a), (b).]

Mandatory exclusion. Under the mandatory exclusion provisions of the Social Security Act, an individual or entity *must* be excluded from participation in any federal health care program if convicted of any of the following: (1) a criminal offense related to the delivery of an item of service under Medicare or under any state health care program; (2) a criminal offense relating to neglect or abuse of patients in connection with the delivery of a health care item or service; (3) a felony relating to fraud, theft, embezzlement, breach of fiduciary responsibility, or other financial misconduct relating to health care; or (4) a felony relating to the unlawful manufacture, distribution, prescription, or dispensing of a controlled substance. [Soc. Sec. Act § 1128(a); 42 C.F.R. § 1001.101.]

The minimum period of a mandatory exclusion is five years. If, however, the individual has (before, on, or after such date) been convicted on one previous occasion of one or more offenses for which an exclusion may be imposed under Soc. Sec. Act § 1128(a), the period of the exclusion must be at least 10 years. An exclusion will be permanent if the individual has been convicted on two or more other occasions of one or more offenses for which an exclusion may be effected under Soc. Sec. Act § 1128(a). [Soc. Sec. Act § 1128(a), (c).]

Permissive exclusion. The OIG *may* exclude individuals or entities for any of the reasons described in Soc. Sec. Act § 1128(b). The exclusion period varies based on the offense. [Soc. Sec. Act § 1128(b), (c) (3).]

Payment of claims after exclusion. If a patient submits Part B claims for services furnished by an excluded practitioner, Medicare will pay the first claim submitted and immediately notify the beneficiary of the exclusion. CMS will not pay for items or services furnished by an excluded individual or entity, or under the medical direction or on the prescription of an excluded physician or other authorized individual, more than 15 days after the date on the notice to the enrollee, or after the effective date of the exclusion, whichever is later. Additionally, payment will be made for up to 30 days after the date of the exclusion for inpatient hospital and skilled nursing facility services furnished to patients admitted before the effective date of the suspension, and for home health and hospice care furnished under a plan established before the effective date of the suspension. [42 C.F.R. § 1001.1901(c) (1)–(3).]

Voluntary Self-Disclosure Protocols

In 2013 the OIG published a voluntary provider self-disclosure protocol (SDP), which established a process for health care providers to voluntarily identify, disclose, and resolve instances of potential fraud involving the federal health care programs. Providers should conduct an initial assessment to substantiate that there is noncompliance with program requirements before making a disclosure to the OIG. In addition, a disclosing provider should conduct an internal financial assessment and prepare a report of its findings to estimate the monetary impact of the disclosed matter. Providers that disclose under the SDP should do so with the intention of resolving their overpayment liability exposure for the conduct identified. [*OIG Letter, Recommendations for Provider Self-Disclosure*, April 17, 2013.]

In settling the matter, the OIG's general practice is to require a minimum multiplier of 1.5 times the single damages, although in each case, it determines whether a higher multiplier is appropriate. For kickback-related submissions accepted into the SDP, the OIG will require a minimum $50,000 settlement. For all other matters accepted into the SDP, the OIG will require a minimum $10,000 settlement amount to resolve the matter. [*OIG Letter, Recommendations for Provider Self-Disclosure*, April 17, 2013.]

Open Payments

Manufacturers of covered drugs, devices, biologics or medical supplies are required to annually submit information regarding payments or other transfers of value made to physicians and teaching hospitals. Applicable manufacturers or group purchasing organizations are also required to disclose all ownership and investment interests in the applicable manufacturer or applicable group purchasing organization that were held by a physician or an immediate family member of a physician. [Soc. Sec. Act § 1128G; 42 C.F.R. § § 403.904, 403.906.] CMS has organized these reporting requirements into an Open Payments program. [http://www.cms.gov/openpayments/index.html.]

[¶ 730] Provider Participation Agreements

To qualify for payment for its services to Medicare beneficiaries, a provider must: (1) undergo a survey and be certified by the state agency or accrediting organization to be in compliance with legal and regulatory requirements; and (2) sign a participation agreement with CMS. The participation agreement includes the conditions required for the provider to maintain compliance and continue certification.

The law defines a "provider of services," for purposes of signing a participation agreement, as a hospital, a critical access hospital (CAH), a skilled nursing facility (SNF), a home health agency (HHA), a hospice, a comprehensive outpatient rehabilitation facility, certain funds for payments for physicians and other practitioners provided by hospitals, a clinic, a rehabilitation agency, a public health agency, or a community health center with respect to partial hospitalization services. [Soc. Sec. Act § 1866(e)(1), (e)(2), (u).]

The term "supplier" means a physician or other practitioner, a facility, or other entity (other than a provider of services) that furnishes items or services used in care and treatment under the Medicare statute and can bill Medicare for Part B services. [Soc. Sec. Act § 1861(d); 42 C.F.R. § 400.202; *State Operations Manual*, Pub. 100-07, Ch. 2, § 2002.] "Suppliers" include all physician specialities, dentists, optometrists, podiatrists, chiropractors, independently practicing occupational and physical therapists, suppliers of diagnostic tests, suppliers of radiology services, multi-speciality clinics, independent laboratories, mammography screening centers, independent diagnostic testing facilities, audiologists, independently billing psychologists, ambulatory surgical centers (ASCs), supplier specialties, suppliers of durable medical equipment (DME), and others. [*Medicare Claims Processing Manual*, Pub. 100-04, Ch. 1, § 30.3.12.1.]

Screening requirements. All Medicare providers are required to undergo screening before initial enrollment and revalidate their compliance with enrollment requirements every five years; suppliers of durable medical equipment, prosthetics, orthotics, and supplies must revalidate every three years. A Medicare contractor is required to screen all initial provider and supplier applications and any applications received in response to a revalidation request and assign them to a level of limited, moderate, or high. [Soc. Sec. Act § 1866(j)(2)(D)(iii); 42 C.F.R. §§ 424.57(g), 424.515, 424.518.]

Essentials of Provider Agreements

To participate in the Medicare program, a provider of services must sign an agreement with the Secretary:

    (1) to limit its charges to beneficiaries to the costs of noncovered services and to the deductible, coinsurance, and other charges allowed under federal law (see "Allowable Charges" below);

    (2) to make adequate provision for the refund of amounts incorrectly collected from beneficiaries;

    (3) to disclose the hiring of any individual who, at any time during the year preceding employment, was employed in a managerial, accounting, auditing, or similar capacity by the provider's Medicare administrative contractor;

    (4) to release, upon request, patient data to a quality improvement organization (QIO) (see ¶ 710) reviewing the provider;

    (5) to bill other primary payers before billing Medicare in accordance with statutory and regulatory requirements concerning alternate insurance coverage (see ¶ 636); and

    (6) to admit surveyors from the state health agency or accrediting organization to assess their compliance with conditions of participation.

[Soc. Sec. Act § 1866(a)(1); 42 C.F.R. §§ 489.20, 489.30.]

Hospitals. The conditions of participation and provisions of the provider agreement for hospitals include the following additional requirements:

¶730

(1) to either furnish directly or make arrangements for all Medicare care and services (other than physician and certain health care practitioner services) (see ¶ 635);

(2) to maintain an agreement with a QIO for the review of admissions, quality, and diagnostic information (see ¶ 710);

(3) not to charge for services rejected by a QIO on the basis of quality of care;

(4) to participate in TRICARE, CHAMPVA (Civilian Health and Medical Program of the Veterans Administration), and Veterans Administration programs (42 C.F.R. §§ 489.25, 489.26);

(5) to make available to beneficiaries directories of participating physicians in the area and identify any qualified participating physicians in the area, whenever a referral is made to a nonparticipating physician;

(6) to accept as payment in full any payments made by risk-basis health maintenance organizations on behalf of their Medicare enrollees if the payments made are at the level traditional Medicare would have paid (42 C.F.R. § 422.214);

(7) to provide beneficiaries with a written notice, at the time of admission to the facility, explaining the beneficiary's right to Medicare benefits (see below) and right to appeal a discharge from the hospital (42 C.F.R. § 489.27);

(8) to report quality data in accordance with the HHS Secretary's requirements;

(9) to comply with the requirements of Soc. Sec. Act § 1866(f) relating to maintaining written policies and procedures respecting advance directives;

(10) if the hospital has a financial interest in an entity to which patients are discharged, it must disclose the nature of the financial interest, the number of its patients who require home health services, and the percentage of such individuals who received such services from such entity;

(11) to provide the HHS Secretary with information regarding the volume of patients, as required by Soc. Sec. Act § 1886(d)(12);

(12) to be a participating provider of medical care both (1) under the contract health services program funded by the Indian Health Service (IHS) and operated by the IHS, and Indian tribes, or tribal organizations, and (2) any program funded by the IHS and operated by an urban Indian organization with respect to the purchase of items or services for an eligible urban Indian;

(13) if not otherwise subject to the Occupational Safety and Health Act of 1970, to comply with the Bloodborne Pathogens standard under 29 C.F.R. § 1910.1030;

(14) in the case of hospitals with emergency departments, to meet the responsibilities imposed by the law with respect to treating emergency cases (see below under "Treatment of Emergency Cases—Antidumping Rules") (42 C.F.R. § 489.24); and

(15) for individuals receiving observation services as an outpatient for more than 24 hours, to explain to the individual no more than 36 hours after the start of services (or, if sooner, upon release) that he or she has the status of an outpatient receiving observation services rather than as an inpatient and why; the implications of that status on, for example, cost-sharing requirements and subsequent eligibility for coverage for SNF services; and other appropriate information.

[Soc. Sec. Act § 1866(a)(1).] Additional terms are required for CAHs, SNFs, HHAs, and hospice programs.

Treatment of Emergency Cases—Antidumping Rules

Each hospital provider agreement must include a clause requiring the provider to comply with the Emergency Medical Treatment & Labor Act (EMTALA), which is intended to ensure public access to emergency services regardless of ability to pay. [Soc. Sec. Act §§ 1866(a)(1)(I), 1867; 42 C.F.R. §§ 489.20(l), 489.24.]

Under the EMTALA "antidumping" provision, a hospital must provide for an appropriate medical screening examination (within the capability of the hospital's emergency department) for any individual who comes to the emergency department and requests a medical examination or treatment, regardless of whether that individual is a Medicare beneficiary. The screening examination must be sufficient to determine whether an emergency medical condition exists or whether the individual is in active labor. If a patient has an emergency condition or is in active labor, the hospital must provide the treatment necessary to stabilize his or her condition. For a woman in active labor, stabilization requires delivery of both the newborn and the placenta. [Soc. Sec. Act § 1867(a), (e)(3), (h).]

Transfer. The transfer of an emergency room patient whose condition has not been stabilized is not appropriate unless either: (1) the patient (or a person acting on the patient's behalf) requests a transfer in writing; or (2) a physician has certified that the medical benefits to be obtained from treatment available at the receiving hospital outweigh the risks of transfer and that the receiving facility has the space and personnel necessary to treat the patient. [Soc. Sec. Act § 1867(c); 42 C.F.R. § 489.24(e)(2)(iv), (f).]

Records. Each hospital must post a sign in its emergency department specifying patients' rights with respect to examination and treatment for emergency medical conditions and women in labor. [Soc. Sec. Act § 1866(a)(1)(I), (N)(iii).]

Policies and procedures. A hospital must have written policies and procedures in place to respond to situations in which a particular specialty is not available or the on-call physician cannot respond because of circumstances beyond the physician's control, and to provide that emergency services are available to meet the needs of individuals with emergency medical conditions. [42 C.F.R. § 489.24(j).]

Delay in treatment. Medicare-participating hospitals must not delay required screening and the stabilization of an emergency in order to: (1) obtain insurance information; (2) seek, or direct a patient to seek, authorization to provide screening or stabilizing services from the individual's health plan, managed care organization, or insurance company; or (3) prepare an Advance Beneficiary Notice and obtain a beneficiary signature. Appropriate screening and stabilization must be provided first. [42 C.F.R. § 489.24(d)(4).]

Refusal to consent. If an individual intends to leave the hospital before the screening examination, the hospital should offer further medical examination and treatment, inform the individual of the benefits of such examination and treatment, and take all reasonable steps to obtain written informed consent to refuse such examination and treatment. The hospital must document any refusal of treatment and its actions or efforts to comply with EMTALA requirements and provide treatment. [42 C.F.R. § 489.24(d)(3).]

Sanctions. If a hospital knowingly and willfully, or negligently, fails to handle emergency treatment cases, it may have its provider agreement with Medicare terminated. In addition, the Secretary may impose civil money penalties against the hospital and responsible physician, and the law provides for civil actions against a hospital (but not against physicians). [Soc. Sec. Act § 1867(d).]

Except when a delay would jeopardize the health and safety of individuals, the Secretary is required to request a QIO review before making a compliance determination that would terminate a hospital's Medicare participation because of EMTALA violations. [Soc. Sec. Act § 1867(d)(3); 42 C.F.R. § 489.24(h).]

Notifying Beneficiaries of Medicare Rights

Within two days of admission, hospitals must provide each Medicare beneficiary with a written statement (using language approved by the Secretary) explaining the beneficiary's Medicare rights, i.e., the "Important Message from Medicare." The explanation of rights must include: (1) rights to inpatient hospital services and post-hospital services; (2) the circumstances under which the beneficiary will and will not be liable for charges for a continued stay at the hospital; (3) the beneficiary's right to appeal a determination that a continued inpatient hospital stay is not covered (including practical steps to initiate such an appeal); and (4) the beneficiary's liability for payment for services if the determination is upheld on appeal. The hospital must give the patient a second copy of the notice not more than two days before discharge. [Soc. Sec. Act § 1866(a)(1)(M); 42 C.F.R. § 405.1205; *Medicare Claims Processing Manual*, Pub. 100-04, Ch. 30, § 200.3.1.]

Provider Policies on Advance Directives

Hospitals and other health care facilities must maintain written policies and procedures relating to an advance directive (a written instruction, such as a living will or durable power of attorney for health care), which expresses a patient's wishes relating to the provision of care when the individual is incapacitated. Each facility must: (1) inform Medicare and Medicaid patients of their rights under state law to make an advance directive, and (2) explain the written policies of the organization respecting the implementation of such rights. [Soc. Sec. Act § 1866(a)(1)(Q), (f).]

Allowable Charges

A provider agreement requires a provider of services to limit its charges to beneficiaries to the costs of noncovered services and to the deductible and coinsurance (copayment) charges allowed under federal law and regulations. Under Medicare law and regulations, the provider may charge a beneficiary the following amounts:

(1) Providers may charge beneficiaries for the Part A inpatient hospital deductible and coinsurance, which consist of: (a) the amount of the inpatient hospital deductible or, if less, the actual charges for the services (see ¶ 220); (b) the amount of inpatient hospital coinsurance applicable for each day the individual is furnished inpatient hospital services after the 60th day during a benefit period (see ¶ 224); and (c) the post-hospital extended care services coinsurance amount (see ¶ 242). [42 C.F.R. §§ 489.30–489.32.]

(2) Providers may charge beneficiaries for the Part B deductible and coinsurance, which consist of an annual deductible and a coinsurance of 20 percent of the Medicare-approved Part B payment amount in excess of that deductible (see ¶ 335 for further details and exceptions). [Soc. Sec. Act § 1833(b); 42 C.F.R. § 489.30.] For outpatient hospital services, allowable deductible charges depend on whether the hospital can determine the beneficiary's deductible status.

(3) Providers may charge beneficiaries for the blood deductible, which consists of charges for the first three pints of blood or units of packed red blood cells furnished during a calendar year (see ¶ 220). [Soc. Sec. Act § 1833(b).]

(4) Providers may not charge a deductible for certain services not subject to deductible. Many preventive services are not subject to any copayment or deductible (see ¶ 335). [Soc. Sec. Act § 1861.]

(5) For costlier services requested by a beneficiary, the difference between the provider's customary charges for services covered under Medicare and the costlier services may be charged. Whenever a provider is permitted to charge for an item or service, it may not charge the Medicare beneficiary or another person more than the amount customarily charged by the provider for such an item or service. [Soc. Sec. Act § 1866(a)(2)(B).]

Deposits and Prepayment Requests

A provider agreement contains specific requirements concerning prepayment. Under these provisions, the provider agrees not to:

(1) require an individual entitled to hospital insurance benefits to prepay in part or in whole for inpatient services as a condition of admittance, except when it is clear upon admission that payment under Part A cannot be made;

(2) deny covered inpatient services to an eligible individual on the ground of inability or failure to pay a requested amount at or before admission;

(3) evict, or threaten to evict, an individual for inability to pay a deductible or a coinsurance amount required under Medicare; and

(4) charge an individual for: (a) an agreement to admit or readmit the individual on some specified future date for covered inpatient services, (b) the individual's failure to remain an inpatient for any agreed-upon length of time, or (c) the individual's failure to give advance notice of departure from the provider's facilities.

[42 C.F.R. § 489.22.]

Providers must not require advance payment of the inpatient deductible or coinsurance as a condition of admission. Additionally, providers may not require that the beneficiary prepay any Part B charges as a condition of admission, except when prepayment from non-Medicare patients is required. In such cases, only the deductible and coinsurance may be collected. [Pub. 100-04, Ch. 2, § 10.3.]

A hospice is prohibited from discontinuing care to a patient because of his or her inability to pay. [Soc. Sec. Act § 1861(dd)(2)(D).]

Termination of Provider Agreements

A provider may terminate its participation in the Medicare program voluntarily, or its participation may be terminated by the Secretary for cause. [Soc. Sec. Act § 1866(b).] A provider whose participation is terminated for cause has the right to administrative appeal and judicial review but has no right to delay of the termination pending the hearing. [Soc. Sec. Act § 1866(h); 42 C.F.R. §§ 498.5, 498.20.]

In general, no Medicare payment will be made to a provider after the effective date of the termination. However, in the case of inpatient hospital services (including inpatient psychiatric hospital services) and SNF services, payments may be made for up to 30 days for services furnished to an individual who is admitted to the institution before the effective date of the termination. Similarly, home health services and hospice care furnished under a plan established before the termination date of the participation agreement will be covered for up to 30 days after termination. [Soc. Sec. Act §§ 1128(c)(2), 1866(b)(3); 42 C.F.R. § 489.55.]

[¶ 735] Role of Medicaid

Although the Medicaid program is administered separately from Medicare, Medicaid is required to pay the Medicare premiums, deductibles, and/or coinsurance amounts for certain Medicare beneficiaries. Medicare beneficiaries eligible for Medicaid cost-sharing assistance are called "qualified Medicare beneficiaries" or "dual eligibles." [Soc. Sec. Act § 1905(p).]

Medicaid pays all Medicare cost-sharing for dual-eligible beneficiaries with incomes up to 100 percent of the federal poverty level (FPL). Medicaid pays the Part B premiums for dual eligibles with incomes between 100 and 120 percent of FPL, referred to as specified low-income beneficiaries. To the extent that funds are available, Medicaid must pay a portion of the Part B premium for Medicare beneficiaries with incomes between 120 percent and 135 percent of FPL, called "qualifying individuals." Section 211 of the Medicare Access and CHIP Reauthorization Act of 2015 (MACRA) (P.L. 114-10) made the qualifying individual program permanent. [Soc. Sec. Act § § 1902(a)(10)(E)(iv), 1933(g).]

States also may pay Medicare Part A and Part B premiums under "buy-in" agreements with Medicare for beneficiaries who do not qualify for qualified Medicare beneficiary status. [Soc. Sec. Act § § 1818(g), 1843.]

Prescription drug benefit. Medicaid agencies assist in the determination of eligibility for the Medicare low-income subsidies under the prescription drug benefit (see ¶ 508) by notifying CMS of each Medicaid applicant or recipient who is eligible for the low-income subsidy for Medicare Part D cost-sharing. States are required to provide this information as a condition of receiving federal Medicaid assistance. [Soc. Sec. Act § 1935.]

[¶ 740] "Medigap" Insurance

Medicare beneficiaries enrolled in "original Medicare," the traditional fee-for-service Medicare plan, may purchase Medicare supplement policies, also called "Medigap" policies. These policies are private insurance policies used to pay some of the health care costs that Medicare does not cover, such as copayments, coinsurance, and deductibles. [Soc. Sec. Act § 1882(g)(1), (o)(1); 42 C.F.R. § 403.205.]

Types of Medigap Policies

There are several standard types of Medigap policies, each designated with a letter of the alphabet: A, B, C, D, F, G, K, L, M, and N. Each policy type must be the same for every insurance company. For instance, a Medigap policy type A must offer the same coverage no matter which insurance company is offering the plan. Each plan type also has a specific set of benefits, which enables consumers to compare policies on the basis of price and the company's reputation. In Massachusetts, Minnesota, and Wisconsin, however, different standardized Medigap plans are available. [Choosing a Medigap Policy: A Guide to Health Insurance for People with Medicare.]

The basic (core) benefits are included in plans with designation A through G, M, and N. Plan A covers only the core benefits, and Plan G offers the most benefits. Plans designated M and N are identical to plans designated with a category D except that they pay more of Medicare's copayments. Two plans, K and L, may be sold with a high deductible option.

Core benefits. Except for policies K and L, all Medigap policies must cover: (1) Part A copayments; (2) 365 days of hospital coverage after Part A benefits have been used; (3) payment of Part B copayments after the Part B deductible has been paid; and (4) the first three pints of blood (or the equivalent in packed cells) per calendar year unless the patient or a donor has donated the amount of blood used. Effective for policies issued or renewed on of after June 1, 2010, hospice services must be included as a core benefit. [*Notice*, 74 FR 18807, April 24, 2009.]

Optional benefits. Policies B through G offer varying combinations of: (1) the inpatient hospital deductible; (2) the Part B deductible; (3) coinsurance payments for skilled nursing facility services; (4) Part B excess charges; (5) emergency care during foreign travel; and (6) preventive care not covered under Medicare. Preventive services and at-home recovery are no longer included as optional benefits in policies issued on or after June 1, 2010. [*Notice*, 74 FR 18807, April 24, 2009.]

Benefit packages. Two high-deductible Medigap benefit packages, Policies K and L, offer less than the core benefits. [Soc. Sec. Act § 1882(s)(3)(C); Choosing a Medigap Policy: A Guide to Health Insurance for People with Medicare.]

All issuers of Medigap policies are required to offer either Policy C or F in addition to Policy A. [Soc. Sec. Act § 1882(o)(5).]

Standards for Medigap Policies

Medicare supplement policies are required to meet certain specified federal standards, as outlined in Social Security Act section 1882, and National Association of Insurance Commissioners (NAIC) model standards. [Soc. Sec. Act § 1882; 42 C.F.R. § 403.206; *Notice*, 74 FR 18807, April 24, 2009.]

Federal law requires a standardized description of policies to avoid confusion when comparing policies from different companies and guaranteed renewability of policies to prevent cancellation for any reason other than nonpayment of premiums. In addition, certain "out clauses," such as denial of benefits for preexisting conditions when one Medigap policy is replaced with another, are prohibited. [Sec. Sec. Act § 1882(o)(3), (o)(4), (q).]

Beginning January 1, 2020, a Medigap plan that provides coverage of the Part B deductible may not be sold or issued to a newly eligible Medicare beneficiary. [Soc. Sec. Act § 1882(z).]

Prescription drug coverage. As of January 1, 2006, when the Medicare prescription drug (Part D) benefit became effective, no new Medigap policies may cover prescription drugs, but Medigap policies that covered prescription drugs before that date may be renewed. [Soc. Sec. Act § 1882(v)(2)(B).]

Preexisting conditions. Issuance of new Medigap policies is guaranteed without any preexisting condition exclusion for the following Medicare beneficiaries:

(1) persons whose coverage under an employee welfare plan terminates;

(2) persons enrolled in a Medicare Advantage (MA) plan (see ¶ 400 *et seq.*) who disenroll for permissible reasons (plan termination or a move out of the plan area);

(3) persons enrolled in risk- or cost-based health maintenance organizations (HMOs) or other qualifying plans who disenroll for permissible reasons;

(4) persons whose enrollment in a Medigap policy ceases because of insurer bankruptcy or insolvency;

(5) persons previously enrolled under a Medigap policy who terminate enrollment in the Medigap policy, enroll for the first time in MA, an HMO, or other qualifying plan, and subsequently terminate such enrollment within 12 months;

(6) persons previously enrolled in a Medigap policy who are enrolled in MA, are terminated involuntarily within the first 12 months from such an enrollment, and who, without an intervening enrollment, enroll with a similar organization, provider, plan, or program (for whom the subsequent enrollment is considered an initial enrollment, such as in (5)) [Soc. Sec. Act § 1882(s)(3)(F)]; and

(7) persons who enroll in MA or in the Program of All-Inclusive Care for the Elderly (PACE) under section 1894 of the Social Security Act when first reaching Medicare eligibility but then disenroll within 12 months.

¶740

[Soc. Sec. Act § 1882(s)(3)(B).]

The preexisting condition exclusion may not be imposed on a beneficiary during the six-month period that begins on the first day of the month in which the individual has reached age 65 and is enrolled in Medicare Part B, if the beneficiary had six continuous months of creditable coverage on the date of application. Persons with fewer than six months of coverage are entitled to have the period of any preexisting condition exclusion reduced by any period of creditable coverage. [Soc. Sec. Act § 1882(s)(2)(A).]

An insurer may not impose an exclusion based on a preexisting condition for individuals enrolling in Medicare Part D (see ¶ 500). Insurers are prohibited from discriminating in the pricing of such policies on the basis of the individual's health status, claims experience, receipt of health care, or medical condition. [Soc. Sec. Act § 1882(s)(3)(A).]

Genetic information. The Genetic Information Nondiscrimination Act of 2008 (GINA) (P.L. 110-233) prohibits Medigap insurers from obtaining or using genetic information for underwriting purposes to make decisions whether to enroll an individual, exclude conditions as preexisting, or set premiums to be charged. Genetic information includes the results of a genetic testing on an individual or family member (dependent or other relative as close as great-grandparents and certain cousins) and the manifestation of a disease in a family member of the insured. [Soc. Sec. Act § 1882(s)(2)(E) and (F), (x).]

Penalties

It is a criminal offense to engage in fraudulent activities connected with the sale of Medigap policies, including: making false statements and misrepresentations; falsely claiming certification by the federal government; selling policies that duplicate Medicare benefits, including selling to MA beneficiaries; and mailing into a state Medigap policies that have been disapproved by that state. Violation of these provisions is a felony, entailing maximum penalties of $25,000, five years' imprisonment, or both. [Soc. Sec. Act § 1882(d); 42 C.F.R. § 402.105(c).]

Chapter 8– PAYMENT RULES

[¶ 800] Introduction

Medicare's method of paying for services provided to a beneficiary varies according to whether the services are furnished under Part A, Part B, Part C, or Part D. Providers of most Part A services are reimbursed by Medicare under various prospective payment systems. Providers of most Part B services are reimbursed by Medicare under various fee schedules. Providers of managed care services are paid by Part C organizations, which are funded by Medicare, and providers of prescription drugs are paid by Part D plans, which are also funded by Medicare.

Part A Payment

Payments made to most hospitals are made under the inpatient prospective payment system (IPPS) for services covered by Medicare Part A, which covers institutional services (see ¶ 810). PPS payments are made for a hospital's inpatient operating and capital-related costs at predetermined, specific rates for each hospital discharge. Prospective payment systems also have been established for home health agencies (see ¶ 830), hospital outpatient services (combining elements of Part A and Part B; see ¶ 820), skilled nursing facilities (see ¶ 835), inpatient rehabilitation facilities (see ¶ 837), long-term care hospitals (see ¶ 815), inpatient hospital services furnished in psychiatric hospitals and units (see ¶ 840), and end-stage renal disease facilities (see ¶ 845). Other institutional providers and services not covered by a PPS are paid on the basis of "reasonable costs." Medicare payment is made directly to the provider that furnished the services.

Part B Payment

Part B services provided by physicians and other health care practitioners generally are paid on the basis of a physician fee schedule (see ¶ 855 and ¶ 860). Other suppliers of services and equipment paid under Part B are paid on the basis of different fee schedules (see, for example, the discussions about the clinical laboratory, ambulance, and durable medical equipment fee schedules at ¶ 875, ¶ 880, and ¶ 882) or on a "reasonable charge" basis (not covered in this book). Medicare payment is made to the physician or supplier who furnished the services if assignment has been accepted (see ¶ 868). Otherwise, the payment is made to the beneficiary, who then has the obligation to pay the physician or supplier.

Part C Payment

Medicare Advantage organizations are risk-bearing entities that can issue, within designated geographic areas, health plans offering a specific set of benefits at a uniform premium and uniform level of cost-sharing to each Medicare beneficiary who chooses to enroll in a such a plan under Medicare Part C, which is called the Medicare Advantage (MA) program. The payment rules for MA organizations are at ¶ 408. The MA program:

- allows beneficiaries to choose among health maintenance organizations, preferred provider organization plans, fee-for-service plans, and medical savings account plans for their health coverage;

- offers plans designed to provide coverage to people with special needs, i.e., dually eligible for Medicaid and Medicare, institutionalized, or diagnosed with a specified chronic illness or disability;

- provides a wider range of benefit choices available to enrollees, including prescription drug benefits;

- provides for regional plans that provide private plan options to many more beneficiaries, especially in rural areas;

- bases payments for local and regional MA plans on competitive bids rather than administered pricing; and

- establishes uniform grievance and appeals procedures, as well as notice and timeliness procedures to ensure the beneficiary's rights are protected and understood.

[Soc. Sec. Act § 1851.]

Part D Payments

On January 1, 2006, Medicare began to cover the cost of prescription drugs under Medicare Part D. Currently, beneficiaries entitled to Part A and enrolled in Part B, and enrollees in MA private fee-for-service plans or medical savings account plans are eligible for the prescription drug benefit. Medicare Part D is covered at ¶ 500 *et seq.*

Accountable Care Organizations

Medicare services also may be delivered through accountable care organizations (ACOs), groups of service and supplier providers that work together to manage and coordinate care for Medicare fee-for-service beneficiaries. An ACO is typically a network of provider groups, often affiliated with a hospital, that work together and are jointly responsible for the cost and quality of care provided to Medicare beneficiaries. ACOs must meet certain criteria to be designated as an ACO. If an ACO meets specified quality performance standards it may receive a portion of the shared savings. ACOs are discussed at ¶ 853.

[¶ 810] Inpatient Hospital Services

The inpatient hospital prospective payment system (IPPS) applies to all short-term, acute-care hospitals unless they are specifically excluded from the IPPS. Under the IPPS, Medicare provides a single payment amount to hospitals for each hospital discharge, identified by the diagnosis-related group (DRG) into which each discharge is classified. [42 C.F.R. § § 412.1, 412.2(a).]

DRG Classifications

Under the IPPS, all patient illnesses and injuries resulting in admission to a hospital are classified into different DRGs, which are clinically coherent and relatively homogeneous with respect to resources used by a hospital. [Soc. Sec. Act § 1886(a); 42 C.F.R. § 412.1 *et seq.*]

Each DRG (i.e., each type of illness or injury) is paid at a set rate that is weighted geographically. Cases are classified into DRGs based on a principal diagnosis, additional or secondary diagnoses, surgical procedures, and the age, sex, and discharge status of the patient. The amount paid under the IPPS is based upon the DRG for each discharge, regardless of the number of services received or the length of the patient's stay in the hospital, and includes all inpatient operating costs. The DRG payment covers all items and services provided by the hospital to the patient. If the hospital's costs are less than that payment, the hospital keeps the difference; if the hospital's costs are more than the set rate, the hospital absorbs the loss. Not included in the DRG are services provided by the patient's physician, which are covered under Part B (see ¶ 855). [Soc. Sec. Act § 1886(a); 42 C.F.R. § 412.1 *et seq.*]

IPPS Payment Adjustments

The base payment rate to an individual hospital may be adjusted in a number of ways, usually in the form of a percentage add-on payment, including the following:

- If the hospital treats a disproportionate share of low-income patients or is located in an urban area, has 100 or more beds, and can demonstrate that more that 30 percent of its revenue is derived from state and local government payments for indigent care provided to patients not covered by Medicare or Medicaid, it will receive a disproportionate share hospital (DSH) adjustment. [Soc. Sec. Act § 1886(d)(5)(F); 42 C.F.R. § 412.106(c)(2).] Starting in fiscal year (FY) 2014, hospitals' Medicare DSH payments are reduced to reflect lower uncompensated care costs relative to increases in the number of insured. [Soc. Sec. Act § 1886(r).]

- If the hospital is an approved teaching hospital, it will receive an indirect medical education (IME) adjustment. This percentage varies depending on the ratio of residents to beds. [Soc. Sec. Act § 1886(d)(5)(B); 42 C.F.R. § 412.105.]

- If a particular case involves certain approved new medical technology, additional payments may be made. [Soc. Sec. Act § 1886(d)(5)(K); 42 C.F.R. §§ 412.87, 412.88.]

- If the hospital stay is unusually long or costly, the hospital may be eligible for an additional "outlier" payment. [Soc. Sec. Act § 1886(d)(5)(A); 42 C.F.R. §§ 412.80–412.86.]

See ¶ 847 for a discussion of payment issues that apply to certain rural hospitals.

Inpatient Quality Data Reporting Program

Under the Inpatient Quality Reporting (IQR) program, beginning in FY 2015, IPPS hospitals that do not submit required quality data on specific quality indicators to the Medicare program each year have their applicable hospital market basket percentage increase reduced by one-fourth. In previous years the reduction was 2 percentage points. [Soc. Sec. Act § 1886(b)(3)(B)(viii); 42 C.F.R. § 412.64(d)(2).]

In the FY 2017 final rule, CMS added four new claims-based measures for the FY 2019 payment determination and subsequent years (three clinical episode-based payment measures and one communication and coordination-of-care measure) and removed 15 measures for the FY 2019 payment determination and later. [*Final rule*, 81 FR 56762, Aug. 22, 2016.]

Hospital Inpatient Value-Based Purchasing Program

The Hospital Inpatient Value-Based Purchasing (VBP) program adjusts payments to hospitals for inpatient services based on their performance on an announced set of measures. [Soc. Sec. Act § 1886(o)(1); 42 C.F.R. § 412.162.]

The HHS Secretary announces performance standards, including levels of achievement and improvement, 60 days before the beginning of a performance period. The Secretary will also provide for an assessment for each hospital for each performance period. The assessment must result in an appropriate distribution of value-based incentive payments among hospitals achieving different levels of hospital performance scores, with hospitals achieving the highest hospital performance scores receiving the largest value-based incentive payments. [Soc. Sec. Act § 1886(o); 42 C.F.R. §§ 412.160–412.167.]

Hospital Readmissions Reduction

The Hospital Readmissions Reduction Program (HRRP) reduces reimbursement to certain hospitals that have excess readmissions for certain conditions. For FY 2017 and later, the reduction is based on a hospital's risk-adjusted readmission rate during a three-year period for acute myocardial infarction, heart failure, pneumonia, chronic obstructive pulmonary disease, total hip arthroplasty/total knee arthroplasty, and coronary artery bypass graft. A "readmission" refers to an admission to an acute-care hospital paid under the IPPS within 30 days of a discharge from the same or another acute-care hospital. [Soc. Sec. Act § 1886(q); 42 C.F.R. §§ 412.152, 412.154; *Final rule*, 81 FR 56762, Aug. 22, 2016.]

Hospital-Acquired Conditions

Section 3008 of the Patient Protection and Affordable Care Act (ACA) (P.L. 111-148) established the Hospital-Acquired Condition (HAC) Reduction Program to provide an incentive for hospitals to reduce HACs. Beginning FY 2015, the HAC Reduction Program requires the Secretary to adjust payments to applicable hospitals that rank in the worst-performing quartile of all subsection (d) hospitals with respect to risk-adjusted HAC quality measures. These hospitals have their payments reduced to 99 percent of what would otherwise have been paid for such discharges. [Soc. Sec. Act § 1886(p); 42 C.F.R. § 412.172.]

Hospital-Acquired Conditions Present on Admission Indicator program. The Hospital-Acquired Conditions Present on Admission Indicator program is intended to prevent certain avoidable or preventable HACs, including infections that occur during a hospital stay. If a selected condition that was not present on admission (POA) manifests during the hospital stay, it is considered a HAC and the case is paid as though the secondary diagnosis was not present. [Soc. Sec. Act § 1886(d)(4)(D).]

The list of HACs for which CMS does not pay after FY 2015 includes the following:

(1) foreign object retained after surgery;

(2) air embolism;

(3) blood incompatibility;

(4) stages III and IV pressure ulcers;

(5) falls and trauma, including fracture, dislocation, intracranial injury, crushing injury, or burn;

(6) manifestations of poor glycemic control;

(7) catheter-associated urinary tract infection;

(8) vascular catheter-associated infection;

(9) surgical site infection after coronary bypass graft surgery;

(10) surgical site infection following bariatric surgery for obesity;

(11) surgical site infection following certain orthopedic procedures;

(12) surgical site infection following cardiac implantable electronic device;

(13) deep vein thrombosis and pulmonary embolism following certain orthopedic procedures; and

(14) iatrogenic pneumothorax with venous catheterization.

[*Final rule*, 79 FR 49854, Aug. 22, 2014.]

Hospital Closure

To preserve resident positions that would otherwise be lost when a hospital with an approved medical residency program closes on or after March 23, 2008, the HHS Secretary is required to redistribute unused medical resident positions to other hospitals. [Soc. Sec. Act § 1886(h)(4)(H)(vi); 42 C.F.R. § 412.105(f)(1)(ix)(A).] In addition, if a hospital's "reference resident level" is less than the applicable resident limit, the resident limit will be reduced by 65 percent of the difference between the resident limit and the reference resident level. [Soc. Sec. Act § 1886(h)(8); 42 C.F.R. § 412.105(f)(1)(iv)(B)(2).]

Three-Day Payment Window

Under the three-day payment window, a hospital (or an entity that is wholly owned or wholly operated by the hospital) subject to the IPPS must include on the claim for a Medicare beneficiary's inpatient stay the diagnoses, procedures, and charges for all outpatient diagnostic services and admission-related outpatient nondiagnostic services that are furnished to the beneficiary on the date of admission to the hospital and during the three calendar days immediately preceding the date of admission. [Soc. Sec. Act § 1886(a)(4); 42 C.F.R. § 412.2(c)(5); *Medicare Claims Processing Manual*, Pub. 100-04, Ch. 3, § 40.3.]

"Two Midnight" Rule

Under the "two midnight" rule, effective for admissions on or after October 1, 2013, if a physician expected a beneficiary's surgical procedure, diagnostic test, or other treatment to require a stay in the hospital lasting at least two midnights and admitted the beneficiary to the hospital based on that expectation, it was presumed to be appropriate that the hospital receive Medicare Part A payment. Hospital services spanning less than two midnights would be provided on an outpatient basis unless there was clear documentation in the medical record that the procedure was designated by CMS as an inpatient-only service or that the physician's order clearly stated an expectation of a stay spanning more than two midnights. [42 C.F.R. §§ 412.3(d), 419.22(n); *Final rule*, 78 FR 50496, Aug. 19, 2013.]

In the FY 2017 IPPS final rule, CMS applied an adjustment to the FY 2017 payment rates to permanently prospectively remove the 0.2 percent reduction to the rate that was put in place in FY 2014 to offset the estimated increase in IPPS expenditures associated with the projected increase in inpatient encounters that was expected to result from the new inpatient admission guidelines under the two-midnight policy. In addition, CMS made a temporary one-time prospective increase to the FY 2017 standardized amount, the hospital specific payment rates, and the national capital federal rate to address the effects of the 0.2 percent reduction to the rate for the two-midnight policy in effect for FYs 2014, 2015, and 2016. [*Final rule*, 81 FR 56762, Aug. 22, 2016.]

Hospitals Excluded from Inpatient PPS

Certain hospitals are exempt from the IPPS, including psychiatric hospitals and units, rehabilitation hospitals and units, pediatric hospitals, long-term care hospitals, and certain cancer hospitals. Hospitals exempt from the IPPS either are reimbursed on a reasonable cost basis but are subject to a ceiling on the rate of increase in inpatient costs or have their own prospective payment system. [Soc. Sec. Act § 1886(b)(1)(C), (j); 42 C.F.R. § 412.23.]

[¶ 815] Long-Term Care Hospitals

CMS pays for both the operating and capital-related costs of hospital inpatient stays in long-term care hospitals (LTCHs) under Part A based on prospectively set rates. LTCHs are hospitals that are primarily engaged in providing inpatient services by or under the supervision of a physician to Medicare beneficiaries with medically complex conditions who require a long hospital stay. LTCH facilities must have an average inpatient length of stay greater than 25 days (or 20 days for certain hospitals focusing on cancer treatment) and further meet the requirements for hospitals set forth in Soc. Sec. Act § 1861(e). These facilities generally provide extended medical and rehabilitative care for patients who may suffer from multiple acute or chronic conditions. [Soc. Sec. Act § 1861(ccc)(1)–(3).]

Requirements for LTCHs

LTCHs are required to do the following:

(1) have a documented patient review process that includes pre-admission screening, validation within 48 hours of admission that patients meet admission criteria, and periodic evaluation of each patient's need for continued care in the LTCH and assessment of the available discharge options;

(2) have active physician involvement with patients through an organized medical staff, with physicians available on-site every day to review patients' progress and consulting physicians on call and able to be at the patient's bedside within a moderate period of time; and

(3) have interdisciplinary teams of health care professionals, including physicians, to prepare and implement an individualized treatment plan for each patient.

[Soc. Sec. Act § 1861(ccc)(4).]

Moratorium on new LTCHs. A moratorium on the establishment of new Medicare-participating LTCHs, the addition of LTCH satellite facilities to an existing LTCH, and any increase in the number of certified beds in existing LTCHs and LTCH satellites, applies from April 1, 2014, through September 30, 2017. The moratorium provides exceptions for the establishment of new LTCHs and LTCH satellite facilities; however, no exceptions are provided for increases in the number of certified beds in existing LTCHs and LTCH satellites. [Pathways to SGR Reform Act of 2013 (P.L. 113-67) 1206(b), as amended by Protecting Access to Medicare Act of 2014 (P.L. 113-93) § 112(b); 42 C.F.R. § 412.23(e)(6)–(8); *Letter to State Survey Agency Directors*, S&C: 15-03, Jan. 9, 2015.]

Long-Term Care Hospital PPS Payment Methodology

CMS publishes the LTCH prospective payment system (PPS) annual update in the *Federal Register* by September 1st of each year. [42 C.F.R. § 412.535; *Final rule*, 81 FR 56762, Aug. 22, 2016.] Payment under the LTCH PPS is made on a per-discharge basis. Each patient case is classified according to the principal diagnosis, secondary diagnoses, procedures performed during the stay, and discharge status of the patient. The patient's case is classified by MS-LTC-DRG, based on the relative costliness of treatment for patients in the group, similar to classification under IPPS. [42 C.F.R. § 412.513.]

The amount of the prospective payment is based on the standard federal rate, established under 42 C.F.R. § 412.523 and adjusted for the MS-LTC-DRG relative weights, differences in area wage levels, cost of living in Alaska and Hawaii, high-cost outliers, and other special payment provisions.

Productivity adjustment. Section 3401(c) of the Patient Protection and Affordable Care Act (ACA) (P.L. 111-148) amended the annual update to the standard federal rate under Soc. Sec. Act § 1886(m) to add a productivity adjustment for discharges in 2012 and later. The productivity adjustment is the same one applied to inpatient hospital services under Soc. Sec. Act § 1886(b)(3)(B)(xi)(II). The application of this productivity adjustment may result in the annual update being less than 0.0 for a year and may result in payment rates under the LTCH PPS for a year being less than such payment rates for the preceding year. [Soc. Sec. Act § 1886(m)(3).]

Also pursuant to section 3401(c) of the ACA, updates for 2010 through 2019 are subject to an "other adjustment"; the adjustment for 2017, 2018, and 2019 is 0.75 percentage point. [Soc. Sec. Act § 1886(m)(3)(A)(ii), (m)(4).]

Section 411(e) of the Medicare and CHIP Reauthorization Act of 2015 (MACRA) (P.L. 114-10) set the annual update for fiscal year 2018, after the application of these adjustments, at 1.0 percent. [Soc. Sec. Act § 1886(m)(3)(C).]

Site-neutral IPPS payment amount. Effective for discharges in cost reporting periods beginning during fiscal year 2018 or later, patients with stays longer than three days in an intensive care unit or on a ventilator for more than 96 hours will qualify for the traditional increased rate received by LTCHs. All other cases will be reimbursed at a site-neutral rate, which is the same level as an inpatient facility stay. [Soc. Sec. Act § 1886(m)(6); 42 C.F.R. § 412.522.]

For discharges during cost reporting periods beginning between October 1, 2015 and September 30, 2017, payment for discharges under this rule will be paid using a blended payment rate, determined as 50 percent of the site neutral payment rate amount and 50 percent of the standard prospective payment rate amount for the discharge. [Soc. Sec. Act § 1886(m)(6)(B); 42 C.F.R. § 412.522(c)(3).]

Patient shifting and the "25 percent rule." CMS may reduce the payments to an LTCH if more than 25 percent of its Medicare patients were transferred from hospitals co-located with the LTCH or a satellite facility (the "25 percent rule"). A legislative moratorium to the 25 percent rule applies through September 30, 2017. Grandfathered LTCHs are permanently exempt from the 25 percent rule. [21st Century Cures Act (P.L. 114-255) § 15006(a); 42 C.F.R. § 412.538.]

One-Day Payment Window

LTCHs are subject to a one-day payment window, the "24-hour rule," for preadmission services related to the inpatient stay. In other words, outpatient diagnostic services and most nonphysician services provided during the calendar day immediately preceding the date of admission to an LTCH (excluding ambulance services and maintenance renal dialysis services) are included in the standard payment. A preadmission service is related to the inpatient stay if:

(1) it is diagnostic (including clinical diagnostic laboratory tests);

(2) it is nondiagnostic when furnished on the date of the beneficiary's inpatient admission; or

(3) it is nondiagnostic when furnished on the calendar day preceding the date of the beneficiary's inpatient admission and the hospital does not attest that such service is unrelated to the beneficiary's inpatient admission.

[42 C.F.R. § 412.540.]

LTCH Outlier Payments

The high-cost outlier is an adjustment to the applicable LTCH PPS payment rate for LTCH stays with unusually high costs that exceed the typical cost for cases with a similar case-mix. It equals 80 percent of the difference between the estimated cost of the case and the outlier threshold, and it is made in addition to the applicable LTCH PPS payment rate. [42 C.F.R. § 412.525(a).]

LTCHs are paid adjusted rates for outlier patients who have short stays. Short-stay outliers are cases with a length of stay up to and including five-sixths of the geometric average length of stay for each MS-LTC-DRG. The short-stay outlier adjustment allows Medicare to reimburse LTCHs for costly short-stay outlier patients and yet pay less for cases that do not receive a full episode of care at the LTCH and should not be reimbursed at the full MS-LTC-DRG payment rate. [42 C.F.R. § 412.529(a)–(c).]

LTCH PPS Interrupted Stay Policy

An interruption of stay occurs when a Medicare inpatient is transferred upon discharge to an acute-care hospital, an inpatient rehabilitation facility (IRF), a skilled nursing facility (SNF), or the patient's home for treatment or services that are not available in the LTCH, and returns to the same LTCH. CMS has divided interruption of stay into two categories, a "three-day or less interruption of stay" and a "greater than three-day interruption of stay." [42 C.F.R. § 412.531(a); *Medicare Claims Processing Manual*, Pub. 100-04, Ch. 3, § 150.9.1.2.]

Three or fewer days. If an interruption of stay of three or fewer days occurs during an episode of care, the entire stay is paid as a single discharge from the LTCH and CMS makes only one LTC-DRG payment for all portions of a long-term care stay. The LTCH must provide services either directly or "under arrangements" with the other provider. The LTCH is responsible for paying the other provider for the costs of services. [42 C.F.R. § 412.531 (b) (1) (ii) (A).]

Greater than three-day interruption of stay. A greater than three-day interruption of stay is defined as a stay in a LTCH during which a Medicare inpatient is discharged from the LTCH to an acute-care hospital, IRF, or SNF for a period of greater than three days but returns to the LTCH within the applicable fixed-day period:

- between four and nine consecutive days for a discharge to an acute care hospital;
- between four and 27 consecutive days for a discharge to an IRF; and
- between four and 45 consecutive days for a discharge to a SNF.

[42 C.F.R. § 412.531 (a) (2) (i)–(iii).] In such cases, CMS will make one LTC-DRG payment for all portions of a long-term care stay and will separately pay the acute-care hospital, IRF, or SNF in accordance with their respective payment systems. [42 C.F.R. § 412.531 (b) (1) (ii) (B), (c).]

If, however, the applicable fixed-day time frames are exceeded, the subsequent admission to the LTCH is considered a new stay and the LTCH will receive two separate PPS payments. [42 C.F.R. § 412.531 (b) (4).] For example, if an LTCH patient is discharged to an acute-care hospital and is readmitted to the LTCH on any day up to and including the ninth day following the original day of discharge from the LTCH, one MS-LTC-DRG payment will be made. If the patient is readmitted to the LTCH from the acute-care hospital on the tenth day after the original discharge or later, Medicare will pay for the second admission as a separate stay with a second MS-LTC-DRG assignment. [42 C.F.R. § 412.531 (b) (4) (i).]

Outlier payments. Interrupted stays at an LTCH are subject to the short-stay and high-cost outlier rules. If the total number of days of a patient's stay before and following an interruption of stay is at or below five-sixths of the geometric average length of stay of the MS-LTC-DRG, CMS will make a short-stay outlier payment. An additional payment will be made if the patient's stay qualifies as a high-cost outlier. [42 C.F.R. § 412.531 (b) (2), (3).]

LTCH Quality Reporting Program

Section 3004 (a) of the ACA required the establishment of the LTCH quality reporting program (QRP). Beginning in FY 2014, LTCHs that do not report the quality data are subject to a 2.0 percentage point reduction to the annual update of the standard federal rate. [Soc. Sec. Act § 1886 (m) (5); 42 C.F.R. § § 412.523 (c) (4), 412.560 (b) (2).]

In addition, section 2 of the Improving Medicare Post-Acute Care Transformation Act of 2014 (IMPACT Act) (P.L. 113-185), required post-acute care (PAC) providers, including LTCHs, to report standardized patient assessment data, data on quality measures, and data on resource use and other measures. Data measures include: (1) functional status, cognitive function, and changes in function and cognitive function; (2) skin integrity and changes in skin integrity; (3) medication reconciliation; (4) incidence of major falls; and (4) accurately communicating the individual's health information and care preferences. LTCHs were required to begin reporting on most quality measures by October 1, 2016, and must begin reporting on patient assessment data no later than October 1, 2018. [Soc. Sec. Act § 1899B.]

For the FY 2018 payment determination and subsequent years LTCHs must report on the following measures: (1) Medicare Spending Per Beneficiary-PAC LTCH QRP; (2) Discharge to Community-PAC LTCH QRP; and (3) Potentially Preventable 30-Day Post-Dis-

¶815

charge Readmission Measure for the PAC LTCH QRP. CMS also established one new quality measure to meet the requirements of the IMPACT Act for the FY 2020 determination and subsequent years, Drug Regimen Review Conducted with Follow-Up for Identified Issues-PAC LTCH QRP. [*Final rule*, 81 FR 56762, Aug. 22, 2016.]

[¶ 820] Hospital Outpatient Services

Outpatient services are covered under Medicare Part B and paid under the outpatient prospective payment system (OPPS). Under the OPPS, predetermined amounts are paid for designated services furnished to Medicare beneficiaries. [Soc. Sec. Act § 1833(t); 42 C.F.R. § 419.2.]

The OPPS is applicable to any hospital participating in the Medicare program, except for: critical access hospitals (CAHs); hospitals located in Maryland and paid under the Maryland All-Payer Model; hospitals located outside of the 50 states, the District of Columbia, and Puerto Rico; and Indian Health Service (IHS) hospitals. [42 C.F.R. § 419.20.]

Services subject to the OPPS. CMS makes payment under the OPPS for the following services:

(1) designated hospital outpatient services;

(2) certain Medicare Part B services furnished to hospital inpatients who are either not entitled to benefits under Part A or who have exhausted their Part A benefits but are entitled to benefits under Part B of the program;

(3) partial hospitalization services furnished by community mental health centers (CMHCs);

(4) antigens, splints and casts, and the hepatitis B vaccine furnished by a home health agency (HHA) to patients who are not under an HHA plan or treatment or by a hospice program furnishing services to patients outside the hospice benefit; and

(5) an initial preventive physical examination performed within first 12 months of Part B coverage.

[42 C.F.R. § 419.21.]

Services excluded from the OPPS. 42 C.F.R. § 419.22 excludes a number of services from payment under the OPPS, except when packaged as a part of a bundled payment. Section 603 of the Bipartisan Budget Act of 2015 (P.L. 114-74) requires that certain items and services furnished by certain off-campus hospital outpatient departments will no longer be paid under the OPPS beginning January 1, 2017. These services will instead be paid under the Medicare physician fee schedule. [Soc. Sec. Act § 1833(t)(1)(B)(v); 42 C.F.R. §§ 419.22(v), 419.48(a).]

Site-of-service price transparency. To facilitate price transparency with respect to items and services for which payment may be made either to a hospital outpatient department or to an ambulatory surgical center (ASC), the HHS Secretary must, beginning in 2018, make available to the public via a searchable Internet website, with respect to an appropriate number of such items and services: (1) the estimated payment amount for the item or service under the OPPS and the ASC PPS (see ¶ 825); and (2) the estimated amount of beneficiary liability applicable to the item or service. [Soc. Sec. Act § 1834(t), as added by 21st Century Cures Act (P.L. 114-255) § 4011.]

Determining a Payment Under OPPS

The unit of payment under the OPPS is the ambulatory payment classification (APC) system. CMS assigns individual services to APCs based on similar clinical characteristics and similar costs. CMS assigns to each APC group an appropriate weighting factor to reflect the relative geometric mean costs for the services within the APC group compared to the geometric mean costs for the services in all APC groups. The APC weights are converted to payment rates through the application of a conversion factor. [Soc. Sec. Act § 1833 (t) (3), (5); 42 C.F.R. § § 419.31, 419.32 (c).]

The items and services in an APC group are those that are recognized as contributing to the cost of the procedures or services. Items and services within a group cannot be considered comparable with respect to the use of resources if the highest median cost for an item or service within the group is more than two times greater than the lowest median cost for an item or service within the group, referred to as the "two times rule." The Secretary may make an exception to the two-times limit in unusual cases such as low-volume items and services. [Soc. Sec. Act § 1833 (t) (2); 42 C.F.R. § 419.31 (a).]

To account for geographic differences in input prices, the labor portion of the payment rate is further adjusted by the hospital wage index for the area where payment is being made. [42 C.F.R. § § 419.31 (c), 419.43 (c).]

Items and services included in the APC payment rate. Within each APC, payment for dependent, ancillary, supportive, and adjunctive items and services is packaged into payment for the primary independent service. In general, these packaged costs may include, but are not limited to, the following items and services, the payment for which is packaged or conditionally packaged into the payment for the related procedures or services:

- use of an operating suite, procedure room, or treatment room;

- use of recovery room;

- observation services;

- anesthesia; certain drugs, biologics, and other pharmaceuticals; medical and surgical supplies and equipment; surgical dressings; and devices used for external reduction of fractures and dislocations;

- supplies and equipment for administering and monitoring anesthesia or sedation;

- intraocular lenses (IOLs);

- ancillary services;

- capital-related costs;

- implantable items used in connection with diagnostic x-ray tests, diagnostic laboratory tests, and other diagnostic tests;

- durable medical equipment that is implantable;

- implantable and insertable medical items and devices, including, but not limited to, prosthetic devices (other than dental) that replace all or part of an internal body organ (including colostomy bags and supplies directly related to colostomy care), including replacement of these devices;

- costs incurred to procure donor tissue other than corneal tissue;

- image guidance, processing, supervision, and interpretation services;

- intraoperative items and services;

- drugs, biologics, and radiopharmaceuticals that function as supplies when used in a diagnostic test or procedure (including, but not limited to, diagnostic radiopharmaceuticals, contrast agents, and pharmacologic stress agents);

¶820

- drugs and biologics that function as supplies when used in a surgical procedure (including, but not limited to, skin substitutes and similar products that aid wound healing and implantable biologics);

  - certain clinical diagnostic laboratory tests; and

  - certain services described by add-on codes.

[42 C.F.R. § 419.2(b).]

Hospitals subject to the OPPS are paid for certain items and services that are outside the scope of OPPS on a reasonable cost or other basis. The following costs are outside the scope of OPPS:

- direct graduate medical education;

- nursing and allied health programs;

- interns and residents not in approved teaching programs;

- teaching physicians' charges for Part B services in hospitals that elect cost-based payment for teaching physicians;

- anesthesia services furnished to hospital outpatients by qualified nonphysician anesthetists such as certified registered nurse anesthetists and anesthesiologists' assistants employed by the hospital or obtained under arrangements;

- bad debts for uncollectible deductible and coinsurance amounts;

- organ acquisition costs paid under Part B; and

- corneal tissue acquisition or procurement costs for corneal transplant procedures.

[42 C.F.R. § 419.2(c).]

Adjustments and Additional Payments Under the OPPS

Hospitals may receive payments in addition to standard OPPS payments.

Outlier payments. Medicare provides for additional "outlier" payments to hospitals when they provide exceptionally costly outpatient services. CMS makes an outlier payment when a hospital's charges, adjusted to cost, exceed a fixed multiple of the OPPS payment as adjusted by pass-through payments. [Soc. Sec. Act § 1833(t)(5); 42 C.F.R. § 419.43(d).]

To qualify for an outlier payment in calendar year (CY) 2017, the cost of a service must exceed: (1) 1.75 times the APC payment rate, and (2) a fixed dollar outlier threshold of $3,825. The outlier payment for a particular service will equal 50 percent of the amount by which the cost of furnishing the service exceeds 1.75 times the APC payment rate. [*Final rule with comment period*, 81 FR 79562, Nov. 14, 2016.] Outlier payments made to CMHCs for services provided on or after January 1, 2017, are subject to a cap, applied at the individual CMHC level, so that each CMHC's total outlier payments for the calendar year do not exceed 8 percent of that CMHC's total per diem payments for the calendar year. [42 C.F.R. § 419.43(d)(7).]

Transitional pass-through payments. The OPPS provides for additional payments, called transitional pass-through payments, for certain innovative medical devices, drugs, and biologics for a period of two to three years. CMS makes a transitional pass-through payment for the following drugs and biologics that are furnished as part of an outpatient hospital service: (1) orphan drugs; (2) cancer therapy drugs and biologics; (3) radiopharmaceutical drugs and biologic products; and (4) new medical devices, drugs, and biologics. The purpose of transitional pass-through payments is to allow for adequate payment of new and innovative technology until there is enough data to incorporate the costs for these items into the base APC group. [Soc. Sec. Act § 1833(t)(6); 42 C.F.R. §§ 419.64, 419.66.]

Certain cancer hospitals. CMS adjusts OPPS payments to certain cancer hospitals—those exempted by law from payment under the inpatient prospective payment system for covered hospital outpatient services provided in CY 2017. If a cancer hospital has a payment-to-cost ratio (PCR) for CY 2017 that is below a target PCR, the hospital will receive an additional payment so that final payment is equal to the target PCR. The target PCR is defined as the weighted average PCR for other hospitals furnishing services under the OPPS determined from available cost reports. [Soc. Sec. Act § 1833(t)(18); 42 C.F.R. § 419.43(i); *Final rule with comment period*, 81 FR 79562, Nov. 14, 2016.]

Hold-harmless status for certain cancer hospitals and children's hospitals. If payments for outpatient department services furnished by cancer hospitals and children's hospitals are lower than those they would have received under previous policies, CMS provides additional payments to make up the difference. [Soc. Sec. Act § 1833(t)(7)(D)(ii); 42 C.F.R. § 419.70(d)(3).]

Small rural hospital adjustment. Medicare makes an OPPS payment adjustment for rural sole community hospitals and essential access community hospitals. For 2017, the adjustment represents a 7.1 percent payment increase to these small rural hospitals. The adjustment is for all services and procedures paid under the OPPS, excluding separately payable drugs and biologics, devices paid under the pass-through payment policy, and items paid at charges reduced to costs. [Soc. Sec. Act § 1833(t)(13)(B); 42 C.F.R. § 419.43(g); *Final rule with comment period*, 81 FR 79562, Nov. 14, 2016.]

Copayment/Coinsurance Under the OPPS

Under the OPPS, coinsurance is defined as the percent of the Medicare-approved amount that beneficiaries pay for a service furnished in the hospital outpatient department (after they have met the Part B deductible—see ¶ 335). Copayment is defined as the set dollar amount that beneficiaries pay under the OPPS and is capped at the Part A deductible for that year. In 2017, the Part A deductible will be $1,316 per APC, meaning a beneficiary will never pay more than this amount for any outpatient procedure provided. [42 C.F.R. §§ 419.40(c), 419.41(c)(4); *Notice*, 81 FR 80060, Nov. 11, 2016.]

The coinsurance percentage is calculated as the difference between the program payment percentage and 100 percent. The coinsurance percentage in any year is defined for each APC group as the greater of the ratio of the APC group unadjusted copayment amount to the annual APC group payment rate, or 20 percent. [Soc. Sec. Act § 1833(t)(3)(B), (t)(8)(C); 42 C.F.R. § 419.40.]

The Secretary must reduce the national unadjusted coinsurance amount each year so that the effective coinsurance rate for a covered service in the year does not exceed 40 percent of the APC payment rate. For a covered service furnished in a year, the national unadjusted coinsurance amount cannot be less than 20 percent of the payment rate amount. [Soc. Sec. § 1833(t)(3)(B)(ii) and (t)(8)(C); 42 C.F.R. § 419.41(c)(4)(iii).]

The coinsurance amount for the APC or APCs for a drug or biologic furnished on the same day is aggregated with the coinsurance amount for the APC that reflects the administration of the drug or biologic furnished on that day and treated as the coinsurance amount for one APC. [42 C.F.R. § 419.41(c)(4)(i)(B).]

Coinsurance for new procedures. APCs for new procedures may be adopted when the new procedures do not fit well into another APC. When an APC is added that consists of HCPCS codes for which there was no 1996 charge data to calculate the unadjusted coinsurance amount, coinsurance is based on the minimum unadjusted coinsurance, which is 20 percent of the APC payment amount. Additional payments for outlier cases and for certain medical devices, drugs, and biologics, and transitional corridor payments will not affect the coinsurance amounts. [Soc. Sec. § 1833(t)(3)(B)(iii); *Final rule*, 65 FR 18434, 18487, April 7, 2000.]

Hospital election to reduce coinsurance. A hospital may elect to reduce coinsurance for any or all APC groups on a calendar-year basis by selecting the minimum coinsurance amount; however, it may not reduce coinsurance for some, but not all, services within the same APC group. If a hospital reduces a coinsurance amount, it must notify its Medicare administrative contractor by December 1 of the preceding year by documenting the applicable APCs and the coinsurance amount that the hospital has selected. The reduced coinsurance may not be less than 20 percent of the APC payment rate. The hospital may advertise that it has reduced the level of coinsurance identifying the specific outpatient services to which the reduction is applicable. Coinsurance reductions are not allowed in physicians' offices or other ambulatory settings. [Soc. Sec. Act § 1833(t)(8)(B); 42 C.F.R. § 419.42.]

Coinsurance waiver for preventive services. Deductibles and copayments for preventive services paid under the OPPS are waived. Preventive services are defined as: screening and preventive services currently listed in Soc. Sec. Act § 1861(ww)(2); preventive "wellness" physical examinations; and personalized preventive plan services. For coinsurance to be waived, preventive services must be given a grade of "A" or "B" by the United States Preventive Services Task Force. [Soc. Sec. Act § 1833(a), (b)(1).] See ¶ 369 for a discussion of Part B coverage of preventive services.

Hospital Outpatient Quality Reporting Program

Providers of outpatient services must report quality of care data to avoid a 2.0 percent decrease in their annual market basket payment adjustments as part of the Hospital Outpatient Quality Reporting (OQR) Program. [Soc. Sec. Act § 1833(t)(17)(a)(i).]

Validation requirement. To ensure that hospitals are accurately reporting quality of care measures for chart-abstracted data, CMS may validate one or more measures by reviewing documentation of patient encounters submitted by selected participating hospitals. CMS requires hospitals to achieve a minimum 75 percent reliability score based on this validation process to receive the full OPPS update. [42 C.F.R. § 419.46(e).]

Quality measures. For the payment determination year of CY 2020 and later, CMS adopted a total of seven new measures, two of which are claims-based measures and five of which are Outpatient and Ambulatory Surgery Consumer Assessment of Healthcare Providers and Systems (OAS CAHPS) survey-based measures. The two claims-based measures are Admissions and Emergency Department (ED) Visits for Patients Receiving Outpatient Chemotherapy Measure and Hospital Visits After Hospital Outpatient Surgery Measure. [*Final rule with comment period*, 81 FR 79562, Nov. 14, 2016.]

Separately Payable Drugs, Biologics, and Radiopharmaceuticals

The costs of drugs, biologics, and radiopharmaceuticals are generally included in the payment for the procedure during which they were administered. For CY 2017, drugs, biologics, and radiopharmaceuticals with a per-administration cost less than or equal to $110 will be packaged, and items with an estimated per-administration cost greater than $110 will receive separate payment (the packaging threshold was $100 in 2016). [Soc. Sec. Act § 1833(t)(16)(B); *Final rule with comment period*, 81 FR 79562, Nov. 14, 2016.]

In CY 2017, CMS will pay for separately payable drugs and biologics at the average sale price (ASP) plus 6 percent. [*Final rule with comment period*, 81 FR 79562, Nov. 14, 2016.]

Specified covered outpatient drugs. Payment for "specified covered hospital outpatient department drugs" must be based on the average acquisition cost of the drug for a certain year, i.e., the adjusted ASP. A "specified covered outpatient department drug" is a covered outpatient drug for which a separate APC has been established and that is (1) a radiopharmaceutical or (2) a drug or biologic that qualified for "pass-through" payments on or before December 31, 2002. The term "specified covered outpatient department drug" does not include a drug or biologic for which payment was first made on or after January 1, 2003, under the transitional pass-through payment provision in Soc. Sec. Act § 1833(t)(6); a drug or biologic for which a temporary HCPCS code has not been assigned; or, during 2004 and 2005, an orphan drug. [Soc. Sec. Act § 1833(t)(14); *Final rule*, 80 FR 70298, Nov. 6, 2015.]

[¶ 825] Ambulatory Surgical Centers

CMS pays for surgical procedures provided in freestanding or hospital-based ambulatory surgical centers (ASCs) using a payment system based on the hospital outpatient prospective payment system (OPPS). Under the system, CMS reimburses ASCs for any covered individual "surgical procedure." ASC covered surgical procedures are those that are separately paid under the OPPS, that would not pose a significant risk to beneficiary safety, and for which standard medical practice dictates that the beneficiary would not typically be expected to require active medical monitoring and care at midnight following the procedure. [Soc. Sec. Act § 1833(i)(1), (2); 42 C.F.R. § 416.166.]

Like the OPPS, the ASC payment system sets payments for individual services using a set of relative weights, a conversion factor (or average payment amount), and adjustments for geographic differences in input prices. Medicare pays ASCs 80 percent of the lesser of: (1) the actual charge for the services; or (2) the geographically adjusted payment rate determined by CMS. The beneficiary pays the remaining 20 percent, as the Part B deductible and coinsurance amount applies to services provided at an ASC. [42 C.F.R. §§416.167, 416.171, 416.172.]

Medicare pays for the related physician services under the physician fee schedule (see ¶ 855). [42 C.F.R. § 416.163(b).] See ¶ 386 for a discussion of Medicare coverage of ASC services.

Reporting of ASC Quality Data

Under the ASC quality reporting (ASCQR) program, ASCs must retain and report data on several measures of the quality of care provided. ASCs that do not maintain and report this data as required will have the increase in their payments reduced by 2 percent. [Soc. Sec. Act § 1833(i)(2)(D)(iv), (i)(7)(A); 42 C.F.R. § 416.300.]

In the calendar year 2017 OPPS final rule, CMS decided not to add any new measures for the 2018 and 2019 payment determination. For the calendar year (CY) 2020 payment determination and later, ASCs must collect and report quality of care data for the following measures: (1) patient burn; (2) patient fall; (3) wrong site, wrong side, wrong patient, wrong procedure, wrong implant; (4) hospital transfer/admission; (5) prophylactic intravenous antibiotic timing; (6) safe surgery checklist use; (7) ASC facility volume data on selected surgical procedures; (8) influenza vaccination coverage among health care personnel; (9) endoscopy/polyp surveillance: appropriate follow-up interval for normal colonoscopy in average risk patients; (10) endoscopy/polyp surveillance for colonoscopy intervals for patients with a history of adenomatus polyps; (11) improvement in patient's visual function within 90 days following cataract surgery; (12) facility seven-day risk-standardized hospital visit rate after outpatient colonoscopy; (13) normothermia outcome; (14) unplanned anterior vitrectomy; and (15) five measures collected using the Outpatient and Ambulatory Surgical

Center Consumer Assessment of Healthcare Providers and Systems (OAS CAHPS) survey. [*Final rule with comment period*, 81 FR 79562, Nov. 14, 2016.]

[¶ 827] Hospice Reimbursement

With the exception of payment for physician services, Medicare payment for hospice care is made at one of four predetermined rates for each day that a Medicare beneficiary is under the care of the hospice. Because the rates are prospective, there are no retroactive adjustments other than the application of the statutory "caps" on overall payments made at the end of the fiscal year (FY) and on payments for inpatient care. The rate paid for any particular day varies depending on the level of care furnished to the beneficiary. The four levels of care into which each day of care is classified are:

> (1) Routine Home Care—Revenue code 0651;
>
> (2) Continuous Home Care—Revenue code 0652;
>
> (3) Inpatient Respite Care—Revenue code 0655; and
>
> (4) General Inpatient Care (Nonrespite)—Revenue code 0656.

For each day that a Medicare beneficiary is under the care of a hospice, the hospice is reimbursed an amount applicable to the type and intensity of the services furnished to the beneficiary for that day. [42 C.F.R. § 418.302(a), (b); *Medicare Claims Processing Manual*, Pub. 100-04, Ch. 11, § 30.1.]

The hospice payment on a continuous care day varies depending on the number of hours of continuous services provided. The continuous home care rate is divided by 24 to yield an hourly rate. The number of hours of continuous care provided during a continuous home care day is then multiplied by the hourly rate to yield the continuous home care payment for that day. A minimum of eight hours of care must be furnished on a particular day to qualify for the continuous home care rate. [42 C.F.R. § 418.302(e)(4).]

On any day on which the beneficiary is not an inpatient, the hospice is paid the routine home care rate, unless the patient receives continuous care for at least eight hours. Subject to certain limitations, on any day on which the beneficiary is an inpatient in an approved facility for inpatient care, the appropriate inpatient rate (general or respite) is paid depending on the category of care furnished. [42 C.F.R. § 418.302(e)(3) and (4), (f).]

Annual update of payment rates. The hospice payment update percentage for FY 2017 is 2.1 percent. This percentage is based on an estimated 2.7 percent inpatient hospital market basket update, reduced by a 0.3 percentage point productivity adjustment and by 0.3 percentage point mandated by section 3401(g) of the Patient Protection and Affordable Care Act (ACA) (P.L. 111-148). [Soc. Sec. Act § 1814(i)(1)(C); *Final rule*, 81 FR 52144, Aug. 5, 2016.]

CMS publishes general hospice payment rates annually to be used for revenue codes 0651, 0652, 0655, and 0656. These rates must then be adjusted by the Medicare administrative contractor based on the beneficiary's locality. [42 C.F.R. § 418.306; Pub. 100-04, Ch. 11, § 30.2.]

Hospice per diem payment rates for the FY 2017 period from October 1, 2016, through September 30, 2017, for hospices that submit quality data, are as follows: continuous home care $964.63, inpatient respite care $170.97, and general inpatient care (non-respite) $734.94. FY 2017 hospice payment rates for routine home care for hospices that submit quality data are $190.55 for days 1 through 60 and $149.82 for days 61 and later. [*Final rule*, 81 FR 52144, Aug. 5, 2016.]

Aggregate cap amount. The total amount of payments made for hospice care provided by (or under arrangements made by) a hospice program for an accounting year may not exceed the "cap amount" for the year multiplied by the number of Medicare beneficiaries in the hospice program in that year. [Soc. Sec. Act § 1814(i)(2)(A); 42 C.F.R. § 418.309.]

Until FY 2016, the cap year was from November 1 to October 31 of the following year. Starting with FY 2017, the cap accounting year is aligned with the federal FY; therefore, the 2017 cap year started on October 1, 2016, and will end on September 30, 2017. The hospice aggregate cap amount for the cap year ending September 30, 2017, is set at $28,404.99. The hospice must refund any payments in excess of the cap. [42 C.F.R. § 418.309; *Final rule*, 81 FR 52144, Aug. 5, 2016; *Medicare Benefit Policy Manual*, Pub. 100-02, Ch. 9, § 90.2.]

Hospice Quality Reporting Program

Beginning with FY 2014, CMS will reduce the hospice market basket update by 2.0 percentage points for any hospice that does not comply with quality data submission requirements. Hospices are required to complete and submit an admission Hospice Item Set (HIS) and a discharge HIS for each patient admission to hospice, regardless of payer or patient age. [Soc. Sec. Act § 1814(i)(5); 42 C.F.R. § 418.312.]

In the FY 2017 final rule, CMS established two new updates to the Hospice Quality Reporting Program (HQRP) to go into effect beginning with the FY 2019 payment determination. The first measure set, Hospice Visits When Death is Imminent, addresses whether patient and caregiver needs were met by hospice staff in the last days of a patient's life. The first measure of the set assesses the percentage of patients that were visited by providers at least once in the last three days of life, while the second measure assesses the percentage that received at least two visits from social workers, chaplains or spiritual counselors, licensed practical nurses, or hospice aides in the last seven days of life. The second measure set, Hospice and Palliative Care Composite Process Measure—Comprehensive Assessment at Admission, focuses on the hospice admission assessment by evaluating the number of individual care processes completed upon admission for each patient stay. [*Final rule*, 81 FR 52144, Aug. 5, 2016.]

Reimbursement for Hospice Services Performed by Physicians

The following services performed by hospice physicians and nurse practitioners are included in the hospice rates described above: (1) general supervisory services of the medical director; and (2) participation in the establishment of plans of care, supervision of care and services, periodic review and updating of plans of care, and establishment of governing policies by the physician member of the interdisciplinary group. [42 C.F.R. § 418.304(a).]

For other services, the contractor pays the hospice an amount equivalent to 100 percent of the physician fee schedule (see ¶ 855) for those physician services furnished by hospice employees or under arrangements with the hospice. [42 C.F.R. § 418.304(a).]

Independent attending physician. Services of the patient's attending physician, if he or she is not an employee of the hospice or providing services under arrangements with the hospice, are not considered hospice services. These services are reimbursed under the physician fee schedule. [Soc. Sec. Act § 1861(dd)(2)(B); 42 C.F.R. § 418.304(c); Pub. 100-04, Ch. 11, § 40.1.3.]

Nurse practitioners. Medicare pays for attending physician services provided by nurse practitioners to Medicare beneficiaries who have elected the hospice benefit and who have selected a nurse practitioner as their attending physician, even if the nurse practitioner is not a hospice employee. Payment for nurse practitioner services are made at 85 percent of the physician fee schedule amount. [42 C.F.R. § 418.304(e).]

Care plan oversight services. Medicare makes separate payment for physician care plan oversight services under the following conditions: (1) the services require recurrent physician supervision of therapy involving 30 or more minutes of the physician's time per month; and (2) payment is made to only one physician per patient for services furnished during a calendar month period. The physician must have furnished a service requiring a face-to-face encounter with the patient at least once during the six-month period before the month for which care plan oversight payment is first billed. [42 C.F.R. § 414.39(b)(1), (b)(2).]

Payment for pre-election evaluation. A physician on staff of a hospice may be paid to evaluate a patient who has not yet elected hospice care to determine the patient's need for pain and symptom management and for hospice care and to help with advance care planning. [Soc. Sec. Act § 1812(a)(5); 42 C.F.R. § 418.304(d).]

[¶ 830] Home Health Agencies

Under the home health prospective payment system (HH PPS), a standardized payment, subject to several adjustments, is made for each 60-day episode of care a beneficiary receives from a home health agency (HHA). [Soc. Sec. Act § 1895; 42 C.F.R. § 484.205(a).] See ¶ 250–¶ 268 for a discussion of Part A coverage of home health services.

Split percentage payment. Generally, payment for a home health episode of care is made in two stages. The HHA may make a request for anticipated payment (RAP) at the beginning of the episode to receive a percentage of the amount expected to be payable for the episode. The balance, including any adjustments, is paid at the end of the episode of care. The anticipated payment is 60 percent for an initial episode of care and 50 percent for each subsequent episode. [42 C.F.R. § 484.205(b).]

If a physician-signed plan of care is not available at the time the HHA requests an initial payment, it can be based on verbal orders from a physician that are copied into the plan of care, including a description of the patient's condition and the services to be provided by the HHA. An accompanying attestation must be signed and dated by the registered nurse or qualified therapist responsible for furnishing or supervising the ordered service in the plan of care. [42 C.F.R. § 409.43(c).]

The remainder of the adjusted payment will be made when care or the episode is completed. Before submitting that claim, HHAs are required to: (1) have received a physician's certification of the beneficiary's homebound status and need for home care; and (2) have a plan of care signed by a physician. [42 C.F.R. § 409.43(c)(3); *Medicare Claims Processing Manual*, Pub. 100-04, Ch. 10, § 10.1.10.4.]

2017 payment rates. The calendar year (CY) 2017 national standardized 60-day episode payment rate for an HHA that submits quality data is $2,989.97; the rate for an HHA that does not submit quality data is $2,931.63. These rates include rebasing adjustments to the national, standardized 60-day episode payment rate, the national per-visit rates, and the nonroutine medical supply (NMS) conversion factor, as required by section 3131 of the Patient Protection and Affordable Care Act (ACA) (P.L. 111-148). [Soc. Sec. Act § 1895(b)(3)(A)(iii); *Final rule*, 81 FR 76702, Nov. 3, 2016.]

Adjustments to Standard HH PPS Payment

The base unit of payment under the Medicare HH PPS is a national, standardized 60-day episode payment rate. CMS adjusts the national, standardized 60-day episode payment rate by a case-mix relative weight to explain the relative resource utilization of different patients and a wage index value based on the site of service for the beneficiary. The basic pay rate per 60 days of care is subject to adjustments based on: (1) low utilization; (2) a partial period of care; and (3) outlier visits. [Soc. Sec. Act § 1895(b); 42 C.F.R. § § 484.205, 484.220.]

Case-mix adjustment. The case-mix index is a scale that measures the relative difference in resource intensity among different groups in the clinical model. It factors for significant variation in costs among different units of services. [Soc. Sec. Act § 1895(b)(4); 42 C.F.R. § 484.220.]

Outlier adjustment. The outlier adjustment provides additional payment to an HHA when the cost of providing care to a beneficiary exceeds a threshold amount. The outlier payment is a proportion of the amount of estimated costs beyond a threshold defined by CMS. The total amount of outlier payments to a specific HHA for a year may not exceed 10 percent of the total payments to the specific agency under the HH PPS for the year. [Soc. Sec. Act § 1895(b)(5); 42 C.F.R. § § 484.205(e), 484.240.]

Partial episode payment adjustment. An HHA receives a partial period of care adjustment if a 60-day episode is interrupted by an intervening event, such as (1) a beneficiary-elected transfer to another HHA; or (2) discharge with goals met or no expectation of return to home health and the beneficiary is readmitted to home health during the 60-day episode. The original 60-day episode payment is adjusted to reflect the length of time the beneficiary remained under the care of the original HHA based on the first billable visit date through and including the last billable visit date. [42 C.F.R. § § 484.205(d), 484.235.]

Low-utilization payment adjustment. A low-utilization payment adjustment (LUPA) applies to beneficiaries who receive four or fewer visits during a 60-day period. LUPA episodes that occur as the only episode or as an initial episode in a sequence of adjacent episodes are adjusted by applying an additional amount to the LUPA payment before adjusting for area wage differences. [42 C.F.R. § § 484.205(c), 484.230.]

Home Health Quality Reporting Program

An HHA must submit data on health care quality to CMS or its home health market basket update will be reduced by 2 percentage points. The reduction applies to reimbursement for the calendar year for which measures were not reported. [Soc. Sec. Act § 1895(b)(3)(B)(v)(I), (II); 42 C.F.R. § § 484.225, 484.250(a).]

HHAs submit Outcome and Assessment Information Set (OASIS) assessments and Home Health Care Consumer Assessment of Healthcare Providers and Systems Survey (HHCAHPS) data to meet the quality reporting requirements, and a subset of the home health quality measures is publicly reported on the Home Health Compare website, http://www.medicare.gov/homehealthcompare/. For CY 2017, CMS will continue to use an HHA's submission of the OASIS data as one form of quality data to meet the requirement that the HHA submit data appropriate for the measurement of health care quality. [*Final rule*, 81 FR 76702, Nov. 3, 2016.]

HHAs that become Medicare certified on or after May 31 of the preceding year are excluded from the OASIS quality reporting requirement and any payment penalty for quality reporting purposes for the following year. Therefore, HHAs that are certified on or after May 31, 2016, are not subject to the 2 percentage point reduction to their market basket update for CY 2017. [*Final rule*, 81 FR 76702, Nov. 3, 2016.]

Pay-for-reporting performance requirement for OASIS quality data. To meet the quality reporting requirements of Soc. Sec. Act § 1895(b)(3)(B)(v) for the reporting period of July 1, 2016 through June 30, 2017, an HHA must score at least 80 percent on the quality assessments only metric of OASIS. For the reporting period of July 1, 2017, through June 30,

2018, and later, an HHA must score at 90 percent on the quality assessments only metric. [*Final rule*, 81 FR 76702, Nov. 3, 2016.]

IMPACT Act. Under the Improving Medicare Post-Acute Care Transformation Act of 2014 (IMPACT Act) (P.L. 113-185), the HHS Secretary must require post-acute care (PAC) providers, including HHAs, to report standardized patient assessment data, data on quality measures, and data on resource use and other measures. Data measures include: (1) functional status, cognitive function, and changes in function and cognitive function; (2) skin integrity and changes in skin integrity; (3) medication reconciliation; (4) incidence of major falls; and (4) accurately communicating the individual's health information and care preferences. [Soc. Sec. Act § 1899B.]

HHAs must begin reporting on certain data by January 1, 2017. An HHA that fails to submit the required data will have its market basket update reduced by 2 percent. [Soc. Sec. Act § 1899B.]

Value-based purchasing. Beginning on January 1, 2016, all Medicare-certified HHAs in selected states will be required to participate in a HH value-based purchasing (HHVBP) model, which requires these entities to compete for payment adjustments under the current PPS reimbursement schedule based on quality performance. The HHVBP model allows for the flexibility to incorporate the IMPACT Act measures in a post-acute care setting. [42 C.F.R. § § 484.300–484.330.]

Home Health Consolidated Billing

All Medicare-covered home health services listed in section 1861(m) of the Social Security Act and ordered by the physician in a plan of care must be billed to Medicare by the HHA that established a 60-day home health episode of care (see ¶ 250). [Soc. Sec. Act § 1842(b)(6)(F); *Medicare Benefit Policy Manual*, Pub. 100-02, Ch. 7, § 40.]

Home Health Advance Beneficiary Notices and Demand Billing

Whenever an HHA believes that home health services ordered by a physician will not be covered by Medicare, the HHA must give the patient oral and written notice of: (1) the extent to which payment may be expected from Medicare, Medicaid, or any other federally funded or aided program known to the HHA; (2) the charges for services that will not be covered by Medicare; (3) the charges that the individual may have to pay; and (4) any changes with respect to items (1) through (3). [42 C.F.R. § 484.10(e).]

An HHA may seek denials for entire claims from Medicare in cases when it knows that all services will not be covered by Medicare. To inform beneficiaries about possible noncovered charges HHAs must use the ABN of Noncoverage, CMS-R-131, and the Home Health Change of Care Notice (HHCCN). [Pub. 100-04, Ch. 30, § § 50.1, 60.1.]

HHAs must use the HHCCN to provide notice to a beneficiary on the first occasion that a "triggering event" occurs. Triggering events include when the HHA: (1) reduces or stops an item and/or service during a spell of illness while continuing others, including when one home health discipline ends but others continue; or (2) ends delivery of all services. [Pub. 100-04, Ch. 30, § 60.3.]

[¶ 835] Skilled Nursing Facilities

Skilled nursing facilities (SNFs) are paid under a prospective payment system (PPS) on a case-mix adjusted, per diem basis. The payment rates represent payment in full (subject to applicable coinsurance) for all routine, ancillary, and capital-related costs associated with furnishing inpatient SNF services to Medicare beneficiaries, other than costs associated with approved educational activities. [Soc. Sec. Act § 1888(e); 42 C.F.R. § 413.335.]

Services and Items Included in SNF PPS

The SNF PPS covers extended care services furnished to an individual after discharge from a hospital in which he or she was an inpatient for not less than three consecutive days, and transfer to a SNF. A SNF is required to submit consolidated Medicare claims for almost all of the services that a resident receives during the course of a covered Part A stay. SNFs are also responsible for billing for physical and occupational therapy and speech-language pathology services that a resident receives during a noncovered stay. With the below exceptions, all items and services furnished by a SNF are paid under the PPS. [Soc. Sec. Act §§ 1842(b)(6)(E), 1861(i), 1862(a)(18), 1888(e)(2)(A).]

Exclusions. The per diem rate does not cover the following costs, for which separate Part B claims must be made:

(1) physician services furnished to individual SNF residents;

(2) certain nurse practitioner, clinical nurse specialist, or physician assistant services;

(3) services of certified nurse-midwives, qualified psychologists, clinical social workers, or certified registered nurse anesthetists;

(4) certain dialysis services (home dialysis supplies and equipment, self-care home dialysis support services, institutional dialysis services and supplies, renal dialysis services), erythropoietin, and ambulance services furnished to an individual in conjunction with renal dialysis services;

(5) telehealth services using the SNF as the originating site;

(6) certain chemotherapy items and administrative services, and radioisotope services;

(7) certain customized prosthetic devices delivered to an inpatient for use during a SNF stay and intended for use after discharge; and

(8) services provided by a rural health clinic (RHC) or a federally qualified health center (FQHC), if the services would have been excluded if furnished by a physician or practitioner who was not affiliated with a RHC or FQHC.

[Soc. Sec. Act § 1888(e)(2)(A)(ii)–(iv).]

FY 2017 SNF PPS Payments

The SNF rate increased 2.4 percent for fiscal year (FY) 2017. The adjusted market basket growth rate of 2.7 percent was reduced by 0.3 percent, in accordance with the multifactor productivity adjustment. The rate was not reduced for forecast error correction. CMS estimates that the rate adjustment will result in an increase of $920 million in aggregate payments to SNFs during FY 2017. [*Final rule*, 81 FR 51969, Aug. 6, 2016.]

Payment for residents with AIDS. SNF payment rates include a special adjustment that is intended to cover the additional services required for any SNF resident with HIV/AIDS—a 128 percent increase in the PPS per diem payment. [Soc. Sec. Act § 1888(e)(12)(A); *Final rule*, 81 FR 51969, Aug. 6, 2016.]

SNF Quality Reporting Program

SNFs are required to submit quality measures and standardized patient assessment data to CMS. SNFs that fail to submit the required quality data to CMS will be subject to a 2 percentage point reduction to the annual market basket percentage update factor for fiscal years beginning with FY 2018. [Soc. Sec. Act §§ 1888(e)(6), 1899B.]

¶835

Measures. Any payment reductions that are taken will begin approximately one year after the end of the data submission period for that FY and approximately two years after CMS first adopts the measure for the SNF quality reporting program (QRP). CMS adopted three measures for the FY 2018 SNF QRP related to (1) the percent of residents with pressure ulcers that are new or worsened; (2) percent of residents experiencing one or more falls with major injury; and (3) percent of patients with an admission and discharge functional assessment and a care plan that addresses function. [*Final rule*, 81 FR 51969, Aug. 6, 2016.]

Reports. Beginning October 1, 2016, SNFs will receive quarterly confidential reports from the HHS Secretary regarding their performance on the hospital readmission measures. By October 1, 2017, the HHS Secretary must post information on SNFs' performance with respect to these measures on the Nursing Home Compare Medicare website. SNFs will have the opportunity to review and submit corrections to the information before it is made public. [Soc. Sec. Act § 1888(g).]

Value-based purchasing program. The HHS Secretary established a SNF value-based purchasing (VBP) program beginning with FY 2019 under which value-based incentive payments are made to SNFs based on performance. The SNF VBP will use the Skilled Nursing Facility 30-Day All-Cause Readmission Measure (SNFRM) to measure and rank SNF performance. High-measuring SNFs will receive an incentive payment. Beginning in 2019, the achievement threshold for quality under the VBP program will be set as the 25th percentile of achievement on VBP program measures. Additionally, CMS set January 1, 2017, through December 31, 2017, as the performance period for the FY 2019 SNF VBP Program. [Soc. Sec. Act § 1888(h); *Final rule*, 81 FR 51969, Aug. 6, 2016.]

Resource Utilization Groups and Minimum Data Set

Resource Utilization Groups (RUG) is a system used to classify SNF residents into mutually exclusive groups based on clinical, functional, and resource-based criteria. RUGs are the basis for the relative payment weights used both for standardization of the SNF PPS rates and subsequently to establish case-mix adjustments to SNF PPS rates for patients with different service use. Care provided directly to, or for, a patient is represented by an index score based on the amount of staff time associated with each group, weighted by salary levels. Each RUG is assigned an index score that represents the amount of nursing time and rehabilitation (therapy) time associated with caring for patients who qualify for the group. RUG IV was finalized in the SNF PPS update for FY 2011 and became effective October 1, 2010. [*Notice*, 75 FR 42886, July 22, 2010.]

RUG IV includes 66 classification groups based on data collected in 2006 and 2007 during the Staff Time and Resource Intensity Verification (STRIVE) study, which was done to identify the level of staffing resources needed to provide quality care to nursing home patients. To determine the appropriate payment rate, SNFs classify each of their patients into a RUG IV group based on assessment data from the Minimum Data Set (MDS) 3.0. [*Final rule*, 74 FR 40288, Aug. 11, 2009.]

Minimum Data Set. MDS 3.0 is used by nursing homes to conduct functional assessments of SNF residents. To determine appropriate payment rates, SNFs use the functional assessments to classify their residents into RUG IV groups. [*Final rule*, 74 FR 40288, Aug. 11, 2009; *Proposed rule*, 74 FR 22208, May 12, 2009; Medicare and Medicaid Extenders Act of 2010 (MMEA) (P.L. 111-309) § 202.]

Swing-Bed Facilities

Swing-bed hospitals have agreements with HHS that allow their inpatient hospital beds to be used for services that would be considered extended care services if provided by a SNF. Swing-bed facilities, including swing-bed rural hospitals, are reimbursed under the SNF

PPS. All updates to rates and wage indices that apply under SNF PPS apply to all swing-bed hospitals. [Soc. Sec. Act § 1888(e)(7).] In addition, all non-critical access hospital (CAH) swing-bed rural hospitals are paid under the SNF PPS, so all rates and wage indexes outlined for the SNF PPS also apply to all non-CAH swing-bed rural hospitals. [Soc. Sec. Act § 1888(e)(7); 42 C.F.R. § 413.114.]

All non-CAH swing-bed rural hospitals are required to complete an MDS 3.0 swing-bed assessment limited to certain demographic, payment, and quality items. [*Final rule*, 74 FR 40288, Aug. 11, 2009.]

[¶ 837] Inpatient Rehabilitation Facilities

An inpatient rehabilitation facility (IRF) is a hospital or hospital unit that has been excluded from the inpatient hospital prospective payment system (IPPS) and serves an inpatient population requiring intensive rehabilitation services for treatment. Patients must require physical and/or occupational therapy, along with other active and ongoing therapeutic intervention of multiple-therapy disciplines such as speech-language pathology or prosthetics/orthotics therapy. [Soc. Sec. Act § 1886(j); 42 C.F.R. §§ 412.23(b), 412.622(a)(3).]

IRF Patient Assessment Instrument

IRFs must use the IRF patient assessment instrument (IRF-PAI) to assess each Medicare Part A fee-for-service and Medicare Advantage IRF patient upon admission and discharge. [Soc. Sec. Act § 1886(j)(2)(D); 42 C.F.R. §§ 412.604(c), 412.606.] The admission assessment is used to place a patient in a case-mix group (CMG). Each CMG is a functional-related group, determined by distinguishing classes of IRF patient discharges on the basis of impairment, age, comorbidities, functional capability of the patient, and other factors that may improve the ability of the functional-related groups to estimate variations in resource use. The CMG determines the base payment rate that the IRF receives for the Medicare-covered Part A services furnished by the IRF during the beneficiary's episode of care. [Soc. Sec. Act § 1886(j)(2); 42 C.F.R. § 412.620.]

IRFs must electronically report patient assessment data for all admission and discharge assessment data, including any interruption in stay data, to CMS. [42 C.F.R. §§ 412.614(b)–(c), 412.618(b).]

IRF Compliance Threshold

One criterion that Medicare uses to classify a hospital or unit of a hospital as an IRF is that a minimum percentage (known as a compliance threshold) of the facility's total inpatient population must require intensive rehabilitative services for the treatment of at least one of 13 medical conditions. The IRF must serve an inpatient population of whom at least 60 percent required intensive rehabilitation services for treatment of one or more of the following conditions:

    (1) stroke;

    (2) spinal cord injury;

    (3) congenital deformity;

    (4) amputation;

    (5) major multiple trauma;

    (6) hip fracture;

    (7) brain injury;

    (8) neurological disorders, including multiple sclerosis, motor neuron diseases, polyneuropathy, muscular dystrophy, and Parkinson's disease;

(9) burns;

(10) active, polyarticular rheumatoid arthritis, psoriatic arthritis, and seronegative arthropathies resulting in significant functional impairment of ambulation and other activities of daily living that have not improved after an appropriate, aggressive, and sustained course of outpatient therapy services or services in other less intensive rehabilitation settings immediately preceding the inpatient rehabilitation admission or that result from a systemic disease activation immediately before admission, but have the potential to improve with more intensive rehabilitation;

(11) systemic vasculidities with joint inflammation, resulting in significant functional impairment of ambulation and other activities of daily living that have not improved after an appropriate, aggressive, and sustained course of outpatient therapy services or services in other less intensive rehabilitation settings immediately preceding the inpatient rehabilitation admission or that result from a systemic disease activation immediately before admission, but have the potential to improve with more intensive rehabilitation;

(12) severe or advanced osteoarthritis (osteoarthrosis or degenerative joint disease) involving two or more major weight-bearing joints (elbow, shoulders, hips, or knees, but not counting a joint with a prosthesis) with joint deformity and substantial loss of range of motion, atrophy of muscles surrounding the joint, and significant functional impairment of ambulation and other activities of daily living that have not improved after the patient has participated in an appropriate, aggressive, and sustained course of outpatient therapy services or services in other less intensive rehabilitation settings immediately preceding the inpatient rehabilitation admission but have the potential to improve with more intensive rehabilitation; or

(13) knee or hip joint replacement, or both, during an acute hospitalization immediately preceding the inpatient rehabilitation stay and also meeting one or more of the following specific criteria: (1) the patient underwent bilateral knee or bilateral hip joint replacement surgery during the acute hospital admission immediately preceding the IRF admission; (2) the patient is extremely obese with a Body Mass Index of at least 50 at the time of admission to the IRF; or (3) the patient is age 85 or older at the time of admission to the IRF.

[42 C.F.R. §§ 412.23(b), 412.29(b).]

IRF PPS Payment Rate

Under the IRF PPS, IRFs receive a predetermined amount per discharge for inpatient services furnished to Medicare Part A beneficiaries. PPS rates encompass the inpatient operating costs and capital costs, including routine and ancillary costs, of furnishing covered rehabilitation services. In addition to payments based on prospective payment rates, IRFs receive payments for the bad debts of Medicare beneficiaries and a payment amount per unit for blood clotting factor provided to Medicare inpatients who have hemophilia. Payment rates are calculated using relative weights to account for variations in resource needs in CMGs. [Soc. Sec. Act § 1886(j)(3)(A); 42 C.F.R. § 412.622.]

Payment adjustments. Facility-level adjustments include area wage adjustments and adjustments for facilities located in rural areas, for treating low-income patients, and for teaching facilities. CMS makes additional payments for outlier cases that incur extraordinarily high costs. [Soc. Sec. Act § 1886(j)(3)(A), (4); 42 C.F.R. § 412.624; *Medicare Claims Processing Manual*, Pub. 100-04, Ch. 3, §§ 140.2.4, 140.2.5.]

2017 update. For fiscal year (FY) 2017, IRF payment rates will increase 1.65 percent, about $145 million. The FY 2017 update reflects a market basket increase of 2.7 percent less a 0.3 percent productivity adjustment and a 0.75 percentage point legislative reduction. Applying the combined budget neutrality factor for the 2017 wage index and the labor-related share results in a standard payment conversion factor of $15,708 for FY 2017, up from $15,478 in FY 2016. The high-cost outlier threshold in FY 2017 is decreased to $7,984 from $8,658 in FY 2016, which will maintain estimated outlier payments at 3 percent of all cases. [*Final rule*, 81 FR 52056, Aug. 5, 2016.]

IRF Quality Reporting Program

Pursuant to section 3004 of the Patient Protection and Affordable Care Act (ACA) (P.L. 111-148), CMS implemented a quality data program for providers paid under the IRF PPS. IRFs that fail to successfully participate in the IRF quality reporting program (QRP) receive a 2.0 percent payment reduction in their IRF market basket update, beginning in FY 2014. This could result in payment decreases for non-complying IRFs if the IRF payment update is less than 2.0 percent in any given year. [Soc. Sec. Act § 1886(j)(7); 42 C.F.R. § 412.634; Pub. 100-04, Ch. 3, § 140.2.11.]

Further, under section 2 of the Improving Medicare Post-Acute Care Transformation Act of 2014 (IMPACT Act) (P.L. 113-185), the HHS Secretary must require IRFs to report standardized patient assessment data, data on quality measures, and data on resource use and other measures. Data measures include: (1) functional status, cognitive function, and changes in function and cognitive function; (2) skin integrity and changes in skin integrity; (3) medication reconciliation; (4) incidence of major falls; and (4) accurately communicating the individual's health information and care preferences. IRFs must begin reporting on most quality measures and data on resource use by October 1, 2016, and patient assessment data no later than October 1, 2018. [Soc. Sec. Act § 1899B.]

The quality measures finalized for the FY 2018 payment determination and subsequent years to meet the resource use and other measure domains are as follows: (1) Medicare spending per beneficiary — post-acute care (PAC) IRF QRP; (2) discharge to community — PAC IRF QRP; and (3) potentially preventable 30-day post-discharge readmission – IRF QRP. To meet the medication reconciliation domain, CMS finalized Drug Regimen Review Conducted with Follow-Up for Identified Issues for the FY 2020 payment determination and subsequent years. [*Final rule*, 81 FR 52056, Aug. 5, 2016.]

In the FY 2017 final rule, CMS also adopted Potentially Preventable within Stay Readmission for IRFs for FY 2018 payment determination and subsequent years. [*Final rule*, 81 FR 52056, Aug. 5, 2016.]

One-Day Payment Window

Under the IRF PPS, IRFs are subject to a one-day payment window, or the "24-hour rule," for pre-admission services. In other words, outpatient diagnostic services and most non-physician services provided during the calendar day immediately preceding the date of admission to an IRF are included in the IRF case-mix group payment. Separate payment is not made for outpatient diagnostic services provided during the 24-hour period prior to admission to an IRF. [Pub. 100-04, Ch. 3, § 140.2.]

IRFs and hospitals reimbursed under IRF PPS are not subject to the three-day payment window for pre-admission services. The three-day payment window applies only to acute inpatient hospitals paid under the inpatient prospective payment system (see ¶ 810). [Pub. 100-04, Ch. 3, § 140.2.]

Accreditation Requirements

IRFs must meet accreditation requirements to ensure the quality of suppliers of durable medical equipment, prosthetics, and supplies (DMEPOS). This rule requires that suppliers be accredited by independent accrediting organizations to meet quality standards to bill the Medicare program for items such as walkers, wheelchairs, and hospital beds furnished to Medicare beneficiaries. [42 C.F.R. § 424.57(c).]

[¶ 840] Psychiatric Hospitals and Units

Inpatient psychiatric services that are furnished in a psychiatric hospital, units in an acute care hospitals, or a critical access hospital are reimbursed under a per diem prospective payment system (PPS). The inpatient psychiatric facility (IPF) PPS is designed to ensure appropriate payment for services to patients with severe mental illness, while providing incentives to IPFs for efficient care of Medicare beneficiaries. [Soc. Sec. Act § 1886(s); 42 C.F.R. § 412.400.]

The IPF PPS does not apply to Veterans Administration hospitals, hospitals reimbursed by Medicare under approved state cost-control systems, hospitals in demonstration projects, or nonparticipating hospitals furnishing emergency psychiatric care. [*Medicare Benefit Policy Manual*, Pub. 100-02, Ch. 2, § 10.3.]

For a discussion of Part B coverage of outpatient mental health services, see ¶ 387. For information on lifetime and "spell of illness" restrictions on inpatient psychiatric hospital coverage, see ¶ 225.

Requirements for IPFs

An IPF is certified under Medicare as an inpatient psychiatric hospital, which means an institution that: (1) is primarily engaged in providing, by or under the supervision of a physician, psychiatric services for the diagnosis and treatment of mentally ill patients; (2) maintains clinical records necessary to determine the degree and intensity of the treatment provided to the mentally ill patient; and (3) meets staffing requirements sufficient to carry out active programs of treatment for individuals who are furnished care in the institution. A distinct part psychiatric unit may also be certified if it meets the clinical record and staffing requirements in 42 C.F.R. § 412.27 for a "psychiatric hospital." [42 C.F.R. §§ 412.23(a), 412.27; Pub. 100-02, Ch. 2, § 10.3.]

For all IPFs, a provisional or admitting diagnosis must be made on every patient at the time of admission, and it must include the diagnosis of comorbid diseases as well as the psychiatric diagnosis. In addition, distinct-part psychiatric units of acute care hospitals are required to admit only those patients whose admission to the unit is required for active treatment of a psychiatric principal diagnosis that is listed in the Fourth Edition, Text Revision of the American Psychiatric Association's Diagnostic and Statistical Manual, or in Chapter Five ("Mental Disorders") of the International Classification of Diseases, Ninth Revision, Clinical Modification and an intensity that can be provided appropriately only in an inpatient hospital setting. [42 C.F.R. § 412.27(a), (c)(1)(ii).]

Services Covered Under the IPF PPS

The IPF must furnish all necessary covered services to an inpatient Medicare beneficiary, either directly or under arrangements. Psychiatric hospital inpatient services payable under the IPF PPS do not include the services of physicians, physician assistants, nurse practitioners, clinical nurse specialists, certified nurse-midwives, qualified psychologists, or certified registered nurse anesthetists. These services are paid by Medicare under applicable provider fee schedule provisions. [42 C.F.R. § 412.404(d).]

Pre-admission services otherwise payable under Medicare Part B and furnished to a beneficiary either on the day of admission or the day preceding admission are paid under the IPF PPS as long as the services are: (1) furnished by the IPF or by an entity wholly owned or wholly operated by the IPF; (2) diagnostic, including clinical diagnostic laboratory tests; or

(3) nondiagnostic when furnished on the date of the beneficiary's inpatient admission, nondiagnostic when furnished on the calendar day preceding the date of the beneficiary's inpatient admission and the hospital does not demonstrate that such services are unrelated to the beneficiary's inpatient admission, and are not ambulance services or maintenance renal dialysis services. [42 C.F.R. § 412.405.]

IPF PPS Payment Methodology

Under the IPF PPS, IPFs receive a predetermined federal per diem base rate for inpatient hospital services furnished to Medicare Part A fee-for-service beneficiaries. The federal per diem payment amount is based on the federal per diem base rate plus applicable adjustments. [42 C.F.R. § 412.422.]

Patient- and facility-level adjustments. The federal per diem payment under the IPF PPS is composed of the federal per diem base rate and certain patient- and facility-level payment adjustments that are associated with statistically significant per diem cost differences. Patient-level adjustments include age, diagnosis-related group (DRG) assignment, comorbidities, and variable per diem adjustments to reflect higher per diem costs in the early days of an IPF stay. Facility-level adjustments include adjustments for the IPF's wage index, rural location, teaching status, a cost-of-living adjustment for IPFs located in Alaska and Hawaii, and the presence of a qualifying emergency department. [42 C.F.R. § 412.424(d).]

The IPF PPS provides additional payment policies for outlier cases, interrupted stays, and a per-treatment adjustment for patients who undergo electroconvulsive therapy (ECT). [42 C.F.R. § 412.424(d)(3).]

ACA productivity adjustments. The Patient Protection and Affordable Care Act (ACA) (P.L. 111-148) § 10319(e) amended the annual update to add a productivity adjustment beginning in fiscal year (FY) 2012. The productivity adjustment is the same one applied to inpatient hospital services under Soc. Sec. Act § 1886(b)(3)(B)(xi)(II). [Soc. Sec. Act § 1886(s)(2)(A)(i).]

The ACA also required the application of an "other adjustment" that reduces updates to the IPF PPS base rate from 2010 through 2019. The adjustment for FYs 2017, 2018, and 2019 will be 0.75 percent. [Soc. Sec. Act § 1886(s)(2)(A)(ii), (s)(3)(E).]

The application of these adjustments may result in the annual percentage increase being less than 0.0 for a year and may result in payment rates under the IPF PPS being less than such payment rates for the preceding year. [Soc. Sec. Act § 1886(s)(2)(B).]

FY 2017 per diem rates. The standard per diem base rate for FY 2017 is $761.37, up from the per diem base rate of $743.73 for FY 2016. The per-treatment rate for ECT is $327.78, compared to $320.19 for FY 2016. [*Notice*, 81 FR 50502, Aug. 1, 2016.]

The IPF PPS provides for gradually reduced per diem rates for consecutive days of an IPF stay. The first day of any psychiatric stay provides IPFs with the highest reimbursement due to costly admitting services; the rate is even higher for IPFs with emergency departments. The payments are adjusted downward from day 2 through day 21 of an IPF stay. For day 22 and thereafter, the variable per diem adjustment remains the same each day for the remainder of the stay. [*Notice*, 81 FR 50502, Aug. 1, 2016.]

IPF Quality Program

Beginning in FY 2014, IPFs are required to submit data on specified quality measures that selected from those endorsed by qualified concensus-based entities or established by a different process. IPFs that do not participate in the program are subject to a 2.0 percent reduction in their annual market basket update. IPFs are required to submit data on specified quality measures to receive a full market basket adjustment. [Soc. Sec. Act § 1886(s)(4); 42 C.F.R. § 412.424(d)(1)(vi).]

Quality measures. CMS added five new measures for the FY 2018 payment determination and later years: (1) Tobacco Use Treatment Provided or Offered at Discharge; (2) Alcohol Use Brief Intervention Provided or Offered; (3) Transition Record with Specified Elements Received by Discharged Patients (Discharges from an Inpatient Facility to Home/Self Care or Any Other Site of Care); (4) Timely Transmission of Transition Record (Discharges from an Inpatient Facility to Home/Self Care or Any Other Site of Care); and (5) Screening for Metabolic Disorders. [*Final rule*, 80 FR 46652, Aug. 5, 2015.]

CMS removed the Patients Discharged on Multiple Antipsychotic Medications measure for the FY 2017 payment determination and later. For the FY 2018 payment determination and later, CMS removed the Post-Discharge Continuing Care Plan and the Post-Discharge Continuing Care Plan Transmitted to the Next Level of Care Provider Upon Discharge measures. [*Final rule*, 80 FR 46652, Aug. 5, 2015.]

Lifetime Limitation on Inpatient Psychiatric Services

Payment may not be made for more than a total of 190 days of inpatient psychiatric hospital services during the patient's lifetime. [42 C.F.R. § 409.62.] This limitation applies only to services furnished in a free-standing psychiatric hospital. It does not apply to inpatient psychiatric services furnished in a distinct part psychiatric unit of an acute care hospital or critical access hospital. [Pub. 100-02, Ch. 2, § 80.]

[¶ 845] End-Stage Renal Disease

End-stage renal disease (ESRD) is permanent kidney failure that is severe enough to require a regular course of dialysis or a kidney transplant to maintain life. The ESRD prospective payment system (PPS) provides a case-mix adjusted single payment to ESRD facilities for renal dialysis services provided in an ESRD facility or in a beneficiary's home. The ESRD PPS covers renal dialysis services and home dialysis services, support, and equipment. [Soc. Sec. Act § 1881(b)(14); 42 C.F.R. §§ 413.172, 413.217.]

For renal dialysis services furnished to Medicare Part B fee-for-service beneficiaries, ESRD facilities receive a predetermined per-treatment payment amount that is the sum of: (1) the per-treatment base rate adjusted for wages, and adjusted for facility-level and patient-level characteristics; (2) any outlier payment; and (3) any training adjustment add-on. In addition to the per-treatment payment amount, the ESRD facility may receive payment for bad debts of Medicare beneficiaries. [42 C.F.R. § 413.230.]

If the beneficiary has incurred the full Part B deductible before the dialysis treatment, Medicare pays a dialysis facility 80 percent of the prospective rate; if the beneficiary did not incur the full deductible before treatment, CMS subtracts the amount applicable to the deductible from the ESRD facility's prospective rate and pays the facility 80 percent of the remainder, if any. [42 C.F.R. § 413.176.]

See ¶ 205 for a discussion of the coverage period for ESRD beneficiaries. Part B coverage of ESRD services is discussed at ¶ 389.

Payment for acute kidney injury dialysis. Pursuant to § 808(b) of the Trade Preferences Extension Act of 2015 (P.L. 114-27), CMS established a payment system for renal dialysis services furnished to beneficiaries with an acute kidney injury (AKI) in or under the supervision of an ESRD facility. An individual with acute kidney injury means a person who has acute loss of renal function and does not receive renal dialysis services for which payment is made under Soc. Sec. Act § 1881(b)(14). [Soc. Sec. Act § 1834(r); 42 C.F.R. §§ 413.370, 413.371.]

Beginning January 1, 2017, the payment amount for AKI dialysis services is the ESRD PPS base rate, as adjusted by the wage index. CMS may apply other adjustments provided under Soc. Sec. Act § 1881(b)(14). The AKI dialysis payment rate applies to renal dialysis services furnished under Medicare Part B by a renal dialysis facility or provider of services paid under Soc. Sec. Act § 1881(b)(14). Other items and services furnished to beneficiaries with AKI that are not considered to be renal dialysis services, but that are related to their dialysis treatment as a result of their AKI, are separately payable. [Soc. Sec. Act § 1834(r); 42 C.F.R. §§ 413.372, 413.373, 413.374.]

Quality Incentive Program for ESRD Services

Under the quality incentive program (QIP), an ESRD facility is required to report to CMS on quality measures. If the provider of services or a renal dialysis facility does not meet those requirements, payments will be reduced by up to 2 percent. Each year, a provider's performance score is based on reported compliance with quality measures, based on data from two years prior to the reimbursement year (for example, 2017 data affects 2019 reimbursement). [Soc. Sec. Act § 1881(h); 42 C.F.R. § 413.177.]

The basic ESRD quality measures include: (1) measures on anemia management that reflect the labeling approved by the Food and Drug Administration for such management and measures on dialysis adequacy; (2) iron management; (3) bone mineral metabolism; (4) vascular access, including maximizing the placement of arterial venous fistula; and (5) to the extent feasible, a measure of patient satisfaction. [Soc. Sec. Act § 1881(h)(2).]

CMS finalized the creation of a new Safety Measure Domain as a third category of measures for payment year (PY) 2019. CMS also reintroduced the National Healthcare Safety Network (NHSN) Dialysis Event reporting measure into the QIP measure set. For PY 2019 CMS created a new NHSN Bloodstream Infection clinical measure topic, which will consist of the new NHSN Dialysis Event reporting measure and the existing NHSN BSI clinical measure. [*Final rule*, 81 FR 77834, Nov. 4, 2016.]

In addition, CMS made two substantive changes to the Hypercalcemia Clinical Measure for PY 2019 and later to ensure that the measure remains in alignment with the measure specifications endorsed by the National Quality Forum. First, CMS added plasma as an acceptable substrate in addition to serum calcium. Second, CMS amended the denominator definition to include patients regardless of whether any serum calcium values were reported at the facility during the three-month study period. [*Final rule*, 81 FR 77834, Nov. 4, 2016.]

Reimbursement for ESRD Drugs

Medicare Part B pays for drugs medically necessary in the treatment of patients for ESRD if they are furnished in approved ESRD facilities. [42 C.F.R. § 410.50.]The drugs and biologics include but are not limited to:

(1) drugs and biologics included under the composite rate as of December 31, 2010;

(2) former separately billable Part B injectable drugs;

(3) oral or other forms of injectable drugs used for the treatment of ESRD formerly billed under Part D; and

(4) oral or other forms of drugs and biologics without an injectable form.

Note, however, that payment under the ESRD PPS for ESRD-related oral-only drugs has been postponed until January 1, 2025. [Achieving a Better Life Experience Act of 2014 (ABLE Act) (P.L. 113-295) § 204; 42 C.F.R. § 413.174(f)(5), (6).]

Effective January 1, 2016, new injectable or intravenous products are included in the ESRD PPS bundled payment. [42 C.F.R. § 413.234(b).]

Physician Reimbursement for ESRD Services

Physicians and practitioners managing patients on dialysis are paid a "monthly capitation payment" (MCP) for most outpatient dialysis-related physician services furnished to a Medicare ESRD beneficiary regardless of the volume of the services provided. Under the MCP method, the Medicare administrative contractor (MAC) pays an MCP amount for each patient to cover all professional services furnished by the physician, except those listed as exclusions from MCP. The payment amount varies based on the number of visits provided within each month and the age of the ESRD beneficiary. [42 C.F.R. § 414.314.]

Exclusions from MCP. The MCP does not apply to the following physician services, which are paid according to the physician fee schedule:

(1) administration of hepatitis B vaccine;

(2) covered physician services furnished by another physician when the patient is not available to receive the outpatient services as usual, for example, when the patient is traveling out of town;

(3) covered physician services furnished to hospital inpatients, including services related to inpatient dialysis, by a physician who elects not to continue to receive the MCP during the period of inpatient stay;

(4) surgical services;

(5) interpretation of tests that have a professional component;

(6) complete evaluation for renal transplantation;

(7) evaluation of potential living transplant donors;

(8) the training of patients to perform home hemodialysis, self-hemodialysis, and the various forms of self-peritoneal dialysis;

(9) non-renal related physician's services; and

(10) all physician services that pre-date the initiation of outpatient dialysis.

[42 C.F.R. § 414.314(b)(1); *Medicare Claims Processing Manual*, Pub. 100-04, Ch. 8, § 140.]

"Initial method" of payment. Physicians may elect a different method of reimbursement under a modified version of the former "initial method." Under this method, physicians may be paid for their services to patients in the form of an "add-on" payment. To be eligible for payment under this method, all physicians in a facility must elect this method of payment for all the ESRD facility patients they serve. [42 C.F.R. § § 414.310(e), 414.313.]

Self-dialysis training services. Physicians are paid for providing self-dialysis training services as a flat fee (subject to deductible and coinsurance requirements) for each patient a physician supervises during the training course. If the training is not completed, the payment amount is proportionate to the time spent in training. [42 C.F.R. § 414.316; Pub. 100-04, Ch. 8, § 140.2.]

Transplants. Surgeons performing renal transplants are paid on a comprehensive payment basis, subject to the deductible and the coinsurance, that covers all surgical services in connection with a renal transplant, including pre-operative and post-operative surgical care and for immunosuppressant therapy supervised by the attending transplant surgeon for 60 days. Medically necessary services rendered after that period are reimbursed under the physician fee schedule. [42 C.F.R. § 414.320.]

[¶ 847] Rural Health Facilities

The Medicare program reimburses rural health facilities for providing health care services to Medicare beneficiaries. Health care entities in low-population rural areas include: (1) critical access hospitals (CAHs), which are rural hospitals with fewer than 25 acute care beds located at least 35 miles from other hospitals; (2) sole community hospitals (SCHs), which are rural hospitals with fewer than 50 acute care beds located at least 50 miles from the nearest hospital; and (3) rural health clinics (RHCs), which are clinics that serve medically underserved communities. Medicare also makes payment adjustments to qualifying low-volume rural hospitals and certain small rural hospitals for which Medicare patients make up a significant percentage of inpatient days or discharges.

Critical Access Hospitals

To qualify as a CAH, a hospital must be located in a county in a rural area or treated as being located in a rural area and (1) located more than a 35-mile drive (or, in the case of mountainous terrain or in areas with only secondary roads available, a 15-mile drive) from a hospital or CAH; or (2) certified before January 1, 2006, by the state as being a necessary provider of health care services to residents in the area. [Soc. Sec. Act § 1820(c)(2).]

Unlike traditional hospitals, which are paid under the inpatient prospective payment system (IPPS), Medicare pays CAHs based on each hospital's reported costs. Each CAH receives 101 percent of its costs for outpatient, inpatient, laboratory services, and certain ambulance services. [42 C.F.R. § 413.70.]

CAHs, which are limited to 25 beds, must provide 24-hour emergency services. Generally, they may not provide acute inpatient care for a period longer than, as determined on an annual average basis, 96 hours per patient. In addition to 25 acute beds, CAHs are allowed to have distinct-part 10-bed psychiatric units and 10-bed rehabilitation units; however, these distinct departments of the CAH are paid through Medicare's various prospective payment systems and are not eligible for cost-based reimbursement. [Soc. Sec. Act § 1820(c)(2); *Medicare Claims Processing Manual*, Pub. 100-04, Ch. 3, § 30.1.]

Sole Community Hospitals

Special reimbursement rules apply to SCHs, which are hospitals located in rural areas and the sole source of care available to residents of the area.

Criteria. To qualify for sole community status under the IPPS, a hospital must be the sole source of inpatient hospital services reasonably available to Medicare Part A beneficiaries in the geographic area. CMS classifies a hospital as a SCH if it meets one of the following conditions:

(1) the hospital is located more than 35 miles from other like hospitals;

(2) the hospital is rural and located between 25 and 35 miles from other like hospitals and meets one of the following criteria:

(a) no more than 25 percent of residents who become hospital inpatients or no more than 25 percent of the Medicare beneficiaries who become hospital inpatients in the hospital's service area are admitted to other like hospitals located within a 35-mile radius of the hospital or, if larger, within its service area;

(b) the hospital has fewer than 50 beds and the Medicare administrative contractor (MAC) certifies that the hospital would have met the criteria in paragraph (2)(a) above were it not for the fact that some beneficiaries or residents were forced to seek care outside the service area due to the unavailability of necessary specialty services at the community hospital; or

(c) because of local topography or periods of prolonged severe weather conditions, the other like hospitals are inaccessible for at least 30 days in each of two out of three years;

(3) the hospital is rural and located between 15 and 25 miles from other like hospitals but because of local topography or periods of prolonged severe weather conditions, the other like hospitals are inaccessible for at least 30 days in each of two out of three years; or

(4) the hospital is rural and because of distance, posted speed limits, and predictable weather conditions, the travel time between the hospital and the nearest like hospital is at least 45 minutes.

[42 C.F.R. § 412.92(a).]

SCHs are paid based on the rate that results in the greatest aggregate payment to them, using either the federal rate or their hospital-specific rate based on their 1982, 1987, 1996, or 2006 costs per discharge. [Soc. Sec. Act § 1886(d)(5)(D)(i); 42 C.F.R. § 412.92(d)(1).]

Rural Health Clinics

RHCs are facilities located in areas that are not urbanized areas (as defined by the Bureau of the Census) and in which there are insufficient numbers of needed health care practitioners (as determined by HHS). Within the previous three-year period, RHCs must have been designated and certified as being in an area with a shortage of personal health services. [Soc. Sec. Act. § 1861(aa)(2); 42 C.F.R. § 405.2401.] See ¶ 382 for a discussion of coverage of RHC services.

A provider-based RHC that is authorized to bill under the reasonable cost system is paid in accordance with 42 C.F.R. Parts 405 and 413 if it is an integral and subordinate part of a hospital, skilled nursing facility, or home health agency participating in Medicare and operated with other departments of the provider under common licensure, governance, and professional supervision. Independent RHCs that are authorized to bill under the reasonable cost system are paid on the basis of an all-inclusive rate for each beneficiary visit for covered services, as determined by the MAC. [42 C.F.R. § 405.2462(a), (b); Pub. 100-04, Ch. 9, § 20.1.]

Low-Volume Hospitals

Medicare provides an additional payment to qualifying rural hospitals for the higher incremental costs associated with a low volume of discharges. To qualify for the adjustment for fiscal years (FYs) 2011 through 2017, a hospital must have fewer than 1,600 Medicare discharges during the FY, based on the hospital's Medicare discharges from the most recently available MedPAR data, and must be located more than 15 road miles from the nearest subsection (d) hospital. For low-volume hospitals with 200 or fewer Medicare discharges, the adjustment is an additional 25 percent for each Medicare discharge. For low-volume hospitals with Medicare discharges of more than 200 and fewer than 1,600, the adjustment for each Medicare discharge is an additional percent calculated using the formula (4/14)—(number of Medicare discharges/5600). [Soc. Sec. Act § 1886(d)(12), as amended by Medicare Access and CHIP Reauthorization Act of 2015 (MACRA) (P.L. 114-10) § 204; 42 C.F.R. § 412.101.]

Medicare-Dependent Hospital Program

The Medicare-Dependent Hospital program, which provides increased Medicare reimbursement to certain small rural hospitals for which Medicare patients make up a significant percentage of inpatient days or discharges, has been in existence since 1987. It has been extended a number of times, most recently through October 1, 2017. [Soc. Sec. Act § 1886(d)(5)(G)(i), as amended by MACRA § 205(a); 42 C.F.R. § 412.108.]

A hospital is classified as a Medicare-dependent, small rural hospital if it is located in a rural area and meets the following conditions:

(1) the hospital has 100 or fewer beds during the cost reporting period;

(2) the hospital is not also classified as a SCH; and

(3) at least 60 percent of the hospital's inpatient days or discharges were attributable to individuals entitled to Medicare Part A benefits during at least two of the last three most recent audited cost reporting periods for which the Secretary has a settled cost report. If the cost reporting period is for less than 12 months, the hospital's most recent 12-month or longer cost reporting period before the short period is used.

[42 C.F.R. § 412.108(a)(1).]

[¶ 850] Federally Qualified Health Centers

Section 10501(i)(3)(A) of the Affordable Care Act (ACA) (P.L. 111-148) established a new system of payment for the costs of federally qualified health center (FQHC) services under Medicare Part B based on prospectively set rates. The FQHC prospective payment system (PPS) is based on an average of reasonable costs of FQHCs and pays FQHCs the lesser of their actual charges for services or a single encounter-based rate for professional services furnished per beneficiary per day. [Soc. Sec. Act § 1834(o).] Part B coverage of FQHC services is described at ¶ 382.

Except for preventive services, for which Medicare pays 100 percent, beneficiaries pay a coinsurance amount of 20 percent of the lesser of the FQHC's actual charge or the PPS encounter rate. No deductible is applicable to FQHC services. [Soc. Sec. Act § 1833(a)(1)(Z), (b)(4); 42 C.F.R. § 405.2462(d).]

FQHC PPS Payment Rates

FQHCs billing under the PPS receive a single, per diem rate based on the prospectively set rate for each beneficiary visit for covered services. CMS calculates a per diem rate by dividing total FQHC costs by total FQHC daily encounters to establish an average per diem cost. The per diem rate is adjusted for the following:

(1) geographic differences in cost based on the geographic practice cost indices (GPCIs) in accordance with the physician fee schedule (see ¶ 855) during the same period, limited to only the work and practice expense GPCIs;

(2) furnishing care to a beneficiary that is a new patient; and

(3) furnishing care to a beneficiary receiving a comprehensive initial Medicare visit (an initial preventive physical examination or an initial annual wellness visit) or a subsequent annual wellness visit.

[Soc. Sec. Act § 1834(o); 42 C.F.R. §§ 405.2462(c), 405.2464(b).]

Beginning January 1, 2017, the previous year's rate will be increased by the percentage increase in a market basket of FQHC goods and services as created by regulations, or if such an index is not created, by the percentage increase in the Medicare Economic Index for the year. [Soc. Sec. Act § 1834(o)(2)(B); 42 C.F.R. § 405.2467.]

Supplemental payments. FQHCs under contract with Medicare Advantage (MA) organizations are eligible for supplemental payments for covered services furnished to enrollees in MA plans to cover any difference between their payments from the MA plan and what they would receive under: (1) the PPS rate if the FQHC is authorized to bill under the PPS; or (2) the Medicare outpatient per visit rate as set annually by the Indian Health Service for grandfathered tribal FQHCs. [Soc. Sec. Act § 1833(a)(3)(B); 42 C.F.R. § 405.2469.]

[¶ 853] Accountable Care Organizations

Accountable care organizations (ACOs) are groups of service and supplier providers that work together to manage and coordinate care for Medicare fee-for-service (FFS) beneficiaries. The program, as required by Patient Protection and Affordable Care Act (ACA) (P.L. 111-148) § 3022, is an alternative payment system that rewards provider groups for promoting accountability for patients, coordinating items and services under Medicare Part A and Part B, and encouraging investment in infrastructure and redesigned care processes to ensure high quality and efficient delivery. ACOs are generally networks of provider groups, often affiliated with a hospital, that work together and are jointly responsible for the cost and quality of care provided to Medicare beneficiaries. ACOs must meet certain criteria and specified quality performance standards to receive a portion of the shared savings they create. [Soc. Sec. Act § 1899(a)–(b); 42 C.F.R. §§ 425.10, 425.100.]

Eligibility to participate. The following types of providers of services and suppliers are eligible to participate in the program: (1) ACO professionals in group practice arrangements; (2) networks of individual practices of ACO professionals; (3) partnerships or joint venture arrangements between hospitals and ACO professionals; (4) hospitals employing ACO professionals; (5) critical access hospitals (CAHs) that bill under Method II; (6) rural health clinics (RHCs); (7) federally qualified health centers (FQHCs); and (8) teaching hospitals that have elected to receive payment on a reasonable cost basis for the direct medical and surgical services of their physicians. [Soc. Sec. Act § 1899(b)(1); 42 C.F.R. § 425.102.]

Participation requirements. There are a number of requirements that ACOs must satisfy to participate. ACOs must:

(1) agree to be accountable for the quality, cost, and overall care of Medicare fee-for-service beneficiaries;

(2) agree to participate for at least a three-year period;

(3) have a formal legal structure allowing them to receive and distribute payments;

(4) include enough primary-care ACO professionals to accommodate no fewer than 5,000 beneficiaries;

(5) provide the HHS Secretary with information regarding ACO professionals as deemed appropriate;

(6) have leadership and management in place to support clinical and administrative systems;

(7) define processes to promote evidence-based medicine and patient engagement, report on quality and cost measures, and coordinate care through the use of methods such as telehealth, remote patient monitoring, and other enabling technologies; and

(8) demonstrate to the Secretary that they meet patient-centeredness criteria, such as patient and caregiver assessments and individualized care plans.

[Soc. Sec. Act § 1899(b)(2); 42 C.F.R. §§ 425.104–425.112.]

Providers that participate in models under Soc. Sec. Act § 1115A or any other program or demonstration project that involves shared savings or the independence at home medical practice pilot program under Soc. Sec. Act § 1866E are ineligible to participate as ACOs. [Soc. Sec. Act § 1899(b)(4); 42 C.F.R. § 425.114.] The Secretary assigns beneficiaries to an ACO based on the utilization of primary care services. [Soc. Sec. Act § 1899(c); 42 C.F.R. §§ 425.400–425.404.]

For performance year 2017 and later, the ACO must have an ACO participant agreement with each ACO participant. In addition, an ACO's agreement with an ACO provider/supplier regarding such items and services must satisfy certain requirements. [42 C.F.R. § 425.116.]

Before the start of an agreement period, before each performance year thereafter, and at such other times as specified by CMS, the ACO must submit to CMS an ACO participant list and an ACO provider/supplier list. [42 C.F.R. § 425.118.]

An ACO may be sanctioned if it attempts to keep costs down by avoiding high-risk patients. Furthermore, the Secretary may terminate an agreement with an ACO if the organization does not meet the Secretary's quality-performance standards. [Soc. Sec. Act § 1899(d)(3), (4).]

ACOs, on behalf of their ACO providers/suppliers who are eligible professionals, must submit quality measures using a CMS web interface to qualify on behalf of their EPs for the Physician Quality Reporting System incentive (see ¶ 855) under the Shared Savings Program. For 2017 and later reporting years, ACO must submit all of the CMS web interface measures under 42 C.F.R. § 425.500 to satisfactorily report on behalf of their eligible clinicians for purposes of the quality performance category of the Quality Payment Program. [Soc. Sec. Act § 1899(b)(3); 42 C.F.R. §§ 425.500, 425.504, 425.508.]

ACO Shared Savings and Losses

ACO participants continue to receive payment under the traditional Medicare FFS program under Parts A and B. Only if an ACO meets certain quality and savings requirements and has per capita costs for beneficiaries that are below specified benchmarks and above a minimum savings rate will the ACO qualify for shared savings, which will be based on the quality score it receives. [Soc. Sec. Act § 1899(d)(1); 42 C.F.R. §§ 425.500–425.506.]

ACOs are able to choose whether to be involved in a one-sided or a two-sided risk model. The one-sided model, referred to as Track 1, allows for the sharing of savings, only, while the two-sided models, Tracks 2 and 3, provide for the sharing of both savings and losses for the duration of an ACO contract with Medicare. [42 C.F.R. §§ 425.600, 425.604, 425.606.]

One-sided model. An ACO may operate under the one-sided model for agreement periods after the initial agreement period; however, it may not operate under the one-sided model for a second agreement period unless the immediately preceding agreement period was under the one-sided model and the ACO meets criteria for ACOs seeking to renew their agreements. [42 C.F.R. § 425.600(b).]

To qualify for shared savings under the one-sided model, an ACO must meet or exceed its minimum savings rate, which is determined on a sliding scale based on the number of beneficiaries assigned to the ACO. An ACO that meets all the requirements for receiving shared savings payments under the one-sided model will receive a shared savings payment of up to 50 percent of all savings under the updated benchmark, as determined on the basis of its quality performance. The amount of shared savings an eligible ACO receives under the one-sided model may not exceed 10 percent of its updated benchmark. [42 C.F.R. § 425.604.]

Two-sided models. Under the two-sided models, for each performance year, CMS determines whether the estimated average per capita Medicare expenditures under the ACO for Medicare fee-for-service beneficiaries for Part A and Part B services are above or below the updated benchmark. To qualify for a shared savings payment under Tracks 2 or 3, or to be responsible for sharing losses with CMS, an ACO's average per capita Medicare expenditures under the ACO for Medicare fee-for-service beneficiaries for Part A and Part B services for the performance year must be below or above the updated benchmark, respectively, by at least the minimum savings or loss rate. [42 C.F.R. §§ 425.606(a), 425.610(a).]

Under Track 2, for agreement periods beginning in 2016 and later, the ACO must choose from the three options for establishing the minimum sharing rate (MSR)/minimum loss rate (MLR) for the duration of the agreement period. An ACO that meets all the requirements for receiving shared savings payments under Track 2 will receive a shared savings payment of up to 60 percent of all the savings under the updated benchmark, and the payment cap is 15 percent of an ACO's benchmark. For an ACO that is required to share losses with the Medicare program for expenditures over the updated benchmark, the amount of shared losses, which may not exceed 60 percent, is determined based on the inverse of its final sharing rate. There is a cap on the amount of shared losses an ACO is liable for: 5 percent of the benchmark for the first performance year of participation in Track 2, 7.5 percent in the second year, and 10 percent in the third and later performance years. [42 C.F.R. § 425.606.]

An ACO that meets all the requirements for receiving shared savings payments under Track 3 will receive a shared savings payment of up to 75 percent of all the savings under the updated benchmark. The sharing loss rate must be between 40 and 70 percent, and the amount of shared losses for which an eligible ACO is liable may not exceed 15 percent of its updated benchmark. [42 C.F.R. § 425.610.]

[¶ 855] Physician Fee Schedule

Physicians are paid by Medicare on the basis of a national physician fee schedule. The physician fee schedule applies to all "physicians' services" (see ¶ 350 for the meaning of "physician") and certain services performed by other health care professionals. Specifically, the fee schedule applies to the following:

(1) professional services of doctors of medicine and osteopathy (including osteopathic practitioners), doctors of optometry, doctors of podiatry, doctors of dental surgery and dental medicine, and chiropractors (see ¶ 350);

(2) services and supplies furnished as an incident to a physician's professional service (see ¶ 351), excluding drugs, which are separably payable (see ¶ 362);

(3) outpatient physical and occupational therapy services and outpatient speech-language pathology services furnished by a therapist (not a provider such as a hospital, other facility, or agency) (see ¶ 381);

(4) diagnostic x-ray tests and other diagnostic tests (see ¶ 353), except diagnostic laboratory tests paid under a separate fee schedule (see ¶ 875);

(5) x-ray, radium, and radioactive isotope therapy, including materials and services of technicians (see ¶ 354);

(6) antigens (see ¶ 362); and

(7) preventive services (see ¶ 369).

[Soc. Sec. Act § 1848(j)(3); 42 C.F.R. § 414.2.]

How the Physician Fee Schedule Works

Under the physician fee schedule, Medicare generally pays 80 percent of the lower of: (1) the fee schedule amount; or (2) the actual charge billed by the physician or other health care practitioner (the other 20 percent is paid by the patient as coinsurance—see ¶ 335). The fee schedule payment amount for a service is determined by a formula that takes into consideration the relative value unit (RVU) for the service, the conversion factor (CF) for the year, and the geographic adjustment factor (GAF) for the service. The net effect of the physician fee schedule is that, in any particular geographical area, only one fee may be paid for each allowable service. [Soc. Sec. Act §§ 1833(a), 1848(a)(1), (b)(1); 42 C.F.R. §§ 414.20, 414.21.]

Relative value unit. The Social Security Act requires CMS to establish payments under the physician fee schedule based on national uniform RVUs that account for the relative resources used in furnishing a service. CMS establishes RVUs for three categories of resources:

(1) work required, which reflects the relative time and intensity associated with furnishing a service;

(2) practice expense (PE), which reflects the costs of maintaining a practice (such as renting office space, buying supplies and equipment, and staff costs); and

(3) malpractice insurance expense.

[Soc. Sec. Act § 1848(c)(1)(S); 42 C.F.R. § 414.22.]

Geographic adjustment factor. The GAF compares the relative value of physicians' work effort in each of the different fee schedule areas to the national average of that work effort. CMS uses a geographic practice cost index (GPCI) to establish the GAF for every Medicare payment locality for each of the three components (work, PE, and malpractice). The GPCIs are applied in the calculation of a fee schedule payment amount by multiplying the RVU for each component times the GPCI for that component. [Soc. Sec. Act § 1848(e); 42 C.F.R. § 414.26.]

Soc. Sec. Act § 1848(e)(1)(E) provides for a 1.0 floor for the work GPCIs. The Medicare Access and CHIP Reauthorization Act of 2015 (MACRA) (P.L. 114-10) extended the 1.0 work floor for work GPCIs through December 31, 2017. [Soc. Sec. Act § 1848(e)(1)(E).]

Conversion factor. The sum of the geographically adjusted RVUs is multiplied by a dollar CF. Soc. Sec. Act § 1848(d) specifies the formula by which the CF is updated on an annual basis. For 2016 through 2019, the CF will be 0.5 percent, and for 2020 through 2025, it will be 0.0 percent. [Soc. Sec. Act § 1848(d); 42 C.F.R. § 414.30.]

Facility-Based Physicians

There are two parts to Medicare payment for the services of physicians who are hospital-based (e.g., radiologists, anesthesiologists, pathologists, teaching physicians, and interns and residents) or otherwise facility-based. The portion of the physician's activities representing services that are not directly related to an identifiable part of the medical care of the individual patient is the "provider component." Payment for provider component services can be made only to a provider and is included in the provider's prospective payment system rate. The "professional component" services, which relate to the portion of the physician's activities that is directly related to the medical care of the individual patient, are generally paid under the physician fee schedule. [*Medicare Claims Processing Manual*, Pub. 100-04, Ch. 6, § 80; Ch. 12, § 60; Ch. 13, § 20.1.]

¶855

Another distinction is made between the technical and professional components. The technical component is for nonphysician work, including the taking of a test. The professional component includes the physician's professional services, such as the interpretation of a test. [42 C.F.R. § 414.40(b)(2).]

Medicare pays for physician services furnished to beneficiaries in providers on a fee schedule basis if the following requirements are met: (1) the services are personally furnished for an individual beneficiary by a physician; (2) the services contribute directly to the diagnosis or treatment of an individual beneficiary; (3) the services ordinarily require performance by a physician; and (4) in the case of radiology or laboratory services, the additional requirements in 42 C.F.R. §§ 415.120 or 415.130 are met. [42 C.F.R. § 415.102(a); Pub. 100-04, Ch. 12, § 80.]

Anesthesiologists. For anesthesia services performed, medically directed, or medically supervised by a physician, Medicare pays the lesser of the actual charge or the anesthesia fee schedule amount. Payment for anesthesiologists factors in time units as well as relative values. [42 C.F.R. § 414.46; Pub. 100-04, Ch. 12, § 50.]

Radiologists. A radiologist's services are paid under the physician fee schedule if the services are "patient services" and they are identifiable, direct, and discrete diagnostic or therapeutic services furnished to an individual patient, such as interpretation of x-ray plates, angiograms, myelograms, pyelograms, or ultrasound procedures. For interpretations to be paid, a radiologist must prepare a written report for inclusion in the patient's medical record maintained by the hospital. [42 C.F.R. § 415.120(a); Pub. 100-04, Ch. 13, § 20.1.]

Pathologists. A pathologist's services are paid under the physician fee schedule if the services meet the conditions for payment in 42 C.F.R. § 415.102 and are one of the following services: (1) surgical pathology services; (2) specific cytopathology, hematology, and blood banking services that have been identified as requiring performance by a physician and are listed in program operating instructions; (3) clinical consultation services; or (4) clinical laboratory interpretive services meeting some of the same requirements for clinical consultative services. [42 C.F.R. § 415.130(b).]

Physicians in teaching hospitals. A physician in a teaching hospital personally furnishing Part B physician services is paid under the physician fee schedule on the same basis as physicians providing those services in other settings. Payment is made only if a physician in a teaching hospital supervising residents is present during the "key portion" of the service or procedure. [42 C.F.R. § 415.172.]

The services of a resident in an approved teaching program provided as part of that program are covered as inpatient hospital services and not as physician services, even if the resident is licensed as a physician under state law. Consequently, payment for their services is made to the hospital under Part A; however, separate payment may be made for residents for low- and mid-level evaluation and management services if the conditions for the non-presence of a teaching physician are met. [42 C.F.R. § 415.200.]

Assistants at surgery. The law permits payment under Part B for a physician assistant at surgery in a teaching hospital only under certain conditions. When payment is authorized for the services of assistants at surgery, Medicare will pay no more than 16 percent of the fee schedule amount otherwise payable to the primary physician for the global surgical service involved. In a teaching hospital setting, Medicare does not pay for assistant-at-surgery services when a resident physician at the hospital could have assisted but did not. [Soc. Sec. Act §§ 1842(b)(7)(D)(i), 1848(i)(2); 42 C.F.R. § 415.190(c); Pub. 100-04, Ch. 12, § 20.4.3.]

¶855

Payment for "Incident to" Services and Drugs

Services provided by the physician's staff that are incident to the physician's services are paid under the physician fee schedule as if the physician had personally furnished the services. [42 C.F.R. § 414.34 (b).]

Office medical supplies are considered to be part of a physician's practice expense, and payment for them is included in the practice expense portion of the payment to the physician for the medical or surgical service to which they are incidental. [42 C.F.R. § 414.34 (a) (1).]

Services of certain health care practitioners (e.g., nurse practitioners, physician assistants, etc.) can be billed and paid separately (see ¶ 366). When this occurs, no payment is made to the physician.

Drugs supplied by physician offices are separably payable (see ¶ 885). [42 C.F.R. §§ 405.517, 414.36.]

Global Payments for Surgery

The global surgical package includes all necessary services normally furnished by a surgeon before, during, and after a procedure. The Medicare-approved amount includes payment for the following services related to the surgery when furnished by the physician who performs the surgery: (1) pre-operative visits; (2) intra-operative services; (3) complications following surgery; (4) post-operative visits; (5) post-surgical pain management (by the surgeon); (6) supplies (except for splints and casting supplies); and (7) miscellaneous services (changes and removal of tubes, intravenous lines, catheters, and dressings and removal of operative pack, cutaneous sutures and staples, lines, wires, tubes, drains, casts, and splints). [Soc. Sec. Act § 1848(c) (1) (A) (ii); Pub. 100-04, Ch. 12, § 40.1.]

Duration of a global period. The global period for major surgeries includes the day immediately before the day of surgery, the day of surgery, and 90 days following the day of surgery. The period for minor surgeries includes the day of surgery and a post-operative period that varies from 0 to 10 days. [Pub. 100-04, Ch. 12, § 40.1.]

Services not included in the global surgical package. Procedure code modifiers are used to identify the most common services not included in the global fee, such as (1) evaluation and management services on the day before major surgery or the day of major surgery that result in the initial decision to operate; (2) return trips to the operating room during the post-operative period; (3) unrelated procedures or visits during the post-operative period; (4) significant evaluation and management on the day of a procedure (including critical care); and (5) post-operative critical care. [Pub. 100-04, Ch. 12, § 40.2.]

Telehealth Services

Medicare pays a physician or practitioner located at a distant site that furnishes a telehealth service the same amount that would have been paid for the service under the physician fee schedule had it been furnished without the use of a telecommunications system. The consultation may be billed only by the consulting practitioner, and payments made to the practitioner at the distant site may not be shared with the referring practitioner or telepresenter. [Soc. Sec. Act § 1834(m) (2) (A); 42 C.F.R. § 414.65(a).]

The facility fee for the originating site is updated by the Medicare Economic Index. Only the originating site may bill for the originating site facility fee and only on an assignment-related basis. [Soc. Sec. Act § 1834(m) (2) (B); 42 C.F.R. § 414.65(b); Pub. 100-04, Ch. 12, § 190.6.]

The payment for the professional service and originating site facility fee is subject to coinsurance and deductible requirements. [42 C.F.R. § 414.65(c).]

Physician Incentive Programs

CMS increases or decreases payments to physicians to provide various incentives, including:

- physicians that participate in the Medicare program receive a higher amount for the services they provide to Medicare beneficiaries; the physician fee schedule payment amount applicable to nonparticipating physicians, suppliers, and practitioners is 5 percent less than that for participating practitioners or suppliers, pursuant to Soc. Sec. Act § 1848(a)(3);

- under the Physician Quality Reporting System (PQRS), through 2018 a negative adjustment applies for failing to satisfactorily submit data on PQRS quality measures;

- eligible professionals (EPs) that do not meaningfully use certified electronic health record (EHR) technology will have their Medicare physician fee schedule amount reduced for each year from 2015 through 2018 (see ¶ 717);

- the value-based payment modifier, which provides for differential payment under the physician fee schedule, is based on the quality of care furnished compared to cost during a performance period; and

- bonus payments for practitioners in underserved areas.

MACRA consolidates and replaces the EHR meaningful use program, PQRS, and the value-based payment modifier into the new Merit-Based Incentive Payment System (MIPS) program. MACRA will sunset the three programs at the end of 2018. [MACRA § 101(b), (c).]

In addition, under MACRA, starting in 2019, the amounts paid to individual providers will be subject to adjustment through one of two mechanisms, depending on whether the physician chooses to participate in an Advanced Alternative Payment Model (APM) program or MIPS. [MACRA § 101(c), (e)(2).]

MIPS. Providers who opt to participate in MIPS will receive payments that are subject to positive or negative performance adjustments. The performance adjustment for an individual provider will depend on that provider's performance compared to a threshold. [Soc. Sec. Act § 1848(q), as added by MACRA § 101(c)(1).]

APMs. An APM requires participation in an entity that assumes a meaningful financial risk, reporting of quality measures, and use of certified EHR technology. From 2019 through 2024, eligible professionals receiving a substantial portion of their revenue from APMs will receive a lump-sum payment after each year equal to 5 percent of their Medicare payments in that year. [Soc. Sec. Act § 1833(z), as added by MACRA § 101(e)(2).]

Physician Quality Reporting System. PQRS measures address various aspects of care, such as prevention, chronic- and acute-care management, procedure-related care, resource utilization, and care coordination, and can be reported for measures groups created for specific conditions. Starting with calendar year 2015, a negative adjustment to physician fee schedule payments applies to services for which a professional does not satisfactorily submit data on quality measures. The adjustment in 2016, 2017, and 2018 will result in a 98 percent payment. [Soc. Sec. Act § 1848(a)(8)(A); 42 C.F.R. § 414.90(e).]

An EP or group practice that wishes to participate in the PQRS must report information on the individual PQRS quality measures or measures groups identified by CMS in a form and manner specified by CMS. The details are posted on the CMS website: https://www.cms.gov/Medicare/Quality-Initiatives-Patient-Assessment-Instruments/PQRS/index.html. Instead of reporting quality measures, an EP may choose to participate in a qualified clinical data registry. [Soc. Sec. Act § 1848(m)(3); 42 C.F.R. § 414.90(c)(5).]

Value-based payment modifier. The value-based payment modifier provides for differential payment starting in 2015 to groups of physicians and starting in 2017 to all physicians and groups of physicians under the physician fee schedule based on the quality of care furnished compared to cost during a performance period. The modifier is based upon a comparison of the composite of quality of care measures and a composite of cost measures. [Soc. Sec. Act § 1848(p); 42 C.F.R. §§ 414.1200, 414.1275.]

Bonus payments for practitioners in underserved areas. Medicare pays a bonus of 10 percent to physicians who furnish covered services to Medicare beneficiaries in areas designated as Health Professional Shortage Areas (HPSAs). The bonus is added to whatever would otherwise be paid under the fee schedule and applies to both urban and rural HPSAs. [Soc. Sec. Act § 1833(m); 42 C.F.R. § 414.67(a).]

Information on Amounts Paid to Individual Physicians

On January 17, 2014, CMS changed its policy on requests made under the Freedom of Information Act (FOIA) for information on amounts paid to individual physicians under the Medicare program. Effective March 18, 2014, CMS will make case-by-case determinations as to whether exemption 6 of FOIA applies to a given request by weighing the balance between the privacy interest of individual physicians and the public interest in disclosure of such information. [*Notice*, 79 FR 3205, Jan. 17, 2014.]

[¶ 860] Nonphysician Practitioners

As discussed at ¶ 351, separate Medicare coverage is provided for several kinds of nonphysician practitioners. Health care practitioners such as nurse practitioners (NPs) are authorized to bill Medicare separately when they perform specialized services or stand in the place of a physician. At one time, however, the services of nonphysician practitioners were covered only as "incident to" a physician's services and payment for their services was included in Medicare's payment to the physician. The Medicare payment amount for nonphysician practitioners is normally a certain percentage of the physician fee schedule for the same services (or less if their actual charges are less).

Assignment. Medicare claims for payment for services of nonphysician practitioners such as PAs, NPs, clinical nurse specialists (CNSs), certified nurse-midwives (CNMs), and certified registered nurse anesthetists (CRNAs) may only be submitted on an assignment basis (see ¶ 868). [42 C.F.R. §§ 410.74(d)(2), 410.75(e)(2), 410.76(e)(2), 410.77(d)(2), 414.60(c).]

Physician Assistants, Nurse Practitioners, and Nurse-Midwives

The Medicare payment amount for the services of NPs, CNSs, and physician assistants (PAs) (other than assistant-at-surgery services) is based on 85 percent of the fee schedule payment for physicians furnishing the same service. [Soc. Sec. Act §§ 1833(a)(1)(O), 1842(b)(18); 42 C.F.R. §§ 414.52(d), 414.56(c).]

Physician assistants. PAs must have their own "nonphysician practitioner" national provider identifier (NPI). The NPI is used for identification purposes only when billing for PA services because only an appropriate PA employer or a provider/supplier for whom the PA furnishes services as an independent contractor can bill for PA services. [Soc. Sec. Act § 1842(b)(6)(C); 42 C.F.R. § 410.74(a)(2)(v); *Medicare Claims Processing Manual*, Pub. 100-04, Ch. 12, § 110.4.]

Nurse practitioners and clinical nurse specialists. Payment may be made directly to a NP or CNS for their professional services when furnished in collaboration with a physician. NPs and CNSs must have their own "nonphysician practitioner" NPI number for billing purposes. [Pub. 100-04, Ch. 12, § 120.3.]

Certified nurse-midwives. CNMs services are paid at 80 percent of the lesser of: (1) the actual charge for the services, or (2) 100 percent of the physician fee schedule amount. [Soc. Sec. § 1833(a)(1)(K); 42 C.F.R. § 414.54(b).]

Payment for CNM services is made directly to CNMs for their professional services and for services furnished incident to their professional services. [Pub. 100-04, Ch. 12, § 130.1.]

Global surgical payments. When a PA, NP, or CNS furnishes services to a patient during a global surgical period, Medicare administrative contractors must determine the level of PA, NP, or CNS involvement in furnishing part of the surgeon's global surgical package. PA, NP, or CNS services furnished during a global surgical period are paid at 80 percent of the lesser of the actual charge or 85 percent of what a physician is paid under the physician fee schedule. [Pub. 100-04, Ch. 12, §§ 110.1, 120.]

When a CNM is providing most of the care to a Medicare beneficiary that is part of a global service and a physician also provides a portion of the care for this same global service, the fee paid to the CNM is based on the portion of the global fee that would have been paid to the physician for the service provided by the CNM. [Pub. 100-04, Ch. 12, § 130.2.]

Certified Registered Nurse Anesthetists

Anesthesia services furnished by a qualified nonphysician anesthetist (including both CRNAs and anesthesia assistants (AAs) are paid at the lesser of the actual charge, the physician fee schedule, or the anesthesia fee schedule. [Soc. Sec. Act § 1833(a)(1)(H), (l); 42 C.F.R. § 414.60.]

Payment may be made to the qualified nonphysician anesthetist who furnished the anesthesia services or to a hospital, physician, group practice, or ambulatory surgical center with which the anesthetist has an employment or contractual relationship. [Soc. Sec. Act § 1842(b)(18); 42 C.F.R. § 414.60; Pub. 100-04, Ch. 12, § 140.2.]

Medicare does not pay for CRNA services when an anesthesiologist is personally involved in the case unless it is determined to be medically necessary for both to be involved. [42 C.F.R. § 414.46(c)(1)(iv).]

Teaching CRNAs. A teaching CRNA is reimbursed 100 percent of the physician fee schedule amount if the teaching CRNA, who is not under medical direction of a physician, is present with the student nurse anesthetist for the pre- and post-anesthesia services included in the anesthesia base units payment and is continuously present during anesthesia time in a single case with a student nurse anesthetist. If the teaching CRNA is involved with two concurrent anesthesia cases, he or she can be involved only with those two concurrent cases and may not perform services for other patients. [Medicare Improvements for Patients and Providers Act of 2008 (MIPPA) (P.L. 110-275) § 139(b); 42 C.F.R. § 414.61.]

Clinical Psychologists and Social Workers

Clinical psychologists are paid 80 percent of the lesser of: (1) the actual charge for the services; or (2) 100 percent of the amount determined for corresponding services under the physician fee schedule. [Soc. Sec. Act § 1833(a)(1)(L); 42 C.F.R. § 414.62.] Direct payment may be made to clinical psychologists under Part B for professional services, and they are required to accept assignment for all Medicare claims for their services. [Pub. 100-04, Ch. 1, § 30.3.1; Ch. 12, §§ 170, 170.1.]

Clinical social workers. For therapeutic and other diagnostic services, clinical social workers are paid 80 percent of the lesser of: (1) the actual charge for the services; or (2) 75 percent of the amount determined for payment of a clinical psychologist. [Soc. Sec. Act § 1833(a)(1)(F).]

¶860

Physical Therapists, Occupational Therapists, and Speech-Language Pathologists

The Medicare physician fee schedule is the method of payment for outpatient physical therapy, occupational therapy, speech-language pathology services. [Soc. Sec. Act § 1834 (k); Pub. 100-04, Ch. 5, § 10.] Outpatient therapists may bill Medicare directly for their services. [Soc. Sec. Act § § 1832 (a) (2) (C), 1833 (a) (8).]

Functional reporting. Therapists must comply with reporting requirements to receive payment for furnished therapy services. At the outset of treatment, therapists are required to report on the projected goal for treatment using modifiers that describe the percentage of impairment. [42 C.F.R. § § 410.59 (a) (4), 410.60 (a) (4), 410.62 (a) (4); Pub. 100-04, Ch. 5, § 10.6.]

Therapy caps. Annual per-beneficiary limitations apply to the amount of expenses that can be considered as incurred expenses for outpatient therapy services under Part B. There is one therapy cap for outpatient occupational therapy services and another separate therapy cap for physical therapy and speech-language pathology services combined. [Soc. Sec. Act § 1833 (g).]

The annual therapy cap for 2017 is $1,980 for physical therapy and speech-language pathology services combined; there is a separate cap of $1,980 for occupational therapy services. [*Final rule*, 81 FR 80170, Nov. 15, 2016.]

Therapy caps apply to outpatient therapy services furnished in all settings, including critical access hospitals and the once-exempt outpatient hospital setting. [42 C.F.R. § § 410.59 (e) (1) (iv), 410.60 (e) (1) (iv) and (e) (3); *Final rule*, 79 FR 67548, Nov. 13, 2014; Pub. 100-04, Ch. 5, § 10.3.]

Limitations on beneficiary liability. The limitations on beneficiary liability provisions of Soc. Sec. Act § 1879 apply when a claim for services is denied for exceeding the therapy caps. [Soc. Sec. Act § 1833 (g) (5) (D).]

Exceptions to therapy caps. An exceptions process for the therapy caps for when the provision of additional therapy services is medically necessary will be in effect through December 31, 2017. [Soc. Sec. Act § 1833 (g) (5), as amended by Medicare Access and CHIP Reauthorization Act of 2015 (MACRA) (P.L. 114-10) § 202 (a).]

A request for an exception to the therapy cap on claims that are over the cap amount must contain an appropriate modifier (such as the KX modifier) indicating that the services are medically necessary as justified by documentation in the medical record. [Soc. Sec. Act § 1833 (g) (5) (B).]

Requests for an exception to therapy caps with respect to expenses that would be incurred for outpatient therapy services that exceed an annual threshold of (1) $3,700 for occupational therapy services or (2) $3,700 for physical therapy and speech-language pathology therapy services combined, are subject to a manual medical review. [Soc. Sec. Act § 1833 (g) (5) (C).] MACRA required the Secretary to implement a process for targeted medical review in place of the manual medical review process. [Soc. Sec. Act § 1833 (g) (5) (E), as added by MACRA § 202 (b).]

[¶ 865] Actual Charge Restrictions

To protect beneficiaries from excessive charges by Medicare physicians and suppliers, the Medicare program has several rules that limit how much beneficiaries can be charged (actual charge restrictions). These rules apply only to physicians and suppliers who do not accept assignment, including "nonparticipating" physicians and suppliers (see ¶ 870 for an explanation of the Participation Program). Payments to physicians and suppliers who accept assignment are governed by separate rules (see ¶ 868). If these actual charge restrictions did not exist, a physician or supplier who does not accept assignment would be free to set any amount as the actual charge and could require the beneficiary to pay that amount. Medicare would, as usual, pay 80 percent of the amount it determines to be allowable, and the beneficiary would have to pay the difference between the Medicare payment amount and the physician's or supplier's actual charge.

The Limiting Charge

As discussed at ¶ 868, when assignment is accepted, a physician agrees to the Medicare-approved charge as the full charge and bills the patient only the 20 percent coinsurance amount not paid by Medicare. Physicians, suppliers, or other practitioners who do not accept assignment are subject to a "limiting charge" that places restrictions on how much they are allowed to charge a Medicare patient. [Soc. Sec. Act § 1848(g).]

The limiting charge is 115 percent of the fee schedule amount for "nonparticipating" physicians and suppliers, which is 95 percent of the physician fee schedule amount for each service. [Soc. Sec. Act § § 1834(b)(5)(B), 1848(a)(3) and (g)(2)(C); 42 C.F.R. § 414.48.]

In cases when a payment basis other than the physician fee schedule is used, the 115 percent limiting charge is applied to the recognized payment amount for nonparticipating providers, which is defined by the statute as 95 percent of the applicable payment basis. [Soc. Sec. Act § 1848(g)(2)(D); 42 C.F.R. § 414.48(b).]

The limiting charge applies to all of the following services and supplies, regardless of who provides or bills for them, if they are covered by the Medicare program:

- physicians' services;

- services and supplies furnished incident to a physician's services that are commonly furnished in a physician's office;

- outpatient physical or occupational therapy services furnished by an independently practicing therapist;

- diagnostic tests; and

- radiation therapy services (including x-ray, radium, and radioactive isotope therapy, and materials and services of technicians).

[*Medicare Claims Processing Manual*, Pub. 100-04, Ch. 1, § 30.3.12.3.]

Example • • • _____

Carla visits Dr. Kent for a series of medical tests and services for which Dr. Kent would charge private-pay patients $800. The physician fee schedule amount for those services is $510. Carla has paid the Part B deductible for the year.

(1) If Dr. Kent is a participating physician, Medicare will pay Dr. Kent $408 and Carla will pay the $102 coinsurance (that is, 20 percent of $510).

(2) If Dr. Kent is a nonparticipating physician, the Medicare-approved amount is 5 percent less than the fee schedule ($485), and the Medicare payment amount is $388 (80 percent of the reduced approved amount).

(a) If Dr. Kent accepts assignment and, thus, agrees to accept the reduced Medicare-approved amount as his full charge, Medicare will pay Dr. Kent $388 and Carla will pay the other $97.

(b) If Dr. Kent does not accept assignment and wants to charge Carla more than the reduced Medicare-approved amount, Dr. Kent may not charge Carla more than 15 percent over the reduced Medicare-approved amount (i.e., 15 percent over $485, or $557.75). The

Medicare-approved payment amount ($388) is sent to Carla, and Carla is responsible for paying the other $169.75.

Medicare secondary payments. The rules for calculating Medicare secondary benefits apply regardless of whether the limiting charge applies. However, when the limiting charge is less than the actual charge, the limiting charge will be considered to be the actual charge as well as the plan's allowable charge. [*Medicare Secondary Payer Manual*, Pub. 100-05, Ch. 5, § 40.7.4.]

A nonparticipating physician/supplier that does not take assignment must reduce charges to the beneficiary to reflect the Medicare limiting charge. A physician who charges a patient more than the limiting charge must refund the difference. [Soc. Sec. Act § 1848(g)(1)(A)(iv).]

If a physician knowingly and willfully bills above the limiting charge, the Secretary may apply sanctions, including: (1) barring the physician from participating in the Medicare program for up to five years; and (2) imposing a civil money penalty or assessment. [Soc. Sec. Act § 1842(j)(1)(A), (j)(2).] The Secretary may use any penalties so collected to reimburse the beneficiary for the overcharge. [Soc. Sec. Act § 1842(j)(4).]

Other Actual Charge Restrictions

While a number of limitations on actual charges became obsolete with the adoption of the physician fee schedule and the limiting charge, other actual charge restrictions affect how much health care providers may charge or bill Medicare beneficiaries.

Services not reasonable or necessary. When a physician furnishes otherwise-covered services on an unassigned basis to a Medicare beneficiary and Medicare determines that those services were not covered because they were not reasonable or necessary, the physician is required to refund to the beneficiary any payments collected for those services (including deductible and coinsurance amounts). A program payment, however, may be made to the physician if neither the physician nor the patient knew, or could reasonably have been expected to know, that Medicare would not pay for the items and services provided. [Soc. Sec. Act §§ 1834(a)(18)(A), 1842(l)(1)(A); 42 C.F.R. § 411.408(a).]

Elective surgery on an unassigned basis. When a physician performs an elective surgical procedure on an unassigned basis for a Medicare beneficiary, and the charge for that procedure is at least $500, the physician must refund to the patient any payment collected above the Medicare allowed charge for the procedure unless the physician discloses to the beneficiary in advance the difference between (1) the physician's estimated charge; (2) the estimated Medicare payment; and (3) the excess of the physician's actual charge over the estimated Medicare payment. A physician who knowingly and willfully fails to make a required refund for an elective surgery procedure may be subject to civil money penalties or may be suspended from program participation. The Secretary is required to monitor elective surgery claims to assure that required refunds are being made. [Soc. Sec. Act § 1842(m).]

[¶ 868] Assignment

An assignment is an agreement between a physician or supplier and a Medicare beneficiary. Under the terms of the assignment, the beneficiary transfers to the physician or supplier his right to Medicare benefits for the services received and the physician or supplier accepts the Medicare-approved charge as the full charge for the items or services provided. The physician or supplier submits a claim for payment for the services rendered to the Medicare administrative contractor (MAC). If the MAC approves the charges, Medicare pays the physician or supplier the Medicare-approved "fee schedule" amount (see ¶ 855) and the beneficiary is responsible for paying the coinsurance and any remaining deductible (see ¶ 335). [Soc. Sec. Act § 1842(b)(3)(B)(ii); 42 C.F.R. § 424.55; *Medicare Claims Processing Manual*, Pub. 100-04, Ch. 1, § § 30.2 and 30.3.]

Some physicians and suppliers do not accept assignment and some beneficiaries may want Medicare to sent payment directly to them. In these situations, a Medicare payment is sent directly to the beneficiary after an itemized bill is submitted to the MAC on the appropriate form (Form CMS-1500). The beneficiary is responsible for paying the physician or supplier (see also ¶ 900). [42 C.F.R. § § 424.50–424.56; Pub. 100-04, Ch. 1, § 30.3.]

Signature of patient. The signature of the patient on the billing form, or that of a person qualified to sign on his or her behalf, is necessary to assign payment of benefits to the physician or supplier. The signature should be obtained on the billing form, on the provider's records, or, in the case of a prolonged illness, on a special statement having the effect of a general consent to assignment. [Pub. 100-04, Ch. 1, § 50.1.3.]

Mandatory Assignment

Certain practitioners who provide services under the Medicare program are required to accept assignment for all Medicare claims for their services. This means that they must accept the Medicare allowed amount as payment in full for their practitioner services. The beneficiary's liability is limited to any applicable deductible plus the 20 percent coinsurance. Assignment is mandated for the following claims:

- clinical diagnostic laboratory services and physician lab services (see Soc. Sec. Act § 1833(h)(5)(C));

- physician services to individuals dually entitled to Medicare and Medicaid;

- services of physician assistants, nurse practitioners, clinical nurse specialists, nurse-midwives, certified registered nurse anesthetists, clinical psychologists, clinical social workers, registered dietitians/nutritionists, and anesthesiologist assistants (see 42 C.F.R. § § 410.74(d)(2), 410.75(e)(2), 410.76(e)(2), 414.60(c); Pub. 100-04, Ch. 12, § § 110–170);

- mass immunization roster billers (billing only for influenza and pneumococcal vaccinations and administrations, services not subject to the deductible or the 20 percent coinsurance);

- ambulatory surgical center services (no deductible and 25 percent coinsurance for colorectal cancer screening colonoscopies applies);

- home dialysis supplies and equipment paid under Method II for dates of service before January 1, 2011 (see Pub. 100-04, Ch. 1, § 30.3.8);

- drugs and biologics (see 42 C.F.R. § 414.707(b); Pub. 100-04, Ch. 17, § 50);

- ambulance services (see 42 C.F.R. § 414.610(b); Pub. 100-04, Ch. 15, § 10.4);

- competitive bidding items of durable medical equipment, prosthetics, orthotics, and supplies (42 C.F.R. § 414.408) and upgrades from a competitive bid item to a non-bid item; and

- telehealth services (see 42 C.F.R. § 414.65(d)).

[Pub. 100-04, Ch. 1, § 30.3.1; Ch. 36, § § 40, 40.11, 40.12.]

Accepting assignment is not mandatory for the services of physicians, independently practicing physical and occupational therapists, or for the suppliers of radiology services or diagnostic tests. [Pub. 100-04, Ch. 1, § 30.3.1.]

Limitation on Physician/Supplier Charges to Beneficiaries

By submitting the claims form with the beneficiary's assignment authorization, the physician or supplier agrees to accept the Medicare-approved charge as the full charge for the items or services provided. A physician or supplier agrees not to charge the beneficiary for services for which Medicare pays 100 percent of the approved amount. In addition, the physician or supplier agrees to collect only: (1) the difference between the Medicare-approved amount and the Medicare Part B payment; (2) any applicable deductible; and (3) any applicable coinsurance amount for which Medicare does not pay 100 percent of the approved amount. [42 C.F.R. § 424.55(b); Pub. 100-04, Ch. 1, § 30.3.2.] If the physician or supplier is dissatisfied with the amount of the Medicare-approved charge, the remedy is to request a review and hearing with the MAC. The physician may not ask the beneficiary for more money. [Soc. Sec. Act § 1842(b)(3)(B)(ii).]

If a beneficiary has private insurance in addition to Medicare (e.g., a Medigap policy— see ¶ 740), the physician or supplier who has accepted assignment is in violation of the assignment agreement if that physician or supplier bills or collects from the beneficiary or the private insurer an amount that, when added to the Medicare benefit received, exceeds the approved charge. [Pub. 100-04, Ch. 1, § 30.3.2.]

Physicians and suppliers who do not accept assignment also are limited on the amount they may charge beneficiaries. This "limiting charge" is 115 percent of the Medicare-approved charge for nonparticipating physicians and suppliers (see ¶ 865).

A physician or supplier who accepts assignment for some services (that is, on a case-by-case basis) is not ordinarily precluded from billing the patient for other services; however, a physician or supplier may not accept assignment for some services and claim payment from the beneficiary for other services he or she performed for that same beneficiary at the same place on the same occasion. [Pub. 100-04, Ch. 1, § 30.3.2.]

Exception. When a physician is required to accept assignment for certain services as a condition for any payment or for Medicare payment to be made (for example, for clinical diagnostic laboratory services (see ¶ 875) and the services of physician assistants (see ¶ 860)), the physician may accept assignment for those services while billing on an unassigned basis for other services the physician furnishes at the same place and on the same occasion. [Pub. 100-04, Ch. 1, § 30.3.2.]

Prohibition Against Reassignment

While a beneficiary may assign his or her right to Medicare payment for Medicare services received, providers, physicians, and suppliers generally may not reassign the right to receive payments assigned to them. [Soc. Sec. Act §§ 1815(c), 1842(b)(6); 42 C.F.R. §§ 424.73(a), 424.80(a); Pub. 100-04, Ch. 1, § 30.2.2.]

Any person who accepts an assignment of benefits under Medicare and "knowingly, willfully, and repeatedly" violates the assignment agreement is guilty of a misdemeanor and subject to a fine of not more than $2,000, imprisonment of up to six months, or both. Further, if the prohibition against assignment or reassignment is violated, CMS may terminate a provider agreement or revoke the party's right to receive assigned benefits. [Soc. Sec. Act § 1128A; 42 C.F.R. §§ 424.74, 424.82; Pub. 100-04, Ch. 1, § 30.2.15.]

A power of attorney may not be used to circumvent the prohibition against reassignment. [Soc. Sec. Act § 1842(b)(6); 42 C.F.R. § 424.73(a).]

Exceptions. There are several exceptions to the reassignment prohibition. Medicare payment may be made to the employer of a physician or other practitioner providing services if the physician or practitioner is required as a condition of his or her employment to turn over the fee to his or her employer and, if the services are provided in a hospital, clinic, or other facility, payment may be made to the facility if there is a contractual arrangement between the physician or other person and the facility under which the facility submits the bill for the services. [Soc. Sec. Act § 1842(b)(6); 42 C.F.R. § 424.80(b)(1); Pub. 100-04, Ch. 1, § 30.2.7.]

There is an additional exception to the prohibition against reassignment—the "indirect payment procedure" for entities that provide payment under a complementary health benefit plan. The coverage that such a plan provides is complementary to Medicare benefits and covers only the amount by which the Part B payment falls short of the approved charge for the service under the plan. ("Medigap" plans are examples of this type of plan.) Under this exception, payment may be made to an entity that provides coverage of the services under a complementary health benefits plan under the circumstances described at 42 C.F.R. § 424.66. [Pub. 100-04, Ch. 1, § 30.2.8.3.]

Medicare payment may be made to a substituting physician when the patient's first physician arranges for substitution services by a second physician because the first physician is unavailable to provide the services and the services are not provided by the second physician over a continuous period longer than 60 days. [Soc. Sec. Act § 1842(b)(6)(D); Pub. 100-04, Ch. 1, § 30.2.11.]

For other exceptions to the prohibition against assignment and reassignment, see regulations beginning at 42 C.F.R. § 424.70 and Pub. 100-04, Ch. 1, § 30.2.1.

[¶ 870] Participation Program for Physicians and Suppliers

Under Medicare's "Participating Physicians and Suppliers Program," physicians and suppliers are encouraged to sign a participation agreement with the HHS Secretary binding them to accept assignment (see ¶ 868) for services provided to all Medicare patients for the following calendar year. [Soc. Sec. Act § 1842(h)(1).]

Participation agreements run on a calendar-year basis and are normally effective for one year. They are automatically renewed unless cancelled. Once the year has begun, physicians and suppliers will not be permitted to enter or drop out of the program until the end of the year. However, a newly licensed physician, a physician who begins a practice in a new area, or a new supplier who begins a new business may enter into a participation agreement for the remainder of the year. [Soc. Sec. Act § 1842(h)(1); *Medicare Claims Processing Manual*, Pub. 100-04, Ch. 1, § 30.3.12.]

WK Note: The "participation" program relates only to how physicians or suppliers are paid; it does not affect whether the services provided are covered. Thus, for coverage purposes, it makes no difference whether the physician or supplier providing the items or services is "participating" or "nonparticipating."

Incentives to Participate in Medicare

The "participation program" provides incentives to encourage physicians and suppliers to participate in Medicare. These include the following:

(1) the establishment and free distribution of participating physician and supplier directories (see discussion below) (Soc. Sec. Act § 1842(h)(4));

(2) toll-free telephone numbers through which beneficiaries may obtain the names, addresses, specialties, and telephone numbers of participating physicians and suppliers (Soc. Sec. Act § 1842(h)(2));

(3) electronic transmission of claims to Medicare contractors (Soc. Sec. Act § 1842(h)(3));

(4) higher payment rates (nonparticipating physicians are paid 95 percent of the payment rates applied to participating physicians) (Pub. 100-04, Ch. 1, § 30.3); and

(5) limitations on the actual charges that can be billed by nonparticipating physicians, including important refund and disclosure rules (Pub. 100-04, Ch. 1, § 30.3.12.3).

[Pub. 100-04, Ch. 1, § 30.3.12.1 (I).]

Directory of Participating Physicians and Suppliers

At the beginning of each year CMS publishes local directories containing the names, addresses, specialties, and telephone numbers of all local "participating" physicians and suppliers. These directories, called "Medicare Participating Physicians/Suppliers Directories" (abbreviated MEDPARD), are made available at all Social Security and Medicare administrative contractor (MAC) offices and at some senior citizen organization centers. MACs are required to mail directories to beneficiaries at no charge upon request. [Soc. Sec. Act § 1842(h) (2), (4), (5) (A).]

Each time a payment explanation (the Medicare Summary Notice) is sent to beneficiaries with respect to claims made on an unassigned basis, the Secretary is required to remind them about the existence of the participation program, the charge limits applicable to nonparticipants, the local MAC's toll-free telephone number, and an offer to help the beneficiary locate a participating physician or supplier. [Soc. Sec. Act § 1842(h) (7).]

Hospitals and critical access hospitals are required to make available to patients the directory of participating physicians for the area. [Soc. Sec. Act § 1866(a) (1) (N).]

[¶ 872] Private Non-Medicare Contracts with Health Care Practitioners

CMS allows Medicare beneficiaries and their physicians (and certain nonphysician practitioners) to enter into private contracts for health care services outside the Medicare system. A physician or practitioner may opt out of Medicare for a two-year period by entering into a private contract with a Medicare beneficiary and submitting an affidavit. Services furnished under such private contracts are not covered services under Medicare, and no Medicare payment will be made for such services either directly or indirectly, except in limited cases. [Soc. Sec. Act § § 1802(b) (1), 1862(a) (19); 42 C.F.R. § § 405.405, 405.410.]

Physicians who may opt out of Medicare include dentists, podiatrists, and optometrists. Practitioners who may opt out include: (1) physician assistants, nurse practitioners, and clinical nurse specialists; (2) certified registered nurse anesthetists; (3) certified nurse-midwives; (4) clinical social workers; (5) clinical psychologists; and (6) registered dietitians or nutrition professionals. [Soc. Sec. Act § 1802(b) (6).]

Medicare's limiting charge (see ¶ 865) does not apply to private contract arrangements. [Soc. Sec. Act § 1802(b) (4).] Also, a physician or practitioner who opts out is not required to submit claims on behalf of beneficiaries. [*Medicare Benefit Policy Manual*, Pub. 100-02, Ch. 15, § 40.]

Pursuant to Soc. Sec. Act § 1842(b) (5), the HHS Secretary posted information concerning opt-out physicians and practitioners on the HHS website at go.cms.gov/optoutinfo.

Requirements for Private Physician Contracts

For an opt out to be effective, the contract between the beneficiary and physician/practitioner must be in writing and signed by the beneficiary before any item or service is provided, and not at a time when the beneficiary is facing an emergency or urgent health care situation. It also must clearly state whether the physician or practitioner is excluded from Medicare under Soc. Sec. Act § § 1128, 1156, or 1892. [Soc. Sec. Act § 1802(b) (2); 42 C.F.R. § 405.415.]

By signing the contract, the beneficiary:

(1) agrees not to submit a claim (or to request that the physician or practitioner submit a claim) for the items or services, even if they are otherwise covered by Medicare;

(2) agrees to be responsible, through insurance or otherwise, for payment and understands that no reimbursement will be provided;

(3) acknowledges that no limits under Title XVIII (including the limiting charge) apply to amounts that may be charged for such items or services;

(4) acknowledges that Medigap plans under Soc. Sec. Act § 1882 do not, and other supplemental insurance plans may elect not to, make payments for the items and services because payment is not made by Medicare; and

(5) acknowledges that the beneficiary has the right to have the items or services provided by other physicians or practitioners for whom payment would be made by Medicare.

[Soc. Sec. Act § 1802(b)(2)(B); 42 C.F.R. § 405.415.]

Opt-out period. Opt outs last two years and are automatically extended for additional two-year periods unless the physician or practitioner provides notice to the Secretary 30 days before the end of the previous two-year period that he or she does not want to exend the contract. [Soc. Sec. Act § 1802(b)(3); 42 C.F.R. §§ 405.400, 405.405(b), 405.410(c).]

Physician affidavit. For the private contract to be effective, the physician or practitioner must sign and file with the HHS Secretary an affidavit stating that for the opt-out period he or she will not submit any claims to Medicare nor receive any payment from Medicare for items or services provided to any Medicare beneficiary. [Soc. Sec. Act § 1802(b)(3); 42 C.F.R. § 405.420.]

Enforcement. A physician or practitioner who knowingly and willfully submits a claim to Medicare or receives any payment from Medicare during the affidavit's opt-out period will lose the rights provided under the private contract provision for the remainder of the period and will not be eligible to receive Medicare payments for the remainder of the period. [Soc. Sec. Act § 1802(b)(3)(C); 42 C.F.R. § 405.435(a).]

Medicare payment may be made for the claims submitted by a beneficiary for the services of an opt-out physician or practitioner when the physician or practitioner did not privately contract with the beneficiary for services that were not emergency care services or urgent care services and were furnished no later than 15 days after the date of a notice by the Medicare administrative contractor that the physician or practitioner has opted out of Medicare. [42 C.F.R. § 405.435(c).]

Emergency or urgent care. A physician or practitioner who has opted out of Medicare does not need to enter into a private contract to furnish emergency care services or urgent care services to a Medicare beneficiary. Accordingly, a physician or practitioner will not have failed to maintain opt out if he or she furnishes emergency care services or urgent care services to a Medicare beneficiary with whom the physician or practitioner has not previously entered into a private contract. In such circumstances, the physician or practitioner must submit a claim and may collect no more than the Medicare limiting charge, in the case of a physician, or the deductible and coinsurance, in the case of a practitioner. [42 C.F.R. § 405.440; Pub. 100-02, Ch. 15, § 40.28.]

Terminating opt outs and appeals. A physician or practitioner may terminate an opt out by satisfying certain notification and refund requirements. Further, a physician or practitioner who is dissatisfied with a determination by CMS that a physician or practitioner has failed to properly opt out, failed to maintain opt out, failed to timely renew opt out, failed to privately contract, or failed to properly terminate opt out may utilize the enrollment appeals process currently available for providers and suppliers addressed in 42 C.F.R. Part 498. [42 C.F.R. §§405.445, 405.450(a).]

[¶ 875] Clinical Diagnostic Laboratory Tests

Generally, outpatient clinical diagnostic laboratory tests, except provider-based laboratories performing clinical diagnostic laboratory tests for their own inpatients, are paid according to fee schedules established by the HHS Secretary. This includes clinical laboratory tests performed in a physician's office and by an independent laboratory or a hospital laboratory for its outpatients. [Soc. Sec. Act §1833(h)(1).]

An independent laboratory, however, may not bill the Medicare administrative contractor for the technical component (TC) of physician pathology services furnished to a hospital inpatient or outpatient. [42 C.F.R. §415.130(d).]

Payment for clinical diagnostic laboratory test services. Most clinical diagnostic laboratory tests are paid under the clinical laboratory fee schedule pursuant to Soc. Sec. Act §1833(h)(1). The amount paid is at 80 percent (or 100 percent, in the case of such tests for which payment is made on an assignment-related basis) of the lesser of the fee schedule amount, the limitation amount for that test determined under Soc. Sec. Act §1833(h)(4)(B), or the actual charges. [Soc. Sec. Act §1833(a)(1)(D), (a)(2)(D).]

In the case of any diagnostic laboratory test that is not paid on the basis of a fee schedule, the HHS Secretary may negotiate a payment rate with the person or entity performing the test that would be considered the full charge for the test. Part B pays 100 percent of the negotiated rate. [Soc. Sec. Act §1833(a)(1)(D)(ii), (h)(6).]

Different payment rules apply beginning January 1, 2018 (see Payment for Laboratory Services Beginning January 1, 2018, below).

Other methods of payment. Certain outpatient laboratory services can be paid in other ways, including:

- under the physician fee schedule (see *Medicare Claims Processing Manual*, Pub. 100-04, Ch. 16, §§100, 100.2);

- at 101 percent of reasonable cost for critical access hospitals only;

- under the outpatient prospective payment system (OPPS) when packaged into the payment for related procedures (see 42 C.F.R. §419.2(b)); or

- the reasonable charge payment method.

[Pub. 100-04, Ch. 16, §10.2.]

Mandatory assignment. Payment for clinical diagnostic tests performed by clinical laboratories, excluding tests performed by rural health clinics (RHCs), may be made only on an assignment-related basis. If a person repeatedly bills beneficiaries for clinical diagnostic laboratory tests on other than an assignment-related basis, he or she will be subject to exclusion from the program and civil money penalties. [Soc. Sec. Act §1833(h)(5)(C), (D).]

Deductibles. The usual Part B deductible does not apply to clinical diagnostic laboratory tests paid (1) under Soc. Sec. Act §1833(a)(1)(D)(i) or (a)(2)(D)(i) on an assignment-related basis, or to a provider having an agreement under Soc. Sec. Act §1866; or (2) for tests furnished before January 1, 2018, on the basis of a negotiated rate. [Soc. Sec. Act §1833(b)(3).]

Calculation of Payment Under the Clinical Laboratory Fee Schedule

Each fee schedule is set at 60 percent of the prevailing charge levels for each area, as adjusted annually to reflect changes in the Consumer Price Index for All Urban Consumers (U.S. city average), and subject to such other adjustments as the HHS Secretary determines are justified by technological changes or the need to adequately compensate for emergency services or high utilization of sophisticated equipment and skilled personnel. Laboratories in sole community hospitals are paid 62 percent of the prevailing charge level. [Soc. Sec. Act § 1833(h)(2).]

Fee schedule adjustments. Section 3401(l) of the Patient Protection and Affordable Care Act (ACA) (P.L. 111-148) provided for a productivity adjustment to the clinical laboratory fee schedule, effective for services in 2011 and later. The productivity adjustment is the same one applied to inpatient hospital services under Soc. Sec. Act § 1886(b)(3)(B)(xi)(II). The application of this productivity adjustment may not result in the annual percentage increase being less than 0.0 for a year. [Soc. Sec. Act § 1833(h)(2)(A)(iv)(I).]

Also pursuant to section 3401(l) of the ACA, updates for 2011 through 2015 were subject to an additional reduction of 1.75 percentage points, which could result in an adjustment to the fee schedule being less than 0.0 for a year and the payment rates for a year being less than the rates for the preceding year. In addition, the Secretary was required to reduce by 2 percent the fee schedules otherwise determined under Soc. Sec. Act § 1833(h)(2)(A)(i) for 2013, and such reduced fee schedules serve as the base for 2014 and subsequent years. [Soc. Sec. Act § 1833(h)(2)(A)(iv).]

Fee schedule ceiling. Medicare law imposes a ceiling (called the "national limitation amount") on the amount that may be paid under a fee schedule. The ceiling is set at 74 percent of the median of all fee schedules established for that test for that laboratory setting. In the case of new tests for which no limitation amount has previously been established, the ceiling is 100 percent of the median. [Soc. Sec. Act § 1833(h)(4)(B).]

Fees for specimen collection and travel. In addition to the fee schedule amount, CMS will pay: (1) a nominal additional fee for the costs in collecting the sample on which a clinical diagnostic laboratory test was performed; and (2) a fee to cover the transportation and personnel expenses for trained personnel to travel to the location of an individual who is homebound or an inpatient in an inpatient facility other than a hospital to collect the sample. [Soc. Sec. Act § 1833(h)(3)(A); Pub. 100-04, Ch. 16, §§ 60.1, 60.2.]

Automated laboratory tests. Clinical laboratory tests are covered under Medicare if they are reasonable and necessary for the diagnosis or treatment of an illness or injury. Because of the numerous technological advances and innovations in the clinical laboratory field and the increased availability of automated testing equipment, no distinction generally is made in determining payment for individual tests because of either (1) the site where the service is performed; or (2) the method of the testing process used, whether manual or automated. Whether the test is performed manually or with automated equipment, the services are considered similar and the payment is the same. [Pub. 100-04, Ch. 16, § 90.1.]

Multiple procedure payment reduction. CMS applies a multiple procedure payment reduction (MPRR) to the TC of certain cardiovascular and ophthalmology diagnostic tests. For diagnostic cardiovascular services, full payment is made for the procedure with the highest TC payment, and payment is reduced by 25 percent for the TC for each additional procedure furnished to the same patient on the same day. For diagnostic ophthalmology services, full payment is made for the procedure with the highest TC payment, and payment is reduced by 20 percent for the TC for each additional procedure furnished to the same patient on the same day. [*Final rule*, 77 FR 68891, Nov. 16, 2012.]

Payment for Laboratory Services Beginning January 1, 2018

Section 216 of the Protecting Access to Medicare Act of 2014 (PAMA) (P.L. 113-93), which added Soc. Sec. Act § 1834A, required CMS to implement a new Medicare payment system for clinical diagnostic laboratory tests based on private payer rates beginning January 1, 2017; CMS issued regulations changing the effective date to January 1, 2018. [42 C.F.R. § 414.507.] For tests furnished on or after January 1, 2018, that are paid under § 1834A, the amount paid will be 80 percent (or 100 percent, in the case of such tests for which payment is made on an assignment-related basis) of the lesser of the amount determined under § 1834A or the actual charges.

Advanced diagnostic laboratory tests. An "advanced diagnostic laboratory test" is a clinical diagnostic laboratory test covered under Medicare Part B that is offered and furnished only by a single laboratory and not sold for use by a laboratory other than the single laboratory that designed the test or a successor owner of that laboratory, and meets certain other criteria. [42 C.F.R. § 414.502.]For advanced diagnostic laboratory tests, the payment rate is based upon the test's actual list charge, up to 130 percent of the weighted medial private payer rate. [42 C.F.R. § 414.522.]

Reporting of payment rates. Beginning January 1, 2016, and every three years thereafter, each "applicable laboratory" is required to report to CMS, with respect to a laboratory test for the previous 12-month period, the following: (1) the payment rate that was paid by each private payer (health insurance issuers, group health plans, Medicare Advantage plans, and Medicaid managed care organizations) for the test during the period; and (2) the volume of such tests for each such payer for that period. An "applicable laboratory" is defined as a laboratory that derives the majority of its revenues from Soc. Sec. Act § § 1834A, 1833(h) (the clinical laboratory fee schedule), or 1848 (the physician fee schedule). [Soc. Sec. Act § 1834A(a); 42 C.F.R. § 414.504.]

The applicable laboratory must then report this data to CMS between January 1 and March 31 of the following year, to be used in calculating the clinical laboratory fee schedule for three years beginning the subsequent year. Therefore, data collected between January 1 and June 30, 2016, will be reported between January 1 and March 31, 2017, for rate years 2018 through 2020. [42 C.F.R. § 414.504; *Final rule*, 81 FR 41036, June 23, 2016.]

Payment. For clinical diagnostic laboratory tests furnished on or after January 1, 2018, the payment amount under Soc. Sec. Act § 1834A will be equal to the weighted median for the test for the period, as determined by the Secretary based on the information reported under Soc. Sec. Act § 1834A(a). Reductions from the implementation of the private payer rate will be phased in from 2018 through 2023. [Soc. Sec. Act § 1834A(b); 42 C.F.R. § 414.507.]

Different rules apply to new tests and new advanced diagnostic tests. [Soc. Sec. Act § 1834A(c), (d); 42 C.F.R. § § 414.508, 414.522.]

Who May Bill for Laboratory Tests

In most cases, only the person or entity that performed or supervised performance of a clinical diagnostic laboratory test can receive payment. Thus, a physician will not be paid for a test unless the physician (or another physician with whom the physician shares his or her practice) personally performed or supervised the performance of the test. Similarly, in most cases a laboratory that refers tests to another laboratory will cannot receive payment. There is an exception for hospitals when the tests are performed under arrangements made by the hospital and the referring laboratory meets certain conditions and does not have a financial relationship with the referring physician. [Soc. Sec. Act § § 1833(h)(5)(A), 1887.]

¶875

Payment for clinical diagnostic laboratory tests normally can be made only if the physician ordering the tests is also the physician treating the patient. [42 C.F.R. § 410.32(a).]

When a laboratory bills for a test on the basis of a physician referral, the laboratory is required to include the name and national provider identifier of the referring physician and indicate whether the referring physician is an investor in the laboratory. [Soc. Sec. Act § 1833(q).]

Prohibition on referrals to related labs. Physicians (and their immediate relatives) are generally prohibited from referring laboratory tests to labs with which the physician has a financial relationship (see ¶ 720). [Soc. Sec. Act § 1877(a)–(g).]

Prohibition on Mark-Up of Clinical Laboratory Services

If a physician bills for a laboratory test performed by an outside laboratory and identifies both the laboratory and the amount the laboratory charged, payment for the test will be based on the lower of the following amounts:

(1) the outside laboratory's reasonable charge for the service; or

(2) the amount that the laboratory charged the physician for the service.

[42 C.F.R. § 405.515(b).]

If the bill or request for payment does not indicate that the test was personally performed or supervised either by the physician who submitted the bill or another physician with whom that physician shares his or her practice and if the outside laboratory and the amount the laboratory charged are not identified, payment will be based on the lowest charge at which the Medicare administrative contractor estimates the test could have been secured from a laboratory serving the physician's locality. [42 C.F.R. § 405.515(c).]

[¶ 880] Ambulance Fee Schedule

Ambulance services, except for services furnished by certain critical access hospitals (CAHs), are reimbursed under a fee schedule payment system. Under the fee schedule, Medicare-covered ambulance services are paid based on the lower of the actual billed amount or the ambulance fee schedule amount. [Soc. Sec. Act § 1834(l); 42 C.F.R. §§ 414.601, 414.610(a).]

The fee schedule payment for ambulance services equals a base rate for the level of service plus a separate payment for mileage to the nearest appropriate facility and applicable adjustment factors. Oxygen and other items and services provided as part of the transport are included in the base payment rate and are not separately payable. [Soc. Sec. Act § 1834(l); 42 C.F.R. § 414.610(a); *Medicare Claims Processing Manual*, Pub. 100-04, Ch. 15, § 20.1.1.]

Ground ambulance service. To compute the fee schedule amount for ground ambulance services, the conversion factor (CF), an amount that serves as a nationally uniform base rate, is multiplied by the applicable relative value units (RVUs) for each level of service to produce a service-level base rate. The service-level base rate is then adjusted by the geographic adjustment factor (GAF) (equal to the practice expense (PE) portion of the geographic practice cost index (GPCI) for the physician fee schedule for each ambulance fee schedule locality area). The lesser of the actual charge or the GAF adjusted base rate amount is added to the lesser of the actual mileage charges or the payment rate per mile, multiplied by the number of miles that the beneficiary was transported. [42 C.F.R. § 414.610(c)(1), (c)(4).]

Air ambulance service. The base payment rate for the applicable type of air ambulance service is adjusted by the GAF and, when applicable, by the appropriate rural adjustment factor, to determine the amount of payment. Air ambulance services have no CF or RVUs. This amount is compared to the actual charge. The lesser of the charge or the adjusted GAF rate amount is added to the payment rate per mile, multiplied by the number of miles that the beneficiary was transported. [42 C.F.R. § 414.610(c)(2).]

Adjustments to Ambulance Fee Schedule Amounts

Soc. Sec. Act § 1834(l)(12)(A) provides for a "super rural bonus," a percent increase in the base rate of the fee schedule for transportation originating in a qualified rural area. The payment amount for the ground ambulance base rate is increased by 22.6 percent where the point of pickup is in a rural area determined to be in the lowest 25 percent of rural population arrayed by population density. Section 203(b) of the Medicare Access and CHIP Reauthorization Act of 2015 (MACRA) (P.L. 114-10) extended this bonus through December 31, 2017. [Soc. Sec. Act § 1834(l)(12)(A); 42 C.F.R. § 414.610(c)(5)(ii).]

Soc. Sec. Act § 1834(l)(13)(A) also provides for temporary increases to ground ambulance services. For covered ground ambulance transports that originate in a rural area or in a rural census tract of a metropolitan statistical area (MSA), the fee schedule amount is increased by 3 percent, and for covered ground ambulance transports that do not originate in a rural area or in a rural census tract of an MSA, the fee schedule amounts are increased by 2 percent. Most recently, MACRA extended these payment add-ons for services furnished through December 31, 2017. [Soc. Sec. Act § 1834(l)(13)(A); 42 C.F.R. § 414.610(c)(1)(ii).]

Productivity adjustment. Section 3401(j) of the Patient Protection and Affordable Care Act (ACA) (P.L. 111-148) amended the annual update under Soc. Sec. Act § 1834(l)(3)(B) to add a productivity adjustment for ambulance services, effective for services in 2011 and later. The productivity adjustment is the same one applied to inpatient hospital services under Soc. Sec. Act § 1886(b)(3)(B)(xi)(II). The application of this productivity adjustment may result in the annual percentage increase being less than 0.0 for a year and may result in payment rates under the ambulance fee schedule for a year being less than such payment rates for the preceding year. [Soc. Sec. Act § 1834(l)(3)(C).]

ESRD beneficiaries. The ambulance fee schedule amount normally paid for non-emergency basic life support services to transport beneficiaries with end-stage renal disease for dialysis services is reduced by 10 percent if furnished by a provider or renal dialysis facility. [Soc. Sec. Act § 1834(l)(15); 42 C.F.R. § 414.610(c)(8).]

Transporting multiple patients. The allowable amount per beneficiary for a single ambulance transport when more than one patient is transported simultaneously is based on the total number of patients (both Medicare and non-Medicare) on board:

(1) If two patients are transported at the same time in one ambulance to the same destination, the adjusted payment allowance for each Medicare beneficiary is 75 percent of the single-patient allowed amount applicable to the level of service furnished a beneficiary, plus 50 percent of the total mileage payment allowance for the entire trip.

(2) If three or more patients are transported at the same time in one ambulance to the same destination, the adjusted payment for each Medicare beneficiary is 60 percent of the single-patient allowed amount applicable to the level of service furnished that beneficiary. A single payment allowance for mileage, however, will be prorated by the number of patients on board.

[42 C.F.R. § 414.610(c)(6); *Medicare Benefit Policy Manual*, Pub. 100-02, Ch. 10, § 10.3.10.]

"Patient Transportation"

Ambulance services are separately reimbursable only under Part B. Once a beneficiary is admitted to a hospital, CAH, or skilled nursing facility (SNF), it may be necessary to transport the beneficiary to another hospital or other site temporarily for specialized care while the beneficiary maintains inpatient status with the original provider. This movement of the patient is considered "patient transportation" and is covered as an inpatient hospital or CAH service under Part A and as a SNF service when the SNF is furnishing it as a covered SNF service and Part A payment is made for that service. Because the service is covered and payable as a beneficiary transportation service under Part A, the service cannot be classified and paid for as an ambulance service under Part B. This includes intra-campus transfers between different departments of the same hospital, even when the departments are located in separate buildings. Such intra-campus transfers are not separately payable under the Part B ambulance benefit. [Pub. 100-04, Ch. 15, § 10.4.]

[¶ 882] Payment for Durable Medical Equipment, Prosthetics, Orthotics, and Other Supplies

Medicare pays for durable medical equipment, prosthetics, orthotics, and other supplies (DMEPOS) based on regional fee schedules. Payment for those items equals 80 percent of the lower of the actual charge for the durable medical equipment (DME) or the fee schedule amount. [Soc. Sec. Act § 1834(a)(1), (h)(1).]

Fee schedule classes. DMEPOS are categorized into the following classes, with a separate fee schedule for each class:

- inexpensive or routinely purchased items;
- items requiring frequent and substantial servicing;
- certain customized items;
- oxygen and oxygen equipment;
- prosthetic and orthotic devices;
- capped rental items; and
- transcutaneous electrical nerve stimulants (TENS) units.

[Soc. Sec. Act § 1834(a); 42 C.F.R. § 414.210(b).]

Blood-testing strips and glucose monitors. The payment amount for diabetic testing supplies, including test strips, that are not mail-order items are the same as the single payment amounts established under the national mail order competition for diabetic supplies under Soc. Sec. Act § 1847, when such single payment amounts are implemented. [Soc. Sec. Act § 1834(a)(1)(H).]

Productivity adjustment. Pursuant to § 3401(m) of the Patient Protection and Affordable Care Act (ACA) (P.L. 111-148), for 2011 and later, the annual payment update for DME is reduced by the productivity adjustment applicable to hospital inpatient services. The application of this productivity adjustment may result in the annual percentage increase being less than 0.0 for a year and may result in payment rates for DME for a year being less than such payment rates for the preceding year. [Soc. Sec. Act § 1834(a)(14)(L) and (h)(4).]

Maintenance, Servicing, and Replacement of DME

Generally, Medicare pays the reasonable and necessary charges for maintenance and servicing of beneficiary-owned equipment. Reasonable and necessary charges are those made for parts and labor not otherwise covered under a manufacturer's or supplier's warranty. The contractor establishes a reasonable fee for labor associated with repairing, maintaining, and servicing the item. Payment is made for replacement parts in a lump sum based on the contractor's consideration of the item. [42 C.F.R. § 414.210(e)(1).]

¶882

Exceptions. No payments are made for maintenance and servicing of the following: (1) items requiring frequent and substantial servicing; (2) capped rental items that are not beneficiary owned; and (3) oxygen equipment. [42 C.F.R. § 414.210(e)(3).]

Replacement. If an item of DME or a prosthetic or orthotic device paid for under the DMEPOS fee schedule has been in continuous use by the patient for the equipment's reasonable useful lifetime (of at least five years) or if the contractor determines that the item is lost, stolen, or irreparably damaged, the beneficiary may elect to obtain a new piece of equipment. If the beneficiary elects to obtain replacement oxygen equipment, payment is made in accordance with 42 C.F.R. § 414.226(a). If the beneficiary elects to obtain a replacement capped rental item, payment is made in accordance with 42 C.F.R. § 414.229(a)(2) or (a)(3). For all other beneficiary-owned items, if the beneficiary elects to obtain replacement equipment, payment is made on a purchase basis. [42 C.F.R. § 414.210(f).]

Prior Authorization Process for Certain DME

Pursuant to section 1834(a)(15) of the Social Security Act, the Secretary developed a list of DMEPOS that, based on prior payment experience, were determined to be frequently subject to unnecessary utilization, as well as a prior authorization process for these items. [42 C.F.R. § 414.234; *Final rules*, 80 FR 81674, Dec. 30, 2015; 81 FR 93636, Dec. 21, 2016.]

The Master List of Items Frequently Subject to Unnecessary Utilization includes items listed on the DMEPOS fee schedule with an average purchase fee of $1,000 (adjusted annually for inflation using Consumer Price Index for All Urban Consumers (CPI-U)) or greater or an average rental fee schedule of $100 (adjusted annually for inflation using CPI-U) or greater that also meet one of the following two criteria:

(1) the item has been identified as having a high rate of fraud or unnecessary utilization in a report that is national in scope from 2007 or later published by the Office of Inspector General or the General Accountability Office; or

(2) the item is listed in the 2011 or later Comprehensive Error Rate Testing (CERT) program's Annual Medicare Fee-For-Service Improper Payment Rate Report DME and/or DMEPOS Service Specific Reports.

The Master List is self-updating annually, and items remain on it for 10 years. [42 C.F.R. § 414.234(b).]

To balance minimizing provider and supplier burden with CMS's need to protect the Medicare program, CMS is initially implementing prior authorization for a subset of items on the Master List. CMS publishes in the *Federal Register* and posts on the CMS prior authorization website a list of items, the Required Prior Authorization List, which is selected from the Master List, that require prior authorization as a condition of payment. [42 C.F.R. § 414.234(c); *Final rules*, 80 FR 81674, Dec. 30, 2015; 81 FR 93636, Dec. 21, 2016.]

Before furnishing the item and submitting the claim for processing, a prior authorization requester must submit evidence that the item complies with all applicable Medicare coverage, coding, and payment rules. After receipt of all applicable required Medicare documentation, CMS or one of its review contractors will conduct a medical review and communicate a decision that provisionally affirms or non-affirms the request. A provisional affirmation prior authorization decision is a condition of payment. [42 C.F.R. § 414.234(d), (e).]

DME Competitive Acquisition Program

For items furnished on or after January 1, 2011, the DME fee schedule amounts may be adjusted, and for items furnished on or after January 1, 2016, the fee schedule amounts must be adjusted, based on information on the payment determined as part of implementation of the competitive bidding programs for certain DMEPOS items, as required by Soc. Sec. Act § 1847(a) and (b) (excluding information on the payment determined in accordance with the special payment rules at 42 C.F.R. § 414.409). If adjustments do occur, inherent reasonableness will not apply. [42 C.F.R. § 414.210(g).]

The implementing regulations created a six-month transition period, from January 1, 2016 through June 30, 2016. During the transition period, applicable items and services furnished had a payment adjustment equal to 50 percent of the adjusted payment amount established under this section and 50 percent of the unadjusted fee schedule amount. [42 C.F.R. § 414.210(g)(9)(1).] The transition period was extended by section 16007 of the 21st Century Cures Act (P.L. 114-255) to June 30, 2016 to December 31, 2016, with the full implementation applying to items and services furnished with dates of service on or after January 1, 2017. The HHS Secretary is required to conduct a study and issue a report on the impact of the payment adjustments on the number of DME suppliers and the availability of DME to Medicare Part A and Part B beneficiaries. [21st Century Cures Act § 16007.]

Inexpensive or Routinely Purchased Items

DME is "inexpensive" if the average purchase price of it did not exceed $150 from July 1986 through June 1987. DME is routinely purchased if it was acquired by purchase on a national basis at least 75 percent of the time from July 1986 through June 1987. Included in the definition of inexpensive or routinely purchased equipment are accessories used in conjunction with a nebulizer, aspirator, or ventilator that is either a continuous airway pressure device or a respiratory assist device with bi-level pressure capability. [Soc. Sec. Act § 1834(a)(2)(A); 42 C.F.R. § 414.220(a); *Medicare Claims Processing Manual*, Pub. 100-04, Ch. 20, § 130.2.]

Payment for inexpensive or routinely purchased items is made on a rental basis or in a lump-sum purchase amount that is based on the national limited payment amount (the cost of purchasing the DME in a national market), as updated by changes in the Consumer Price Index. If rental rather than lump-sum purchase is chosen, the total amount of rental payments may not exceed the allowed lump-sum purchase amount. [Soc. Sec. Act § 1834(a)(2)(B)(iv), (C); 42 C.F.R. § 414.220(b); Pub. 100-04, Ch. 20, § 30.1.]

Payment for TENS units is made on a purchase basis with the purchase price determined using the methodology for purchase of inexpensive or routinely purchased items. The payment amount for TENS computed under 42 C.F.R. § 414.220(c)(2), however, is reduced. [Soc. Sec. Act § 1834(a)(1)(D); 42 C.F.R. § 414.232(a).]

Customized Items

To be considered a customized item for payment purposes, a covered item (including a wheelchair) must be uniquely constructed or substantially modified for a specific beneficiary according to the description and orders of a physician and be so different from another item used for the same purpose that the two items cannot be grouped together for pricing purposes. [Soc. Sec. Act § 1834(a)(4); 42 C.F.R. § 414.224(a).] According to the *Medicare Claims Processing Manual*, customized items are rarely necessary and rarely furnished. [Pub. 100-04, Ch. 20, § 130.4.]

Payment is made on a lump sum basis for the purchase of a customized item based on the DME Medicare administrative contractor's (MAC) individual consideration and judgment of a reasonable payment amount for each customized item. The MAC's individual consideration takes into account written documentation on the costs of the item including at least the cost of labor and materials used in customizing an item. [Soc. Sec. Act § 1834(a)(4); 42 C.F.R. § 414.224(b).]

Oxygen and Oxygen Equipment

National limited monthly payment rates are calculated and paid as the monthly fee schedule amounts for the following classes of items: (1) stationary oxygen equipment (including stationary concentrators) and oxygen contents (stationary and portable); (2) portable equipment only (gaseous or liquid tanks); (3) oxygen generating portable equipment only; (4) stationary oxygen contents only; and (5) portable oxygen contents only. [42 C.F.R. § 414.226(c) (1).]

Medicare pays for rental of oxygen equipment based on a monthly fee schedule amount during the period of medical need, but for no longer than a period of continuous use of 36 months. Medicare does not pay for purchases of this type of equipment. [Soc. Sec. Act § 1834(a) (5); 42 C.F.R. § 414.226(a) (1), (d) (1) and (2); Pub. 100-04, Ch. 20, § § 30.6, 30.6.2.]

Medicare pays for purchase of oxygen contents based on a monthly fee schedule amount until medical necessity ends. [42 C.F.R. § 414.226(a) (2), (d) (3) and (4); Pub. 100-04, Ch. 20, § 30.6.3.]

Payment for oxygen equipment after rental cap. A supplier that furnishes oxygen equipment after the 36-month rental cap must (1) continue to furnish the equipment during any period of medical need for the remainder of the reasonable useful lifetime of the equipment in accordance with 42 C.F.R. § 414.210(f) (1); or (2) arrange for furnishing the oxygen equipment with another supplier if the beneficiary relocates to an area outside the supplier's normal service area. [Soc. Sec. Act § 1834(a) (5) (F) (ii); 42 C.F.R. § 414.226(f) (1).]

A supplier that furnishes liquid or gaseous oxygen equipment (stationary or portable) for the 36th continuous month must (1) continue to furnish the oxygen contents necessary for the effective use of the liquid or gaseous equipment during any period of medical need for the remainder of the reasonable useful lifetime established for the equipment in accordance with 42 C.F.R. § 414.210(f) (1); or (2) arrange for furnishing the oxygen contents with another supplier if the beneficiary relocates to an area outside the supplier's normal service area. [Soc. Sec. Act § 1834(a) (5) (F) (ii); 42 C.F.R. § 414.226(f) (2).]

For the first six-month period after the 36-month rental period ends, the contractor makes no payment for maintenance and servicing of oxygen equipment other than liquid and gaseous equipment (stationary and portable). For each succeeding six-month period, payment may be made during the first month of that period for routine maintenance and servicing of the equipment in the beneficiary's home (including an institution used as the beneficiary's home). The supplier must visit the beneficiary's home to inspect the equipment during the first month of the six-month period. [42 C.F.R. § 414.210(e) (5).]

Capped Rental Items

For rented DME not subject to the payment provisions of 42 C.F.R. § § 414.220 through 414.228, during the first three months of use, payment is limited to 10 percent of the "recognized purchase price"; thereafter, payment is limited to 7.5 percent of the recognized purchase price. [Soc. Sec. Act § 1834(a) (7) (A) (i) (II); 42 C.F.R. § 414.229(b) (2); Pub. 100-04, Ch. 20, § 30.5.1.]

For power-driven wheelchairs, payment equals 15 percent of the recognized purchase price for the first three months and 6 percent of the recognized purchase price for the remaining months. [Soc. Sec. Act § 1834(a) (7) (A) (i) (III); 42 C.F.R. § 414.229(b) (3).]

The purchase price is based on the national limited payment amount (the cost of purchasing the DME in a national market), as updated by changes in the Consumer Price Index. [Soc. Sec. Act § 1834(a) (8); 42 C.F.R. § 414.229(c) (3).]

¶882

Replacement. If the reasonable lifetime (five years) of an item has been reached during a continuous period of medical need, or the contractor determines that the item is lost or irreparably damaged, payment for replacement may be made on either a rental or a purchase basis. [Soc. Sec. Act § 1834(a)(7)(C); Pub. 100-04, Ch. 20, § 50.1.]

Complex rehabilitative power-driven wheelchairs. Suppliers must offer beneficiaries the option to purchase complex rehabilitative power-driven wheelchairs at the time the equipment is initially furnished. Medicare pays on a lump-sum purchase basis if the beneficiary chooses this option. [Soc. Sec. Act § 1834(a)(7)(A)(iii); 42 C.F.R. § 414.229(d)(1), (h).]

Ownership after rental. Medicare pays for most capped rental items during the period of medical need, but no longer than a period of continuous use of 13 months. On the first day after the 13th continuous month, the supplier must transfer title of the item to the beneficiary. [Soc. Sec. Act § 1834(a)(7)(A)(i)(I), (ii); 42 C.F.R. § 414.229(f).]

Prosthetic Devices and Prosthetics/Orthotics

Medicare pays for prosthetic devices (excluding parenteral and enteral nutrition, nutrients, supplies, and equipment) and prosthetics and orthotics (excluding intraocular lenses and medical supplies furnished by a home health agency) on a lump sum basis. [Soc. Sec. Act § 1834(h)(1)(A), (4); 42 C.F.R. § 414.228(a); Pub. 100-04, Ch. 20, § 30.4.] Ostomy supplies, tracheostomy supplies, and urologicals are reimbursed as inexpensive or other routinely purchased DME under Soc. Sec. Act § 1834(a)(2). [Soc. Sec. Act § 1834(h)(1)(E).]

The payment rules of Soc. Sec. Act § 1834(h) apply to reimbursement for therapeutic shoes for diabetics. [Soc. Sec. Act § 1833(o)(2); 42 C.F.R. § 414.228(c).]

Parenteral and Enteral Nutrition, Splints, Casts, and Certain Intraocular Lenses

For parenteral and enteral nutrition (PEN) items and services, splints and casts, and intraocular lenses (IOLs) inserted in a physician's office on or after April 1, 2014, Medicare pays for the items and services on the basis of 80 percent of the lesser of: (1) the actual charge for the item or service; or (2) the fee schedule amount for the item or service, as determined in accordance with 42 C.F.R. §§ 414.104 through 414.108. [Soc. Sec. Act § 1842(s)(2); 42 C.F.R. § 414.102(a).]

CMS or the contractor determines fee schedules for these items, and CMS designates the specific items and services in each category through program instructions. For 2011 and later for PEN items and services and for 2015 and later for splints and casts and IOLs inserted in a physician's office, the fee schedule amounts of the preceding year are updated by the percentage increase in the CPI-U for the 12-month period ending with June of the preceding year. [Soc. Sec. Act § 1842(s)(1)(B)(ii); 42 C.F.R. § 414.102(b), (c).]

PEN. Payment is made in a lump sum for PEN nutrients and supplies that are purchased and on a monthly basis for equipment that is rented. The fee schedule amounts may be adjusted based on information on the payment determined as part of the DME competitive acquisition program using the methodologies described in 42 C.F.R. § 414.210(g). [Soc. Sec. Act § 1842(s)(3); 42 C.F.R. §§ 414.104(a), 414.105; Pub. 100-04, Ch. 20, § 30.7.]

Splints and casts. Medicare pays for splints and casts in a lump sum. The fee schedule amount for payment for an item or service furnished in 2014 was the reasonable charge amount for 2013, updated by the percentage increase in the CPI-U for the 12-month period ending with June of 2013. [42 C.F.R. § 414.106; Pub. 100-04, Ch. 20, § 170.]

Certain IOLs. Medicare pays for IOLs inserted in a physician's office in a lump sum. The fee schedule amount for payment for an IOL furnished in 2014 was the national average allowed charge for the IOL furnished in calendar year 2012, updated by the percentage increase in the CPI-U for the 24-month period ending with June of 2013. [42 C.F.R. § 414.108.]

[¶ 885] Payment for Drugs and Biologics

Payment for drugs (other than prescription drugs) furnished by physicians usually is based on the lower of the actual charge or the manufacturer's average sales price (ASP). This payment policy is applicable to drugs furnished to Medicare beneficiaries that are not "paid for on a cost or prospective payment basis." [Soc. Sec. Act §§ 1842(o), 1847A; 42 C.F.R. §§ 414.900, 414.904; *Medicare Claims Processing Manual*, Pub. 100-04, Ch. 17, § 20.1.]

Drugs furnished incident to a physician's services fall within this category. [42 C.F.R. §§ 405.517(a)(3), 414.36.] Incident-to services and supplies are defined as services and supplies (including drugs and biologics that are not usually self-administered by the patient) furnished as an incident to a physician's professional service that commonly are furnished in physicians' offices and either rendered without charge or included in the physicians' bills. [Soc. Sec. Act § 1861(s)(2)(A).] See ¶ 855 for an explanation of Part B payment for incident-to items and services.

Outpatient surgery. Beginning January 1, 2014, the following are packaged into the outpatient prospective payment system (OPPS) rate:

- drugs, biologics, and radiopharmaceuticals that function as supplies when used in a diagnostic test or procedure (including, but not limited to, diagnostic radiopharmaceuticals, contrast agents, and pharmacologic stress agents); and

- drugs and biologics that function as supplies when used in a surgical procedure (including, but not limited to, skin substitutes and similar products that aid wound healing and implantable biologic).

[42 C.F.R. § 419.2(b).]

Assignment. All billing for drugs and biologics covered under Part B must be on an assignment-related basis. Sanctions may be imposed against violators. [Soc. Sec. Act § 1842(o)(3).]

Use of Average Sales Price Methodology

The payment allowance limit for Medicare Part B drugs and biologics that are not paid on a cost or prospective payment basis is 106 percent of the ASP. [42 C.F.R. § 414.904(a)(2).]

The payment allowance limits for end-stage renal disease (ESRD) drugs when separately billed by freestanding and hospital-based ESRD facilities, specified covered outpatient drugs, and drugs and biologics with pass-through status under the OPPS are paid based on 106 percent of the ASP. [42 C.F.R. § 414.904(d)(2); Pub. 100-04, Ch. 17, § 20.1.2.]

Except for infusion drugs, payment limits are updated quarterly. The payment amount is subject to coinsurance and deductibles. [Soc. Sec. Act § 1847A(b)(5); 42 C.F.R. § 414.904(f), (h).]

Price substitution. When the Inspector General finds that the ASP exceeds the widely available market price (WAMP) or the average manufacturer price (AMP) by an applicable threshold percentage, CMS must substitute the payment amount for the drug or biologic. [42 C.F.R. § 414.904(d)(3).]

Payment at 103 percent of the AMP for a billing code will occur when the following conditions are met:

(1) the ASP for the billing code has exceeded the AMP for the billing code by 5 percent or more in two consecutive quarters, or three of the previous four quarters immediately preceding the quarter to which the price substitution would be applied;

(2) the AMP for the billing code is calculated using the same set of National Drug Codes used for the ASP for the billing code;

(3) 103 percent of the AMP is less than the 106 percent of the ASP for the quarter in which the price substitution would be applied; and

(4) the drug and dosage form represented by the Healthcare Common Procedure Coding System (HCPCS) code are not reported by the Food and Drug Administration (FDA) on its Current Drug Shortage List to be in short supply at the time the ASP payment limits are finalized.

[42 C.F.R. § 414.904(d)(3).]

The applicable percentage threshold for AMP price comparisons is 5 percent. [42 C.F.R. § 414.904(d)(3)(iv).]

Exceptions to the ASP. The following exceptions to the ASP apply:

- The payment limits for hepatitis B vaccine furnished to individuals at high or intermediate risk of contracting hepatitis B, pneumococcal vaccine, and influenza vaccine are calculated using 95 percent of the AWP.

- The payment limits for infusion drugs furnished through a covered item of durable medical equipment (DME) is calculated using 95 percent of the AWP in effect on October 1, 2003.

- For blood and blood products (other than clotting factors), the payment limits are determined in the same manner as they were determined October 1, 2003.

- For an initial period, if data on the sale prices for drugs is not sufficiently available to compute the ASP, the payment limit is based on the wholesale acquisition cost or the applicable Part B drug methodology in effect on October 1, 2003.

[Soc. Sec. Act § 1847A(b)(4); 42 C.F.R. § 414.90(e); Pub. 100-04, Ch. 17, § 20.1.3.]

[¶ 890] Home Infusion Therapy

Section 5012 of the 21st Century Cures Act (P.L. 114-255) provides separate Part B coverage of home infusion therapy beginning in 2021 (see ¶ 390). [Soc. Sec. Act § 1862(s)(2)(GG), (iii).] The 21st Century Cures Act requires the HHS Secretary to implement a payment system under which a single payment is made to a qualified home infusion therapy supplier for items and services furnished by a qualified home infusion therapy supplier in coordination with the furnishing of home infusion drugs. [Soc. Sec. Act § 1834(u).]

A 20 percent copayment will apply to home infusion therapy services. [Soc. Sec. Act § 1833(a)(1)(BB).]

Chapter 9– CLAIMS, PAYMENTS, AND APPEALS

[¶ 900] Claims and Payments

Medicare defines a claim as a filing from a provider, supplier, or beneficiary that includes or refers to a beneficiary's request for Medicare payment and furnishes the Medicare administrative contractor (MAC) with sufficient information to determine whether payment of Medicare benefits is due and the payment amount. [42 C.F.R. §§ 424.5(a)(5), (6).] A claim must contain sufficient identifying information about the beneficiary to allow any missing information to be obtained through routine methods, such as a file check, microfilm reference, mail, or telephone contact based on an address or telephone number in the file. [*Medicare Claims Processing Manual*, Pub. 100-04, Ch. 1, § 50.1.7.]

Payments under Part C Medicare Advantage (MA) plans and Part D prescription drug plans are not subject to the same requirements for submitting claims for payment and appeals that apply to services provided under Parts A and B. For a detailed discussion of payment and appeals under Part C and Part D, see Chapter 4 and Chapter 5, respectively.

Beneficiary Notices

Providers, physicians, and suppliers are required to notify beneficiaries when they believe that Medicare will not cover charges or when services may be terminated. An Advance Beneficiary Notice (ABN) is evidence of beneficiary knowledge about the likelihood of Medicare denial for the purpose of determining financial liability for expenses incurred for services furnished to a beneficiary. An ABN must: (1) be in writing, using approved notice language; (2) cite the particular service or services for which payment is likely to be denied; and (3) cite the notifier's reasons for believing Medicare payment will be denied. [42 C.F.R. § 411.408(f)(1).]

Beneficiaries may select one of several billing options they prefer when notified by the provider that it anticipates Medicare will not cover a service. If the beneficiary signs a request for payment using the ABN, the provider is required to submit a claim. The beneficiary becomes fully responsible for payments after being notified that Medicare may not pay the claim. [Pub. 100-04, Ch. 1, § 60.4.1; Ch. 30, § 50.]

Medicare summary notice. After the MAC processes and either approves or denies the claim, it sends the results to the beneficiary in the form of a Medicare summary notice (MSN). The MSN explains which charges were allowed, any deductible or coinsurance amount, and what Medicare paid on the claim and why. It also explains various features of the Medicare program of interest to the beneficiary. If the claim is denied in whole or in part, the MSN provides the procedures for an appeal (see ¶ 924). The beneficiary is responsible for any applicable deductible or coinsurance (for Part A, see ¶ 220). [Soc. Sec. Act § 1806(a); Pub. 100-04, Ch. 21, §§ 10, 10.1.]

Beginning January 1, 2016, beneficiaries can elect to receive MSNs electronically. [Soc. Sec. Act § 1806(c).]

Submission of Claims

All initial claims for Medicare reimbursement, except claims from small providers, must be submitted electronically (with limited exceptions). Initial Medicare claims are those claims submitted to the appropriate MAC for payment under Part A or Part B for initial processing, including claims sent to Medicare for the first time for secondary payment purposes, resubmitted previously rejected claims, claims with paper attachments, demand bills, claims in situations in which Medicare is secondary and there is only one primary payer, and nonpayment claims. Initial claims do not include adjustments submitted to MACs on previously submitted claims or appeal requests. [Soc. Sec. Act § 1862(a)(22), (h); 42 C.F.R. § 424.32(d)(1)–(3); Pub. 100-04, Ch. 24, § 30.1.]

The Secretary may waive the electronic claims submission requirement in unusual cases as the Secretary finds appropriate. Unusual cases are deemed to exist in the following situations: (1) the submission of dental claims; (2) there is a service interruption in the mode of submitting the electronic claim that is outside the control of the entity submitting the claim, for the period of the interruption; (3) the entity submitting the claim submits fewer than 10 claims to Medicare per month, on average; (4) the entity submitting the claim furnishes services outside of the U.S. territory only; or (5) other extraordinary circumstances precluding submission of electronic claims. [42 C.F.R. § 424.32(d)(4); Pub. 100-04, Ch. 24, § 90.]

Every entity that submits electronic claims to the Medicare program is required to complete an Electronic Data Interchange (EDI) Enrollment Form. New electronic billers must sign and submit the enrollment form before their first billing will be accepted. A provider must obtain a National Provider Identifier (NPI) and furnish that NPI to its MAC before completion of an initial EDI Enrollment Agreement and issuance of an initial EDI number and password by the MAC. [Pub. 100-04, Ch. 24, § 30.1.]

Part A benefits. Hospitals, skilled nursing facilities (SNFs), home health agencies, hospices, and other providers submit claims for payment for items and services rendered under Part A to the MAC. As discussed at ¶ 730, providers charge beneficiaries for applicable deductible and coinsurance amounts as well as for any noncovered or extra services requested by the beneficiary. When a provider knows or believes that no Medicare payment will be made because of the lack of medical necessity or the service or item is excluded from coverage, the provider must notify the beneficiary in writing in the form of an ABN.

Part B benefits. Physicians, practitioners, durable medical equipment suppliers, or outpatient facilities (physician or supplier) that furnish items or services to beneficiaries covered under Part B are required to complete and submit a claim for payment to a MAC. Beneficiaries may not be charged for this service. [Soc. Sec. Act § 1848(g)(4)(A).] Payment will be made to the physician or supplier if the physician or supplier has accepted assignment (see ¶ 868), or to the beneficiary directly if the physician or supplier does not accept assignment. If payment is made to a physician or supplier that is entitled to receive payment on the beneficiary's behalf, the beneficiary is responsible for any applicable deductible or coinsurance requirements (see ¶ 330 and ¶ 335).

Claims forms. Form CMS-1490S, "Patient's Request for Medicare Payment Form," is used only by beneficiaries (or their representatives) who complete and file their own claims. It contains the first six comparable items of data that are on Form CMS-1500 (provider form). When Form CMS-1490S is used, an itemized bill must be submitted with the claim. Beneficiaries use Form CMS-1490S to submit Part B claims only if the service provider refuses to do so. [42 C.F.R. § 424.32(b); Pub. 100-04, Ch. 1, § 70.8.4.]

Under Part B, a claim can be any writing submitted by or on behalf of the beneficiary; however, when the writing constituting a Part B claim is not submitted on a claim form, there must be enough information about the nature of the medical or other health service to enable the MAC to determine that the service was furnished by a physician or supplier. [42 C.F.R. § 424.32(a); Pub. 100-04, Ch. 1, § 50.1.7.]

Physicians and suppliers (except ambulance suppliers) normally submit requests for payment on Form CMS-1500, the "Health Insurance Claim Form," whether or not the claim is assigned. The form is identical to forms used by other health insurance plans in addition to

Medicare. Form CMS-1500 contains a patient's signature line or reference to the patient signature incorporating the patient's request for payment of benefits, authorization to release information, and assignment of benefits. When the billing form is used as the request for payment, there must be a signature, except in limited circumstances. [42 C.F.R. § 424.32(b); Pub. 100-04, Ch. 1, §§ 50.1.1, 70.8.4; Ch. 26, § 10.]

Request for Payment Signature Requirements

For an eligible provider of services to receive payment from Medicare for services furnished to a beneficiary under either Part A or Part B, a written request for payment must be signed by the individual who receives the services. [Soc. Sec. Act §§ 1814(a)(1), 1835(a)(1); 42 C.F.R. §§ 424.32(a)(3), 424.36.]

Signature of beneficiary's representative. If the beneficiary is physically or mentally unable to sign the claim, the following individuals may sign it: (1) the beneficiary's legal guardian; (2) a relative or other individual that receives Social Security or other governmental benefits on behalf of the beneficiary; (3) a relative or other person that arranges for the beneficiary's treatment or takes responsibility for the beneficiary's affairs; (4) a representative of an agency or institution that did not furnish the care in question but that did furnish other care for the beneficiary; (5) a representative of the provider or of the nonparticipating hospital providing the services in question if the provider is unable to have the claim signed in another way outlined above after making reasonable efforts; or (6) an ambulance provider or supplier that provided emergency or non-emergency transport services if certain conditions are met. [42 C.F.R. § 424.36(b).]

Beneficiary not present for the service. If a provider, nonparticipating hospital, or supplier files a claim for services that involved no personal contact between the provider, hospital, or supplier and the beneficiary (for example, a physician sent a blood sample to the provider for diagnostic tests), a representative of the provider, hospital, or supplier may sign the claim on the beneficiary's behalf. [42 C.F.R. § 424.36(c); Pub. 100-04, Ch. 1, § 50.1.3.]

Refusal to sign. A patient on admission to a hospital or SNF may refuse to request Medicare payment and agree to pay for the services out of his or her own funds or from other insurance. If the patient refuses to request Medicare payment, the provider should obtain a signed statement of refusal whenever possible. If the patient is unwilling to sign the statement of refusal, the provider should record that the patient refused to file a request for payment and was unwilling to sign the statement of refusal. [Pub. 100-04, Ch. 1, § 50.1.5.]

Death of beneficiary. If the patient dies before the request for payment is signed, it may be signed by the legal representative of the estate or by any of the persons or institutions (including an authorized official of the provider) who could have signed it had the patient been alive and incompetent. [Pub. 100-04, Ch. 1, § 50.1.3.]

Time Limits for Submitting Claims

Claims must be submitted no later than one calendar year after the date of service. [Soc. Sec. Act §§ 1814(a)(1), 1835(a)(1); 42 C.F.R. § 424.44(a)(1).]

Exceptions to the one-year time limit. The following exceptions apply to the one calendar year time limit for filing fee-for-service claims: (1) administrative error; (2) retroactive Medicare entitlement; (3) retroactive Medicare entitlement involving state Medicaid agencies; and (4) retroactive disenrollment from an MA plan or Program of All-inclusive Care for the Elderly (PACE) provider organization. [42 C.F.R. § 424.44(b).]

When a provider or supplier makes the initial request for an exception to the timely filing limit, the MAC must determine whether a late claim may be honored based on all pertinent documentation submitted by the provider or supplier. [Pub. 100-04, Ch. 1, § 70.7.]

¶900

Prompt Payment of Claims

MACs are required to pay not less than 95 percent of all "clean claims" within 30 days after the clean claims are received. A clean claim is a claim for which payment is not made on a periodic interim payment basis, and one that has no defect, impropriety, or particular circumstance requiring special treatment that prevents timely payment from being made. [Soc. Sec. Act §§ 1816(c)(2)(A) and (B), 1842(c)(2)(A) and (B); Pub. 100-04, Ch. 1, § 80.2.]

If a clean claim payment is not issued, mailed, or otherwise transmitted within the specified time period, the government will be required to pay interest on the amount of payment it should have made, beginning with the day after the required payment date and ending on the date on which the payment is made. [Soc. Sec. Act §§ 1816(c)(2)(C), 1842(c)(2)(C); Pub. 100-04, Ch. 1, § 80.2.2.]

MACs are prohibited from paying electronic claims within 13 days after their receipt. As an incentive to encourage health care providers to submit claims electronically, this prohibition on payment is expanded to 28 days for all other claims. [Soc. Sec. Act §§ 1816(c)(3)(A) and (B), 1842(c)(3)(A) and (B).]

[¶ 902] Certification and Recertification of Medical Necessity

Medicare requires, as a condition of coverage, that the physician who ordered the services certify on the claim form that the services were medically necessary and, in some instances, recertify that the services continue to be required. [42 C.F.R. §§ 424.10(a), 424.13.]

When a certification or recertification is required, it is the responsibility of the provider to obtain the physician's certifying statement. [42 C.F.R. § 424.5(a)(4).] In the case of services furnished by an institutional provider, the provider must maintain on file a written description that specifies the time schedule for certifications and recertifications and indicates whether utilization review of long-stay cases fulfills the requirement for second and subsequent recertifications. [42 C.F.R. §§ 424.13(g), 424.14(e), 424.20(g).]

In certain instances, nonphysician practitioners such as nurse practitioners, clinical nurse specialists, or physician assistants may certify as to medical necessity. The content requirements and time factors related to certifications and recertifications vary according to the items or services furnished and the facility or institution furnishing them. [Soc. Sec. Act § 1814(a)(2).]

Certification Requirements for Part A

Various certification and recertification requirements apply to Part A providers.

Psychiatric hospitals. For psychiatric hospital services, a physician must certify that inpatient services under the supervision of a physician were required and: (1) such treatment can or can be reasonably expected to improve the condition; or (2) inpatient diagnostic study is or was necessary and such services were necessary for such purposes. [Soc. Sec. Act § 1814(a)(2)(A).]

Inpatient hospital services. For inpatient hospital services other than psychiatric hospital services, a physician must certify that such services were required to be given on an inpatient basis for the individual's medical treatment or that inpatient diagnostic study is required and such services are necessary for those purposes. The certification must be furnished no later than the 20th day of the provision of services and should be accompanied by supporting materials. [Soc. Sec. Act § 1814(a)(3).]

Skilled nursing facilities. Certification and recertification for skilled nursing facility (SNF) services must indicate that SNF services are or were required because the individual needs or needed, on a daily basis, skilled nursing care (provided directly by or requiring the supervision of skilled nursing personnel) or other skilled rehabilitation services, which, as a practical matter, can or could only be provided in a SNF or a swing-bed hospital on an inpatient basis. This applies for any of the conditions with respect to which the individual received covered inpatient hospital services. [Soc. Sec. Act § 1814(a)(2)(B); 42 C.F.R. § 424.20.]

Home health. For home health services, a physician must certify that such services were required because the individual is or was confined to the home (except when receiving items or services pursuant to Soc. Sec. Act § 1861(m)(7)) and needs or needed skilled nursing care (other than solely venipucture for the purposes of obtaining a blood sample) on an intermittent basis or physical or speech therapy, or in the case of an individual who has been furnished home health services based on such a need and who no longer has such a need for such care or therapy, continues or continued to need occupational therapy. [Soc. Sec. Act §§ 1814(a)(2)(C), 1835(a)(2)(A); 42 C.F.R. § 424.22.]

The physician who established the plan of care documents must certify that a face-to-face encounter occurred no more than 90 days before the home health start of care or within 30 days of the start of home health care. The face-to-face encounter may occur through telehealth. The physician must also certify as to the necessity for home health services and, when services are to continue for a period of time, recertify as to the continued need for services. [Soc. Sec. Act § 1835(a)(2)(A); 42 C.F.R. § 424.22.] See ¶ 260.

Hospice. For hospice care to be covered by Medicare, the beneficiary's attending physician and the medical director of the hospice must each certify in the first 90-day period that the beneficiary is terminally ill, i.e., that the medical prognosis is that the individual's life expectancy is six months or less if the terminal illness runs its normal course. For a subsequent 90- or 60-day period, the medical director or physician must recertify at the beginning of the period that the individual is terminally ill. [Soc. Sec. Act § 1814(a)(7)(A); 42 C.F.R. § 418.22.]

A hospice physician or hospice nurse practitioner must have a face-to-face encounter with each hospice patient whose total stay across all hospices is anticipated to reach the third benefit period. The face-to-face encounter must occur before, but no more than 30 calendar days before, the third benefit period recertification, and every benefit period recertification thereafter, to gather clinical findings to determine continued eligibility for hospice care. [Soc. Sec. Act § 1814(a)(7)(D); 42 C.F.R. § 418.22(a)(4).]

Critical access hospital. A physician must certify that an individual is reasonably expected to be discharged from a critical access hospital (CAH) or transferred to another hospital within 96 hours of the date of admission to the CAH for the services to be covered under Medicare Part A. The certification is required no less than one day before the claim for payment for such services is submitted. [42 C.F.R. § 424.15.]

Certification Requirements for Part B

Generally, a physician's certification and recertification is required for all Part B medical and other health services except: (1) hospital services and supplies incident to physicians' services rendered to outpatients, including drugs and biologics that cannot be self-administered; and (2) outpatient hospital diagnostic services, including necessary drugs and biologics ordinarily furnished or arranged for by a hospital for the purpose of diagnostic study. [Soc. Sec. Act § 1835(a)(2)(B); 42 C.F.R. § 424.24(a), (g).]

Blood glucose. For each blood glucose test, the physician must certify that the test is medically necessary. A physician's standing order is not sufficient to order a series of blood glucose tests payable under the clinical laboratory fee schedule. [42 C.F.R. § 424.24(f).]

Partial hospitalization services. The physician must certify that the individual would require inpatient psychiatric care if the partial hospitalization services were not provided and that the services were furnished under an individualized written plan of treatment while the individual was under the care of a physician. The plan sets forth: (1) the physician's diagnosis; (2) the type, amount, duration, and frequency of the services; and (3) the treatment goals. [Soc. Sec. Act § 1835(a)(2)(F); 42 C.F.R. § 424.24(e).]

Physical and occupational therapy and speech-language pathology services. The physician must certify (and recertify, when appropriate) that the patient needs or needed physical therapy (including occupational therapy) or speech-language pathology services while the patient is under the care of a physician, nurse practitioner, clinical nurse specialist, or physician assistant, and that the services were furnished under a plan of treatment. [Soc. Sec. Act §§ 1835(a)(2)(C), (D); 42 C.F.R. § 424.24(c).]

Comprehensive outpatient rehabilitation facility services. For payment to be made for comprehensive outpatient rehabilitation facility services, a physician must certify (and recertify, when appropriate) that: (1) the services were required because the individual needed skilled rehabilitation services; (2) the services were furnished while the individual was under the care of a physician; and (3) a written plan of treatment has been established and is reviewed periodically by a physician. [Soc. Sec. Act § 1835(a)(2)(E); 42 C.F.R. § 424.27.]

Durable medical equipment. For durable medical equipment (DME) items that appear on a list of specified covered items that CMS updates annually in the *Federal Register*, the physician must document that the physician, a physician assistant, a nurse practitioner, or a clinical nurse specialist had a face-to-face encounter (including through telehealth) with the individual within six months before an order for DME is written. [42 C.F.R. § 410.38(g).]

[¶ 904] Guarantee of Payment to Hospitals

Under the guarantee of payment provisions, if a hospital or critical access hospital (CAH) acted reasonably and in good faith and did not have knowledge that an individual was not entitled to Medicare benefits but instead assumed that entitlement existed, the hospital or CAH may be paid for: (1) inpatient hospital services furnished to a beneficiary whose eligibility for inpatient hospital benefit days has been exhausted; or (2) inpatient psychiatric hospital services after the 190-day psychiatric lifetime benefit has been exhausted. [Soc. Sec. Act § 1814(e); *Medicare Benefit Policy Manual*, Pub. 100-02, Ch. 5, § 10.1.]

The guarantee provisions are not applicable until the individual has exhausted his or her 60-day lifetime reserve days for inpatient hospital services, except in situations in which the beneficiary is deemed to have elected not to use lifetime reserve days. In these cases, the guarantee of payment generally applies because the reserve days cannot be used. [Soc. Sec. Act § 1814(e); Pub. 100-02, Ch. 5, § 10.1.]

Conditions for payment. Payment may be made for inpatient hospital or inpatient CAH services furnished to a beneficiary after he or she has exhausted the available benefit days if the following conditions are met:

(1) The services were furnished before CMS or the Medicare contractor notified the hospital or CAH that the beneficiary had exhausted the available benefit days and was not entitled to have payment made for those services.

(2) At the time the hospital or CAH furnished the services, it was unaware that the beneficiary had exhausted the available benefit days and could reasonably have assumed that he or she was entitled to have payment made for these services.

(3) Payment would be precluded solely because the beneficiary has no benefit days available for the particular hospital or CAH stay.

(4) The hospital or CAH claims reimbursement for the services and refunds any payments made for those services by the beneficiary or by another person on his or her behalf.

[42 C.F.R. § 409.68.]

Limitation on payment. Payment cannot be made if the hospital has received prior notification that all days of entitlement have been used and, in any event, payment cannot be made beyond the sixth day after the day of admission to the hospital (excluding Saturdays, Sundays, and legal holidays). [Soc. Sec. Act § 1814(e); 42 C.F.R. § 409.68(b).] Benefits paid to a hospital under the guarantee provision are subject to recovery from the beneficiary or third-party payers in the same way as other overpayments are subject to recovery. [Soc. Sec. Act § 1870; 42 C.F.R. § 409.68(c).]

The guarantee of payment provisions extend to inpatient services furnished to individuals who have exhausted their eligibility for inpatient hospital services, but they do not extend to individuals who have no coverage for other reasons; for example, hospitals are not guaranteed payment by Medicare when an individual is not entitled under hospital insurance or when entitlement has been terminated. [Pub. 100-02, Ch. 5, § 10.1.]

[¶ 905] Payments on Behalf of a Deceased Beneficiary

When a beneficiary dies after receiving covered Part B services, whom Medicare pays depends upon on whether the bill has been paid and, if the bill has been paid, who made the payment. [42 C.F.R. §§ 424.62, 424.64.]

Beneficiary dies and bill has been paid. If a beneficiary has received covered services for which he or she could receive direct payment under 42 C.F.R. § 424.53 but dies without receiving Medicare payment and the bill has been paid, Medicare pays the following people in the specified circumstances:

- The person or persons who, without a legal obligation to do so, paid for the services with their own funds, before or after the beneficiary's death.

- The legal representative of the beneficiary's estate if the services were paid for by the beneficiary before he or she died, or with funds from the estate.

- If the deceased beneficiary or his or her estate paid for the services and no legal representative of the estate has been appointed, the survivors, in order of priority.

- If none of the specified relatives survive, no payment is made.

- If the services were paid for by a person other than the deceased beneficiary, and that person died before payment was completed, Medicare does not pay that person's estate. Medicare pays a surviving relative of the deceased beneficiary in accordance with the priorities referenced above. If none of those relatives survive, Medicare pays the legal representative of the deceased beneficiary's estate. If there is no legal representative of the estate, no payment is made.

[Soc. Sec. Act § 1870(e); 42 C.F.R. § 424.62(b), (c).]

For a payment to be made to the person other than the beneficiary, the person who claims payment must: (1) submit a claim on a CMS-prescribed form and include an itemized bill; (2) provide evidence that the services were furnished if the Medicare contractor requests it; and (3) provide evidence of payment of the bill and the identity of the person who paid it. Evidence of payment includes: a receipted bill or a properly completed "Report of Services" section of a claim form showing who paid the bill; a cancelled check; a written statement from the provider or supplier or an authorized staff member; or other probative evidence. [42 C.F.R. § 424.62(e), (f).]

Request for payment signed on behalf of a deceased beneficiary. If a patient dies before he or she can sign the request for payment for Part A or Part B services, the request may be signed on his or her behalf by the legal representative of his or her estate or by a representative payee (a person designated by the Social Security Administration or other governmental agency to receive an incompetent beneficiary's monthly cash benefits), relative, friend, representative of an institution providing him or her care or support, or by a governmental agency providing assistance. Claims for Part B services may be filed by physicians and suppliers without a request for payment signed by the beneficiary when the beneficiary is deceased, the bill is unpaid, and the physician or supplier agrees to accept the Medicare-approved amount as the full charge. [42 C.F.R. § 424.62; *Medicare Claims Processing Manual*, Pub. 100-04, Ch. 1, § § 50.1.3, 50.1.6.]

Beneficiary dies and bill has not been paid. If a beneficiary has received covered services from a Medicare physician or supplier, the beneficiary dies without making an assignment to the physician or supplier, and the bill has not been paid, Medicare pays the physician or supplier if it:

(1) files a claim on a CMS-prescribed form;

(2) upon request from the contractor, provides evidence that the services for which it claims payment were furnished; and

(3) agrees in writing to accept the reasonable charge as the full charge for the services.

[42 C.F.R. § 424.64(c)(1).]

If the physician or other supplier does not agree to accept the reasonable charge as full charge for the service, Medicare will pay any other person who submits all of the following to the Medicare contractor:

(1) a statement indicating that he or she has assumed legal obligation to pay for the services;

(2) a claim on a CMS-prescribed form;

(3) an itemized bill that identifies the claimant as the person to whom the physician or other supplier holds responsible for payment; and

(4) if the contractor requests it, evidence that the services were actually furnished.

[42 C.F.R. § 424.64(c)(2).]

[¶ 906] Overpayments and Underpayments

Overpayments are Medicare payments a provider or beneficiary has received in excess of amounts due and payable under the statute and regulations. Overpayments are defined as "any funds that a person receives or retains under Medicare or Medicaid to which the person, after applicable reconciliation, is not entitled under such title." [Soc. Sec. Act § 1128J(d)(4)(B).]

Providers, suppliers, Medicare Advantage organizations, prescription drug sponsors, and Medicaid managed care organizations that receive an overpayment from Medicare or Medicaid must, by the later of 60 days after the date the overpayment was identified or the date any corresponding cost report is due: (1) report and return the overpayment to the Secretary of HHS, CMS, the state, or the Medicare administrative contractor (MAC), as appropriate; and (2) provide written notification of the reason for the overpayment. [Soc. Sec. Act § 1128J(d).]

Once a determination of an overpayment has been made, the amount is a debt owed by the debtor to the United States government. [Soc. Sec. Act § 1128J(d); *Medicare Financial Management Manual*, Pub. 100-06, Ch. 3, § 10.]

The requirement to report and return overpayments is enforced under the False Claims Act (FCA), which means that the retention of an overpayment beyond the 60-day period exposes a provider to civil money penalties plus treble damages and penalties, even if the provider voluntarily discloses and repays the overpayment after the 60-day period has elapsed. Exposure to the penalties under the FCA exists only if the provider "knew" of the overpayment for more than 60 days. Under the FCA, "knowingly" is defined to include reckless disregard and deliberate ignorance. [Soc. Sec. Act § 1128J(d)(3); 31 U.S.C. § 3729; 28 C.F.R. § 85.3.] In addition, the Office of Inspector General (OIG) may exclude individuals or entities that know of an overpayment and do not report and return it. [Soc. Sec. Act § 1128A(a)(10).]

Examples of individual overpayment cases include: (1) payment for provider, supplier, or physician services after benefits have been exhausted, or when the individual was not entitled to benefits; (2) incorrect application of the deductible or coinsurance; (3) payment for noncovered items and services, including medically unnecessary services or custodial care furnished to an individual; (4) payment based on a charge that exceeds the reasonable charge; (5) duplicate processing of charges or claims; (6) payment to a physician on a nonassigned claim or to a beneficiary on an assigned claim (payment made to wrong payee); (7) primary payment for items or services for which another entity is the primary payer; and (8) payment for items or services rendered during a period of nonentitlement. [Pub. 100-06, Ch. 3, § 10.2.]

Beneficiary Liability for Overpayments

The law provides that any Medicare payment made for a beneficiary's benefit will be considered a payment to the beneficiary, even if the payment is received by someone other than the beneficiary. Accordingly, if the MAC determines that the overpayment cannot be recouped from the provider, physician, or supplier or that the provider, physician, or supplier was without fault with respect to the overpayment, the beneficiary then becomes liable. A provider is deemed to be without fault if, in the absence of evidence to the contrary, the overpayment was made after the fifth year following the year in which notice of the payment was sent to the individual. [Soc. Sec. Act § 1870(a), (b); 42 C.F.R. § 405.350.]

If payment is made directly to the beneficiary, liability always lies with the beneficiary unless recovery is waived under the limitation of liability provision. [Pub. 100-06, Ch. 3, § 70.]

Recovery from beneficiary. In a recovery action, the Secretary will make the proper adjustment by: (1) decreasing any Social Security (or Railroad Retirement) benefits to which the individual is entitled; (2) requiring the individual or his or her estate to refund the amount in excess of the correct amount; (3) decreasing any Social Security payments to the estate of the individual or to any other person on the basis of the wages and self-employment income (or compensation) that were the basis of the payments to the individual; or (4) applying any combination of these adjustments. [Soc. Sec. Act § 1870(b); 42 C.F.R. § 405.352; Pub. 100-06, Ch. 3, § 110.]

If an individual who is overpaid dies before the overpayment has been recovered, the Secretary may initiate a recovery action, as necessary, against any other individual who is receiving cash Social Security benefits on the same earnings record as the deceased overpaid beneficiary. [Soc. Sec. Act § 1870(b).]

Waiver of beneficiary liability. The Secretary may not pursue recovery of the overpayment if the (1) overpaid beneficiary is without fault (or the survivor of the deceased overpaid beneficiary who is liable for repayment of a Medicare overpayment is without fault); and (2) the recovery would be against equity and good conscience or defeat the purposes of titles II or XVIII the Social Security Act. Adjustment or recovery of an incorrect payment against an individual who is without fault is deemed to be against equity and good conscience if the Secretary determines that the payment was incorrect after the fifth year following the year in which notice of the payment was sent to such individual; the Secretary may, however, reduce such five-year period to not less than one year. [Soc. Sec. Act § 1870(c); 42 C.F.R. § § 405.355, 405.358; Pub. 100-06, Ch. 3, § § 70.3, 110.10.]

When collection of a beneficiary overpayment is from a provider (or physicians or other persons who have accepted assignments), after three years, the provider (or the physician or other person) is prohibited from charging the beneficiary for services found by the Secretary to be medically unnecessary or custodial in nature, in the absence of fault on the part of the individual who received the services. The Secretary is authorized to make the presumption before the three years have expired (but not before one year) if to do so would be consistent with the objectives of the Medicare program. [Soc. Sec. Act § § 1842(b)(3)(B)(ii), 1866(a)(1)(B).]

Interest Charges on Overpayments and Underpayments

When a final determination is made that a provider of services under Part A or a physician or supplier that accepted assignment under Part B has received an overpayment or underpayment from Medicare, and payment of the excess or deficit is not made within 30 days of the determination, interest charges will be applied to the balance due. The interest rate on overpayments is determined in accordance with regulations promulgated by the Secretary of the Treasury and is the higher of the private consumer rate or the current value of fund rates prevailing on the date of final determination. No interest is assessed for a period of less than 30 days; interest is calculated in full 30-day periods. Interest is assessed on the principal amount only and is calculated on a simple rather than a compound basis. [Soc. Sec. Act § § 1815(d), 1833(j); 42 C.F.R. § 405.378.]

Suspension, Offset, and Recoupment of Overpayments

Under the Federal Claims Collection Act of 1966, each agency of the federal government must attempt collection of claims for the federal government for money arising out of the activities of the agency in a timely and aggressive manner. The MAC will not be liable for overpayments it makes to debtors in the absence of fraud or gross negligence on its part; however, once the MAC determines an overpayment has been made, it must attempt recovery of overpayments in accordance with CMS regulations. [31 U.S.C. § § 3701–3720A; Pub. 100-06, Ch. 3, § 10.] CMS may, under certain circumstances, suspend, offset, and recoup Medicare payments to providers and suppliers of services to recover overpayments. [42 C.F.R. § 405.371(a).]

Suspension of payments. CMS or a MAC may suspend, in whole or in part, Medicare payments to providers and suppliers: (1) if CMS or the MAC possesses reliable information that an overpayment exists or that the payments to be made may not be correct, although additional information may be needed for a determination; or (2) in cases of suspected fraud, if CMS or the MAC has consulted with the OIG, and, as appropriate, the Department of Justice, and determined that a credible allegation of fraud exists against a provider or supplier, unless there is good cause not to suspend payments. [42 C.F.R. § 405.371(a)(1), (2).]

¶906

Once the determination has been made that a suspension of payments should be put into effect, notice ordinarily will be given to the provider or supplier along with a written statement of the reasons for the suspension. Notice to the provider or supplier is not necessary if: (1) the intended suspension involves fraud or misrepresentation; (2) CMS or the MAC determines that the Medicare Trust Fund would be harmed by giving prior notice; or (3) the intended suspension is the result of the provider's or supplier's failure to submit requested information necessary to determine amounts due the provider or supplier. [42 C.F.R. § 405.372(a).]

If prior notice is required, the MAC must give the provider or supplier 15 days to submit a statement of rebuttal. If, by the end of the period specified in the notice, no rebuttal has been received, the suspension will go into effect automatically. With certain exceptions, the period of suspension is limited to 180 days. [42 C.F.R. § § 405.372(b), (d), 405.374.]

Offset or recoupment. CMS or a MAC may offset or recoup Medicare payments, in whole or in part, if it determines that the provider or supplier to whom payments are to be made has been overpaid. An offset is the recovery by Medicare of a non-Medicare debt by reducing present or future Medicare payments and applying the amount withheld to the indebtedness. A recoupment, on the other hand, refers to the recovery by Medicare of outstanding Medicare debt by reducing present or future Medicare payments and applying the amount withheld to the indebtedness. [42 C.F.R. § § 405.370(a), 405.371(a)(3).]

When CMS or the MAC determines that an offset or recoupment should be put in place, the provider or supplier must receive notice and an opportunity for rebuttal. If no rebuttal statement is received within the time period specified in the notice, the recoupment or offset will go into effect immediately. A recoupment or offset remains in effect until the earliest of the following: (1) the overpayment and any assessed interest are liquidated; (2) the MAC obtains a satisfactory agreement from the provider or supplier for liquidation of the overpayment; or (3) the MAC, on the basis of subsequently acquired evidence or otherwise, determines that there is no overpayment. [42 C.F.R. § 405.373.]

Rebuttals. The rebuttal process occurs before the appeals process and permits the provider a vehicle to indicate why the recoupment or offset should not take place. If the provider or supplier submits a statement as to why a suspension, offset, or recoupment should not be put into effect, CMS or the MAC must, within 15 days from the date the statement is received, consider the statement and determine whether the facts justify the suspension, offset, or recoupment. CMS or the MAC must send written notice of the determination to the provider or supplier, including an explanatory statement of the determination and: (1) in the case of offset or recoupment, the rationale for the determination, or (2) in the case of suspension of payment, specific findings on the conditions upon which the suspension is initiated, continued, or removed. Suspension, offset, or recoupment is not delayed beyond the date stated in the notice to review the statement. Such a determination is not an initial determination and, therefore, is not appealable. [42 C.F.R. § 405.375.]

Requests for reconsidation and redetermination. When a provider or supplier seeks a redetermination by a MAC or reconsideration by a qualified independent contractor (QIC) on an overpayment determination, CMS may not recoup or demand a Medicare overpayment until the decision on the redetermination or reconsideration is rendered. When a valid request for a redetermination or reconsideration has been received from a provider, the MAC will cease recoupment or not begin recoupment at the normally scheduled time (41 days from the date of the initial overpayment demand for the redetermination and 76 days for the reconsideration). Interest paid to a provider or supplier whose overpayment is reversed at subsequent levels of appeal will accrue from the date of the original determination. [Soc. Sec. Act § 1893(f)(2); 42 C.F.R. § § 405.379(a), (d); Pub. 100-06, Ch. 3, § § 200, 200.3.]

Once both the redetermination and reconsideration are completed and CMS prevails, collection activities, including demand letters and internal recoupment, may resume. [Pub. 100-06, Ch. 3, § 200.]

Extended repayment schedule. If the repayment of an overpayment within 30 days would constitute a hardship, a provider or supplier can enter into a plan with the Secretary to repay the overpayment over a period of six to 36 months (or, in the case of extreme hardship, no longer than five years). [Soc. Sec. Act § 1893(f)(1); 42 C.F.R. §§ 401.607(c)(2), 405.379(h).]

[¶ 915] Limitation of Liability

Medicare law provides financial relief to beneficiaries, providers, practitioners, physicians, and suppliers by permitting Medicare payment to be made, or requiring refunds to be made, for certain services and items for which Medicare payment would otherwise be denied. This is referred to as "the limitation on liability provision." The purpose of this provision is to protect beneficiaries and other claimants from liability in denial cases under certain conditions when services they received are found to be excluded from coverage for one of the reasons specified below. [Soc. Sec. Act § 1879; *Medicare Claims Processing Manual*, Pub. 100-04, Ch. 30, §§ 20, 20.1.1.]

Services for which the limitation on liability provisions apply. The limitation on liability (LOL) of claims payment and beneficiary indemnification provisions are applicable only to claims for beneficiary items or services submitted by providers or suppliers, including physicians or other practitioners, or entities other than providers, that furnish health care services under Medicare and that have taken assignment. The LOL provisions are triggered by two factors: (1) the provider, practitioner, physician, supplier, or beneficiary must not have known or could not reasonably have been expected to know that items or services were not covered; and (2) the denied claims were for one of the following items or services:

(1) services and items or additional preventive services that are found not to be reasonable and necessary for the diagnosis or treatment of illness or injury or to improve the functioning of a malformed body member under section 1861(a)(1)(A) of the Social Security Act;

(2) pneumococcal vaccine and its administration, influenza vaccine and its administration, and hepatitis B vaccine and its administration, furnished to an individual who is at high or intermediate risk of contracting hepatitis B, which are not reasonable and necessary for the prevention of illness;

(3) in the case of hospice care, services and items that are not reasonable and necessary for the palliation or management of terminal illness;

(4) clinical care items and services provided with the concurrence of the Secretary and, with respect to research and experimentation conducted by, or under contract with, the Medicare Payment Advisory Commission or the Secretary, that are not reasonable and necessary;

(5) services and items that, in the case of research conducted pursuant to Soc. Sec. Act § 1142, are not reasonable and necessary to carry out the purposes of the governing law;

(6) screening mammography that is performed more frequently than is covered under Soc. Sec. Act § 1834(c)(2) or that is not conducted by a facility described in Soc. Sec. Act § 1834(c)(1)(B), and screening pap smears and screening pelvic exams performed more frequently than is provided for under Soc. Sec. Act § 1861(nn);

(7) screening for glaucoma that is performed more frequently than is provided under Soc. Sec. Act § 1861(uu);

(8) prostate cancer screening tests that are performed more frequently than is covered under Soc. Sec. Act § 1861(oo);

(9) colorectal cancer screening tests that are performed more frequently than is covered under Soc. Sec. Act § 1834(d);

(10) the frequency and duration of home health services (see ¶ 250) that are in excess of normative guidelines established by the Secretary;

(11) a drug or biological specified in Soc. Sec. Act § 1847A(c)(6)(C) for which payment is made under Part B that is furnished in a competitive area that is not furnished by an entity under a contract under Soc. Sec. Act § 1847B;

(12) an initial preventive physical examination that is performed more than one year after the date the individual's first coverage period begins under Part B;

(13) cardiovascular screening blood tests that are performed more frequently than is covered under Soc. Sec. Act § 1861(xx)(1);

(14) a diabetes screening test that is performed more frequently than is covered under Soc. Sec. Act § 1861(yy)(1);

(15) ultrasound screening for abdominal aortic aneurysm that is performed more frequently than is provided for under Soc. Sec. Act § 1861(s)(2)(AA);

(16) kidney disease education services that are furnished in excess of the number of sessions covered under Soc. Sec. Act § 1861(ggg);

(17) personalized prevention plan services that are performed more frequently than is covered under Soc. Sec. Act § 1861(hhh)(1);

(18) custodial care under Soc. Sec. Act § 1862(a)(9) (see ¶ 625);

(19) inpatient hospital services or extended care services if payment is denied solely because of an unintentional, inadvertent, or erroneous action that resulted in the beneficiary's transfer from a certified bed in a skilled nursing facility (SNF) or hospital (Soc. Sec. Act § 1879(e));

(20) home health services determined to be noncovered because the beneficiary was not homebound or did not require intermittent skilled nursing care; and

(21) hospice care (see ¶ 270) determined to be noncovered because the beneficiary was not "terminally ill" (as required by Soc. Sec. Act § 1861(dd)(3)(A), as referenced by Soc. Sec. Act § 1879(g)(2)).

[Soc. Sec. Act §§ 1862(a)(1) and (a)(9), 1879; Pub. 100-04, Ch. 30, §§ 20, 20.1.1.]

Services not subject to the LOL provisions. Medicare payment under the LOL provision cannot be made when Medicare coverage is denied on any basis other than one of the provisions of the law specified above. There are certain claims that may appear to involve a question of medical necessity, as described in section 1862(a)(1) of the Social Security Act, but Medicare payment denial is based on a different statutory provision. Under these circumstances, Medicare payment under the LOL provision cannot be made because the denial is not based on one of the statutory provisions specified above. [Pub. 100-04, Ch. 30, § 20.2.]

Third-party payers. The waiver of liability provision applies to third-party payers. Accordingly, a provider, practitioner, or supplier that is determined liable may not seek payment from a third-party payer without being subject to recovery action that could occur if it sought payment from the beneficiary. [Pub. 100-04, Ch. 30, § 30.2.2.]

¶915

Determination of Liability

The Medicare administrative contractor determines whether the provider, physician, or beneficiary is liable for the overpayment and whether to waive liability. [*Medicare Financial Management Manual*, Pub. 100-06, Ch. 3, § 70.] In addition, quality improvement organization (QIO) determinations (see ¶ 710) are conclusive for payment purposes as to whether the provider and the beneficiary knew or could reasonably be expected to have known that services were excluded because of the reasonableness, medical necessity, and appropriateness of placement at an acute level of patient care. [42 C.F.R. § 476.86(a)(4).]

There are three possible outcomes of a determination of liability.

(1) If the beneficiary had knowledge (or could have been expected to know) of the noncoverage of services for the reasons specified above, the ultimate liability will rest with the beneficiary.

(2) When neither the beneficiary nor the provider, practitioner, or supplier knew or reasonably could have been expected to know that services were not covered, the government will accept liability.

(3) When the beneficiary did not have such knowledge, but the provider, practitioner, or supplier knew, or could have been expected to know, of the exclusion of the items or services, the liability for the charges for the denied items or services rests with the provider, practitioner, or supplier.

[Pub. 100-04, Ch. 30, § 20.]

If the Medicare program accepts liability and makes payment, CMS will put the provider and beneficiary on notice that the service was noncovered and, in any subsequent cases involving similar situations and further stays or treatments (or similar types of cases in the instance of the provider), will consider that the provider and beneficiary had knowledge that payment would not be made. [Soc. Sec. Act § 1879(a).]

If the provider did not exercise due care, but there was good faith on the part of the beneficiary, liability will shift to the provider. The provider can appeal the contractor's decision as to coverage of the services and whether it exercised due care. If the provider received reimbursement from the beneficiary, the program will indemnify the beneficiary (although deductibles and coinsurance apply). Medicare treats the indemnification as an overpayment against the provider and recoups the amount of the payment through an offset against any amounts otherwise payable to the provider. [Soc. Sec. Act § 1879(b), (d); Pub. 100-04, Ch. 30, § § 20, 30.1.1, 30.2.2.]

Waiver of Beneficiary Liability

The waiver of liability provision provides that the beneficiary will not have to pay for noncovered services if the beneficiary did not know, and did not have reason to know, that the services were not covered. The contractor presumes that the beneficiary did not know that services are not covered unless the evidence indicates that written notice was given to the beneficiary by the QIO, the Medicare contractor, the utilization review committee responsible for the provider that furnished the services, or the provider, practitioner, or supplier that furnished the service. [Soc. Sec. Act § 1879(a); 42 C.F.R. § § 411.404, 411.408(f); Pub. 100-04, Ch. 30, § § 30.1, 30.1.1, 30.1.2.]

If the contractor waives the beneficiary's liability for the services, liability shifts either to the government or to the provider—depending upon whether the provider utilized due care in applying Medicare policy in its dealings with the beneficiary and the government. [Soc. Sec. Act § 1879(a), (b), and (c); 42 C.F.R. § 411.402; Pub. 100-04, Ch. 30, § 30.2.1; Pub. 100-06, Ch. 3, § § 70, 70.1.]

¶ 915

Waiver of Provider Liability

The issue of whether a practitioner or other supplier is liable for payment for services not covered by Medicare arises only when the beneficiary has been found not liable. A physician's or supplier's liability will not be waived for noncovered services unless the physician or supplier accepted assignment for the services (see ¶ 868). [42 C.F.R. § 411.400(a); Pub. 100-06, Ch. 3, § § 70.3, 90.]

For the initial determination, the practitioner or other supplier is presumed to have had the requisite knowledge of likely Medicare denial of payment for denied services or items and will be liable unless the practitioner or supplier gave the beneficiary a proper Advance Beneficiary Notice (ABN) that Medicare will likely deny payment for the service or item to be furnished. A provider, practitioner, or supplier will not be held liable when the provider, practitioner, or supplier indicates on the claim that the beneficiary has been given an ABN before the items or services were furnished. In that case, the Medicare contractor will hold the beneficiary liable for the denied services or items at the initial determination because the notice constitutes proof that the beneficiary and the practitioner or supplier had prior knowledge that Medicare payment would be denied for the service or item in question. When the beneficiary and the practitioner or other supplier are found to have had the requisite knowledge of likely Medicare denial, the beneficiary is held liable. [Pub. 100-04, Ch. 30, § § 30.2.1, 40.1.1.]

A provider, practitioner, or supplier that furnished services that constitute custodial care or are not reasonable and necessary is considered to have known that the services were not covered if:

- the Medicare contractor had informed the provider, practitioner, or supplier that the services furnished were not covered, or that similar or reasonably comparable services were not covered;

- the utilization review committee for the provider or the beneficiary's attending physician had informed the provider that these services were not covered;

- before the services were furnished, the provider, practitioner, or supplier informed the beneficiary that the services were not covered or the beneficiary no longer needed covered services; or

- the provider, practitioner, or supplier could have been expected to have known that the services were excluded from coverage based on the receipt of CMS notices, including manual issuances, bulletins, or other written guides or directives from Medicare contractors, including: (1) QIO screening criteria and preadmission review; (2) *Federal Register* publications containing notice of national coverage decisions or of other specifications regarding noncoverage of an item or service; and (3) knowledge of acceptable standards of practice by the local medical community.

[42 C.F.R. § 411.406.] A provider, practitioner, or supplier that is determined liable for all or a portion of the charges for noncovered items and services furnished a beneficiary may appeal such a decision by the contractor. [Pub. 100-04, Ch. 30, § 30.2.2.]

[¶ 920] Medicare Entitlement and Enrollment Appeals

The Social Security Administration (SSA) makes an initial determination on an application for Medicare benefits and entitlement of an individual to receive Medicare benefits. Entitlement concerns whether an individual has a right to Medicare benefits, not whether a particular item or service is covered or how much Medicare pays for it. Any individual dissatisfied with the SSA's initial determination as to whether he or she is *entitled to* or *enrolled in* Medicare may request reconsideration of the determination in the same manner provided for Social Security (or Railroad Retirement) benefit claims if the requirements for obtaining a reconsideration are met. [20 C.F.R. § 404.909; 42 C.F.R. 405.904(a).]

The SSA mails written notice of the government's determination that an individual is not eligible for Medicare to the individual at his or her last known address. An initial determination becomes final and binding on the parties unless reconsideration is requested or the determination is reopened and revised within the specified time limits. [20 C.F.R. §§ 404.904, 404.905.]

The claimant (or his or her representative) may request a reconsideration of this determination by letter or on a special form available at any district Social Security office. The request for a reconsideration should be in writing and filed at a district office within 60 days from the date of receipt of the original adverse determination. [20 C.F.R. § 404.909.]

The SSA reviews the evidence considered in making the initial determination and any other evidence received and makes its determination on the preponderance of the evidence. The reconsideration is binding unless a request for a hearing is made within the stated time period and a decision is made, the expedited appeals process is used, or the determination is revised. The SSA mails a written notice of the reconsidered determination stating the specific reasons for the determination and the right to a hearing before an administrative law judge (ALJ). [20 C.F.R. §§ 404.900(b), 404.913(a), 404.920, 404.921, 404.922.]

Following the reconsideration, the individual may request a hearing before an ALJ under the Medicare appeal rules. If the individual is dissatisfied with the ALJ decision, he or she may request the Medicare Appeals Council to review the case. If dissatisfied with the Medicare Appeals Council decision, the individual is entitled to file a suit in federal district court. [42 C.F.R. § 405.904(a).]

[¶ 924] Medicare Part A and B Claims Appeals

There are four levels of administrative appeals to challenge a coverage or payment decision under Part A or Part B. The first level of appeal is a redetermination made by the Medicare administrative contractor (MAC). The second administrative appeal is a "reconsideration," conducted by a qualified independent contractor (QIC). The third level of appeal is to an administrative law judge (ALJ), and the final administrative review is conducted by the Medicare Appeals Council. [Soc. Sec. Act §§ 1869(b)–(d).]

For beneficiaries that have enrolled in Medicare Advantage plans, specific requirements have been established with respect to administrative determinations, reconsiderations, appeals, and judicial review. These requirements are outlined at ¶ 403. For beneficiaries enrolled in Part D, the voluntary prescription drug benefit, administrative determinations, appeals, grievances, and judicial review are discussed at ¶ 515–¶ 516.

Initial Determinations

When a medical service provider, supplier, or beneficiary submits a bill containing a request for payment for benefits, the MAC will make an initial determination approving, denying, or partially denying the claim. The MAC will notify the beneficiary of its initial determination with a Medicare summary notice (MSN) and the provider or supplier with an electronic or paper remittance advice (RA) describing the action taken. The MSN states in detail the basis for the determination, informs beneficiaries of the right to appeal the determination if they are dissatisfied, and provides instructions on how to obtain information on the specific provision of the policy, manual, or regulation used in making the determination or redetermination. [Soc. Sec. Act § 1869(a)(4); 42 C.F.R. §§ 405.920, 405.921.]

An initial determination on claims made by or on behalf of a beneficiary includes, but is not limited to, determinations with respect to:

(1) coverage of furnished items and services;

(2) if the beneficiary, physician, or supplier who accepts assignment knew or could reasonably be expected to know that the items or services were not covered;

(3) whether the deductible is met;

(4) computation of the coinsurance amount;

(5) the number of inpatient hospital days used for inpatient hospital, psychiatric hospital, or post-hospital extended care;

(6) periods of hospice care used;

(7) requirements for certification and plan of treatment for physician services, durable medical equipment, therapies, inpatient hospitalization, skilled nursing care, home health, hospice, and partial hospitalization services;

(8) the beginning and ending of a spell of illness;

(9) the medical necessity of the services, or the reasonableness or appropriateness of placement of an individual at an acute level of patient care made by the quality improvement organization (QIO) on behalf of the MAC;

(10) any other issues affecting the amount of benefits payable, including underpayments;

(11) a determination with respect to the waiver of liability provision;

(12) if a particular claim is not payable to Medicare based on the application of Medicare Secondary Payer (MSP) provisions;

(13) under MSP provisions, that Medicare has a recovery claim against a provider, supplier, or beneficiary for services or items that were already paid by the Medicare program, except when the recovery claim is based on failure to file a proper claim;

(14) if a claim is not payable to a beneficiary for the services of a physician who has opted out; and

(15) under the MSP provisions, that Medicare has a recovery claim if Medicare is pursuing recovery directly from an applicable plan (defined as liability insurance, no-fault insurance, or a workers' compensation law or plan).

[42 C.F.R. § 405.924(b).]

An initial determination also includes a determination made by a QIO that: (1) a provider can terminate services provided to an individual when a physician certified that failure to continue the provision of those services is likely to place the individual's health at significant risk; or (2) a provider can discharge an individual from that provider. [42 C.F.R. § 405.924(c).] See ¶ 926 for a discussion of expedited appeals of provider service terminations to QIOs. See also ¶ 710 for a discussion of beneficiary complaints and appeals to QIOs regarding quality of care issues.

Parties to initial determinations. The parties to the initial determination are: (1) the beneficiary who files a claim for payment under Medicare Part A or Part B or has had a claim for payment filed on his or her behalf, or in the case of a deceased beneficiary, when there is no estate, any person obligated to make or entitled to receive payment, except that payment by a third-party payer does not entitle that entity to party status; (2) a supplier who has accepted assignment for items or services furnished to a beneficiary that are at issue in the claim; (3) a provider of services who files a claim for items or services furnished to a beneficiary; and (4) an applicable plan for an initial determination under 42 C.F.R. § 405.924(b)(16) where Medicare is pursuing recovery directly from the applicable plan. [42 C.F.R. § 405.906(a).]

Deadlines for making initial determinations. Initial determinations must be concluded no later than the 45-day period beginning on the day the claim is received. [Soc. Sec. Act § 1869(a)(2)(A).]

Parties to Redeterminations, Reconsiderations, ALJ Hearings, and Medicare Appeals Council Reviews

Parties to a redetermination, reconsideration, hearing, and Medicare Appeals Council review are: (1) the parties to the initial determination, except when a beneficiary has assigned appeal rights pursuant to 42 C.F.R. § 405.912; (2) a Medicaid state agency (see 42 C.F.R. § 405.908); (3) a provider or supplier that has accepted an assignment of appeal rights from the beneficiary pursuant to 42 C.F.R. § 405.912; (4) a nonparticipating physician not billing on an assigned basis who may be liable to refund monies collected for services furnished to the beneficiary because those services were denied due to their exclusion from coverage; and (5) a nonparticipating supplier not billing on an assigned basis who may be liable to refund monies collected for items furnished to the beneficiary. [42 C.F.R § 405.906(b).]

Except for an initial determination with respect to an applicable plan under 42 C.F.R § 405.924(b)(16), if a provider or supplier is not a party to an initial determination, it may appeal an initial determination related to services it rendered to a beneficiary who subsequently dies if there is no other party available to appeal the determination. [42 C.F.R § 405.906(c).]

Redeterminations

A person or entity that may be a party to a redetermination in accordance with 42 C.F.R. § 405.906(b) that is dissatisfied with an initial determination may request a redetermination by a MAC. [Soc. Sec. Act § 1869(a)(3); 42 C.F.R. § 405.940.]

A request for redetermination must be filed with the MAC indicated on the notice of the initial determination. The request for redetermination must be in writing and should be made on a standard CMS form. A written request that is not made on a standard form is accepted if it contains the required elements, i.e., the beneficiary's name, health insurance claim number, the specific services or items for which the redetermination is being requested and the dates the services or items were furnished, and the name and signature of the party or the party's representative. [42 C.F.R. § 405.944(a), (b).]

The request for redetermination must be filed within 120 calendar days after receipt of an initial determination (presumed to be five days after the date of the notice), unless the MAC grants the appellant an extension to the filing deadline. [Soc. Sec. Act § 1869(a)(3)(C)(i); 42 C.F.R. § 405.942(a), (b).]

The request for redetermination must include an explanation of why the party disagrees with the MAC's determination and should include any evidence that the MAC should consider in making the redetermination. If parties cannot submit relevant documentation along with their redetermination requests, then they can provide later submissions. When a party submits additional evidence after filing the request for redetermination, however, the MAC's 60 calendar-day decision-making time frame is automatically extended 14 calendar days for each submission. [42 C.F.R. § 405.946.]

MACs are required to process all redeterminations within 60 calendar days. The time frame may be extended when: a MAC grants an extension of the 120-day deadline for filing a request for redetermination, multiple parties request a redetermination, or a party submits evidence after the request for redetermination is filed. [Soc. Sec. Act § 1869(a)(3)(C)(ii); 42 C.F.R. § 405.950.]

Written notice of the redetermination affirming, in whole or in part, the initial determination must be mailed to the parties. For decisions that are affirmations, in whole or in part, of the initial determination, the redetermination must be written in a manner calculated to be understood by a beneficiary and contain, among other explanations and information, a summary of the rationale of the redetermination, rules for submitting evidence and missing documentation, and the right to a reconsideration and the procedures to request a reconsideration. For decisions that are full reversals of the initial determination, the redetermination must be in writing, contain a clear statement indicating that the redetermination is wholly favorable, and include any other requirements specified by CMS. [Soc. Sec. Act § 1869(a)(5); 42 C.F.R. §§ 405.954, 405.956.]

The redetermination is binding on all parties unless a timely appeal is filed, the redetermination is revised, or the expedited appeals process is used. [42 C.F.R. § 405.958.]

Reconsiderations

A person or entity that is a party to a redetermination made by a MAC and is dissatisfied with that determination may request a reconsideration, regardless of the amount in controversy. A reconsideration is an independent, on-the-record review of an initial determination, including the redetermination and all the issues related to payment of the claim, performed by a QIC. A QIC may reconsider an initial determination only after the MAC has performed a redetermination of the initial determination. [Soc. Sec. Act § 1869(c)(3)(B); 42 C.F.R. §§ 405.960, 405.968(a).]

A reconsideration is final and binding on all parties unless a timely appeal is filed and a higher appeal overturns the reconsideration decision or the reconsideration is reopened and revised by the QIC. [42 C.F.R. §§ 405.974(b)(3), 405.978.]

If the initial determination involves a finding as to whether an item or service is reasonable and necessary, the QIC's reconsideration must involve consideration by a panel of physicians or other appropriate health care professionals and be based on clinical experience, the patient's medical records, and medical, technical, and scientific evidence of record, to the extent applicable. When the claim pertains to the furnishing of treatment by a physician, or the provision of items and services by a physician, the reviewing professional must be a physician. National coverage determinations (NCDs), CMS rulings, and applicable laws and regulations are binding on the QIC. [42 C.F.R. § 405.968.]

Request for reconsideration. A request for reconsideration must be in writing and filed with the QIC indicated on the notice of redetermination within 180 calendar days after receipt of the notice of redetermination (presumed to be five days after the date of the notice). The written request should be on a standard CMS form. A written request that is not made on a standard CMS form is accepted if it contains the beneficiary's name, Medicare health insurance claim number, specific services and items for which the reconsideration is being requested, name and signature of the party or the representative of the party, and the name of the MAC that made the redetermination. [42 C.F.R. §§ 405.962(a), 405.964; Pub. 100-04, Ch. 29, § 320.1.]

Time frame for reconsideration. QICs must complete their reconsiderations within 60 calendar days of receiving a timely filed request. [42 C.F.R. § 405.970(a).] However, when a party submits additional evidence after filing the request for redetermination, the QIC's 60 calendar-day decision-making time frame is automatically extended by up to 14 calendar days for each submission. [Soc. Sec. Act § 1869(c)(3)(C); 42 C.F.R. §§ 405.966(b), 405.970(b)(3).]

Escalation. If the QIC does not issue its decision within the 60-calendar-day deadline, the parties may submit a written request directing the QIC to escalate the appeal to an ALJ. When a QIC receives an escalation request, it has five days to complete its reconsideration and notify the parties of its decision or acknowledge the escalation request and forward the case file to the ALJ. [42 C.F.R. § 405.970(d),(e).]

Expedited access to judicial review. A beneficiary, provider, or supplier may obtain expedited access to judicial review (EAJR) after the QIC completes a reconsideration if the review entity determines that the Medicare Appeals Council does not have the authority to decide the question of law or regulation relevant to the matters in controversy and there is no material issue of fact to dispute. The requester has 60 calendar days from the date of certification to bring a civil action in federal court. [42 C.F.R. § 405.990(a), (c), (h).]

Administrative Law Judge Review

The third level of the claims appeal process, which follows a QIC reconsideration, is a review by an ALJ. [42 C.F.R. § 405.1000.]

Parties to an ALJ hearing. Any party to the QIC's reconsideration may request a hearing before an ALJ. The party who filed the request for hearing and all other parties to the reconsideration are parties to the ALJ hearing. [42 C.F.R. § 405.1008.]

CMS or its MAC may enter an appeal at the ALJ level as a party unless an unrepresented beneficiary brings the appeal. CMS will have all the rights of a party, including the right to call witnesses, submit additional evidence within the time frame specified by the ALJ, and seek review of a decision adverse to CMS. The ALJ may not require CMS or a MAC to enter a case as a party or draw any adverse inferences if CMS or a MAC decides not to enter as a party. [42 C.F.R. § 405.1012.] CMS or a MAC also will be allowed to participate in an ALJ hearing, including oral hearing, at the request of an ALJ, CMS, or a MAC. [42 C.F.R. § 405.1010.]

Amount-in-controversy requirement. To be entitled to a hearing before an ALJ, the party must meet the amount-in-controversy requirements. Claims may be aggregated to meet the amount in controversy if they involve common issues of law and fact and delivery of similar or related services. Effective for requests for ALJ hearings filed on or after January 1, 2017, the amount-in-controversy threshold amount is $160. [Soc. Sec. Act § 1869(b)(1)(E); 42 C.F.R. § 405.1006(b); *Notice*, 81 FR 65651, Sept. 23, 2016.]

Request for an ALJ hearing. ALJ hearing requests must be in writing and include: (1) the name, address, and Medicare health insurance claim number of the beneficiary whose claim is being appealed; (2) the name and address of the appellant, when the appellant is not the beneficiary; (3) the name and address of designated representatives; (4) the document control number assigned to the appeal by the QIC; (5) the dates of service; (6) the reasons the appellant disagrees with the QIC's reconsideration or other determination being appealed; and (7) a statement of any additional evidence to be submitted and the date it will be submitted. [42 C.F.R. § 405.1014(a).]

Requests for ALJ review must be filed with the entity specified in the QIC's reconsideration within 60 calendar days of receipt of the notice of the reconsideration. [42 C.F.R. § 405.1014(b).]

Evidence. Generally, parties must submit all written evidence they wish to have considered at the hearing with the request for hearing (or within 10 calendar days of receiving the notice of hearing). Any evidence submitted by a provider, supplier, or beneficiary represented by a provider or supplier that is not submitted prior to the issuance of the QIC's reconsideration determination must be accompanied by a statement explaining why the evidence was not previously submitted to the QIC or to a prior decision maker. However, these requirements do not apply to oral testimony given at a hearing or evidence submitted by an unrepresented beneficiary. [42 C.F.R. § 405.1018.]

¶924

The hearing. The ALJ hearing results in a new decision by an independent reviewer and a decision based on the hearing. The ALJ conducts the hearing in person, by video-teleconference, or by telephone. The ALJ will conduct a *de novo* review (i.e., an in-depth review conducted as if for the first time) and issue a decision based on the hearing record. If the beneficiary or his or her representative waives the right to appear at the hearing, the ALJ will make a decision based on the evidence that is in the file and any new evidence that may have been submitted for consideration. [42 C.F.R. § 405.1000(b), (d), (e).]

The issues before the ALJ include all the issues brought out in the initial determination, redetermination, or reconsideration that were not decided entirely in a party's favor. In addition, the ALJ may consider a new issue at the hearing if he or she notifies all of the parties about the new issue any time before the start of the hearing. The new issues may result from the participation of CMS at the ALJ level of adjudication and from any evidence and position papers submitted by CMS for the first time to the ALJ. The ALJ may consider a new issue only if its resolution could have a material impact on the claim or claims that are the subject of the request for hearing and is permissible under the rules governing reopening of determinations and decisions. [42 C.F.R. § 405.1032(a), (b).]

ALJs are bound by all NCDs whether based on Soc. Sec. Act § 1862(a)(1) or on other grounds, as well as the Medicare Act, applicable regulations, and CMS rulings. ALJs also must give substantial deference to nonbinding CMS and MAC policies such as local coverage determinations, manual instructions, and program memoranda, and if the ALJ declines to follow a policy in a particular case, his or her decision must explain the reasons. [42 C.F.R. §§ 405.1060(a)(4), (b), 405.1062.]

Time frame for ALJ's decision. The ALJ must issue a decision, dismissal order, or remand to the QIC within 90 calendar days of when the request for hearing is received by the entity specified in the QIC's notice of reconsideration. When an appellant escalates an appeal from the QIC level to the ALJ level, the proceedings before the ALJ are not subject to the 90-calendar-day limit. In these cases, ALJs must complete their action within 180 calendar days of receipt of the escalation request, unless the 180-calendar-day period has been extended. When CMS is a party to the hearing and a party requests discovery against another party, these adjudication periods are tolled. [42 C.F.R. § 405.1016.]

Notice of ALJ's decision. The notice of the ALJ's decision must be in writing, in a manner that is understood by the beneficiary, and must include: (1) the specific reasons for the determination, including, to the extent appropriate, a summary of the clinical or scientific evidence used in making the determination; (2) the procedures for obtaining additional information concerning the decision; and (3) notification of the right to appeal the decision and instructions on how to initiate the appeal. [42 C.F.R. § 405.1046(b).]

Escalation. If the ALJ does not issue a decision within the deadline, the parties may escalate the case to the next level of appeal. A party may request Medicare Appeals Council review if: (1) the party files a written request with the ALJ to escalate the appeal to the Medicare Appeals Council after the adjudication period has expired, and (2) the ALJ does not issue a decision, dismissal order, or remand order within the later of five calendar days of receiving the request for escalation or five calendar days from the end of the applicable adjudication period. [42 C.F.R. § 405.1104.]

If the ALJ is not able to issue a decision, dismissal order, or remand order within the time period, he or she sends notice to the appellant acknowledging receipt of the request for escalation and confirming that the ALJ is not able to issue a decision, dismissal order, or remand order within the statutory time frame. If the ALJ does not act on a request for escalation within the time period or does not send the required notice to the appellant, the

QIC decision becomes the decision that is subject to Medicare Appeals Council review. [42 C.F.R. § 405.1104, 405.1106(b).]

Escalation affects the next level's deadlines for making a decision. For example, although the decision-making deadline for the Medicare Appeals Council is generally 90 days, if a case is escalated from the ALJ to the Medicare Appeals Council, the Medicare Appeals Council has 180 calendar days from receipt of a request for escalation to complete its action. [42 C.F.R. § 405.1100(d).]

Medicare Appeals Council Review

A party to the ALJ hearing may request a Medicare Appeals Council review by filing a written request for review with the Medicare Appeals Council or appropriate ALJ office within 60 calendar days after receiving the ALJ's decision. The request should be made on a standard form but will be accepted if it contains the required elements. [42 C.F.R. §§ 405.1102(a), 405.1106(a), 405.1112(a).]

In addition, any time within 60 calendar days after the date of an ALJ decision or dismissal, the Medicare Appeals Council may decide on its own motion to review the ALJ's action. CMS or any of its MACs also may refer a case to the Medicare Appeals Council for it to consider reviewing under this authority any time within 60 calendar days of an ALJ's decision or dismissal. [42 C.F.R. § 405.1110(a).]

The review. The Medicare Appeals Council conducts a *de novo* review of an ALJ decision and limits its review to the evidence contained in the record of the proceedings before the ALJ. If the hearing decision identifies a new issue that the parties were not afforded an opportunity to present at the ALJ level, the Medicare Appeals Council considers any evidence related to that issue that is submitted with the request for review. If the Medicare Appeals Council determines that additional evidence is necessary to resolve the issues in the case and the hearing record indicates that the previous decision makers have not attempted to obtain the evidence, it may remand the case to an ALJ to obtain the evidence and issue a new decision. [42 C.F.R. §§ 405.1108(a), 405.1122(a), 405.1126(a).] A party also may request to appear before the Medicare Appeals Council to present oral argument. [42 C.F.R. § 405.1124.]

If the Medicare Appeals Council is reviewing a case that was escalated from the ALJ level, it will decide the case based on the record constructed by the QIC and any additional evidence that was entered into the record by the ALJ before the case was escalated. The Medicare Appeals Council may remand the case to an ALJ to consider or obtain evidence and issue a new decision if it: (1) receives additional evidence with the request for escalation that is material to the question to be decided; or (2) determines that additional evidence is needed to resolve the issues in the case. [42 C.F.R. §§ 405.1122(b), 405.1126(a).]

Final action. Subject to the limitations on Medicare Appeals Council consideration of additional evidence, it issues a final action or remands a case to the ALJ for further proceedings within 90 calendar days of receipt of the appellant's request for review, unless the 90-day period is extended. [42 C.F.R. § 405.1100(c).] The Medicare Appeals Council may adopt, modify, or reverse the ALJ hearing decision or recommended decision. It mails a copy of its decision to all the parties. [42 C.F.R. § 405.1128.]

The Medicare Appeals Council's decision is final and binding on all parties unless a federal district court issues a decision modifying the decision or it is revised as the result of a reopening. [42 C.F.R. § 405.1130.]

Escalation. If the Medicare Appeals Council does not issue a decision or dismissal or remand the case to an ALJ within the applicable time frame, the appellant may request that

¶924

the appeal, other than an appeal of an ALJ dismissal, be escalated to the federal district court. If the Medicare Appeals Council is unable to issue a decision or dismissal or remand within five calendar days of the receipt of the request or five calendar days of the end of the applicable adjudication period, it will send a notice to the appellant acknowledging receipt and confirming that it is not able to issue a decision, dismissal, or remand within the statutory time frame. A party may file an action in a federal district court within 60 calendar days after it receives the Medicare Appeals Council's notice. [42 C.F.R. § 405.1132.]

Judicial Review

A party dissatisfied with the Medicare Appeals Council review may request court review of the decision if the amount in controversy meets the threshold and all of the above administrative remedies have been exhausted. For requests filed on or after January 1, 2017, the minimum amount-in-controversy required for beneficiaries to qualify for judicial review of determinations by an ALJ is $1,560; the requirement for 2016 was $1,500. [Soc. Sec. Act §§ 1155(b)(4), 1869(b)(1)(E); *Notices*, 81 FR 65651, Sept. 23, 2016; 80 FR 57827, Sept. 25, 2015.]

The party must file the complaint in the U.S. district court for the judicial district in which the party resides or where the individual, institution, or agency has its principal place of business, within 60 calendar days after the date it receives notice of the Medicare Appeals Council's decision or notice that the Medicare Appeals Council is not able to issue a final decision, dismissal order, or remand order. If the party does not reside within any judicial district, or if the individual, institution, or agency does not have its principal place of business within any such judicial district, the civil action must be filed in the District Court of the United States for the District of Columbia. [42 C.F.R. §§ 405.1130, 405.1132, 405.1134, 405.1136.]

Standard of review. In general, federal courts will liberally construe the Medicare Act to include rather than exclude coverage and any doubts are resolved in favor of coverage. The courts, however, are required to give deference to CMS's actions. The federal court may hold unlawful or set aside agency action, findings, and conclusions that are found to be: (1) arbitrary or capricious; (2) an abuse of discretion; (3) not in accordance with the law; or (4) not supported by substantial evidence. [Administrative Procedure Act, 5 U.S.C. § 706.] Judicial review of administrative determinations of Medicare cases is limited by the substantial evidence rule. The finding of the Secretary as to any fact, if supported by substantial evidence, is considered conclusive. [Soc. Sec. Act § 205(g); 42 C.F.R. § 405.1136(f).]

Assignment of Appeal Rights

Only a provider or supplier that is not a party to the initial determination and that furnished an item or service to the beneficiary may seek assignment of appeal rights from the beneficiary for that item or service. An individual or entity that is not a provider or supplier may not be an assignee. [42 C.F.R. § 405.912(a), (b).]

The assignee must waive the right to collect payment for the item or service for which the assignment of appeal rights is made. If the assignment is revoked, the waiver of the right to collect payment remains valid. In addition, a waiver of the right to collect payment remains in effect regardless of the outcome of the appeal decision. The assignee, however, is not prohibited from recovering payment associated with coinsurance or deductibles or when an Advance Beneficiary Notice (ABN) is properly executed. [42 C.F.R. § 405.912(d).]

When a valid assignment of appeal rights is executed, the assignor transfers all appeal rights involving the particular item or service to the assignee. These rights include, but are not limited to, obtaining information about the claim to the same extent as the assignor; submitting evidence; making statements about facts or law; and making any request, or giving or receiving any notice about, appeal proceedings. When an assignment of appeal rights is revoked, the rights to appeal revert to the assignor. [42 C.F.R. § 405.912(f)–(g).]

Appointment of Representatives

An appointed representative may act on behalf of an individual or entity in exercising his or her right to an initial determination or appeal. Appointed representatives do not have party status and may take action only on behalf of the individual or entity that they represent. [42 C.F.R. § 405.910(a).]

If the requestor is the beneficiary's legal guardian, no appointment is necessary, and the requestor is defined as the authorized representative. [*Medicare Claims Processing Manual*, Pub. 100-04, Ch. 29, § 270.1.1.]

A representative may be appointed at any point in the appeals process. To file an appeal, the representative must file a copy of the Appointment of Representative (AOR) form or other written instrument with the appeal request. [42 C.F.R. § 405.910(c); Pub. 100-04, Ch. 29, § 270.1.2.]

Duration of appointment. Unless revoked, an appointment is considered valid for one year from the date that the AOR form or other conforming written instrument contains the signatures of both the party and the appointed representative. If the initial determination involves a MSP recovery, an appointment signed in connection with the party's efforts to make a claim for third-party payment is valid for the duration of any later appeal. [42 C.F.R. § 405.910(e); Pub. 100-04, Ch. 29, § 270.1.5.]

Authority and responsibilities of appointed representative. An appointed representative has an affirmative duty to inform the party of the scope and responsibilities of the representation and of the status of the appeal and the results of actions taken, including, notification of appeal determinations, decisions, and further appeal rights. The representative must also disclose to the beneficiary any financial risk and liability of a non-assigned claim that the beneficiary may have. An appointed representative may, on behalf of the party, obtain appeals information about the claim to the same extent as the party, submit evidence, make statements about facts and law, and make any request, or give or receive, any notice about the appeal proceedings. [42 C.F.R. § 405.910(g), (h).]

Fees. An appointed representative may charge a fee, if approved by the Secretary, for an appeal before the Secretary; however, no fees may be charged against the Medicare trust funds, and services rendered below the ALJ level are not considered proceedings before the Secretary. [42 C.F.R. § 405.910(f)(1)–(2).]

Representation by provider or supplier. A provider, physician, or supplier cannot represent a beneficiary if there is a conflict of interest under the waiver of liability provision (i.e., if there is a question as to who knew or had reason to know that the services would not be covered) (see ¶ 915). A provider, physician, or supplier cannot impose any financial liability on the beneficiary in connection with such a representation. [Soc. Sec. Act § 1869(b)(1)(B); 42 C.F.R. § 405.910(f)(3).]

An appeal request filed by a provider or supplier must include a signed statement that no financial liability is imposed on the beneficiary in connection with the representation. If applicable, the appeal request also must include a signed statement that the provider or supplier waives the right to payment from the beneficiary for services or items regarding issues related to items and services considered under the limitation on liability provisions. [42 C.F.R. § 405.910(g)(2).]

¶924

[¶ 926] Expedited Appeals of Provider Service Terminations

Expedited determination and reconsideration procedures are available to beneficiaries when a home health agency, skilled nursing facility, hospice, or comprehensive outpatient rehabilitation facility informs the beneficiary of a decision that Medicare coverage of their services is about to end. [42 C.F.R. § 405.1200(a)(1).]

Termination of Medicare-covered service is considered a discharge of a beneficiary from a residential provider of services or a complete cessation of coverage at the end of a course of treatment, regardless of whether the beneficiary agrees that the services should end. A termination does not include a reduction in services, nor does it include the termination of one type of service by the provider if the beneficiary continues to receive other Medicare-covered services from the provider. [42 C.F.R. § 405.1200(a)(2).]

The provider of the service must deliver valid written notice to the beneficiary of the decision to terminate covered services no later than two days before the proposed end of the services. The provider must use a standardized notice as specified by CMS and include the date the services are to terminate and the date financial liability is to begin, as well as a description of the beneficiary's right to an expedited determination. Quality improvement organizations (QIOs) conduct the expedited determination, and qualified independent contractors (QICs) conduct the expedited reconsideration. [42 C.F.R. §§ 405.1200(b), 405.1202, 405.1204.]

QIO's Expedited Redetermination

A beneficiary has a right to an expedited determination by a QIO for services furnished by a nonresidential provider if he or she disagrees with the provider that services should be terminated and a physician certifies that failure to continue the provision of the services may place the beneficiary's health at significant risk. For services furnished by a residential provider or a hospice, a beneficiary has a right to an expedited determination if he or she disagrees with the provider's decision to discharge him or her. Coverage of provider services continues until the date and time designated on the termination notice, unless the QIO reverses the provider's service termination decision. [42 C.F.R. § 405.1202(a), (c).]

A beneficiary must submit a request for an expedited determination to the QIO in the state in which he or she is receiving the services, in writing or by telephone, by than noon of the calendar day following receipt of the notice of termination. The beneficiary, or his or her representative, must be available to answer questions or supply information that the QIO may request to conduct its review. The beneficiary may, but is not required to, submit evidence to be considered by a QIO in making its decision. [42 C.F.R. § 405.1202(b).]

When a beneficiary requests an expedited determination by a QIO, the burden of proof rests with the provider to demonstrate that termination of coverage is the correct decision, based either on medical necessity or other Medicare coverage policies. [42 C.F.R. § 405.1202(d).]

Within 72 hours of receiving the request for an expedited determination, the QIO must notify the beneficiary, the beneficiary's physician, and the provider of services of its determination of whether termination of Medicare coverage is the correct decision. [42 C.F.R. § 405.1202(e)(6).]

QIC Expedited Reconsiderations

A beneficiary who is dissatisfied with a QIO's expedited determination may request an expedited reconsideration by a QIC. The request for reconsideration must be submitted to the appropriate QIC in writing or by telephone no later than noon of the calendar day following initial notification of receipt of the QIO's determination. When a beneficiary requests an expedited reconsideration in accordance with the required deadline, the provider may not bill the beneficiary for any disputed services until the QIC makes its determination. [42 C.F.R. § 405.1204(a), (b), (f).]

On the day the QIC receives the request for reconsideration, it must notify the QIO that made the expedited determination and the provider of services of the request. When a QIC notifies a QIO that a beneficiary has requested an expedited reconsideration, the QIO must supply all information that the QIC needs to make its expedited reconsideration as soon as possible, but no later than by close of business of the day that the QIC notifies the QIO of the request for an expedited reconsideration. At a beneficiary's request, the QIO must furnish the beneficiary with a copy of, or access to, any documentation that it sends to the QIC. A provider may, but is not required to, submit evidence to be considered by a QIC in making its decision. If a provider fails to comply with a QIC's request for additional information beyond that furnished to the QIO for purposes of the expedited determination, the QIC makes its reconsideration decision based on the information available. [42 C.F.R. § 405.1204(c)–(e).]

QICs must provide their reconsideration decisions no later than 72 hours after receiving the appeal request and related medical records. The decisions must be provided by telephone and in writing to the provider of services, the beneficiary requesting the appeal, and the attending physician of the beneficiary. [42 C.F.R. § 405.1204(c).]

See ¶ 710 for a discussion of QIO coverage determinations and reconsideration determinations related to: (1) reasonableness, medical necessity (including the need for using assistants at cataract surgery), and appropriateness of the services furnished or proposed to be furnished (for example, whether treatment was appropriate for the condition); (2) appropriateness of the setting in which the services were, or are proposed to be, furnished; (3) financial liability for the services; and (4) diagnosis-related group (DRG) validation reviews.

Hospital Inpatient Expedited Determinations

A beneficiary has a right to request an expedited determination by the QIO when a hospital, acting directly or through its utilization review committee, with physician concurrence, determines that inpatient care is no longer necessary. [42 C.F.R. § 405.1206(a).] If the hospital acting directly or through its utilization review committee believes that the beneficiary does not require further inpatient hospital care but is unable to obtain the agreement of the physician, it may request an expedited determination by the QIO. [42 C.F.R. § 405.1208(a).]

A beneficiary who wishes to exercise his or her right to an expedited determination must submit a request no later than the day of discharge. The request must be made in writing or by telephone to the QIO that has an agreement with the hospital. Upon request by the QIO, the beneficiary, or his or her representative, must be available to discuss the case and may, but is not required to, submit written evidence to be considered by a QIO in making its decision. [42 C.F.R. § § 405.1206(b)(1)–(3).]

When the QIO issues an expedited determination, it must notify the beneficiary, physician, and hospital of its decision by telephone, followed by a written notice that includes: (1) the basis and rationale for the determination; (2) an explanation of the Medicare payment consequences of the determination, including the date the beneficiary becomes fully liable for the services; and (3) information about the beneficiary's right to a reconsideration of the QIO's determination, including how to request a reconsideration and the time period for doing so. [42 C.F.R. § § 405.1206(d)(8), 405.1208(d).] When the hospital requests a determination, the QIO must make a determination and notify the beneficiary, hospital, and physician within two working days of the hospital's request and receipt of any pertinent information submitted by the hospital. [42 C.F.R. § 405.1208(c)(4).]

The QIO determination is binding upon the beneficiary, physician, and hospital, except: (1) if the beneficiary is still an inpatient in the hospital and is dissatisfied with the determination, he or she may request a QIC reconsideration (see discussion above), or (2) if the beneficiary is no longer an inpatient in the hospital and is dissatisfied with this determination, the determination is subject to the general claims appeal process (see ¶ 924). [42 C.F.R. §§ 405.1206(g), 405.1208(e).]

[¶ 928] NCD and LCD Appeals

The term "national coverage determination" (NCD) means a determination by the HHS Secretary with respect to whether a particular item or service is covered under the Medicare program (see ¶ 390). However, an NCD does not include a determination of what code, if any, is assigned to a particular item or service covered or a determination with respect to the amount of payment made for a particular item or service so covered. The term "local coverage determination" (LCD) means a determination by a contractor under Part A or Part B concerning whether a particular item or service is covered on a Medicare administrative contractor-wide basis in accordance with Social Security Act section 1862(a)(1)(A), which sets the reasonable and necessary standard for covered services. [Soc. Sec. Act § 1869(f)(1)(B), (f)(2)(B).]

Avenues of appeals. The right to challenge NCDs and LCDs is distinct from the existing rights that beneficiaries have for appealing Medicare claims (see ¶ 924). [42 C.F.R. § 426.310(a).]

There are two avenues of appeals for LCDs and NCDs: reconsideration and review. The main differences between an LCD/NCD review and an LCD/NCD reconsideration are the avenue an individual chooses to take to initiate a change to a coverage policy and who may initiate the review. The reconsideration process allows any individual, not just an aggrieved party, to submit new evidence for reconsideration of an LCD or NCD. The review process permits only an "aggrieved party" to file a complaint to initiate the review of an LCD or NCD. [*Final rule*, 68 FR 63692, Nov. 7, 2003.] The Secretary established specific procedures for filing a written complaint for a review of an LCD and separate procedures for filing a written complaint for a review of an NCD (see 42 C.F.R. §§ 426.400 *et seq.*; 426.500 *et seq.*).

Mediation for disputes related to LCDs. CMS established a mediation process to mediate disputes between groups representing providers of services, suppliers, and the medical director for a Medicare administrative contractor whenever the regional administrator involved determines that there is a systematic pattern and a large volume of complaints from such groups regarding decisions of the director or there is a complaint from the co-chair of the advisory committee of that contractor to the regional administrator regarding the dispute. [Soc. Sec. Act § 1869(i).]

LCD/NCD Reviews

Under CMS's appeals process for NCDs and LCDs, beneficiaries who qualify as aggrieved parties can challenge NCDs and LCDs by filing a complaint. An aggrieved party is defined as a Medicare beneficiary who is entitled to benefits under Part A, enrolled under Part B, or both (including an individual enrolled in fee-for-service Medicare, a Medicare Advantage plan, or another Medicare managed care plan), and is in need of coverage for a service that is the subject of an applicable LCD (in the relevant jurisdiction) or NCD, as documented by the beneficiary's treating physician. The HHS Departmental Appeals Board (DAB) conducts NCD reviews and administrative law judges (ALJs) review LCDs. [Soc. Sec. Act § 1869(f)(1), (2), (5); 42 C.F.R. §§ 426.110, 426.300, 426.320.]

Only LCDs or NCDs (including deemed NCDs) that are currently effective may be challenged. The following items are not reviewable:

(1) pre-decisional materials, including draft LCDs, template LCDs or suggested LCDs, and draft NCDs, including NCD memoranda;

(2) retired LCDs or withdrawn NCDs;

(3) LCD or NCD provisions that are no longer in effect due to revisions or reconsiderations;

(4) interpretive policies that are not an LCD or NCD;

(5) contractor decisions that are not based on Soc. Sec. Act § 1862(a)(1)(A);

(6) contractor claims processing edits;

(7) payment amounts or methodologies;

(8) procedure coding issues, including determinations, methodologies, definitions, or provisions;

(9) contractor bulletin articles, educational materials, or website frequently asked questions;

(10) any Medicare Advantage organization or managed care plan policy, rule, or procedure;

(11) an individual claim determination; or

(12) any other policy that is not an LCD or an NCD as set forth in 42 C.F.R. § 400.202.

[42 C.F.R. § 426.325.]

LCD review. An aggrieved party may initiate a review of an LCD by filing a timely written complaint that meets the requirements and includes all the necessary elements with the office designated by CMS on the Medicare website. [42 C.F.R. § 426.400.]

After a complete review of a coverage challenge, the applicable adjudicator is required to issue a description of the appeal rights or provide notice that the decision is pending. An ALJ's decision must include one of the following findings: (1) the provision of the LCD is valid under the reasonableness standard; (2) the provision of the LCD is not valid under the reasonableness standard; (3) the complaint regarding the LCD is dismissed, with a rationale for the dismissal; or (4) the LCD record is complete and adequate to support the validity of the LCD provisions under the reasonableness standard. [42 C.F.R. §§ 426.447, 426.450, 426.462, 426.482.]

An aggrieved party, CMS, or a CMS contractor may appeal the ALJ's decision if it states that a provision of the LCD is valid under the reasonableness standard or the complaint is dismissed. If the DAB determines the appeal is acceptable, it will permit the party that did not file the appeal an opportunity to respond, hear oral arguments, review the LCD record and the parties' arguments, and issue a written decision either upholding, modifying, or reversing the ALJ decision or remanding the ALJ decision for further proceedings. [42 C.F.R. §§ 426.465, 426.476(a).]

NCD review. An aggrieved party may initiate a review of an NCD by filing with the DAB a timely written complaint that meets applicable requirements. [42 C.F.R. § 426.500.] The DAB's decision must include one of the following: (1) a determination that the provision of the NCD is valid under the reasonableness standard; (2) a determination that the provision of the NCD is not valid under the reasonableness standard; (3) a statement dismissing the complaint regarding the NCD and a rationale for the dismissal; or (4) a determination that the NCD record is complete and adequate to support the validity of the NCD provisions under the reasonableness standard. [42 C.F.R. § 426.550.]

After the DAB makes a decision regarding an NCD complaint, it sends a written notice of the decision to each party stating the outcome of the review and informing each party to the determination of his or her rights to seek further review if he or she is dissatisfied with the determination, and the time limit under which an appeal must be requested. CMS may not appeal a DAB decision. [42 C.F.R. § § 426.562, 426.566.]

A decision by the DAB constitutes a final agency action and is subject to judicial review. A party may bypass DAB review in favor of judicial review if he or she alleges an absence of material issues of the facts in dispute and the only issue concerns the constitutionality of the law or the validity of the regulation. [Soc. Sec. Act § 1869(f)(3); 42 C.F.R. § 426.560(a).]

NCD Reconsiderations

When an NCD currently exists, any individual or entity may request that CMS reconsider any provision of that NCD by filing a complete formal request for reconsideration. CMS will consider accepting a request for reconsideration if the requestor submits evidence of one of the following:

- additional scientific evidence that was not considered in the most recent review; or

- plausible arguments that the conclusion reached in the last review along with a sound premise that new evidence may change the conclusion.

[Notice, 78 FR 48167, Aug. 7, 2013.]

CMS considers a request to complete and formal only if the following conditions are met:

- the requester provides a final letter of request and clearly identifies the request as a "Formal Request for NCD Reconsideration";

- the requester identifies the scientific evidence that he or she believes supports the request for reconsideration; and

- the written request includes and supports any additional Medicare Part A or Part B benefit categories in which the requester believes the item or service falls.

The request for reconsideration must be submitted electronically. CMS will usually make a decision within 60 days. [Notice, 78 FR 48167, Aug. 7, 2013.]

[¶ 930] Recovery Audit Contractor, Cost Report, Status, Exclusion, and Suspension Appeals

Provider and supplier appeals include appeals of recovery audit contractor (RAC) determinations, provider status determinations, and suspension and exclusion from participation in Medicare and other federal health care programs. Cost report reviews pertain only to certain providers, such as hospitals, critical access hospitals, and skilled nursing facilities, because those providers are required to submit annual cost reports.

Recovery Audit Contractor Appeals

Although RACs do not make initial determinations, as Medicare contractors, they are able to reopen claims based on their audits of providers' claims to detect improper payments. [Soc. Sec. Act § 1893(h); Final rule, 74 FR 65296, Dec. 9, 2009.] Appeals of RAC determinations regarding fee-for-service claims are handled with other overpayment determinations under the fee-for-service Medicare appeals process (see ¶ 924). [Medicare Financial Man-

agement Manual, Pub. 100-06, Ch. 4, §§ 100.6, 100.7.] For a discussion of RAC responsibilities, see ¶ 711.

Administrative Review of Disputed Cost Reports

Hospitals and certain other providers that participate in the Medicare program are required to submit an annual accounting of the costs they incur to operate their facilities, including direct patient costs for Medicare and non-Medicare patients and operating costs such as depreciation, capital-related costs, and other expenses. The cost report is the vehicle for reporting costs and income to CMS.

Appeals of cost report determinations must follow specific administrative procedures found at 42 C.F.R. § 405.1801 *et seq.* If the amount in dispute is less than $10,000, review is available through the Medicare administrative contractor (MAC), which will appoint a hearing officer or a panel of hearing officers. [42 C.F.R. § 405.1809.]A provider that is dissatisfied with the outcome of this review may request review by a CMS official. [42 C.F.R. § 405.1834.]

PRRB review. Any provider of services that has filed a timely cost report may appeal an adverse final decision of the MAC to the Provider Reimbursement Review Board (PRRB) if the amount at issue is $10,000 or more. Groups of providers may appeal adverse final decisions of the MAC to the PRRB when the matters at issue share a common question of fact or law and the total amount in controversy, in the aggregate, is $50,000 or more. Providers also may appeal to the PRRB on a late cost report decision by the MAC if the amount involved is $10,000 or more. The appeal must be filed within 180 days after the provider receives notice of the MAC's or Secretary's final determination. [Soc. Sec. Act § 1878(a), (b); 42 C.F.R. § 405.1835(a)(2), (a)(3).]

CMS review. A party to a PRRB appeal or CMS may request a CMS Administrator review, or the CMS Administrator, at his or her discretion, may immediately review any decision of the PRRB related to: (1) a hearing decision; (2) a dismissal of a request for hearing; (3) a decision for an expedited judicial review, but only to the question of whether there is PRRB jurisdiction over a specific matter at issue in the decision (the Administrator may not review the PRRB's determination in a decision of its authority to decide a legal question relevant to the matter at issue); or (4) any other final decision of the PRRB. [42 C.F.R. § 405.1875(a), (c).]

Judicial review. A provider has a right to obtain judicial review of a final decision of the PRRB, or of a timely reversal, affirmation, or modification by the Administrator, by filing a civil action within 60 days of receipt of the decision. When judicial review is sought, the amount in controversy is subject to annual interest beginning on the first day of the first month that begins after the 180-day period following the notice of the Medicare contractor's final determination. [Soc. Sec. Act § 1878(f)(1), (2); 42 C.F.R. § 405.1877.]

Providers also have the right to obtain judicial review of any action of the MAC involving a question of law or regulations relevant to the matters in controversy, whenever the PRRB determines (on its own motion or at the request of the provider) that it is without authority to decide the question. [Soc. Sec. Act § 1878(f)(1).]

Appeals of Provider Status Determinations

CMS makes the initial determination as to whether a provider or supplier meets the conditions for participation or coverage in the Medicare program. Providers and suppliers may appeal adverse decisions to an administrative law judge (ALJ) and the Departmental Appeals Board (DAB). [Soc. Sec. Act § 1866(h); 42 C.F.R. § 498.5.] The determinations and

¶930

appeals procedures are outlined in 42 C.F.R. Part 498 and are applicable to these and other status determinations.

Appeals Concerning Suspensions and Fines

The Secretary has the authority (see ¶ 720), delegated to the HHS Inspector General, to exclude from participation in the Medicare program, or impose sanctions upon, entities or individuals if they are determined to have committed certain program abuses. An excluded entity or individual is entitled to reasonable notice of an opportunity for hearing by the Secretary. Any practitioner, provider, or supplier that has been suspended, whose services have been excluded from coverage, or that has been sanctioned is entitled to a hearing before an ALJ. Any suspended or excluded practitioner, provider, or supplier dissatisfied with a hearing decision may request a DAB review and has a right to seek judicial review of the DAB's decision by filing an action in federal district court. [Soc. Sec. Act § 1128(f); 42 C.F.R. § 498.5(i).]

Any person adversely affected by a determination of the Secretary with respect to the imposition of a civil money penalty may obtain review of the determination in a U.S. Court of Appeals (see ¶ 720). [Soc. Sec. Act § 1128A(e).]

Topical Index

→ *References are to paragraph numbers*

END

FATHERS AND SONS

THE AUTHOR ON THE NOVEL

CONTEMPORARY REACTIONS

ESSAYS IN CRITICISM

SECOND EDITION

A NORTON CRITICAL EDITION

IVAN TURGENEV

FATHERS AND SONS

SECOND EDITION

THE AUTHOR ON THE NOVEL
CONTEMPORARY REACTIONS
ESSAYS IN CRITICISM

*Edited with a substantially
new translation by*

RALPH E. MATLAW
UNIVERSITY OF CHICAGO

W · W · NORTON & COMPANY
NEW YORK · LONDON

Published simultaneously in Canada by Penguin Books Canada Ltd., 2801 John
Street, Markham, Ontario L3R 1B4
Printed in the United States of America.

Second Edition

Library of Congress Cataloging-in-Publication Data
Turgenev, Ivan Sergevich, 1818–1883.
[Ottsy i deti. English]
Fathers and sons / Ivan Turgenev; edited with a substantially new
translation by Ralph E. Matlaw.—2nd ed.
p.   cm.— (A Norton critical edition)
Translation of: Ottsy i deti.
Includes selections from Turgenev's correspondence, together with
critical essays.
Bibliography: p. 345
1. Turgenev, Ivan Sergevich, 1818–1883. Ottsy i deti.
2. Turgenev, Ivan Sergevich, 1818–1883 Criticism and
interpretation. I. Turgenev, Ivan Sergevich, 1818–1883.
Correspondence. English. Selections. 1989. II. Matlaw, Ralph E.
III. Title.
PG3421.08   1989   88-17841

ISBN 0-393-95795-0

W. W. Norton & Company, Inc., 500 Fifth Avenue, New York, N.Y. 10110
W. W. Norton & Company Ltd., 37 Great Russell Street, London WC1B 3NU

1 2 3 4 5 6 7 8 9 0

Contents

v

The Contemporary Reaction

Essays in Criticism

Preface

Translating Turgenev's novel poses many problems, beginning with the title. The literal translation is *Fathers and Children*. But "sons" in English better implies the notion of spiritual and intellectual generations conveyed by the Russian *deti*. It is almost impossible to reproduce the rich yet firm texture of the prose. At the same time Turgenev is distinctly old-fashioned, so that a new translation into contemporary English would distort the work. The solution adopted was to use the translation made by Constance Garnett at the turn of the century, which has a comparable quaint but dated charm, and to revise it with three aims in mind: first, to correct many errors and omissions that were the results of the text Mrs. Garnett used, the rapidity of her work, and occasional misinterpretation; second, to change some of the locutions that are too outmoded or too British into others that are less distracting and more comprehensible to the reader; and third, to recast sentence structure when Mrs. Garnett followed the Russian too closely, to the detriment of English style.

No book published in Russia has ever aroused a critical storm as violent and acrimonious as that around *Fathers and Sons*. The controversy is not yet over. It has flared up in a new form in the Soviet Union, and in various ways it engages the attention of all who write on Turgenev, so that it becomes a central problem for those who study Russian intellectual life in the second half of the nineteenth century (see Mathewson's eloquent statement on the plight of the writer in meeting the demands of the Russian reading public). The background material is vast, and in one sense necessary only to the specialist, since the novel itself dramatizes the issues so well. The bibliography offers some possibilities for exploring the historical background. In the notes to the text I have indicated some of Turgenev's specific jibes at certain contemporary ideas, and I have grouped a considerable amount of the background material under the heading "The Contemporary Reaction," where the reader may follow these ideas and trace the attempts to justify or condemn Turgenev's work by the most important writers of his day, Turgenev's own involvement and defense of his intentions occupied him for the remainder of his life and embittered and angered him. The excerpts from his correspondence and his own defense of the novel reprinted here indicate this but also show his concern for revising the work to increase its clarity and its artistic polish.

To the western reader many of these problems do not seem so significant nor even entirely germane to the novel. Writers like Prosper Mérimée and Henry James were happy to pay tribute to Turgenev as a fellow artist—he is, after all, the most European of all nineteenth-century Russian writers in form and subject. But the vast literature on Turgenev has dealt comparatively little with those aspects of his work.

Still, an overwhelming proportion of criticism on *Fathers and Sons* deals with its main figure and turns into Bazarov criticism instead. This is entirely understandable since Bazarov so thoroughly dominates the novel, but such criticism has a disturbing tendency to turn into psychological or socio-political speculation on that personage at the expense of literary analysis of a character in a novel. There has been no way of avoiding such material, the more so as it would have falsified the historical significance of the novel if it had been omitted. It is particularly evident in Turgenev's letters and Pisarev's article, and to a lesser extent in Strakhov's more balanced review of the book, Garnett's article, and my own piece. For matters of craft and composition, the reader may refer to Freeborn's analysis of the structure, to Justus's treatment of nature as a thematic device as well as a descriptive one in the novel, and to Pustovoyt's discussion of various stylistic features and compositional devices characteristic of Turgenev.

The first Essays in Criticism are so arranged that the reader with little or no background may obtain a fairly complete picture of Turgenev, his art, and the particular historical and aesthetic problems of *Fathers and Sons*. Mirsky's is a concise summary of Turgenev's life and art, Yarmolinsky's of the circumstances attendant upon the publication of the novel. The background of the critical controversy that raged around the novel and the more permanent features of the book are discussed in the other essays.

There has been no attempt made to make the transliteration of names consistent in the entire volume. Since the names are readily identifiable this should present no problem. In the text and in the translations prepared for this edition, the *a* or *aya* at the end of family names in the feminine has properly been omitted, so that Anna Sergeevna's last name is Odinstov, and I have bitten my thumb at the "emancipated lady" and left her as Kukshin. No accentuation has been provided for the Russian names, nor have I followed the practice of indicating the possible implications of the names. Yet I cannot refrain from pointing out that the hero's name—Bazarov—is most appropriate, for it contains and symbolizes those ideas bruited during the 1860s in the intellectual marketplace.

RALPH E. MATLAW
DECEMBER 1965

Preface to the Second Edition

Since the appearance of the first edition, a considerable body of criticism has appeared, stimulated more by the century of Turgenev's death than by the impetus of structuralism. Even the latter, however, has had an influence on Turgenev studies, as reflected in several commentaries on narrative techniques, semiotic indicators, and prose structure. Most of these require working with the Russian text, but they are also reflected in the essays newly reprinted here and in items added to the Bibliography. I have eliminated three essays that now seem less relevant to the novel. I am indebted to Professor Walter Arndt of Dartmouth College for a score or so of the corrections made in the text of the novel and elsewhere.

RALPH E. MATLAW
APRIL 1988

The Text of
Fathers and Sons

The Translation by Constance Garnett,
Revised by Ralph E. Matlaw

Fathers and Sons

Dedicated to the memory of
VISSARION GRIGOR'EVICH BELINSKY [1]

I

"Well, Peter, not in sight yet?" was the question asked on May
20th, 1859,[2] by a gentleman a little over forty, in a dusty coat
and checked trousers, who came out hatless to the low
porch of the posting station at S——. He was addressing his servant, a chubby young fellow, with whitish down on his chin, and
little lack-lustre eyes.

The servant, in whom everything—the turquoise ring in his ear,
the pomaded streaky hair, and the civility of his movements—
indicated a man of the new, advanced generation, glanced condescendingly along the road, and replied:

"No, sir; definitely not in sight."

"Not in sight?" repeated his master.

"Not in sight," responded the man a second time.

His master sighed and sat down on a little bench. We will introduce him to the reader while he sits, his feet tucked under him,
gazing thoughtfully round.

His name was Nikolai Petrovich Kirsanov. He had twelve miles
from the posting station, a fine property of two hundred souls, or,
as he expressed it—since he had arranged the division of his land
with the peasants, and started a "farm"—of nearly five thousand
acres.[3] His father, a general who had fought in 1812, a half-edu-

1. Belinsky (1811–48), the most gifted critic
Russia produced in the nineteenth century, was
the idol of young liberals in the 1830's and
1840's. He enthusiastically reviewed Turgenev's early work. The dedication thus immediately implies a work dedicated to the highest
ideals of liberal or progressive thought. See
Turgenev's letter to A. V. Toporov, November
25 (December 8), 1882.
2. The novel is deliberately set before the
liberation of the serfs, which took place February 19, 1861 (old style). The Julian calendar,
used in Russia until 1917, was twelve days behind the Gregorian calendar in use in the

West. February 19 was therefore March 3 new
style.
3. Kirsanov's action marks him as a liberal
landowner, choosing to ameliorate the serfs' lot
on his own initiative. He had substituted quitrent (obrok)—a fixed sum of money to be paid
annually by each peasant—for the indentured
service—*barshchina* (In France *corvée*)—the
owner could demand from his serfs. The quitrent required far less of the serfs' time. Kirsanov
has also divided his property into that part reserved for his own and those plots farmed by
the serfs to provide their own food and earn
their quitrent.

cated, coarse, but not ill-natured man, a typical Russian, had worked hard all his life, first in command of a brigade, then of a division; and constantly lived in the provinces where, by virtue of his rank, he played a fairly important part. Nikolai Petrovich was born in the south of Russia like his elder brother, Pavel, of whom more hereafter. He was educated at home till he was fourteen, surrounded by cheap tutors, free-and-easy but toadying adjutants, and other regimental and staff people. His mother, one of the Kolyazin family, as a girl called *Agathe*, but as a general's wife Agafokleya Kuzminishna Kirsanov, was one of those "lady commandants." She wore sumptuous caps and rustling silk dresses; in church she was the first to advance to the cross; she talked a great deal in a loud voice, let her children kiss her hand in the morning, and gave them her blessing at night—in fact, she got everything out of life she could. Nikolai Petrovich, as a general's son—though so far from being distinguished by courage that he even earned the label "lily-livered"— was intended, like his brother Pavel, to enter the army; but he broke his leg on the very day when the news of his orders arrived, and, after being in bed two months, retained a slight limp to the end of his life. His father gave him up as a bad job, and let him go into the civil service. He took him to Petersburg as soon as he was eighteen, and placed him in the university. His brother happened about the same time to be made an officer in the Guards. The young men started living together in one set of rooms, under the remote supervision of a cousin on their mother's side, Ilya Kolyazin, an official of high rank. Their father returned to his division and his wife, and only rarely sent his sons large quarto sheets of grey paper, scrawled over in a bold clerkly hand. The bottom of these quarto sheets were adorned by the words, "Peater Kirsanof, Major-General,"[4] enclosed carefully in scroll-work. In 1835 Nikolai Petrovich was graduated from the university, and in the same year General Kirsanov was put on the retired list after an unsuccessful parade, and came to Petersburg with his wife to live. He was about to take a house near the Taurus Garden and had joined the English club, but he died suddenly of a stroke. Agafokleya Kuzminishna soon followed him; she could not accustom herself to the dull life in the capital; she was consumed by the boredom of existence in retirement. Meanwhile Nikolai Petrovich had already, in his parents' lifetime and to their no slight chagrin, had time to fall in love with the daughter of his landlord, a petty official, Prepolovensky. She was pretty, and, what is called an "intellectual miss," she used to read serious articles in the "Science" sections of the journals. He married her as soon as the term of mourning was over; and leaving the civil service in which his father had by favor procured him a post, was perfectly blissful with his Masha, first in a country villa near the

---

4. A phonetic transcription that indicates the general is not too literate.

Forestry Institute, afterwards in town in a pretty little flat with a clean staircase and a rather chilly drawing-room; and then in the country, where he finally settled for good, and where in a short time a son, Arkady, was born to him. The young couple lived very happily and peacefully; they were scarcely ever apart; they read together, sang and played duets together on the piano; she tended her flowers and looked after the poultry-yard; he sometimes went hunting, and busied himself with the estate, while Arkady grew and grew in the same happy and peaceful way. Ten years passed like a dream. In 1847 Kirsanov's wife died. He almost succumbed to this blow; in a few weeks his hair turned grey; he was getting ready to go abroad, if possible to distract his mind . . . but then came the year 1848.[5] He returned willy-nilly to the country, and, after a rather prolonged period of inactivity, occupied himself with the reorganisation of his estate. In 1855 he brought his son to the university; he spent three winters with him in Petersburg, hardly going out anywhere, and trying to make acquaintance with Arkady's young companions. The last winter he had not been able to go, and here we see him in the May of 1859, already quite grey, stoutish, and rather bent, waiting for his son, who had just taken his degree, as once he had taken it himself.

The servant, out of a feeling of propriety, and perhaps, too, not anxious to remain under the master's eye, had gone to the gate, and was smoking a pipe. Nikolai Petrovich bent his head, and began staring at the crumbling steps; a big mottled chicken walked sedately towards him, treading firmly with its great yellow legs; a muddy cat gave him an unfriendly look, curled up affectedly on the railing. The sun was scorching; from the half-dark passage of the posting station came an odor of hot rye-bread. Nikolai Petrovich fell to dreaming. "My son . . . a graduate . . . Arkasha . . ." were the ideas that continually revolved in his head; he tried to think of something else, and again the same thoughts returned. He remembered his dead wife. . . . "She did not live to see it!" he murmured sadly. A plump, blue-grey pigeon flew into the road, and hurriedly went to drink from a puddle near the well. Nikolai Petrovich began looking at it, but his ear had already caught the sound of approaching wheels.

"It sounds as if they're coming, sir," announced the servant, popping in from the gateway.

Nikolai Petrovich jumped up, and fixed his eyes on the road. A carriage with three posting-horses harnessed abreast appeared; in the carriage he caught a glimpse of the blue band of a student's cap, the familiar outline of a dear face.

"Arkasha! Arkasha!" shouted Kirsanov, and he ran waving his hands. . . . A few instants later, his lips were pressed to the beardless, dusty, sunburnt cheek of the youthful graduate.

5. The revolution of 1848 initiated the most reactionary phase of Nicholas I's reign. It became practically impossible for Russians to travel abroad.

II

"Let me shake myself first, daddy," said Arkady, in a voice hoarse from travelling, but cheerful and youthful, as he gaily responded to his father's caresses; "I am covering you with dust."

"Never mind, never mind," repeated Nikolai Petrovich, smiling tenderly, and twice he struck the collar of his son's cloak and his own great-coat with his hand. "Let me have a look at you; let me have a look at you," he added, moving back from him, but immediately he went with hurried steps towards the yard of the station, calling, "This way, this way; and horses at once."

Nikolai Petrovich seemed far more excited than his son; he seemed a little bewildered, a little timid. Arkady stopped him.

"Daddy," he said, "let me introduce you to my good friend, Bazarov, about whom I have so often written to you. He has been so kind as to promise to stay with us."

Nikolai Petrovich turned around quickly, and going up to a tall man in a long, loose, rough coat with tassels, who had only just got out of the carriage, he warmly pressed the bare red hand, which the latter did not at once hold out to him.

"I am heartily glad," he began, "and very grateful for your kind intention of visiting us. . . . May I know your name and patronymic." [6]

"Evgeny Vassilyev," answered Bazarov, in a lazy but manly voice; and turning back the collar of his rough coat, he showed Nikolai Petrovich his whole face. It was long and lean, with a broad forehead, a nose flat at the base and sharp at the tip, large greenish eyes, and drooping side whiskers of a sandy color; it was animated by a tranquil smile, and showed self-confidence and intelligence.

"I hope, dear Evgeny Vassilyich, it won't be boring for you with us," continued Nikolai Petrovich.

Bazarov's thin lips moved just perceptibly, though he made no reply, but merely took off his cap. His long, thick dark-blond hair did not hide the prominent bumps of his large skull.

"Well, Arkady," Nikolai Petrovich began again, turning to his son, "shall the horses be put to at once, or would you like to rest?"

"We will rest at home, daddy; tell them to harness the horses."

"At once, at once," his father assented. "Hey, Peter, do you hear?

6. The patronymic is formed by adding the appropriate suffix to one's father's given name, and Russians normally address each other by name and patronymic rather than as Mr. or Mrs. plus family name. In speaking to close friends, children, or inferiors the patronymic is usually omitted. Bazarov gives the short popular form of his patronymic, thereby exaggerating his lower origin. The use of the family name alone, particularly for female characters, as later in this book, and without Mr., Miss, or Mrs. can convey various shades of characters' (or author's) behavior and attitudes.

Get things ready, my good boy; look sharp."

Peter, who as an advanced servant had not kissed the young master's hand, but only bowed to him from a distance, again vanished through the gateway.

"I came here with the carriage, but there are three horses for your coach too," said Nikolai Petrovich fussily, while Arkady drank some water from an iron dipper brought him by the woman in charge of the station, and Bazarov lit a pipe and went up to the driver, who was taking out the horses; "there are only two seats in the carriage, and I don't know how your friend . . ."

"He will go in the coach," interposed Arkady in an undertone. "You must not stand on ceremony with him, please. He's a splendid fellow, so simple—you will see."

Nikolai Petrovich's coachman brought the horses round.

"Come, hurry up, bushy beard!" said Bazarov, addressing the driver.

"Do you hear, Mityukha," put in another driver, standing by with his hands thrust behind him into the opening of his sheepskin coat, "what the gentleman called you? It's bushy beard you are too."

Mityukha only gave a jerk to his hat and pulled the reins off the heated shaft-horse.

"Look sharp, look sharp, lads, lend a hand," cried Nikolai Petrovich; "there'd be something to drink our health with!"

In a few minutes the horses were harnessed; the father and son were installed in the carriage; Peter climbed up on to the box; Bazarov jumped into the coach, and nestled his head down into the leather cushion; and both the vehicles rolled away.

III

"So here you are, a graduate at last, and come home again," said Nikolai Petrovich, touching Arkady now on the shoulder, now on the knee. "At last!"

"And how is uncle, quite well?" asked Arkady who, in spite of the genuine, almost childish delight filling his heart, wanted as soon as possible to turn the conversation from an emotional to a more commonplace level.

"Quite well. He was thinking of coming with me to meet you, but for some reason or other he gave up the idea."

"And how long have you been waiting for me?" inquired Arkady.

"Oh, about five hours."

"Dear old dad!"

Arkady turned round quickly to his father, and resoundingly kissed him on the cheek. Nikolai Petrovich gave vent to a low chuckle.

"I have got such a capital horse for you!" he began. "You will see. And your room has been freshly papered."

"And is there a room for Bazarov?"

"We will find one for him too."

"Please, dad, be nice to him. I can't tell you how I prize his friendship."

"Have you made friends with him lately?"

"Yes, quite lately."

"Ah, that's how it is I did not see him last winter. What does he study?"

"His chief subject is the natural sciences. But he knows everything. Next year he wants to take his M. D."

"Ah! he's in the medical faculty," observed Nikolai Petrovich, and he was silent for a little. "Peter," he went on, stretching out his hand, "aren't those our peasants driving along?"

Peter looked where his master was pointing. Several carts harnessed with unbridled horses were moving rapidly along a narrow by-road. In each cart there were one or at most two peasants in sheepskin coats, unbuttoned.

"Yes, sir," replied Peter.

"Where are they going,—to the town?"

"To the town, I suppose. To the pot-house [7]," he added contemptuously, turning slightly towards the coachman, as though appealing to him. But the latter did not stir a muscle; he was a man of the old stamp, and did not share the modern views of the younger generation.

"I have had a lot of bother with the peasants this year," pursued Nikolai Petrovich, turning to his son. "They won't pay their rent. What is one to do?"

"But are you satisfied with your hired laborers?"

"Yes," said Nikolai Petrovich between his teeth. "They are being set against me, that's the mischief; and they don't do their best as yet. They spoil the tools. But they have tilled the land pretty fairly. When things have settled down a bit, it will be all right. Do you take an interest in farming now?"

"You've no shade; that's a pity," remarked Arkady, without answering the last question.

"I have had a great awning put up on the north side over the balcony," observed Nikolai Petrovich; "now we can even have dinner in the open air."

"It'll be rather too like a summer villa. . . . Still, that's all non-

---

7. The pot-house (*kabak*) was a kind of small inn or hut, something like a bar, where peasants would go to drink.

sense. But what air there is here! How delicious it smells! Really I fancy there's nowhere such fragrance in the world as in these regions! And the sky, too."

Arkady suddenly stopped short, cast a stealthy look behind him, and said no more.

"Of course," observed Nikolai Petrovich, "you were born here, and so everything is bound to strike you in a special——"

"Come, dad, it makes no difference where a man is born."

"Still——"

"No; it makes absolutely no difference."

Nikolai Petrovich gave a sidelong glance at his son, and the carriage went on half-a-mile further before the conversation was renewed between them.

"I don't remember whether I wrote to you," began Nikolai Petrovich, "your old nurse, Egorovna, is dead."

"Really? Poor thing! Is Prokofich still living?"

"Yes, and not a bit changed. Grumbles as much as ever. In fact, you won't find many changes in Marino."

"Do you still have the same bailiff?"

"Well, to be sure, there is a change there. I decided not to keep about me any freed serfs who had been house servants, or, at least, not to entrust them with duties of any responsibility." (Arkady glanced towards Peter.) *"Il est libre, en effet,"* [8] observed Nikolai Petrovich in an undertone; "but, you see, he's only a valet. Now I have a bailiff, a townsman; he seems a practical fellow. I pay him two hundred and fifty rubles a year. But," added Nikolai Petrovich, rubbing his forehead and eyebrows with his hand, which was always an indication with him of inward embarrassment, "I told you just now that you would not find changes at Marino. . . . That's not quite correct. I think it my duty to prepare you, even though . . ."

He hesitated for an instant, and then went on in French.

"A severe moralist would regard my openness as improper; but, in the first place, it can't be concealed, and secondly, you are aware I have always had special ideas as regards the relation of father and son. Though, of course, you would be right in blaming me. At my age . . . In short . . . that . . . that girl, about whom you have probably heard already . . ."

"Fenichka?" asked Arkady easily.

Nikolai Petrovich blushed. "Don't mention her name aloud, please. . . . Well . . . she is living with me now. I have installed her in the house . . . there were two little rooms there. But that can

8. "He is free, actually."

all be changed."

"Goodness, daddy, what for?"

"Your friend is going to stay with us . . . it would be awkward . . ."

"Please, don't be uneasy on Bazarov's account. He's above all that."

"Well, but you, too," added Nikolai Petrovich. "The little lodge is so horrid—that's the worst of it."

"Goodness, dad," interposed Arkady, "it's as if you were apologising; I wonder you're not ashamed."

"Of course, I ought to be ashamed," answered Nikolai Petrovich, blushing more and more.

"Nonsense, dad, nonsense; please don't!" Arkady smiled affectionately. "What a thing to apologise for!" he thought to himself, and his heart was filled with a feeling of indulgent tenderness for his kind, soft-hearted father, mixed with a sense of a certain secret superiority. "Please stop," he repeated once more, instinctively revelling in a consciousness of his own advanced and emancipated condition.

Nikolai Petrovich glanced at him from under the fingers of the hand with which he was still rubbing his forehead, and there was a pang in his heart. . . . But at once he blamed himself for it.

"Here are our fields at last," he said, after a long silence.

"And that in front is our forest, isn't it?" asked Arkady.

"Yes. Only I have sold the timber. This year they will cut it down."

"Why did you sell it?"

"The money was needed; besides, that land is to go to the peasants."

"Who don't pay you their quitrent?"

"That's their affair; besides, they will pay it some day."

"I am sorry about the forest," observed Arkady, and he began to look about him.

The country through which they were driving could not be called picturesque. Fields upon fields stretched all along to the very horizon, now sloping gently upwards, then dropping down again; here and there groves were to be seen, and winding ravines, planted with low, scanty bushes, recalling vividly the representation of them on the old-fashioned maps of Catherine's time. They came upon little streams too with hollow banks; and tiny lakes with narrow dykes; and little villages, with low hovels under dark and often tumble-down thatch roofs, and slanting barns with walls woven of brushwood and gaping doorways beside neglected threshing-floors; and churches, some brick-built, with stucco peeling off in patches, others wooden, with crosses fallen askew, and overgrown graveyards. Slowly Arkady's heart sank. To complete the picture, the peasants they met were all in tatters and on the sorriest little nags; the willows, with their trunks stripped of bark, and broken branches, stood like ragged beggars along the roadside; lean and shaggy cows looking pinched by hunger, were greedily tearing at the grass along the ditches. They looked as though they had just been snatched out of the murderous clutches of some threatening monster; and the piteous state of the weak, starved beasts in the midst of the lovely spring day, called up, like a white phantom, the endless, comfortless winter, with its storms, and frosts, and snows. . . . "No," thought Arkady, "this is not rich land; it does not impress one by prosperity or industriousness; it can't, it can't go on like this, reforms are absolutely necessary . . . but how is one to carry them out, how is one to begin?"

Such were Arkady's reflections; . . . but even as he reflected, the spring regained its sway. Everything around shone golden green, everything—trees, bushes, grass—glistened and stirred gently in wide waves under the soft breath of the warm wind; from all sides flooded the endless trilling music of the larks; the peewits were calling as they hovered over the low-lying meadows, or noiselessly ran over the tussocks of grass; the rooks strutted among the half-grown short spring-corn, standing out black against its tender green; they disappeared in the already whitening rye, only from time to time their heads peeped out amid its grey waves. Arkady gazed and gazed, and his reflections grew slowly fainter and passed away. . . . He flung off his coat and turned to his father, with a face so bright and boyish, that the latter gave him another hug.

"We're not far off now," remarked Nikolai Petrovich; "we have only to get up this hill, and the house will be in sight. We shall get on together splendidly, Arkasha; you shall help me in farming the estate, if it isn't a bore to you. We must draw close to one another now, and learn to know each other thoroughly, mustn't we?"

"Of course," said Arkady; "but what an exquisite day it is to-day!"

"To welcome you, my dear boy. Yes, it's spring in its full loveliness. Though I agree with Pushkin—do you remember in *Evgeny Onegin*—

> 'To me how sad thy coming is,
> Spring, spring, the time of love!
> What . . .' [9]

"Arkady!" called Bazarov's voice from the coach, "send me a match; I've nothing to light my pipe with."

---

9. Pushkin's "novel in verse" (1823–31) is the classic of Russian literature, and Pushkin is its greatest poet.

Nikolai Petrovich stopped, while Arkady, who had begun listening to him with some surprise, though with sympathy, too, made haste to pull a silver matchbox out of his pocket and sent it to Bazarov by Peter.

"Will you have a cigar?" shouted Bazarov again.

"Thanks," answered Arkady.

Peter returned to the carriage, and handed him with the matchbox a thick black cigar, which Arkady began to smoke promptly, diffusing about him such a strong and pungent odor of cheap tobacco, that Nikolai Petrovich, a life-long nonsmoker, was forced to turn away his head, as imperceptibly as he could for fear of wounding his son.

A quarter of an hour later, the two carriages drew up before the steps of a new wooden house, painted grey, with a red iron roof. This was Marino, also known as New-Wick, or, as the peasants had nicknamed it, Lackland Farm.

IV

No crowd of house-serfs ran out on to the steps to meet the masters; only a little girl of twelve appeared alone. After her there came out of the house a young lad, very like Peter, dressed in a coat of grey livery, with white armorial buttons, the servant of Pavel Petrovich Kirsanov. Without speaking, he opened the door of the carriage, and unbuttoned the apron of the coach. Nikolai Petrovich with his son and Bazarov walked through a dark and almost empty hall, from behind the door of which they caught a glimpse of a young woman's face, into a drawing-room furnished in the latest style.

"Here we are at home," said Nikolai Petrovich, taking off his cap, and shaking back his hair. "The main thing now is to have supper and rest."

"A meal would not come amiss, certainly," observed Bazarov, stretching, and he dropped on to a sofa.

"Yes, yes, let us have supper, supper directly." Nikolai Petrovich, with no apparent reason, stamped his foot. "And here just at the right moment comes Prokofich."

A man about sixty entered, white-haired, thin, and swarthy, in a brown dress-coat with brass buttons, and a pink neckerchief. He grinned, went up to kiss Arkady's hand, and bowing to the guest, retreated to the door, and put his hands behind him.

"Here he is, Prokofich," began Nikolai Petrovich; "he's come back to us at last. . . . Well, how does he look to you?"

"As well as could be, sir," said the old man, and was grinning again, but he quickly knitted his bushy brows. "You wish supper to be served?" he said impressively.

"Yes, yes, please. But won't you like to go to your room first, Evgeny Vassilyich?"

"No, thanks; no reason to. Only give orders for my little box to be taken there, and this garment, too," he added, taking off his frieze overcoat.

"Certainly. Prokofich, take the gentleman's coat." (Prokofich, with an air of perplexity, picked up Bazarov's "garment" in both hands, and holding it high above his head, retreated on tiptoe.) "And you, Arkady, are you going to your room for a minute?"

"Yes, I must wash," answered Arkady, and was just moving towards the door, but at that instant there came into the drawing-room a man of medium height, dressed in a dark English suit, a fashionable low cravat, and patent leather shoes, Pavel Petrovich Kirsanov. He looked about forty-five: his close-cropped, grey hair shone with a dark lustre, like new silver; his face, bilious but free from wrinkles, was exceptionally regular and pure in line, as though carved by a light and delicate chisel, and showed traces of remarkable beauty; specially fine were his shining, black, almond-shaped eyes. The whole figure of Arkady's uncle, with its elegant and aristocratic cast, had preserved the gracefulness of youth and that air of striving upwards, away from earth, which for the most part is lost after a man's twenties.

Pavel Petrovich took out of his trouser pocket his beautiful hand with its long pink nails, a hand which seemed still more beautiful against the snowy whiteness of the cuff, buttoned with a single, big opal, and gave it to his nephew. After a preliminary handshake in the European style, he kissed him thrice after the Russian fashion, that is to say, he touched his cheek three times with his perfumed moustaches, and said "Welcome."

Nikolai Petrovich presented him to Bazarov; Pavel Petrovich greeted him with a slight inclination of his supple figure, and a slight smile, but he did not give him his hand, and even put it back into his pocket.

"I had begun to think you were not coming to-day," he began in a musical voice, rocking gently and with a shrug of the shoulders, as he showed his splendid white teeth. "Did anything happen on the road?"

"Nothing happened," answered Arkady; "we were rather slow. But we're as hungry as wolves now. Hurry up Prokofich, dad; and I'll be back directly."

"Stay, I'm coming with you," cried Bazarov, pulling himself up suddenly from the sofa. Both the young men went out.

"Who is that?" asked Pavel Petrovich.

"A friend of Arkasha's; according to him a very clever fellow."

"Is he going to stay with us?"

"Yes."

"That unkempt creature?"

"Why, yes."

Pavel Petrovich drummed with his finger-nails on the table. "I fancy Arkady *s'est dégourdi,*" [1] he remarked. "I'm glad he has come back."

At supper there was little conversation. Bazarov especially said nothing, but he ate a great deal. Nikolai Petrovich related various incidents in what he called his career as a farmer, talked about the impending government measures, about committees, deputations' [2] the need for introducing machinery, etc. Pavel Petrovich paced slowly up and down the dining-room (he never ate supper), sometimes sipping from a glass of red wine, and less often uttering some remark or rather exclamation, such as "Ah! aha! hm!" Arkady told some news from Petersburg, but he was conscious of a little awkwardness, that awkwardness which usually overtakes a youth when he has just ceased to be a child and has come back to a place where they are accustomed to regard him and treat him as a child. He made his sentences quite unnecessarily long, avoided the word "daddy," and even sometimes replaced it by the word "father," mumbled, it is true, between his teeth; with an exaggerated carelessness he poured into his glass far more wine than he really wanted, and drank it all off. Prokofich did not take his eyes off him, and kept chewing his lips. After supper they all separated at once.

"Your uncle's a queer fish," Bazarov said to Arkady, as he sat in his dressing-gown by his bedside, smoking a short pipe. "Only fancy such style in the country! His nails, his nails—you could send them to an exhibition!"

"Why, of course, you don't know," replied Arkady. "He was a great swell in his own day, you know. I will tell you his story one day. He was very handsome, you know, used to turn all the women's heads."

"Oh, that's it, is it? So he keeps it up in the memory of the past. It's a pity there's no one for him to fascinate here, though. I kept staring at his exquisite collars. They're like marble, and his chin's shaved simply to perfection. Come, Arkady Nikolaich, isn't that ridiculous?"

"Perhaps it is; but he's a splendid man, really."

"An antique survival! But your father's a capital fellow. He wastes his time reading poetry, and doesn't know much about farming, but he's a good-hearted fellow."

"My father has a heart of gold."

1. "has become more easy going."
2. Created and headed by Alexander II for considering problems of the emancipation of the
serfs.

"Did you notice how shy he is?"

Arkady shook his head as though he himself were not shy.

"It's something astonishing," pursued Bazarov, "these elderly romantics! They develop their nervous systems to the breaking point . . . so balance is lost. But good-night. In my room there's an English washstand, but the door won't fasten. Anyway, that ought to be encouraged—an English washstand stands for progress!"

Bazarov went away, and a sense of great happiness came over Arkady. Sweet it is to fall asleep in one's own home, in the familiar bed, under the quilt worked by loving hands, perhaps a dear nurse's hands, those kind, tender, untiring hands. Arkady remembered Egorovna, and sighed and wished her peace in heaven. . . . For himself he made no prayer.

Both he and Bazarov were soon asleep, but others in the house were awake long after. His son's return had agitated Nikolai Petrovich. He lay down in bed, but did not put out the candles, and his head propped on his hand, he fell into deep thought. His brother was sitting long after midnight in his study, in a wide Hambs armchair before the fireplace, on which there smouldered some faintly glowing embers. Pavel Petrovich was not undressed, only red Chinese slippers without heels had replaced the patent leather shoes on his feet. He held in his hand the latest issue of *Galignani*,[3] but he was not reading; he gazed fixedly into the grate, where a bluish flame flickered, dying down, then flaring up again. . . . God knows where his thoughts were rambling, but they were not rambling in the past only; the expression of his face was concentrated and surly, which is not the way when a man is absorbed solely in recollections. And in a small back room there sat on a large chest a young woman in a blue dressing jacket with a white kerchief thrown over her dark hair, Fenichka. She was half listening, half dozing, and often looked across towards the open door through which a child's crib was visible, and the regular breathing of a sleeping baby could be heard.

V

The next morning Bazarov woke up earlier than any one and went out of the house. "Oh, my!" he thought, looking about him, "the little place isn't much to boast of!" When Nikolai Petrovich had divided the land with his peasants, he had had to build his new manor-house on ten acres of perfectly flat and barren land. He had built a house, offices, and farm buildings, laid out a garden, dug a pond, and sunk two wells; but the young trees had not done well, very little water had collected in the pond, and that in the wells tasted brackish. Only one arbor of lilac and acacia had

3. A daily newspaper, *Galignani's Messenger*, published in English in Paris.

grown fairly well; they sometimes had tea and dinner in it. In a few minutes Bazarov had traversed all the little paths of the garden; he went into the cattle-yard and the stable, routed out two farm-boys, with whom he made friends at once, and set off with them to a small swamp about a mile from the house to look for frogs.

"What do you want frogs for, sir?" one of the boys asked him.

"I'll tell you what for," answered Bazarov, who possessed the special faculty of inspiring confidence in people of a lower class, though he never tried to win them, and behaved very casually with them; "I shall cut the frog open, and see what's going on in his insides, and then, as you and I are much the same as frogs, only that we walk on legs, I shall know what's going on inside us, too."

"And what do you want to know that for?"

"So as not to make a mistake, if you're taken ill, and I have to cure you."

"Are you a doctor, then?"

"Yes."

"Vaska, do you hear, the gentleman says you and I are the same as frogs—that's funny!"

"I'm afraid of frogs," observed Vaska, a boy of seven, with a head as white as flax, and bare feet, dressed in a grey smock with a stand-up collar.

"What is there to be afraid of? Do they bite?"

"There, get into the water, philosophers," said Bazarov.

Meanwhile Nikolai Petrovich, too, had waked up, and gone in to see Arkady, whom he found dressed. The father and son went out on to the terrace under the shelter of the awning; near the balustrade, on the table, among great bunches of lilac, the samovar was already boiling. A little girl came up, the same who had been the first to meet them at the steps on their arrival the evening before. In a shrill voice she said—

"Fedosya Nikolaevna is not quite well; she cannot come; she gave orders to ask you, will you please to pour out tea yourself, or should she send Dunyasha?"

"I will pour out myself, myself," interposed Nikolai Petrovich hurriedly. "Arkady, how do you take your tea, with cream, or with lemon?"

"With cream," answered Arkady; and after a brief silence, he uttered interrogatively, "Daddy?"

Nikolai Petrovich looked at his son with embarrassment.

"Well?" he said.

Arkady dropped his eyes.

"Forgive me, dad, if my question seems unsuitable to you," he began, "but you yourself, by your openness yesterday, encourage me to be open . . . you will not be angry . . .?"

"Go on."

"You give me confidence to ask you. . . . Isn't the reason Fen . . . isn't the reason she will not come here to pour out tea, because I'm here?"

Nikolai Petrovich turned slightly away.

"Perhaps," he said, at last, "she supposes . . . she is ashamed."

Arkady turned a rapid glance on his father.

"She has no need to be ashamed. In the first place, you are aware of my views" (it was very pleasant for Arkady to utter that word); "and, secondly, could I be willing to hamper your life, your habits, in the least thing? Besides, I am sure you could not make a bad choice; if you have allowed her to live under the same roof with you, she must be worthy of it; in any case, a son cannot judge his father,—least of all, I, and least of all such a father who, like you, has never hampered my liberty in anything."

Arkady's voice had been shaky at the beginning; he felt himself magnanimous, though at the same time he realised he was delivering something like a lecture to his father; but the sound of one's own voice has a powerful effect on any man, and Arkady brought out his last words resolutely, even with emphasis.

"Thanks, Arkasha," said Nikolai Petrovich thickly, and his fingers again strayed over his eyebrows and forehead. "Your suppositions are just in fact. Of course, if this girl had not deserved. . . . It is not a frivolous caprice. It's not easy for me to talk to you about this; but you will understand that it is difficult for her to come here, in your presence, especially the first day of your return."

"In that case I will go to her," cried Arkady, with a fresh rush of magnanimous feeling, and he jumped up from his seat. "I will explain to her that she has no need to be ashamed before me."

Nikolai Petrovich, too, got up.

"Arkady," he began, "be so good . . . how can . . . there . . . I have not told you yet . . ."

But Arkady no longer listened to him, and dashed away from the terrace. Nikolai Petrovich looked after him, and sank into his chair overcome by confusion. His heart began to throb. Did he at that moment realise the inevitable strangeness of the future relations between him and his son? Was he conscious that Arkady would perhaps have shown him more respect if he had never touched on this subject at all? Did he reproach himself for weakness?—it is hard to say; all these feelings stirred within him, but as sensations—and vague sensations—while the flush did not leave his face, and his heart throbbed.

There was the sound of hurrying footsteps, and Arkady came

on to the terrace. "We have made friends, father!" he cried, with an expression of a kind of affectionate and good-natured triumph on his face. "Fedosya Nikolaevna is really not quite well to-day, and she will come a little later. But why didn't you tell me I had a brother? I should have kissed him last night, as I have kissed him just now."

Nikolai Petrovich wanted to say something, wanted to get up and open his arms. Arkady flung himself on his neck.

"What's this, embracing again?" sounded the voice of Pavel Petrovich behind them.

Father and son were equally rejoiced at his appearance at that instant; there are touching positions, from which one nevertheless longs to escape as soon as possible.

"Why should you be surprised at that?" said Nikolai Petrovich gaily. "Think what ages I have been waiting for Arkasha. I've not had time to get a good look at him since yesterday."

"I'm not at all surprised," observed Pavel Petrovich; "I feel not indisposed to embrace him myself."

Arkady went up to his uncle, and again felt on his cheeks the touch of his perfumed moustache. Pavel Petrovich sat down to the table. He wore an elegant morning suit in the English style, and a gay little fez on his head. This fez and the carelessly tied little cravat carried a suggestion of the freedom of country life, but the stiff collars of his shirt—not white, it is true, but striped, as is correct in morning dress—stood up as inexorably as ever against his well-shaved chin.

"Where's your new friend?" he asked Arkady.

"He's not in the house; he usually gets up early and goes off somewhere. The main thing is, we mustn't pay any attention to him; he doesn't like ceremony."

"Yes, that's obvious." Pavel Petrovich began deliberately spreading butter on his bread. "Is he going to stay long with us?"

"Perhaps. He came here on the way to his father's."

"And where does his father live?"

"In our province, sixty-five miles from here. He has a small property there. He was formerly an army doctor."

"Tut, tut, tut! To be sure, I kept asking myself, 'Where have I heard that name, Bazarov?' Nikolai, do you remember in our father's division there was a surgeon Bazarov?"

"I believe there was."

"Yes, yes, to be sure. So that surgeon was his father. Hm!" Pavel Petrovich twitched his moustaches. "Well, and what precisely is Mr. Bazarov himself?" he asked, deliberately.

"What is Bazarov?" Arkady smiled. "Would you like me, uncle, to tell you what he really is?"

"If you will be so good, nephew."

"He's a nihilist."

"How?" inquired Nikolai Petrovich, while Pavel Petrovich lifted a knife in the air with a small piece of butter on its tip, and remained motionless.

"He's a nihilist," repeated Arkady.

"A nihilist," said Nikolai Petrovich. "That's from the Latin, *nihil, nothing*, as far as I can judge; the word must mean a man who . . . who accepts nothing?"

"Say, 'who respects nothing,' " put in Pavel Petrovich, and he set to work on the butter again.

"Who regards everything from the critical point of view," observed Arkady.

"Isn't that just the same thing?" inquired Pavel Petrovich.

"No, it's not the same thing. A nihilist is a man who does not bow down before any authority, who does not take any principle on faith, whatever reverence that principle may be enshrined in."

"Well, and is that good?" interrupted Pavel Petrovich.

"That depends, uncle. Some people it will do good to, but some people will suffer for it."

"Indeed. Well, I see it's not in our line. We are old-fashioned people; we imagine that without *principes* (Pavel Petrovich pronounced the word softly, in the French way; Arkady, on the other hand, pronounced it harshly, "*pryntsip*," emphasizing the first syllable), without *principes* taken as you say on faith, there's no taking a step, no breathing. *Vous avez changé tout cela.*[4] God give you good health and the rank of a general, while we will be content to look on and admire, worthy . . . what was it?"

"Nihilists," Arkady said, speaking very distinctly.

"Yes. There used to be Hegelists, and now there are nihilists. We shall see how you will exist in a void, in a vacuum; and now please ring, brother Nikolai Petrovich; it's time I had my cocoa."

Nikolai Petrovich rang the bell and called "Dunyasha!" But instead of Dunyasha, Fenichka herself came on to the terrace. She was a young woman about three-and-twenty, all soft and white, with dark hair and eyes, red, childishly pouting lips, and little delicate hands. She wore a neat print dress; a new blue kerchief lay lightly on her round shoulders. She carried a large cup of cocoa, and setting it down before Pavel Petrovich, she was overwhelmed with confusion; the hot blood rushed in a wave of crimson under the delicate skin of her pretty face. She dropped her eyes, and stood at the table, leaning a little on the very tips of her fingers. It seemed as though she were ashamed of having come in, and at the same time felt that she had a right to come.

---

4. "You've changed all that." The sentence following, up to "general," a common locution for good wishes, was originally a line in Griboedor's play *Woe from Wit* (1824).

Pavel Petrovich knitted his brows severely while Nikolai Petrovich looked embarrassed.

"Good morning, Fenichka," he muttered through his teeth.

"Good morning to you," she replied in a voice not loud but resonant, and with a sidelong glance at Arkady, who gave her a friendly smile, she went away softly. She walked with a slightly rolling gait, but even that suited her.

For some minutes silence reigned on the terrace. Pavel Petrovich sipped his cocoa; suddenly he raised his head. "Here is Sir Nihilist coming to honor us," he said in an undertone.

Bazarov was in fact approaching through the garden, stepping over the flower-beds. His linen coat and trousers were besmeared with mud; clinging marsh weed was twined round the crown of his old round hat; in his right hand he held a small bag; in the bag something alive was moving. He quickly drew near the terrace, and said with a nod, "Good morning, gentlemen; sorry I was late for tea; I'll be back directly; I must just put these captives away."

"What have you there—leeches?" asked Pavel Petrovich.

"No, frogs."

"Do you eat them—or breed them?"

"For experiment," said Bazarov indifferently, and he went off into the house.

"So he's going to cut them up," observed Pavel Petrovich. "He has no faith in *principes*, but he has faith in frogs."

Arkady looked compassionately at his uncle; Nikolai Petrovich shrugged his shoulders stealthily. Pavel Petrovich himself felt that his witticism was unsuccessful, and began to talk about husbandry and the new bailiff, who had come to him the evening before to complain that a laborer, Foma, "was deboshed," and quite unmanageable. "He's such an Æsop," he said among other things; "in all places he had protested himself a worthless fellow; he's not a man to keep his place; he'll walk off in a huff like a fool."

VI

Bazarov came back, sat down to the table, and began hastily drinking tea. The two brothers looked at him in silence, while Arkady stealthily watched first his father and then his uncle.

"Did you walk far from here?" Nikolai Petrovich asked at last.

"Where you have a little swamp near the aspen grove. I started some half-dozen snipe; you might slaughter them, Arkady."

"Aren't you a hunter?"

"No."

"Is your special study physics?" Pavel Petrovich in his turn inquired.

"Physics, yes; and the natural sciences in general."

"They say the Teutons have lately had great success in that line."

"Yes; the Germans are our teachers in it," Bazarov answered carelessly.

Pavel Petrovich had used the word "Teutons" instead of Germans, with ironical intention; no one noticed it, however.

"Have you such a high opinion of the Germans?" said Pavel Petrovich, with exaggerated courtesy. He was beginning to feel a secret irritation. His aristocratic nature was revolted by Bazarov's absolute nonchalance. This surgeon's son was not only unintimidated, he even gave abrupt and indifferent answers, and in the tone of his voice there was something coarse, almost insolent.

"The scientists there are a clever lot."

"Quite so. But you probably have a less flattering opinion of Russian scientists?"

"Very likely."

"That's very praiseworthy self-abnegation," Pavel Petrovich declared, drawing himself up, and throwing his head back. "But did not Arkady Nikolaich tell us just now that you recognize no authorities? Don't you believe in them?"

"But why should I accept them? And what is there to believe in? They talk sense, I agree, that's all."

"And do all Germans talk sense?" uttered Pavel Petrovich, and his face assumed an expression as detached, and remote, as if he had withdrawn to some cloudy height.

"Not all," replied Bazarov, with a short yawn. He obviously did not care to continue the discussion.

Pavel Petrovich glanced at Arkady, as he wanted to say to him, "Your friend's polite, I must say." "For my own part," he began again, not without some effort, "I am so unregenerate as not to like Germans. I won't even mention Russian Germans; we all know what sort of creatures they are. But even German Germans are not to my liking. In former days there were some here and there; they had—well, Schiller, to be sure, *Goetthe* . . . my brother —he takes a particularly favorable view of those two . . . But now they are all some sort of chemists and materialists. . . ."

"A good chemist is twenty times as useful as any poet," broke in Bazarov.

"Oh, indeed," commented Pavel Petrovich, and, as though falling asleep, he barely raised his eyebrows. "You don't recognize art then, I suppose?"

"The art of making money or of 'shrinking hemorrhoids'!" cried Bazarov, with a contemptuous laugh.

"Indeed, sir indeed. You are pleased to jest, I see. You reject everything, then? Granted. That means you believe only in science?"

"I have already informed you that I believe in nothing; and what is science—science in the abstract? There are sciences, as there are trades and vocations; but abstract science doesn't exist at all."

"Very good. Well, and do you maintain the same negative attitude in regard to the other conventions accepted as social customs?"

"What is this, an examination?" asked Bazarov.

Pavel Petrovich turned slightly pale. . . . Nikolai Petrovich thought it his duty to interrupt the conversation.

"We will discuss this subject in greater detail some day, my dear Evgeny Vassilyich; we will get to know your views, and express our own. For my part I am very glad you are studying the natural sciences. I have heard that Liebig has made some wonderful discoveries in soil fertilization. You can be of assistance to me in my agricultural work; you can give me some useful advice."

"I am at your service, Nikolai Petrovich; but Liebig is far beyond our heads! You have to learn the alphabet and then begin to read, but we haven't started our ABC's yet."

"You certainly are a nihilist, I see," thought Nikolai Petrovich. "Still, you will allow me to apply to you on occasion," he added aloud. "And now, brother, I think it's time for us to have a talk with the bailiff."

Pavel Petrovich rose from his chair.

"Yes," he said, without looking at any one; "it's a misfortune to live five years in the country like this, far from mighty intellects! You turn into a fool directly. You try not to forget what you've been taught, but there—poof!—it turns out that it's all rubbish, and you're told that sensible men have nothing more to do with such foolishness, and that you, if you please, are an antiquated old fogey. What's to be done? Young people, of course, are cleverer than we are!"

Pavel Petrovich turned slowly on his heels, and slowly left. Nikolai Petrovich went after him.

"Is he always like that?" Bazarov coolly asked Arkady, as soon as the door had closed behind the two brothers.

"Listen, Evgeny, you really were too sharp with him," remarked Arkady. "You offended him."

"Yes, I'll pamper them, these provincial aristocrats! Why, that's all vanity, dandy habits, fatuity. He should have continued his career in Petersburg, if that's his bent. But there, enough of him! I've found a rather rare species of a water-beetle, *Dytiscus marginatus*, do you know it? I will show you."

"I promised to tell you his story," began Arkady.

"The story of the beetle?"

"Come, don't, Evgeny. The story of my uncle. You will see he's not the sort of man you fancy. He deserves pity rather than ridicule."

"I don't dispute it; but why are you so concerned about him?"

"One ought to be just, Evgeny."

"How does that follow?"

"No; listen . . ."

And Arkady told him his uncle's story. The reader will find it in the following chapter.

VII

Pavel Petrovich Kirsanov was educated first at home, like his younger brother, and afterwards in the Corps of Pages. From childhood he was distinguished by remarkable good looks; moreover he was self-confident, somewhat ironical, and amusingly caustic; he could not fail to please. As soon as he received his commission as an officer, he began to be seen everywhere. He was much admired in society, and he indulged himself, played the fool, even gave himself airs, but that too was attractive in him. Women went mad about him; men called him a fop, and were secretly jealous of him. He lived, as has been related already, in an apartment with his brother, whom he loved sincerely, though he was not at all like him. Nikolai Petrovich was a little lame, he had small, pleasant rather melancholy features, small, black eyes, and thin, soft hair; he enjoyed loafing, but he also enjoyed reading, and was timid in society. Pavel Petrovich did not spend a single evening at home, prided himself on his audacity and agility (he was just making gymnastics fashionable among young men in society), and had read in all five or six French books. At twenty-eight he was already a captain; a brilliant career awaited him. Suddenly everything changed.

At that time, there was occasionally seen in Petersburg society a woman who has even not been forgotten today, Princess R——. She had a well-educated, well-bred, but rather stupid husband, and no children. She used to go abroad suddenly and suddenly return to Russia, and in general led an eccentric life. She had the reputation of being a frivolous coquette, abandoned herself eagerly to every sort of pleasure, danced to exhaustion, laughed and jested with young men, whom she received in the dim light of her drawing-room before dinner; while at night she wept and prayed, found no peace anywhere, and often paced her room till morning, wringing her hands in anguish, or sat, pale and cold, reading the Psalms. Day came, and she was again transformed into a grand lady; again she went out, laughed, chattered, and simply flung herself headlong into anything which could afford her the slightest distraction. She had a wonderful figure, her hair, gold-colored and heavy as gold, fell below her knees, but no one would have called her a beauty; in her whole face the only good point was her eyes, and not even the eyes themselves—they were grey, and not large—but their glance was swift and deep, unconcerned to the point of audacity, and pensive to the point of despondence—an enigmatic glance. Something extraordinary shone in them, even while her tongue babbled the emptiest of inanities. She dressed exquisitely. Pavel Petrovich met her at a ball, danced the mazurka with her, in the course of which she did not utter a single sensible word, and fell passionately in love with her. Being accustomed to make conquests, in this instance, too, he soon attained his object, but his easy success did not damp his ardor. On the contrary, he was still more agonizingly, closely attached to this woman, in whom, even when she surrendered herself completely, there always seemed something still to remain mysterious and unattainable, which none could penetrate. What was hidden in that soul—God knows! It seemed as though she were in power of mysterious forces, incomprehensible even to herself; they seemed to play on her at will; her limited intellect could not master their caprices. Her whole behavior presented a series of inconsistencies; she wrote the only letters which could have awakened her husband's just suspicions to a man who was almost a stranger to her; while her love always had an element of melancholy; she ceased to laugh and to jest with the man she chose, she listened to him, and gazed at him with a look of bewilderment. Sometimes, for the most part suddenly, this bewilderment passed into chill horror; her face assumed a wild, death-like expression; she locked herself up in her bedroom, and her maid, by listening at the keyhole, could hear her smothered sobs. More than once, as he went home after a tender meeting, Kirsanov felt within him that heartrending, bitter vexation which follows definite failure.

"What more do I want?" he asked himself, while his heart was heavy. He once gave her a ring with a sphinx engraved on the stone.

"What's that?" she asked; "a sphinx?"

"Yes," he answered, "and that sphinx is you."

"I?" she asked, and slowly raising her enigmatical glance upon him. "Do you know that's awfully flattering?" she added with a meaningless smile, while her eyes still kept the same strange look.

Pavel Petrovich suffered even while Princess R—— loved him; but when she cooled toward him, and that happened rather quickly, he almost went out of his mind. He was on the rack, and he was jealous; he gave her no peace, followed her about everywhere; she grew sick of his persistent pursuit, and went abroad. He resigned his commission in spite of the entreaties of his friends and the exhortations of his superiors, and followed the princess; he spent four years in foreign lands, sometimes pursuing her, at others intentionally losing sight of her. He was ashamed of himself, he was disgusted with his own lack of spirit . . . but nothing availed. Her image, that incomprehensible, almost meaningless, but bewitching image, was deeply rooted in his heart. At Baden he once more regained his old footing with her; it seemed as though she had never loved him so passionately . . . but in a month it was all over: the flame flickered up for the last time and went out forever. Foreseeing inevitable separation, he at least wanted to remain her friend, as though friendship with such a woman were possible. . . . She secretly left Baden, and from that time steadily avoided Kirsanov. He returned to Russia, and tried to take up the threads of his former life again; but he could not get back into the former groove. He wandered from place to place like a man possessed; he still went into society; he still retained the habits of a man of the world; he could boast of two or three fresh conquests; but he no longer expected anything special of himself or of others, and he undertook nothing. He aged and his hair turned grey; to spend his evening at the club, in jaded boredom, and to argue in bachelor society became a necessity for him—a bad sign, as we all know. He did not even think of marriage, of course. Ten years passed in this way; they passed by colorless and fruitless—and quickly, fearfully quickly. Nowhere does time fly past as in Russia; in prison they say it flies even faster. One day at dinner at the club, Pavel Petrovich heard of the Princess R——'s death. She had died at Paris in a state bordering on insanity. He rose from the table, and a long time he paced about the rooms of the club, or stood stockstill near the card-players, but he did not go home earlier than usual. Some time later he received a packet addressed to him; it contained the ring he had given the princess. She had drawn lines in the shape of a cross over the sphinx and sent him word that the solution of the enigma was the cross.

This happened at the beginning of the year 1848, at the very time when Nikolai Petrovich came to Petersburg, after the loss of his wife. Pavel Petrovich had scarcely seen his brother since the latter had settled in the country; the marriage of Nikolai Petrovich had coincided with the very first days of Pavel Petrovich's acquaintance with the princess. When he came back from abroad, he had gone to him with the intention of staying with him a couple of months, to enjoy gazing at his happiness, but he had only succeeded in standing a week of it. The difference in the positions of the two brothers was too great. In 1848, this difference had grown less; Nikolai Petrovich had lost his wife, Pavel Petrovich had lost his memories; after the death of the princess he tried not to think of her. But to Nikolai, there remained the sense of a well-spent life, his son was growing up under his eyes; Pavel, on the contrary, a lonely bachelor, was entering upon that indefinite twilight period of regrets that are akin to hopes, and hopes that are akin to regrets, when youth is over, while old age has not yet come.

This time was harder for Pavel Petrovich than for any other man; in losing his past, he lost everything.

"I will not invite you to Marino now," Nikolai Petrovich said to him one day, (he had called his property by that name in honor of his wife Mary); "you were bored there even when my wife was alive, and now I think you would simply languish away."

"I was stupid and fidgety then," answered Pavel Petrovich; "since then I have grown quieter, if not wiser. On the contrary, now, if you will let me, I am ready to settle with you for good."

Instead of answering Nikolai Petrovich embraced him; but a year and a half passed after this conversation, before Pavel Petrovich made up his mind to carry out his intention. When he once settled in the country, however, he did not leave it, even during the three winters which Nikolai Petrovich spent in Petersburg with his son. He began to read, chiefly English; in general he arranged his whole life in the English style, rarely saw the neighbors, and only went out to the election of marshals, where he was generally silent, only occasionally annoying and alarming land-owners of the old school by his liberal sallies, and not associating with the representatives of the younger generation. Both the latter and the former considered him "stuck up"; and both parties respected him for his fine aristocratic manners; for the rumors of his conquests; for the fact that he was very well dressed and always stayed in the best room in the best hotel; for the fact that he generally dined well, and had once even dined with Wellington at Louis Philippe's table; for the fact that he always took everywhere with him a real silver dressing-case and a portable bath; for the fact that he always smelt of some unusual, amazingly "aristocratic" scent; for the fact that he played whist in masterly fashion, and always lost; and lastly, they respected him also for his incorruptible honesty. Ladies considered him enchantingly romantic, but he did not cultivate ladies' acquaintance. . . .

"So you see, Evgeny," observed Arkady, as he finished his

story, "how unjustly you judge my uncle! To say nothing of his having more than once helped my father out of difficulties, given him all his money—the property, perhaps you don't know, wasn't divided—he's glad to help any one, among other things he always sticks up for the peasants; it's true, when he talks to them he frowns and sniffs eau de cologne. . . ."

"His nerves, no doubt," put in Bazarov.

"Perhaps; but his heart is in the right place. And he's far from being stupid. What useful advice he has given me, especially . . . especially in regard to relations with women."

"Aha! a scalded cat fears cold water, we know that!"

"In short," continued Arkady, "he's profoundly unhappy, believe me; it's a sin to despise him."

"But who does despise him?" retorted Bazarov. "Still, I must say that a man who stakes his whole life on one card—a woman's love—and when that card fails, turns sour, and lets himself go till he's fit for nothing, is not a man, but a male. You say he's unhappy; you know best; but he hasn't got rid of all his fads. I'm convinced that he seriously considers himself worthwhile because he reads that wretched *Galignani*, and once a month saves a peasant from a flogging."

"But remember his education, the age in which he grew up," observed Arkady.

"Education?" broke in Bazarov. "Every man must educate himself, just as I've done, for instance. . . . And as for the age, why should I depend on it? Let it rather depend on me. No, my dear fellow, that's all shallowness, dissoluteness! And what about all these mysterious relations between a man and woman? We physiologists know what these relations are. Study the anatomy of the eye a bit; where does the enigmatical glance you talk about come in there? That's all romanticism, nonsense, rot, artiness.[5] We'd better go and look at the beetle."

And the two friends went off to Bazarov's room, which was already pervaded by a sort of medico-surgical odor mingled with the smell of cheap tobacco.

VIII

Pavel Petrovich did not stay long at his brother's interview with his bailiff, a tall, thin man with a sweet consumptive voice and knavish eyes, who to all Nikolai Petrovich's remarks answered,

5. Bazarov echoes N. A. Dobrolyubov (1836–61), a radical critic after whom he is in part drawn. The radical, or civic, critics flourished in the middle of the nineteenth century. Their primary interest in literature was its social and political content, its expression of progressive ideas, and its reflection of "reality." They became spokesmen for a particular kind of political opinion, called by some "liberal," since under tsarist censorship it was easier to discuss politics under the guise of literary criticism than in its purer state.

"Certainly, sir, of course, sir" and tried to make the peasants out to be thieves and drunkards. The estate had only recently been put on to the new reformed system, and the new mechanism, creaking like an ungreased wheel, cracking like homemade furniture of unseasoned wood. Nikolai Petrovich did not lose heart, but he often sighed and sank into thought; he felt that things could not go on without money, and his money was almost all gone. Arkady had spoken the truth; Pavel Petrovich had more than once helped his brother; more than once, seeing him struggling and cudgelling his brains, at a loss which way to turn, Pavel Petrovich moved deliberately to the window and thrusting his hands into his pockets, muttered between his teeth, *"mais je puis vous donner de l'argent,"* [6] and gave him money; but to-day he had none himself, and he preferred to withdraw. The petty details of agricultural management depressed him; besides, it constantly struck him that Nikolai Petrovich, for all his zeal and industry, did not set about things in the right way, though he would not have been able to point out precisely where Nikolai Petrovich's mistake lay. "My brother's not practical enough," he reasoned to himself; "they cheat him." Nikolai Petrovich, on the other hand, had the highest opinion of Pavel Petrovich's practical ability, and always asked his advice. "I'm a soft, weak fellow, I've spent my life in the country," he used to say; "while you haven't seen so much of the world for nothing, you see through people; you have an eagle eye." In answer to which Pavel Petrovich would only turn away, but did not contradict his brother.

Leaving Nikolai Petrovich in his study, he walked along the corridor which separated the front part of the house from the back; when he had reached a low door, he stopped in hesitation, then pulling his moustaches, he knocked at it.

"Who's there? Come in," sounded Fenichka's voice.

"It is I," said Pavel Petrovich, and he opened the door.

Fenichka jumped up from the chair on which she was sitting with her baby, and giving him into the arms of a girl who at once carried him out of the room, she hastily straightened her kerchief.

"Pardon me, if I disturbed you," began Pavel Petrovich, without looking at her; "I only wanted to ask you . . . they are sending into the town to-day, I think . . . please order some green tea for me."

"Certainly," answered Fenichka; "how much do you want to buy?"

"Oh, half a pound will be enough, I imagine. You have made

6. "But I can give you money."

a change here, I see," he added, with a rapid glance round him, which glided over Fenichka's face too. "The curtains here," he explained, seeing she did not understand him.

"Oh, yes, the curtains; Nikolai Petrovich was so good as to give them to me; but they have been put up a long while now."

"Yes, and it's a long while since I have been to see you. It is very pleasant here now."

"Thanks to Nikolai Petrovich's kindness," murmured Fenichka.

"Are you more comfortable here than in the little lodge you used to have?" inquired Pavel Petrovich, politely, but without the slightest smile.

"Certainly, it's better, sir."

"Who has been put in your place now?"

"The laundry-maids are there now."

"Ah!"

Pavel Petrovich fell silent. "Now he will go," thought Fenichka; but he did not go, and she stood before him motionless, hesitatingly moving her fingers.

"Why did you send your little one away?" said Pavel Petrovich at last. "I like children; do let me see him."

Fenichka blushed all over with confusion and delight. She was afraid of Pavel Petrovich; he scarcely ever spoke to her.

"Dunyasha," she called: "will you bring Mitya, please." (Fenichka did not treat any one in the house familiarly.) "But wait a minute, I have to put something on him," Fenichka moved towards the door.

"That doesn't matter," remarked Pavel Petrovich.

"I will be back directly," answered Fenichka, and she went out quickly.

Pavel Petrovich was left alone, and this time he looked round with special attention. The small low-pitched room in which he found himself was very clean and snug. It smelt of the freshly painted floor and of camomile and hydromel. Along the walls stood chairs with lyre-shaped backs, bought by the late general on his campaign in Poland; in one corner was a little bedstead under a muslin canopy beside an iron-clamped chest with a rounded lid. In the opposite corner a little lamp was burning before a big dark image of St. Nikolai the wonder-worker; a tiny porcelain egg hung by a red ribbon from the protruding gold halo down to the saint's breast; by the windows there were glass jars of last year's jam carefully tied down, shining green; on their paper covers Fenichka herself had written in big letters "Gusberry"; Nikolai Petrovich was particularly fond of that preserve. A cage with a bobtailed siskin hung on a long cord from the ceiling; the bird was constantly chirping and hopping about, the cage was constantly shaking and swinging, while hempseeds fell with a light tap on to the floor. On the wall, between two windows, above a small chest of drawers, hung some rather bad photographs of Nikolai Petrovich in various attitudes, taken by an itinerant photographer; there also hung a photograph of Fenichka herself, which was an absolute failure; it was an eyeless face wearing a forced smile, in a dark frame, nothing more could be made out; while above Fenichka, General Ermolov, in a Circassian cloak, scowled menacingly at the Caucasian mountains in the distance, from beneath a little pincushion which fell right on to his brows.

Five minutes passed; bustling and whispering could be heard in the next room. Pavel Petrovich took up a greasy book from the chest of drawers, an odd volume of Masalsky's *Musketeers*, and turned over a few pages. . . . The door opened, and Fenichka came in with Mitya in her arms. She had put on him a little red smock with an embroidered collar, had combed his hair and washed his face; he was breathing heavily, his whole body working, and his little hands waving in the air, as is the way with all healthy babies; but his elegant smock obviously impressed him: an expression of pleasure was reflected in every part of his chubby little figure. Fenichka had put her own hair in order, too, and had arranged her kerchief better; but she might well have remained as she was. And really is there anything in the world more captivating than a beautiful young mother with a healthy baby in her arms?

"What a roly-poly!" said Pavel Petrovich graciously and he tickled Mitya's little double chin with the tip of the long nail of his forefinger. The baby stared at the siskin, and chuckled.

"That's uncle," said Fenichka, bending her face down to him and lightly bouncing him, while Dunyasha quietly set in the window a smouldering incense cone putting a half-penny under it.

"How many months old is he?" asked Pavel Petrovich.

"Six months; it will soon be seven, on the eleventh."

"Isn't it eight, Fedosya Nikolaevna?" put in Dunyasha, with some timidity.

"No, seven; what an idea!" The baby chuckled again, stared at the chest, and suddenly caught hold of his mother's nose and mouth with all his five little fingers. "Saucy mite," said Fenichka, not drawing her face away.

"He resembles my brother," observed Pavel Petrovich.

"Who else should he be like?" thought Fenichka.

"Yes," continued Pavel Petrovich, as though speaking to himself; "there's an unmistakable likeness." He looked attentively, almost mournfully, at Fenichka.

"That's uncle," she repeated, in a whisper this time.

"Ah! Pavel! so this is where you are!" Nikolai Petrovich's voice was suddenly heard.

Pavel Petrovich turned hurriedly round and frowned; but his brother looked at him with such delight, such gratitude that he could not help responding to his smile.

"You've a splendid little fellow," he said, and looking at his watch. "I came in here to speak about some tea."

And, assuming an expression of indifference, Pavel Petrovich went out of the room.

"Did he come of himself?" Nikolai Petrovich asked Fenichka.

"Yes, sir; he knocked and came in."

"Well, and has Arkasha been in to see you again?"

"No. Hadn't I better move into the lodge, Nikolai Petrovich?"

"Why so?"

"I wonder whether it wouldn't be best just for the first."

"N—no," Nikolai Petrovich brought out hesitatingly, rubbing his forehead. "We ought to have done it before. . . . How are you, fatty?" he said, suddenly brightening, and going up to the baby, he kissed him on the cheek; then he bent a little and pressed his lips to Fenichka's hand, which lay white as milk upon Mitya's little red smock.

"Nikolai Petrovich! what are you doing?" she whispered, dropping her eyes, then slowly raised them. Very charming was the expression of her eyes when she looked up as it were from under her brows, and smiled tenderly and a little foolishly.

Nikolai Petrovich had made Fenichka's acquaintance in the following manner. He had once happened three years before to stay a night at an inn in a remote district town. He was agreeably struck by the cleanness of the room assigned to him, the freshness of the bed-linen. Surely the woman of the house must be a German, was the idea that occurred to him; but she proved to be a Russian, a woman of about fifty, neatly dressed, with a pleasant, clever face and discreet speech. He entered into conversation with her at tea; he liked her very much. Nikolai Petrovich had at that time only just moved into his new home, and not wishing to keep serfs in the house, he was on the lookout for hired servants; the woman of the inn on her side complained of the small number of visitors to the town and the hard times; he proposed to her to come into his house in the capacity of housekeeper; she consented. Her husband had long been dead, leaving her an only daughter, Fenichka. Within a fortnight Arina Savishna (that was the new housekeeper's name) arrived with her daughter at Marino and installed herself in the little lodge. Nikolai Petrovich's choice proved a successful one. Arina brought order into the household. As for Fenichka, who was at that time seventeen, no one spoke of her, and scarcely any one saw her; she lived quietly and modéstly, and only on Sundays Nikolai Petrovich noticed in the parish church, somewhere on the side, the delicate profile of her white face. More than a year passed thus.

One morning, Arina came into his study, and bowing low as usual, she asked him if he could do anything for her daughter, who had got a spark from the stove in her eye. Nikolai Petrovich, like all stay-at-homes had studied simple cures and even ordered a homœpathic medicine chest. He at once told Arina to bring the patient to him. Fenichka was much frightened when she heard the master had sent for her; however, she followed her mother. Nikolai Petrovich led her to the window and took her head in his two hands. After thoroughly examining her red and swollen eye, he prescribed a fomentation, which he made up himself at once, and tearing his handkerchief in pieces, he showed her how to apply it. Fenichka listened to all he had to say, and then started to leave. "Kiss the master's hand, silly girl," said Arina. Nikolai Petrovich did not give her his hand, and in confusion himself kissed her bent head on the part. Fenichka's eye was soon well again, but the impression she had made on Nikolai Petrovich did not pass quickly. He kept thinking of that pure, tender, timidly raised face; he felt that soft hair on the palms of his hands, and saw those innocent, slightly parted lips, through which pearly teeth gleamed with moist brilliance in the sunshine. He began to watch her with greater attention in church, and tried to get into conversation with her. At first she was shy of him, and one day meeting him at the approach of evening in a narrow footpath through a field of rye, she ran into the tall thick rye, overgrown with cornflowers and wormwood, so as not to meet him face to face. He caught sight of her little head through a golden network of ears of rye, from which she was peeping out like a little animal, and called affectionately to her:

"Good-evening, Fenichka! I don't bite."

"Good-evening," she whispered, not coming out of her ambush.

By degrees she began to be more at home with him, but was still shy in his presence, when suddenly her mother, Arina, died of cholera. What was to become of Fenichka? She inherited from her mother a love for order, regularity, and sedateness; but she was so young, so alone. Nikolai Petrovich was himself so good and considerate. . . . It's needless to relate the rest. . . .

"So my brother came in to see you?" Nikolai Petrovich questioned her. "He knocked and came in?"

"Yes sir."

"Well, that's a good thing. Let me give Mitya a swing."

And Nikolai Petrovich began tossing him almost up to the ceiling, to the huge delight of the baby, and to the considerable uneasiness of the mother, who every time he flew up stretched her arms up towards his little bare legs.

Pavel Petrovich went back to his elegant study, its walls covered with handsome bluish-grey wall paper, with weapons hanging upon a colorful Persian rug nailed to the wall; with walnut furniture, upholstered in dark green velveteen, with a renaissance-style bookcase of old black oak, with bronze statuettes on the magnificent desk, with a fireplace. He threw himself on the sofa, clasped his hands behind his head, and remained without moving, looking at the ceiling almost in despair. Whether he wanted to hide from the very walls that which was reflected in his face, or for some other reason, he got up, drew the heavy window curtains, and again threw himself on the sofa.

IX

On that same day Bazarov too became acquainted with Fenichka. He was walking with Arkady in the garden, and explaining to him why some of the trees, especially the young oaks had not done well.

"You ought to plant silver poplars here mostly, and firs, and perhaps lindens, adding loam. The arbor there has done well," he added, "because it's acacia and lilac; they're good fellows, they don't need much care. Why, there's some one in here."

In the arbor Fenichka was sitting with Dunyasha and Mitya. Bazarov stood still, while Arkady nodded to Fenichka like an old friend.

"Who's that?" Bazarov asked him as soon as they had passed by. "What a pretty girl!"

"Whom are you speaking of?"

"You know who; only one of them was pretty."

Arkady, not without embarrassment, explained to him briefly who Fenichka was.

"Aha!" remarked Bazarov; "your father's got good taste, one can see. I like him, your father, by George! He's a good fellow. We ought to get acquainted though," he added, and turned back towards the arbor.

"Evgeny!" Arkady cried after him in dismay; "mind what you are about, for mercy's sake."

"Don't get excited," said Bazarov; "I've been around, I'm not a country bumpkin."

Going up to Fenichka, he took off his cap.

"Allow me to introduce myself," he began, with a polite bow. "I'm a friend of Arkady Nikolaevich's and a harmless person."

Fenichka got up from the garden seat and looked at him without speaking.

"What a splendid baby!" continued Bazarov; "don't be uneasy, my praises have never brought ill-luck yet. Why are his cheeks so flushed? Is he cutting teeth?"

"Yes sir," said Fenichka; "he has cut four teeth already, and now the gums are swollen again."

"Show me, and don't be afraid, I'm a doctor."

Bazarov took the baby up in his arms, and to the great astonishment both of Fenichka and Dunyasha the child made no resistance, and was not frightened.

"I see, I see. . . . It's nothing, everything's all right, he'll have a good set of teeth. If anything goes wrong, tell me. And are you quite well yourself?"

"Quite, thank God."

"Thank God,—that's the great thing. And you?" he added, turning to Dunyasha.

Dunyasha, a very prim girl in the master's house, and a gigglebox outside the gates, only snorted in answer.

"Well, that's all right. Here's your mighty knight."

Fenichka received the baby in her arms.

"How good he was with you!" she commented in an undertone.

"Children are always good with me," answered Bazarov; "I have a way with them."

"Children know who loves them," remarked Dunyasha.

"Yes, they certainly do," Fenichka said. "Why, Mitya will not go to some people for anything."

"Will he come to me?" asked Arkady, who, after standing in the distance for some time, had gone up to the arbor.

He tried to entice Mitya to come to him, but Mitya threw his head back and started to squeal, to Fenichka's great confusion.

"Another day, when he's had time to get used to me," said Arkady indulgently, and the two friends walked away.

"What's her name?" asked Bazarov.

"Fenichka . . . Fedosya," answered Arkady.

"And her patronymic? One must know that too."

"Nikolaevna."

"*Bene*. What I like in her is that she's not too embarrassed. Some people, I suppose, would think ill of her for it. What nonsense! What is there to embarrass her? She's a mother—she's in the right."

"She is all right," observed Arkady,—"but my father. . . ."

"And he's in the right too," put in Bazarov.

"Well, no, I don't think so."

"I suppose an extra heir's not to your liking?"

"How can you not be ashamed to attribute such ideas to me!" retorted Arkady hotly; "I don't consider my father wrong from that point of view. I think he ought to marry her."

"Oho-ho!" responded Bazarov tranquilly. "What magnanimous fellows we are! You still attach significance to marriage; I did not expect that of you."

The friends walked a few paces in silence.

"I have looked at your father's entire establishment," Bazarov began again. "The cattle are inferior, the horses are broken down; the buildings also aren't much, and the workmen seem to be confirmed loafers; while the bailiff is either a fool or a knave, I haven't quite found out which yet."

"You are rather hard on everything to-day, Evgeny Vassilevich."

"And the good peasants are taking your father in for sure. You know the Russian proverb, 'The Russian peasant will cheat God Himself.' "

"I begin to agree with my uncle," remarked Arkady; "you certainly have a poor opinion of Russians."

"As though that mattered! The only good point in a Russian is his having the lowest possible opinion of himself. What does matter is that two and two make four, and the rest is all nonsense.

"And is nature nonsense?" said Arkady, looking pensively at the bright-colored fields in the distance, in the beautiful soft light of the sun, which was no longer high in the sky.

"Nature, too, is nonsense in the sense you understand it. Nature's not a temple, but a workshop, and man's the workman in it." [7]

At that instant, the long drawn notes of a violoncello floated out to them from the house. Some one was playing Schubert's *Expectation* with much feeling, though with an unpracticed hand, and the sweet melody flowed through the air like honey.

"What's that?" cried Bazarov in amazement.

"It's my father."

"Your father plays the violoncello?"

"Yes."

---

7. Bazarov quotes from Chernyshevsky's dissertation *The Aesthetic Relations of Art to Reality* (1855), the bible of the radicals. Chernyshevsky maintained that art is only an imitation of reality, and reality is always superior to it.

"And how old is your father?"

"Forty-four."

Bazarov suddenly burst into laughter.

"What are you laughing at?"

"Really, a man of forty-four, a *paterfamilias* in this out-of-the-way district, playing on the violoncello!"

Bazarov went on laughing; but much as he revered his mentor, this time Arkady did not even smile.

X

About a fortnight passed. Life at Marino went on its accustomed course, while Arkady played the sybarite, and Bazarov worked. Every one in the house had grown used to him, to his careless manners, and his curt and abrupt speeches. Fenichka, in particular, was so far at home with him that one night she sent to wake him up; Mitya had convulsions; and he came, and, half joking, half-yawning as usual, stayed two hours with her and relieved the child. On the other hand Pavel Petrovich had grown to detest Bazarov with all the strength of his soul; he regarded him as stuck-up, impudent, cynical, and plebeian; he suspected that Bazarov had no respect for him, that he had all but contempt for him—him, Pavel Kirsanov! Nikolai Petrovich was rather afraid of the young "nihilist," and doubted whether his influence over Arkady was for the good; but he was glad to listen to him, and was glad to be present at his scientific and chemical experiments. Bazarov had brought a microscope with him, and busied himself with it for hours on end. The servants, too, took to him, though he made fun of them; they felt that he was one of themselves just the same, not a master. Dunyasha was always ready to giggle with him, and used to cast significant and stealthy glances at him when she ran by "like a quail"; Peter, an extremely vain and stupid man, forever wearing an affected frown on his brow, a man whose whole merit consisted in the fact that he looked civil, could spell out a page of reading, and brushed his coat frequently—even he smirked and brightened up as soon as Bazarov paid him any attention; the boys on the farm simply ran after the "doctor" like puppies. Old Prokofich was the only one who did not like him; he served him at table with a surly face, called him a "mule skinner" and "a humbug"; and maintained that with his side whiskers he looked like a pig in a bush. Prokofich in his own way was quite as much of an aristocrat as Pavel Petrovich.

The best days of the year had come—the first days of June. The weather kept fine; in the distance, it is true, cholera was threatening again, but the inhabitants of that province had had time to get used to its visits. Bazarov used to get up very early and go out for two or three miles, not for a walk—he couldn't bear walking without an object—but to collect specimens of plants and insects. Sometimes he took Arkady with him. On the way home an argument usually sprang up, and Arkady was usually vanquished in it, though he said more than his companion.

One day they had somehow lingered rather late; Nikolai Petrovich went to meet them in the garden, and as he reached the arbor he suddenly heard the quick step and voices of the two young men. They were walking on the other side of the arbor, and could not see him.

"You don't know my father well enough," said Arkady.

Nikolai Petrovich concealed himself.

"Your father's a nice man," said Bazarov, "but he's behind the times; his day is done."

Nikolai Petrovich listened intently. . . . Arkady made no answer.

The man whose day was done remained motionless for a couple of minutes, and plodded slowly home.

"The day before yesterday I saw him reading Pushkin," Bazarov was continuing meanwhile. "Explain to him, please, that that's entirely useless.[8] He's not a boy, you know; it's time to throw up that rubbish. And what an idea to be a romantic these days! Give him something sensible ro read."

"What ought I to give him?" asked Arkady.

"Oh, I think Büchner's *Stoff und Kraft*[9] to begin with."

"I think so too," observed Arkady approvingly, "*Stoff und Kraft* is written in popular language. . . ."

"So it seems," Nikolai Petrovich said the same day after dinner to his brother, as he sat in his study, "you and I are behind the times, our day's over. Well, well. Perhaps Bazarov is right; but one thing hurts, I confess; I did hope, precisely now, to get on close, intimate terms with Arkady, and it turns out I'm left behind, and he has gone forward, and we can't understand one another."

"But how has he gone forward? And in what way is he so superior to us?" cried Pavel Petrovich impatiently. "It's that signor, that nihilist, who's knocked all that into his head. I hate that doctor fellow; in my opinion, he's simply a quack; I'm convinced, for all his frogs, he's not got very far even in physics."

"No, brother, you mustn't say that; Bazarov is clever, and knows his subject."

8. Bazarov again echoes Dobrolyubov, who maintained that Pushkin wrote only for the educated class and that few people were interested in him.

9. "Matter and Force." Actually, *Force and Matter* (1855), Russian translation 1860. Ludwig Büchner was the brother of Georg, the German dramatist.

"And his conceit's something revolting," Pavel Petrovich broke in again.

"Yes," observed Nikolai Petrovich, "he is conceited. But there's no doing without that, it seems; only that's what I did not take into account. I thought I was doing everything to keep up with the times; I have done well by the peasants, I have started a farm so that I am positively called a "Red" all over the province; I read, I study, I try in every way to keep abreast with the requirements of the day—and they say my day's over. And, brother, I begin to think that it is."

"Why so?"

"I'll tell you why. This morning I was sitting reading Pushkin. . . . I remember, it happened to be *The Gypsies* . . . all of a sudden Arkady came up to me, and, without speaking, with such kindly compassion on his face, as gently as if I were a baby, took the book away from me, and laid another before me—a German book . . . smiled, and went away, carrying Pushkin off with him.

"Upon my word! What book did he give you?"

"This one here."

And Nikolai Petrovich pulled the famous treatise of Büchner, in the ninth edition, out of his coat-tail pocket.

Pavel Petrovich turned it over in his hands. "Hm!" he growled. "Arkady Nikolaevich is taking your education in hand. Well, did you try reading it?"

"Yes, I tried it."

"Well, what did you think of it?"

"Either I'm stupid, or it's all—nonsense. I must be stupid, I suppose."

"Haven't you forgotten your German?" queried Pavel Petrovich.

"I understand the German."

Pavel Petrovich again turned the book over in his hands, and glanced from under his brows at his brother. Both were silent.

"Oh, by the way," began Nikolai Petrovich, obviously wishing to change the subject, "I've got a letter from Kolyazin."

"Matvey Ilyich?"

"Yes. He has come to inspect the province. He's a bigwig now, and writes to me that, as a relation, he should like to see us, and invites you and me and Arkady to the town."

"Are you going?" asked Pavel Petrovich.

"No; are you?"

'No, I won't go either. Much object there would be in dragging oneself over thirty miles on a wild-goose chase. *Mathieu* wants to show himself in all his glory. The hell with him! he will have the whole province doing him homage; he can get on without us. A grand dignity, indeed, a privy councillor! If I had stayed in the service, if I had trudged on in that stupid harness, I should have been a general-adjutant by now. Besides, you and I are behind the times, you know."

"Yes, brother; it's time, it seems, to order a coffin and cross one's arms on one's breast," remarked Nikolai Petrovich, with a sigh.

"Well, I'm not going to give in quite so soon," muttered his brother. "I've got a tussle with that doctor fellow before me, I have a premonition."

A tussle came off that same day at evening tea. Pavel Petrovich came into the drawing-room, all ready for the fray, irritable and determined. He was only waiting for an excuse to fall upon the enemy; but for a long while an excuse did not present itself. As a rule, Bazarov said little in the presence of the "old Kirsanovs" (that was how he spoke of the brothers), and that evening he felt out of humor, and drank off cup after cup of tea without a word. Pavel Petrovich was all aflame with impatience; his wishes were fulfilled at last.

The conversation turned on one of the neighboring landowners. "Trash, a rotten little aristocrat," observed Bazarov indifferently. He had met him in Petersburg.

"Allow me to ask you," began Pavel Petrovich, and his lips were trembling, "according to your ideas, have the words 'trash' and 'aristocrat' the same meaning?"

"I said 'rotten little aristocrat,'" replied Bazarov, lazily swallowing a sip of tea.

"Precisely so, sir; but I imagine you have the same opinion of aristocrats as of rotten little aristocrats. I consider it my duty to inform you that I do not share that opinion. I venture to say that every one knows me for a man of liberal ideas and devoted to progress; but, exactly for that reason, I respect aristocrats—real aristocrats. Kindly remember, sir" (at these words Bazarov lifted his eyes and looked at Pavel Petrovich), "kindly remember, sir," he repeated, with acrimony—"the English aristocracy. They do not abate one iota of their rights, and for that reason they respect the rights of others; they demand the fulfillment of obligations in dealing with them, and for that reason they fulfill their own obligations. The aristocracy has given freedom to England, and supports it for her."

"We've heard that song a good many times," replied Bazarov; "but what are you trying to prove by that?"

"I am tryin' to prove by that, sir" (when Pavel Petrovich was angry he intentionally clipped his words in this way, though, of course, he knew very well that such forms are not strictly grammatical. In this whim could be discerned a survival of the habits of the times of Alexander I. The exquisites of those days, on the rare occasions when they spoke their own language, made use of such slipshod forms; as much as to say, "We, of course, are genuine Russians, at the same time we are grandees, who are at liberty to neglect the rules of scholars"); I am tryin' to prove by that, sir, that without the sense of personal dignity, without self-respect—and these two sentiments are well developed in the aristocrat—there is no secure foundation for the social . . . *bien public* . . . the social fabric. Character, sir—that is the chief thing; a man's character must be firm as a rock, since everything is built on it. I am very well aware, for instance, that you are pleased to consider my habits, my dress, my neatness, in short, ridiculous; but all that proceeds from a sense of self-respect, from a sense of duty—yes sir, yes sir, of duty. I live in the country, in the wilds, but I will not lower myself. I respect the dignity of man in myself."

"Let me ask you, Pavel Petrovich," said Bazarov; "you respect yourself, and sit with your arms folded; what sort of benefit does that do to the *bien public?* If you didn't respect yourself, you'd do just the same."

Pavel Petrovich turned white. "That's a different question. It's absolutely unnecessary for me to explain to you now why I sit with my arms folded, as you are pleased to express yourself. I wish only to tell you that aristocracy is a *principe*, and in our days none but immoral or silly people can live without *principes*. I said that to Arkady the day after he came home, and I repeat it now. Isn't it so, Nikolai?"

Nikolai Petrovich nodded his head.

"Aristocracy, Liberalism, progress, principles," Bazarov was saying meanwhile; "if you think of it, what a lot of foreign . . . and useless words! No Russian needs them, even as a gift."

"What is good for something according to you? According to you we are outside humanity, outside its laws. Come—the logic of history demands . . . ."

"But what's that logic to us? We can get on without it too."

"How do you mean?"

"Why, this. You don't need logic, I hope, to put a piece of bread in your mouth when you're hungry. What are these abstractions to us?"

Pavel Petrovich flung up his hands.

"I don't understand you, after that. You insult the Russian people. I don't understand how it's possible not to acknowledge *principes*, rules! By virtue of what do you act then?"

"I've told you already, uncle, that we don't recognize any authorities," put in Arkady.

"We act by virtue of what we recognize as useful," observed Bazarov. "At the present time, negation is the most useful of all—and we deny——"

"Everything?"

"Everything!"

"What, not only art and poetry . . . but even . . . horrible to say . . ."

"Everything," repeated Bazarov, with indescribable composure.

Pavel Petrovich stared at him. He had not expected this; while Arkady fairly blushed with delight.

"Allow me, though," began Nikolai Petrovich. "You deny everything; or, speaking more precisely, you destroy everything . . . But one must construct too, you know."

"That's not our business now. . . . The ground has to be cleared first."

"The present condition of the people requires it," added Arkady, with dignity; "we are bound to carry out these requirements, we have no right to yield to the satisfaction of our personal egoism."

This last phrase apparently displeased Bazarov; there was a flavor of philosophy, that is to say, romanticism about it, for Bazarov called philosophy, too, romanticism, but he did not think it necessary to correct his young disciple.

"No, no!" cried Pavel Petrovich, with sudden energy. "I'm not willing to believe that you, gentlemen, know the Russian people really, that you are the representatives of their requirements, their aspirations! No; the Russian people is not what you imagine it. It holds tradition sacred; it is a patriarchal people; it cannot live without faith . . ."

"I'm not going to dispute that," Bazarov interrupted. "I'm even ready to agree that in *that* you're right."

"But if I am right. . . ."

"It still proves nothing."

"It just proves nothing," repeated Arkady, with the confidence of a practised chess-player, who has forseen an apparently dangerous move on the part of his adversary, and so is not at all taken aback by it.

"How does it prove nothing?" muttered Pavel Petrovich, astounded. "You must be going against the people then?"

"And what if we are?" cried Bazarov. "The people imagine that when it thunders the prophet Elijah's riding across the sky in his chariot. What then? Are we to agree with them? Besides, the people's Russian; but am I not Russian, too?"

"No, you are not Russian, after all you have just been saying!

I can't acknowledge you as Russian."

"My grandfather ploughed the land," answered Bazarov with haughty pride. "Ask any one of your peasants which of us—you or me—he'd readily acknowledge as a fellow-countryman. You don't even know how to talk to them."

"While you talk to him and despise him at the same time."

"Well, suppose he deserves contempt. You find fault with my attitude, but who told you that it's accidental in me, that it's not a product of that very national spirit, in the name of which you wage war?"

"To be sure! Much we need nihilists!"

"It is not for us to decide whether they're needed or not. Why, even you suppose you're not a useless person."

"Gentlemen, gentlemen, no personalities, please!" cried Nikolai Petrovich, getting up.

Pavel Petrovich smiled, and laying his hand on his brother's shoulder, forced him to sit down again.

"Don't be uneasy," he said; "I shall not forget myself, just through that sense of dignity which is made fun of so mercilessly by Mr. . . . by the doctor. Let me ask," he resumed, turning again to Bazarov; "perhaps you suppose, that your doctrine is a novelty? That is quite a mistake. The materialism you advocate has already been in vogue more than once, and has always proved insufficient . . ."

"A foreign word again!" broke in Bazarov. He was beginning to feel angry, and his face assumed a peculiar coarse coppery hue. "In the first place, we advocate nothing; that's not our way . . ."

"What do you do, then?"

"I'll tell you what we do. Formerly, not long ago, we used to say that our officials took bribes, that we had no roads, no commerce, no real justice . . ." [1]

"Well yes, yes, you are accusers;—that's what it's called, I think. I too agree with many of your denunciations, but . . ."

"Then we figured out that talk, perpetual talk, and nothing but talk about our social sores, was not worthwhile, that it all led to nothing but banality and doctrinairism. We saw that even our clever ones, so-called advanced people and accusers, were no good; that we were occupied by nonsense, talked about some sort of art, unconscious creativeness, parliamentarianism, the legal profession, and the devil knows what all, while it's a question of daily bread, while we're stifling under the grossest superstition, while all our corporations come to grief simply because there

---

1. Bazarov now echoes in part Dobrolyubov's article "What is Oblomovitis?" (1859), an obtuse sermon on Goncharov's tragi-comic novel *Oblomov*. Dobrolyubov found the cause for Oblomov's sloth in the institution of serfdom!

aren't enough honest men to carry them on, while the very emancipation our Government's busy upon will hardly come to any good, because peasants are glad to rob even themselves to get drunk at the pot-house."

"Yes," interposed Pavel Petrovich, "yes; you become convinced of all this, and decided not to undertake anything seriously yourselves."

"We decided not to undertake anything," repeated Bazarov grimly. He suddenly felt vexed with himself for having been so expansive before this gentleman.

"But to confine yourselves to abuse?"

"To confine ourselves to abuse."

"And that is called nihilism?"

"And that is called nihilism," Bazarov repeated again, this time with peculiar rudeness.

Pavel Petrovich puckered up his face a little. "So that's it!" he observed in a strangely composed voice. "Nihilism is to cure all our woes, and you, you are our heroes and saviors. But why do you abuse others, even those accusers? Don't you do as much talking as every one else?"

"Whatever faults we have, we do not err in that way," Bazarov muttered between his teeth.

"What, then? Do you act, or what? Are you preparing for action?"

Bazarov made no answer. Something like a tremor passed over Pavel Petrovich, but he at once regained control of himself.

"Hm! . . . Action, destruction . . ." he went on. "But how destroy without even knowing why?"

"We shall destroy, because we are a force," observed Arkady.

Pavel Petrovich looked at his nephew and smiled.

"Yes, a force is not to be called to account," said Arkady, drawing himself up.

"Unhappy boy!" groaned Pavel Petrovich; he was positively incapable of restraining himself any longer. "If you could only realise *what* you are supporting in Russia with your vile sententiousness. No; it's enough to try the patience of an angel! Force! There's forces both in the savage Kalmuck and in the Mongolian; but what is it to us? What is precious to us is civilization; yes, yes, honored sir, its fruits are precious to us. And don't tell me those fruits are worthless; the poorest scribbler, *un barbouilleur*, the man who plays dance music for five farthings an evening, is of greater use than you, because they are the representatives of civilization, and not of brute Mongolian force! You fancy yourselves advanced people, and all the while you are fit only for the Kalmuck's hovel! Force! And recollect, you forcible gentlemen, that you're only four men and a half, and the others are millions, who won't let you trample their sacred traditions under foot, who will crush you!"

"If we're crushed, serves us right," observed Bazarov. "But that's an open question. We are not so few as you suppose."

"What? You seriously suppose you can overcome a whole people?"

"All Moscow was burnt down, you know, by a penny candle," answered Bazarov.

"Yes, yes. First a pride almost Satanic, then ridicule—that, that's what it is attracts the young, that's what gains an ascendancy over the inexperienced hearts of boys! Here's one of them sitting beside you, ready to worship the ground under your feet. Look at him! (Arkady turned away and frowned.) And this plague has spread far already. I have been told that in Rome our artists never set foot in the Vatican. Raphael they almost regard as a fool, because, if you please, he's an authority; yet they themselves are disgustingly impotent and sterile, men whose imagination does not soar beyond 'Girls at a Fountain,' however they try! And even the girls are miserably drawn. They are fine fellows to your mind, are they not?"

"To my mind," retorted Bazarov, "Raphael's not worth a brass farthing; and they're no better than he."

"Bravo! bravo! Listen, Arkady . . . that's how young men of to-day ought to express themselves! And if you come to think of it, how could they fail if they followed you! In old days, young men had to study; they didn't want to be called dunces, so they had to work hard whether they liked it or not. But now, they need only say, 'Everything in the world is nonsense!' and the trick's done. Young men are delighted. And, to be sure, they were simply blockheads before, and now they have suddenly turned nihilists."

"Your vaunted sense of personal dignity has given way," remarked Bazarov phlegmatically, while Arkady flared up, and his eyes were flashing. "Our argument has gone too far; it's better to cut it short, I think. I shall be quite ready to agree with you," he added, getting up, "when you bring forward a single institution in our present mode of life, in family or in social life, which does not call for complete and unqualified repudiation."

"I will bring forward millions of such institutions," cried Pavel Petrovich—"millions! Well—the village commune, for instance."

A cold smile curved Bazarov's lips. "Well, as regards the village commune," he commented; "you had better talk to your brother. He has seen by now, I should fancy, what sort of thing the village commune is in fact—its common guarantee, its sobriety, and other features of the kind."

"The family, then, the family as it exists among our peasants!" cried Pavel Petrovich.

"And that subject, too, I imagine, it will be better for yourselves not to go into detail. You've perhaps heard of the father-in-law's rights with the bride? Take my advice, Pavel Petrovich, allow yourself two days to think about it; you're not likely to find anything on the spot. Go through all our classes, and think well over each, while Arkady and I will . . ."

"Will go on turning everything into ridicule," broke in Pavel Petrovich.

"No, will go on dissecting frogs. Come, Arkady; good-bye, gentlemen!"

The two friends walked off. The brothers were left alone, and at first they only looked at one another.

"So that," began Pavel Petrovich, "so that's what our young men of this generation are! They are like that—our successors!"

"Our successors!" repeated Nikolai Petrovich, with a dejected sigh. He had been sitting on thorns, all through the argument, and had done nothing but glance stealthily, with a sore heart, at Arkady. "Do you know what I was reminded of, brother? I once had a dispute with our late mother; she shouted, and wouldn't listen to me. At last I said to her, 'Of course, you can't understand me; we belong,' I said, 'to two different generations.' She was dreadfully offended, while I thought, 'It can't be helped. It's a bitter pill, but she has to swallow it.' You see, now, our turn has come, and our successors can say to us, 'You are not of our generation; swallow your pill.'"

"You are really too generous and modest," replied Pavel Petrovich. "I'm convinced, on the contrary, that you and I are far more in the right than these young gentlemen, though we do perhaps express ourselves in old-fashioned language, *vieilli*, and have not the same insolent conceit. . . . And the swagger of the young men nowadays! You ask one, 'Do you take red wine or white?' 'It is my custom to prefer red!' he answers, in a deep bass, with a face as solemn as if the whole universe had its eyes on him at that instant. . . ."

"Do you care for any more tea?" asked Fenichka, putting her head in at the door; she had not been able to make up her mind to come into the drawing-room while there was the sound of voices in dispute there.

"No, you can tell them to take the samovar," answered Nikolai Petrovich, and he got up to meet her. Pavel Petrovich said *"bon soir"* to him abruptly, and went away to his study.

XI

Half an hour later Nikolai Petrovich went into the garden to his favorite arbor. He was overtaken by melancholy thoughts. For the first time he realized clearly the distance between him and his son; he foresaw that every day it would grow wider and wider. In vain, then, had he sometimes spent whole days in the winters at Petersburg over the latest books; in vain had he listened to the talk of the young men; in vain had he rejoiced when he succeeded in putting in his word, too, in their heated discussions. "My brother says we are right," he thought, "and apart from all vanity, I do think myself that they are further from the truth than we are, though at the same time I feel there is something behind them we have not got, some superiority over us. . . . Is it youth? No, not only youth. Doesn't their superiority consist in there being fewer traces of the slave owner in them than in us?"

Nikolai Petrovich's head sank despondently, and he passed his hand over his face.

"But to renounce poetry?" he thought again; "to have no feeling for art, for nature . . ."

And he looked round, as though trying to understand how it was possible to have no feeling for nature. Evening was already approaching; the sun was hidden behind a small copse of aspens which lay a quarter of a mile from the garden; its shadow stretched endlessly across the still fields. A peasant on a white nag went at a trot along the dark, narrow path close beside the copse; his whole figure was clearly visible even to the patch on his shoulder, in spite of his being in the shade; the white horse's legs flashed by distinctly and pleasantly. The sun's rays for their part made their way into the copse, and piercing through its thickets, threw such a warm light on the aspen trunks that they looked like pines, and their leaves were almost a dark blue, while above them rose a pale blue sky, faintly tinged by the glow of sunset. The swallows flew high; the wind had quite died away, belated bees buzzed slowly and drowsily among the lilac blossom; a swarm of midges hung like a cloud over a solitary branch which stood out against the sky. My God, how beautiful!" thought Nikolai Petrovich, and his favorite verses came to his lips; he remembered Arkady's *Stoff und Kraft*—and was silent, but still he sat there, still he gave himself up to the sorrowful consolation of solitary thought. He was fond of reverie; his country life had developed the tendency in him. How short a time ago, he had been dreaming like this, waiting for his son at the posting station, and what changes had already occurred since that day; their relations that were then undefined, were defined now—and how defined! Again his late wife came back to his imagination, but not as he had known her for many years, not as the good domestic housewife, but as a young girl with a slim figure, innocently inquiring eyes, and a tight braid on her childish neck. He remembered how he had seen her for the first time. He was still a student then. He had met her on the staircase of his lodgings, and, jostling by accident against her, he tried to apologize, and could only mutter, "*Pardon, monsieur,*" while she bowed, smiled, and suddenly seemed frightened, and ran away, though at the bend of the staircase she had glanced rapidly at him, assumed a serious air, and blushed. Afterwards, the first timid visits, the half-words, the half-smiles, and embarrassment; and melancholy, and yearnings, and at last that breathing rapture. . . . Where had it all vanished? She became his wife, he had been happy as few on earth are happy. . . . "But," he mused, "these sweet first moments, why could not one live an eternal, immortal life in them?"

He did not try to make his thought clear to himself; but he felt that he longed to keep that blissful time by something stronger than memory; he longed to feel his Marya near him again, to have the sense of her warmth and breathing, and already he could fancy that over him. . . .

"Nikolai Petrovich," came the sound of Fenichka's voice close by him; "where are you?"

He started. He felt no pang, no shame. He never even admitted the possibility of comparison between his wife and Fenichka, but he was sorry she had thought of coming to look for him. Her voice at once brought back to him his grey hairs, his age, the present. . . .

The enchanted world into which he had already stepped, which already rose out of the dim mists of the past, was shaken—and vanished.

"I'm here," he answered; "I'm coming, run along." "There it is, the traces of the slave owner," flashed through his mind. Fenichka peeped into the arbor at him without speaking, and disappeared; while he noticed with astonishment that the night had come on while he had been dreaming. Everything around was dark and hushed, and Fenichka's face had glimmered so pale and slight before him. He got up, and was about to go home; but the emotion stirred in his heart could not be soothed at once, and he began slowly walking about the garden, sometimes looking at the ground at his feet, and then raising his eyes towards the sky where swarms of stars were already twinkling. He walked a great deal, till he was almost tired out, while the restlessness within him, a kind of yearning, vague, melancholy restlessness, still was not appeased. Oh, how Bazarov would have laughed at him, if he had known what was passing within him then! Arkady himself would have condemned him. He, a man forty-four years old, an agronomist and a farmer, was shedding tears, causeless tears; this was a hundred times worse than the violoncello.

Nikolai Petrovich continued to walk, and could not make up his mind to go into the house, into that snug and peaceful nest, which looked out at him so hospitably from all its lighted windows; he had not the force to tear himself away from the darkness, the garden, the sense of the fresh air in his face, from that melancholy, that restless craving.

At a turn in the path, he was met by Pavel Petrovich. "What's the matter with you?" he asked Nikolai Petrovich; "you are as pale as a ghost; you are not well; why don't you go to bed?"

Nikolai Petrovich explained to him briefly his state of feeling and moved away. Pavel Petrovich went to the end of the garden, and he too grew thoughtful, and he too raised his eyes towards the heavens. But nothing was reflected in his beautiful dark eyes except the light of the stars. He was not born a romantic, and his fastidiously dry and sensuous soul, with its French tinge of misanthropy, was not capable of dreaming. . . .

"Do you know what?" Bazarov was saying to Arkady the same night. "I've got a splendid idea. Your father was saying to-day that he had received an invitation from your illustrious relative. Your father's not going; let us be off to X——; you know that that gentleman invited you too. See what fine weather it is; we'll take a ride about and look at the town. We'll enjoy ourselves for five or six days and that's that!"

"And you'll come back here again?"

"No; I must go to my father's. You know, he lives about twenty miles from X——. I haven't seen him for a long time nor my mother; I have to please the old folks. They're good people, especially my father; he's awfully funny. I'm their only child too."

"And will you be long with them?"

"I don't suppose so. It will be dull, I suppose."

"And you'll come to us on your way back?"

"I don't know . . . I'll see. Well, what do you say? Shall we go?"

"If you like," observed Arkady languidly.

In his heart he was highly delighted with his friend's suggestion, but he thought it a duty to conceal his feeling. He was not a nihilist for nothing!

The next day he set off with Bazarov to X———. The younger part of the household at Marino were sorry at their going; Dunyasha even cried . . . but the old folks breathed more easily.

XII

The town of X———to which our friends set off was in the jurisdiction of a governor who was still young, at once a progressive and a despot, as often happens in Russia. Before the end of the first year of his government, he had managed to quarrel not only with the marshal of nobility, a retired captain of the guards, who kept open house and a stud of horses, but even with his own subordinates. The feuds arising from this at last assumed such proportions that the ministry in Petersburg had found it necessary to send down a trusted personage with a commission to investigate it all on the spot. The choice of the authorities fell upon Matvey Ilyich Kolyazin, the son of the Kolyazin under whose protection the brothers Kirsanov had once found themselves. He, too, was a "young man"; that is to say, he had not long passed forty, but he was already on the high road to becoming a statesman, and wore a star on each side of his breast—one, to be sure, a foreign star, of the undistinguished kind. Like the governor, whom he had come to pass judgment upon, he was reckoned a progressive; and though he was already a bigwig, he was not like the majority of bigwigs. He had the highest opinion of himself; looked with approval, listened condescendingly, and laughed so good-naturedly, that at first he might even be taken for "a jolly good fellow." On important occasions, however, he knew, as the saying is, how to make the fur fly. "Energy is essential," he used to say then, *"l'énergie est la première qualité d'un homme d'état;"* [2] and for all that, he was usually taken in, and any moderately experienced official could turn him round his finger. Matvey Ilyich used to speak with great respect of Guizot, and tried to impress every one with the idea that he did not belong to the class of *routiniers* and high-and-dry bureaucrats, that not a single important phenomenon of social life passed unnoticed by him. . . . All such phrases were very familiar to him. He even followed, with dignified indifference, it is true, the development of contemporary literature; so a grown-up man who meets a procession of small boys in the street will sometimes walk after it. In reality, Matvey Ilyich had not got much beyond those political men of the days of Alexander I, who used to prepare for an evening party at Madame Svetchin's by reading a page of Con-

2. "energy is the first requisite for a statesman."

dillac; [3] only his methods were different, more modern. He was an adroit courtier, a great schemer, and nothing more; he had no special aptitude for affairs, and no intellect, but he knew how to manage his own business successfully; no one could get the better of him there, and, to be sure, that's the principal thing.

Matvey Ilyich received Arkady with the good-nature, we might even call it playfulness, characteristic of the enlightened higher official. He was astonished, however, when he heard that the cousins he had invited had remained at home in the country. "Your father was always a queer fellow," he remarked, playing with the tassels of his magnificent velvet dressing-gown, and suddenly turning to a young official in a most discreetly buttoned-up uniform, he cried, with an air of concentrated attention, "What?" The young man, whose lips were glued together from prolonged silence, rose and looked in perplexity at his chief. But, having nonplussed his subordinate, Matvey Ilyich paid no further attention to him. Our higher officials are fond of nonplussing their subordinates as a rule; the methods to which they have recourse to attain that end are rather various. The following one, among others, is in great vogue, *"is quite a favourite,"* as the English say; a high official suddenly ceases to understand the simplest words, assuming total deafness. He will ask, for instance, "What's to-day?"

He is respectfully informed, "To-day's Friday, your Ex-s-s-s-lency."

"Eh? What? What's that? What do you say?" the great man repeats with intense attention.

"To-day's Friday, your Ex—s—s—lency."

"Eh? What? What's Friday? What Friday?"

"Friday, your Ex—s—s—s—lency, the day of the week."

"What, do you pretend to teach me, eh?"

Matvey Ilyich was a higher official all the same, though he was reckoned a liberal.

"I advise you, my dear boy, to go and call on the Governor," he said to Arkady; "you understand, I don't advise you to do so because I adhere to old-fashioned ideas about the necessity of paying respect to authorities, but simply because the Governor's a decent fellow; besides, you probably want to become acquainted with society here. . . . You're not a bear, I hope? And he's giving a grand ball the day after to-morrow."

"Will you be at the ball?" inquired Arkady.

3. Sofya Petrovna Svechin (1782–1859) was a leader in the religious mysticism fashionable in the later part of Alexander I's reign (died 1825). Her work, republished while the novel was being written, was much discussed. Etienne Condillac (1715–80), French philosopher, would provide arguments against her views.

"He's giving it in my honor," answered Matvey Ilyich, almost pityingly. "Do you dance?"

"I dance, but badly."

"That's a pity! There are pretty girls here, and it's a disgrace for a young man not to dance. Again, I don't say that through any old-fashioned ideas; I don't in the least imagine that a man's wit lies in his feet, but Byronism is ridiculous, *il a fait son temps.*" [4]

"But, uncle, it's not through Byronism at all, I . . ."

"I will introduce you to the ladies here; I will take you under my wing," interrupted Matvey Ilyich, and he laughed complacently. "You'll find it warm, eh?"

A servant entered and announced the arrival of the president of the government administration, a mild-eyed old man, with wrinkled lips who loved nature passionately, especially on a summer day, when, in his words, "every little bee takes a little bribe from every little flower." Arkady withdrew.

He found Bazarov at the inn where they were staying and was a long while persuading him to go with him to the Governor's. "Well, it can't be helped," said Bazarov at last. "It's no good doing things by halves. We came to look at the gentry; let's look at them!" The Governor received the young men affably, but he did not ask them to sit down, nor did he sit down himself. He was in an everlasting fuss and hurry; in the morning he used to put on a tight uniform and a stiff cravat; he never finished eating or drinking, for he was constantly busy administering. He was nicknamed Bourdaloue in the province, not after the renowned French preacher, but as a hint at *burda,* swill. He invited Kirsanov and Bazarov to his ball, and within a few minutes invited them a second time, regarding them as brothers, and calling them Kaisarov.

They were on their way home from the Governor's when suddenly a short man, in a Slavophile jacket,[5] leaped out of a trap that was passing them, and with a shout, "Evgeny Vassilyich!" dashed up to Bazarov.

"Ah! it's you, Herr Sitnikov," observed Bazarov, continuing to step along on the pavement; "by what fate did you come here?"

"Fancy, absolutely by chance," he replied, and turning to the trap, he waved his hand several times, and shouted, "Follow, follow us!—My father had business here," he went on, hopping across the gutter, "and so he asked me. . . . To-day I heard of your arrival, and have already been to see you. . . ." (The friends did, in fact, on returning to their room find a card with the corners

4. "has had its day."
5. The Slavophiles maintained that Russia should reject the West and go back to its own traditions and cultural roots. Among their more nonsensical acts was the attempt to dress in supposedly "native" Russian clothes.

turned down, bearing the name of Sitnikov, on one side in French, on the other in Slavonic characters.) "I hope you are not coming from the Governor's?"

"It's no use hoping; we come straight from him."

"Ah! in that case I will call on him too. . . . Evgeny Vassilvich, introduce me to your . . . to the . . ."

"Sitnikov, Kirsanov," grumbled Bazarov, not stopping.

"I am greatly flattered," began Sitnikov, walking sidewise, smirking, and hurriedly pulling off his really far too elegant gloves. "I have heard so much. . . . I am an old acquaintance of Evgeny Vassilyich and, I may say—his disciple. I am indebted to him for my regeneration. . . ."

Arkady looked at Bazarov's disciple. There was an expression of worry and tension imprinted on the small but pleasant features of his well-groomed face; his small eyes, that seemed squeezed in, had a fixed and uneasy look, and his laugh, too, was uneasy— a sort of short, wooden laugh.

"Would you believe it," he continued, "when Evgeny Vassilyich said for the first time that it was not right to recognize any authorities, I felt such enthusiasm . . . as though my eyes were opened! Here, I thought, at last I have found a man! By the way, Evgeny Vassilyich, you positively must call on a lady here who is really capable of understanding you, and for whom your visit would be a real feast; you have heard of her, I suppose?"

"Who is she?" Bazarov brought out unwillingly.

"Kukshin, *Eudoxie*, Evdoksya Kukshin. She's a remarkable nature, *émancipée* in the true sense of the word, an advanced woman. Do you know what? We'll all go together to see her now. She lives only two steps from here. We'll have lunch there. You have not lunched yet, have you?"

"No; not yet."

"Well, that's capital. She has separated, you understand, from her husband; she is not dependent on any one."

"Is she pretty?" Bazarov cut in.

"N . . . no, one couldn't say that."

"Then, what the devil are you asking us to see her for?"

"Fie; you must have your joke. . . . She will give us a bottle of champagne."

"Oh, that's it. One can see the practical man at once. By the way, is your father still in the liquor business?"

"Yes," said Sitnikov, hurriedly, and laughed shrilly. "Well? Will you come?"

"I really don't know."

"You wanted to see people, go along," said Arkady in an undertone.

in creating Bazarov I was not only not angry with him, but felt "an attraction, a sort of disease" [1] toward him, so that Katkov was at first horrified and saw in him the apotheosis of *The Contemporary* and as a result convinced me to delete not a few traits that would have mellowed him, which I now regret. Of course he crushes "the man with the fragrant mustache" and others! That is the triumph of democracy over the aristocracy. With hand on heart I feel no guilt toward Bazarov and could not give him an unnecessary sweetness. If he is disliked as he is, with all his ugliness, it means that *I* am at fault and was not able to cope with the figure I chose. It wouldn't take much to present him as an ideal; but to make him a wolf and justify him just the same—that was difficult. And in that I probably did not succeed; but I only want to fend off the reproach that I was exasperated with him. It seems to me, on the contrary, that the feeling opposite to exasperation appears in everything, in his death, etc. But *basta così*—we'll talk more when we see each other.

I haven't become addicted to mysticism and will not be; in my relations to God I share Faust's opinion:

> Wer darf ihn nennen,
> Und wer bekennen:
> Ich glaub' ihn!
> Wer empfinden
> Und sich unterwinden
> Zu sagen: Ich glaub' ihn nicht! [2]

Moreover, that feeling in me has never been a secret to you. * * *

To *Ludwig Pietsch* [3]
Karlsruhe, January 22 (*February* 3), 1869
[Original in German]

Dear Friend:

Your letter evoked in my heart a mixed feeling of pity, gratefulness, and adoration! Quite seriously! A man as busy as you, to whom time is so valuable, to occupy himself with the painstaking, nerve-irritating work of revision [of the translation of *Fathers and Sons* into German]! That is a great proof of friendship!

---

1. A quotation from Griboedov's play *Woe from Wit* (1825), (act 4, scene 4) [*Editor*].
2. Why may name him/And who confess/"I believe in him!"/Who can feel/And dare/To say "I don't believe in him!" [*Editor*].
3. Ludwig Pietsch (1824–1911), a German journalist and writer, who helped popularize Turgenev in Germany [*Editor*].

So far as the translation is concerned you naturally have complete *carte blanche!* If you wish, you can have Bazarov marry Odintsov; I won't protest! On the contrary!

Bazarov has the habit of expressing himself contemptuously: he calls his old coat *"une loque," "ein Fetzen,"* [4]—use whatever word you like. * * *

To Ludwig Pietsch
Baden-Baden, May 22 (*June* 3), 1869
[Original in German]

* * * You write that you have to do reviews of *Fathers and Sons.* Splendid! Do one of them that is cool and strict toward it, but do express in it your incomprehension and amazement that the young generation in Russia took the portrait of Bazarov as an insulting caricature and a slanderous satire. Show instead that I portrait the fellow entirely too heroically—idealistically (which is *true*) and that Russian youth has entirely too sensitive a skin. Precisely through Bazarov I was (and still am) bespattered with mud and filth. So much abuse and invective, so many curses have been heaped on my head that was consigned to all the spirits of Hell (Vidocq, Judas bought for money, fool, ass, adder, *spittoon*—that was the *least* that I was called) that it would be a satisfaction for me to show that other nations see the matter in a different light. I dare ask you for such publicity because it corresponds completely to the truth and, of course, in no way contradicts your convictions. Otherwise I would not have troubled you. If you wish to fulfill my request, do so quickly, so that I could add a translation of the most important parts of the review to my literary reminiscences, which are to appear soon.[5] * * *

To P. V. Annenkov
Baden-Baden, December 20, 1869 (*January* 1, 1870)

* * * I have reread my article "Apropos of *Fathers and Sons*" and, just think, I feel that every word seems to have poured out of my soul. It seems that one must either not speak the truth or—what is more likely—that no author understands completely what he is doing. There is a kind of contradiction here which one cannot resolve oneself no matter how one approaches it. It is clearer for an outsider. * * *

---

4. "A rag, a tatter" [*Editor*].
5. The request was fulfilled. See Turgenev's

"Apropos of *Fathers and Sons*" [*Editor*].

To Ya. P. Polonsky [6]
Baden-Baden, December 24, 1869 (January 5, 1870)
* * * It seems that everyone is dissatisfied with my little article "Apropos of *Fathers and Sons*." From this I gather that one shouldn't always speak the truth; since each word in that article is the truth itself, so far as I am concerned, of course. * * *

To I. P. Borisov
Baden-Baden, December 24, 1869 (January 5, 1870)
* * * It seems that my little article on *Fathers and Sons* has satisfied no one. Just think I will disown my fame, like Rostopchin did the burning of Moscow. Annenkov has even scolded me roundly. And yet every word in it is the sacred truth, at least in my judgment. It seems that an author doesn't always know himself what he is creating. My feelings toward Bazarov—my own personal feelings—were of a confused nature (God only knows whether I loved him or hated him), nevertheless the figure came out so specific that it immediately entered life and started acting by itself, in its own manner. In the final analysis what does it matter what the author himself thinks about his work. He is one thing and the work is another; but I repeat, my article was as sincere as a confession. * * *

To A. F. Onegin
Baden-Baden, December 27, 1869 (January 8, 1870)
* * * You don't like my little article "Apropos of *Fathers and Sons*." In Russia they abuse it terribly: they see in it something like apostasy on my part from my own service in approaching the "nihilists" and so forth. But why don't you like it? I hope you will not doubt that every word in it, every letter, is true. Consequently you, as a positive man, must look upon it as a fact—bluntly, to look down upon it: that's how a man jumps in a given instance, that's how he could grapple, that's what he expressed—what can you not like about it? * * *

To A. P. Filosofov
Bougival, August 18, (30), 1874
* * * You write that in Bazarov I wanted to present a caricature of current youth. You repeat that—forgive the blunt expression—silly reproach. Bazarov is my favorite child, for whom I quarreled

6. Ya. P. Polonsky (1819–98), an important Russian poet [*Editor*].

with Katkov, on whom I expended all the colors at my disposal, Bazarov, that bright man, that hero—a caricature? But apparently it cannot be helped. As Louis Blanc, despite all his protestations, is still constantly accused of bringing about the national work-shops (ateliers nationaux), so they ascribed to me the desire to offend youth by a caricature. For a long time now I have reacted to that accusation with contempt. I did not expect that I would have to renew that feeling in reading your letter. * * *

To A. P. Filosofov
Bougival, September 11 (23), 1874

* * * You began with Bazarov: I, too, shall start with him. You seek him in real life, but you won't find him. I shall tell you why. Times have changed. Bazarovs are not necessary now. For current social activity neither special talents nor even special intelligence is needed—nothing great, outstanding, too individual-istic. Assiduity and patience are necessary. One must know how to sacrifice oneself without any ado; one must know how to humble oneself and not to abhor petty and obscure, even lowly work—I choose the word "lowly" in the sense of simple, straightforward, terra à terre. What, for example, could be more lowly than to teach a peasant to read, to help him, to found hospitals, etc.? What does talent and even erudition have to do with that? Only the heart is necessary, the ability to sacrifice one's egoism—one cannot even speak of a calling here (not to mention Mr. V. D.'s decoration). A feeling of duty, the glorious feeling of patriotism in the true sense of that word—that's all that's necessary.

And yet Bazarov is still a figure, a prophet, a huge figure endowed with a certain charm, not devoid of a certain aureole: all that is out of place now, and it is silly to speak of heroes or artists of work. . . . Yet your search for Bazarov—"the real one" —nevertheless expresses, unconsciously perhaps, the thirst for beauty, of a special kind, of course. All these dreams must be given up. * * *

To M. E. Saltykov [7]
Paris, January 3 (15), 1876

* * * Well, now I'll say a couple of words about Fathers and Sons too, since you mentioned it. Do you really suppose that I have not thought of everything you have reproached me with?

---

7. M. E. Saltykov-Schedrin (1826–89), Russia's leading satirist of that era and a major novelist [Editor].

"No, I'm not a Slavophile though, of course . . ."

"No, no, no. You are a Slavophile. You're an advocate of patriarchal despotism. You want to have the whip in your hand!"

"A whip's an excellent thing," remarked Bazarov; "but we've got to the last drop."

"Of what?" interrupted Evdoksya.

"Of champagne, most honored Avdotya Nikitishna, of champagne—not of your blood."

"I can never listen calmly when women are attacked," pursued Evdoksya. "It's awful, awful. Instead of attacking them, you'd better read Michelet's book, *De l'amour*.[1] That's marvelous! Gentlemen, let us talk of love," added Evdoksya, letting her arm fall languidly on the rumpled sofa cushion.

A sudden silence followed. "No, why should we talk of love," said Bazarov; "but just now you mentioned Odintsov . . . That was what you called her, I think? Who is that lady?"

"She's charming, charming!" piped Sitnikov. "I will introduce you. Clever, rich, a widow. It's a pity, she's not yet advanced enough; she ought to see more of our Evdoksya. I drink to your health, *Eudoxie!* Let us clink glasses! *Et toc, et toc, et tin-tin-tin! Et toc, et toc, et tin-tin-tin!!*"

"Victor, you're a rascal."

The lunch dragged on a long while. The first bottle of champagne was followed by another, a third, and even a fourth. . . . Evdoksya chattered without pause; Sitnikov seconded her. They discussed at length the question whether marriage was a prejudice or a crime, and whether men were born equal or not, and precisely what individuality consists in. Things reached the point that Evdoksya, flushed from the wine she had drunk, tapped with her blunt nails on the keys of a discordant piano, and began to sing in a hoarse voice, first gipsy songs, and then Seymour Schiff's song, "Granada lies slumbering"; while Sitnikov tied a scarf round his head, and represented the dying lover at the words—

> "And thy lips to mine
> In burning kiss entwine."

Finally Arkady could not stand it. "Gentlemen, this has turned into something like Bedlam," he remarked aloud. Bazarov, who had at rare intervals put in an ironical word in the conversation— he paid more attention to the champagne—yawned loudly, got up, and, without taking leave of their hostess, he walked out with Arkady. Sitnikov jumped up and followed them.

"Well, what do you think of her?" he inquired, skipping

1. *On Love*, (1859).

obsequiously from right to left of them. "I told you, you see, a remarkable personality! If we only had more women like that! She is, in her own way, a highly moral phenomenon."

"And is your pop's establishment also a highly moral phenomenon?" asked Bazarov, pointing to a pot house which they were passing at that instant.

Sitnikov again went off into a shrill laugh. He was greatly ashamed of his origin, and did not know whether to feel flattered or offended at Bazarov's unexpected familiarity.

XIV

A few days later the Governor's ball took place. Matvey Ilyich was the real "hero of the occasion." The marshal of nobility declared to one and all that he had come simply out of respect for him; while the Governor, even at the ball, even while he remained perfectly motionless, was still "administering." The affability of Matvey Ilyich's demeanor could only be equalled by its dignity. He was gracious to all, to some with a shade of aversion, to others with a shade of respect; he appeared *"en vrai chevalier français"* [2] before the ladies, and was continually giving vent to a hearty, sonorous, unshared laugh, such as befits a high official. He slapped Arkady on the back, and called him loudly "little nephew"; vouchsafed Bazarov—who was attired in a rather old evening coat—a sidelong glance in passing—absentminded but condescending—and an indistinct but affable grunt, in which nothing could be distinguished but "I . . ." and "very much"; offered Sitnikov a finger and a smile, though with his head already averted; even to Kukshin, who made her appearance at the ball with dirty gloves, no crinoline, and a bird of Paradise in her hair, even to Kukshin he said *"enchanté."* There were hordes of people, and no lack of dancing men; the civilians were for the most part standing close along the walls, but the officers danced assiduously, especially one of them who had spent six weeks in Paris, where he had mastered various daring interjections like—*"zut,"* "Ah, *fichtr-re,"* *"pst, pst, mon bibi,"* and such. He pronounced them to perfection with genuine Parisian *chic*, and at the same time he said *"si j'aurais"* for *"si j'avais,"* *"absolument"* in the sense of "certainly" [3] expressed himself, in fact, in the Great Russo-French jargon which the French ridicule so when they have no reason for assuring us that we speak their language like angels, *"comme des anges."*

Arkady, as we are aware, danced badly, while Bazarov did not

2. "a real French cavalier."
3. That is, incorrectly uses the present conditional instead of the indicative imper-fect for "if I had," and *absolument* for emphasis.

dance at all; they both took up their position in a corner, Sitnikov joined them. With an expression of contemptuous scorn on his face, and giving vent to spiteful comments, he looked insolently about him, and really seemed to be enjoying himself. Suddenly his face changed, and turning to Arkady, he said, with some show of embarrassment it seemed, "Odintsov is here!"

Arkady looked round, and saw a tall woman in a black dress standing at the door of the room. He was struck by the dignity of her carriage. Her bare arms lay gracefully beside her slender waist; gracefully some light sprays of fuchsia drooped from her shining hair on to her sloping shoulders; her clear eyes looked out from under a somewhat protruding white brow, with a tranquil and intelligent expression—tranquil it was precisely, not pensive—and on her lips was a scarcely perceptible smile. A kind of gracious and gentle force emanated from her face.

"Do you know her?" Arkady asked Sitnikov.

"Intimately. Would you like me to introduce you?"

"Please . . . after this quadrille."

Bazarov's attention, too, was directed to Odintsov.

"That's a striking figure," he remarked. "Not like the other females."

After waiting till the end of the quadrille, Sitnikov led Arkady up to Odintsov; but he hardly seemed to be intimately acquainted with her; he was embarrassed in his sentences, while she looked at him in some surprise. But her face assumed an expression of pleasure when she heard Arkady's surname. She asked him whether he was not the son of Nikolai Petrovich.

"Exactly so."

"I have seen your father twice, and have heard a great deal about him," she went on; "I am glad to meet you."

At that instant some adjutant flew up to her and begged for a quadrille. She consented.

"Do you dance then?" asked Arkady respectfully.

"Yes, I dance. Why do you suppose I don't dance? Do you think I am too old?"

"Really, how could I possibly. . . . But in that case, let me ask you for the mazurka."

Odintsov smiled graciously. "Certainly," she said, and she looked at Arkady, not exactly with an air of superiority, but as married sisters look at very young brothers. Odintsov was a little older than Arkady—she was twenty-nine—but in her presence he felt himself a schoolboy, a little student, so that the difference in age between them seemed of more consequence. Matvey Ilyich approached her with a majestic air and ingratiating speeches. Arkady moved away, but he still watched; he could not take his eyes off her even during the quadrille. She talked with as much ease to her partner as to the grand official, quietly turned her head and eyes, and twice laughed softly. Her nose—like almost all Russian noses—was a little thick; and her complexion was not perfectly clear; Arkady made up his mind, for all that, that he had never before met such an attractive woman. He could not get the sound of her voice out of his ears; the very folds of her dress seemed to hang upon her differently from all the rest—more gracefully and amply—and her movements were particularly smooth and natural at the same time.

Arkady felt some timidity in his heart when at the first sounds of the mazurka he sat down beside his partner. He had prepared to enter into a conversation with her, but he only passed his hand through his hair, and could not find a single word to say. But his timidity and agitation did not last long; Odintsov's calm communicated itself to him too: before a quarter of an hour had passed he was telling her freely about his father, his uncle, his life in Petersburg and in the country. Odintsov listened to him with polite sympathy, slightly opening and closing her fan; his chatter was broken off when partners came for her; Sitnikov, by the way, asked her twice. She would come back, sit down again, take up her fan, and her bosom did not even heave more rapidly, while Arkady fell to chattering again, permeated by the happiness of being near her, talking to her, looking at her eyes, her lovely brow, her whole sweet, dignified, clever face. She said little herself but her words showed a knowledge of life; from some of her observations, Arkady gathered that this young woman had already felt and thought much. . . .

"Who is that you were standing with?" she asked him, "when Mr. Sitnikov brought you to me?"

"Did you notice him?" Arkady asked in his turn. He has a splendid face, hasn't he? That's a certain Bazarov, my friend."

Arkady fell to discussing "his friend." He spoke of him in such detail, and with such enthusiasm, that Odintsov turned towards him and looked attentively at him. Meanwhile, the mazurka was drawing to a close. Arkady felt sorry to part from his partner; he had spent nearly an hour so happily with her! He had, it is true, during the whole time continually felt as though she were condescending to him, as though he ought to be grateful to her . . . but young hearts are not weighed down by that feeling.

The music stopped. "*Merci*," said Odintsov, getting up. "You promised to come and see me; bring your friend with you. I shall be very curious to see a man who has the courage to believe in nothing."

The Governor came up to Odintsov, announced that supper was

ready and, with a careworn face, offered her his arm. As she moved away, she turned to give a last smile and nod to Arkady. He bowed low, looked after her (how graceful her figure seemed to him, draped in the greyish lustre of black silk!), and thinking, "This very minute she has already forgotten my existence," was conscious of an exquisite humility in his soul.

"Well?" Bazarov questioned him, as soon as he had gone back to him in the corner. "Did you have a good time? A gentleman has just been talking to me about that lady; he said, 'She's—ooh la la!' but the gentleman seems a fool. What do you think, is she really—ooh la la?"

"I don't quite understand that definition," answered Arkady.

"Oh, come! What innocence!"

"In that case, I don't understand your gentleman. Odintsov is very sweet, no doubt, but she behaves so coldly and severely, that . . ."

"Still waters . . . you know!" put in Bazarov. "That's just what gives it piquancy. You like ices, I expect?"

"Perhaps," muttered Arkady. "I can't give an opinion on that. She wishes to make your acquaintance, and has asked me to bring you to see her."

"I can imagine how you've described me! But you did very well. Take me. Whatever she may be—whether she's simply a provincial lioness, or *émancipée* after Kukshin's fashion—anyway she's got a pair of shoulders such as I've not set eyes on for a long while."

Arkady was wounded by Bazarov's cynicism, but—as often happens—he reproached his friend not precisely for what he did not like in him . . .

"Why are you unwilling to allow freethinking in women?" he said in a low voice.

"Because, my boy, as far as my observations go, the only freethinkers among women are frights."

The conversation ended with that. Both young men went away immediately after supper. The were pursued by a nervously malicious, but somewhat fearful laugh from Kukshin; her vanity had been deeply wounded by neither of them having paid any attention to her. She stayed later than any one at the ball, and after three o'clock in the morning she was dancing a polka-mazurka with Sitnikov in the Parisian style. This edifying spectacle was the final event of the Governor's ball.

XV

"Let's see what species of mammalia this person belongs to," Bazarov said to Arkady the following day, as they mounted the staircase of the hotel in which Odintsov was staying. "I scent out something wrong here."

"I'm surprised at you!" cried Arkady. "What? You, you, Bazarov, clinging to the narrow morality, which . . ."

"What a strange fellow you are!" Bazarov cut him short, carelessly. "Don't you know that 'something wrong' means 'something right' in my dialect and for me? It means there's something to be gained. Didn't you tell me yourself this morning that she made a strange marriage, though, to my mind, to marry a rich old man is by no means a strange thing to do, but, on the contrary, very sensible. I don't believe the gossip of the town; but I should like to think, as our cultivated Governor says, that it's well-grounded."

Arkady make no answer, and knocked at the door. A young servant in livery conducted the two friends into a large room, badly furnished, like all rooms in Russian hotels, but filled with flowers. Soon Odintsov herself appeared in a simple morning dress. She seemed still younger by the light of the spring sunshine. Arkady presented Bazarov, and noticed with secret amazement that he seemed embarrassed, while Odintsov remained perfectly tranquil, as she had been the previous day. Bazarov himself was conscious of being embarrassed, and was irritated by it. "There's something—frightened of a petticoat!" he thought, and lolling in an easy-chair, quite like Sitnikov, he began talking with an exaggerated appearance of ease, while Odintsov kept her clear eyes fixed on him.

Anna Sergeyevna Odintsov was the daughter of Sergey Nikolaevich Loktev, famous for his good looks, his speculations, and his gambling, who after cutting a figure and making a sensation for fifteen years in Petersburg and Moscow, finished by ruining himself completely at cards, and was forced to retire to the country, where he died soon after, leaving a very small property to his two daughters—Anna, a girl of twenty, and Katya, a child of twelve. Their mother, who came of an impoverished line of princes — the Kh—s —had died in Petersburg when her husband was in his heyday. Anna's position after her father's death was very difficult. The brilliant education she had received in Petersburg had not fitted her for putting up with the cares of the household and estate management—for an obscure existence in the country. She knew positively no one in the whole neighborhood, and there was no one she could consult. Her father had tried to avoid all contact with the neighbors, he despised them in his way, and they despised him in theirs. She did not lose her head, however, and promptly sent for a sister of her mother's, Princess Avdotya Stepanovna Kh——, a spiteful and arrogant old lady, who, on installing herself in her niece's house, appropriated all the best rooms for her own use, scolded and grumbled from morning till night, and would not go a walk even in the garden unattended by her one serf, a surly footman in a threadbare pea-green livery with light blue trimming and a three-cornered hat. Anna put up patiently with all her aunt's whims, gradually set to work on her sister's education, and was, it seemed, already getting reconciled to the idea of wasting her life in the wilds. . . . But destiny had decreed another fate for her. She chanced to be seen by Odintsov, a very wealthy man of forty-six, an eccentric hypochondriac, stout, heavy, and sour, but not stupid, and not ill-natured; he fell in love with her, and offered her his hand. She consented to become his wife, and he lived six years with her, and on his death settled all his property upon her. Anna Sergeyevna remained in the country for nearly a year after his death; then she went abroad with her sister, but only stopped in Germany; she got tired of it and came back to live at her favorite Nikolskoe, which was nearly thirty miles from the town of X———. There she had a magnificent, splendidly furnished house and a beautiful garden, with conservatories; her late husband had spared no expense to gratify his fancies. Anna Sergeyevna very rarely went to town, generally only on business, and even then she did not stay long. She was not liked in the province; there had been a fearful outcry at her marriage with Odintsov, all sorts of improbabilities were told about her: it was asserted that she had helped her father in his cardsharping tricks, and even that she had gone abroad for excellent reasons, that it had been necessary to conceal the lamentable consequences . . . "You understand?" the indignant gossips would wind up. "She has gone through fire and water," was said of her; to which a noted provincial wit usually added: "And through brass pipes." All this talk reached her; but she turned a deaf ear to it; there was much independence and a good deal of determination in her character.

Odintsov sat leaning back in her easy-chair, and listened to Bazarov with folded hands. He, contrary to his habit, was talking a good deal, and obviously trying to interest her—again a surprise for Arkady. He could not make up his mind whether Bazarov was attaining his object. It was difficult to conjecture from Anna Sergeyevna's face what impression was being made on her; it retained the same expression, gracious and refined; her beautiful eyes shined with attention, but quiet attention. Bazarov's bad manners had impressed her unpleasantly for the first minutes of the visit like a bad smell or a discordant sound; but she saw at once that he was nervous, and that even flattered her. Nothing was repulsive to her but vulgarity, and no one could have accused

Bazarov of vulgarity. Arkady was fated to meet with surprises that day. He expected Bazarov to talk to a clever woman like Odintsov about his opinions and his views; she had herself expressed a desire to listen to the man "who dares to have no belief in anything"; but, instead of that, Bazarov talked about medicine, about homœpathy, and about botany. It turned out that Odintsov had not wasted her time in seclusion; she had read several good books, and expressed herself in excellent Russian. She turned the conversation upon music; but noticing that Bazarov did not appreciate art, she quietly brought it back to botany, even though Arkady was just launching into a discourse upon the significance of national melodies. Odintsov treated him as though he were a younger brother; she seemed to appreciate his good-nature and youthful simplicity and that was all. For over three hours a lively conversation was kept up, ranging freely over various subjects.

The friends at last got up and began to take leave. Anna Sergeyevna looked cordially at them, held out her beautiful white hand to both, and, after a moment's thought, said with a doubtful but delightful smile, "If you are not afraid of being bored gentlemen, come and see me at Nikolskoe."

"Oh, Anna Sergeyevna," cried Arkady, "I shall think it the greatest happiness . . ."

"And you, Monsieur Bazarov?"

Bazarov only bowed, and a last surprise was in store for Arkady; he noticed that his friend was blushing.

"Well?" he said to him in the street; "are you still of the same opinion—that she's ooh la la?"

"Who can tell? See how frigid she's made herself!" retorted Bazarov; and after a brief pause he added, "She's a perfect duchess, a regal personage. She only needs a train behind, and a crown on her head."

"Our duchesses don't speak Russian like that," remarked Arkady.

"She's seen ups and downs, my dear boy; she's know what it is to be hard up!"

"Anyway, she's charming," observed Arkady.

"What a magnificent body," Bazarov continued. "Perfect for the dissecting-table."

"For God's sake, stop Evgeny! that's beyond everything."

"Well, don't get angry, you baby. I meant it's first-rate. We must go to stay with her."

"When?"

"Well, why not the day after to-morrow. What is there to do here? Drink champagne with Kukshin? Listen to your cousin, the Liberal dignitary? . . . Let's be off the day after to-morrow. By the way, too—my father's little place is not far from there. This Nikolskoe's on the S—— road, isn't it?"

"Yes."

"*Optime*, why hesitate? Leave that to fools and smart alecs. I tell you, it's a splendid body!"

Three days later the two friends were driving along the road to Nikolskoe. The day was bright, and not too hot, and the sleek posting-horses trotted smartly along, switching their tied and plaited tails. Arkady looked at the road, and not knowing why, he smiled.

"Congratulate me," cried Bazarov suddenly, "to-day's the 22nd of June, my guardian angel's day. Let's see how he will watch over me. To-day· they expect me home," he added, dropping his voice. . . . "Well, they can go on expecting. . . . What does it matter!"

XVI

The estate on which Anna Sergeyevna lived stood on the slope of an exposed hill, a short distance from a yellow stone church with a green roof, white columns, and a fresco over the principal entrance representing the "Resurrection of Christ" in the "Italian" style. Sprawling in the foreground of the picture was a swarthy warrior in a helmet, specially conspicuous for his rotund contours. Behind the church an extensive village stretched in two rows, with chimneys peeping out here and there above the thatched roofs. The manor-house was built in the same style as the church, the style known among us as that of Alexander I; the house, too, was painted yellow, and had a green roof, and white columns, and a pediment with an escutcheon on it. The architect had designed both buildings with the approval of the deceased Odintsov, who could not endure—as he expressed it—idle and arbitrary innovations. The house was enclosed on both sides by the dark trees of an old garden; an avenue of pruned pines led up to the entrance.

Our friends were met in the hall by two tall footmen in livery; one of them at once ran for the butler. The butler, a stout man in a black dress coat, promptly appeared and led the visitors by a staircase covered with rugs to a special room, in which two bedsteads were already prepared for them, and all the necessaries. It was clear that order reigned supreme in the house; everything was clean, everywhere there was a peculiar pleasant fragrance, just as there is in the reception rooms of ministers.

"Anna Sergeyevna requests you to join her in half an hour," the butler announced; "are there any orders meanwhile?"

"No orders," answered Bazarov; "perhaps you will be so good as to trouble yourself to bring me a glass of vodka."

"Yes, sir," said the butler, looking somewhat perplexed, and he withdrew, his boots creaking as he walked.

"What *grand genre!*" remarked Bazarov. "That's what it's called in your set, isn't it? She's a duchess, and that's all there is to it."

"A fine duchess," retorted Arkady, "at the very first meeting she invited such great aristocrats as you and me to stay with her."

"Especially me, a future doctor, and a doctor's son, and a village sexton's grandson. . . . You know, I suppose, I'm the grandson of a sexton? Like the great Speransky," [4] added Bazarov after a brief pause, contracting his lips. "At any rate she likes to be comfortable; oh, doesn't she, this lady! Oughtn't we to put on evening dress?"

Arkady only shrugged his shoulders . . . but he, too, was conscious of a little nervousness.

Half an hour later Bazarov and Arkady went together into the drawing-room. It was a large lofty room, furnished rather luxuriously but without particular taste. Heavy, expensive furniture stood in the ordinary stiff arrangement along the walls, which were covered with cinnamon-colored paper patterned in gold; the late Odintsov had ordered the furniture from Moscow through a friend and agent of his, a liquor dealer. Over the center sofa hung a portrait of a flabby light-haired man—and it seemed to look with displeasure at the visitors. "It must be *himself*," Bazarov whispered to Arkady, and wrinkling his nose, he added, "Hadn't we better bolt . . .?" But at that instant the lady of the house entered. She wore a light barège dress; her hair smoothly combed back behind her ears gave a girlish expression to her pure and fresh face.

"Thank you for keeping your promise," she began. "You must stay a little while with me; it's really not bad here. I will introduce you to my sister; she plays the piano well. That is a matter of indifference to you, Monsieur Bazarov; but you, I think, Monsieur Kirsanov, are fond of music. Besides my sister I have an old aunt living with me, and one of our neighbors comes in sometimes to play cards; that makes up all our circle. And now let us sit down."

Odintsov delivered all of this little speech with peculiar precision, as though she had learned it by heart; then she turned to Arkady. It appeared that her mother had known Arkady's mother, and had even been her confidante in her love for Nikolai Petrovich. Arkady began talking with great warmth of his dead mother; while Bazarov fell to turning over albums. "How tame I've be-

---

4. The son of a priest, educated in a seminary, M. M. Speransky (1772–1839) was an outstanding statesman, responsible for a new code of law (1832) and many other major achievements. He was the first plebeian to rise to such eminence in Russia.

come!" he thought to himself.

A beautiful wolfhound with a blue collar ran into the drawing-room, tapping on the floor with her nails, and after her entered a girl of eighteen,[5] black-haired and dark-skinned, with a rather round but pleasing face, and small dark eyes. In her hands she held a basket filled with flowers.

"This is my Katya," said Odintsov, indicating her with a motion of her head. Katya made a slight curtsey, placed herself beside her sister, and began picking out flowers. The wolfhound, whose name was Fifi, went up to both of the visitors, in turn wagging her tail, and thrusting her cold nose into their hands.

"Did you pick all that yourself?" asked Odintsov.

"Yes," answered Katya.

"Is auntie coming to tea?"

"Yes."

When Katya spoke, she had a very charming smile, sweet, timid, and candid, and looked up from under her eyebrows with a sort of humorous severity. Everything about her was still youthfully fresh; the voice, and the bloom on her whole face, and the rosy hands, with white palms, and the rather narrow shoulders. . . . She was constantly blushing and catching her breath.

Odintsov turned to Bazarov. "You are looking at pictures out of politeness, Evgeny Vassilyich," she began. "That does not interest you. You had better come closer to us, and let us have a discussion about something."

Bazarov came closer. "What subject have you decided upon for discussion?" he said.

"Whatever you like. I warn you, I am dreadfully argumentative."

"You?"

"Yes. That seems to surprise you. Why?"

"Because, as far as I can judge, you have a calm, cool character, and one must be impulsive to be argumentative."

"How can you have had time to understand me so soon? In the first place, I am impatient and obstinate—you should ask Katya; and secondly, I am very easily carried away."

Bazarov looked at Anna Sergeyevna. "Perhaps; you know best. And so you are in the mood for a discussion—by all means. I was looking through the views of the Saxon mountains in your album, and you remarked that that couldn't interest me. You said so, because you suppose me to have no feeling for art, and in fact I haven't any; but these views might be interesting to me from a geological standpoint, for the formation of the mountains, for instance."

5. According to Turgenev's earlier statement, she was eight years younger than her sister, hence twenty-one.

"Excuse me; but as a geologist, you would sooner have recourse to a book, to a special work on the subject and not to a drawing."

"The drawing shows me at a glance what would be spread over ten pages in a book."

Anna Sergeyevna was silent for a little.

"And so you haven't the least artistic feeling?" she observed, putting her elbow on the table, and by that very action bringing her face nearer to Bazarov. "How can you get on without it?"

"Why, what is it needed for, may I ask?"

"Well, at least to enable one to study and understand men."

Bazarov smiled. "In the first place, experience of life does that; and in the second, I assure you, studying separate individuals is not worth the trouble. All people resemble each other, in soul as in body; each of us has brain, spleen, heart, and lungs made alike; and the so-called moral qualities are the same in all; the slight variations are of no importance. A single human specimen is sufficient to judge all the rest. People are like trees in a forest; no botanist would think of studying each individual birch tree." [6]

Katya, who was arranging the flowers, one at a time in a leisurely fashion, lifted her eyes to Bazarov with a puzzled look, and meeting his rapid and careless glance, she crimsoned up to her ears. Anna Sergeyevna shook her head.

"Like trees in a forest," she repeated. "Then according to you there is no difference between the stupid and the clever person, between the good-natured and ill-natured?"

"No, there is a difference, just as between the sick and the healthy. The lungs of a consumptive patient are not in the same condition as yours and mine, though they are made on the same plan. We know approximately what physical diseases come from; moral diseases come from bad education, from all the nonsense people's heads are stuffed with from childhood up, from the deformed state of society; in short, reform society, and there will be no diseases."

Bazarov said all this with an air as though he were all the while thinking to himself, "Believe me or not, it's all the same to me!" He slowly passed his fingers over his side whiskers, while his eyes strayed about the room.

"And you conclude," observed Anna Sergeyevna, "that when society is reformed, there will be no stupid nor wicked people?"

"At any rate, in a proper organization of society, it will be absolutely the same whether a man is stupid or clever, wicked

6. Bazarov is again paraphrasing Cherny-shevsky's A.M. dissertation, *The Aesthetic Relationship of Art and Reality* (1855), which became the bible of the so-called "Radical Critics" and their partisans.

or good."

"Yes, I understand; they will all have the same spleen."

"Precisely so, madam."

Odintsov turned to Arkady. "And what is your opinion, Arkady Nikolaevich?"

"I agree with Evgeny," he answered.

Katya looked up at him from under her eyelids.

"You amaze me, gentlemen," commented Odintsov, "but we will talk together again. But now I hear my aunt coming in to tea; we must spare her."

Anna Sergeyevna's aunt, Princess Kh——, a thin little woman with a pinched-up face, drawn together like a fist, and staring, ill-natured-looking eyes under a grey wig, came in, and, scarcely bowing to the guests, she dropped into a wide velvet covered arm-chair, upon which no one but herself was privileged to sit. Katya put a footstool under her feet; the old lady did not thank her, did not even look at her, merely moving her hands under the yellow shawl which almost covered her feeble body. The Princess liked yellow; her cap, too, had bright yellow ribbons.

"How have you slept, aunt?" inquired Odintsov, raising her voice.

"That dog in here again," the old lady muttered in reply, and noticing Fifi was making two hesitating steps in her direction, she cried, "Ss—ss!"

Katya called Fifi and opened the door for her.

Fifi dashed out delighted, in the expectation of being taken out for a walk; but when she was left alone outside the door, she began scratching on it and whining. The princess scowled. Katya was about to go out. . . .

"I expect tea is ready," said Odintsov.

"Come, gentlemen; aunt, will you go in to tea?"

The princess got up from her chair without speaking and led the way out of the drawing-room. They all followed her into the dining-room. A little page in livery drew an arm-chair covered with cushions, also devoted to the princess's use, back from the table with a scraping sound; she sank into it; Katya in pouring out the tea handed her first a cup emblazoned with a heraldic crest. The old lady put some honey in her cup (she considered it both sinful and extravagant to drink tea with sugar in it, though she never spent a farthing herself on anything), and suddenly asked in a hoarse voice, "And what does Prince Ivan write?"

No one answered her. Bazarov and Arkady soon guessed that they paid no attention to her, though they treated her respectfully.

"They put up with her for *appearances*, because she's princely breed," thought Bazarov. . . .

After tea, Anna Sergeyevna suggested that they go out for a walk; but it began to rain a little, and the whole party, with the exception of the princess, returned to the drawing-room. The neighbor, the devoted card-player, arrived; his name was Porfiry Platonich, a stoutish, greyish man with short, spindly legs, very polite and ready to entertain. Anna Sergeyevna, who talked more and more principally with Bazarov, asked him whether he'd care to play an old-fashioned game of preference with them. Bazarov assented, saying that he ought to prepare himself beforehand for the duties awaiting him as a country doctor.

"Be careful," observed Anna Sergeyevna; "Porfiry Platonich and I will beat you. And you, Katya," she added, "play something for Arkady Nikolaevich; he is fond of music, and we can listen, too."

Katya went unwillingly to the piano; and Arkady, though he certainly was fond of music, unwillingly followed her; it seemed to him that Odintsov was sending him away, and already, like every young man at his age, he felt a vague and oppressive emotion surging up in his heart, like the forebodings of love. Katya raised the lid of the piano, and without looking at Arkady, asked in a low voice:

"What am I to play you?"

"Whatever you like," answered Arkady indifferently.

"What sort of music do you like best?" repeated Katya without changing her attitude.

"Classical," Arkady answered in the same tone of voice.

"Do you like Mozart?"

"Yes, I like Mozart."

Katya pulled out Mozart's *Sonata-Fantasia in C minor*. She played very well, though rather overcorrectly and drily. She sat upright and immovable, her eyes fixed on the notes and her lips tightly compressed, and only at the end of the sonata her face glowed, her hair came loose, and a little lock fell on to her dark brow.

Arkady was particularly struck by the last part of the sonata, the part in which, in the midst of the captivating gaiety of the careless melody, the pangs of such mournful, almost tragic suffering, suddenly break in. . . . But the ideas stirred in him by Mozart's music had no reference to Katya. Looking at her, he simply thought, "Well, that young lady doesn't play badly, and she's not bad-looking either."

When she had finished the sonata, Katya, without taking her hands from the keyboard, asked, "Is that enough?" Arkady declared that he could not venture to trouble her further, and began talking to her about Mozart. He asked her whether she had chosen that sonata herself, or someone had recommended it to her. But Katya answered him in monosyllables; she withdrew into herself, went back into her shell. When this happened to her, she did not very quickly come out again; her face even assumed at such times an obstinate, almost stupid expression. She was not exactly shy, but diffident, and rather overawed by her sister, who had educated her, and who, of course, did not even suspect it. Arkady was reduced at last to calling Fifi, who had returned, and with an affable smile patting her on the head to save face. Katya set to work again upon her flowers.

Bazarov meanwhile was kept revoking. Anna Sergeyevna played cards in masterly fashion; Porfiry Platonich, too, could hold his own in the game. Bazarov lost a sum which, though trifling in itself, was not altogether pleasant for him. At supper Anna Sergeyevna again turned the conversation on botany.

"Let us go for a walk to-morrow morning," she said to him. "I want you to teach me the Latin names of the wild flowers and their species."

"What use are the Latin names to you?" asked Bazarov.

"Order is needed in everything," she answered.

"What an exquisite woman Anna Sergeyevna is!" cried Arkady, when he was alone with his friend in the room assigned to them.

"Yes," answered Bazarov, "a female with brains. Yes, and she's seen life too."

"In what sense do you mean that, Evgeny Vassilich?"

"In a good sense, a good sense, my dear friend, Arkady Nikolaevich! I'm convinced she manages her estate capitally too. But what's splendid is not her, but her sister."

"What, that little dark thing?"

"Yes, that little dark thing. She now is fresh and untouched, and shy and silent, and anything you like. She's worth educating and developing. You might make something fine out of her; but the other's—a stale loaf."

Arkady made no reply to Bazarov, and each of them got into bed with his own thoughts.

Anna Sergeyevna, too, thought of her guests that evening. She liked Bazarov for the absence of gallantry in him, and even for his sharply defined views. She found in him something new, which she had not chanced to meet before, and she was curious.

Anna Sergeyevna was a rather strange creature. Having no prejudices of any kind, having no strong convictions even, she never gave way or went out of her way for anything. She had seen many things very clearly; she had been interested in many things, but nothing had completely satisfied her; indeed, she hardly desired complete satisfaction. Her intellect was at the same time inquiring and indifferent; her doubts were never soothed to forgetfulness, and they never grew strong enough to distract her. Had she not been rich and independent, she would perhaps have thrown herself into the struggle, and have known passion. But life was easy for her, though she was bored at times, and she went on passing day after day with deliberation, never in a hurry, placid, and only rarely disturbed. Dreams sometimes danced in rainbow colors before her eyes even, but she breathed more freely when they died away, and did not regret them. Her imagination indeed overstepped the limits of what is reckoned permissible by conventional morality; but even then the blood flowed as quietly as ever in her fascinatingly graceful, tranquil body. Sometimes coming out of her fragrant bath all warm and languorous, she would fall to musing on the insignificance of life, the sorrow, the labor, the malice of it. . . . Her soul would be filled with sudden daring, and would flow with generous ardor, but a draft would blow from a half-closed window, and Anna Sergeyevna would shrink into herself, and feel plaintive and almost angry, and there was only one thing she cared for at that instant—to get away from that horrid wind.

Like all women who have not succeeded in loving, she wanted something, without herself knowing what. Strictly speaking, she wanted nothing; but it seemed to her that she wanted everything. She could hardly endure the late Odintsov (she had married him out of calculation, though probably she would not have consented to become his wife if she had not considered him a good man), and had conceived a secret repugnance for all men, whom she could only figure to herself as slovenly, heavy, drowsy, and feebly importunate creatures. Once, somewhere abroad, she had met a handsome young Swede, with a chivalrous expression, with honest blue eyes under a broad brow; he had made a powerful impression on her, but it had not prevented her from going back to Russia.

"A strange man this doctor!" she thought as she lay in her luxurious bed on lace pillows under a light silk coverlet. . . .

Anna Sergeyevna had inherited from her father a little of his inclination for luxury. She had deeply loved her sinful but good-natured father, and he had idolized her, used to joke with her in a friendly way as though she were an equal, and to confide in her fully, to ask her advice. She scarcely remembered her mother.

"This doctor is a strange man!" she repeated to herself. She stretched, smiled, clasped her hands behind her head, then ran her eyes over two pages of a stupid French novel, dropped the book—and fell asleep, all clean and cool, in her clean and fragrant linen.

The following morning Anna Sergeyevna went off botanizing with Barazov directly after breakfast, and returned just before lunch; Arkady did not go off anywhere, and spent an hour or so with Katya. He was not bored with her; she herself offered to repeat yesterday's sonata; but when Odintsov came back at last, when he caught sight of her, he felt an instantaneous pang at his heart. She came through the garden with a rather tired step; her cheeks were glowing and her eyes shining more brightly than usual under her round straw hat. In her fingers she was twirling the thin stalk of a wildflower, a light mantle had slipped down to her elbows, and the wide gray ribbons of her hat were clinging to her bosom. Bazarov walked behind her, self-confident and careless as usual, but the expression on his face, cheerful and even friendly as it was, did not please Arkady. Muttering "Good-morning!" between his teeth, Bazarov went away to his room, while Odintsov shook Arkady's hand abstractedly, and also walked past him.

"Good-morning!" thought Arkady. . . . "As though we had not seen each other already to-day!"

XVII

Time, it is well known, sometimes flies like a bird, sometimes crawls like a worm; but man is wont to be particularly happy when he does not even notice whether it passes quickly or slowly. It was in that way Arkady and Bazarov spent a fortnight at Odintsov's. The good order she had established in her house and in her life partly contributed to this result. She adhered strictly to this order herself, and forced others to submit to it. Everything during the course of the day was done at a fixed time. In the morning, precisely at eight o'clock, every one assembled for tea; from morning tea till lunch time every one did what he pleased; the mistress herself was engaged with her bailiff (the estate was on the quitrent system), her butler, and her head housekeeper. Before dinner everyone met again for conversation or reading; the evening was devoted to walking, cards, and music; at half-past ten Anna Sergeyevna retired to her own room, gave her orders for the following day, and went to bed. Bazarov did not like this measured, somewhat ostentatious punctuality in daily life, "like moving along rails," he pronounced it to be; the footmen in livery, the decorous butlers offended his democratic sentiments. He declared that if one went so far, one might as well dine in the English style at once—

in tail-coats and white ties. He once spoke plainly upon the subject to Anna Sergeyevna.

Her attitude was such that no one hesitated to speak his mind freely before her. She heard him out; and then her comment was, "From your point of view, you are right—and perhaps, in that respect, I am too much of a lady; but there's no living in the country without order, one would be devoured by ennui," and she continued to go her own way. Bazarov grumbled, but the very reason life was so easy for him and Arkady at Odintsov's was that everything in the house "moved on rails." For all that, a change had taken place in both young men since the first days of their stay at Nikolskoe. Bazarov, in whom Anna Sergeyevna was obviously interested, though she seldom agreed with him, began to show signs of unrest, unprecedented in him; he was easily put out of temper, and unwilling to talk, he looked irritated, and could not sit still in one place, just as though something were urging him on; while Arkady, who had definitely decided in himself that he was in love with Odintsov, began to yield to a gentle melancholy. This melancholy did not, however, prevent him from becoming friendly with Katya; it even helped him to get on friendly, affectionate terms with her. "*She* does not appreciate me? So be it . . . But here is a good creature, who does not repulse me," he thought, and his heart again knew the sweetness of magnanimous emotions. Katya vaguely realized that he was seeking a sort of consolation in her company, and did not deny him or herself the innocent pleasure of a half-shy, half-confidential friendship. They did not talk to each other in Anna Sergeyevna's presence; Katya always shrank into herself under her sister's sharp eyes; while Arkady, as befits a man in love, could pay attention to nothing else when near the object of his passion; but he was happy only with Katya. He felt that he was unable to interest Odintsov; he was shy and at a loss when he was left alone with her, and she did not know what to say to him: he was too young for her. With Katya, on the other hand, Arkady felt at home; he treated her condescendingly, did not discourage her from expressing the impressions made on her by music, reading novels, verses, and other such trifles without noticing or realizing that these *trifles* were what interested him too. Katya, on her side, did not try to drive away his melancholy. Arkady was at his ease with Katya, Odintsov with Bazarov, and thus it usually came to pass that the two couples, after being a little while together, went off on their separate ways, especially during the walks. Katya *adored* nature, and Arkady loved it, though he did not dare to acknowledge it; Odintsov was rather indifferent to the beauties of nature, like Bazarov. The almost continual separation of the two friends was not without its consequences; the relations between them began to change. Bazarov gave up talking to Arkady about Odintsov, even gave up abusing her "aristocratic ways"; true, he praised Katya as before, and only advised him to restrain her sentimental tendencies, but his praises were hurried, his advice dry, and in general he talked less to Arkady than before . . . he seemed to avoid him, seemed ill at ease with him.

Arkady observed it all, but he kept his observations to himself.

The real cause of all this "newness" was the feeling inspired in Bazarov by Odintsov, a feeling which tortured and maddened him, and which he would at once have denied, with scornful laughter and cynical abuse, if any one had ever so remotely hinted at the possibility of what was taking place in him. Bazarov had a great love for women and for feminine beauty; but love in the ideal, or, as he expressed it, romantic sense, he called gibberish, unpardonable imbecility; he regarded chivalrous sentiments as something like deformity or disease, and had more than once expressed his wonder that Toggenburg and all the minnesingers and troubadors had not been put into a lunatic asylum. "If a woman takes your fancy," he used to say, "try to gain your end; but if you can't—well, turn your back on her—there are lots of good fish in the sea." Odintsov had taken his fancy; the rumors about her, the freedom and independence of her ideas, her unmistakable liking for him, all seemed to be in his favor, but he soon saw that with her he would not "gain his ends," and he found, to his own bewilderment, that it was beyond his power to turn his back on her. His blood was on fire as soon as he thought of her; he could easily have mastered his blood, but something else was taking root in him, something he had never admitted, at which he had always jeered, at which all his pride revolted. In his conversations with Anna Sergeyevna he expressed more strongly than ever his calm contempt for everything romantic; but when he was alone, with indignation he recognized the romantic in himself. Then he would set off to the forest and walk with long strides about it, breaking the twigs that came in his way, and cursing under his breath both her and himself; or he would get into the hay-loft in the barn, and, obstinately closing his eyes, try to force himself to sleep, in which, of course, he did not always succeed. Suddenly his fancy would bring before him those chaste hands twining one day about his neck, those proud lips responding to his kisses, those intellectual eyes dwelling with tenderness—yes, with tenderness—on his, and his head went round, and he forgot himself for an instant, till indignation boiled up in him again. He caught himself in all sorts of "shameful" thoughts, as though he were driven on by a devil mocking him. Sometimes it seemed to him that there was a change taking place in Odintsov too; that there were signs in the expression of her face of something special; that, perhaps . . . but at that point he would stamp, or grind his teeth, and shake his fist in his own face.

And yet Bazarov was not altogether mistaken. He had struck Odintsov's imagination; he interested her, she thought a great deal about him. In his absence, she was not dull, she was not impatient for his coming, but she always grew more lively on his appearance; she liked to be left alone with him, and she liked talking to him, even when he irritated her or offended her taste, her refined habits. She was eager, as it were, both to put him to the test and to analyze herself.

One day walking in the garden with her, he suddenly announced, in a surly voice, that he intended going to his father's place very soon. . . . She turned pale, as though something had given her a pang, and such a pang, that she was amazed and pondered long after what it could mean. Bazaróv had spoken of his departure with no idea of putting her to the test, of seeing what would come of it; he never "fabricated." On the morning of that day he had an interview with his father's bailiff, who had taken care of him when he was a child, Timofeich. This Timofeich, a little old man of much experience and astuteness, with faded yellow hair, a weather-beaten red face, and tiny tear-drops in his puckered eyes, unexpectedly appeared before Bazarov, in his shortish overcoat of stout greyish-blue cloth, girt with a strip of leather, and in tarred boots.

"Hello, oldtimer; how are you?" cried Bazarov.

"How do you do, Evgeny Vassilyich?" began the little old man, and he smiled with delight, so that his whole face was all at once covered with wrinkles.

"What have you come for? They sent for me, eh?"

"Heavens, sir, how could we?" mumbled Timofeich. (He remembered the strict injunctions he had received from his master on starting.) "I was sent to town on business, and I heard news of your honor, so here I turned off on my way, that's to say—to have a look at your honor . . . as if we could think of disturbing you!"

"Come, don't lie!" Bazarov cut him short. "Do you mean to tell me this is the road to the town?" Timofeich hesitated, and made no answer. "Is my father well?"

"Thank God, yes."

"And my mother?"

"Anna Vlasyevna too, glory be to God."

"They are waiting for me, I suppose?"

The little old man held his tiny head on one side.

"Ah, Evgeny Vassilyich, how they wait for you, it makes one's heart ache to see them; it really does."

"Oh, all right, all right, don't carry on! Tell them I'm coming soon."

"Yes, sir," answered Timofeich, with a sigh.

As he went out of the house, he pulled his cap down on his head with both hands, clambered into a wretched-looking racing droshky, and went off at a trot, but not in the direction of the town.

That same evening, Odintsov was sitting in her own room with Bazarov, while Arkady walked up and down the hall listening to Katya's playing. The princess had gone upstairs to her own room; she could not bear guests as a rule, and "especially this new riff-raff lot," as she called them. In the common rooms she only sulked; but she made up for it in her own room by breaking out into such abuse before her maid that the cap danced on her head, wig and all. Odintsov was well aware of all this.

"How is it you are proposing to leave us?" she began; "how about your promise?"

Bazarov started. "What promise, madam?"

"Have you forgotten? You meant to give me some lessons in chemistry."

"It can't be helped! My father expects me; I can't loiter any longer. However, you can read Pelouse et Frémy, *Notions générales de chimie*; it's a good book, and clearly written. You will find everything you need in it."

"But do you remember; you assured me a book cannot take the place of . . . I've forgotten how you put it, but you know what I mean . . . do you remember?"

"It can't be helped!" repeated Bazarov.

"Why go away?" said Odintsov, dropping her voice.

He glanced at her. Her head had fallen on to the back of her easy-chair, and her arms, bare to the elbows, were folded on her bosom. She seemed paler in the light of the single lamp covered with a perforated paper shade. An ample white gown hid her completely in its soft folds; even the tips of her feet, also crossed, were hardly seen.

"And why stay?" answered Bazarov.

Odintsov turned her head slightly. "You ask why? Have you not enjoyed yourself here? Or do you suppose you will not be missed here"

"I am sure I won't be."

Odintsov was silent a minute. "You are wrong in thinking that. But I don't believe you. You could not have said that seriously." Bazarov still sat immovable. "Evgeny Vassilyich, why don't you speak?"

"Why, what am I to say to you? In general it's not worth missing people, and me less than most."

"Why so?"

"I'm a practical, uninteresting person. I don't know how to talk."

"You are fishing for compliments, Evgeny Vassilyich."

"That's not a habit of mine. Don't you know yourself that I've nothing in common with the elegant side of life, the side you prize so much?"

Odintsov bit the corner of her handkerchief.

"You may think what you like, but I shall be dull when you go away."

"Arkady will remain," remarked Bazarov. Odintsov shrugged her shoulders slightly. "I shall be dull," she repeated.

"Really? In any case you will not feel dull for long."

"What makes you suppose that?"

"Because you told me yourself that you are only dull when your regular routine is interrupted. You have ordered your existence with such impeccable regularity that there can be no place in it for dullness or sadness . . . for any unpleasant emotions."

"And do you consider I am so impeccable . . . that's to say, that I have ordered my life with such regularity?"

"I should think so. Here's an example: in a few minutes it will strike ten, and I know beforehand that you will drive me away."

"No; I'm not going to drive you away, Evgeny Vassilyich. You may stay. Open that window. . . . I feel somewhat stifled."

Bazarov got up and gave the window a push. It flew open with a crash. . . . He had not expected it to open so easily; besides, his hands were shaking. The soft, dark night looked in to the room with its almost black sky, its faintly rustling trees, and the fresh fragrance of the pure open air.

"Draw the blind and sit down," said Odintsov; "I want to have a chat with you before you go away. Tell me something about yourself; you never talk about yourself."

"I try to talk to you upon useful subjects, Anna Sergeyevna."

"You are very modest . . . But I should like to know something about you, about your family, about your father, for whom you are forsaking us."

"Why is she talking like that?" thought Bazarov.

"All that's not in the least interesting," he uttered aloud, "especially for you; we are obscure people. . . ."

"And you regard me as an aristocrat?"

Bazarov lifted his eyes to Madame Odintsov.

"Yes," he said, with exaggerated sharpness.

She smiled. "I see you know me very little, though you do maintain that all people are alike, and it's not worth while to study them. I will tell you my life some time or other . . . but first you tell me yours."

"I know you very little," repeated Bazarov. "Perhaps you are right; perhaps, really, every one is a riddle. You, for instance; you avoid society, you are oppressed by it, and you have invited two students to stay with you. With your intellect, with your beauty, why do you live in the country?"

"What? What was it you said?" Odintsov interposed eagerly. "With my . . . beauty?"

Bazarov scowled. "Never mind that," he muttered; "I meant to say that I don't exactly understand why you have settled in the country."

"You don't understand it. . . . But you explain it to yourself in some way?"

"Yes . . . I assume that you remain continually in the same place because you indulge yourself, because you are very fond of comfort and ease, and very indifferent to everything else."

Odintsov smiled again. "You would absolutely refuse to believe that I am capable of being carried away by anything?"

Bazarov glanced at her from under his brows.

"By curiosity, perhaps; but not otherwise."

"Really? Well, now I understand why we are such friends; you are just like me, you see."

"We are such friends . . ." Bazarov uttered in a hollow voice.

Bazarov got up. The lamp burnt dimly in the middle of the dark, fragrant, isolated room; from time to time the blind was shaken, and there flowed in the disturbing freshness of the night; its mysterious whisperings were heard. Odintsov did not move a single limb; hidden emotion gradually possessed her. It communicated itself to Bazarov. He was suddenly conscious that he was alone with a young and lovely woman. . . .

"Where are you going?" she said slowly.

He answered nothing, and sank into a chair.

"And so you consider me a placid, pampered, spoiled creature," she went on in the same voice, never taking her eyes off the window. "While I know about myself that I am unhappy."

"You unhappy? What for? Surely you can't attach any importance to idle gossip?"

Odintsov frowned. It annoyed her that he had given *that* meaning to her words.

"Such gossip does not even amuse me, Evgeny Vassilyich, and I am too proud to allow it to disturb me. I am unhappy because . . . I have no desires, no passion for life. You look at me incredulously; you think that's said by an 'aristocrat,' who is all in lace, and sitting in a velvet armchair. I don't conceal the fact: I love what you call comfort, and at the same time I have little desire to live. Explain that contradiction as best you can. But all that's romanticism in your eyes."

Bazarov shook his head. "You are in good health, independent, rich; what more would you have? What do you want?"

"What do I want?" echoed Odintsov, and she sighed. "I am very tired, I am old, I feel as if I have lived very long. Yes, I am old," she added, softly drawing the ends of her lace over her bare arms. Her eyes met Bazarov's eyes, and she faintly blushed. "I already have so many memories behind me: my life in Petersburg, wealth, then poverty, then my father's death, marriage, then the inevitable foreign tour. . . . So many memories, and nothing to remember, and before me, before me—a long, long road, and no goal. . . . I have no wish to go on."

"Are you so disillusioned?" asked Bazarov.

"No, but I am dissatisfied," Odintsov replied, dwelling on each syllable. "I think if I could interest myself strongly in something. . . ."

"You want to fall in love," Bazarov interrupted her, "and you can't love; that's where your unhappiness lies."

Odintsov began to examine the sleeve of her lace.

"Is it true I can't love?" she said.

"I should say not! Only I was wrong in calling that an unhappiness. On the contrary, any one's more to be pitied when such a mischance befalls him."

"Mischance, what?"

"Falling in love."

"And how do you come to know that?"

"By hearsay," answered Bazarov angrily.

"You're flirting," he thought; "you're bored, and teasing me for want of something to do, while I . . . ." His heart really seemed as though it were being torn to pieces.

"Besides, you are perhaps too exacting," he said, bending his whole frame forward and playing with the fringe of the chair.

"Perhaps. My idea is everything or nothing. A life for a life. Take mine, give up yours, and that without regret or turning back. Or else better have nothing."

"Well?" observed Bazarov; "those are fair terms, and I'm surprised that so far you . . . have not found what you wanted."

"And do you think it would be easy to give oneself up wholly to anything whatever?"

"Not easy, if you begin reflecting, waiting and attaching value to yourself, prizing yourself, I mean; but to give oneself up without reflection is very easy."

"How can one help prizing oneself? If I am of no value, who could need my devotion?"

"That's not my affair; that's somebody else's business to assess my value. The chief thing is to be able to yield oneself."

Odintsov bent forward from the back of her chair. "You speak," she began, "as though you had experienced all that."

"It happened to come up, Anna Sergeyevna; all that, as you know, is not in my line."

"But you could yield yourself?"

"I don't know. I shouldn't like to boast."

Odintsov said nothing, and Bazarov was mute. The sounds of the piano floated up to them from the drawing-room.

"How is it Katya is playing so late?" observed Odintsov.

Bazarov got up. "Yes, it is really late now; it's time for you to go to sleep."

"Wait a little; why are you in a hurry? . . . I want to say something to you."

"What is it?"

"Wait a little," whispered Odintsov. Her eyes rested on Bazarov; it seemed as though she were examining him attentively.

He walked across the room, then suddenly went up to her, hurriedly said, "Good-bye," squeezed her hand so that she almost screamed, and was gone. She raised her crushed fingers to her lips, breathed on them, and suddenly, impulsively getting up from her low chair, she moved with rapid steps towards the door, as though she wished to bring Bazarov back. . . . A maid came into the room with a decanter on a silver tray. Odintsov stood still, told her she could go, and sat down again, and again sank into thought. Her hair slipped loose and fell in a dark coil down her shoulders. Long after the lamp was still burning in Anna Sergeyevna's room, and for long she stayed without moving, only from time to time chafing her hands, nipped by the cold of the night.

And Bazarov came back to his bedroom two hours later with his boots wet with dew, dishevelled and glum. He found Arkady at the writing table with a book in his hands, his coat buttoned up to the throat.

"You're not in bed yet?" he said in a tone, it seemed, of annoyance.

"You stopped a long while with Anna Sergeyevna this evening," remarked Arkady, not answering him.

"Yes, I stopped with her all the while you were playing the piano with Katerina Sergeyevna."

"I did not play. . ." Arkady began, and he stopped. He felt the tears were coming into his eyes, and he did not like to cry before his sarcastic friend.

XVIII

The following morning when Odintsov came down to morning tea, Bazarov sat a long while bending over his cup, then suddenly he glanced up at her. . . . She turned to him as though he had touched her, and he thought that her face had become a little paler during the night. She soon went off to her own room, and did not appear till lunch. It rained from early morning; there was no possibility of going for a walk. The whole company assembled in the drawing-room. Arkady took up the latest issue of a journal and began reading it aloud. The princess, as was her habit, at first expressed amazement on her face, as though he were doing something improper, then glared angrily at him; but he paid no attention to her.

"Evgeny Vassilyich," said Anna Sergeyevna, "come to my room. . . . I want to ask you. . . . You mentioned a manual yesterday. . . ."

She got up and went to the door. The princess looked round with an expression that seemed to say, "Look at me, look at me: see how shocked I am!" and again glared at Arkady; but he raised his voice, and exchanging glances with Katya, near whom he was sitting, he went on reading.

Odintsov went to her study with rapid steps. Bazarov followed her quickly, not raising his eyes, and only catching with his ears the delicate swish and rustle of her silk gown gliding before him. Odintsov sank into the same easy-chair in which she had sat the previous evening, and Bazarov took up the same position as before.

"Well, what was the name of that book?" she began, after a brief silence.

"Pelouse et Frémy, *Notions générales*," answered Bazarov. "I might however also recommend to you Ganot, *Traité élémentaire de physique expérimentale*. In that book the illustrations are clearer, and in general that text-book . . ."

Odintsov stretched out her hand.

"Evgeny Vassilyich, I beg your pardon, but I didn't invite you in here to discuss text-books. I wanted to renew last night's conversation. You went away so suddenly. . . . You won't get bored?"

"I am at your service, Anna Sergeyevna. But what were we talking about last night?"

Odintsov flung a sidelong glance at Bazarov.

"We were talking of happiness, I believe. I told you about myself. By the way, I just used the word 'happiness.' Tell me why it is that even when we are enjoying music, for instance, or a fine evening, or a conversation with sympathetic people, it all seems an intimation of some measureless happiness existing apart somewhere rather than actual happiness—such, I mean, as we ourselves are in possession of? Why is it? Or perhaps you have no feeling like that?"

"You know the saying, 'The grass is always greener. . . .' " replied Bazarov; "besides, you told me yesterday you are discontented. I certainly never have such ideas come into my head."

"Perhaps they seem ridiculous to you?"

"No; but they don't come into my head."

"Really? Do you know, I should very much like to know what you think about?"

"What? I don't understand."

"Listen; I have long wanted to speak openly to you. There's no need to tell you—you are conscious of it yourself—that you are not an ordinary man; you are still young—all life is before you. What are you preparing yourself for? What future awaits you? I mean to say—what object do you want to attain? What are you going forward to? What is in your heart? In short, who are you, what are you?"

"You surprise me, Anna Sergeyevna. You are aware that I am studying natural sciences, and who I . . ."

"Well, who are you?"

"I have explained to you already that I am going to be a district doctor."

Anna Sergeyevna made an impatient movement.

"What do you say that for? You don't believe it yourself. Arkady might answer me in that way, but not you."

"Why, in what is Arkady . . ."

"Stop! Is it possible you could content yourself with such a humble career, and aren't you always maintaining yourself that you don't believe in medicine? You—with your ambition—a district doctor! You answer me like that to put me off, because you have no confidence in me. But, do you know, Evgeny Vassilyich, that I could understand you; I have been poor and ambitious myself, like you; I have been perhaps through the same trials as you."

"That is all very well, Anna Sergeyevna, but you must pardon me for . . . I am not in the habit of talking freely about myself at any time as a rule, and between you and me there is such a gulf . . ."

"What sort of gulf? You mean to tell me again that I am an aristocrat? No more of that, Evgeny Vassilyich; I thought I had proved to you . . ."

"And even apart from that," broke in Bazarov, "what could induce one to talk and think about the future, which for the most part does not depend on us? If a chance turns up of doing something—so much the better; and if it doesn't turn up—at least one will be glad one didn't gossip idly about it beforehand."

"You call a friendly conversation idle gossip? . . . Or perhaps you consider me as a woman unworthy of your confidence? I know you despise us all."

"I don't despise you, Anna Sergeyevna, and you know it."

"No, I don't know anything . . . but let us suppose so. I understand your disinclination to talk of your future career; but as to what is taking place within you now . . ."

"Taking place!" repeated Bazarov, "as though I were some sort of government or society! In any case, it is utterly uninteresting; and besides, can a man always speak of everything that 'takes place' in him?"

"Why, I don't see why you can't speak freely of everything you have on your mind."

"Can you?" asked Bazarov.

"Yes," answered Anna Sergeyevna, after a brief hesitation. Bazarov bowed his head. "You are more fortunate than I am."

Anna Sergeyevna looked at him questioningly. "As you please," she went on, "but still something tells me that we have not come together for nothing; that we shall be good friends. I am sure this —what should I say, constraint, reticence in you will vanish at last."

"So you have noticed reticence . . . as you expressed it . . . constraint?"

"Yes."

Bazarov got up and went to the window. "And would you like to know the reason of this reticence? Would you like to know what is passing within me?"

"Yes," repeated Odintsov, with a sort of dread she did not at the time understand.

"And you will not be angry?"

"No."

"No?" Bazarov was standing with his back to her. "Let me tell you then that I love you like a fool, like a madman. . . . There, you've forced it out of me."

Odintsov put both her hands out before her; but Bazarov was leaning with his forehead pressed against the window pane. He breathed hard: his whole body was visibly trembling. But it was not the tremor of youthful timidity, not the sweet alarm of the first declaration that possessed him; it was passion struggling in him, strong and painful—passion not unlike hatred, and perhaps akin to it . . . Odintsov felt both afraid and sorry for him.

"Evgeny Vassilyich!" she said, and there was the ring of unconscious tenderness in her voice.

He turned quickly, flung a devouring look at her, and snatching both her hands, he drew her suddenly to his breast.

She did not at once free herself from his embrace, but an instant later she was standing far away in a corner, and looked at Bazarov from there. He rushed at her. . . .

"You have misunderstood me," she whispered hurriedly, in alarm. It seemed that if he had made another step she would have screamed. . . . Bazarov bit his lips, and went out.

Half an hour after a maid gave Anna Sergeyevna a note from Bazarov; it consisted simply of one line: "Am I to go to-day, or can I stop till to-morrow?"

"Why should you go? I did not understand you—you did not understand me," Anna Sergeyevna answered him, but to herself she thought: "I did not understand myself either."

She did not show herself till dinner time, and kept walking to and fro in her room with her arms behind her back, stopping sometimes at the window, sometimes at the looking-glass, and slowly rubbing her handkerchief over her neck, on which she still seemed to feel a burning spot. She asked herself what had induced her to "force" his confidence, in Bazarov's words, and whether she had suspected nothing. . . . "I am to blame," she decided aloud, "but I could not have foreseen this." She fell to musing, and blushed crimson, remembering Bazarov's almost bestial face when he had rushed at her. . . .

"Or?" she uttered suddenly, and she stopped short and shook back her curls. . . . She caught sight of herself in the glass; her head thrown back, with a mysterious smile on the half-closed, half-opened eyes and lips, told her, it seemed, in a flash something at which she herself was confused. . . .

"No," she made up her mind at last. "God knows what it would lead to; you can't toy with him; peace is the best thing in the world, anyway."

Her peace of mind was not shaken; but she felt gloomy, and even shed a few tears once, though she could not have said why —certainly not for the insult done her. She did not feel insulted; she was more inclined to feel guilty. Under the influence of various vague emotions, the sense of life passing by, the desire of novelty, she had forced herself to go up to a certain point, forced herself to glance behind it, and had seen behind it not even an abyss, but a void . . . or something hideous.

XIX

Though Odintsov's self-control was great, and superior as she was to every kind of prejudice, she felt awkward when she went into the dining-room to dinner. The meal went off fairly successfully, however. Porfiry Platonovich made his appearance and told various anecdotes; he had just come back from the town. Among other things, he informed them that Governor Swill had ordered his secretaries on special commissions to wear spurs, in case he might send them off anywhere for greater speed on horseback. Arkady talked in an undertone to Katya, and diplomatically attended to the princess's wants. Bazarov maintained a grim and obstinate silence. Odintsov looked at him twice, not stealthily, but straight in the face, which was bilious and forbidding, with downcast eyes, and contemptuous determination stamped on every feature, and thought: "No . . . no . . . no." . . . After dinner she went with the whole company into the garden, and seeing that Bazarov wanted to speak to her, she took a few steps to one side and stopped. He went up to her, but even then did not raise his eyes, and said in a hollow voice:

"I must apologize to you, Anna Sergeyevna. You must be in a fury with me."

"No, I'm not angry with you, Evgeny Vassilyich," answered Odintsov; "but I am sorry."

"So much the worse. Anyway, I'm sufficiently punished. My position, you will certainly agree, is most foolish. You wrote to me, 'Why go away?' But I cannot stay, and don't wish to. Tomorrow I shall be gone."

"Evgeny Vassilyich, why are you . . ."

"Why am I going away?"

"No; I didn't mean to say that."

"You can't bring back the past, Anna Sergeyevna . . . and this was bound to come about sooner or later. Consequently I must go. I can only conceive of one condition upon which I could remain; but that condition can never be. Excuse my impertinence, but you don't love me, and you never will love me, I suppose?"

Bazarov's eyes glittered for an instant under their dark brows.

Anna Sergeyevna did not answer him. "I'm afraid of this man," flashed through her brain.

"Good-bye, then," said Bazarov, as though he guessed her thought, and he went back into the house.

Anna Sergeyevna walked slowly after him, and calling Katya to her, she took her arm. She did not leave her side till quite evening. She did not play cards, and was constantly laughing, which did not at all accord with her pale and perplexed face. Arkady was bewildered, and looked on at her as all young people look on—that is to say, he was constantly asking himself, "What is the meaning of that?" Bazarov shut himself up in his room; he came back to tea, however. Anna Sergeyevna longed to say something friendly to him, but she did not know how to approach him. . . .

An unexpected incident relieved her from her embarrassment; the butler announced the arrival of Sitnikov.

It is difficult to do justice in words to the strange figure cut by the young apostle of progress as he fluttered into the room, like a quail. With his characteristic impudence, he had made up his mind to go into the country to visit a woman whom he hardly knew, who had never invited him; but with whom, according to information he had gathered, such talented and intimate friends were staying, he was nevertheless trembling to the marrow of his bones; and instead of bringing out the apologies and compliments he had learned by heart beforehand, he muttered some absurdity about Evdoksya Kukshin having sent him to inquire after Anna Sergeyevna's health, and Arkady Nicolaevich's too, having always spoken to him in the highest terms. . . . At this point he faltered and lost his presence of mind so completely that he sat down on his own hat. However, since no one turned him out, and Anna Sergeyevna even presented him to her aunt and her sister, he soon recovered himself and began to chatter volubly. The introduction of the commonplace is often an advantage in life; it relieves over-strained feelings, and sobers too self-confident or self-forgetful emotions by recalling its close kinship with them. With Sitnikov's appearance everything somehow became duller and emptier; they all even ate a more solid supper, and retired to bed half an hour earlier than usual.

"I might now repeat to you," said Arkady, lying in bed, to Bazarov, who was also undressed, "what you once said to me, 'Why are you so melancholy? One would think you had fulfilled some sacred duty.'" For some time past a sort of pretense of free-and-easy banter had sprung up between the two young men, which is always an unmistakable sign of secret displeasure or unexpressed suspicions.

"I'm going to my father's tomorrow," said Bazarov.

Arkady raised himself and leaned on his elbow. He felt both surprised, and for some reason or other pleased. "Ah!" he commented, "and is that why you're sad?"

Bazarov yawned. "You'll get old if you know too much."

"And Anna Sergeyevna?" persisted Arkady.

"What about Anna Sergeyevna?"

"I mean, will she let you go?"

"I'm not her hired hand."

Arkady grew thoughtful, while Bazarov lay down and turned with his face to the wall.

Some minutes went by in silence. "Evgeny!" cried Arkady suddenly.

"Well?"

"I will leave with you to-morrow, too."

Bazarov made no answer.

"Only I will go home," continued Arkady. "We will go together as far as Khokhlovsky, and there you can get horses at Fedot's. I should be delighted to make the acquaintance of your people, but I'm afraid of being in their way and yours. You are coming to us again later, of course?"

"I've left all my things with you," Bazarov said, without turning round.

"Why doesn't he ask me why I am going, and just as suddenly as he?" thought Arkady. "In reality, why am I going, and why is he going?" he pursued his reflections. He could find no satisfactory answer to his own question, though his heart was filled with some bitter feeling. He felt it would be hard to part from this life to which he had grown so accustomed; but for him to remain alone would be rather odd. "Something has passed between them," he reasoned to himself; "what good would it be for me to hang on after he's gone? She's utterly sick of me; I'm losing the last that remained to me." He began to imagine Anna Sergeyevna to himself, then other features gradually eclipsed the lovely image of the young widow.

"It's a pity about Katya too!" Arkady whispered to his pillow, on which a tear had already fallen. . . . All at once he shook back his hair and said aloud:

"What the devil made that fool of a Sitnikov turn up here?"

Bazarov at first stirred a little in his bed, then pronounced the following: "You're still a fool, my boy, I see. Sitnikovs are indispensable to us. I—do you understand? I need dolts like him. It's not for the gods to bake bricks, in fact!" . . .

"Oho!" Arkady thought to himself, and then in a flash all the fathomless depths of Bazarov's conceit dawned upon him. "Are you and I gods then? At least, you're a god; am not I a dolt then?"

"Yes," repeated Bazarov gloomily; "you're still a fool."

Odintsov expressed no special surprise when Arkady told her the next day that he was going with Bazarov; she seemed tired and absorbed. Katya looked at him silently and seriously; the princess went so far as to cross herself under her shawl so that he could not help noticing it. Sitnikov, on the other hand, was completely disconcerted. He had only just come in to lunch in a new and fashionable get-up, not on this occasion of a Slavophile cut; the evening before he had astonished the servant assigned to him by the amount of linen he had brought with him, and now all of a sudden his comrades were deserting him! He took a few tiny steps, doubled back like a hunted hare at the edge of a copse, and abruptly, almost with dismay, almost with a wail, announced that he intended to go too. Odintsov did not attempt to detain him.

"I have a very comfortable carriage," added the unfortunate young man, turning to Arkady; "I can take you, while Evgeny Vassilyich can take your coach, so it will be even more convenient."

"But, really, it's not at all in your way, and it's a long way to my place."

"That's nothing, nothing; I've plenty of time; besides, I have business in that direction."

"Liquor?" asked Arkady, rather too contemptuously.

But Sitnikov was reduced to such desperation that he did not even laugh as usual. "I assure you, my carriage is exceedingly comfortable," he muttered; "and there will be room for all."

"Don't wound Monsieur Sitnikov by a refusal," commented Anna Sergeyevna.

Arkady glanced at her, and bowed his head significantly.

The visitors started off after lunch. As she said good-bye to Bazarov, Odintsov held out her hand to him, and said, "We shall meet again, shall we not?"

"As you command," answered Bazarov.

"In that case, we shall."

Arkady was the first to go out to the porch; he got into Sitnikov's carriage. The butler tucked him in respectfully, but he could have hit him with pleasure, or have burst into tears. Bazarov took his seat in the coach. When they reached Khokhlovsky, Arkady waited till Fedot, the keeper of the posting-station, had put in the horses, and going up to the coach he said, with his old smile, to Bazarov, "Evgeny, take me with you; I want to come to you."

"Get in," Bazarov uttered through his teeth.

Sitnikov, who had been walking to and fro round the wheels of his carriage, whistling briskly, could only gape when he heard these words; while Arkady coolly pulled his luggage out of the carriage, took his seat beside Bazarov, and bowing politely to his former fellow-traveler, he called, "Whip up!" The coach rolled away, and was soon out of sight . . . Sitnikov, utterly nonplussed, looked at his coachman, but the latter was flicking his whip about the tail of the off horse. Then Sitnikov jumped into the carriage, and thundering at two passing peasants, "Put on your caps, idiots!" he drove to town where he arrived very late, and where, next day, at Kukshin's, he dealt very severely with two "disgusting stuck-up churls."

When he was seated in the coach by Bazarov, Arkady pressed his hand warmly, and for a long while he said nothing. It seemed as though Bazarov understood and appreciated both the pressure and the silence. He had not slept at all the previous night, and had not smoked, and had eaten scarcely anything for several days. His profile, already thinner, stood out darkly and sharply under his cap, which was pulled down to his eyebrows.

"Well, brother," he said at last, "give us a cigar. But look, tell me, is my tongue yellow?"

"Yes, it is," answered Arkady.

"Hm . . . and the cigar is tasteless. The machine's out of gear."

"You really have changed lately," observed Arkady.

"It's nothing! We shall soon be all right. One thing's a bother—my mother's so tender-hearted; if you don't grow as round as a tub, and eat ten times a day, she's quite upset. My father's all right, he's known all sorts of ups and downs himself. No, I can't smoke," he added, and he flung the cigar into the dust of the road.

"Do you think it's fifteen miles?" asked Arkady.

"Yes. But ask this sage here." He indicated the peasant sitting on the box, a laborer of Fedot's.

But the sage only answered, "Who's to know—miles hereabout aren't measured," and went on swearing in an undertone at the shaft horse for "kicking with her head-piece," that is, jerking her head.

"Yes, yes," began Bazarov; "it's a lesson to you, my young friend, an instructive example. The devil knows what nonsense it is. Every man hangs on a thread, the abyss may open under his feet any minute, and yet he must go and invent all sorts of discomforts for himself, and spoil his life."

"What are you alluding to?" asked Arkady.

"I'm not alluding to anything; I'm saying straight out that we've both behaved like fools. What's the use of talking about it! Still, I've noticed in hospital practice, the man who's furious at his illness—he's sure to get over it."

"I don't quite understand you," observed Arkady; "I should have thought you had nothing to complain of."

"And since you don't quite understand me, I'll tell you this—to my mind, it's better to break stones on the highroad than to let a woman have the mastery of even the end of one's little finger. That's all . . ." Bazarov was on the point of uttering his favorite word, "romanticism," but he checked himself, and said, "nonsense. You don't believe me now, but I tell you; you and I have been in feminine society, and very nice we found it; but to leave society like that is as pleasant as a dip in cold water on a hot day. A man hasn't time to attend to such trifles; a man must be savage, says an

excellent Spanish proverb. Now, you, I suppose, my sage friend,"
he added, turning to the peasant sitting on the box—"you've a
wife?"

The peasant showed both the friends his dull blear-eyed face.
"A wife? Yes. How else?"

"Do you beat her?"

"My wife? Anything can happen. We don't beat her without good
reason!"

"That's excellent. Well, and does she beat you?"

The peasant gave a tug at the reins. "That's a strange thing to
say, master. You like your joke. . . ." He was obviously offended.

"You hear, Arkady Nikolaevich! But we have taken a beating
. . . that's what comes of being educated people."

Arkady gave a forced laugh, while Bazarov turned away, and
did not open his mouth again the whole journey.

The fifteen miles seemed a whole thirty to Arkady. But at last,
on the slope of a gently rising knoll appeared the tiny village
where Bazarov's parents lived. Beside it, in a small copse of young
birch, could be seen a tiny house with a thatched roof. Two
peasants stood with their hats on at the first hut, abusing each
other. "You're a big pig," said one; "and worse than a little sucking
pig."

"And your wife's a witch," retorted the other.

"From their unconstrained behavior," Bazarov remarked to
Arkady, "and the playfulness of their retorts, you can guess that
·my father's peasants are not too much oppressed. Why, there he is
himself coming out on the porch of his house. They must have heard
the bells. It's him; it's him—I know his figure. Oho ho! how grey he's
grown though, poor fellow!"

XX

Bazarov leaned out of the carriage, while Arkady thrust his
head out behind his companion's back, and caught sight on the
small porch of the little manor-house of a tall, gaunt man with
dishevelled hair, and thin aquiline nose, dressed in an old military
frock coat not buttoned up. He was standing, his legs wide apart,
smoking a long pipe and squinting his eyes to keep the sun out
of them.

The horses stopped.

"Arrived at last," said Bazarov's father, still going on smoking
though the pipe was fairly dancing up and down between his
fingers. "Come, get out; get out; let me hug you."

He began embracing his son. . . . "Enyusha, Enyusha," a trembling woman's voice was heard. The door was flung open, a plump,
short, little old woman in a white cap and a short, striped jacket,

appeared on the threshold. She oh'd, swayed, and would certainly have fallen, had not Bazarov supported her. Her small plump hands were instantly entwined round his neck, her head was pressed to his breast, and there was a complete hush. The only sound heard was her broken sobs.

Old Bazarov breathed hard and squinted his eyes up more than ever.

"There, that's enough, that's enough, Arisha! stop," he said, exchanging a glance with Arkady, who remained motionless near the coach, while the peasant on the box even turned his head away; "that's not necessary at all, please stop."

"Ah, Vassily Ivanovich," faltered the old woman, "for what ages, my dear one, my darling, Enyusha," . . . and, not unclasping her hands, she drew her wrinkled face, wet with tears and working with tenderness, a little away from Bazarov, and gazed at him with blissful and comic-looking eyes, and again fell on his neck.

"Well, well, to be sure, that's all in the nature of things," commented Vassily Ivanovich, "only we'd better come indoors. Here's a visitor come with Evgeny. You must excuse it," he added, turning to Arkady, and made a slight bow; "you understand, a woman's weakness; and well, a mother's heart . . ."

But his lips and eyebrows, too, were twitching, and his beard was quivering . . . he was obviously trying to control himself and appear almost indifferent.

"Let's come in, mother, really," said Bazarov, and he led the enfeebled old woman into the house. Putting her into a comfortable armchair, he once more hurriedly embraced his father and introduced Arkady to him.

"Heartily glad to make your acquaintance," said Vassily Ivanovich, "but you mustn't expect great things; everything here in my house is done in a plain way, on a military footing. Arina Vlasyevna, calm yourself, pray; what weakness! The gentleman our guest will think ill of you."

"My dear sir," said the old lady through her tears, "I haven't the honor of knowing your name and patronymic . . ."

"Arkady Nikolaich," put in Vassily Ivanovich solemnly, in a low voice.

"You must excuse a silly old woman like me." The old woman blew her nose, and bending her head to right and to left, carefully wiped one eye after the other. "You must excuse me. You see, I thought I should die, that I should not live to see my da . . . arling."

"Well, here we have lived to see him, madam," put in Vassily Ivanovich. "Tanyushka," he turned to a barelegged little girl of thirteen in a bright red cotton dress, who was timidly peeping in at the door, "bring your mistress a glass of water—on a tray, do you hear?—and you, gentlemen," he added, with a kind of old-fashioned playfulness "let me ask you into the study of a retired old veteran."

"Just let me embrace you once more, Enyusha," moaned Arina Vlasyevna. Bazarov bent down to her. "Why, what a handsome fellow you have grown!"

"Well, I don't know about being handsome," remarked Vassily Ivanovich, "but he's a man, as the saying is, *ommfay*.[7] And now I hope, Arina Vlasyevna, that having satisfied your maternal heart, you will turn your thoughts to satisfying the appetites of our dear guests, because, as you're aware, even nightingales can't be fed on fairy tales."

The old lady got up from her chair. "This minute, Vassily Ivanovich, the table shall be laid. I will run myself to the kitchen and order the samovar to be brought in; there will be everything, everything. Why, I have not seen him, not given him food or drink these three years; is that nothing?"

"There, mind, good mother, bustle about; don't put us to shame; while you, gentlemen, I beg you to follow me. Here's Timofeich come to pay his respects to you, Evgeny. He, too, I daresay, is delighted, the old dog. Eh, aren't you delighted, old dog? Be so good as to follow me."

And Vassily Ivanovich went bustling forward, scraping and flapping with his slippers trodden down at heel.

His whole house consisted of six tiny rooms. One of them—the one to which he led our friends—was called the study. A thick-legged table, littered over with papers black with the accumulation of ancient dust as though they had been smoked, occupied the entire space between two windows; on the walls hung Turkish firearms, whips, swords, two maps, anatomical charts of some sort, a portrait of Hufeland,[8] a monogram woven in hair in a black frame, and a glass-framed diploma; a leather sofa, torn and worn into hollows here and there, was placed between two enormous cupboards of Karelian birchwood; books, boxes, stuffed birds, jars, and phials were huddled together in confusion on the shelves; in one corner stood a broken galvanic battery.

"I warned you, my dear guest," began Vassily Ivanovich, "that we live, so to say, bivouacking. . . ."

"There, stop that, what are you apologizing for?" Bazarov interrupted. "Kirsanov knows very well we're not Crœsuses, and that you don't have a palace. Where are we going to put him, that's

---

7. That is, *homme fait*—"a real man."   8. A German physician (1762–1836).

the question?"

"To be sure, Evgeny; I have a capital room there in the little lodge; he will be very comfortable there."

"Have you had a lodge put up then?"

"Of course, sir, where the bathhouse is, sir," put in Timofeich.

"That is, next to the bathhouse," Vassily Ivanovich added hurriedly. "It's summer now . . . I will run over there at once, and make arrangements; and you, Timofeich, meanwhile bring in their things. You, Evgeny, I shall of course offer my study. *Suum cuique.*"[9]

"There you have him! A comical old chap, and the kindest," remarked Bazarov, as soon as Vassily Ivanovich had gone. "Just such a queer fish as yours, only in another way. He chatters too much."

"And your mother seems an awfully nice woman," observed Arkady.

"Yes, there's no humbug about her. You'll see what a dinner she'll give us."

"They didn't expect you to-day, sir; they didn't buy any beef," observed Timofeich, who was just dragging in Bazarov's box.

"We shall get on very well without beef. It's no use crying for the moon. Poverty, they say, is no vice."

"How many serfs has your father?" Arkady asked suddenly.

"The estate's not his, but mother's; there are fifteen serfs, if I remember."

"Twenty-two in all," Timofeich added, with an air of displeasure.

The flapping of slippers was heard, and Vassily Ivanovich reappeared. "In a few minutes your room will be ready to receive you," he cried triumphantly. "Arkady . . . Nikolaich? I think that is right? And here is your attendant," he added, indicating a short-cropped boy, who had come in with him in a blue coat with ragged elbows and a pair of boots which did not belong to him. "His name is Fedka. Again, I repeat, even though my son tells me not to, you mustn't expect great things. He knows how to fill a pipe, though. You smoke, of course?"

"I generally smoke cigars," answered Arkady.

"And you do very sensibly. I myself give the preference to cigars, but in these isolated parts it is exceedingly difficult to obtain them."

"There, that's enough humble pie," Bazarov interrupted again. "You'd much better sit here on the sofa and let us have a look at you."

Vassily Ivanovich laughed and sat down. His face was very

9. "To each his own."

much like his son's, only his brow was lower and narrower, and his mouth rather wider, and he was forever restless, shrugging up his shoulder as though his coat cut him under the arms, blinking, clearing his throat, and gesticulating with his fingers, while his son was distinguished by a kind of nonchalant immobility.

"Humble pie!" repeated Vassily Ivanovich. "You must not imagine, Evgeny, that I want to appeal, so to speak, to our guest's sympathies by making out we live in such a wilderness. Quite the contrary, I maintain that for a thinking man nothing is a wilderness. At least, I try as far as possible not to get rusty, so to speak, not to fall behind the age."

Vassily Ivanovich drew out of his pocket a new yellow silk handkerchief, which he had had time to snatch up on the way to Arkady's room, and flourishing it in the air, he proceeded: "I am not now alluding to the fact that, for example, at the cost of considerable sacrifice for me I have put my peasants on the quit-rent-system and given up my land to them on half profits. I regarded that as my duty; common sense itself enjoins such a proceeding, though other proprietors do not even dream of it; I am alluding to the sciences, to education."

"Yes; I see you have here *The Friend of Health* [1] for 1855," remarked Bazarov.

"It's sent me by an old comrade out of friendship," Vassily Ivanovich made haste to answer; "but we even have, some idea of phrenology, for instance," he added, addressing himself principally, however, to Arkady, and pointing to a small plaster head on the cupboard, divided into numbered squares; "we are not unacquainted even with Schönlein and Rademacher."

"Why, do people still believe in Rademacher in this province?" asked Bazarov.

Vassily Ivanovich cleared his throat. "In this province. . . . Of course, gentlemen, you know best; how could we keep pace with you? You are here to take our places. In my day, too, there was some sort of a Humoralist school, Hoffmann, and Brown too with his vitalism—they seemed very ridiculous to us, but, of course, they too had been great men at one time or other. Some one new has taken Rademacher's place with you; you bow down to him, but in another twenty years it will be his turn to be laughed at."

"For your consolation I will tell you," observed Bazarov, "that nowadays we laugh at medicine altogether, and don't bow down to any one."

"How's that? Why, you're going to be a doctor, aren't you?"

1. A medical journal. The two worthy physicians next mentioned were renowned German professors in the elder Bazarov's heyday.

"Yes, but the one fact doesn't prevent the other."

Vassily Ivanovich poked his third finger into his pipe, where a little smouldering ash was still left. "Well, it may be it may be—I am not going to argue. What am I? A retired army-doctor, *volla-too*;[2] now I've turned into an agronomist. I served in your grandfather's brigade," he addressed himself again to Arkady; "yes sir, yes sir, I have seen many sights in my day. And I was thrown into all kinds of society, brought into contact with all sorts of people! I myself, the man you see before you now, have felt the pulse of Prince Wittgenstein and of Zhukovsky![3] They were in the southern army, on the fourteenth,[4] you understand" (and here Vassily Ivanovich pursed his lips significantly). "Well, well, but my work was on the sideline; stick to your lancet, and let everything else go hang! Your grandfather was a very honorable man, a real soldier."

"Confess, now, he was a real blockhead," remarked Bazarov, lazily.

"Ah, Evgeny, how can you use such an expression! Do consider. . . . Of course, General Kirsanov was not one of the . . ."

"Come, drop him," broke in Bazarov; "I was pleased as I was driving along here to see your birch copse; it has shot up splendidly."

Vassily Ivanovich brightened up. "And you must see what a little garden I've got now! I planted every tree myself. I've fruit, and raspberries, and all kinds of medicinal herbs. However clever you young gentlemen may be, old Paracelsus spoke the holy truth: *in herbis, verbis et lapidibus*.[5] . . . I've retired from practice, you know, of course, but two or three times a week it will happen that I'm brought back to my old work. They come for advice—I can't drive them away. Sometimes the poor have recourse to me for help. And indeed there are no doctors here at all. There's one of the neighbors here, a retired major, only fancy, he doctors the people too. I asked, 'Has he studied medicine?' And they told me, 'No, he's not studied; he does it more out of philanthropy.' . . . Ha! ha! ha! out of philanthropy! What do you think of that? Ha! ha! ha!"

"Fedka, fill me a pipe!" said Bazarov rudely.

---

2. That is, *et voilà tout*—"and that's all."
3. A Russian field marshal, who distinguished himself during the war of 1812 and then commanded the armies in the South of Russia (1818–28). V. A. Zhukovsky (1783–1852) was Russia's leading poet at the beginning of the nineteenth century.
4. An allusion to the Decembrist Revolt (1825), a badly organized and conducted revolt by aristocratic officers, aimed at establishing a liberal constitution and abolishing serfdom. It was put down in a matter of hours, and many of the participants, the flower of the Russian aristocracy, were banished. The militant part of the conspiracy was headed by P. I. Pestel and involved those serving in the armies in the South.
5. "Through herbs, words, and minerals."

"And there's another doctor here who just got to a patient," Vassily Ivanovich persisted in a kind of desperation, "when the patient was already *ad patres;* [6] the servant didn't let the doctor speak; 'you're no longer needed,' he told him. He hadn't expected this, got confused, and asked, 'What, did your master hiccup before his death?' 'Yes sir.' 'Did he hiccup much?' 'Yes sir.' 'Ah, well, that's all right,' and off he set back again. Ha! ha! ha!"

The old man was alone in his laughter; Arkady forced a smile on his face. Bazarov only stretched. The conversation went on in this way for about an hour; Arkady had time to go to his room, which turned out to be the anteroom attached to the bathhouse, but was very snug and clean. At last Tanyusha came in and announced that dinner was ready.

Vassily Ivanovich was the first to get up. "Come, gentlemen. You must be magnanimous and pardon me if I've bored you. I daresay my good wife will satisfy you better."

The dinner, though prepared in haste, turned out to be very good, even abundant; only the wine was not quite up to the mark; it was almost black sherry, bought by Timofeich in the town from a merchant he knew and had a faint coppery, or perhaps resinous taste, and the flies were a great nuisance. On ordinary days a serf-boy used to keep driving them away with a large green branch; but on this occasion Vassily Ivanovich had sent him away through dread of the criticism of the younger generation. Arina Vlasyevna had had time to dress; she had put on a high cap with silk ribbons and a pale blue flowered shawl. She broke down again as soon as she caught sight of her Enyusha, but her husband had no need to admonish her; she made haste to wipe away her tears herself, for fear of spotting her shawl. Only the young men ate anything; the master and mistress of the house had dined long ago. Fedka waited at table, obviously encumbered by the novelty of boots; he was assisted by a woman of a masculine cast of face and one eye, by name Anfisushka, who performed the duties of housekeeper, poultry-woman, and laundress. Vassily Ivanovich walked up and down during the whole of dinner, and with a perfectly happy, positively beatific countenance, talked about the serious anxiety he felt at Napoleon III's policy, and the intricacy of the Italian question. Arina Vlasyevna took no notice of Arkady; leaning on her little closed fist, her round face, to which the full cherry-colored lips and the little moles on the cheeks and over the eyebrows gave a very simple, good-natured expression, she did not take her eyes off her son, and kept sighing;

6. "to the fathers" (that is, died).

she was dying to know for how long he had come, but she was afraid to ask him.

"What if he stays for two days," she thought, and her heart sank. After the roast Vassily Ivanovich disappeared for an instant, and returned with an opened half-bottle of champagne. "Here," he cried, "though we do live in the wilds, we have something to make merry with on festive occasions!" He filled three champagne glasses and a little wineglass, proposed the health of "our inestimable guests," and at once tossed off his glass in military fashion. He made Arina Vlasyevna drink her wineglass to the last drop. When the time came in due course for preserves, Arkady, who could not bear anything sweet, thought it his duty, however, to taste four different kinds which had been freshly made, all the more as Bazarov flatly refused them and began at once smoking a cigar. Then tea arrived—with cream, butter, and biscuits; then Vassily Ivanovich took them all into the garden to admire the beauty of the evening. As they passed a garden seat he whispered to Arkady—

"This is the spot where I love to philosophise as I watch the sunset; it suits a recluse like me. And there, a little farther off, I have planted some of the trees beloved of Horace."

"What trees?" asked Bazarov, overhearing.

"Why acacias, of course."

Bazarov began to yawn.

"I imagine it's time our travellers were in the arms of Morpheus," observed Vassily Ivanovich.

"That is, it's time for bed," Bazarov put in. "That's a sound idea. It is time, certainly."

As he said good-night to his mother, he kissed her on the forehead, while she embraced him, and stealthily behind his back she gave him her blessing three times. Vassily Ivanovich conducted Arkady to his room, and wished him "as refreshing repose as I enjoyed at your happy age." And Arkady did in fact sleep excellently in his bathhouse; there was a smell of mint in it, and two crickets behind the stove rivalled each other in their drowsy chirping. Vassily Ivanovich went from Arkady's room to his study, and perching on the sofa at his son's feet, he was looking forward to chatting with him; but Bazarov at once sent him away, saying he was sleepy, and did not fall asleep till morning. With wide open eyes he stared vindictively into the darkness; the memories of childhood had no power over him; and besides, he had not yet had time to get rid of his recent bitter impressions. Arina Vlasyevna first prayed to her heart's content, then she had a long, long conversation with Anfisushka, who stood stockstill before her mistress, and fixing her solitary eye upon her, communicated in a mysterious whisper all her observations and conjectures in regard to Evgeny Vassilyich. The old lady's head was giddy with happiness and wine and cigar smoke: her husband tried to talk to her, but with a wave of his hand gave it up in despair.

Arina Vlasyevna was a genuine Russian gentlewoman of the olden times; she ought to have lived two centuries before, in the days of old Muscovy. She was very devout and emotional, believed in fortune-telling, charms, dreams, and omens of every possible kind; she believed in the prophecies of holy fools, in house-spirits, in wood-spirits, in unlucky meetings, in the evil eye, in popular remedies, she ate specially prepared salt on Holy Thursday, and believed that the end of the world was near; she believed that if on Easter Sunday the candles did not go out during the all night mass, then there would be a good crop of buckwheat, and that a mushroom will not grow after a human eye has seen it; she believed that the devil likes to be where there is water, and that every Jew has a blood-stained spot on his breast; she was afraid of mice, of snakes, of frogs, of sparrows, of leeches, of thunder, of cold water, of drafts, of horses, of goats, of red-haired people, and black cats and she regarded crickets and dogs as unclean beasts; she never ate veal, doves, crayfishes, cheese, asparagus, artichokes, hares, nor water-melons, because a cut water-melon suggested the head of John the Baptist, and she could not speak of oysters without a shudder; she was fond of eating—and fasted rigidly; she slept ten hours out of the twenty four—and never went to bed at all if Vassily Ivanovich had so much as a headache; she had never read a single book except *Alexis or the Cottage in the Forest;* [7] she wrote one, or at the most two letters in a year, but knew what she was about in running the household, preserving, and jam-making, though she never touched a thing with her own hands, and was generally disinclined to move from her place. Arina Vlasyevna was very kindhearted, and in her way not at all stupid. She knew that the world is divided into masters whose duty it is to command, and simple folk whose duty it is to serve them—and so she felt no repugnance to servility and prostrations to the ground; but she treated those in subjection to her kindly and gently, never let a single beggar go away empty-handed, and never spoke ill of any one, though she was fond of gossiping now and then. In her youth she had been pretty, had played the clavichord, and spoken French a little; but in the course of many years' wanderings with her husband, whom she had married against her will, she had grown stout, and forgotten both music and French. She loved and feared

7. A sentimental novel by Ducray–Dumesnil (1761–1819), very popular in the first third of the nineteenth century in Russia.

her son unutterably; she had given up the management of the property to Vassily Ivanovich—and now did not interfere in anything; she used to groan, flutter her handkerchief, and raise her eyebrows higher and higher with horror as soon as her old husband began to discuss the impending government reforms and his own plans. She was apprehensive, constantly expecting some great misfortune, and began to weep as soon as she remembered anything sorrowful. . . . Such women are not common nowadays. God knows whether we ought to rejoice!

XXI

On getting up Arkady opened the window, and the first object that met his view was Vassily Ivanovich. In an Oriental dressing-gown girt round the waist with a pocket-handkerchief he was industriously digging in his garden. He perceived his young visitor, and leaning on his spade, he called, 'The best of health to you! How have you slept?"

"Splendidly,' answered Arkady.

"Here am I, as you see, like some Cincinnatus,[8] marking out a bed for late turnips. The time has come now—and thank God for it!—when every one ought to obtain his sustenance with his own hands; it's useless to reckon on others; one must labor oneself. And it turns out that Jean-Jacques Rousseau was right. Half an hour ago, my dear young gentleman, you might have seen me in a totally different position. One peasant woman, who complained of looseness—that's how they express it, but in our language, dysentery—I . . . how can I express it best? I administered opium; and for another I extracted a tooth. I proposed an anæsthetic to her . . . but she would not consent. All that I do *gratis—anamatyer* [9] I'm used to it, though; you see, I'm a plebeian, *homo novus*—not one of the old stock, not like my spouse. . . . Wouldn't you like to come this way into the shade, to breathe the morning freshness a little before tea?"

Arkady went out to him.

"Welcome once again," said Vassily Ivanovich, raising his hand in a military salute to the greasy skull-cap which covered his head. "You, I know, are accustomed to luxury, to amusements, but even the great ones of this world do not disdain to spend a brief space under a cottage roof."

"Good heavens," protested Arkady, "as though I were one of the great ones of this world! And I'm not accustomed to luxury."

"Pardon me, pardon me," rejoined Vassily Ivanovich with a polite

---

8. Cincinnatus returned to his farm after saving the Roman army and state. He culti- vated the land with his own hands.
9. That is, *en amateur*—"as a hobby."

simper. "Though I am laid on the shelf now, I have knocked about
the world too—I can tell a bird by its flight. I am something of
a psychologist, too, in my own way, and a physiognomist. If I had
not, I will venture to say, been endowed with that gift, I should
have come to grief long ago; I should have stood no chance, a
poor man like me. I tell you without flattery, I am sincerely
delighted at the friendship I observe between you and my son. I
have just seen him; he got up as he usually does—no doubt you
are aware of it—very early, and went for a ramble about the
neighborhood. Permit me to inquire—have you known my son
long?"

"Since last winter."

"Indeed. And permit me to question you further—but hadn't
we better sit down? Permit me, as a father, to ask without reserve,
what do you think of my Evgeny?"

"Your son is one of the most remarkable men I have ever met,"
Arkady answered emphatically.

Vassily Ivanovich's eyes suddenly opened wide, and his cheeks
were suffused with a faint flush. The spade fell out of his hand.

"And so you expect," he began . . .

"I'm convinced," Arkady put in, "that your son has a great
future before him; that he will do honor to your name. I've been
certain of that ever since I first met him."

"How . . . how was that?" Vassily Ivanovich articulated with
an effort. His wide mouth was relaxed in a triumphant smile,
which would not leave it.

"Would you like me to tell you how we met?"

"Yes . . . and altogether. . . ."

Arkady began to tell his tale, and to talk of Bazarov with
even greater warmth, even greater enthusiasm than he had done
on the evening when he danced the mazurka with Odintsov.

Vassily Ivanovich listened and listened, blew his nose, rolled
his handkerchief up into a ball in both his hands, cleared his
throat, ruffled up his hair, and at last could stand it no longer;
he bent down to Arkady and kissed him on his shoulder. "You
have made me completely happy," he said, never ceasing to
smile. "I ought to tell you, I . . . idolize my son; I won't speak
of my old wife—we all know what mothers are!—but I dare not
show my feelings before him, because he doesn't like it. He is
averse to every kind of demonstration of feeling; many people even
find fault with him for such firmness of character, and regard it
as a proof of pride or lack of feeling, but men like him ought
not to be judged by the common standard, ought they? And
here, for example, many another in his place would have been a
constant drag on his parents; but he, would you believe it, has

never from the day he was born taken a farthing more than he could help, that's God's truth!"

"He is a disinterested, honest man," observed Arkady.

"Exactly so; he is disinterested. And I don't only idolize him, Arkady Nikolaich, I am proud of him, and the height of my ambition is that some day there will be the following lines in his biography: 'The son of a simple army-doctor, who was, however, capable of divining his greatness betimes, and spared nothing for his education . . .' " The old man's voice broke.

Arkady pressed his hand.

"What do you think," inquired Vassily Ivanovich, after a short silence, "it won't be in medicine that he will attain the celebrity you anticipate for him?"

"Of course not in medicine, though even in that department he will be one of the leading scientific men."

"In what then, Arkady Nikolaich?"

"It would be hard to say now, but he will be famous."

"He will be famous!" repeated the old man, and he sank into a reverie.

"Arina Vasyevna sent me to call you in to tea," announced Anfisushka, coming by with an immense dish of ripe raspberries.

Vassily Ivanovich started. "And will there be cooled cream for the raspberries?"

"Yes, sir."

"Cold now, mind! Don't stand on ceremony, Arkady Nikolaich; take some more. How is it Evgeny doesn't come?"

"I'm here," Bazarov's voice was heard from Arkady's room.

Vassily Ivanovich turned round quickly. "Aha! you wanted to pay a visit to your friend; but you were too late, *amice*, and I have already had a long conversation with him. Now we must go in to tea, mother summons us. By the way, I want to have a little talk with you.

"What about?"

"There's a peasant here; he's suffering from icterus. . . ."

"You mean jaundice?"

"Yes, a chronic and very obstinate case of icterus. I prescribed centaury and St. John's wort, ordered him to eat carrots, and gave him soda; but all that's merely *palliative* measures; we need something more drastic. Though you do laugh at medicine, I am certain you can give me practical advice. But we will talk of that later. Now come in to tea."

Vassily Ivanovich jumped up briskly from the garden seat, and hummed from *Robert le Diable*—[1]

---

1. A popular opera (1831) by Meyerbeer (1791–1864).

"The rule, the rule we 'set ourselves,
To live, to live for pleasure!"

"Singular vitality!" observed Bazarov, going away from the window.

It was midday. The sun was burning hot behind a thin veil of unbroken whitish clouds. Everything was hushed; there was no sound but the cocks crowing provocatively at one another in the village, producing in every one who heard them a strange sense of drowsiness and ennui; and somewhere, high up in a tree-top, the incessant plaintive cheep of a young hawk. Arkady and Bazarov lay in the shade of a small haystack, putting under themselves a couple of armfuls of dry and rustling but still greenish and fragrant grass.

"That aspen," began Bazarov, "reminds me of my childhood; it grows at the edge of the clay-pits where the brickshed used to be, and in those days I believed firmly that that clay-pit and aspen possessed a peculiar talismanic power; I never felt bored near them. I did not understand then that I was not bored because I was a child. Well, now I'm grown up, the talisman's lost its power."

"How long did you live here altogether?" asked Arkady.

"Two years on end; then we travelled about. We led a roving life, wandering from town to town for the most part."

"And has this house been standing long?"

"Yes. My grandfather built it—my mother's father."

"Who was he—your grandfather?"

"Devil knows. Some second-major. He served with Suvorov, and was always telling stories about the the crossing of the Alps. He was probably lying."

"So that's why you have a portrait of Suvorov hanging in the drawing-room. I like these little houses like yours; they're so warm and old-fashioned; and there's always a special sort of scent about them."

"A smell of lamp-oil and clover," Bazarov remarked, yawning. "And the flies in those dear little houses. . . . Faugh!"

"Tell me," began Arkady, after a brief pause, "were they strict with you when you were a child?"

'You can see what my parents are like. They're not the strict sort."

"Do you love them, Evgeny?"

"I do, Arkady."

"How they love you!"

Bazarov was silent for a while. "Do you know what I'm thinking about?" he brought out at last, clasping his hands behind his head.

"No. What is it?"

"I'm thinking life is a happy thing for my parents. My father at sixty is fussing around, talking about 'palliative' measures, doctoring people, playing the bountiful master with the peasants—having a fine time, in short; and my mother's happy too; her day's so chockful of duties of all sorts, and sighs and groans that she's no time even to think of herself; while I . . ."

"While you?"

"I think; here I lie under a haystack. . . . The tiny space I occupy is so infinitely small in comparison with the rest of space, in which I am not, and which has nothing to do with me; and the period of time in which it is my lot to live is so petty beside the eternity in which I have not been, and shall not be. . . . And in this atom, this mathematical point, the blood circulates, the brain works and wants something. . . . Isn't it hideous? Isn't it petty?"

"Allow me to remark that what you're saying applies to men in general."

"You are right," Bazarov cut in. "I was going to say that they now—my parents, I mean—are absorbed and don't trouble themselves about their own insignificance, its stench doesn't sicken them . . . while I . . . I feel nothing but weariness and malice."

"Malice? Why malice?"

"Why? How can you ask why? Have you forgotten?"

"I remember everything, but still I don't admit that you have any right to be malicious. You're unlucky, I'll allow, but . . ."

"Pooh! then you, Arkady Nikolaevich, I can see, regard love like all modern young men; cluck, cluck, cluck you call to the hen, but if the hen comes near you, you take to your heels! I'm not like that. But that's enough of that. What can't be helped, it's shameful to talk about." He turned over on his side. "Aha! there goes a valiant ant dragging off a half-dead fly. Take her, brother, take her! Don't pay attention to her resistance; it's your privilege as an animal to be free from the sentiment of pity—make the most of it—not like us conscientious self-destructive animals!"

"You shouldn't say that, Evgeny! When have you destroyed yourself!"

Bazarov raised his head. "That's the only thing I pride myself on. I haven't crushed myself, so a skirt can't crush me. Amen! It's all over! You shall not hear another word from me about it."

Both friends lay for some time in silence.

"Yes," began Bazarov, "man's a strange animal. When one gets a view from the side, sort of, or from a distance at the dull life our 'fathers' lead here, one thinks, What could be better? You eat and drink, and know you are acting in the most reasonable, most judicious manner. But no, boredom will devour you. One wants to have to do with people if only to abuse them."

"One ought so to order one's life that every moment in it should be of significance," Arkady affirmed reflectively.

"I dare, say! What's of significance is sweet, however mistaken; one could make up one's mind to what's insignificant even. But pettiness, pettiness, that's what's insufferable."

"Pettiness doesn't exist for a man so long as he refuses to recognise it."

"H'm . . . what you've just said is a 'commonplace in reverse.' "

"What? What do you mean by that term?"

"I'll tell you: to say that education is beneficial, for instance, that's a commonplace; but to say that education is injurious, that's a commonplace in reverse. There's more style about it, so to say, but in reality it's one and the same."

"And the truth is—where, which side?"

"Where? Like an echo I answer, 'Where?' "

"You're in a melancholy mood today, Evgeny."

"Really? The sun must have softened me, I suppose, and one shouldn't eat so many raspberries either."

"In that case, a nap's not a bad thing," observed Arkady.

"Certainly; only don't look at me; every man's face is stupid when he's asleep."

"But isn't it all the same to you what people think of you?"

"I don't know what to say to you. A real man ought not to care; a real man is one whom it's no use thinking about, whom one must either obey or hate."

"That's strange! I don't hate anybody," observed Arkady, after a moment's thought.

"And I hate so many. You are a soft-hearted, sluggish creature; how could you hate any one? . . . You're timid; you don't rely on yourself much."

"And you," interrupted Arkady, "do you rely on yourself very much? Do you have a high opinion of yourself?"

Bazarov paused. "When I meet a man who can hold his own beside me," he said, dwelling on every syllable, "then I'll change my opinion of myself. Yes, hatred! You said, for instance, to-day as we passed our bailiff Philip's cottage—it's the one that's so nice and clean—well, you said Russia will attain perfection when the poorest peasant has a hut like that, and every one of us ought to work to bring it about. . . . And I felt such a hatred for this poorest peasant, this Philip or Sidor, for whom I'm to be ready to jump out of my skin, and who won't even thank me for it . . . and what do I need his thanks for? Why, suppose he does live in a clean hut, while I'm pushing up daisies,—well what comes after that?"

"Enough, Evgeny . . . to listen to you to-day one would be driven to agree with those who reproach us for lack of principles."

"You talk like your uncle. There are no general principles— you've not made out that even yet! There are feelings. Everything depends on them."

"How so?"

"Why, just so. Take me, for instance. I maintain a negative attitude, by virtue of my sensations; I like to deny—my brain's made on that plan, and that's all! Why do I like chemistry? Why do you like apples?—also by virtue of our sensations. It's all the same thing. Men will never penetrate deeper than that. Not every one will tell you that, and, in fact, I won't tell you so another time."

"What, and is honesty a matter of the senses?"

"I should say so."

"Evgeny!" Arkady was beginning in a dejected voice . . .

"Well? What? You don't like it?" broke in Bazarov. "No, brother. If you've made up your mind to mow down everything, don't spare your own legs. But we've philosophized enough. 'Nature wafts the silence of sleep,' said Pushkin."

"He never said anything of the sort," protested Arkady.

"Well, if he didn't, as a poet he might have—and ought to have said it. By the way, he must have been a military man."

"Pushkin was never a military man!"

"Why, on every page of him there's, 'To arms! to arms! for Russia's honor!' "

"Why, what stories you invent! I declare, it's outright calumny."

"Calumny? My, what a grave matter! What a word he's found to frighten me with! Whatever charge you make against a man, you may be certain he deserves twenty times worse than that in reality."

"We had better go to sleep," said Arkady, vexed.

"With the greatest pleasure," answered Bazarov. But neither of them slept. A feeling almost of hostility came over both young men. Five minutes later, they opened their eyes and glanced at one another in silence.

"Look," said Arkady suddenly, "a dry maple leaf has come off and is falling to earth; its movement is exactly like a butterfly's flight. Isn't it strange? Gloom and death—like brightness and life."

"Oh, my friend, Arkady Nikolaich!" cried Bazarov, "one thing

I beg of you; no fine talk."

"I talk as best I can. . . . And, I declare, it's perfect despotism. An idea came into my head; why shouldn't I utter it?"

"Yes; and why shouldn't I utter my ideas? I think that fine talk's positively indecent."

"And what is decent? Abuse?"

"Ha! ha! I see you really do intend to walk in your uncle's footsteps. How pleased that idiot would have been if he had heard you!"

"What did you call Pavel Petrovich?"

"I called him, very justly, an idiot."

"But this is intolerable!" cried Arkady.

"Aha! family feeling spoke there," Bazarov commented coolly. "I've noticed how obstinately it sticks to people. A man's ready to give up everything and break with every prejudice; but to admit, for instance, that his brother, who steals handkerchiefs, is a thief —that's too much for him. And when one comes to think of it: *my* brother, *mine*—and no genius . . . that's an idea no one can swallow."

"It was a simple sense of justice spoke in me and not family feeling at all," retorted Arkady passionately. "But since that's a sense you don't understand, since you haven't that *sensation*, you can't judge it."

"In other words, Arkady Kirsanov is too exalted for my comprehension. I bow down before him and say no more."

"Don't, please, Evgeny; we shall really quarrel at last."

"Ah, Arkady! do me a favor, let's really quarrel for once till we're both laid out dead, until we're destroyed."

"But then perhaps we should end by . . ."

"Fighting?" put in Bazarov. "So what? Here, on the hay, in these idyllic surroundings, far from the world and people's eyes, it wouldn't matter. But you'd be no match for me. I'd have you by the throat in a minute."

Bazarov spread out his long, tough fingers. . . . Arkady turned round and prepared, as though in jest, to resist. . . . But his friend's face struck him as so vindictive—there was such menace in grim earnest in the smile that distorted his lips and in his glittering eyes, that he instinctively felt afraid.

"Ah! so this is where you have got to!" the voice of Vassily Ivanovich was heard at that instant, and the old army-doctor appeared before the young men, garbed in a home-made linen pea-jacket, with a straw hat, also home-made, on his head. "I've been looking and looking for you. . . . Well, you've picked out a capital place, and you're excellently employed. Lying on the 'earth, gazing up to 'heaven.' Do you know, there's a special significance in that?"

"I never gaze up to heaven except when I want to sneeze," growled Bazarov, and turning to Arkady he added in an undertone. "Pity he interrupted us."

"Well, that's enough," whispered Arkady and stealthily pressed his friend's hand. But no friendship can long survive such collisions.

"I look at you, my youthful friends," Vassily Ivanovich was saying meantime, shaking his head, and leaning his folded arms on some sort of cunningly bent stick of his own making, with a Turk's figure for a top,—"I look, and I cannot refrain from admiration. You have so much strength, such youth in bloom, such abilities, such talents! Positively, Castor and Pollux." [2]

"Get along with you—going off into mythology!" commented Bazarov. "You can see at once that he was a great Latinist in his day! Why, I seem to remember, you gained the silver medal for Latin prose—didn't you?"

"The Dioscuri, the Dioscuri!" repeated Vassily Ivanovich.

"Come, enough, father; don't get sentimental."

"Once in a great while it's surely permissible," murmured the old man. "However, I have not been seeking for you, gentlemen, to pay you compliments; but with the object, in the first place, of announcing to you that we shall soon be dining; and secondly, I wanted to prepare you, Evgeny. . . . You are a sensible man, you know the world, and you know what women are, and consequently you will excuse. . . . Your mother wished to have a Te Deum sung on the occasion of your arrival. You must not imagine that I am inviting you to attend this thanksgiving—it is finished now; but Father Alexey . . ."

"The parson?"

"Well, yes, the priest; he . . . is to dine with us. . . . I did not anticipate this, and did not even approve of it . . . but it somehow came about . . . he did not understand me. . . . And, well . . . Arina Vlasyevna . . . Besides, he's a worthy, reasonable man."

"He won't eat my share at dinner, I suppose?" queried Bazarov.

Vassily Ivanovich laughed. "How you talk!"

"Well, that's all I ask. I'm ready to sit down to table with any man."

Vassily Ivanovich set his hat straight. "I was certain before I spoke," he said, "that you were above any kind of prejudice. Here am I, an old man of sixty-two, and I have none." (Vassily Ivanovich did not dare to confess that he had himself desired the thanksgiving service. He was just as religious as his wife.) "And Father Alexey very much wanted to make your acquaintance. You will like

---

2. Mythological heroes, sons of Zeus and Leda, inseparable friends. They are the Dioscuri.

him, you'll see. He's no objection even to cards, and he sometimes—but this is between ourselves . . . positively smokes a pipe."

"All right. We'll have a round of whist after dinner, and I'll
clean him out."

"He! he! he! We shall see! That remains to be seen."

"What? Are you up to your old tricks?" said Bazarov, with a
peculiar emphasis.

Vassily Ivanovich's bronzed cheeks were suffused with an uneasy flush.

"For shame, Evgeny. . . . Let bygones be bygones. Well, I'm
ready to acknowledge before this gentleman I had that passion in
my youth; and I have paid for it too! How hot it is, though! Let
me sit down with you. I won't be in your way, I hope?"

"Oh, not at all," answered Arkady.

Vassily Ivanovich lowered himself, sighing, into the hay. "Your
present quarters remind me, my dear sirs," he began, "of my
military bivouacking existence, the dressing stations, somewhere like
this under a haystack, and we were thankful even for that." He
sighed. "I have had many, many experiences in my life. For
example, if you will allow me, I will tell you a curious episode
of the plague in Bessarabia."

"For which you got the Vladimir cross?" put in Bazarov. "We
know, we know. . . . By the way, why is it you're not wearing it?"

"Why, I told you that I have no prejudices," muttered Vassily
Ivanovich (he had only the evening before had the red ribbon
picked off his coat), and he proceeded to relate the episode of
the plague. "Why, he's fallen asleep," he whispered all at once
to Arkady, pointing to Evgeny, and winking good-naturedly. "Evgeny! get up," he went on aloud. "Let's go in to dinner."

Father Alexey, a good-looking stout man with thick, carefully combed hair, with an embroidered girdle round his lilac
silk cassock, appeared to be a man of much tact and adaptability.
He made haste to be the first to offer his hand to Arkady and
Bazarov, as though understanding beforehand that they did not
want his blessing, and he behaved himself in general without constraint. He neither derogated from his own dignity, nor gave
offence to others; he vouchsafed a passing smile at the seminary
Latin, and stood up for his bishop; drank two small glasses of
wine, but refused a third; accepted a cigar from Arkady, but did
not proceed to smoke it, saying he would take it home with him.
The only thing not quite agreeable about him was a way he had
of constantly raising his hand with care and deliberation to catch
the flies on his face, sometimes succeeding in smashing them. He
took his seat at the card table, expressing his satisfaction at doing

so in measured terms, and ended by winning two and a half rubles from Bazarov in paper money; [3] they had no idea of even reckoning in silver in the house of Arina Vlasyevna. . . . She was sitting, as before, near her son (she did not play cards), her cheek, as before, propped on her little fist; she only got up to order some new dainty to be served. She was afraid to caress Bazarov, and he gave her no encouragement, he did not invite her caresses; and besides, Vassily Ivanovich had advised her not to "trouble" him too much. "Young men are not fond of that sort of thing," he declared to her. (It's needless to say what the dinner was like that day; Timofeich in person had galloped off at early dawn for a special variety of Circassian beef; the bailiff had gone off in another direction for turbot, gremille, and crayfish; for mushrooms alone forty-two kopecks had been paid the peasant women in copper); but Arina Vlasyevna's eyes, bent steadfastly on Bazarov, did not express only devotion and tenderness; in them was to be seen sorrow also, mingled with awe and curiosity; there was to be seen too a sort of humble reproachfulness.

Bazarov, however, was in no mood to analyse the exact expression of his mother's eyes; he seldom turned to her, and then only with some short question. Once he asked her for her hand "for luck"; she gently laid her soft, little hand on his rough, broad palm.

"Well," she asked, after waiting a little, "has it been any use?"

"Worse luck than ever," he answered, with a careless laugh.

"He plays too rashly," pronounced Father Alexey, as it were compassionately, and he stroked his beard.

"Napoleon's rule, good Father, Napoleon's rule," put in Vassily Ivanovich, leading an ace.

"It brought him to St. Helena, though," observed Father Alexey, as he trumped the ace.

"Wouldn't you like some currant tea, Enyusha?" inquired Arina Vlasyevna.

Bazarov merely shrugged his shoulders.

"No!" he said to Arkady the next day, "I'm off from here tomorrow. I'm bored; I want to work, but I can't work here. I will come to your place again; I've left all my apparatus there, too. In your house one can at any rate shut oneself up. While here my father repeats to me, 'My study is at your disposal—nobody shall interfere with you,' and all the time he himself is never a step away. And I'm somehow ashamed to shut myself away from him.

3. A silver ruble (roughly fifty cents), the monetary standard, was worth three and a half paper rubles. There are one hundred kopeks in either ruble.

It's the same thing, too, with mother. I hear her sighing the other side of the wall, and when I go in to her, there is nothing to say to her."

"She will be very much grieved," observed Arkady, "and so will he."

"I shall come back again to them."

"When?"

"Why, when on my way to Petersburg."

"I feel particularly sorry for your mother."

"Why's that? Has she won your heart with berries or what?"

Arkady dropped his eyes. "You don't understand your mother, Evgeny. She's not only a very good woman, she's very clever really. This morning she talked to me for half-an-hour, and so sensibly, interestingly."

"I suppose she was expatiating upon me all the while?"

"We didn't talk only about you."

"Perhaps; an outsider sees more clearly. If a woman can keep up half-an-hour's conversation it's always a hopeful sign. But I'm going, all the same."

"It won't be very easy for you to break it to them."

"No, it won't be easy. Some demon drove me to tease my father to-day; he had one of his rent-paying peasants flogged the other day, and quite right too—yes, yes, you needn't look at me in such horror—he did quite right, because he's a terrible thief and drunkard; only my father had no idea that I, as they say, was cognizant of the facts. He was very embarrassed, and now, I'll have to upset him more than ever. . . . . Never mind! Never say die! He'll get over it!"

Bazarov said, "Never mind"; but the whole day passed before he could make up his mind to inform Vassily Ivanovich of his intentions. At last, when he was just saying good-night to him in the study, he observed, with a feigned yawn—

"Oh . . . I was almost forgetting to tell you. . . . Send to Fedot's for our horses to-morrow."

Vassily Ivanovich was dumfounded. "Is Mr. Kirsanov leaving us, then?"

"Yes; and I'm going with him."

Vassily Ivanovich positively reeled. "You are going?"

"Yes . . . I must. Make the arrangements about the horses, please."

"Very good. . . ." faltered the old man; "to Fedot's . . . very good . . . only . . . only . . . How is it?"

"I must go to stay with him for a little time. I will come back here again later."

"Ah! For a little time . . . very good." Vassily Ivanovich drew out his handkerchief, and, blowing his nose, doubled up almost to the ground. "Well . . . everything shall be done. I had thought you were to be with us . . . a little longer. Three days. . . . After three years, it's rather little; rather little, Evgeny!"

"But, I tell you, I'm coming back directly. It's necessary for me to go."

"Necessary. . . . Well! Duty before everything. So, you want the horses sent ahead? Very good. Arina and I, of course, did not anticipate this. She has just begged some flowers from a neighbor; she meant to decorate the room for you." (Vassily Ivanovich did not even mention that every morning almost at dawn he took counsel with Timofeich, standing with his bare feet in his slippers, and pulling out one dog's-eared ruble note after another, with trembling fingers, charged him with various purchases, with special reference to good things to eat, and to red wine, which, as far as he could observe, the young men liked very much.) "Freedom is the most important thing; that's my rule. . . . I don't want to hamper you . . . not . . ."

He suddenly ceased, and made for the door.

"We shall soon see each other again, father, really."

But Vassily Ivanovich, without turning round, merely waved his hand and was gone. When he got back to his bedroom he found his wife in bed, and began to say his prayers in a whisper, so as not to wake her up. She woke, however. "Is that you, Vassily Ivanovich?" she asked.

"Yes, mother."

"Have you come from Enyusha? Do you know, I'm afraid of his not being comfortable on that sofa. I told Anfisushka to put him your travelling mattress and the new pillows; I should have given him our feather-bed, but I seem to remember he doesn't like too soft a bed. . . ."

"Never mind, mother; don't worry yourself. He's all right. Lord, have mercy on me, a sinner," he went on with his prayer in a low voice. Vassily Ivanovich was sorry for his old wife; he did not mean to tell her over night what a sorrow there was in store for her.

Bazarov and Arkady set off the next day. From early morning all was dejection in the house; Anfisushka let the tray slip out of her hands; even Fedka was bewildered, and finished by taking off his boots. Vassily Ivanovich was more fussy than ever; he was obviously trying to put on a brave front, talked loudly, and stamped with his feet, but his face looked haggard, and his eyes were continually avoiding his son. Arina Vlasyevna was crying quietly; she was utterly crushed, and could not have controlled herself at all if her husband had not spent two whole hours early in the morning exhorting her. When Bazarov, after repeated promises to come back certainly not later than in a month's time, tore himself at last from the embraces detaining him, and took his seat in the coach; when the horses had started, the bell was ringing, and the wheels were turning round, and when it was no longer any good to look after them, and the dust had settled, and Timofeich, all bent and tottering as he walked, had crept back to his little room; when the old people were left alone in their little house, which seemed suddenly to have shrunken and grown decrepit too, Vassily Ivanovich, after a few more moments of hearty waving of his handkerchief on the porch, sank into a chair, and his head dropped on to his breast. "He has cast us off; he has forsaken us," he faltered; "forsaken us; he was dull with us. All by myself, like a finger, now, all by myself!" he said several times and each time thrust his hand out with the index finger separated from the rest. Then Arina Vlasyevna went up to him, and, leaning her grey head against his grey head, said, "There's no help for it, Vasya! A son is a piece cut off. He's like the falcon that flies home and flies away at his pleasure; while you and I are like mushrooms in the hollow of a tree, we sit side by side, and don't move from our place. Only I remain unchanged for you, forever, as you for me."

Vassily Ivanovich took his hands from his face and clasped his wife, his friend, more firmly than he had clasped her even in his youth; she comforted him in his grief.

XXII

In silence, only rarely exchanging a few insignificant words, our friends travelled as far as Fedot's. Bazarov was not altogether pleased with himself. Arkady was displeased with him. He was feeling, too, that causeless melancholy which is only known to very young people. The coachman changed the horses, and getting up on to the box, inquired, "To the right or to the left?"

Arkady started. The road to the right led to the town, and from there home; the road to the left led to Odintsov's.

He looked at Bazarov.

"Evgeny," he queried; "to the left?"

Bazarov turned away. "What folly is this?" he muttered.

"I know it's folly," answered Arkady. . . . "But what does that matter? It's not the first time."

Bazarov pulled his cap down over his brows. "As you like," he said at last. "Turn to the left," shouted Arkady.

The coach rolled away in the direction of Nikolskoe. But having resolved on folly, the friends were even more obstinately silent than before, and seemed positively angry.

The friends could perceive that they had acted injudiciously in giving way so suddenly to a passing impulse merely by the way the butler met them on the steps of Odintsov's house. They were evidently not expected. They sat for a rather long while, in the drawing-room looking rather foolish. Odintsov came in to them at last. She greeted them with her customary politeness, but was surprised at their hasty return, and, so far as could be judged from the deliberation of her gestures and words, she was not over-pleased at it. They hastened to announce that they had only called on their way, and had to go farther, to the town, within four hours. She confined herself to a slight exclamation, begged Arkady to remember her to his father, and sent for her aunt. The princess appeared very sleepy, which gave her wrinkled old face an even more ill-natured expression. Katya was not well; she did not leave her room. Arkady suddenly realised that he was at least as anxious to see Katya as Anna Sergeyevna herself. The four hours were spent in insignificant discussion of one thing and another; Anna Sergeyevna both listened and spoke without a smile. It was only at the very parting that her former friendliness seemed, as it were, to revive.

"I have an attack of spleen just now," she said; "but you must not pay attention to that, and come again—I say this to both of you—some time later."

Both Bazarov and Arkady responded with a silent bow, took their seats in the coach, and without stopping again anywhere went straight home to Marino, where they arrived safely on the evening of the following day. During the whole course of the journey neither one nor the other even mentioned the name of Odintsov; Bazarov in particular scarcely opened his mouth, and kept staring to the side away from the road, with a kind of exasperated intensity.

At Marino every one was exceedingly delighted to see them. The prolonged absence of his son had begun to make Nikolai Petrovich uneasy; he uttered a cry of joy, and bounced up and down on the sofa, dangling his legs, when Fenichka ran to him with sparkling eyes, and informed him of the arrival of the "young gentlemen"; even Pavel Petrovich was conscious of some degree of agreeable excitement, and smiled condescendingly as he shook hands with the returned wanderers. Talk and questions followed; Arkady talked most, especially at supper, which was prolonged long after midnight. Nikolai Petrovich ordered up several bottles of porter which had just been sent from Moscow, and himself went on such a spree that his cheeks were crimson, and he kept laughing a half-childish, half-nervous little chuckle. Even the servants were infected by the general gaiety. Dunyasha ran up and down like one possessed, and was continually slamming doors; while Peter was still attempting to strum a Cossack waltz on the guitar after two in the morning. The strings gave forth a sweet and plaintive sound in the still air; but with the exception of a small preliminary flourish, nothing came of the cultured valet's efforts; nature had given him no more musical talent than it had anything else.

Yet things were not going overharmoniously at Marino, and poor Nikolai Petrovich was having a bad time. Difficulties on the farm multiplied every day, dreary senseless difficulties. Trouble with the hired laborers had become insupportable. Some asked for their wages to be settled or for an increase of wages, while others made off with the wages they had received in advance: the horses fell sick; the harness fell to pieces as though it were burnt, the work was done carelessly; a threshing machine that had been ordered from Moscow turned out to be useless because of its great weight, another was ruined the first time it was used; half the cattle sheds were burnt down through an old blind woman on the farm going with a burning brand in windy weather to fumigate her cow . . . the old woman, it is true, maintained that the whole mischief could be traced to the master's plan of introducing newfangled cheeses and dairy-products. The overseer suddenly turned lazy and began to grow fat, as every Russian grows fat when he gets a snug berth. When he caught sight of Nikolai Petrovich in the distance, he would fling a stick at a passing pig or threaten a half-naked urchin to show his zeal, but the rest of the time he was generally asleep. The peasants who had been put on the quitrent system did not bring their money at the time due and stole the forest-timber; almost every night the keepers caught peasants' horses in the meadows of the "farm," and sometimes forcibly bore them off. Nikolai Petrovich first set a monetary fine for damages, but the matter usually ended after the horses had been kept a day or two on the master's forage by their returning to their owners. To top it all, the peasants began quarrelling among themselves; brothers asked for a division of property, their wives could not get on together in one house; all of a sudden the squabble, as though at a given signal, came to a head, and they would come running to the counting-house steps, and crawling to the master, often drunken and with battered face, demanding justice and judgment; then arose an uproar and clamor, the shrill wailing of the women mixed with the curses of the men. Then one had to examine the contending parties, and shout oneself hoarse, knowing all the while that one could never anyway arrive at a just decision. . . . There were not hands enough for the harvest; a neighboring petty landowner with the most benevolent countenance contracted to supply him with reapers for a commission of two rubles an acre, and cheated him in the most shameless fashion; his peasant women demanded unheard-of sums, and the corn meanwhile went to waste; and here they were not getting on with the mowing, and there the Council of Guardians threatened and demanded prompt payment, in full, of interest due. . . .

"I can do nothing!" Nikolai Petrovich cried more than once in despair. "I can't flog them myself, and as for calling in the police captain, my principles don't allow it, but you can do nothing with them without the fear of punishment!"

"*Du calme, du calme,*" Pavel Petrovich would remark to this, but even he hummed to himself, frowning and tugged at his moustache.

Bazarov held aloof from these "wranglings," and indeed as a guest it was not for him to meddle in other people's business. The day after his arrival at Marino, he set to work on his frogs, his infusoria, and his chemical compositions, and was forever busy with them. Arkady, on the contrary, thought it his duty, if not to help his father, at least to make a show of being ready to help him. He listened to him patiently, and once offered him some advice, not with any idea of its being acted upon, but to show his interest. Farming did not arouse any aversion in him; he used even to dream with pleasure of agricultural work, but at this time his brain was swarming with other ideas. Arkady, to his own astonishment, thought incessantly of Nikolskoe; in former days he would simply have shrugged his shoulders if any one had told him that he could ever feel dull under the same roof as Bazarov—and that roof his father's! But he actually was dull and longed to get away. He tried to go on long walks till he was tired, but that was no use. In conversation with his father one day, he found out that Nikolai Petrovich had in his possession rather interesting letters, written by Odintsov's mother to his wife, and he gave him no rest till he got hold of the letters, for which Nikolai Petrovich had to rummage in twenty different drawers and boxes. Having gained possession of these half-crumbling papers, Arkady felt soothed, as it were, just as though he had caught a glimpse of the goal towards which he ought now to go. "I mean that for both of you," he was constantly whispering—she had added that herself! "I'll go, I'll go, hang it all!" but he recalled the last visit, the cold reception, and the embarrassment he had felt and timidity got the better of him. The "go-ahead" feeling of youth, the secret desire to try his luck, to prove his own worth without the protection of any one whatever, finally won out. Before ten days had passed after his return to Marino, on the pretext of studying the working of the Sunday schools, he galloped off to town again, and from there to Nikolskoe. Constantly urging the driver on, he flew along, like a young officer riding to battle; and he felt both frightened and light-hearted, and was breathless with impatience. "The chief thing is—one mustn't think," he kept repeating to himself. His driver happened to be a lad of spirit; he halted before every public house, saying, "A drink or not a drink?" but, to make up for it, when he had drunk he did not spare his horses. At last the lofty roof of the familiar house came in sight. . . . "What am I doing?" flashed through Arkady's head. "Well, there's no turning back now!" The three horses galloped in unison; the driver whooped and whistled at them. And now the bridge was groaning under the hoofs and wheels, and now the avenue of pruned pines seemed running to meet them. . . . There was a glimpse of a woman's pink dress against the dark green, a young face peeped out from under the light fringe of a parasol. . . . He recognised Katya, and she recognised him. Arkady told the driver to stop the galloping horses, leaped out of the carriage, and went up to her. "It's you!" she murmured, gradually flushing all over; "let us go to my sister, she's here in the garden; she will be pleased to see you."

Katya led Arkady into the garden. His meeting with her struck him as a particularly happy omen; he was as delighted to see her, as though she were very close to him. Everything had happened so splendidly; no butler, no formal announcement. At a turn in the path he caught sight of Anna Sergeyevna. She was standing with her back to him. Hearing footsteps, she turned slowly round.

Arkady began to feel confused again, but the first words she uttered soothed him at once. "Welcome back, runaway!" she said in her even, caressing voice, and came to meet him, smiling and squinting, frowning to keep the sun and wind out of her eyes. "Where did you pick him up, Katya?"

"I have brought you something, Anna Sergeyevna," he began, "which you certainly don't expect."

"You have brought yourself; that's best of all."

XXIII

Having seen Arkady off with ironical compassion, and given him to understand that he was not in the least deceived as to the real object of his journey, Bazarov shut himself up in complete solitude; he was overtaken by a fever for work. He did not dispute now with Pavel Petrovich, especially as the latter assumed an excessively aristocratic demeanor in his presence, and expressed his opinions more in inarticulate sounds than in words. Only on one occasion Pavel Petrovich fell into a controversy with the *nihilist* on the subject of the question then much discussed of the rights of the nobles of the Baltic province; but suddenly he stopped of his own accord, remarking with chilly politeness, "However, we cannot understand one another; I, at least, have not the honor of understanding you."

"I should think not!" cried Bazarov. "A man's capable of understanding anything—how the ether vibrates, and what's going on in the sun—but how any other man can blow his nose differently from him, that he's incapable of understanding."

"What, is that supposed to be clever?" observed Pavel Petrovich inquiringly, and he went off to one side.

However, he sometimes asked permission to be present at Bazarov's experiments, and once even placed his perfumed face, washed with the very best soap, to the microscope to see how a transparent infusoria swallowed a green speck, and busily munched it with two very rapid sort of clappers which were in its throat. Nikolai Petrovich visited Bazarov much oftener than his brother; he would have come every day, as he expressed it, to "study," if his worries on the farm had not kept him too busy. He did not hinder the young scientist; he would sit down somewhere in a corner of the room and look on attentively, occasionally permitting himself a discreet question. During dinner and supper he would try to turn the conversation to physics, geology, or chemistry, seeing that all other topics, even agriculture, to say nothing of politics might lead, if not to collisions, at least to mutual unpleasantness. Nikolai Petrovich surmised that his brother's dislike for Bazarov had not diminished at all. An unimportant incident, among many others, confirmed his surmises. Cholera began to appear here and there in the neighborhood, and even "carried off" two persons from Marino itself. One night Pavel Petrovich fell very ill. He was in torment till morning, but did not have recourse to Bazarov's skill. And when he met him for the following day, in reply to his question, "Why he had not sent for him?" answered, still quite pale, but scrupulously brushed and shaved, "Why, I seem to recollect you said yourself you didn't believe in medicine." So the days went by. Bazarov went on working obstinately and grimly . . . and meanwhile there was in Nikolai Petrovich's house one creature to whom, if he did not open his heart he at least was glad to talk. . . . That creature was Fenichka.

He used to meet her for the most part early in the morning, in the garden, or the yard; he never went to her room to see her, and she had only once been to his door to inquire—ought she to let Mitya have his bath or not? It was not only that she confided in him, that she was not afraid of him—she was positively freer and more at her ease in her behavior with him than with Nikolai Petrovich himself. It is hard to say how it came about; perhaps it was because she unconsciously felt the absence in Bazarov of anything aristocratic, of all that superiority which at once attracts and frightens. In her eyes he was both an excellent doctor and a simple man. She looked after her baby without constraint in his presence; and once when she was suddenly attacked with giddiness and headache, she took a spoonful of medicine from his hand. Before Nikolai Petrovich she kept, as it were, at a distance from Bazarov; she acted in this way not from hypocrisy, but from a kind of feeling of propriety. She was more afraid of Pavel Petrovich than ever; for some time he had begun to watch her, and would suddenly make his appearance, as though he sprang out of the earth behind her back, in his English suit, with his immovable vigilant face, and his hands in his pockets. "It's like being doused with cold water," Fenichka complained to Dunyasha, and the latter sighed in response, and thought of another "heartless" man. Bazarov, without the least suspicion of the fact, had become the *cruel tyrant* of her heart.

Fenichka liked Bazarov; but he liked her too. His face was positively transformed when he talked to her; it assumed a bright, almost kind expression, and his habitual nonchalance was replaced by a sort of jesting attentiveness. Fenichka was growing prettier every day. There is a time in the life of young women when they suddenly begin to expand and blossom like summer roses; this time had come for Fenichka. Everything furthered it, even the prevailing July heat. Dressed in a light white dress, she herself seemed lighter and whiter; she was not tanned by the sun; while the heat, from which she could not shield herself, spread a slight flush over her cheeks and ears, and, shedding a soft indolence over her whole body, was reflected in a dreamy languor in her pretty eyes. She was almost unable to work; her hands seemed to fall naturally into her lap. She scarcely walked at all, and was constantly sighing and complaining with comic helplessness.

"You should go swimming more often," Nikolai Petrovich told her. He had made a large bathing place covered with an awning in one of his ponds which had not yet quite dried up.

"Oh, Nikolai Petrovich! You die by the time you get to the pond, and you die again on the way back. There's no shade in the garden at all."

"That's true, there's no shade," replied Nikolai Petrovich, rubbing his forehead.

One day at seven o'clock in the morning, Bazarov, returning from a walk, came upon Fenichka in the lilac arbor, which was long past flowering, but was still thick and green. She was sitting on the garden seat, and had as usual thrown a white kerchief over her head; near her lay a whole heap of red and white roses still wet with dew. He said good morning to her.

"Ah! Evgeny Vassilyich!" she said, and lifted the edge of her kerchief a little to look at him, in doing which her arm was bared to the elbow.

"What are you doing here?" said Bazarov, sitting down beside her. "Are you making a bouquet?"

"Yes, for the table at lunch. Nikolai Petrovich likes it."

"But it's a long while yet to lunch time. What a heap of flowers!"

"I gathered them now, because it will be hot then, and one can't go out. This is the only time you can breathe. I feel quite weak from the heat. I'm really afraid that I'm going to be ill."

"What an idea! Let me feel your pulse." Bazarov took her hand, felt for the evenly beating pulse, but did not even begin to count its throbs. "You'll live a hundred years!" he said, dropping her hand.

"Ah, God forbid!" she cried.

"Why? Don't you want a long life?"

"Well, but a hundred years! We had a grandmother of eighty-five—and what a martyr she was! Black, deaf, bent, and coughing all the time; nothing but a burden to herself. That's a dreadful life!"

"So it's better to be young?"

"Well, isn't it?"

"But why is it better? Tell me!"

"How can you ask why? Why, while I'm young, I can do everything—go and come and carry, and needn't ask any one for anything. . . . What can be better?"

"And to me it's all the same whether I'm young or old."

"How do you say—it's all the same? What you say is impossible."

"Well, judge for yourself, Fedosya Nikolaevna, what good is my youth to me. I live alone, a poor wretch . . ."

"That always depends on you."

"It doesn't all depend on me! At least, some one ought to take pity on me."

Fenichka glanced sidelong at Bazarov, but said nothing. "What's this book you have?" she asked after a short pause.

"That? That's a scientific book, very difficult."

"And are you still studying? And don't you find it dull? You know everything already, I'd say."

"It seems not everything. You try to read a little."

"But Í don't understand anything here. Is it Russian?" asked Fenichka, taking the heavily bound book in both hands. "How thick it is!"

"Yes, it's Russian."

"All the same, I won't understand anything."

"Well, I didn't give it to you for you to understand it. I wanted to look at you while you were reading. When you read, the end of your little nose moves so nicely."

Fenichka, who had set to work to spell out in a low voice the article on "Creosote" she had chanced upon, laughed and threw down the book . . . it slipped from the seat to the ground.

"I like it, too, when you laugh," observed Bazarov.

"Nonsense!"

"I like it when you talk. It's just like a little brook babbling."

Fenichka turned her head away. "What a person you are for talk!" she commented, picking the flowers over with her finger. "And how can you care to listen to me? You have talked with such clever ladies."

"Ah, Fedosya Nikolaevna, believe me; all the clever ladies in the world are not worth your little elbow."

"Come, there's another invention!" murmured Fenichka, clasping her hands.

Bazarov picked the book up from the ground.

"That's a medical book; why did you throw it away?"

"Medical?" repeated Fenichka, and she turned to him again. "Do you know, ever since you gave me those drops—do you remember?—Mitya has slept so well! I really can't think how to thank you; you are so good, really."

"But you have to pay doctors," observed Bazarov with a smile. "Doctors, you know yourself, are grasping people."

Fenichka raised her eyes, which seemed still darker from the whitish reflection cast on the upper part of her face, and looked at Bazarov. She did not know whether he was joking or not.

"If you please, we shall be delighted. . . . I must ask Nikolai Petrovich . . ."

"Why, do you think I want money?" Bazarov interrupted. "No; I don't want money from you."

"What then?" asked Fenichka.

"What?" repeated Bazarov. "Guess!"

"A likely person I am to guess!"

"Well, I'll tell you; I want . . . one of those roses."

Fenichka laughed again, and even clapped her hands, so amusing Bazarov's request seemed to her. She laughed, and at the same time felt flattered. Bazarov was looking intently at her.

"By all means," she said at last; and bending down to the seat, she began picking over the roses. "Which will you have—a red or white one?"

"Red—and not too large."

She sat up again. "Here, take it," she said, but at once drew back her outstretched hand, and, biting her lips looked towards the entrance of the arbor, then listened.

"What is it?" asked Bazarov. "Nikolai Petrovich?"

"No . . . He went to the fields . . . besides, I'm not afraid of him . . . but Pavel Petrovich . . . I fancied . . ."

"What?"

"I fancied he was coming here. No . . . it was no one. Take it." Fenichka gave Bazarov the rose.

"Why are you afraid of Pavel Petrovich?"

"He always scares me. It's not what he says but he has a way of looking knowingly. And I know you don't like him. Do you remember, you always used to quarrel with him? I don't know what your quarrel was about, but I could see you turn him about like this and like that."

Fenichka showed with her hands how in her opinion Bazarov turned Pavel Petrovich about.

Bazarov smiled. "But if he were to get the upper hand," he asked, "would you stand up for me?"

"How could I stand up for you? But no, no one will get the better of you."

"Do you think so? But I know a hand which could overcome me if it liked."

"What hand?"

"Why, don't you know, really? Smell, how delicious this rose smells you gave me."

Fenichka stretched her little neck forward, and put her face close to the flower. . . . The kerchief slipped from her head on to her shoulders; her soft mass of dark, shining, slightly ruffled hair was visible.

"Wait a minute; I want to smell it with you," said Bazarov. He bent down and kissed her vigorously on her parted lips.

She started, pushed him back with both her hands on his breast, but pushed feebly, and he was able to renew and prolong his kiss.

A dry cough was heard behind the lilac bushes. Fenichka instantly moved away to the other end of the seat. Pavel Petrovich showed himself, made a slight bow, and saying with a sort of malicious despondence, "You are here," he retreated. Fenichka at once gathered up all her roses and went out of the arbor. "It was wrong of you, Evgeny Vassilyich," she whispered as she went. There was a note of genuine reproach in her whisper.

Bazarov remembered another recent scene, and he felt both shame and contemptuous annoyance. But he at once shook his head, ironically congratulated himself "on his formal assumption of the part of the gay Lothario," and went off to his own room.

Pavel Petrovich went out of the garden, and made his way with deliberate steps to the copse. He stayed there rather a long while; and when he returned to lunch, Nikolai Petrovich inquired anxiously whether he were quite well—his face had such a dark look.

"You know, I sometimes suffer bilious attacks," Pavel Petrovich answered calmly.

XXIV

Two hours later he knocked at Bazarov's door.

"I must apologize for hindering you in your scientific pursuits," he began, seating himself on a chair near the window, and leaning with both hands on a handsome walking-stick with an ivory knob (he usually walked without a stick), "But I am compelled to beg you to spare me five minutes of your time . . . no more."

"All my time is at your disposal," answered Bazarov, over whose face something quickly passed as soon as Pavel Petrovich crossed the threshold.

"Five minutes will be enough for me. I have come to put a single question to you."

"A question? What is it about?

"I will tell you, if you will kindly hear me out. At the commencement of your stay in my brother's house, before I had denied myself the pleasure of conversing with you, I heard your opinions on many subjects; but so far as my memory serves, neither between us, nor in my presence, was the subject of single combats and duelling in general broached. Allow me to hear what are your views on that subject?"

Bazarov, who had risen to meet Pavel Petrovich, sat down on the edge of the table and folded his arms.

"My view is," he said, "that from the theoretical standpoint, duelling is absurd; from the practical standpoint, now—it's quite a different matter."

"That is, you mean to say, if I understand you right, that whatever your theoretical views on duelling, you would not in practice allow yourself to be insulted without demanding satisfaction?"

"You have guessed my meaning absolutely."

"Very good sir. I am very glad to hear you say so. Your words relieve me from a state of uncertainty."

"Of indecision, you mean to say."

"That is all the same, sir; I express myself so as to be understood; I . . . am not a seminary rat. Your words save me from a rather deplorable necessity. I have made up my mind to fight you."

Bazarov opened his eyes wide. "Me?"

"Absolutely."

"But what for, pray?"

"I could explain the reason to you," began Pavel Petrovich, "but I prefer to be silent about it. To my taste, your presence here is superfluous; I cannot endure you; I despise you; and if that is not enough for you . . ."

Pavel Petrovich's eyes glittered . . . Bazarov's, too, were flashing.

"Very well, sir," he assented. "No need for further explanations. You have taken a notion to try your chivalrous spirit upon me. I might refuse you this pleasure, but—so be it!"

"I am sensible of my obligation to you," replied Pavel Petrovich; "and may reckon then on your accepting my challenge without compelling me to resort to violent measures."

"That means, speaking without allegories, to that stick?" Bazarov remarked coolly. "That is precisely correct. It's quite unnecessary for you to insult me. As a matter of fact, it would not be quite safe. You may remain a gentleman. . . . I accept your challenge, too, like a gentleman."

"Excellent," observed Pavel Petrovich, putting his stick in the corner. "We will say a few words directly about the conditions of our duel; but I should like first to know whether you think it necessary to resort to the formality of a trifling dispute, which might serve as a pretext for my challenge?"

"No; it's better without formalities."

"I think so myself. I presume it is also out of place to go into the real grounds of our difference. We cannot endure one another. What more is necessary?"

"What more, indeed?" repeated Bazarov ironically.

"As regards the conditions of the meeting itself, seeing that we shall have no seconds—for where could we get them?"

"Exactly so; where could we get them?"

"Then I have the honor to lay the following proposition before you: The combat to take place early to-morrow, at six, let us say, behind the copse, with pistols, at a distance of ten paces . . ."

"At ten paces? [4] That will do; we hate one another at that distance."

"We might have it eight," remarked Pavel Petrovich.

"We might, why not?"

"To fire twice; and, to be ready for any result, let each put a letter in his pocket, in which he accuses himself of his end."

"Now, that I don't approve of at all," observed Bazarov. "There's a slight flavor of the French novel about it, something not very plausible."

---

4. The distance indicates that Pavel means this duel to result in one of the combatants' death. Twelve paces would be adequate even for a very serious duel. It represents the final line to which an adversary may advance before firing, though he may fire at any time while approaching it.

"Perhaps. You will agree, however, that it would be unpleasant to incur a suspicion of murder?"

"I agree. But there is a means of avoiding that painful reproach. We shall have no seconds, but we can have a witness."

"And whom, allow me to inquire?"

"Why, Peter."

"What Peter?"

"Your brother's valet. He's a man who has attained the acme of contemporary culture, and he will perform his part with all the *comme il faut* necessary in such cases."

"I believe you are joking, sir."

"Not at all. If you think over my suggestion, you will be convinced that it's full of common sense and simplicity. You can't hide a candle under a bushel; but I'll undertake to prepare Peter in a fitting manner, and bring him on to the field of battle."

"You persist in jesting," Pavel Petrovich declared, getting up from his chair. "But after the courteous readiness you have shown me, I have no right to insist further. . . . And so, everything is arranged. . . . By the way, perhaps you have no pistols?"

"Why should I have pistols, Pavel Petrovich? I'm not a warrior."

"In that case, I offer you mine. You may rest assured that it's five years since I shot with them."

"That's a very comforting piece of news."

Pavel Petrovich took up his stick. . . . "And now, my dear sir, it only remains for me to thank you and to leave you to your studies. I have the honor to take leave of you."

"Till we have the pleasure of meeting again, my very dear sir," said Bazarov, conducting his visitor to the door.

Pavel Petrovich went out, while Bazarov remained standing a minute before the door, and suddenly exclaimed, "Well, I'll be damned! How fine, and how foolish! A pretty farce we've been through! Like trained dogs dancing on their hind-paws. But to decline was out of the question; why, I do believe he'd have struck me, and then . . ." (Bazarov turned white at the very thought; all his pride was up in arms at once)—"then it might have come to my strangling him like a kitten." He returned to his microscope, but his heart was beating and the composure necessary for making observations had disappeared. "He caught sight of us today," he thought; "but would he really act like this on his brother's account? And as if a kiss were so important. There must be something else in it. Bah! isn't he perhaps in love with her himself? To be sure, he's in love himself; of course he's in love; it's as clear as day. What a complication! It's a nuisance!" he decided at last; "it's bad any way you look at it. In the first place, to risk a bullet through one's brains, and in any case to go away; and then Arkady . . . and that ladybug, Nikolai Petrovich. It's a bad job."

The day passed in a kind of peculiar stillness and languor. Fenichka gave no sign of her existence; she sat in her little room like a mouse in its hole. Nikolai Petrovich had a careworn air. He had just heard that blight had begun to appear in his wheat, upon which he had in particular rested his hopes. Pavel Petrovich overwhelmed every one, even Prokofich, with his icy courtesy. Bazarov began a letter to his father, but tore it up, and threw it under the table.

"If I die," he thought, "they will find it out; but I'm not going to die. No, I shall struggle along in this world a good while yet." He gave Peter orders to come to him on important business the next morning as soon as it was light. Peter imagined that he wanted to take him to Petersburg with him. Bazarov went to bed late, and all night long he was tormented by disordered dreams . . . Odintsov kept appearing in them, now she was his mother, and she was followed by a kitten with black whiskers, and this kitten seemed to be Fenichka; then Pavel Petrovich took the shape of a big forest with which he had to fight anyway. Peter woke him up at four o'clock; he dressed at once, and went out with him.

It was a lovely, fresh morning; tiny flecked clouds hovered overhead like little lambs in the pale clear blue; a fine dew lay in drops on the leaves and grass, and sparkled like silver on the spiders' webs; the damp, dark earth seemed still to keep traces of the rosy dawn; from the whole sky poured the songs of larks. Bazarov walked as far as the copse, sat down in the shade at its edge, and only then disclosed to Peter the nature of the service he expected of him. The refined valet was scared to death; but Bazarov soothed him by the assurance that he would have nothing to do but stand at a distance and look on, and that he would not incur any sort of responsibility. "And meantime," he added, "only think what an important part you have to play!" Peter threw up his hands, looked down, and leaned against a birch-tree, his face turning green.

The road from Marino skirted the copse; a light dust lay on it, untouched by wheel or foot since the previous day. Bazarov unconsciously stared along this road, picked and gnawed a blade of grass, while he kept repeating to himself, "What a piece of foolery!" The chill of the early morning made him shiver twice. . . . Peter looked at him dejectedly, but Bazarov only smiled; he was not afraid.

The tramp of horses' hoofs was heard along the road. . . . A peasant came into sight from behind the trees. He was driving before him two horses hobbled together, and as he passed Bazarov he·

looked at him rather strangely, without doffing his cap, which it was easy to see disturbed Peter, as an unlucky omen. "There's some one else up early too," thought Bazarov; "but he at least got up for work, while we . . ."

"I think he's coming, sir," Peter whispered suddenly.

Bazarov raised his head and saw Pavel Petrovich. Dressed in a light check jacket and snow-white trousers, he was walking rapidly along the road; under his arm he carried a box wrapped up in green cloth.

"I beg your pardon, I believe I have kept you waiting," he observed, bowing first to Bazarov, then to Peter, whom he treated respectfully at that instant, as representing something in the nature of a second. "I was unwilling to wake my man."

"It doesn't matter, sir," answered Bazarov; "we've only just arrived ourselves."

"Ah! so much the better!" Pavel Petrovich took a look round. "There's no one in sight; no one hinders us. We can proceed?"

"Let us proceed."

"You do not, I presume, desire any fresh explanations?"

"No, I don't."

"Would you like to load?" inquired Pavel Petrovich, taking the pistols out of the box.

"No; you load, and I will measure out the paces. My legs are longer," added Bazarov with a smile. "One, two, three."

"Evgeny Vassilyich," Peter babbled with an effort (he was shaking as though he were in a fever), "say what you like, I am going farther off."

"Four . . . five . . . Move away, my good fellow, move away; you may get behind a tree even, and stop up your ears, only don't shut your eyes; and if any one falls, run and pick him up. Six . . . seven . . . eight . . ." Bazarov stopped. "Is that enough?" he said, turning to Pavel Petrovich; "or shall I add two paces more?"

"As you like," replied the latter, pressing down the second bullet.

"Well, we'll add two more paces." Bazarov drew a line on the ground with the toe of his boot. "There's the barrier then. By the way, how many paces may each of us go back from the barrier? That's an important question too. That point was not discussed yesterday."

"I imagine, ten," replied Pavel Petrovich, handing Bazarov both pistols. "Will you be so good as to choose?"

"I will be so good. But, Pavel Petrovich, you must admit our combat is singular to the point of absurdity. Only look at the countenance of our second."

"You are disposed to laugh at everything," answered Pavel

Petrovich. "I acknowledge the strangeness of our duel, but I think it my duty to warn you that I intend to fight seriously. A *bon entendeur, salut!*" [5]

"Oh! I don't doubt that we've made up our minds to make away with each other; but why not laugh too and unite *utile dulci?* [6] You talk to me in French, while I talk to you in Latin."

"I am going to fight in earnest," repeated Pavel Petrovich, and he walked off to his place. Bazarov on his side counted off ten paces from the barrier, and stood still.

"Are you ready?" asked Pavel Petrovich.

"Perfectly."

"We can approach one another."

Bazarov moved slowly forward, and Pavel Petrovich, his left hand thrust in his pocket, walked towards him, gradually raising the muzzle of his pistol. . . . "He's aiming straight at my nose," thought Bazarov, "and doesn't he blink down it carefully, the ruffian! Not an agreeable sensation, though. I'm going to look at his watch chain."

Something whizzed sharply by his very ear, and at the same instant there was the sound of a shot. "I heard it, so it must be all right," had time to flash through Bazarov's brain. He took one more step, and without taking aim pressed the trigger.

Pavel Petrovich gave a slight start, and clutched at his thigh. A stream of blood began to trickle down his white trousers.

Bazarov flung aside the pistol, and went up to his antagonist. "Are you wounded?" he said.

"You had the right to call me up to the barrier," said Pavel Petrovich, "the wound is a trifle. According to our agreement, each of us has the right to one more shot."

"Well, excuse me, that'll do for another time," answered Bazarov, catching hold of Pavel Petrovich, who was beginning to turn pale. "Now I'm not a duellist but a doctor, and I must have a look at your wound before anything else. Peter, come here, Peter, where have you gone to?"

"That's all nonsense . . . I need no one's aid," Pavel Petrovich declared jerkily, "and . . . we must . . . again . . ." He tried to pull at his moustache, but his hand failed him, his eyes grew dim, and he lost consciousness.

"Here's something new! A fainting fit! What next!" Bazarov cried involuntarily, as he laid Pavel Petrovich on the grass. "Let's have a look at what's wrong." He pulled out a handkerchief, wiped away the blood, and began feeling round the wound. . . . "The bone's not touched," he muttered through his teeth; "the bullet

---

5. "A word to the wise is sufficient."
6. "The useful with the pleasant" (Horace, *Ars poetica*).

went through but not too deep; one muscle, *vastus externus*, grazed. He'll be dancing about in three weeks! . . . And to faint! Oh, these nervous people, how I hate them! Look, what a delicate skin!"

"Is he killed?" the quavering voice of Peter came rustling behind his back.

Bazarov looked round. "Go for some water as quick as you can, my good fellow, and he'll outlive us yet."

But the advanced servant apparently did not understand his words, and did not stir. Pavel Petrovich slowly opened his eyes. "He is dying!" whispered Peter, and he began crossing himself.

"You are right. . . . What an imbecile countenance!" remarked the wounded gentleman with a forced smile.

"Well, go for the water, damn you!" shouted Bazarov.

"No need. . . . It was a momentary *vertige*. . . . Help me to sit up. . . . there, that's right. . . . I only need something to bind up this scratch, and I can reach home on foot, or else you can send a droshky for me. The duel, if you are willing, shall not be renewed. You have behaved honorably . . . to-day, to-day—observe."

"There's no need to recall the past," rejoined Bazarov; "and as regards the future, it's not worth while for you to trouble your head about that either, for I intend being off without delay. Let me bind up your leg now; your wound's not serious, but it's always best to stop bleeding. But first I must bring this corpse to his senses."

Bazarov shook Peter by the collar, and sent him for a droshky.

"Mind, you don't frighten my brother," Pavel Petrovich said to him; "don't dream of informing him."

Peter flew off; and while he was running for a droshky, the two antagonists sat on the ground and said nothing. Pavel Petrovich tried not to look at Bazarov; he did not want to be reconciled to him in any case; he was ashamed of his own haughtiness, of his failure; he was ashamed of the whole position he had brought about, even while he felt it could not have ended in a more favorable manner. "At any rate, he won't be hanging around," he consoled himself by reflecting, "and that's something to be thankful for." The silence continued, a distressing and awkward silence. Both of them were ill at ease. Each was conscious that the other understood him. That is pleasant to friends, and very unpleasant to those who are not friends, especially when it is impossible either to have things out or to separate.

"Have I bound up your leg too tight?" inquired Bazarov at last.

"No, not at all; it's splendid," answered Pavel Petrovich; and after a brief pause, he added, "There's no deceiving my brother; we shall have to tell him we quarreled over politics."

"Very good," assented Bazarov. "You can say I insulted all Anglomaniacs."

"That will do splendidly. What do you imagine that man thinks of us now?" continued Pavel Petrovich, pointing to the same peasant who had driven the hobbled horses past Bazarov a few minutes before the duel, and going back again along the road, took off his cap at the sight of the "masters."

"Who knows?" answered Bazarov. "It is quite likely he thinks nothing. The Russian peasant is that mysterious stranger about whom Mrs. Radcliffe [7] used to talk so much. Who is to understand him! He doesn't understand himself!"

"Ah! so that's your idea!" Pavel Petrovich began; and suddenly he cried, "Look what your fool of a Peter has done! Here's my brother galloping up to us!"

Bazarov turned round and saw the pale face of Nikolai Petrovich, who was sitting in the droshky. He jumped out of it before it had stopped, and rushed up to his brother.

"What does this mean?" he said in an agitated voice. "Evgeny Vassilyich, please, what is this?"

"Nothing," answered Pavel Petrovich; "you have been alarmed for nothing. I had a little dispute with Mr. Bazarov, and I have had to pay for it a little."

"But what was it all about, for God's sake!"

"How can I tell you? Mr. Bazarov alluded disrespectfully to Sir Robert Peel. I must hasten to add that I am the only person to blame in all this, while Mr. Bazarov has behaved most honorably. I called him out."

"But you're covered with blood, good heavens!"

"Well, did you suppose I had water in my veins? But this blood-letting is positively beneficial to me. Isn't that so, doctor? Help me to get into the droshky, and don't give way to melancholy. I shall be quite well to-morrow. That's it; splendid. Drive on, coachman."

Nikolai Petrovich walked after the droshky; Bazarov remained where he was. . . .

"I must ask you to look after my brother," Nikolai Petrovich said to him, "till we get another doctor from the town."

Bazarov nodded his head without speaking. In an hour's time Pavel Petrovich was already lying in bed with a skillfully bandaged leg. The whole house was alarmed; Fenichka became ill. Nikolai Petrovich kept stealthily wringing his hands, while Pavel Petrovich laughed and joked, especially with Bazarov; he had put on a fine cambric night shirt, an elegant morning jacket, and a fez, did not allow the blinds to be drawn down, and humorously complained of the necessity of being kept from food.

Towards night, however, he began to be feverish; his head ached.

---

7. Ann Radcliffe (1764–1823), writer of extremely popular "gothic" novels.

The doctor arrived from the town. (Nikolai Petrovich would not listen to his brother, and indeed Bazarov himself did not wish him to; he sat the whole day in his room, looking bilious and vindictive, and only went in to the invalid for as brief a time as possible; twice he happened to meet Fenichka, but she shrank away from him with horror.) The new doctor advised cooling drinks; he confirmed, however, Bazarov's assertion that there was no danger. Nikolai Petrovich told him his brother had wounded himself by accident, to which the doctor responded, "Hm!" but having twenty-five silver rubles slipped into his hand on the spot, he observed, "You don't say so! Well, it's a thing that often happens, to be sure."

No one in the house went to bed or undressed. Nikolai Petrovich kept going in to his brother on tiptoe, retreating on tiptoe again; the latter dozed, moaned a little, told him in French, *Couchez-vous,*[8] and asked for drink. Nikolai Petrovich sent Fenichka twice to take him a glass of lemonade; Pavel Petrovich gazed at her intently, and drank off the glass to the last drop. Towards morning the fever had increased a little; there was slight delirium. At first Pavel Petrovich uttered incoherent words; then suddenly he opened his eyes, and seeing his brother near his bed bending anxiously over him, he said, "Don't you think, Nikolai, Fenichka has something in common with Nellie?"

"What Nellie, Pavel dear?"

"How can you ask? Princess R——. Especially in the upper part of the face. *C'est de la même famille.*" [9]

Nikolai Petrovich made no answer, while inwardly he marveled at the persistence of old passions in man. "Just see when its come to the surface," he thought.

"Ah, how I love that light-headed creature!" moaned Pavel Petrovich, clasping his hands mournfully behind his head. "I can't bear any insolent upstart to dare to touch . . ." he whispered a few minutes later.

Nikolai Petrovich only sighed; he did not even suspect to whom these words referred.

Bazarov presented himself before him at eight o'clock the next day. He had already had time to pack, and to set free all his frogs, insects, and birds.

"You have come to say good-bye to me?" said Nikolai Petrovich, getting up to meet him.

"Yes."

"I understand you, and approve of you fully. My poor brother, of course, is to blame; and that's why he was punished. He told me himself that he made it impossible for you to act otherwise. I

8. "Go to sleep."   9. "It is kindred."

believe that you could not avoid this duel, which . . . which to some extent is explained by the almost constant antagonism of your respective views." (Nikolai Petrovich began to get a little mixed up in his words.) "My brother is a man of the old school, hot-tempered and obstinate. . . . Thank God that it has ended as it has. I have taken every precaution to avoid publicity."

"I'm leaving you my address, in case there's any fuss," Bazarov remarked casually.

"I hope there will be no fuss, Evgeny Vassilyich. . . . I am very sorry your stay in my house should have such a . . . such an end. It is the more distressing to me since Arkady . . ."

"I shall be seeing him, I expect," replied Bazarov, in whom "explanations" and "protestations" of every sort always aroused a feeling of impatience; "in case I don't, I beg you to say good-bye to him for me, and accept the expression of my regret."

"And I beg . . ." answered Nikolai Petrovich. But Bazarov went off without waiting for the end of his sentence.

When he heard of Bazarov's going, Pavel Petrovich expressed a desire to see him, and shook his hand. But even then he remained as cold as ice; he realized that Pavel Petrovich wanted to play a magnanimous role. He did not succeed in saying good-bye to Fenichka; he only exchanged glances with her at the window. Her face struck him as looking dejected. "She'll come to grief, perhaps," he said to himself. . . . "But who knows? she'll pull through somehow, I daresay!" Peter, however, was so overcome that he wept on his shoulder, till Bazarov damped him by asking if he'd a constant supply of water laid in for his eyes; while Dunyasha was obliged to run away into the wood to hide her emotion. The originator of all this woe got into a light cart, lit a cigar, and when at the third mile, at the bend in the road, the Kirsanovs' estate, with its new house, could be seen in a long line, he merely spat, and muttering "Damned aristocrats!" wrapped himself closer in his cloak.

Pavel Petrovich was soon better; but he had to remain in bed for a week or so. He bore his captivity, as he called it, pretty patiently, though he took great pains over his toilette, and had everything scented with eau-de-cologne. Nikolai Petrovich used to read him the journals; Fenichka waited on him as before, brought him lemonade, bouillon, boiled eggs, and tea; but she was overcome with secret dread whenever she went into his room. Pavel Petrovich's unexpected action had alarmed every one in the house, and her more than any one; Prokofich was the only person not agitated by it; he discoursed upon how gentlemen in his day used to fight, but "only with real gentlemen; low curs like that they ordered horsewhipped in the stable for their insolence."

Fenichka's conscience scarcely reproached her; but she was

tormented at times by the thought of the real cause of the quarrel; and Pavel Petrovich, too, looked at her so strangely . . . so that even when her back was turned she felt his eyes upon her. She grew thinner from constant inward agitation, and, as is usually the way, became still more charming.

One day—the incident took place in the morning—Pavel Petrovich felt better, and moved from his bed to the sofa, while Nikolai Petrovich, having satisfied himself he was better, went off to the threshing floor. Fenichka brought him a cup of tea, and setting it down on a little table, was about to withdraw. Pavel Petrovich detained her.

"Where are you going in such a hurry, Fedosya Nikolaevna?" he began; "are you busy?"

"No, sir . . . I have to pour out tea."

"Dunyasha will do that without you; sit a little while with a sick man. By the way, I must have a little talk with you."

Fenichka sat down on the edge of an easy-chair, without speaking.

"Listen," said Pavel Petrovich, tugging at his moustaches; "I have long wanted to ask you something; you seem somehow afraid of me?"

"I, sir?"

"Yes, you. You never look at me, as though your conscience were not at rest."

Fenichka crimsoned, but looked at Pavel Petrovich. He impressed her as looking strange, and her heart began throbbing slowly.

"Is your conscience at rest?" he questioned her.

"Why should it not be at rest?" she faltered.

"Goodness knows why! Besides, whom can you have wronged? Me? That is not likely. Any other people in the house here? That, too, is something incredible. Can it be my brother? But you love him, don't you?"

"I love him."

"With your whole soul, with your whole heart?"

"I love Nikolai Petrovich with my whole heart."

"Truly? Look at me, Fenichka." (It was the first time he had called her that name.) "You know, it's a great sin to lie!"

"I am not lying, Pavel Petrovich. Not love Nikolai Petrovich— I shouldn't care to live after that."

"And will you never give him up for any one?"

"For whom could I give him up?"

"For whom indeed! Well, how about that gentleman who has just gone away from here?"

Fenichka got up. "My God, Pavel Petrovich, what are you torturing me for? What have I done to you? How can such things be said!" . . .

"Fenichka," said Pavel Petrovich, in a sorrowful voice, "you know I saw . . ."

"What did you see, sir?"

"Well, there . . . in the arbor."

Fenichka crimsoned to her hair and to her ears. "How was I to blame for that?" she articulated with an effort.

Pavel Petrovich raised himself up. "You were not to blame? No? Not at all?"

"I love Nikolai Petrovich, and no one else in the world, and I shall always love him!" cried Fenichka with sudden force, while sobs rose in her throat. "As for what you saw, at the Last Judgment I will say I'm not to blame, and wasn't to blame for it, and I would rather die at once if people can suspect me of such a thing against my benefactor, Nikolai Petrovich."

But here her voice broke, and at the same time she felt that Pavel Petrovich was snatching and pressing her hand. . . . She looked at him, and was fairly petrified. He had turned even paler than before; his eyes were shining, and what was most marvelous of all, one large solitary tear was rolling down his cheek.

"Fenichka!" he was saying in a strange whisper; "love him, love my brother! He is such a kind, good man! Don't give him up for any one in the world; don't listen to any one else! Think what can be more terrible than to love and not be loved! Never leave my poor Nikolai!"

Fenichka's eyes were dry, and her terror had passed away, so great was her amazement. But what were her feelings when Pavel Petrovich, Pavel Petrovich himself, put her hand to his lips and kept it there without kissing it, only heaving convulsive sighs from time to time. . . .

"Goodness," she thought, "isn't it some attack coming on him?" . . .

At that instant his whole ruined life was stirred up within him.

The staircase creaked under rapidly approaching footsteps. . . . He pushed her away from him, and let his head drop back on the pillow. The door opened, and Nikolai Petrovich entered, cheerful, fresh, and ruddy. Mitya, as fresh and ruddy as his father, in nothing but his little shirt, was bouncing on his chest, catching the big buttons of his rough country coat with his little bare toes.

Fenichka simply flung herself upon him, and clasping him and her son together in her arms, dropped her head on his shoulder. Nikolai Petrovich was surprised; Fenichka, the reserved and staid Fenichka, had never given him a caress in the presence of a third person.

"What's the matter?" he said, and, glancing at his brother, he gave her Mitya. "You don't feel worse?" he inquired, going up to Pavel Petrovich.

He buried his face in a cambric handkerchief. "No . . . not at all . . . on the contrary, I am much better."

"You were in too great a hurry to move on to the sofa. Where are you going?" added Nikolai Petrovich, turning round to Fenichka; but she had already closed the door behind her. "I was bringing in my young hero to show you; he's been crying for his uncle. Why has she carried him off? What's wrong with you, though? Has anything passed between you, eh?"

"Brother!" said Pavel Petrovich solemnly.

Nikolai Petrovich started. He felt dismayed, he could not have said why himself.

"Brother," repeated Pavel Petrovich, "give me your word that you will carry out my one request."

"What request? Tell me."

"It is very important; the whole happiness of your life, as I see it, depends on it. I have been thinking a great deal all this time over what I want to say to you now. . . . Brother, do your duty, the duty of an honest and generous man; put an end to the scandal and bad example you are setting—you, the best of men!"

"What do you mean, Pavel?"

"Marry Fenichka. . . . She loves you; she is the mother of your son."

Nikolai Petrovich stepped back a pace, and flung up his hands. "Do you say that, Pavel? You whom I have always regarded as the most determined opponent of such marriages! You say that? Don't you know that it has simply been out of respect for you that I have not done what you so rightly call my duty?"

"You were wrong to respect me in that case," Pavel Petrovich responded, with a weary smile. "I begin to think Bazarov was right in accusing me of being an aristocrat. No, dear brother, don't let us worry ourselves about appearances and the world's opinion any more; we are old folks now and resigned; it's time we laid aside vanity of all kinds. Let us, just as you say, do our duty; and mind, we shall get happiness that way into the bargain."

Nikolai Petrovich rushed to embrace his brother.

"You have opened my eyes completely!" he cried. "I was right in always declaring you the wisest and kindest-hearted fellow in the world, and now I see you are just as reasonable as you are noble-hearted."

"Easy, easy," Pavel Petrovich interrupted him; "don't hurt the leg of your reasonable brother, who at close upon fifty has been fighting a duel like an ensign. So, then, it's a settled matter;

Fenichka is to be my . . . *belle soeur.*" [1]

"My dearest Pavel! But what will Arkady say?"

"Arkady? He'll be in ecstasies, you may depend upon it! Marriage is against his principles, but then the sentiment of equality in him will be gratified. And, after all, what sense have class distinctions *au dix-neuvième siècle?*" [2]

"Ah, Pavel, Pavel, let me kiss you once more! Don't be afraid, I'll be careful."

The brothers embraced each other.

"What do you think, should you not inform her of your intention now?" queried Pavel Petrovich.

"Why be in a hurry?" responded Nikolai Petrovich. "Has there been any conversation between you?"

"Conversation between us? *Quelle idée!*" [3]

"Well, that is all right then. First of all, you must get well, and meanwhile there's plenty of time. We must think it over well, and consider . . ."

"But your mind is made up, I suppose?"

"Of course, my mind is made up, and I thank you from the bottom of my heart. I will leave you now; you must rest; any excitement is bad for you. . . . But we will talk it over again. Sleep well, dear heart, and God bless you!"

"What is he thanking me like that for?" thought Pavel Petrovich, when he was left alone. "As though it did not depend on him! I will go away as soon as he is married, somewhere a long way off— to Dresden or Florence, and will live there till I drop."

Pavel Petrovich moistened his forehead with eau de cologne, and closed his eyes. His handsome, emaciated head, the glaring daylight shining full upon it, lay on the white pillow like the head of a dead man. . . . And indeed he was a dead man.

XXV

At Nikolskoe Katya and Arkady were sitting in the garden on a turf seat in the shade of a tall ash tree; Fifi had placed herself on the ground near them, giving her slender body that graceful curve which is known among hunters as "the hare bend." Both Arkady and Katya were silent; he was holding a half-open book in his hands, while she was picking out of a basket the few crumbs of bread left in it and throwing them to a small family of sparrows, who with the frightened impudence peculiar to them were hopping and chirping at her very feet. A faint breeze stirring in the ash leaves kept slowly moving pale-gold flecks of sunlight back and forth over Fifi's tawny back and the shady path; a patch

---

1. "sister-in-law."
2. "in the nineteenth century."

3. "What an idea!"

of unbroken shade fell upon Arkady and Katya; only from time to time a bright streak gleamed on her hair. Both were silent, but the very way in which they were silent, in which they were sitting together, was expressive of confidential intimacy; each of them seemed not even to be thinking of his companion, while secretly rejoicing in his presence. Their faces, too, had changed since we saw them last; Arkady looked more tranquil, Katya brighter and more daring.

"Don't you think," began Arkady, "that the ash has been very well named in Russian *yasen*; no other tree is so lightly and clearly *(yasno)* transparent against the air as it is."

Katya raised her eyes to look upward, and assented "Yes", while Arkady thought, "Well, this one does not reproach me for *talking finely*."

"I don't like Heine,[4]" said Katya, glancing towards the book which Arkady was holding in his hands, "either when he laughs or when he weeps; I like him when he's thoughtful and melancholy."

"And I like him when he laughs," remarked Arkady.

"That's the relics of your old satirical tendencies left in you." ("Relics!" thought Arkady—"if Bazarov had heard that?") "Wait a little; we shall transform you."

"Who will transform me? You?"

"Who?—my sister; Porfiry Platonovich, whom you've given up quarrelling with; auntie, whom you escorted to church the day before yesterday."

"Well, I couldn't refuse! And as for Anna Sergeyevna, she agreed with Evgeny in a great many things, you remember?"

"My sister was under his influence then, just as you were."

"As I was? Do you find that I've shaken off his influence now?" Katya did not speak.

"I know," pursued Arkady, "you never liked him."

"I can have no opinion about him."

"Do you know what, Katerina Sergeyevna, every time I hear that answer I disbelieve it. . . . There is no man that every one of us could not have an opinion about! That's simply a way of getting out of it."

"Well, I'll say then, I don't. . . . It's not exactly that I don't like him, but I feel that he's of a different order from me, and I am different from him . . . and you, too, are different from him."

"How's that?"

"How can I tell you? . . . He's a wild animal, and you and I are tame."

4. German poet (1797–1856).

"Am I tame too?"

Katya nodded.

Arkady scratched his ear. "Let me tell you, Katerina Sergeyevna, do you know, that's really an insult?"

"Why, would you like to be wild."

"Not wild, but strong, energetic."

"It's no good wishing for that. . . . Your friend, you see, doesn't wish for it, but he has it."

"Hm! So you imagine he had a great influence on Anna Sergeyevna?"

"Yes. But no one can keep the upper hand of her for long," added Katya in a low voice.

"Why do you think that?"

"She's very proud. . . . I didn't mean that . . . she values her independence a great deal."

"Who doesn't value it?" asked Arkady, and the thought flashed through his mind, "What good is it?" "What good is it?" occurred to Katya too. When young people are often together on friendly terms, they are constantly stumbling on the same ideas.

Arkady smiled, and coming slightly closer to Katya, he said in a whisper, "Confess that you are a little afraid of her."

"Of whom?"

"Her," repeated Arkady, significantly.

"And how about you?" Katya asked in her turn.

"I am too, observe I said I am, *too*."

Katya threatened him with her finger. "I wonder at that," she began; "my sister has never felt so friendly to you as just now; much more so than when you first came."

"Really!"

"Why, haven't you noticed it? Aren't you glad of it?"

Arkady grew thoughtful.

"How have I succeeded in gaining Anna Sergeyevna's good opinion? Wasn't it because I brought her your mother's letters?"

"Both that and other causes, which I won't tell you."

"Why?"

"I won't say."

"Oh! I know; you're very obstinate."

"Yes, I am."

"And observant."

Katya gave Arkady a sidelong look. "Perhaps that irritates you? What are you thinking of?"

"I am wondering how you come to be as observant as you really are. You are so shy, so distrustful; you keep every one at a distance."

"I have lived alone a great deal; that drives one to reflection.

But do I really keep every one at a distance?"

Arkady flung a grateful glance at Katya.

"That's all very well," he pursued; "but people in your position —I mean in your circumstances—don't often have this faculty; it is as hard for them as it is for sovereigns to get at the truth."

"But, you see, I am not rich."

Arkady was taken aback, and did not at once understand Katya. "Why, of course, the property's all her sister's!" struck him suddenly; the thought was not unpleasing to him. "How nicely you said that!" he commented.

"What?"

"You said it nicely, simply, without being ashamed or posturing. By the way, I imagine there must always be something special, a kind of pride of a sort in the feeling of any man, who knows and says he is poor."

"I have never experienced anything of that sort, thanks to my sister. I only referred to my position just now because it happened to come up."

"Well; but you must admit that you have a share of that pride I spoke of just now."

"For instance?"

"For instance, you—forgive the question—you wouldn't marry a rich man, I fancy, would you?"

"If I loved him very much. . . . No, I think even then I wouldn't marry him."

"There! you see!" cried Arkady, and after a short pause he added, "And why wouldn't you marry him?"

"Because unequal matches even appear in songs."

"You want to rule, perhaps, or . . .

"Oh, no! why should I? On the contrary, I am ready to obey; only inequality is hard to bear. To respect oneself and obey, that I can understand, that's happiness; but a subordinate existence . . . No, I've had enough of that as it is."

"Enough of that as it is," Arkady repeated after Katya. "Yes, yes," he went on, "you're not Anna Sergeyevna's sister for nothing; you're just as independent as she is; but you're more reserved. I'm certain you wouldn't be the first to give expression to your feeling, however strong and holy it might be . . ."

"Well, what would you expect?" asked Katya.

"You're equally clever; and you've as much, if not more, character than she."

"Don't compare me with my sister, please," interposed Katya hurriedly; "that's too much to my disadvantage. You seem to forget my sister's beautiful and clever and . . . you in particular, Arkady Nikolaevich, ought not to say such things, and with such a serious face, too."

"What do you mean by 'you in particular'—and what makes you suppose I am joking?"

"Of course, you are joking."

"You think so? But what if I'm convinced of what I say? If I believe I have not even put it strongly enough?"

"I don't understand you."

"Really? Well, now I see; I certainly took you to be more observant than you are."

"How?"

Arkady made no answer, and turned away, while Katya looked for a few more crumbs in the basket, and began throwing them to the sparrows; but she moved her arm too vigorously, and they flew away, without stopping to pick them up.

"Katerina Sergeyevna!" began Arkady suddenly; "it's of no consequence to you, probably; but, let me tell you, I put you not only above your sister, but above every one in the world."

He got up and went quickly away, as though he were frightened at the words that had fallen from his lips.

Katya let her two hands drop together with the basket on to her lap, and with bent head she stared a long while after Arkady. Gradually a crimson flush came faintly over her cheeks; but her lips did not smile, and her dark eyes had a look of perplexity and some other, as yet undefined, feeling.

"Are you alone?" she heard the voice of Anna Sergeyevna near her; "I thought you came into the garden with Arkady."

Katya slowly raised her eyes to her sister (elegantly, even exquisitely dressed, she was standing in the path and tickling Fifi's ears with the tip of her open parasol), and slowly replied, "Yes, I'm alone."

"So I see," she answered with a smile; "I suppose he has gone to his room."

"Yes."

"Have you been reading together?"

"Yes."

Anna Sergeyevna took Katya by the chin and lifted her face up.

"You have not been quarrelling, I hope?"

"No," said Katya, and she quietly removed her sister's hand.

"How solemnly you answer! I expected to find him here, and meant to suggest his coming for a walk with me. He keeps asking me. They have sent you some shoes from the town; go and try them on; I noticed only yesterday your old ones are quite shabby. In general you don't think enough about such things, and you have such charming little feet! Your hands are nice too . . . though they're large; so you must make the most of your little feet. But you're not vain."

Anna Sergeyevna went farther along the path with a light rustle of her beautiful gown; Katya got up from the grass, and, taking Heine with her, went away too—but not to try on her shoes.

"Charming little feet!" she thought, as she slowly and lightly mounted the stone steps of the terrace, which were burning with the heat of the sun; "charming little feet you call them. . . . Well, he shall be at them."

But all at once a feeling of shame came upon her, and she ran swiftly upstairs.

Arkady was going along the corridor to his room; the butler overtook him, and announced that Mr. Bazarov was in his room.

"Evgeny!" murmured Arkady, almost with dismay; "has he been here long?"

"Mr. Bazarov arrived this minute, sir, and gave orders not to announce him to Anna Sergeyevna, but to show him straight up to you."

"Can any misfortune have happened at home?" thought Arkady, and running hurriedly up the stairs, he at once opened the door. The sight of Bazarov at once reassured him, though a more experienced eye might very probably have discerned signs of inward agitation in the sunken, though still energetic face of the unexpected visitor. With a dusty cloak over his shoulders, with a cap on his head, he was sitting at the window; he did not even get up when Arkady flung himself with noisy exclamations on his neck.

"This is unexpected! What good luck brought you?" he kept repeating, bustling about the room like one who both imagines himself and wishes to show himself delighted. "I suppose everything's all right at home; every one's well, eh?"

"Everything's all right, but not every one's well," said Bazarov. "Don't be a chatterbox, but send for some kvass for me, sit down, and listen while I tell you all about it in a few, but, I hope, pretty vigorous sentences."

Arkady quieted down, and Bazarov described his duel with Pavel Petrovich. Arkady was very much surprised, and even grieved, but he did not think it necessary to show this; he only asked whether his uncle's wound was really not serious; and on receiving the reply that it was most interesting, but not from a medical point of view, he gave a forced smile, but at heart he felt both wounded and as it were ashamed. Bazarov seemed to understand him.

"Yes, my dear fellow," he commented, "you see what comes

of living with feudal people. You turn feudal yourself, and find yourself taking part in knightly tournaments. Well, so I set off 'to the fathers,' " [5] Bazarov wound up, "and I've turned in here on the way. . . . to tell you all this, I should say, if I didn't think a useless lie stupid. No, I turned in here—the devil only knows why. You see, it's sometimes a good thing for a man to take himself by the scruff of the neck and pull himself up, like. a radish out of its bed; that's what I've been doing of late. . . . But I wanted to have one more look at what I'm giving up, at the bed where I've been planted."

"I hope those words don't refer to me," responded Arkady with some emotion; "I hope you don't think of giving me up?"

Bazarov turned an intent, almost piercing look upon him.

"Would that be such a grief to you? It strikes me *you* have given me up already, you look so fresh and smart. . . . Your affair with Anna Sergeyevna must be getting on successfully."

"What do you mean by my affair with Anna Sergeyevna?"

"Why, didn't you come here from the town on her account, little bird? By the way, how are those Sunday schools getting on? Do you mean to tell me you're not in love with her? Or have you already reached the stage of discretion?"

"Evgeny, you know I have always been open with you; I can assure you, I will swear to you, you're making a mistake."

"Hm! That's a new story," remarked Bazarov in an undertone. "But there is no reason for you to get excited, it's a matter of absolute indifference to me. A romantic would say, 'I feel that our paths are beginning to part,' but I will simply say that we're tired of each other."

"Evgeny . . ."

"My dear soul, there's no great harm in that. One gets tired of much more than that in this life. And now I suppose we'd better say good-bye, hadn't we? Ever since I've been here I've had such a loathsome feeling, just as if I'd been reading Gogol's letter to the governor of Kaluga's wife.[6] By the way, I didn't tell them to unhitch the horses."

"Upon my word, this is too much!"

"Why?"

"I'll say nothing of myself; but that would be highly discourteous to Anna Sergeyevna, who will certainly wish to see you."

"Oh, you're mistaken there."

5. Bazarov mockingly (and ominously) recalls the *ad patres* of p. 95 (note 6).
6. Gogol's letter of June 6, 1846, was deleted from his *Selected Correspondence With Friends* and first appeared in 1860, that is, a year after the purported setting of the novel, under the title "What a Governor's Wife Is." Like the original volume, which had aroused Belinsky's ire, it offended both radicals and liberals with its sententiousness.

"On the contrary, I am certain I'm right," retorted Arkady. "And what are you pretending for? If it comes to that, haven't you come here on her account yourself?"

"That may be so, but you're mistaken anyway."

But Arkady was right. Anna Sergeyevna desired to see Bazarov, and sent word to him by the butler. Bazarov changed his clothes before going to her; it turned out that he had packed his new suit so as to be able to get it out easily.

Odintsov did not receive him in the room where he had so unexpectedly declared his love to her, but in the drawing-room. She held her finger tips out to him cordially, but her face betrayed an involuntary sense of tension.

"Anna Sergeyevna," Bazarov hastened to say, "before everything else I must set your mind at rest. Before you is a mortal who has come to his senses long ago, and who hopes other people, too, have forgotten his follies. I am going away for a long while; and though, as you will allow, I'm by no means a very soft creature, it would be anything but cheerful for me to carry away with me the idea that you remember me with repugnance."

Anna Sergeyevna sighed deeply, like one who has just climbed up a high mountain, and her face was lit up by a smile. She held out her hand a second time to Bazarov, and responded to his pressure.

"Let bygones be bygones," she said. "I am all the readier to do so because, speaking in all conscience, I was to blame then, too, for flirting or something like that. In a word, let us be friends as before. That was a dream, wasn't it? And who remembers dreams?"

"Who remembers them? And besides, love . . . you know, is a purely imaginary feeling."

"Really? I am very glad to hear that."

So Anna Sergeyevna spoke, and so spoke Bazarov; they both supposed they were speaking the truth. Was the truth, the whole truth, to be found in their words? They could not themselves have said, and much less could the author. But a conversation followed between them precisely as though they completely believed one another.

Anna Sergeyevna asked Bazarov, among other things, what he had been doing at the Kirsanovs'. He was on the point of telling her about his duel with Pavel Petrovich, but he checked himself with the thought that she might imagine he was trying to make himself interesting, and answered that he had been at work all the time.

"And I," observed Anna Sergeyevna, "had a fit of depression at first, goodness knows why; I even made plans for going abroad, fancy! . . . Then it passed off, your friend Arkady Nikolaich came, and I fell back into my old routine, and took up my real part again."

"What part is that, may I ask?"

"The character of aunt, guardian, mother—call it what you like. By the way, do you know I used · not quite to understand your close friendship with Arkady Nikolaich; I thought him rather insignificant. But now I have come to know him better, and to see that he is clever. . . . And he's young, he's young . . . that's the great thing . . . not like you and me, Evgeny Vassilyich."

"Is he still as shy in your company?" queried Bazarov.

"Why, was he?" . . . Anna Sergeyevna began, and after a brief pause she went on: "He has grown more confiding now; he talks to me. He used to avoid me before. Though, indeed, I didn't seek his society either. He and Katya are great friends."

Bazarov felt irritated. "A woman can't help being crafty, of course!" he thought. "You say he used to avoid you," he said aloud, with a chilly smile; "but it is probably no secret to you that he was in love with you?"

"What! he too?" fell from Anna Sergeyevna's lips.

"He too," repeated Bazarov, with a submissive bow. "Can it be you didn't know it, and I've told you something new?"

Anna Sergeyevna dropped her eyes. "You are mistaken, Evgeny Vassilyich."

"I don't think so. But perhaps I ought not to have mentioned it." "And don't you try telling me lies again," he added to himself.

"Why not mention it? But I imagine that in this, too, you are attributing too much importance to a passing impression. I begin to suspect you are inclined to exaggeration."

"We had better not talk about it, Anna Sergeyevna."

"Oh, why?" she retorted; but she herself led the conversation into another channel. She was still ill at ease with Bazarov, though she had told him and assured herself that everything was for-gotten. While she was exchanging the simplest remarks with him, even while she was jesting with him, she was conscious of a faint spasm of dread. So people on a steamer at sea talk and laugh carelessly, for all the world as though they were on dry land; but let only the slightest hitch occur, let the least sign be seen of anything out of the common, and at once on every face there emerges an expression of peculiar alarm, betraying the constant consciousness of constant danger.

Anna Sergeyevna's conversation with Bazarov did not last long. She began to seem absorbed in thought, answered abstractedly, and suggested at last that they should go into the hall, where they found the princess and Katya. "But where is Arkady Nikolaich?" inquired the lady of the house; and on hearing that he had not shown himself for more than an hour, she sent for him. He was not very quickly found; he had hidden himself in the very thickest part of the garden, and with his chin propped on his clasped hands, he was sitting lost in meditation. They were deep and serious meditations, but not mournful. He knew Anna Sergeyevna was sitting alone with Bazarov, but he felt no jealousy as once he had; on the contrary, his face slowly brightened; he seemed to be at once wondering and rejoicing, and resolving on something.

XXVI

The deceased Odintsov had not liked innovations, but he had tolerated "a certain play of ennobled taste," and had in consequence put up in his garden, between the hothouse and the lake, something like a greek portico, made of Russian brick. Along the dark wall at the back of this portico or gallery were six niches for statues, which Odintsov had proceeded to order from abroad. These statues were to represent Solitude, Silence, Meditation, Melancholy, Modesty, and Sensibility. One of them, the goddess of Silence, with her finger on her lip, had been sent and put up; but on the very same day some boys on the farm had broken her nose; and though a plasterer of the neighborhood undertook to make her a new nose "twice as good as the old one," Odintsov ordered her to be taken away, and she was still to be seen in the corner of the threshing barn, where she had stood many long years, a source of superstitious terror to the peasant women. The front part of the portico had long been overgrown with thick bushes; only the pediments of the columns could be seen above the dense green. In the portico itself it was cool even at midday. Anna Sergeyevna did not like to visit this place ever since she had seen a snake there; but Katya often came and sat on the wide stone seat under one of the niches. Here, in the midst of the shade and coolness, she used to read and work, or to give herself up to that sensation of perfect peace, doubtless known to each of us, the charm of which consists in the half-unconscious, silent listening to the vast current of life that flows forever both around us and within us.

The day after Bazarov's arrival Katya was sitting on her favorite stone seat, and beside her Arkady was sitting again. He had besought her to come with him to the portico.

There was still about an hour to lunch time; the dewy morning had already given place to sultry day. Arkady's face retained the expression of the preceding day; Katya had a preoccupied look. Her sister had called her into her room directly after their morning tea, and after some preliminary caresses, which always scared Katya a little, she had advised her to be more guarded in her behavior with Arkady, and especially to avoid solitary talks with him, which had supposedly attracted the notice of her aunt and the entire household. Besides this, even the previous evening Anna Sergeyevna had not been herself; and Katya herself had felt ill at ease, as though she were conscious of some fault in herself. As she yielded to Arkady's entreaties, she said to herself that it was for the last time.

"Katerina Sergeyevna," he began with a sort of bashful easiness. "since I've had the happiness of living in the same house with you, I have discussed a great many things with you; but meanwhile there is one, very important . . . for me . . . one question, which I have not touched upon up till now. You remarked yesterday that I have been changed here," he went on, at once catching and avoiding the questioning glance Katya was turning upon him. "I certainly have changed a great deal, and you know that better than any one else—you to whom I really owe this change."

"I? . . . Me? . . ." said Katya.

"I am not now the conceited boy I was when I came here," Arkady went on. "I've not reached twenty-three for nothing; as before, I want to be useful, I want to devote all my powers to the truth; but I no longer look for my ideals where I did; they present themselves to me . . . much closer to hand. Up till now I did not understand myself; I set myself tasks which were beyond my powers. . . . My eyes have been opened lately, thanks to one feeling. . . . I'm not expressing myself quite clearly, but I hope you understand me."

Katya made no reply, but she ceased looking at Arkady.

"I suppose," he began again, this time in a more agitated voice, while above his head a chaffinch sang its song unheeding among the leaves of the birch—"I suppose it's the duty of every one to be open with those . . . with those people who . . . in fact, with those who are near to him, and so I . . . I resolved . . ."

But here Arkady's eloquence deserted him; he lost the thread, stammered, and was forced to be silent for a moment. Katya still did not raise her eyes. She seemed not to understand what he was leading up to in all this, and to be waiting for something.

"I foresee I shall surprise you," began Arkady, pulling himself together again with an effort, "especially since this feeling relates in a way . . . in a way, notice . . . to you. You reproached me, if you remember, yesterday with a want of seriousness," Arkady went on, with the air of a man who has got into a bog, feels that he is sinking further and further in at every step, and yet hurries onwards in the hope of crossing it as soon as possible;

"that reproach is often aimed . . . often falls . . . on young men even when they cease to deserve it; and if I had more self-confidence . . . " ("Come, help me, do help me!" Arkady was thinking, in desperation; but, as before, Katya did not turn her head.) "If I could hope . . ."

"If I could feel sure of what you say," was heard at that instant the clear voice of Anna Sergeyevna.

Arkady was still at once, while Katya turned pale. Close by the bushes that screened the ·portico ran a little path. Anna Sergeyevna was walking along it escorted by Bazarov. Katya and Arkady could not see them, but they heard every word, the rustle of their clothes, their very breathing. They walked on a few steps, and, as though on purpose, stood still just opposite the portico.

"You see," pursued Anna Sergeyevna, "you and I made a mistake; we are both past our first youth, I especially so; we have seen life, we are tired; we are both—why affect not to know it?—clever; at first we interested each other, curiosity was aroused . . . and then . . ."

"And then I grew stale," put in Bazarov.

"You know that was not the cause of our misunderstanding. But however that may be, we had no need of one another, that's the chief point; there was too much . . . what shall I say? . . . that was alike in us. We did not realize it all at once. Now, Arkady . . ."

"Do you need him?" queried Bazarov.

"Hush, Evgeny Vassilyich. You tell me he is not indifferent to me, and it always seemed to me he liked me. I know that I might well be his aunt, but I don't wish to conceal from you that I have come to think more often of him. In such youthful, fresh feeling there is a special charm . . ."

"The word *fascination* is most usual in such cases," Bazarov interrupted; suppressed spleen could be heard in his choked though hollow voice. "Arkady was mysterious over something with me yesterday, and didn't talk either of you or of your sister. . . . That's a serious symptom."

"He is just like a brother with Katya," commented Anna Sergeyevna, "and I like that in him, though, perhaps, I ought not to have allowed such intimacy between them."

"That idea is prompted by . . . your feelings as a sister?" Bazarov brought out, drawling.

"Of course . . . but why are we standing still? Let us go on. What a strange talk we are having, aren't we? I would never have believed I should talk to you like this. You know, I am afraid of you . . . and at the same time I trust you, because in reality you are so good."

"In the first place, I am not in the least good; and in the second place, I have lost all significance for you, and you tell me I am good . . . It's like laying a wreath of flowers on the head of a corpse."

"Evgeny Vassilyich, we.are not responsible . . ." Anna Sergeyevna began; but a gust of wind blew across, set the leaves rustling, and carried away her words. "Of course, you are free . . ." Bazarov declared after a brief pause. Nothing more could be distinguished; the steps retreated . . . everything was still.

Arkady turned to Katya. She was sitting in the same position, but her head was bent still lower. "Katerina Sergeyevna," he said with a shaking voice, and clasping his hands tightly together, "I love you forever and irrevocably, and I love no one but you. I wanted to tell you this, to find out your opinion of me, and to ask for your hand, since I am not rich, and I feel ready for any sacrifice. . . . You don't answer me? You don't believe me? Do you think I speak lightly? But remember these last days! Surely for a long time past you must have known that everything—understand me—everything else has vanished long ago and left no trace? Look at me, say one word to me . . . I love . . . I love you . . . believe me!"

Katya glanced at Arkady with a bright and serious look, and after long hesitation, with the faintest smile, she said, "Yes."

Arkady leaped up from the stone seat. "Yes! You said Yes, Katerina Sergeyevna! What does that word mean? Only that I do love you, that you believe me . . . or . . . or . . . I daren't go on . . ."

"Yes," repeated Katya, and this time he understood her. He snatched her large beautiful hands, and, breathless with rapture, pressed them to his heart. He could scarcely stand on his feet, and could only repeat, "Katya, Katya . . ." while she began weeping in a guileless way, smiling gently at her own tears. He who has not seen those tears in the eyes of the beloved, does not yet know to what a point, faint with shame and gratitude, a man may be happy on earth.

The next day, early in the morning, Anna Sergeyevna sent to ask Bazarov to her boudoir, and with a forced laugh handed him a folded sheet of notepaper. It was a letter from Arkady; in it he asked for her sister's hand.

Bazarov quickly scanned the letter, and made an effort to control himself, that he might not show the malignant feeling which was instantaneously aflame in his breast.

"So that's how it is," he commented; "and you, I fancy, only yesterday imagined he loved Katerina Sergeyevna as a brother. What do you intend to do now?"

"What do you advise me?" asked Anna Sergeyevna, still laughing.

"Well, I suppose," answered Bazarov, also with a laugh, though he felt anything but cheerful, and had no more inclination to laugh than she had; "I suppose you ought to give the young people your blessing. It's a good match in every respect; Kirsanov's position is passable, he's the only son, and his father's a good-natured fellow, he won't try to thwart him."

Odintsov walked up and down the room. By turns her face flushed and grew pale. "You think so," she said. "Well, I see no obstacles . . . I am glad for Katya . . . and for Arkady Nikolaevich too. Of course, I will wait for his father's answer. I will send him in person to him. But it turns out, you see, that I was right yesterday when I told you we were both old people. . . . How was it I saw nothing? That's what amazes me!" Anna Sergeyevna laughed again, and quickly turned her head away.

"The younger generation have grown awfully sly," remarked Bazarov, and he, too, laughed. "Good-bye," he began after a short silence. "I hope you will bring the matter to the most satisfactory conclusion; and I will rejoice from a distance."

Odintsov turned quickly to him. "You are not going away? Why should you not stay *now*? Stay . . . it's enjoyable to talk to you . . . one seems walking on the edge of a precipice. At first one feels timid, but one gains courage as one goes on. Do stay."

"Thanks for the suggestion, Anna Sergeyevna, and for your flattering opinion of my conversational talents. But I think I have already been moving too long in a sphere which is not my own. Flying fish can hold out for a time in the air, but soon they must splash back into the water; allow me, too, to paddle in my own element."

Odintsov looked at Bazarov. His pale face was twitching with a bitter smile. "This man loves me!" she thought, and she felt pity for him, and held out her hand to him with sympathy.

But he, too, understood her. "No!" he said, stepping back a pace. "I'm a poor man, but I've never taken charity so far. Good-bye, and good luck to you."

"I am certain we are not seeing each other for the last time," Anna Sergeyevna declared with an involuntary gesture.

"Anything may happen!" answered Bazarov, and he bowed and went away.

"So you are thinking of making yourself a nest?" he said the same day to Arkady, as he packed his box, crouching on the floor. "Well, it's a fine thing. But you needn't have been so foxy. I expected something from you in quite another quarter. Perhaps, though, it took you by surprise yourself?"

"I certainly didn't expect this when I parted from you," answered Arkady; "but why are you so foxy yourself, calling it 'a fine thing,' as though I didn't know your opinion of marriage."

"Ah, my dear friend," said Bazarov, "how you talk! You see what I'm doing; there seems to be an empty space in the box, and I am putting hay in; that's how it is in the box of our life; we would stuff it up with anything rather than have a void. Don't be offended, please; you remember, no doubt, the opinion I have always had of Katerina Sergeyevna. Many a young lady's called clever simply because she can sigh cleverly; but yours can hold her own, and, indeed, she'll hold it so well that she'll have you under her thumb—to be sure, though, that's quite as it ought to be." He slammed the lid to, and got up from the floor. "And now, I say again, good-bye, for it's useless to deceive ourselves—we are parting for good, and you know that yourself . . . you have acted sensibly; you're not made for our bitter, rough, lonely existence. There's no daring, no hate in you, but you've the dash of youth and the fire of youth. Your sort, you gentry, can never get beyond refined submission or refined indignation, and that's a mere trifle. You won't fight—and yet you fancy yourselves gallant chaps—but we mean to fight. But what's that! Our dust would get into your eyes, our mud would bespatter you, and you're not yet up to our level, you're admiring yourselves unconsciously, you like to upbraid yourself; but we're sick of that—we want something else! we want to smash other people! You're a good fellow; but you're a mild, liberal gentleman for all that—*ay volla-too,* as my parent is fond of saying."

"You are parting from me for ever, Evgeny," sadly responded Arkady; "and have you nothing else to say to me?"

Bazarov scratched the back of his head. "Yes, Arkady, yes, I have other things to say to you, but I'm not going to say them, because that's romanticism—that means, mawkishness. And you get married as soon as you can; and build your nest, and have lots of children. They'll be clever because they'll be born at a better time than you and me. Aha! I see the horses are ready. Time's up! I've said good-bye to every one. . . . What now? embracing, eh?"

Arkady flung himself on the neck of his former mentor and friend, and the tears fairly gushed from his eyes.

"That's what comes of being young!" Bazarov commented calmly. "But I rest my hopes on Katerina Sergeyevna. You'll see how quickly she'll console you!"

"Good-bye, friend!" he said to Arkady when he had got into the light cart, and, pointing to a pair of jackdaws sitting side by side on the stable roof, he added, "That's for you! follow that example."

"What does that mean?" asked Arkady.

"What? Are you so weak in natural history, or have you forgotten that the jackdaw is a most respectable family bird? An example to you! . . . Good-bye, signor!"

Bazarov had spoken truly. In talking that evening with Katya, Arkady completely forgot about his former teacher. He already began to follow her lead, and Katya was conscious of this, and not surprised at it. He was to set off the next day for Marino, to see Nikolai Petrovich. Anna Sergeyevna was not disposed to put any constraint on the young people, and only on account of the proprieties did not leave them by themselves for too long together. She magnanimously kept the princess out of their way; the latter had been reduced to a state of tearful frenzy by the news of the proposed marriage. At first Anna Sergeyevna was afraid the sight of their happiness might prove rather trying to herself, but it turned out quite the other way; this sight not only did not distress her, it interested her, it even softened her at last. Anna Sergeyevna felt both glad and sorry at this. "It is clear that Bazarov was right," she thought; "it has been curiosity, nothing but curiosity, and love of ease, and egoism . . ."

"Children," she said aloud, "what do you say, is love a purely imaginary feeling?"

But neither Katya nor Arkady even understood her. They were shy with her; the fragment of conversation they had involuntarily overheard haunted their minds. But Anna Sergeyevna soon set their minds at rest; and it was not difficult for her—she had set her own mind at rest.

XXVII

Bazarov's old parents were all the more overjoyed by their son's arrival, as it was quite unexpected. Arina Vlasyevna was so flustered, and kept running backwards and forwards in the house, that Vassily Ivanovich compared her to a "hen partridge"; the short tail of her abbreviated jacket did, in fact, give her something of a birdlike appearance. He himself merely growled and gnawed the amber mouthpiece of his pipe, or, clutching his neck with his fingers turned his head round, as though he were trying whether it were properly screwed on, then all at once he opened his wide mouth and went off into a perfectly noiseless chuckle.

"I've come to you for six whole weeks, old thing," Bazarov said to him. "I want to work, so please don't hinder me now."

"You shall forget my face completely, that's how I'll hinder you!" answered Vassily Ivanovich.

He kept his promise. After installing his son as before in his study, he almost hid himself away from him, and kept his wife from all superfluous demonstrations of tenderness. "On Enyusha's first visit, my dear soul," he said to her, "we bothered him a little; we must be wiser this time." Arina Vlasyevna agreed with her husband, but that was small compensation since she saw her son only at meals, and was now absolutely afraid to address him. "Enyushenka," she would say sometimes—and before he had time to look round, she was nervously fingering the tassels of her reticule and faltering, "Never mind, never mind, I only——" and afterwards she would go to Vassily Ivanovich and, her cheek in her hand, would consult him: "If you could only find out, darling, which Enyusha would like for dinner to-day—borsch or *shchi*?" [7]—"But why didn't you ask him yourself?"—"Oh, he will get sick of me!" Bazarov, however, soon ceased to shut himself up; the fever of work fell away, and was replaced by dreary boredom or vague restlessness. A strange weariness began to show itself in all his movements; even his walk, firm and impetuously bold, was changed. He gave up walking in solitude, and began to seek company; he drank tea in the drawing-room, strolled about the kitchen-garden with Vassily Ivanovich, and smoked with him in silence; once even asked after Father Alexey. Vassily Ivanovich at first rejoiced at this change, but his joy was not long-lived. "Enyusha's breaking my heart," he complained in secret to his wife: "it's not that he's discontented or angry—that would be nothing; he's sad, he's sorrowful—that's what's so terrible. He's always silent. If he'd only abuse us; he's growing thin, he's lost his color."—"Mercy on us, mercy on us!" whispered the old woman; "I would put an amulet on his neck, but, of course, he won't allow it." Vassily Ivanovich several times attempted in the most circumspect manner to question Bazarov about his work, about his health, and about Arkady. . . . But Bazarov's replies were reluctant and casual; and, once noticing that his father was gradually leading up to something in conversation, he said to him in a tone of vexation: "Why do you always seem to be walking round me on tiptoe? That way's worse than the old one."—

7. The standbys of Russian cooking. Both are thick soups—borsch (literally *borshch*) is made with beets, *shchi* with cabbage. Both are served with sour cream. Borsch contains, among other things, beef, sausage, and potatoes; *shchi* is identical with the *pot-au-feu*, or boiled beef, except for the sour cream and a tablespoon of chopped dill.

"There, there, I meant nothing!" poor Vassily Ivanovich answered hurriedly. So his political hints remained fruitless. He hoped to awaken his son's sympathy one day by beginning, apropos the approaching emancipation of the peasantry, to talk about progress; but the latter responded indifferently: "Yesterday I was walking past the fence, and I heard the peasant boys here, instead of some old ballad, bawling a popular tune. That's what progress is."

Sometimes Bazarov went into the village, and in his usual bantering tone entered into conversation with some peasant: "Come," he would say to him. "expound your views on life to me, friend; you see, they say all the strength and future of Russia lies in your hands, a new epoch in history will be started by you—you give us our real language and our laws." The peasant either answered nothing or articulated a few words of this sort, "Well, we'll try . . . because, you see, that's the extent of the land . . ."

"You explain to me what your *mir* (world) [8] is," Bazarov interrupted; "and is it the same *mir* that is said to rest on three fishes?"

"It's the earth that rests on three fishes," the peasant would declare soothingly, in a kind of patriarchal, good-natured singsong; "and as against ours, that's to say, the *mir*, we know there's the master's will; because you are our fathers. And the stricter the master's rule, the better for the peasant."

After listening to such a reply one day, Bazarov shrugged his shoulders contemptuously and turned away, while the peasant sauntered slowly homewards.

"What was he talking about?" inquired another peasant of middle age and surly aspect, who at a distance from the door of his hut had been following his conversation with Bazarov.— "Arrears? eh?"

"Arrears, no indeed, mate!" answered the first peasant, and now there was no trace of patriarchal singsong in his voice; on the contrary, there was a certain scornful gruffness to be heard in it: "Oh, he clacked away about something or other; wanted to stretch his tongue a bit. Of course, he's a gentleman; what does he understand?"

"What should he understand!" answered the other peasant, and jerking back their caps and pushing down their belts, they proceeded to deliberate upon their work and their wants. Alas! Bazarov, shrugging his shoulders contemptuously, that self-confident Bazarov, who knew how to talk to peasants (as he had

8. Bazarov plays on two meanings of *mir*: the world, and the village commune. The ignorant folk believed myths that the world was supported by three fish.

boasted in his dispute with Pavel Petrovich), did not even suspect that in their eyes he was all the while something of the nature of a buffoon.

He found employment for himself at last, however. One day Vassily Ivanovich bound up a peasant's wounded leg in his presence, but the old man's hands trembled, and he could not manage the bandages; his son helped him, and from that time began to take a share in his practice, though at the same time he was constantly sneering both at the remedies he himself advised and at his father, who hastened to make use of them. But Bazarov's jeers did not in the least perturb Vassily Ivanovich; they were positively a comfort to him. Holding his greasy dressing-gown across his stomach with two fingers, and smoking his pipe, he used to listen with enjoyment to Bazarov; and the more malicious his sallies, the more good-naturedly did his delighted father chuckle, showing every one of his black teeth. He used even to repeat these sometimes flat or pointless retorts, and would, for instance, for several days without rhyme or reason, constantly repeat, "No great shakes!" simply because his son, on hearing he was going to matins, had made use of that expression. "Thank God! he has got over his melancholy!" he whispered to his wife; "how he gave it to me to-day, it was splendid!" Moreover, the idea of having such an assistant made him ecstatic and filled him with pride. "Yes, yes," he would say to some peasant woman in a man's coat, and a cap shaped like a horn, as he handed her a bottle of Goulard's extract or a box of white ointment, "you ought to thank God every minute, my good woman, that my son is staying with me; you will be treated now by the most scientific, most modern method. Do you know what that means? The Emperor of the French, Napoleon, even, has no better doctor." And the peasant woman, who had come to complain that her "stiches were rising" (the exact meaning of these words, however, she was not able to explain herself), merely bowed low and rummaged in her bosom, where four eggs lay tied up in the corner of a towel.

Bazarov once even pulled out a tooth for a passing pedlar; and though this tooth was an average specimen, Vassily Ivanovich preserved it as a curiosity, and incessantly repeated, as he showed it to Father Alexey, "Just look, what a fang! The force Evgeny has! The pedlar seemed to leap into the air. If it had been an oak, he'd have rooted it up!"

"Most promising!" Father Alexey would comment at last, not knowing what answer to make, and how to get rid of the ecstatic old man.

One day a peasant from a neighboring village brought his brother who was ill with typhus to Vassily Ivanovich. The unhappy man, lying face down on a truss of straw, was dying; his body was covered with dark patches, he had long ago lost consciousness. Vassily Ivanovich expressed his regret that no one had taken steps to procure medical aid sooner, and declared there was no hope. And, in fact, the peasant did not get his brother home again; he died in the cart.

Three days later Bazarov came into his father's room and asked him if he had any caustic.

"Yes; what do you want it for?"

"I must have some . . . to burn a cut."

"For whom?"

"For myself."

"What, yourself? Why is that? What sort of a cut? Where is it?"

"Look here, on my finger. I went to-day to the village, you know, where they brought that peasant with typhus fever. They were just going to do an autopsy for some reason or other, and I've had no practice of that sort for a long while."

"Well?"

"Well, so I asked the district doctor about it; and so I cut myself."

Vassily Ivanovich all at once turned quite white, and, without uttering a word, rushed to his study, from which he returned at once with a bit of caustic in his hand. Bazarov was about to take it and go away.

"For mercy's sake," said Vassily Ivanovich, "let me do it myself."

Bazarov smiled. "What a devoted practitioner!"

"Don't laugh, please. Show me your finger. The cut is not a large one. Do I hurt?"

"Press harder; don't be afraid."

Vassily Ivanovich stopped. "What do you think, Evgeny; wouldn't it be better to burn it with hot iron?"

"That ought to have been done sooner; even the caustic is useless, really, now. If I've taken the infection, it's too late now."

"How . . . too late. . . ." Vassily Ivanovich could scarcely articulate the words.

"I should think so! It's more than four hours ago."

Vassily Ivanovich burnt the cut a little more. "But had the district doctor no caustic?"

"No."

"How was that, good Heavens? A doctor not have such an indispensable thing as that!"

"You should have seen his lancets," observed Bazarov as he walked away.

Up till late that evening, and all the following day, Vassily Ivanovich kept catching at every possible excuse to go into his son's room; and though far from referring to the cut—he even tried to talk about the most irrelevant subjects—he looked so persistently into his face, and watched him in such trepidation, that Bazarov lost patience and threatened to go away. Vassily Ivanovich gave him his promise, that he would not worry, the more readily as Arina Vlasyevna, from whom, of course, he kept it all secret, was beginning to worry him as to why he did not sleep, and what had come over him. For two whole days he held himself in, though he did not at all like the look of his son, whom he kept watching stealthily, . . . but on the third day, at dinner, he could bear it no longer. Bazarov sat with downcast looks, and had not touched a single dish.

"Why don't you eat, Evgeny?" he inquired, putting on an expression of the most perfect carelessness. "The food, I think, is very nicely cooked."

"I don't want anything, so I don't eat."

"Have you no appetite? And your head," he added timidly; "does it ache?"

"Yes. Of course, it aches."

Arina Vlasyevna sat up and was all alert.

"Don't be angry, please, Evgeny," continued Vassily Ivanovich; "won't you let me feel your pulse?"

Bazarov got up. "I can tell you without feeling my pulse; I'm feverish."

"Has there been any shivering?"

"Yes, there has been shivering too. I'll go and lie down, and you can send me some lime-flower tea. I must have caught cold."

"To be sure, I heard you coughing last night," observed Arina Vlasyevna.

"I've caught cold," repeated Bazarov, and he went away.

Arina Vlasyevna busied herself about the preparation of lime-flower tea, while Vassily Ivanovich went into the next room and clutched at his hair in silent desperation.

Bazarov did not get up again that day, and passed the whole night in heavy, half-unconscious torpor. After midnight, opening his eyes with an effort, he saw by the light of a lamp his father's pale face bending over him, and told him to go away. The old man begged his pardon, but he quickly came back on tiptoe, and half-hidden by the cupboard door, he gazed persistently at his son. Arina Vlasyevna did not go to bed either, and leaving the study door just open a very little, she kept coming up to it to listen "how Enyusha was breathing," and to look at Vassily Ivanovich. She could see nothing but his motionless bent back, but even that afforded her some faint consolation. In the morning Bazarov tried to get up; he was seized with giddiness, his nose began to bleed; he lay down again. Vassily Ivanovich waited on him in silence; Arina Vlasyevna went in to him and asked him how he was feeling. He answered, "Better," and turned to the wall. Vassily Ivanovich gesticulated at his wife with both hands; she bit her lips so as not to cry, and went away. The whole house seemed suddenly darkened; every one looked gloomy; there was a strange hush; a shrill cock was carried away from the yard to the village, unable to comprehend why he should be treated so. Bazarov continued to lie turned to the wall. Vassily Ivanovich tried to address him with various questions, but they fatigued Bazarov, and the old man sank back into his arm-chair, motionless, only cracking his finger-joints now and then. He went for a few minutes into the garden, stood there like a statue, as though overwhelmed with unutterable bewilderment (the expression of bewilderment never left his face all through), and went back again to his son, trying to avoid his wife's questions. She caught him by the arm at last, and passionately, almost menacingly, said, "What is wrong with him?" Then he came to himself, and forced himself to smile at her in reply; but to his own horror, instead of a smile, he found himself taken somehow by a fit of laughter. He had sent at daybreak for a doctor. He thought it necessary to inform his son of this, for fear he should be angry.

Bazarov suddenly turned over on the sofa, bent a fixed dull look on his father, and asked for drink.

Vassily Ivanovich gave him some water, and as he did so felt his forehead. It seemed on fire.

"Old thing," began Bazarov, in a slow, drowsy voice; "I'm in a bad way; I've got the infection, and in a few days you'll have to bury me."

Vassily Ivanovich staggered back, as though some one had aimed a blow at his legs.

"Evgeny!" he faltered; "what do you mean! . . . God have mercy on you! You've caught cold!"

"Enough!" Bazarov interrupted deliberately. "A doctor can't be allowed to talk like that. There's every symptom of infection; you know yourself."

"Where are the symptoms . . . of infection, Evgeny? . . . Good Heavens!"

"What's this?" said Bazarov, and, pulling up his shirt-sleeve, he showed his father the ominous red patches coming out on his arm.

Vassily Ivanovich was shaking and chill with terror.

"Supposing," he said at last, "even supposing . . . if even there's something like . . . infection . . ."

"Pyæmia," put in his son.

"Well, well . . . something of the epidemic . . ."

"*Pyæmia*," Bazarov repeated sharply and distinctly; "have you forgotten your text-books?"

"Well, well—as you like. . . . Anyway, we will cure you!"

"Come, that's humbug. But that's not the point. I didn't expect to die so soon; it's a most unpleasant incident, to tell the truth. You and mother ought to make the most of your strong religious belief; now's the time to put it to the test." He drank off a little water. "I want to ask you about one thing . . . while my head is still under my control. To-morrow or next day my brain, you know, will send in its resignation. I'm not quite certain even now whether I'm expressing myself clearly. While I've been lying here, I've kept fancying red dogs were running round me, while you were making them point at me, as if I were a woodcock. Just as if I were drunk. Do you understand me all right?"

"I assure you, Evgeny, you are talking perfectly correctly."

"All the better. You told me you'd sent for the doctor. You did that to comfort yourself . . . comfort me too; send a messenger . . ."

"To Arkady Nikolaich?" put in the old man.

"Who's Arkady Nikolaich?" said Bazarov, as though in doubt. . . . "Oh, yes! that little bird! No, let him alone; he's turned jackdaw now. Don't be surprised; that's not delirium yet. You send a messenger to Odintsov, Anna Sergeyevna; she's a lady with an estate. . . . Do you know?" (Vassily Ivanovich nodded.) "Evgeny Bazarov, say, sends his greetings, and sends word he is dying. Will you do that?"

"Yes, I will do it. . . . But is it a possible thing for you to die, Evgeny? . . . Think only! Where would divine justice be after that?"

"I know nothing about that; only you send the messenger."

"I'll send this minute, and I'll write a letter myself."

"No, why? Say I send greetings; nothing more is necessary. And now I'll go back to my dogs. Strange! I want to fix my thoughts on death, and nothing comes of it. I see a kind of blur . . . and nothing more."

He turned heavily back to the wall again; while Vassily Ivanovich went out of the study, and struggling as far as his wife's bedroom, simply dropped down on to his knees before the holy pictures.

The doctor, the same district doctor who had had no caustic, arrived, and after looking at the patient, advised them to persevere with waiting it out, and at that point said a few words of the chance of recovery.

"Have you ever chanced to see people in my state not set off for the Elysian Fields?" asked Bazarov, and suddenly snatching the leg of a heavy table that stood near his sofa, he swung it round, and pushed it away. "There's strength, there's strength," he murmured; "it's here still, and I must die! . . . An old man at least has time to be weaned from life, but I . . . Well, go and try to disprove death. Death will disprove you, and that's all! Who's crying there?" he added, after a short pause.—"Mother? Poor thing! Whom will she feed now with her exquisite borsch? You, Vassily Ivanovich, whimpering too, I do believe! Why, if Christianity's no help to you, be a philosopher, a Stoic, or what not! Why, didn't you boast you were a philosopher?"

"Me a philosopher!" wailed Vassily Ivanovich, while the tears fairly streamed down his cheeks.

Bazarov got worse every hour; the progress of the disease was rapid, as is usually the way in cases of surgical poisoning. He still had not lost consciousness, and understood what was said to him; he was still struggling. "I don't want to lose my wits," he muttered, clenching his fists; "what rot it all is!" And at once he would say, "Come, take ten from eight, what remains?" Vassily Ivanovich wandered about like one possessed, proposed first one remedy, then another, and ended by doing nothing but cover up his son's feet. "Try cold pack . . . emetic . . . mustard plasters on the stomach . . . bleeding," he would murmur with an effort. The doctor, whom he had entreated to remain, agreed with him, ordered the patient to drink lemonade, and for himself asked for a pipe and something "warming and strengthening"—that is to say vodka. Arina Vlasyevna sat on a low stool near the door, and only went out from time to time to pray. A few days before, a looking-glass had slipped out of her hands and been broken, and this she had always considered an omen of evil; even Anfisushka could say nothing to her. Timofeich had gone off to Odintsov's.

The night passed badly for Bazarov. . . . He was in the agonies of high fever. Towards morning he was a little easier. He asked Arina Vlasyevna to comb his hair, kissed her hand, and swallowed two gulps of tea. Vassily Ivanovich revived a little.

"Thank God!" he kept declaring; "the crisis is coming, the crisis is at hand!"

"There, to think now!" murmured Bazarov; "what a word can do! He's found it; he's said 'crisis,' and is comforted. It's an astounding thing how man believes in words. If he's told he's a fool, for instance, though he's not thrashed, he'll be wretched; call him a clever fellow, and he'll be delighted if you go off without paying him."

This little speech of Bazarov's, recalling his old "retorts," moved Vassily Ivanovich greatly.

"Bravo! well said, very good!" he cried, making as though he were clapping his hands.

Bazarov smiled mournfully.

"So what do you think," he said; "is the crisis over, or coming?"

"You are better, that's what I see, that's what gives me joy," answered Vassily Ivanovich.

"Well, that's good; joy never comes amiss. And to her, do you remember, did you send?"

"To be sure I did."

The change for the better did not last long. The disease resumed its onslaughts. Vassily Ivanovich was sitting by Bazarov. It seemed as though the old man were tormented by some special anguish. Several times he was on the point of speaking—and could not.

"Evgeny!" he brought out at last; "my son, my beloved, dear son!"

This unfamiliar mode of address produced an effect on Bazarov. He turned his head a little, and, obviously trying to fight against the load of oblivion weighing upon him, he articulated: "What is it, father?"

"Evgeny," Vassily Ivanovich went on, and he fell on his knees before Bazarov, though the latter had closed his eyes and could not see him. "Evgeny, you are better now; please God, you will get well, but make use of this time, comfort your mother and me, perform the duty of a Christian! What it means for me to say this to you, it's awful; but still more awful . . . for ever and ever, Evgeny . . . think a little, what. . . ."

The old man's voice broke, and a strange look passed over his son's face, though he still lay with closed eyes.

"I won't refuse, if that can be any comfort to you," he brought out at last; "but it seems to me there's no need to be in a hurry. You say yourself I am better."

"Oh, yes, Evgeny, better certainly; but who knows, it is all in God's hands, and in doing the duty . . ."

"No, I will wait a bit," broke in Bazarov. "I agree with you that the crisis has come. And if we're mistaken, well! they give the sacrament to men who are unconscious, you know."

"Evgeny, I beg."

"I'll wait a little. And now I want to go to sleep. Don't disturb me." And he laid his head back in its former position.

The old man rose from his knees, sat down in the arm-chair, and clutching his beard, began biting his fingers . . .

The sound of a light carriage on springs, that sound which is peculiarly impressive in the wilds of the country, suddenly struck his ears. Nearer and nearer rolled the light wheels; now even the neighing of the horses could be heard. . . . Vassily Ivanovich jumped up and ran to the little window. There drove into the courtyard of his little house a carriage with seats for two, harnessed with four horses. Without stopping to consider what it could mean, with a rush of a sort of senseless joy, he ran out on to the steps. . . . A groom in livery was opening the carriage doors; a lady in a black veil and a black mantle was getting out of it . . .

"I am Odintsov," she said. "Is Evgeny Vassilyich still alive? Are you his father? I have a doctor with me."

"Benefactress!" cried Vassily Ivanovich, and snatching her hand, he pressed it convulsively to his lips, while the doctor brought by Anna Sergeyevna, a little man in spectacles, of German physiognomy, stepped very deliberately out of the carriage. "Still alive, my Evgeny is alive, and now he will be saved! Wife! wife! . . . An angel from heaven has come to us. . . ."

"What does it mean, good Lord!" faltered the old woman, running out of the drawing-room; and, comprehending nothing, she fell on the spot in the passage at Anna Sergeyevna's feet, and began kissing her garments like a mad woman.

"What are you doing!" protested Anna Sergeyevna; but Arina Vlasyevna did not heed her, while Vassily Ivanovich could only repeat, "An angel! an angel!"

"*Wo ist der Kranke?* and where is the patient?" said the doctor at last, with some impatience.

Vassily Ivanovich recovered himself. "Here, here, follow me, *werthester Herr College,*" [9] he added through old associations.

"Ah!" articulated the German, grinning sourly.

Vassily Ivanovich led him into the study. "The doctor from Anna Sergeyevna Odintsov," he said, bending down quite to his

9. "Honored colleague."

son's ear, "and she herself is here."

Bazarov suddenly opened his eyes. "What did you say?"

"I say that Anna Sergeyevna is here, and has brought this gentleman, a doctor, to you."

Bazarov moved his eyes about him. "She is here. . . . I want to see her."

"You shall see her, Evgeny; but first we must have a little talk with the doctor. I will tell him the whole history of your illness since Sidor Sidorich" (this was the name of the district doctor) "has gone, and we will have a little consultation."

Bazarov glanced at the German. "Well, talk away quickly, only not in Latin; you see, I know the meaning of *jam moritur*.[1]

"*Der Herr scheint des Deutschen mächtig zu sein,*"[2] began this new follower of Æsculapius, turning to Vassily Ivanovich.

"*Ich.* . . . *gabe* . . . We had better speak Russian," said the old man.

"*Ach* so! so that's how it is. . . . To be sure . . ." and the consultation began.

Half-an-hour later Anna Sergeyevna, conducted by Vassily Ivanovich, came into the study. The doctor had had time to whisper to her that it was hopeless even to think of the patient's recovery.

She looked at Bazarov . . . and stood still in the doorway, so greatly was she impressed by the inflamed, and at the same time deathly face, with its dim eyes fastened upon her. She was simply dismayed, with a sort of cold and suffocating fear; the thought that she would not have felt like that if she had really loved him flashed instantaneously through her brain.

"Thanks," he said painfully, "I did not expect this. It's a good deed. So we have seen each other again, as you promised."

"Anna Sergeyvena has been so kind," began Vassily Ivanovich . . .

"Father, leave us alone. Anna Sergeyevna, you will allow it, I fancy, now?"

With a motion of his head, he indicated his prostrate helpless frame.

Vassily Ivanovich went out.

"Well, thanks," repeated Bazarov. "This is royally done. Monarchs, they say, visit the dying too."

"Evgeny Vassilyich, I hope—"

"Ah, Anna Sergeyevna, let us speak the truth. It's all over with me. I'm under the wheel. So it turns out that it was useless to think of the future. Death's an old joke, but it comes fresh to every one. So far I'm not afraid . . . but there, unconsciousness

1. "Is dying now."

2. "The gentleman seems to master the German language."

will come, and then it's all over!——" he waved his hand feebly. "Well, what do I have to say to you . . . that I loved you? There was no sense in that even before, and less than ever now. Love is a form, and my own form is already breaking up. I better say how lovely you are! And now here you stand, so beautiful . . ."

Anna Sergeyevna gave an involuntary shudder.

"Never mind, don't be uneasy. . . . Sit down there . . . Don't come close to me; you know, my illness is catching."

Anna Sergeyevna swiftly crossed the room, and sat down in the arm-chair near the sofa on which Bazarov was lying.

"Noble-hearted!" he whispered. "Oh, how near, and how young, and fresh, and pure . . . in this loathsome room! . . . Well, good-bye! live long, that's the best of all, and make the most of it while there is time. You see what a hideous spectacle; the worm half crushed, but writhing still. And, you see, I thought too: I'd break down so many things, I wouldn't die, why should I, there were problems to solve, and I was a giant! And now all the problem for the giant is how to die decently, though that makes no difference to any one either . . . Never mind; I'm not going to turn my tail."

Bazarov fell silent, and began feeling with his hand for the glass. Anna Sergeyevna gave him a drink, not taking off her glove, and drawing her breath apprehensively.

"You will forget me," he began again; "the dead's no companion for the living. My father will tell you what a man Russia is losing. . . . That's nonsense, but don't contradict the old man. Whatever toy will comfort the child . . . you know. And be kind to mother. People like them aren't to be found in your great world if you look by daylight with a candle. . . . I am needed by Russia. . . . No, it's clear, I am not needed. And who is needed? The shoemaker's needed, the tailor's needed, the butcher . . . gives us meat . . . the butcher . . . wait a little, I'm getting mixed. . . . There's a forest here . . ."

Bazarov put his hand to his brow.

Anna Sergeyevna bent down to him. "Evgeny Vassilyich, I am here . . ."

He at once took his hand away, and raised himself.

"Good-bye," he said with sudden force, and his eyes gleamed with their last light. "Good-bye. . . . Listen . . . you know I didn't kiss you then. . . . Breathe on the dying lamp, and let it go out . . ."

Anna Sergeyevna put her lips to his forehead.

"Enough!" he murmured, and dropped back on to the pillow. "Now . . . darkness . . ."

Anna Sergeyevna went softly out. "Well?" Vassily Ivanovich

asked her in a whisper.

"He has fallen asleep," she answered, hardly audibly. Bazarov was not fated to awaken. Towards evening he sank into complete unconsciousness, and the following day he died. Father Alexey performed the last rites of religion over him. When they anointed him, when the holy oil touched his breast, one eye opened, and it seemed as though at the sight of the priest in his vestments, the smoking censers, the light before the ikon, something like a shudder of horror passed over the death-stricken face. When at last he had breathed his last, and there arose a universal lamentation in the house, Vassily Ivanovich was seized by a sudden frenzy. "I said I should rebel," he shrieked hoarsely, with his face inflamed and distorted, shaking his fist in the air, as though threatening some one; "and I rebel, I rebel!" But Arina Vlasyevna, all in tears, hung upon his neck, and both prostrated themselves. "Side by side," Anfisushka related afterwards in the servants' room, "they drooped their poor heads like lambs at noonday . . ."

But the heat of noonday passes, and evening comes and night, and then, too, the return to the kindly refuge, where sleep is sweet for the weary and heavy laden. . . .

XXVIII

Six months had passed by. White winter had come with the cruel stillness of unclouded frosts, the thick-lying, crunching snow, the rosy rime on the trees, the pale emerald sky, the caps of smoke above the chimneys, the clouds of steam rushing out of the doors when they are opened for an instant, with the fresh faces, that look stung by the cold, and the hurrying trot of the chilled horses. A January day was drawing to its close; the cold of evening was more keen than ever in the motionless air, and a lurid sunset was rapidly dying away. There were lights burning in the windows of the house at Marino; Prokofich in a black frock coat and white gloves, with a special solemnity laid the table for seven. A week before in the small parish church two weddings had taken place quietly, and almost without witnesses—Arkady and Katya's, and Nikolai Petrovich and Fenichka's; and on this day Nikolai Petrovich was giving a farewell dinner to his brother, who was going away to Moscow on business. Anna Sergeyevna had gone there also directly after the ceremony was over, after making very handsome presents to the young people.

Precisely at three o'clock they all gathered about the table. Mitya was placed there too; with him appeared a nurse in a cap of glazed brocade. Pavel Petrovich took his seat between Katya and Fenichka; the husbands took their places beside their wives. Our friends had changed of late; they all seemed to have grown stronger and better looking; only Pavel Petrovich was thinner, which gave an even more elegant and *grand seigneur* air to his expressive features. . . . And Fenichka, too, was different. In a fresh silk gown, with a wide velvet head-dress on her hair, with a gold chain round her neck, she sat with respectful immobility, respectful towards herself and everything surrounding her, and smiled as though she would say, "I beg your pardon; I'm not to blame." And not she alone—all the others smiled, and also seemed apologetic; they were all a little awkward, a little sorry, and in reality very happy. They all helped one another with humorous attentiveness, as though they had all agreed to rehearse a sort of artless comedy. Katya was the most composed of all; she looked confidently about her, and it could be seen that Nikolai Petrovich was already dotingly fond of her. At the end of dinner he got up, and his glass in his hand, turned to Pavel Petrovich.

"You are leaving us . . . you are leaving us, dear brother," he began; "not for long, to be sure; but still, I cannot help expressing what I . . . what we . . . how much I . . . how much we. . . . There, the worst of it is, we don't know how to make speeches. Arkady, you speak."

"No, daddy, I've not prepared anything."

"As though I were so well prepared! Well, brother, I will simply say, let me embrace you, wish you all good luck, and come back to us as quickly as you can!"

Pavel Petrovich exchanged kisses with every one, of course not excluding Mitya; in Fenichka's case, he kissed also her hand, which she had not yet learned to offer properly, and drinking off the glass which had been filled again, he said with a deep sigh, "May you be happy my friends! *Farewell!*" This English finale passed unnoticed; but all were touched.

"To the memory of Bazarov," Katya whispered in her husband's ear, as she clinked glasses with him. Arkady pressed her hand warmly in response, but he did not venture to propose this toast aloud.

This would seem to be the end. But perhaps some of our readers would care to know what each of the characters we have introduced is doing in the present, the actual present. We are ready to satisfy him.

Anna Sergeyevna has recently married, not for love but out of good sense, with one of the future leaders of Russia, a very clever man, a lawyer, with vigorous practical sense, a strong will, and remarkable eloquence—still young, good-natured, and cold as ice. They live in the greatest harmony together, and will live perhaps to attain complete happiness . . . perhaps love. The Princess K— is dead, forgotten the day of her death. The Kirsanovs, father and son, have settled down at Marino; their fortunes are beginning to mend. Arkady has become zealous in the management of the estate, and the "farm" now yields a fairly good income. Nikolai Petrovich has been made one of the mediators appointed to carry out the emancipation reforms, and works with all his energies; he is forever driving about over his district; delivers long speeches (he maintains the opinion that the peasants ought to be "brought to comprehend things," that is to say, they ought to be reduced to a state of exhaustion by the constant repetition of one and the same words); and yet, to tell the truth, he does not give complete satisfaction either to the refined gentry, who talk with *chic* or with melancholy of the *emancipation* (pronouncing it as though it were French), nor to the uncultivated gentry, who unceremoniously curse "tha' 'muncipation.'" He is too soft-hearted for both sets. Katerina Sergeyevna has a son, little Nikolai, while Mitya runs about merrily and talks fluently. Fenichka, Fedosya Nikolaevna, after her husband and Mitya, adores no one so much as her daughter-in-law, and when the latter is at the piano, she would gladly spend the whole day at her side. A passing word of Peter. He has grown perfectly rigid with stupidity and dignity, pronounces all his *e*'s as *u*'s but he too is married, and received a respectable dowry with his bride, the daughter of a market-gardener of the town, who had refused two excellent suitors, only because they had no watch; while Peter not only had a watch—he had a pair of patent leather shoes.

In Dresden, on the Brühl Terrace, between two and four o'clock—the most fashionable time for walking—you may meet a man about fifty, quite grey, and looking as though he suffered from gout, but still handsome, elegantly dressed, and with that special stamp which is gained only by moving in the higher strata of society. That is Pavel Petrovich. From Moscow he went abroad for the sake of his health, and has settled for good at Dresden, where he associates mostly with the English and with passing Russians. With English people he behaves simply, almost modestly, but with dignity; they find him rather a bore, but respect him for being, as they say, *"a perfect gentleman."* With Russians he is more free and easy, gives vent to his spleen, and makes fun of himself and them, but that is done by him with great amiability, negligence, and propriety. He holds Slavophile views;

it is well known that in the highest society this is regarded as *très distingué!* He reads nothing in Russian, but on his writing table there is a silver ash-tray in the shape of a peasant's plaited shoe. He is much run after by our tourists. Matvey Ilyich Kolyazin, happening to be "in temporary opposition," paid him a majestic visit on his way to take the waters in Bohemia; while the natives, with whom, however, he is very little seen, positively grovel before him. No one can so readily and quickly obtain a ticket for the court chapel, for the theatre and such things as *der Herr Baron von Kirsanoff.* He does as much good as he can; he still makes some little noise in the world; it is not for nothing that he was once a great society lion, but life is a burden to him . . . a heavier burden than he suspects himself. One need but glance at him in the Russian church, when, leaning against the wall on one side, he sinks into thought, and remains long without stirring, bitterly compressing his lips, then suddenly recollects himself, and begins almost imperceptibly to cross himself. . . .

Kushkin, too, went abroad. She is in Heidelberg, and is now studying not natural science but architecture, in which, according to her own account, she has discovered new laws. She still fraternizes with students, especially with the young Russians studying physics and chemistry, with whom Heidelberg is crowded, and who astound the naïve German professors at first by the soundness of their views of things, later astound the same professor no less by their complete inactivity and absolute idleness. In company with two or three such young chemists, who don't know oxygen from nitrogen, but are filled with scepticism and self-conceit, and with the great Elisyevich, too, Sitnikov now roams about Petersburg, also getting ready to be great, and, according to himself, continues Bazarov's "work." There is talk that some one recently gave him a beating; but he paid the fellow back: in an obscure little article, hidden in an obscure little journal, he has hinted that the man who beat him was a coward. He calls this irony. His father bullies him as before, while his wife regards him as a fool . . . and a literary man.

There is a small village graveyard in one of the remote corners of Russia. Like almost all our graveyards it presents a wretched appearance; the ditches surrounding it have long been overgrown; the grey wooden crosses lie fallen and rotting under their once painted gables; the tombstones are all displaced, as though some one were pushing them up from beneath; two or three ragged trees scarcely give scant shade; the sheep wander unchecked among the tombs . . . But among them is one untouched by man, untrampled by beast, only the birds perch upon it and sing at daybreak. An iron railing runs round it; two young fir-trees have been planted, one at each end. Evgeny Bazarov is buried in this tomb. Often from the little village not far off, two quite feeble old people come to visit it—a husband and wife. Supporting one another, they move to it with heavy steps; they go up to the railing, fall down, and remain on their knees, and long and bitterly they weep, and intently they gaze at the mute stone, under which their son is lying; they exchange some brief word, wipe away the dust from the stone, set straight a branch of a fir-tree, and pray again, and cannot tear themselves from this place, where they seem to be nearer to their son, to their memories of him. . . . Can it be that their prayers and their tears are fruitless? Can it be that love, sacred, devoted love, is not all-powerful? Oh, no! However passionate, sinning, and rebellious the heart hidden in the tomb, the flowers growing over it peep serenely at us with their innocent eyes; they tell us not of eternal peace alone, of that great peace of "indifferent" nature;[3] they tell us, too, of eternal reconciliation and of life without end.

August, 1861.

---

3. A citation from Pushkin. See p. 321.

The Author on the Novel

IVAN TURGENEV

Apropos of *Fathers and Sons*†

I was sea-bathing in Ventnor, a small town on the Isle of Wight—it was in August of 1860—when I first thought of *Fathers and Sons*, that tale thanks to which I lost—and apparently forever—the younger Russian generation's friendly disposition toward me. I have frequently heard and read in critical articles that in my works I "started with an idea"; some praised me for it, others, on the contrary, blamed me; for my part I must confess that I never attempted "to create a figure" unless I had a living character rather than an idea, to whom appropriate elements were gradually added and mixed in. Since I do not possess a great deal of free invention, I always needed solid ground on which I could step firmly. That is precisely what occurred with *Fathers and Sons*. At the basis of the main character, Bazarov, there lay the figure of a young provincial doctor that had struck me. (He died shortly before 1860.) This remarkable man embodied in my view that barely nascent still fermenting principle that was later called nihilism. The impression that man made on me was very strong and at the time not entirely clear: at first, I could not myself make him out clearly, and I intently listened and examined everything around me as though I wanted to verify the justness of my own feelings. I was disturbed by the following fact: I did not even find a hint in any work of our literature of what I seemed to see everywhere; against my will I was beset by doubts: was I not chasing a phantom? I remember that on the Isle of Wight there lived at the same time a certain Russian gifted with extremely fine tastes and a remarkable sensitivity to what the late Apollon Grigoriev called the "Waft" of the era. I communicated to him the thoughts that occupied me and with speechless amazement heard the following remark: "But haven't you already presented a similar type in Rudin?"[1] I remained silent: what could I say? Rudin and Bazarov—one and the same type!

Those words had such an effect on me that during the course of several weeks I avoided any consideration of the work I had conceived; however, after I returned to Paris I again took it up—the *plot* gradually took shape in my mind: I wrote the first chapters during the course of the winter, but finished the tale in Russia, in the countryside, in the month of July. In the autumn I read it to several friends, corrected a few things, elaborated others, and in March 1862 *Fathers and Sons* appeared in *The Russian Herald*.

† From "Literary and Autobiographical Reminiscences," I. S. Turgenev, *Polnoe sobranie sochinenij*, Moscow, 1967, xiv, pp. 97–109. Translated by Ralph E. Matlaw. First published in 1869.

1. The hero of Turgenev's first novel, *Rudin* (1856) [*Editor*].

I will not expatiate on the impression made by that tale; I will only say that when I returned to St. Petersburg, the very day of the notorious fires in the Apraksin Palace, the word "nihilist" had already been taken up by thousands of voices, and the first exclamation that burst from the lips of the first acquaintance I encountered on the Nevsky was "See what *your* nihilists are doing! They are burning Petersburg!" My impressions at that time though of various sorts were all similarly oppressive. I noted the coldness, practically indignation, of many people close and sympathetic to me; I was congratulated, almost embraced by people belonging to a camp repugnant to me, by enemies. I was troubled, and embittered and grieved by that, but my conscience was clear: I knew very well that my attitude toward the character I had introduced was not only honorable and free of prejudice but even sympathetic;[2] for I valued the calling of an artist, of a literary man too highly to be hypocritical in such a matter. The word "valued" is even not quite appropriate here: I simply could not and cannot work differently; and in the final analysis there was no reason for me to do so. My critics called my tale a "broadside pamphlet," mentioned "exasperated," "wounded" egoism; but why would I write a pamphlet on Dobrolyubov,[3] whom I had hardly met, but whom I esteemed highly as a man and as a talented writer? Whatever modest opinion I might have of my talent, I would nevertheless have considered and do consider the writing of a pamphlet, a "pasquil" beneath it and unworthy of it. As for "wounded" egoism, I will only note that Dobrolyubov's article about my last work before *Fathers and Sons*—about *On the Eve* (and he properly considered himself the spokesman of public opinion)—that the article, which appeared in 1861, is full of the warmest praise, which, in all conscience, it does not merit. But the critics found it necessary to present me as a humiliated pamphleteer: *"leur siège etait fait"*[4]—and even this year I could read the following lines in Appendix #1 to *The Cosmos* (p. 96): "Finally everyone knows that the pedestal on which Mr. Turgenev stood was destroyed chiefly by Dobrolyubov . . ." and later (p. 98) my "bitterness" is mentioned, which the critic, however, understands—and "perhaps even forgives."

Critics in general do not quite correctly conceive what goes on in an author's soul, what precisely causes his joys and sorrows, his stirrings, his successes and failures. For example, they do not even suspect the existence of that pleasure that Gogol mentions and which consists in chastising oneself and one's shortcomings in depicted characters one has

---

2. I permit myself to cite the following excerpt from my diary: "July 30, Sunday. An hour and a half ago I finally finished my novel . . . I do not know whether it will be successful. *The Contemporary* will probably treat me with contempt because of Bazarov and will not believe that during the whole time I was writing I was involuntarily attracted to him." [*The Contemporary* was a leading periodical, in which the ideas repeated by Bazarov appeared—*Editor*.]

3. See n. 5, p. 25.

4. "They have taken their stand" [*Editor*].

created. They are completely convinced that all an author does is to "convey his ideas"; they do not wish to believe that to reproduce the truth, the reality of life accurately and powerfully, is the literary man's highest joy, even if that truth does not correspond to his own sympathies. I will permit myself to cite a small example. I am an inveterate and incorrigible Westerner[5] and I have never in any way concealed it, nor do I do so now; nevertheless despite that, I derived particular satisfaction in depicting in Panshin (in A *Nest of Noblemen*) all the comical and vulgar aspects of Westernism; I made the Slavophile Lavretsky "destroy him at every point." Why did I do that—I, who consider Slavophile doctrine false and barren? Because *in this instance, as I saw it that was precisely* how life turned out and above all I wanted to be honest and truthful. In drawing the character of Bazarov I excluded everything artistic from his sympathies, I endowed him with harshness and an unceremonious tone—not out of a blind desire to insult the younger generation (!!!),[6] but simply as a result of observing my acquaintance Dr. D. and people like him. "That is how that *life* turned out,"— experience again told me—perhaps mistakenly, but, I repeat, scrupulously; there was no reason for hair-splitting, and I had to depict him precisely *that way*. My personal inclinations meant nothing here; but no doubt many of my readers would be amazed if I told them that I share almost all of Bazarov's convictions with the exception of those on art. Yet I am assured that I was on the side of the "fathers" . . . I, who in the character of Pavel Kirsanov even erred against artistic truth and overdid it, practically turned his faults into caricature, made him comic![7]

The whole reason for the misunderstandings, the whole "fault" so to speak consisted in that the Bazarov type created by me was not able to pass through gradual stages, as other literary types ordinarily do. It was not his lot—as it was Onegin's or Pechorin's[8]—to experience a period of idealization, of sympathetic exaltation. At the moment of the *new* man's—Bazarov's—appearance, the author treated him critically . . .

---

5. The two opposing camps in Russia were the Westerners, who thought that Russians should emulate European civilization, and the Slavophiles, who wanted to depend on native traditions [*Editor*].

6. Among many proofs of my "spite against youth" one critic even brought forth the fact that I made Bazarov lose at cards to Father Alexey. "He just doesn't know how to wound and humiliate enough! He doesn't even know how to play cards!" There is absolutely no doubt that if I had made Bazarov win, the same critic would triumphantly exclaim: "Isn't it clear? The author wants to suggest that Bazarov is a cheat!"

7. Foreigners simply cannot understand the merciless reproaches directed at me for Bazarov. *Fathers and Sons* was translated into German several times. This is what one critic writes, reviewing the latest translation that ap-

peared in Riga ([?] *Zeitung*, Thursday, June 10, Supplement 2, page 3): "The unprejudiced reader will be completely puzzled how the radical Russian younger generation could become so frenzied about a representative of its convictions and strivings as Turgenev depicted Bazarov that it subjected Turgenev to formal disgrace and covered him with abuse. One might rather have thought that every young radical would rather have recognized with a feeling of joyous satisfaction his own portrait and the portrait of his partisans in so proud an image, gifted with such a strength of character, such total independence from everything petty, vulgar, slothful, and false." [Turgenev quotes the German original before translating into Russian—*Editor*.]

8. In Pushkin's *Eugene Onegin* and Lermontov's *Hero of Our Time* [*Editor*.]

objectively. That led many astray and, who knows, perhaps that was, if not a mistake, at least unfair. The Bazarov type was at least entitled to as much idealization as his predecessors. I just said that the author's relation to his created character led the reader astray: the reader is always uneasy, doubts, even vexation seizes him if an author treats an invented character like a living human being, that is, he sees and presents his bad and good traits, and most of all, if he doesn't show a clear sympathy or antipathy toward his own offspring. The reader is ready to take offense: he has to clear his own path rather than follow an established one. "Why should I trouble myself?" the reader involuntarily begins to think— "books exist for distraction not for breaking one's head; and what would it have cost the author to say how I should think about a particular figure—what he himself thinks of him!" And if the author's relation to that figure is of even vaguer character, if the author doesn't know himself whether he loves the created character or not (as happened to me in regard to Bazarov, since that "involuntary attraction" which I mention in my diary is not love)—then things are altogether bad. The reader is ready to attribute fictitious sympathies or fictitious antipathies to the author, only in order to escape from unpleasant "vagueness."

"Neither Fathers nor Sons," a witty lady said to me after reading my book, "that is the real title of your book—and you are a nihilist yourself." A similar opinion was expressed even more forcefully after the publication of Smoke. I won't undertake a refutation; perhaps the lady even told the truth. In the work of composition (to judge by myself) each does not what he wishes but what he can—and in so far as it succeeds I suppose that works of belles-lettres must be judged en gros and while demanding strict conscientiousness from the author, other aspects of his activity should be considered I won't say unconcernedly but calmly. But much as I would like to oblige my critics, I cannot consider myself guilty of a lack of conscientiousness.

I have gathered a rather curious collection of letters and other documents relating to Fathers and Sons. Comparing them is not without some interest. While some accuse me of insulting the younger generation, of being out of touch, of obscurantism, inform me that "they burn my photographs with contemptuous laughter"—others, on the other hand, indignantly reproach me with grovelling before that same younger generation. "You are crawling at Bazarov's feet," one correspondent exclaims. "You only pretend to condemn him; in reality you ingratiate yourself with him, and await a single careless smile of his as a favor!" I remember that one critic, in forceful and eloquent expressions addressed directly at me, presented me and Mr. Katkov[9] as two conspirators who devised their despicable plot, their calumny against younger Russian forces in the quiet of an isolated study. It was an effective

9. See n. 2, p. 176.

picture! In fact, this is how that "conspiracy" took place. When Mr. Katkov received from me the manuscript of *Fathers and Sons*, of whose contents he had not even an inkling, he felt bewildered.[1] The type of Bazarov seemed to him "practically an apothesis of *The Contemporary*," and I would not have been surprised if he had refused to publish my tale in his journal. "*Et voila comme on ecrit l'histoire!*"[2] one might exclaim. But can such minor matters really be inflated by so sonorous a name?

On the other hand, I understand the reasons for the anger my book aroused in a certain faction. They are not groundless, and I accept— without false humility—part of the reproaches made to me. The term "nihilist," which I launched, was at that time used by many who only sought an incident, an excuse, to stop a movement that had taken possession of Russian society. The term was not used by me as a reproach nor with the intent to insult; but as an exact and appropriate expression of a fact that had materialized, a historical fact; it was turned into a weapon of denunciation, of irrevocable condemnation,—almost as a brand of shame. Several unfortunate events that took place at that time further nurtured suspicions that were arising and seemed to confirm the apprehensions that were spreading, justifying the efforts and fussing of our "saviors of the Fatherland" . . . since "saviors of the Fatherland" appeared among us as in Rus[3] at that time. The tide of public opinion, still so vague with us, turned . . . but a shadow was cast on my name. I do not deceive myself, I know that that shadow will not disappear from my name. But other people, before whom I all too deeply feel my insignificance, might utter the great words "*Perissent nos noms, pourvu que la chose publique soit sauvée!*"[4] Imitating them I too could console myself with the notion that my book was of some use. That compensates me for the unpleasantness of undeserved reproaches. And really what does it signify? Twenty or thirty years from now who will remember all these storms in a teacup and my name, with or without a shadow cast upon it?

But enough about me—and it is time to stop these sporadic reminiscences which, I fear, will hardly satisfy readers. I only wish, before

1. I hope Mr. Katkov will not complain to me for citing several places from a letter he wrote to me at the time. "Even if Bazarov isn't raised to an apotheosis," he wrote, "one must still admit that somehow he accidentally landed on a very high pedestal. He really crushes everything around him. Everything before him is either tinsel, or feeble and immature. Was that the impression one would have wished? One feels in the tale that the author wanted to characterize a principle he was little sympathetic to, but he seemed to waiver in his tone and unconsciously came under its sway. Some sort of constraint is felt in the author's relationship to the tale's hero, some sort of uneasiness and stiffness. The author somehow loses his head before him, he doesn't like him, but he is even more afraid of him!" Further, Mr. Katkov regrets that I didn't make Odintsov treat Bazarov ironically, etc.—all in the same tone! It is clear that one of the "conspirators" was not entirely satisfied with the work of the other.
2. "And that's how history is written!" [*Editor*].
3. The term for Ancient Russia [*Editor*].
4. That is, "Let our names perish as long as our common cause is saved."

signing off, to say a few words to my young contemporaries, my colleagues who embark on the slippery field of literature. I have already stated and am ready to repeat that I am not blinded so far as my own position is concerned. My twenty-five years' "service of the muses" ended in the gradual disenchantment of the reading public and I do not foresee any reason why it should reverse its view. New times have come, new people are required; literary old timers are like the army's—almost always cripples—and blessed are those that retire in time! Without a hortatory tone, to which, actually, I have no right, I intend to pronounce my parting words in the tones of an old friend who is listened to with half-condescending, half-impatient attention, if only he does not become excessively long-winded. I shall try to avoid that.

And so, my young colleagues, I address myself to you.

> *Greift nur hinein in's volle Menschenleben!—*

I would say to you in the words of our common teacher, Goethe,—

> *Ein jeder lebt's—nicht vielen ist's bekannt,*
> *Und wo ihr's packt—da ist's interessant!*[5]

Only talent gives one the power for that "apprehension," that "catching" of life, and one cannot grant oneself talent; but mere talent is in itself insufficient. Constant communion with the sphere you undertake to reproduce is required, honesty, implacable honesty toward one's own feelings is required, and, finally, education is required, knowledge is required! "Aha! We understand! We see what you're driving at!" many will perhaps exclaim here. "Potugin's ideas—Ci-vi-li-za-tion, *prenez mon ours!*"[6] Such exclamations do not surprise me; but neither will they make me renounce one iota of what I said. Learning is not only light, according to the Russian proverb—it is freedom as well. Nothing liberates man as much as learning, and nowhere is freedom as necessary as in art, in poetry: not for nothing are the arts called "liberal," free, even in bureaucratic language. Can a man "seize," "catch" what surrounds him if he is tied up inside? Pushkin felt that deeply; not for nothing did he write in his immortal sonnet, that sonnet that every beginning writer should memorize and remember like a commandment;

> . . . Go by a *free* road,
> Where your *free* mind draws you.

The lack of such freedom, incidentally, also explains why not one of the Slavophiles, despite their undoubted talent,[7] ever created anything

---

5. That is, "Put your hand right in (I cannot translate it any better) into the depths of human life! Everyone lives by it, few know it and wherever you grab it, there it will be interesting."
6. "The same old story!" Potugin is Turgenev's spokesman in the novel *Smoke* (1866) [*Editor*].
7. One cannot, of course, reproach the Slavophiles with ignorance, with inadequate education; but for achieving an artistic result one needs—to use the latest terminology—the in-

that is alive; not one of them was able to remove his rose-tinted glasses even for a minute. But the saddest example of the lack of true freedom stemming from the lack of true knowledge is seen in Count L. N. Tolstoy's latest work (*War and Peace*), which at the same time through its creative, poetic gifts most likely stands at the head of everything produced in European literature since 1840. No! Without veracity, without education, without freedom in the broadest sense—toward one's self, toward one's preconceived ideas and systems, even toward one's people, one's history—a true artist is inconceivable; without that air you cannot breathe.

So far as a final result, a final appraisal of a so-called literary career is concerned, here too one must remember Goethe's words

Sind's Rosen—nun sie werden blühen.[1]

There are no unacknowledged geniuses just as there are no services that lie beyond their alloted time. "Sooner or later everyone finds his niche," the late Belinsky used to say. One can be grateful if one has contributed all one's mite in one's time and place. Only the chosen ones are in a position to convey to posterity not only the content but also the *form* of their thoughts and views, their personality which, generally speaking, doesn't concern the public. Ordinary individuals are condemned to disappear in the whole, to be swallowed up in its stream; but they augmented its force, broadened and deepened its course—what more could they want?

I put down my pen . . . One more bit of advice to young writers and one last request. My friends, never justify yourself no matter how you may be slandered; don't try to clear up misunderstandings, don't try either to say "the final word" or to listen to it. Do your work—everything will sort itself out later. In any case, first let a long period of time pass—and then look at all the rubbish of the past from the historical point of view, as I have tried to do now. Let the following example serve to guide you. Only once in the course of my literary career did I try to "establish the facts." Namely, when the editors of *The Contemporary* started to assure its subscribers in print that they had'dispensed with me for my wretched convictions (while in fact *I* would not publish there—despite their pleas—for which I have documentary proof), I could not keep up my character, and publicly proclaimed what was involved, and of course, suffered a complete fiasco! The younger generation became even more indignant with me . . . "How dared I raise my hand against its idol! What does it matter that I was right! I should have kept quiet!" That lesson was useful to me; I hope that it will be useful to you as well.

---

teraction of many *factors*. The factor Slavo-philes lack is freedom; others lack education, still others talent, etc.

8. "If they are roses—they will bloom."

And my request consists of the following: guard our language, our splendid Russian language, transmitted to us by our predecessors, at whose head Pushkin again shines! Treat that powerful weapon respectfully; in able hands it can achieve marvels! Even those who don't care for "philosophical abstractions" and "poetic tenderness," practical people for whom language is only a means for expressing a thought, like a simple lever,—even to them I say: at least respect the laws of mechanics, extract the maximum use of everything. Or else, scanning some pale, confused, feebly long-winded verbiage, a reader involuntarily will think that you have exchanged a *lever* for some primitive props, that you are returning to the infancy of mechanics itself . . .

But enough, otherwise I too will become verbose.

1868–1869
Baden-Baden

From Turgenev's Letters †

P. V. Annenkov to Turgenev [1]

September 26 (October 9), 1861.

* * * In Moscow I took your novel from Katkov [2] and read it carefully. In my opinion it is a masterful thing in exposition and finish, surpassing in its external form everything written by its author till now. That is the general consensus rather than my own or somebody's in particular, and therefore you may rest secure on that score. Bazarov is something else. There are different opinions about him as a result of a single cause: the author himself is somewhat constrained about him and doesn't know what to consider him—a productive force in the future or a stinking abscess of an

† From I. S. Turgenev, *Pis'ma v 13–i tomakh*, Moscow, 1961 to date, Vols. 4, 7, and 8, and I. S. Turgenev, *Sobranie sochineniy*, Moscow, 1949, Vol. XI (letters of 1874–1882). Translated by Ralph E. Matlaw.

All dates are given in both old and new style. The first is the Julian calendar used in Russia until 1917, the second the Gregorian used in the West. In the nineteenth century the Julian calendar was 12 days behind the Gregorian, and in the twentieth it was 13 days behind. The liberation of the serfs, February 19, 1861, thus took place on March 3 in our calendar, and the October Revolution is annually commemorated in the Soviet Union on November

7. Almost all Turgenev's letters bear the double date.
1. This important letter, to which Turgenev frequently alludes, was published only recently in *Russkaya Literatura*, 1958, No. 1, pp. 147–49. P. V. Annenkov (1813–87) was a critic of the mid-century and friend to many leading writers, including Turgenev. His reminiscences of that period are his most important and lasting work [*Editor*].
2. M. N. Katkov (1818–87), publisher of *The Russian Herald*, where *Fathers and Sons* appeared. Katkov became increasingly conservative and by the 1860's the journal was already considered reactionary [*Editor*].

empty culture, of which one should rid oneself quickly. Bazarov cannot be both things at the same time, yet the author's indecisiveness sways the reader's thoughts too from one pole to the other. In the form that he (that is, Bazarov) appears now, he is able at one and the same time to flatter pleasantly all negators of Tryapichkin's ilk, creating for them an honored ideal, at which they will gaze very willingly, and, on the other hand, he is capable of arousing the loathing of people who work, have faith in science and in history. He is two-faced, like Janus, and each party will see only that facet which comforts it most or which it is most capable of understanding. That's precisely what I have already seen in practice. Katkov is horrified by that force, power, superiority to the crowd, and ability to subjugate people which he noted in Bazarov; he says it is *The Contemporary* raised to an apotheosis, and despairs for thought and science when people like the author of the tale instead of fighting with the corrupting tendency, strike the colors before it, yield before it, give up, venerate in thought its empty, phosphorescent, and deceptive lustre. Another person, Katkov's direct opposite, daring to do battle with him on that score, am I. In clear conscience, that gentleman, on the contrary, sees in Bazarov the same Mongol, Genghis Khan, etc., that the real ones were; his animal brute force is not only not attractive, but increases one's repulsion toward him and is tainted with sterility. The whole type *in toto* is a condemnation of the savage society wherein he could be born, and if that type becomes known to foreigners, it will be used by them as proof of that coarse, nomadic, brutal condition in which our state finds itself, though it has a gloss of books from the Leipzig Fair. That's the kind of nonsense and disagreement Bazarov already produces now.

And you, friend, are responsible for it just the same.

Let us assume that Katkov's eyes start in fear and that I, on the contrary, am completely correct, which I do not doubt for a minute, but you really did cast a Plutarchian aura over Bazarov, because you did not even give him that "burning, diseased egotism" that distinguishes the entire generation of nihilists. An inveterate romantic may still be without "egotism" among us, but is this possible for the latest negator? That is a real trait, after all, and its absence will have the effect of making people doubt that Bazarov belongs to this world, relating him to a heroic cycle, to kinship with Ossian turned inside out, etc. In order to show the other side of the character, that splendid scene with Arkady on the haystack is not enough; occasionally or at least at some time, the Sitnikov in Bazarov must creep out too. Only through venomous egotism can Bazarov be tied to reality—that artery from the real world to his navel—and there is no reason for cutting it off. For that matter it's easy to alleviate the situation if, while maintaining all his contempt for Sitnikov, he at some time mentions to Arkady that one must preserve the Sitnikovs on the basis of the rules promulgated by Prince Vorontsov, who replied to complaints about the abominations of a certain police inspector, "I know that he is a scoundrel but he has one important merit—he is genuinely devoted to me." Finally, in one of the conversations between Bazarov and Pavel Petrovich, one of them mentions Cavour, directly citing a passage in *The Contemporary*. I think that has to be changed: one must not approach such a special phenomenon of life so directly and indiscriminately. The tale reflects the guiding idea of life but not its actual statement, expression, mannerisms. Speaking entirely in the Hegel manner, that's *schlechte Realität*.[3] But having said all that, at the same time I figuratively kiss your brow for creating that type, which discloses your usual feeling for social phenomena and which is destined to teach, to sober, to make our era pensive, though, of course, our era will undergo all these with a certain amount of stubbornness.

My second remark concerns the splendid Anna Sergeyevna. That type is drawn so delicately by you that its future judges will hardly be able to understand it completely. Only in one place does it become obscure, namely in chapter XXV, where in a conversation with Bazarov a new inclination toward Arkady on A. S.'s part is expressed. The traits are so minute here that strong mental magnifying glasses are needed for understanding them, and not everyone is obliged to have them. I think one ought to hint at her new psychological state with some sort of striking turn, otherwise it'll turn out something like a Japanese snuffbox, which contains miniature trees with fruit, ponds, and boats; and that's the more annoying since the general tone of the tale is sharp, in relief, and its progress completely solid. And so far as the scene with Bazarov after receiving Arkady's request for permission to marry Katya is concerned, it is simply unbearable. It's something like Prince Kuchumov or current Russian dramatic literature in general where there is talk for talk's sake and where a kind of repellent, tepid, and fetid psychology reigns. Change that scene any way you like, let it be the mutual gaiety of the conversants, one of whom laughs out of malice and the other out of despair, but change it without fail if you value my respect.

And having said that, I congratulate you on an excellent tale, which proves that its author is still in full possession of his creative power, and that's what was most important of all for me to discover. It will create a great stir—you can expect that. It will not

---

3. "Bad actuality" [*Editor*].

raise the question of talent and artistic merit but rather whether its author is the historian or ringleader of the party. Serious writers have always given birth to such questions among their contemporaries and that sort of argument around a well-known name always proves the importance and significance of that name. There is no point in speaking of the many splendid details in that tale, and it is so absorbing that while reading it you think the first line stands next to the last one—the middle is swallowed up so quickly! I have heard that Countess Lambert [4] is dissatisfied with the novel: don't believe it. The world into which you led her is so terrible that she has confused its hideousness with the hideousness of the creative work—that's how I explain her judgment to myself. So, it seems, I have conscientiously fulfilled the task placed before me, and would like to know to what extent you yourself share my opinions, which, for that matter, are far from incontrovertible. * * *

To P. V. *Annenkov*

Paris, October 1 (13), 1861

Dear Pavel Vasil'evich:

Please accept my sincere thanks for your letter in which you express your frank opinion of my tale. It made me very glad, the more so as my confidence in my own work was badly shaken. I agree completely with all your observations (the more so since V. P. Botkin [5] also finds them just), and tomorrow I will begin work on corrections and revisions, which apparently will be of considerable scope, and I have already written Katkov to that effect. I still have a great deal of time at my disposal. Botkin, who is apparently getting better, also made several apt suggestions to me and differs with you in only one thing: he does not like Anna Sergeyevna much. But I think that I know how to bring that whole business into proper balance. When I finish my work I will send it to you, and you pass it on to Katkov. But enough about that and once again my sincere and warm thanks. * * *

To M. N. *Katkov*

Paris, October 1 (13), 1861

Dear Mikhail Nikiforovich:

Forgive me for bombarding you with letters, but I wanted to forewarn you that as a result of letters I received from Annenkov and the remarks of Botkin to whom I read my tale here, the

4. A close friend of Turgenev's (died 1883). He valued her literary opinions [Editor].
5. Literary critic, author, member of liberal sets Turgenev frequented, and a lifelong friend (1810–69) [Editor].

revisions of *Fathers and Sons* will be more extensive than I had anticipated, and will occupy me approximately two weeks, during which time you will receive a careful list of all omissions and additions. And therefore I repeat my request *not to publish an excerpt* and also to hold on to the manuscript, that is, not to let others read it. I hope that as a result of my corrections the figure of Bazarov will become clear to you and will not create in you the impression of an apotheosis, which was not my idea at all. Other figures will gain, too, I think. In short, I consider my piece not completely finished, and since I have expended a great deal of work on it I would like to issue it in the best possible form. * * *

To M. N. Katkov
Paris, October 27 (November 8), 1861

Dear Mikhail Nikoforovich:

On the advice of friends and on my own conviction, which probably coincides with yours, I think that under the current circumstances [6] the publication of *Fathers and Sons* should be put off for some time, the more so since the censorship may create difficulties now. And therefore I ask you to delay publication, which, however, does not prevent me from sending you the substantial changes and corrections I have made. In any case, rest assured that *Fathers and Sons* will appear—if at all—nowhere other than in *The Russian Herald*. Drop me a note so that I will know that you have received this letter. I also repeat my request to hold on to the manuscript and not let others read it. * * *

To M. N. Katkov
Paris, October 30 (November 11), 1861

Dear Mikhail Nikoforovich:

I recently wrote you, but after your letter which I received yesterday I consider it necessary to write a couple of words in reply. I agree with your comments, with almost all of them, particularly about *Pavel Petrovich* and Bazarov himself. So far as Odintsov is concerned, the unclear impression produced by that character indicates to me that here, too, I have to take more pains. (Incidentally, the *argument* between Pavel Petrovich and Bazarov has been completely revised and shortened.)

* * * I cannot agree with one thing: Odintsov ought not to be ironic with Bazarov, nor should the peasant stand higher than he,

6. Turgenev refers to student demonstrations in the fall of 1861 and the arrests that followed. The censors would be far more strict and would strike anything that mentioned or implied the disorders or radical thought among students [*Editor*].

though Bazarov himself is empty and barren. Perhaps my view of Russia is more misanthropic than you suppose: in my mind he is the real hero of our time. A fine hero and a fine time you'll say. But that's how it is.

I repeat my request to keep my product hidden. * * *

To F. M. Dostoevsky

Paris, March 18 (30), 1862

Dear Fedor Mikhailovich:

I cannot tell you to what extent your opinion of *Fathers and Sons* has made me happy. It isn't a question of satisfying one's pride but in the assurance that you haven't made a mistake and haven't missed the mark, and that labor hasn't been wasted. That was the more important for me since people whom I trust very much (I am not talking about Kolbasin) seriously advised me to throw my work into the fire—and only recently (but this is confidential) Pisemsky [7] wrote me that Bazarov is a complete failure. How can one then not doubt oneself and be led astray? It is hard for an author to feel *immediately* to what extent his idea has come to life, and whether it is true, and whether he has mastered it, etc. In his own work he is lost in the woods.

You have probably experienced this more than once yourself. And therefore thank you again. You have so completely and subtly grasped what I wanted to express through Bazarov that I simply throw my hands up in amazement—and in pleasure. It's as if you had entered my soul and felt even what I didn't consider necessary to express. God grant that this indicates not only the keen penetration of a master but also the simple comprehension of a reader—that is, God grant that everyone realize at least a part of what you have seen! Now I am at ease about the destiny of my tale: it has done its work and I have nothing to repent for.

Here is another proof of the extent to which you familiarized yourself with that character: in the meeting between Arkady and Bazarov, at that place where, according to you, something was missing, Bazarov made fun of *knights* and Arkady listened to him with secret horror, etc. I struck it out and now I regret it: [8] in general I rescribbled and revised a great deal under the influence of unfavorable comments, and the sluggishness you noticed may, per-

---

7. A. F. Pisemsky (1820–81), an outstanding novelist and playwright [*Editor*].
8. The passage was in chapter XXV and was later reintroduced. It reads, "he became terrified and somehow ashamed. Bazarov seemed to understand him. 'Yes, friend,' he said, 'that's what it is to live with feudal people. You become feudal yourself and start participating in jousting tournaments. Well, sir . . .' [*Editor*].

haps, have come from that.

I have received a pleasant letter from Maykov and will answer him. I shall be roundly cursed—but that has to be waited out, like a summer rain. * * *

To A. N. Maykov [9]
Paris, March 18 (30), 1862

Dear Apollon Nikolaevich:

I'll tell you straight out, like a peasant, "God grant you health for your kind and good letter!" You've comforted me greatly. I have not lacked confidence in a single one of my things as strongly as in that very one. The remarks and judgments of people whom I am accustomed to believe were extremely unfavorable. But for Katkov's persistent demands *Fathers and Sons* would never have appeared. Now I can say to myself that I couldn't have written complete nonsense if people like you and Dostoevsky stroke my head and say "Good, little man, we'll give you a 'B'." The image of a student who has solidly passed an examination is much more accurate than your image of the triumphant man, and let me tell you that your comparing yourself to a pigmy is worthless. No, you are a fellow artist, extending your hand in brotherly gesture to your friend. And I reply to your embrace with mine, to your greeting with a warm greeting and with gratitude. You have really set me at ease. Not in vain did Schiller say

Wer für die Besten seiner Zeit gelebt—
Der hat gelebt für alle Zeiten.[1]

* * *

To A. A. Fet [2]
Paris, March 19 (31), 1862

* * * I have not yet received a copy of my tale, but three letters have already arrived about the thing from Pisemsky, Dostoevsky, and Maykov. The first abuses the main character, the other two enthusiastically praise everything. That made me rejoice, because I was full of doubts. I think I wrote you that people whom I trust advised me to burn my work. But I tell you without flattery

---

9. A. N. Maykov (1821–97), a poet and friend of Turgenev's [*Editor*].
1. "He who has lived for the best men of his time/Has lived for all time." The quotation is

not accurate [*Editor*].
2. A. A. Fet (1820–92), one of Russia's most sensitive and delicate lyric poets, who was also a hard-fisted, reactionary landowner [*Editor*].

that I await your opinion in order to ascertain definitely what I should think. I argue with you at every step, but I firmly believe in your esthetic sense and in your taste. * * *

To A. A. Fet

Paris, April 6 (18), 1862

First of all, dear Afanasy Afanas'evich, thank you for your letter—and my thanks would be greater if you didn't consider it necessary to put on kid gloves. Believe me, I have borne and am able to bear the harshest truth from my friends. And so, despite your euphemisms, you don't like *Fathers and Sons.* I bow my head, since there is nothing to be done about it, but I want to say a few words in my defense, though I know how unseemly and pointless it is. You ascribe the whole trouble to *tendentiousness reflection,* in short, to reason. But in reality, you had only to say that the craft was inadequate. It seems that I am more naïve than you assume. Tendentiousness! But let me ask you, what kind of tendentiousness in *Fathers and Sons?* Did I want to abuse Bazarov or or to extol him? *I do not know that myself,* since I don't know whether I love him or hate him! There you have tendentiousness! Katkov took me to task for making Bazarov into an apotheosis. You also mention *parallelism.* But where is it, permit me to ask you, and where are these *pairs,* believers and nonbelievers? Does Pavel Petrovich believe or not? I wouldn't know since I simply wanted to portray in him the type of the Stolypins, the Rossets, and other Russian ex-lions. It is a strange thing: you blame me for parallelism, but others write me "Why isn't Anna Sergeyevna a lofty person, to contrast her more fully with Bazarov? Why aren't Bazarov's old people completely patriarchical? Why is Arkady banal, and wouldn't it be better to portray him as an upright young man who is carried away for a moment? What purpose does Fenichka serve, and what conclusions can be drawn from her?" I'll tell you one thing, I drew all those characters as I would draw mushrooms, leaves, and trees. They were an eyesore to me and so I started to sketch them. But it would be strange and amusing to dismiss my own impressions simply because they resemble tendentiousness. I don't want you to draw the conclusion from that that I am a courageous fellow. On the contrary: what can be concluded from my words is even more injurious to me: it's not that I have been too shrewd, but that I was not capable enough. But truth above all. But actually—*omnia vanitas.* * * *

To K. K. Sluchevsky [3]

Paris, April 14 (26), 1862

I hasten to answer your letter, for which I am very grateful to you, dear Sluchevsky. One must value the opinion of youth. In any case I very much want there to be no misunderstandings about my intentions. I'll answer point by point.

1) The first reproach is reminiscent of the accusation made against Gogol and others, why they did not introduce *good* people among the others. Bazarov crushes all the other characters in the novel just the same (Katkov thought I presented an apotheosis of *The Contemporary* in him). The qualities given to him are not accidental. I wanted to make a tragic figure out of him—there was no place for tenderness here. He is honest, upright, and a democrat to his fingertips—and you fail to find *good* sides in him? He recommends *Stoff and Kraft* precisely as a *popular* book, that is, an empty one; the duel with Pavel Petrovich is introduced precisely as graphic proof of the emptiness of elegantly noble knighthood, presented almost in an exaggeratedly comic way. And how could he decline it? After all, Pavel Petrovich would have hit him. I think Bazarov constantly beats Pavel Petrovich and not the other way around. And if he is called a "nihilist" that word must be read as "revolutionary."

2) What you said about Arkady, the rehabilitation of the fathers, etc., only proves—alas!—that I was not understood. *My entire tale is directed against the nobility as the leading class.* Look at Nikolai Petrovich, Pavel Petrovich, and Arkady. Weakness and languor, or limitations. Esthetic feelings made me choose precisely *good* representatives of the nobility, in order to prove my theme the more surely: if the cream is bad what will the milk be like? It would be coarse, *le pont aux ânes* [4]—and untrue to take functionaries, generals, exploiters, etc. All the real *negators* I have known, without exception (Belinsky, Bakunin, Herzen, Dobrolyubov, Speshnev, etc.), came from comparatively good and honest parents. A great idea is contained therein: it removes from the *men of action*, the negators, every suspicion of *personal* dissatisfaction, personal irritation. They go their way only because they are more sensitive to the demands of national life. Countess Sal'yas [5] is wrong when she says that characters like Nikolai Petrovich and Pavel Petrovich are our grandfathers: I am Nikolai Petrovich, as are Ogarev and thousands of others; Stolypin,

3. K. K. Sluchevsky (1837–1904) was voicing the objections of Russian students studying in Heidelberg. He was already then known as a poet. [*Editor*]

4. "Trite" [*Editor*].
5. Countess Sal'yas (1810–81) wrote novels, criticism, and children's stories under the pseudonym Evgeniya Tur [*Editor*].

Esakov, Rosset, our contemporaries too—are Pavel Petrovich. They are the best of the nobility and were chosen by me for precisely that reason, in order to prove their bankruptcy. To present grafters on the one hand and ideal youth on the other—let others draw that picture. I wanted something larger. In one place (I struck it because of the censorship), Bazarov says to Arkady, that very Arkady in whom your Heidelberg friends see *a more successful type:* "Your father is an honest fellow. But even if he were the worst grafter you wouldn't go any farther than noble resignation or flaring up because you're a little nobleman."

3) My God! You consider Kukshin, that caricature, *most successful* of all! One should not even answer that. Odintsov *falls in love* as little with Arkady as with *Bazarov*—how can you fail to see that? She, too, is the representative of our idle, dreaming, curious and cold epicurean young ladies, our female nobility. Countess Sal'yas understood *that* character completely clearly. At first she would like to stroke the wolf's fur (Bazarov's), so long as he doesn't bite, then stroke the little boy's curls—and continue to recline, all clean, on velvet.

4) Bazarov's death (which Countess Sal'yas calls *heroic* and therefore criticizes) should, I think, have added the last stroke to his tragic figure. And our young people find it, too, accidental! I close with the following remark: if the reader does not come to love Bazarov with all his coarseness, heartlessness, pitiless dryness and sharpness—if he does not come to love him, I repeat —I am at fault and have not attained my aim. But I did not want to "sugar-coat" him, to use his own words, though through that I would have had the young on my side immediately. I did not want to purchase popularity through those kinds of concessions. Better to lose the battle (and apparently I have lost it) than to win it through a trick. I dreamt of a figure that was grim, wild, huge, half grown out of the ground, powerful, sardonic, honest—and doomed to destruction nevertheless—since it nevertheless still stands only at the threshold of the future— I dreamt of some sort of strange *pendant* to Pugachev,[6] etc.— and my young contemporaries tell me, shaking their heads: "You, friend, have made a mistake and have even insulted us: your Arkady has turned out better, you should have taken greater pains with him." I can only "Take off my hat and bow low" as in the gypsy song. Up to now only two people, Dostoevsky and Botkin, have understood Bazarov completely, that is, under-

---

6. *"Pendant"*—"counterpart, offshoot." Pugachev was the Cossack leader of a major uprising against Catherine II in 1773, finally crushed in a battle with Russia's most brilliant general, Suvorov [*Editor*].

stood my intentions. I shall try to send you a copy of my tale. But now *basta* about that. * * *

A. I. Herzen to Turgenev [7]

London, April 9 (21), 1862

* * * You grew very angry at Bazarov, out of vexation lampooned him, made him say various stupidities, wanted to finish him off "with lead"—finished him off with typhus, but nevertheless he crushed that empty man with fragrant mustache and that watery gruel of a father and that blancmange Arkady. Behind Bazarov the characters of the doctor and his wife are sketched masterfully—they are completely alive and live not in order to support your polemic but because they were born. Those are real people. It seems to me that, like an amiable rowdy, you took offense at the insolent, airy, bilious exterior, at the plebeian-bourgeois turn, and taking that as an insult, went further. But where is the explanation for his young soul's turning callous on the outside, stiff, irritable? What turned away everything tender, expansive in him? Was it Büchner's book?

In general it seems to me that you are unfair toward serious, realistic experienced opinion and confound it with some sort of coarse, bragging materialism. Yet that isn't the fault of materialism but of those "Neuvazhay-Korytos" [8] who understand it in a brutish way. Their idealism is repulsive too.

The Requiem at the end, with the further moving toward the immortality of the soul is good, but dangerous: you'll slip into mysticism that way.

There for the moment are some of the impressions I've gathered on the wing. I do not think that the great strength of your talent lies in *Tendenzschriften*.[9] In addition, if you had forgotten about all the Chernyshevskys in the world while you were writing it would have been better for Bazarov. * * *

To A. I. Herzen

Paris, April 16 (28), 1862

My dear Alexander Ivanovich:

I reply to your letter immediately—not in order to defend myself, but to thank you, and at the same time to declare that

7. A. I. Herzen (1812–70), a leading Russian writer, philosopher, and journalist in revolutionary causes, spent the last twenty years of his life in exile in London, publishing the most influential Russian newspaper (*The Bell*) of the time. He was a close friend of Turgenev's [*Editor*].

8. "Disrespect-pigtrough." A comical name that figures on a list of peasants in Gogol's novel *Dead Souls* (1842). He "was run over by a careless cart as he lay sleeping in the middle of the road" [*Editor*].

9. "Polemics" [*Editor*].

That's why I did not want to disappear from the face of the earth without having finished my large novel, [*Virgin Soil*], which, so far as I can judge, would clarify many misunderstandings and would place me in the position where I really should be put. I don't wonder, incidentally, that Bazarov has remained an enigma for many people. I can hardly figure out how I wrote him. There was a *fatum* [fate] there—please don't laugh—something stronger than the author himself, something independent of him. I know one thing: there was no preconceived idea, no tendentiousness in me then. I wrote naïvely, as if I was struck myself by what came out. You refer to the disciple's teacher.[8] But it was precisely after *Fathers and Sons* that I became estranged from that circle, where, strictly speaking, I was never a member, and would have considered it stupid and shameful to write or to work for it. Tell me honestly, can a comparison to Bazarov be insulting to anyone? Do you not yourself notice that he is the most sympathetic of my characters? "A certain delicate fragrance" is added by readers. But I am ready to confess (and already did so in print in my *Reminiscences*) that I had no right to give our reactionary rabble the chance to pick up a catchword, a name. The writer in me should have sacrificed that to the citizen, and therefore I consider fair both the alienation of youth from me and all sorts of reproaches heaped on me. The problem rising then was more important than artistic truth, and I should have known it in advance. * * *

To A. V. Toporov
Paris, November 26 (*December* 8), 1882

* * * Incidentally, I forgot one important thing: under the heading *Fathers and Sons*, you must *without fail* put in brackets:

Dedicated to the memory of Vissarion Grigor'evich Belinsky. Don't forget. * * *

---

8. Bazarov's "teacher" is Chernyshevsky or Dobrolyubov, and the circle is that of the journal *The Contemporary* [*Editor*].

The Contemporary Reaction

DMITRY I. PISAREV

Bazarov†

Turgenev's new novel affords us all those pleasures which we have learned to expect from his works. The artistic finish is irreproachably good: the characters and situations, the episodes and scenes are rendered so graphically and yet so unobtrusively, that the most arrant repudiator of art will feel on reading the novel a kind of incomprehensible delight which can be explained neither by the inherent interest of the narrated events, nor by the striking truth of the fundamental idea. The fact is that the events are not particularly entertaining and that the idea is not startlingly true. The novel has neither plot nor denouement, nor a particularly well-considered structure; it has types and characters, it has episodes and scenes, and above all through the fabric of the narration we see the personal, deeply felt involvement of the author with the phenomena he has portrayed. And these phenomena are very close to us, so close that our whole younger generation with its aspirations and ideas can recognize itself in the characters of this novel. By this I do not mean to say that in Turgenev's novel the ideas and aspirations of the younger generation are depicted just as the younger generation itself understands them: Turgenev regards these ideas and aspirations from his own point of view, and age and youth almost never share the same convictions and sympathies. But if you go up to a mirror which while reflecting objects also changes their color a little bit, then you recognize your own physiognomy in spite of the distortions of the mirror. We see in Turgenev's novel contemporary types and at the same time we are aware of the changes which the phenomena of reality have undergone while passing through the consciousness of the artist. It is interesting to observe the effects on a man like Turgenev of the ideas and aspirations stirring in our younger generation and manifesting themselves, as do all living things, in the most diverse forms, seldom attractive, often original, sometimes misshapen.

Such an investigation may have profound significance. Turgenev is one of the best men of the last generation; to determine how

† "Bazarov," D. I. Pisarev, in *Sochineniya*, 2 (Moscow), 1955), 7–50. Translated by Lydia Hooke. Pisarev (1840–68), the most radical critic of the 1860's, published his review of *Fathers and Sons* within a month of the novel's appearance, and was in part responsible for the controversy that arose over the work. This essay is somewhat atypical of his work, where he usually sacrificed his genuine critical insight to further "The Destruction of Aesthetics," as he entitled one of his essays.

he looks at us and why he looks at us thus and not otherwise is to find the reason for that conflict which is apparent everywhere in our private family life; this same conflict which so often leads to the destruction of young lives and which causes the continual moaning and groaning of our old men and women, who have not been able to fit the deeds and ideas of their sons and daughters to their own mold. As you can see, this is a task of vital importance, substantial and complex; I probably will not be able to cope with it but I am willing to try.

Turgenev's novel, in addition to its artistic beauty, is remarkable for the fact that it stirs the mind, leads to reflection, although, it does not solve a single problem itself and clearly illuminates not so much the phenomena depicted by the author as his own attitudes toward these phenomena. It leads to reflection precisely because everything is permeated with the most complete and most touching sincerity. Every last line in Turgenev's latest novel is deeply felt; this feeling breaks through against the will and realization of the author himself and suffuses the objective narration, instead of merely expressing itself in lyric digressions. The author himself is not clearly aware of his feelings; he does not subject them to analysis, nor does he assume a critical attitude toward them. This circumstance gives us the opportunity to see these feelings in all their unspoiled spontaneity. We see what shines through and not just what the author wants to show us or prove. Turgenev's opinions and judgments do not change our view of the younger generation or the ideas of our time by one iota; we do not even take them into consideration, we will not even argue with them; these opinions, judgments, and feelings, expressed in inimitably lifelike images, merely afford us material for a characterization of the older generation, in the person of one of its best representatives. I shall endeavor to organize this material and, if I succeed, I shall explain why our old people will not come to terms with us, why they shake their heads and, depending on the individual and the mood, are angry, bewildered, or quietly melancholy on account of our deeds and ideas.

II

The action of the novel takes place in the summer of 1859. A young university graduate, Arkady Nikolaevich Kirsanov, comes to the country to visit his father, accompanied by his friend, Evgeny Vassilyich Bazarov, who, evidently, exerts a strong influence on his young comrade's mode of thought. This Bazarov, a man of strong mind and character, occupies the center of the novel. He is the representative of our young generation; he possesses those personality traits which are distributed among the masses in small quantities; and the image of this man clearly and distinctly stands out in the reader's imagination.

Bazarov is the son of a poor district doctor; Turgenev says nothing about his life as a student, but it must be surmised that this life was poor, laborious, and difficult; Bazarov's father says of his son that he never in his life took an extra kopeck from them; to tell the truth, it would have been impossible to take very much even if he had wanted to; consequently, if the elder Bazarov says this in praise of his son, it means that Evgeny Vassilyich supported himself at the university by his own labor, eking out a living by giving cheap lessons and at the same time finding it possible to prepare himself ably for his future occupation. Bazarov emerged from this school of labor and deprivation a strong and stern man; the course of studies in natural and medical sciences which he pursued developed his innate intelligence and taught him never to accept any idea and conviction whatsoever on faith; he became a pure empiricist; experience became for him the sole source of knowledge, his own sensations—the sole and ultimate proof. "I maintain a negative attitude," he says, "by virtue of my sensations; I like to deny—my brain's made on that plan, and that's all! Why do I like chemistry? Why do you like apples?—also by virtue of our sensations. It's all the same thing. Men will never penetrate deeper than that. Not everyone will tell you that, and, in fact, I won't tell you so another time." As an empiricist, Bazarov acknowledges only what can be felt with the hands, seen with the eyes, tasted by the tongue, in a word, only what can be examined with one of the five senses. All other human feelings he reduces to the activity of the nervous system; consequently, the enjoyment of the beauty of nature, of music, painting, poetry, the love of a woman do not seem to him to be any loftier or purer than the enjoyment of a copious dinner or a bottle of good wine. What rapturous youths call an ideal does not exist for Bazarov; he calls all this "romanticism," and sometimes instead of the word "romanticism" he uses the word "nonsense." In spite of all this, Bazarov does not steal other people's handkerchiefs, he does not extract money from his parents, he works assiduously and is even not unwilling to do something useful in life. I have a presentiment that many of my readers will ask themselves: what restrains Bazarov from foul deeds and what motivates him to do anything useful? This question leads to the following doubt: is not Bazarov pretending to himself and to others? Is he not showing off? Perhaps in the depths of his soul he acknowledges much of what he repudiates aloud, and perhaps it is precisely what he thus acknowledges which secretly saves him from moral degradation and moral worthlessness. Although Bazarov is nothing to me, although I, perhaps, feel no sympathy for him, for the sake of abstract justice, I shall endeavor to answer this question and refute this silly doubt.

You can be as indignant as you please with people like Bazarov, but you absolutely must acknowledge their sincerity. These people can be honorable or dishonorable, civic stalwarts or inveterate swindlers, depending on circumstances and their personal tastes. Nothing but personal taste prevents them from killing or stealing and nothing but personal taste motivates such people to make discoveries in the realms of science and social life. Bazarov would not steal a handkerchief for the same reason that he would not eat a piece of putrid beef. If Bazarov were starving to death, then he probably would do both. The agonizing feeling of an unsatisfied physical need would conquer his aversion to the smell of rotting meat and to the secret encroachment on other people's property. In addition to direct inclination, Bazarov has one other guiding principle in life—calculation. When he is sick, he takes medicine, although he feels no direct inclination to swallow castor oil or assafetida. He acts thus through calculation: he pays the price of a minor unpleasantness in order to secure greater comfort in the future or deliverance from a greater unpleasantness. In a word, he chooses the lesser of two evils, although he feels no attraction even to the lesser evil. This sort of calculation generally proves useless to average people; they are calculatingly cunning and mean, they steal, become entangled and wind up being made fools of anyway. Very clever people act differently; they understand that being honorable is very advantageous and that every crime, from a simple lie to murder, is dangerous and consequently inconvenient. Thus very clever people can be honorable through calculation and act openly where limited people would equivocate and lay snares. By working tirelessly, Bazarov is following his direct inclination and taste, and, furthermore, acts according to the truest calculation. If he had sought patronage, bowed and scraped, acted meanly instead of working and conducting himself proudly and independently, he would have been acting against his best interests. Careers forged through one's own work are always more secure and broader than a career built with low bows or the intercession of an important uncle. By the two latter means, it is possible to wind up as a provincial or even a metropolitan bigwig, but since the world began, no one has ever succeeded in becoming a Washington, Copernicus, Garibaldi, or Heinrich Heine through such means. Even Herostratus built his career by his own efforts and did not find his way into history through patronage. As for Bazarov, he does not aspire to become a provincial bigwig: if his imagination sometimes pictures the future, then this future is somehow indefinitely broad; he works without a goal, in order to earn his crust of bread or from love of the process of work, but, nevertheless, he vaguely feels that given the caliber of his mind his work will not pass without a trace and will lead to something. Bazarov is exceedingly full of self-esteem, but this self-esteem is u nnoticeable as a direct consequence of his vastness. He is not interested in the trifles of which commonplace human relationships are composed; it would be impossible to insult him with obvious disdain or to make him happy with signs of respect; he is so full of himself and stands so unshakably high in his own eyes that he is almost completely indifferent to other people's opinions. Kirsanov's uncle, who closely resembles Bazarov in his cast of mind and character, calls his self-esteem "satanic pride." This expression is well-chosen and characterizes our hero perfectly. In truth, it would take nothing short of a whole eternity of constantly expanding activity and constantly increasing pleasures to satisfy Bazarov, but to his misfortune, Bazarov does not believe in the eternal existence of the human personality. "You said, for instance," he says to his friend Arkady, "to-day as we passed our bailiff Philip's cottage—it's the one that's so nice and clean—well, you said Russia will attain perfection when the poorest peasant has a hut like that, and every one of us ought to work to bring it about. . . . And I felt such a hatred for this poorest peasant, this Philip or Sidor, for whom I'm to be ready to jump out of my skin, and who won't even thank me for it . . . and what do I need his thanks for? Why, suppose he does live in a clean hut, while I am pushing up daisies,—well, what comes after that?"

Thus Bazarov, everywhere and in everything, does only what he wishes or what seems to him to be advantageous or convenient. He is ruled only by his whims or his personal calculations. Neither over himself, nor outside himself, nor within himself does he recognize a moderator, a moral law or principle; ahead— no exalted goal; in his mind—no high design, and yet he has such great capacities.—But this is an immoral man! A villain, a monster!—I hear the exclamations of indignant readers on all sides. Well, all right, a villain and a monster; abuse him further; abuse him more, persecute him with satire and epigrams, indignant lyricism and aroused public opinion, the fires of the Inquisition and the executioners' axes—and you will neither rout him out nor kill this monster, nor preserve him in alcohol for the edification of the respectable public. If Bazarovism is a disease, then it is a disease of our time, and must be endured to the end, no matter what palliatives and amputations are employed. Treat

Bazarovism however you please—that is your business; but you will not be able to put a stop to it; it is just the same as cholera.

III

The disease of an age first infects the people who by virtue of their mental powers stand higher than the common level. Bazarov, who is possessed by this disease, is distinguished by his remarkable mind and consequently produces a strong impression on people who come into contact with him. "A real man," he says, "is one whom it's no use thinking about, whom one must either obey or hate." This definition of a real man precisely fits Bazarov himself: he continually seizes the attention of the people surrounding him at once; some he frightens and antagonizes; others he conquers, not so much with arguments as with the direct force, simplicity, and integrity of his ideas. As a remarkably intelligent man, he has never yet met his equal. " 'When I meet a man who can hold his own beside me,' he said, dwelling on every syllable, 'then I'll change my opinion of myself.' "

He looks down on people and rarely even takes the trouble to conceal his half-disdainful, half-patronizing attitude toward those who hate him and those who obey him. He loves no one; although he does not break existing ties and relationships, he does not move a muscle to renew or maintain these relationships, nor does he soften one note in his harsh voice or sacrifice one cutting joke or witty remark.

He acts thus not in the name of a principle, not in order to be completely frank at every moment, but simply because he considers it completely unnecessary to lay any restraint whatsoever on himself; for the same motive from which Americans throw their legs over the backs of chairs and spit tobacco juice on the parquet floors of elegant hotels. Bazarov needs no one, fears no one, loves no one and consequently spares no one. Like Diogenes he is almost ready to live in a barrel and because of this grants himself the right to tell people to their faces the harsh truth, simply because it pleases him to do so. We can distinguish two sides to Bazarov's cynicism—an internal and an external one; a cynicism of thought and feeling and a cynicism of manner and expression. An ironic attitude toward emotion of any sort, toward dreaminess, lyrical transports and effusions, is the essence of the internal cynicism. The rude expression of this irony, and a causeless and purposeless harshness in the treatment of others relates to external cynicism. The first depends on the cast of mind and general world view; the second is conditioned by purely external conditions of development; the traits of the society in which the subject under consideration lived. Bazarov's derisive attitude toward the softhearted Kirsanov follows from the basic characteristic of the general Bazarov type. His rude clashes with Kirsanov and his uncle arise from his individual traits. Bazarov is not only an empiricist, he is also an uncouth rowdy, who has known no life other than the homeless, laborious, sometimes wildly dissipated life of the poor student. In the ranks of Bazarov's admirers there will undoubtedly be those who will be enraptured by his coarse manners, the vestiges of student life, who will imitate these manners, which are, in any case, a shortcoming and not a virtue, who will perhaps even exaggerate his harshness, gracelessness, and abruptness. In the ranks of Bazarov's enemies there will undoubtedly be those who will pay particular attention to these ugly features of his personality and will use them to reproach the general type. Both of these groups would be mistaken and would only be displaying their profound incomprehension of the real matter. We may remind them of Pushkin's lines:

> One may be a man of sense
> Yet consider the beauty of his fingernails.

It is possible to be an extreme materialist, a complete empiricist and at the same time look after your toilet, treat your acquaintances politely, be amiable in conversation and a perfect gentleman. I say this for the benefit of those readers who attribute great significance to refined manners, who look with aversion on Bazarov, as on a man who is *mal élevé* [1] and *mauvais ton*.[2] He really is *mal élevé* and *mauvais ton*, but this really has no relevance to the essence of the type and speaks neither against it nor in its favor. Turgenev decided to choose as a representative of the Bazarov type an uncouth man; of course as he delineated his hero, he did not conceal or try to gloss over his awkwardness. Turgenev's choice can be explained by two motives: first, the character's personality, the tendency to deny ruthlessly and with complete conviction everything which others consider exalted and beautiful, is most often engendered by the drab conditions of a life of labor; from hard labor the hands coarsen, so do the manners and emotions; the man grows stronger and banishes youthful dreaminess, rids himself of lachrymose sensitivity; it is not possible to daydream at work, the attention is directed on the business at hand, and after work one must rest and really satisfy one's physical needs and one has no time for dreams. This man has become used to looking on dreams as on a whim, peculiar to idleness and aristocratic pampering; he has begun to consider moral sufferings to be products of daydreams; moral aspirations

---

1. "Badly brought up" [*Editor*].   2. "Ill-bred" [*Editor*].

and actions as imagined and ridiculous. For him, the laboring man, there exists only one, eternally recurring care: today he must think about how not to starve tomorrow. This simple care, terrible in its simplicity, overshadows everything else for him, secondary anxieties, the petty troubles and cares of life; in comparison with this care the artificial products of various unsolved problems, unresolved doubts, indefinite relations which poison the lives of secure, idle people seem to him to be trivial and insignificant.

Thus the proletarian laborer, by the very process of his life, independently of the process of reflection, arrives at practical realism; from lack of leisure he forgets how to dream, to pursue an ideal, to aspire to an unattainably lofty goal. By developing the laborer's energy, labor teaches him to unite thought and deed, an act of will with an act of the mind. The man who has learned to rely on himself and on his own capacities, who has become used to accomplishing today what he conceived yesterday, begins to look with more or less obvious disdain on people who dream of love, of useful activity, of the happiness of the whole human race, and yet are not capable of lifting a finger to improve even a little whether he be doctor, artisan, pedagogue, or even a writer (it is possible to be a writer and at the same time a man of action), feels a natural, indefinable aversion to phrase making, to waste of words, to sweet thoughts, to sentimental aspirations, and in general to all pretensions not based on real tangible forces. This aversion to everything estranged from life and everything that has turned into empty phrases is the fundamental characteristic of the Bazarov type. This fundamental characteristic is engendered in precisely those various workshops where man, sharpening his mind and straining his muscles, struggles with nature for the right to live in the wide world. On these grounds, Turgenev had the right to take his hero from one of these workshops and to bring him into the society of cavaliers and ladies, in a work apron, with dirty hands, and a gloomy and preoccupied gaze. But justice forces me to put forward the proposition that the author of *Fathers and Sons* acted thus not without an insidious intention. This insidious intention is the second motive to which I referred earlier. The fact is that Turgenev, evidently, looks with no great favor on his hero. His soft, loving nature, striving for faith and sympathy, is jarred by corrosive realism; his delicate esthetic sensibility, not devoid of a large dose of aristocratism, takes offense at the faintest glimmer of cynicism; he is too weak and sensitive to bear dismal repudiations; he must become reconciled with existence, if not in the realm of life, at least in the realm of thought, or, more precisely, dreams. Like a nervous woman or the plant "touch-me not," Turgenev shrinks from the slightest contact with the bouquet of Bazarovism.

This feeling, an involuntary antipathy toward this tenor of thought, he presented to the reading public in a specimen as ungraceful as possible. He knows very well that there are very many fashionable readers in our public and, counting on the refinement of their aristocratic tastes, he did not spare the coarse details, with the evident desire of debasing and vulgarizing not only his hero but the cast of ideas which form the defining characteristic of the type. He knows very well that the majority of his readers will say of Bazarov that he is badly brought up and that it would be impossible to have him in a respectable drawing room; they will go no further or deeper; but speaking with such people, a talented artist and honorable man must be extremely careful out of respect for himself and the idea which he is upholding or refuting. Here one must hold one's personal antipathy in check since under some conditions it can turn into the involuntary slander of people who do not have the opportunity to defend themselves with the same weapons. * * *

* * * Arkady's uncle, Pavel Petrovich, might be called a small-scale Pechorin; he sowed some wild oats in his time and played the fool but finally began to tire of it all; he never succeeded in settling down, it just was not in his character; when he reached the time of life when, as Turgenev puts it, regrets resemble hopes and hopes resemble regrets, the former lion moved in with his brother in the country, surrounded himself with elegant comfort and turned his life into a peaceful vegetation. The outstanding memory of Pavel Petrovich's noisy and brilliant life was his strong feeling for a woman of high society, a feeling which had afforded him much pleasure, and afterward, as is almost always the case, much suffering. When Pavel Petrovich's relations with this woman were severed, his life became perfectly empty.

"He wandered from place to place like a man possessed;" Turgenev writes, "he still went into society; he still retained the habits of a man of the world; he could boast of two or three fresh conquests; but he no longer expected anything special of himself or of others, and he undertook nothing. He aged and his hair turned grey; to spend his evenings at the club in jaded boredom, and to argue in bachelor society became a necessity for him— a bad sign as we all know. He did not even think of marriage, of course. Ten years passed in this way. They passed by colorless and fruitless—and quickly, fearfully quickly. Nowhere does time fly past as in Russia; in prison they say it flies even faster."

An acrimonious and passionate man, endowed with a versatile mind and a strong will, Pavel Petrovich is sharply distinguished from his brother and from his nephew. He does not succumb to the influence of other people; he himself dominates the people around him and he hates those people from whom he suffers a rebuff. He has no convictions, truth to tell, but he has habits by which he sets great store. From habit he speaks of the rights and duties of the aristocracy, and from habit proves in arguments the necessity for *principles.* He is used to the ideas which are held by society and he stands up for these ideas, just as he stands up for his comfort. He cannot bear it when someone refutes his ideas, although, at bottom, he has no heartfelt attachment to them. He argues with Bazarov much more energetically than does his brother, and yet Nikolai Petrovich suffers much more from his merciless repudiations. In the depths of his soul, Pavel Petrovich is just as much of a skeptic and empiricist as Bazarov himself; in practical life he always acted and acts as he sees fit, but in the realm of thought he is not able to admit this to himself and thus he adheres in words to doctrines which his actions continually contradict. It would be well if uncle and nephew were to exchange convictions, since the first mistakenly ascribes to himself a belief in *principes* and the second just as mistakenly imagines himself to be an extreme skeptic and a daring rationalist. Pavel Petrovich begins to feel a strong antipathy toward Bazarov from their first meeting. Bazarov's plebeian manners rouse the indignation of the outdated dandy; his self-confidence and unceremoniousness irritate Pavel Petrovich as a lack of respect for his elegant person. Pavel Petrovich sees that Bazarov does not allow him to predominate over himself and this arouses in him a feeling of vexation on which he seizes as a diversion amidst the profound boredom of country life. Hating Bazarov himself, Pavel Petrovich is outraged by all his opinions, he carps at him, forces him into arguments, and argues with the zealous enthusiasm which is displayed by people who are idle and easily bored.

And what does Bazarov do amidst these three personalities? First of all, he endeavors to pay them as little attention as possible and spends the greater part of his time at work; he roams about the neighborhood, collects plants and insects, dissects frogs, and occupies himself with his microscope; he regards Arkady as a child, Nikolai Petrovich as a good-natured old man or, as he puts it, an old romantic. His feeling toward Pavel Petrovich is not exactly amicable; he is annoyed by the element of haughtiness in him, but he involuntarily tries to conceal his irritation under the guise of disdainful indifference. He does not want to admit to himself that he can be angered by a "provincial aristocrat," yet his passionate nature outs, frequently he replies vehemently to Pavel Petrovich's tirades and does not immediately succeed in gaining control over himself and once more shutting himself up in his derisive coldness. Bazarov does not like to argue or, in general, to express his opinions and only Pavel Petrovich is sometimes able to draw him into a significant discussion. These two strong characters react with hostility to each other; seeing these two men face to face it is easy to be reminded of the struggle between two successive generations. Nikolai Petrovich, of course, is not capable of being an oppressor: Arkady Nikolaevich, of course, is incapable of struggling against familial despotism; but Pavel Petrovich and Bazarov could, under certain conditions, be clear representatives: the former of the congealing, hardening forces to the past, the latter of the liberating, destructive forces of the present.

On whose side are the artist's feelings? This vitally important question may be answered definitely: Turgenev does not fully sympathize with any of his characters; his analysis does not miss one weak or ridiculous trait; we see how Bazarov senselessly repudiates everything, how Arkady revels in his enlightenment, how Nikolai Petrovich is as timid as a fifteen-year-old boy, and how Pavel Petrovich shows off and is angry that he has not won the admiration of Bazarov, the only man whom he respects, despite his hatred of him.

Bazarov talks nonsense—this is unfortunately true. He bluntly repudiates things which he does not know or understand: poetry, in his opinion is rubbish; reading Pushkin is a waste of time; to be interested in music is ludicrous; to enjoy nature is absurd. It is very possible that he, a man stifled by a life of labor, lost or never had time to develop the capacity to enjoy the pleasant stimulation of the visual and auditory nerves, but it does not follow from this that he has a rational basis for repudiating or ridiculing this capacity in others. To cut other people down to fit your own measure is to fall into narrow-minded intellectual despotism. To deny completely arbitrarily one or another natural and real human need is to break with pure empiricism.

Bazarov's tendency to get carried away is very natural; it can be explained, first by the one-sidedness of his development, and secondly by the general character of the time in which we live. Bazarov knows natural and medical sciences thoroughly: with their assistance he has rid himself of all prejudices; however, he has remained an extremely uneducated man; he has heard something or other about poetry, something or other about art, and not troubling to think, he passed abrupt sentence on these subjects which were unknown to him. This arrogance is generally a characteristic of ours; it has its good sides such as intellectual courage, but on the other hand, of course, it leads at times to flagrant errors. The general character of the time is practicality: we all want to live by the rule that fine words butter no parsnips. Very energetic people often exaggerate the prevailing tendency; on these grounds, Bazarov's overly indiscriminate repudiations and the very one-sidedness of his development are tied directly to the prevailing striving for tangible benefits. We have become tired of the phrases of the Hegelians, our heads have begun to spin from soaring around in the clouds, and many of us, having sobered up and come down to earth, have gone to the other extreme and while banishing dreaminess have started to persecute simple feelings and even purely physical sensations, like the enjoyment of music. There is no great harm in this extremity, but it will not hurt to point it out; and to call it ludicrous does not mean to join the ranks of the obscurantists and old romantics. Many of our realists are up in arms against Turgenev because he does not sympathize with Bazarov and does not conceal his hero's blunders from the reader; many express the desire that Bazarov had been presented as an irreproachable man, a knight of thought without fear and reproach, and that thereby the superiority of realism to all other schools of thought would thus have been proved to the reading public. In my opinion, realism is indeed a fine thing; but let us not, in the name of this very realism, idealize either ourselves or our movement. We coldly and soberly regard all that surrounds us; let us regard ourselves just as coldly and soberly; all around us is nonsense and backwardness, but, God knows, we are far from perfect. What we repudiate is ridiculous but the repudiators have also been known, at times, to commit colossal follies; all the same, they stand higher than what they repudiate, but this is no great honor; to stand higher than flagrant absurdity does not yet mean to become a great thinker. But we, the speaking and writing realists, are now too carried away by the mental struggle of the moment, by this fiery skirmish with backward idealists, with whom it is not even worthwhile to argue; we, in my view, have gotten too carried away to maintain a skeptical attitude toward ourselves and to submit to rigorous analysis the possibility that we might have fallen into the dust of the dialectic battles which go on in journalistic pamphlets and in everyday life. Our children will regard us skeptically, or, perhaps, we ourselves will learn our real value and will begin to look *à vol d'oiseau* [3] on our present beloved ideas. Then we will regard the past from the height of the present; Turgenev is now regarding the present from the height of the past. He does not follow us, but tranquilly gazes after us and

---

3. "As the crow flies," that is, "straight." Pisarev seems to think it means to have a "bird's eye view" [*Editor*].

describes our gait, telling us how we quicken our pace, how we jump across ditches, how now and then we stumble over rough places in the road.

There is no irritation in the tone of his description; he has simply grown tired of moving on; the development of his own world view has come to an end, but his capacity to observe the movement of another person's thought process, to understand and reproduce all its windings, has remained in all its fullness and freshness. Turgenev himself will never be a Bazarov, but he has pondered this type and gained an understanding of it so true that not one of our young realists has yet achieved it. There is no apotheosis of the past in Turgenev's novel. The author of *Rudin* and "Asya," who laid bare the weaknesses of his generation and who revealed in A *Hunter's Sketches* a whole world of wonders which had been taking place right in front of the eyes of this very generation, has remained true to himself and has not acted against his conscience in his latest work. The representatives of the past, the "fathers," are depicted with ruthless fidelity; they are good people, but Russia will not regret these good people; there is not one element in them which would be worth saving from the grave and oblivion, but still there are moments when one can sympathize more fully with these fathers than with Bazarov himself. When Nikolai Petrovich admires the evening landscape he appears more human than Bazarov who groundlessly denies the beauty of nature to every unprejudiced reader.

"And is nature nonsense?" said Arkady, looking pensively at the bright-colored fields in the distance, in the beautiful soft light of the sun, which was no longer high in the sky.

"Nature, too, is nonsense in the sense you understand it. Nature's not a temple, but a workshop, and man's the workman in it."

In these words, Bazarov's repudiation has turned into something artificial and has even ceased to be consistent. Nature is a workshop and man is a worker in it—with this idea I am ready to agree; but when I carry this idea further, I by no means arrive at the conclusion which Bazarov draws. A worker needs rest and rest does not only mean heavy sleep after exhausting labor. A man must refresh himself with pleasant sensations; life without pleasant sensations, even if all the vital needs are satisfied, turns into unbearable suffering. The consistent materialists, like Karl Vogt, Moleschotte, and Büchner do not deny a day-laborer his glass of vodka, nor the well-to-do classes the use of narcotics. They indulgently regard even the excessive use of such substances, although they acknowledge that such excesses are harmful to the health. If a worker found pleasure in spending his free time lying on his back and gazing at the walls and ceiling of his workshop, then every sensible man would say to him: gaze on, dear friend, stare as much as you please, it won't harm your health but don't you spend your working hours staring or you will make mistakes. Why then, if we permit the use of vodka and narcotics, should we not tolerate the enjoyment of beautiful scenery, mild air, fresh verdure, the gentle play of form and color? Bazarov, in his persecution of romanticism, with incredible suspiciousness seeks it in places where it never has existed. Taking arms against idealism and destroying its castles in the air, he himself, at times, becomes an idealist, that is, he begins to prescribe to man how he should enjoy himself and how he should regulate his own sensations. Telling a man not to enjoy nature is like telling him to mortify his flesh. The more harmless sources of pleasure there are, the easier it is to live in the world, and the whole task of our generation is precisely to decrease the sum of suffering and increase the strength and amount of pleasure. Many will retort that we live in such a difficult time that it is out of the question to think about pleasure; our job, they will say, is to work, to eradicate evil, disseminate good, to clear a site for the great building where our remote descendants will feast. All right, I agree that we are compelled to work for the future, since the fruit we have sown can ripen only after several centuries; let us suppose that our goal is very lofty, still this loftiness of goal affords very little comfort in everyday unpleasantnesses. It is doubtful whether an exhausted and worn-out man will become gay and contented from the thought that his great-great-grandson will enjoy his life. Comforting oneself in the hard moments of life with a lofty goal is, if you will, just the same as drinking unsweetened tea while gazing on a piece of sugar hung from the ceiling. For people without exceedingly vivid imaginations, these wistful upward looks do not make the tea any tastier. In precisely the same way, a life consisting exclusively of work is not to the taste and beyond the powers of contemporary man. Thus, with whatever viewpoint you regard life, you will still be brought up against the fact that pleasure is absolutely indispensable. Some regard pleasure as a final goal; others are compelled to acknowledge pleasure as a very important source of the strength necessary for work. This is the sole difference between the epicureans and stoics of our day.

Thus, Turgenev does not fully sympathize with anyone or anything in his novel. If you were to say to him: "Ivan Sergeevich, you do not like Bazarov, but what would you prefer?" he would not answer the question. He would not wish the younger generation to share their fathers' ideas and enthusiasms. Neither the fathers nor the sons satisfy him, and in this case, his repudiation is more profound and more serious than the repudiations of those people, who, having destroyed everything that existed before them, imagine that they are the salt of the earth and the purest expression of total humanity. These people are perhaps right in their destruction, but in their naïve self-adoration or in their adoration of the type which they consider that represents, lies their limitation and one-sidedness. The forms and types with which we can be contented and feel no need to look further have not yet been and perhaps never will be created by life. People who give up their intellectual independence and substitute servile worship for criticism, by giving themselves over completely to one or another prevailing theory, reveal that they are narrow, impotent, and often harmful people. Arkady is capable of acting in this way, but it would be completely impossible for Bazarov, and it is precisely this trait of mind and character which produces the captivating power of Turgenev's hero. The author understands and acknowledges this captivating power, despite the fact that neither in temperment nor in the conditions of his development does he resemble his nihilist. Furthermore, Turgenev's general attitudes toward the phenomena of life which make up his novel are so calm and disinterested, so devoid of slavish worship of one or another theory, that Bazarov himself would not have found anything timid or false in these attitudes. Turgenev does not like ruthless negations, but, nevertheless, the personality of the ruthless negator appears as a powerful one—and commands the involuntary respect of every reader. Turgenev has a propensity for idealism, but, nevertheless, not one of the idealists in his novel can be compared to Bazarov either in strength of mind or in strength of character. I am certain that many of our journalistic critics will want, at all costs, to find in Turgenev's novel a repressed urge to debase the younger generation and prove that the children are worse than their parents, but I am just as certain that the readers' spontaneous feelings, unfettered by the necessity of supporting a theory, will approve Turgenev and will find in his work not a dissertation on a particular theme, but a true, deeply felt picture of contemporary life drawn without the slightest attempt at concealment of anything. If a writer belonging to our younger generation and profoundly sympathizing with the "Bazarov school" had happened upon Turgenev's theme, then, of course, the picture would have been drawn otherwise and the colors would have been applied differently. Bazarov would not have been portrayed as an awkward student dominating the people around him through the natural strength of his healthy mind; he, perhaps, would have been turned into the embodiment of the ideas which make up the essence of this type; he, perhaps, would have manifested in his personality the clear expression of the author's tendencies, but it is doubtful whether he would have been Bazarov's equal in faithfulness to life and roundness of characterization. My young artist would have said to his contemporaries of his work: "This, my friends, is what a fully developed man must be like! This is the final goal of our efforts!" But Turgenev just says calmly and simply: "This is the sort of young people there are nowadays!" and does not even try to conceal the fact that such young people are not completely to his taste. "How can this be?" many of our contemporary journalists and publicists will cry. "This is obscurantism!" Gentlemen, we could answer, why should Turgenev's personal sensations concern you? Whether he likes such people or does not like them is a matter of taste; if, for instance, feeling no sympathy for the type, he were to slander it, then every honorable man would have the right to unmask him, but you will not find such slander in the novel: even Bazarov's awkwardnesses, to which I already alluded, are perfectly satisfactorily explained by the circumstances of his life and constitute, if not an essential requirement, at least a very frequently encountered trait of people of the Bazarov type. It would, of course, have been much more pleasant for us, the young people, if Turgenev had concealed and glossed over the graceless rough places in Bazarov, but I do not think that an artist who indulged our capricious desires could better capture the phenomena of reality. Both virtues and shortcomings are more clearly apparent when regarded from a detached point of view, and, for this reason, a detached, severely critical view of Bazarov proves, at present, to be much more fruitful than indiscriminate admiration or slavish worship. By regarding Bazarov detachedly as is possible only for a man who is "behind the times" and not involved in the contemporary movement of ideas; by examining him with the cold, probing gaze which is only engendered by long experience of life, Turgenev has justified his hero and valued him at his true worth. Bazarov has emerged from this examination as a pure and a strong man. Turgenev did not find one essential indictment against this type, and thus his voice, the voice of a man who finds himself in a camp which is inconsistent with his age and his views of life, has an especially important and decisive meaning. Turgenev did not grow fond of Bazarov, but he acknowledged his strength and his superiority and offered him a full tribute of respect.

This is more than sufficient to absolve Turgenev's novel from

the powerful charge of being behind the times; it is even sufficient to compel us to acknowledge his novel as practically
useful for the present age.

VI

Bazarov's relations with his comrade throw a bright streak of
light on his character: Bazarov has no friends, since he has not
yet met a man "who could hold his own" with him; Bazarov
stands alone at the cold heights of sober thought and he is not
oppressed by his isolation, he is completely engrossed in himself and in his work; observations and experiments on living
nature, observations and experiments on living people fill for him
the emptiness of his life and insure him against boredom. He
does not feel the need to look for sympathy and understanding
in another person; when some thought occurs to him, he simply
expresses it, paying no attention whether his listeners agree
with his opinion, or whether his ideas please them. Most frequently he does not even feel the need to express himself; he
thinks to himself and, from time to time, lets drop a cursory
remark, which is usually seized upon with respectful eagerness by
his proselytes and pupils like Arkady. Bazarov's personality is
self-contained and reserved, since it finds practically no kindred
elements either outside or around itself. This reserve of Bazarov's
has a dampening effect on the people who would like to see
tenderness and communicativeness from him, but there is nothing
artificial or premeditated in this reserve. The people who surround Bazarov are insignificant intellectually and can in no way
move him, thus he is either silent or speaks in abrupt aphorisms,
or breaks off an argument he has begun because he recognizes
its ludicrous uselessness. If you put an adult in the same room
with a dozen children, you will probably feel no surprise if the
adult does not begin to converse with his roommates about his
humanistic, social, and scientific convictions. Bazarov does not
put on airs before other people, he does not consider himself
a man of genius misunderstood by his contemporaries; he is
merely obliged to regard his acquaintances from above because
these acquaintances only come up to his knees; what else can
he do? Is he to sit on the floor so that he will be the same
height as they? He cannot pretend to be a child just so that
the children will share their immature ideas with him. He involuntarily remains in isolation, and this isolation does not oppress
him because he is young and strong and occupied with the
seething activity of his own thoughts. The process of these thoughts
remains in the shadows; I doubt whether Turgenev was in a
position to render the description of this process: in order to

portray it, he would have had to live through it in his own head, he would have had to himself become Bazarov, but we can be sure that this did not happen to Turgenev, because anyone who had even once, even for a few minutes, looked at things through Bazarov's eyes would have remained a nihilist for the rest of his life. In Turgenev, we see only the results at which Bazarov arrived, we see the external side of the phenomena; that is, we hear what Bazarov says and we know how he acts in life. how he treats various people. But we do not find a psychological analysis or a coherent compendium of Bazarov's thoughts; we can only guess what he thought and how he formulated his convictions to himself. By not initiating the reader into the secret of Bazarov's intellectual life, Turgenev may cause bewilderment among the segment of the public which is not used to filling in through their own mental efforts what is not stated or written in the works of a writer. The inattentive reader may come to the conclusion that Bazarov has no internal substance and that his entire nihilism consists of an interweaving of daring phrases snatched from the air and not created by independent thought. It is possible to say positively that Turgenev himself does not fully understand his hero, and does not trace the gradual development and maturation of his ideas only because he cannot and does not want to render Bazarov's thoughts as they would have arisen in his hero's mind. Bazarov's thoughts are expressed in his deeds, in his treatment of people; they shine through and it is not difficult to make them out, if only the reader carefully organizes the facts and is aware of their causes.

Two episodes fill in the details of this remarkable personality: first, his treatment of the woman who attracts him; secondly, his death.

I will consider both of these, but first I consider it not out of place to turn my attention to other, secondary details.

Bazarov's treatment of his parents will predispose some readers against the character, and others against the author. The former, becoming carried away by sentimental feelings, will reproach Bazarov for callousness; the latter, becoming carried away by their attachment to the Bazarov type, will reproach Turgenev for injustice to his hero and for a desire to show him in a disadvantageous light. Both sides, in my opinion, would be completely wrong. Bazarov really does not afford his parents the pleasures which the good old people were expecting from his visit to them, but between him and his parents there is not one thing in common. * * *

In town, at the governor's ball, Arkady becomes acquainted with a young widow, Anna Sergeyevna Odintsov; while dancing the mazurka with her, he happens to mention his friend Bazarov and excites her interest with his rapturous description of his friend's daring intellect and decisive character. She invites him to visit her and asks him to bring Bazarov. Bazarov, who had noticed her the instant she appeared at the ball, speaks to Arkady about her, involuntarily intensifying the usual cynicism of his tone, partially in order to conceal both from himself and from Arkady the impression that this woman has made on him. He willingly agrees to visit Odintsov with Arkady and explains his pleasure to himself and to Arkady by his hope of beginning a pleasant intrigue. Arkady, who has not failed to succumb to Odintsov's charms, takes offense at Bazarov's jocular tone, but, of course, Bazarov pays not the slightest attention and keeps on talking about Odintsov's beautiful shoulders, he asks Arkady whether this lady is really "ooh la la!", he says that still waters run deep and that a cold woman is just like ice cream. As he approaches Odintsov's apartments Bazarov feels a certain agitation and, wanting to overcome it, at the beginning of the visit behaves unnaturally informally and, according to Turgenev, sprawls in his chair just like Sitnikov. Odintsov notices Bazarov's agitation and, partially guessing its cause, calms our hero down with the gentle affability of her manner, and the young people's unhurried, diverse, and lively conversation continues for three hours. Bazarov treats her with special respect; it is evident that he is not indifferent to what she thinks of him, to the impression he is making; contrary to his usual habit, he speaks quite a lot, tries to interest his listener, does not make cutting remarks and even, carefully avoiding topics of general concern, discusses botany, medicine, and other subjects he is well-versed in. As the young men take their leave, Odintsov invites them to visit her in the country. Bazarov bows silently to indicate his acceptance and flushes. Arkady notices all this and is astonished by it. After this first meeting with Odintsov, Bazarov endeavors to speak of her in his former jocular tone, but the very cynicism of his expressions belies an involuntary, repressed respect. It is evident that he admires this woman and wishes to come into friendship with her; he jokes about her because he does not want to speak seriously with Arkady, either about this woman or about the new sensations which he notices in himself. Bazarov could not fall in love with Odintsov at first sight or after their first meeting; such things only happen to very shallow people in very bad novels. He was simply taken by her beautiful, or as he himself puts it, splendid body; her conversation did not destroy the general harmony of impressions, and this was enough at first to reinforce his desire to know her better. Bazarov has not yet formulated a theory about love. His student years, about which Turgenev does not say a word, probably did not pass without some affair of the heart; Bazarov, as we shall see later on, proves to be an experienced man, but, in all probability, he has had to do with women who were completely uneducated and far from refined and, consequently, incapable of strongly interesting his intellect or stirring his nerves; when he meets Odintsov he sees that it is possible to speak to her as an equal and senses that she possesses the versatile mind and firm character which he is conscious of and likes in himself. When Bazarov and Odintsov speak to each other they are able, intellectually speaking, to look each other in the eye over the fledgling Arkady's head and this instinctive mutual understanding affords them both pleasant sensations. Bazarov sees an elegant figure and involuntarily admires it; beyond this figure he discerns innate strength and unconsciously begins to respect this strength. As a pure empiricist, he enjoys the pleasant sensation and gradually becomes so accustomed to it, that when the time comes to tear himself away, it is difficult and painful for him to do so. Bazarov does not subject love to an ,analysis because he feels no mistrust in himself. He goes to the country to see Odintsov, with curiosity and without the slightest fear, because he wants to have a closer look at this pretty woman, wants to be with her and to spend a few days pleasantly. In the country, fifteen days pass imperceptibly; Bazarov talks with Anna Sergeyevna a lot, argues with her, expresses himself fully, and finally begins to feel for her a kind of malicious, tormenting passion. Such passion is most frequently engendered in energetic men by women who are beautiful, intelligent, and cold. The beauty of the woman stirs the blood of her admirer; her mind allows her to understand and to subject to subtle psychological analysis the feelings which she does not share or even sympathize with; her coldness insures her against getting carried away, and by increasing the obstacles, increases the man's desire to overcome them. Looking at such a woman, a man involuntarily thinks: she is so beautiful, she speaks so well about emotion, at times she becomes so animated when she expresses her subtle psychological analysis or listens to my deeply felt speeches. Why are her feelings so obstinately silent? How can I touch her to the quick? Can it be that her whole being is concentrated in her brain? Can it be that she is only amusing herself with impressions and is not capable of becoming carried away by them? Time passes in strenuous efforts to puzzle out the vital enigma; the intellect labors alongside the passions; heavy, torturous sensations appear; the whole romance of the relationship between a man and a woman takes on the strange character of a struggle. Becoming acquainted with Odintsov, Bazarov thought to amuse himself with a pleasant intrigue; knowing her better, he felt respect for her but began to see that he had little hope of success; if he had not managed to become strongly attached to Odintsov, he simply would have dismissed her with a shrug and immediately have occupied himself with the practical observation that the world is very large and there are many women in it who are easier to handle; he tried to act in such a way but he did not have the strength to shrug off Odintsov. Common sense advised him to abandon the whole affair and go away so as not to torment himself in vain, but his craving for pleasure spoke more loudly than his common sense and Bazarov remained. He was angry and he was conscious of the fact that he was committing a folly but, nevertheless, went on committing it, because his desire to live for his pleasure was stronger than his desire to be consistent. This capacity consciously to behave stupidly is an enviable virtue of strong and intelligent people. A dispassionate and dried-up person always acts according to logical calculations; a timid and weak person tries to deceive himself with sophistry and assure himself of the rightness of his desires and actions; but Bazarov has no need for such trickery; he says to himself straightforwardly: this is stupid, but nevertheless, I will do what I want, and I do not want to torment myself over it. When it becomes necessary I will have the time and strength to do what I must. A wholehearted, strong nature is manifested in this capacity to become completely carried away: a healthy, incorruptible mind is expressed in this capability to recognize as folly the passion which has consumed the whole organism.

Bazarov's relationship with Odintsov is brought to an end by a strange scene which takes place between them. She draws him into a discussion about happiness and love; with the curiosity peculiar to cold and intelligent women she questions him about what is taking place within him, she extracts a confession of love from him, with a trace of involuntary tenderness she utters his name; then, when stunned by the sudden onslaught of sensation, and new hopes, he rushes to her and clasps her to his breast, she jumps away in fear to the other end of the room and assures him that he had misunderstood her, that he was mistaken.

Bazarov leaves the room and with this their relationship comes to an end. He leaves her house the day after this incident; afterward, he sees Anna Sergeyevna twice, even visits her in the company of Arkady, but for both of them past events prove to be irrevocably past, and they regard each other calmly and speak together in the tones of reasonable and sedate people. Nevertheless, it saddens Bazarov to look on his relationship with Odintsov as on an episode from his past; he loves her and, while he does not allow himself to complain, suffer, or play the rejected lover, he becomes irregular in his way of life, now throwing himself into his work, now falling into idleness, now merely becoming bored and grumbling at the people around him. He does not want to talk about it to anyone, he does not even acknowledge to himself that he feels something resembling anguish and yearning. He becomes angry and sour because of his failure, it annoys him to think that happiness beckoned to him but then passed on and it annoys him to feel that this event has made an impression on him. All this would have worked itself out in his organism, he would again have taken up his work and cursed in the most energetic manner damnable romanticism and the inaccessible lady who had led him by the nose, and would have lived as he had before, occupied with the dissection of frogs and the courting of less unconquerable beauties. But Turgenev did not bring Bazarov out of his gloomy mood. Bazarov suddenly dies, not from grief, of course, and the novel comes to an end, or, more precisely, sharply and unexpectedly breaks off. * * *

The description of Bazarov's death is one of the best passages in Turgenev's novel; indeed, I doubt whether anything more remarkable can be found in the whole body of his work. It would be impossible for me to quote an excerpt from this magnificent episode; it would destroy the integrity of the effect; I should really quote the whole ten pages, but I do not have the space; furthermore, I hope that all my readers have read or will read Turgenev's novel. Thus, without quoting a single line, I shall endeavor to trace and explicate Bazarov's mental state from the beginning to the end of his illness. Bazarov cuts his finger while dissecting a corpse and does not have the opportunity to cauterize the cut immediately with a caustic stone or iron. Only after four hours does Bazarov come to his father's room and cauterize the sore spot, without concealing either from himself or from Vassily Ivanovich that this measure is useless if the infected matter from the corpse has entered the blood. Vassily Ivanovich knows as a doctor how great the danger is, but he cannot bring himself to look it in the face and tries to deceive himself. Two days pass, Bazarov steels himself, he does not go to bed, but he has fever and chills, loses his appetite, and suffers from a severe headache. His father's sympathy and questions irritate him because he knows that all this will not help and that the old man is pampering himself and diverting himself with empty illusions. It vexes him to see a man, and a doctor besides, not daring to view the matter in its proper light. Bazarov spares Arina Vlasyevna; he tells her that he has caught cold; on the third day he goes to bed and asks for lime tea. On the fourth day he turns to his father and straightforwardly and seriously tells him that he will die soon, shows him the red spots on his body which are a sign of infection, gives him the medical term for his illness, and coldly refutes the timid objections of the broken old man. Nevertheless, he wants to live, he is sorry to give up his self-awareness, his thoughts, his strong personality, but this pain at parting with his young life and untried power expresses itself not in a gentle melancholy but in a bitter, ironic vexation, in his scornful attitude toward himself, an impotent being, and toward the crude, meaningless accident which has trampled and crushed him. The nihilist remains true to himself to the last moment.

As a doctor, he has seen that infected people always die and he does not doubt the immutability of this law, despite the fact that it condemns him to death. In precisely the same way, he does not replace his gloomy world view by another more comforting one in a crucial moment: neither as a doctor nor as a man does he comfort himself with mirages. * * *

The author sees that Bazarov loves no one, because around him all is petty, stupid, and flabby, while he himself is fresh, intelligent, and strong; the author sees this and, in his mind, relieves his hero of the last undeserved reproach. Turgenev has studied Bazarov's character, he has pondered its elements and the conditions of its development, and he has come to see that for him there can be neither occupation nor happiness. He lives as an isolated figure and dies an isolated figure, and a useless isolated figure besides, dies as a hero who has nowhere to turn, nothing to draw breath on, nothing to do with his mighty powers, no one to love with a powerful love. As there is no reason for him to live, we must observe how he dies. The whole interest, the whole meaning of the novel is contained in the death of Bazarov. If he had turned coward, if he had been untrue to himself, it would have shed a completely different light on his whole character; he would have appeared to have been an empty braggart from whom it would be impossible to expect fortitude or decisivness in a time of need; the whole novel would have been turned into a slander on the younger generation, an undeserved reproach; with such a novel, Turgenev would have been saying: look here, young people, here is an example: even the best of you is no good. But Turgenev, as an honorable man and a true artist, could not have brought himself to tell such a grievous lie. Bazarov did not become abased, and the meaning of the novel emerged as follows: today's young people become carried away and go to extremes; but this very tendency to get carried away points to fresh strength and incorruptible intellect; this strength and this intellect, without any outside assistance or influence, will lead these young people on to the right road and will support them in life.

Whoever has found this splendid thought in Turgenev's novel could not help but express his deep and warm gratitude to this great artist and honorable citizen of Russia.

But all the same, the Bazarovs have a bad time of it in this life, although they make a point of humming and whistling. There is no occupation, no love—consequently, there is no pleasure either.

They do not know how to suffer, they will not complain, but at times they feel only that all is empty, boring, drab, and meaningless.

But what is to be done? Is it possible to infect ourselves on purpose just in order to have the satisfaction of dying beautifully and tranquilly? No! What is to be done? We must live while we are alive, eat dry bread if there is no roast beef, know many women if it is not possible to love a woman, and, in general, we must not dream about orange trees and palms, when under foot are snowdrifts and the cold tundra.

N. N. STRAKHOV

Fathers and Sons†

* * * In order to be completely consistent to the very end, Bazarov refrains from preaching, as another form of empty chatter. And in reality, preaching would be nothing other than the admission of the rights of thought and the force of ideas. Preaching would be that justification which, as we have seen, was superfluous for Bazarov. To attach importance to preaching would mean to admit intellectual activity, to admit that men are ruled not by the senses and need, but also by thought and the words in which it is vested. To start preaching would mean to start going into abstractions, would mean calling logic and history to one's aid, would mean to concern oneself with those things already admitted to be trifles in their very essence. That is why Bazarov is not fond of arguments, disputation, and does not attach great value to them. He sees that one cannot gain much by logic; he tries instead to act through his

† From N. Strakhov, *Kriticheskiya stat'i,* 1 (Kiev, 1908), 1–39. Translated by Ralph E. Matlaw. The article first appeared in Dostoev-sky's periodical *Time* in April, 1862. Strakhov (1828–96) was a philosopher and literary critic, and a close friend of Tolstoy's and Dostoevsky's.

personal example, and is sure that Bazarovs will spring up by themselves in abundance, as certain plants spring up where their seeds are. Pisarev understands that position very well. He says, for example: "Indignation at stupidity and baseness in general is understandable, though it is for that matter as fruitful as indignation at autumn dampness or winter cold." He judges Bazarov's tendency in the same way: "If Bazarovism is a disease, then it is a disease of our time, and must be endured to the end, no matter what palliatives and amputations are employed. Treat Bazarovism however you please—that is your business; but you will not be able to put a stop to it; it is just the same as Cholera."

Therefore it is clear that all the chatterer-Bazarovs, the preacher-Bazarovs, the Bazarovs occupied only with their Bazarovism rather than with deeds are on the wrong road, which will lead them to endless contradictions and stupidities, that they are far less consistent and stand much lower than Bazarov.

Such is the stern cast of mind, the solid store of thoughts Turgenev embodied in Bazarov. He clothed that mind with flesh and blood, and fulfilled that task with amazing mastery. Bazarov emerged as a simple man, free of all affectation, and at the same time firm and powerful in soul and body. Everything in him fits his strong character unusually well. It is quite noteworthy that he is *more Russian*, so to speak, than all the rest of the characters in the novel. His speech is distinguished by its simplicity, appropriateness mockery, and completely Russian cast. In the same way he approaches the common people more easily than any other character in the novel and knows better than they how to behave with them.

Nothing could correspond so well as this to the simplicity and straight forwardness of the view Bazarov professes. A man who is profoundly imbued with certain convictions, who is their complete embodiment, must without fail also turn out natural and therefore close to his native traditions and at the same time a strong man. That is why Turgenev, who up to this point had created divided characters, so to speak, for example, the Hamlet of the Shchigry District, Rudin, and Lavretsky,[1] finally attained the type of an undivided personality in Bazarov. Bazarov is the first strong character, the first whole character, to appear in Russian literature from the sphere of so called educated society. Whoever fails to value that, whoever fails to understand the importance of that phenomenon, had best not judge our literature. Even Antonovich [2]

1. Characters in the story by that name (1849), the novels *Rudin* (1856), and *Nest of Noblemen* (1859) [*Editor*].

2. Reviewer for *The Contemporary* [*Editor*].

noticed it, as one may see by the following strange sentence: "Apparently Turgenev wanted to portray in his hero what is called a *demonic or Byronic character, something on the order of Hamlet.*" Hamlet—a demonic character! That indicated a confused notion of Byron and Shakespeare. Yet actually *something of a demonic order* does emerge in Turgenev's work, that is, a figure rich in force, though that force is not pure.

In what does the action of the novel really consist?

Bazarov together with his friend Arkady Kirsanov arrives in the provinces from Petersburg. Both are students who have just completed their courses, one in the medical academy, the other at the university. Bazarov is no longer a man in his first youth; he has already acquired a certain reputation, has managed to present his mode of thought; while Arkady is still completely a youth. The entire action of the novel takes place during one vacation, perhaps for both the first vacation after completing their courses. For the most part the friends visit together, in the Kirsanov family, in the Bazarov family, in the provincial capital, in the village of the widow Odintsov. They meet many people, whom they either meet for the first time or have not seen for many years. To be precise, Bazarov had not gone home in three years. Therefore there occurs a variegated collision of their new views, brought from Petersburg, with the views of the people they meet. The entire interest of the novel is contained in these collisions. There are very few events and little action in it. Toward the end of the vacation Bazarov dies, almost by accident, becoming infected from a decomposing body, and Kirsanov marries, having fallen in love with Odintsov's sister. With that the entire novel ends.

In this Bazarov appears completely the hero, despite the fact that there is apparently nothing brilliant or striking in him. The reader's attention is focused on him from the first, and all the other characters begin to turn about him as around the main center of gravity. He is least of all interested in other characters, but the others are all the more interested in him. He does not try to attach anyone to himself and does not force himself on them, and yet wherever he appears he arouses the greatest attention and becomes the main object of feelings and thoughts, love and hatred.

In setting off to spend time with his parents and with friends Bazarov had no particular aim in mind. He does not seek anything and does not expect anything from that trip. He simply wants to rest and travel. At the most he sometimes wants to *look at people*. But with that superiority he has over those around him and as a result of their all feeling his strength, these characters themselves seek closer relations with him and involve him in a drama he did not at all want and did not even anticipate.

He had hardly appeared in the Kirsanov family when he immediately arouses irritation and hatred in Pavel Petrovich, respect mixed with fear in Nikolai Petrovich, the friendly disposition of Fenichka, Dunyasha, the servants' children, even of the baby Mitya, and the contempt of Prokofich. Later on, things reach the stage that he is himself carried away for a moment and kisses Fenichka, and Pavel Petrovich challenges him to a duel. "What a piece of foolery!" Bazarov repeats, not at all having expected such *events*.

The trip to town, its purpose to *look at people*, also is not without consequences for him. Various characters begin to mill around him. Sitnikov and Kukshin, masterfully depicted characters of the false progressive and the false emancipated woman, begin to court him. Of course they do not disconcert him; he treats them with contempt and they only serve as a contrast, from which his mind and force, his total integrity emerge still more sharply and in greater relief. But here the stumbling block, Anna Sergeyevna Odintsov, is also met. Despite his coolness Bazarov begins to waver. To the great amazement of his worshipper Arkady he is even embarrassed once, and on another occasion blushes. Without suspecting any danger, however, firmly confident of himself, Bazarov goes to visit Odintsov, at Nikolskoe. And he really does control himself splendidly. And Odintsov, like all the other characters, becomes interested in him, as she probably had not become interested in anyone else in her whole life. The matter ends badly, however. Too great a passion is aroused in Bazarov, while Odintsov's inclination does not rise to real love. Bazarov leaves almost completely rejected and again begins to be amazed at himself and to upbraid himself. "The devil knows what nonsense it is! Every man hangs on a thread, the abyss may open under his feet any minute, and yet he must go and invent all sorts of discomforts for himself, and spoil his life."

But despite these wise comments, Bazarov continues involuntarily to spoil his life just the same. Even after that lesson, even during his second visit to the Kirsanovs, he is carried away with Fenichka and is forced to fight a duel with Pavel Petrovich.

Apparently Bazarov does not at all desire and does not expect a love affair, but the love affair takes place against his iron will; life, which he had thought he would rule, catches him in its huge wave.

Near the end of the story, when Bazarov visits his father and mother, he apparently is somewhat bewildered after all the shocks he had undergone. He was not so bewildered that he could not be cured, that he would not rise again in full force after a short while. But nevertheless the shadow of sorrow which lay over that iron man even at the beginning becomes deeper toward the end. He loses the desire to work, loses weight, begins to make fun of the peasants no longer in a friendly way but rather sardonically. As a result, it turns out that this time he and the peasant fail to understand each other, while formerly mutual understanding was possible up to a point. Finally, Bazarov begins to improve and becomes interested in medical practice. The infection of which he dies nevertheless seems to testify to inadequate attention and agility, to a momentary diversion of his spiritual forces.

Death is the last test of life, the last accident that Bazarov did not expect. He dies, but to the very last moment he remains foreign to that life with which he came into conflict so strangely, which bothered him with such *trifles*, made him commit such *fooleries* and, finally killed him as result of such an *insignificant* cause.

Bazarov dies altogether the hero and his death creates a shattering impression. To the very end, to the last flash of conscience, he does not betray himself by a single word nor by a single sign of cowardice. He is broken, but not conquered.

Thus despite the short time of action in the novel and despite his quick death, Bazarov was able to express himself completely and completely show his force. Life did not destroy him—one cannot possibly draw that conclusion from the novel—but only gave him occasions to disclose his energy. In the readers' eyes Bazarov emerges the victor from his trials. Everyone will say that people like Bazarov can do much, and that with such strength one may expect much from them.

Strictly speaking, Bazarov is shown only in a narrow frame and not with all the sweep of human life. The author says practically nothing about his hero's development, how such a character could have been formed. In precisely the same way, the novel's rapid ending leaves the question "would Bazarov have remained the same Bazarov, or in general what development awaited him in the future" as a complete puzzle. And yet silence on the first as on the second question has, it seems to me, its reason in realistic basis. If the hero's gradual development is not shown, it is unquestionably because Bazarov did not become educated through the gradual accumulation of influences but, on the contrary, by a rapid, sharp break. Bazarov had not been home for three years. During that time he studied, and now suddenly he appears before us imbued with everything he has managed to learn. The morning after his arrival he already goes forth after frogs and in general he continues his *educational* life at every convenient opportunity. He is a man of theory, and theory created him, created him imperceptibly, without events, without anything that one might have related, created him with a single intellectual turnabout.

Bazarov soon dies. That was necessary to the artist in order to make the picture simple and clear. Bazarov could not long remain in his present tense mood. Sooner or later he would have to change and stop being Bazarov. We have no right to complain to the author that he did not choose a broader task and limited himself to the narrower one. He decided to stop at a single step in his hero's development. Nonetheless the *whole man*, not fragmentary traits, appear at that step of his development, as generally happens in development. In relation to the fullness of character the author's task is splendidly fulfilled.

A living, whole man is caught by the author in each of Bazarov's actions and movements. Here is the great merit of the novel, which contains its main idea, and which our hurried moralizers did not notice. Bazarov is a theoretician; he is a strange and sharply one-sided person; he preaches unusual things; he acts eccentrically; he is a schoolboy in whom the coarsest *affectation* is united with profound sincerity; as we said before, he is a man foreign to life; that is, he himself avoids life. But a warm stream of life courses beneath all these external forms. With all his sharpness and the artificiality of his actions Bazarov is a completely live person, not a phantom, not an invention but real flesh and blood. He rejects life yet at the same time lives profoundly and strongly.

After one of the most wonderful scenes in the novel, namely, after the conversation in which Pavel Kirsanov challenges Bazarov to a duel and the latter accepts the challenge and agrees on its terms, Bazarov, amazed by the unexpected turn of events and the strangeness of the conversation, exclaims: "Well, I'll be damned! How fine, and how foolish! A pretty farce we've been through! Like trained dogs dancing on their hind paws." It would be difficult to make a more caustic remark. And yet the reader feels that the conversation Bazarov so characterizes was in reality a completely live and serious conversation; that despite all the deformity and artificiality of its form, the conflict of two energetic characters has been accurately expressed in it.

The poet shows us the same thing with unusual clarity through the whole novel. It may constantly be seen that the characters and particularly Bazarov *put on a farce* and that like trained dogs they *dance on their hind legs*. Yet beneath this appearance, as beneath a transparent veil, the reader clearly discerns that the feelings and actions underlying it are not at all canine but purely and profoundly human.

That is the point of view from which the action and events of the novel may best be evaluated. Beneath the rough, deformed, artificial, and affected forms, the profound vitality of all the phenomena and characters brought to the scene is heard. If Bazarov, for example, possesses the reader's attention and sympathy, he does so because in reality all these words and actions flow out of a living soul, not because each of his words is sacred and each action fair. Apparently Bazarov is a proud man, terribly egoistic and offending others by his egoism. But the reader makes his peace with that pride because simultaneously Bazarov lacks all smugness and self-satisfaction; pride brings him no joy. Bazarov treats his parents carelessly and curtly. But no one could suspect him, in that instance, of pleasure in the feeling of his personal superiority or the feeling of his power over them. Still less can he be reproached for abusing that superiority and that power. He simply refuses tender relationship with his parent and refuses it incompletely. Something strange emerges: he is uncommunicative with his father, laughs at him, sharply accuses him either of ignorance or tenderness. And yet the father is not only not offended but rather happy and satisfied. "Bazarov's jeers did not in the least perturb Vassily Ivanovich; they were positively a comfort to him. Holding his greasy dressing-gown across his stomach with two fingers, and smoking his pipe, he used to listen with enjoyment to Bazarov; and the more malicious his sallies, the more good-naturedly did his delighted father chuckle, showing every one of his black teeth." Such are the wonders of love. Soft and good-natured Arkady could never *delight* his father as Bazarov does his. Bazarov himself, of course, feels and understands that very well. Why should he be tender with his father and betray his inexorable consistency!

Bazarov is not at all so dry a man as his external actions and the cast of his thoughts might lead one to believe. In life, in his relations to people, Bazarov is not consistent (with himself); but in that very thing his vitality is disclosed. He likes people. "Man is a strange being," he says, noticing the presence of that liking in himself, "he wants to be with people, just to curse them, so long as he can be with them." Bazarov is not an abstract theoretician who solves all problems and is completely calmed by that solution. In such a case he would be a monstrous phenomenon, a caricature, not a man. That is why Bazarov is easily excited, why everything vexes him, everything has an effect on him, despite all his firmness and consistency in words and actions. This excitement does not betray his view and his intentions at all; for the most part it only arouses his bile and vexes him. Once he says the following to his friend Arkady: "You said, for instance, to-day as we passed our bailiff Philip's cottage—it's the one that's so nice and clean—well, you said Russia will attain perfection when the poorest peasant has a house like that, and every one of us ought to work to bring it about. And I felt such a hatred for this poorest peasant, this Philip or Sidor, for whom I'm to be ready to jump out of my skin, and * * * what do I need his thanks for? Why, suppose he does live in a clean hut, while the nettles are growing out of me,—well, what comes after that?" What a terrible, shocking speech, isn't it?

A few minutes later Bazarov does still worse: he discloses a longing to choke his tender friend Arkady, to choke him for no particular reason and in the guise of a pleasant trial already spreads wide his long and hard fingers.

Why does all this not arm the reader against Bazarov? What could be worse than that? And yet the impression created by these incidents does not serve to harm Bazarov. So much so that even Antonovich (striking proof!) who with extreme diligence explains everything in Bazarov on the bad side in order to prove Turgenev's sly intention to blacken Bazarov—completely left that incident out!

What does this mean? Apparently Bazarov, who so easily meets people, takes such lively interest in them, and so easily begins to feel rancor toward them, suffers more from that rancor than those for whom it is destined. That rancor is not the expression of destroyed egoism or insulted self-esteem, it is the expression of suffering, and oppression created by the absence of love. Despite all his views, Bazarov eagerly seeks love for people. If that desire appears as rancor, that rancor only represents the reverse of love. Bazarov cannot be a cold, abstract man. His heart demands full-ness and demands feeling. And so he rages at others but feels that he should really rage at himself more than at them.

From all this it at least becomes apparent what a difficult task Turgenev undertook in his latest novel and how successfully in our view he carried it out. He depicted life under the deadening in-fluence of theory; he gave us a living being, though that man apparently embodied himself in an abstract formula without leav-ing a remnant behind. Through this, if one were to judge the novel superficially, it is not very comprehensible, presents little that is appealing, and seems to consist entirely of an obscure logical con-struction. But in reality, it is actually marvelously clear, unusually attractive, and throbs with warm life.

There is practically no need to explain why Bazarov turned out and had to turn out a theoretician. Everyone knows that our *real* representatives, that the "carriers of thought" in our generation, have long ago renounced being *practical*, that active participation in the life around them had long ago become impossible. From that point of view Bazarov is a direct and immediate imitator of Onegin, Pechorin, Rudin, and Lavretsky. Exactly like them he lives in the mental sphere for the time being and spends his spiritual forces on it. But the thirst for activity has reached the final, ex-treme point in him. His entire theory consists in the direct demand for action. His mood is such that he inevitably would come to grips with that action at the first convenient possibility.

The characters surrounding Bazarov unconsciously feel the living man in him. That is why so many attachments turn upon him, far more than on any other character in the novel. Not only do his father and mother remember him and pray for him with infinite and inexpressible tenderness; in other characters too the memory of Bazarov is accompanied by love; in a moment of happiness Katya and Arkady drink "to Bazarov's memory."

Such is Bazarov's image for us, too. He is not a hateful being who repels through his shortcomings; on the contrary, his gloomy figure is grandiose and attractive.

"What then is the idea of the novel?" Lovers of bare and exact conclusions will ask. Does Bazarov present a subject for imitation according to you? Or should his failure and roughness on the contrary teach the Bazarovs not to fall into the errors and extremes of the real Bazarov? In short, is the novel written *for* the young generation or *against* it? Is it progressive or reactionary?

If the question so insistently concerns the author's intentions, what he wanted to teach and what he wanted to have unlearned, then it seems these questions would have to be answered as follows: Turgenev does in fact want to be instructive, but he chooses tasks far higher and more difficult than you suppose. It is not a difficult thing to write a novel with a progressive or reactionary tendency. But Turgenev had the pretension and daring to create a novel that had *all possible* tendencies. The worshipper of eternal truth and eternal beauty, he had the proud aim of showing the eternal in the temporary and to write a novel neither progressive nor reactionary but, so to speak, *constant*. In this instance he may be compared to a mathematician who tries to find some important theorem. Let us assume that he has finally found that theorem. Would he not be terribly amazed and disconcerted if he were suddenly approached with the question whether his theorem was progressive or reactionary? Does it conform to the *modern* spirit or does it obey the *old*?

He could only answer such questions thus: your questions make no sense and have no bearing on my findings: my theorem is an *eternal truth*.

> Alas! In life's furrows
> By Providence's secret will
> Generations are the fleeting harvest
> They rise, ripen and fall;
> Others come in their wake . . .

The change of generations is the outward theme of the novel. If Turgenev did not depict all fathers and sons, or not *those* fathers and sons who would like to be different, he splendidly described fathers *in general* and children *in general* and the relationship between those two generations. Perhaps the difference between generations has never been as great as it is at the present, and therefore their relationship too appears to be particularly acute. However that may be, in order to measure the difference between objects the same measure must be used for both; in order to draw a picture all objects must be described from a point of view common to all of them.

That single measure, that general point of view for Turgenev is *human life* in its broadest and fullest meaning. The reader of his novel feels that behind the mirage of external actions and scenes there flows such a profound, such an inexhaustible current of life, that all these actions and scenes, all the characters and events are insignificant in comparison to that current.

If we understand Turgenev's novel that way, then, perhaps the moral we are seeking will also be disclosed to us more clearly. There is a moral, even a very important one, for truth and poetry are very instructive.

If we look at the picture presented by the novel more calmly and at some distance, we note easily that though Bazarov stands head and shoulders above all the other characters, though he majestically passes over the scene, triumphant, bowed down to, respected, loved, and lamented, there is nevertheless something that taken as a whole stands above Bazarov. What is that? If we examine it attentively, we will find that that higher something is not a character but that *life* which inspires them. Above Bazarov stands that fear, that love, those tears he inspires. Above Bazarov is that scene he passes through. The enchantment of nature, the charm of art, feminine love, family love, parents' love, *even* religion, all that—living, full, powerful—is the background against which Bazarov is drawn. That background is so clear and sparkling that Bazarov's huge figure stands out clearly but at the same time gloomily against it. Those who think that for sake of a supposed condemnation of Bazarov the author contrasts to him one of his characters, say Pavel Petrovich, or Arkady, or Odintsov, are terribly wrong. All these characters are insignificant in comparison to Bazarov. And yet their life, the human element in their feelings is not insignificant.

We will not discuss here the description of nature, of Russian nature, which is so difficult to describe and in describing which Turgenev is such a master. It is the same in this as in previous novels. The sky, air, fields, trees, even horses, even chicks—everything is caught graphically and exactly.

Let's simply take people. What could be weaker or more insignificant than Bazarov's young friend Arkady? He apparently submits to every passing influence; he is the most ordinary of mortals. And yet he is extremely nice. The magnanimous agitation of his young feelings, his nobility and purity are emphasized by the author with great finesse and are clearly depicted. Nikolai Petrovich, as is proper, is the real father of his son. There is not a single clear trait in him and the only good thing is that he is a man, though a very simple man. Further, what could be emptier than Fenichka? The author writes "The expression of her eyes was charming, particularly when she seemed to gaze up from beneath her brow and smiled kindly and a little stupidly." Pavel Petrovich himself calls her an *empty creature*. And yet that silly Fenichka attracts almost more adorers than the clever Odintsov. Not only does Nikolai Petrovich love her, but in part Pavel Petrovich falls in love with her as does Bazarov himself. And yet that love and falling in love are real and valuable human feelings. Finally, what is Pavel Petrovich—a dandy, a fop with gray hair, completely taken up with his concern for his toilette? But even in him, despite the apparent distortion there are living and even energetic vibrations of the heartstrings.

The farther we go in the novel, the nearer to the end of the drama, the more gloomy and tense does Bazarov's figure become, while the background becomes clearer and clearer. The creation of such figures as Bazarov's mother and father is a real triumph of talent. Apparently nothing could be less significant and useless than these people who have lived out their time and who become decrepit and disfigured in the new life with all their prejudices of old. And yet what richness of *simple* human feeling! What depth and breadth of spiritual life among the most ordinary life that does not rise a jot above the lowest level.

When Bazarov becomes ill, when he rots alive and inexorably undergoes the cruel battle with illness, life around him becomes more tense and clear in proportion to his becoming gloomier. Odintsov comes to say farewell to Bazarov! She had probably done nothing generous in her life and will not do so again all her life. So far as the father and mother are concerned, it would be difficult to find anything more touching. Their love bursts forth like some sort of lightning, for a moment striking the reader. From their simple hearts there seem to be torn infinitely sad hymns, some sort of limitlessly deep and tender outcries that irresistibly touch the soul.

Bazarov dies amidst that light and that warmth. For a moment a storm flares up in his father's soul. It is harder to imagine anything more fearful. But it soon dies down and everything again becomes bright. Bazarov's very grave is illuminated by light and peace. Birds sing over it and tears are poured on it.

So there it is, there is that secret moral which Turgenev put in his work. Bazarov turns away from nature; Turgenev does not reproach him for it; he only depicts nature in all its beauty. Bazarov does not value friendship and rejects romantic love; the author does not reproach him for it; he only describes Arkady's friendship toward Bazarov and his happy love for Katya. Bazarov denies close bonds between parents and children; the author does not reproach him for it; he only develops a picture of parental love before us. Bazarov shuns life; the author does not present him as a villain for it; he only shows us life in all its beauty. Bazarov repudiates poetry; Turgenev does not make him a fool for it; he only depicts him with all the fullness and penetration of poetry.

In short, Turgenev stands for the eternal principles of human life; for those fundamental elements which can endlessly change their forms but actually always remain unchangeable. But what have we said? It turns out that Turgenev stands for those things all poets stand for, that every real poet must stand for. And, consequently, in this case Turgenev put himself above any reproach for ulterior motives; whatever the particular circumstances he chose for his work may be, he examines them from the most general and highest point of view.

All his attention is concentrated on the general forces of life. He has shown us how these forces are embodied in Bazarov, in that same Bazarov who denies them. He has shown us if not a more powerful then a more apparent, clearer embodiment of those forces in those simple people who surround Bazarov. Bazarov is a titan, rising against mother earth; no matter how great his force it only testifies to the greatness of the forces that begot him and fed him, but it does not come up to mother earth's force.

However it may be, Bazarov is defeated all the same. He is not defeated by the characters and occurrences of life but by the very idea of that life. Such an ideal victory over him is only possible if he is done all justice, if he is exalted to his appropriate grandeur. Otherwise the victory would have no force or meaning.

In his *Government Inspector* Gogol said there was a single honorable character in the play—laughter. One might say similarly about *Fathers and Sons* that it contains one character who stands higher than the others and even higher than Bazarov—*life*. That life that rises above Bazarov would apparently be smaller and lower to the extent that the main hero of the novel, Bazarov, would be portrayed smaller and lower.

APOLLON GRIGOREV

[Nihilists] †

* * * Now the matter has become clear once and for all. It is not a question of Pushkin's "rattlings" or the "vulgarity" of certain of his poems (like "The Hero," for example)—it is not at all a question of the "kingdom of darkness," supposedly described only satirically by Ostrovsky,[1]—now the matter consists of matter, that is, in that:

1. *Art* is nonsense, useful only to arouse dormant human energy to something more substantial and important, and swept away as soon as any kind of positive results are attained.

2. *Nationality*—that is, certain national organisms—is also nonsense, which must disappear during the amalgamation the result of which will be a world where the moon is joined to the earth.

3. *History* (this had been said two years ago completely clearly) is nonsense, a senseless canvas of inept errors, shameful blindness and the most amusing enthusiasms.

4. *Science*—except for its exact and positive sides, expressed in the branches of mathematics and natural science—is the greatest nonsense, the ravings of fruitlessly stultifying human heads.

5. *Thought* is a completely senseless process, useless and quite conveniently replaced by the good teachings of the five—excuse me!—six clever little books.

But any person who is accustomed to the noxious process of thinking will involuntarily repeat Galileo's words "And yet it does turn!" Since even these results, that in the final analysis deny thought any meaning, are in themselves the results of thought—whatever it may be, it is thinking nevertheless and not the digestive process. ("And perhaps the digestive process too?" You will ask me again to note.)

Certain "generalizations" so reluctantly used by the adepts of our nihilism, which they flee and fear as the devil fears holy water, were nevertheless present at the conception of their theories. In order to say "I dissect frogs," or "I make soap" [as in Ustryalov's parody of *Fathers and Sons*], certain generalizations, albeit nega-

---

† From A. A. Grigorev, *Sochineniya*, edited by N. N. Strakhov, St. Petersburg, 1876, pp. 626–27. Translated by Ralph E. Matlaw. This is a section of an article, "Paradoxes of Organic Criticism," that appeared in Dostoevsky's *The Epoch* in 1864. Grigorev (1822–64) was a brilliant though eccentric critic extolling tradi-tional Russian life, and a good poet.
1. A. N. Ostrovsky (1823–86), leading Russian dramatist. His early plays, dealing with the merchant world, were "analyzed" by Dobrolyubov in a long article entitled "The Kingdom of Darkness" (1859) [*Editor*].

tive ones, are necessary—to wit, to elevate disbelief in any other knowledge than particular knowledge into a principle. These very words are insincere in Bazarov and childishly vulgar in his parody. On Bazarov's lips they simply cover a certain intellectual despair, a despair of conscience that has been scalded several times and consequently fears cold water, conscience that had been stopped short by several insubstantial systems that tried grandiosely though not completely successfully to contain all of universal life in a single principle. Such a completely comprehensible moment of consciousness, considered ideal by Bazarov and ideal by nihilism too, has a completely legitimate place in the general process of human consciousness,—and therefore though I laugh wholeheartedly at the facts, that is, at one foolish representative or another of so-called nihilism, I do not permit myself to laugh at the general stream, at the general spirit christened with that name—whether successfully or not—and am still less capable of denying the organic-historical necessity of that eructation of materialism in new forms. But that this organic-historical eructation is no more than a passing moment—no dreams about white blackamoors will dissuade me of that.

Thought, science, art, nationality, history are not at all steps in some sort of progress, a husk swept away by the human spirit as soon as it has attained some positive results, but the eternal, organic work of eternal forces inherent in him as an organism. It seems to be a very simple and clear thing, and yet that's just what one has to explain in our day, as if it were something completely new . . . and yet it would seem, it is completely simple and clear, so simple and clear that the most organic view that emerges immediately from it is nothing other than a simple, untheoretical view of life and its manifestations or expression in science, art, and the history of nations. * * *

ALEXANDER HERZEN

Bazarov Once Again†

First Letter

Instead of a letter, dear friend, I am sending you a dissertation, and an unfinished one at that. After our conversation I reread

---

† From Alexander Herzen, *Sobranie sochine-niy*, XX (Moscow, 1954–61), 335–40. Translated by Lydia Hooke. In this essay of 1868 Herzen undertook to show other forms of civic action than those the nihilists proclaimed. In particular he emphasized the "fathers' " activity in publishing, at home and abroad, and their salutary effect on social development in Russia.

Pisarev's article on Bazarov, which I had completely forgotten, and I am very glad of it; that is, not that I had forgotten it, but that I reread it.

This article confirms my own viewpoint. In its one-sidedness it is truer and more remarkable than its adversaries thought.

Whether Pisarev understood Turgenev's Bazarov correctly does not concern me. What is important is that he recognized *himself* and *others like him* in Bazarov and supplied what was lacking in the book. The less Pisarev kept to the mold in which the angry parent sought to fit the refractory son, the more freely does he project his own ideal on him.

"But why should Pisarev's ideal interest us? Pisarev is an incisive critic, he wrote much, he wrote about everything, sometimes on subjects he knew, but all this does not give his ideal the right to claim general consideration."

But the point is that this is not just his personal ideal, but the ideal that was cherished by the young generation *before* Turgenev's Bazarov and *after him* and which was embodied, not only by various characters in stories and novels, but also by real people who endeavored to base their actions and words on Bazarovism. I have heard and seen a dozen times what Pisarev is talking about; he has artlessly given away the heartfelt idea of a whole group; he has focused diffuse rays on one point and with them illuminated the original Bazarov.

Bazarov is more than an outsider to Turgenev, but to Pisarev he is more than a brother; for heuristic purposes, of course, we should choose the viewpoint which regards Bazarov as its *desideratum*.

Pisarev's adversaries were frightened by his imprudence; they repudiated Turgenev's Bazarov as a caricature and even more vehemently rejected his transfigured double; they were displeased that Pisarev had made a fool of himself, but this does not mean that he had misunderstood Bazarov.

Pisarev knows the heart of his Bazarov to the core. He even confesses for him: "Perhaps," he says, "in the depths of his soul Bazarov acknowledges much of what he repudiates aloud and perhaps it is precisely what he thus acknowledges which secretly saves him from moral degradation and moral worthlessness." We consider this immodesty, peering so deeply into the soul of another, to be very significant.

Pisarev further characterizes his hero as follows: "Bazarov is exceedingly full of self-esteem, but this self-esteem is unnoticeable [it is clear that this is not Turgenev's Bazarov] as a direct consequence of his vastness." Bazarov could be satisfied only by "a *whole eternity of constantly expanding activity and constantly in-creasing pleasures."* [1]

Bazarov, everywhere and in everything, does what he pleases or what seems to him to be advantageous or convenient. He is ruled only by his whims or his personal calculations. Neither over himself, nor outside himself, nor within himself does he recognize a moderator . . . ahead—no exalted goal; in his mind—no high design, and yet he has such great capacities. . . . If Bazarovism is a *disease*, then it is the disease of our time, and must be endured to the end no matter what palliatives and amputations are employed.

[Bazarov] looks down on people and rarely even takes the trouble to conceal *his half disdainful, half patronizing attitude* toward those who hate him and those who obey him. He loves no one. . . . he considers it completely unnecessary to lay any restraint whatsoever on himself . . .

His cynicism has two aspects, an internal and an external one, a cynicism of thought and feeling and a cynicism of manner and expression. An ironic attitude toward emotion of any sort, toward dreaminess, lyrical transports and effusions, is the essence of the internal cynicism. The rude expression of this irony, and a cause-external cynicism. . . . Bazarov is not only an empiricist, he is less and purposeless harshness in the treatment of others relates to also an uncouth rowdy . . . In the ranks of Bazarov's admirers there will undoubtedly be those who will be enraptured by his coarse manners, . . . which are, in any case, a shortcoming and not a virtue.[2]

. . . [Such people are] most often engendered by the drab conditions of a life of labor; from hard labor the hands coarsen, so do the manners and emotions; the man grows stronger and banishes youthful dreaminess, rids himself of lachrymose sensi-tivity; it is not possible to daydream at work . . . This man has become used to looking on dreams as on a whim, peculiar to idleness and aristocratic pampering; . . . moral aspirations and actions as imagined and ridiculous. . . . [He feels an] aversion to phrase making.

1. Youth likes to express itself in various ex-travagant conceits and to strike the imagination with infinitely large images. The last sentence reminds me of Karl Moor, Ferdinand, and Don Carlos [in Schiller's plays].
2. This prediction came true. This mutual in-teraction of people and books is a strange thing. A book takes its whole shape from the society that spawns it, then generalizes the material, renders it clearer and sharper, and as a con-sequence reality is transformed. The originals become caricatures of their own sharply drawn portraits and real people take on the character of their literary shadows. At the end of the last century all German men were a little like Werther, all German women like Charlotte; at the beginning of this century, the university Werthers began to turn into "robbers," Schill-er's, not real ones. Young Russians were almost all out of [Chernyshevsky's] *What's to be done?* after 1862, with the addition of a few of Ba-zarov's traits.

Then Pisarev introduces Bazarov's family tree: the Onegins and the Pechorins begat the Rudins and Bel'tovs.[3] The Rudins and Bel'tovs begat Bazarov. (Whether the Decembrists were omitted purposely or not, I do not know.)[4]

Weary, bored people are replaced by people yearning for action, life rejects them both as unfit and incomplete. "At times they will have to suffer, but they will never succeed in accomplishing deeds. Society is deaf and implacable toward them. They are not capable of accommodating themselves to its conditions, not one of them ever attained the rank of *head of a department*. Some console themselves by becoming professors and working for the future generation." There is no doubt of the negative service they perform. They increase the number of people *incapable* of practical action, consequently, this practical action itself or, more precisely, the forms which it usually takes at present, slowly but surely are lowered in the opinion of society.

It seemed (after the Crimean campaign) that Rudinism was coming to an end, that the epoch of fruitless dreaming and yearning was to be followed by an epoch of tireless and useful activity. But the mirage was dispelled. The Rudins did not become practical men, from them came a new generation, which regards its predecessors with *reproach and mockery*. 'What are you complaining about, what are you seeking, what do you ask of life? No doubt, you want happiness? That's not much, is it? Happiness must be won. If you have the power, take it. If not— *be silent*, things are bad enough without you.' A gloomy, intense energy is manifested in the younger generation's *unfriendly* attitude toward its mentors. In its concepts of good and evil this generation was like the best people of the preceding generation, their sympathies and antipathies were the same, they *desired one and the same thing*, but the people of the past *fussed and bustled about*. The people of the present do not fuss, they seek nothing, they submit to no compromises and they *place their hopes on nothing*. They are just as impotent as the Rudins, but they have acknowledged their impotence.

'I cannot act now,' thinks each of these new people, 'I will not even try, I *disdain everything around me* and I will not conceal my disdain. I shall enter the battle against evil only when I feel myself to be strong.' Since they cannot act, these people begin to think and analyze . . . superstitions and authorities are shattered and their world view becomes completely devoid of various illusory notions. They are not concerned with whether society is following them; they are full of themselves, of their

3. Leading character of Herzen's novel *Whose Fault?* [*Editor*].
4. The four characters named are the protagonists of novels by Pushkin, Lermontov, Turgenev, and Herzen. They formed a historic series of the "superfluous man" in Dobrolyubov's interpretation. The Decembrists were real, the participants in the abortive revolt of December, 1825 [*Editor*].

inner life. In a word, the Pechorins have *the will but not the knowledge*, the Rudins have *the knowledge but not the will*, the Bazarovs have *both the knowledge and the will*. Thought and deed merge in one stable whole.

Everything is here, if there are no errors, both characterization and classification—all is concise and clear, the sum is tallied, the account is rendered, and from the point of view from which the author approached the problem everything is perfectly correct.

But we do not accept this account, we protest against it from our premature and unready graves. We are not Karl V and do not wish to be buried alive.[5]

The fates of the *fathers and sons* are strange! Clearly Turgenev did not introduce Bazarov to pat him on the head; it is also clear that he had wanted to do something for the benefit of the fathers. But, juxtaposed to such pitiful and insignificant fathers as the Kirsanovs, the stern Bazarov captivated Turgenev and, instead of spanking the son, he flogged the fathers.

This is why it happened that a portion of the younger generation recognized itself in Bazarov. But we do not recognize ourselves at all in the Kirsanovs; just as we do not recognize ourselves in the Manilovs and Sobakeviches,[6] although the Manilovs and Sobakeviches existed right up to the time of our youth and exist today.

There is no lack of moral abortions living at the same time in different strata of society, and in its different tendencies; without doubt, they represent more or less general types, but they do not present the sharpest and most characteristic aspects of their generation—the aspects which most express its intensiveness. Pisarev's Bazarov, in one sense, is to some degree the extreme type of what Turgenev called the sons, while the Kirsanovs are the most insignificant and vulgar representatives of the fathers.

Turgenev was more of an artist in his novel than people think and because of this he lost his way, and, in my view, this is very fortunate—he was going into one room, stumbled into another, but into a better one.

What good would it have done to send Bazarov to London? The despicable Pisemsky did not stint on travel funds for his agitated monsters.[7] We, perhaps, would have proved to him, on the banks of the Thames, that it is possible, without attaining the rank of *head of a department*, to be of just as much use as any *head of a department*, that society is not always deaf and implacable when a protest

---

5. Charles V, Emperor of the Holy Roman Empire, abdicated in 1555 and retired to a monastery [Editor].
6. Characters in Gogol's *Dead Souls* [Editor].
7. In Pisemsky's anti-nihilist novel *The Agi-*tated Sea (1863) "nihilists" come to London to confront Russian political emigrants with their ostensible failure to do something worthwhile [Editor].

strikes the right note, that the job sometimes does get done, that the Rudins and Bel'tovs sometimes do have the will and steadfastness and that, recognizing the impossibility of the action for which they were yearning, they gave up *much*, went to a strange land and "without fussing or bustling around" started to print Russian books and disseminate Russian propaganda.

The influence of the Russian press in London from 1856 to the end of 1863—is not only a practical fact, but a historical one as well. It is impossible to erase it, it must be accepted.

In London, Bazarov would have seen that only from a distance does it seem as if we are waving our hands in the air, and that, actually, we are working with them. Perhaps he would have replaced his anger with favor and would have ceased to regard us "with reproach and mockery."

I openly admit that this throwing of stones at one's predecessors is repugnant to me. . . . I repeat what I have said before. (*My Past and Thoughts*, volume IV): "I would like to save the younger generation from historical ingratitude and even from historical errors. It is time that father Saturn refrained from making a snack of his children, but it is also time that the children stop following the example of the Kamchadals who kill their old men."

Essays in Criticism

D. S. MIRSKY

Turgénev[†]

Iván Sergéyevich Turgénev was born on October 28, 1818, in Orël. His father, a handsome but impoverished squire who had served in the cavalry, was married to an heiress older than himself. She had had a very unhappy childhood and girlhood and adored her husband, who never loved her. This combined with the control of a large fortune to make of Mme Turgénev an embittered and intolerable domestic tyrant. Though she was attached to her son, she treated him with exasperating despotism, and with her serfs and servants she was plainly cruel. It was in his mother's house that the future author of *A Sportsman's Sketches* saw serfdom in its least attractive form.

In 1833 Turgénev entered the University of Moscow, but remained there only one year, for in 1834 his mother moved to Petersburg and he went over to the other university. He studied under Púshkin's friend, Professor Pletnëv, and had occasion to meet the great poet himself. His first verses were published in Pletnëv's, formerly Púshkin's, *Sovreménnik* (1838). This connection with the "literary aristocracy" is of importance: alone of all his contemporaries, Turgénev had a living link with the age of poetry. After taking his degree he went to Berlin to complete his philosophical education at the university that had been the abode and was still the temple of Hegel—the divinity of the young generation of Russian idealists. Several of them, including Stankévich and Granóvsky, Turgénev met at Berlin, and henceforward he became the friend and ally of the Westernizers. His three years at Berlin (1838–41) imbued him with a lifelong love for Western civilization and for Germany. When in 1841 he returned to Russia he at first intended to devote himself to a university career. As this did not come off, he entered the Civil Service, but there also he remained only two years, and after 1845 abandoned all pursuits except literature. His work at first was chiefly in verse, and in the midforties he was regarded, chiefly on the strength of the narrative poem *Parásha* (1843), as one of the principal hopes of the young generation in poetry.

In 1845 Turgénev fell out with his mother, who ceased to give him money, and for the following years, till her death, he had to live the life of a literary Bohemian. The reason for Mme Turgénev's

† From D. S. Mirsky, *A History of Russian Literature from Its Beginnings to 1900*, edited by Francis J. Whitfield, New York: 1958. Pp. 193–208.

displeasure was partly that she resented her son's leaving the Civil Service and becoming a scribbler of a dangerous, revolutionary kind, but especially that she strongly disapproved of his infatuation for the famous singer Pauline García (Mme Viardot). This infatuation proved to be the love of his life. Mme Viardot tolerated it and liked Turgénev's company, and so he was able most of his life to live near her. In 1847 he went abroad, following her, and returned only in 1850, at the news of his mother's dangerous illness. On her death he found himself the possessor of a large fortune.

Meanwhile Turgénev had abandoned verse for prose. In 1847 Nekrásov's *Sovreménnik* started the publication of the short stories that were to form A *Sportsman's Sketches*. They appeared in book form in 1852, and this, together with the publication, about the same time, of other stories, gave Turgénev one of the first places, if not the first, among Russian writers. A *Sportsman's Sketches* was a great social as well as literary event. On the background of the complete silence of those years of reaction, the *Sketches*, seemingly harmless if taken one by one, produced a cumulative effect of considerable power. Their consistent presentation of the serf as a being, not only human, but superior in humanity to his masters, made the book a loud protest against the system of serfdom. It is said to have produced a strong impression on the future Emperor Alexander II and caused in him the decision to do away with the system. Meanwhile the authorities were alarmed. The censor who had passed the book was ordered to leave the service. Shortly after that an obituary notice of Gógol by Turgénev, written in what seemed to the police a too enthusiastic tone, led to his arrest and banishment to his estate, where he remained eighteen months (1852–3). When he was released he came to Petersburg already in the full glory of success. For several years he was the *de facto* head of Petersburg literature, and his judgment and decisions had the force of law.

The first years of Alexander II's reign were the summer of Turgénev's popularity. No one profited more than he from the unanimity of the progressive and reforming enthusiasm that had taken hold of Russian society. He was accepted as its spokesman. In his early sketches and stories he had denounced selfdom; in *Rúdin* (1856) he paid homage to the idealism of the elder generation while exposing its inefficiency; in A *Nest of Gentlefolk* (1859) he glorified all that was noble in the old Orthodox ideals of the old gentry; in *On the Eve* (1860) he attempted to paint the heroic figure of a young girl of the new generation. Dobrolyúbov and Chernyshévsky, the leaders of advanced opinion, chose his works for the texts of their journalistic sermons. His art answered to the demands of everyone. It was civic but not "tendentious." It painted life as it was, and chose for its subjects the most burning problems of the day. It was full of truth and, at the same time, of poetry and beauty. It satisfied Left and Right. It was the mean term, the middle style for which the forties had groped in vain. It avoided in an equal measure the pitfalls of grotesque caricature and of sentimental "philanthropy." It was perfect. Turgénev was very sensitive to his success, and particulárly sensitive to the praise of the young generation and of advanced opinion, whose spokesman he appeared, and aspired, to be.

The only thing he had been censured for (or rather, as everyone believed in the photographic veracity of Turgénev's representation of Russia, it was not he, but Russian life, that was found fault with) was that while he had given such a beautiful succession of heroines, he had failed to give a Russian hero; it was noticed that when he had wanted a man of action, he had chosen a Bulgarian (Insárov in *On the Eve*). This led the critics to surmise that he believed a Russian hero an impossibility. Now Turgénev decided to make up for this shortcoming and give a real Russian man of action—a hero of the young generation. This he did in Bazárov, the nihilist hero of *Fathers and Sons* (1862). He created him with love and admiration, but the result was unexpected. The radicals were indignant. This, they said, was a caricature and no hero. This nihilist, with his militant materialism, with his negation of all religious and aesthetic values and his faith in nothing but frogs (the dissection of frogs was the mystical rite of Darwinian naturalism and anti-spiritualism), was a caricature of the young generation drawn to please the reactionaries. The radicals raised a hue and cry against Turgénev, who was proclaimed to have "written himself out." A little later, it is true, a still younger and more extreme section of radicals, in the person of the brilliant young critic Pisarev, reversed the older radicals' verdict, accepted the name of nihilist, and recognized in Bazárov the ideal to be followed. But this belated recognition from the extreme Left did not console Turgénev for the profound wound inflicted on him by the first reception given to Bazárov. He decided to abandon Russia and Russian literature. He was abroad when *Fathers and Sons* appeared and the campaign against him began. He remained abroad in the shade of Mme Viardot, at first in Baden-Baden and after 1871 in Paris, and never returned to Russia except for short periods. His decision to abandon literature found expression in the fragment of lyrical prose *Enough*, where he gave full play to his pessimism and disillusionment. He did not, however, abandon literature, and continued writing to his death. But in by far the greater part of his later work he turned away from contemporary Russia, so distasteful and unresponsive to him, towards

242 · D. S. Mirsky

the times of his childhood, the old Russia of before the reforms. Most of his work after 1862 is either frankly memoirs, or fiction built out of the material of early experience. He was loath, however, to resign himself to the fate of a writer who had outlived his times. Twice again he attempted to tackle the problems of the day in big works of fiction. In *Smoke* (1867) he gave full vent to his bitterness against all classes of Russian society; and in *Virgin Soil* (1877) he attempted to give a picture of the revolutionary movement of the seventies. But the two novels only emphasized his growing estrangement from living Russia, the former by its impotent bitterness, the latter by its lack of information and of all sense of reality in the treatment of the powerful movement of the seventies. Gradually, however, as party feeling, at least in literature, sank, Turgénev returned into his own (the popularity of his *early* work had never diminished). The revival of "æsthetics" in the later seventies contributed to a revival of his popularity, and his last visit to Russia in 1880 was a triumphant progress.

In the meantime, especially after he settled in Paris, Turgénev became intimate with French literary circles—with Mérimée, Flaubert, and the young naturalists. His works began to be translated into French and German, and before long his fame became international. He was the first Russian author to win a European reputation. In the literary world of Paris he became an important personality. He was one of the first to discern the talent of the young Maupassant, and Henry James (who included an essay on Turgénev in a volume on *French* novelists) and other beginning writers looked up to him as to a master. When he died, Renan, with pardonable lack of information, proclaimed that it was through Turgénev that Russia, so long mute,[1] had at last become vocal. Turgénev felt much more at home among his French confreres than among his Russian equals (with most of whom, including Tolstóy, Dostoyévsky, and Nekrásov, he sooner or later quarreled), and there is a striking difference between the impressions he produced on foreigners and on Russians. Foreigners were always impressed by the grace, charm and sincerity of his manner. With Russians he was arrogant and vain, and no amount of hero-worship could make his Russian visitors blind to these disagreeable characteristics.

Soon after his last visit to Russia Turgénev fell ill. He died on August 22, 1883, in the small commune of Bougival, on the Seine below Paris.

Turgénev's first attempt at prose fiction [2] was in the wake of

---

1. One will remember the words of Carlyle on "mute Russia" written in 1840, three years after the death of Púshkin.

2. For the poetic work of Turgénev see Chapter V; for his dramatic work, Chapter VII.

Lérmontov, from whom he derived the romantic halo round his first Pechórin-like heroes (*Andréy Kólosov, The Duelist, Three Portraits*) and the method of the intensified anecdote (*The Jew*). In *A Sportsman's Sketches*, began in 1847, he was to free himself from the romantic conventions of these early stories by abandoning all narrative skeleton and limiting himself to "slices of life." But even for some time after that date he remained unable in his more distinctly narrative work to hit on what was to become his true manner. Thus, for instance, *Three Meetings* (1852) is a story of pure atmosphere woven round a very slender theme, saturated in its descriptions of moonlit nights, with an excess of romantic and "poetical" poetry. *The Diary of a Superfluous Man* (1850) is reminiscent of Gógol and of the young Dostoyévsky, developing as it does the Dostoyevskian theme of humiliated human dignity and of morbid delight in humiliation, but aspiring to a Gógol-like and very un-Turgenevian verbal intensity. (The phrase "a superfluous man" had an extraordinary fortune and is still applied by literary and social historians to the type of ineffective idealist portrayed so often by Turgénev and his contemporaries.) At last *Mumú* (1854), the well-known story of the deaf serf and his favorite dog, and of how his mistress ordered it to be destroyed, is a "philanthropic" story in the tradition of *The Greatcoat* and of *Poor Folk*, where an intense sensation of pity is arrived at by methods that strike the modern reader as illegitimate, working on the nerves rather than on the imagination.

A Sportsman's Sketches, on the other hand, written in 1847–51, belongs to the highest, most lasting, and least questionable achievement of Turgénev and of Russian realism. The book describes the casual and various meetings of the narrator during his wanderings with a gun and a dog in his native district of Bólkhov and in the surrounding country. The sketches are arranged in a random order and have no narrative skeleton, containing nothing but accounts of what the narrator saw and heard. Some of them are purely descriptive, of scenery or character; others consist of conversation, addressed to the narrator or overheard. At times there is a dramatic *motive,* but the development is only hinted at by the successive glimpses the narrator gets of his personages. This absolute matter-of-factness and studious avoidance of everything artificial and made-up were the most prominent characteristics of the book when it appeared—it was a new genre. The peasants are described from the outside, as seen (or overseen) by the narrator, not in their intimate, unoverlooked life. As I have said, they are drawn with obviously greater sympathy than the upper classes. The squires are represented as either vulgar, or cruel, or ineffective. In the peasants, Turgénev emphasized their humanity, their imaginativeness, their poetical and artistic giftedness, their sense of dignity, their intelligence. It was in this quiet and unobtrusive way that the book struck the readers with the injustice and ineptitude of serfdom. Now, when the issue of serfdom is a thing of the past, the *Sketches* seem once more as harmless and as innocent as a book can be, and it requires a certain degree of historical imagination to reconstruct the atmosphere in which they had the effect of a mild bombshell.

Judged as literature, the *Sketches* are frequently, if not always, above praise. In the representation of rural scenery and peasant character, Turgénev never surpassed such masterpieces as *The Singers* and *Bézhin Meadow*.[3] *The Singers* especially, even after *First Love* and *Fathers and Sons*, may claim to be his crowning achievement and the quintessence of all the most characteristic qualities of his art. It is the description of a singing-match at a village pub between the peasant Yáshka Túrok and a tradesman from Zhízdra. The story is representative of Turgénev's manner of painting his peasants; he does not one-sidedly idealize them; the impression produced by the match, with its revelation of the singers' high sense, of artistic values, is qualified by the drunken orgy the artists lapse into after the match is over and the publican treats Yáshka to the fruit of his victory. *The Singers* may also be taken as giving Turgénev's prose at its highest and most characteristic. It is careful and in a sense artificial, but the impression of absolute ease and simplicity is exhaled from every word and turn of phrase: It is a carefully *selected* language, rich, but curiously avoiding words and phrases, crude or journalese, that might jar on the reader. The beauty of the landscape painting is due chiefly to the choice of exact and delicately suggestive and descriptive words. There is no ornamental imagery after the manner of Gógol, no rhetorical rhythm, no splendid cadences. But the sometime poet's and poets' disciple's hand is evident in the careful, varied, and unobtrusively perfect balance of the phrases.

The first thing Turgénev wrote after the *Sketches* and *Mumú* was *The Inn*. Like *Mumú* it turns on the unjust and callous treatment of serfs by their masters, but the sentimental, "philanthropic" element is replaced for the first time in his work by the characteristic Turgenevian atmosphere of tragic necessity. *The Inn* was followed in 1853–61 by a succession of masterpieces. They were divided by the author himself into two categories: novels and *nouvelles* (in Russian, *romány* and *póvesti*). The difference between the two forms in the case of Turgénev is not so much one of size or scope as that the novels aim at social significance and

3. It is interesting to note that these pieces are precisely those Henry James singles out for particular praise.

at the statement of social problems, while the *nouvelles* are pure and simple stories of emotional incident, free from civic preoccupations. Each novel includes a narrative kernel similar in subject and bulk to that of a *nouvelle,* but it is expanded into an answer to some burning problem of the day. The novels of this period are *Rúdin* (1856), *A Nest of Gentlefolk* (1859), *On the Eve* (1860), and *Fathers and Sons* (1862); the *nouvelles, Two Friends* (1854), *A Quiet Spot* (1854), *Yákov Pásynkov* (1855), *A Correspondence* (1856), *Faust* (1856), *Ásya* (1858), and *First Love* (1860). It will be noticed that the civic novels belong chiefly to the age of reform (1856–61), while the purely private *nouvelles* predominate in the reactionary years that precede it. But even "on the eve" of the Emancipation, Turgénev could be sufficiently detached from civic issues to write the perfectly uncivic *First Love.*

The novels of Turgénev are, thus, those of his stories in which he, voluntarily, submitted to the obligation of writing works of social significance. This significance is arrived at in the first place by the nature of the characters, who are made to be representative of phases successively traversed by the Russian intellectual. Rúdin is the progressive idealist of the forties; Lavrétsky, the more Slavophil idealist of the same generation; Eléna, in *On the Eve,* personifies the vaguely generous and active fermentation of the generation immediately preceding the reforms; Bazárov, the militant materialism of the generation of 1860. Secondly, the social significance is served by the insertion of numerous *conversations* between the characters on topics of current interest (Slavophilism and Westernism, the ability of educated Russian to act, the place in life of art and science, and so on). These conversations are what especially distinguished Turgénev's novels from his *nouvelles.* They have little relation to the action, and not always much more to the character of the representative hero. They were what the civic critics seized upon for comment, but they are certainly the least permanent and most dating part of the novels. There frequently occur characters who are introduced with no other motive but to do the talking, and whom one would have rather wished away. But the central, representative characters—the heroes—are in most cases not only representative, but alive. Rúdin, the first in date, is one of the masterpieces of nineteenth-century character drawing. An eminent French novelist (who is old-fashioned enough still to prefer Turgénev to Tolstóy, Dostoyévsky, and Chékhov) has pointed out to me the wonderfully delicate mastery with which the impression produced by Rúdin on the other characters and on the reader is made gradually to change from the first appearance in the glamour of superiority to the bankruptcy of his pusillanimous breach with Natália, then to the gloomy glimpse of the undone and degenerate man, and to the redeeming flash of his heroic and ineffective death on the barricades of the faubourg St. Antoine. The French writer thought this delicate change of attitude unique in fiction. Had he known more Russian, he would have realized that Turgénev had merely been a highly intelligent and creative pupil of Pushkin's. Like Pushkin in *Evgeny Onegin*, Turgénev does not analyze and dissect his heroes, as Tolstóy and Dostoyévsky would have done; he does not uncover their souls; he only conveys their atmosphere, partly by showing how they are reflected in others, partly by an exceedingly delicate and thinly woven aura of suggestive accompaniment—a method that at once betrays its origin in a *poetic* novel. Where Turgénev attempts to show us the *inner* life of his heroes by other methods, he always fails—the description of Eléna's feelings for Insárov in *On the Eve* is distinctly painful reading. Turgénev had to use all the power of selfcriticism and self-restraint to avoid the pitfall of false poetry and false beauty.

Still, the characters, constructed though they are by means of suggestion, not dissection, are the vivifying principle of Turgénev's stories. Like most Russian novelists he makes character predominate over plot (and it is the characters that we remember. The population of Turgénev's novels (apart from the peasant stories) may be classified under several heads. First comes the division into the Philistines and the elect. The Philistines are the direct descendants of Gógol's characters—heroes of *póshlost*, self-satisfied inferiority. Of course there is not a trace in them of Gógol's exuberant and grotesque caricature; the irony of Turgénev is fine, delicate, unobtrusive, hardly at all aided by any obvious comical devices. On the other side are the elect, the men and women with a sense of values, superior to those of vegetable enjoyment and social position. The men, again, are very different from the women. The fair sex comes out distinctly more advantageously from the hands of Turgénev. The strong, pure, passionate, and virtuous woman, opposed to the weak, potentially generous, but ineffective and ultimately shallow man, was introduced into literature by Púshkin, and recurs again and again in the work of the realists, but nowhere more insistently than in Turgénev's. His heroines are famous all the world over and have done much to spread a high reputation of Russian womanhood. Moral force and courage are the keynote to Turgénev's heroine—the power to sacrifice all worldly considerations to passion (Natália in *Rúdin*), or all happiness to duty (Líza in *A Nest of Gentlefolk*). But what goes home to the general reader in these women is not so much the height of their moral beauty as the extraordinary *poetical* beauty woven round them by the delicate and perfect art of their begetter.

Turgénev reaches his highest perfection in this, his own and unique art, in two of the shorter stories, A *Quiet Spot* and *First Love*. In the first, the purely Turgenevian, tragic, poetic, and rural atmosphere reaches its maximum of concentration, and the richness of suggestion that conditions the characters surpasses all he ever wrote. It transcends mere fiction and rises into poetry, not by the beauty of the single words and parts, but by sheer force of suggestion and saturated significance. *First Love* stands somewhat apart from the rest of Turgénev's work. Its atmosphere is cooler and clearer, more reminiscent of the rarefied air of Lérmontov. The heroes—Zinaída and the narrator's father (who is traditionally supposed to portray the author's own father)—are more *animal* and vital than Turgénev usually allows his heroes to be. Their passions are tense and clear-cut, free from vagueness and idealistic haze, selfish, but with a selfishness that is redeemed by self-justifying vitality. Unique in the whole of his work, *First Love* is the least relaxing of Turgénev's stories. But, characteristically, the story is told from the point of view of the boy admirer of Zinaída and of his pangs of adolescent jealousy for his rival and father.

At the height of his popularity, in 1860, Turgénev wrote a famous essay on *Hamlet and Don Quixote*. He considered these characters as the two prototypes of the elect intellectual portion of mankind, which was divided into self-conscious, introspective, and consequently ineffective, Hamlets, and enthusiastic, single-minded, courageous at the risk of seeming ridiculous, Quixotes. He himself and the great majority of his heroes were Hamlets. But he had always wanted to create Quixotes, whose freedom from reflection and questioning would make them efficient, while their possession of higher values would raise them above the Philistines. In the later forties the critics, who had taken note of the consistent inefficiency of Turgénev's heroes, clamored for him to produce a more active and effective hero. This he attempted in *On the Eve*. But the attempt was a failure. He made his hero a Bulgarian patriot, Insárov. But he failed to breathe into him the spirit of life. Insárov is merely a strong, silent puppet, at times almost ludicrous. In conjunction with the stilted and vapid Eléna, Insárov makes *On the Eve* distinctly the worst of all Turgénev's mature work.

The best of the novels and ultimately the most important of Turgénev's works is *Fathers and Sons*, one of the greatest novels of the nineteenth century. Here Turgénev triumphantly solved two tasks that he had been attempting to solve: to create a living masculine character not based on introspection, and to overcome the contradiction between the imaginative and the social theme. *Fathers and Sons* is Turgénev's only novel where the social problem is distilled without residue into art, and leaves no bits of undigested journalism sticking out. Here the delicate and poetic narrative art of Turgénev reaches its perfection, and Bazárov is the only one of Turgénev's men who is worthy to stand by the side of his women. But nowhere perhaps does the essential debility and feminineness of his genius come out more clearly than in this, the best of his novels. Bazárov is a strong man, but he is painted with admiration and wonder by one to whom a strong man is something abnormal. Turgénev is incapable of making his hero triumph, and to spare him the inadequate treatment that would have been his lot in the case of success, he lets him die, not from any natural development of the nature of the subject, but by the blind decree of fate. For fate, blind chance, crass casualty, presides over Turgénev's universe as it does over Hardy's, but Turgénev's people submit to it with passive resignation. Even the heroic Bazárov dies as resigned as a flower in the field, with silent courage but without protest.

It would be wrong to affirm that after *Fathers and Sons* Turgénev's genius began to decline, but at any rate it ceased to grow. What was more important for his contemporaries, he lost touch with Russian life and thus ceased to count as a *contemporary* writer, though he remained a permanent classic. His attempts again to tackle the problems of the day in *Smoke* (1867) and in *Virgin Soil* (1877) only emphasized his loss of touch with the new age. *Smoke* is the worst-constructed of his novels: it contains a beautiful love story, which is interrupted and interlarded with conversations that have no relation to its characters and are just dialogued journalism on the thesis that all intellectual and educated Russia was nothing but smoke. *Virgin Soil* is a complete failure, and was immediately recognized as such. Though it contains much that is in the best manner of Turgénev (the characters of the bureaucratic-aristocratic Sipyágin family are among his best satirical drawings), the whole novel is disqualified by an entirely uninformed and necessarily false conception of what he was writing about. His presentation of the revolutionaries of the seventies is like an account of a foreign country by one who had never seen it.

But while Turgénev had lost the power of writing for the times, he had not lost the genius of creating those wonderful love stories which are his most personal contribution to the world's literature. Pruned of its conversations, *Smoke* is a beautiful *nouvelle*, comparable to the best he wrote in the fifties, and so is *The Torrents of Spring* (1872). Both are on the same subject: a young man loves a pure and sweet young girl but forsakes her for a mature and lascivious woman of thirty, who is loved by many and for whom he is the plaything of a fleeting passion. The characters of Irína, the older woman in *Smoke*, and of Gemma, the Italian girl in *The Torrents of Spring*, are among the most beautiful in the whole of his gallery. *The Torrents of Spring* is given a retrospective setting, and in most of the other stories of this last period the scene is set in the old times of pre-Reform Russia. Some of these stories are purely objective little tragedies (one of the best is *A Lear of the Steppes*, 1870); others are non-narrative fragments from reminiscences, partly continuing the manner and theme of *A Sportsman's Sketches*. There are also the purely biographical reminiscences, including interesting accounts of the author's acquaintance with Púshkin and Belínsky and the remarkable account of *The Execution of Troppmann* (1870), which in its fascinated objectivity is one of the most terrible descriptions ever made of an execution.

There had always been in Turgénev a poetic or romantic vein, as opposed to the prevailing realistic atmosphere of his principal work. His attitude to nature had always been lyrical, and he had always had a lurking desire to transcend the limits imposed on the Russian novelist by the dogma of realism. Not only did he begin his career as a lyrical poet and end it with his *Poems in Prose*, but even in his most realistic and civic novels the construction and atmosphere are mainly lyrical. *A Sportsman's Sketches* includes many purely lyrical pages of natural description, and to the period of his highest maturity belongs that remarkable piece *A Tour in the Forest* (1857), where for the first time Turgénev's conception of indifferent and eternal nature opposed to transient man found expression in a sober and simple prose that attains poetry by the simplest means of unaided suggestion. His last period begins with the purely lyrical prose poem *Enough* and culminates in the *Poems in Prose*. At the same time the fantastic element asserts itself. In some stories (*The Dog, Knock! Knock! Knock!* and *The Story of Father Alexis*) it appears only in the form of a suggestion of mysterious presences in an ordinary realistic setting. The most important of these stories is his last, *Clara Mílich* (1883), written under the influence of spiritualistic readings and musings. It is as good as most of his stories of purely human love, but the mysterious element is somewhat difficult to appreciate quite whole-heartedly today. It has all the inevitable flatness of Victorian spiritualism. In a few stories Turgénev freed himself from the conventions of realistic form and wrote such things as the purely visionary *Phantoms* (1864) and *The Song of Triumphant Love* (1881), written in the style of an Italian *novella* of the sixteenth century. There can be no greater contrast than between these and such stories of Dostoyévsky as *The Double* or *Mr. Prokhárchin*. Dostoyévsky, with the material of sordid reality, succeeds in building fabrics of weird fantasy. Turgénev, in spite of all the paraphernalia introduced, never succeeded in freeing himself from the second-rate atmosphere of the medium's consulting room. *The Song of Triumphant Love* shows up his limitation of another kind—the inadequacy of his language for treating subjects of insufficient reality. This limitation Turgénev shared with all his contemporaries (except Tolstóy and Leskóv). They did not have a sufficient feeling of words, of language as language (as Púshkin and Gógol had had), to make it serve them in unfamiliar fields. Words for them were only signs of familiar things and familiar feelings. Language had entered with them on a strictly limited engagement—it would serve only in so far as it had not to leave the everyday realities of the nineteenth century.

The same stylistic limitation is apparent in Turgénev's last and most purely lyrical work, *Poems in Prose* (1879–83). (Turgénev originally entitled them *Senilia*; the present title was given them with the author's silent approval by the editor of the *Messenger of Europe*, where they first appeared.) They are a series of short prose fragments, most of them gathered round some more or less narrative kernel. They are comparable in construction to the objectivated lyrics of the French Parnassians, who used visual symbols to express their subjective experience. Sometimes they verge on the fable and the apologue. In these "poems" is to be found the final and most hopeless expression of Turgénev's agnostic pessimism, of his awe of unresponsive nature and necessity, and of his pitying contempt for human futility. The best of the "poems" are those where these feelings are given an ironic garb. The more purely poetical ones have suffered from time, and date too distinctly from about 1880—a date that can hardly add beauty to anything connected with it. The one that closes the series, *The Russian Language*, has suffered particularly—not from time only, but from excessive handling. It displays in a condensed form all the weakness and ineffectiveness of Turgénev's style when it was divorced from concrete and familiar *things*. The art of eloquence had been lost.

Turgénev was the first Russian writer to charm the Western reader. There are still retarded Victorians who consider him the only Russian writer who is not disgusting. But for most lovers of Russian he has been replaced by spicier food. Turgénev was very nineteenth century, perhaps the most representative man of its latter part, whether in Russia or west of it. He was a Victorian, a man of compromise, more Victorian than any one of his Russian contemporaries. This made him so acceptable to Europe, and this has now made him lose so much of his reputation there. Turgénev struck the West at first as something new, something typically Russian. But it is hardly necessary to insist today on the fact that he is not in any sense representative of Russia as a whole. He was representative only of his class—the idealistically educated middle gentry, tending already to become a non-class intelligentsia—and of his generation, which failed to gain real touch with Russian realities,[4] which failed to find itself a place in life and which, ineffective in the sphere of action, produced one of the most beautiful literary growths of the nineteenth century. In his day Turgénev was regarded as a leader of opinion on social problems; now this seems strange and unintelligible. Long since, the issues that he fought out have ceased to be of any actual interest. Unlike Tolstóy or Dostoyévsky, unlike Griboyédov, Púshkin, Lérmontov, and Gógol, unlike Chaadáyev, Grigóriev, and Herzen—Turgénev is no longer a teacher or even a ferment. His work has become pure art—and perhaps it has won more from this transformation than it has lost. It has taken a permanent place in the Russian tradition, a place that stands above the changes of taste or the revolutions of time. We do not seek for wisdom or guidance in it, but it is impossible to imagine a time when *The Singers, A Quiet Spot, First Love,* or *Fathers and Sons* will cease to be among the most cherished of joys to Russian readers.

AVRAHM YARMOLINSKY
Fathers and Children†

Always ill at ease when it came to traffic with abstract ideas, principles, opinions, Turgenev felt sure of himself only when he was dealing with what is visible, audible, tangible. "When I don't have to do with concrete figures," he wrote, "I am entirely lost and I don't know where to turn. It always seems to me that exactly the opposite of what I say could be asserted with equal justice. But if I am speaking of a red nose and blonde hair, then the hair is blonde and the nose red; no amount of reflection will change that."

Belinsky had said at the outset of Turgenev's career that while he was extremely observant, he had no imagination. The young author had agreed with this judgment wholeheartedly. To the end he was possessed by a self-distrust which led him to lean heavily upon what the world offered to his observation. George Moore went to the root of the matter when he said that Turgenev had the illuminative rather than the creative imagination and that

---

4. What Turgénev was in touch with were not the raw realities of Russian life, but only their reflection in the minds of his generation of intellectuals.

† From Avrahm Yamolinsky, *Turgenev, The*

Man, His Art and His Age, New York, 1959. Copyright 1959 by Avrahm Yarmolinsky. Published by The Orion Press. Reprinted by permission of Adam Yarmolinsky.

he "borrowed" his stories, leaving them, as far as structure went, much as he found them.

Turgenev confessed that he envied the English their secret of making a successful plot, an ability which he found lacking in himself as in so many Russian writers. He had a prodigious memory, which served him well. He liked to insist that his characters were not invented, but discovered. He stalked them with the patience, the eagerness, and the skill with which he pursued his woodcock and his partridge. Indeed, it appears that he almost invariably drew from living models and that his fictions were fathered by experience rather than by fancy. He told a friend that it was his custom, after meeting a stranger, to set down in his notebook any peculiarities he had observed. He studied Lavater's [1] work on physiognomy from cover to cover. Drawing rooms, railway carriages, reading rooms were his favorite observatories. He did not hesitate to incorporate verbatim in his story, "The Brigadier," a private letter which he found among his mother's papers. If he had had his choice, he once remarked, he would have been a writer like Gibbon. The novelist had the historian's need for documentation.

A writer of fiction, he held, dare not be a dilettante. He must maintain close contact with life. To represent it truthfully and fairly, without philosophizing about it or trying to improve it—that was the greatest happiness for the artist. But since reality "teemed" with adventitious matter, the novelist's gift, he insisted, lay in the ability to eliminate all superfluities, so as to render only that which, in the light of his knowledge and understanding, appeared significant, characteristic, what Turgenev liked to call *typical*. He believed that the writer, while aiming at the universal, must deal with the particular, and he quoted Johann Merck enthusiastically: "With the ancients everything was local, of the moment, and thus it became eternal." Annenkov said that he represented "the personified flair of contemporaneity" in Russian literature. Looking back at his novels toward the close of his life, Turgenev wrote: "I strove, within the limits of my power and ability, conscientiously and impartially to represent and incarnate in appropriate types both what Shakespeare called 'the body and pressure of the time' and the rapidly changing countenance of the educated Russians, who have been the predominant object of my observations."

In the case of *Fathers and Children*, as in most of his writings, the germ came to Turgenev not in the form of a situation or an idea, but in that of a person. Chancing to meet in a railway train a provincial doctor who, talking shop, had

---

1. J. K. Lavater (1741–1801), philosopher and writer on physiognomy [*Editor*].

something to say on the subject of anthrax, the novelist was struck by the man's rough, matter-of-fact, candid manner. (He was to end his days in Siberia.) It flashed upon the novelist that here was a representative of a type, one which was to become known as the Nihilist. An individual of a similar cast, also a physician, was among the Russians he encountered on the Isle of Wight. As he looked about him, he seemed to see everywhere signs pointing to the emergence of that type. But finding no trace of it in the fiction of the day, he wondered if he were not chasing a ghost.

The notion of building a novel around this figure occurred to him during his stay at Ventnor in August, 1860. In the fall, when he was back in Paris, the idea returned with renewed force, and he found himself increasingly absorbed in it. By October the stuff for his new novel was all in his head, but, he wrote, "the spark which must kindle everything has not yet blazed up."

It was presumably about this time that he began to get up for his characters the "dossiers" without which he could not begin work on a novel. He was in the habit, as he told Henry James among others, of setting down "a sort of biography of each of his characters, and everything that they had done and that had happened to them up to the opening of the story." As in the case of *On the Eve*, he kept a diary for one of the characters, but this time it was not the journal of a minor figure, but of the protagonist, Bazarov.

When that delightful period was over during which the figures for his novel floated like nebulæ through his mind, and once he had a good grasp of his characters, Turgenev's final move, according to James, was the arduous business of devising the action which would lead them to reveal their inner natures. In *Fathers and Children* the novelist put Bazarov through his paces by taking this brusque commoner on a visit to a house of gentlefolk; by leading him into arguments with his two middle-aged, cultivated hosts; by making him fall hopelessly in love with a beautiful lady, indolent and undersexed; by involving him in a stupid, almost comical duel with one of his hosts; by engaging him in talk with his earnest, apish, pliant disciple; by sending him home to see his pathetic old parents; by bringing upon him an untimely death, the result of an infection contracted at a rural post-mortem.

The method he followed here is his habitual one—realization of the characters not by analysis of their consciousness, but by exhibition of their behavior. Like so many of his fellow craftsmen, he exalted into a dogma his way of working. When he was brooding over the plan for *Fathers and Children* he set down for a literary protégé this precept: "The writer must be a psychologist, but a secret one: he must sense and know the roots of phenomena, but offer only the phenomena themselves,—as they blossom or wither." Ten years earlier he had said, in the course of a critique, much the same thing in other words: "The psychologist must disappear in the artist, as the skeleton is concealed within the warm and living body, for which it serves as a firm but invisible support."

From the moment when we first see Bazarov taking his time about offering his bare red hand to his host, and turning down the collar of his nondescript coat to show his long, thin face, with its sandy side-whiskers and cool green eyes, to the moment, a few months later, when the dying atheist raises one eyelid in horror as the priest administers the last sacrament, we are in the presence of a figure that dwarfs all around him and carries the whole weight of the story. It is also a figure that shows the fullest measure of Turgenev's powers of characterization. He believed that a novelist must be "objective," concerned to represent the world about him rather than his response to it, that his art required an interest in and a cumulative knowledge of other people's lives, as well as an understanding of the forces that shaped them. Bazarov, the tough-minded, hard-fisted medic, with his brutal honesty, his faith in a crudely empirical science that he uses as a cudgel wherewith to hit out at the genteel culture he abominates, this professed "Nihilist," is an example of what the objective method can achieve. In some respects, he is perhaps fashioned after an image at the back of Turgenev's mind, the image of the man he admired and could not be.

During the winter he was at work on the first chapters, and on July 19, 1861, he was writing to Countess Lambert from Spasskoye that in about two weeks he expected to taste "the only joy in a writer's life," to wit, "penning the last line." He finished the novel on July 30. In later years he asserted that he had written it seemingly without volition, almost surprised at what came from his pen.

The agony of revision followed, the most troublesome he had known, or so he claimed. At first buoyed up with confidence in his tale, he became more and more doubtful of it as he received his friends' comments. Countess Lambert had nothing good to say for it. "People in whom I have great faith," he wrote, "advised me to throw my work into the fire." As with *On the Eve*, he had the impulse, which he did not obey, to take this advice. Katkov, the editor of *The Russian Herald*, in which *Fathers and Children* was to appear, was displeased to see that the author adulated "the younger generation" (a euphemism for the radicals) and placed Bazarov on a pedestal. Turgenev wrote back to say that it was not his intention to present an apotheosis of his protagonist and that he would try to remove that impression. He added that in his opinion Bazarov, though "empty and sterile," was nevertheless "the hero of our time." He went over and over the text, cutting, adding, altering.

What increased his uncertainty was the news of student riots in Petersburg and Moscow. Under these circumstances was it proper, he wondered, to bring out a novel that had a bearing, however remote, on the political situation? He pleaded with Katkov for a postponement of publication until spring, arguing that he found it necessary to revise the work thoroughly and unhurriedly—"to replow it," as he phrased it. The author's hemmings and hawings went on until the exasperated Annenkov, who had undertaken to see the manuscript through the press, was ready to wash his hands of it. Turgenev declared that the novel was published only because "the merchant demanded delivery of the goods he had bought" and because he himself needed money.

Fathers and Children made its appearance in the issue of *The Russian Herald* for February, 1862, and shortly afterward was published separately with a dedication to the memory of Belinsky. When in the spring of the year Turgenev returned to Petersburg from Paris, he found the capital excited by a number of conflagrations which razed a section of the city and which rumor put at the door of revolutionary incendiaries. An acquaintance, meeting him on the Nevsky, exclaimed: "See what *your* Nihilists are doing! They're setting Petersburg on fire!" Turgenev had not invented the term—it was first used by St. Augustine to denote unbelievers—any more than he had invented the type, but his employment of the word and his projection of the character made for the vogue of both. Eventually he came to regret having provided what he called "our reactionary rabble" with a convenient term for their *bête noire*. The word was also used loosely by the general public. A girl wanting a new frock was likely to face her parents with the threat of turning Nihilist if they didn't come round. Where, as in Russia, literature has great prestige, the novelist is peculiarly able to become the arbiter of fashion in personality. The novel was read by everyone, from the Empress down to people who had not opened a book since their school days, and before long one discovered at least a dash of Bazarov in every young man of independent spirit.

Turgenev's conscious attitude toward his protagonist was ambiguous. He noted in his diary an hour and a half after finishing the novel that while writing it he had felt "an involuntary attraction" toward his hero. He said the same thing in a letter to Herzen a few weeks after publication. "If the reader doesn't love Bazarov, with all his coarseness, heartlessness, pitiless dryness and brusqueness," he had written a fortnight earlier to the young versifier, Sluchevsky, "it's my fault—I haven't achieved my purpose." About the same time, however, he wrote to Fet that he did not know if he loved or hated Bazarov, and defending himself against the accusation of having produced a tendentious work, he claimed that he had drawn his character as he might have sketched "mushrooms, leaves, trees," things he had seen until, in the Russian phrase, they had "calloused his eyes." In 1869 he asserted publicly that he shared Bazarov's convictions, except for his view of the arts. Privately he admitted that in saying this he had gone too far. Unquestionably the admiration the author felt for his hero went hand in hand with a desire to preserve the values that this iconoclast rejected. We have Turgenev's word for it that Nikolay Kirsanov, one of the two landed proprietors who represent the older generation, is a self-portrait.

One of Bazarov's sentiments was undoubtedly shared by his creator—dislike of the nobility. Turgenev's treatment of it in this novel afforded him the satisfaction of the flagellant. "My entire tale," reads the letter to Sluchevsky quoted above, "is directed against the gentry as a leading class." Look at these Kirsanovs, both young and old, and what do you find? "Weakness, flabbiness, inadequacy." And these are gentlefolk of the better sort. "If the cream is bad, what can the milk be like?" How well he knew these people—their good intentions, their feeble achievements, their tender sensibilities, so readily touched by a line of verse, a point of honor, enchanted memories of a dead love, the glow of a setting sun which makes the aspens look like pines! But the knowledge that made for contempt fed his sympathy, too, and Nikolay Kirsanov, at least, is a lovable fellow.

Throughout, his craftsmanship is at its best. Even the minor characters are deftly sketched in. The description of Bazarov's illness gave Chekhov, himself a physician, the sensation of having "caught the infection from him." Bathed in an atmosphere of tenderness and pathos, the passages about Bazarov's parents are among the most moving in literature. As he wrote the last lines, in which the old couple are shown visiting the grave of their only son, Turgenev had to turn away his head, so that his tears would not blot the manuscript, and even in such a dry-eyed age as ours, there must be readers who do not finish the paragraph without blinking.

True, the comings and goings crowded into the few weeks during which the action unfolds seem somewhat contrived. The structure of the novel lacks the formal beauty of *A Nest of Gentlefolk* and *On the Eve*. The touching passage at the close is flawed by the last few lines, with their suggestion of a half-hearted piety. These blemishes are negligible, however, in a work of such wide validity. *Fathers and Children* is a novel to which Turgenev gave his full powers: his intuitions, his insights, the fruit of his contacts with a variety of men and women, his reflections on experience, his sense of the pathos of the human condition. Rudin and Lavretzky can each be fully understood only in the context of his age and his country. Bazarov, while unmistakably Russian, is a universal and a profoundly attractive figure. * * *

SIR ISAIAH BERLIN

Fathers and Children: Turgenev and the Liberal Predicament†

* * *

Young Man to Middle-Aged Man: 'You had content but no force.'
Middle-Aged Man to Young Man: 'And you have force but no content.'
From a contemporary conversation[1]

This is the topic of Turgenev's most famous, and politically most interesting, novel *Fathers and Children*. It was an attempt to give flesh and substance to his image of the new men, whose mysterious, implacable presence, he declared, he felt about him everywhere, and who inspired in him feelings that he found difficult to analyse. 'There was', he wrote many years later to a friend, '—please don't laugh—some sort of *fatum*, something stronger than the author himself, something independent of him. I know one thing: I started with no preconceived idea, no "tendency"; I wrote naïvely, as if myself astonished at what was emerging.'[2] He said that the central figure of the novel, Bazarov, was mainly modelled on a Russian doctor whom he met in a train in Russia. But Bazarov has some of the characteristics of Belinsky too. Like him, he is the son of a poor army doctor, and he possesses some of Belinsky's brusqueness, his directness, his intolerance, his liability to explode at any sign of hypocrisy, of solemnity, of pompous conservative, or evasive liberal, cant. And there is, despite Turgenev's denials, something of the ferocious, militant, anti-aestheticism of Dobrolyubov too. The central topic of the novel is the confrontation of the old and the young, of

† © Oxford University Press 1972. Reprinted from *Fathers and Children*: The 1970 Romanes Lecture by Isaiah Berlin (1972) by permission of Oxford University Press. Footnotes curtailed.

1. The original epigraph to *Fathers and Chil-dren* which Turgenev later discarded. See A. Mazon, *Manuscrits parisiens d'Ivan Tourgué-nev*, Paris, 1930, pp. 64–5.
2. From a letter to Saltykov-Shchedrin, 15 January 1876.

liberals and radicals, traditional civilization and the new, harsh positivism which has no use for anything except what is needed by a rational man. Bazarov, a young medical researcher, is invited by his fellow student and disciple, Arkady Kirsanov, to stay at his father's house in the country. Nicolai Kirsanov, the father, is a gentle, kindly, modest country gentleman, who adores poetry and nature, and greets his son's brilliant friend with touching courtesy. Also in the house is Nicolai Kirsanov's brother, Paul, a retired army officer, a carefully dressed, vain, pompous, old-fashioned dandy, who had once been a minor lion in the *salons* of the capital, and is now living out his life in elegant and irritated boredom. Bazarov scents an enemy, and takes deliberate pleasure in describing himself and his allies as 'nihilists', by which he means no more than that he, and those who think like him, reject everything that cannot be established by the rational methods of natural science. Truth alone matters: what cannot be established by observation and experiment is useless or harmful ballast—'romantic rubbish'—which an intelligent man will ruthlessly eliminate. In this heap of irrational nonsense Bazarov includes all that is impalpable, that cannot be reduced to quantitative measurement—literature and philosophy, the beauty of art and the beauty of nature, tradition and authority, religion and intuition, the uncriticized assumptions of conservatives and liberals, of populists and socialists, of landowners and serfs. He believes in strength, will-power, energy, utility, work, in ruthless criticism of all that exists. He wishes to tear off masks, blow up all revered principles and norms. Only irrefutable facts, only useful knowledge, matter. He clashes almost immediately with the touchy, conventional Paul Kirsanov: 'At present', he tells him, 'the most useful thing is to deny. So we deny.' 'Everything?' asks Paul Kirsanov. 'Everything.' 'What? Not only art, poetry . . . but even . . . too horrible to utter . . .' 'Everything.' 'So you destroy everything . . . but surely one must build, too?' 'That's not our business . . . First one must clear the ground.' The fiery revolutionary agitator Bakunin, who had just then escaped from Siberia to London, was saying something of this kind: the entire rotten structure, the corrupt old world, must be razed to the ground, before something new can be built upon it; what this is to be is not for us to say; we are revolutionaries, our business is to demolish. The new men, purified from the infection of the world of idlers and exploiters and its bogus values—these men will know what to do. The French anarchist Georges Sorel once quoted Marx as saying 'Anyone who makes plans for after the revolution is a reactionary.'[3] This went beyond the position of Turgenev's radical critics of the *Contemporary Review*; they did have a programme of sorts: they

---

3. Sorel declares that this passage occurs in a letter which, according to the economist Lujo Brentano, Marx wrote to one of his English friends, Professor Beesly (*Réfléxions sur la vi-* *olence*, 7th edn, Paris, 1930, p. 199, n. 2). I have not found it in any published collection of Marx's letters.

were democratic populists. But faith in the people seems just as irrational to Bazarov as the rest of the 'romantic rubbish'. 'Peasants?' he says, 'They are prepared to rob themselves in order to drink themselves blind at the inn.' A man's first duty is to develop his own powers, to be strong and rational, to create a society in which other rational men can breathe and live and learn. His mild disciple Arkady suggests to him that it would be ideal if all peasants lived in a pleasant, whitewashed hut, like the head man of their village. 'I have conceived a loathing for this . . . peasant,' Bazarov says, 'I have to work the skin off my hands for him, and he won't so much as thank me for it; anyway, what do I need his thanks for? He'll go on living in his whitewashed hut, while weeds grow out of me.' Arkady is shocked by such talk; but it is the voice of the new, hard-boiled, unashamed materialism. Nevertheless Bazarov is at his ease with peasants, they are not self-conscious with him even if they think him an odd sort of member of the gentry. Bazarov spends his afternoon in dissecting frogs. 'A decent chemist', he tells his shaken host, 'is twenty times more use than any poet.' Arkady, after consulting Bazarov, gently draws a volume of Pushkin out of his father's hands, and slips into them Büchner's *Kraft und Stoff*,[4] the latest popular exposition of materialism. Turgenev describes the older Kirsanov walking in his garden: 'Nikolai Petrovich dropped his head, and passed his hand over his face. "But to reject poetry," he thought again, "not to have a feeling for art, for nature . . ." and he cast about him, as if trying to understand how it was possible not to have a feeling for nature.' All principles, Bazarov declares, are reducible to mere sensations. Arkady asks whether, in that case, honesty is only a sensation. 'You find this hard to swallow?' says Bazarov. 'No, friend, if you have decided to knock everything down, you must knock yourself down, too! . . .' This is the voice of Bakunin and Dobrolyubov: 'one must clear the ground.' The new culture must be founded on real, that is materialist, scientific values: socialism is just as unreal and abstract as any other of the 'isms' imported from abroad. As for the old aesthetic, literary culture, it will crumble before the realists, the new, tough-minded men who can look the brutal truth in the face. 'Aristocracy, liberalism, progress, principles . . . what a lot of foreign . . . and useless words. A Russian would not want them as a gift.' Paul Kirsanov rejects this contemptuously; but his nephew Arkady cannot, in the end, accept it either. 'You aren't made for our harsh, bitter, solitary kind of life,' Bazarov tells him, 'you aren't insolent, you aren't nasty, all you have is the audacity, the impulsiveness of youth, and that is of no use in our business. Your type, the gentry, cannot get beyond noble humility, noble indignation, and that is nonsense. You won't, for instance, fight, and yet you think yourselves terrific. We want

4. Turgenev calls it *Stoff und Kraft*.

to fight . . . Our dust will eat out your eyes, our dirt will spoil your clothes, you haven't risen to our level yet, you still can't help admiring yourselves, you like castigating yourselves, and that bores us. Hand us others—it is them we want to break. You are a good fellow, but, all the same, you are nothing but a soft, beautifully bred, liberal boy . . .'

Bazarov, someone once said, is the first Bolshevik; even though he is not a socialist, there is some truth in this. He wants a radical change and does not shrink from brute force. The old dandy, Paul Kirsanov, protests against this: 'Force? There is force in savage Kalmucks and Mongols, too . . . What do we want it for? . . . Civilization, its fruits, are dear to us. And don't tell me they are worthless. The most miserable dauber . . . the pianist who taps on the keys in a restaurant . . . they are more useful than you are, because they represent civilization and not brute Mongol force. You imagine that you are progressive; you should be sitting in a Kalmuck wagon!' In the end, Bazarov, against all his principles, falls in love with a cold, clever, well-born society beauty, is rejected by her, suffers deeply, and not long after dies as a result of an infection caught while disserting a corpse in a village autopsy. He dies stoically, wondering whether his country had any real need of him and men like him; and his death is bitterly lamented by his old, humble, loving parents. Bazarov falls because he is broken by fate, not through failure of will or intellect. 'I conceived him', Turgenev later wrote to a young student, 'as a sombre figure, wild, huge, half-grown out of the soil, powerful, nasty, honest, but doomed to destruction because he still stands only in the gateway to the future . . .'[5] This brutal, fanatical, dedicated figure, with his unused powers, is represented as an avenger for insulted human reason; yet, in the end, he is crushed by heartless nature, by what the author calls the cold-eyed goddess Isis who does not care for good or evil, or art or beauty, still less for man, the creature of an hour; he struggles to assert himself; but she is indifferent; she obeys her own inexorable laws.

Fathers and Children was published in the spring of 1862 and caused the greatest storm among its Russian readers of any novel before or, indeed, since. What was Bazarov? How was he to be taken? Was he a positive or a negative figure? A hero or a devil? He is young, bold, intelligent, strong, he has thrown off the burden of the past, the melancholy impotence of the 'superfluous men' beating vainly against the bars of the prison house of Russian society. The critic Strakhov in his review spoke of him as a character conceived on a heroic scale. Many years later Lunacharsky described him as the first 'positive' hero in Russian literature. Does he then symbolize progress? Freedom? Yet his hatred of art and culture, of the entire world of liberal values, his cynical

5. Letter to Sluchevsky, 26 April 1862.

asides—does the author mean to hold these up for admiration? Even before the novel was published his editor, Mikhail Katkov, protested to Turgenev. This glorification of nihilism, he complained, was nothing but grovelling at the feet of the young radicals. 'Turgenev', he said to the novelist's friend Annenkov, 'should be ashamed of lowering the flag before a radical, or saluting him as an honourable soldier.' Katkov declared that he was not deceived by the author's apparent objectivity: 'There is concealed approval lurking here . . . this fellow, Bazarov, definitely dominates the others and does not encounter proper resistance,' and he concluded that what Turgenev had done was politically dangerous. Strakhov was more sympathetic. He wrote that Turgenev, with his devotion to timeless truth and beauty, only wanted to describe reality, not to judge it. He too, however, spoke of Bazarov as towering over the other characters, and declared that Turgenev might claim to be drawn to him by an irresistible attraction, but it would be truer to say that he feared him. Katkov echoes this: 'One gets the impression of a kind of embarrassment in the author's attitude of the hero of his story . . . It is as if the author didn't like him, felt lost before him, and, more than this, was terrified of him!'

The attack from the Left was a good deal more virulent. Dobrolyubov's successor, Antonovich, accused Turgenev in the *Contemporary* of perpetrating a hideous and disgusting caricature of the young. Bazarov was a brutish, cynical sensualist, hankering after wine and women, unconcerned with the fate of the people; his creator, whatever his views in the past, had evidently crossed over to the blackest reactionaries and oppressors. And, indeed, there were conservatives who congratulated Turgenev for exposing the horrors of the new, destructive nihilism, and thereby rendering a public service for which all men of decent feeling must be grateful. But it was the attack from the Left that hurt Turgenev most. Seven years later he wrote to a friend that 'mud and filth' had been flung at him by the young. He had been called fool, donkey, reptile, Judas, police agent. And again, 'While some accused me of . . . backwardness, black obscurantism, and informed me that "my photographs were being burnt amid contemptuous laughter", yet others indignantly reproached me with kowtowing to the . . . young. "You are crawling at Bazarov's feet!" cried one of my correspondents. "You are only pretending to condemn him. Actually you scrape and bow to him, you wait obsequiously for the favor of a casual smile." . . . A shadow has fallen upon my name.' At least one of his liberal friends who had read the manuscript of *Fathers and Children* told him to burn it, since it would compromise him for ever with the progressives. Hostile caricatures appeared in the left-wing press, in which Turgenev was represented as pandering to the fathers, with Bazarov as a leering Mephistopheles, mocking his disciple Arkady's love for his father. At best, the author was drawn as a bewildered figure simultaneously attacked by frantic democrats from the Left and threatened by armed fathers from the Right, as he stood helplessly between them. But the Left was not unanimous. The radical critic Pisarev came to Turgenev's aid. He boldly identified himself with Bazarov and his position. Turgenev, Pisarev wrote, might be too soft or tired to accompany us, the men of the future; but he knows that true progress is to be found not in men tied to tradition, but in active, self-emancipated, independent men, like Bazarov, free from fantasies, from romantic or religious nonsense. The author does not bully us, he does not tell us to accept the values of the 'fathers'. Bazarov is in revolt; he is the prisoner of no theory; that is his attractive strength; that is what makes for progress and freedom. Turgenev may wish to tell us that we are on a false path, but in fact he is a kind of Balaam: he has become deeply attached to the hero of his novel through the very process of creation, and pins all his hopes to him. 'Nature is a workshop, not a temple' and we are workers in it; not melancholy day-dreams, but will, strength, intelligence, realism—these, Pisarev declares, speaking through Bazarov, these will find the road. Bazarov, he adds, is what parents today see emerging in their sons and daughters, sisters in their brothers. They may be frightened by it, they may be puzzled, but that is where the road to the future lies.

Turgenev's familiar friend, Annenkov, to whom he submitted all his novels for criticism before he published them, saw Bazarov as a Mongol, a Genghiz Khan, a wild beast symptomatic of the savage condition of Russia, only 'thinly concealed by books from the Leipzig Fair'. Was Turgenev aiming to become the leader of a political movement? 'The author himself . . . does not know how to take him,' he wrote, 'as a fruitful force for the future, or as a disgusting boil on the body of a hollow civilization, to be removed as rapidly as possible.' Yet he cannot be both, 'he is a Janus with two faces, each party will see only what it wants to see or can understand.' Katkov, in an unsigned review in his own journal (in which the novel had appeared), went a good deal further. After mocking the confusion on the Left as a result of being unexpectedly faced with its own image in nihilism, which pleased some and horrified others, he reproaches the author for being altogether too anxious not to be unjust to Bazarov, and consequently of representing him always in the best possible light. There is such a thing, he says, as being too fair; this leads to its own brand of distortion of the truth. As for the hero, he is represented as being brutally candid: that is good, very good; he believes in telling the whole truth, however upsetting to the poor, gentle Kir-sanovs, father and son, with no respect for persons or circumstances: most admirable; he attacks art, riches, luxurious living, yes, but in the name of what? Of science and knowledge? But, Katkov declares, this is simply not true. Bazarov's purpose is not the discovery of scientific truth, else he would not peddle cheap popular tracts—Büchner and the rest—which are not science at all, but journalism, materialist propaganda. Bazarov (he goes on to say) is not a scientist; this species scarcely exists in Russia in our time. Bazarov and his fellow nihilists are merely preachers: they denounce phrases, rhetoric, inflated language—Bazarov tells Arkady not to talk so 'beautifully'—but only in order to substitute for this their own political propaganda; they offer not hard scientific facts, in which they are not interested, with which, indeed they are not acquainted, but slogans, diatribes, radical cant. Bazarov's dissection of frogs is not genuine pursuit of the truth, it is only an occasion for rejecting civilized and traditional values which Paul Kirsanov, who in a better-ordered society—say England—would have done useful work, rightly defends. Bazarov and his friends will discover nothing; they are not researchers; they are mere ranters, men who declaim in the name of a science which they do not trouble to master; in the end they are no better than the ignorant, benighted Russian priesthood from whose ranks they mostly spring, and far more dangerous.

Herzen, as always, was both penetrating and amusing. 'Turgenev was more of an artist in his novel than people think, and for this reason lost his way, and, in my opinion, did very well. He wanted to go to one room, but ended up in another and a better one.' The author clearly started by wanting to do something for the fathers, but they turned out to be such nonentities that he 'became carried away by Bazarov's very extremism; with the result that instead of flogging the son, he whipped the fathers. Nature sometimes follows art: Bazarov affected the young as Werther, in the previous century, influenced them, like Schiller's *The Robbers*, like Byron's Laras and Giaours and Childe Harolds in their day. Yet these new men, Herzen added in a later essay, are so dogmatic, doctrinaire, jargon-ridden, as to exhibit the least attractive aspect of the Russian character, the policeman's—the martinet's—side of it, the brutal bureaucratic jackboot; they want to break the yoke of the old despotism, but only in order to replace it with one of their own. The 'generation of the forties', his own and Turgenev's, may have been fatuous and weak, but does it follow that their successors—the brutally rude, loveless, cynical, philistine young men of the sixties, who sneer and mock and push and jostle and don't apologize—are necessarily superior beings? What new principles, what new constructive answers have they provided? Destruction is destruction. It is not creation.

In the violent babel of voices aroused by the novel, at least five attitudes can be distinguished. There was the angry right wing which thought that Bazarov represented the apotheosis of the new nihilists, and sprang from Turgenev's unworthy desire to flatter and be accepted by the young. There were those who congratulated him on successfully exposing barbarism and subversion. There were those who denounced him for his wicked travesty of the radicals, for providing reactionaries with ammunition and playing into the hands of the police; by them he was called renegade and traitor. Still others, like Dimitri Pisarev, proudly nailed Bazarov's colors to their mast and expressed gratitude to Turgenev for his honesty and sympathy with all that was most living and fearless in the growing party of the future. Finally there were some who detected that the author himself was not wholly sure of what he wanted to do, that his attitude was genuinely ambivalent, that he was an artist and not a pamphleteer, that he told the truth as he saw it, without a clear partisan purpose.

This controversy continued in full strength after Turgenev's death. It says something for the vitality of his creation that the debate did not die even in the following century, neither before nor after the Russian Revolution. Indeed, as lately as ten years ago the battle was still raging amongst Soviet critics. Was Turgenev for us or against us? Was he a Hamlet blinded by the pessimism of his declining class, or did he, like Balzac or Tolstoy, see beyond it? Is Bazarov a forerunner of the politically committed, militant Soviet intellectual, or a malicious caricature of the fathers of Russian communism? The debate is not over yet.[6]

Turgenev was upset and bewildered by the reception of his book. Before sending it to the printer, he had taken his usual precaution of seeking endless advice. He read the manuscript to friends in Paris, he altered, he modified, he tried to please everyone. The figure of Bazarov suffered several transformations in successive drafts, up and down the moral scale as this or that friend or consultant reported his impressions. The attack from the Left inflicted wounds which festered for the rest of his life. Years later he wrote 'I am told that I am on the side of the "fathers"—I, who in the person of Paul Kirsanov, actually sinned against artistic truth, went too far, exaggerated his defects to the point of travesty, and made him ridiculous!' As for Bazarov, he was 'honest, truthful, a democrat to his fingertips'. Many years later, Turgenev told the anarchist Kropotkin that he loved Bazarov 'very, very much . . . I will show you my diaries—you will see how I wept when I ended the book with Bazarov's death.' 'Tell me honestly,' he wrote to one of his most caustic critics, the satirist Saltykov (who complained that the word 'nihilist' was

6. The literature, mostly polemical, is very extensive, [and] represents the continuing controversy, in which Lenin's scathing reference to the similarity of Turgenev's views to those of German right-wing social democrats is constantly quoted both for and against the conception of Bazarov as a prototype of Bolshevik activists. There is an even more extensive mass of writing on the question of whether, and how far, Katkov managed to persuade Turgenev to amend his text in a 'moderate' direction by darkening Bazarov's image. That Turgenev did alter his text as a result of Katkov's pleading is certain; he may, however, have restored some, at any rate, of the original language when the novel was published as a book. His relations with Katkov deteriorated rapidly; Turgenev came to look on him as a vicious reactionary and refused his proffered hand at a banquet in honour of Pushkin in 1880; one of his favorite habits was to refer to the arthritis which tormented him as Katkovitis (*Katkovka*).

used by reactionaries to damn anyone they did not like), 'how could anybody be offended by being compared to Bazarov? Do you not yourself realize that he is the most sympathetic of all my characters?' As for 'nihilism', that, perhaps, was a mistake. 'I am ready to admit . . . that I had no right to give our reactionary scum the opportunity to seize on a name, a catchword; the writer in me should have brought the sacrifice to the citizen—I admit the justice of my rejection by the young and of all the gibes hurled at me . . . The issue was more important than artistic truth, and I ought to have foreseen this.' He claimed that he shared almost all Bazarov's views, all save those on art. A lady of his acquaintance had told him that he was neither for the fathers, nor for the children, but was a nihilist himself; he thought she might be right. Herzen had said that there had been something of Bazarov in them all, in himself, in Belinsky, in Bakunin, in all those who in the forties denounced the Russian kingdom of darkness in the name of the West and science and civilization. Turgenev did not deny this either. He did, no doubt, adopt a different tone in writing to different correspondents. When radical Russian students in Heidelberg demanded clarification of his own position, he told them that 'if the reader does not love Bazarov, as he is—coarse, heartless, ruthlessly dry and brusque . . . the fault is mine; I have not succeeded in my task. But to "melt him in syrup" (to use his own expression)—that I was not prepared to do . . . I did not wish to buy popularity by this sort of concession. Better lose a battle (and I think I have lost this one), than win it by a trick.' Yet to his friend the poet Fet, a conservative landowner, he wrote that he did not himself know if he loved Bazarov or hated him. Did he mean to praise or denigrate him? He did not not know. And this is echoed eight years later: 'My personal feelings [towards Bazarov] were confused (God only knows whether I loved him or hated him!).' To the liberal Madame Filosofova he wrote, 'Bazarov is my beloved child; on his account I quarrelled with Katkov . . . Bazarov, that intelligent, heroic man—a caricature?!' And he added that this was 'a senseless charge'. He found the scorn of the young unjust beyond endurance. He wrote that in the summer of 1862 'despicable generals praised me, the young insulted me.' The socialist leader Lavrov reports that he bitterly complained to him of the injustice of the radicals' change of attitude towards him. He returns to this in one of his late *Poems in Prose*: 'Honest souls turned away from him. Honest faces grew red with indignation at the mere mention of his name.' This was not mere wounded *amour propre*. He suffered from a genuine sense of having got himself into a politically false position. All his life he wished to march with the progressives, with the party of liberty and protest. But, in the end, he could not bring himself to accept their brutal contempt for art, civilized behavior, for everything that he held dear in European culture. He hated their dogmatism, their arrogance, their destructiveness, their appalling ignorance of life. He went abroad, lived in Germany and France, and returned to Russia only on flying visits. In the West he was universally praised and admired. But in the end it was to Russians that he wished to speak. Although his popularity with the Russian public in the sixties, and at all times, was very great, it was the radicals he most of all wanted to please. They were hostile or unresponsive.

* * *

RALPH E. MATLAW

Fathers and Sons†

Perhaps the most suggestive insight ever made into *Fathers and Sons* was V. E. Meyerhold's attempt to cast the poet Vladimir Mayakovsky in the role of Bazarov for a film version contemplated in 1929. Among those who remember the young Mayakovsky's early appearances in films, Yuri Olesha described his face as "sad, passionate, evoking infinite pity, the face of a strong and suffering man." It is a little hard to imagine Mayakovsky with side-whiskers (Bazarov, after all, presumably wears these to resemble more closely his intellectual prototype, the studious and sickly N. A. Dobrolyubov), but apart from that one could not conceive of a better reincarnation of Bazarov than Mayakovsky. For Mayakovsky, in his flamboyant and tragic life, and frequently in his verse, was or would have been if Bazarov had not already staked out a claim to that title, the arch example of the phenomenon we now call "the angry young man."

The term, with due allowance for the changes of a century and of cultures, points to two fundamental aspects of Bazarov that underlie both his attractive and repulsive traits for most

† From Ralph E. Matlaw, ed., *Fathers and Sons: A Norton Critical Edition* (New York: Norton, 1966), pp. 274–78.

readers—his immaturity and his position as an outsider in "a world he never made." And these, in turn, point to the psychological and social verities that secure so high place for *Fathers and Sons* in modern literature. The second of these has a specifical historical context and prototype, V. G. Belinsky, to whom the novel is dedicated. Bazarov's portrait, like Belinsky's career, is associated with and typifies two important notions in Russian intellectual history. The first is the rise of the "intelligentsia," a term, apparently of Rusian invention, that designates intellectuals of all persuasions dedicated in one form or another to the improvement of life in Russia, and so carries far greater ethical implications than the mere word "intellectual." The second is that of the *raznochintsy*, literally "persons of various classes," a term applied to those members of classes other than the gentry, usually the clergy or the minor and provincial professional and bureaucratic classes, who sought to pursue a career other than the one their background would normally indicate. Frequently they became members of the intelligentsia, usually after considerable privation. Unlike members of the gentry like Herzen or Turgenev, who could always turn to other sources if necessary, they were entirely dependent upon their intellectual labors, whether as tutors, journalists, writers, or in other pursuits, and from their difficult position derived no small part of their exaltation and indefatigability. While there were factions and enmities within the intelligentsia, all its members were in principle agreed on one point: opposition to the conditions of life around them. Clearly connected with these conditions is the intrusion of the *raznochintsy* into literature, until 1830 or so the exclusive purview of the gentry, who were all too eager to avoid the imputation of professionalism. In style and in tone a sharp shift may be observed, and no one better exemplifies this change in real life than Belinsky or in literature than Bazarov.

Intellectual equality, unfortunately,. offered no social prerogatives. Beyond his intellectual circles and his normal habitat, the major cities, even in the rapidly changing society of the mid-nineteenth century, the *raznochinets* was an outsider, if not an upstart. Bazarov, with his enormous sensitivity and vanity, feels out of place at the Governor's Ball and at Odintsov's estate (the wording of his request for vodka amazes the butler). He frequently and deliberately emphasizes his plebeian origin, as in the ironic reference to his similarity to the great Speransky, his sharp reaction to his father's apologies, his feelings about Pavel Kirsanov, and in numerous turns of speech that the English translation cannot convey completely. As for Pavel Kirsanov, we need only think of Prince André's disdain for Speransky in *War and Peace* to judge the gulf that in Pavel's mind separates Bazarov from him. To the aristocrat who has cultivated and refined his privileged position, the democratic virtue of being a self-made man does not appear so laudable. And from this point of view Bazarov's contempt for Pavel Petrovich, "snobism in reverse," to adapt Bazarov's witticism, is another manifestation of his discomfort when out of his class. Still, as Bazarov makes clear, his prospects are very meager, and it leads to great bitterness. Outside the "establishment," which he cannot tolerate, there is no opposition party, not even a real hierarchy, and the consciousness of insuperable obstacles leads to Bazarov's great "anger." As Turgenev chose to present the matter it appears more as a social than political theme, but its motive force is just as operative. The point may profitably be compared to a similar one in *The Red and The Black* where, in Stendhal's happier imagination, Julien Sorel rises to the top, only to insist perversely at his trial on his peasant origin and to accuse his jury of seeking "to punish in me and to discourage forever that class of young men who, born in an inferior station and in a sense burdened with poverty, have the good fortune to secure a sound education, and the audacity to mingle with what the pride of rich people calls society."

The second component is more directly implied in the novel's title as the conflict between generations, apparently an inherent problem in human nature, though manifesting itself in different forms and in different degrees. *Fathers and Sons* presents it in particularly sharp form. Nikolai Kirsanov tells his brother of the remark he made to his mother, "Of course you can't understand me. We belong to different generations," and is now resigned to his turn having come to "swallow the pill." Bazarov's father similarly remembers how he scoffed at the earlier generation, accepts Bazarov's ridiculing his outdated notions, but as a matter of course indicates that in twenty years Bazarov's idols too will be replaced. The intensity of rejection, however, does differ and is a sign of the times. For Bazarov replies "For your consolation I will tell you that nowadays we laugh at medicine altogether, and don't bow down to anyone," which his father simply cannot comprehend. Normally, the problem of generations is resolved by time: the sons gradually move toward their permanent positions, give over being "angry young men," and become husbands and fathers, angry or not. It is perhaps the hardest subject of all to handle, as the reaction to the end of *War and Peace* with its assertion of domestic permanence, and, in *Fathers and Sons*, the quick taming of Arkady Kirsanov prove: the world of struggle and aspiration is more interesting to contemplate that that of fixity and acceptance. The "angry young man" cannot remain so, and is something of an anomaly if not of outright ridicule, when he maintains that view as paterfamilias.

Bazarov denies the values of normal human behavior, but when his theory is put to a single test it collapses. Bazarov falls in love and can no longer return to his former mode. Turgenev permits him to maintain his character by shifting the problem of generations to its ultimate form, that of death. This condition, at least, Bazarov must accept: "An old man at least has time to be weaned from life, but I . . . . Well, go and try to disprove death. Death will disprove you, and that's all!" And in his illness Bazarov compresses into a brief period that acceptance of traditional values—family, love, life itself—that otherwise would accrue slowly and undramatically, in the process to some extent attenuating the strident expression of his former views.

But this only occurs at the end. Throughout the novel the high-mindedness, dedication, and energy that make Bazarov tower over the other characters are occasionally expressed with an immaturity bordering on adolescent revolt. The ideas themselves thus in part express the temperament of the "sons." Superficially the state may seem to apply more readily to Arkady, but it is far more ingrained in Bazarov. There are such remarks as "Bazarov drew himself up haughtily. 'I don't share anyone's ideas: I have my own,' " and "When I meet a man who can hold his own beside me, then I'll change my opinion of myself," his deliberately offensive manners, his sponging on and abuse of Kukshin and Sitnikov, his trifling with Fenichka and his jejune declaration to Odintsov. In short, the attempt to impose his own image on the world and to reshape the world accordingly. It is a point Turgenev made quite explicit in his draft for *Virgin Soil*:

> There are *Romantics of Realism* * * * They long for a reality and strive toward it, as former Romantics did toward the ideal. In reality they seek not poetry—that is ludicrous for them—but something grand and meaningful; and that's nonsense: real life is prosaic and should be so. They are unhappy, distorted, and torment themselves with this very distortion as something completely inappropriate to their work. Moreover, their appearance —possible only in Russia, always with a *sermonizing* or educational aspect—is necessary and useful: they are preachers and prophets in their own way, but complete prophets, contained and defined in themselves. Preaching is an illness, a hunger, a desire; a healthy person cannot be a prophet or even a preacher. Therefore I put something of *that* romanticism in Bazarov too, but only Pisarev noticed it.[5]

The two problems of youth and anger, or maturity and acceptance, come to a head in Bazarov's involvement with Odintsov, the

---

1. André Mazon, "L'élaboration d'un roman de Turgenev: *Terres vierges.*" *Revue des études slaves*, V (1925), 87–88.

central episode in the novel, which also serves as a kind of structural dividing line between the political (or social) and the psychological. The discussions of nihilism and contemporary politics, that phase of the battle between the generations dominates the opening of the novel but is practically concluded when Bazarov and Arkady leave Odintsov in Chapter Nineteen. From this point on an opposite movement assumes primary importance: Bazarov's and Arkady's liberation from involvement with theories and the turn toward life itself, that is, toward those people and things in the characters' immediate existence. It entails a shift from scenes and formulations essentially intellectual to others that are more ruminative, inwardly speculative, communicating psychological states and feelings rather than ideas. With it, Bazarov's views and behavior assume a different cast, far more personal, more indicative of his real needs and dissatisfactions. His speeches about necessary reforms now turn into expressions of personal desire ("I felt such a hatred for this poorest peasant, this Philip or Sidor, for whom I'm to be ready to jump out of my skin, and who won't even thank me for it"), his rigorous materialism into the purely Pascalian speech on man's insignificance as a point in time and space. His brusqueness and former contempt for decorum now are so tempered that he accepts a challenge to a duel, has a frock coat easily accessible as he returns to Odintsov, and practices elaborate politeness as she visits him on his deathbed. The end with Bazarov's disquisition on strength, life, and necessity strike the reader as rather mawkish and hollow, for the words now have if not a false, at least a commonplace ring. Indeed, the great effect of the ending is achieved not through Bazarov's speeches but by communicating the despair of his parents.

In the final analysis Turgenev could neither condemn nor yet wholly redeem Bazarov without falsifying or diminishing the portrait. On the last page of the novel he instead implies the reconciliation of the character with a larger, permanent order of things, expressed in terms of the touchstone and overriding image of the novel—nature. The concluding words "[the flowers] tell us, too, of eternal reconciliation and of life without end" do not at all tend toward mysticism, as Herzen claimed and Turgenev denied, but affirm that "the passionate, sinning,[2] and rebellious heart" buried beneath the ground has finally come to terms with permanent reality. The passage is secular rather than religious: life is "without end" not "eternal"; it is life on earth, not in the hereafter.

2. Perhaps "erring" conveys the spirit rather than the letter of the word better than "sinning" does.

PROSPER MÉRIMÉE

Ivan Turgénev†

The name of Turgenev is popular in France today; each of his works is awaited with the same eagerness and read with the same pleasure in Paris and in St. Petersburg. He is considered one of the leaders of the realist school. This may be criticism or praise, but I do not think he belongs to any school; he follows his own inspiration. Like all good novelists, he has devoted himself to the study of the human heart, an inexhaustible mine despite its being exploited for so long a time. A delicate, exact observer, sometimes to the point of minutiae, he creates his characters as a painter and a poet at the same time. Their passions and the features of their faces are equally familiar to him. He knows their habits and their gestures; he hears them speak and gives a stenographic report of their conversation. Such is the art with which he creates a physical and moral whole from all the parts, that the reader sees a portrait rather than a imaginary tableau. Thanks to his faculty for condensing his observations in some manner and of giving them precise form, Turgenev does not shock us more than nature when he presents an abnormal and extraordinary case to us. In his novel *Fathers and Sons* he shows us a young lady who has large hands and small feet. Ordinarily there is a certain harmony among the extremities of the human frame, but exceptions are rarer in nature than in novels. Why does that nice Katya have large hands? The author saw her thus and, through his love for truth, had the indiscretion of saying so. Why is Hamlet fat and out of breath? Ought one to agree with an ingenious German professor that Hamlet, being uncertain of his resolutions, could only have a lymphatic temperament and *therefore* a disposition toward stoutness? But Shakespeare had not read Cabanis,[1] and I would prefer to think that in representing the prince of Denmark that way he had in mind the actor who was to play that role, if it did not seem still more probable to me that the poet had a figure of his imagination before him,

---

† From Prosper Mérimée, *Oeuvres complètes*, XII (Paris, 1932), 241–45. Translated by Ralph E. Matlaw. The article originally appeared as a preface to a collection of Turgenev in 1868. Mérimée translated a number of works from Russian, including several stories by Turgénev.
1. P. J. G. Cabanis (1757–1808), French physician and philosopher, wrote on the relation of morality to the physique [*Editor*].

who presented himself "in the mind's eye" clearly, and completely finished. Souvenirs, associations of ideas that one cannot account for to oneself, involuntarily obsess the man who has the habit of studying nature. In his fiction he gathers at a glance a host of details united by some mysterious tie that he feels but that he cannot perhaps explain. Let us note again that the resemblance, the life in a portrait, frequently depends on a detail. I remember hearing Sir Thomas Lawrence, certainly one of the great portrait painters of this century, profess this theory. He said: "Choose a trait in your sitter's face; copy it faithfully, even servilely; later you can embellish all the others. You will have made a good likeness and the sitter will be satisfied."

Painter of the most handsome aristocracy of Europe, Lawrence took great care in choosing the trait to be copied servilely. Turgenev is no more flattering than a photographer, and has none of the weaknesses toward the children of their imagination common to novelists. He gives birth to them with their faults, lets them be seen with their ridiculous aspects, leaves to his reader the task of adding up the good and the bad and consequently coming to a conclusion. Still less does he seek to offer us his characters as types of a certain passion or as the representatives of a certain idea, a practice that has been in use for a long time. With his delicate mode of analysis he does not see general types; he knows only individuals. And really, does a man who has only a single passion or who follows a single idea without deviation, does such a man exist in nature? He would surely be much more formidable than the man *of a single book* that Terence feared.

That impartiality, that love for truth which is the distinguishing trait of Turgenev, never abandons him. It is difficult today, in writing a novel whose characters are our contemporaries, not to be led to treat some of those great questions which agitate our modern societies, or at least to disclose one's views on the revolutions that operate in *mores*. However, one could not say whether Turgenev regrets the passing of society in Alexander I's day or whether he prefers that of Alexander II to it. In his novel *Fathers and Sons* he has brought on himself the anger of the young and of the old. One and the other claim to be slandered. He has only been impartial, and this the factions will hardly forgive. I will add that one must be careful not to take Bazarov for the representative of progressive youth or Pavel Kirsanov as the perfect model of the old order. These are two figures that we have seen somewhere. They no doubt exist, but they are not personifications either of the old or new of this century. One might well wish that all young men had as much verve as Bazarov and all the old men sentiments as noble as Pavel Kirsanov's.

Turgenev banishes great crimes from his novels, and one must not look for tragic scenes in them. There are few events in his novels. Nothing more simple than their plot, nothing that more resembles ordinary life, and this too is one of the consequences of his love for truth. The progress of civilization tends to make the violence of our modern society disappear, but it has not been able to change the passions that hide in the human heart. The form they assume is softened or, if you like, worn out, like a coin that has circulated a long time. In society, even in the demi-monde, one hardly ever sees Macbeths or Othellos any more. However, there are always ambitious and jealous people, and the torments that Othello undergoes before strangling Desdemona have been endured by some Parisian bourgeois before asking for a legal separation. I knew a clerk who no doubt had not seen "a dagger, the handle pointed toward him" in a diabolic hallucination, but who constantly saw before his eyes the office manager's gilt-studded armchair, and that armchair moved him to slander his superior to obtain his place. It is in "these private dramas" as it is called today that Turgenev's talent takes pleasure in and excels. * * *

HENRY JAMES

[Ivan Turgénev]†

* * * The germ of a story, with him, was never an affair of plot—that was the last thing he thought of: it was the representation of certain persons. The first form in which a tale appeared to him was as the figure of an individual, or a combination of individuals, whom he wished to see in action, being sure that such people must do something very special and interesting. They stood before him definite, vivid, and he wished to know and to show, as much as possible of their nature. The first thing was to make clear to himself what he did know, to begin with; and to this end he wrote a sort of biography of each of his characters, and everything that they had done and had happened to them up to the opening of the story. He had their *dossier*, as

---

† The first paragraph is from *Partial Portraits*, London and New York: Macmillan & Co., 1888. The last two paragraphs are from the Preface to *The Portrait of a Lady* in the *Novels and Tales of Henry James*, New York Edition, Volume III, Charles Scribner's Sons, 1908.

the French say, and as the police have that of every conspicuous criminal. With this material in his hand he was able to proceed; the story all lay in the question, What shall I make them do? He always made them do things that showed them completely; but, as he said, the defect of his manner and the reproach that was made him was his want of "architecture"—in other words, of composition. The great thing, of course, is to have architecture as well as precious material, as Walter Scott had them, as Balzac had them. If one reads Turgénev's stories with the knowledge that they were composed—or rather that they came into being—in this way, one can trace the process in every line. Story, in the conventional sense of the word—a fable constructed, like Wordsworth's phantom, "to startle and waylay" —there *is* as little as possible. The thing consists of the motions of a group of selected creatures, which are not the result of a preconceived action, but a consequence of the qualities of the actors. Works of art are produced from every possible point of view, and stories, and very good ones, will continue to be written in which the evolution is that of a dance—a series of steps, the more complicated and lively the better, of course, determined from without and forming a figure. This figure will always, probably, find favor with many readers, because it reminds them enough, without reminding them too much, of life. * * *

* * * "I have always fondly remembered a remark that I heard fall years ago from the lips of Ivan Turgenieff in regard to his own experience of the usual origin of the fictive picture. It began for him almost always with the vision of some person or persons, who hovered before him, soliciting him, as the active or passive figures, interesting him and appealing to him just as they were and by what they were. He saw them, in that fashion, as *disponibles*,[1] saw them subject to the chances, the complications of existence, and saw them vividly, but then had to find for them the right relations, those that would most bring them out; to imagine, to invent and select and piece together the situations most useful and favorable to the sense of the creatures themselves, the complications they would be most likely to produce and to feel.

"To arrive at these things is to arrive at my 'story'," he said, "and that's the way I look for it. The result is that I'm often accused of not having 'story' enough. I seem to myself to have as much as I need—to show my people, to exhibit their relations with each other; for that is all my measure. If I watch them long enough I see them come together, I see them *placed*, I see them

---

1. "Disposable" [*Editor*].

engaged in this or that act and in this or that difficulty. How they look and move and speak and behave, always in the setting I have found for them, is my account of them—of which I dare say, alas, *que cela manque souvent d'architecture*.[2] But I would rather, I think, have too little architecture than too much—when there's danger of its interfering with my measure of the truth. The French of course like more of it than I give—having by their own genius such a hand for it; and indeed one must give all one can. As for the origin of one's wind-blown germs themselves, who shall say, as you ask, where they come from? We have to go too far back, too far behind, to say. Isn't it all we can say that they come from every quarter of heaven, that they are *there* at almost any turn of the road? They accumulate, and we are always picking them over, selecting among them. They are the breath of life—by which I mean that life, in its own way, breathes them upon us. They are so, in a manner prescribed and imposed—floated into our minds by the current of life. That reduces to imbecility the vain critic's quarrel, so often, with one's subject, when he hasn't the wit to accept it. Will he point out then which other it should properly have been?—his office being, essentially *to* point out. *Il en serait bien embarrassé*[3]! Ah, when he points out what I've done or failed to do I give him up my 'architecture'," my distinguished friend concluded, "as much as he will." * * *

A. P. CHEKHOV

Letter to A. S. Suvorin, February 24, 1893 †

* * * My God! What a magnificent thing *Fathers and Sons* is! It simply makes you desperate. Bazarov's illness is so powerfully done that I turned weak and had a feeling as if I had been infected by him. And Bazarov's death? And the old people? And Kukshin? God knows how he does it. It is sheer genius. I don't like *On the Eve* except Helen's father and the ending. That ending is full of tragedy. "The Dog" is very good; its language is amazing. Please read it if you've forgotten it. "Asya" is very nice, "The Quiet Spot" is crumpled and doesn't satisfy. I don't like *Smoke* at all. A *Nest of Noblemen* is weaker than *Fathers and Sons*, but the ending is almost a marvel. Besides the old woman in Bazarov, that is, Evgeny's mother and mothers in

2. "That that frequently lacks structure" [*Editor*].
3. "He'd be hard put to do it" [*Editor*].

† From A. P. Chekhov, *Sobranie sochineniy*, XII (Moscow, 1960–64); 17–18. Translated by Ralph E. Matlaw.

general, particularly the fashionable ladies, who all resemble each other, by the way (Liza's mother, Helen's mother), and Lavretsky's mother, the former serf, and in addition the simple women, all of Turgenev's women and young ladies are unbearable with their artificiality and, forgive me, falseness. Liza, Helen—these aren't Russian young ladies but some sort of Pithians, with their pronouncements, their excessive pretensions. Irina in *Smoke*, Odintsov in *Fathers and Sons*, in general the lionesses, ardent, appetizing, insatiable, seeking something—they're all nonsense. When you think of Tolstoy's Anna Karenin, all these young ladies of Turgenev's with their tempting shoulders vanish. Women of the negative sort, where Turgenev lightly caricatures them (Kukshin), or makes merry with (the description of balls), are wonderfully drawn and so successfully come off in him that, as the saying goes, you can't find a flaw in it. The descriptions of nature are good, but—I feel that we are already becoming disaccustomed to that kind of description and that something else is needed. * * *

EDWARD GARNETT

[Bazarov]†

* * * What, then, is Bazarov?

Various writers have agreed in seeing in him only "criticism, pitiless, barren, and overwhelming analysis, and the spirit of absolute negation," but this is an error. Representing the creed which has produced the militant type of Revolutionist in every capital of Europe, *he is the bare mind of Science first applied to Politics.* His own immediate origin is German Science interpreted by that spirit of logical intensity, Russian fanaticism, or devotion to the Idea, which is perhaps the distinguishing genius of the Slav. But he represents the roots of the modern Revolutionary movements in thought as well as in politics, rather than the branches springing from those roots. Inasmuch as the early work of the pure scientific spirit, knowing itself to be fettered by the superstitions, the confusions, the sentimentalities of the Past, was necessarily destructive, Bazarov's primary duty was to Destroy. In his essence, however, he stands for *the sceptical conscience of modern Science.* His watchword is *Reality*, and not Negation, as everybody in pious horror

† From Edward Garnett, *Turgenev, A Study*, London, 1917, pp. 116–26. Reprinted by permission of William Collins Ltd. and David Garnett.

hastened to assert. Turgenev, whose first and last advice to young writers was, "You need truth, remorseless truth, as regards your own sensations," was indeed moved to declare, "Except Bazarov's views on Art, I share almost all his convictions." The crude materialism of the 'sixties was not the basis of the scientific spirit, it was merely its passing expression; and the early Nihilists who denounced Art, the Family and Social Institutions were simply freeing themselves from traditions preparatory to a struggle that was inevitable. Again, though Bazarov is a Democrat, perhaps his kinship with the people is best proved by the contempt he feels for them. He stands forward essentially as an Individual, with the "isms" that could aid him, mere tools in his hand; Socialist, Communist or Individualist, in his necessary phases he fought this century against the tyranny of centralized Governments, and next century he will be fighting against the stupid tyranny of the Mass. Looking at Bazarov, however, as a type that has played its part and vanished with its generation, as a man he is a new departure in history. His appearance marks the dividing-line between two religions, that of the Past—Faith, and that growing religion of to-day—Science. His is the duty of breaking away from all things that men call Sacred, and his savage egoism is essential to that duty. He is subject to neither Custom nor Law. He is his own law, and is occupied simply with the fact he is studying. He has thrown aside the ties of love and duty that cripple the advance of the strongest men. He typifies Mind grappling with Nature, seeking out her inexorable laws. Mind in pure devotion to the What Is, in startling contrast to the minds that follow their self-created kingdoms of What Appears and of What Ought to Be. He is therefore a foe to the poetry and art that help to increase Nature's glamour over man by alluring him to yield to her; for Bazarov's great aim is to see Nature at work behind the countless veils of illusions and ideals, and all the special functions of belief which she develops in the minds of the masses to get them unquestioning to do her bidding. Finally, Bazarov, in whom the comfortable compromising English mind sees only a man of bad form, bad taste, bad manners and overwhelming conceit, finally, Bazarov stands for Humanity awakened from century-old superstitions and the long dragging oppressive dream of tradition. Naked he stands under a deaf, indifferent sky, but he feels and knows that he has the strong brown earth beneath his feet.

This type, though it has developed into a network of special branches to-day, it is not difficult for us to trace as it has appeared and disappeared in the stormy periods of the last thirty years. Probably the genius and energy of the type was chiefly devoted to positive Science, and not to Politics; but it is sufficient to glance at the Revolutionary History, in theory and action, of the Continent to see that every movement was inspired by the ideas of the Bazarovs, though led by a variety of leaders. Just as the popular movements for Liberty fifty years earlier found sentimental and *romantic* expression in Byronism, so the popular movements of our time have been realistic in idea, and have looked to Science for their justification. Proudhon, Bakunin, Karl Marx, the Internationals, the Russian Terrorists, the Communists, all have a certain relation to Bazarov, but his nearest kinsmen in these and other movements we believe have worked, and have remained, obscure. It was a stroke of genius on Turgenev's part to make Bazarov die on the threshold unrecognized. He is Aggression, destroyed in his destroying. And there are many reasons in life for the Bazarovs remaining obscure. For one thing, their few disciples, the Arkadys, do not understand them; for another, the whole swarm of little interested persons who make up a movement are more or less engaged in personal interests, and they rarely take for a leader a man who works for his own set of truths, scornful of all cliques, penalties and rewards. Necessarily, too, the Bazarovs work alone, and are given the most dangerous tasks to accomplish unaided. Further, they are men whose brutal and breaking force attracts ten men where it repels a thousand. The average man is too afraid of Bazarov to come into contact with him. Again, the Bazarovs, as Iconoclasts, are always unpopular in their own circles. Yesterday in political life they were suppressed or exiled, and even in Science they were the men who were supplanted before their real claim was recognized, and to-day, when order reigns for a time, the academic circles and the popular critics will demonstrate that Bazarov's existence was a mistake, and the crowd could have got on much better without him.

The Crowd, the ungrateful Crowd! though for it Bazarov has wrested much from effete or corrupt hands, and has fought and weakened despotic and bureaucratic power, what has its opinion or memory to do with his brave heroic figure? Yes, heroic, as Turgenev, in indignation with Bazarov's shallow accusers, was betrayed into defining his own creation, Bazarov, whose very atmosphere is difficulty and danger, who cannot move without hostility carrying as he does destruction to the old worn-out truths, contemptuous of censure, still more contemptuous of praise, he goes his way against wind and tide. Brave man, given up to his cause, whatever it be, it is his joy *to stand alone*, watching the crowd as it races wherever reward is and danger is not. It is Bazarov's life to despise honours, success, opinion, and to let nothing, not love itself, come between him and his inevitable course, and, when death comes, to turn his face to the wall, while in the street below he can hear the voices of men cheering the popular hero who has last arrived. The Crowd! Bazarov is the antithesis of the cowardice of the Crowd. That is the secret why we love him.

III

As a piece of art *Fathers and Children is* the most powerful of all Turgenev's works. The figure of Bazarov is not only the political centre of the book, against which the other characters show up in their respective significance, but a figure in which the eternal tragedy of man's impotence and insignificance is realized in scenes of a most ironical human drama. How admirably this figure dominates everything and everybody. Everything falls away before this man's biting sincerity. In turn the figureheads of Culture and Birth, Nicolai and Pavel representing the Past; Arkady the sentimentalist representing the Present; the father and mother representing the ties of family that hinder a man's life-work; Madame Odintsov embodying the fascination of a beautiful woman—all fall into their respective places. But the particular power of *Fathers and Children*, of epic force almost, arises from the way in which Turgenev makes us feel the individual human tragedy of Bazarov in relation to the perpetual tragedy everywhere in indifferent Nature. In *On the Eve* Turgenev cast his figures against a poetic background by creating an atmosphere of War and Patriotism. But in *Fathers and Children* this poetic background is Nature herself, Nature who sows, with the same fling of her hand, life and death springing each from each, in the same rhythmical cast of fate. And with Nature for the background, there comes the wonderful sense conveyed to the reader throughout the novel, of the generations with their fresh vigorous blood passing away quickly, a sense of the coming generations, whose works, too, will be hurried away into the background, a sense of the silence of Earth, while her children disappear into the shadows, and are whelmed in turn by the inexorable night. While everything in the novel is expressed in the realistic terms of daily commonplace life, the characters appear now close to us as companions, and now they seem like distant figures walking under an immense sky; and the effect of Turgenev's simply and subtly drawn landscapes is to give us a glimpse of men and women in their actual relation to their mother earth and the sky over their heads. This effect is rarely conveyed in the modern Western novel, which deals so much with purely indoor life; but the Russian novelist gained artistic force for his tragedies by the vague sense ever present with him of the enormous distances of the vast steppes, bearing on their bosom the peasants' lives, which serve as a sombre background to the life of the isolated individual figures with which he is dealing. Turgenev has availed himself of this hidden note of tragedy, and with the greatest art he has made Bazarov, with all his ambition opening out before him, and his triumph awaited, the eternal type of man's conquering egoism conquered by the pin-prick of death. Bazarov, who looks neither to the right hand nor to the left, who delays no longer in his life-work of throwing off the mind-forged manacles; Bazarov, who trusts not to Nature, but would track the course of her most obscure laws; Bazarov, in his keen pursuit of knowledge, is laid low by the weapon he has selected to wield. His own tool, the dissecting knife, brings death to him, and his body is stretched beside the peasant who had gone before. Of the death scene, the great culmination of this great novel, it is impossible to speak without emotion. The voice of the reader, whosoever he be, must break when he comes to those passages of infinite pathos where the father, Vassily Ivanovitch, is seen peeping from behind the door at his dying son, where he cries, "Still living, my Yevgeny is still living, and now he will be saved. Wife, wife!" And where, when death has come, he cries, "I said I should rebel. I rebel, I rebel!" What art, what genius, we can only repeat, our spirit humbled to the dust by the exquisite solemnity of that undying simple scene of the old parents at the grave, the scene where Turgenev epitomizes in one stroke the infinite aspiration, the eternal insignificance of the life of man.

Let us end here with a repetition of a simple passage that, echoing through the last pages of *Fathers and Children*, must find an echo in the hearts of Turgenev's readers: " 'To the memory of Bazarov,' Katya whispered in her husband's ear, . . . but Arkady did not venture to propose the toast aloud." We, at all events, can drink the toast to-day as a poor tribute in recompense for those days when Turgenev in life proposed it, and his comrades looked on him with distrust, with coldness and with anger.

RICHARD FREEBORN

[The Structure of *Fathers and Sons*]†

* * * Turgenev has said that he was first prompted to write about a hero of the type of Bazarov by the example of a young provincial doctor of his acquaintance who had died, presumably, about the

† From Richard Freeborn, *Turgenev: The Novelist's Novelist*, London, 1960, pp. 68–74. Copyright 1960 by Oxford University Press.

Reprinted by permission of the Clarendon Press, Oxford.

year 1859. When he mentioned his intention to a friend whom he met on the Isle of Wight in August 1860, he was amazed to hear this gentleman reply: 'But surely you have already presented a similar type in—Rudin?' Turgenev adds: 'I was speechless: what was there to say? Rudin and Bazarov—one and the same type? . . . These words had such an effect on me that for several weeks I avoided all thought of the work on which I had embarked. . . . The gentleman's remark, however, is not so extraordinary as it may appear at first sight. It simply serves to underline the fact that Bazarov, like Rudin, was conceived as a hero designed to have more intellectual interest than Lavretsky, for instance, or Yelena. Like Rudin, he was intended to dominate the fiction, although— unlike the Rudin of the original version—he was conceived as a tragic figure whose tragedy would be climaxed by his death.[1]

Fathers and Children tells the story of Bazarov's return from the university in the company of his young friend, Arkady Kirsanov. They both stay for a while on the Kirsanovs' estate, where the contrast between the Fathers and the Children is initiated in the arguments between Pavel Petrovich Kirsanov and the hero, and later they visit the local town, where Bazarov meets the heroine, Odintsova. This meeting initiates the major love theme of the novel, but the action is by no means devoted exclusively to the development of it. Subsequently Bazarov visits his parents, spends a short while with them and then, to their understandable dismay, returns to the Kirsanovs' estate where the argument between Fathers and Children is concluded by the duel between him and Pavel Petrovich. Later Bazarov returns to his parents, where he decides to help his father, a retired army doctor, in his practice. Here he contracts typhus after performing an autopsy on a peasant killed by the disease and finally succumbs to it himself. As can be seen, there is more story content in *Fathers and Children* than in the previous novels, but this does not alter the fact that it is the characterization of the central figure which provides the interest of the fiction.

The objectivity of the work is remarkable on two counts. Firstly, in portraying Bazarov Turgenev has achieved a masterly portrait of a type—the type of the 'new man' of the sixties, the *raznochinets* intellectual or 'nihilist'—with whose political and social views he was manifestly out of sympathy. Secondly, the novel possesses an

---

1. Hjalmar Boyesen records Turgenev as saying (originally in 'A visit to Turgenev', *The Galaxy*, xvii (1874), 456–66: 'I was once out for a walk and thinking about death. . . . Immediately there rose before me the picture of a dying man. This was Bazarov. The scene produced a strong impression on me and as a consequence the other characters and the action itself began to take form in my mind.' Quoted from the Russian in 'K biografii I. S. Turgeneva', *Minuvshiye gody*, 1908, No. 8, p. 70. Turgenev writes to the same effect in his letter to Sluchevsky of April 1862.

organic unity, in which there are no narrative devices that obtrude into the fiction to distort, however slightly, the final impression of naturalness. This is not to say that *Fathers and Children* is merely a factual document or chronicle, unenlivened by the author's technique as an artist. It simply means that the technique has been perfected to the point where such devices as the use of commentator (in *Rudin* and *A Nest of the Gentry*) or devices such as diary extracts and letters (as in *On the Eve*) are no longer necessary in the delineation of character. The emphasis now falls squarely on the scenic, pictorial objectivity of the narrative and the artistic composition of the work, leaving the impression that the novel is 'telling itself', as it were, almost without the author's agency or participation.

In every respect this is more obviously 'a novel of ideas' than *On the Eve*, although the ideological independence of each minor character is linked, without being in any sense compromised or diminished, to the development of the central figure, Bazarov, in a more compelling manner than were Shubin and Bersenev to Yelena. This is due to the fact that in *Fathers and Children* the minor characters are not only spokesmen or embodiments of ideas or ideological attitudes, but they are also representatives of a particular social class with specific class attitudes; and Bazarov, opposed to them, is not only an opponent of their ideas, but a spokesman for a new, emergent social class which is to usurp the political and social authority of the older generation. In his previous novels Turgenev had not delineated class distinctions so clearly, but in *Fathers and Children* he carefully welds the social and political issues, the ideological and class attitudes, into the structure of his novel, creating a remarkable organic unity. The result is the most artistically perfect, structurally unified and ideologically compelling of Turgenev's novels.

Arkady Kirsanov and his father, Nikolay Petrovich Kirsanov, are introduced in detail to the reader at the very beginning of the novel. All the other characters—Pavel Petrovich Kirsanov, Odintsova, Bazarov's parents and such lesser characters as Fenichka (the peasant girl who has borne Nikolay Petrovich an illegitimate son), Kukshina and Sitnikov, the talkative representatives of the younger generation—are introduced into the fiction to the accompaniment of biographical and other information sufficient to explain their significance. The exception is again the unknown quantity, the hero, whose characterization is to provide the interest of the novel. Bazarov is not introduced to the reader by means of any biographical excerpt which might set his character in perspective; he is introduced, and his background lightly sketched in, by the remarks made about him by the other characters (particularly during the conversation between Arkady and Pavel Petrovich in Chapter V). While these remarks serve to provide information about Bazarov without which the reader might not be able to understand his significance for the fiction, they also serve to illustrate the contrasting nature of Bazarov, arising from his different social background. There are, of course, intimations in the fiction that Bazarov is 'different' from the other characters, but Turgenev does not rely on his omniscient position as author of the fiction to emphasize this 'difference'. On the contrary, he allows it to be made clear by the natural contrast that arises initially from the fact that Bazarov enters the fiction unexplained and by the more definite contrast which is provided through Bazarov's contact with the other characters.

Bazarov is further highlighted in the fiction by the fact that the novel is so constructed as to isolate him from the other characters. This is achieved by giving the other characters not only biographical backgrounds, or information sufficient to make their backgrounds comprehensible, but also specific 'places' in the fiction. Each character, with the exception of Bazarov, has his or her own 'place' or situation in the fiction: Nikolay, Arkady, Pavel—the poverty-stricken Mar'ino; Odintsova, Katya—the luxurious Nikol'skoye; the elderly Bazarovs—their humble estate; Sitnikov, Kukshina—the background of the town. With the exception of Bazarov and Arkady, all these characters remain in their own particular 'places' and are only comprehensible in relation to their 'places' (Odintsova and Sitnikov, admittedly, can be said to abandon their 'places' for short episodes—Odintsova to the town and to visit Bazarov on his death-bed, Sitnikov to Nikol'skoye (Chapter XIX)—but it is still true that they are only comprehensible in relation to their own 'places'). Moreover, each 'place' in the fiction and its occupants has the purpose of illuminating, by contrast, an aspect of the hero. Pavel Petrovich in Mar'ino illuminates the ideological aspect of Bazarov's significance for the fiction, the problem of the socio-political conflict between the generations; Sitnikov and Kukshina in the town illuminate the superiority of Bazarov by comparison with other members of the younger generation; Odintsova in Nikol'skoye illuminates the essential personality of the hero as a man, the duality in his nature; Bazarov's parents illuminate his egoism, the personal, as distinct from the ideological, barrier dividing the generations, and his individual insignificance as a human being, for their adoration of him is carefully offset by his own pessimistic musings on his destiny. Each 'place' in the fiction can therefore be seen as a stage in the process of the hero's characterization, and the stages are graded to elaborate and deepen the hero's portrait. Finally, Arkady ceases to play an active part in the fiction (after becoming involved in his love-story with Katya), and Bazarov is isolated as the central figure of the novel's action. In this way it can be seen that Turgenev emphasizes the tragedy of Bazarov's isolation, both as a social type and as a human being, by emphasizing his isolation within the fiction itself.

The process of characterization is also structurally integrated with the pattern of love-stories which, loosely speaking, supplies the plot of the novel and illustrates the ideological issues at stake. There are, in all, four different love-stories: (*a*) Nikolay-Fenichka; (*b*) Pavel-Fenichka, involving Bazarov; (*c*) Bazarov-Odintsova; (*d*) Arkady-Katya. All these love-stories express in one way or another an aspect of the conflict between the Fathers and the Children. The first love-story, between the land-owner and the peasant girl, implies at once the underlying social problem of the day: the relationship between land-owner and peasant on the eve of the Emancipation in 1861 (the action of the novel, it may be noted, occurs in 1859). The nature of this particular relationship between Nikolay and Fenichka also illustrates the moral failure of the older generation, of the Fathers, and it is a point at issue, in the early stage of the novel, between Nikolay and his son. The second love-story (it scarcely obtrudes as a love-story, but it must not be overlooked) is of considerably greater importance for the structure of the novel. So far as the external action of the novel is concerned, the fact that Pavel Petrovich sees Bazarov kissing Fenichka (Chapter XXIII) simply supplies him with grounds for challenging Bazarov to a duel. But the inner meaning of this episode must also be noted. The ideological conflict has already occurred (Chapters VI and X); the contrast with the members of the younger generation has been made (Chapters XII and XIII); the relationship with Odintsova has already been explored and has reached a climax (Chapters XV-XVIII), though it has not yet been abandoned; Bazarov's awareness of his own significance as a human being and his tragic destiny, despite the great future hoped for by his parents, has been made explicit in his conversation with Arkady on his parents' estate (Chapter XXI). Bazarov is now ready to reject the ideological and social precepts of the *dvoryanstvo*, the gentry; his desire to provoke a fight with Arkady in Chapter XXI foreshadows his readiness to accept the challenge that Pavel Petrovich offers him in Chapter XXIV. Yet the fact that they fight the duel ostensibly over Fenichka, the peasant girl, shows the way in which the ideological issues are welded into the structure of the novel. For Bazarov's readiness to fight the duel must be understood in the light of the fact that he is prepared not only to reject the *dvoryanstvo,* but also to devote his life to working for the peasants. His interest in Fenichka may be purely personal, but it is also given ideological significance. Similarly, Pavel Petrovich's readiness to offer the challenge must be understood in relation to the fact that for him Fenichka bears a resemblance to a certain Princess R. . . . out of passion for whom he had ruined his career and had been obliged to retire to the splendid isolation of Mar'ino (the predicament of the 'superfluous man' *par excellence*), and in relation to the fact that the crux of his earlier argument with Bazarov (Chapter X) had been the problem of the peasantry, whom he had claimed to understand better than Bazarov. His interest in Fenichka is also a mixture of the personal and the ideological. The subsequent duel represents the climax in the personal and ideological conflict between the two generations; and the defeat of Pavel Petrovich is not simply the defeat of the older generation by the younger, it is also the defeat of the gentry, the *dvoryanstvo,* by the new class of the *raznochintsy.*

The third love-story, between Odintsova and Bazarov, is clearly the most interesting, both because it concerns two people of widely differing social status and because it serves, like all the major love-stories in Turgenev's fiction, as a means of illustrating the differing personalities of the two characters. It is, however, Bazarov who emerges more successfully from this contrast. Odintsova is almost as passive a participant in the relationship as was Insarov in *On the Eve.* But, unlike the Yelena-Insarov relationship, the relationship between Odintsova and Bazarov does not absorb the whole of the fiction. There is no definite continuity to it and it is allowed to languish, in contrast to the fourth love-story, between Arkady and Katya, which is both the most conventional in the sense that it is between two young people of similar social status and the most conventional in the sense that it has a happy outcome.

It is in the different relationships involved in these love-stories that an enlargement of both structure and content in *Fathers and Children* as compared with the previous novels is to be discerned. In *Rudin,* for instance, there had been a suggestion of triangular form about the central love-story (Rudin-Natal'ya-Volyntsev), but the Rudin-Natal'ya relationship had been the most important relationship in the fiction, paralleled by the love-story between Lezhnyov and Aleksandra Lipina. In the relationship between Rudin and Natal'ya, however, there had been no explicit suggestion of social inequality, although Rudin was banished from Dar'ya Lasunskaya's house because he was not felt to be 'suitable' for her daughter; yet, despite his lack of rank, he was of the same class.

In *A Nest of the Gentry* the major love-story between Lavretsky and Liza had been connected with the Liza-Panshin, Liza-Lemm relationships, but these latter had had little bearing on the central theme of the novel. Similarly, although Lavretsky's social standing was compromised by the fact that his mother was of peasant extraction, in other points of genealogy he was Liza's social equal. In *On the Eve* Shubin and Bersenev had been united by similar feelings for Yelena, but the love-story between Yelena and Insarov had been quite independent of them. In the social sense, the inequality between Yelena and Insarov was partly camouflaged by the fact that he was given Bulgarian nationality, although Kurnatovsky was thought to be socially more. fitting for Yelena, and it can be seen that her parents' reaction to her marriage was one of shock not at the fact that Insarov was a Bulgarian but because he was of more modest social origins. In general, therefore, it can be said that in these three novels there had been a single love-story which was at the centre of the fiction and only in *On the Eve* did the relationship infer a marked social inequality. But in *Fathers and Children* there is a multiplication of love-stories in the structure of the novel, and all the love-stories, with the exception of the Arkady-Katya relationship, involve social inequalities. Inevitably this means that the novel embraces an enlarged view of Russian society, for all classes in Russian society are exemplified by this means: the gentry (*dvoryanstvo*), the new men (*raznochintsy*), and the peasantry. The single love-story in the earlier novels, standing at the centre of the fiction and absorbing the greater part of its interest, had not permitted such an enlarged view.

Yet, in structural terms, the main feature of *Fathers and Children* is the figure of Bazarov. The action of the novel hinges upon him almost exclusively. He is present in practically every scene of the novel, and it is his movement within the fiction that serves to link together the different 'places' or foci of interest which comprise the setting of the novel. Simultaneously, these 'places' and their occupants contribute, stage by stage, to the process of his characterization. A natural unity of form and content is thus achieved, which is the most striking development in Turgenev's exploration of the novel-form. The portrait of Bazarov that finally emerges from the novel is one that transcends all other issues in the fiction. Beginning on May 20th 1859, the action of the novel portrays Bazarov during approximately the last three or four months of his life. His portrait acquires finally a tragic grandeur, culminating in his death which is a moment unequalled in Turgenev's fiction. * * *

RUFUS W. MATHEWSON, JR.
[The Artist and His Relation to the Truth of His Work]†

* * * The crux of the dispute [between the liberal writers and the radical critics] is in the effort to locate the center of the creative process. For the liberals it is unquestionably fixed in the sovereign moral intelligence of the artist. For the radical it is elsewhere—in life which can always be invoked to challenge a novel's formal design, in ethical obligations which arise from the needs and suffering of the masses, or in a doctrinal truth which alone directs the writer to "the significant" in experience.

In asserting their independence from the views and aspirations of other men—above all from the tactical needs of an underground political movement—the artists were merely insisting on minimal conditions for the performance of their work, which they conceived as the discovery of the whole truth about human experience. "Truth," unadorned and without qualification, became a battle cry of the group. "My hero is truth," Tolstoy shouted at Sevastopol, refusing to falsify for patriotic purposes any of the human beings he observed there. Art's truth, Turgenev felt, was a special personal vision of experience to which the artist dedicated himself as to a holy mission. The critics simply did not understand the creative process:

> They do not imagine that enjoyment . . . which consists of punishing oneself for the shortcomings . . . in the people one invents; they are fully convinced that an author unfailingly creates only that which conducts his ideas, they do not want to believe that to reproduce powerfully and accurately the truth, the realness of life, is the greatest happiness for a writer even if this truth does not coincide with his own sympathies.[1]

Formal discipline is no end in itself—art is not a game—but a means to this greater end. Political truth is not false but "one-sided," simply one aspect of the totality of man's experience. The goal is the rendering, compactly but completely, of the whole of

---

† From Rufus W. Mathewson, *The Positive Hero in Russian Literature*, New York, 1958, pp. 111–17, 135–36. Copyright 1958 by Columbia University Press. Reprinted by permission of the publishers, Columbia University Press. The title for this section of a chapter entitled "Rebuttal I" is provided from a preceding section.
1. From Chapter 5, "A propos de *Fathers and Sons*," in his *Literary Reminiscences* dated 1868–80 (*Polnoe sobranie schinenii* [St. Petersburg, 1913], X, 104).

the human condition as one's characters share it. The writer does not address himself to the "significant" truth or to the useful truth or to the probable truth, but to the whole of its gnarled and knotty substance. Chekhov, the last and often the most perceptive spokesman for the writers, makes it clear that no limitation within the writer's awareness must be allowed to infringe on the fidelity of his image. Since it is in the artist's mind that order and meaning are discovered in experience, he must clearly be independent (though not necessarily unaware) of the imperatives derived from other disciplines, if he is to meet this challenging and exhausting standard of "absolute and honest truth."

In a sense the writers' claim to autonomy is based on the notion that the act of creation is in itself an act of discovery. Art maintains its own outposts on the frontiers of experience, conducts its own explorations according to its own rules, and presents its findings to the public without referral to any authority outside the writer's conscience. Art bears comparison in this connection with a scientific experiment. Lionel Trilling has compared the fabricated world of the work of art—Marianne Moore's "imaginary garden" —with the artificial situation of the experiment, "which is devised to force or foster a fact into being." [2] Both wings of Russian realism accepted some such view of the creative process. But there is a significant difference between them on this point. It is not that either group really rigged the experiment or allowed the unrestricted play of the experimenter's subjectivity. The distinction is rather to be found in differing stands of selectivity regulating the amount and kinds of data to be taken under consideration. The liberal in spite of his prejudices and pedispositions seemed always inclined to permit more data—in terms of variety of character and situation—as raw material to be tested in his experiment. The radical favored smaller amounts with a larger share pretested by other disciplines. To the extent that this was so, the outcome always tended to be predetermined in this kind of fiction, as Chernyshevsky's novel clearly indicated.

The writer's effort to remain true to the logic of the data, and to organize them without damage or distortion, gave rise more than once to the peculiar situation in which the writer struggled desperately, and sometimes unsuccessfully, to control the outcome of his story, and asked in bewilderment what had gone wrong when he failed. Gogol's Chichikov (*Dead Souls*), Tolstoy's Levin (*Anna Karenina*), Dostoevsky's Myshkin (*The Idiot*)—all represent intentions unfulfilled. It may be argued that Raskolnikov's questionable conversion violates the logic of the data, and the writer's

---

2. Lionel Trilling, "Introduction," in James, *The Princess Casamassima*, I, xiv.

better judgment, too, as it is revealed in his working notes for the novel's conclusions: "Raskolnikov goes to shoot himself."[3] Ivan Karamazov's state of suspension, far from fulfillment but as far from defeat, does not express the author's explicit beliefs as we know them to be. In all these cases the writer has created someone as strong and assertive as himself, with an independent identity and destiny. Turgenev is painfully honest and frankly at sea about his relation to Bazarov. True to his precept: to present "the whole of the living human face," he found himself unable to say, after he had done so, that Bazarov was the creature of his hopes, or even whether "I love him or hate him."[4] Working out of this ambivalence, Turgenev endowed Bazarov with a striking combination of good and bad qualities: he has in his make-up "coarseness," "heartlessness," "ruthless dryness and sharpness," yet he is "strong," "honorable, just, and a democrat to the tip of his toes." These, at least, are some of the qualities Turgenev discovered in him after the fact. But they were not the result of a calculated balancing of vices and virtues during the act of creation itself. At that moment his governing intention was to exclude arbitrary manipulation and to submit to the logic of his invention. He has described his curious feeling of helplessness before his creation:

> It seems that an author himself does not know what he is creating; my feelings for Bazarov—my personal feelings—were of a confused nature (whether I loved him or hated him, the Lord knows!), nevertheless the image came out so defined that he immediately stepped into life and started to act in his own particular way. In the end what does it matter what a writer thinks of his work. It is a thing in itself and he is a thing in himself.[5]

Turgenev would have been a happier man if he had really believed in the separate existences of author and hero. He was never able to disclaim responsibility for Bazarov entirely, but he achieved a degree of detachment that enabled him to penetrate to the real reasons for the clamorous and discordant reception of "his favorite child." The danger lay in his own ambiguity:

> If the writer's attitude toward his characters is not defined . . . if the author himself doesn't know whether he loves the character he has set forth . . . then it is thoroughly bad. The reader is prepared to attach to the author imaginary sympathies or imaginary antipathies, if only to escape from the unpleasant "uncertainty."[6]

3. F. M. Dostoevsky, *Iz arkhiva F. M. Dostoevskogo. Prestuplenie i nakazanie: neizdannye materialy* ed. I. I. Glivenko (Moscow-Leningrad, 1931), p. 216.

4. Letter to A. A. Fet, dated April 6/18, 1862.
5. Letter to I. P. Borisov, January 5, 1870.
6. From the *Literary Reminiscences* in *Polnoe sobranie sochinenii*, X, 106.

Fathers and Sons fell, as Turgenev put it, "like oil on the fire." [7] In this superheated time readers "read through" the novel and groped for direct, immediate identification with the life around them. There was neither the leisure nor the tolerance to honor his real purpose as he explained it to Dostoevsky: "Nobody, it seems, suspects that I tried to present . . . a tragic figure—and everybody comments: why is he so sinister? or why is he so good?" [8]

Turgenev was a victim of the partisan view of truth held by the political extremists on both sides, a view impatient of paradox or ambiguity, hence unwilling to accept the complexity or the contradictions of tragedy. In the radicals' universe allowance was made for obstacles and setbacks but not for doubt or bewilderment. They felt that much larger sectors of the available truth were known than the liberal writers believed. And, in any case, important new discoveries would not, in all likelihood, be made by freely ranging writer-explorers. The writer, in the radical prescription, was expected to deal far more with the given—to illustrate the known, not to seek the unknown. Behind the words "typical," "healthy," "progressive," and "necessary" lay the certainty that such words had fixed and exclusive definitions, and, still further in the background, the implication that these definitions, constituting the essential truth, must be accepted by—or even imposed on—writers.

In deciding what truth is for the writer, certain judgments must be made about what aspects of the truth of human life or what moments in man's life cycle are of greatest fictional interest. For the great Russian novelists ideas and doctrine were not excluded, but were contained in character, and made a function of the whole man. The truth of fiction for them embraced all varieties of love, friendship, and hatred, had as its permanent backdrop the perspective of growth, decay, and death, and, because of the artist's elevation above, and independence from, his characters, included the human facts of fallibility, error, and failure. The radicals, on the other hand, were interested in ideological man. In their view of literary truth—and undoubtedly in their own private moral code—character was a function of doctrine, and men generally were most "interesting" when seen in active response to their social situation. Against the liberal creed of knowledge of life for its own sake whatever the consequences, the radicals opposed an ideology, a body of organized knowledge designed to affect men's future social behavior in a specific way. Since the doctrine was known to be valid, its spokesmen in art could not be permitted to fail, or if they did, for personal reasons, they became simply uninteresting or untypical in the radicals' special use of those words. For the

7. Letter to P. V. Annenkov, June 8, 1862.   8. Letter to F. M. Dostoevsky, April 22, 1862.

liberal with his eye focused on the individual in all his observable relations with life, this doctrinal view of man was, as Tolstoy put it, "one-sided." Turgenev was undoubtedly reacting against this view when he enjoined young writers to steer clear of any and all "dogma." Also, since an ideological view of the world involved a calculation about the future, literary truth for the radicals must contain that diagram of what is to come, as they discerned it in present events. According to the canons of realism, the future, seen either as the inevitable or as the desirable, must remain an unknown. Possibilities might be stated, but any effort to force character into one of these possibilities had unhappy results, as we have seen in the case of Chichikov, Raskolnikov, Levin, and others. * * *

* * * Turgenev, whose indictment of the radical is far gentler than his friend Herzen's, had, nevertheless, to acknowledge the presence of a towering arrogance in the radical type.[9] In Bazarov this quality provides the outlet for his admirable courage and energy and is, at the same time, a crippling malformation of his character. When his doctrinal supports have been worn away and shown to be inadequate, Bazarov lapses fleetingly into Nietzschean image of himself as a kind of superman, before he collapses under the weight of his swollen ego.[1] When charged with falsification and slander on this point, Turgenev looked beyond Herzen's concrete explanations and sought to explain it in general, psychological terms:

> What kind of artist would I be (I don't say man) if I did not understand that self confidence, exaggeration of expression . . . and posing, even a certain cynicism, constitute inevitable attributes of youth.[2]

IRVING HOWE
Turgenev: The Politics of Hesitation†

* * * If Rudin has partly been created in Turgenev's own image, Bazarov, the hero of *Fathers and Sons*, is a figure in opposition to

9. Even Chernyshevsky acknowledges this. But with Rakhmetov, his self-assurance and his abruptness in personal relations are seen as a refreshingly direct and time-saving manner which all his friends understand and appreciate. [Rakhmetov is the hero of Chernyshevsky's novel *What Is To Be Done? Editor*].
1. Turgenev makes it clear in a letter to K. K. Sluchevski that the slip of a knife that kills

Bazarov is not an accident but part of a coherent tragic design (Letter of April 14/26, 1862).
2. Letter to A. P. Filosofov, August 18/30, 1874.
† From Irving Howe, *Politics and the Novel*, New York, 1957, pp. 129–33. Copyright 1957 by Irving Howe. Reprinted by permission of the publishers, Horizon Press, Inc.

that image. The one rambles idealistic poetry, the other grumbles his faith in the dissection of frogs; the one is all too obviously weak, the other seems spectacularly strong. Yet between the two there is a parallel of social position. Both stand outside the manor-house that is Russia, peering in through a window; Rudin makes speeches and Bazarov would like to throw stones but no one pays attention, no one is disturbed. They together might, like Dostoevsky's Shatov and Kirillov, [in *The Possessed*] come to a whole man; but they are not together, they alternate in Russian life, as in Russian literature, each testifying to the social impotence that has made the other possible.

Like all of Turgenev's superfluous men, Bazarov is essentially good. Among our more cultivated critics, those who insist that the heroes of novels be as high-minded as themselves, it has been fashionable to look with contempt upon Bazarov's nihilism, to see him as a specimen of Russian boorishness. Such a reading is not merely imperceptive, it is humorless. Would it really be better if Bazarov, instead of devoting himself to frogs and viscera, were to proclaim about Poetry and the Soul? Would it be better if he were a metaphysician juggling the shells of Matter and Mind instead of a coarse materialist talking nonsense about the irrelevance of Pushkin?

For all that Bazarov's nihilism accurately reflects a phase of Russian and European history, it must be taken more as a symptom of political desperation than as a formal intellectual system. Bazarov is a man ready for life, and cannot find it. Bazarov is a man of the most intense emotions, but without confidence in his capacity to realize them. Bazarov is a revolutionary personality, but without revolutionary ideas or commitments. He is all potentiality and no possibility. The more his ideas seem outmoded, the more does he himself seem our contemporary.

No wonder Bazarov feels so desperate a need to be rude. There are times when society is so impervious to the kicks of criticism, when intellectual life softens so completely into the blur of gentility, that the rebellious man, who can tolerate everything but not being taken seriously, has no alternative to rudeness. How else is Bazarov to pierce the elegant composure of Pavel Petrovich, a typically "enlightened" member of the previous generation who combines the manners of a Parisian litterateur with an income derived from the labor of serfs. Bazarov does not really succeed, for Pavel Petrovich forces him to a duel, a romantic ceremony that is the very opposite of everything in which Bazarov believes. During the course of the duel, it is true, Pavel Petrovich must yield to Bazarov, but the mere fact that it takes place is a triumph for the old, not the new. Bazarov may regard Pavel

Petrovich as an "archaic phenomenon," but the "archaic phenomenon" retains social power.

The formal components of Bazarov's nihilism are neither unfamiliar nor remarkable: 19th century scientism, utilitarianism, a crude materialism, a rejection of the esthetic, a belief in the powers of the free individual, a straining for tough-mindedness and a deliberate provocative rudeness. These ideas and attitudes can gain point only if Bazarov brings them to political coherence, and the book charts Bazarov's journey, as an uprooted plebeian, in search of a means of expression, a task, an obligation. On the face of it, Bazarov's ideas have little to do with politics, yet he is acute enough to think of them in political terms; he recognizes that they are functions of his frustrated political passion. "Your sort," he says to his mild young friend Arkady, "can never get beyond refined submission or refined indignation, and that's no good. You won't fight—and yet you fancy yourselves gallant chaps—but we mean to fight . . . We want to smash other people! You're a capital fellow; but you're a sugary liberal snob for all that . . ." This is the language of politics; it might almost be Lenin talking to a liberal parliamentarian. But even as Bazarov wants to "smash other people" he senses his own helplessness: he has no weapons for smashing anything. "A harmless person," he calls himself, and a little later, "A tame cat."

In the society of his day, as Turgenev fills it in with a few quick strokes, Bazarov is as superfluous as Rudin. His young disciple Arkady cannot keep pace with him; Arkady will marry, have a houseful of children and remember to be decent to his peasants. The older generation does not understand Bazarov and for that very reason fears him: Arkady's father, a soft slothful landowner, is acute enough, however, to remark that Bazarov is different: he has "fewer traces of the slaveowner." Bazarov's brief meeting with the radicals is a fine bit of horseplay, their emptyheaded chatter being matched only by his declaration, as preposterous as it is pathetic: "I don't adopt anyone's ideas; I have my own." At which one of them, in a transport of defiance, shouts: "Down with all authorities!" and Bazarov realizes that among a pack of fools it is hard not to play the fool. He is tempted, finally, by Madame Odintzov, the country-house Delilah; suddenly he finds his awkward callow tongue, admitting to her his inability to speak freely of everything in his heart. But again he is rejected, and humiliated too, almost like a servant who has been used by his mistress and then sent packing. Nothing remains but to go home, to his good sweet uncomprehending mother and father, those remnants of old Russia; and to die.

Turgenev himself saw Bazarov in his political aspect:

> If he [Bazarov] calls himself a nihilist, one ought to read—
> a revolutionary . . . I dreamed of a figure that should be gloomy,
> wild, great, growing one half of him out of the soil, strong,
> angry, honorable, and yet doomed to destruction—because as
> yet he still stands on the threshold of the future. I dreamed of a
> strange parallel to Pugatchev. And my young contemporaries
> shake their heads and tell me, "You have insulted us . . . It's a
> pity you haven't worked him out a little more.' There is nothing
> left for me but, in the words of the gipsy song, "to take off my
> hat with a very low bow."

Seldom has a writer given a better cue to the meaning of his
work, and most of all in the comparison between Bazarov and
Pugatchev, the leader of an 18th century peasant rebellion who
was hanged by a Tzar. Pugatchev, however, had his peasant fol-
lowers, while Bazarov . . . what is Bazarov but a Pugatchev without the peasants?

It is at the end of *Fathers and Sons* that Turgenev reaches his
highest point as an artist. The last twenty-five pages are of an
incomparable elevation and intensity, worthy of Tolstoy and Dostoevsky, and in some respects, particularly in their blend of tragic
power and a mute underlying sweetness, superior to them. When
Bazarov, writhing in delirium, cries out, "Take ten from eight,
what's left over?" we are close to the lucidity of Lear in the
night. It is the lucidity of final self-confrontation, Bazarov's lament
over his lost, his unused powers: "I was needed by Russia . . .
No, it's clear, I wasn't needed . . ." Nothing so thoroughly under-
cuts his earlier protestations of self-sufficiency as this last outcry.

This ending too has failed to satisfy many critics, even one
so perceptive as Prince Mirsky, who complains that there is something arbitrary in Bazarov's death. But given Russia, given Bazarov, how else *could* the novel end? Too strong to survive in
Russia, what else is possible to Bazarov but death? The accident of
fate that kills him comes only after he has been defeated in every
possible social and personal encounter; it is the summation of those
encounters. The "arbitrariness" of Bazarov's death comes as a bitterly
ironic turning of his own expectations. Lying lonely and ignored in
a corner of Russia, this man who was to change and destroy everything ends in pitiful helplessness. Political and not political, the
ending is the only one that was available to Turgenev at the time
he wrote.

JAMES H. JUSTUS

Fathers and Sons: The Novel as Idyll†

One of the most striking successes of *Fathers and Sons* is not its rather reluctant political statement, which at best reveals the division of Turgenev's mind, but the unambiguous theme of the "goodness" of nature. In a day when the concept has become philosophically banal, this achievement is all the more remarkable. However positively Bazarov preaches his nihilism, however influentially he sways disciples, however rabidly he hints of the Advent, he remains a powerless, unused talent. Arguing that he remains so because "the time is not yet at hand" is to beg the question. Moreover, Turgenev drops sufficient clues to suggest that Bazarov's fault is not in the "when" of Russia's destiny but in the "how" of his own nature.

By the time he seeks out Anna Sergyevna, observing what a "tame cat" he is becoming, the threat (or promise) of any significant influence he may have on society at large is passed; and with that passing goes the political interest Bazarov may have whipped up earlier in the reader. Yet structurally the novel gains, not loses, interest after this climax at Nikolskoe. Obviously, Turgenev's story of a young revolutionary is concerned with a more comprehensive and at the same time more personal rebellion than that which a single-dimensioned political reading can give. What we face is nothing less than the very life, the focus, of the novel: the search for self-definition.

That which sets in relief the world view of the Fathers and records, both explicitly and implicitly, the progress of the world view of the Sons is external nature, a symbolic system observable in the varying degrees to which the two opposing world views conflict and reconcile. To see nature serving a more artistic purpose than mere scene-painting is not to deny the politics in the novel; rather, the methods by which Turgenev uses nature (particularly the suggestion of the mystic "Mother Russia" or "native soil" idea) enhance the tragedy which he foresees—the loss of communication between the generations and the ultimate rupture in revolution.

Throughout *Fathers and Sons* there is greater emphasis on the conflict between generations than between bourgeoisie and proletariat. Conflict of the latter type, inevitable though it is, is

† From *Western Humanities Review*, XV (1961), 259–65. Reprinted by permission of James H. Justus and the editors.

less explicit, that is, it has less ideological affection, sorrow, or even concern for the peasant who will be caught up in it than, say, Conrad's *Under Western Eyes* or even James's *Princess Casamassima*. In Turgenev's novel the hurt is both something less and something more—families dissolved by ideological postulates. Intellectually powerful as the political issues are, they are vapid compared with the moral-emotional episodes in the homes of the Fathers. These scenes are memorable not because of their vigor—as Dostoyevsky's memorable scenes are apt to be—but because of quiet, undertoned pathos. And much of this pathos is created by the repetitive use of nature symbols.

Superficially the great world of nature is associated with the Fathers, the guardians and lovers of the land, which includes the recognizable objects of an agrarian society: aspens, swallows, bees, lilac blossoms, gardens of roses, sunsets. This is the natural milieu of both Arkady and Bazarov, an environment from which they have wrenched themselves but to which they return. Though it is a harsh land with its satisfactions dearly earned, it is also a gentle land, which supports a society of individuals who show mutual respect and love and abide by the canons of traditional manners and faith.

Almost mournfully Turgenev seems to permit the naturalistic, scientific Sons to better their Fathers in argument and in their vision of a new Russia—mournfully because his heart-felt sympathy is attached to the dying class in spite of its "vanity, dandy habits, fatuity . . . perpetual talk . . . about art, unconscious creativeness, parliamentarism, trial by jury" and its sometimes hollow adherence to the principle of man's dignity.

Perhaps the single most affecting scene occurs immediately after the explosive dinner argument between Bazarov and Pavel Petrovitch. After the arrogant young nihilist challenges Pavel to take two days to think of an institution that "does not call for complete and unqualified destruction," Nikolai, overtaken by melancholy, retires in the dying day to his favorite arbor to reflect on the chasm that separates him from his son. Not even the violence of Bazarov's gibes when they are pertinent nor the shallow discipleship of Arkady when it is most excusable can overshadow the dramatic force of this scene in which Nikolai comprehends the nature of the tension. He wants to agree with his son and up to a point applauds his world view:

> . . . I feel there is something behind them we have not got, some superiority over us. . . . Is it youth? No; not only youth. Doesn't their superiority consist in there being fewer traces of the slave-owner in them than in us?

But how far must he go to bridge the widening chasm? He is already known as a "Red Radical" over the province for his soft policies toward the peasants; he reads and studies, trying to keep abreast of developments. But all this is not enough. His methods smack of reform, when the young men have little patience with anything short of revolution.

But even the image of revolution, of sheer energy unleashed, is not so hateful to Nikolai as the Sons' underlying assumption that a chemist is "twenty times as useful as any poet," a materialism that ignores and even denounces the values of poetry, art, and nature:

> And he looked round, as though trying to understand how it was possible to have no feeling for nature. . . . The sun's rays from the farther side fell full on the copse, and piercing through its thickets, threw such a warm light on the aspen trunks that they looked like pines, and their leaves were almost a dark blue, while above them rose a pale blue sky, faintly tinged by the glow of sunset. . . . "How beautiful, my God!" thought Nikolai Petrovitch, and his favorite verses were almost on his lips . . . but still he sat there, still he gave himself up to the sorrowful consolation of solitary thought. He was fond of dreaming; his country life had developed the tendency in him.

Here is more than scene-painting. Couched in even more religious terms than the references to religion itself, this episode is Turgenev's most explicit use of nature as a symbolic system embodying the deepest values of the Fathers. Despite the depressing presence of streams with hollow banks, hovels with tumble-down roofs, barns with gaping doorways and neglected threshing-floors, and tattered peasants, these values are stubbornly insisted on and equated with the Fathers' native soil. At such times the scenes take on an almost sacramental cast.

Vassily Ivanovitch, even though a provincial doctor, is also identified with the Russian soil and landscape. He reads authorities in order to keep up with advances in healing, and though he understands the fad of discarding idols for more advanced ones, he cannot understand his son's concept of laughing at medicine altogether. With obvious relief he turns to Bazarov's comment on the growth of his birch trees.

> "And you must see what a little garden I've got now! I planted every tree myself. I've fruit, and raspberries, and all kinds of medicinal herbs."

After tea Vassily takes them to his garden "to admire the beauty of the evening" and whispers to Arkady,

"At this spot I love to meditate, as I watch the sunset; it suits a recluse like me. And there, a little farther off, I have planted some of the trees beloved of Horace."

This initial impression of Bazarov's father is reinforced time and time again; Arkady sees him garbed in an Oriental dressing gown industriously digging in the garden, regaling his visitor with his plans for late turnips, and citing Rousseau's philosophy of the necessity for man's obtaining "his sustenance with his own hands." And later, when he unknowingly interrupts a hostile fight between Arkady and Bazarov in the shade of a haystack, he can see only a Castor-and-Pollux pair "excellently employed," with a special "significance" in their lying on the earth and gazing up to heaven.

II

But the Fathers' orientation to the natural world, a source of both their strength and inefficacy, does not constitute a simple opposition to the crude scientism and anti-esthetic pragmatism of the Sons. Ultimately the Sons' ideology is fuzzy and narrow, separated as it is from the deceptively simple agrarian world view. Paradoxically, it is this simple orientation that proves multidimensional, capable of absorbing both Bazarov's aggressive and Arkady's passive revolutionary airs. Both Sons consistently underrate their Fathers' world. Bazarov cannot channel his arrogance, rudeness, and frustration into political coherence (Arkady hardly tries) and so cannot overcome the settled, all-encompassing, and pervading social coherence of the Fathers. With considerable skill Turgenev traces the Sons' progress from the stages of rebellion against this social coherence to at least a partial reconciliation with it, and his methods are enhanced by the framework of nature which gives authority to this agrarian world view. Significant or not, the Sons' references to objects of nature outnumber those of the Fathers. Some are, of course, openly negative: a flourishing denial of the symbols means a denial of the entire system, which must be destroyed and built anew, presumably in an image yet to be found. On the night before the duel Bazarov has a dream in which Pavel Petrovitch takes "the shape of a great wood, with which he had yet to fight." And the same dark image recurs on his deathbed, where after his fitful siege of self-confronting, he sees the final struggle: "There's a forest here. . . ."

But the negative responses to nature—or those which take the form of "disordered dreams"—are surely no less indicative of the massive strength of the Fathers' world (and indeed of the Sons' unconscious involvement in it) than the more obvious garden scenes with the Fathers. The battle lines are not simply Sons versus Fathers but, more importantly, Sons versus Themselves. They possess too much of their Fathers' world to dismiss it successfully, even though it is a dying world, for to dismiss it outright is to deny themselves the self-definition they both crave. It is this tension that ideologically tilts the outcome to the Fathers and dramatically signifies Turgenev's theme. Without this inner tension, the story would be simply another tale of young ideals clashing against old ones. As it is, this novel is essentially a modification of the traditional story of the young hero who sets out in search of his fortune, which (according to Lionel Trilling in his essay on *The Princess Casamassima*) is "What the folktale says when it means that the hero is seeking himself." In *Fathers and Sons* it is a painful progress, and the opposing forces are not a series of physical obstacles but the ponderous irrationality of an entire social system. The irony in such a modern modification is that this society into which Arkady and Bazarov are plunged is not new to their experience. They have not only been there before; it is part of themselves. In one sense of their return, they do battle with themselves to attain a fully satisfactory self-definition.

Arkady, prone as he is to accept all premises and conclusions of Bazarov, still permits himself to recognize the symbols of the land; and in spite of that land's "endless, comfortless winter, with its storms, and frosts, and snows," he feels swayed by a familiar spring:

> All around was golden green, all—trees, bushes, grass—shone and stirred gently in wide waves under the soft breath of the warm wind; from all sides flooded the endless trilling music of the larks; . . . the rooks strutted among the half-grown short spring-corn . . . only from time to time their heads peeped out amid its grey waves.

This is the natural attraction of the land—dramatically juxtaposed against Arkady's own denial that it is his birthplace which creates this special feeling. (In the same connection he can exclaim: "What air . . . ! How delicious it smells! Really I fancy there's nowhere such fragrance . . . !") Later, countering Bazarov's declaration that "two and two make four, and the rest is all foolery," Arkady asks, "And is nature foolery?" and notes the "bright-colored fields in the distance, in the beautiful soft light of the sun. . . ."

III

Once back under the family roof, influence of the old order increases as Bazarov's declines. Finally, as a gesture, he offers to help his father with the difficult problems of the farm; doubtless the involvement would have been deeper immediately but for his preoccupation with Katya. At Nikolskoe the major scenes occur out-of-doors, primarily in various parts of the garden. Here under ash trees he and Katya feed sparrows and relax into a "confidential intimacy" where they admit that Bazarov's influence on them and Anna has passed. In the same garden but hidden "in the very thickest part," he loses himself in meditation and "at once wondering and rejoicing" he resolves to marry Katya. It is a significant scene, for it constitutes his final break with what is essentially an alien spirit; his alliance with Katya ushers in a domestic period of acceptance. It discards revolution, but not reform.

Bazarov, on the other hand, is the strong character but simultaneously the most decisively divided. His pastime is natural history, psychologically a more acceptable deference to the old order than the more esthetic, wasteful nature-observing of the others. His frog-cutting contributes to his scientific-medical knowledge. Only occasionally he permits himself observations, and then often from a pragmatic impulse. He explains to Arkady that poplars and spruce firs do better than oaks. To assure Anna that studying a single human specimen is enough to judge the entire race he makes an analogy quite in character: "People are like trees in a forest; no botanist would think of studying each individual birch-tree." His walks more often take him to the forest, and he naps regularly in the barn's hayloft. And in a rare self-revealing speech to Arkady he says:

> "That aspen-tree . . . reminds me of my childhood; it grows at the edge of the clay-pits where the bricks were dug, and in those days I believed firmly that that clay-pit and aspen-tree possessed a peculiar talismanic power; I never felt dull near them. I did not understand then that I was not dull, because I was a child. Well, now I'm grown up, the talisman's lost its power."

Unusually loquacious, Bazarov broods on his "loathsome pettiness." Contrasting himself to his parents, who "don't trouble themselves about their own nothingness; it doesn't sicken them," he mutters: "I feel nothing but weariness and anger." Part of his frustration derives from his unfortunate, unrealized love for Anna, and in self-pity he advises an ant dragging off a half-dead fly,

> "Take her, brother, take her! Don't pay attention to her resistance; it's your privilege as an animal to be free from the sentiment of pity—make the most of it—not like us conscientious self-destructive animals!"

His conversation with Fenichka, which culminates in their kissing, takes place in the lilac arbor; and the duel which Pavel instigates as a result of it occurs at dawn on a fresh morning, when the most salient part of the picture is the singing of the larks. Hearing of Arkady's coming marriage, he calls his friend a jackdaw, "a most respectable family bird," and later advises him with more gravity:

> "And you get married as soon as you can; and build your nest, and get children to your heart's content. They'll have the wit to be born in a better time than you and me."

Despite Bazarov's death-bed pledge to himself and to Anna ("Never mind; I'm not going to turn tail"), he realizes that any number of men are more important to Russia than he. He solves his last problem of "how to die decently," but Turgenev makes it clear that the giant succumbs in the end to the same natural processes as the pygmy Fathers and in fact on the Fathers' own terms. However wretched the graveyard with its rotting wooden crosses and scrubby shade trees, birds perch on Bazarov's tomb and sing while his parents pray. And conventional as Turgenev's personal conclusion to the tale may be, it underscores the rebellious principle quite apart from political considerations. Here is one whose self was not only divided but at war and whose reconciliation and submission to the basic pattern, the natural life, come inexorably:

> However passionate, sinning, and rebellious the heart hidden in the tomb, the flowers growing over it peep serenely at us with their innocent eyes; they tell us not of eternal peace alone, of that great peace of "indifferent" nature; they tell us, too, of eternal reconciliation and of life without end.

It is not correct to say that Bazarov's reconciliation is entirely unsought, a matter of physical necessity. Long before his death he deliberately returns, giving up dissection of frogs for the healing of humans, pleasing his parents in his perverse manner, and indulging them in their "toys," which are part of the old order.

That Turgenev as a conscious craftsman intends his novel to bear its theme partly through external nature as a referent can be deduced from his many pertinent allusions to Rousseau, Emerson, Pushkin, and even Fenimore Cooper's Natty Bumpo. But, more important, he communicates the stature of Nikolai and Vassily through identification with the land that can produce stability, affection, and even growth, as well as tradition-bound inadequacies in social and political matters. For Arkady and Bazarov, their radical notions at first dispossess them from such a heritage; but despite this open rejection, the reader can follow consistently their alliance to it through a patterned thematic thread of nature references, an alliance that the two characters recognize and admit only sporadically. The movement is reunion with and reconciliation to the mainstream of humanity, and with all its faults, that mainstream is the world of the Fathers.

P. G. PUSTOVOYT

Some Features of Composition in *Fathers and Sons*†

Dialogue plays so large a role in Turgenev's novels that it would be incorrect to consider it simply as a technical device of the writer's. The increasing role of dialogue is determined by the themes and the intellectual content of his works. In general, dialogue is the most appropriate form in the sociological novel to raise philosophical arguments on the large questions preoccupying the author's contemporary society. It makes it possible to develop actual political problems, and to cast light on them from various points of view. Finally, in dialogue characters are disclosed and discovered and appear as active agents and participants in ideological conflict.

In the novel *Fathers and Sons* dialogues are above all passionate political and philosophical arguments. Unlike his opponents, Bazarov is brief and lapidary in arguments. He does not conquer and overwhelm his opponents through long arguments and philosophical tirades as Rudin did but in laconic, pregnant replies, apt, full of meaning, appropriately expressed in aphorisms. Bazarov does not attempt to speak beautifully, he does not try "to pin down words like butterflies." And yet Bazarov emerges the victor in almost all the arguments, since his replies, thrown off almost as if in passing, are jammed full of profound thoughts and testify to the hero's colossal erudition, his knowledge of life, his resourcefulness and cleverness. Bazarov's replies may be turned into a complete system of opinions. A definite democratic scheme underlies every reply. For example, the replies "peasants are glad to rob even themselves to get dead drunk at the pot-house" or "when it thunders

† From P. G. Pustovoyt, *Roman I. S. Turgeneva "Ottsy i deti" i ideynaya bor'ba 60–x godov XIX veka*, Moscow, 1960, pp. 224–39. Translated by Ralph E. Matlaw. Much of the enormous literature on Turgenev in the Soviet Union rehashes the political and intellectual background. A smaller body of work deals with Turgenev's style and methods. This essay has been chosen as representative of the quality and tenor of Soviet criticism of *Fathers and Sons*.

the common folk think Elijah the Prophet is riding through the heavens in a chariot" clearly express the educational plans formulated in Chernyshevsky's and Dobrolyubov's articles in *The Contemporary* at the end of the 1850's, and embodied in many of N. Uspensky's stories about common folk, which usually appeared in the opening pages of that periodical. Bazarov's reply "The art of making money or 'Shrink Hemorrhoids' " has been explained by N. K. Brodsky as a reference by Bazarov for polemical purposes to two works by a writer of the 1860's, I. T. Kokorev, reviewed by Chernyshevsky and Dobrolyubov. It is easy to prove that the main hero's other replies ("Raphael isn't worth a plugged nickel," "a good chemist is twenty times more useful than any poet") are based on the rich real material of the epoch.

In order to make Bazarov's speech in the dialogues broad and to make it express the hero's ideas in concentrated form, Turgenev makes Bazarov use proverbs and sayings, idiomatic expressions, and other forms of phraseology more frequently than other characters ("a scalded cat fears cold water," "that's not the whole story," "as the ale is drawn it must be drunk"). And yet it would be incorrect to consider the aphoristic and idiomatic quality of Bazarov's speech in argumentation as its only characteristic feature. Turgenev endowed his main hero with the capacity for oratorical speech in addition to these very real and characteristic marks of Bazarov's speech, which reveal in him the genuine democrat who tries to make himself understood by common folk. Thus, in Chapter Ten of the novel, in the argument with Pavel Petrovich, Bazarov does not limit himself to the brief and devastatingly apt replies ("We've heard that song a good many times," that is, he criticizes Pavel Petrovich's discussion of the English aristocracy; or "The ground has to be cleared first"), but he also delivers a fairly long critical tirade against liberal phrasemongering:

> Then we figured out that talk, perpetual talk, and nothing but talk about our social sores was not worthwhile, that it all led to nothing but banality and doctrinairism. We saw that even our clever ones, so-called advanced people and accusers, were no good; that we were occupied by nonsense, talked about some sort of art, unconscious creativeness, parliamentarism, the legal profession, and the devil knows what all, while it's a question of daily bread, while we're stifling under the grossest superstition, while all our corporations come to grief simply because there aren't enough honest men to carry them on . . .[1]

1. The reader will note that Pustovoyt has omitted the last part of the sentence: "while the very emancipation our Government's busy upon will hardly come to any good, because peasants are glad to rob even themselves to get drunk at the pot-house" [*Editor*].

The syntactical construction of that sentence is itself enough to prove that before us is not an ordinary district doctor but an orator, a tribune, a leader of a certain party (that is, the presence of parallel constructions: "We figured out," "we saw," and before that "we said"; repeated conjunctions "that" and "while"). If we examine the content of Bazarov's angry tirade it becomes clear that Turgenev did not shut his hero's lips, did not limit his participation in arguments to witticisms, but permitted him to express himself "at the top of his voice," that is, as he might have expressed himself before a large mass of his partisans.

Bazarov knows how to ridicule and parry Pavel Petrovich's country squire's drawing-room manner of speech with its countless formulas of servile-courtier politeness and ingratiation like "I haven't the honor of knowing," "permit me to be so curious as to ask," "will you be so kind as." Thus, for example, when Pavel Petrovich in his usual elegant manner, which he considered a mark of special chic, offers Bazarov with solemn grandioseness to "be so good as to choose (pistols)" Bazarov answers him calmly but with deadly irony "I will be so good." Such are some of the characteristics of dialogue in Turgenev's *Fathers and Sons*.

The portraits of characters play a vital, though not the most important, role in Turgenev's novels in general and in *Fathers and Sons* in particular. Turgenev very carefully studies a character's bearing, his exterior, and his gestures before engraving it on the artistic work. Turgenev wrote "I define characters as for a play: so and so, aged such and such, dresses this way, bears himself this way. Sometimes a certain gesture occurs to me and I immediately put down: passes his hand over his hair or pulls at his moustache. And I do not start to write until he becomes an old acquaintance for me, until I see him and hear his voice. And so with all the characters." In Turgenev's works, the characters are portrayed in many different ways. Upon close examination at least three types of portraits emerge from the variety offered.

The first is a detailed portrait with a description of the height, hair, face, and eyes of the hero and also several characteristic individual traits designed for the reader's visual impression. As a rule this sort of portrait is accompanied in Turgenev by little commentaries by the author, which distinguishes Turgenev's manner from, say, Goncharov's. This type of portrait appears as early as *The Hunter's Sketches*, for example the portrait of Yashka the Turk in "The Singers":

a lean and well-built man of twenty-three, dressed in a long-skirted blue nankeen coat. He looked like a dashing factory worker and, it seems, could hardly boast of good health. His sunken cheeks, large, restless gray eyes, straight nose with fine moving nostrils, a white, sloping brow, with flaxen curls pushed back from it, large but handsome and expressive lips—*his entire face revealed an impressionable and passionate man.*[2]

Natalia Lasunsky in *Rudin*, Lavretsky in *A Nest of Noblemen*, Shubin in *On the Eve* are other examples. * * * In *Fathers and Sons* the portraits of Bazarov and Odintsov are executed in a similar way. Here, for example, is the portrait of Bazarov in the second chapter:

> "Nikolai Petrovich turned around quickly and going up to a *tall* man in a *long*, loose, rough coat with tassels, who had only just got out of the carriage, he warmly pressed the *bare red* hand, which the latter did not at once hold out to him. . . . answered Bazarov, in a *lazy* but *manly* voice; and turning back the collar of his rough coat, he showed Nikolai Petrovich his whole face. It was *long* and *lean*, with a *broad* forehead, a nose flat at the base and *sharp* at the tip, *large greenish* eyes, and *drooping* side whiskers of a *sandy* color."

Then the author's explanations occur: "It was animated by a tranquil smile, and showed self-confidence and intelligence."

It is easy to note that dominant psychological trait of the hero is in the present case already defined through the portrait. With the aid of numerous precise details and commentary on the general impression given, Turgenev really creates that "physical and moral union" noted by Prosper Mérimée. The further description of the hero's exterior may continue even after the definition of the dominant psychological traits: the following details are added to the basic portrait of Bazarov: "his *long, thick, dark-blond* hair did not hide the prominent bumps of his *large skull*."

The portrait of Odintsov in the fourteenth chapter is presented in the same kind of relief and in the same clear images:

> Arkady looked round, and saw a tall woman in a *black* dress standing at the door of the room. He was struck by the dignity of her carriage. Her *bare* arms lay gracefully beside her *slender* waist; gracefully some *light* sprays of fuchsia drooped from her *shining* hair on to her *sloping* shoulders; her *clear* eyes looked out from under a somewhat *protruding white* brow, with a tranquil and intelligent expression—tranquil it was precisely, not pensive —and on her lips was a *scarcely perceptible* smile. A kind of *gracious* and *gentle* force emanated from her face.

---

2. Italics in the quoted text are Pustovoyt's throughout, except *Victor* on p. 307, Turgenev's indication that Kukshin pronounced his name in French rather than in Russian [*Editor*].

Here too, after explaining what sort of impression the figure of Odintsov should produce on the reader, Turgenev does not stop describing the exterior of his heroine; he goes on to remark that

> her nose—like almost all Russian noses—was a little thick; and her complexion was not perfectly clear; Arkady made up his mind, for all that, that he had never before met such an attractive woman.

Second. In Turgenev's novels we encounter satirical portraits in some respects similar to Gogol's manner. These consist of portraits with extensive use of the background, characterizing the figure by oblique means. The author's commentary on the satirical portrait sometimes does not limit itself to a simple indication of one quality or another in the figure, but develops into a whole picture. * * *

In *Fathers and Sons*, the clearest satiric portraits approximating Gogol's manner, gradually disclosing the essence of character by oblique means, are those of Kukshin and Sitnikov. The portrait of Kukshin is created against a broad background, consisting of several concentric circles that increasingly strengthen the satiric element. Turgenev begins Chapter Thirteen, devoted to Kukshin, by describing the city, then discusses the city's streets, then the little house "in the Moscow style" where Madame Kukshin lives, then adduces details like the "visiting card nailed on askew," the "bell-handle," the "some one who was not exactly a servant nor exactly a companion, in a cap—unmistakable tokens of the progressive tendencies of the mistress." It is perfectly clear that the background heralds to the reader nothing great and grandiose but testifies to some sort of unfounded pretense on the part of the inhabitant of this place; while the author's comment on "the progressive tendencies of the mistress" clearly has an ironic ring.

Continuing to develop the device of oblique characterization, Turgenev moves to a narrower concentric circle of observation and presents a detailed description of Kukshin's room: "Papers, letters, thick issues of Russian journals, for the most part uncut [a very characteristic detail!], lay at random on the dusty tables; cigarette ends lay scattered everywhere." It suffices to remember how in *Dead Souls* Gogol gradually discloses the image of Manilov by means of the furnishings (the exposed house, the abandoned pond, the room, the book with a bookmark on page 14), to become convinced that Turgenev successfully uses Gogol's device of oblique characterization.

The figure Turgenev chooses as the object of his satire usually appears in the novel, as in Gogol, after a distinctive descriptive overture, after the corresponding background has been drawn and when the reader has already formed a definite impression about him or her on the basis of the preceding description of setting an environment aroung the figure. Turgenev draws Kukshin's portrait only after discussing the city, its streets, the house, and the room in which she lives:

> "On a leather-covered sofa a lady, still young, was reclining. Her fair hair was rather dishevelled; she wore a silk gown, not altogether tidy, heavy bracelets on her short arms, and a lace handkerchief on her head. She got up from the sofa, and carelessly drawing over her shoulders a velvet cape trimmed with yellowish ermine, she said languidly, "good-morning, *Victor.*"

Underlining a series of incongruities in Kukshin's external appearance (young—rather dishevelled; in a silk gown—not altogether tidy; bracelets—on short arms), a series of deprecatory details ("round eyes, between which was a forlorn little turned-up red nose," "when she laughed, the gum showed above her upper teeth," "fingers brown with tobacco stains," etc.), Turgenev adds force to the author's comments to the portrait. In this case it is no longer a casual author's remark or a reply as, for example, the one about Bazarov's face "It was animated by a tranquil smile and expressed self-confidence and intelligence."

In describing Kukshin the commentaries grow into an extensive satirical characterization which is presented as it were not only through the author but also through another character, in this instance Bazarov. The author and Bazarov seem to fuse into a single character to convey the satiric judgment on Kukshin: "Bazarov frowned. There was nothing repulsive in the little plain person of the emancipated woman; but the expression of her face produced a disagreeable effect on the spectator. One felt impelled [it is hard to say who was impelled: the author or Bazarov, or everyone, including the reader] to ask her, 'What's the matter; are you hungry? Or bored? Or shy? What are you fidgeting about?' Both she and Sitnikov always had the same uneasy air. She was extremely unconstrained and at the same time awkward; she obviously regarded herself a good-natured, simple creature, and all the while, whatever she did, it always struck one that it was just what she did not want to do; everything with her seemed, as children say, done on purpose, that's to say, not simply, not naturally." We note that the satiric portrait of the imitative nihilist is presented before the dialogue in which her negative essence is disclosed.

Sitnikov's portrait is created through separate satirical brush strokes and subtle details that characterize him accurately. He is a man of small stature, he doesn't get out of the carriage but *leaps* out, *dashes* toward Bazarov like a shot although there is no reason either for shouting or for hurrying, immediately starts to *fidget* around Bazarov, *hops* over the ditch, runs now at the right of Bazarov, now at the left, advances somehow sideways, laughs *shrilly*, smiles *subserviently*, etc. "An expression of *worry* and *tension*," Turgenev writes in Chapter Twelve, was "imprinted on the *small* but *pleasant* features of his *well-groomed* face; his small eyes, that seemed *squeezed in*, had a fixed and uneasy look, and his laugh, too, was uneasy—a sort of short, wooden laugh." The words "but pleasant" are neutralized to such an extent by the preceding "worry and tension" and subsequent "well-groomed face" that they must be taken as the author's malicious irony toward his character. Sitnikov's portrait is concluded with the following stroke: in Kukshin's room Sitnikov "by now was lolling in an armchair, one leg in the air."

When a definite impression of these caricature-like nihilists has been created through their portraits, an impression Shchedrin later so aptly called one of "flap-ears playing the fool," Turgenev discloses their foolishness in detail through dialogue and action.

In the *third place*, a portrait that contradicts the inner content of the person is very characteristic for Turgenev. The variations of that kind of portrait are determined by the nature of the contrast between that which the author emphasizes in the exterior of the person and what he later discloses his essence to be. * * * The exterior [of Pavel Petrovich] emphasizes his aristocracy and European polish, satirical traits creep into the description of the character's external anglomania, while the essence of Pavel Petrovich is not disclosed by satiric means. * * *

Several critics of Turgenev's work are inclined to consider the figure of Pavel Petrovich satirical in general, relying upon Turgenev's own words "I raised his faults to the point of making them a caricature, I made him laughable." Actually, of course, the matter is not quite so. Turgenev criticises very sharply but not by satirical means Pavel Petrovich's principles and convictions with the exception of his views on dueling and the duel itself. The bankruptcy of Pavel Petrovich's pompous speeches about reforms, government steps, committees, and deputies is exposed with "the thunder of indignation." Turgenev notes his character's complete inactivity without satire. But Turgenev permits obvious satirical strokes to appear in depicting Pavel Pavlovich's anglomania and external aristocracy. This was clearly expressed in his portrait and gave various satirical journals an opportunity to parody precisely that part of the character.

Pretensions to something special and original are seen in the figure's dress and in his manners: the English *suit*, the stylish cravate, various fezzes, his custom of speaking while gently rocking, moving his shoulders, his European "shake-hands," etc.

Actually Pavel Petrovich did not create and could not create anything new and original, since the social force he represented was disappearing from the historical arena in the 1860's, yielding its place to the progressively developing democratic forces that were gathering strength. Turgenev understood that both Pavel Petrovich and Nikolay Petrovich became outmoded people, and even had his Bazarov say that their song had been sung. However, this could not please Turgenev who was a moderate liberal and therefore in dismissing the principles of liberals of the 1860's the author avoided satire. * * *

Bazarov's parents may serve as clear examples of transitional or mixed portraits. The portrait of Bazarov's father appears in Chapter Twenty as follows:

> Bazarov leaned out of the carriage, while Arkady thrust his head out behind his companion's back, and caught sight on the small porch of the little manor-house of a *tall, gaunt* man with *dishevelled* hair, and a *thin aquiline* nose, dressed in an *old military* frock coat not buttoned up. He was standing, his legs wide apart, smoking a *long* pipe and squinting his eyes to keep the sun out of them.

Here everything reminds one of the manner in which the first type of portrait is drawn (that of Bazarov, for example), but there are no author's comments in the portrait of the father. On the other hand, Turgenev later pays considerable attention to the device of oblique characterization—he presents a detailed description of Vassily Ivanovich's study:

> A thick-legged table, littered over with papers black with the accumulation of ancient dust as though they had been smoked, occupied the entire space between two windows; on the walls hung Turkish firearms, whips, swords, two maps, anatomical charts of some sort, a portrait of Hufeland, a monogram woven in hair in a black frame, and a glass-framed diploma; a leather sofa, torn and worn into hollows here and there was placed between two enormous cupboards of Karelian birchwood; books, boxes, stuffed birds, jars, and phials were huddled together in confusion on the shelves; in one corner stood a broken galvanic battery.

Speaking more accurately, the reader sees a museum of an ancient Aesculapius, whose archaic exhibits testify to former enthusiasm in equal degree for medicine and hunting, rather than the study of a contemporary scholar and practitioner, keeping up with recent discoveries in science. Even more, it testifies to the desolation and backwardness reigning in Vassily Ivanovich's house. After such a description of Bazarov's father's study, it is clear that such details as "dishevelled hair," "old military frock coat not buttoned up," "legs wide apart" are not amassed accidentally in the portrait.

Before turning to the portrait of Arina Valasyevna, Bazarov's mother, Turgenev traces a distinctive background in Gogol's style: "at last, on the slope of a gently rising knoll, appeared the *tiny village* where Bazarov's parents lived. Beside it, in a *small copse* of young birch, could be seen a *tiny* house with a thatched roof."

One should draw attention to the use of diminutives, through which the author creates in the reader an impression of something pitiful and insignificant. In the same way and with the help of similar diminutives, the author paints a portrait "of a real Russian little gentlewoman of the former, ancient days"; "the door was flung open, *plump, short, little old woman in white cap and a short little striped jacket* appeared on the threshold. She oh'd, swayed, and would certainly have fallen had not Bazarov supported her. Her *small plump hands* were instantly entwined around his neck."

Later on, details in the external appearance of the sentimental old woman that lower the portrait are increased ("crumpled and adoring face," "blissful and comic-looking eyes") and the author seems, as it were, to create a second portrait (but now no longer in full), at which he himself looks with good-natured, kindly irony: "leaning, on her little closed fist, her *round* face, to which the *full, cherry-colored lips and the little moles* on the cheeks and over the eyebrows gave a very simple, good-natured expression, she did not take her eyes off her son, and kept sighing."

Other forms of characterization do not play a primary role in Turgenev's novels and are not distinguished from the specific traits that strike one. Thus, characterization of a figure in action is almost identical in Turgenev with Goncharov's procedure. A. Mazon correctly writes that Turgenev "conceived a novel as a succession of scenes, connected one to the other by means of a simple plot." Therefore there are no extravagances and unexpected situations in Turgenev's novels. Thereby Turgenev distinguishes himself, among others, from Dostoevsky, in whose novels the actions and behavior of characters is given before they are characterized, and therefore at times seem strange and unexpected (for instance in *The Possessed* and *The Idiot*).

The conflict of "fathers" and "sons," the characters of each of the groups, to a certain extent of course are disclosed in their actions: Bazarov's duel with Pavel Petrovich, his behavior toward Odintsov, his clash and break with Arkady, Arkady's marriage to Katya. Finally Bazarov's infection and death is presented by the author as the result of selfless, noble, but unconsidered action by the hero.

As a rule the action of Turgenev's characters is not accompanied by such long and at times tormenting reflections as frequently occurs in Dostoevsky (it suffices to mention Raskol'nikov). Nor do Turgenev's novels contain extensive "interior monologues" characteristic of Tolstoy's heroes. This fact is explained by Turgenev's special view of the role and place of psychology in the artist's creative process. As early as 1852 Turgenev published in *The Contemporary* a review, "A few Words on Ostrovsky's New Play *The Poor Bride*." Firmly protesting against the dramatist's excessive fragmentation of characters, Turgenev wrote: "In our view Mr. Ostrovsky creeps, so to speak, into the soul of every character he creates; but we permit ourselves to remark to him that this unquestionably useful operation should be completed by the author as a preliminary step. His characters must be in his complete power when he presents them to us. We will be told that that is psychology; very well, but the psychologist must disappear in the artist, as the skeleton disappears beneath the living body, which it serves as a solid but invisible support." This Turgenev affirmed before he wrote his novels. But even later, in a letter to A. A. Fet apropos of Tolstoy's *War and Peace* Turgenev didn't change his view of psychological analysis in an artistic work. He wrote,

> The second part of *The Year 1805* is also weak: how petty and sly that all is, and is Tolstoy really not fed up with those eternal reflections, 'Am I coward, or not' . . . And the historical additions . . . is a puppet show and charlatanism while the psychology— all those sharply pointed boots of Alexander, Speransky's laugh —are nonsense. . . . these delicate reflections, meditations and observations on one's own feeling are boring. * * *

From what has been said several conclusions may be made concerning Turgenev's principles of psychological analysis of characters.

In the first place, in order not to destroy the unity of the created figures, not to fragment characters and not to harm the artistry of the work, the writer must not carry on the analysis of the character psychology before the reader's eyes. All that is accomplished earlier by the writer, who offers the reader only the psychological results. We note that the psychological picture of Bazarov is presented precisely that way in *Fathers and Sons*. Odintsov evaluates Arkady's qualities in accordance with the same psychological principles after the falling out with Bazarov.

In the second place, the device of presenting the psychological process itself ("the dialectic of the soul") a characteristic feature of Tolstoy's art, is completely unacceptable and foreign to Turgenev's heart.

In the third place, opposing the fragmentation of psychological characterization into particularities, Turgenev fights for the wholeness and clarity of the general psychological portrait of the hero, for the careful choice and artistic filtering of the fundamental, primary psychological traits of the character.

All these conclusions find support in the writer's artistic practice. In the psychological tales and socio-psychological novels, where the psychological characterization plays a corresponding role, Turgenev made use of internal monologues, as well as diaries and letters and reminiscences and dreams and indirect speech—that is, all the existing components of psychological characterization, as an artistic device. He artfully alternated that artistic device with others—characterization by portrait, speech, and dialogue.

In those novels, like *Fathers and Sons*, that clearly express the dominating importance of the political, there was no great need for psychological characterization. Therefore it does not occupy so large a place in the novel *Fathers and Sons* as it does, for example, in *A Nest of Noblemen* or *First Love*. This permits us to limit ourselves to general observations on this artistic device.

ALEXANDER FISCHLER

The Garden Motif and the Structure of Turgenev's *Fathers and Sons*†

It has taken the better part of a century to shift the focus of critical attention from the *raznochintsy* and assorted contemporaries whom Turgenev was alleged to have satirized in *Fathers and Sons* to the characters of the novel itself, notably to Bazarov as fictional hero. In recent years, it has even been possible to argue that the oft analyzed death of Bazarov was less a commentary on the character or the times than the culminating point of a tragic plot, carefully devised along the lines of classical tragedy; that, once politics are set aside, the novel turns out to be centered on

† From *Novel* 9.3 (Spring 1976): 243–55.

love; and that the natural environment is far more significant than the political in allowing us to understand the characters.[1] It ought to be possible by now to ignore, if not to challenge, a tacit assumption which runs throughout Turgenev criticism, namely, that his plots are scarcely worth studying since, by his own admission—recorded and consecrated by no less an authority than Henry James—the works are dominated by character and lacking in *architecture* (plot, story or, as James puts it, "composition").[2]

Just as Turgenev was misleading at home in defending his Bazarov against political attacks "from the left and the right," so he was misleading abroad in slighting his own interest in composition before his Western novelist friends who, as he knew and told James, had made composition their main stock in trade. He was obviously much less concerned with form than either James or Flaubert, and he indeed had much less respect for story than Stendhal and Balzac. He took broad license in the genre from Gogol, the English novelists of the eighteenth century, and, of course, Cervantes, with the result that his plots did not quite conform to the realistic canons in vogue by the middle of the nineteenth century. However, and this in fact is the gist of his remarks to James, the very presentation which he allowed to seem archaic brought out the contemporaneity of his characters and their problems. Stylization calls attention to itself: this, of course, is one of the foundations of rhetoric. Besides, Turgenev's stylization tolerated a great range of ironic devices and could give characters a mythic dimension not readily available to a James or a Flaubert. The *manque d'architecture* in his works, which Turgenev confessed, is at the most an apology for frequent reliance on structural devices and conventions. Obviously, it did not always serve him well, but, obviously also, *Fathers and Sons* is a notable exception: here, the uneasy coexistence of the old and the new, the artificial and the "natural" was in perfect accord with the main themes the author had chosen.

The narrative technique of the novel underlines the fact that the problems raised are insoluble, that rifts revealed can be mended "only by time"; indeed, the entire novel culminates in this old adage. And the progression is just as unoriginal: it is insured by the horse-and-carriage method, with an explicitly omniscient narrator holding the reins. The pauses are carefully and obviously contrived. On the very first page, the author invites us to leave Nikolai Kirsanov, "his feet tucked under him,"

---

1. The arguments appear, respectively, in Frank F. Seeley, "Theme and Structure in *Fathers and Sons*," *Annali*, Sezione Slava, XII (Naples 1970), [83]–104; Ralph E. Matlaw, "Turgenev's Novels and *Fathers and Sons*," in his first edition of the novel (New York: Norton Critical Edition, 1966), pp. 261–78; James H. Justus, "*Fathers and Sons*: The Novel as Idyll," *ibid.*, pp. 307–14 (reprinted from *Western Humanities Review*, XV [1961], 259–65). All references to *Fathers and Sons* in the text will be to the Norton Critical Edition, Matlaw, trans. and ed. (for the sake of consistency, some name spellings were regularized).

2. Henry James, quoted by Matlaw, p. 283; the most detailed statement by James on Turgenev, bringing together earlier remarks, serves as Introduction to Volume I of *The Novels and Stories of Ivan Turgenev*, the complete translated edition (New York: Charles Scribner's Sons, 1903), used here for all quotations other than those from *Fathers and Sons*.

at the posting station of S——. so that he may explain his background and why he is anxiously awaiting the return of his son. On the road between the station and Marino, a few pages later, he stops the horses in scarcely more subtle fashion to provide, in one cart, a match to light Bazarov's pipe and, in the other, relief for Arkady from the lyric effusions of his father. Throughout the novel, Turgenev does not miss an opportunity to create fortuitous interruptions and fortunate intrusions at moments of high drama. The drama prepared at every changing of the horses and crossing of the roads must be transformed, so the author himself will suggest in the epilogue, into *prostodushnaia komediia*, "artless comedy"—life itself or a play in which the author's strings no longer matter. In such comedy, the naive pursuit of happiness by the characters remaining on stage blends with timeless designs, overwhelming what momentarily stood out and was disturbing because of its alien, fortuitous or fateful appearance. Architecture, indeed, almost in its "real estate sense," fixes the fathers in time and place within this novel; but *architecture* of a subtle, literary kind fixes the sons as well: within a few chapters, they are reduced to shuttling back and forth between their "estates," and even the detours to the bedlam of the city or to its antipode, the ordered realm of Nikolskoe, merely confirm their confinement to native grounds, two points "in the same district." Turgenev obviously enjoyed and meant for his readers to enjoy every twist and turn along a road which, in the end, had to become the straight and narrow: he measured out every segment in versts as well as in days, counting pauses for drink, noting the landmarks, especially the human landmarks along the way, and he took up as often as possible the challenge of animating them for the measured moment. What could be more contrived and yet more full of life than, at the end of Chapter XX, the portrait-presentation of Arina Vlasyevna, Bazarov's mother, ruling over her household?

Far from allowing "composition" to be secondary to character, as he claimed he had done throughout his works, and far from sacrificing character in this novel to political considerations, as he was accused of doing, Turgenev sacrificed character to literary tradition following established guidelines. From the Western handbook of composition, he had chosen one of the oldest rhetorical *topoi*, the *locus amoenus*, using its variants to evolve his plot, and using its traditional thematic associations to suggest an answer to the contemporary problems he had raised as well as to determine the stature of his main protagonist. An examination of the garden pattern in *Fathers and Sons* shows that Turgenev performed the sacrifice of his characters as ritualistically as possible. At the same time that he was anchoring the novel in reality, ending the action and the composition in "August 1861," he gave the characters mythic dimensions, thus sparing himself the task of passing judgment upon them. The fact that we can nonetheless look upon the novel as a

monument of nineteenth-century realism suggests classical guidelines
may indeed facilitate passage through the "gate of horn."

One must first note that Bazarov belongs to a special category of
protagonists, the tragic protagonist or even the nature hero. He fits there
less because of his famous assertion that nature is his "workshop," than
because of his repeatedly underlined mysterious bonds with the natural
surroundings. He is associated with nature not only by brute strength
and passion, but by vaguer, though not necessarily less awesome bonds
of sympathy: the world responds to him, follows him, at least so long
as he chooses to practice and accept association, that is, throughout the
first part of the novel. He is born with a gift for harmony with the
creation, yet, as he himself points out to Arkady, it is a gift of limited
usefulness: one may derive strength from nature so long as one yields
to it through naïve faith, so long as one is willing to believe in the
talismanic virtue of an aspen tree by a clay pit; but, when the magic is
lost, one must drift to the inevitable end. Nonetheless, even when
Bazarov's bond to nature ceases being a means for coping with the world,
his fate remains associated with it by the structure of the novel. He is
a nature hero, and, by ironic extension, he is even a nature "god": he
appears on the stage in spring (May 1859) to offer the traditional challenge to an existing order already undermined by inner and outer turmoil;
he is defeated (except perhaps in the duel with Pavel Kirsanov, the living-
dead representative of the old order who, in many respects, is a projection
of himself), then largely through his own acquiescence and even com-
plicity, he dies in August, at the height of summer, a traditional time
for the death of gods; in mid-winter, six months later, the living celebrate
their own survival in a double marriage ceremony that unites the young
with the young as well as the "old" with the young, and this is followed
by a farewell dinner for the erstwhile antagonist, Pavel Kirsanov, which
culminates in a libation offered "To the memory of Bazarov"; finally,
in the last lines of the novel which close two full revolutions of the cycle
bringing things to the "present," August 1861, it is suggested to us that
Bazarov's spirit has passed into the flowers on his grave which tell "of
eternal reconciliation and of life without end"—evidently, the irony
associated with him throughout the novel, Romantic or circumstantial,
has exhausted itself here, on the edge of timelessness where everything
is necessarily antithetical to what the living, vital Bazarov had stood for.[3]

Such a glance at Bazarov's career stresses merely one aspect of his
presentation, the one most clearly relevant to the current investigation.
Other aspects, no less stylized and no less ironic, can be identified to
cast him in a Romantic hero role: the dark rebel (with "pride almost
Satanic," as Pavel Petrovich points out), the spirit of negation whose

---

3. Bazarov is also associated with the smaller cycle of day and night after his death; appropriately,
his last words are "Now . . . darkness . . ." (see end of Ch. XXVII).

deathbed is visited by an ineffectual "angel." The roles are complementary. Just as Turgenev's realism (using the term in an extremely narrow sense of "contemporaneity," with a tinge of "relevance") must emerge from fusion of the traditional and the actual, so the stature of his protagonist is enhanced by triumph over the personal inconsistencies, the social inadequacies, the more-or-less tragic flaws, and the seemingly overwhelming figures with which the novelist associates him and with which he must struggle to seem great.

* * *

Distance in time, for us, makes it possible to marvel at the attempt [to create godlike heroes for his time] and, in particular, at the sustained artistic effort evident in the creation of Bazarov. Not only his career, but the entire plot of the novel is linked with the seasons. Bazarov himself governs only the tragic segment, spring to mid-summer; he is survived, however, by young and old who complete the cycle. The old are forced to resign themselves to tragedy ("Side by side," says the one-eyed Anfisuchka, "they drooped their heads like lambs at noonday"); they have almost nothing left beyond a graveyard plot to tend. But the young inherit the land to be fruitful and to multiply. If one reads the novel without expecting to find a political oracle in its pages, the concluding "cultivate your garden" seems not only an appropriate message, but the only one possible, the only one which the death-transcending cyclical view would tolerate.

Turgenev evidently sought to insure the palatability of the message by structuring the novel in large part on a garden motif urbanely, at times even ironically, presented to his readers. Though Russian soil is considered implicitly, Marino is the garden whose cultivation is topical throughout the novel, the only reasonable gauge of progress and adjustment in the world opened for the readers. Of course, to see a beautiful garden here at all required a sympathetic or proprietary interest, preferably supplemented, as in the case of Nikolai Petrovich and his son Arkady, by a good deal of sentimentality. One notes besides, already in the initial presentation, that both are a little dazzled by the May sun. An objective viewer, like Bazarov, immediately notes that Marino is a very sorry estate, an originally poor design, poor executed and poorly kept up. Yet there is at the heart of Marino a garden in the conventional sense, a place where nature was not frustrated and hence produced an arbor of acacias and lilacs which, particularly in the spring, is indeed an approximation of paradise.[4] Here Nikolai Petrovich can come to seek

---

4. This is the first detailed presentation of the *locus amoenus* in the novel, and one may note that it is conventional down to the small, realistic detail of the vegetation, the lilac and acacia. For the history and tradition of the *locus* and the related earthly and enchanted gardens, see Ernst R. Curtius, *European Literature and the Latin Middle Ages* (New York: Harper & Row, 1963), Ch. X, "The Ideal Landscape," pp. 181–202; and A. Bartlett Giamatti, *The Earthly Paradise and Renaissance Epic* (Princeton, N.J.: Princeton University Press,

release from an overwhelming sense of disjointedness in time, brought home to him by the acrimonious debate between Arkady and Bazarov on the one hand and by his brother Pavel on the other. Here he can review things in what seems like a proper perspective, accommodate uncertain hopes for the future with present sympathies and even friendly shades that rise out of the past. The arbor, in fact, enhances everything that had always appeared to him intrinsically and unquestionably beautiful and good, notably poetry and nature. The setting sun not only creates beauty, but confirms its permanence (through the cycles again); here the past reaches out reassuringly to the present, love conquers time, Nikolai Petrovich's late, beloved Marya waits in the shadow to come to his aid. But the promise of the dark turns out to be Fenichka, paradigm of flesh and blood, "the present" come to inquire about him. At a time of less storm and stress, the sight would have brought Nikolai Petrovich back into the house; in this instance however, it merely seems to prevent absolute communion with nature, leaving him to his uncertainties.

Though unconfirmed, Nikolai Petrovich's view of nature as foundation of permanence and source of beauty is allowed to stand. From the very beginnings of Western literature, the *locus amoenus* and the related myths of Golden Age and Paradise had been the means for expressing precisely this view, not the ground for testing it. The garden is a privileged ground, a place for escape, and we should not be surprised that even Bazarov, for whom it is a mere *locus*, "a workshop," and for whom testing and challenging are a way of life, will turn instinctively (and ironically) to the same arbor for distraction. As a geomorphological concept, the garden is a microcosm of nature, foreshortening its laws to uphold *what ought to be*: the perpetual spring that reigns within does not threaten the full cycle beyond. And yet, as James Justus pointed out in commenting on this scene, even in the realm of *what is*, nature is viewed as idyllic, "as a symbolic system embodying the deepest values of the Fathers."[5]

For Nikolai Petrovich, the Marino arbor is the Romantic version of the *locus amoenus*, a setting where a recalcitrant but sympathetic Nature (the flowers around, the stars above) is called to witness vague fears and longings, and where at the age of forty-four a man may yet shed "causeless tears" in the dark. The setting is equally sympathetic to all. Pavel Petrovich appears, and, having learned the reason for his brother's ghost-like appearance, he "went to the end of the garden, and he too grew thoughtful, and he too raised his eyes towards the heavens. But nothing was reflected in his beautiful dark eyes except the light of the stars. He was not born a romantic, and his fastidiously dry and sensual soul, with

---

1966), in particular the Introduction, Ch. I, and the bibliographies following each.   5. See Justus' essay in this edition [*Editor*].

its French tinge of misanthropy, was not capable of dreaming. . . ." (p. 46). Pavel Petrovich, Turgenev explained a few pages earlier, is at home in his elegant study, not in the garden, though in the study he cannot conjure up sympathetic influences from the dark either.[6]

* * *

Turgenev was obviously sensitive to the traditions he had adopted as bases for his novel. If anything, the action performed against the garden background had demonstrated how easy it is to defeat a nihilist who, by definition, sides with the dark, seeks what is not, and reaches for what lies beyond reach (we recall that the dying Bazarov's main worry is that he will enter "darkness" unconscious). Born for the garden, he cannot rest there, and yet he has no attainable goal beyond it. We are not surprised to find his greatest temptation in Nikolskoe, the enchanted garden, where the show or the promise of ideals fulfilled arrests him for a while and subjects him to the dominion of a power other than his own. All and nothing blend in the enchanted garden: Bazarov is in his own element. But there is a clue here also to the uses of the garden tradition for a mid-nineteenth-century Russian novelist. The tradition offered two clearly distinct strains which we may call in context the "arkadian" and the "bazarian": where the one led to the message and morality of cultivation and to cyclical permanence, the other led to a tragic ending after utter inability to fit the unsorted and overabundant supply to yet unformulated demand (to rephrase Turgenev's own, correct assessment of his hero's failure with his contemporaries). A. Bartlett Giamatti has told us that the enchanted garden assumed prominence in the Renaissance because it represented ambiguity and allowed conflicting forces to stand facing each other with no possibility for a reconciliation: it would have been out of place. The conflicts Giamatti situates in the great garden poems of the Renaissance can be made parallel to those which were the contemporary background in Turgenev's novels. Thus, "the conflict between classical heritage and Christian culture" has its counterpart in the conflict between Westernizers and Slavophiles; the conflict "between Love and Duty" persists; for Bazarov, the rival pair "woman and God" would have to be adapted, perhaps by substituting Science for God; the conflict between "illusion and reality" persists as well, tending in this novel to define itself more narrowly in terms of "Romanticism and realism," without much precision in either category.

Finally, it can of course be argued that Turgenev had a personal affinity for the ambiguous, enchanted garden, for exile, and for contempt, one that was to become even stronger in the years following publication of *Fathers and Sons*, allegedly because of its reception. This

6. The scene has a later parallel: in his father's study, Bazarov, who has no hold on his native ground, stares vindictively into the dark; "the memories of childhood had no power over him".

particular affinity suggests that he spoke the truth when he repeatedly asserted his sympathy for Bazarov. But the sympathy of the author evidently could not save the character from either his fate or his critics. The left and the right had good grounds for condemning the novel from a political point of view, since, by using the garden motif as key to its structure, Turgenev had fallen back upon a device that precluded political commitment, demanded ambiguity, focused hopes and aspirations, but, at the same time, frustrated them with inaccessibility. It was, nonetheless, a device that enhanced the presentation of themes and characters; indeed, when we consider the artistic achievement in *Fathers and Sons*, we must concur with what Curtius says to sum up the merits of the garden motif: "The finest fruit ripens on espaliers."

KATHRYN FEUER

Fathers and Sons: Fathers and Children†

* * *

The social-political interpretation of *Fathers and Sons* has been widespread. It was most recently articulated by Isaiah Berlin in his Romanes Lectures, published as *Fathers and Children*, where he calls the "central topic of the novel . . . the confrontation of the old and the young, of liberals and radicals, traditional civilization and the new, harsh positivism which has no use for anything except what is needed by a rational man." Ralph Matlaw, in his preface to the valuable Norton Critical Edition, explains that he has chosen the widely used English title "Fathers and Sons" rather than the literal "Fathers and Children" because " 'Sons' in English better implies the notions of spiritual and intellectual generations conveyed by the Russian *deti*." Matlaw, with the majority of non-Soviet critics, see Turgenev as having drawn on the specific details and data of the debate between Russian liberals and radicals for the portrayal of a not merely political but universal theme, the eternal conflict of generations.

Yet can our interpretation of the novel stop here? Only, I believe, at the cost of ignoring its deepest layer of meaning and thus missing its consummate achievement. The most perceptive discussion of *Fathers and Sons* that I have read is also, regrettably, very brief, an "introduction" to the novel by René Wellek. Wellek begins by explaining and paying tribute to the admirable "concrete social picture" of an era and its disputes which Turgenev presents. Calling "the eternal conflict between the old

† From *The Russian Novel from Pushkin to Pasternak*, ed. John Garrard Yale UP 1983, pp. 68–69, 71–74. Footnotes omitted. Reprinted by permission of Yale University Press.

and the young . . . one of the main themes of the book," nevertheless, he asserts, *Fathers and Sons* "goes beyond the temporal issues and enacts a far greater drama: man's deliverance to fate and chance, the defeat of man's calculating reason by the greater powers of love, honor, and death." "Man's deliverance to fate and chance" is indeed, I would submit, one central theme of the novel, but to see this clearly we must go a step further in the rejection of traditional interpretations. We must dispense with the notion that the novel portrays the conflict of generations and recognize that instead it portrays love between generations, the triumph of love over tension and conflict; that its essential core is the intertwining of two great themes, affectionate continuity from parent to child and child to parent and "man's deliverance to fate and chance," that is, man's knowledge of his own mortality. It is to this novel that Turgenev gave the title *Fathers and Children*, which is, moreover, a novel far more profound in its political implications than we have heretofore realized.

This reading of the book can best be elucidated by beginning at its conclusion, at the almost unbearable closing picture of Bazarov's aged parents kneeling and weeping at his grave. Waste, futility, and anguish are overwhelming, but then comes a dramatic reversal, and the novel ends with a declaration of hope:

> Can it be that their prayers, their tears, will be fruitless? Can it be that love, sacred, dedicated love will not be all-powerful? Oh no! However passionate, guilty, rebellious the heart concealed in the grave, the flowers growing over it gaze at us serenely with their innocent eyes: not only of eternal peace do they speak to us, of that great peace of "indifferent" nature; they speak also of eternal reconciliation and of life without end. . . . [chap. 28]

This passage is remarkable, almost incomprehensible as a conclusion to all that has gone before it in the novel; the incongruity has been described best by Wellek: "Turgenev puts here 'indifferent nature' in quotation marks, but as early as in A *Sportsman's Sketches* (*Zapiski okhotnika*) he had said: 'From the depths of the age-old forests, from the everlasting bosom of waters the same voice is heard: "You are no concern of mine," says Nature to Man.' " And he adds, with reference to *Fathers and Sons*: "There is no personal immortality, no God who cares for man; nature is even a disease beyond reason—this seems the message Turgenev wants to convey." The contradictory quality of the last sentence of the novel has been noted by many readers, yet Wellek alone has commented on the particular peculiarity of Turgenev's having written " 'indifferent' nature" with the adjective in quotation marks, seeming to imply rejection of the idea of nature's indifference, an implication almost insulting to the reader, so opposite is it to text of *Fathers and Sons* and to the major body of Turgenev's writings over the preceding quarter of a century.

The quotation marks can be read another way, however, as meaning not "so called" or "not really" but denoting—literally—a quotation, in this case a quotation from Pushkin, from the last lines of one of his best-known poems, "Whether I wander along noisy streets" ("Brozhu li Ya vdol ulits shumnykh"):

> And let indifferent nature
> Shine in her eternal beauty.

That Turgenev could have had the poem in mind is not difficult to suppose. For most writers there are other writers whose lines, paragraphs, works, exist as part of their consciousness, touchstones which may only occasionally be specified but whose presence is constant. For Turgenev, Pushkin was such a writer. The last stanza of the poem, indeed, is a major passage in the conclusion of one of Turgenev's most important early works, "Diary of a Superfluous Man" ("Dnevnik lishnego cheloveka"). Moreover, Pushkin's poetry is an important presence in *Fathers and Sons*: as a thematic element, as an emotional vector, as an emblem for the existence of beauty.

* * *

Pushkin's poem is about death and about the poet's morbidly haunted awareness of the random uncertainty of the time when it will come and the utter certainty of its coming. What we find in *Fathers and Sons*, I suggest, is the onset of Pushkin's malady in Bazarov, as a direct consequence of his love for Odintsova. Once this love has infected him, he becomes haunted by the knowledge of his own mortality. It has always been recognized that Bazarov's love crippled him, although some readers see Odintsova's rejection as the decisive event. I am proposing here that the effect of love on Bazarov was not some sort of general demoralization coming from a recognition that his nature does not correspond with his ideology, but a specific effect, the one I have called Pushkin's malady: an obsession with the knowledge of his own mortality.

Throughout the first fourteen chapters of the novel Bazarov is a triumphant expression of the life-force, a man exuberantly intelligent and supremely self-confident, caring for no one's good opinion but his own. He is liked by the peasants, works assiduously, takes pride in being Russian, exhibits a zest for life in a variety of ways: his pleasure in Fenichka's "splendid" baby, his eagerness for a visit to town, his appreciation of pretty women. His serious concerns are positive. He scorns upbringing or the "age we live in" as excuses for weakness: "As for our times—why should I depend on that? Let my times depend on me" (chap. 7).

In chapter 15 the crucial transition occurs. When Bazarov and Arkadi first call on Odintsova, Arkadi sees that "contrary to his habit Bazarov was talking a good deal and obviously trying to interest" Odintsova.

Then, as they leave, when Odintsova expresses the polite hope that they may visit her estate: "Bazarov only bowed and—a last surprise for Arkadi; he noticed that his friend was blushing." Shortly after, when Arkadi comments on Odintsova's beauty, Bazarov agrees: "A splendid body! Perfect for the dissection table." And three days later, as the friends are driving to Odintsova's estate: " 'Congratulate me,' Bazarov suddenly exclaimed, 'today is June 22nd, my guardian angel's day. Well, we'll see how he'll take care of me.' "

What has happened here? Bazarov has called on his "guardian angel"; whether he realizes it or not he is aware for the first time of his vulnerability to death; he is subconsciously asking Pushkin's question: "Is the hour already near?" He will continue to ask the question until he dies, and his preoccupation, usually just below the surface though sometimes bursting forth in bitter outrage, will be expressed in the imagery of disease or death, which first enters his consciousness and conversation in the moment we have witnessed: "A splendid body! Perfect for the dissection table."

In chapter 16 he illustrates a nonmedical argument to Odintsova by an analogy with "the lungs of a consumptive." In chapter 17, when he has acknowledged his passion to himself, this love "tortured and possessed him," for he regarded such feelings "as something like deformity or disease." In chapter 18, when Odintsova asks whether happiness exists, Bazarov can answer only: "You know the proverb: it's always better where we don't exist." A little later, when she tries to question him about his plans and ambitions, he answers ominously: "What's the point of talking or thinking about the future, which for the most part doesn't depend on us?"

Immediately after this exchange come Bazarov's declaration of his love and Odintsova's refusal. Now the images of disease increase: in Bazarov's speech there is a movement from the sense of vulnerability to that of fatality. Moreover, new motifs appear: insecure megalomania supersedes self-confidence, hostility to Arkadi replaces condescending but genuine friendship. In chapter 19 he agrees to Arkadi's accusation of elitism: " 'Is it that *you're* a god while I'm just one of the blockheads?' 'Yes,' Bazarov repeated weightily, 'you're still stupid.' " Besides increasing in number, Bazarov's images of disease and death are now applied to himself: "The machine's become unstuck." Then, still in chapter 19, Bazarov articulates the first unequivocal statement of his intimation: "Every man hangs on a thread; the abyss can open up beneath him at any moment. . . ."

Soon after, his preoccupation with his "approaching . . . anniversary" breaks forth more explicitly:

"I think, here I am, lying under a haystack . . . the tiny, cramped spot I occupy is so minute in comparison with the rest of the universe, where I don't exist and where I don't matter; and the space of time allotted for me to live in is a mere moment in that eternity of time where I was not and will not be. . . . And in this atom, in this mathematical dot, the blood circulates, the brain works, there's even a desire for something. . . . How outrageous it is! How petty!"

[chap. 21]

Bazarov now gives way to impotent fury, vindictiveness, malice:

"Ha! There's a fine fellow of an ant, dragging off a half-dead fly. Take her, brother, take her. It doesn't matter that she resists, make use of her as you will."

When Bazarov lauds hatred, "How strange!" Arkadi observes, "why I don't hate anyone." "And I hate so many," Bazarov replies:

"Hatred! Well, for example take yesterday—as we were passing our bailiff, Phillip's cottage—and you said that Russia will attain perfection when every last muzhik has such a place to live, and that every one of us ought to work to bring that about. . . . And I felt such a hatred for your every last muzhik. . . . Yes, he'll be living in a white cottage, while the nettles are growing out of me. . . ."

"Ah, Arkadi, do me a favor, let's have a fight, a real fight, till we're laid out in our coffins, till we destroy each other."

This attack on Arkadi has been triggered by his comment on a dead leaf falling to earth, fluttering like a butterfly: "Gloom and death," he remarks, "and at the same time gaiety and life!" What seems to enrage Bazarov is that Arkadi can accept the unity of life and death, can see death as a part of life rather than as its negation.

Bazarov's bravery during the duel with Pavel Kirsanov only underlines the depth and inner intensity of his preoccupation with death. It is not the concrete incident in which his life is endangered which obsesses the death-haunted man; it is the subliminal question, when and where, which accompanies him whether wandering noisy streets or lounging beneath a haystack.

After his departure from the Kirsanovs Bazarov pays a brief visit to Odintsova; once again the imagery of death is related to himself. When Odintsova tells him that he is a "good man," he replies: "That's the same as laying a wreath of flowers on the head of a corpse" (chap. 26). Is there also a presentiment of fatality in Bazarov's parting words to her? When she tells him she is sure they will meet again (as of course they do, at Bazarov's deathbed), he answers: "In this world, anything may happen!" Such an interpretation of his words is prepared by the grim pun with which he has just before informed Arkadi that he is stopping by at Odintsova's on his way home: "Well, so I've set off 'to the fathers.' " As Matlaw points out, Bazarov here "mockingly (and ominously) recalls the '*ad patres*' used by Bazarov's father earlier [in chap. 20] as an expression for death."

Bazarov goes home for six weeks to settle down to work. Are the lethargy and melancholy that soon overtake him further evidence of his morbid preoccupation? It hardly matters. Soon, whether by accident or suicide, he *is* dying and, as when he faced death in the duel, his behavior is calm and courageous. The fear has dissolved, once it has become recognized reality. On one occasion he does rebel: he takes hold of a heavy table and manages to swing it around: " 'Strength, real strength,' he murmured. 'It's all still here, and yet I must die! . . . Well, go and try to refute death. She'll refute you, and that's that!' " (chap. 27). Bazarov is no longer haunted by wondering: the question of the date of the "approaching . . . anniversary" has been answered and we have come to the scene of Bazarov's grave, to the grieving parents, to Turgenev's assertion that the flowers speak of eternal reconciliation and not just of " 'indifferent' nature," and so back to Pushkin's poem.

* * *

MICHAEL HOLQUIST

Bazarov and Sečenov: The Role of Scientific Metaphor in *Fathers and Sons*†

Valentin Kataev tells a marvelous story of how the great Mejerchol'd once developed a plan for putting *Fathers and Sons* on the screen: "The film was to have begun with a diagram of the human chest— white ribs and, behind them, as if behind dungeon bars, a human heart, beating at first steadily and rhythmically as the law of blood circulation demands, then fluttering and leaping until it stops in a last convulsion . . . Bazarov draws a charcoal circle on his chest around the place where his heart beats. With horror he notices that it is love, passion, desire that makes his heart contract . . .".

Mejerchol'd's interpretation of the novel refuses to take Bazarov's Nihilism seriously: "Bazarov a Nihilist? Nonsense [*vzdor*]!". He sees Bazarov not as an ideologue but as a poet; and he even planned to have Bazarov's role in the film played by Majakovskij himself. The film was never made, which is unfortunate because it might have helped to clear up a certain ambivalence that has grown up around Turgenev's reputation. I believe Mejerchol'd was absolutely right in perceiving that Bazarov is more poet than scientist, a position I wish to extend in this paper, in the hope that it not only will provide yet another interpretation of *Fathers and Sons*, but will in some small measure add to the growing body of work that seeks to offset the currently reigning clichés about Turgenev's status as a writer in the distinctively Russian literary tradition.

† Reprinted from *Russian Literature* by permission of Elsevier Science Publishers.

As Isaiah Berlin made clear in his 1970 Romanes lecture, Turgenev's "artistic reputation is not in question; it is as a social thinker that he is still today the subject of a continuing dispute." The most serious charge against Turgenev of this kind would seem to have been made by D. S. Mirsky: "There had always been in Turgenev a poetic or romantic vein . . . his attitude to nature had always been *lyrical* . . . even in his most realistic and civic novels the construction and atmosphere are mainly lyrical". What this vision of Turgenev's achievement results in is the ineluctable conclusion that ". . . In his day Turgenev was regarded as a leader of opinion on social problems. *Now* this seems strange and unintelligible. Long since the issues that he fought out have ceased to be of any actual interest". And then comes the inevitable and invidious comparison: "Unlike Tolstoy or Dostoevsky", or virtually any other important figure of nineteenth century Russian literary culture—"Turgenev is no longer a teacher . . . his work has become pure art . . .".

Not only is Turgenev not a novelist, he is more precisely not a *Russian* novelist. I take this to mean that he is unlike Tolstoj or Dostoevskij insofar as he is not a *thinker*: he is precisely what the most characteristic strand of Russian criticism would have most vigorously objected to, i.e., someone, who is *only* an artist, someone who provides merely aesthetic pleasure. And insofar as this is true of Turgenev, he will be perceived as not doing the work of Russian literature as defined by the great Belinskij, whose views continue to shape ideas about the extra aesthetic importance of the artist.

The irony of such a view will become apparent if we remember facts so familiar that their importance is often overlooked. Not only is *Fathers and Sons* dedicated to Turgenev's old friend Belinskij, the still-invoked conscience of the Russian intelligentsia, but it was as well a central document in the intellectual—not *only* the artistic or political—life of Russia during one of its most formative periods.

The conception of Turgenev as exclusively an artist of a particularly refined sort is usually combined with an indictment of him as a failed man of action. The implication of such a view is that the only area other than literature itself for such a lyricist to demonstrate his seriousness was politics, an area in which Turgenev clearly did not excel. Mirsky in a rather curious echo of Vulgar Sociologism, sums up this view by suggesting that in political importance, Turgenev was "representative of his class . . . and of his generation, which failed to gain real touch with Russian realities . . . and which, ineffective in the sphere of action, produced one of the most beautiful literary growths of the nineteenth century." Finding in Turgenev "merely" beauty, it is inevitable that Mirsky concludes by saying, "We do not seek wisdom [in Turgenev]". Turgenev, in other words, is the literary equivalent of the proverbial dumb blonde.

To dispute the Mirskian view of Turgenev as an ineffectual aesthete would require a principled study of the kind only a thoroughly trained Turgenev scholar might carry out. I am not in the position to make such a study. Nevertheless, I would like at least to hint at a relation between Turgenev and *one* of the major intellectual currents of the modern period, the mind/body duality that has haunted us since at least Descartes. My purpose will be to suggest the further point that Turgenev may be perceived not only as an artist, but *in* his artistry, as a certain kind of *thinker*. A thinker not so much about politics as such, but about the politics competing discourses represent as they express competing social currents in the history of the Russian language. In what follows, then, I will try very quickly to sketch two arguments: Turgenev *is* similar to other novelists and in particular to those Russian novelists from whose company Mirsky would exclude him, in that he uses the medium of the novel to think through important extra-literary problems. One reason we so often fail to see the intellectual, analytical side of Turgenev is because it is assumed the only scope for such activity was the immediate political situation of nineteenth century Russia. But there were other and arguably much more historically important trends of thought—and action—abroad in the same period, and it is in at least one of these, in at least one of his works (*Fathers and Sons*) that Turgenev's importance both as a thinker and as a figure whose work had consequences in real life should rather be sought.

The particular debate in which Turgenev played such a role is the one concerning the relation between the science of physiology, on the one hand, idealistic concepts of personhood and individuality, on the other. This is a problem that occupies some of the best minds—both scientific and literary—throughout the late eighteenth and all of the nineteenth century, indeed up to the present time. My argument may be stated in a number of theses, which I will first list, and then go on to specify.

1) Turgenev occupies a distinctive place in the history of nineteenth century European literature insofar as certain of his works (particularly *Fathers and Sons*) mark a crucial stage in the movement toward a new perception of nature (and therefore of the place of man in nature) that begins to manifest itself in the middle decades of the nineteenth century, a movement charted in literary history between the poles conventionally called Romanticism, and, at the other extreme, Naturalism.

2) His place in that movement, in order to be appreciated, must be calibrated not only within the closed system of literary history, but rather as a border incident between literary and extra-literary discourses (particularly those of the body sciences).

3) The extra-aesthetic language which is most helpfully invoked if we are seeking Turgenev's unique place in the history of the novel is, then, *scientific*, not, as is so often assumed, political; and more specifically it is the language of a physiologically grounded *psychology* that was in the

process of formation during the early and middle years of the nineteenth century.

4) The specific way Bazarov and his famous frogs are used in *Fathers and Sons* is as a means for testing what was this new scientific psychology's major claim, i.e. that thinking is an illusion based on an erroneous division between mind and body. This view held that all aspects of human existence previously ascribed to the individual person's intentions, to his unique soul or psyche, were merely extra-individual manifestations of physiological processes in the human organism. As Bazarov tells the little peasant boys in Chapter V, when they ask him why he is catching frogs: "I shall cut the frog open and see what's going on in his inside, and then, as you and I are much as frogs (only we walk on two legs), I shall know what's going on inside us too".

5) *Fathers and Sons*, then, is a kind of literary laboratory for testing certain nineteenth century claims of science. But since Turgenev is a much subtler thinker than, let us say, Zola, Turgenev's version of the *roman expérimental* is not a laboratory modelled on those in the Rue Gay-Lussac, with their electrical generators and Bunsen burners, but rather a *language* laboratory. What we get is not a naive application of methods in physiology, nor do we get an equally naive attempt to "attack" such methods. No, Turgenev sees that at the heart of the new somatic definition of man lurks a theory of language—an attempt to get out of words and to the *things themselves*. What he does is to translate the latent content of scientism into a set of discursive practices which he then tests against other forms of discourse in his novel.

6) Finally, Turgenev may indeed have been ineffectual in the realm of politics. But in the realm of science he was to have at least one important actual consequence: By raising certain questions about Bazarov's physiological theories *in* his novel, *outside* the novel he caused Bazarov's double, the great physiologist Ivan Sečenov (1829–1905) to ask certain questions whose answers were to have a powerful and lasting effect on later concepts of the somatic structure of the brain and the way that structure relates to human psychology. Although Sečenov is precisely Bazarov's contemporary, then, I shall be arguing that if we were to apply Turgenev's own symbolic genealogy, it could be said that Sečenov is son to Bazarov's father.

But before we can see the relation between Turgenev and Sečenov— and the implications of such a relationship for any attempt to assess Turgenev's role as novelist—we must deal with a few preliminary considerations.

At a merely anecdotal level, nothing could be simpler than to define relations between Sečenov and Turgenev: each respected the other; both at one time or another belonged to the circle around the journal *Sovremennik*; both spent great stretches of time in Germany and France absorbing the very latest ideas across a broad spectrum of interests, and both shared an almost British liberalism that made their politics appear slightly unreal or wildly eccentric to their more millenarian fellow Slavs. The connection between the two appears even more ineluctable to anyone who has seen the famous photo of Sečenov, taken in 1861, the year Turgenev completes *Fathers and Sons*: we see a fierce-eyed, hirsute young man sitting at his work table in the Medico-Surgical Academy, complete with Bunsen burner, electrical charging mechanism and a laboratory clamp from which are suspended—of course—three frogs. It is less the portrait of an individual man than it is the icon of an era, one of those rare instances that let us actually *see* the otherwise invisible historical forces shaping whole eras.

But if we reach for the deeper meaning Sečenov and Turgenev had for each other, we shall have to go beyond their merely personal associations and look (very briefly) into the way each responded to the new challenges raised by Nineteenth Century science to traditional assumptions about man's place in nature. It is the cognitive revolution that took place between a time when nature was felt to reflect *man*, and a later time in which man was conceived as little more than a reflection of *nature* that makes the local relationship of Turgenev and Sečenov of particular interest.

Of all the pejoratives Bazarov uses, none in his eyes is more damning than "romantic". He means by this not merely that Romantics are old-fashioned because they prize the past: as a naturalist, he seeks as well to invoke by this term the particular romantic sense of *nature* that dominated Europe in the late eighteenth, early nineteenth century.

* * *

In March of 1860, at the very time Turgenev was at work on *Fathers and Sons*, Sečenov began a series of lectures at the St. Petersburg Medico-Surgical Academy. These lectures produced a sensation among not only the students, but all Petersburg. As the historian M. N. Šaternikov puts it: "Both the form and the contents of Sečenov's lectures produced an immense impression, not only on the academic world, but also on intellectual society in general. [His] manner of speaking was simple and convincing; his method of exposition was absolutely new. With youthful enthusiasm and deep faith in the all-conquering power of Science and Reason . . . he spoke not only of what had already been achieved, also of what was yet to be done . . . [he produced a large number of students and] we may confidently assert that Sečenov is the initiator of the Russian school of physiologists". (I should add that Sečenov's work continues to be ranked very high, even in the West: in Boring's definitive *History of Experimental Psychology* it is said that Sečenov was "far ahead of West European thought", and the eminent cyberneticist Walter Rosenblith has called Sečenov "a too little appreciated forebear of Norbert Weiner".)

But the aspect of Sečenov's achievement I wish to stress has less to do with his specific work on the brain. What I wish to emphasize, rather, is what Šaternikov has in mind when he says "The remarkable demonstration with which [Sečenov] illustrated his lectures acquainted students with the most recent techniques of scientific experiment and *taught* them to use the *language of facts*". It is not Sečenov as a kind of *Urfigur* for Bazarov, but rather Sečenov's "language of facts" that is significant for understanding Turgenev's novelistic practice. It is Scientism as a *language*, as a discursive practice claiming a unique relation to truth that Turgenev will test in his fiction.

In order to proceed with this argument, we shall want to keep two prior assumptions in mind. First, that an interplay between science and literature is possible because both are, in the end, exercises in language. Secondly, that the novel is preeminently the literary genre whose constitutive feature is an artistically organized diversity of social speech types, particularly *Fathers and Sons* in which the major thematic and structural emphasis is on the ideology of Scientism as it is expressed in the speech practice of the Nihilists.

Turning to the text of *Fathers and Sons*, we will notice first of all the most *obvious* level at which Turgenev contrasts different languages. These would include the large number of what might be called *phatic* scenes: those encounters in which characters explain to other characters the peculiar meanings of their different idiolects. In Chapter XV we are aware of the growing differences between Arkadij and Bazarov when the latter reproaches the former for interpreting literally his statement about Odincova's situation to the effect that "something is wrong here". Bazarov must explain to his young friend that "something wrong" (*ne ladno*) means "something *right* in my dialect and for me . . .". In the following chapter, Bazarov, impressed by the haughty demeanor of Odincova's butler, says to Arkadij, "What *grand genre*! . . . That's what it's called in your set (*u vas*), isn't it—". When Odincova invites Bazarov for a walk she says "I want you to teach me the Latin names of the wildflowers". And Bazarov seeks to mark off the difference between them by insisting on the fact they speak different languages: "What use are the Latin names to you?" he asks with his usual rudeness.

* * *

We could go on with this demonstration that self-conscious speech patterns that mark off distinct ideological positions are important building blocks in Turgenev's novel, with the corollary that when differences in *language* are dramatized, it is to dramatize *ideological* differences.

He is convinced his own truth is timeless because it is extralinguistic, scientific. What scientific means in his value system can be gathered from its opposite, the set of conventions and beliefs Bazarov castigates as Romantic: Romantic means Puškin, it means literature, it means metaphors. It means, in other words, inaccurate or deceptive *language*. Poetry can become outmoded because it is in a language that is false. Bazarov holds that science is a system that is true to the extent it is free from the confusions of language. It is he, the polar opposite of the underground man, who holds up the extralinguistic proposition that $2 \times 2 = 4$ as the ultimate argument for the truth of science.

What he fails to perceive, of course—what the whole *movement* of scientism failed to perceive—was that the extension of purely intrinsic scientific laws to *extrinsic* considerations such as ethics or politics—*was itself a metaphoric move*. It was an attempt to organize *social* life by *scientific* principles, i.e. to translate one system of signs into another: same but different, the classical definition of metaphor. In translating the laws of science into ideological practice, Scientism gives up the extrahistorical claim to truth attaching to mathematical signs. Their extra-scientific claims for science become subject to all the confusions and historicity of natural languages, the limitations of which for anyone seeking to express extrahistorical, ultimate truths are all too obvious.

Bazarov, like the underground man, is sick, and Turgenev is extremely acute in diagnosing Bazarov's disease: he is suffering from an illness that is the opposite of Dostoevskij's anti-hero, who suffered from an excess of "consciousness"; Bazarov, on the contrary, suffers from an *uncon*sciousness of the metaphoric nature of language. Speaking of his blindness as a disease is a metaphor, but so is Bazarov's sickness in the novel: the great proponent of the concept that men are no more than the sum of the cells and chemicals of their physical bodies is himself brought down by an illness contracted from his dissection of a corpse, i.e. a body that is *indeed* no more than its physical makeup. But the truth—the non-scientific truth—which this metaphor points to, is that Bazarov's disease is blindness to the metaphoric heart of his scientific ideology.

One way this is made apparent in the novel is in Bazarov's use of scientific metaphors. As the science he feels to be most scientific is physiology, it is not surprising that body imagery dominates his rhetoric. For instance, Arkadij—in defending his uncle—tells the story of Pavel Petrovič's hopeless romance for Princess R——: Bazarov answers with an uncharacteristically long speech:

> And what about all these mysterious relations between a man and a woman? We physiologists know what these relations are. Study the anatomy of the eye a bit, where does the enigmatical glance you talk about come in there. That's all romanticism, nonsense, rot, and artsy nonsense [chudožestvo]. Much better if we go and look at a beetle.

What he's saying, of course, is that physiological mechanisms are *true*, but they may become layered over with false metaphors, especially the kind to which lovers are notoriously drawn. There is a truth of the physical on the one hand, and the fiction of a self that is more than sum of its cellular activities, on the other.

The interesting thing, of course, is that Bazarov's example of a bodily organ is precisely the one that constitutes the novel's most obsessively recurring metaphor: everyone in the book is characterized by the quality of his eyes. The only place where there seems to be a one-to-one fit between appearance and reality is in eye metaphors. The bailiff at Mar'ino is a cheat so his eyes are of course "knavish" [plutovskie]. When Katja is confused by Arkadij's blurted declaration of his love, her eyes accurately reflect that confusion: "her dark eyes had a look of perplexity". The constantly flustered and anxious-to-please Sitnikov's eyes are "small and seemed squeezed in a fixed and uneasy look". Eyes, as a Romantic would say, are the windows of the soul, external physical signs accurately reflecting internal psychological truths. What Turgenev is doing here (as he does in his treatment of other parts of the anatomy, such as Kukšina's nose, Katja's feet, or Odincova's shoulders) is using the human body as lyrical poets had earlier used *landscape*. It is a selfconscious and highly sophisticated variant of the somatic sympathetic fallacy: instead of merely the landscape of nature reflecting inner psychological states (spring/young love), the whole body becomes such a metaphor (a lesson that will not be lost on Tolstoj).

The greatest twist on this metaphoric use of metaphor is Bazarov's own use of metaphor: as he lies dying, he metamorphoses into a romantic of the kind his Scientism previously had caused him to scorn. He spouts nothing but metaphors: a naturalist might explain away his reference to himself as a worm "half crushed but writhing still" as a last attempt on Bazarov's part to deny the difference between animals and humans. But only a poet would exploit light imagery as Bazarov does in his final speech: He says to Odincova, "be good to my parents, you'll not find any like them in your world even if you look by daylight with a candle . . .". Turgenev as author quite wickedly conflates his own imagery in his authorial voice with Bazarov's imagery: Turgenev as author says Bazarov's eyes "gleamed with their last light", but has Bazarov say in his own voice, "Goodbye . . . breathe on the dying lamp and let it go out . . . Enough . . . Now, Darkness": It is a poet's death: Mejerchol'd was quite right to want Majakovskij to play the role in his projected film of the novel.

Bazarov reverses in his biography the direction taken by the movement from Romanticism to Naturalism: he is a naturalist who metamorphoses into a romantic poet.

*　*　*

DAVID LOWE

Characterization in *Fathers and Sons*: Groups†

* * *

Broadly speaking, the two major sources of information about characters in *Fathers and Sons* include (1) information that any given character provides about himself and (2) information provided by other characters and the narrator. If we begin with the second group of sources, we can distinguish three general types of information about characters in *Fathers and Sons*: (a) what seem to be minimally evaluative, maximally objective surface descriptions of appearance, actions, and reactions, (b) overtly evaluative remarks about behavior, and (c) information relating to heredity and environment.

Surface descriptions tend to focus on hair, facial expression, clothing, and body language. Such descriptions are not applied in equal measure to all characters. If Arkady, Nikolay, and Katya seem pale, for instance, that is for a good reason: we learn relatively little about their looks. They are literally rather faceless characters. (Note that this is entirely in keeping with their function as comedic heroes and heroines.) Details of dress are everywhere important, especially in the case of Bazarov and Pavel. Bazarov's and Pavel's contrasting modes of dress—the former's lack of attention to it, the latter's fastidious concern for his toilette—are very much reflections of the essence of their personalities.

Kurlyandskaia makes some very apt observations about Turgenev's descriptions of actions and reactions. First, she points out that in Turgenev's world, the more intense a character's emotions, the more immobile his response.[1] The examples that she gives are from *A Nest of Gentlefolk*, but several instances in *Fathers and Sons* come immediately to mind. When Arkady first announces that Bazarov is a nihilist, Pavel freezes:

> "What?" asked Nikolay Petrovich, and Pavel Petrovich poised his knife in the air with a piece of butter on the tip of the blade and remained immobile.

Or consider Bazarov's state just after his declaration of love for Odintsova: "Odintsova extended both her hands to him, but Bazarov pressed his forehead against the windowpane". This leads naturally into Kurlyandskaia's second observation: many of the verbs that Turgenev uses to describe behavior and reactions indicate external reflections of inner emotions.[2] Nikolay sighs, blushes, wipes his brow. Odintsova lowers her

† From David Lowe, *Fathers and Sons*, Ann Arbor: Ardis, c. 1983. Reprinted by permission of Ardis Publishers.

1. G. B. Kuliandskaia, *Khudozhestvennyi me-tod Turgeneva-romanista* (Tula, 1972), 196–197.

2. Kurliandskaia, 158.

voice, bites the corner of her handkerchief, frowns. These are but a few examples of a phenomenon occurring on every page of *Fathers and Sons*. Here, in connection with surface information, we confront the question of Turgenev's use of psychological analysis, or as some critics maintain, his avoidance of it.

Most commentators argue that Turgenev's is a superficial psychology. Mazon, for instance, writes of the weakness of Turgenev's psychological portrayal:

> The author is satisfied with catching these [psychological] motifs in their external manifestations, in the acts of the heroes, in their words and gestures. He does not attempt to penetrate beyond the surface of phenomena.[3]

* * *

Turgenev's surface psychology is an integral part of his general novelistic technique, which is, improbably enough, cinematic at heart. *Fathers and Sons*, in particular, seems almost to have been written for the screen. Character in the novel is developed through individual scenes. As Matlaw points out, *Fathers and Sons* is a novel

> illustrating that the only requirement for Turgenev's purpose is a series of scenes each of which reveals character in a different way, illuminates it from a different angle or perspective, or demonstrates still another facet of its personality.[4]

Batyuto goes so far as to call these individual scenes "frames," and with good reason.[5] They follow each other in lightning succession, often without any transition. More importantly, and something that Batyuto does not remark, the frames often are arranged so as to create a montage effect, by virtue of which each frame acquires additional meaning because of its juxtaposition to preceding and succeeding ones. (Here we are in fact dealing with one of Eisenstein's most influential film discoveries.[6]) Consider, for instance, the conclusion of Chapter IV, where Pavel sits alone in his room late at night and muses:

> God knows where his thoughts wandered: the expression on his face was concentrated and gloomy, which does not occur when a person is occupied exclusively with reminiscences.

3. A. Mazon, *Parizhskie rukopisi I. S. Turgeneva* (M-L, 1931), 59; quoted in A. G. Tseitlin, *Masterstvo Turgeneva-romanista* (M, 1958), 103. The former is a translation of A. Mazon, *Manuscrits parisien d'Ivan Tourguénev: notices et extraits* (Paris, 1930).

4. Ralph E. Matlaw, "Turgenev's Novels: Civic Responsibility and Literary Predilection," *Harvard Slavic Studies*, IV (1957), 257.

5. A. Batiuto, *Turgenev-romanist* (L, 1972), 205.

6. See Sergei Eizenshtein, "Montazh 1938," *Izbrannye sochineniia v 6-i tomakh* (M, 1964), II, 156, where Eizenshtein observes that "two pieces of any kind, when placed next to each other, inevitably unite to form a new concept arising out of their juxtaposition as a new quantity." Other relevant works in the same volume include "Vertikal'nyi montazh" (189–268) and "Montazh attraktsionov" (269–273).

The very next sentence, without even a paragraph break, describes Fenechka sitting in her room, her gaze directed at her baby's bed. The juxtaposition of these two scenes suggests an indirect and troubled link between Pavel and Fenechka. Such a technique is possible only in the novel or on the screen: it would be impossible on the stage, where transitions from one scene to another can never be quite instantaneous. Furthermore, Turgenev's descriptions of facial expressions are the equivalent of the cinematic close up. In general, Turgenev tends to show in his novels just what we might see on the screen. If Dostoevsky is an eminently dramatic novelist,[7] Turgenev may be properly called a cinematic novelist. All this may seem far removed from a discussion of Turgenev's psychology, but the point is that although Turgenev limits himself largely to surface reflections of a character's inner life (precisely what we would see on a screen), it does not follow that his use of psychology cannot be sophisticated or revealing. Consider Bazarov's leaning his feverish brow against the window pane, Fenechka's rushing into Nikolay's arms after Pavel has accused her of not loving her benefactor, or Katya's bemused raising of her eyes when Bazarov proclaims that individuals differ from each other no more than does one tree in a forest from another. Such quick external details are infinitely telling. Turgenev ought not to be faulted for his general extrinsic approach to psychological portaiture: it has yet to be demonstrated that anyone—writer, psychologist, or bio-chemist—can explain or describe adequately the workings of the human mind. Turgenev is well aware of the X-factor in human behavior, and he chooses not to describe the indescribable.

* * *

The narrator supplies us with two basic types of information about characters' thoughts and motivations: definitive and qualified analyses. In some cases he waxes omniscient, telling us precisely what is transpiring inside a person's mind. An example of this is the lengthy description of Bazarov's inner struggle with "romanticism" (ch. XVII). Elsewhere the narrator only seems to guess at a given individual's motivations or thoughts; note, for instance, the narrator's multiple conjectures about what Nikolay may be thinking and feeling when Arkady runs off to introduce himself to Fenechka. In many of the qualified descriptions Russian words meaning "as if" (*slovno, budto, kak budto*) abound. In general the narration in *Fathers and Sons* is inconsistent: the narrator wavers between authorial omniscience and the limited first-person point of view of a faceless participant in the novel. One might argue that there are two narrative *personae* in *Fathers and Sons*: one an author-narrator who clearly stands above the work as its creator and who even occasionally addresses his reader directly—as a reader (*chitatel*), and another

---

7. This is one of the basic theses of George Steiner's *Tolstoy or Dostoevsky: An Essay in the Old Criticism* (New York, 1959).

who seems to be an unidentifiable, passive participant in and witness to the events he describes. Note, for instance, the narrator's impressions of Kukshina:

> She spoke and moved very easily and at the same time awkwardly: she obviously considered herself an affable and simple creature, yet no matter what she did, it seemed to you that it was exactly what she had not wanted to do.

Here the narrator seems to be on a par with Arkady and Bazarov rather than above them, creating them and the scene. This narrator describes surface phenomena; the other narrator indulges in motivational analysis. In short, Turgenev's narration is not as "objective" as some critics would have us believe: it occasionally calls attention to itself. Consider, for instance, Chapter VII, which Arkady narrates to Bazarov, although in fact we hear it from the narrator: "And Arkady told him his uncle's story. The reader will find it in the next chapter." Most of the next chapter is clearly *not* narrated by the naive, inarticulate Arkady, who takes over the narration at the phrase " 'And so you see, Evgeny,' said Arkady, finishing up his story, 'how unjustly you judge Uncle!' "

* * *

The third category of information about characters—details relating to heredity and environment—is also a function of Turgenev's psychological technique. An individual's pre-history, as Reeve observes, is meant to reveal his character.[8] Matlaw argues that Turgenev does not manage to show the formation of personality, that he only reveals it,[9] but in the case of Pavel's prehistory, Matlaw would seem to overstate the case. Pavel's personality is reshaped by his encounter with Princess R., and we observe that transformation, or perhaps we should say deformation. Every major protagonist, with the crucial exception of Bazarov, has a pre-history of some sort, but some are more detailed than others. The particulars of Fenechka's and Katya's past, for instance, are skimpy: this dearth of detail may well be a reflection of what Fisher calls Turgenev's tendency "to ignore the psychology of types that are essentially alien to him."[1]

Especially important for characterization through environment is a character's choice of surroundings. Pavel's elegantly appointed room is an aspect of his person, as is Bazarov's father's cozily cluttered home. Similar environmental details are provided for Odintsova, Kukshina, and Fenechka, while Bazarov lacks any environment that is distinctly his own, and this very lack of a personalized setting is significant.[2]

8. F. D. Reeve, "Fathers and Children," in *The Russian Novel* (New York, 1966), 135.
9. Matlaw, 258.
1. V. M. Fisher, "Povest' i roman u Turgeneva," in *Tvorchestvo Turgeneva: Sbornik statei*, I. u. Rozanov and Iu. M. Sokolov, eds. (M,

1920), 36.
2. The use of environment for purposes of characterization is hardly original with Turgenev. It occurs often in the works of French realists: Balzac and Stendhal, for instance, both inundate readers with minute depictions of

All the types of information discussed so far may be related either directly by the narrator or by one or another of the persons in the novel. Most of the time it is the narrator himself who purveys information (except in the case of dialogue, of course), although Turgenev does occasionally narrate scenes or parts of them from the point of view of one of the participants. This type of indirect narration is largely restricted to Arkady. In many of the scenes in which he is present he is our observer. It is largely through his eyes that we see the land surrounding Marino; Pavel's pre-history, though not narrated by Arkady himself, is ostensibly from his point of view (Chapter VII); it is from Arkady's vantage point that we first observe Odintsova; much of the scene in Odintsova's hotel room is reported from Arkady's perspective, and many of the scenes between Arkady and Katya are told substantially from his point of view. Our initial perceptions of Bazarov are filtered through Arkady's eyes. Turgenev relies on Arkady because he is the most naive of the major characters. (Bazarov is perhaps more naive in a certain sense, but to use him as a point of view would render him less enigmatic.)

* * *

Pavel and Bazarov both undergo radical pesonality changes as a result of confrontations with "fatal" women. Pavel's pre-history, related in the inserted novella (*vstavnaia novella*) which comprises most of Chapter VII, serves as an ironic foreshadowing of Bazarov's experiences with Odintsova. Reducing Chapter VII to its relevant essentials, we recall that Pavel, a frivolous young nobleman, plays the rake and enchants everyone with his manner, which is "self-assured, faintly ironical, and somehow amusingly caustic." A brilliant career awaits him, but his prospects of success are altered drastically by his encounter with the Princess R., with whom he promptly falls in love after meeting her at a ball. Pavel, "accustomed to easy conquests," quickly achieves his desired ends, but he is amazed to discover that his ardor fails to cool. He pursues the Princess R., who is alternately in and out of love with him, all over Europe. Their affair ends in Baden: "Within a month it was all over: the fire flared up for the last time and went out forever." Pavel returns to Russia a changed man. He eventually retires to his brother's estate, where he looks after his personal toilette, rarely goes out into society, and leads a solitary, joyless existence. An unrequited love has destroyed him.

Bazarov can only mock Pavel's tragedy:

All the same, I hold that a man who has staked his whole life on the card of a woman's love, and then, when he has lost, turns sour and

---

buildings, rooms, toilette, and so on. In Russian literature the device surfaces as early as *Evgeny Onegin*, where Pushkin provides a detailed portrait of Onegin's study. Partly because of the influence of the physiological sketch—

French in origin—the technique of characterization via surroundings became standard in the works of Russian authors from the late 1830s on.

allows himself to drift—a creature like that is not a man, but just a male animal.

Irrational, passionate love is nonsense to Bazarov: "And what are these mysterious relations between men and women? We physiologists know what these relations are." But, in perhaps the most striking instance of analogy in the novel, Bazarov's confrontation with Odintsova and the irrational repeats the main outlines of Pavel's pre-history.

Like Pavel, Bazarov displays a self-assured, ironical, caustic manner, though unlike Pavel, he does not precisely enchant everyone. Like Pavel, he is a man of whom others entertain great expectations. Arkady tells Bazarov's father, for instance: "I am certain . . . that a great future awaits your son, that he will do honor to your name." Odintsova also senses Bazarov's enormous potential, and on his death bed Bazarov himself admits that he had thought of himself as a giant (*gigant*). But Bazarov's potentially great career is cut short by his experience with Odintsova, whom, significantly, he first meets at a ball, just as Pavel had met Princess R. at a ball. There is sufficient textual evidence to assume that up to his meeting with Odintsova Bazarov's relations with women had been not unlike Pavel's:

> Bazarov was a great admirer of women and female beauty, but love in the ideal, or as he expressed it, romantic sense, he called lunacy, unpardonable idiocy . . . "If you like a certain woman," he would say, "try to get what you want; and if you can't—well, so what, drop her—there are other women."

And, though he fails to "get what he wants (*dobitsia tolku*)," he finds, as had been Pavel's experience with Princess R., that he lacks the resolution to drop Odintsova. Instead, even after his humiliating rejection by her ("You have misunderstood me" she whispers), Bazarov, not unlike Pavel, returns to the family estate to lick his wounds and brood. As Bazarov is dying he asks that Odintsova come to see him, and his last words are saturated with romantic pathos: "Blow out the dying lamp, and let it go out . . . Enough! . . . Now . . . darkness . . ." The imagery is a visual echo of the dying fire imagery surrounding Pavel's last encounter with Princess R. in Baden.

Neither Pavel nor Bazarov is open to esthetic pleasure. In Chapter XI the narrator describes Nikolay's pleasantly melancholy meditations as he looks at the stars of a summer sky. Pavel's emotions are then contrasted:

> Pavel Petrovich reached the end of the garden, and he also sank into meditation, and also raised his eyes to the heavens. But there was nothing reflected in his beautiful dark eyes except the light of the stars. He was not born a romantic. . . .[3]

3. James Justice, "*Fathers and Sons:* The Novel as Idyll," *Western Humanities Review*, XV (1961), 261, writes that "the fathers are associated with the soil, land, and nature." While this is true of Nikolay Petrovich and Vasily Ivanovich, it is decidedly not so with Pavel, who, significantly, is not a father.

In an analogous scene at Bazarov's parents' estate, Vasily, coming across Bazarov and Arkady lying in the hay, remarks: "Lying on the 'earth,' looking at the 'sky' . . . You know—there's a special meaning to that." Bazarov cuts him off: "I only look at the sky when I want to sneeze." This instance of scenic parallelism serves to underline an indifference to the wonder, mystery, and beauty of nature—an indifference that Pavel and Bazarov have in common. An additional demonstration of Bazarov's lack of awe before nature is his too-often-quoted "Nature is not a temple, but a workshop." Finally, the narrator at one point states explicitly that Bazarov is essentially indifferent to the beauties of nature.

That Pavel is not especially attracted to art is everywhere apparent: in his youth he read but five or six French novels. In his arguments with Bazarov he specifically mentions that it is his brother Nikolay who is so taken with German poetry. [4] His beautifully appointed room is more likely a reflection of his social status and Anglomania than of any particular esthetic sensibilities. Bazarov is not merely uninterested in art: his utilitarian principles make him denigrate its value. "A decent chemist is twenty times more useful than any poet," he proclaims in one of his more militant (and clichéd) moments. In a less martial mood he admits to Odintsova that he has no feeling for art, at the same time wondering why anyone needs such feelings. [5]

* * *

4. Michael Nierle, *Die Naturschilderung und ihre Funktionen in Verdichtung und Prosa von I. S. Turgenev* (Verlag Gehlen: Bad Homburg v.d.H., 1969), 249, suggests that Nikolay *and* Pavel love Schiller and Goethe. Similarly, he states that Bazarov *and* Arkady share an enthusiasm for Büchner. Thus, even though on page 248 of his work Neirle says that the problem of the generations in *Fathers and Sons* is one located within generations rather than between them, he goes on to misread the text, attributing a non-existent similarity of views to Pavel and Nikolay, Bazarov and Arkady.
5. In the so-called "Paris manuscript," Bazarov is even more hostile to art. He sees "no use in artists" (449). Turgenev excised the remark, perhaps because it introduces a note of tension into the novel too early.

The so-called "Paris manuscript" is a holding of the Bibliothèque Nationale in Paris. It is Turgenev's final draft (*belovoi avtograf*) of the novel, containing the deletions and additions that Turgenev made after having sent the first draft around for his friends to read and comment on. Therefore it is a valuable document for a study of the novel's gestation. When a photocopy of it was made available to Soviet scholars a minor upheaval ensued in

Soviet Turgenev scholarship. One of the more bilious traditions in Soviet scholarship had been that Katkov had castrated the novel before publishing it in *Russkii vestnik*. An examination of the Paris manuscript made it clear that Turgenev himself had made the changes which had so long been attributed to Katkov. Several Soviet critics were thus placed in a rather embarrassing situation. See Charles Moser, *Antinihilism in the Russian Novel of the 1860s* (The Hague, 1964), 82–83, for a more extensive treatment of this laughable development. P. G. Pustovoit, *Roman I. S. Turgeneva "Ottsy i deti" i ideinaia bor'ba 60-kh godov XIX veka* (M, 1960), 108–115, goes on at length about Katkov's brazenness; in a later work, *Roman I. S. Turgeneva "Ottsy i deti": Literaturnyi kommentarii* (M, 1964), Pustovoit admits in a footnote on page 100 that he, Gutiar, Stasov, Brodsky, and Batiuto were dead wrong about Katkov's supposed villainy.

Volume VIII of *PSSP*, 446–478, includes all the variants in the Paris manuscript. In citing those variants the following scheme will be used: the first number indicates the page on which the variant may be found; the second, after a slash, refers to the page of the canonical text to which the variant relates.

Even in their disagreements, Pavel and Bazarov display similar attitudes. They argue about the virtues of the Russian *narod*,[6] but in fact both are profoundly contemptuous of the peasantry. Pavel sniffs eau de cologne when he speaks to them, and Bazarov hates "Filip and Sidor," to whose betterment he is supposed to devote himself. The sources of their contempt are different. As Boyd points out: "Pavel Petrovich's contempt is that of a master for his slaves, while Bazarov is exasperated by their indolence and apathy."[7] But the end results are the same: by the close of the novel the peasants call Bazarov a gentleman (*barin*), thus putting him, as far as they are concerned, in the same camp with Pavel.[8]

A final minor but amusing instance of parallelism between Bazarov and Pavel involves card playing. Pavel is admired in the neighborhood because he "plays whist in a masterly fashion and always loses". Bazarov plays whist twice in the course of the novel, once with Odintsova and Porfiry Platonych (Ch. XVI) and once with his father and the priest (XXI): he loses consistently.[9]

If Bazarov and Pavel are so alike in their pride, exclusion from the world of esthetic pleasure, and lack of a rewarding inner life (except vis-à-vis their love lives), why are they the opponents in the novel? One answer is that they are nonetheless ideologically opposed to each other, although their respective ideologies are anything but cohesive and coherent. A more substantial answer, however, draws on the fundamental laws of magnetism: likes repel. We can see how the axiom is corroborated in the novel if we recall that Pavel and Bazarov accuse each other of the same thing—limitless and unfounded vanity.

* * *

Some scholars have tried to show parallels between Odintsova and Princess R. Byaly, for instance, argues that the characterization of both heroines is based on antitheses and mystery.[1] In this way, he reasons, "Turgenev confronts his Bazarov with the real existence of what had been for him no more than a fiction, 'romanticism, nonsense, rot,

---

6. *Narod* does not have an exact English equivalent. It is close to the German "Volk." Usually translated as "the people," in works of nineteenth-century Russian literature it refers to the peasantry.
7. Alexander F. Boyd, "A Landscape with Figures: Ivan Turgenev and *Fathers and Sons*," *Aspects of the Russian Novel* (Totowa, N.J., 1972), 79.
8. Seas of ink have been spilled over the question of Bazarov's relation to the peasantry. This is an especially touchy issue for Soviet critics. They interpret Bazarov's last confrontation with the peasants variously. Some argue Turgenev is blinded by his class consciousness in

this scene, others admit that Bazarov's doubts about the peasants are an accurate reflection of the attitudes of Pisarev and Nikolay Uspensky. For a detailed treatment of peasants in the works of Turgenev see B. M. Sokolov, "Muzhiki v izobrazhenii Turgeneva," *Tvorchestvo Turgeneva* (Odessa, 1919), 194–233.
9. Turgenev, in "Apropos of *Fathers and Sons*," notes that the radicals attacked him for making Bazarov lose at cards. Had he allowed Bazarov to win, Turgenev is certain that he would have been attacked for portraying Bazarov as a cardsharp (XIV, 100).
1. G. A. Bialyi, *Roman Turgeneva "Ottsy i deti"* (M-L, 1963), 77.

art.' "[2] Similarly, Blair argues that Odintsova is "a realistic version of the melodramatic caricature of Princess R."[3] This is to confuse structural and stylistic parallels, however, with insubstantial similarities of character. Odintsova and Princess R. play analogous roles in the lives of Bazarov and Pavel, but they have little in common as personality types. Batyuto asks: "In point of fact, is there much in common between the calm and well-balanced, 'clear as daylight' genteel-epicurean Odintsova and the tortured, mysterious, at times almost mad Princess R.?"[4] Their temperaments are as different as night and day. We cannot deny that Odintsova at times displays the frantic, hysterical tendencies that are typical of Princess R., who is flighty during the day and racked by anguish at night. Odintsova paces nervously around her room after Bazarov's confession, but the point is that such behavior is unusual for her; her calm is rarely shattered for any length of time, while Princess R. is manic-depressive by nature.

It should be noted that oblique, "hereditary" links between Princess R. and Odintsova can be established by going outside the novel in search of prototypes. Batyuto, for instance, links Princess R. to the heroine of "A Correspondence": both heroines enslave the men who love them. [5] Then, by appealing to Kiyko's work on "A Correspondence," Batyuto goes on to suggest Pauline Viardot as a prototype for both Princess R. and Odintsova. But one may with equal justification posit Mariya Alexandrovna, the heroine of "A Correspondence," as a forerunner of Odintsova: like Odintsova, she is an emancipated woman of sorts who lives in the country with her sister. She refuses the roles traditionally assigned a woman by bourgeois society—wife, mother, housemaker— and the neighbors think of her as a wild woman. So we may conclude that although Princess R. and Odintsova play similar structural roles in *Fathers and Sons*, and although they share a common prototype, their natures are very different. The characters in the novel to whom Odintsova is closest in temperament are Pavel and Bazarov.

Odintsova shares with Pavel an attachment to order and superficial stability. The neighbors respect Pavel for the fact that even though he has retired to the provinces, he has not let himself go to seed. His dress and conduct continue to be impeccable. Similarly, Odintsova pays considerable attention to dress and scheduling. Life at Nikolskoe follows a preordained pattern. When Bazarov objects to this rigidity, Odintsova defends herself by saying:

> You are right from your point of view—and perhaps, in this case, I am the genteel noblewoman; but one cannot live in the country without order; boredom would overtake one.

2. Bialyi, 77.
3. Joel Blair, "The Architecture of Turgenev's *Fathers and Modern Fiction Studies*, Vol. 19,
No. 4 (Winter 1973–74), 559.
4. Batiuto, 260.
5. Batiuto, 261–263.

In addition, the imagery surrounding Pavel and Odintsova underscores the fact that they are both spiritually dead. Odintsova sleeps "all pure and frigid in her clean and fragrant linen." In the Paris manuscript we find Odintsova "pure as marble." A few lines later there is a description of her motionless sleep. The emphasis is clear: Odintsova is calm and cold—a corpse. The portrait of Pavel recuperating after the duel employs similar imagery:

> Pavel Petrovich moistened his forehead with eau-de-cologne and closed his eyes. His handsome, wasted head, illuminated by the brilliant daylight, lay on the white pillow like the head of a corpse . . . Indeed, he was a corpse.

Odintsova shares with Pavel and Bazarov an indifference to nature, music, and the arts in general. The narrator points out, for instance, that she *and* Bazarov are immune to the charms of nature. It is Katya who plays the piano while Odintsova plays whist with Bazarov—the card playing yet another motif linking Pavel, Bazarov, and Odintsova. Furthermore, like the two men, Odintsova is endowed with strength of will and an overriding concern for spiritual freedom. As she thinks about the affair with Bazarov that might have been, she concludes: "No . . . God knows where it might have led, it's nothing to be joked with, peace (*spokoystvie*) is still better than anything on earth." Similarly, Bazarov tells Arkady:

> If you don't quite understand me, then I'll tell you the following: in my opinion, it's better to break stones on the roadway than to allow a woman to possess so much as the tip of your finger.

Bazarov, Pavel, and Odintsova all belong to the camp of the strong, the egoistic, and the sterile. There are, of course, differences among the three. Whereas Pavel's and Odintsova's coldness and indifference are thoroughgoing and genuine, Bazarov's are untested, and once they are challenged, they prove eminently assailable. His strong will and egoism, however, are constants in his personality, and they ally him with Pavel and Odintsova. All these characters impress us with their strength. We are not shown its sources, but the emanations of that psychic energy are everywhere discernible. These characters all have the power to influence other people: Bazarov is the novel's most influential protagonist, but Odintsova has Katya and Bazarov under her thumb through some of the novel, and Nikolay and Fenechka live in dread of Pavel's censure. These strong individuals react intensely—even violently—to the other protagonists in their own camp. Pavel and Bazarov fight a duel. Bazarov embraces Odintsova like a wild animal, or so it seems to her. All the members of this group are egoists, as a result of which they are the observed, rather than observers within the novel. In formal terms this means that individual scenes are hardly ever narrated from their point of view. Their self-preoccupation does not permit genuine interest in anyone or anything outside of themselves.

* * *

A Chronology
of Turgenev's Life

(The first date represents the Russian Calendar, the second the Western. See note to Turgenev's Letters).

1818   October 28 (November 9). Born in Orel.

1819–27   Raised on the estate Spasskoe.

1827–34   Moves to Moscow, matriculates at Moscow University, 1833.

1834   Transfers to St. Petersburg University. Father dies.

1837   Graduates from university.

1838–41   European jaunt, attends University of Berlin. Returns to Russia in May (June), 1841.

1842   Passes examination for M.A. at St. Petersburg University, but does not finish required dissertation.

1843   Publishes his first narrative poem. Meets Belinsky. Meets Pauline Viardot, French singer, to whom he remained devoted till his death.

1847–50   Publication of A Hunter's Sketches and stay in Paris with the Viardots. Returns to Russia in June, 1850. Mother dies November 16 (28), 1850.

1852   Under arrest April 16 (28)–May 15 (27) for laudatory obituary on Gogol. Lionized (in jail and elsewhere) by society and intellectuals.

1852–53   "Exiled" to Spasskoe under police surveillance.

1856   Publishes Rudin. Goes abroad July 21 (August 2).

1858   Returns to Russia.

1859   Publishes Nest of Noblemen. Goes abroad.

1860   Publishes On the Eve, First Love. Goes abroad.

1861   Returns to Russia. Finishes Fathers and Sons. Goes abroad.

1862   Publishes Fathers and Sons (February). Visits Russia.

1863   Settles in Baden-Baden with the Viardots. Will make six visits to Russia in the next eight years.

1867   Publishes Smoke.

1869   Publishes Reminiscences and Collected Works.

1870   Publishes A King Lear of the Steppes.

1872 Publishes *Spring Freshets*. A *Month in the Country* (1850, published 1855), first performed in Moscow.

1875 Jointly with the Viardots buys estate in Bougival near Paris.

1877 Publishes *Virgin Soil*.

1879 Honorary degree from Oxford University.

1880 In Russia, participates in Pushkin festival. More or less makes peace with Tolstoy and Dostoevsky.

1882 Publishes "Poems in Prose," prepares new collected edition. Becomes ill.

1883 Dies in Bougival September 3 after terrible agonies (cancer), during which he for a while kept a detailed diary of the course of the disease. At one point near the end he hurled an inkwell at Pauline Viardot, an act of plagiarism (from Luther) and of ingratitude to the source of his inspiration for thirty-five years.

Selected Bibliography

A complete English bibliography may be found in *Turgenev in English. A checklist of works by and about him* compiled by Riss Yachnin and David H. Stam. New York, The New York Public Library, 1962.

Blair, Joel. "The Architecture of Turgenev's *Fathers and Sons.*" *Modern Fiction Studies*, 1973–74.

Børtnes, Jostein. "The Poetry of Prose: The Art of Parallelism in Turgenev's *Fathers and Sons.*" *Scando-Slavica*, 1984.

Burns, Virginia M. "The Structure of the Plot of *Fathers and Sons.*" *Russian Literature*, 1974.

Cecil, David Lord. *Poets and Story-tellers.* London, 1949.

Fathers and Sons: Textual Strategies. Ed. Josué V. Harari. Ithaca: Cornell UP, 1979.

Folejewski, Zbigniew. "The Recent Storm around Turgenev as a Point in Soviet Aesthetics." *Slavic and East European Journal*, 1962.

Hindus, Milton. "The Duels in Turgenev and Mann. *Comparative Literature*, 1959.

Freeborn, Richard. *Turgenev: The Novelist's Novelist.* London, 1960.

Gettman, Royal A. *Turgenev in England and America.* Urbana, Illinois, 1941.

Gifford, Henry. *The Hero of His Time: A Theme in Russian Literature.* London, 1950.

Granjard, Henri. *Ivan Tourguénev et les courants politiques et sociaux de son temps.* Paris, 1954.

Hare, Richard. *Portrait of Russian Personalities Between Reform and Revolution.* New York, 1958.

Herschkowitz, Harry. *Democratic Ideas in Turgenev's Novels.* New York, 1932.

Lloyd, J. A. T., *Ivan Turgenev.* London, 1942.

Magarshack, David. *Turgenev, A Life.* New York, 1954.

Matlaw, Ralph E. "Turgenev's Novels: Civic Responsibility and Literary Predilection." *Harvard Slavic Studies*, 1957.

New Zealand Slavonic Journal. I. S. Turgenev. 1983.

Reeve, Franklin D. "Fathers and Children." *The Russian Novel.* New York, 1966.

Patrick H. Waddington. Turgenev's Sketches for *Fathers and Sons. New Zealand Slavonic Journal*, 1984.

Wilson, Edmund. "Turgenev and the Life-Giving Drop." In *Turgenev's Literary Reminiscences.* New York, 1958.

Yarmolinsky, Avrahm. *Turgenev: The Man, His Art and His Age.* New York, 1959.

Zhitova, Vera. *The Turgenev Family.* London, 1947.

NORTON CRITICAL EDITIONS